Ernst & Ernst
GAAP

Ernst & Ernst
GAAP

STOCK LIFE COMPANIES

Ernst & Ernst INSURANCE INDUSTRY COMMITTEE

COPYRIGHT © 1974 ERNST & ERNST

Printed in the United States of America
Library of Congress Catalog Card Number 74-19844

Summary
of Contents

Foreword   vii
Preface   ix
Detailed Table of Contents   xiii

Part I / *Introduction*

1 Background of the Financial Reporting Problem   3
2 Life Insurance Operations   13
3 Ordinary Products and Prices   29
4 Income Concepts   50
5 Revenue Recognition   60
6 Adverse Deviation and Lock-in   71

Part II / *Benefits*

7 Fundamentals of Adjusted Reserves   91
8 Mortality and Withdrawals   112
9 Investment Yields   138
10 Dividends   159
11 Reserve Grading and Other Compromises   178
12 Calculation Techniques   201

Part III / *Expenses*

13 Life Insurance Company Cost Accounting   227
14 Composition of Acquisition Costs   243
15 Deferral of Acquisition Costs   262
16 Amortization of Acquisition Costs   288
17 Development, Maintenance, and Other Costs   315

Part IV / *Other Lines of Business*

18 Industrial Insurance   331
19 Individual Health Insurance   349
20 Credit and Group Insurance   379
21 Variable Products   407
22 Reinsurance   424

Part V / *Special Problems*

23 Deferred and Uncollected Premiums   449
24 Recoverability and Loss Recognition   465
25 Restricted Participating Business   477
26 Deferred Taxes   498
27 Business Combinations   527
28 Conversion Mechanics   557

Part VI / *Perspectives on GAAP*

29 Financial Statements   571
30 A Few Audit Considerations   576
31 Using GAAP   584
32 Whither GAAP?   595

Appendixes

A Present Values and Related Concepts   599
B Taxes on Investment Income   620
C Crazy Quilt Life   627
D Mortality Fluctuation Reserves   647
E Actuaries' Responsibilities   650

Chapter References   655
Selected Bibliography   659
List of Tables   669
Index   677

Foreword

Late in the 1960s it became apparent to our firm that life insurance companies might have to adopt a new set of accounting principles for certain public reporting purposes. Some of the ideas then being advanced seemed to offer advantages; others appeared to hold serious disadvantages. No one, however, could judge with certainty because the ideas had not been tested against the complexities of life insurance operations. So, in our view, there was a distinct possibility that principles which might be acceptable in theory would in practice prove to be unrealistic.

It was against this backdrop that our firm, drawing on years of experience with its many insurance clients, decided to study the effects of these theories. Our goal was to develop a body of facts which would help lead to sound and practical accounting principles and practices. That decision was to consume the attention of our life insurance specialists for the better part of six years. This volume reports the findings of their massive and unique study.

Preface

Although this book is the product of the Ernst & Ernst Insurance Industry Committee, it was decided that I should bear the main burden of blame for it. To make my culpability manifest, it was decided that a personal preface would be in order. Guilt is symbolized by use of the term "I". Use of the term "we" means that I'm speaking for our Insurance Industry Committee.

I'm embarrassed by the size of this book. On the other hand, I'm convinced that we've come about as far as we can with broad generalizations. It's time to give the generalizations some flesh and blood, and this book is a modest attempt to do that. If nothing else, the book may demonstrate that some important details have been overlooked or neglected in the process of generalizing. Hopefully the book will also help deal with the details, which at times are nettlesome indeed.

The book is studded with suggestions and recommendations. To repeat a line from our 1970 book on natural reserves, the suggestions and recommendations are in the nature of hypotheses awaiting empirical validation. Life insurance accounting has entered into a period of experimentation, and this book is necessarily experimental.

Which raises one other point. The life insurance audit guide devotes a scant 32 pages to "principles of accounting". This book mainly represents an attempt to interpret the principles set forth in those 32 pages. That suggests how much interpreting needs to be done. Until opinion and practice have had time to evolve toward common understandings, decisions are going to be made (and I'm certain, *have* been made) that hindsight is going to prove wrong. That

seems unavoidable until the necessary hindsight is acquired.

The answer to the problem is not to stick with the status quo, however. Progress always exacts its price, and in this case part of the price is uncertainty. The answer, it seems to me, is to go slowly, learn the subject thoroughly, be decently conservative, and agonize properly over every significant point. I don't think that anyone has to apologize for a good job even if, a few years hence, events suggest it might have been done differently.

One night a year or so ago one of our younger staff members was helping me assemble some actuarial data for Crazy Quilt Life, our model office. After gazing at formulas and computer output for a while he sighed and asked, "Is it true that actuaries walk on water?" I assured him they were at least ankle deep, but pointed out that neither the life insurance business nor our research project could survive without them. He asked if actuaries were as smart as accountants. I told him I certainly hoped so since they seemed to be developing generally accepted accounting principles. Finally he asked if actuaries have a sense of humor. I told him to read the audit guide and find out for himself.

It's very fortunate that actuaries rose to the challenge of the audit guide. Without their considerable talents the guide would have been a disaster. That doesn't mean the guide is perfect; far from it. It only means that the guide is defensible, and considering the complexity of life insurance accounting, that's saying a lot.

It's fair to say that before the audit guide, accounting was of only incidental concern to actuaries. Now it's a major concern, and all users of life insurance company financial statements may be thankful for that.

The main stumbling block to early publication of the audit guide was disagreement over old-fashioned basic principles—what is revenue, what are profits, and so on. As a somewhat withered veteran of nine years in the accounting profession, I guess I should realize that there are no immutable laws governing such matters. But I wish there had been more to go on. Vulnerability on basic principles invited endless arguments and the invitation was readily accepted. Vulnerability on basic principles also invited compromise, and the audit guide is very definitely a package of compromises. There's nothing wrong with compromise when the truth does not cry out for recognition, and there are few shrieking truths in life insurance accounting. But everyone winds up slightly dissatisfied. And everyone I know, including myself, is at least slightly dissatisfied. I fully expect another quantum leap in life insurance accounting some years hence when we achieve a more common understanding of, and agreement on, the basic principles.

What has the audit guide done for the users of financial statements? For one thing, it's made it impossible for management to hide behind a statutory loss or an optimistic rule-of-thumb adjustment. That's a very valuable service to investors. A GAAP loss is not easy to explain. Perhaps GAAP results will even have some value to regulators as an early-warning device.

Secondly, the guide has provided at least a foundation for developing reasonably comparable financial statements for stock life companies. I hasten to add that complete comparability is unlikely ever to be achieved. But reasonable comparability is a big step forward.

And thirdly, the guide proves that the life insurance industry, the actuarial profession, and the accounting profession can work together for progress in financial reporting. So far as the public interest is concerned, that may be the most important contribution the audit guide has made.

The best way to use this book is not to read it, thereby avoiding a lot of aggravation. The next best thing to do is use it as a reference work. The least desirable thing to do is read it from cover to cover. Only confirmed masochists should do the latter.

The book is supposed to be a textbook, a reference work, and in some cases a harangue. Harangues are generally resorted to when reason fails.

As a textbook this volume might be useful in teaching the subject of life insurance accounting. However, the book is pretty much limited to generally accepted accounting principles for stock life insurance companies. It assumes a knowledge of the principles of life insurance and of statutory accounting practices. These subjects are well covered in commercial texts.

As a reference work the book might be useful in developing approaches to the resolution of specific problems. It goes without saying, though, that there is nothing sacred about what the book recommends or suggests or illustrates. Discretion is the better part of valor in using this book to solve problems.

A reader will readily be able to identify a harangue when he encounters one. In most cases the word "therefore" or "accordingly" will tip him off. It's amazing how much apparent authority these terms can lend a discussion when all else fails. "The book says 'therefore', therefore it must be." Perhaps a better attitude would be, "The book says 'therefore', therefore it probably isn't." Accordingly, we suggest the reader proceed with great caution when he encounters these particular terms of circumvention.

If the reader is not familiar with basic actuarial science he might consider reading Appendix A, "Present Values and Related Concepts", before tackling the rest of the book. Theory and technique are inextricably interwoven in life insurance accounting. The reader who seeks to grasp the main points without bothering with the arithmetic is not going to have much success.

The book is designed for a diverse audience and diverse uses. Accountants may occasionally chafe because of some things that are intuitively obvious to them. They are respectfully requested to consider the needs of actuaries. Actuaries will no doubt be very impatient with the way actuarial topics are handled. They are respectfully requested to consider gaps (no pun intended) in accountants' knowledge of actuarial science.

The book is likely to be heavy going despite occasional attempts to be light-hearted, and for this we apologize. We couldn't find a way to simplify the subject, which unavoidably reflects the complexity of the industry.

Many hundreds of people assisted in the preparation of this book. Significant contributions were made by life insurance executives, actuaries, accountants, security analysts, professors, regulatory officials, industry trade association executives, and others. Many of them are listed in the bibliography. To all, our heartfelt thanks. They deserve the credit for whatever is good about the book. I accept the blame for whatever is bad about it.

This project could not have been carried out without the dedicated help of a fine group of Project Assistants. Our thanks for performance beyond the call of duty to Masako Guthrie, Carol Iorizzo, Marilyn Marais, Elizabeth Navas, Reiko Schroeder, Eleanor Taub, and John Woods.

And a special expression of gratitude to my wife Diane, who devoted about 2,000 hours to project work and who has tolerated a preoccupied husband for five years.

The project has taken about 15,000 hours of my time, 25,000 hours of staff support, and about 3,000 hours of computer time. In addition, other Ernst & Ernst personnel spent about 20,000 hours on matters relating to the project and industry representatives contributed at least as much time. The project involved about 1,000,000 miles of travel, 10,000 outgoing letters, 5,000 incoming letters, and over 1,000 conversations. The project files include some 500,000 pages of documents, about 200,000,000 words. I drank about 1,000 cups of coffee while writing the book,

mainly to stay awake. (The reader may need about as many while reading the book, mainly for the same reason.)

The project is probably the biggest specialized accounting research effort ever undertaken. And yet we've just scratched the surface of the subject. This suggests the vastness and complexity of the subject. It also suggests that accounting research is still in its infancy.

I should be grateful that the project is over. Indeed, it will be pleasant to spend an evening on the town with a congenial actuary without lusting after his insights; to read something more ebullient than the *Study Notes* for the actuarial examinations; and generally to assume a more conventional position in the pecking order. Five years of heavy research are enough for anyone.

But the project has been a remarkable experience, and it is with some sadness that I take leave of it. It has been exhilarating to draw some order out of chaos. Some would argue, with considerable justification, that I have the process reversed. Whichever view prevails, the fact remains that the project has been the experience of a lifetime.

Robert Posnak
New York
May 31, 1974

Detailed Contents

Part I / *Introduction*

1 BACKGROUND OF THE FINANCIAL
  REPORTING PROBLEM   3

Statutory Accounting   3
  Brief History of the Convention Statement   4
  Objectives of Statutory Accounting   5
  Statutory Accounting and "Generally
    Accepted" Accounting   6
Pressures for "Adjusted Earnings"   6
  Property and Liability Precedents   7
  Security Analysts   7
  The Stock Market   8
  Holding Companies and Diversification   8
  Securities and Exchange Commission   8
  New York Stock Exchange   9
Development of the Audit Guide   9
  The 1970 Exposure Draft   9
  The Revised Audit Guide   11
The Ernst & Ernst Research Project   11
  Problem   11
  Objectives   11
  General Research Methods   11
  Findings, Conclusions, and Recommendations   12
  Organization of the Book   12

2 LIFE INSURANCE OPERATIONS   13

Crazy Quilt Life   13
  Historical Summary   13
  Capital and Surplus   14
  Organization   14
  Top Management   15
Marketing   17
  Ordinary Agencies   17
  Combination Agencies   18
  Products   18
Underwriting Operations   19
  Underwriting   20
  Medical Operations   20

Group Operations   20
  Group Sales and Service   20
  Products   21
  Group Underwriting   21
Actuarial Operations   21
  Individual Actuarial   21
  Group Actuarial   22
  Product Development   23
Investment Operations   23
Administration   28
  Insurance Services   28
  Controller   28
  Treasurer   28
  Systems   28
  Corporate Services   28
Financial Reporting   28

3 ORDINARY PRODUCTS AND PRICES   29

Nonparticipating Permanent Insurance   29
  Equation Approach to Pricing   29
  Asset Share Accumulation Approach to Pricing   30
  Anderson Accumulation Approach to Pricing   30
  Cash Values and Reserves   32
Nonparticipating Term Insurance   35
  Level Term   35
  Renewability   36
  Convertibility   38
  Decreasing Term   39
Participating Permanent Insurance   43
  Premiums   43
  Dividends   44
  Rate Test   46
Individual Fixed Annuities   47
Specialty Policies and Supplemental Benefits   47

4 INCOME CONCEPTS   50

Nature of the Life Insurance Transaction   50
  The Sales Aspect   50
  The Service Aspect   52
Recognizing Revenues and Profits   53

Installment Sales Method	53
Pure Service Method	54
Comparison of Methods	54
Professional Literature	55
Overview of the Audit Guide	56
Economic Value	56
Discount Rates	57
Crazy Quilt Life	57

5 REVENUE RECOGNITION	**60**
Premium Revenues	60
Long-Duration Contracts	60
Short-Duration Contracts	63
The "When Due" Provision	65
Disclosure	65
Reserves and Premiums	65
Life Reserves	66
Casualty-Type Business	68
Miscellaneous Revenue Items	68
Investment Income	68
Deposit-Type Items	70

6 ADVERSE DEVIATION AND LOCK-IN	**71**
Adverse Deviation	71
Audit Guide References to Adverse Deviation	71
The Release-from-Risk Concept	73
Implementing the Release-from-Risk Concept	73
Interpretations of the Audit Guide	75
Effect of the Two Interpretations	76
Need for a Consistent Interpretation	78
Toward a Consistent Interpretation	79
"Prudent Best Estimates"	81
Role of Surplus in Degree of Conservatism	81
Future Development of Release-from-Risk Theory	82
Lock-In	82
References to Lock-In	82
Problems with the Principle	83
Theory of the Lock-In Principle	83
Practical Reasons for Lock-In	84
Implementing Lock-In	85
Exceptions to Lock-In	87

Part II / *Benefits*

7 FUNDAMENTALS OF ADJUSTED RESERVES	**91**
Terminology	91
Adjusted Reserves	91
Valuation Premiums	92
Reserve Assumptions	92
What Assumptions Encompass	92
Responsibility for Reserve Assumptions	93
General Criteria for Reserve Assumptions	93
General Approach Toward Choosing Reserve Assumptions	94
Crazy Quilt Life	95
Valuation Premiums	98
Audit Guide References to Valuation Premiums	98
American Academy Guidelines for Valuation Premiums	99

Illustration of Relationships	100
Effect on Profit	102
Crazy Quilt Life	102
Constancy of Percentage Relationships	103
Adjusted Reserves	106
Calculation of Factors	107
Profit Patterns	107
Expense Reserves	108
Adjusted Benefit Reserves	109
Disclosure	111

8 MORTALITY AND WITHDRAWALS	**112**
Mortality	112
Audit Guide Provisions as to Mortality	112
Principal Mortality Tables	113
Experience Tables	113
Effect on Reserves	116
Effect on Profits	117
Provisions for Adverse Deviation	121
Another View of Adverse Deviation	125
Term Renewal Mortality	125
The "When Paid" Assumption	126
Settlement Options	126
Miscellaneous Ordinary Benefits and Coverages	127
Disclosure	127
Term Conversions	127
Calculating the Cost of Conversion	127
Operation of the Conversion Mechanism	128
Effect on Reserves	129
Combined Renewal and Conversion	130
Separate Conversion Reserves	130
Group Conversions	130
Disclosure	131
Withdrawals	131
Audit Guide Provisions	131
Withdrawal Tables	131
Nonforfeiture Benefits	132
Effect on Reserves	134
Effect on Profits	134
Provisions for Adverse Deviation	134
The "When Terminated" Assumption	136
Term Renewals	136
Term Conversions	136
Disclosure	137
Mortality Fluctuation Reserves	137

9 INVESTMENT YIELDS	**138**
Interest Assumptions in General	138
Audit Guide Provisions	138
Nature of Interest	139
Significance of the Interest Assumption	141
Influences on the Interest Assumption	142
Provision for Adverse Deviation	143
Inflation and the Interest Assumption	144
Elements of the Interest Assumption	144
Gross Investment Income	144
Investment Expenses	146
Taxes on Investment Income	147

Yield Calculation	150
Selecting Interest Assumptions	150
Influence of Trends	150
Interest Models	153
Taxes on Investment Income	153
Plan Differentiation	153
Policy Loans	155
Capital Gains and Losses	156
Audit Guide Provisions	156
The Problem with Capital Gains and Losses	157
Lack of a Solution	157
Revaluations	157
Gains and Losses on Other than Stocks and Bonds	158
Securities Valuation Reserve	158
Disclosure	158

10 DIVIDENDS — 159

Basics of the Par Adjustment	159
"No Earnings Restrictions"	159
"Scales Unrelated to Actual Earnings"	159
"Specified Policy Dividends"	160
"Provided for Ratably"	160
"Planned Contractual Benefit"	160
Significance of Dividends	160
Dividend Scales and Adjusted Reserves	160
Dividend Assumptions	162
Adjusted Reserves	166
Changes in the Scale	166
Nature of a Change in Dividend Scale	166
Revising Reserves for Revised Dividend Scales	168
Use of Statutory Reserves	169
Recoverability and Loss Recognition	169
Adjusted Benefit Reserves	170
Dividend "Benefits"	170
Profit Tests	170
Reserve Assumptions	171
Provisions for Adverse Deviation	173
Adjusted Reserves	173
Separating the Dividend Component	173
Dividend Liabilities	175
Dividends Payable	175
Dividend Options	176
Coupons and Pure Endowments	176
Paid-up Additions	177
Disclosure	177

11 RESERVE GRADING AND OTHER COMPROMISES — 178

Reserve Grading	178
Reasons for Grading	178
Audit Guide Provisions	179
Mechanics of Grading	179
Effects of Grading	182
Grading Guidelines	189
Relationship to Statutory Reserve Method	193
Disclosure	196
Paid-up Business	197
Averaging	198
Substituted Statutory Basis	198

Single Valuation Basis	198
Statutory	198
Supplemental Benefits	198
Waiver of Premium	198
Accidental Death	200
Substandard	200
Miscellaneous Coverages	200
Supplemental Contracts	200

12 CALCULATION TECHNIQUES — 201

Incidence Assumptions	201
Nature of the Incidence Problem	201
Policy Anniversary	202
Mortality	202
Withdrawals	203
Nonforfeiture Benefits	203
Dividends	203
Conversions	204
Valuation Premiums	204
Fractional Premiums	204
Interest	204
Expenses	204
Intermediate Reserves	204
Reserve Accumulation	204
Mean of Beginning and Ending Reserves	205
Deferred and Uncollected Premiums	206
Continuous-Premium Intermediate Reserves	206
Similarity to Means and Mid-Terminals	208
Mean Reserves	208
Mid-Terminal Reserves	208
Expense Reserves	209
Assumed Incidence of Expenses	209
Annual-Premium Case Intermediate Reserves	209
Continuous-Premium Cases	210
Intermediate Reserve Formulas	211
Decrement Rates	211
Benefits	211
Expenses	212
Reserve Factors	212
Definitions and Formulas	213
Crazy Quilt Life Formulas	219
Definitions and Formulas	219
Reserve Factors	224

Part III / *Expenses*

13 LIFE INSURANCE COMPANY COST ACCOUNTING — 227

Terminology	227
Basic Cost Accounting Concepts	228
The Costing Object	228
The Flow of Costing Objects	229
Classification of Costs	230
Unit Costs	232
Life Insurance Functional Costs	232
Nature of Functional Costs	232
The LOMA Functional Cost Program	233
Actuarial Approaches to Cost Accounting	237
Cost Accounting and Income Determination	241
Functional Costs and Inventoriable Costs	242

14 COMPOSITION OF ACQUISITION COSTS	243
Variability and Attribution	243
Variability	244
Attribution	246
Applicability of Process Costing Concepts	247
LOMA Suggestions	247
Selling Costs	247
First-Year Commissions and Commission Equivalents	247
Agents' Stock Options	251
Renewal-Year Commissions and Commission Equivalents	252
Sales Support	254
Mail Order Solicitation Costs	256
Selection Costs	259
Issue Costs	259
Indirect Costs	260
Nature of Indirect Costs	260
Allocating Indirect Costs to New Business Functions	260
"Reasonable Conservatism"	261
Latitude Allowed by the Audit Guide	261
15 DEFERRAL OF ACQUISITION COSTS	262
Cost Analysis	262
Line-of-Business Allocations	262
New Business Functional Costs	263
Meeting the Attribution Criteria	265
Variability Tests	268
Renewal-Year Acquisition Costs	269
Commissions and Commission Equivalents	270
Term Renewals	271
Term Conversions	272
Approximation Techniques	273
Cost Accumulation	273
Relationship to Income Statement Format	273
Estimates for Prior Years	274
Allocations to Blocks of Business	276
Reasons for Allocation	276
Allocation Principles	278
Riders	278
Allocation Techniques	279
Joint Costs	280
Comparisons with Assumed	283
Final Expression of Acquisition Costs	286
Disclosure	286
16 AMORTIZATION OF ACQUISITION COSTS	288
Nature of Amortization	288
Rational and Systemic Allocation	288
Matching Premiums and Acquisition Costs	289
Sum-of-the-Years'-Premiums Method	289
Interest on Acquisition Costs	290
Arguments for Recognizing Interest	290
Arguments Against Recognizing Interest	290
A Matter of Choice	290
Effect of Interest	291
Persistency Adjustments	293
Audit Guide Requirements	293
Adjustments without Recalculation	294
Adjustments with Recalculation	295
Guidelines for Persistency Adjustments	295
Conflict with Lock-in	296
Conflict with Release-from-Risk Concept	296
Worksheet Methods	296
Advantages and Disadvantages	296
Amortization without Interest	296
Amortization with Interest	299
Renewal-Year Acquisition Costs	300
Calendar-Year Adjustments	301
Estimates for Prior Years	302
Summary Worksheet	304
Acquisition Cost Factors	304
Assignment of Costs	305
Valuation Premiums	305
Calculation of Factors	305
Application of Factors	305
Special Problems with Factors	305
Effects of Withdrawals and Mortality	305
Minor Lines of Business	306
Individual Fixed Annuities	307
Arbitrary Grading	307
General Guidelines	308
Relationship to Reserve Grading	309
Some Comparisons	309
Disclosure	309
17 DEVELOPMENT, MAINTENANCE, AND OTHER COSTS	315
Development Costs	315
Nature of Development Costs	315
Types of Development Costs	315
Some Arguments for Deferral	315
Some Arguments against Deferral	316
APB Opinion No. 17	316
Agency Development	317
Ratebook Development	318
Costs of Developing a New Line of Business	318
Development of Specialized Markets	319
Administrative Systems	320
Summary	320
Disclosure	320
Maintenance and Settlement Costs	320
Nature of Maintenance and Settlement Costs	321
Relationship to Cost Accounting	321
Reasons for Reserving	321
Calculating Reserves	321
When Reserves are Needed	321
Practical Approaches	323
Effect of Interest	324
Effect of Withdrawals	324
Effect of Grading	325
Effect of Inflation	325
Relationship to Recoverability Tests	326
"Single-Reserve" Factors	326
Disclosure	326
Investment Expenses	327
Nature of Investment Expenses	328
Reasonableness	328
Disclosure	328
Overhead	328

Part IV / *Other Lines of Business*

18 INDUSTRIAL INSURANCE — 331
Products and Marketing — 331
  Marketing — 331
  Underwriting — 332
  Products — 333
  Pricing — 333
Benefit Reserves — 336
  Assumptions — 337
  Differential Nonforfeiture Costs — 337
  Calculation Techniques — 338
  Grading — 340
  Paid-up Business — 340
Expenses — 340
  Accounting Records — 340
  The "Times" System — 343
  Deferral of Acquisition Costs — 344
  Amortization of Acquisition Costs — 347
  Maintenance and Settlement Expenses — 347
Disclosure — 348

19 INDIVIDUAL HEALTH INSURANCE — 349
Commercial Forms — 349
  Revenue — 349
  Composition of Acquisition Costs — 350
  Casualty Approach — 350
  Crazy Quilt Life — 350
  "Heaped" Acquisition Costs — 352
  Property-Liability Practice — 352
  Claim Reserves — 352
  Disclosure — 352
Noncancellable Business — 352
  Pricing — 353
  Revenue — 356
  Benefit Reserve Assumptions — 356
  Benefit Reserve Calculations — 358
  Grading to Statutory — 363
  Reserve Behavior — 363
  Claim Liabilities — 364
  Composition of Acquisition Costs — 364
  Deferral and Amortization — 366
  Arbitrary Amortization Cutoff — 368
  Maintenance Costs — 368
  Unearned Premiums — 371
  Uncollected Premiums — 374
  Statutory as an Approximation — 374
  Disclosure — 375
Guaranteed Renewable Business — 376
Return-of-Premium Business — 376
  Product Design — 376
  Risk — 376
  Acquisition and Other Costs — 377
  Liabilities for Incurred Claims — 377
  Active Life Reserves — 377
  Disclosure — 378

20 CREDIT AND GROUP INSURANCE — 379
Credit Insurance — 379
  Types of Business — 379

  Statutory Reserves — 380
  Benefit Patterns — 380
  Audit Guide Provisions — 381
  Long-Term Business — 382
  Single-Premium Non-Bank Business — 383
  Single-Premium Bank-Type Business — 385
  Coinsurance — 386
  Level Term Business — 387
  Outstanding Balance Business — 387
  Adverse Deviation — 388
  Crazy Quilt Life — 388
  Income Statement Classifications — 389
  Disclosure — 390
Group Term Life and Health Insurance — 392
  Group Products — 393
  Group Pricing — 393
  Experience Rating — 394
  Cost Accounting — 395
  Reserves — 397
  Retention Business — 397
  Pooled Business — 404
Group Annuities — 404

21 VARIABLE PRODUCTS — 407
Variable Annuities — 407
  Product Design — 407
  Statutory Reserves — 408
  Operation of a Separate Account — 408
  Revenue — 408
  Deferral of Acquisition Costs — 408
  Amortization of Acquisition Costs — 410
  "First-Year" vs. "Renewal" — 410
  Other Revenue Sources for Matching Purposes — 412
  General Overhead — 412
  Development Costs — 412
  Reserves — 412
  Separate Account Surplus — 412
  Presentation and Disclosure — 413
Variable Life Insurance — 413
  Product Design — 413
  Pricing — 414
  General Account vs. Separate Account — 414
  Revenue — 414
  Variable Life Valuation — 414
  Assumptions — 416
  Impact of Assumptions — 416
  Presentation and Disclosure — 422
Index-Linked Products — 422

22 REINSURANCE — 424
Reinsurance in General — 424
  Yearly Renewable Term — 424
  Coinsurance — 425
  Modified Coinsurance — 426
  Non-Proportional Reinsurance — 426
  Recapture — 427
  Experience Rating — 428
  Special Reinsurance Agreements — 429
  "Cost of Reinsurance" — 429
Accounting for Normal Agreements — 429
  Treatment of Reinsurance "Cost" — 430

Yearly Renewable Term	430
Further Comments on YRT Reserves	431
Implicit Expense Allowances	432
YRT Refunds	433
Coinsurance	435
Modified Coinsurance	436
Coinsurance Refunds	438
Recapture	441
Non-Proportional Reinsurance	443
Other Lines of Business	443
Unauthorized Reinsurance	443
Disclosure	443
Accounting for Special Agreements	443
Audit Guide Provisions	443
Definition of a "Special Agreement"	444
Limitation of Risk	444
Disproportionate Expense Allowances	444
Optional Recapture	444
Outright Sale	445
Disclosure	445
Reinsurance Assumed	445
Yearly Renewable Term	445
Coinsurance and Modified Coinsurance	445
Special Agreements	446
Contingency Reserves	446
Disclosure	446

Part V / *Special Problems*

23 DEFERRED AND UNCOLLECTED PREMIUMS	449
Nature of Ordinary Life Deferred and Uncollected Premiums	449
Deferred and Uncollected Premiums as an Asset	449
Deferred and Uncollected Premiums as a Reserve Correction	449
Statutory Accounting Tradition	449
Cost of Collection in Excess of Loading	450
Deferred and Uncollected Premiums in the Context of Adjusted Statements	451
Calculation of Deferred and Uncollected Premiums	453
Relationship to Mean Reserves	453
Computing Statutory Deferred and Uncollected Net Premiums	453
Computing Adjusted Deferred and Uncollected Valuation Premiums	453
Cost of Collection on Gross Deferred and Uncollected Premiums	455
Crazy Quilt's Calculation of Cost of Collection	455
Interest on the Cost of Collection Adjustment	461
Some Other Considerations	461
Accounting Separately for Acquisition Costs	461
Mid-Terminal Reserves	462
Uncollected Group Premiums	464
The "When Due" Provision	464

24 RECOVERABILITY AND LOSS RECOGNITION	465
Audit Guide Provisions	465
Issue-Year Recoverability Tests	466

Test Frames	466
Test Elements	468
New Companies	469
Test Methods	469
Calculating a Deficiency	470
Recording a Deficiency	471
Special Problems	471
Practical Considerations	472
Disclosure	472
Loss Recognition	473
Defining a "Line of Business"	473
Indicators of a Deficiency	473
Elements of a Deficiency Calculation	474
Recording a Deficiency	474
Special Problems	474
Disclosure	476

25 RESTRICTED PARTICIPATING BUSINESS	477
Audit Guide Provisions	477
Percentage Restrictions	477
Flat Amount Per $1,000	477
Greater of Percentage or Amount	478
100 Percent Restriction	478
"Inure to Stockholders"	478
Comparison with Type 1 Company	478
Types of Restrictions	478
Regulatory Restrictions	479
Charter Restrictions	479
Contractual Restrictions	479
Self-Imposed Restrictions	479
Interpreting the Restrictions	479
The New York Law	480
Management Fee Concept	480
Ultimate Ownership of Surplus	481
Current Restrictions on Surplus	481
Company Intent	482
Importance of the Interpretation	482
General Guidelines for Interpretations	483
Separation of Statutory Accounts	483
General Approaches	483
Degrees of Separation	484
Crazy Quilt Life	485
Accounting for the Restriction	489
Stockholder Charge Mode	489
Treatment of Dividends	490
Reserve Assumptions	490
Cost Allocations	492
Deferred Taxes	493
Shifting Stockholder Charge Modes	493
Testing the Method Adopted	494
Par Deficits	494
Financial Statement Presentations	495
Income Statement	495
Surplus Statement	496
Balance Sheet	496
Notes to Financial Statements	496

26 DEFERRED TAXES	498
Life Insurance Taxation	498
Brief History of Life Insurance Taxation	498
Phases of Taxation	499

Crazy Quilt Life 506
Principles of Deferred Tax Accounting 506
Accounting Principles Board Opinion No. 11 507
Timing Differences 507
Applying Opinion No. 11 508
Categories of Tax Situations 509
The Future-Category Assumption 511
Changes in Facts and Circumstances 511
Special Deductions 513
Operations Losses 515
Policyholders' Surplus 518
Deferred Tax Calculations 518
Grouping of Timing Differences 518
Gross Change and Net Change Methods 520
Crazy Quilt Life 524
Disclosure 524

27 BUSINESS COMBINATIONS 527
Poolings 527
Consistency and Opinion No. 16 527
*Poolings Involving Non-Life Insurance
Companies* 527
*Poolings Involving Life Insurance
Companies Only* 529
Purchases 530
Purchases of Life Insurance Companies 531
Crazy Quilt's Strategy for Acquisitions 531
The Purchase of McCabe Life 532
Purchase Valuations 534
Valuation of Policy Reserves 534
Determination of Acquisition Cost 536
Amortization of Acquisition Cost 541
Special Problems in Valuing Insurance in Force 545
*Implications of Not Assigning Part of the
Purchase Price to Insurance in Force* 547
Value of Agency Plant 548
Goodwill 551
Other Approaches 552
Inter-Company Relationships 552
Accounting for New Business 552
Inter-Company Profits 553
20-To-50 Percent Equity Investments 553
Reporting the Equity in Statutory Earnings 554
Cost in Excess of Book Value 554
Inconsistent Adjusted Accounts 554
Consolidation Policies 555
Stock Companies Controlled by Mutual
Companies 555
Wholly-Owned Subsidiaries 555
Partially-Owned Subsidiaries 555
Disclosure 556

28 CONVERSION MECHANICS 557
Administering a Conversion 557
Organization of the Conversion Effort 557
Conversion Timetable 557
Planning Meetings 557
Documentation 558
Reserve Models 558
A General Approach 559

Health Insurance Models 565
Subsidiaries 565
Recording Conversion Adjustments 565
Working Papers 565
Reconciliations 568

Part VI / *Perspectives on GAAP*

29 FINANCIAL STATEMENTS 571
Presentation Methods 571
Adjusted Primary Statements 571
Disclosure 571
Required Disclosures 572
Desirable Disclosures 572
Annual Reports 572
Description of the Conversion 572
Interim Statements 573
Provisions of APB Opinion No. 28 573
Acquisition Costs 574
Development Costs 574
Changes in Estimates 574
Benefit Reserves 574
Capital Gains and Losses 575
Income Taxes 575
SEC Reporting 575

30 A FEW AUDIT CONSIDERATIONS 576
Independent Audits 576
Established Companies 576
New Companies 576
Reasonableness Reviews 577
Participation of Actuaries 578
Audit Guide Provisions 578
Independent Actuaries 579
Coordination with Auditors 580
Actuaries' Letters 581
Citations of Actuary's Participation 582
Statements of the Actuarial Profession 582
Internal Audits 582
Internal Controls and Procedures 583
Data Integrity 583
Cost Effectiveness 583
Liaison 583
Other Possibilities 583
Boards and Audit Committees 583

31 USING GAAP 584
Evaluating GAAP Earnings 584
Knowledgeable Analysts 585
Coherent Principles 585
Disclosure 585
Some Approaches to Analysis 586
Line-of-Business Analysis 586
Return on Sales 588
Return on Equity 589
Rules of Thumb 589

Dollars-Per-Thousand Method	590
AIFA Method	591
Management Uses of GAAP	593
Analyzing Business in Force	593
Earnings by Source	593
Corporate Models	593
Profit Planning	593
Valuing Business in Force	593
Agency Evaluation	594
Incentive Compensation	594
Cost Accounting	594
Maximizing Returns from GAAP	594

32 WHITHER GAAP?	595

Appendixes

A. PRESENT VALUES AND RELATED CONCEPTS	599
Statutory Reserves	599
Net Level Premiums	600
Net Level Reserves	602
Modified Reserves	603
Cash Values	606
Adjusted Premiums	606
Terminal Cash Values	607
Gross Premiums	607
Deaths and Terminations	608
Other Assumptions	609
Projection of Cash Flow	609
Asset Shares	609
Level Annual Equivalents	609
Break-Even Premiums	610
Natural Reserves	611
Present Value of Book Profits	612

Interest on Reserve	612
Book Profits Discounted at Assumed Investment Earnings Rate	614
Book Profits Discounted at a Risk Rate	614
Value of Insurance In Force	617
Gross Premium Reserves	617
Comparing Actual and Assumed	618

B. TAXES ON INVESTMENT INCOME	620
Source Data for Illustrations	620
Company Taxed on T	620
Company Taxed on 1/2 (G+T)	620
Company Taxed on G	624
Nontaxable Investment Income	624
Interest on Statutory Reserve	624
Discounting Future Tax Payments	626

C. CRAZY QUILT LIFE	627
Individual Lines	627
Supplemental Benefits	645
Variable Annuities	646
Commercial Individual Health Insurance	646
Group Insurance and Annuities	646
Credit Insurance	646

D. MORTALITY FLUCTUATION RESERVES	647

E. ACTUARIES' RESPONSIBILITIES	650
Introduction	650
Clarifying Statement	650
Opinions	651
Actuarial Report	652
Statement of Actuarial Opinion	653
Other Actuarial Statements	653

Part I

Introduction

1

Background of the Financial Reporting Problem

San Juan is popularly regarded as one of the playgrounds of the Western World, particularly in the winter. The weather is balmy, the surf is gentle, and the women are tall, tan, and occasionally young and lovely, vaguely in the tradition of the girl from Ipanema. And in this idyllic setting, in December of 1972, while thousands of erstwhile observers of the insurance scene shivered apprehensively on the frozen tundras to the north, the Accounting Principles Board approved publication of *Audits of Stock Life Insurance Companies.*

But no one resented the APB's choice of a vacation spot for its December meeting. The APB was phasing out of existence after many difficult years of unstinting and (curmudgeons to the contrary) *successful* work on behalf of the business community, and the Board deserved pleasant surroundings in its twilight months. Further, after all the squabbling over the life insurance audit guide in recent years, it was somehow fitting and proper that the guide be given unction in a setting somewhat removed from the field of battle.

Wall Street was elated by the APB's vote of approval. Security analysts were quick to herald the dawn of a new day in the market for life insurance stocks. They generally felt that the market had not discounted the development in advance, and that resolution of the "earnings problem" would cause institutional resistance to fade and prices to rise phoenix-like from the ashes of a long bear market. (At the time of this writing, life stock prices had yet to resurrect.)

Security analysts tend to be enthusiastic by nature and training, and since the audit guide is oriented primarily to investors, their enthusiasm is understandable. But they were not alone. Few vigorous dissents to the guide as a whole could be heard from any

quarter. This may seem surprising in view of the fact that earlier versions of the guide stimulated often acrimonious debate. But the guide as finally published represents a remarkable set of compromises among various conflicting interests. Nobody was completely satisfied, but almost everybody had won a point and was unwilling to jeopardize it.

Adoption of the audit guide was seemingly simple and straightforward. But while the act of adoption was simple, the history that lay behind it was complex, turbulent, and fascinating. A knowledge of that history is important to a full understanding of the guide.

What follows is a brief history of statutory accounting, early attempts to "adjust" the earnings of life insurance companies, development of the life insurance audit guide, and the Ernst & Ernst life insurance accounting research project.

Statutory Accounting *

This book presupposes a basic knowledge of life insurance and statutory accounting practices. By "statutory accounting practices" is meant that body of accounting practices applicable to insurance companies which are prescribed or permitted under statutes and/or administrative guidelines of the various states. All accountants who have been associated with life insurance company financial statements

---

* Most of the material in this section is based upon two unpublished doctoral dissertations: Sterling Surrey's *The Development of the Convention Form of Life Insurance Statement* (University of Pennsylvania, 1949) and Robert H. Raymond's *Financial Statements of Life Insurance Companies* (Michigan State University, 1964).

know what is meant by "statutory accounting practices."

What is not so well known is the history of statutory accounting and some of the ways in which the philosophies underlying statutory accounting conflict with the philosophies underlying "generally accepted accounting principles".

An understanding of the traditions and philosophies underlying statutory accounting is fundamental to an appreciation of the fact that statutory accounting is here to stay. The indispensability of statutory accounting to the regulatory process is recognized in this book. All too often statutory accounting has been cavalierly dismissed as "inadequate". Such an attitude betrays a somewhat narrow point of view, since "inadequacy" is obviously being measured in terms of a special set of interests which statutory accounting was never designed to serve.

This is not to say, of course, that statutory accounting is an appropriate basis for preparing general-purpose financial statements. The term "general-purpose financial statements" is technically incorrect; both statutory financial statements and "adjusted" financial statements are specialized accounting statements in the sense that they are prepared for different purposes, and one purpose cannot be presumed to reign supreme. Nevertheless, in the context of this chapter, the term "general-purpose statements" is used to designate statements prepared in conformity with generally accepted accounting principles.

Brief History of the Convention Statement

For all practical purposes, life insurance company financial reporting began in 1828, when an act of the New York legislature required "all monied corporations" [1] to file annual reports with the state comptroller on a prescribed form (which was, in reality, simply a questionnaire). The form was not designed specifically for life insurance companies. In any case, only one insurance company (New York Life and Trust Company) reported to the comptroller through 1847, and that company adopted its own form of reporting, i.e., it did not follow the prescribed form.

In 1837 Massachusetts passed a law requiring all domestic insurers to file annual reports in a prescribed form. In 1848, New York adopted a form specifically designed for insurance companies and extended the reporting requirement to all domestic insurers, and in 1849 the New York comptroller, complaining (justly) about practices of some foreign insurers, sponsored

legislation to require out-of-state companies doing business in New York to file annual reports.

In 1851, a New York act prescribed the first reporting form designed specifically for life insurance companies. Various new forms were developed by New York and prescribed for life insurance financial reporting in the 1850s.

All of the forms used during the period 1828–1851 had certain peculiarities. They were not balance sheets, but were generally in the nature of questionnaires. Some of the forms attempted to develop a kind of balance sheet, but assets and liabilities did not balance (due primarily to the inclusion of insurance in force as a liability). Also, the nature of accrual accounting was not clearly understood. A kind of charge and discharge statement was required in some cases; the report reflected cash receipts and disbursements and was used to reconcile assets, but the assets would not reconcile when, for example, interest was accrued.

In 1859 Elizur Wright, the Massachusetts insurance commissioner, sponsored legislation requiring companies to report insurance reserves on the basis of net premium valuations and to disclose the assumptions used in such valuations.*

Wright was a remarkable individual and is often referred to as "the father of life insurance". He sponsored nonforfeiture legislation—nonforfeiture values were rarely provided prior to Wright's tenure—and compiled enormous tables of factors for reserve valuation purposes. He also maintained a registry book in which was listed every policy issued by Massachusetts companies and the reserve thereon so every policyholder could come to Wright's office and look up "his" reserve, upon which the nonforfeiture value was based. In Surrey's words, "Mr. Wright was an unusual insurance commissioner. He insisted that the rights of the policyholders superseded those of the insurance companies." [2]

The New York Insurance Department was created in 1859 and soon developed a new reporting form which replaced the "liability" for insurance in force with an account entitled "amount required to safely reinsure all outstanding risks." The concept of the re-

---

* One British company had furnished reports to Wright showing the present value of all future benefits less the present value of future gross premiums as liabilities; Wright objected on the basis that loadings should be reserved for future expenses and contingencies. When reserves were converted to a net premium basis, Wright found the company insolvent. But the company had filed the required report, and that was all the law required of foreign insurers at the time.

serve as an accounting requirement gained ground. In the early 1860s Wright and the New York commissioner began a series of meetings to develop identical reserve valuation standards. Wright felt the New York commissioner's proposals were too liberal; eventually a compromise was struck and written into New York law in 1869. Massachusetts failed to enact such legislation because "the Massachusetts Commissioner [apparently Wright's successor] did not use his influence." [3] Reserve valuation standards continued to vary by state.

In the 1860s various insurance commissioners (notably those in New York and Massachusetts) began to express concern over the "quality" of assets. And for good reason; by 1870 companies were reporting agents' balances equal to as much as 55 percent of total assets. In 1871 Massachusetts required that agents' balances, loans or advances to officers, stationery and similar items be non-admitted. Other states prescribed similar treatment of such items.

The failure of two New York companies in 1870 focused further attention on financial reporting. States continued to experiment with reporting forms and accounting practices. By 1871, all of the 14 states which had enacted insurance legislation required all companies doing business in a given state to file financial statements in that state. Most of the states had unique reporting requirements and unique valuation standards. Obviously this diversity of practice greatly inconvenienced insurance companies and hampered regulation.

For these and other reasons, a National Convention of Insurance Commissioners (which evolved into the National Association of Insurance Commissioners) was convened in 1871 to develop certain uniform regulatory standards. In 1875 a uniform "Convention" reporting blank was adopted for use in all states, and standards of asset and reserve valuation were established.

The Convention Statement adopted in 1875 remained basically unchanged until 1951. There were relatively minor revisions of the Convention Statement in 1895, 1914, 1925, and 1939. In 1895 a "gain and loss" exhibit was added, and the exhibit stimulated controversy for years. The gain and loss exhibit attempted to trace sources of gain or loss in terms of loading, mortality, interest, and surrenders; all such gains or losses were reckoned using reserve requirements as a starting point. In the 1906 meeting of the insurance commissioners, one commissioner stated that, in examining a life insurance company, an examiner "tried to make up a gain and loss exhibit, and he was only a million and a half dollars out of

balance." [4] Another speaker complained that "all companies estimate some items in the exhibit . . . some estimate what others calculate, while calculating what others estimate, and . . . excepting those who enter a balance unaccounted for, every company has an item which represents a forced balance." [5]

One main problem with the Convention Statement was the necessity to maintain ledger accounts on the cash basis. This posed no particular problem with respect to the balance sheet, since various worksheet entries could be made to bring the balance sheet accounts to an accrual basis. But the "income statement" was a cash-basis statement required to reconcile *ledger* assets (which were on a cash basis). Only by agonizing effort could an accrual-basis income statement be prepared. The 1939 Convention Statement added an exhibit very similar to today's analysis of operations by line of business; the exhibit was needed to reconcile surplus. The fact remains, however, that an income statement, as such, was of slight interest to the insurance commissioners; they were interested in measuring solvency and reviewing management's accountability in terms of cash received and disbursed.

In 1951 the Convention Statement was modified to the form in use today; revisions since 1951 have been minor. The 1951 revision appears to have been prompted by the joint efforts of the American Life Convention and the Life Insurance Association of America, whose objective was "to have a statement which is, as nearly as may be, in the form generally used by other corporations and as understandable to the public as the intricacies of our business permit." [6] The NAIC adopted many of the recommendations of the ALC and the LIAA, but not all of them. The 1951 revision resulted in a vastly improved reporting format, but the substance of the prior Convention Statement was unchanged. In terms of basic accounting practices, today's Convention Statement is the same as it was a century ago.

Objectives of Statutory Accounting

Today's Convention Statement is in substance the same as it was a century ago because its principal function has not changed. The Convention Statement is essentially a formula for the computation of "legal surplus"—assets minus liabilities and capital stock equals surplus, and surplus is, in Robert Raymond's words, a "first-line indicator of solvency." [7]

Again in Raymond's words,

Ultra-conservatism is built into the [balance sheet], apparently on the theory that if a company can show an excess of assets over liabilities and capital stock under the restrictions imposed, state officials may justifiably assume that the company has sufficient resources to carry out the provisions of every policy in force . . . However, it is not accurate to say that a liquidation postulate is followed.[8]

A liquidation concept is not followed because many companies would otherwise be rendered insolvent. For example, unrealized losses in fixed debt portfolios at the end of 1969 would have resulted in a great many insolvencies if bonds and mortgages were valued at market. Even statutory accounting, designed primarily to measure solvency, has been forced to compromise with some of the principles of going-concern accounting.

There is no point in belaboring the obvious. Insurance commissioners want overwhelming evidence that life insurance companies will be able to fulfill their obligations under contracts in force, and statutory accounting is a principal means by which such evidence is obtained.

There are other less obvious objectives of statutory accounting. One commissioner attending the 1896 Convention pleaded for the cost of acquiring new business to be reported in the anual statement. Said he: "I would wish to have the truth set forth in great red letters, so that every policyholder and everyone else in the United States could see the extravagant and outrageous commissions that insurance companies are paying for new business. I want to see the companies made ashamed of the record they are making on these questions." [9] Such concern with the public weal is no doubt partly responsible for the fact that acquisition costs are not deferred—even as non-admitted assets, a procedure which would not affect legal surplus, the "first-line indicator of solvency."

Statutory Accounting and "Generally Accepted" Accounting

If surplus is a first-line indicator of solvency, then statutory accounting is necessarily oriented toward valuation. Generally accepted accounting principles, on the other hand, appear to be oriented primarily toward allocation of revenues, costs, and expenses. The implications of these conflicting orientations are profound. In one case, the income statement (or the income and surplus statements combined) is a repository for adjustments arising in the balance sheet valuation process. In the other case, the balance sheet is a repository for adjustments arising in the process of allocating revenues, costs, and expenses to accounting periods. This is, of course, a vast over-simplification, but the important thing is to recognize the differing accounting consequences of the two points of view.

Given the concept that statutory accounting must be preserved, then a different basis of accounting must be superimposed, as it were, on statutory accounting if general-purpose financial statements are to be prepared. This means that the financial statements cannot articulate very well; profits computed on one basis are available for distribution only to the extent that they have been computed on another basis. This is the price that must be paid when statutory financial statements are adjusted.

It should be recognized, however, that such a situation is not unique. There is, of course, precedence for this in property and liability insurance accounting. Also, companies owning subsidiaries in foreign countries must frequently allocate some portion of profits to surplus reserves which under the laws of the given foreign country are unavailable for distribution. Such restrictions on distribution of surplus may be disclosed, but they have no effect on earnings determinations. In point of fact, earning power need bear no relationship to surplus currently distributable. While it would be intellectually satisfying to know that life insurance earnings flow unfettered into surplus and are immediately available for distribution, this condition is not a prerequisite to presenting an income statement prepared on a different basis than that which underlies the computation of distributable surplus.

Pressures for "Adjusted Earnings"

Many statutory accounting practices have long been regarded as being at variance with generally accepted accounting principles. Thus independent accountants have historically rendered qualified opinions on financial statements of stock life insurance companies.

Yet until recently there has been no concert of opinion on what to do about the variances. This created an impossible situation for stock life insurance companies: they were unable to obtain unqualified opinions on the financial statements they published and were unable to take any action to permit the rendering of an unqualified opinion.

The fact that accountants would not, or could not, render unqualified opinions on life insurance company financial statements was not of great moment to the life insurance industry until the 1950s. During that period life insurance stocks began to be actively traded, and interest of investors in life insurance company financial statements grew apace. New companies were formed in record numbers. Because a "generally accepted" measure of a company's progress was not available, security analysts developed certain methods of approximating earnings which might be reported if generally accepted accounting principles were applied to life insurance company financial statements. Unfortunately these methods did not take quality into account and typically reported as current net income (unreduced for deferred taxes) the present value of future profits on new business, which profits, as often as not, never materialized.

The inevitable happened. Disenchantment set in and the market for life stocks plummeted in the mid-1960s. It has never really recovered. The market became too sophisticated to invest in life insurance stocks on the basis of faith and security analysts' often optimistic estimates of "adjusted earnings".

Property and Liability Precedents

Since the 1930s A. M. Best Company has reported "adjusted earnings" of property and liability insurance companies in various reports. Best's recognized that property and liability companies are required to charge off acquisition costs while maintaining full unearned premium reserves; thus arose the concept of the equity in the unearned premium reserve.

In 1957 the AICPA Committee on Insurance Accounting and Auditing began working on an audit guide for property and liability insurance companies and proposed, among other things, that acquisition costs be deferred and charged to expense only as related premium income is earned. It has been argued that the Committee did not communicate adequately with insurance industry representatives in preparing the audit guide. In any event, certain top-level individuals from industry disagreed strongly with the Committee's views, and the audit guide was nine years in preparation. In 1966 the audit guide, which still propounded the view that acquisition costs should be deferred, was published in spite of continued dissent by certain industry representatives. The audit guide has served as a guide to practice by CPAs since its publication.

Security Analysts

Security analysts, who recognized that some of the same limitations applicable to statutory property and liability insurance accounting applied also to statutory life insurance accounting, quickly developed methods of "adjusting" life insurance company financial statements. One of the pioneers in this effort was Shelby Cullom Davis, who is reputed to have developed the "dollars per thousand" method. The dollars per thousand method is so called because it involves adding to statutory earnings an estimate, expressed as so many dollars per thousand of the increase in insurance in force, of the present value of future profits of such increase.

Adjusted earnings as computed by security analysts are generally regarded as contributing significantly to the rise of life stocks—and the resulting welter of new companies—in the 1950s and early 1960s. But adjusted earnings reported by the analysts were not uniform. Different analysts had different ideas as to what the increase in new business was worth. Other analysts, sensing that the dollars per thousand method was perhaps less than perfect, developed new methods only to have something different to sell. In any case, there were over 30 different approaches to adjusting earnings in 1964, which could, of course, result in over 30 different earnings figures for any given company.

In 1965 the New York Association of Insurance and Financial Analysts appointed a committee to study the problem and, hopefully, to develop a uniform method of adjusting earnings which could be used by all analysts. In 1969 the Association published the results of the Committee's four years of work. The method proposed in the report involved, among other things, separate adjustments for acquisition costs and reserve interest, based upon information contained in the Convention Statement. A. M. Best Company, which was represented on the Committee, adopted the method for use in its Insurance Securities Research Service reports and offered to provide companies with an independent calculation of adjusted earnings according to the Association method for use as supplementary data in annual reports.

The AICPA rejected the AIFA method as a basis for formal financial reporting. However, many companies began reporting adjusted earnings, generally calculated by Best's, as supplementary data. The AIFA method came to be widely used by security analysts.

The AIFA method of adjusting earnings was a vast improvement over the welter of competing adjustment methods which were found in practice before the AIFA method was available. And it may fairly be said that the AIFA's work stimulated the AICPA and others to accelerate their efforts to resolve the industry's financial reporting problems.

The Stock Market

While security analysts were striving mightily to develop a method of expressing life insurance earnings in a manner which would permit reasonable comparability with earnings reported by other industries, the stock market was responding with a mighty yawn. Best's Stock Index shows that the market index for life insurance stocks peaked at 460 (1941–43 = 10) in 1964, fell to 240 in 1966, and was at the 330 level in June 1973. Relative to the general indexes, life insurance stocks haven't done well at all.

Opinion differs as to why this is so. But there is general agreement that the "earnings dilemma"—that is, uncertainty over how to report earnings and skepticism toward the various formula methods—has had something to do with the market's dismal performance.

Thus pressures grew to develop a method of adjusting life insurance company earnings that would be acceptable to independent accountants and would therefore stand a reasonable chance of acceptance by the financial community. The "financial community", so far as life insurance stocks are concerned, is dominated by institutional investors, who tend to be quite sophisticated in their methods of investment analysis and who, among other things, demand reliable earnings figures.

Holding Companies and Diversification

In the late 1960s the insurance holding company phenomenon was born. Insurers diversified into non-insurance activities (for various reasons which are beyond the scope of this book) and the depressed prices of life stocks made life insurance companies attractive to acquisition-minded noninsurance corporations. Accountants were faced with a new problem: how to combine "generally-accepted" financial statements of noninsurance companies with the statutory financial statements of insurance companies. They were often combined, but the financial statements were frequently accompanied by accountants' opinions that can only be called torturous. The desire to provide a consistent framework for reporting on such diversified enterprises added to the pressures to develop generally accepted accounting principles for stock life insurance companies.

Securities and Exchange Commission

In 1964 the Securities and Exchange Commission published Article 7A of Regulation S–X. Article 7A, applicable to life insurance companies, called basically for statutory-basis statements in filings with the Commission.

Also in 1964 the Commission sought to extend its jurisdiction over securities traded in the over-the-counter market. Substantially all life insurance company shares were traded over the counter at that time, and the life insurance industry mounted a concerted effort to defeat the Commission's proposals. Although the Commission did not propose to modify basic statutory accounting practices, numerous industry representatives raised charges that the Commission was attempting to do so. The Commission's proposals to extend its jurisdiction over insurance securities were defeated following the 1964 Hearings to Amend the Securities Acts. New responsibilities in the area of investor protection were assigned to state insurance commissioners, with the caveat that if any state failed to discharge its responsibilities adequately, the Commission would assume them.

Notwithstanding this setback for the SEC, many life insurance companies had registered stock and many continued to do so. Thus many life insurance companies came under the Commission's jurisdiction. Regulation S–X required statutory-basis statements, but the Commission recognized that life insurance accounting was not regarded as "generally accepted" by all accountants and permitted CPAs to qualify their opinions on life insurance company financial statements.

In 1968 the Wheat Report, *Disclosures to Investors,* was published and, among other things, called for an early resolution of the life insurance company adjusted earnings problem. While recognizing that the AICPA was working on the problem (and apparently committed to waiting for the AICPA to act), the Commission began to permit companies to report adjusted earnings, evaluating and passing upon such proposals on a case-by-case basis. In 1968 a large life insurance holding company (whose shares are traded on the New York Stock Exchange) deferred acquisition costs in financial statements filed with the Commission. In 1969 additional life insurance companies filing financial statements with the Commission made adjustments for acquisition costs, and another large life insurance holding company (whose shares are also traded on the New York Stock Exchange) adjusted reserves for interest and mortality. In 1970 still more life insurance companies filed adjusted statements with the Commission, pursuant to a 1970 exposure draft of the life insurance audit guide (the 1970 draft is discussed later in this chapter). The Commission called a temporary halt to the filing of adjusted statements in 1971, but in 1972 the Commission withdrew its ban, and several more companies filed adjusted statements with the Commission.

In early 1974 a revision of Article 7A was released by the Commission. The revision provides that "financial statements filed after June 30, 1974 . . . shall be prepared in accordance with generally accepted accounting principles."

New York Stock Exchange

The New York Stock Exchange has always demanded that financial statements be prepared on the basis of generally accepted accounting principles. The Exchange has taken a dim view toward qualifications as to accounting principles in accountants' opinions on financial statements of life insurance holding companies whose shares are listed. Such companies, while relatively few in number, are large and influential. While the Exchange did grant some temporary exemptions from its normal requirements, there's little question that the Exchange applied a good deal of pressure on the listed companies to prepare their financial statements in such a manner as to obtain unqualified opinions from their independent accountants.

Development of the Audit Guide *

In 1966 the AICPA Committee on Insurance Accounting and Auditing began work on the life insurance audit guide. Thus began an odyssey of Homeric proportions. Only in 1973 did the AICPA Committee's difficult journey come to an end with publication of *Audits of Stock Life Insurance Companies.*

An "audit guide" is seemingly innocuous. All it tries to do is apply accounting principles and auditing standards to a specialized industry, primarily for the guidance of independent accountants.** In other

words, an audit guide is simply designed to help the auditor formulate his opinion on the financial statements of a specialized company.

Therein lies the rub. Most specialized companies (including stock life insurance companies) whose shares are publicly traded engage independent accountants who render opinions on their financial statements. To the extent that a specialized company wishes to have an unqualified opinion on its financial statements, it must prepare the statements on the basis of the guidelines set forth in the applicable audit guide. There are numerous forces at work to induce specialized companies to seek unqualified opinions. The financial community views unqualified opinions favorably.

Companies whose financial statements are not accompanied by unqualified opinions are frequently at a competitive disadvantage in the stock market. The New York Stock Exchange generally requires unqualified opinions on the financial statements of listed companies. The Securities and Exchange Commission, besides preferring unqualified opinions on the financial statements of companies whose shares are registered with the Commission, promulgates accounting principles required to be followed by registrants, and such principles are heavily influenced by pronouncements of the accounting profession.

Of some 200 stock life insurance companies and life insurance company complexes whose shares are publicly traded, the financial statements of approximately 80 percent are audited. The shares of approximately 10 percent are traded on the New York Stock Exchange.[10] A majority of these companies is subject to the jurisdiction of the Securities and Exchange Commission. Clearly, then, the independent accountant's opinion has considerable significance to the stock company segment of the life insurance industry. Because the independent accountant's opinion is heavily influenced by the life insurance audit guide, stock life insurance companies have an intense interest in what the guide contains.

The 1970 Exposure Draft

In December 1970 the AICPA Committee released an exposure draft of the proposed life insurance audit

---

*This section is adapted, with permission, from an article by Robert L. Posnak entitled "Perspectives on Life Insurance Financial Reporting" contained in Vol. XL, No. 1 (March 1973) of *The Journal of Risk and Insurance.*

** Audit guides have been prepared for a sizeable number of specialized industries and several more are in progress. Recent audit guides have been introduced by the comment that "This audit guide is published for the guidance of members

of the [American Institute of Certified Public Accountants] in examining and reporting on financial statements" of a company that falls within the specialized industry. The comment is made also that members of the Institute "may be called upon to justify departures" from the recommended practices.

guide which, among other things, propounded use of the "natural reserve" method of accounting by life insurance companies. The natural reserve method described in the exposure draft essentially involves the deferral and amortization of acquisition costs and recalculation of policy reserves based on assumptions inherent in the gross premiums.

This approach was not developed by the accounting profession. The concept was first suggested by Gary Corbett, FSA, Vice President and Actuary of SAFECO Life Insurance Company, in a paper circulated privately in December 1969 and January 1970 to actuaries and accountants. The approach was further developed by the Joint Committee on Financial Reporting Principles of the American Life Convention and the Life Insurance Association of America, which was established in 1967 to bring the industry's point of view to bear in the preparation of the audit guide. Finally, a research paper prepared in March 1970 (followed by a book in August 1970) by Ernst & Ernst argued for the natural reserve approach with, however, some significant constraints on the definition of acquisition costs and the choice of reserve assumptions.

The natural reserve approach was adopted in a matter of months. There was little opportunity for reflection on the method. The 1970 exposure draft was released and some 36 companies adopted the natural reserve method or some variation thereof in their 1970 annual reports,[11] on the assumption that the final version of the audit guide would correspond with the exposure draft.

The period of exposure lasted until May 1971. Over 800 pages of comments were received, most of which were favorable. The most noteworthy response was made by the Joint Actuarial Committee on Financial Reporting, which had been hastily constituted late in 1970 by the Society of Actuaries, the American Academy of Actuaries, the Conference of Actuaries in Public Practice, and the Canadian Institute of Actuaries.

In what now ranks as a landmark contribution to actuarial literature, the Joint Actuarial Committee propounded the "release-from-risk" theory of reserving, which was devised by Richard Horn, FSA, Vice President and Actuary of Security Life and Accident Company. Natural reserves were seen to be a special case of a family of reserves associated with the release-from-risk system, which is basically defined as a system of reserves which results in recognizing profits in proportion to the release from risk of adverse deviation from actuarial assumptions as to mortality, interest, expense, and withdrawal.*

The Joint Actuarial Committee asked that a range of reserve methods be permitted, including the natural reserve method. If only one method were permitted, the Joint Actuarial Committee indicated a preference for the percentage-of-completion method, which is generally regarded as the most conservative application of release-from-risk theory.[12]

In the months following the close of the exposure period the AICPA Committee deliberated at length on the comments received, particularly the comments by the Joint Actuarial Committee, which continued to work with the AICPA Committee. The Joint ALC-LIAA Committee also continued to cooperate with the AICPA Committee. But it became apparent that the exposure draft was not likely to be modified significantly; it was expected that the guide would be released in time for many more companies to implement its provisions in 1971. At this point the applicability of the exposure draft to mutual companies was not clear.

Meantime, a number of parties at interest had been studying the exposure draft and had concluded that the guidelines set forth in the draft were insufficient to prevent abuse. Further, several companies had apparently interpreted the exposure draft somewhat liberally in preparing their 1970 financial statements. In an extraordinary memorandum to the Securities and Exchange Commission in November 1971, executives of four life insurance companies (two stock and two mutual) argued that the exposure draft invited abusive practices and that companies should be prohibited from implementing it. At the same time, a major accounting firm repudiated the exposure draft and suggested, in its stead, a percentage-of-completion method of its own devising. The SEC then advised the industry that companies subject to its jurisdiction that had not already published adjusted statements would be prohibited from doing so until the audit guide was finalized. (The SEC lifted its ban in 1972.)

Also in late 1971 and early 1972, a series of articles highly critical of the exposure draft appeared in the insurance press. Some of the articles were less than carefully reasoned, but they further stirred controversy by the very fact that they had been published.

* The release-from-risk concept is explored in greater detail in Chapters 4 and 6.

The Revised Audit Guide

Late 1971 and early 1972 was an emotional period for the AICPA Committee, but the turmoil proved to be worthwhile. The revised audit guide, issued early in 1973, incorporates many new safeguards against abuse. The Joint ALC-LIAA Committee contributed importantly to the revision. Several of the constraints suggested in the Ernst & Ernst book were written into the revision, together with some sophisticated actuarial concepts of risk and release-from-risk. In essence, the revision strikes a compromise between the natural reserve method propounded in the first exposure draft and the percentage-of-completion method proposed by the Joint Actuarial Committee.*

Not everyone is satisfied with the compromise. Some would still prefer that a pure percentage-of-completion approach be used. Others prefer the original natural reserve approach. For two very important reasons, however, the compromise is likely to endure. First, there is no technical imperative calling for either of the approaches; both approaches have theoretical support and deserve equal recognition. Second, industry is divided on the issue; a compromise is necessary to achieve general acceptance. In large measure, general acceptance by the financial community is a prerequisite for accounting principles to become "generally accepted".

The audit guide applies only to stock companies. Mutual companies are not subject to the provisions of the guide because of disagreements over the nature and purpose of mutual company financial statements and the applicability of generally accepted accounting principles to such statements. (The question of mutual company accounting and its relationship to generally accepted accounting principles is being dealt with by an AICPA task force at the time of this writing.)

The Ernst & Ernst Research Project

In the summer of 1968 Ernst & Ernst's Insurance Industry Committee proposed that a member or members of Ernst & Ernst's professional staff be assigned to study, in depth, the nature and effects of life insurance company financial reporting practices and the relationship of such practices to generally accepted accounting principles. In September 1968 Richard T. Baker, Ernst & Ernst's Managing Partner, authorized Robert L. Posnak to undertake the research project commencing in November 1968.

---

* The method propounded in the audit guide is sometimes referred to as the "intermediate release-from-risk" approach.

Initially it was thought that one year would be sufficient to carry out the project. As the complexity—both technical and political—of the subject became apparent, the scope of the project was gradually expanded. The project took five years. This book is a report on the findings and conclusion of the research.

Problem

The general subject matter of the project, as stated in 1968, was as follows:

The problem giving rise to this research project is the fact that the application of generally accepted accounting principles to life insurance companies has not definitively been determined. Underlying this general problem is the problem that the nature and practices of the life insurance business are not adequately understood from the accounting point of view.

Objectives

The initial objectives of the project were (1) to develop and portray an insight into life insurance company operations from an accounting viewpoint, (2) to determine methods for reporting on financial position and results of operations, and (3) to relate the preceding to generally accepted accounting principles.

In addition, in recognition of the many conflicting points of view on the subject—among actuaries, accountants, regulatory officials, life insurance management, and others—another initial objective of the project was to attempt to reconcile such conflicting points of view.

The final initial objective of the project was to contribute to the work of the AICPA Committee on Insurance Accounting and Auditing.

As time passed, three other objectives were adopted —developing materials and techniques for training the staff of Ernst & Ernst in the subject matter of the project, assisting clients in resolving problems relating to conversions to generally accepted accounting principles, and developing methods of implementing the life insurance audit guide.

General Research Methods

The basic research methods used in carrying out the project included review and analysis of relevant published and unpublished materials, extensive interviews and correspondence with informed parties at interest, issuance for comment of various memoranda on significant issues, and creation of a large and complex model office for the purpose of analyzing various approaches to life insurance accounting in a reasonably credible environment.

Findings, Conclusions, and Recommendations

It is not feasible to summarize the findings, conclusions, and recommendations of the research in a paragraph or two.

Perhaps the overall conclusion of the project can be expressed as follows: The life insurance audit guide is a worthy and imperfect document. Its worthiness should be appreciated and its imperfections should be clearly understood. The guide deserves acceptance by the financial community, but acceptance should be accompanied by full knowledge of the guide's limitations.

Organization of the Book

Part I of this book provides some background on the development of the life insurance audit guide and on some of the basic theoretical considerations underlying the guide.

Part II deals with accounting for life insurance benefits, and Part III deals with accounting for acquisition and other costs. Parts II and III are heavily oriented to individual ordinary insurance, which provides a controlled frame of reference for the discussion. Part IV is devoted to other lines of business.

Part V deals with some of the knottier special problems related to implementation of the audit guide.

Part VI offers some suggestions on working with the audit guide to independent accountants, actuaries, security analysts, and general management.

Several appendixes have been added to provide material of interest which is beyond the scope of any of the individual chapters.

2

Life Insurance Operations

Life insurance operations are so complex and so varied that it is difficult to generalize about them. The diversity of products, territories, goals, histories, capabilities, and personalities is such that almost every company is somewhat unique in its approaches to the various functions which comprise life insurance "operations".

But it is necessary to understand life insurance operations to deal successfully with life insurance accounting. This is particularly true with respect to generally accepted accounting principles. Statutory accounting is governed by a body of laws, rules, forms, and customs that together provide a kind of instruction list for preparation of a set of statutory statements. There is no such instruction list for preparation of financial statements that conform with generally accepted accounting principles. Thus, for example, it is not sufficient merely to follow the rule of charging off operating costs as incurred; it is necessary to analyze the source and nature of such costs to determine how they should be accounted for; and to do this it is necessary to understand the operations in respect of which the costs are incurred.

While it may not be feasible to generalize about life insurance operations, perhaps a brief examination of the operations of a hypothetical company would be useful.

Crazy Quilt Life

Throughout the remainder of this book, frequent reference is made to "Crazy Quilt Life", a model office developed in connection with the Ernst & Ernst Life Insurance Accounting Research Project to test various approaches to life insurance accounting in a reasonably credible environment.

Crazy Quilt Life is an assembly of information from many sources—computerized production and in-force models created especially for purposes of the research project, simulations of operations of real companies, manually-prepared models based on subjective choices of matters thought to be of interest, etc. Further, Crazy Quilt is set up in such a way as to be almost anything that one wants it to be. For example, the model is comprised of hundreds of sub-models, constructed in such a way that a single line of business, or indeed a single plan-year-age combination or a single year of issue, can be regarded as a company unto itself. The methods employed to construct Crazy Quilt Life are described in some detail in Appendix C.

Thus, while it has its moments of coherence, Crazy Quilt is essentially a patchwork of ideas and testing situations. The model was dubbed "Crazy Quilt" because Webster's definition of the term seemed appropriate:

CRAZY QUILT. n. 1: a patchwork quilt made without a design or pattern. 2: an incoherently pieced-together entity.[1]

Historical Summary

Crazy Quilt Life was incorporated in the State of Domicile on July 1, 1941 with paid-in capital of $10 million and began doing business on that date, offering ordinary and industrial policies in 10 states. Ordinary operations were conducted on the general agency plan.

Table 2–1.

SUMMARY OF GROWTH OF CRAZY QUILT LIFE,
1941–1971 (STATUTORY BASIS)

| | | 000 | | | 000,000 | |
| | Gain | | | Total | Ordinary and Industrial Life Insurance | |
Year	From Operations	Assets	Capital And Surplus	Premiums and Considerations	Written	In Force
1941	$ (1,290)	$ 9,154	$ 8,475	$ 971	$ 33	$ 30
1945	(806)	14,673	5,012	7,203	88	212
1950	528	46,346	5,553	17,701	129	533
1955	858	117,604	5,953	29,575	148	885
1960	2,949	207,700	15,297	37,401	178	1,137
1965	2,391	317,799	36,758	61,760	438	1,917
1966	1,780	337,875	35,733	69,959	508	2,207
1967	2,371	370,129	36,828	79,509	581	2,540
1968	(30)	411,122	44,238	88,783	649	2,904
1969	1,067	455,245	30,148	98,539	724	3,306
1970	11,189	504,482	37,599	110,657	810	3,758
1971	10,244	565,555	43,165	122,894	887	4,249

As time passed Crazy Quilt began selling new lines of business—individual annuities in 1952, group in 1956, individual health in 1960, credit in 1968, and variable annuities in 1968. At December 31, 1971, management was investigating variable life. The Company also had expanded into 49 states by 1971, all but New York. Further, the Company gradually moved toward the branch office plan of operation. After 1950, all new sales offices were branch offices, with the result that a majority (55 percent) of the business produced in 1971 was produced by branch offices.

Growth in new business volume was erratic but over the 31 years from 1941 to 1971 averaged 9 percent. At December 31, 1971, Crazy Quilt Life had $4.2 billion of ordinary and industrial insurance in force and assets of $566 million. In 1971 ordinary and industrial new business written was $887 million, total premium income was $123 million, and gain from operations was $10 million. Growth of the Company is summarized in Table 2–1.

Crazy Quilt has resisted all temptations to diversify, form a holding company, or list its stock on the New York Stock Exchange. Its only subsidiaries as of December 31, 1971 were a broker-dealer, set up in 1968 in connection with establishing a separate account for variable annuities, and a life insurance subsidiary, McCabe Life Insurance Company, acquired on January 1, 1971, for $5 million in cash and $12 million in Crazy Quilt stock.

The State of Domicile, located approximately midway between New York and California, has adopted many of the laws and practices of those two states.

Capital and Surplus

Crazy Quilt's capital and surplus accounts are summarized in Table 2–2. In recent years unassigned surplus has been severely depleted by two events: a strengthening of reserves in the amount of $10 million in 1969, and a charge to surplus of $14 million in 1971 representing the excess of the cost of McCabe Life Insurance Company over the statutory net worth of McCabe.

Crazy Quilt's stock is traded over-the-counter. The stock has always been relatively widely held. The price of the stock has ebbed and flowed with the market for life insurance stocks in general.

Organization

Crazy Quilt Life's organization chart as of December 31, 1971 is shown in Table 2–3. It will be observed that Crazy Quilt's organization is a little ponderous. That's mainly because layers of administrators have been tacked on as the need arose. Because of increasing size and the addition of new lines of business, the need arose fairly frequently.

At December 31, 1971, Crazy Quilt's management was considering a revision of its organizational structure which would involve an "office of the president" and a realignment of executive responsibility. The office of the president would, in effect, consist of a three-man team whose joint responsibilities would

Table 2–2.

SUMMARY OF STATUTORY CAPITAL AND SURPLUS ACCOUNTS
OF CRAZY QUILT LIFE, 1941–1971 (000 Omitted)

Year	Transaction	Common Stock Number of Shares	Common Stock Amount	Paid-In Surplus	Unassigned Surplus
1941	Common stock ($2.50 par value) issued for cash at $10 a share	1,000	$ 2,500	$ 7,500	
1960	Split 5 for 1 (to $.50 par value)	4,000			
1964	Common stock ($.50 par value) issued for cash at $47.00 a share	213	106	9,894	
1966	Change par value to $2.50 a share		10,426	(10,426)	
1968	Common stock ($2.50 par value) issued for cash at $70.00 a share	143	357	9,643	
1969	Change par value to $5.00 a share		13,390	(13,390)	
1971	Common stock ($5.00 par value) issued in connection with acquisition of McCabe Life Insurance Company at $91.00 a share	133	667	11,478	
	1% stock dividend (market, $2,989,000)	55	275		$ (275)
1941 to 1971	Cumulative net gain from operations				55,938
	Cumulative realized capital gains, net of taxes				5,931
	Cumulative unrealized capital gains				188
	Non-admitted assets				(5,510)
	Mandatory securities valuation reserve				(13,966)
	Reserve strengthening				(10,451)
	Excess of cost over book value of purchased subsidiary				(13,902)
	Unauthorized reinsurance				(14)
	Cumulative cash dividends to stockholders				(17,200)
	Miscellaneous				6
		5,544	$27,721	$14,699	$ 745

be to establish policy, devise broad strategies for the future, establish profit plans, and monitor overall progress in relation to such profit plans. Responsibility for day-to-day operations would be centered in three senior executive vice presidents—insurance services, investments, and administrative controls. It was recognized that such a plan was ambitious for a company with assets of only $566 million, but Crazy Quilt wanted to begin providing for a future that looked quite promising.

Nevertheless, the organization depicted in Table 2–3 is the organization Crazy Quilt had to work with in 1971, and that organization is the basis of the discussions which follow.

Top Management

Based on the number of boxes at the top of the organization chart, there seems to be plenty of room at the top at Crazy Quilt.

The Board of Directors has four standing committees. The Finance Committee approves all investment transactions, establishes investment policy, and oversees relationships with the investment community. The Executive Committee passes upon all other policy matters except those having to do with auditing, personnel, and compensation. The Audit Committee, comprised entirely of outside directors, establishes policies with regard to internal auditing and internal

Table 2–3.

CRAZY QUILT LIFE ORGANIZATION CHART

Directors	20
Home Office Employees	820
Regional Claim Office Employees	52
Field Clerical Employees	107
General Agents	31
Branch Managers	42
District Supervisors	12
Other Field Managers	38
Agents	970
Combination Agents	101
Group Field Representatives	17
Brokers	4,215

control, and hears reports from the general auditor, independent accountants, and state insurance examiners. The Personnel Committee sets general personnel and compensation policies, approves compensation to executives of vice-presidential rank or higher, proposes incentive compensation plans for executives, and monitors Crazy Quilt's progress in minority hiring.

Some of the policies "established" by the various committees must be reviewed and approved by the full Board, but that is usually routine.

The Chairman of the Board, which in Crazy Quilt's case is a full-time job, deals mainly with broad policy matters, long-range planning, relations with the investment community, social responsibility, and, of course, he monitors the performance of the President and the Company as a whole. Because of the consumerist movements of recent years, Crazy Quilt's concern about financial public relations, and the increasingly legalistic business environment, both the Vice President for Public Relations and the General Counsel report directly to the Chairman. The General Auditor reports administratively to the Chairman but renders his audit reports directly to the Audit Committee, which alone has the power to discharge him. The Chairman's background is finance.

The President is kind of a super executive vice president, having responsibility for all day-to-day operations. Five Executive Vice Presidents report to him, as does the President of McCabe Life, a subsidiary. Because of Crazy Quilt's traditional concern for the welfare of employees, the Vice President for Personnel reports directly to the President. The Vice President for Planning also reports to the President, for two reasons: the President is heavily dependent on Crazy Quilt's profit plans, which are drawn up and administered largely by that vice president; and the President consults frequently with the Chairman on long-range planning. Partly because his background is in sales and marketing, the President spends a great deal of his time in the marketing area.

Marketing

Responsibility for Crazy Quilt Life's marketing operations is divided between two executive vice presidents. Marketing of group life, health, and pension business and credit life and health business are the responsibility of the Vice President of Group Sales and Service, who reports to the Exective Vice President for Group Operations. Everything else— ordinary, industrial, individual annuities, variable

annuities, and individual health—is the responsibility of the Executive Vice President for Marketing, to whom two Senior Vice Presidents—one for Ordinary Agencies and one for Combination Agencies—are responsible. Two staff executives, the Vice President for Advertising and Promotion and the Vice President for Market Research, also report to the Executive Vice President for Marketing.

Ordinary Agencies

Crazy Quilt operates on both the general agency and branch office plans and has, in addition, numerous brokerage arrangements, primarily with agents of mutual companies.

The proportion of business written by branch offices has steadily increased, from zero in 1941 to 55 percent in 1971. Initially Crazy Quilt found it expedient to recruit experienced general agents. Then, using general agency business as a base, the Company began building a branch office operation which it was felt would give management greater control over marketing operations.

In 1941 general agents were essentially independent businessmen whom the Company compensated largely by commissions based on production. As time passed the general agents became increasingly dependent; the relationship between the Company and the general agents changed. Crazy Quilt began paying certain office expenses, providing recruiting and training allowances, and furnishing pension benefits to agents. The distinction between general agencies and branch offices began to blur, and by 1971 there were few substantive differences between the two.

Crazy Quilt's general agents are paid overrides on all business produced by sub-agents. Personal-producing general agents are paid normal selling commissions but no overrides on their own business. Production in excess of a defined quota is rewarded by a production bonus; favorable persistency is rewarded by a persistency bonus. Most overrides on general agency business are vested; the pattern varies with respect to vesting of sub-agents' commissions. Crazy Quilt pays sub-agents directly, for the most part.

Branch offices are normally managed by salaried branch managers, assisted, in the case of larger branches, by one or more assistant managers. Managers perform many of the functions of a general agent. However, none of the branch managers produces business personally. Branch managers also receive production and persistency bonuses, generally in the form of commissions. Commissions to agents on branch office business are usually not vested until the agent has produced persistent business at an acceptable level for five years. Crazy Quilt owns a few branch office buildings and leases space for the others.

Brokers are actively recruited. Most brokerage business comes from mutual company agents who need a facility for placing nonparticipating business when a nonparticipating product is demanded by a prospect. Brokers are paid commissions that are roughly equivalent to direct commissions plus overrides. Commissions on brokerage business are usually vested.

Crazy Quilt finances its agents by various means. Commissions are often annualized; or outright advances to agents are made; or agents are given a minimum salary until their production results in sufficient commission income for the agent to get along.

Crazy Quilt has observed the tendency in the industry in recent years to provide agents with additional sources of income, such as mutual funds and property-liability business. Crazy Quilt has not followed that approach. The Company believes its agents are not able to absorb the additional technical background required to sell such products. The Company prefers instead to emphasize basic life and health insurance products and promote a mastery of those products among its agents. In effect, Crazy Quilt is fearful that the introduction of additional products would dilute the efforts of agents and render them less productive over-all. In any event, the average income of Crazy Quilt's agents is quite high by industry standards, as a result of which it is not considered critical that they be given additional sources of income.

Crazy Quilt's home office marketing organization is fairly typical. Agency administration functions— contracts, financing, etc.—are performed by an "agency secretary". Separate offices within the agency division deal with new agency development (for example, determining where to locate new branch offices), recruiting and training, and brokerage sales. Because of their unique characteristics, health insurance sales and variable annuity sales are also administered by separate offices. Crazy Quilt has a number of "field superintendents" scattered throughout the nation whose responsibilities include liaison between agents and the home office, regional sales meetings, regional training programs, etc. Finally, a field office evaluation unit constantly monitors the quality of business produced by each general agency and branch office. The field office evaluation unit is in the nature of a special "controllership" function within the agency division.

Marketing operations are supported by an advertising and promotion function, which includes advertising for agents as well as general product advertising. In addition, market research is performed by a separate office. A special conservation unit also reports to the Vice President for Market Research.

Combination Agencies

Crazy Quilt has long sold insurance by the debit system in certain Southern states. In 1941 most of the business was weekly premium. By 1971 combination agents were selling weekly premium debit business, monthly premium debit business, and—whenever possible—regular ordinary products for which premiums are billed by the home office.

All combination agencies are branch offices managed by salaried district managers, which are comparable to ordinary branch managers. Agents are compensated by a complicated system of advances, salaries, and commissions. They are compensated for production by means of paying them a multiple of the weekly increase in their debits. They are compensated for collection services by means of a straight percentage of premiums collected. And their weekly income is subject to a floor. All of the agents' earnings are channeled into a "sales core", which is essentially a memorandum account; the amount in the "core" is paid out over time. The practical effect of this technique is to smooth agents' earnings. The Company records expense only as earnings are paid out to agents.

In most respects the home office organization is the same as the ordinary organization. However, because of the significant amounts of cash collected by agents and flowing through district offices, and because of the administrative complications arising from a debit system, special field accounting and field service units are employed to train field clerical personnel, audit debits, monitor cash transfers, etc. The agency auditing function is designed to maintain continuous control over all debits and related cash receipts. The Company's General Auditor also performs independent audits of selected district offices.

Products

Products marketed by Crazy Quilt Life's ordinary agencies currently or in the past include participating whole life, nonparticipating whole life, limited-payment life, endowments, decreasing term, renewable term, term riders, waiver of premium, and accidental

Table 2–4.

LIFE INSURANCE PRODUCTION BY CRAZY QUILT LIFE'S AGENTS, 1941–1971 (000 omitted)

| | Ordinary | | | | | | |
| | Whole Life | | Limited-Payment Life | | Term | | |
Year	Participating *	Nonparticipating **		Endowments	Level	Decreasing	Industrial
Volumes sold:							
1941	$ 2,000	$ 6,250	$ 7,250	$ 7,000	$ 2,500		$ 7,500
1945	5,850	19,500	19,500	14,950	11,050		16,700
1950	11,990	34,880	18,530	19,620	23,980		19,300
1955	12,700	43,180	16,510	11,430	43,180		19,800
1960	17,050	57,350	12,400	6,200	40,300	$ 21,700	21,200
1965	36,090	160,400	32,080		52,130	120,300	30,000
1966	42,210	187,600	37,520		56,280	145,390	31,500
1967	48,600	216,000	43,200		64,800	167,400	32,800
1968	54,450	235,950	48,400		72,600	193,600	33,800
1969	60,930	264,030	54,160		74,470	223,410	34,800
1970	68,310	296,010	60,720		83,490	250,470	35,850
1971	75,141	325,611	66,792		91,839	280,170	36,000
First-year premiums received:							
1941	64	161	232	357	26		107
1945	185	497	620	770	116		379
1950	373	834	572	1,025	217		440
1955	352	1,026	486	599	364		458
1960	428	1,179	344	325	288	135	480
1965	804	3,102	757		311	742	668
1966	938	3,629	885		335	895	700
1967	1,070	4,179	1,019		385	1,027	732
1968	1,199	3,916	1,121		413	1,185	757
1969	1,342	4,422	1,255		424	1,367	780
1970	1,444	5,330	1,407		475	1,573	897
1971	1,588	5,865	1,548		523	1,760	972

* Excluding dividend additions.
** Excluding term conversions and reinsurance.

death; medical expense and loss-of-time policies; individual fixed annuities; and individual variable annuities. An ordinary agent occasionally initiates a group contract, but in such cases a group field representative is called in as soon as contact is made.

All term products are convertible, and Crazy Quilt's agents actively encourage conversion. The Company provides commission incentives to stimulate conversions.

Products marketed by combination agents are principally nonparticipating industrial limited-payment life policies with a standard package of supplemental benefits included with every policy. Monthly debit ordinary life and health coverages are modifications of the regular ordinary life and individual health products; weekly premium health coverages are not available. Of course, combination agents can also sell the products sold by ordinary agents.

Life insurance production by ordinary agents and brokers and combination agents, measured in terms of volume and first-year premiums, is summarized in Table 2–4. Production of fixed annuities (measured in terms of stipulated payments received) and health insurance (measured in terms of annualized premiums) is shown in Table 2–5.

Underwriting Operations

Underwriting and issue functions for all new business sold by ordinary agents and brokers and combination agents are headed by the Senior Vice President for Underwriting, who reports to the Executive Vice President—Actuarial. Two vice presidents report to the Senior Vice President for Underwriting: the Vice President for Underwriting and the Vice President and Medical Director.

Table 2–5.

ANNUITY AND HEALTH INSURANCE PRODUCTION BY CRAZY QUILT LIFE'S AGENTS, 1941–1971
(000 Omitted)

Year	Annual Income of Fixed Annuities Sold (First Sold In 1952)	First-Year Stipulated Payments on New Variable Annuities (First Sold In 1968)	New Annualized Premiums on Loss-of-Time Policies (First Sold in 1963)	Total Annualized Premiums on Medical Expense Policies (First Sold in 1960)
1955	$ 214			
1960	261			$3,299
1965	675		$1,382	2,570
1966	788		1,678	2,422
1967	909		2,271	2,914
1968	1,017	$1,009	2,567	2,719
1969	1,139	5,732	2,863	2,658
1970	1,277	7,364	2,452	3,273
1971	1,404	8,576	2,453	2,241

Underwriting

There are three underwriting departments—one for ordinary life and annuities, one for industrial life, and one for individual health insurance. A large policy issue department issues all policies regardless of type.

A significant proportion of ordinary life and individual health insurance, and substantially all industrial life insurance, are issued nonmedically. The Company requires inspection reports for most ordinary life insurance. Substandard business is accepted but not encouraged; the proportion of substandard business issued is negligible.

The Company's retention on any one life is $150,000. Necessary reinsurance arrangements are made by the ordinary life underwriting department. Crazy Quilt has automatic yearly renewable term, coinsurance, and modified coinsurance treaties with various large reinsurers. The Company also has facultative treaties with most of the same reinsurers.

Medical Operations

The Vice President and Medical Director assists in formulating underwriting policy and consults with the underwriting department on large cases involving significant medical risks. In addition, he participates in training programs and conducts limited research in medical impairments and other medical topics directly relevant to Crazy Quilt's operations.

Group Operations

The marketing, servicing, and underwriting of group insurance is a complex and inter-related set of operations. In recognition of this, Crazy Quilt has a separate organization for those group functions, headed by the Executive Vice President for Group Operations.

However, group actuarial operations, including experience rating, report to the Company's Senior Vice President and Actuary. This is discussed in the next section.

Group Sales and Service

Although Crazy Quilt's ordinary agents occasionally initiate a group sale, most group life, health, and pension business is sold through salaried group field representatives who solicit business from brokers and frequently contact larger potential clients themselves. In addition to their salaries, field representatives are given commissions for business they sell. The group field representatives are supervised by a relatively small number of regional managers whose compensation is based on the same principles as the compensation of field representatives. Most recruiting and training of field representatives is done by home office personnel.

Field service offices perform most of the administrative services for group policyholders, including enrollments, interpretation of contract provisions, etc.

Table 2–6.

GROUP INSURANCE PRODUCTION BY CRAZY QUILT LIFE, 1956–1971 (000 Omitted)

Year	True Group Life— Total Premiums	Health— Total Premiums	Annuities —Deposits Received	Group Credit Life— Single Premiums	Health— Single Premiums
1956	$ 3	$ 19			
1960	13	79			
1965	2,414	4,862	$ 220		
1966	2,801	6,139	364		
1967	3,800	6,668	360		
1968	4,601	6,548	804	$1,000	$1,000
1969	4,555	6,094	1,260	1,400	1,400
1970	4,858	5,924	1,163	1,700	1,860
1971	5,167	7,191	413	3,000	2,856

Credit life and health insurance is marketed mainly through the field representatives, who call on auto dealers, furniture dealers, mobile home dealers, banks, finance companies, and so on. Because credit coverages are themselves so specialized, a separate credit sales unit coordinates the marketing of credit business. Similarly, because of the complexity of pension business, a separate pension services unit consults with the field force on all pension cases and performs important administrative functions in connection with pension business.

Finally group records—which are extensive—are maintained by a records unit. The records unit also prepares premium billings for cases administered by the home office and accounts for all premiums received.

All group sales and service departments report to the Vice President for Group Sales and Services.

Crazy Quilt's group insurance volumes are summarized in Table 2–6 for the period from 1956, when the Company first entered the group business, to 1971.

Products

Crazy Quilt offers regular group term life and health insurance on a retention basis and, for smaller cases, on a non-retention pooled basis. The Company also offers group permanent coverages, and other franchise cases are usually sold through field representatives, typically in concert with a broker. Pensions on both the deposit administration basis and the immediate participation guarantee basis are offered.

Group Underwriting

All group underwriting and issue functions are performed by one large department headed by the Vice President for Group Underwriting.

Underwriting is virtually a continuous process. Almost all group policies must be underwritten every year; Crazy Quilt offers few rate guarantees beyond one year. The group underwriting department receives detailed reports monthly on major cases and pores over the data to spot deteriorating situations; such information is essential in underwriting specific cases upon renewal as well as developing insights into the trend of the Company's group results as a whole.

Group contracts are standardized to the extent possible, but almost every contract has some unique feature. Contracts are processed by a separate unit. Policies and certificates are issued by another unit.

Actuarial Operations

Crazy Quilt Life's Senior Vice President and Actuary (who reports to the Executive Vice President—Actuarial) presides over three extremely important operations: individual actuarial operations, group actuarial operations, and product development.

Individual Actuarial

The Vice President and Associate Actuary has responsibility for three departments that support individual insurance operations—ordinary life actuarial, industrial life actuarial, and individual health actuarial. Responsibilities of the departments include rate testing, rate books, dividend calculations, mortality studies, morbidity studies, persistency studies, valuations, certain monitoring functions, and other such duties. In addition, the departments furnish necessary actuarial advice to nonactuarial departments and assist in preparation of the Convention Statement.

The actuarial research and development department performs risk analysis, makes special studies

Table 2–7.

DISTRIBUTION OF CRAZY QUILT LIFE'S NEW INVESTMENTS AND NEW MONEY YIELDS, 1941–1971

Year	Bonds				Common Stocks	Mortgage Loans	Real Estate	Policy Loans	Total
	Municipal	Government	Industrial and Miscellaneous	Total					
Distribution of new investments:									
1941	-0-%	-0-%	100%	100%	-0-%	-0-%	-0-%	-0-%	100%
1945	-0-	17	50	67	-0-	32	-0-	1	100
1950	2	12	36	50	4	40	2	4	100
1955	2	14	41	57	2	35	2	4	100
1960	3	14	42	59	3	30	1	7	100
1965	1	15	46	62	5	28	1	4	100
1966	1	15	44	60	5	27	1	7	100
1967	1	17	51	69	6	19	1	5	100
1968	1	17	51	69	7	16	2	6	100
1969	1	17	51	69	8	14	1	8	100
1970	1	17	51	69	8	14	1	8	100
1971	1	17	52	70	7	14	1	8	100
Gross yields on new investments:									
1941	—	—	2.95	2.95	—	—	—	—	2.95
1945	—	2.34	2.72	2.65	—	4.70	—	5.00	4.25
1950	2.00	2.32	2.71	2.57	6.90	4.60	10.50	5.00	3.81
1955	2.50	2.80	3.13	3.03	4.40	4.90	10.50	5.00	3.93
1960	3.75	3.99	4.54	4.37	3.50	6.30	11.00	5.00	5.05
1965	3.25	4.23	4.55	4.43	3.00	5.80	11.50	5.00	4.87
1966	3.80	4.68	5.22	5.08	4.10	6.00	11.50	5.00	5.38
1967	4.00	4.90	5.66	5.43	3.30	6.50	11.50	5.00	5.62
1968	4.50	5.33	6.31	6.03	3.30	7.00	11.50	5.00	6.04
1969	5.00	5.50	7.50	6.98	3.50	7.50	11.50	5.00	6.97
1970	5.00	5.50	8.00	7.38	4.00	7.50	12.00	5.00	7.25
1971	5.00	5.25	7.71	7.09	3.90	7.50	12.00	5.00	6.82
Net * yields on new investments:									
1941	—	—	2.85	2.85	—	—	—	—	2.85
1945	—	2.24	2.62	2.55	—	4.20	—	4.50	3.83
1950	1.90	2.22	2.61	2.47	6.80	4.10	4.00	4.50	3.40
1955	2.40	2.70	3.03	2.93	4.30	4.40	4.00	4.50	3.55
1960	3.65	3.89	4.44	4.27	3.40	5.80	4.50	4.50	4.72
1965	3.15	4.13	4.45	4.33	2.90	5.30	4.50	4.50	4.57
1966	3.70	4.58	5.12	4.98	4.00	5.50	5.00	4.50	5.05
1967	3.90	4.80	5.56	5.33	3.20	6.00	5.00	4.50	5.31
1968	4.40	5.23	6.21	5.93	3.20	6.50	5.00	4.50	5.72
1969	4.90	5.40	7.40	6.88	3.40	7.00	5.00	4.50	6.68
1970	4.90	5.40	7.90	7.28	3.90	7.00	5.50	4.50	6.96
1971	4.90	5.15	7.61	6.99	3.80	7.00	5.50	4.50	6.54

* Gross yields less all investment expenses and taxes but excluding Federal income taxes.

(such as experience under converted term policies), works constantly on improving various actuarial techniques, and studies all new developments in the profession in terms of their implications for Crazy Quilt. In addition, the actuarial research and development department participated heavily in Crazy Quilt's conversion to generally accepted accounting principles.

Group Actuarial

The group actuarial department (headed by a vice president) provides important information to group underwriting with respect to risk patterns and emerging experience in the group business, group expenses, retention formulas, and so on.

The department maintains all experience rating

Table 2–8.

PORTFOLIO YIELD RATES FOR CRAZY QUILT LIFE, 1941–1971

Year	Bonds Gross	Net	Common Stocks Gross	Net	Mortgage Loans Gross	Net	Real Estate Gross	Net	Policy Loans Gross	Net	All Investments—Weighted Total Gross	Net	Industry Net Rate
1941	2.95%	2.85%									2.95%	2.85%	3.42%
1942	2.89	2.79									2.89	2.80	3.44
1943	2.89	2.79			4.79%	4.29%					3.04	2.91	3.33
1944	2.83	2.73			4.73	4.23			5.00%	4.50%	3.14	2.98	3.23
1945	2.81	2.71			4.72	4.22			5.00	4.50	3.13	2.97	3.11
1946	2.79	2.69			4.62	4.12			5.00	4.50	3.19	3.00	2.93
1947	2.74	2.64			4.55	4.05			5.00	4.50	3.17	2.97	2.88
1948	2.73	2.63			4.53	4.03			5.00	4.50	3.22	3.02	2.96
1949	2.72	2.62			4.55	4.05			5.00	4.50	3.27	3.06	3.06
1950	2.70	2.60	6.89%	6.79%	4.56	4.06	10.50%	4.00%	5.00	4.50	3.41	3.15	3.13
1951	2.74	2.64	6.57	6.47	4.60	4.10	10.50	4.00	5.00	4.50	3.53	3.23	3.18
1952	2.79	2.69	6.26	6.16	4.64	4.14	10.50	4.00	5.00	4.50	3.61	3.29	3.28
1953	2.88	2.78	6.12	6.02	4.70	4.20	10.50	4.00	5.00	4.50	3.71	3.38	3.36
1954	2.85	2.75	5.38	5.28	4.77	4.27	10.50	4.00	5.00	4.50	3.76	3.40	3.46
1955	2.90	2.80	5.14	5.04	4.87	4.37	10.50	4.00	5.00	4.50	3.88	3.47	3.51
1956	3.01	2.91	5.04	4.94	4.82	4.32	10.50	4.00	5.00	4.50	3.96	3.56	3.63
1957	3.22	3.12	5.03	4.93	5.02	4.52	10.62	4.12	5.00	4.00	4.18	3.76	3.75
1958	3.36	3.26	4.69	4.59	5.15	4.65	10.72	4.22	5.00	4.50	4.25	3.87	3.85
1959	3.63	3.53	4.30	4.20	5.34	4.84	10.77	4.27	5.00	4.50	4.52	4.08	3.96
1960	3.82	3.72	4.08	3.98	5.54	5.04	10.80	4.30	5.00	4.50	4.68	4.26	4.11
1961	4.00	3.90	3.81	3.71	5.65	5.15	10.83	4.33	5.00	4.50	4.81	4.38	4.22
1962	4.08	3.98	3.77	3.67	5.73	5.23	10.86	4.36	5.00	4.50	4.87	4.45	4.34
1963	4.12	4.02	3.63	3.53	5.77	5.27	10.88	4.38	5.00	4.50	4.91	4.49	4.45
1964	4.19	4.09	3.62	3.52	5.82	5.32	10.99	4.49	5.00	4.50	4.99	4.56	4.53
1965	4.27	4.17	3.45	3.35	5.83	5.33	11.06	4.56	5.00	4.50	5.03	4.61	4.61
1966	4.55	4.45	3.60	3.50	5.85	5.35	11.14	4.64	5.00	4.50	5.19	4.77	4.73
1967	4.92	4.82	3.51	3.41	5.96	5.46	11.21	4.71	5.00	4.50	5.35	4.97	4.82
1968	5.42	5.32	3.43	3.33	6.12	5.62	11.27	4.77	5.00	4.50	5.66	5.25	4.95
1969	6.12	6.02	3.47	3.37	6.32	5.82	11.31	4.81	5.00	4.50	6.03	5.65	5.12
1970	6.67	6.57	3.61	3.51	6.50	6.00	11.45	4.95	5.00	4.50	6.34	5.98	5.30
1971	6.76	6.66	3.68	3.58	6.63	6.13	11.54	5.04	5.00	4.50	6.45	6.04	5.45

records, calculates reserves, and calculates experience rating refunds. This function was separated from group operations for reasons of internal control.

In selling pension cases, Crazy Quilt offers two options with respect to actuarial services: either the client can retain its own consulting actuaries, or Crazy Quilt will furnish actuarial services for a fee. Group actuaries provide actuarial services to pension clients that request them.

Product Development

The Vice President for Product Development investigates the feasibility and cost of new products and, together with the General Counsel, drafts new policy forms. Substantially all new product ideas are channeled through this department.

Investment Operations

As befits the importance of the investment function, investment operations are headed by an executive vice president. Reporting to the Executive Vice President for Investments are three vice presidents, each of whom presides over a major aspect of the Company's investment program:

▶ Commercial and industrial development,
▶ Mortgage loans and real estate, and
▶ Bonds and stocks.

All purchases and sales of investments must be ratified by the Finance Committee of the Board of Directors. Investment policy is established by the full Board, usually based upon recommendations of the Finance Committee.

Table 2–9.

CONDENSED STATUTORY BALANCE SHEET FOR CRAZY QUILT LIFE AT DECEMBER 31, 1971 (000 Omitted)

ADMITTED ASSETS

Bonds—at amortized cost	
U. S. Government	$ 68,494
Municipals	7,133
Industrial and other	205,483
	281,110
Common stocks—at market	42,390
Mortgage loans	134,083
Real estate—at cost	
Investment	11,779
Company-occupied	4,356
	16,135
Less allowances for depreciation	4,333
	11,802
Policy loans	44,989
Cash	5,600
Investment in life insurance subsidiary	3,243
Deferred and uncollected premiums	10,897
Other assets	1,670
Separate account assets	29,771
	$565,555

LIABILITIES, RESERVES, AND CAPITAL

Insurance reserves:	
Life and annuity	$442,311
Health	13,076
	455,387
Claims	8,612
Dividends	1,399
Dividend accumulations	2,281
Supplementary contracts not involving life contingencies	1,628
Experience rating refunds	3,216
Deposit administration and annuity accumulation funds	2,585
Federal income taxes	1,856
Other liabilities	1,675
Liability for unauthorized reinsurance	14
Mandatory securities valuation reserve	13,966
Separate account liabilities	29,771
	522,390
Capital:	
Common stock, par value $5.00 a share—	
5,544,000 shares issued and outstanding	27,721
Additional paid-in capital	14,699
Unassigned surplus	745
	43,165
	$565,555

The Company's investment policies have, of course, changed over the years, as have the policies of the entire industry. The Company's new investments over the years are summarized in Table 2–7. Information on portfolio yield rates is summarized in Table 2–8.

The yields shown in Tables 2–7 and 2–8 reflect dividends, interest, rents, and similar items of investment income; realized and unrealized capital gains and losses are excluded. Crazy Quilt's capital gains history is discussed in Chapters 10 and 25.

There is a fair degree of interaction between the investment departments and the actuarial departments. In testing rates Crazy Quilt's actuaries always consult with investment officers to obtain information on the probable course of interest rates. Further, and

Table 2–10.

CONDENSED STATUTORY SUMMARY OF OPERATIONS AND STATEMENT OF CAPITAL AND SURPLUS
FOR CRAZY QUILT LIFE FOR YEAR ENDED DECEMBER 31, 1971 (000 Omitted)

SUMMARY OF OPERATIONS

Revenue:	
Premiums and considerations:	
Life and annuity	$ 97,620
Health	21,990
Proceeds left on deposit	1,017
Deposit administration and annuity accumulation funds received	413
Reserve transfers under modified coinsurance agreements	179
Management fees and miscellaneous	1,676
Investment income, less expenses and taxes of $1,897,000	30,433
	153,328
Benefits paid or provided:	
Life and annuity:	
Death benefits	17,055
Matured endowments	5,558
Annuity benefits	7,997
Disability benefits	481
Surrender benefits	9,779
Payments on supplementary contracts	1,261
Dividend accumulations surrendered	258
Dividends to policyholders	1,438
Experience rating refunds to group policyholders	508
Miscellaneous	1,057
Increase in reserves	34,426
Health:	
Health insurance benefits	10,597
Experience rating refunds to group policyholders	481
Increase in reserves	2,185
	93,081
	60,247
Insurance expenses:	
Commissions	19,254
Taxes, licenses and fees	3,366
General insurance expenses	25,410
Increase in loading on deferred and uncollected premiums	207
	48,237
Gain from operations before Federal income taxes	12,010
Federal income taxes	1,766
NET GAIN FROM OPERATIONS	$ 10,244

STATEMENT OF CAPITAL AND SURPLUS

	Common Stock		Paid-in Surplus	Unassigned Surplus
	Number of Shares	*Amount*		
Balance, January 1, 1971	5,356	$26,779	$ 3,221	$ 7,598
Additions (deductions):				
Net gain from operations				10,244
Realized capital gains, less applicable taxes				263
Change in unrealized appreciation of common stocks				3,184
Change in non-admitted assets				(490)
Change in mandatory securities valuation reserve				(3,592)
Change in liability for unauthorized reinsurance				115
Stock issued in connection with purchase of subsidiary	133	667	11,478	
Cost in excess of net admitted asset value of subsidiary purchased				(13,902)
Dividends to shareholders:				
Cash—$.435				(2,400)
Stock—1%	55	275		(275)
BALANCE, DECEMBER 31, 1971	5,544	$27,721	$14,699	$ 745

Table 2-11.

AFTER-TAX STATUTORY GAIN FROM OPERATIONS BY LINE OF BUSINESS FOR CRAZY QUILT LIFE, 1941–1971 (000 Omitted)

Year	Total	Corporate Account	Industrial	Ordinary Life	Total and Permanent Disability	Additional Accidental Death	Individual Annuities	Supplementary Contracts	Group Life Insurance	Group Annuities	Accident and Health Group	Accident and Health Other
1941	$(1,290)	$ 122	$(222)	$(1,185)	$ (5)	$Nil		$ Nil				
1942	(823)	286	(229)	(880)	(1)	Nil		2				
1943	(879)	304	(248)	(960)	18	8		Nil				
1944	(818)	322	(262)	(909)	13	14		3				
1945	(806)	336	(232)	(905)	2	30		(9)				
1946	(639)	351	(209)	(318)	10	19		8				
1947	(340)	370	(178)	(526)	25	45		24				
1948	1,068	391	(59)	644	27	40		24				
1949	654	338	(21)	210	62	60		4				
1950	528	311	(36)	112	105	50		(14)				
1951	670	372	(14)	215	116	104	$ (35)	(87)				
1952	(394)	375	16	(961)	137	93	(6)	(48)				
1953	58	373	(156)	(417)	163	87	52	(42)				
1954	616	366	(216)	64	220	123	65	(6)				
1955	858	327	(143)	462	164	80	84	(115)	$ (2)		$ (6)	
1956	1,935	320	(84)	1,347	181	135	109	(67)				
1957	2,652	304	1	1,925	207	107	151	(48)	Nil		3	
1958	2,543	560	28	1,615	150	85	135	(34)	Nil		2	
1959	2,979	604	52	1,956	123	94	160	(17)	Nil		4	
1960	2,949	616	84	1,813	163	88	188	1	Nil	$ 4	5	$ (10)
1961	3,326	595	117	1,923	157	81	214	(6)	(126)	(1)	(97)	467
1962	4,954	663	118	3,319	228	83	172	(28)	(15)		197	216
1963	3,463	624	125	2,447	236	92	164	Nil	10		52	(289)
1964	3,662	859	131	1,916	153	63	181	232	120		107	(106)
1965	2,391	972	100	941	185	40	196	20	(5)	(1)	41	(98)
1966	1,780	1,120	119	345	171	75	219	(43)	2	(14)	(64)	(148)
1967	2,371	888	172	545	196	89	299	17	108	(2)	224	(166)
1968	(30)	1,229	260	(1,567)	240	115	(570)	(31)	218	4	158	(88)
1969	1,067	1,371	316	(833)	208	89	(715)	(47)	279	(104)	330	173
1970	11,189	2,415	497	6,957	411	249	(934)	(46)	596	39	465	537
1971	10,244	2,663	533	5,820	335	279	(845)	(124)	527	(39)	222	872

NOTE—May not add across due to rounding.

Table 2–12.

ENTRIES TO STATUTORY UNASSIGNED SURPLUS FOR CRAZY QUILT LIFE, 1941–1971 (000 Omitted)

Year	Net Gain From Operations	Realized Capital Gains, Less Taxes	Change in Unrealized Capital Gains	Change in Non-Admitted Assets	Change in Mandatory Securities Valuation Reserve	Change in Liability for Unauthorized Reinsurance	Reserve Strengthening	Excess Cost of Subsidiary	Dividends to Stockholders	Miscellaneous	Net Surplus Change
1941	$ (1,290)			$ (90)	$ (144)						$ (1,524)
1942	(823)										(823)
1943	(879)	$ 80		(10)	(80)						(889)
1944	(818)	4		(20)	(35)						(869)
1945	(806)	18		(30)	(63)						(881)
1946	(639)	54		(40)	(107)						(732)
1947	(340)	26		(50)	(101)						(465)
1948	1,068	19		(70)	(119)					$6	904
1949	654	4		(70)	(123)						465
1950	528	170	$ 104	(80)	(347)						375
1951	670	71	46	(100)	(174)						513
1952	(394)	59	33	(130)	(361)						(793)
1953	58	117	90	(150)	(406)						(291)
1954	616	217	745	(160)	(1,026)						392
1955	858	302	500	(170)	(913)						577
1956	1,935	135	62	(170)	(214)						1,748
1957	2,652	(66)	(532)	(180)	191						2,065
1958	2,543	376	1,747	(190)	(1,980)				$ (400)		2,096
1959	2,979	(111)	(1,436)	(200)	911				(400)		1,743
1960	2,949	240	(713)	(220)	34				(600)		1,690
1961	3,326	386	707	(210)	(1,230)				(600)		2,379
1962	4,954	292	(476)	(210)	(229)				(800)		3,531
1963	3,463	683	1,621	(210)	(2,138)				(800)		2,619
1964	3,662	434	335	(230)	(1,059)				(1,000)		2,142
1965	2,391	440	1,049	(240)	(1,653)				(1,200)		787
1966	1,730	(2,100)	(655)	(280)	1,629				(1,400)		(1,026)
1967	2,371	1,196	4,087	(310)	(4,650)				(1,600)		1,094
1968	(30)	1,376	(615)	(350)	(1,170)				(1,800)		(2,589)
1969	1,067	1,392	(8,608)	(390)	4,900		$(10,451)		(2,000)		(14,090)
1970	11,189	(146)	(1,087)	(460)	283	$(129)			(2,200)		7,450
1971	10,244	263	3,184	(490)	(3,592)	115		$(13,902)	(2,675)		(6,853)

perhaps more subtly, the investment portfolio is frequently reviewed jointly by actuarial and investment officers to ensure that there is a reasonable correlation between the maturities of assets and the expected pattern of maturities of reserve liabilities.

Administration

A life insurance company produces, among other things, a great deal of paper. In Crazy Quilt's case the torrent of paper is so great that no fewer than 33 departments are required to handle it. They report through five vice presidents to the Executive Vice President for Finance and Administration.

Insurance Services

Policyholder service and all claims functions are administered by the Vice President for Insurance Services. In addition to a sizeable home office claims staff, several regional offices are utilized to process group claims.

Controller

Crazy Quilt's Vice President and Controller is not unlike the controller of any other large company, except for the fact that actuaries assist in preparing certain portions of the Convention Statement and except for the presence of four somewhat unique departments: cost accounting, which administers the Company's functional cost program (discussed in Chapter 13); premium accounting, which controls premium updating inputs to data processing and monitors suspense accounts; commission accounting, which oversees preparation of agents' statements and commission checks; and variable annuity accounting, which takes care of the unique accounting requirements of that product.

The Vice President and Controller personally directed the Company's conversion to generally accepted accounting principles.

Treasurer

The Vice President and Treasurer performs normal treasury functions and, in Crazy Quilt's case, is the principal administrator of the Company's variable annuity program.

Systems

The Vice President for Systems oversees all data processing operations (which are very substantial) and systems work.

All of the Company's data processing work is done in the home office. A consolidated functions system is used for ordinary life insurance and annuities, and variants of the system are used for industrial life and individual health insurance. Investment accounting is extensively automated, and numerous sophisticated calculation and projection programs have been developed for use by the Company's actuaries, marketing personnel, and planning executives. All general ledgers and journals are automated, as is the compilation of the Convention Statement.

Corporate Services

Printing, purchasing, communications, and general office services—duplicating, mail, supplies, etc.—are headed up by the Vice President for Corporate Services. Certain employee welfare operations, such as the Company cafeteria, are also supervised by him.

Financial Reporting

Crazy Quilt Life must file financial statements in all of the states in which it does business. In addition, the Company must file financial statements with the Securities and Exchange Commission and publishes financial statements in its annual report to shareholders. In years past all such statements have been prepared on the basis of statutory accounting practices.

Tables 2–9 and 2–10 show condensed statutory balance sheet, summary of operations, and capital and surplus accounts, respectively, for the year 1971. After-tax statutory gain from operations by line of business for the 31 years from 1941 to 1971 is shown in Table 2–11, and entries to unassigned surplus during the 31-year period are summarized in Table 2–12.

Gain from operations by line of business reported in Table 2–11 reflects two practices that may be unique to Crazy Quilt Life. Each line of business retains its own surplus and earns investment income on surplus. The "corporate account" reflects investment income on contributed capital plus cash transfers for the stockholder charge against participating earnings plus realized capital gains less dividends to stockholders and less allocable federal income taxes. As Table 2–11 shows, Crazy Quilt's statutory earnings history has been erratic indeed. Some of the reasons why will be explored in chapters to come.

3

Ordinary Products and Prices

Pricing in the life insurance business is one of the most arcane of arts and taxes the ingenuity of even the best of actuaries. On the one hand is competition. While opinion differs as to the extent of price competition in life insurance, the fact is that pressure from agents forces a company to keep a close eye on what competitors are charging. On the other hand is an uncertain future. While errors in pricing industrial products are quickly discerned and can usually be quickly corrected, errors in pricing life insurance products may not be discernible for a generation. The only happy thing about a deferred error is that the actuary may be retired by the time it appears, and assuming that his pension is guaranteed, he may thus escape the slings and arrows of outraged management.

A brief discussion cannot possibly do justice to the subject of pricing, but a few comments on basic pricing techniques are clearly needed because pricing inevitably influences the accounting process (as will be seen in later chapters).* Ordinary products are discussed in this chapter; other products are discussed in Part IV ("Other Lines of Business").

Nonparticipating Permanent Insurance

There are two basic theoretical approaches to the calculation of nonparticipating gross premiums: the "equation" approach and the "accumulation" approach. Under the equation approach, "natural" premiums are computed directly from assumed experience; profit margins are introduced by specific addi-

---

* Readers who are unfamiliar with fundamental present value concepts may wish to review Appendix A before reading this chapter.

tion to the natural premium or by using conservative assumptions. Under the accumulation approach, a trial premium bearing no necessary relationship to assumed experience is projected along with the assumed experience, and the trial premium is adjusted to meet profit objectives based on the results of the projection.

Equation Approach to Pricing

Crazy Quilt Life used the equation approach for many of its premium calculations in the 1940s and 1950s. In developing its first ratebook in 1941, for example, the Company computed premiums for its whole life policy issued to males age 45 by

▸ Selecting an interest rate realistic in the circumstances (2.75 percent),
▸ Using a mortality table representative of current experience (1930–1939 select and ultimate),
▸ "Stealing" a cash value scale from a competitor's ratebook (which defined the valuation basis),
▸ Developing expense assumptions,
▸ Selecting a conservative lapse assumption because there were few guidelines to follow (the withdrawal table selected assumed first-year lapses of 25 percent),
▸ Computing the present value, using the assumed interest rate and a double decrement table, of deaths, surrenders, and expenses,
▸ Computing the present value of a life annuity due of $1 using the same interest, mortality, and withdrawal factors,
▸ Dividing the present value of future benefits by the present value of the life annuity due, and
▸ Adding a more or less arbitrary amount for profit.

The net result of the foregoing process may be summarized as follows (per $1,000 of insurance originally issued):

Present value of death benefits	$147.52
Present value of surrenders	92.88
Present value of expenses	84.08
Present value of benefits and expenses	$324.48
Present value of life annuity due of $1	$ 9.37
Level annual equivalent of benefits and expenses	$ 34.63
Addition for profit net of percentage expenses	.35
Gross premium	$ 34.98

The Company limited its provision for profit to 1 percent because it found itself in a severe competitive bind. In 1941 it was competing with companies whose rates originated in years of higher interest rates; in 1941 the prospect for higher interest rates was dismal. Further, the larger companies generally had lower unit expenses. The fact is that the premium before profit loading was higher than the gross premium of many larger companies. So the profit loading had to be nominal for competitive reasons. Crazy Quilt's agents had a difficult enough time selling the policy as it was.

Crazy Quilt sometimes computed premiums in the manner indicated above, but without providing specifically for profit. Instead, the Company would assume experience somewhat more adverse than it really expected. In that case any profit was buried in the premium assumptions.

The advantage of the equation approach is that it permits premiums to be computed directly without extensive trial-and-error testing. The disadvantages are that it is not practical to vary certain assumptions by calendar year, and profit margins are not readily related to the investment in new business; nor does the equation approach indicate the incidence of profits.

Asset Share Accumulation Approach to Pricing

Under one version of the asset share approach, a trial premium is selected, assumptions are chosen, and a projected cash flow is prepared. The accumulation of assets per $1,000 in force is compared with a prospective valuation (for example, the statutory reserve) at selected points in time. Any necessary modification of the gross premium is then made based on inspection of the data.

Crazy Quilt used the asset share approach in de-veloping some of its early ratebooks. An example of the approach is shown in Table 3–1. An asset share calculation for the 1948–1951 ratebook edition of the Company's nonparticipating whole life policy for a male age 45 is shown. After selecting a proposed premium from a competitor's ratebook and drawing up a set of assumptions, assumed cash receipts and disbursements were accumulated at the assumed investment earnings rate, and the accumulation per policy in force (the "asset share") was compared with the mean net level statutory reserve at each of the first 30 durations. The result was a computed "asset share surplus", defined as the assets per $1,000 in force minus the reserve per $1,000 in force.

Crazy Quilt defined its profit objective in terms of an asset share before taxes equivalent to 120 percent of the statutory reserve at the 20th duration. In the case of the policy shown in Table 3–1, the asset share equals 125 percent of the statutory reserve in the 20th year. Crazy Quilt therefore decided to adopt the premium.

However, the calculations indicated that positive statutory surplus would not appear until the 12th year. This was unsatisfactory. As a result, the Company switched to the Commissioners Reserve Valuation Method in 1948.

Suppose the Company decided that the premium must be revised upward or downward. Would the process have to be repeated to determine the effect of the modification? No, because the change in the asset share caused by a $1.00 change in the premium is readily computed. Thus, the effect of a change in the premium is quickly determinable without recalculating the asset shares.

The sizeable asset share surplus that eventually accumulates is based on the assumption that surplus is not withdrawn. In the typical situation, surplus is invested in new business rather than left to accumulate at the investment earnings rate. That's one reason why it is of little significance to project an asset share beyond the 20th or 30th duration.

The principal advantage of the asset share accumulation approach is that it offers some idea of the incidence of profits. It also permits premiums to be modified more conveniently than the equation approach. The principal disadvantage of the approach is that it does not readily accommodate modern methods of defining profit objectives.

Anderson Accumulation Approach to Pricing

The Anderson accumulation method, introduced in

Table 3–1.

ASSET SHARE, RESERVE, AND ASSET SHARE SURPLUS FOR WHOLE LIFE POLICY ISSUED TO MALE AGE 45—1948–1951 RATEBOOK—PER $1,000 UNIT

Calendar Year	Fund, January 1	Interest, June 30	July 1 Premiums	Deaths	Surrenders	Expenses	Fund	Interest, December 31	Fund, December 31	In Force	Asset Share	Mean Net Level Reserve	Asset Share Surplus
1			$33.95	$1.10		$51.12	$(18.27)	$(.27)	$(18.54)	.99860	$ (18.57)	$ 26.00	$(44.57)
2	$(18.54)	$(.28)	28.79	2.35		5.99	1.63	.02	1.65	.84688	1.95	49.00	(47.05)
3	1.65	.02	26.41	2.74	$ .41	4.28	20.65	.31	20.96	.77648	26.99	71.00	(44.01)
4	20.96	.31	24.73	3.28	1.39	3.37	37.96	.57	38.53	.72671	53.02	94.00	(40.98)
5	38.53	.57	23.38	3.89	1.92	2.59	54.08	.81	54.89	.68657	79.95	117.00	(37.05)
6	54.89	.82	22.08	4.57	2.64	2.44	68.14	1.01	69.15	.64778	106.75	139.00	(32.25)
7	69.15	1.03	20.81	5.03	3.26	2.31	80.39	1.20	81.59	.61048	133.65	162.00	(28.35)
8	81.59	1.21	19.61	5.25	3.80	2.18	91.18	1.36	92.54	.57483	160.99	185.00	(24.01)
9	92.54	1.38	18.45	5.48	4.26	2.05	100.58	1.50	102.08	.54074	188.78	208.00	(19.22)
10	102.08	1.52	17.35	5.73	4.65	1.93	108.64	1.62	110.26	.50811	217.00	231.00	(14.00)
11	110.26	1.64	16.29	5.97	4.98	.92	116.32	1.73	118.05	.47688	247.55	254.00	(6.45)
12	118.05	1.76	15.28	6.23	5.24	.87	122.75	1.83	124.58	.44696	278.73	277.00	1.73
13	124.58	1.85	14.31	6.48	5.41	.81	128.04	1.91	129.95	.41829	310.67	300.00	10.67
14	129.95	1.93	13.38	6.72	5.56	.76	132.22	1.97	134.19	.39082	343.35	323.00	20.35
15	134.19	2.00	12.49	6.94	5.66	.71	135.37	2.02	137.39	.36451	376.92	345.00	31.92
16	137.39	2.05	11.52	7.10	6.82	.67	136.37	2.13	138.40	.33575	412.21	368.00	44.21
17	138.40	2.06	10.60	7.17	6.74	.62	136.53	2.03	138.56	.30865	448.92	390.00	58.92
18	138.56	2.06	9.74	7.21	6.61	.57	135.97	2.02	137.99	.28314	487.36	412.00	75.36
19	137.99	2.05	8.92	7.20	6.44	.52	134.80	2.01	136.81	.25917	527.88	434.00	93.88
20	136.81	2.04	8.16	7.16	6.24	.48	133.13	1.98	135.11	.23667	570.88	455.00	115.88
21	135.11	2.01	7.44	7.08	6.14	.44	130.90	1.95	132.85	.21560	616.19	477.00	139.19
22	132.85	1.98	6.77	6.97	5.87	.40	130.90	1.95	130.27	.19591	664.95	498.00	166.95
23	130.27	1.94	6.14	6.84	5.57	.37	125.57	1.87	127.44	.17752	717.89	518.00	199.89
24	127.44	1.90	5.56	6.68	5.26	.33	122.63	1.83	124.46	.16039	775.98	536.00	237.98
25	124.46	1.85	5.01	6.52	4.93	.30	119.57	1.78	121.35	.14445	840.08	558.00	282.08
26	121.35	1.81	4.46	6.31	5.37	.27	115.67	1.72	117.39	.12825	915.32	577.00	338.32
27	117.39	1.75	3.95	6.07	4.93	.24	111.85	1.67	113.52	.11342	1,000.88	596.00	404.88
28	113.52	1.69	3.49	5.81	4.50	.22	108.17	1.61	109.78	.09988	1,099.12	615.00	484.12
29	109.78	1.63	3.03	5.52	4.67	.19	104.06	1.55	105.61	.08660	1,219.52	633.00	586.52
30	105.61	1.57	2.62	5.19	4.16	.17	100.28	1.49	101.77	.07469	1,362.57	650.00	712.57

1959, has had a significant impact on the pricing of nonparticipating insurance. The Anderson method (which is practicable only with the assistance of a computer) involves determination of book profit or loss (using an arbitrary premium) for each policy year and the discounting of such profits and losses at a predetermined yield rate. The trial premium is then adjusted in such a manner as to produce the desired yield rate.*

Crazy Quilt Life uses an application of the Anderson method in pricing current issues. A review of the techniques employed in pricing the nonparticipating 20-pay life contract (for a male age 45) represented in Crazy Quilt's 1970–1971 ratebook will suggest some of the more important aspects of the method.

Crazy Quilt chose a trial premium and a corresponding set of cash values by inspecting the ratebooks of other large companies. It then put together a set of reasonable assumptions as to interest, mortality, persistency, and expense and decided on using net level reserves (1958 CSO at 3 1/2 percent interest).

The Company then projected the trial premium ($37.64 per $1,000) and the assumed experience for the life of the contract and discounted the resulting pre-tax book profits at 12 percent, which expresses Crazy Quilt's profit objective. The projection is summarized in Table 3–2.

Crazy Quilt found that the calculations produced a small positive present value, namely 26 cents. All that would have been required is zero, which would mean that the first-year investment of surplus, $49.84, is paid back with interest at 12 percent. Since Crazy Quilt's profit objective was satisfied, and since the premium was competitive, the rate tested in Table 3–2 was used in the Company's 1970–1971 ratebook.

Suppose, however, the projection indicated a negative present value of, say, $5.00. The Company could approach the problem in several ways. Calculations indicate that the effect of raising the premium by $1.00 per $1,000 would increase the present value of future profits by $4.09. So the Company might raise the premium by $1.22 ($5.00 ÷ $4.09). This may not be feasible for competitive reasons. The Company might look next to expenses. It might try to pare

$5.00 from first-year expenses, but it is very doubtful that this much could be saved. The effect of reducing expenses by $1.00 per $1,000 annually is to increase the present value of future profits by $6.01. So the Company could also achieve its profit objective by cutting annual per-$1,000 expenses by 83 cents ($5.00 ÷ $6.01). Unfortunately this is rarely feasible, particularly in the age of inflation. As a last resort, the Company might simply accept a lower yield, i.e., less profit. In practice, the final action might involve raising the premium slightly, cutting commissions slightly, accepting a lower profit, and generally hoping for the best. In any case, a good deal of agonizing will precede the decision.*

One of the principal advantages of the Anderson method is that it is possible to compute the yield on the "investment" of financial statement surplus, which in the case of the illustrated 20-pay life policy amounts to $49.84. Since discounting profits after the first year at 12 percent results in a value slightly greater than the "investment" of $49.84, it is apparent that the investment of surplus yields slightly over 12 percent.**

If raw cash flows were projected—in other words, if the reserve were omitted from the projection (in which case there would be no interest income, which is computed with respect to assets equal to the reserve)—the present value of such cash flows would be different. This is because interest on the reserve and increases in the reserve are reflected in calendar year profits, and the present values of these two elements differ.

Crazy Quilt always projects results for the life of the contract. Most companies use a shorter period—say 30 years—for projection purposes. In the situation shown in Table 3–2, the profits after 30 years are immaterial in terms of present values and nothing would be lost by ignoring such subsequent profits. The practical effect would be to introduce some small measure of conservatism into the calculations.

Cash Values and Reserves

Prior to 1948 the cash value for a permanent life insurance policy (and for a term policy of more than 20 years) was computed with reference to the reserve.

---

*This is a grossly oversimplified explanation of the Anderson method. The method calls for two basic yield rates, one applicable to surplus invested in new business and one for surplus invested in agency development, and requires an unusually complex series of calculations. The method is described in detail in James C. H. Anderson's article, "Gross Premium Calculations and Profit Measurement for Nonparticipating Insurance," *TSA* XI (1959).

*Crazy Quilt's president indicates that Table 3–2 is not representative. He states that modification was required about 90 percent of the time and confesses to having squirmed often and uneasily while deciding what modifications to make.

**The actual computed yield rate is 12.1 percent.

Table 3-2.

PROJECTION OF TRIAL PREMIUM AND ASSUMED EXPERIENCE FOR 20-PAY LIFE ISSUED TO MALE AGE 45—1970-1971 RATEBOOK—PER $1,000 OF ORIGINAL ISSUE

Calendar Year	Premiums	Interest on Reserves	Deaths	Surrenders	Increase in Reserves	Expenses	Pre-Tax Profit	Present Value Of Profits at 12% Annual	Present Value Of Profits at 12% Cumulative	Effect on Cumulative Present Value of $1 Annual Change In Premium Per $1,000	Effect on Cumulative Present Value of $1 Annual Change In Expense Per $1,000
1	$37.64	$ .88	$ .93	$ —	$ 30.30	$57.13	$(49.84)	$(49.84)	$(49.84)	$(.29)	$1.00
2	30.81	2.30	1.98	$ .36	17.78	4.29	8.71	7.78	(42.06)	.35	1.73
3	29.19	3.39	2.30	1.27	19.95	3.15	5.91	4.71	(37.35)	.91	2.35
4	27.94	4.51	2.68	1.92	18.96	3.01	5.87	4.18	(33.17)	1.40	2.88
5	26.72	5.57	3.00	2.75	17.52	2.88	6.14	3.90	(29.27)	1.81	3.33
6	25.80	6.59	3.30	2.63	17.37	2.78	6.31	3.58	(25.69)	2.16	3.72
7	24.90	6.93	3.65	3.19	16.31	2.68	6.00	3.04	(22.65)	2.46	4.05
8	24.01	7.11	3.97	3.73	15.27	2.59	5.57	2.52	(20.13)	2.73	4.34
9	23.14	7.83	4.22	4.24	14.26	2.49	5.76	2.33	(17.80)	2.95	4.59
10	22.29	8.50	4.50	4.71	13.26	2.40	5.93	2.13	(15.67)	3.15	4.80
11	21.45	9.13	4.87	5.13	12.24	1.67	6.67	2.15	(13.52)	3.32	4.99
12	20.62	9.70	5.41	5.54	11.15	1.61	6.61	1.90	(11.62)	3.47	5.14
13	19.79	10.21	6.10	5.90	9.99	1.55	6.46	1.66	(9.96)	3.59	5.28
14	18.96	10.67	6.77	6.23	8.83	1.48	6.32	1.45	(8.51)	3.70	5.39
15	18.14	11.08	7.37	6.53	7.67	1.42	6.22	1.27	(7.24)	3.80	5.49
16	17.31	11.42	7.90	6.78	6.54	1.36	6.15	1.12	(6.12)	3.87	5.58
17	16.50	11.71	8.35	6.99	5.45	1.30	6.12	1.00	(5.12)	3.94	5.65
18	15.69	11.95	8.79	7.19	4.38	1.24	6.05	.88	(4.24)	4.00	5.71
19	14.89	12.14	9.20	7.34	3.33	1.18	5.99	.78	(3.46)	4.05	5.76
20	14.10	12.28	9.53	7.41	2.34	1.12	5.97	.70	(2.76)	4.09	5.80
21		12.15	9.84	5.04	(7.75)	.21	4.82	.50	(2.26)	4.09	5.84
22		11.76	10.17	4.87	(8.18)	.20	4.70	.43	(1.83)	4.09	5.87
23		11.35	10.51	4.70	(8.62)	.20	4.56	.38	(1.45)	4.09	5.90
24		10.87	10.80	6.79	(11.30)	.19	4.39	.32	(1.13)	4.09	5.92
25		10.31	11.03	6.44	(11.51)	.18	4.18	.28	(.85)	4.09	5.94
26		9.65	11.13	10.15	(15.71)	.18	3.91	.23	(.62)	4.09	5.96
27		8.89	11.03	9.35	(15.26)	.16	3.61	.19	(.43)	4.09	5.97
28		8.12	10.75	10.30	(16.38)	.15	3.31	.15	(.28)	4.09	5.98
29		7.35	10.34	9.32	(15.45)	.14	3.00	.13	(.15)	4.09	5.99
30		6.61	9.94	8.38	(14.54)	.12	2.70	.10	(.05)	4.09	5.99
31		5.93	9.58	7.51	(13.68)	.11	2.40	.08	(.03)	4.09	6.00
—		—	—	—	—	—	—	—	—	—	—
56		Nil	Nil	—	Nil	Nil	Nil	Nil	.26	—	6.01

Table 3–3.

ASSET SHARES, CASH VALUES, AND RESERVES FOR WHOLE LIFE POLICY ISSUED TO MALE AGE
45—1948-1951 RATEBOOK—PER $1,000 OF INSURANCE IN FORCE

Calendar Year	Asset Share	1941 CSO 2½% Cash Value		1941 CSO 2½% Reserve	
		Next Terminal	Discounted For 6 Months' Interest	Net Level	CRVM
1	$ (19)	$ -0-	$ -0-	$ 26	$ 4
2	2	6	6	49	27
3	27	30	30	71	50
4	53	53	52	94	73
5	80	77	76	117	97
6	107	101	100	139	120
7	134	125	123	162	143
8	161	149	147	185	167
9	189	173	170	208	190
10	271	197	194	231	214
11	248	221	218	254	237
12	279	244	240	277	261
13	311	268	264	300	284
14	343	292	288	323	308
15	377	315	310	345	331
16	412	338	333	368	354
17	449	361	356	390	376
18	487	384	378	412	399
19	528	407	401	434	421
20	571	439	432	455	443

The cash value was equivalent to the reserve less a "surrender charge" (which was subject to a statutory maximum) designed to compensate the company (and persisting policyholders) for expenses and losses occasioned by surrender. The surrender charge would grow smaller and smaller with the passage of time until the cash value equaled the reserve after, say, 15 or 20 years.

It was widely recognized that the reserve was not necessarily a fair measure of a policyholder's equitable interest in his policy. Further, in the early 1940s many companies undertook to strengthen reserves because of declining interest rates, which would have proved inconvenient if cash values were defined in terms of the reserve. The strengthening was a safety measure, not a form of recognition that a policyholder had a greater equity in his policy. If anything, the reverse was true.

After extensive study by an NAIC committee, therefore, all jurisdictions adopted the Standard Nonforfeiture Law effective in 1948. The Law prescribes that minimum cash values should be equivalent to the present value (at 3 1/2 percent) of future benefits

(based on the 1941 CSO* Table) less the present value of future adjusted premiums. The present value of future adjusted premiums is subject to a maximum: the present value of future benefits, plus 2 percent of the face amount, plus 40 percent of the adjusted premium itself for the first policy year, plus 25 percent of the lesser of the adjusted premium for the first policy year or the adjusted premium for a whole life policy issued at the same age. This provision sets a limit on the extent to which a company can charge the policyholder for acquisition costs, surrender expenses, etc.

In theory, the cash value on a nonparticipating policy need bear no relationship to the reserve. In practice, there is a relationship, because (1) the mortality assumption must as a practical matter be the same **, (2) additional reserves must be set up when cash values exceed reserves, and (3) for a number of rea-

*Use of the 1958 CSO Table became mandatory in 1966.

**A mortality basis other than the prescribed table can be used to calculate cash values, but the result must be a cash value at least as great as the statutory minimum.

sons, many companies grade the cash value into the reserve after a period of years, making sure, of course, that the premium level is sufficient to justify that high a cash value.

Table 3–3 reproduces an asset share calculation for a whole life policy (issued to a male age 45) represented in Crazy Quilt Life's 1948–1951 ratebook. The asset shares for the first 20 years are reproduced in Table 3–3, and the cash value and the reserve are shown for comparison.

The asset shares do not necessarily represent values which can be withdrawn by a policyholder without any impact on the company, for several reasons. First, any profits must come out of the asset share. Second, the withdrawing policyholder may tend to be healthier than persisting policyholders, and the asset share reflects average experience which could be disturbed by such a withdrawal.* Third, surrender may involve a capital loss if the company is forced to sell securities at depressed prices to pay the surrender.

From the persisting policyholder's point of view, the asset shares should be increased for surrender values paid as well as the associated processing expense. This is because a persisting policyholder should not be required to bear the cost of surrender (that is, the difference between accumulated funds and the cash value) of a withdrawing policyholder.

For various reasons, therefore, the asset share does not necessarily represent the withdrawing policyholder's equitable interest in his policy, nor does it necessarily represent the amount that could be withdrawn without affecting the company and the persisting policyholders.

Nevertheless, Table 3–3 is indicative that

▶ A loss is occasioned on surrender during the first several policy years,
▶ The cash value is inevitably higher than an equitable interest in assets for the first few years,
▶ The cash value need never equate with the reserve, and
▶ A surrender at any time will create a bookkeeping "gain from terminations" because the reserve is in this case greater than the cash value at all durations.

In addition, it will be observed that while the cash value and the CRVM reserve are based on the same mortality table and interest rate, the cash value is always less. In effect, this means that the acquisition cost allowance is greater in the case of the cash value

*However, any such disturbance has never been proven.

than in the case of the CRVM reserve. This is true even though the cash values are higher than the minimum (1941 CSO, 3 1/2 percent) specified in the Standard Nonforfeiture Law (as that law stood in 1948).

Nonparticipating Term Insurance

As everyone knows, term insurance is (a) the cheapest form of insurance for the policyholder, (b) the least profitable for the insurance company, and (c) the easiest for the layman to understand.

This suggests the limitations of common knowledge, because term insurance can be (a) the most expensive form of insurance for the policyholder, (b) the most profitable for the insurance company, and (c) the most difficult for laymen to understand.

The circumstances under which term can be most expensive for the policyholder is perhaps best left to explication by competent life underwriters, and the mysterious process by which term is rendered more profitable than permanent is perhaps best left to darkle. The present discussion is concerned primarily with explaining some of the financial mechanics of term insurance, particularly some of the more unusual characteristics that have implications for accounting.

Level Term

Nonparticipating one-year term insurance without the right of renewal or conversion is in fact a model of simplicity. Supplementary contracts aside, the contract is discharged within one policy year and no more than two calendar years. From an accounting point of view there is possibly some distortion when the policy year straddles two calendar years, depending on the incidence of claims and expenses. But the distortion is short-lived and is not unlike the distortion which arises when a one-year fire insurance policy is in force over a year-end.* If life insurance companies sold nothing but one-year nonrenewable and nonconvertible term policies, there would be no accounting problems to speak of.

Problems arise when the period of coverage lengthens. Most individual term insurance policies sold in

*In fact, for all practical purposes the policy could be accounted for much like a fire policy is accounted for. Interest is inconsequential, expenses are heaped at the beginning, and claim cost can usually be presumed to be approximately equal through the term. An unearned premium approach, with recognition of the "equity" in the unearned premium, would probably work well enough.

the United States are for durations greater than one year. The problems compound when the privileges of renewability and convertibility are added. As respects shorter-term coverages—for example, five-year and ten-year term—it is common to provide for renewal and conversion. As respects long-term coverages—for example, term-to-65—it is common to provide the conversion privilege.

Crazy Quilt offers a five-year term policy renewable at age 65 and convertible to age 70 (these limits were raised from 60 and 65, respectively, beginning with the 1965–1967 ratebook).

In pricing the policy, the Company first determines the estimated cost of average mortality and subjectively "loads" the average cost to recognize that there may be some adverse selection involved—that is, people in poorer health will tend to buy the lowest-premium form of insurance, i.e., term. Then the Company estimates the cost of extra mortality on renewal; it is obvious that individuals whose health has deteriorated are more likely to renew than people with continuing good health. Finally, the Company estimates the cost of the conversion feature. This is difficult, because (1) there is little solid evidence that conversion results in extra mortality where a company encourages conversion, as Crazy Quilt does, and (2) it appears that until the renewal privilege runs out, people in poor health will tend to renew rather than convert to a higher-premium permanent policy. Nevertheless, the policy is renewable to 65 and convertible to 70; it follows that impaired lives will convert when the alternative is no coverage at all, and that very high extra mortality can be expected at the older ages. Since some percentage of policies sold today will wind up converted to permanent policies under these adverse conditions, and since the premium rates at the time of conversion are not loaded for extra mortality associated with conversion—that is, they are the regular published rates *—then some charge must be made for the cost of conversion.

Renewability

In developing premiums for the 1968–1969 ratebook version of its five-year renewable and convertible term policy, Crazy Quilt found that expected extra mortality on renewal was quite significant. Re-

*A permanent impairment existing at the time of selling the original term policy is also reflected in the premium for the policy to which the policyholder converts. The substandard classification cannot be changed, however; the rate on the permanent policy would be the regular premium plus an extra premium based on the original impairment.

viewing its own experience as well as that of other companies, Crazy Quilt developed its own mortality table for renewable term business. Table 3–4 shows a comparison between renewable term mortality and standard mortality for a male age 45.

It will be observed from Table 3–4 that extra mortality associated with term renewals is projected to 150 percent in the later renewal periods.

As one might expect, the Company found the cost of expected extra mortality to be material:

| | Per $1,000 Issued | |
	Gross Amount	Present Value
Projected death claims on term plan throughout all periods of coverage	$67.52	$37.72
Projected death claims using standard mortality assumptions	53.46	31.28
	$14.06	$ 6.44

In projecting premiums for this plan, Crazy Quilt estimates the proportion of policyholders that will renew and provides for renewals in the assumed lapse rates. Thus, although the policy being sold is a five-year term plan, in the case of a male age 45 Crazy Quilt treats the policy as if its term extended 25 years (that is, the policy is renewable to age 65, so the last renewal would expire at attained age 70). The gross premium per $1,000 (ignoring the policy fee of $15) charged during each renewal period, and the extra mortality anticipated in each such period, is shown in Table 3–5.

Although each renewal represents a new contract, Crazy Quilt incorporates the probability of renewal in its rate tests and treats all renewals as if they were part of a single contract term. Of course, the premium changes with each renewal. Since the premium is not level, the charge for extra mortality incorporated in the premium is not level either. The level annual equivalent of the cost of extra mortality is $1.21. Prorating the cost to the premiums results in a charge ranging from 88 cents in the first five-year period to $4.26 in the last, as follows:

Attained Age	Annual Gross Premium	Gross Premium Without Regard for Cost of Extra Mortality*	12% Loading for Cost of Extra Mortality
45	$ 8.27	$ 7.39	$ .88
50	11.48	10.25	1.23
55	16.67	14.89	1.78
60	25.99	23.21	2.78
65	39.88	35.62	4.26

*This is computed simply by dividing the annual gross premium by 112 percent.

Table 3–4.

COMPARISON OF MORTALITY ASSUMED FOR RENEWABLE TERM POLICY (RENEWABLE TO AGE 65) WITH MORTALITY ASSUMED FOR WHOLE LIFE POLICY ISSUED STANDARD—MALE AGE 45—1968–1969 RATEBOOK

Duration	Assumed Renewable Term Death Rate	Assumed Whole Life Death Rate	Ratio of Renewable Term Death Rate to Whole Life Death Rate
1	.00180	.00180	100%
2	.00259	.00259	100
3	.00307	.00307	100
4	.00383	.00383	100
5	.00443	.00443	100
6	.00773	.00672	115
7	.00857	.00745	115
8	.00744	.00821	115
9	.01037	.00902	115
10	.01142	.00992	115
11	.01364	.01091	125
12	.01501	.01201	125
13	.01653	.01322	125
14	.01819	.01455	125
15	.01999	.01599	125
16	.02636	.01757	150
17	.02892	.01928	150
18	.03168	.02112	150
19	.03465	.02310	150
20	.03788	.02525	150
21	.04142	.02761	150
22	.04532	.03021	150
23	.04962	.03308	150
24	.05436	.03624	150
25	.05949	.03766	150

Table 3–5.

5-YEAR RENEWABLE AND CONVERTIBLE TERM GROSS PREMIUMS AND COST OF EXTRA MORTALITY ON RENEWAL—MALE AGE 45—1968–1969 RATEBOOK—PER $1,000 ORIGINALLY ISSUED

Renewal Period	Attained Age	Annual Gross Premium Per $1,000 Exclusive of $15 Policy Fee	Present Value Per $1,000 At Issue of Gross Premiums	Present Value Per $1,000 At Issue of Cost of Extra Mortality	Present Value of Gross Premiums Without Regard For Cost of Extra Mortality	Ratio of Present Value of Cost of Extra Mortality to Present Value of Gross Premium Without Regard for Cost of Extra Mortality
At issue	45	$ 8.27	$29.33	$ -0-	$29.33	
1	50	11.48	13.94	1.38	12.56	11.0%
2	55	16.67	9.07	1.72	7.35	23.4
3	60	25.99	4.43	1.80	2.63	68.4
4	65	39.88	3.48	1.54	1.94	79.4
			$60.25	$6.44	$53.81	12.0%
Present value of $1 life annuity due for 25 periods			$ 5.33	$5.33	$ 5.33	
Level annual equivalent			$11.30	$1.21	$10.09	

As Table 3–5 indicates, there is no extra mortality cost in the first five years. But an extra premium is charged for the privilege. Immediately after receiving the first premium a theoretical reserve begins to accumulate for the cost of extra mortality. This is because the present value of future extra mortality costs is greater than the present value of future premiums attributable to the renewal privilege *. However, a reserve is not required for purposes of the statutory statement.

Convertibility

In studying mortality under term conversions, Crazy Quilt found that mortality was considerably more adverse than standard in the first year after conversion and graded rapidly to a level only slightly worse than standard. Expressed as a percentage of standard mortality, the following pattern of conversion mortality emerged:

Year Following Conversion	Ratio of Conversion Mortality To Standard Mortality
1	170%
2	130
3	120
4–15	115
16 on	110

Crazy Quilt combined all of its conversion experience in developing these ratios, including conversion experience under term policies that were convertible but not renewable. In the case of the five-year term plan it was recognized that a policyholder who expects to die would renew rather than convert because the premium is lower and the death benefit remains the same. Therefore the ratios are probably overstated somewhat for the five-year term plan, since some part of the extra mortality otherwise associated with conversion would be experienced in connection with the renewal privilege. Nevertheless, lacking breakdowns as to the original plans underlying the conversions, the Company felt obliged to use the information it had. The effect was to assess the cost of conversion in the form of an average charge against convertible policies, irrespective of the relative costs that might be assessed based upon the unique experience of each convertible plan.

In deciding how to compute the cost of conversion, Crazy Quilt wrestled at length with the problem of whether the plan to which the term policy is converted (the "conversion policy") should produce (1) zero profit or (2) a normal profit following the conversion. After due consideration it was decided that provision would be made for an approximately normal profit on the conversion policy following conversion. This had the effect of increasing the cost of conversion relative to a zero-profit policy, since no profits were to be used to offset the cost of conversion.

How to compute the cost of conversion?

The expected extra mortality was known; so were the expense savings (on conversion, there is no underwriting expense and there are some savings in selling and issue expenses as well *). At first blush it would only seem necessary to substitute mortality and expenses on conversion policies for standard experience and run a rate test of a standard policy using the modified assumptions. The difference between the present value of profits on the conversion policy and the present value of profits on the standard policy would measure the cost of conversion.

However, it was known that persistency of conversion policies was better than standard. People in poor health do not lapse their policies, and a sizeable proportion of people converting could be presumed to be in poor health.

So new persistency, mortality, and expense assumptions were introduced into the profit tests for several standard plans. The present value of profits on conversion policies was then compared with the present value of profits on standard policies, and the difference was taken to be the cost of conversion. Such a comparison for a whole life policy issued to a male age 50 under Crazy Quilt's 1970–1971 ratebook is shown in Table 3–6.

The cost of conversion at age 50 was computed to be $4.23. Crazy Quilt next had to determine the probability of conversion. It did this by examining its conversion experience and developing a table of conversion probabilities for each issue age and duration.

In rate testing, the assumed cost of conversion was computed by multiplying the cost of conversion by the probability of conversion. For example, if 15 percent of plans issued at age 45 were expected to convert at age 50, the cost of conversion was computed as 15 percent of $4.23, or 63 cents.

Table 3–7 shows the profit test for Crazy Quilt's 5-year renewable and convertible term policy (1970–1971 ratebook) issued to a male age 35. Insurance in

---

*Some companies weight the extra cost more toward the premiums in the later renewal periods. There is no single method of providing for such cost. In practice, companies usually adopt very practical methods.

*This depends in part on the company's philosophy in allocating selling and issue expenses.

Table 3–6.

CALCULATION OF COST OF CONVERSION OF 5-YEAR TERM PLAN TO NONPARTICIPATING WHOLE LIFE POLICY AT AGE 50—1970–1971 RATEBOOK—PER $1,000 CONVERTED

	Present Value at the Assumed Investment Earnings Rate (Identical in All Cases)		
	Standard Policy	*Converted Policy*	*Cost of Conversion*
Premiums	$285.87	$327.01	$41.14
Death claims	125.47	170.31	44.84
Surrenders	60.53	63.55	3.02
Acquisition costs:			
First year	54.95	50.91	(4.04)
Renewal	13.18	14.80	1.62
Maintenance expenses	15.47	15.40	(.07)
	269.60	314.97	45.37
Profit	$ 16.27	$ 12.04	$ 4.23

force is stated net of non-renewals; hence there is a disproportionate decrease in insurance in force in each renewal year. Acquisition costs (principally commissions and issue expense) are indicated in each renewal year. Conversions are assumed to occur every fifth year, on the average; the related costs of conversion are shown.

Some would say that there is no adverse mortality on conversion so long as the renewal option is operative; this was discussed earlier in this chapter. Because of the nature of the underlying mortality data and Crazy Quilt's method of applying the data, Crazy Quilt opted to be conservative and assume adverse mortality on renewal *and* conversion. The former is reflected in the projected deaths shown in Table 3–7; the latter is reflected in the cost of conversion.

Statutory reserves accumulated under this type of term plan are generally quite small. This is another way of saying that assets associated with the plan are relatively immaterial. Hence the use of a high discount rate does not drastically alter the present value of profits. Use of a discount rate of 12 percent results in a present value of profits per $1,000 issued of $1.81, a healthy sum indeed considering that Crazy Quilt's basic profit objective requires only that the present value of profits at 12 percent must equal zero.

Note that this plan produces statutory losses in the later years. This is due primarily to the fact that statutory reserves do not provide for extra mortality on renewal or the cost of conversion.

Decreasing Term

A great deal of decreasing term insurance is sold in the United States. In general, decreasing term insurance is designed to furnish maximum insurance in the early years when protection is needed most but the capacity to pay premiums is limited. The premium is usually level while the face amount decreases year by year.

Therein lies a problem, because in the later years the same premium buys much less protection, and persistency may suffer. It is not unusual for the persistency rate to increase in the later years.* When the face amount approaches zero, there is little incentive to pay premiums.

For that reason some decreasing term policies provide for a premium-paying period somewhat shorter than the term of coverage (for example, a premium-paying period of 20 years for a 25-year decreasing term policy). Alternatively, the face amount may eventually be frozen at some amount. This was what Crazy Quilt finally did. The Company first offered 25-year decreasing term insurance in its 1957–1961 ratebook, and the amount gradually decreased to zero by the end of the 25th year. But industry experience indicated that terminations would soar in the last five years or so. Therefore, beginning with its 1962–1969 ratebook, Crazy Quilt froze the coverage at 21.3 percent of the initial face amount in the last four years. In addition, the rate of decrease was made more gradual.

*As a matter of fact, there is some tendency for termination rates to turn upward in the later years for all kinds of contracts, term and permanent, as the need for insurance lessens with advancing age and, in the case of permanent insurance, as the cash value begins to approach the face amount.

Table 3-7.

PROJECTION OF TRIAL PREMIUM AND ASSUMED EXPERIENCE FOR 5-YEAR RENEWABLE AND CONVERTIBLE TERM FOR MALE AGE 35—1970–1971 RATEBOOK—PER $1,000 OF ORIGINAL ISSUE

Calendar Year	Insurance In Force	Premiums	Interest on Reserves	Deaths	Cost of Conversion	Increase in Reserves	Acquisition Costs	Maintenance Expenses	Pre-Tax Profits	Cumulative Present Value At 12%	Effect on Cumulative Present Value of Profits (At 12%) of $1 Annual Change — In Premium Per $1,000	In Expense Per $1,000
1	$1,000	$4.90	$.04	$ .38		$1.53	$9.29	$.71	$(6.96)	$(6.96)	$ (.15)	$1.00
2	799	3.91	.09	.76		(.10)		.57	2.77	(4.49)	.50	1.71
3	686	3.36	.08	.80		(.11)		.50	2.26	(2.70)	.99	2.26
4	617	3.02	.07	.85		(.17)		.45	1.97	(1.29)	1.39	2.70
5	554	2.72	.06	.87		(.27)		.40	1.78	(.16)	1.71	3.05
6	432	2.65	.06	.89	$ (.03)	.14	.98	.35	.39	.06	1.88	3.30
7	405	2.49	.06	.93		.14		.33	1.15	.64	2.06	3.50
8	384	2.36	.06	1.00		.02		.31	1.08	1.13	2.22	3.68
9	363	2.23	.05	1.09		(.11)		.30	1.02	1.54	2.36	3.82
10	344	2.11	.05	1.19		(.24)		.28	.93	1.88	2.47	3.95
11	240	2.03	.04	1.16	.05	.04	.67	.24	(.08)	1.85	2.52	4.03
12	220	1.86	.04	1.10		.10		.22	.48	1.99	2.58	4.09
13	201	1.70	.05	1.16		(.01)		.20	.40	2.09	2.63	4.14
14	184	1.56	.04	1.22		(.12)		.18	.32	2.17	2.67	4.18
15	170	1.44	.04	1.28		(.21)		.17	.23	2.21	2.70	4.22
16	113	1.36	.03	1.15	.13	.01	.41	.14	(.45)	2.13	2.71	4.24
17	107	1.29	.03	1.00		.11		.13	.09	2.15	2.73	4.26
18	103	1.24	.04	1.05		.02		.13	.08	2.16	2.74	4.27
19	100	1.21	.04	1.12		(.06)		.12	.06	2.17	2.75	4.28
20	97	1.17	.03	1.19		(.15)		.12	.04	2.17	2.76	4.30
21	81	1.40	.03	1.29	Nil	.16	.40	.13	(.53)	2.12	2.77	4.30
22	77	1.34	.04	1.38		.12		.12	(.25)	2.09	2.78	4.31
23	74	1.29	.04	1.45		.03		.12	(.27)	2.07	2.78	4.32
24	71	1.24	.04	1.53		(.07)		.11	(.30)	2.05	2.79	4.32
25	68	1.19	.03	1.62		(.18)		.11	(.33)	2.03	2.79	4.33
26	37	.98	.03	1.32	1.77	(.11)	.26	.08	(2.31)	1.89	2.79	4.33
27	35	.94	.03	1.01		.09		.08	(.21)	1.88	2.79	4.33
28	33	.89	.03	1.06		.01		.07	(.23)	1.87	2.80	4.33
29	31	.85	.03	1.11		(.06)		.07	(.25)	1.86	2.80	4.33
30	30	.80	.02	1.15		(.13)		.07	(.27)	1.85	2.80	4.34
31	24	.99	.02	1.10	Nil	(.08)	.25	.07	(.33)	1.84	2.80	4.34
32	23	.93	.02	1.04		(.02)		.07	(.14)	1.83	2.80	4.34
33	21	.87	.02	1.06		(.02)		.06	(.22)	1.83	2.80	4.34
34	20	.81	.01	1.08		(.02)		.06	(.29)	1.82	2.80	4.34
35	18	.75	.01	1.09		(.02)		.06	(.36)	1.81	2.80	4.34
36	-0-	-0-	.01	.55		(.26)		-0-	(.29)	1.81	2.80	4.34

Table 3–8.

ORIGINAL FACE AMOUNTS AND INSURANCE IN FORCE FOR 25-YEAR DECREASING TERM BUSINESS

Year	000		Original Face Amount of Policies In Force	Ratio of In-Force to Original Face Amount
	New Business	Insurance In Force		
Issues of all years:				
1957	$ 5,050	$ 4,972	$ 5,047	99%
1958	7,050	10,724	11,004	97
1959	13,800	21,975	22,677	97
1960	21,700	38,738	40,211	96
1961	32,040	62,449	65,195	96
1962	48,250	97,649	102,337	95
1963	70,060	149,060	156,676	95
1964	96,860	219,134	231,108	95
1965	120,300	301,288	319,361	94
1966	145,390	395,824	422,044	94
1967	167,400	497,534	534,032	93
1968	193,600	610,120	659,295	93
1969	223,410	735,345	799,795	92
1970	250,470	869,133	951,705	91
1971	280,170	1,015,951	1,120,585	91
Issues of 1957 only:				
1957	$ 5,050	$ 4,972	$ 5,047	99%
1958		3,783	3,957	96
1959		3,107	3,359	92
1960		2,698	3,018	89
1961		2,392	2,775	86
1962		2,034	2,451	83
1963		1,829	2,298	80
1964		1,654	2,170	76
1965		1,492	2,055	73
1966		1,352	1,960	69
1967		1,098	1,681	65
1968		991	1,611	62
1969		890	1,543	58
1970		790	1,471	54
1971		698	1,407	50

Select mortality savings. Crazy Quilt noted that statutory reserves resulted in some peculiar profit patterns on decreasing term business. The main reason seemed to be that the tabular cost of mortality, computed at ultimate mortality rates, was charged against the reserve (effectively reducing the reserve increase) while select mortality was actually experienced for a number of years. The net result was to flow through to income the difference between select mortality and ultimate mortality. After the selection period wore off, of course, ultimate rates were experienced and ultimate rates were charged against the reserve as tabular cost. There were therefore no more selection savings to flow through to income. This phenomenon is experienced with respect to all classes of business, of course, but it seems to be more pronounced in the case of decreasing term business, due to the fact that face amount is high in the early years, when select mortality is experienced, and low in the later years, when ultimate mortality is experienced.

Volume credits. Some companies carry decreasing term business at a constant "volume credit", for example, 50 or 60 percent of the initial face amount. Crazy Quilt decreases its decreasing term "scientifically", that is, by adjusting each in-force policy annually. The reason is that in Crazy Quilt's case the assumption of a constant relationship doesn't work very well, due mainly to the rapid growth in the line of business. In 1971, for example, insurance in force was equal to 91 percent of the original face amount of

Table 3–9.

PROJECTION OF TRIAL PREMIUM AND ASSUMED EXPERIENCE FOR 25-YEAR CONVERTIBLE DECREASING
TERM—COMPOSITE OF ALL AGES—1970–1971 RATEBOOK—PER $1,000 OF ORIGINAL ISSUE

Calendar Year	Units In Force	Insurance In Force	Premiums	Interest on Reserves	Deaths	Cost of Conversion	Increase in Reserves	Expenses	Pre-Tax Profits	Cumulative Present Value of Profits at 12%	Yield on Invested Surplus	Present Value of Future Profits per Unit In Force At Investment Earnings Rate	12%
1	.999	$985	$6.28	$.04	$ .51		$1.52	$12.28	$(7.99)	$(7.99)		$18.77	$13.90
2	.816	782	5.20	.11	1.05		.62	.80	2.83	(5.46)		20.82	15.41
3	.722	671	4.63	.14	1.12		.50	.62	2.53	(3.44)		21.34	15.79
4	.657	592	4.21	.16	1.18		.36	.56	2.28	(1.82)		21.29	15.76
5	.608	529	3.90	.18	1.20		.25	.52	2.11	(.48)	9.0%	20.80	15.39
6	.517	433	3.25	.18	1.14	$.08	(.26)	.44	2.04	.68	15.6	21.88	16.11
7	.486	391	3.06	.16	1.09		.06	.41	1.66	1.52	19.1	21.05	15.58
8	.460	356	2.89	.15	1.12		(.01)	.39	1.55	2.22	21.4	19.88	14.85
9	.439	324	2.76	.15	1.13		(.05)	.37	1.46	2.81	22.9	18.48	13.92
10	.421	296	2.65	.14	1.16		(.11)	.36	1.38	3.31	23.9	16.89	12.80
11	.376	251	2.42	.13	1.17	.01	(.25)	.32	1.30	3.72	24.6	16.28	12.37
12	.362	228	2.33	.12	1.20		(.18)	.31	1.12	4.05	25.1	14.60	11.13
13	.348	206	2.24	.11	1.26		(.22)	.30	1.00	4.30	25.4	12.98	9.90
14	.334	184	2.14	.10	1.31		(.26)	.29	.90	4.51	25.6	11.45	8.71
15	.319	163	2.04	.09	1.32		(.27)	.28	.81	4.68	25.8	9.96	7.51
16	.262	123	1.66	.07	1.20	.68	(.49)	.23	.11	4.70	25.8	12.32	9.80
17	.250	106	1.58	.05	1.06		(.21)	.22	.57	4.79	25.9	11.18	9.06
18	.238	91	1.50	.04	1.00		(.19)	.21	.53	4.87	25.9	10.05	8.31
19	.227	76	1.42	.04	.93		(.15)	.20	.48	4.93	25.9	8.91	7.52
20	.215	62	1.35	.03	.84		(.10)	.19	.45	4.98	26.0	7.74	6.68
21	.200	47	1.26	.03	.73	Nil	(.03)	.17	.41	5.03	26.0	6.62	5.86
22	.188	40	1.18	.03	.64		.02	.16	.39	5.06	26.0	5.28	4.80
23	.176	37	1.11	.03	.62		(.01)	.15	.36	5.09	26.0	3.80	3.35
24	.164	35	1.03	.03	.64		(.07)	.14	.34	5.12	26.0	2.14	2.05
25	.150	32	.94	.02	.64	Nil	(.13)	.13	.32	5.14	26.0	.28	.28
26	-0-	-0-	-0-	.01	.32		(.36)	-0-	.04	5.14	26.0	-0-	-0-

policies then in force. Table 3–8 sets forth the relationship between insurance in force and original face amounts for Crazy Quilt.

Generally reserve factors for decreasing term insurance are applied to "units" of insurance rather than insurance in force. In Crazy Quilt's case, a "unit" of decreasing term insurance is defined as $1,000 of face amount of original issue. Reserve factors themselves recognize the decrease in insurance in force. Thus reserve valuations are not affected by the particular method used to report volume credits.

Rate test. Table 3–9 shows selected information from the composite profit test for the 25-year decreasing term policy in Crazy Quilt's 1970-1971 ratebook. The method of testing is for the most part the same method as was used for 5-year term (see Table 3–7), with three exceptions:

▶ The test is a "composite" of all issue ages tested, incorporating the projection for each issue age weighted by the distribution of expected issues. Detailed tests were conducted for ages 25, 35, and 45, which were deemed to reasonably represent the central ages for all issues. That is, age 25 was used to represent issues from ages 0–29 (but most of the issues fell in the range 20–29); age 35 was used to represent issues from ages 30–39; and age 45 was used to represent issues from ages 40 to 55 (the highest age at which the policy could be issued; however, the bulk of the issues fell in the range 40–49). For purposes of constructing the composite, the assumed distribution of new business was as follows:

Age 25	30%
Age 35	40
Age 45	30
All ages	100%

▶ Yield on invested surplus of $7.99 is computed as soon as earnings turn positive. In effect, earnings are applied to pay off the investment and produce a return on the investment, which over the life of the block of business is 26 percent compounded. (The yield is found by an automated trial and error technique.)

▶ The present value of future statutory profits per unit of insurance in force, computed on two interest bases, at the end of each calendar year is shown. This is calculated by discounting projected profits arising after the year-end and dividing by the units then in force. The information is valuable in de-

termining how much per $1,000 a block of business will be "worth" at each point in time.

Participating Permanent Insurance

The pricing of participating insurance can be very simple or it can be enormously complex, depending on a stock company's attitude toward the product and depending in part on state law.

Some stock companies regard participating insurance as a product that must be made available mainly to accommodate prospects that insist on it; the alternative is to deprive agents of some income. In short, participating insurance is regarded as a necessary evil. Under these conditions it would not be unusual for the company to price the business as if it were nonparticipating. The only difference is that dividends anticipated would be introduced into the rate test as another form of benefit.

At the opposite extreme are stock companies that regard participating insurance as a unique product, to be priced and administered in much the same way as mutual companies price and administer their participating products. Such companies typically view their participating business as a separate "branch" of the company, and some states require that this view be taken by limiting the extent to which earnings on participating business can inure to the benefit of stockholders (a subject which is discussed at length in Chapter 25). Under these conditions a company would keep track of actual earnings on participating business and attempt to modify the dividend scale frequently so as to distribute such earnings to policyholders. Dividends thus assume the nature of a profit-sharing device rather than a benefit.*

Crazy Quilt's practices lean toward the view that dividends are a profit-sharing device.

Premiums

Crazy Quilt establishes premiums on participating business in a manner which gives every reasonable assurance that each class** of policies will be self-

---

*Another view holds that dividends represent an adjustment of cost to the policyholder rather than a sharing of profits. This difference in viewpoint has some practical significance for mutual companies but not for stock companies.

**A "class" of policies, for this purpose, may be defined as a group of participating policies that will tend to experience similar results and which can therefore equitably be combined for purposes of tallying up actual experience and distributing earnings in the form of dividends.

Table 3–10.

COMPUTATION OF 15TH-YEAR DIVIDEND ILLUSTRATED FOR PARTICIPATING WHOLE LIFE POLICY ISSUED TO MALE AGE 35—1968–1969 RATEBOOK—PER $1,000 IN FORCE

Mortality contribution:

Face amount	$1,000	
Terminal reserve per $1,000	259	
Net amount at risk	$ 741 (a)	
1958 CSO mortality rate	.00760	
Approximate actual ultimate mortality rate	.00606	
Margin	.00154 (b)	
Contribution [(a) × (b)]		$1.14

Interest contribution:

Initial reserve per $1,000	$ 241 (a)	
Distribution interest rate	.0400	
Statutory reserve interest rate	.0250	
Margin	.0150 (b)	
Contribution [(a) × (b)]		3.62

Loading contribution:

Gross premium	$21.85	
Statutory net premium	17.67	
Statutory loading	$ 4.18 (a)	
Formula expenses	$ .99 (b)	
Contribution [(a) − (b)]		3.19
TOTAL DIVIDEND		**$7.95**

supporting, i.e., will not show a loss. This involves charging premiums that provide for the greatest adversity that can reasonably be expected. Such premiums are calculated in a manner which recognizes the types of assumptions described by Horace Bassford in 1942:

1. The interest rate used for determining the gross premiums should be the lowest rate which might reasonably be experienced over an extended period.

2. [The] mortality table must contain sufficient margin to cover the highest long-range level of mortality that may, within reason, be experienced over the lifetime of the policy [and should contain additional margins] to allow for the accumulation of sufficient surplus to provide for exceptionally high but temporary mortality.

3. Unit expense rates [should be] increased to provide a margin for possible increases in expense.[1]

Dividends

There are several methods of calculating dividends, but all of them have one thing in common: they attempt to take into account all sources of gain or loss attributable to each class of policies and distribute such gains and losses equitably to each policyholder in the class. As suggested above, premiums are established based on assumptions that provide for the greatest adversity that can reasonably be expected, which is another way of saying that there is a very high probability that the business will produce profits. The dividend is designed to return a large portion of profits to policyholders in proportion to their contributions to such profits.

Crazy Quilt uses the "classic" contribution system (first developed in 1863), which is essentially a three-factor formula which equitably distributes savings from mortality, interest, and expense. The reserve valuation bases—the valuation mortality assumption, the valuation interest assumption, and statutory loading—are taken to be the assumed rates for purposes of computing dividends. The dividend represents the amount by which actual experience is more favorable, in the aggregate, than assumed experience as represented by the valuation assumptions.

It can be seen, therefore, that choice of a reserve valuation basis will have an effect on the incidence of dividend payments to any individual policyholder. The aggregate value of dividends for all years to a class of policyholders will, in theory, be the same regardless of the valuation basis.

Mortality is expressed on an ultimate basis both for the assumed rate and the experience rate. In other words, an *ultimate* experience rate is used to represent actual experience in the dividend calculation.

Table 3–11.

DIVIDEND SCALE ILLUSTRATED FOR PARTICIPATING WHOLE LIFE POLICY ISSUED TO MALE AGE 35—1968–1969 RATEBOOK—PER $1,000 IN FORCE

End of Policy Year	Illustrated Dividend	End of Policy Year	Illustrated Dividend	End of Policy Year	Illustrated Dividend
1	$ 1.08	23	$12.39	45	$19.67
2	1.52	24	12.74	46	19.87
3	1.96	25	13.10	47	20.07
4	2.43	26	13.47	48	20.27
5	2.89	27	13.83	49	20.47
6	3.37	28	14.21	50	20.67
7	3.87	29	14.59	51	20.88
8	4.36	30	14.99	52	21.09
9	4.87	31	15.38	53	21.30
10	5.40	32	15.78	54	21.51
11	5.94	33	16.17	55	21.73
12	6.49	34	16.57	56	21.95
13	7.06	35	16.96	57	22.17
14	7.63	36	17.34	58	22.39
15	7.95	37	17.70	59	22.61
16	8.79	38	18.06	60	22.84
17	9.39	39	18.39	61	23.07
18	10.01	40	18.72	62	23.30
19	10.67	41	18.91	63	23.53
20	11.33	42	19.10	64	23.77
21	11.69	43	19.29	65	Endowment
22	12.04	44	19.48		

Savings from selection are not normally distributed as gains from mortality; such savings are used, instead, as a credit against high first-year expenses. Mortality savings are generally distributed to individuals based on the net amount at risk, i.e., the face amount less the reserve. This is consistent with the method by which the tabular cost of mortality is computed for reserve purposes.

Excess interest is theoretically the difference between the interest rate actually experienced and the tabular interest rate used for reserve purposes. The difference in the rate is applied to the reserve. The experience rate is computed as an average.

Expenses create a problem. As indicated above, select mortality savings are generally credited against first-year expenses, but a negative balance still remains. This negative balance is amortized over a reasonable period.

It is intuitively obvious that a dividend is rarely, if ever, "earned" in the first year (and sometimes it isn't "earned" for several years). Nevertheless, most companies pay dividends before a positive asset share surplus emerges. A few pay first-year dividends, usually contingent on payment of the second year's premium. Such dividends must be borrowed from surplus. The basic reason for paying such early dividends is to prevent lapses.

The computation of the expected 15th-year dividend for Crazy Quilt's participating whole life policy (1968–1969 ratebook) issued to a male age 35 is illustrated in Table 3–10. Calculations of the mortality and interest contributions are self-explanatory. The loading contribution is in the nature of a balancing item and is often manipulated; when added to the mortality and interest contributions, it provides the level of dividend that profit tests or asset shares show to be reasonable. Put another way, the expense formula will rarely reproduce actual expenses. It allows for amortizing acquisition expenses, "smoothing" the dividend scale, and otherwise making the scale reasonable.

The entire dividend scale for age 35 is shown in Table 3–11. These dividends are illustrated to prospective policyholders on the basis that current experience as to mortality, interest, and expense will

Table 3–12.

RATE TEST FOR PARTICIPATING WHOLE LIFE POLICY ISSUED TO MALE AGE 35—1969–1970
RATEBOOK—PER $1,000 ORIGINALLY ISSUED

Calendar Year	Insurance In Force	Premiums	Deaths	Surrenders	Expenses	Dividends Scale (Per $1,000 In Force)	Dividends *	Net Cash Flow
1	$1,000	$24.66	$ .38	$-0-	$41.19	$ 1.08	$ .90	$(17.81)
2	879	21.69	.82	1.08	3.33	1.52	1.27	15.19
3	825	20.36	.92	1.48	2.62	1.96	1.54	13.80
4	799	19.73	1.04	1.19	2.50	2.43	1.85	13.15
5	774	19.11	1.20	1.53	2.42	2.89	2.13	11.83
6	757	18.70	1.53	1.25	2.35	3.37	2.43	11.14
7	740	18.28	1.87	1.48	2.30	3.87	2.72	9.91
8	723	17.87	2.05	1.70	2.25	4.36	3.00	8.87
9	707	17.46	2.23	1.92	2.20	4.87	3.27	7.84
10	690	17.05	2.42	2.12	2.15	5.40	3.54	6.82
11	674	16.65	2.61	2.32	2.10	5.94	3.80	5.82
12	658	16.25	2.82	2.50	2.05	6.49	4.06	4.82
13	641	15.86	3.05	2.68	2.00	7.06	4.30	3.83
14	625	15.46	3.29	2.84	1.95	7.63	4.53	2.85
15	609	15.07	3.56	3.01	1.91	8.20	4.74	1.85
16	593	14.68	3.85	3.15	1.86	8.79	4.95	.87
17	577	14.29	4.16	3.29	1.81	9.39	5.14	(.11)
18	561	13.90	4.47	3.40	1.76	10.01	5.33	(1.06)
19	545	13.51	4.78	3.52	1.71	10.67	5.52	(2.02)
20	529	13.12	5.11	3.63	1.67	11.33	5.68	(2.97)
21	513	12.73	5.45	3.72	1.62	11.69	5.68	(3.74)
22	497	12.34	5.82	3.79	1.57	12.04	5.67	(4.51)
23	481	11.95	6.21	3.86	1.52	12.39	5.64	(5.28)
24	460	11.44	6.58	5.87	1.47	12.74	5.54	(8.02)
25	440	10.93	6.92	5.85	1.40	13.10	5.44	(8.68)
26	419	10.43	7.26	5.84	1.34	13.47	5.33	(9.34)
27	399	9.94	7.60	5.79	1.28	13.83	5.21	(9.94)
28	380	9.46	7.94	5.72	1.22	14.21	5.08	(10.50)
29	360	8.98	8.26	5.63	1.16	14.59	4.94	(11.01)
30	341	8.51	8.56	5.53	1.10	14.99	4.80	(11.48)
–	–	–	–	–	–	–	–	–
–	–	–	–	–	–	–	–	–
–	–	–	–	–	–	–	–	–
66	Nil	Nil	Nil	Nil	Nil	-0-	-0-	Nil
Present value at investment earnings rate of gross amounts for all years	$282.41	$77.34	$57.43	$74.53		$66.23	$ 6.88

* The present value of the dividend payable at the end of the year is assumed to be paid at the beginning of the policy year. Hence the amount shown for the first year, $.90, is the scale, $1.08, times the percentage of policyholders expected to persist into the second year, 88 percent, times the present value factor, which at 5 percent (the discount rate used in this case) is 95 percent.

obtain indefinitely. This is all that is permitted by law. If future experience differs significantly from current experience, the dividend scale will be revised.*

* However, the timing of the revisions do not necessarily coincide with the timing of changes in experience. Some companies wait many years before revising scales; a few never revise them, preferring to retain excess earnings more or less indefinitely.

Rate Test

Table 3–12 shows the rate test for the participating policy whose dividends are displayed in Table 3–11. It will be observed that premiums and the indicated dividend scale produce some pre-tax profits. Because participating policyholders pay higher premiums than nonparticipating policyholders they thereby assume a much greater portion of the risk of future adversity than do nonparticipating policyholders. Therefore Crazy Quilt does not require a rate of return on participating business as high as the rate of return targeted for nonparticipating business. In fact, Crazy Quilt essentially ignores the traditional rate of return calculations and instead provides for profits on the order of about 10 percent of profits before dividends, which in Crazy Quilt's case happens to coincide with restrictions imposed by state law (which are discussed in Chapter 25). In the case of the policy shown in Table 3–12, the indicated percentage of profits accruing to stockholders is 9.4 percent, as follows:

Present value of net cash flow	$ 6.88
Present value of net cash flow before dividends:	
Present value of net cash flow	$ 6.88
Present value of dividends	66.23
Total	$73.11
Ratio of present value of net cash flow to present value of net cash flow before dividends	9.4%

Individual Fixed Annuities

Individual annuities are much like ordinary life insurance policies, and the pricing techniques are usually much the same. The assumptions used differ, of course; for example, ordinary mortality tables are normally not appropriate for annuities.

Table 3–13 shows the rate test for Crazy Quilt's single-premium nonrefund immediate annuity (1970–1971 ratebook) issued to a male annuitant age 65. The test period stretches out to age 110, since the mortality table being used extends to that age (ordinary life tables usually terminate at age 100, at which time the contract would endow if the policyholder were alive).

No surrenders are shown in the rate test because the contract is a pure annuity. Note that while the total premium is received immediately, expenses—primarily administrative expenses—continue for the life of the contract.

The present value of profits at the investment earnings rate, $84.37, consists of the following components:

	Present Value
Premiums	$1,288.31
Less:	
Annuity benefits	1,082.00
First-year expenses	106.41
Expenses subsequent to the first year	15.53
	1,203.94
	$ 84.37

The reserve covers the annuity benefits and the gross premium received in the first year is available for first-year expenses, but the only income available to absorb expenses in subsequent years is excess interest.

Even if Crazy Quilt had no first-year expenses it would still report a statutory loss on the business. The first-year statutory reserve, $1,331.40, is in excess of the total premium and interest received ($1,326.49). This is because the business is priced on the basis of an interest assumption of 6 percent, while the reserves are based on a 3 percent assumption. This suggests the tremendous surplus problem that single-premium business can cause.

Nevertheless, in Crazy Quilt's case, the expected profitability of the business (profits discounted at 12 percent are $25.24) makes the investment of surplus worthwhile.

Specialty Policies and Supplemental Benefits

A wide variety of "specialty" policies and supplemental benefits are sold in the life insurance industry, but most of them have characteristics similar to the products already discussed in this chapter or to be discussed in Part IV of the book.

To take a few examples, a family policy is really a package of coverages on separate people; the insurance may be permanent or term or both. The various coverages would be priced more or less the same as if they were sold to separate people.

A term rider (level or decreasing) would be priced in much the same fashion as a comparable direct coverage. A disability income rider or waiver of premium benefit would be priced in essentially the same fashion as a loss of time policy (discussed in Chapter 19). Accidental death coverage would be priced like term coverage, the only difference being the substitution of a mortality table limited to deaths by accident.

Supplementary contracts not involving life contingencies are merely interest-bearing deposits. Supple-

Table 3–13.

RATE TEST FOR SINGLE-PREMIUM IMMEDIATE NO-REFUND ANNUITY ISSUED TO MALE AGE 65—1970–1971 RATEBOOK—PER UNIT ($83.33 MONTHLY IN ANNUAL INCOME) ISSUED

Calendar Year	Units in Force	Premium	Interest on Reserve	Annuity Benefits	(Increase) or Decrease Reserve	Expenses	Pre-Tax Profits	Present Value of Profits at Investment Earnings Rate	12%
1	.993	$1,288.31	$38.18	$ -0-	$(1,331.40)	$106.41	$(111.32)	$(111.32)	$(111.32)
2	.979		75.68	118.34	64.21	1.76	19.79	18.66	17.67
3	.963		71.91	116.56	65.05	1.73	18.67	16.62	14.88
4	.944		68.06	114.50	67.39	1.70	19.25	16.17	13.70
5	.920		64.03	111.96	71.27	1.66	21.68	17.17	13.79
6	.890		59.78	108.72	74.78	1.61	24.23	18.10	13.74
7	.857		55.41	104.90	75.30	1.56	24.25	17.10	12.30
8	.823		51.07	100.89	73.73	1.50	22.41	14.90	10.13
9	.787		46.83	96.67	71.90	1.43	20.63	12.94	8.33
10	.750		42.70	92.26	69.78	1.37	18.85	11.16	6.80
11	.711		38.71	87.66	67.39	1.30	17.14	9.56	5.52
12	.670		34.86	82.89	64.69	1.23	15.43	8.13	4.43
13	.628		31.18	77.95	61.78	1.16	13.85	6.88	3.56
14	.586		27.68	72.86	58.55	1.08	12.29	5.76	2.81
15	.542		24.37	67.66	55.11	1.00	10.82	4.78	2.22
16	.498		21.26	62.38	51.45	.93	9.40	3.92	1.72
17	.453		18.38	57.04	47.63	.85	8.12	3.20	1.32
18	.409		15.71	51.70	43.66	.77	6.90	2.56	1.01
19	.365		13.29	46.41	39.60	.69	5.79	2.03	.75
20	.322		11.10	41.21	35.52	.61	4.80	1.59	.56
21	.281		9.15	36.15	31.46	.54	3.92	1.22	.41
22	.242		7.43	31.30	27.47	.46	3.14	.92	.29
23	.205		5.94	26.71	23.64	.40	2.47	.69	.21
24	.171		4.67	22.43	20.00	.33	1.91	.50	.14
25	.139		3.60	18.50	16.62	.27	1.45	.36	.10
26	.112		2.72	14.96	13.54	.22	1.08	.25	.06
27	.087		2.01	11.84	10.80	.18	.79	.17	.04
28	.067		1.45	9.15	8.41	.14	.57	.12	.03
29	.050		1.02	6.89	6.39	.10	.42	.08	.02
30	.036		.69	5.04	4.71	.07	.29	.05	.01
31	.025		.46	3.56	3.37	.05	.22	.04	.01
32	.017		.29	2.44	2.33	.04	.14	.02	Nil
33	.011		.18	1.60	1.55	.02	.11	.02	Nil
34	.007		.11	1.01	.99	.01	.08	.01	Nil
35	.004		.06	.60	.60	.01	.05	.01	Nil
36	.002		.03	.34	.35	.01	.03	Nil	Nil
37	.001		.02	.18	.19	Nil	.03	Nil	Nil
38	.001		.01	.09	.10	Nil	.02	Nil	Nil
39	Nil		Nil	.04	.05	Nil	.01	Nil	Nil
40	Nil		Nil	.02	.02	Nil	-0-	-0-	Nil
41	Nil		Nil	.01	.01	Nil	-0-	-0-	-0-
42-45	Nil		Nil	Nil	Nil	Nil	Nil	-0-	-0-
								$ 84.37	$ 25.24

mentary contracts involving life contingencies are in the nature of single-premium annuities.

Many practical compromises are made in pricing supplemental benefits, perhaps to a greater degree than is true of the underlying coverages. Often, for example, a company will simply select competitive premiums for waiver of premium and accidental death coverages and not bother to test them. This is partly because such coverages are typically not material in terms of a company's overall operations and partly because the rates commonly used are believed *ipso facto* to produce satisfactory profits.

4

Income
Concepts*

In the long and turbulent history of the development of the life insurance audit guide, the subject of revenue recognition resulted in more brouhahas than any other subject.

The reason is that there is no perfect theoretical precedent for accounting for something as unique as the life insurance transaction. So theories and theoreticians abounded. Various parties at interest developed their own concepts of revenue and were inevitably able to find partial support for their concepts either by reference to the characteristics of the life insurance product or by reference to accounting principles applied in other industries.

The problem was especially serious because the definition of revenue and the timing of its recognition in the accounts largely determine the pattern of reported profits. That's because costs are matched with revenue; the incidence of revenue recognition tends to define (and hence control) the incidence of expense recognition; and what's left over is profit, which tends naturally to follow the incidence of revenue recognition.

Of all the theories advanced, none stood supreme. The theory finally adopted for purposes of the life insurance audit guide is an amalgamation of many theories—in short, a compromise. But the theory meets the subjective tests of fairness, reasonableness, rationality, and practicality and is fundamentally faithful to the underlying economic substance of life insurance transactions. The theory is consistent with the general framework of accounting theory.

*Most of the material in this chapter has been adapted, with permission, from an article by Robert L. Posnak entitled "Perspectives on Life Insurance Financial Reporting" contained in Vol. XL, No. 1 (March 1973) of *The Journal of Risk and Insurance.*

Nature of the Life Insurance Transaction

To the extent possible, a method of accounting for revenues should reflect the economic substance of the transaction being accounted for. Before discussing the extent to which the life insurance audit guide fulfills this general requirement, it is necessary to explore the nature of the life insurance transaction. The term "life insurance transaction" is here used to denote the sale of a life insurance policy and all of the events subsequent to the sale.

The sale of a block of life insurance policies is followed by a series of events that may continue for a generation or more. The long-term nature of the life insurance transaction lies at the heart of the financial reporting problem. The problem, simply stated, is this: how much revenue and expense—and hence how much profit—should be recognized in the accounts in each accounting period?

There are some fairly well-defined rules in accounting for recognizing revenues and profits on outright sales of tangible and intangible property. The rules for recognizing revenues and profits on service contracts are less well-defined. And the rules for recognizing revenues and profits on transactions that have aspects of both a sale and a service contract are fuzzy indeed.

The Sales Aspect

As everyone knows, life insurance does not have the speculative appeal of a glamour stock or the ego satisfaction (not to mention the tangibility) of a new motorcycle. While life insurance is called "life" insurance, the fact remains that the principal event being insured against is death, a gloomy prospect at best. People do not rush out to buy protection against their demise. So a life insurance policy must be aggressively sold.

That the sale is primary is self-evident. Life insurance companies proudly announce new business volumes. Investors in life insurance stocks regard growth as the principal indicator of success (assuming, of course, that new business is deemed to be of respectable quality). Up to 80 percent of the operating expenses of a life insurance company is typically devoted to the acquisition of new business. The energies and intellections of top management are generally dedicated in large measure to growth, which means sales. The investment of funds, the payment of a death claim, the processing of a conversion, the actuary's job —all depend upon, and are subsequent to, the sale. In the sense that the sale is all-important, life insurance companies are not dissimilar from their commercial and industrial brethren.

Services rendered to policyholders after the sale are quite passive. In terms of services rendered directly to policyholders, all the company must do is wait for a surrender or a claim. Policyholder service, record-keeping, and processing functions are routine and basically nominal in character and cost. In fact, "service" is something of a misnomer. "Service" usually connotes effort. The furnishing of a guarantee is not necessarily synonymous with the furnishing of a service.

The company is vitally interested in mortality, and mortality is determined to a significant degree at the point of sale as part of the underwriting process. So is persistency. At the point of sale the company must have every reasonable assurance that the premium charged—which is not subject to an increase—will be adequate to cover benefits and expenses over the life of the contract and yield a reasonable profit.

The sale of a block of life insurance policies is followed by a stream of future cash inflows and outflows, the net present value of which represents a store of value. This store of value is of great interest to investors and other users of general-purpose financial statements. It is similar, in terms of economic fundamentals, to the profits deriving from the sale of a product. Of course, the profits deriving from the sale of a product are generally immediately available for distribution, constructive or otherwise, to shareholders, while it may take a long time to convert the profits on a block of life insurance policies to cash available for distribution. But availability of liquid funds for cash distributions to shareholders bears no necessary relationship to operating performance.

Fairness and relevance of a life insurance accounting method should be considered, at least in part, in terms of the financial reporting practices of noninsurance entities, i.e., commercial and industrial businesses. The typical commercial and industrial transaction gives rise to a completed sale and an immediate earnings figure. Life insurance companies have sales, too, but recognition of much of the profit has historically been deferred to the future. One of the dilemmas in life insurance financial reporting is the failure of the stock market to recognize fully this deferred profit. Stock life insurance companies must compete with industrial and commercial companies for investor funds; industrial and commercial companies, by and large, do not have deferred profits on current sales. The potential disadvantage to stock life companies—and investors in life stocks—is obvious.

The potential disadvantage can be readily illustrated. Assume that the present value, at issue, of the profits on a block of life insurance policies is $12 million. Assume further that the accounting method being employed recognizes profits of $500,000 in the first year, with the balance to be recognized in future years. A multiple of 24 must be applied to reported earnings to determine the economic value added by the sale. Any multiple for growth is extra. If, for example, the company's growth rate and risk characteristics call for a multiple of 10, the final price-earning ratio is theoretically 24 times 10, or 240. Realistically, the stock market will not support such a multiple.*

All of the foregoing considerations argue strongly for treating the sale as a sale, which would involve recognition of the present value of future profits in the year of the sale.**

There are, however, three extremely important factors relating to subsequent years that prohibit accounting for the sale as a completed transaction:

---

*Price-earnings ratios are not the province of accountants, of course. Nevertheless accountants must keep equity among companies in mind, and that includes the extent to which reported earnings correlate, or do not correlate, with changes in economic value. The concept of economic value may be ambiguous, but ambiguity does not destroy the importance of the concept. The simple example given merely expresses the economic value problem in terms familiar to everyone, i.e., stock market dynamics.

**Recognition of the present value of future profits was the objective of the "dollars-per-thousand" method of adjusting statutory profits used in the past by many security analysts. For additional comments on recognizing the present value of future profits for accounting purposes, see Gary M. Winkle, *An Examination of External Financial Reporting Practices of Life Insurance Companies,* unpublished dissertation, Florida State University, December 1970.

▶ The company does not have an enforceable claim on future premium payments. Premiums are paid entirely at the discretion of the policyholder. The "receivable" from a policyholder is an installment receivable of so contingent a nature that the company cannot regard the sale as completed until it has received all of the considerations. In effect, the sale is a unique form of installment sale.

▶ While the company must satisfy itself in advance that the premium charged will be adequate over the long term, there nevertheless exists the risk that it will not be adequate. The risk is that experience as to mortality, surrenders, lapses, expenses, and investment income will prove to be more adverse than expected. While the services rendered after the time of sale may be fairly passive, the fact remains that the guarantees under the contract extend over a long period of time, and are only completed over time. At any point in time, some percentage of the total package of guarantees has been completed, and some percentage of the corresponding risk of adversity has consequently been released. Until the contract terminates (or, more correctly, until a block of contracts terminates)—a percentage of the guarantees remains uncompleted and the corresponding risk of adversity remains unreleased.

▶ While services rendered to policyholders in subsequent years are quite passive, the investing function is usually quite active. From the company's point of view, an investment return that is just sufficient to fulfill contract guarantees* is a minimal accomplishment (and is, in fact, embodied in the guarantees themselves). Profit attaches to the function only to the extent that investment return is better than required to fulfill the guarantees. Such excess investment return reflects effort, and the profits, if any, associated with such effort are earned only as the excess is realized.

A life insurance transaction is a unique combination of an installment sale (and the nature of the "installment plan" is itself unique), a package of uncompleted guarantees (as opposed to "services"), and a package of risks that follow the guarantees. The investment function is part and parcel of the package of guarantees, and the investment return in excess of that required to support the guarantees is the real measure of investment performance. The accounting method employed must recognize all of these elements of the transaction.

*In this chapter no distinction is made between a "guarantee" and a "promise".

The Service Aspect

While the performance of a life insurance policy guarantee does not involve the degree of effort commonly associated with service contracts, such as construction contracts, the fact remains that a life insurance company is in the business of providing insuring and investing services to policyholders. The life insurance service is unique, but that doesn't make it any less of a service. And profits should be recognized only insofar as the services are performed.

What service does the life insurance company really perform? If experience as to mortality, interest, lapse, expense, etc. always corresponded with experience assumed in calculating, testing, or otherwise establishing the gross premiums, the insurance pool would be risk-free. The insurance company would be entitled to collect nothing more than a nominal administrative fee and a low, risk-free rate of interest on any monies advanced to finance sales. This would also be true if experience were always more favorable than the underlying assumptions. So long as experience will demonstrably fall within the assumptions, the insurance company undertakes no risk.

The real service performed by a life insurance company is the assumption of the risk that experience will prove to be adverse, that is, will deviate unfavorably from the underlying assumptions. In the real world, such adversity is more than a possibility; it is a probability which can, within limits, be quantified. The insurance company really earns its keep insofar as this risk-taking function is performed. And this function is performed over time. As time passes, a portion of the risk of adversity is "released", and corresponding profits can properly be recognized.*

Profits, in other words, comprise (1) an administrative fee for making money transfers, keeping records, etc., plus (2) interest at a risk-free rate on cash advances, plus (3) appropriate fees for assuming the risk of adverse experience, whether the actual experience is favorable or adverse. In theory, such risk charges (net of actual deviations from expected values) constitute the primary source of income to a life insurance company. Economic reward follows economic risk, and a life insurance company should be appropriately compensated for the risk it assumes.

Allocation of these elements of income to accounting periods inevitably involves subjective determina-

*This is a vastly oversimplified discussion of adverse deviation and release-from-risk concepts. These subjects are explored in some detail in Chapter 6.

tions, but the difficulty of making such allocations does not compromise the fact that they must be made.

Recognizing Revenues and Profits

The method by which the sales and service aspects of the life insurance transaction can both be accommodated by one accounting model is simple in concept but difficult in practice. The method involves recognizing premiums as revenue when received and providing reserves on a basis that recognizes the risk of adverse deviation from assumed experience.

Installment Sales Method

If the life insurance transaction were to be considered as a completed sale, the journal entry to be made at the time of sale would be as follows, conceptually:

	Dr	Cr
Present value of gross premiums	XXX	
Present value of benefits and expenses		XXX
Profit account		XXX

As time passes, each of the above elements of the transaction would accrue interest at the rate used to determine the present values. If profits were distributed immediately, there would be no further gain or loss to be recognized. If profits were retained, such profits would earn interest and the interest would be recognized as additional income in the years in which it is earned.

This assumes, however, that actual experience precisely follows assumed experience. Where experience as to mortality, interest, surrender, lapse, and expense varies from that assumed, miscellaneous gains or losses (depending on whether the variance is favorable or unfavorable) will be recognized periodically.

Installment nature of premiums. Generally, receivables are recognized in a company's balance sheet when the company has an enforceable claim to them. Of course, a company does not have an enforceable claim on gross premiums; they are paid entirely at the will of the policyholder. Each premium represents a separate exchange transaction: the policyholder exchanges his premium for continued insurance coverage under the terms of his insurance contract; payment of the premium is a condition precedent to continued coverage. There is no precedence in accounting for recording such a transaction as a completed sale. At some point in the future, accounting may

move closer to recording estimated changes in economic values, but until that happens there seems to be no authority for reflecting the present value of future gross premiums in the balance sheet.*

This means that premiums should be recognized as revenue as they are received. This conforms with time-honored rules of installment accounting.

The reserving process. Use of the installment method of recognizing revenue is straightforward enough; revenue equals premiums collected.

But revenue is not generated without incurring a related cost. And the measurement of periodic costs to be associated with periodic revenue is anything but a straightforward process.

In accounting theory, costs should be allocated to periodic revenue in proportion to the recognition of revenue. If 10 percent of revenue is recognized during an accounting period, then 10 percent of total costs should also be recognized as expense during the period. The difference between recognized revenue and recognized expense is profit—presumably 10 percent of total profits.

Costs are not incurred uniformly, of course; initial expenses usually far exceed initial premiums, later benefits usually far exceed later premiums, and the incidence of benefits and expenses is typically not level in any event. Therefore a reserve, or combination of reserves, must be utilized to control the allocation of costs and, hence, to control the emergence of profits.

An accounting-oriented reserve may be considered to consist of three elements: a reserve for acquisition costs (which will generally be negative, i.e., an asset), a reserve for benefits (which will generally be positive, i.e., a liability), and a reserve for maintenance and settlement expenses (which will also generally be positive). The acquisition cost reserve is the mechanism employed for amortizing early acquisition costs in proportion to the receipt of premium revenue. The benefit reserve is the device employed to allocate benefit costs equitably against premium revenue. And the maintenance and settlement expense reserve is employed to allocate such expenses proportionally against revenue. Actual cash outlays and reserve changes interact to form a pattern of costs that fulfills the installment accounting requirement that costs be allocated pro rata to revenue.

*This is a simplification. These are certain special situations in which the present value of future gross premiums would in fact be recognized, but such special situations are beyond the scope of this chapter; they are discussed in Chapter 24.

However, at any point in time the ultimate total cost can only be estimated. A company may in good faith expect that Linton B withdrawals will be experienced, that mortality will follow the 1955–1960 Select and Ultimate Table, that interest at a rate of 5 percent will be earned, and that expenses can be accurately predicted. The company could calculate reserves based on such "best estimates". But Linton C terminations, 110 percent of expected mortality, 4 percent interest, and inflated expenses could be experienced. In that event, the reserving method could well result in reporting profits in the early years and losses in the later years.

To the extent that the risk of adverse deviation from best estimates can reasonably be estimated, there is little justification for ignoring the risk in the accounting process. In fact, ignoring the risk in the accounting process can be regarded as an abusive practice.

Some believe that the probability of favorable experience offsets the probability of adverse experience, and that best estimates simply recognize this offsetting tendency. But the risk is really one-sided, because if the probabilities always offset, the insurance company's *raison d'être* would all but disappear. That the risk is one-sided is true in logic as well as in reality.

Therefore, provision for the risk of adverse deviation from best estimates should be an inherent part of the reserving process. This means that the valuation premium would generally be higher than if the reserves were based only on best estimates. Profits would be recognized to the extent of the difference between the gross premium and the valuation premium. Profits would also be recognized as the risk of adverse deviation passes, that is, as the portion of the reserve attributable to the provision for adverse deviation is no longer needed. The determination of how much of the risk of deviation has expired in each accounting period, and therefore how much of the reserve can be released, is primarily the responsibility of the trained actuary.

Pure Service Method

If a life insurance transaction is deemed to be entirely a risk undertaking—if, in other words, the sales aspect of the transaction is ignored—then profits are allocated to accounting periods in proportion to the release from the risk of adverse deviation. This would be accomplished by (1) setting the valuation premium equal to the gross premium, (2) defining a fixed-point best estimate of future experience, and (3) defining estimates of the annual risk of deviation from the best estimates. (In practice, the fixed-point estimate and the annual-deviation estimate would generally be combined in one estimate.) Profits would emerge in two steps, conceptually. First, the difference between actual experience and "best estimate" experience would emerge. Such difference would then be allocated to the risk of deviation and held in suspense—that is, retained in the reserve—until the risk of deviation passes. As risk is released annually, an amount of profit corresponding to the defined value of the risk is also released.

It should be noted that each of the risks of adverse deviation—mortality, interest, withdrawal and expense—must be defined and quantified separately. In effect, expected profits must be distributed to the various elements of risk and released into the income statement as the risk passes. If the profit thus released is actually needed to absorb the cost of adverse deviations, then of course no profit is reported during the period. If the adverse deviation fails to materialize, then profit is reported during the period.

The reserve mechanism is used to distribute profits to risk factors and release such profits as the risks pass. Obviously there are no fixed rules for determining (1) the value of each risk factor and (2) the pattern of release from risk. Thus the actuary is given substantial leeway in determining how much profit should be reported in each accounting period. Some believe that such latitude would lead to incomparability among companies and possibly abuse in some cases.

Certain professional groups have been working on a set of guidelines for evaluating and quantifying the risk of adverse deviation for accounting purposes; this is discussed in Chapter 6. It is fair to say, however, that qualified professional actuaries operating in their individual capacities will have a most significant influence on the reported profits of life insurance companies.

Comparison of Methods

The fundamental difference between the installment sales approach and the service approach is that in the former case the valuation premium may be less than the gross premium while in the latter case the gross premium is equal to the valuation premium. The need to quantify and provide for the risks of adverse deviation is applicable in either case.

In effect, the installment sales approach simply adds another dimension to the service approach: the company is given some credit for having sold the policy. This "selling profit" emerges as the difference between the valuation premium and the gross premium. It emerges, in other words, essentially as a level percentage of the gross premium. Under the service approach, such selling profits are allocated—perhaps arbitrarily—to risk factors, to be released in proportion to the release from risk.

Because a life insurance company is clearly a marketing organization, and because of the importance of the sale, a life insurance company is entitled to recognize a selling profit. Because a life insurance company is in the business of assuming the risk of adverse deviation from assumed experience, profits, if any, specifically attributable to this risk function should be recognized only as the function is performed. The installment sales approach described above satisfies both of these criteria. It comprehends, but is not subject to the limitations of, the service approach. Because it ignores the importance of the sale, the service approach in its pure state does not appear to be entirely faithful to the nature of a life insurance company's operations.

Professional Literature

Pronouncements of the accounting profession that bear on life insurance accounting are scanty. There are pronouncements which deal with certain specific types of service contracts, such as construction contracts, leases, and the like. But all such service contracts differ significantly from the life insurance contract. It is necessary to look to some of the more basic professional literature for guidance.

Pervasive measurement principles. According to Statement No. 4 of the Accounting Principles Board,

Revenue is generally recognized when . . . (1) the earning process is complete or virtually complete, and (2) an exchange has taken place . . . Revenue from services rendered is recognized under this principle when services have been performed and are billable.[1]

In the case of a life insurance policy, an exchange takes place when a premium is paid by a policyholder (this was discussed earlier in this chapter). "Services" are "billable" at about the same time; the maximum time lag between billing and receipt is the grace period.

It can readily be seen, therefore, that the only substantive questions to be resolved in selecting a method of recognizing life insurance revenue are the questions of "when . . . the earning process is complete or nearly

complete" and "when services have been performed".

According to Statement No. 4, "All of the profit-directed activities of an enterprise that comprise the process by which revenue is earned may be called the *earning process . . . earning . . .* refers to the activities that give rise to the revenue." [2] As suggested earlier in this chapter, analysis of the life insurance transaction indicates that "the activities that give rise to the revenue" are, from the point of view of the company, heavily concentrated in the period preceding and encompassing the sale. "The profit-directed activities" of a life insurance company are oriented to the sale. There is little question that in terms of the economic substance of the transaction, revenue is "earned" quite early in the life of a block of business.

Some have argued, however, that "services" are only performed over time. By way of an analogy, they point to the following statement in Statement No. 4:

Amounts for rent or magazine subscriptions received in advance are not treated as revenue of the period in which they are received but as revenue of the future period or periods in which they are "earned".[3]

Again, it must be recognized that "guarantees" are not the same as "services". Statement No. 4 puts the term "earned" in quotation marks in the foregoing passage because the term can only be defined in context; its meaning is not clear-cut. "Earning" follows effort, as a rule, and the performance of a guarantee under a life insurance contract usually involves relatively little effort. The fact that guarantees remain to be performed in the future has no necessary relationship to the services, or work, actually performed. And it is work performed by the company that properly forms the basis for measuring revenue "earned".

It is to be hoped that no one will take the position that a life insurance policy is the same thing as a magazine subscription or a rental agreement. Lest prevailing rules on subscriptions, rental agreements, dancing schools, and the like be regarded as applicable by default, it is worth quoting again from literature of the accounting profession:

Sometimes strict adherence to the pervasive measurement principles produces results that are considered by the accounting profession as a whole to be unreasonable in the circumstances or possibly misleading. Accountants approach their task with a background of knowledge and experience. The perspective provided by this background is used as the basis for modifying accounting treatments when strict application of the pervasive measurement principles yields results that do not appear reasonable to the profession as a whole.[4]

The Board recognizes that there are exceptional cases where receivables are collectible over an extended period of time and, because of the terms of the transactions or other conditions, there is no reasonable basis for estimating the degree of collectibility.[5]

Inasmuch as premiums are not "receivables" (in that the company has no enforceable claim on them), the life insurance transaction easily qualifies as an "exceptional case". In addition, of course, premiums are usually "collectible over an extended period of time". There appears to be no precedent for recording the life insurance sale as a completed transaction.

Under the installment method, according to Statement No. 4,

The proceeds collected measure revenue . . . Expenses are measured at an amount determined by multiplying the cost of the asset sold by the ratio of the proceeds collected to the total selling price.[6]

The foregoing description also describes the essence of the installment method of life insurance accounting, except that "cost of asset sold" is replaced by a combination of deferred acquisition costs and a provision for future benefits and expenses. The modifying convention of conservatism is applied by providing adequately for the risk of adverse experience in performing future contract guarantees.

Overview of the Audit Guide

The accounting method embodied in the life insurance audit guide is substantially in conformity with the installment sales method as hereinbefore described. Premiums are generally recognized as revenue during the premium-paying period. The valuation premium need not be equal to the gross premium. The probability of adverse deviation from best estimates must be provided for in the reserving process.

However, nowhere in the audit guide can one find a reference to installment accounting. Instead the guide provides that premiums should generally be recognized as revenue "when due",[7] which amounts to the same thing. The guide specifically requires that adverse deviation be provided for in reserve assumptions.

The net result of the accounting method embodied in the audit guide is consistent with the substance of the life insurance transaction, is compatible with what is known about accounting theory, and does not conflict with pronouncements of the accounting profession.

The method, conscientiously applied, will also result in fair and relevant financial statements.

Economic Value

Perhaps the primary reason that the method will result in fair and relevant financial statements is that the method is reasonably consistent with concepts of economic value. The ambiguity of "economic value" is such as to preclude the recording of changes in economic value directly. But there is little question that the concept of economic value, ambiguous or not, influences the accounting process indirectly. It has to do this. The accountant who fails to keep economic value in mind when he prepares, or reports on, the financial statements of a business entity also fails the investor, the lender, and other users of financial statements. All users of financial statements are interested in measures of economic progress, and the ultimate measure of economic progress during a period is the change in economic value during that period.

The economic value of a tangible business asset may be measured in several ways. One measure would be the fair value of the asset. Another would be the discounted value of expected future net cash receipts attributable to the asset. In theory, the two values should be about the same.

An intangible business asset is not much different. The fair value of a block of insurance in force at the moment of issue, for example, is approximately equivalent to the present value of expected future net cash receipts attributable to the block of business. At the moment of issue, neither the reserve nor any other bookkeeping device affects the computation of such present value.

Subsequent to the moment of issue the reserve directly affects measurements of present value. This is because assets equivalent to the reserve must be set aside; "future net cash receipts" include net additions to, or deductions from, the assets related to the reserve. Changes in the reserve are measured with reference to the level of the reserve. The higher the reserve, the higher the aggregate future decreases in the reserve. A decrease in the reserve is equivalent to a release of assets. The greater the total of such future asset releases, the higher the present value of the releases. Thus, the theoretical fair value of a block of insurance in force at any point in time may be viewed as the present value of future net cash receipts where increases and decreases in the reserve are deemed to be equivalent to cash outflows and inflows, respectively.

These concepts are of more than academic interest. They affect the determination of prices to be paid for blocks of business or entire companies. They are frequently taken into account in determining the issue price of the stock of a new company. In a few regulatory jurisdictions they are used in determining whether an applicant for a charter is sound enough to qualify for the charter. Hopefully they are taken into account in security analysis; in fact, the dollars-per-thousand adjustment technique seeks to measure present value in the manner described above.

It might be said that these concepts are generally accepted in the world of economic decision-making. It follows that accounting should at least give a nod in their direction. The function of accounting, after all, is "to provide quantitative information, primarily financial in nature, about economic entities that is intended to be useful in making economic decisions".[8]

Discount Rates

The present value of future profits on a block of insurance in force at any point in time after the moment of issue is calculated by projecting future book profits and discounting such profits to a present value. The discount rate used is a function of (1) risk and (2) the purpose of the calculation. In the typical investment situation, the discount rate theoretically reflects the yield rates available on investment opportunities with comparable risk characteristics. This, of course, does not imply that alternative investment opportunities can be found which have identical risk characteristics. Determination of an appropriate discount rate is subjective to a significant degree. Nevertheless, the central tendency of the discount rate is to place the proposed investment on an equal footing with other possible investments—to yield a comparable measure of economic value.*

It is fairly typical to find discount rates in the range of 8–15 percent used in discounting profits of life insurance companies. The illustrations which follow assume a discount rate of 12 percent. That does not imply that 12 percent would necessarily be used. The illustration of present values is indicative, not conclusive, as to the "appropriate" level of present values. That does not alter the significance of the concept.

*The subjectivity of the discount rate, and the inherent uncertainty involved in forecasting the profits to which the rate is applied, explain why "economic values" *per se* are generally not recorded in financial accounting unless they are embodied in an exchange transaction.

Crazy Quilt Life

Crazy Quilt Life was described in Chapter 2, and additional information on it will be found in Appendix C.

Table 4–1 shows reported profits and the change in economic values for the 31-year period of Crazy Quilt Life's history on two bases: statutory and adjusted. "Change in economic values" is equivalent to reported profits, which are assumed to be distributed immediately to shareholders, plus the change in the present value at 12 percent of profits to be recognized in future years. All values are pre-tax.

It will be noted that the pattern of statutory profits, besides being erratic, rarely correlates well with the change in economic values. On the other hand, reported profits computed by using adjusted reserves do follow the general pattern of changes in economic value. This similarity of patterns is very important. It means that reported adjusted profits are reasonably indicative of the trend of changes in economic values. From the point of view of the user of the financial statements, this is important information indeed, for reasons which should be obvious to everyone.

Most of the critics of the life insurance audit guide have complained that the guide would invite abuse unless guidelines almost as severe as statutory accounting rules were written into the guide. In some cases it appeared that the critics had confused the objectives of the audit guide with the objectives of statutory accounting rules. The solvency standards implicit in statutory accounting are not necessarily appropriate for general-purpose financial statements that purport to measure operating performance.

This is not to say that general-purpose financial statements can ignore questions of solvency; any respectable measurement of operating performance should indicate a deteriorating financial situation. But ensuring solvency is not the principal objective of general-purpose financial statements, whereas it most assuredly is the principal objective of statutory statements. Statutory solvency standards, including statutory accounting practices, remain in full force and effect, and it is entirely appropriate that the audit guide concern itself primarily with reasonable and realistic measures of operating performance.

The effect of superimposing the provisions of the audit guide on the statutory framework is suggested by Table 4–2. Assets equivalent to statutory reserves must be retained irrespective of the level of adjusted reserves. The interest on assets equal to the difference in reserves is available as an additional safety margin.

Table 4–1.

PRESENT VALUE OF FUTURE PROFITS AND REPORTED PROFITS (1) USING STATUTORY RESERVES AND (2) USING ADJUSTED RESERVES FOR BUSINESS ISSUED BY CRAZY QUILT LIFE (000 omitted)

	Using Statutory Reserves				*Using Adjusted Reserves*			
	Present Value of Future Profits			*Reported Profits Plus Change in*	*Present Value of Future Profits*			*Reported Profits Plus Change in*
Year	*At End of Year*	*Change*	*Reported Profits **	*Present Value of Future Profits*	*At End of Year*	*Change*	*Reported Profits **	*Present Value of Future Profits*
1941	$ 1,000	$ 1,000	$ (778)	$ 222	$ 390	$ 390	$ (14)	$ 376
1942	2,261	1,261	(831)	430	962	572	10	582
1943	3,853	1,592	(880)	712	1,767	805	56	861
1944	5,663	1,810	(795)	1,015	2,746	979	159	1,138
1945	7,904	2,241	(784)	1,457	4,001	1,255	328	1,583
1946	10,535	2,631	(637)	1,994	5,577	1,576	506	2,082
1947	13,409	2,874	(415)	2,459	7,421	1,844	646	2,490
1948	14,643	1,234	869	2,103	8,961	1,540	769	2,309
1949	16,635	1,992	431	2,423	10,822	1,861	854	2,715
1950	19,151	2,516	339	2,855	12,970	2,148	1,017	3,165
1951	22,030	2,879	453	3,332	15,347	2,377	1,277	3,654
1952	26,215	4,185	(696)	3,489	17,930	2,583	1,510	4,093
1953	30,405	4,190	(112)	4,078	20,728	2,798	1,746	4,544
1954	34,654	4,249	392	4,641	23,702	2,974	1,943	4,917
1955	38,711	4,057	1,087	5,144	26,719	3,017	2,146	5,163
1956	42,400	3,689	1,855	5,544	29,617	2,898	2,377	5,275
1957	45,060	2,660	2,378	5,038	31,404	1,787	2,736	4,523
1958	47,731	2,671	2,673	5,344	33,139	1,735	3,045	4,780
1959	50,379	2,648	3,032	5,680	34,788	1,649	3,412	5,061
1960	53,238	2,859	3,143	6,002	36,465	1,677	3,711	5,388
1961	56,544	3,306	3,060	6,366	38,354	1,889	3,892	5,781
1962	58,721	2,177	4,637	6,814	40,699	2,345	3,942	6,287
1963	62,694	3,973	3,372	7,345	43,552	2,853	4,365	7,218
1964	68,047	5,353	2,618	7,971	46,857	3,305	4,744	8,049
1965	75,107	7,060	1,623	8,683	50,597	3,740	5,211	8,951
1966	83,460	8,353	1,340	9,693	54,928	4,331	5,650	9,981
1967	92,944	9,484	1,312	10,796	59,729	4,801	6,230	11,031
1968	105,218	12,274	(2,283)	9,991	63,855	4,126	7,055	11,181
1969	117,200	11,982	(837)	11,145	67,754	3,899	8,158	12,057
1970	128,311	11,111	(165)	10,946	70,858	3,104	9,546	12,650
1971	140,009	11,698	152	11,850	73,433	2,575	10,818	13,393

* Assuming immediate distribution to shareholders. Any profits retained in the business would of course earn interest, which would increase reported profits.

The last amount column in Table 4–2 shows the profits which would be reported if the model distributed every dollar it could legally distribute. As the last column in Table 4–2 indicates, the interest differential represents a sizeable hedge against adversity. This is in addition to the present value of future profits, which is also a kind of safety margin.

Any further conservatism would seem to be unwarranted in the case of general-purpose financial statements. Any further conservatism would lead to measurements of operating performance that represent little, if any, improvement over statutory statements. In fact, since statutory statements do not purport to measure operating performance while general-purpose statements do, it might be said that any further conservatism would represent an abusive practice from the point of view of the users of the financial statements.

Table 4–2.

EFFECT OF STATUTORY RESERVES ON ADJUSTED STATEMENTS FOR CRAZY QUILT LIFE (000 omitted)

Year	Level of Statutory Reserves	Level of Adjusted Reserves *	Interest on Statutory Reserves	Interest on Adjusted Reserves	Interest Differential	Theoretical Adjusted Profits **	"Zero Statutory Surplus" Reported Profits	Interest Differential As Percentage of Theoretical Adjusted Profits
1941	$ 451	$ (323)	$ 6	$ (4)	$ 10	$ (14)	$ (4)	—%
1942	1,397	(253)	26	(8)	34	10	44	340
1943	2,974	326	63	1	62	56	118	111
1944	5,264	1,570	120	28	92	159	251	58
1945	8,431	3,499	201	74	127	328	455	39
1946	12,536	6,296	308	144	164	506	670	32
1947	17,621	10,118	445	242	203	646	849	31
1948	22,466	14,838	596	371	225	769	994	29
1949	28,483	20,191	770	530	240	854	1,094	28
1950	35,466	26,224	991	719	272	1,017	1,289	27
1951	43,337	32,960	1,251	939	312	1,277	1,589	24
1952	53,400	40,438	1,568	1,190	378	1,510	1,888	25
1953	64,080	48,793	1,941	1,474	467	1,746	2,213	27
1954	75,340	57,953	2,340	1,792	548	1,943	2,491	28
1955	86,970	67,902	2,776	2,153	623	2,146	2,769	29
1956	98,727	78,442	3,281	2,586	695	2,377	3,072	29
1957	110,584	89,174	3,849	3,082	767	2,736	3,503	28
1958	122,599	99,973	4,467	3,624	843	3,045	3,888	28
1959	134,764	110,826	5,153	4,221	932	3,412	4,344	27
1960	147,176	121,639	5,874	4,843	1,031	3,711	4,742	28
1961	158,169	130,665	6,536	5,401	1,135	3,892	5,027	29
1962	167,043	139,027	7,070	5,863	1,207	3,942	5,149	31
1963	176,198	145,907	7,553	6,270	1,283	4,365	5,648	29
1964	186,056	152,209	8,075	6,645	1,430	4,744	6,174	30
1965	197,272	158,183	8,691	7,038	1,653	5,211	6,864	32
1966	209,565	164,195	9,497	7,525	1,972	5,650	7,622	35
1967	223,512	170,833	10,553	8,163	2,390	6,230	8,620	38
1968	242,627	177,581	11,981	8,952	3,029	7,055	10,084	43
1969	263,104	185,164	13,777	9,879	3,898	8,158	12,056	48
1970	286,658	194,089	15,846	10,929	4,917	9,546	14,463	52
1971	313,546	204,366	17,703	11,756	5,947	10,818	16,765	55

* Net of deferred acquisition costs.
** Assuming immediate distribution.

5 Revenue Recognition

The space (fewer than five pages) devoted in the life insurance audit guide to principles of revenue recognition belies the effort devoted to the subject. Probably no other subject has stirred as much argument. It is probable that the life insurance audit guide would have been issued much sooner—perhaps a year sooner—were it not for substantive disagreements over the nature of revenue and the timing of its recognition.

The theoretical aspects of revenue recognition are discussed in Chapter 4, as are the principles that were finally adopted. What follows is a discussion of the provisions of the audit guide.

Premium Revenues

The life insurance audit guide identifies premiums as revenue and interest as an adjustment of costs. This conclusion is implicit in the language of the guide.[1]

In theory, says the guide, "premium revenues should be recognized over the life of the contract in proportion to performance under the contract".[2] In practice, however, premiums should be recognized "when due" with the exception of certain health insurance coverages and certain short-duration term coverages.

The guide deals with revenue recognition for each of the major types of insurance contracts. The reason is that while performance is supposed to be the basis for recognizing revenue, performance is well-nigh impossible to measure. So detailed and somewhat arbitrary rules were adopted which it was felt would give recognition, at least indirectly, to the principal functions and services associated with each type of contract.

In discussing revenue the guide makes two basic distinctions between types of insurance contracts: long-duration and short-duration. Premiums on long-duration contracts are to be recognized as revenue when due, i.e., essentially over the premium-paying period. Premiums on short-duration contracts are to be recognized as revenue over the life of the contracts.

Long-Duration Contracts

Long-duration insurance contracts include the following, which are specifically discussed in the guide:

Permanent life insurance and endowment contracts:
  Whole life.
  Limited-payment life.
  Endowment.
Annuities.
Long-duration term insurance contracts for which premiums "are collected throughout the life of the contract." [3]
Health insurance contracts "which are expected to be in force for a reasonable period of time and for which elements of expense or benefit costs are not level." [4]

Whole-life contracts.   In the case of whole-life contracts (or contracts substantially equivalent to whole-life contracts), the guide concludes that there is "no predominant function or service . . . [providing] . . . a measure of the composite of all functions or services" and that premiums should be recognized as revenues levelly over the lives of the contracts. "This level recognition of premium revenues is satisfactorily accomplished by recognizing premiums as revenues when due." [5]

Recognition of whole-life premiums as revenues

when due will not always result in a level recognition of revenue. For example, so-called "modified life" policies provide for a reduced level of premiums for a certain number of years, followed by a higher level of premiums. In that case, the level-recognition criterion would be violated if premiums were recognized as revenue when due.

The spirit of the audit guide calls for recognition of premiums as revenue when due regardless of any modifications of gross premiums such as the one discussed above. This is because the guide strains to justify the recognition of revenues when due; the discussion of level recognition is designed mainly to lend partial support to the "when due" basis. This will become clearer as this discussion proceeds.

Limited-payment life contracts. Although providing that revenues on limited-payment life contracts should also "be recognized in relation to performance under the contract," [6] level recognition of premium revenues over the life of the contracts is not required. Although the guide does not specifically state that premiums should be recognized as revenue when due, it is clear from the discussion that this is what is intended.

Some arguments are advanced to support the "when due" approach, but they are not persuasive. For example, the guide states that "performance . . . is significantly greater during the premium-paying period than after such period." [7] It is difficult to extend this reasoning to very short premium-paying periods, such as, for example, single-premium business. It is apparent that the guide is predisposed toward recognizing premiums as revenues when due and spreading profits out by use of the reserve mechanism, that is, by providing for the risk of adverse deviation in establishing reserve assumptions:

If, after providing for mortality, withdrawals, expenses, . . . and the risk of adverse deviation . . . , there is any remaining gross premium in excess of the valuation premium, it is properly recognized over the premium-paying period in recognition of the higher level of services and functions performed during that period. Because of the provision for risk of adverse deviation from estimates of mortality, withdrawals, investment yield, and expenses over the life of the contract, this method should provide operating results that are both reasonable and conservative.[8]

Endowment contracts. The guide does not specifically discuss endowment contracts but instead treats them as being the same as whole-life or limited-payment life contracts. There is, of course, a difference—a life contract extends essentially for the whole of life while an endowment contract matures on a specified date. Nevertheless, the applicable principles are the same—premiums should be recognized as revenue when due.

Annuities. "The reasoning underlying the accounting described for recognition of premium revenue from whole-life and limited-payment life insurance contracts also applies to annuity contracts; therefore, annuity considerations should be recognized as revenue when due." [9]

Long-duration term contracts. The guide provides that premiums on term contracts may be recognized as revenue when due "in instances where premiums are collected throughout the life of the . . . contract *and* where the contract is of sufficient duration as to make it unclear as to the relative significance of the protection service as opposed to the sales, collection, investment and conservation services necessary to establish and retain the pooling of individual risks." [10] (Emphasis supplied.)

Thus there are two requirements to satisfy in order to recognize premiums on term contracts as revenue when due:

▸ Premiums must be payable (not necessarily levelly) for the life of the contract, and
▸ The contract must be of "sufficient duration."

Single-premium term contracts would apparently never qualify for "when due" treatment. As a practical matter, single-premium ordinary, industrial, and group term insurance contracts of long duration are rarely sold. When they are, however, the apparent technical restriction written into the audit guide presents a difficult problem, which is discussed later in this chapter under the caption "Short-Duration Contracts".

Cash values are applied as single term insurance premiums in connection with the extended term insurance nonforfeiture option, but it is reasonable to treat the premium as a settlement measured at the expected cost of the extended term insurance. This avoids what could otherwise be a very knotty problem. Dividends are sometimes applied as a single premium to purchase one-year term insurance, but the period of coverage is so short and the amounts involved so immaterial that the "when due" approach can safely be used.

The real problem is defining what constitutes "sufficient duration". A level-premium long-term contract such as term to 70 is much like permanent insurance and presents no particular problem; such a contract is obviously of "sufficient duration".

How about one-year contracts? five-year contracts? ten-year contracts?

If a term contract is renewable and/or convertible, it should normally be regarded as being of sufficient duration to qualify for the "when due" approach. That's because a renewable term policy represents a continuum; there is a quantifiable probability that a policy will persist to the end of the last renewal period. The same general reasoning applies to convertible term policies.

For term policies that are neither renewable nor convertible, an arbitrary cutoff point must be used. Five years seems to be an appropriate tentative basis for classifying such contracts as short-term or long-term; if the contract is for five years or more, it should be regarded as being of sufficient duration to qualify for the "when due" approach. Beyond five years the slope of mortality begins to be important, and the contract begins to assume some of the characteristics of permanent insurance.

The audit guide specifies that premiums on short-term contracts should be recognized in proportion to insurance in force. This makes no allowance for increasing mortality rates. So when the slope of mortality becomes significant, the contract should be deemed to meet the test of sufficient duration regardless of the term of the contract.

Group term life insurance is usually of the short-term variety. Because premiums are normally paid monthly, the reserves on such business are usually nominal. Some companies hold unearned gross premiums on such business for statutory purposes, in which case the audit guide requirements are automatically met. Where a company holds unearned valuation premiums, the profit loading in the unearned premium is released, and this would apparently constitute a technical violation of the audit guide's requirements, but only with respect to group business not subject to experience rating; for experience-rated business, most or all of the additional profits would apparently flow to the experience rating refund liability. (Group business is discussed in detail in Chapter 20.) In any event, the amounts involved are likely to be so insignificant that either gross or net reserves would usually be acceptable.

As a practical matter, the audit guide's provisions with respect to term contracts are directed primarily to single-premium credit life insurance; there was much sentiment for prohibiting the recognition of all revenues—and hence a disproportionate share of the profits—when such single premiums are "due". Singling out credit insurance for special treatment would have been quite arbitrary; hence the rules were framed in terms of all term insurance. But the practical effect of the restrictions is essentially limited to credit insurance.

Riders and supplemental benfits. The accounting for premium revenues on term and disability income riders and supplemental benefits (such as waiver of premium, accidental death, payor benefit, guaranteed insurability, and substandard extras) should follow the accounting for premium revenues on the underlying contract, i.e., premiums should be recognized as revenue when due. Normally such riders and supplemental benefits would qualify for such treatment on their own merits; but even in those few cases in which there is some question as to whether they do in fact so qualify, they should be treated the same. The reason is partly theoretical (the contract is best viewed as an integral whole*) and partly practical (the amount of work usually required to segregate the various items of revenue and expense is not justified).

Long-term health contracts. As indicated previously, there is a two-part test which health contracts must satisfy to qualify as long-duration contracts. The audit guide provides that "the accounting for accident and health insurance policies, which are expected to be in force for a reasonable period of time *and* for which elements of expense or benefit costs are not level, should follow the same principle of accounting as followed for whole-life insurance. Accordingly, premium revenues should be recognized over the premium-paying period." [11] (Emphasis supplied.)

Noncancellable and guaranteed renewable health insurance contracts qualify as long-duration contracts for the same reasons as permanent insurance and renewable term contracts qualify. They are almost always "expected to be in force for a reasonable period of time" and benefit costs are not level (hence additional reserves must usually be carried). Further, there is usually a front-end bulge in expenses for selection, issue, and commissions and other selling expenses (or, in the case of mail-order companies, solicitation costs).

It is true, of course, that renewal rates on guaranteed renewable business are not guaranteed as to timing or amount, and some have suggested that this makes guaranteed renewable business similar to group insurance or property-liability insurance. Unlike group or property-liability coverages, however, guaranteed

---

*For example, only one policy is sold, underwritten, and issued, and many of the expenses apply to the entire contract, not discrete parts of it.

renewable contracts are not cancellable, and this feature allies them more closely to noncancellable coverages than to group or property-liability coverages.

Group health insurance, collectively renewable contracts, and cancellable individual contracts can apparently be treated as long-duration or short-duration contracts, depending on the pattern of costs. Even though such contracts are cancellable, companies usually expect a sizeable number to be renewed from year to year. So the requirement that there must be an expectation that the policies will "be in force for a reasonable period of time" is easily satisfied. Expenses are often somewhat higher in the first year, particularly when commissions are not level. Benefits, however, tend to be "level", i.e., a constant percentage of premiums, since premiums can be adjusted to correspond with loss experience.*

But group health, collectively renewable, and cancellable individual health contracts are so similar to property-liability coverages that they should be regarded as short-duration contracts in most cases, regardless of whether expenses are level or not. This means that "gross premiums should be recognized as revenues on a pro rata basis over the period covered by the premium".[12] This in turn means that unearned gross premiums rather than unearned net premiums should be held in reserve, thus resulting in a pro rata recognition of premiums as revenue "over the period covered by the premium". The only difference between the two reserves is the treatment of any profit loading. The use of unearned net premiums results in recognizing the profit loading as income in the period in which the premium is due. The use of unearned gross premiums results in recognizing the profit loading as income in the period in which the premium itself is taken into revenue.

Sometimes acquisition costs on cancellable health coverages are sufficiently large that one year's premiums are insufficient to absorb them; they must be amortized. Obviously it is necessary to assume that a significant portion of the business will be "in force for a reasonable period of time". In that case the short-duration approach should still be used; acquisition costs should be amortized in a manner which recognizes the portion of the gross premium taken into income in each period.

---

*However, a theoretical tendency toward a constant loss ratio is all there is. Obviously loss ratios differ from year to year, and sometimes group rates are guaranteed for a period of time, during which time losses might fluctuate significantly. The rating problem is somewhat similar to property-liability rating.

(The decision as to whether to hold unearned net or unearned gross premiums on health contracts is discussed at length in Chapter 19. Amortization of health insurance acquisition costs is also discussed in that chapter.)

Again, as in the case of short-duration term contracts, the audit guide's provisions with respect to health contracts are directed primarily to single-premium credit health contracts. And again, rather than single out single-premium credit health contracts for arbitrary restriction, general criteria were established for all health contracts. The practical effect of the restrictions has reference primarily to single-premium credit health insurance.

Short-Duration Contracts

It was suggested in the preceding discussion that all single-premium term life insurance contracts, nonrenewable and nonconvertible term contracts of less than five years' duration, group term life insurance, group health insurance, and collectively renewable and cancellable individual health insurance contracts should normally be regarded as short-duration contracts for purposes of revenue recognition. In addition, the audit guide specifically refers to credit life and health insurance as generally requiring short-duration treatment.

So short-duration contracts might be summarized as follows:

> Term insurance contracts:
> Single-premium.
> Short-duration.
> Health insurance contracts which are not expected to be in force for a reasonable period of time and for which elements of expense and benefit costs are level; also, by specific mention, all credit health insurance contracts.

Term insurance contracts. As mentioned earlier, the life insurance audit guide seems to require that all single-premium term insurance contracts be treated as short-duration contracts. Only where premiums are "collected throughout the life of the term contract" [13] might it be appropriate to recognize premiums as revenue when due.

For term insurance contracts accounted for as short-duration contracts, the guide provides that "gross premium revenues . . . should be recognized in proportion to the amounts of insurance in force." [14] Thus, if the contract is a level term contract, premiums would be recognized as revenue levelly.

Problems arise when the contract is of long duration. While the amount of insurance in force may be level, the cost of mortality per unit of insurance in force increases. In other words, the claims to be covered by level premium revenues will tend to be less than revenues in the early durations and more than revenues in the later durations. Yet it is clear from the guide's discussion of cost recognition that unearned premium reserves—the cumulative difference between premiums received and premiums recognized as revenue—should normally be held in respect of such business in lieu of actuarially computed reserves.[15]

There are apparently only two acceptable methods of resolving the problem: (1) hold an additional reserve for the excess premiums recognized as revenue, or (2) modify the revenue recognition pattern so as to recognize premium revenues in proportion to the expected claim pattern. The first approach would be technically consistent with the audit guide's requirements as to term life contracts; the second approach would at least be consistent with the guide's provisions as to credit health contracts, which provisions accord recognition to the fact that claim costs per unit of insurance in force are not relatively constant.

There is one other approach that appears to violate the intent of the guide, and that is to treat single-premium term contracts of long duration in the same manner as single-premium permanent insurance contracts. Under this approach, premiums would be recognized as revenues when due and actuarially computed reserves would be established.

It does appear that the guide intended the single-premium restriction to apply only to short-duration contracts:

Examples of term contracts where the predominant service is protection, include credit life insurance and other types of single or limited payment contracts of a relatively short duration.[16]

Thus the examples refer to contracts which are single- or limited-payment contracts *and* are of short duration, while the general requirements for reporting premiums as revenue when due specify that premiums must be "collected throughout the life of the contract" and the contract must be "of sufficient duration". The examples are not consistent with the general requirements.

It was mentioned earlier that the principal objective of the audit guide's provisions applicable to revenue recognition on term contracts was to restrict the amount of revenues and profits that could be

recognized in the year of issue with respect to single-premium credit insurance contracts. In view of this, and in view of the examples discussed in the guide, apparent conflicts in the guide should be resolved by recognizing revenues on single-premium term contracts in the following manner:

▸ Premiums on single-premium or limited-payment ordinary and industrial term contracts should be recognized as revenue when due if (1) the contracts are of five years' duration or more or (2) the slope of mortality is significant. Actuarial reserves should be computed.

▸ Premiums on single-premium or limited-payment ordinary and industrial term contracts should be recognized in proportion to amounts of insurance in force if (1) the contracts are of less than five years' duration and (2) the slope of mortality is insignificant.

▸ Premiums on single-premium or limited-payment credit and group contracts should be recognized as revenue in proportion to the amounts of insurance in force if (1) the contracts are of less than five years' duration and (2) the slope of mortality is not significant. Unearned gross premiums are held in lieu of actuarial reserves.

▸ Premiums on single-premium or limited-payment credit and group contracts should be recognized as revenue on the basis of the anticipated claim pattern where (1) the contracts are of five years' duration or more or (2) the slope of mortality is significant.

For short-duration term contracts for which premiums are payable approximately in proportion to the amounts of insurance in force—for example, credit life insurance for which premiums are payable monthly on the basis of the outstanding balance—then the audit guide's requirements for revenue recognition are automatically met. However, if the slope of mortality is significant, premium revenues should be recognized on the basis of the anticipated claim pattern even if premiums are payable in proportion to insurance in force; any amounts not recognized as revenue should be reported as an unearned premium reserve.

Health insurance contracts. Premiums on group, collectively renewable, and cancellable individual health contracts should be recognized as revenue "on a pro rata basis over the period covered by the premium".[17] This was discussed earlier in this chapter. The indicated treatment is substantially in conformity with practices of property-liability companies.

In the case of credit health insurance, claim costs typically are not relatively fixed per unit of coverage, even with respect to short-duration contracts. Sometimes the claim cost per unit increases fairly rapidly. As a result, claims often do not occur in a pattern that corresponds with the nominal amount of insurance in force. In such cases the audit guide requires that "gross premiums should be recognized as revenues over the stated period of the contract in reasonable relationship to the anticipated claims" [18] rather than on the basis of amounts of insurance in force. Methods of accomplishing this are discussed in Chapter 20.

The "When Due" Provision

As mentioned repeatedly in this chapter, premiums on long-duration insurance contracts are, according to the audit guide, supposed to be recognized as revenue "when due". What does this mean?

First of all, it means that changes in deferred premiums technically should not be recorded as revenue. Deferred premiums are not "due".

However, it does seem to mean that the change in *uncollected* premiums should be recognized as revenue. Uncollected premiums are "due".

Some of them, however, will never be received by the company. The policyholder has no obligation to pay premiums due. Coverage during the grace period is really an additional benefit allocable to premiums already received.

An amount corresponding to the valuation premium component of uncollected premiums is set aside in the reserve. However, any profit loading in uncollected premiums is not reserved for. Therefore, a company that treats uncollected premiums as revenue, and recognizes any profits in uncollected premiums, should establish an allowance for profits attributable to premiums that will never be collected.

Deferred and uncollected premiums are discussed in Chapter 23. It is argued in Chapter 23 that deferred and uncollected premiums represent reserve adjustments and that premium revenues should be reported on the basis of cash received. The "when due" provision should therefore be interpreted to refer to premiums received, adjusted to exclude amounts allocable to premium deposit funds, premiums paid in advance, and advance premiums.

Group uncollected premiums which are valid claims on group policyholders should be recognized as receivables and the change therein should be recorded as revenue.

Disclosure

Heretofore life insurance companies have generally referred to premium revenue as "premiums" or "premium income" in their income statements.[19] Such premiums are neither written, collected, nor earned, being an amalgam of cash received, increases in deferred and uncollected premiums, and adjustments for advance premiums.

Property-liability companies have generally referred to premium revenues as "premiums earned" in their income statements.[20]

Life insurance companies should preferably use the term "premiums" as the income statement caption for premium revenues. It is a satisfactory all-inclusive term. Revenue accounting policies and practices should, of course, be described in notes to the financial statement.

The income statement and the applicable notes might thus read somewhat as follows:

INCOME STATEMENT:

Revenue:	
Premiums:	
Life, less reinsurance ceded of $XXX	$XXX
Health, less reinsurance ceded of $XXX	XXX
	XXX
Gross investment income	XXX
Miscellaneous	XXX
TOTAL REVENUE	XXX

NOTES TO FINANCIAL STATEMENTS:

Accounting policies note:
Premiums for long-duration insurance contracts are reported as revenue when received. Premiums for short-duration insurance contracts are reported as revenue when earned.

Other note:
Premium revenues applicable to long-duration life and health insurance contracts aggregated $XXX and $XXX, respectively, in 19XX.

Reserves and Premiums

There has long been controversy over the nature of a life insurance reserve—whether a reserve is in the nature of deferred revenue, or whether it is in the nature of an accrued expense.

There is also some controversy over the treatment of reserves on casualty-type business. Assuming for the moment that an increase in life reserves should be recorded as an expense item, the question remains as to whether the increase in unearned premium reserves on casualty-type business sold by life insurance companies should be reflected as an adjustment of premiums, the practice followed by property-liability companies, or as an expense item, the practice usually followed by life insurance companies.

Life Reserves

Under the deferred revenue concept, life insurance reserves are deemed to represent unearned premiums plus unearned investment income, held for release into operations as benefits and expenses are actually incurred. In other words, (1) benefits and expenses do not "accrue", (2) benefits and expenses are effectively charged to operations as they occur, and (3) revenue is recognized in the accounts in a manner that can reasonably be expected to cover such periodic benefits and expenses. Reserve changes would be recorded as an adjustment of revenue, somewhat as follows:

Premiums	XXX
Interest	XXX
Increase in reserves	(XXX)
EARNED REVENUE	XXX

Under the accrued expense concept, revenue is recognized without any necessary or sufficient relationship to the reserve, pro rata portions of expense are accrued to match the revenue thus recognized, and the reserve becomes, in effect, an accrued expense account. Premiums and investment income are reported as revenue items and the increase in reserves is reported as an item of expense.

Thus, under the deferred revenue concept revenue is allocated to expense, while under the accrued expense concept, expense is allocated to revenue.

In terms of fundamental concepts, it doesn't seem to matter whether the reserve is regarded as a deferred revenue account or an accrued expense account. In both cases the reserve is a kind of balancing account designed to produce a pattern of derivative profits which conform at least roughly to predetermined concepts of services rendered. Definition of services rendered is the central problem in both cases.

The accrued expense concept, however, introduces some troublesome problems with respect to the format of the income statement. The problems can best be discussed with reference to an illustration. In Table 5–1 will be found a 31-year summary of the statements of operations for the American Experience block of business (i.e., issues of 1941–1947) issued by Crazy Quilt Life. It will be observed that the block of business grows for seven years and is then closed off. It will also be observed that additions to the benefit reserves are positive (i.e., a charge to operations) until 1960 and then turn negative (i.e., a credit to operations) as the reserves begin to reverse. Similarly, additions to expense reserves are negative (i.e., a credit to operations) until 1947, after which the reserves begin reversing (which results in a charge to operations). In the latter case, reversals of the reserve after 1947 represent amortization of acquisition costs primarily.*

Questions which arise are as follows:

1. Is an increase in the benefit reserve (a) a reduction of revenue or (b) an increase in expense?

2. Is a decrease in the benefit reserve (a) an increase in revenue or (b) a "negative expense"?

3. Is an increase in the expense** reserve (a) a negative expense or (b) an increase in revenue?

4. Is a decrease in the expense reserve (a) an expense or (b) a reduction of revenue?

Some believe that changes in the benefit reserve represent revenue adjustments, and that the net result is to report net revenue which is matchable against benefits incurred during the period. They believe that consistent reporting of a negative expense (such as would occur when a reserve begins to reverse) is illogical.

It should be noted, however, that a consistently negative expense is not without precedence in accounting. A deferred tax credit which reverses over time operates in much the same manner as a benefit reserve.

Furthermore, acquisition cost reserves create problems. It could be argued that only the benefit reserve changes should be reflected as revenue adjustments, with changes in the expense reserves applied to increase or decrease reported expenses. This seems inconsistent with the concept that revenue should be recognized to meet benefits and expenses as they occur.

Treating the changes in the expense reserve as revenue adjustments is possible, but the result is peculiar and perhaps illogical. In the first year, for example, reported revenue would jump from $840,000 to $1,734,000. This means that additional revenue is, in effect, being accrued to take care of the high level of expenses incurred. After 1947 the expense reserves

---

*The expense reserves include acquisition cost reserves and reserves for maintenance and settlement expenses. The reserves for maintenance and settlement expense exert a relatively minor influence, however.

**For purposes of this discussion it is assumed that the expense reserve is negative, i.e., an "asset".

Table 5-1.

CONDENSED STATEMENTS OF OPERATIONS FOR THE AMERICAN EXPERIENCE BLOCK OF BUSINESS

(000 omitted)

	Insurance (000,000 omitted)		Premiums	Interest on Adjusted Reserve	Change in Adjusted Reserve		Death Benefits	Surrender Benefits	Matured Endowments	Other Benefits	Expenses	Pre-Tax Profits
	Sold	In Force			Benefit Reserve	Expense Reserve						
1941	$25	$ 25	$ 844	$ (4)	$ 571	$ (894)	$ 12			$ 3	$1,162	$ (14)
1942	35	55	1,837	(8)	1,206	(1,135)	55			8	1,685	10
1943	47	92	3,065	1	2,001	(1,422)	119			16	2,296	56
1944	56	135	4,450	28	2,861	(1,617)	170	$ 37		27	2,841	159
1945	71	188	6,127	74	3,877	(1,948)	232	104		42	3,566	328
1946	83	247	8,012	144	4,981	(2,184)	358	205		65	4,225	506
1947	92	309	9,970	242	6,097	(2,275)	531	340		94	4,779	646
1948		273	8,980	393	5,228	930	665	520		117	1,217	696
1949		253	8,410	575	4,703	800	752	754		136	1,145	695
1950		236	7,942	751	4,155	746	799	1,038		154	1,099	702
1951		221	7,503	917	3,688	742	789	1,251		171	1,034	745
1952		206	7,090	1,073	3,272	715	784	1,448		184	969	791
1953		195	6,718	1,219	2,895	702	849	1,629		172	890	800
1954		185	6,357	1,353	2,510	674	933	1,806		164	826	797
1955		174	6,006	1,480	2,140	645	998	1,968		160	760	815
1956		164	5,669	1,620	1,803	618	1,060	2,098		157	694	859
1957		155	5,345	1,769	1,501	595	1,069	2,213		154	626	956
1958		147	5,042	1,918	1,244	567	1,036	2,322		150	588	1,053
1959		139	4,753	2,072	973	550	1,022	2,427		147	560	1,146
1960		131	4,478	2,214	713	524	1,056	2,514		143	534	1,208
1961		123	4,057	2,285	(1,234)	481	1,099	2,447	$1,697	139	502	1,211
1962		114	3,611	2,272	(1,938)	421	1,100	2,335	2,189	133	462	1,181
1963		105	3,134	2,216	(2,631)	366	1,076	2,160	2,699	124	413	1,143
1964		97	2,638	2,130	(3,217)	303	1,055	1,954	3,101	117	366	1,089
1965		89	2,102	2,018	(3,857)	230	1,025	1,700	3,567	110	317	1,028
1966		80	1,541	1,889	(4,549)	150	993	1,394	4,104	104	265	969
1967		72	972	1,746	(4,881)	62	957	1,078	4,279	97	215	911
1968		69	905	1,702	(710)	79	933	1,093		90	182	940
1969		65	841	1,767	(800)	77	937	1,116		83	173	1,022
1970		62	780	1,826	(892)	66	943	1,149		76	167	1,097
1971		59	722	1,820	(968)	60	954	1,162		69	158	1,107

begin reversing, and it seems just as illogical to report consistently negative revenue items as to report consistently negative expense items.

On the other hand, treating reserve changes as expense adjustments rather than revenue adjustments is not necessarily the answer either. If a benefit reserve is regarded as accrued expense, for example, then logically benefits should be charged against the accrued liability. The benefit expense reported for a period would be a single amount representing the net change in the accrued liability. If an expense reserve is regarded as being in the nature of inventory, then operating expenses reported for a period would likewise be a single amount.

It would seem that as far as financial statement format is concerned, there are problems whether the reserve is regarded as deferred revenue or accrued expense. The problems derive from the unique and all-encompassing character of a "reserve". The treatment of reserve changes could be regarded as a matter of individual preference, and the reporting of individual income statement items could be regarded as a matter of disclosure. However, the life insurance audit guide provides that premiums on long-term contracts should be recognized as revenue when due. To implement this provision, increases in reserves on such business should be treated as expense items.

Substantially all companies report increases in reserves as expense items in their annual reports to shareholders.[21] It is likely that this practice was actually "generally accepted" before the advent of the audit guide.

Casualty-Type Business

Even if increases in life reserves are treated as expense items, there remains the question as to how to record increases in unearned premium reserves on casualty-type business (for example, commercial forms of individual health insurance). Property-liability companies record increases in such reserves as premium adjustments; premium revenue is reported as "earned " rather than when due. Life insurance companies usually treat increases in unearned premium reserves as expense items. The problem of consistency becomes particularly acute when financial statements of a life insurance company are consolidated with financial statements of a property-liability company. Which practice should prevail?

In the case of casualty-type business, there is a long precedent in the property-liability industry for treating increases in unearned premiums on such business as

revenue adjustments. Of course, life insurance companies have a long history of treating increases in unearned premiums as expense items. However, inasmuch as casualty business is much more material to the property-liability industry than to the life insurance industry, the property-liability precedent should prevail.

Further, the life insurance audit guide defines premium revenues on casualty-type business in the property-liability context. Again, in order to implement the audit guide's provisions, premium revenues on casualty-type business should be reported on an earned basis.

Miscellaneous Revenue Items

Premiums are, of course, the largest revenue item in a life insurance company's income statement. But investment income is not to be slighted; it accounted for 21 percent of the life insurance industry's total revenue (statutory basis) in 1972.

In addition, there are numerous other items, traditionally treated as revenue by life insurance companies, that deserve comment.

Investment Income

Interest, dividends, rents, capital gains and losses, and other such items make up a life insurance company's investment income. Capital gains are segregated for special treatment, both in the statutory statements and in financial statements prepared in conformity with generally accepted accounting principles. Capital gains are discussed in Chapter 10. The relationship of investment income to reserve assumptions is also discussed in Chapter 10. This discussion deals only with the nature of investment income and its presentation in the financial statements.

The life insurance audit guide treats investment income as a negative cost rather than as a revenue item. Thus premium revenue is seen to "provide investable funds", and "The investment of such premiums is recognized in the actuarial assumptions and in setting the premiums." [22] And "interest" is discussed in the section of the guide entitled "Recognition of Costs".

In other words, investment income is viewed as one of the determinants of the cost of benefits and expenses. The revenue stream against which benefits and expenses are matched is essentially limited to premiums. Premiums are discounted for anticipated interest, and so are projected benefits and expenses. Interest required to support reserves is charged to expense in each accounting period; such required interest is implicit in the reserve increase for a period. The amount of required interest charged to expense is dependent on the assumptions underlying the reserves.

Investment income as revenue. How then should a life insurance company report investment income that it actually earns?

Some believe that because the audit guide treats investment income as an adjustment of costs, investment income should be allocated to the various items of expense. Thus investment income would be offset against required interest; reserve increases would be reported net of investment income. Any investment income in excess of required interest would serve to reduce expense for the period to an amount that is less than anticipated expense.

Others believe that only investment income in excess of required interest should be regarded as revenue. Under this view, required interest would be eliminated from reserve increases and such required interest would be deducted from investment income, with the balance being shown as revenue for the period.

The audit guide discusses only the interest *assumption* used to calculate reserves. This does not constitute a mandate for accounting for *actual* investment income as an adjustment of expense. Nor does the fact that the guide regards premium revenue as the principal matching base mean that investment income is not revenue.

Further, there is no necessary relationship between investment income earned and required interest. For example, required interest would be charged to operations whether or not investment income is sufficient to cover it. Required interest bears essentially the same relationship to earned investment income as valuation premiums bear to gross premiums. Both required interest and required valuation premiums are included in the reserve increase for the year.

Therefore investment income without reduction for required interest should be regarded as revenue, just as premiums are. Both sources of revenue are required to absorb expenses, including reserve increases.

Investment expenses. Investment income is usually reported as revenue without deduction of investment expenses in most other industries; investment expenses are treated like other expenses and are deducted in a separate section of the income statement, sometimes without specific identification. A few life insurance companies also follow this practice.[23] However, the overwhelming majority of life insurance companies report, as revenue, investment income net of expenses. This results in a certain internal consistency in the statements, since required interest charged to operations is a net figure (the assumed "yield rate should be net of investment expenses"[24]). Precedence and consistency suggest, however, that the gross figure is preferable in reporting investment income in the income statement.

Home office "rent". The practice of charging expense (and crediting revenue) for the rental value of premises owned and occupied by the company is unique to insurance companies. Some have questioned the propriety of this practice, which inflates revenue and expense. They believe that the practice derives from statutory accounting traditions, which should not necessarily influence financial statements prepared in conformity with generally accepted accounting principles.

Others believe that an insurance company is, in effect, a consolidation of two types of operations, investment and insurance; that the investment in home office real estate results from an investment decision, not an insurance decision; and that the distinction between investment income and insurance expense is fitting and proper.

Theory and practice are clearly on the side of those who believe that the rental value of home office premises owned and occupied by the company should *not* be reported as investment income. Furthermore, the insurance operation is dependent on the investment operation to a degree that impairs or destroys the notion that the two operations are separate and distinct. It is questionable whether the practice of recording the rental value of home office premises owned and occupied by the company is in conformity with generally accepted accounting principles.

So the practice should be discouraged. If a company insists on following the traditional statutory accounting practice, then full disclosure of the relevant amounts should be made if the amounts are material.*

Disclosure. Regardless of how investment income is reported in the revenue section of the income statement, the principal sources of investment income and total investment expenses should be disclosed, either in the income statement itself or—preferably—in notes to the financial statements. In addition, significant distortive relationships—such as material amounts of

---

*Other peculiarities of investment income, and the relationship of investment income to reserve assumptions, are discussed in Chapter 10.

real estate revenue and expense—should also be disclosed.

Income statement disclosure might take the following form:

INCOME STATEMENT:

Revenue:	
Premiums	$ XXX
Gross investment income	XXX
Deductions from revenue:	
Investment expenses	XXX

NOTES TO FINANCIAL STATEMENTS:

Accounting policies note:

Investment income is reported as revenue when earned. It is the company's practice to record as investment income the rental value of home office premises owned and occupied by the company and to record as an expense the associated depreciation and other real estate expenses. The components of investment income are as follows:

Interest on bonds	$ XXX
Interest on policy loans	XXX
Dividends on stocks	XXX
Real estate rentals (including $XXX for the rental value of home office premises owned and occupied by the company)	XXX
Other	XXX
	$ XXX

It will be observed that the example assumes that the company follows the practice of reporting as investment income the rental value of home office premises owned and occupied by the company. This in no way constitutes an endorsement of the practice.

Deposit-Type Items

Certain types of receipts commonly classified as revenue by life insurance companies are, in fact, deposits which should be accounted for as such. Deposit items would include the following:

Reserve transfers under modified coinsurance agreements (discussed further in Chapter 22)

Deposits to reserves for active lives for which the life insurance company is not on the risk, such as:

Deposit administration funds

Annuity accumulation funds under immediate participation guarantee arrangements

Supplementary contracts not involving life contingencies

Stipulated payments under variable annuity contracts

Dividends left on deposit at interest

Premium deposit funds received

Premiums paid in advance

In general, receipts of payments on contracts not involving life contingencies should be recorded directly as additions to the related liabilities. There is fundamentally no difference between insurance companies and other financial institutions so far as deposit-type items are concerned. Thus, for example, savings and loan associations do not record deposits as revenue, and neither should a life insurance company. Precedence in accounting clearly calls for omitting deposit-type receipts from the income statement.

Receipts involving life contingencies—such as supplementary contracts involving life contingencies and dividends applied to purchase paid-up additions—are unique to life insurance companies. They are in the nature of premiums and should be recorded as revenue. However, premiums and considerations applicable to a life insurance company's own pension plan should not be recorded as revenue, even though the company holds the reserves. Revenue is not created by a self-insurance arrangement.

6

Adverse
Deviation and
Lock-In

Webster's defines a life insurance reserve as

. . . the amount of funds or assets calculated on net premiums to be necessary for a life insurance company to have at any given time to enable it with interest and premiums paid as they shall accrue to meet all claims on the insurance then in force as they would mature according to the particular mortality table accepted.[1]

While an actuary or a grammarian might possibly take issue with Mr. Webster on that definition, it pretty well states the classic notion of what a reserve is for: a reserve is designed to earmark funds that will be required to pay for the excess of future claims over future premiums and investment income.

The "classic notion" of a reserve is oriented toward solvency considerations. The main thing is to have *enough* on hand at any point in time, and statutory rules prescribe more or less how the amount on hand should be accumulated. It is fair to say that the effect on the income statement of the pattern of accumulation is of secondary concern to regulators, and rightly so.

In converting to generally accepted accounting principles, however, the effect on the income statement of the pattern of reserve accumulation is a consideration of great importance.

Adverse Deviation

From the standpoint of the life insurance audit guide, the primary function of an adjusted reserve is to control the emergence of profits on the books of a life insurance company. The guide does not say this in so many words, of course, but profit allocation is clearly the main objective of the discussion of reserve assumptions. Thus, for example, adjusted reserves on whole-life contracts should be calculated using assumptions that "will *cause* some profits to emerge over the life of the contract." [2] (Emphasis supplied.)

Some would say that the "control" of profit recognition by an accounting device sounds a bit suspicious. But any reserve system "controls" the emergence of profit. One cannot argue with the concept of using reserves to control profit recognition unless one is prepared to do away with reserves and make do with cash flow.

That still leaves the question of how profit emergence should be controlled—that is, within what parameters profits should be accelerated, slowed down, or kept level. No one has the final answer to that, and it is doubtful that anyone ever will. This is mainly because no one knows exactly how to provide for adverse deviation. But provisions for adverse deviation are required by the audit guide, and such provisions can have a very significant impact on the incidence of reported profits—or no impact at all.

Audit Guide References to Adverse Deviation

The most significant reference to adverse deviation in the life insurance audit guide comes in the discussion of revenue recognition. While concluding that there is "no predominant function or service which [provides] a measure of the composite of all functions and services with respect to whole life contracts," [3] the guide does make the point that assumption of the risk of adverse deviation from best estimates of future experience is *"an* essential function or service performed by a life insurance company." [4] (Emphasis supplied.) Therefore the "risks of adverse deviations . . . should be recognized in determining the timing of the recognition of premium revenues and related costs." [5] Premiums are recognized as revenue when they are received, for the most part. That means that the risk of adverse deviation can only be provided for through the reserve mechanism, i.e., in the "timing of the recognition . . . of . . . costs."

Up to this point the guide has spoken of adverse deviation in the context of allocating profits on the basis of release from the risk of adverse deviation. In other words, each risk of adverse deviation— mortality, interest, withdrawal and expense—carries with it a profit component which should be recognized only as the risk passes. The guide then introduces an additional consideration:

The inclusion of a provision for the risk of adverse deviations in arriving at *reasonably conservative* assumptions will cause some profits to emerge over the life of the contract as risks are eliminated.[6] (Emphasis supplied.)

A provision for adverse deviation that is based on assigning a value to the actual risk of deviation would not necessarily result in a "reasonably conservative" assumption. This will be discussed later in this chapter and in various other chapters. But the guide suggests in the passage quoted above that reasonable conservatism should operate as a constraint on provisions for adverse deviation in all cases. The guide is more explicit later in the discussion:

. . . The provisions must be reasonable in relation to the total valuation premium. Conservatism in determining such provisions *should also be considered in relation to the effect of the provision on recognition of profit.* Conservatism with respect to individual assumptions will not necessarily result in conservative recognition of profit.[7] (Emphasis supplied.)

It is clear, therefore, that regardless of the results that would be produced by regarding a provision for adverse deviation as a device for recognizing profits in proportion to the release from risk, the final result must be a "conservative recognition of profit."

Other significant references to adverse deviation and conservatism include the following:

▶ On the role of the actuary: "[The actuary's] responsibility to use assumptions which are 'adequate and appropriate' is consistent with the concept, under generally accepted accounting principles,

that actuarial assumptions be characterized by conservatism which is 'reasonable and realistic'." [8]

▶ On reserve assumptions in general: "The assumptions used, including provision for the risk of adverse deviation, must be reasonably conservative." [9]

▶ On the interest assumption: "Since life insurance involves long-term obligations and investment risks, the assumed interest rate should include provision for the risk of adverse deviation . . . " [10] "While it is not possible to establish a precise limitation or guideline . . . the auditor should be satisfied that the rate used is reasonable and conservative." [11]

▶ On the mortality assumption: "As in the case of other estimates, provision for adverse deviations should be included." [12]

▶ On the withdrawal assumption: "As in the case of interest and mortality estimates, provision for the risk of adverse deviation . . . should be included." [13]

▶ On annuity reserves: "The mortality assumption in annuity reserves involves the most significant risk of adverse deviation. It should be recognized that conservatism in providing reserves for annuity benefits means . . . a lower assumed death rate." [14]

▶ On health insurance: "It should be noted that for coverages which have increasing claim costs, it is not conservative to assume high lapse rates in renewal years." [15]

▶ On new companies: "The auditor may be satisfied if the company uses very conservative provisions for adverse deviations, principally for interest and mortality." [16]

So a provision for adverse deviation is both (1) a means of distributing profits in proportion to release from the risk of adverse deviation, "an essential function or service performed by a life insurance company," and (2) a means of being conservative. But such conservatism must be reasonable and even realistic:

For current issues, [an established] company should use its own [mortality] experience if such experience is credible . . . [established] companies should use published withdrawal tables . . . only if the results produced by the use of such tables are comparable with the company's actual withdrawal experience.[17]

It is obvious that adverse deviation, as presented in the audit guide, is a very fluid concept, simultaneously embracing release-from-risk concepts, conservatism, and realism. Several interpretations of adverse deviation, or a combination of interpretations, are possible. Each interpretation carries with it important implications for the financial statements.

The Release-from-Risk Concept

As mentioned in Chapter 1, the concept of release-from-risk was introduced to the Joint Actuarial Committee on Financial Reporting by Richard Horn and formed the basis for the Committee's *Response* to the December 1970 draft of the life insurance audit guide. Mr. Horn subsequently published an article, "Life Insurance Earnings and the Release from Risk Policy Reserve System", in Volume XXIII (November 1972) of *Transactions of the Society of Actuaries*.

Underlying the release-from-risk concept is a certain view of a life insurance company—that a life insurance company is a risk enterprise and that assumption of risk is synonymous with the service that a life insurance company performs. Thus:

Beyond the general economic and business risks faced by all business, life insurance companies assume the risks underlying their insurance products—specifically, mortality, investment, expense, and withdrawal. . . . the company's hazard, however, lies in deviations from the expected values rather than the expected values themselves. The company must provide for the costs of both the expected values of the risks inherent in their products and the deviations from the expected values . . . The risks of adverse variability in realistically assumed rates of mortality, interest, withdrawal, and expense constitute the hazard of the life insurance endeavor.[18]

Making a provision for the risk of adverse deviation is conceptually easy. It would involve adding a "delta", or margin, to an expected value. Thus, for example, if the best estimate of mortality in a given year is x and the necessary margin for adverse deviation is y, the mortality assumption used in the adjusted reserve calculation would be $x + y$. If actual mortality in the given year is z, which happens to be a little less than x, then reported profits associated with the mortality assumption in the given year would be $x + y - z$. In other words, if x = \$5, y = \$1, and z = \$4, the year's "mortality profits" would be \$2, as follows:

Release from the adjusted reserve of mortality realistically assumed to occur during the year (expected value)	\$5
Mortality actually experienced	4
Favorable deviation from expected value ("mortality profit" under the old natural reserve approach)	1
Release from the adjusted reserve of prior provision for adverse deviation, withheld from income of prior years and no longer needed because the risk has passed	1
"Mortality profit" under the release-from-risk approach	\$2

It can readily be seen that the difference between the old natural reserve approach and the release-from-risk approach lies in the *specificity* of the provision for the risk of adverse deviation. In the case illustrated above, the expected value turned out to contain a provision for adverse deviation which was largely accidental. The specific provision was intentional.

The release-from-risk concept involves the provision for "deltas" representing the risk of adverse deviation with respect to each of the risks. Assuming that expected values are in fact experienced, the earnings of a period are the algebraic sum of

gain from interest risk release,
gain from mortality risk release,
gain from withdrawal risk release,
gain from expense risk release,

plus, to the extent that there remains a difference between the gross premium and the valuation premium after making all the provisions for adverse deviation,

gain from loading.[19]

On this latter point, Mr. Horn suggests that management's view of the nature of a life insurance company might influence the manner in which adverse deviation is provided for and, hence, the manner in which profits emerge. "If the management of a particular company considered its corporation to be primarily a marketing organization," such a company might choose to treat the sale of a life insurance policy as an installment sale, with profits emerging as a level percentage of premiums. "On the other hand, if management regarded its corporation as a mechanism for the sharing and carrying of risk, it might reasonably feel that earnings should emerge only as risk is released." [20] Under this latter approach there would be no gains from loading.

As Mr. Horn points out, the release-from-risk system is a generalized system, of which the two extremes set forth above are special cases. In the usual case, provisions for adverse deviation would be expected to use up some, but not all, of the difference between the gross premium and a valuation premium based on best estimates. In the usual case, then, a portion of the profit emerges as loading (i.e., as a constant percentage of premiums) and a portion emerges in proportion to release from risk (i.e., as adjusted reserves built up to cover the deltas are released). This is the "intermediate release-from-risk" approach.

Implementing the Release-from-Risk Concept

Mr. Horn states that "the adverse variability associated with the expected value of a given risk can be quantified either on the basis of appropriate risk statistics or by determining the margins for variance which the gross premium rate structure implicitly permits." [21] He points out that measures of adverse variability associated with each of the separate risks "could be determined separately with relative ease (assuming the existence of the necessary probability distributions)." [22]

Take, for example, the withdrawal assumption, for which a suitable probability distribution is constructed:

Withdrawal Range	The Probability That Withdrawals Will Fall Within the Range	Cumulative Probability
0–5 %	.01	.01
6–10	.04	.05
11–15	.05	.10
16–20	.15	.25
21–25	.30	.55
26–30	.20	.75
31–35	.10	.85
36–40	.05	.90
41–45	.04	.94
46–50	.03	.97
Over 51	.03	1.00

For this particular table the average withdrawal rate is 26.2 percent. This value might be rounded down to 25 percent and thus become an "expected value" or best estimate.*

Assuming one wishes a 90 percent probability that the assumed withdrawal rate will not be exceeded, one might use 40 percent—an expected value of 25 percent (at which rate the probability of adverse deviation is offset by the probability of favorable deviation) plus a provision for adverse deviation of 15 percent. Note that the provision for adverse deviation ignores the probability of favorable deviation; it is a one-sided provision.

In theory, a similar frequency distribution could be developed for each plan, issue age, year of issue, and assumption. Assuming 100 plans issued at 50 ages with an average spread of durations of 50 years and four assumptions (mortality, interest, withdrawal, and expense), then 1,000,000 frequency distributions would be needed.

*This table is adapted with permission from a report by Gary Corbett dated May 19, 1972, to the members of the Joint Actuarial Committee on Financial Reporting Principles. It should be noted that the purpose and scope of Mr. Corbett's paper differed from the simple illustrative purpose to which the material is put in this discussion.

But that's not all. As Mr. Horn points out, "quantification of the combined risks taken as a whole is considerably more difficult" than quantifying each risk separately, because the separate risks are "nonadditive" and "the separate risks of adverse deviations are somewhat related and interdependent." [23] In the case of the withdrawals discussed above, for example, the probability distribution may change as a function of the interest assumption if one assumes that high interest rates encourage surrenders or vice versa. In turn, the withdrawal assumption would probably affect the mortality assumption, since the probability distribution relating to mortality would presumably recognize the exposure base, i.e., amounts of insurance assumed to be in force. "Various other relationships exist, and the strength of each relationship can vary by duration. If it were considered desirable to recognize possible cyclical trends in adverse deviations, this would add an additional dimension of complexity." [24]

So the complexity of the calculations required to do full justice to the release-from-risk concept would tax the capabilities of even the largest computers. Furthermore, it is extremely doubtful that common probability distributions can be created that will be appropriate to a given company; in fact, some believe that the necessary probability distributions simply cannot be created within acceptable tolerances of precision. There are alternate approaches; Mr. Horn suggests one in the discussion of his paper, pointing out that "An adequate exploration of the theoretical considerations involved in quantifying the risks of adverse deviation would plow a great deal of new ground." [25] In other words, the necessary theory is not available; new ground must be plowed.*

Meantime, what are the actuary and accountant to do? Mr. Horn suggests that adverse deviation can be quantified in a "rather practical manner":

The quantification of the risks of adverse variability can be accomplished in a rather practical manner by allocating all, or a part, of the profit margin contained in the gross premium to the various risk elements. The determination of how much of the profit margin to allocate and the division into the various risk elements would be largely a matter of judgment. The judgment employed in this process would be similar to, or an extension of, the judgment employed in deciding upon

*The Board of Governors of the Society of Actuaries during 1973 approved a study, funded by the Society, of what deltas should be added to best estimates in order to implement the release-from-risk concept. Thus the Society, as well as other actuarial groups, are attempting to plow the necessary new ground.

a set of assumptions to use in establishing gross premiums. As an example, an actuary might feel that the risk of an adverse mortality deviation should be represented by, say, 5 percent of his most realistic estimate of future mortality rates. A similar assignment of amounts for the risks of adverse deviation in the interest rate assumption and the withdrawal rate and expense rate assumptions could likewise be made on the basis of the actuary's judgment. The criterion that would need to be satisfied in each instance, however, would be that the premium calculated on the basis of realistic assumptions plus the amounts assigned to the risks of adverse deviations must be no greater than the gross premium.[26]

In other words, the actuary would use up that portion of the difference between the gross premium and the "best estimate" valuation premium which *in his judgment* adequately provides for adverse deviation. Judgments differ, of course, and the provision for adverse deviation conceivably could range from zero to the entire difference between the gross premium and the valuation premium. The actuary is subject only to the constraint that the valuation premium must not exceed the gross premium (unless, of course, there are inherent losses in the business computed without regard for adverse deviation).

Mr. Horn makes one further point in the discussion of his paper which is most pertinent:

If the AICPA Committee . . . concludes that an intentional degree of conservatism in the . . . [assumptions] . . . is required, then they will in fact be requiring the use of [deltas]. Since [deltas] do not always increase [adjusted] reserves, their impact on earnings may not always be to defer profit emergence . . . [For example,] a mortality rate [delta] that reduced the slope of the mortality curve would . . . tend to anticipate, rather than defer, earnings. It is recommended that the AICPA proceed carefully.[27]

Interpretations of the Audit Guide

Proceeding carefully, the AICPA Committee provided in the life insurance audit guide that

▸ Adverse deviation should be provided for;
▸ The resulting adjusted reserve assumptions should be reasonably conservative;
▸ Such conservatism, besides being reasonable, should be realistic;
▸ Conservatism should be measured in terms of the effect of the provision for adverse deviation on the valuation premium *and* on the pattern of profit recognition; and
▸ Having done all this, adequate recognition is

implicity given to the release-from-risk concept; assumption of the risk of adverse deviation is *an* essential function or service (but not *the* essential function or service) performed by a life insurance company.

Some have interpreted the audit guide to mean that a provision for adverse deviation is primarily a deliberately-introduced margin for conservatism and secondarily a means of implementing the release-from-risk concept. This interpretation is most widely attributed to accountants, although many actuaries also hold the same view.* They point out that while the guide indicates that provision for adverse deviation should be "included" in determining assumptions for mortality, interest, and withdrawal,** the overall effect of the provisions should be a reasonably conservative recognition of profit. In short, while the various individual assumptions would be "considered" individually, it is not mandatory that specific deltas be introduced for each assumption; it is only necessary that the net result be reasonable, realistic, and conservative.

Many other actuaries, however, including the Joint Actuarial Committee on Financial Reporting, believe that adverse deviation as defined in the audit guide is designed primarily to implement the release-from-risk concept and secondarily to introduce a margin for conservatism. Thus, according to the Joint Actuarial Committee:

The Joint Actuarial Committee on Financial Reporting supports the Audit Guide in the policy reserve method adopted but we feel that it is important to state the basis for our support . . . The policy reserve method in the Audit Guide is recognized as the Intermediate Form Release from Risk method by the Joint Actuarial Committee. . . . The . . . Committee feels that the Intermediate Form Release from Risk policy reserve method is appropriate for general purpose financial statements of stock life insurance companies since this reserve method is consistent with generally accepted accounting principles as they now exist.[28]

The Committee on Financial Reporting Principles of the American Academy of Actuaries, whose responsibility it is to provide recommendations—which are binding on Academy members—with respect to actuarial aspects of the audit guide, also holds the

---

*This representation as to the views of most accountants and many actuaries is based on numerous informal discussions with informed accountants and actuaries.

**The guide does not discuss adverse deviation as the concept might apply to expense assumptions.

view that the intent of the audit guide is to implement the release-from-risk concept. The Committee states in an "Interpretation" on its first "Recommendation":

The general theory underlying the disciplining of actuarial assumptions for [adjusted] reserves has been called, by the Joint Actuarial Committee on Financial Reporting, the 'intermediate form of release from risk reserving method' . . . Each actuarial assumption underlying [adjusted] reserves should be chosen with due regard to providing for the risk of adverse deviation, over and above the most likely assumption . . . There should be a reasonable balance among the provisions for risk of adverse deviation, both by type of assumption and by policy year . . . Any specific loading for profit in the actual gross premium is limited to the excess, if any, of the gross premium over the valuation premium based on actuarial assumptions which include appropriate provisions for the risk of adverse deviation . . .[29]

The Committee points out that the result of providing for adverse deviation is to produce an element of profit, which "should be positive," equal to the difference between expected experience and valuation assumptions (modified by the difference between actual and expected reserves released). Such profits "will emerge substantially in proportion to release from risk."[30]

The Committee reconciles the release-from-risk theory with the audit guide's general requirement for conservatism by noting that the release-from-risk theory

. . . provides a way by which quantitative concepts can be used in discussions of the indefinite concept 'conservatism'. It does so by recognizing that no portion of the actual gross profit should be available as a specific loading for profit unless the risks of adverse deviation have been duly provided for in the valuation premium.[31]

The Committee recommends that the relationship between the valuation premium and the gross premium be the principal constraint on actuarial assumptions.

There are, then, two distinct schools of thought as to what the audit guide intends by its references to provisions for adverse deviation:

▶ The main purpose of the provisions is to introduce reasonable conservatism. Conservatism is measured in part by the effect on profit recognition. Specific deltas corresponding to a defined pattern of risk release are not required.

▶ The main purpose of the provisions is to implement the release-from-risk concept. Conservatism is measured in terms of the relationship between the valuation premium and the gross premium. Specific deltas corresponding to a defined pattern of risk release are required and there should be a reasonable balance among the various deltas.

Effect of the Two Interpretations

It might appear that the two interpretations of adverse deviation would lead to the same answer. After all, the only difference between the two is a matter of emphasis.

But a difference in emphasis can have a significant effect. An example may suggest how this can be so.

Assume that the product for which assumptions are being chosen is a $1,000 two-year level-premium endowment, that the gross premium is $475, that mortality and withdrawal are zero, and that interest rates are as follows:

Earnings rate on new investments in preceding year (eventually sustained through the two following years)	7%
Best estimate	7%
Best estimate loaded for reasonable conservatism, determined judgmentally	7% in first year, 6% in second
Rate for which there is a 90% probability that it will not be exceeded	4%

The corresponding valuation premiums would be as follows:

Best estimate	$451.49
Best estimate loaded for reasonable conservatism	455.75
"90%" estimate	471.34

The profits that would be reported in each of the two years under each approach would be as follows:

	Year 1	Year 2	Total
Best estimate	$25.16	$26.92	$52.08
Loaded best estimate	20.60	31.48	52.08
"90%" estimate	18.05	34.03	52.08

In this case reasonable conservatism was applied by use of judgment. The rate that was chosen (7 percent graded to 6 percent) was felt to be consistent with "such factors as actual yields, trends in yields, portfolio mix and maturities, and a company's overall investment experience generally,"[32] as suggested by the audit guide.

For purposes of implementing the release-from-risk concept, however, another approach was used. Examination of interest rate cycles indicated that the probability that the interest rate on new investments would not fall beneath 4 percent was 90 percent, and the actuary quantified the assumption of risk in terms of the 90 percent probability.

In one case, then, reasonable conservatism was applied directly, and sufficient recognition of release-from-risk concepts was believed to be implicit in the margin for conservatism. In the other case, release-from-risk concepts were applied first and the requirement of reasonable conservatism was felt to be satisfied automatically.

It can be seen, therefore, that the result that is obtained can depend in part on one's interpretation of what the audit guide means when it says that adverse deviation be provided for.

A somewhat more significant example of the difference between the two approaches may be found in connection with the withdrawal assumption.

Assume a 10-year term policy with level gross premiums of $50, first-year acquisition costs of $275, zero mortality, zero interest, zero renewal expenses, and withdrawals (all in the first year) as follows:

Best estimate	20%
Loaded best estimate	25
"90%" estimate	50

The valuation premiums that would be associated with the foregoing sets of assumptions would be as follows:

	Benefit Premium	Expense Premium
Best estimate	$ –0–	$33.53
Loaded best estimate	–0–	35.48
"90%" estimate	–0–	50.00

The first-year reserve factors based on the foregoing would be as follows (assuming that first-year lapses occur just prior to the valuation date):

	Benefit Reserve	Expense Reserve
Best estimate	$ –0–	$301.84
Loaded best estimate	–0–	319.36
"90%" estimate	–0–	450.00

Finally, the reserves that would be reported if lapses occurred as expected would be as follows (again assuming that valuation occurs just after lapse):

	Expected Units in Force	Benefit Reserve	Expense Reserve
Best estimate	.800	$ –0–	$241.47
Loaded best estimate	.750	–0–	239.52
"90%" estimate	.600	–0–	225.00

Assume now that the actual lapse rate is 20 percent, the best estimate. In that event, the reserves would be as follows:

	Benefit Reserve	Expense Reserve
Best estimate	$ –0–	$241.47
Loaded best estimate	–0–	255.49
"90%" estimate	–0–	360.00

The profits that would be reported under these conditions would be as follows:

	Year 1	Year 2–10	Total
Best estimate	$ 16.47	$118.53	$135.00
Loaded best estimate	30.49	104.51	135.00
"90%" estimate	135.00	–0–	135.00

It will be observed that, using the "90 percent" estimate, the company winds up deferring more acquisition cost than it incurs and taking in all of the profits in the first year. This would apparently be acceptable under the pure application of release-from-risk theory; the company has defined its risk in terms of the first-year lapse rate, and once the risk has passed, any profits assigned to the risk can be released.

It appears, however, that generally accepted accounting principles would not permit deferral of an amount greater than the amount incurred. In fact, the audit guide is quite specific on this point. "If actual [persistency] experience differs significantly from that assumed, the [acquisition cost] factors should be recomputed." [33] Even if the release-from-risk approach should call for recognizing "withdrawal" profits when the risk passes, the guide's concept of reasonable conservatism would call for recomputation of the factors and, hence, a significant modification of the profit pattern that would be associated with release from the withdrawal risk.

The examples are admittedly extreme. In fact, they are somewhat bizarre. Furthermore, it is conceivable that an individual actuary would set the confidence level, or otherwise define the risk, in such a manner that pure application of release-from-risk theory would essentially duplicate the effect of loading best estimates judgmentally. Nevertheless, it might be said that the range within which the actuary's judgment can be brought to bear is somewhat greater under the release-from-risk approach than under the conservatism approach. A given provision for adverse deviation may not appear particularly reasonable or realistic in terms of the prevailing facts and circumstances, yet it may seem eminently reasonable and realistic in terms of how the company defines the risks underlying its products.

The present situation presents the actuary with something of a problem. Regardless of how he provides for adverse deviation now, his work may be invalidated by future developments in the actuarial profession—specifically, by guidelines that may eventually be mandated by the American Academy of Actuaries. Further, an actuary can't be certain that what he is doing now is consistent with what his fellow professionals are doing; some actuaries are not taking the release-from-risk concept as seriously as other actuaries. Finally, an actuary can't be entirely certain that what he is doing meets the audit guide's criteria that "actuarial assumptions [should] be characterized by conservatism which is 'reasonable and realistic'."

The actuary must "be able to demonstrate that assumptions used in determining actuarial items in a general-purpose statement meet such standards." [34]

Accountants are perhaps somewhat more sanguine about adverse deviation than actuaries are, possibly because they are not thoroughly familiar with the underlying issues. Accountants, moreover, are familiar with the concept of conservatism. Conservatism is, as the American Academy Committee on Financial Reporting Principles, an "indefinite concept," but accountants deal with it all the time. So they would not necessarily object to a provision for adverse deviation that does not fully implement release-from-risk theory. In fact, they might object if a provision for adverse deviation that is fully responsive to a company's definition of risk seemed to be "unduly conservative." [35] While "the choice of actuarial assumptions and the disciplining of that choice are primary responsibilities of the actuarial profession," the choice must be guided by "considerations which are consistent with generally accepted accounting principles." [36] Among other things, this means that the reserve assumptions must be "reasonable and realistic", and the frame of reference within which an accountant judges reasonableness and realism is bound to have an impact on the actuary. To the extent that the accountant's interpretation of adverse deviation differs from the actuary's, he may have a considerably different idea of what is reasonable and realistic and hence in conformity with generally accepted accounting principles. This intensifies the actuary's dilemma. And the accountant has his problems, too; after all, he depends on the actuary to choose the assumptions.

Need for a Consistent Interpretation

One consulting actuary has indicated that where he must recommend the approach to follow to his client, he would recommend "best-estimate" assumptions that have an element of conservatism. Mortality would be based on prior experience (company experience or published data, if appropriate); conservatism would be regarded as implicit in the assumption in that projected improvements would not be recognized. Interest would be graded to an ultimate rate of about 4 percent, in the absence of unusual circumstances. Withdrawals would be based on best estimates with possibly some margins for later durations. With respect to renewal expenses, an inflationary factor might be included depending on the interest assumption; but he would recognize also that for most companies future growth and improved operating methods should introduce some economies. No specific deltas would be required and the level of the valuation premium would not depend on the level of the gross premium. In all cases, however, the actuary would obtain formal expressions of concurrence with the approach from the company and its independent accountants. He also indicates that if his approach proves to be inconsistent with guidelines to be promulgated by the actuarial profession eventually—through the work of the American Academy of Actuaries—then he would conform his approach to those guidelines. This could, of course, result in a restatement in some future year.

One company actuary has studied his company's business, the rate of growth, prior company experience, plans for the future, trends in economic and investment conditions, and other factors and has attempted to translate these data into a pattern of deltas. He concludes that the release-from-risk theory, as he interprets it, is satisfactorily implemented by setting the valuation premium equal to (1) the best-estimate valuation premium plus (2) one-half of the difference between the valuation premium and the gross premium. The 50% provision is effectively a composite provision for specific deltas, and it can be seen that the level of the valuation premium is in part a function of the level of the gross premium.

Meantime, three knowledgeable individuals from

three different accounting firms have interpreted the audit guide's adverse deviation requirement as follows:

Accountant A: If the assumptions are reasonably conservative overall, then they are acceptable. The interest assumption is particularly important in this regard. It is not necessary to build in specific deltas.

Accountant B: There must be conservatism in the assumptions, but specific deltas are not required. The actuary has latitude. The possibility that some accountants may require specific deltas should not be ruled out.

Accountant C: Adverse deviation is generally being viewed as a requirement for conservatism rather than as an implementation of release-from-risk theory. Analysts don't understand the release-from-risk theory and view the margins as a means of introducing conservatism. If interest rates grade to an ultimate rate of about 4 percent and a conservative definition of acquisition costs is used, then the assumptions are probably acceptable.

The need for some degree of consistency in the fundamental interpretation of adverse deviation is obvious. There certainly is room for differences of opinion on how to implement the concept, but there should be no room for difference of opinion on what the concept is.

An analogy of the present situation might be found in depreciation accounting. In the absence of general agreement on the nature of depreciation, one might view it as a method of allocating cost or as a method of reserving funds for replacement of exhausted plant and equipment. One's interpretation of the nature of depreciation would strongly influence how depreciation would be provided. For example, if one viewed depreciation as a method of reserving funds for replacement, depreciation would be based on replacement cost, not historical cost. But accounting literature establishes the principle that depreciation is a rational and systematic allocation of an historical cost. Accountants may differ on how best to allocate the cost rationally and systematically, but they would not differ in their interpretations of what depreciation is. The same degree of consistency is needed in the case of adverse deviation.

Toward a Consistent Interpretation

One might envision three companies with the same product, the same gross premiums, and the same prospects for the future, but three different actuaries who implement release-from-risk theory in three different ways:

Actuary A seeks a 90 percent assurance with respect to each assumption that experience will not prove to be more adverse than the assumption. In effect, he believes that the company's real risk is the risk of ruin from "normal" deviations. He is strongly influenced by his industry's traditional solvency orientation. He believes that he is applying release-from-risk in its purest form. He develops his own frequency distributions.

Actuary B seeks a 60 percent assurance with respect to each assumption that experience will not prove to be more adverse than the assumption. He is influenced by a desire to give some recognition to the upside risk as well as the downside risk, believing that this approach is necessary to produce fair financial statements. He is strongly influenced by the notion of reasonable conservatism, and interprets the release-from-risk theory in such a manner as to implement the notion as he understands it. He too develops his own frequency distributions.

Actuary C decides to go with the quantification of risk that is implicit in the gross premium, and sets the valuation premium equal to the gross, distributing the difference between the gross premium and the "best-estimate" valuation premium to the various individual assumptions in a reasonable manner. He believes this is the most practicable thing to do in the absence of generally accepted frequency distributions and guidelines as to confidence levels.

Each of these approaches might do justice to the release-from-risk theory. In each case the theory is applied conscientiously. In each case, however, the individual actuary is strongly influenced in his implementation of the release-from-risk theory by his own perception of what best serves the purpose of generally accepted accounting principles. Generally accepted accounting principles may be somewhat flexible, but not so flexible as to accommodate all three actuaries.

Precedence in accounting. Many if not most businesses face, in addition to general economic and business risks, risks which are unique to their products. To name a few:

▶ Computer lessors, having invested substantial sums in computer hardware, face the risk that computer technology will render their stock of computers obsolete.

▶ Construction contractors operating on a fixed price face the risk of cost overruns.

▶ Land developers, having sold properties today with a commitment to install improvements later, face the risk that the cost of such improvements will exceed their estimates.

▶ High-technology manufacturers, having invested in expensive specialized machinery, face the risk that technology will render their product obsolete and their investment worthless.

▶ Toy manufacturers, having invested substantial sums in design work and tooling, face the risk of a change in fashion that will eliminate demand for their products.

▶ Auto manufacturers face the risk that cars already sold will have to be called back—a very expensive process—because of some defect that was not apparent at the time of sale.

So while a life insurance company may be viewed as being in the business of assuming risk, so can many other types of companies. Traditionally other types of companies have been viewed as being in business to sell products or services, but a life insurance company can be viewed that way, too. A company's *raison d'être* can vary with one's perspective.

Accountants have normally dealt with perceived risks by introducing a measure of conservatism into the accounting process. Thus a computer lessor might accelerate depreciation of its computer stock; a construction contractor might add a cushion for unexpected costs (in essence, a margin for adverse deviation) in computing the profits to be recognized on a percentage-of-completion basis; a land developer might defer revenues deemed applicable to future development costs, thus providing a cushion to the extent of any profit margins associated with the deferred revenue.

Conservatism is a doctrine, not a rule. It is generally applied more or less subjectively by informed professionals whose concern is the fairness of the financial statements. "Fairness" is measured in terms of a complex set of factors and conditions, such as the interests and needs of investors, the need to report management's accomplishments or failures as promptly and as truthfully as possible, and the need to facilitate capital formation. Accounting that is too liberal, too optimistic, would fail to meet the test of fairness.

*Protection against ruin from castastrophes such as famine or epidemics is not contemplated by any reserve system now extant.

But accounting that is too conservative would also fail to meet the test of fairness. A reserve system that provides, say, 90 percent assurance against ruin from "normal" deviations* would probably be entirely appropriate for statutory purposes, but it is questionable whether a 90 percent reserve would be "fair" in terms of the objectives of general-purpose financial statements. Is operating performance fairly measured only after charging earnings with such additional amounts as are required to protect the company against loss, come what may? There are few if any precedents for this in accounting for profit-making enterprises.

Precedence in accounting suggests that a provision for adverse deviation should be viewed as a reasonable margin for conservatism.

Internal evidence in the audit guide. References to adverse deviation contained in the life insurance audit guide were discussed earlier. Because the guide requires "reasonable and realistic" conservatism, because the guide warns against assumptions that are "unduly conservative," because the effect of the assumptions is to be measured partly in terms of the pattern of profit recognition, and because the guide defines assumption of the risk of adverse deviation as *an* essential function or service but not *the* essential function or service, it seems clear that the guide views a provision for adverse deviation primarily as a margin for conservatism.

Relationship to lock-in principle. It appears that proper implementation of the lock-in principle requires that a provision for adverse deviation be viewed as a margin for conservatism. This is discussed later in this chapter.

Lack of accepted guidelines. Lacking accepted and consistent guidelines for quantifying the risks of adverse deviation, the range within which the actuary's judgment must be brought to bear is too great under the release-from-risk theory in its present stage of development. Consistent interpretation of provisions for adverse deviation as being margins for conservatism would serve to reduce this range to tolerable proportions without in any way affecting the actuary's responsibility to exercise his professional judgment.

Practice to date. In substantially all conversions to generally accepted accounting principles through 1972, provisions for adverse deviation, where made, were interpreted as being margins for conservatism. This approach toward adverse deviation may already be "generally accepted".

Position adopted in this book. This book adopts the point of view that a provision for adverse deviation is primarily a means of introducing a degree of conservatism that is appropriate in the circumstances, and that recognition of income in proportion to release from risk of adverse deviation is a secondary objective of the audit guide's requirements.

This point of view was based partly on the considerations set forth above and partly on the fact that none of the many consulting actuaries whose counsel was sought on the matter were prepared to suggest how the release-from-risk concept should be implemented.

"Prudent Best Estimates"

A letter written late in 1972 by a top-level executive of a very large stock life insurance company states that

I consider that "most likely" means an assumption such that there is an even chance of the actual result falling on either side of "most likely". I have also coined for my own benefit an expression "prudent best estimate", which is a more conservative assumption than "most likely" but only to the extent of the amount of conservatism that would normally be built into any long range estimate in any kind of business. Stated negatively, a "prudent best estimate" *must not be so constructed as to include deliberately a mechanism for the deferral of income recognition.* It will be noted that logically, a "prudent best estimate", as compared to a "most likely" assumption, automatically contains a provision for adverse deviation, however small. (Emphasis supplied.)

"Prudent best estimate" pretty well describes the interpretation of a provision for adverse deviation suggested in this book. There may be differences of opinion as to what is "prudent"—this book argues for a fairly liberal dose of conservatism in setting assumptions—but the letter quoted above is a very succinct statement of the suggested method of providing for adverse deviation.

Role of Surplus in Degree of Conservatism

The author of the letter quoted above also states that, in his opinion,

The real measure of protection against adverse deviations is the combination of the amount which is buried in the reserves [by reason of having provided for adverse deviation] and the amount which is classified as surplus. If the free surplus is very large, the provision for adverse deviation in the reserves may be minimal or zero. If the free surplus is very small, the provision for adverse deviations in the reserves might have to be considerable.

Thus the question is raised as to whether a company's surplus position should have an effect on the extent to which adverse deviation is provided for.

There is little question that a company's general financial condition will have an impact, conscious or otherwise, on provisions for adverse deviations. A company in parlous circumstances will tend to be more conservative than it would be if it were flush with surplus.*

However, any extra provision for adverse deviation because of the company's financial condition is a manifestation of human nature rather than a technical imperative. The extra provision reflects a concern about solvency. But any additional provisions for adverse deviation will not solve a company's solvency problems, which are the responsibility of management and the regulatory authorities. Nor would it be appropriate to create what by its nature would be a contingency reserve and report it as a liability simply because a company has less surplus than it ought to have.** There is little if any precedence for this in accounting.

Provisions for adverse deviation would, under the suggested approach, apparently have to be strengthened each time surplus decreased (even if the decrease resulted from dividends to shareholders that were made possible by successful and relatively deviation-free operations) and weakened each time surplus increased, at least in theory. The result, it appears, would be to create a doubling up of the effect of every transaction that affects surplus.

Surplus from a solvency point of view must necessarily be measured in statutory terms. Adjusted reserves usually produce a sizeable additional surplus which is, of course, restricted. Any provisions for adverse deviation based on the level of surplus should be based on adjusted surplus. That is the surplus that is available to absorb adverse deviation in the context of adjusted reserves. How to reconcile the role of such additional surplus with a provision for adverse deviation based on solvency considerations that must be measured in statutory terms is not readily apparent and may not be possible.

Of most significance, perhaps, is the probability that making provisions for adverse deviations a function of the level of surplus would diminish such comparability as may be possible under a consistent

---

*More precisely, such a company's auditors and consulting actuaries will probably require that it be more conservative.

**It is admittedly sometimes extremely difficult to distinguish between a liability and a contingency reserve, particularly in the insurance business, but the distinction must be made.

approach to interpreting the concept of providing for adverse deviation.

Therefore a company's surplus position should have no *specific* effect on provisions for adverse deviation, which should be made in the form of "prudent best estimates" in all cases. "Prudence" would be measured in terms of all the facts and circumstances affecting the given assumptions, not in terms of the level of surplus, statutory or adjusted.

Future Development of Release-from-Risk Theory

In the discussion of his article "Life Insurance Earnings and the Release from Risk Policy Reserve System" Richard Horn points out that

An adequate exploration of the theoretical considerations involved in quantifying the risks of adverse deviations would plow a great deal of new ground. For example, our traditional techniques for calculating nonparticipating gross premiums involve "realistic" rates of mortality, withdrawal, interest, and expense. Each of these "realistic" rates could be thought of as being the mean value of some undefined probability density function. If we employed an assumed probability density function in place of each "realistic" rate, we could then generate (given adequate computer strength) a gross premium density function. The provision for the risks of adverse deviations contained in a given gross premium could be determined by identifying the patterns of mortality, interest, withdrawal, and expense rates that generated such gross premium . . . Confidence levels could also be determined for a given gross premium from the gross premium probability density function. Perhaps an extension of this approach could be used to determine confidence levels for policy reserves.[37]

One might envision a consistent series of reserves for a given company with confidence levels from, say, 50 percent to 98 percent. A range of, say 90 to 98 percent might be used for statutory purposes (statutes willing) based on the maturity of the company and other factors. A range of, say, 60 to 70 percent might be used for general-purpose statements, again based on an evaluation of the company's situation.

The theories developed in Mr. Horn's remarkable paper have some unusual implications and potentials for pricing, reserving, and possibly the quantification of required levels of surplus. Until consistent and dependable methods of quantifying risks of adverse deviations are developed the release-from-risk theory can affect the accounting process only indirectly. When quantification becomes feasible, one may expect to see

release-from-risk theory influence accounting measurements directly.

Lock-In

According to the life insurance audit guide, reserves on any given block of business should be based generally on assumptions that would have been appropriate at the time the policies were issued. The assumptions should then be "locked in", which means essentially that they should be used forever for the block of business except in cases where future losses inhere in the block of business.

References to Lock-In

References to the lock-in principle in literature published to date are very skimpy. Like the adverse deviation requirement, the lock-in requirement needs to be interpreted.

Audit guide references. The principal reference to the general applicability of the lock-in principle may be found in the guide's discussion of loss recognition. Unless future losses become apparent,

It is anticipated that the original assumptions will continue to be used ("locked-in") during the period in which reserves are accumulated so long as reserves are maintained at a level sufficient to provide for future benefits and expenses. This approach results in variances from original estimates being recognized in the accounting periods in which such variances occur.[38]

Specific references to lock-in are very few:

▸ On interest: "Generally, the interest assumption to be used in computing reserves in conformity with generally accepted accounting principles should be based on the estimate of future interest expected at the time policies are issued." [39]

▸ On mortality: The guide makes one specific reference to the lock-in principle as it might apply specifically to the mortality assumption. With respect to established companies, "For policies issued in previous years, the company's experience or published experience used in the gross premium calculations should be used." [40]

▸ On withdrawals: The guide makes no specific reference to the lock-in principle as it might apply specifically to the withdrawal assumption. Indeed, absent the general requirement discussed above, one might interpret the guide as requiring updated assumptions: "Companies should use published withdrawal tables . . . only if the results produced . . . are comparable with the company's actual withdrawal experience." [41]

▶ On dividends: Under defined circumstances the dividend assumption should be "based upon dividends anticipated or intended in determining gross premiums or as shown by published dividend projections at the date policies are issued." [42]

American Academy references. The Committee on Financial Reporting Principles of the American Academy of Actuaries refers to the lock-in principle in its "Recommendation No. 1" as follows:

Assumptions selected as of the [issue] date should be used in computing the reserves for use in all subsequent financial statements prepared by the company in accordance with generally accepted accounting principles. [43]

Problems with the Principle

The various references to lock-in establish the general principle that original assumptions should be locked in, but the theory underlying the principle is never fully explained. Further, there is a substantive question as to the extent to which adverse deviation should be provided for on older blocks of business. Finally, there is a question as to whether to adhere to the lock-in principle when the results, viewed from the vantage point of hindsight, prove to be unreasonable.

Theory of the Lock-In Principle

There is no completely satisfactory theoretical basis for the lock-in principle, at least in terms of accounting principles.

Usually an asset or liability item that is computed on the basis of anticipated future experience is restated if it appears that future experience will differ significantly from that which was originally assumed, and the effect of such a change in estimates is reported in current and future periods, as provided by Accounting Principles Board Opinion No. 20, "Accounting Changes".

There are three theoretical approaches to explaining the lock-in principle, none of which is complete but each of which sheds light on why the principle was adopted.

Release-from-risk theory. To the extent that the audit guide implements release-from-risk theory, then lock-in is generally consistent with the theory. Assumption of the risk of adverse deviation takes place when a policy is sold. The risk of adverse deviation

must therefore be defined and quantified at the time of issue. What happens thereafter affects profits but does not affect the extent of the risk undertaken originally by the company. Profits are recognized as those risks, as originally assumed, defined, and quantified, are released.

As suggested earlier in this chapter, however, release-from-risk theory has only an indirect influence on the reserving process. To the extent that provisions for adverse deviation are viewed as margins for conservatism, the release-from-risk explanation doesn't work very well; margins for conservatism that are no longer needed should, in theory, be eliminated.

Further, as will be seen, the lock-in principle must be modified in several cases, including situations in which dogged adherence to lock-in produces unreasonable results. If the theory were unqualifiedly sound, such compromises would not be necessary.

Consistency in valuation. So long as fixed-income securities are carried on the basis of amortized cost, the related liabilities should be valued on a consistent basis. Since many bonds, mortgages, etc., are carried at a value which yields something other than the market rate of interest, so must the related liabilities be valued at something other than the market rate of interest. While such consistency is best explained in terms of the interest assumption, there is also a relationship between assets and the mortality and withdrawal assumptions. Presumably asset maturity dates are selected with an eye on the pattern of expected death claims and surrenders.

The consistency argument may explain the lock-in principles for old "layers" of reserves, but it doesn't necessarily justify continuation of the practice with respect to new "layers" of reserves on older blocks of business. After all, premiums received today on business issued 20 years ago are being invested in securities that yield current interest rates, and the future outlook is different today than it was 20 years ago. A case can be made for calculating future reserve requirements on a basis which gives effect to revisions in current and expected future experience.

"Historical cost". An argument can be made that assumptions appropriate at the time of issue represent a kind of historical cost of the product sold, to be allocated over accounting periods in proportion to revenues recognized. The principle involved is somewhat similar to depreciating the historical cost of a piece of equipment. Costs associated with current issues are measured in current prices; any fluctuation in the relationship between revenue and expense flows to income as it occurs.

Under this reasoning entries at the time of sale would be as follows, conceptually:

Premiums receivable	xxx	
Deferred revenue		xxx
Costs incurred	xxx	
Liability for costs incurred		xxx

Deferred revenue would then be recognized in accordance with rules relating to revenue recognition and costs would be written off proportionally.

The foregoing is a useful way to analyze a life insurance transaction, but the fact remains that there is no such thing as an "historical cost" for a liability that is not fixed in fact or amount.

Practical Reasons for Lock-In

In addition to some partial theoretical support for the lock-in principle, there are some compelling practical reasons for it (in addition to the very practical problem that revaluation is a lot of work).

Timing considerations. It's interesting to note that the audit guide, in its only statement of the reasoning underlying the lock-in principle, refers to a very practical consideration. In its discussion of the interest assumption, the guide notes that

Periodically adjusting the reserve interest assumptions for in-force business to reflect changed conditions prospectively is not considered appropriate since the inherent fluctuations in investment yields make it impracticable to determine the proper timing and the extent to which such adjustments should be made.[44]

The guide thus indicates that the practice of revising assumptions frequently raises serious questions as to when the income or loss associated with the revisions was actually earned or incurred. Although such revaluations could be regarded as changes in estimates, thereby qualifying for current and prospective accounting treatment, the consistency and reliability of the financial statements could be so seriously affected that the guide simply prohibits the practice.

Credibility. It is very difficult to obtain sufficient credibility for proposed changes in assumptions. The effort required to support an original set of assumptions is exhaustive, and the same degree of effort would be required to support changes. Similarly, the problems of auditing the initial assumptions are difficult enough; the notion of doing the same thing frequently—say every year—is mind-boggling, and it is doubtful that the cost can be justified.

Immateriality. It is difficult to generalize about the effect of a prospectively-applied change in assumptions, but indications are that the effect would be relatively immaterial in many cases. This is because of the intricate relationships among original valuation premiums, revised valuation premiums, reserve levels, and required interest. The time required to lend credibility to a change in assumptions and the need to be conservative in forecasting distant interest rates, whether in connection with a change in assumptions or not, introduce an additional condition which conduces to immateriality.

By way of illustration, Table 6–1 shows a sample calculation of reserves on a whole life policy holding all assumptions constant except interest. Reserves were calculated (1) on the basis of original interest assumptions and (2) on the basis of assumptions revised every five years for 20 years. It is assumed that actual interest is 5 percent throughout the 20 years, so each revision starts off with 5 percent and grades systematically to a 3 percent ultimate rate. Reserves on hand at the time of a revision are not modified; the effect of revision is allocated to current and future periods in accordance with principles applicable to accounting for changes in estimates. Thus the revised valuation premium for the first revision (in Year 5) was computed as follows:

Present value of future benefits and expenses using revised interest assumptions	$271.69
Adjusted reserve at fifth duration	47.55
Balance to be funded by recomputed valuation premiums	$224.14
Present value of a $1 annuity due for the remaining premium-paying period, computed using revised interest assumptions (originally $11.81)	$ 13.33
Revised valuation premium	$ 16.82

The resulting revised reserves per $1,000, and the related reserve increases, differ little from the original amounts for the first 20 durations. Thereafter the differences increase; suprisingly, though, increases in the revised reserves are greater than increases in the original reserves even though the revised interest assumptions are higher.*

Whether the indicated differences per $1,000 in force are material or not is a matter of judgment. One important consideration in putting the situation in perspective is the relative effects of the revision per

---

*The reader is invited to determine why this is so as a test of his knowledge of the workings of a reserve.

Table 6–1.

ILLUSTRATION OF EFFECT OF CHANGING ASSUMPTIONS VS. KEEPING
ASSUMPTIONS CONSTANT—WHOLE LIFE POLICY ISSUED TO MALE AGE 35

REVISIONS OF INTEREST ASSUMPTIONS

Years	Original Assumptions	First Revision (Year 5)	Second Revision (Year 10)	Third Revision (Year 15)	Fourth Revision (Year 20)
1–5	5.0%				
6–10	4.5	5.0%			
11–15	4.0	4.5	5.0%		
16–20	3.5	4.0	4.5	5.0%	
21–25	3.0	3.5	4.0	4.5	5.0%
26–30	3.0	3.0	3.5	4.0	4.5
31–35	3.0	3.0	3.0	3.5	4.0
36–40	3.0	3.0	3.0	3.0	3.5
41–65	3.0	3.0	3.0	3.0	3.0
New valuation premium	$17.56	$16.82	$15.69	$14.13	$12.12

ADJUSTED RESERVE FACTORS (BENEFITS AND EXPENSES COMBINED) PER $1,000 IN FORCE

Duration	Assumptions Constant — Reserve	Assumptions Constant — Change	Assumptions Revised — Reserve	Assumptions Revised — Change	"Constant" Change More or (Less) than "Revised" Change
5 *	$ 47.55	$15.90	$ 47.55	$15.90	$ -0-
6	63.88	16.33	63.27	15.72	.61
7	80.60	16.72	79.55	16.28	.44
8	97.83	17.23	96.37	16.82	.41
9	115.59	17.76	113.80	17.43	.33
10	133.88	18.29	131.81	18.01	.28
12	170.89	18.55	167.27	18.00	.55
15	228.90	19.70	224.54	19.63	.07
17	267.44	19.10	262.10	19.00	.10
20	326.31	19.90	322.48	20.71	(.81)
22	364.17	18.56	361.47	19.74	(1.18)
25	419.95	18.58	423.76	21.29	(2.71)
27	456.96	18.47	464.72	20.14	(1.67)
30	511.88	18.21	527.45	21.34	(3.13)
35	600.43	17.26	626.85	20.05	(2.79)
40	682.36	15.79	714.57	17.31	(1.52)
45	756.16	13.85	782.70	12.44	1.41
50	815.85	10.65	836.20	9.53	1.12
55	861.70	8.45	877.16	7.53	.92
60	905.91	10.42	916.49	9.24	1.18

* The reserves are the same for Durations 1–5.

$1,000 *originally issued.* If, for example, 50 percent of the business originally issued remains in force through the fifth year, and only 10 percent remains in force through the thirtieth year, then the relative magnitudes of the differences change dramatically, as follows:

	Year 5	Year 30
Percentage in force	50%	10%
Difference per $1,000	$ .61	$(3.13)
Relative magnitude of difference	$ .30	$ (.31)

Implementing Lock-In

In theory, proper application of the lock-in principle would produce financial statements that reproduce the effect of having maintained accounts in accordance with generally accepted accounting principles ever since the company's inception.

That's a fine theory, but it doesn't work very well in practice. There is simply no way to reconstruct what would have been done, say, 30 years ago. Time changes perspective, and hindsight will affect the way in which the lock-in principle is applied regardless of how objective one tries to be. As one insurance company executive said, "You can restate, but you can't relive." [45]

Nor is the use of hindsight inappropriate. Lock-in is a principle, not a rigid rule to be applied blindly. In applying the lock-in principle, as in applying the principle of providing for adverse deviation, judgment and common sense are needed.

What follows are some general comments on applying the lock-in principle. More specific discussions of applying the principle to particular assumptions will be found in subsequent chapters.

Premium assumptions. The life insurance audit guide generally indicates that assumptions should be based on experience that would have been "expected" at the time the policies were issued. Sometimes the guide is even less precise than this, as for example when it states that claim cost assumptions used in calculating health insurance reserves "should be based on realistic estimates of expected claim cost experience at the time premiums are established, or revised, or policies are issued." [46]

Early versions of the audit guide provided that adjusted reserve assumptions should generally be based on assumptions underlying the gross premiums. This provision facilitated implementation of the lock-in principle. Gross premium assumptions for older blocks of business were known or could be approximated. The assumptions provided a good starting point for choosing reserve assumptions. Where a company provided specifically for a profit margin, the assumptions could be used directly as adjusted reserve assumptions. Where a company did not provide specifically for a profit margin, but instead used overly conservative assumptions, the degree of extra conservatism could be estimated and eliminated for purposes of the adjusted reserve assumptions. Where a company simply "lifted" a rate from a competitor's ratebook without testing it, the rate could be tested *ex post facto* using assumptions that would have been realistic at the time. In all cases the assumptions finally chosen could be tested for reasonableness in two ways:

1. A determination of what would have been realistic assumptions at the time in light of the then available information on trends and prospects, and

2. A comparison of the assumed experience with actual experience as it had developed thereafter.

Generally the second test indicated that there were fairly comfortable margins in the original assump-

tions, particularly as regards interest and mortality; and the withdrawal assumption could be adjusted if necessary to reflect actual experience. It is obvious that full advantage could be taken of hindsight in testing the reasonableness of the original assumptions.

There is no reason why the same procedure cannot continue to be used in implementing the lock-in principle under the final version of the audit guide. In fact, the same procedure should be used without exception. A life insurance company makes a major commitment in terms of the assumptions inherent in the gross premiums and, subject always to evidence to the contrary, such assumptions may be regarded as rational and reasonable. They are determined with relative objectivity—i.e., free from the bias introduced in choosing assumptions purely for financial statement purposes. This is particularly true of business sold in years prior to adoption of the audit guide.

Adverse deviation. Using premium assumptions as a basic frame of reference for choosing adjusted reserve assumptions works well if one views a provision for adverse deviation primarily as a margin for conservatism. With respect to prior issues, the conservatism associated with the adjusted reserve assumptions can be judged in terms of experience as it has developed to date. What was reasonable and realistic in 1950, for example, can be seen to have been conservative when viewed from the perspective of 1974.

If provisions for adverse deviation are seen to be primarily a means of implementing the release-from-risk theory, however, it would appear that additional deltas should be provided with respect to early assumptions even if experience demonstrates that the assumptions were conservative. This is because what appears conservative today would have been regarded as best estimates yesterday, and according to release-from-risk theory, best estimates should be "delta-ized" to produce an earnings stream that is consistent with release from the risk of adverse deviation from best estimates.

Thus the application of release-from-risk theory could result in reserve assumptions on issues of prior years that are known to be unduly conservative. The result of undue conservatism with respect to issues of prior years would generally be an undue increase in earnings currently reported on such older blocks of business. It is in recognition of this that the American Academy of Actuaries suggests that, notwithstanding the applicability of release-from-risk theory,

The choice of actuarial assumptions for old blocks of business involves special considerations when a company is preparing its first financial reports in accordance with generally accepted accounting principles. The usual procedure for existing business would be to base actuarial assumptions on those underlying the actual gross premiums, subject to appropriate testing of the adequacy of the gross premiums in the light of current most likely assumptions. In principle, the degree of conservatism in the selection of assumptions should be consistent for both old and new business at the time of transition. The use of a greater degree of conservatism in choosing assumptions for the valuation of business existing at the time of transition would normally increase the stated earnings in the years after the transition and would be inappropriate.[47]

Thus application of release-from-risk theory is modified if the results are seen to be unreasonable. Yet it seems inconsistent to apply the theory in its pure state prospectively; in fact, application of release-from-risk theory in the conservatism context for past issues and in the profit-distribution context for future issues could be regarded as a change in accounting method. Consistent interpretation of the adverse deviation requirement as a requirement to introduce a reasonable measure of conservatism will, in conjunction with the lock-in principle, produce reasonable and consistent results.

Hindsight. There remains a question as to what extent hindsight should be used in applying the lock-in principle to issues of prior years.

If one accepts the notions that (1) a provision for adverse deviation is primarily a margin for conservatism and (2) assumptions underlying the gross premium should generally be used as a basic frame of reference for choosing the adjusted reserve assumptions, then the use of hindsight is entirely proper. It is quite reasonable to test conservatism in the light of how experience has actually developed. The procedure is consistent with the method used to test conservatism with respect to adjusted reserve assumptions for new issues; experience will always be a significant influence on one's judgment about the degree of conservatism used in choosing such assumptions.

A fundamental distinction should be made, however, in applying hindsight to the mortality and interest assumptions, on the one hand, and the withdrawal assumption, on the other. Mortality and interest are estimates based primarily on external events. Given a certain investment policy, a certain underwriting policy, and a given company size and market, then the company's expected experience will be based on a series of developments that lie largely outside the control of the company or its policyholders. In other words, the data upon which the assumptions are based

is essentially impartial with respect to the particular company.

Withdrawals, however, while no doubt influenced by external events, respond much more directly to the actions of the company or its particular body of policyholders. A new product will share the same body of mortality and investment experience as an old product (given the same underwriting standards), but the same thing cannot be said of withdrawal experience. Only time will tell if the product has staying power. Even in the case of established products, persistency depends to a significant degree on the caliber of the agent; this is certainly not true of investment experience and it is probably not true of mortality experience. In other words, expected persistency is in the nature of a guess based on limited and highly individuated information, while expected interest and mortality are in the nature of estimates based on a larger and more objective body of information.

So mortality and interest assumptions for issues of prior years should be those assumptions which underlie the gross premiums, so long as experience that has developed to date is as favorable as, or more favorable than, the assumed experience. The assumptions may be regarded as rational estimates appropriate to a reliable and relatively impartial body of information.

The withdrawal assumption should, however, be modified to correspond reasonably with experience that has actually developed to date. The original assumptions should be regarded as having been tentative and based on a relatively unreliable body of information. Hindsight should be fully applied to determine what would have been a reasonable assumption at the time of issue if sufficient data had been available.

Exceptions to Lock-In

The life insurance audit guide specifies two exceptions to the lock-in principle:

1. When experience deteriorates to the point where a loss is indicated, reserve assumptions should be revised to reflect the new expectations. (This is discussed at length in Chapter 24.)

2. When persistency experience differs radically from that which is assumed, acquisition cost factors should be recomputed to give effect to actual persistency. (This is discussed at length in Chapters 8 and 16.)

There is another case, not discussed in the guide,

in which the lock-in principle would not be applicable. Revised assumptions should be used in connection with an acquisition of an existing block of business or the acquisition of a life insurance company accounted for as a purchase. (This is discussed at length in Chapter 27.)

And there is still one other situation in which it would be appropriate to depart from the lock-in principle. When the basis of valuing assets is materially modified, the basis of valuing reserves should also be modified. (This is discussed at length in Chapter 9.)

Finally, it would be possible for future experience to be so radically more *favorable* than assumed experience that financial statements prepared on the basis of the principles set forth in the audit guide would cease to have meaning. This could happen, for example, if interest rates should quadruple. In such a case, reserve assumptions should be revised. This is of largely theoretical concern at the present time; any revisions of assumptions by reason of radically favorable future experience would not be appropriate with respect to any United States life insurance company in the foreseeable future.

Part II

Benefits

7

Fundamentals of Adjusted Reserves

Specific aspects of adjusted benefit reserves for ordinary life insurance are discussed in Chapters 8 through 12 and other lines of business are discussed in Part IV. This chapter covers some of the more general aspects of adjusted benefit reserves: terminology, assumptions in general, ratebook eras, valuation premiums, reserve factors, and the relationship of adjusted benefit reserves to statutory reserves.

For purposes of discussion, benefits are generally treated as something apart from acquisition costs and other expenses. They are so treated in this book. Benefits and expenses do differ somewhat in character, but the fact is that they are so interrelated, deriving as they do from a single contract and a single integrated set of expectancies, that it is somewhat misleading to consider them in isolation. The reader is cautioned to keep in mind the fact that whatever is said about mortality and persistency has implications for both benefits *and* expenses, and the same may be true of interest under certain circumstances. Further, tests of valuation premium adequacy, recoverability of acquisition costs, and the incidence of profits almost always involve benefits and expenses in combination.

So while benefits and expenses are often discussed separately, it would be well always to think of them as being of the same essence.

Terminology

The lexicon of life insurance accounting is ponderous and complex because of the enormous complexity of the life insurance business in general and the absolutely gargantuan complexity of life insurance accounting in particular. A given term may refer to a great many things or conditions, depending on the context in which it is used. But it is essential to establish a few basic terminological ground rules to govern the discussions which follow.

Adjusted Reserves

In accounting parlance a "reserve" is usually thought of as an appropriation of surplus. In life insurance accounting, a "reserve" usually refers to a liability. It might be preferable to call a life insurance reserve something else to bring the terminology into line with general accounting concepts, but the term "reserve" has such a specific meaning in the life insurance business, and has been around so long, that any attempt to do away with it would no doubt fail.

In a life insurance environment, therefore, the term "reserve" will have two accounting definitions, and the definition that applies in a particular situation will have to be determined from context.

The term "statutory reserve" refers (1) generically, to a reserve computed in accordance with statutory requirements and (2) specifically, to a reserve reported in a company's Convention Statement.

The term "adjusted reserve" has come to refer to a reserve computed for use in financial statements prepared on the basis of generally accepted accounting principles. "Adjusted reserve" is a very unsatisfactory term. It is imprecise and suggests that something is wrong (hence why "adjust"?). But no one has come forward with a more descriptive term *, so the term "adjusted reserve" is used in this book.

*As a matter of possible interest, Ernst & Ernst spent considerable time trying to develop a suitable term, to no avail. The characteristics which the term had to cover—realism, conservatism, sufficient generality to apply descriptively to benefits and expenses, etc.—proved too complex to capture in a single word.

"Natural reserve" was an excellent term, but the early versions of the life insurance audit guide (discussed in Chapter 1) aroused so much controversy that "natural reserve", used throughout those early versions, became a highly emotional term. "Natural reserve" referred to a reserve calculated on the basis of "best-estimate" assumptions. Inasmuch as the term "best estimate" came to have an unsavory connotation, so did the term "natural reserve", and one is hard-pressed to find it used anywhere today.

The audit guide does not take any position on terminology. Indeed, the guide never even refers to "adjusted reserves", but only to "benefit reserves", "valuation reserves", "actuarial valuation", "policy reserves", "reserves determined in conformity with generally accepted accounting principles", and similar generalized terms.

Perhaps a term will come into use eventually that is as satisfying as "natural reserve" used to be. Meantime, "adjusted reserve" will probably have to do.*

Valuation Premiums

The term "net premium" is generally taken to refer to a statutory net premium, i.e., the net premium required to support the statutory reserve.

The term "valuation premium" is a more general term, referring to (1) the portion of the gross premium required to provide for all benefits and expenses or (2) the portion of the gross premium required to support a reserve, adjusted or statutory.

In this book the term "valuation premium" is used generically to mean a valuation premium computed in connection with a conversion to generally accepted accounting principles. The term "adjusted reserve valuation premium" is used to denote the portion of the premium required to support an adjusted reserve (for benefits or expenses or both) after the reserve has been calculated. A valuation premium that is progressing through stages of development to final status as an adjusted reserve valuation premium is referred to as a "trial valuation premium" until it does, in fact, achieve final status.

When the valuation premium required to provide for all benefits and expenses differs from the valuation premium required to support the adjusted reserve (which may not provide for *all* benefits and expenses), such valuation premium is referred to as a "modified valuation premium". The nature and ex-

*Some people use the slang term "GAAP reserve" as a synonym for "adjusted reserve".

tent of modification of a valuation premium will differ according to the purpose for which the valuation premium is being computed; hence the kind of modification referred to in a particular discussion will generally be described in some fashion if its character is not readily apparent.

Reserve Assumptions

The trouble with an assumption is that it's an assumption, a guess about the future. The probability that what actually happens will correspond precisely to what is assumed to happen is, for all practical purposes, nil. So the word "assumption" has an unpleasant ring. Regardless of the care with which an assumption is chosen, it is going to turn out to be wrong.

Of course accountants have been dealing with assumptions for a long time. Depreciation is based on an assumption about the useful life of the item being depreciated. Recognition of profits on construction contracts involves an assumption about costs to be incurred in the future. Carrying inventory at a stated amount in the balance sheet requires an assumption about the future selling prices of the items in stock. Carrying accounts receivable in the balance sheet involves an assumption about their realization. And so on. Accountants can usually deal with uncertainty in a reasonable and prudent manner.

However, as the life insurance audit guide points out,

The actuarial assumptions and estimates used in determining annual revenue and costs applicable to life insurance contracts are extremely significant and involve considerable judgment . . . accounting for life insurance contracts generally involves longer periods of time and substantially more material amounts than those encountered in similar judgments in other businesses.[1]

The importance and all-pervasiveness of assumptions in the life insurance business are such as to make them substantively different from the types of assumptions which accountants historically have had to recognize and give effect to in the accounting process.

What Assumptions Encompass

For purposes of computing adjusted benefit reserves, assumptions about future events must usually be made for at least the following items:

Investment income and expense
Capital gains (implicitly or otherwise)
Normal mortality
Renewal mortality
Conversion mortality
Substandard mortality
Morbidity
Withdrawals
Distribution of surrender options
Differential costs of surrender options
Dividends

Certain expense assumptions also affect benefit assumptions and vice-versa. For example, expense savings on term conversions must usually be offset against extra conversion mortality in computing a "cost of conversion".

Specialty policies and special benefits may require additional assumptions. For example, a policy whose cash values and/or death benefits are linked to the Consumer Price Index would usually require an assumption about the behavior of the Index.

Certain additional assumptions must be made in making the basic assumptions. For example, an assumed distribution of premium modes is normally necessary to develop a withdrawal assumption, since withdrawals differ by mode.

One assumption not included in the foregoing list is the assumed distribution of settlement options and the differential costs of such options. As will be discussed in more detail in the next chapter, this book adopts the position that election of a settlement option other than a lump sum constitutes a new contract (between the insurance company and the beneficiary), and reserves on existing business should not anticipate the effect of a settlement option.

Responsibility for Reserve Assumptions

The life insurance audit guide is quite clear as to who has the responsibility for choosing reserve assumptions: "The choice of actuarial assumptions and the disciplining of that choice are primary responsibilities of the actuarial profession." [2]

That's the way it has to be. "Although the independent auditor may be informed in a general manner about matters of an actuarial nature, he does not purport to act in the capacity of an actuary." [3] Reserve assumptions require the highest level of actuarial judgment, and a high level of actuarial judgment is generally not among an accountant's accomplishments.

However, it is fair to say that actuaries have traditionally applied their judgment in an environment that differs somewhat from generally accepted accounting principles. In pricing, for example, the incidence of profits perhaps means less to the actuary than the present value of profits. In accounting, the incidence of profits is perhaps more important than the present value of profits.

In statutory accounting, the actuary's responsibility "is to see that . . . reserves are adequate and in accordance with statutory requirements." [4] However, as the audit guide points out, adjusted reserves require a "different perspective" [5] on the part of the actuary. Reserves must not only be adequate, they must be in conformity with generally accepted accounting principles. The actuary's perception of "generally accepted accounting principles" is therefore very important. He must be concerned with the incidence of profits and the degree of conservatism in the assumptions, among other things.

The accountant's responsibility is to assist the actuary in perceiving generally accepted accounting principles properly. The accountant must ensure, for example, that his concept of adverse deviation corresponds with the actuary's. The accountant must convey his notions of conservatism, materiality, and fair financial reporting to the actuary. To do this with any chance of success, the accountant must know at least as much about actuarial matters as the actuary knows about generally accepted accounting principles.

So while the responsibility for reserve assumptions is the actuary's, responsibility for the results is shared among the actuary, the accountant, and company management.

General Criteria for Reserve Assumptions

While assumptions for adjusted reserves are primarily the responsibility of the actuary and are chosen in an exercise of his judgment, there are a few general criteria that they must satisfy.

The life insurance audit guide provides a few guidelines. According to the guide, assumptions must

▸ Provide for adverse deviation,
▸ Be characterized by conservatism that is reasonable and realistic,
▸ Not be unduly conservative,
▸ Produce a reasonable valuation premium, and
▸ Produce a reasonable pattern of profits.

In addition, the guide provides a few guidelines in

connection with specific assumptions, which will be discussed in subsequent chapters.

The American Academy of Actuaries Committee on Financial Reporting Principles has also promulgated a few general guidelines, which are binding on members of the Academy. According to "Recommendation No. 1" of the Committee, actuarial assumptions

(a) should be appropriate to the specific circumstances of the company,

(b) should be based on experience or estimated experience which is reasonably applicable to the specific business in the light of all the characteristics of that business and the trends of experience which may reasonably be expected in the future, and

(c) should be so selected that no portion of the actual gross premium would be available as a specific loading for profit unless the risks of adverse deviation are duly provided for in the valuation premium.[6]

Among the elements to be considered by the actuary in choosing the assumptions, according to "Recommendation No. 1", are:

(a) The character and magnitude of the company's business, the types of business which it writes, the age of the company, and its rate of growth.

(b) Prior experience of the company to the extent that the actuary considers it a valid basis for current assumptions, with due regard for the probable consequences of any significant changes in method of operation or plans for the future.

(c) Trends in experience results, economic and investment conditions, government or other external influences, and medical and social developments affecting costs and financial requirements.[7]

Except possibly for the requirement that adverse deviation be explicitly provided for, the Academy Committee's criteria are very similar to the criteria that would normally be used in ratemaking.

General Approach Toward Choosing Reserve Assumptions

The number of possible approaches toward choosing assumptions for adjusted reserves is probably infinite. Nevertheless, there are a few basic steps that should be taken in every case. They are:

1. *Decide on the responsibilities for the work.* This is the first order of business. It is discussed further in Chapter 28.

2. *Decide on a definition of adverse deviation.* This was discussed in Chapter 6 and needs no further elaboration here.

3. *Identify ratebook eras.* A ratebook era—i.e., the period of time covered by each of the company's ratebooks—provides a good starting point for defining "experience eras". Where miscellaneous plans or partial ratebooks have been introduced during interim periods, such miscellaneous plans or partial ratebooks should be merged with the ratebook eras with which they are most logically associated.

4. *Accumulate and array gross premium assumptions for each ratebook era.* This is easier said than done. In the ideal case a company will have records dating back to inception which indicate the pricing assumptions and the way the assumptions were developed. In the usual case, such information, if available at all, will be available only with respect to recent ratebooks. In such cases it will be necessary to estimate the assumptions that would have been used, which isn't as difficult or conjectural as it sounds.

5. *Add any missing assumptions.* Sometimes certain assumptions are ignored in pricing but might be important in computing reserves. Cost of term conversions might be an example. Obviously it would always be necessary to estimate the proper assumption in such cases.

6. *Organize the various ratebook eras into experience eras.* An "experience era" is a period of time during which experience and outlook were sufficiently constant to permit all issues during the period to be regarded as subject to the same assumptions. If a company's ratebooks are sensitive to change—that is, if new ratebooks have been developed fairly frequently—then ratebook eras and experience eras should be the same. If a company's ratebooks have tended to cover long periods of time, this could mean that ratebooks have been issued only when competition forced the company to issue them. If a company has issued new ratebooks very frequently, this could mean that the company has experimented extensively with new policy forms, again for competitive reasons. In such cases ratebook eras should be organized into experience eras. To do this it is obviously necessary to have some good insights into, and good information on, the company's experience.

7. *Compare the ratebook assumptions with key indicators of experience to make certain they are reasonable.* This may already have been done, at least in part, if the ratebook assumptions have been estimated, since a review of experience trends is usually necessary to make the estimates.

8. *Determine the degree of conservatism in the ratebook assumptions.* For older issues the principal danger is that premiums were based on intentionally conservative assumptions and that profits were not specifically provided for. In such cases the extra margin of conservatism should normally be eliminated so that assumptions for older issues are stated on the then best estimates. For newer issues the principal danger is just the reverse.

9. *Make necessary provisions for adverse deviation.* This a matter of high art. It is a problem mainly with respect to newer issues. To the extent that ratebook assumptions are believed to be too optimistic, they would have to be loaded to provide a reasonable degree of conservatism. To the extent that risks can be quantified—i.e., frequency distributions are available—the main problem would be to select a confidence level that is reasonable for measures of operating performance.

10. *Review the tentative assumptions for reasonableness.* This is a highly subjective process for which guidelines cannot readily be offered.

11. *Calculate trial valuation premiums for some key plan-age combinations and compare them with gross premiums.* One of the required tests of reasonableness is that the valuation premium bear a reasonable relationship to the gross premium.

12. *Revise assumptions if the valuation premium exceeds the gross premium.* Provisions for adverse deviation should be eliminated to the extent of any such excess, in proportion to the initial distribution of the provision to the various assumptions. (If the valuation premium based on best estimates still exceeds the gross premium, a loss is indicated and must be provided for. This is discussed in detail in Chapter 24.)

13. *Calculate reserve factors for the key plan-age combinations and project profits.* The life insurance audit guide requires that provisions for adverse deviation be reviewed for reasonableness in relation to the pattern of profit recognition. If, for example, the assumptions produce reserves that create losses in the early years and gains in the later years, or vice-versa (particularly vice-versa), the assumptions may be presumed to be unreasonable even if the valuation premium bears a reasonable relationship to the gross premium. (This test should always be made even if provisions for adverse deviation are not at issue. An unreasonable profit pattern is an unreasonable profit pattern regardless of the assumptions.)

14. *Finalize the assumptions.* One last reasonableness review should be made. Concurrence should be reached among the company, consulting actuaries, and independent accountants.

At this point it should be possible to calculate valuation premiums and reserve factors for all plans and ages for which reserve factors are required.

Other factors—such as whether to grade reserves to statutory over a period of years—would also be considered in the course of choosing assumptions. But the basic procedure normally would not be greatly affected by such other factors.

Crazy Quilt Life

Crazy Quilt Life assigned overall responsibility for its conversion to generally accepted accounting principles to the President. Actuarial aspects of the conversion were the specific responsibility of the Executive Vice President-Actuarial. Ultimately the bulk of the actual actuarial work was done by a task force in the actuarial research and development department.

Crazy Quilt defined adverse deviation along the lines suggested in Chapter 6. Having gotten basic preparations out of the way, Crazy Quilt next proceeded to identify its ratebook eras.

As it turned out, this was relatively easy for Crazy Quilt. Adequate records were available to ascertain the period of years covered by each ratebook issued since the Company's inception in 1941. Furthermore, information was available with respect to assumptions used to calculate or test premiums for each ratebook and, just as important, the *philosophy* underlying the rate tests was documented. Crazy Quilt has always attempted to price its products realistically and introduce a specific profit margin (or compute the implicit profit margin). "Realism" to Crazy Quilt involved a reasonable degree of conservatism, a matter which is discussed at length later.

Inspection of the data indicated that, for pricing purposes, Crazy Quilt had taken into account all items for which assumptions would be required in connection with calculating adjusted reserves except capital gains, the distribution of surrender options, and the differential costs of settlement options.

A summary of Crazy Quilt Life's ordinary life and annuity ratebook eras and a general description of the assumptions related to each era are shown in Table 7–1. Each of the assumptions will be discussed in detail in the chapters that follow.

A review of experience indicated that Crazy Quilt's ratebook eras defined, for all practical purposes, the

Table 7-1.

SUMMARY OF CRAZY QUILT LIFE'S PRINCIPAL ORDINARY LIFE AND ANNUITY RATEBOOK ERAS AND RELATED ASSUMPTIONS

Ratebook Era No.	Years Covered	Products	Normal Mortality	Interest	Withdrawals	Dividends (Par Products Only)	Other Items
LIFE INSURANCE							
1	1941–1947	All	1930–1939 Select and Ultimate Ordinary	Non-par—2.75% level Par—3.5% level	Estimated company experience—similar to Linton B overall	Initial scale	
2	1948–1951	All except endowments	1930–1939 Select and Ultimate Ordinary	Non-par—3.0% level Par—3.5% level	Estimated company experience—similar to Linton B overall	Initial scale	Renewal mortality and conversion costs on term products, estimated from industry data
2a	1948–1961	Endowments	1946–1949 Modified Basic	3.0% level	Estimated company experience—similar to 150% Linton A overall	—	
3	1952–1956	All except par	1946–1949 Modified Basic	3.25% graded to 3.0%	Modified company experience—similar to Linton B overall	—	
3a	1952–1961	Par	1946–1949 Modified Basic	3.5% level	Modified company experience—similar to 150% Linton A overall	Initial scale	
4	1957–1961	All except par	1950–1954 Select and Ultimate Basic	4.0% graded to 3.0%	Modified company experience—similar to Linton B overall	—	
5	1962–1967	All except term and par	1950–1954 Select and Ultimate Basic	4.5% graded to 3.0%	Modified company experience—similar to Linton B overall	Initial scale	Renewal mortality and conversion costs on term products, based on company experience where credible and industry data otherwise
5a	1962–1964	Par	1950–1954 Select and Ultimate Basic	4.5% level	Modified company experience—similar to 150% Linton A overall	—	
5b	1965–1969	Par	1950–1954 Select and Ultimate Basic	5.0% level	Modified company experience—similar to Linton B overall	—	
5c	1962–1967	Level term	1950–1954 Select and Ultimate Basic	4.5% graded to 3.0%	Modified company experience—similar to 250% Linton A overall	—	
5d	1962–1969	Decreasing term	1950–1954 Select and Ultimate Basic	4.5% graded to 3.0%	Modified company experience—similar to Linton B overall	—	
6	1968–1969	All except decreasing term and par	1950–1954 Select and Ultimate Basic	5.5% graded to 3.5%	Modified company experience—similar to Linton B overall	Initial scale	
7	1970–1971	All	1950–1954 Select and Ultimate Basic	Non-par—6.5% graded to 3.5% Par—6.0% level	Modified company experience—similar to Linton B overall	Initial scale	

Table 7–1. Continued

SUMMARY OF CRAZY QUILT LIFE'S PRINCIPAL ORDINARY LIFE AND ANNUITY RATEBOOK ERAS AND RELATED ASSUMPTIONS

ANNUITIES

1	1952–1956	Single-premium	A—49	3.0% level
2	1957–1961	Single-premium	A—49 graded (75%)	3.5% level
3	1962–1967	Single-premium	A—49 graded (60%)	4.5% level
4	1968–1969	Single-premium	A—49 graded (60%)	5.5% level
5	1970–1971	Single-premium	A—49 graded (60%)	6.0% level

Table 7–2.

ARRAY OF RATEBOOK ASSUMPTIONS FOR 1948–1961 ISSUES OF 20-YEAR ENDOWMENT POLICY AND REVIEW OF IMPLICIT PROVISIONS FOR ADVERSE DEVIATION

Assumption Item	Ratebook Assumptions	Experience, 1957–1971
Mortality	Modified 1946–49 Basic Table	On the average, actual about 80% of expected in early years and 85% in later years
Interest	3% level	Portfolio rate (policy year basis) of 3.82% in 1957, moving steadily upward to 6.06% in 1971
Withdrawals	250% of Linton A at Age 10 to Linton A at Age 45; pattern subsequent to first year modified	300% of Linton A at Age 10 to Linton B at Age 45; patterns slightly different after first year
Acquisition costs	81.8% of premiums plus $20.15 per policy plus $2.65 per $1,000	83.3% of premiums plus $21.40 per policy plus $2.80 per $1,000, per 1957 functional cost analysis
Maintenance expenses	9.5% of premiums plus $2.50 per policy	6.0% of premiums plus $4.90 per policy plus $.03 per $1,000 per 1971 functional cost analysis
Cost of processing death claims	$16.25 per claim	$17.05 per claim per 1971 functional cost analysis
Cost of processing surrenders	$9.75 per surrender	$10.25 per surrender per 1971 functional cost analysis

Company's experience eras. The ratebook assumptions were considered reasonable in relation to key experience data. It was decided more or less subjectively that the ratebook assumptions contained adequate provision for adverse deviation.

Crazy Quilt's procedure for choosing assumptions for the 1948–1961 ratebook edition of the 20-year endowment policy is illustrated in Table 7–2. First the Company arrayed each of the various assumptions underlying the rates. Then the Company chose a given year—1957 in this case, representing the mid-range of the issue era weighted for the distribution of new business—and compared experience that had developed since that year with the ratebook assumptions. The comparison indicated that the ratebook assumptions did indeed contain adequate provisions for adverse deviations.

Valuation Premiums

The life insurance audit guide defines "valuation premium" as "that portion of the annual gross premiums required to provide for all benefits and expenses." [8]

However, that definition of a valuation premium is incomplete. The audit guide's definition covers only one of three basic types of valuation premiums, which are:

1. The adjusted reserve valuation premium, which is the valuation premium required to support the adjusted reserve based on the benefits and expenses for which reserve provisions have been made.

2. The modified adjusted reserve valuation premium, which is the adjusted reserve valuation premium plus an additional amount representing items that are not being reserved for but which must be covered by gross premiums. An example might be renewal expenses which, because they are incurred uniformly, are not reserved for. The modified adjusted reserve valuation premium would normally be compared with the gross premium as part of the test of sufficiency and reasonableness of the reserve assumptions. (This is the valuation premium presumably referred to in the audit guide.)

3. The "all-inclusive" valuation premium, which is that amount required to fund all items of cost whether reserved for or not. For example, a portion of acquisition costs may be expensed in the period incurred because of certain accounting requirements, and would therefore not be a part of the adjusted reserve premium.

Audit Guide References to Valuation Premiums

Some of the references to valuation premiums contained in the life insurance audit guide were discussed in Chapter 6. As a matter of convenience those references are repeated here, together with some other references not discussed in Chapter 6.

In determining the risks for adverse deviation, it will be necessary to consider the individual assumptions; however, the provisions must be reasonable in relation to the total valuation premium. [9]

Exactly what is meant by this reference to valuation premiums is not entirely clear. Apparently the guide means that the total modified adjusted reserve valuation premium, which is a composite expression of all the individual assumptions, must be reasonable in relation to the gross premium and that, if such valuation premium is not reasonable, the individual assumptions must be modified so that reasonableness is attained. For example, it would be possible to provide for adverse deviation with respect to each individual assumption, only to produce a modified adjusted reserve valuation premium greater than the gross. In such cases provisions for adverse deviation should be reduced (in proportion to the initial distribution of the provisions to the individual assumptions) until the modified adjusted reserve valuation premium is no greater than the gross premium.

In determining the reasonableness of the assumptions, either individually or as composite factors, the adequacy of the gross premium must be considered. If the valuation premium exceeds the gross premium, a loss is indicated. Such loss should be recognized currently.[10]

This reference is somewhat tricky. As will become clear, the guide is referring here to best-estimate valuation premiums. In other words, if after eliminating all provisions for adverse deviation the modified adjusted reserve valuation premium is still greater than the gross premium, the present value of all deficiencies (i.e., excess of valuation premium over gross premium) should be recognized currently. (This is discussed in detail in Chapter 24.)

In order to use a valuation premium less than the gross premium, the company must demonstrate the reasonableness of the assumptions used based on historical results, current operations, trends, and all other necessary factors to be considered in such judgments. Therefore, the valuation premium based on the assumptions to be used for a block of business should be tested in comparison to the gross premium.[11]

While the modified adjusted reserve valuation premium should normally not exceed the gross premium unless a loss is demonstrably going to occur, neither should such valuation premium be less than the gross premium unless adverse deviation has been provided for in a manner that recognizes the company's particular experience and characteristics. However,

A company should not arbitrarily use the gross premium as the valuation premium if its demonstrated experience and future outlook indicates that such practice is unduly conservative.[12]

In other words, if after providing for adverse devi-

ation the modified adjusted reserve valuation premium is less than the gross premium, such valuation premium should not arbitrarily be revised upward to equal the gross premium.

For companies with narrow profit margins or companies with little experience . . . the use of the gross premium as the valuation premium may be most appropriate.[13] . . . The auditor may be satisfied if [a new] company uses very conservative provisions for adverse deviations, principally for interest and mortality, so as to make the valuation premium approximate the gross premium until the company has demonstrated consistent experience for a reasonable period of time.[14]

It is very important to appreciate that the valuation premium that should be compared with the gross premium is the modified adjusted reserve valuation premium. To illustrate, assume that for a given block of business the gross premium is $100 per unit, the "all-inclusive" valuation premium is $100 (after providing for adverse deviation), and acquisition costs equivalent to a valuation premium of $20 are expensed as incurred because such costs fail to meet the criteria of variability and attribution.* The valuation premium to be compared with the gross premium would be $80, not $100, and the valuation premium would not be revised upward to $100.

As a practical matter, when a company is fairly conservative in its definition of acquisition costs, it would be rare for the modified adjusted reserve valuation premium to be equal to or greater than the gross premium.

American Academy Guidelines for Valuation Premiums

The Committee on Financial Reporting Principles of the American Academy of Actuaries indicates in "Recommendation No. 1" that assumptions for non-participating ordinary and industrial insurance "should be constrained by the relationship, for an entire line of business or a major block of business, of actual gross premiums to three theoretical valuation premiums," namely:

Type One. A Type One valuation premium is a premium based on assumptions selected as of the acquisition [i.e., issue] date which include provisions, selected without regard to the level of the gross premium, for the risks of adverse deviation from most likely assumptions.

Type Two. A Type Two valuation premium is a premium based on most likely assumptions (i.e., without

*The variability and attribution criteria for deferral of acquisition costs are discussed in Chapter 14.

provision for the risks of adverse deviations) selected as of the acquisition date.

Type Three. A Type Three valuation premium is a premium based on assumptions selected as of the acquisition date which substantially reproduce the actual gross premium.[15]

The Academy Committee then suggests that if gross premiums equal or exceed the Type One valuation premiums, the adjusted reserves should be based on the assumptions underlying the Type One valuation premiums. In other words, if after providing for adverse deviation the valuation premium is less than the gross premium, the difference can be recognized as profit.

If the gross premiums are less than the Type One valuation premiums but equal to or greater than the Type Two valuation premiums, the adjusted reserves should be based on the assumptions underlying the Type Three valuation premiums. In other words, if the valuation premiums produced by assumptions that are loaded for adverse deviation are greater than the gross premiums, the assumptions should be revised such that the valuation premiums are substantially equal to the gross premiums.

And finally, if gross premiums are less than the Type Two valuation premiums, the adjusted reserves should be based on the assumptions underlying the Type Two valuation premiums with the valuation premium equal to the gross premium. In other words, if a loss is indicated using best-estimate assumptions, reserves should be based on such best-estimate assumptions.

The constraints on valuation premiums discussed in "Recommendation No. 1" are basically in agreement with comments on valuation premiums contained in the life insurance audit guide. However, "Recommendation No. 1" furnishes what amounts to an important interpretation of the audit guide: the indicated tests should be made in terms of "an entire line of business or a major block of business." Technically this would require the calculation of annual valuation premiums for all plan-year combinations, and if the apppropriate relationships are not obtained, the valuation premiums would have to be calculated again, and again and again until the valuation premiums bear the proper relationship to the gross premiums. This much effort is, of course, not feasible, so the tests would normally be made in terms of key plan-age combinations that are reasonably representative of the company's book of business. Thus it is that "Recommendation No. 1" provides that

In the interest of practicality and the avoidance of unnecessarily burdensome procedures the actuary should feel free to adopt approximate procedures and to make reasonable groupings of policies so long as he is satisfied that the results . . . do not differ materially from the results of applying the Recommendation directly.[16]

The meaning and importance of the recommendation that valuation premium tests be performed in terms of an entire line of business or a major block of business are discussed in Chapter 24.

Illustration of Relationships

Table 7–3 illustrates hypothetical Type One, Type Two, and Type Three valuation premiums for three different situations:

Situation A—Type One (provisions for adverse deviation included) greater than Type Two (best estimates) but less than gross.

Situation B—Type One greater than gross; Type Two less than gross.

Situation C—Type Two greater than gross.

To interpret Table 7–3 it is important to realize that some basic accounting decisions were made with respect to what the valuation premiums had to cover, what to include in the reserves, how to account for development costs, and how to define acquisition costs. These decisions are summarized in the footnotes to Table 7–3.

In Situation A, the Type One valuation premium (and Type One assumptions) would be used for purposes of calculating adjusted reserves. The reserves themselves would include provisions only for the components shown for the adjusted reserve valuation premium. The test for adequacy would be made by comparing the modified adjusted reserve valuation premium with the gross premium; this is because policy-related maintenance expenses, while excluded from the reserves, must be covered by gross premiums. Alternatively, the all-inclusive valuation premium might be compared with the gross premium, on the basis that if it is lower, no further testing or manipulating need be done (putting together a modified adjusted reserve valuation premium constitutes a "manipulation").

Inasmuch as the Type One assumptions and valuation premium are used in Situation A, the key problem to be resolved is the reasonableness of the provisions for adverse deviation made in computing the premium.

The Type Three assumptions and valuation premium would be used in Situation B. Since the Type Three valuation premium is simply the result of "backing out" provisions for adverse deviation included in the Type One valuation premium, the question of the reasonableness of the provisions is

Table 7-3.

ILLUSTRATION OF VARIOUS RELATIONSHIPS AMONG GROSS PREMIUMS AND VALUATION PREMIUMS

	Situation A			Situation B			Situation C			
		$100			$100			$100		
	Type One	Type Two	Type Three	Type One	Type Two	Type Three	Type One	Type Two Variation 1	Variation 2	Type Three
GROSS PREMIUM—whole life policy		$100								
VALUATION PREMIUMS—level annual equivalents:										
All-inclusive valuation premium:										
Deaths	$44	$40	$45	$55	$40	$45	$59	$46	$55	$45
Surrender values	23	20	24	29	20	24	31	24	29	24
Acquisition costs	12	10	13	17	10	13	18	14	17	13
Development costs	5	5	6	8	5	6	9	7	8	6
Policy-related maintenance costs	5	5	6	8	5	6	9	7	8	6
General overhead	5	5	6	8	5	6	9	7	8	6
TOTAL	$94	$85	$100	$125	$85	$100	$135	$105	$125	$100
Adjusted reserve valuation premium:										
Deaths	$44	$40	$45	$55	$40	$45	$59	$46	$55	$45
Surrender values	23	20	24	29	20	24	31	24	29	24
Acquisition costs *	8	7	9	11	7	9	12	9	11	9
Development costs **	-0-	-0-	-0-	-0-	-0-	-0-	-0-	-0-	-0-	-0-
Policy-related maintenance costs ***	-0-	-0-	-0-	-0-	-0-	-0-	-0-	-0-	-0-	-0-
General overhead ****	-0-	-0-	-0-	-0-	-0-	-0-	-0-	-0-	-0-	-0-
TOTAL	$75	$67	$78	$95	$67	$78	$102	$79	$95	$78
Modified adjusted reserve valuation premium:										
Deaths	$44	$40	$45	$55	$40	$45	$59	$46	$55	$45
Surrender values	23	20	24	29	20	24	31	24	29	24
Acquisition costs *	8	7	9	11	7	9	12	9	11	9
Development costs **	-0-	-0-	-0-	-0-	-0-	-0-	-0-	-0-	-0-	-0-
Policy-related maintenance costs ***	5	5	6	8	5	6	9	7	8	6
General overhead ****	-0-	-0-	-0-	-0-	-0-	-0-	-0-	-0-	-0-	-0-
TOTAL	$80	$72	$84	$103	$72	$84	$111	$86	$103	$84

* About one-third of costs incurred expensed due to failure to meet variability and attribution criteria. (This is discussed in Chapter 14.)
** Expensed as incurred. (This is discussed in Chapter 17.)
*** Not reserved for because they are assumed to be uniformly incurred; same impact on income whether reserved for or not. (This is discussed in Chapters 17 and 24.)
**** Regarded as essentially the same as general overhead in other types of business; deemed not to require coverage by margins on existing insurance in force. (This is discussed in Chapters 17 and 24.)

not resolved simply by using the Type Three valuation premium. Reasonableness of the provisions must still be demonstrated.

In Situation C the Type Two assumptions and a valuation premium equal to the gross premium would be used. The principal concern in Situation C is that the best estimates are reasonable, i.e., not overly optimistic.

Notice that in Situation C the wrong conclusion could be drawn with respect to Variation 1 of the Type Two valuation premium if the all-inclusive valuation premium were to be compared with the gross premium. This is because many of the items covered by the all-inclusive valuation premium have been written off or have been judged to be outside the scope of the valuation premium.

Notice also that in Situation C the wrong conclusion could be drawn with respect to Variation 2 of the Type Two valuation premium if the adjusted reserve valuation premium were to be compared with the gross premium. Inclusion of policy-related maintenance costs would cause the valuation premium to exceed the gross premium.

Table 7–3 certainly doesn't cover all of the situations that might be encountered in practice, but it is indicative of the types of analyses that must be made in testing the reasonableness and adequacy of the valuation premium.

Effect on Profit

A comparison of the modified adjusted reserve valuation premium with the gross premium is not the end of the reasonableness tests. The audit guide requires that the reserve assumptions also be tested in relation to the pattern of profit recognition. A reserve is a dynamic quantity, and the fact that a valuation premium is conservative gives no necessary insight into the behavior of a reserve or the related incidence of profits.

To illustrate, assume a two-year single-premium term policy for $1,000 in which the probability of death is 50 percent in Year 1 and 50 percent in Year 2 and that actual mortality is equivalent to assumed; ignore interest and assume that withdrawals are zero. The valuation premium would be $750, the first-year reserve would be $250, and no profit or loss would be reported in respect of mortality:

	Year 1	Year 2	Total
Valuation premium	$ 750	$ -0-	$ 750
Actual mortality cost	(500)	(250)	(750)
Change in reserve	(250)	250	-0-
Gain or (loss)	$ -0-	$ -0-	$ -0-

Assume now that mortality is projected at 75 percent in Year 1 and zero in Year 2 but that actual mortality remains at 50 percent in Year 1 and 50 percent in Year 2. The valuation premium would be the same, $750, but it would be released for the assumed Year 1 mortality since no reserve is required for the assumed zero mortality in Year 2. The result would be a gain in Year 1 and a loss in Year 2:

	Year 1	Year 2	Total
Valuation premium	$750	$ -0-	$750
Actual mortality cost	500	250	750
Gain or (loss)	$250	$(250)	$ -0-

This is a highly exaggerated example of what could happen if one considers valuation premiums in isolation.

Before discussing how to test the reasonableness of the pattern of profit recognition it is first necessary to calculate reserves. Reserve calculations are discussed later in this chapter, and so are techniques of testing the incidence of profits.

Crazy Quilt Life

Crazy Quilt Life calculated trial adjusted reserve valuation premiums that included provisions for benefits, acquisition costs, and policy-related maintenance costs. In other words, Crazy Quilt elected to provide in the reserves for all benefits and expenses required to be covered by future gross premiums. So no modifications of the adjusted reserve valuation premiums were necessary for purposes of comparing the valuation premiums with the gross premiums.

Crazy Quilt generally calculated trial valuation premiums by projecting assumed benefits and expenses and discounting them to a present value using the assumed investment earnings rate; calculating the present value of a $1 annuity due using the same assumptions as to mortality, interest, and withdrawals; and dividing the former by the latter. The general form for the calculation is shown in Table 7–4, using for illustrative purposes the Company's 1948–1961 ratebook edition of the 20-year endowment policy issued to a male age 25, for which the assumptions are outlined in Table 7–2. Further details on Crazy Quilt's method of calculating valuation premiums are given in Appendix A.

Table 7–5 summarizes trial valuation premiums for key plan-age combinations for all ratebook eras. It is important to appreciate at this point that the valuation premiums shown in Table 7–5 are based on taking into account *all* items of cost, including acquisition

Table 7–4.

CALCULATION OF TRIAL VALUATION PREMIUM FOR 20-YEAR ENDOWMENT POLICY ISSUED TO MALE AGE 25—1948–1961 RATEBOOK

	Gross Amount	Present Value at 3%	Level Annual Equivalent
Benefits:			
Projected death claims	$ 17.94	$ 13.18	$ 1.53
Projected surrenders	155.94	109.80	12.76
Projected matured endowments	325.25	180.09	20.92
	499.13	303.07	35.21
Expenses:			
Acquisition costs	66.96	66.96	7.78
Maintenance and overhead	69.72	54.61	6.34
	136.68	121.57	14.12
TOTALS	$635.81	$424.64	$49.33
Present value of $1 annuity due for 20 periods discounted for interest, survivorship, and persistency		$8.608	
VALUATION PREMIUM		$49.33	

costs as defined by the Company. For accounting purposes the Company's definition of acquisition costs had to be modified, as described in Chapter 15. The valuation premiums shown in Table 7–5 are "all-inclusive" valuation premiums.

It will be observed that many of the apparent margins are quite thin. This is suggestive of the degree of conservatism incorporated in the assumptions.

Note too that for 1962–1969 issues of participating whole life, the valuation premium exceeds the gross premium at age 25. This was not adjusted since the other key ages—which together accounted for more than half the expected issues—showed margins greater than the apparent deficiencies for age 25. (The fact that dividends could be adjusted if necessary would also influence what is done with any apparent deficiencies in the case of participating business.)

A review of the difference in margins as between term plans and permanent plans will suggest what is in fact the case. The assumed interest rate is carrying most of the burden of provisions for adverse deviations. Thus the apparent margins on permanent business are slim, while the margins on term business, which is relatively unaffected by interest rates, are fairly healthy.

Having calculated valuation premiums for all plans and ages for which adjusted reserves would be calculated, Crazy Quilt decided to make one last test of reasonableness: a comparison of annualized gross premiums and annualized valuation premiums for all such business in force as of December 31, 1971. Such

a comparison (covering both all-inclusive valuation premiums and the adjusted reserve valuation premiums, which exclude a portion of acquisition costs considered nondeferrable) for ordinary life insurance is shown in Table 7–6. It will be observed that the overall relationships appear reasonable and that no unusual distortion is apparent for any of the blocks of business.

Normally such a test could not be performed until all valuation premiums had been calculated *and* models of insurance in force had been prepared. For the time being it may be assumed that Crazy Quilt has an extremely flexible valuation system that permits it to do things that most companies are unable to do.

Reserve models are discussed in Chapter 28.

Constancy of Percentage Relationships

Normally a valuation premium should bear a constant percentage relationship to the corresponding gross premium. Thus, if a level gross premium is $100 and the valuation premium is $50, the valuation premium should always be equal to 50 percent of the gross premium, whether in Year 1 or Year 50 (unless, of course, valuation premiums have been revised pursuant to the loss recognition requirements of the audit guide).

Where adjusted reserves are graded into statutory reserves in a given year, then the valuation premium in subsequent years will be equal to the statutory net premium. The percentage relationship will therefore

Table 7–5.

COMPARISON OF AVERAGE GROSS PREMIUMS AND TRIAL VALUATION PREMIUMS PER $1,000 FOR CRAZY QUILT LIFE—KEY PLAN-AGE COMBINATIONS

Issue Years	Age	Participating Whole Life Gross	Val'n.	Whole Life Gross	Val'n.	20-Pay Life Gross	Val'n.	20-Year Endowment Gross	Val'n.	5-Year R & C Term* Gross	Val'n.	25-Year Convertible Decreasing Term Gross	Val'n.	Single-Premium Annuities** Gross	Val'n.
1941–1947	25	$22.69	$22.31	$17.95	$16.52	$28.85	$28.10	$48.69	$47.74	$ 8.55	$ 7.03				
	35	29.66	28.85	24.19	22.97	35.49	34.17	49.89	48.65	9.65	7.84				
	45	41.81	40.65	34.98	34.62	45.67	44.54	54.25	53.32	14.40	13.61				
1948–1951	25	22.57	22.09	17.26	15.68	28.85	27.31			7.21	4.82				
	35	30.44	29.44	23.29	21.18	35.02	32.54			8.18	5.94				
	45	43.14	41.36	33.95	31.43	44.30	42.18			12.95	10.46				
1948–1961	25							49.58	49.33						
	35							50.27	49.37						
	45							54.25	53.09						
1952–1956	25			17.26	16.07	28.15	27.28			6.21	4.46				
	35			23.29	21.78	34.26	32.87			7.66	5.76				
	45			33.67	32.30	42.96	42.08			12.56	10.45			$1,590.72	$1,497.94
1952–1961	25	22.53	20.53												
	35	25.88	25.31												
	45	37.24	36.68												
1957–1961	25			15.41	14.47	27.54	26.22			5.90	4.50	$ 3.42	$2.48		
	35			20.90	19.76	32.73	31.46			6.45	5.13	5.42	3.74		
	45			29.85	28.95	41.31	40.00			10.25	8.76	10.47	8.04	1,528.00	1,444.87
1962–1964	25			14.16	13.27	23.13	22.18								
	35			19.81	18.49	29.58	28.07								
	45			28.78	27.70	38.87	37.22								
1962–1967	25	18.79	18.86							5.90	4.64				
	35	24.80	24.14							6.39	5.14				
	45	34.88	34.37							10.18	8.77			1,421.00	1,351.95
1962–1969	25											3.38	2.70		
	35											5.14	3.79		
	45											10.31	8.36		
1965–1969	25	18.68	18.80												
	35	24.66	24.06												
	45	34.64	34.18												
1968–1969	25			13.16	12.30	22.82	20.22			4.57	4.01				
	35			18.12	17.21	28.64	25.78			4.96	4.73				
	45			27.08	26.17	37.78	34.83			8.70	8.79			1,324.23	1,249.65
1970–1971	25	18.02	17.84	12.96	11.87	22.82	19.82			4.40	3.81	3.48	2.77		
	35	23.52	22.64	18.12	16.73	28.64	25.21			4.90	4.49	5.24	3.72		
	45	32.66	32.48	26.83	24.99	37.78	34.09			8.70	8.31	10.48	8.06	1,288.31	1,202.87

* Rates shown are for first five-year period only.
** Age 65 for annuities; unit is $10 of monthly income.

Table 7–6.

COMPARISON OF ANNUALIZED TRIAL ALL-INCLUSIVE VALUATION PREMIUMS AND ANNUALIZED GROSS PREMIUMS FOR ALL ORDINARY LIFE INSURANCE IN FORCE AT DECEMBER 31, 1971 (000 Omitted from Amounts)

	Premium-Paying Business In Force	Annualized Gross Premiums	Annual Statutory Net Premiums	Annualized Adjusted Valuation Premiums				Total	
				Benefits	Expenses Acquisition	Maintenance	Total	Amount	% of Gross
All-inclusive valuation premiums:									
Participating whole life	$ 429,164	$ 9,909	$ 7,105	$ 6,789	$ 1,853	$1,147	$ 3,000	$ 9,789	99%
Whole life:									
Regular plans	1,774,390	34,382	30,827	22,171	7,156	3,375	10,531	32,702	95
Converted plans	84,801	2,342	2,190	1,703	398	166	564	2,267	97
20-pay life	326,317	8,174	7,015	4,875	1,812	1,003	2,815	7,690	94
20-year endowment	36,574	1,474	1,361	1,015	287	89	376	1,391	94
5-year renewable and convertible term	398,942	2,806	1,794	1,342	807	357	1,164	2,506	89
25-year convertible decreasing term	1,015,951	7,060	4,318	2,672	2,033	682	2,715	5,387	76
	$4,066,239	$66,147	$54,610	$40,567	$14,346	$6,819	$21,165	$61,732	93%
Adjusted reserve valuation premiums:									
Participating whole life	$ 429,164	$ 9,909	$ 7,105	$ 6,789	$ 1,409	$1,147	$ 2,556	$ 9,345	94%
Whole life:									
Regular plans	1,774,390	34,382	30,827	22,171	5,429	3,375	8,804	30,975	90
Converted plans	84,801	2,342	2,190	1,703	305	166	471	2,174	93
20-pay life	326,317	8,174	7,015	4,875	1,376	1,003	2,379	7,254	89
20-year endowment	36,674	1,474	1,361	1,015	243	89	332	1,347	91
5-year renewable and convertible term	398,942	2,806	1,794	1,342	578	357	935	2,277	81
25-year convertible decreasing term	1,015,951	7,060	4,318	2,672	1,555	682	2,237	4,909	70
	$4,066,239	$66,147	$54,610	$40,567	$10,895	$6,819	$17,714	$58,281	88%

Table 7–7.

ILLUSTRATION OF CALCULATION OF VALUATION PREMIUMS FOR 5-YEAR RENEWABLE TERM PLAN
ISSUED TO MALE AGE 25—1970-71 RATEBOOK

Present value at issue of:

Deaths	$ 8.29
Conversions	.08
Expenses	14.81
TOTAL BENEFITS AND EXPENSES	$23.18
Premiums	$26.81

Ratio of present value of costs to present value of premiums:

Deaths	30.92%
Conversions	.30
Total benefits	31.22
Expenses	55.24
VALUATION PREMIUM PERCENTAGE	86.46%

Valuation premiums:

Renewal period		Gross Premium	Valuation Premiums — Benefits	Valuation Premiums — Expenses	Valuation Premiums — Total
	1	$ 4.40	$ 1.37	$ 2.43	$ 3.80
	2	4.48	1.40	2.47	3.87
	3	5.00	1.56	2.76	4.32
	4	6.43	2.01	3.55	5.56
	5	8.76	2.73	4.84	7.57
	6	12.32	3.84	6.80	10.64
	7	17.51	5.47	9.67	15.14
	8	26.82	8.38	14.82	23.20
	9	40.70	12.71	22.49	35.20

change at the end of the grading period. This is a special case of the constant relationship principle.*

The most significant implications of the constant relationship principle involve policies whose premiums are not level. For example, premiums on five-year renewable term plans increase in each renewal period. The use of an annuity to calculate the level annual equivalent of benefits and expenses would result in a level valuation premium which, because of changes in the gross premium, would change its percentage relationship to the gross premium every time the gross premium changed—every five years, in this case. The spread between the valuation premium and the gross premium would increase in direct proportion to increases in the gross premium. All other things being equal, the result would be to report diminished profits (and possibly losses) in the early years and greater profits in the later years.

Thus, in the case of business whose premiums are not level, the valuation premium should generally be computed by projecting gross premiums, benefits, and expenses and discounting them to a present value; dividing the present value of benefits and expenses by the present value of gross premiums; and applying the resulting percentage to the gross premiums.

This procedure, and the results, are illustrated in Table 7–7 for Crazy Quilt's 5-year renewable term plan. An issue to a male age 25 (1970–1971 ratebook) is illustrated. The present value of benefits and expenses is 86.46 percent of the present value of premiums, and this percentage is applied to the gross premium in each renewal period to obtain the corresponding adjusted reserve valuation premium.*

Adjusted Reserves

Once the adjusted reserve valuation premiums are finally determined, adjusted reserve factors can be calculated. In the course of calculating factors, profit patterns resulting from the reserves should be tested for reasonableness for some key plan-age combinations. Assuming the results of the testing are favorable, the reserve factors can be finalized and calculated for all in-force business which is to be adjusted.

*It should be noted that the illustration assumes that the 5-year renewable and convertible term policy is here treated as a continuum, i.e., one policy extending through all renewal periods. The reason for this is discussed in the next chapter.

*Reserve grading is discussed in Chapter 11.

Calculation of Factors

The calculation of reserve factors is often thought of as a rather mechanical process, and so it is—but only after the *method* of calculation has been decided on.

There are several ways to calculate reserves: means, mid-terminals, interpolated mid-terminals, and intermediates, among many. Each approach may result in a factor that differs in amount from the other approaches. The various techniques of calculating reserve factors are discussed in Chapter 12.

Crazy Quilt calculated factors using the intermediate reserve approach. In brief, under this approach the mid-policy-year reserve is calculated in such a way as to provide a fund sufficient to cover the next terminal reserve plus benefits assumed to occur in the next six months. In effect, the next terminal reserve and benefits assumed to occur during the next six months are discounted for one-half year's interest, mortality, and withdrawal. Viewed another way, a reserve fund is accumulated up to the date of valuation. This differs from the mean reserve approach, under which the reserve is a simple arithmetic average of the initial reserve and the next terminal reserve, or the mid-terminal reserve approach, under which the reserve is a simple arithmetic average of two terminal reserves.

Calculation of adjusted reserve factors for the 1948–1961 ratebook edition of Crazy Quilt's 20-year endowment policy (male age 25) is summarized in Table 7–8.* Stated simply, the process involves accumulating, at interest, the receipt of valuation premiums and the disbursement of benefits (and, in this case, expenses), using in all cases the assumptions underlying the valuation premium. The result is a fund, computed as of each calendar year-end, which is divided by the units of insurance assumed to be in force; the result is the reserve factor. If in fact the units of insurance in force turn out to be as expected, application of the factors to the in-force volume will yield the expected fund.

Crazy Quilt's methods of calculating reserve factors are explored in detail in Chapter 12 and Appendix A.

Profit Patterns

Having calculated valuation premiums based on assumptions that contain provisions for adverse deviations, and having calculated reserve factors based on those valuation premiums and assumptions, all that

*The assumptions for this plan are outlined in Table 7–2 and the calculation of the valuation premium is summarized in Table 7–4.

remains is to test the resulting reserves in terms of the expected pattern of profit recognition.

This test is pursuant to the requirement of the life insurance audit guide that "conservatism in determining . . . provisions [for adverse deviations] should . . . be considered in relation to the effect of the provision on recognition of profit." [17] Sometimes the effect on profit recognition of a particular provision for adverse deviation can be determined by judgment, i.e., without testing. More often than not, however, some form of testing is likely to be desirable or even necessary.

The type of testing required is not, as is commonly supposed, a test of what will happen to profits if actual experience actually corresponds to the reserve assumptions. Such a test would always produce an apparent profit that is a constant percentage of the gross premium. The valuation premium becomes a "natural premium" in relation to such a test, and the reserve constitutes a "natural reserve". Such a test would not reveal anything that is not already known.

What is required is to test the reserves in relation to a projection of "best-estimate" experience, i.e., a projection of assumptions that do not include an intentional loading for adverse deviation. Only in this way can such a test indicate the effect of conservatism "in relation to the effect of the provision on recognition of profit." Expected profits derive from expected experience, and assumptions loaded for adverse deviation do not necessarily reflect expected experience.

In the case of Crazy Quilt's 1948–1961 edition of the 20-year endowment, the test was fairly simple. A representative year—1957—was chosen for testing. A projection was made which reasonably reflected actual experience from 1957 to 1971 and a rational best estimate of expected experience from 1972 to 1977 (when the 1957 endowments would mature). The adjusted reserves were then inserted into the projection and the resulting expected book profits were generated.

The projection is shown in Table 7–9. It will be observed that persistency was less favorable than expected, which explains the drop in profits in 1958 and 1959 (because the unamortized expense portion of the reserve is written down; this is discussed in Chapter 16). Rising interest rates cure a multitude of sins, however, and excess interest sent profits soaring in the late 1960s and early 1970s. "Excess interest" in this context refers to interest in excess of the rate assumed for rate-testing purposes.

Crazy Quilt decided that the indicated pattern was reasonable. Of the 1971 profit of $7.25, about $6.50 was attributable to excess interest. Since 3 percent was

Table 7–8.

CALCULATION OF RESERVE FACTORS FOR 1948–1961 RATEBOOK EDITION OF 20-YEAR ENDOWMENT
POLICY ISSUED TO MALE AGE 25—PER $1,000 IN FORCE

Calendar Year	Beginning Fund	Valuation Premium Received	Benefits and Expenses Disbursed	Interest Received	Ending Fund	Units in Force	Reserve Factors			
							Net	Benefits	Acquisition Costs	Maintenance Expenses
1	$ -0-	$49.33	$ 67.35	$ (.27)	$ (18.29)	.999605	$(18.30)	$ 35.35	$(54.10)	$ .45
2	(18.29)	39.43	7.32	(.07)	13.75	.799004	17.22	80.08	(62.60)	(.26)
3	13.75	35.85	8.97	.82	41.45	.726399	57.08	121.25	(63.81)	(.36)
4	41.45	34.02	8.57	1.63	68.53	.689365	99.42	161.78	(62.14)	(.22)
5	68.53	32.29	9.68	2.39	93.53	.654166	143.01	203.41	(60.34)	(.06)
6	93.53	30.64	10.70	3.10	116.57	.620691	187.86	246.15	(58.39)	.10
7	116.57	29.07	11.64	3.76	137.76	.588864	234.00	289.99	(56.27)	.28
8	137.76	27.58	12.44	4.36	157.26	.558627	281.57	335.08	(53.99)	.48
9	157.26	26.16	13.19	4.91	175.14	.529900	330.60	381.42	(51.51)	.69
10	175.14	24.81	13.85	5.42	191.52	.502610	381.17	429.07	(48.82)	.92
11	191.52	23.78	12.41	5.91	208.80	.481700	433.62	477.76	(45.35)	1.21
12	208.80	22.79	12.94	6.41	225.06	.461612	487.74	527.84	(41.63)	1.53
13	225.06	21.84	13.43	6.88	240.35	.442308	543.61	579.37	(37.63)	1.87
14	240.35	20.93	13.88	7.32	254.72	.423750	601.31	632.42	(33.34)	2.23
15	254.72	20.05	14.32	7.72	268.17	.405898	660.90	687.01	(28.73)	2.62
16	268.17	19.20	14.75	8.11	280.73	.388712	722.45	743.20	(23.79)	3.04
17	280.73	18.38	15.15	8.47	292.43	.372154	786.04	801.02	(18.47)	3.49
18	292.43	17.60	15.53	8.81	303.31	.356190	851.80	860.60	(12.76)	3.97
19	303.31	16.84	15.89	9.12	313.38	.340786	919.87	922.00	(6.61)	4.48
20	313.38	16.11	16.23	9.40	322.66	.325913	990.36	985.33	-0-	5.03
21	322.66	-0-	327.57	4.91	-0-	-0-	—	—	—	—

considered an appropriate interest rate assumption for endowments issued from 1948–1961, the excess interest earned in 1971 was considered a proper credit to 1971 operations.

Table 7–9 provides for interest at the "best estimate" rate to be earned on assets equivalent to the adjusted reserve. Actually, of course, assets equivalent to statutory reserves must always be held. However, to isolate the effect on profits of a particular adjusted reserve it is necessary to assume that any difference between the statutory reserve and the adjusted reserve is essentially equivalent to appropriated surplus. Interest on such difference may be available as an additional safety margin (assuming the statutory reserve exceeds the adjusted reserve), but the existence of the safety margin should not affect the computation of profits that flow from the use of a particular adjusted reserve.

Crazy Quilt used its portfolio interest rate in preparing Table 7–9. This is because the assumed rate was based on the portfolio rate. Where new money rates have been assumed, it would normally be appropriate to make the test in terms of new money rates. This can be a very difficult problem (for reasons explained in Chapter 9) and would rarely be

done except where a company maintains extremely detailed records of investment income by calendar year of investment. Usually, therefore, a good deal of combining and averaging would be necessary to make the profit tests. Techniques of making the tests in a realistic environment are discussed in Chapter 24.

In fact, it should be understood that any company would make the type of test illustrated in Table 7–9 in terms of broad composites and using highly approximate techniques. The illustration is designed simply to integrate material presented earlier on the 20-year endowment and thus perhaps to make the various interrelated procedures a little more comprehensible.

Finally, the types of problems encountered in testing new or recent issues differ significantly from the types of problems associated with issues of earlier years, for which much of the subsequent experience is known.

Expense Reserves

Up to this point Crazy Quilt has considered expenses in calculating valuation premiums and testing reserve factors. The calculations were designed to test

Table 7–9.

PROJECTION OF EXPECTED BOOK PROFITS FROM 1957 TO 1977 FOR 20-YEAR ENDOWMENT POLICY 1957
ISSUE ISSUED TO MALE AGE 25 USING PROPOSED ADJUSTED RESERVES—1948–1961 RATEBOOK—PER $1,000
ORIGINALLY ISSUED

Calendar Year	Units in Force Expected	Actual	Adjusted Reserve Per Unit in Force	Per Unit Issued	Premiums	Interest on Reserve	Change in Reserve	Benefits	Expenses	Actual Book Profits
1957	.99961	.99970	$ (18.30)	$ (18.29)	$49.58	$ (.34)	$ (18.29)	$ .30	$65.08	$2.15
1958	.79900	.74930	17.22	12.90	37.16	(.10)	31.19	.80	4.01	1.06
1959	.72640	.63647	57.08	36.33	31.57	.99	23.43	5.19	3.48	.46
1960	.68937	.57240	99.42	56.91	28.39	1.94	20.58	5.78	3.33	.64
1961	.65417	.52620	143.01	75.25	26.10	2.83	18.34	6.24	3.19	1.16
1962	.62069	.49422	187.86	92.84	24.51	3.65	17.59	5.82	3.01	1.74
1963	.58886	.46911	234.00	109.77	23.27	4.46	16.93	5.77	2.87	2.16
1964	.55863	.44525	281.58	125.37	22.09	5.24	15.60	6.58	2.75	2.40
1965	.52990	.42258	330.61	139.71	20.96	6.01	14.34	7.34	2.63	2.67
1966	.50261	.40524	381.17	154.47	20.10	6.87	14.76	6.52	2.53	3.16
1967	.48170	.38857	433.63	168.49	19.28	7.87	14.02	7.13	1.95	4.04
1968	.46161	.37640	487.75	183.59	18.68	9.05	15.10	5.90	1.89	4.84
1969	.44231	.36456	543.61	198.18	18.09	10.40	14.59	6.38	1.85	5.67
1970	.42375	.35304	601.31	212.29	17.52	11.83	14.11	6.82	1.81	6.61
1971	.40589	.34182	660.90	225.91	16.96	12.93	13.62	7.25	1.76	7.25
1972*	.38871	.33090	722.45	239.06	16.42	13.61	13.15	7.69	1.72	7.47
1973	.37215	.32025	786.04	251.73	15.90	14.30	12.67	8.11	1.67	7.75
1974	.35618	.30987	815.80	263.94	15.38	15.02	12.21	8.51	1.63	8.05
1975	.34078	.29972	919.87	275.70	14.88	15.72	11.76	8.93	1.58	8.33
1976	.32591	.28979	990.36	286.99	14.39	15.07	11.29	9.33	1.50	7.34
1977	-0-	-0-	—	—	—	7.09	(286.99)	289.78	1.05	3.25

* Actual revised to updated estimates after 1971.

reasonableness, and that objective was considered to be satisfactorily achieved.

Thereafter, however, expenses had to be subjected to additional analysis. Some of the items counted as acquisition costs in the profit tests had to be treated as period costs. This subject is explored in detail in Part III of the book. The remaining comments have to do with adjusted benefit reserves only.

Adjusted Benefit Reserves

One final test of the reserves is to compare adjusted benefit reserves with statutory reserves. Ideally the comparison should be made using net level statutory reserves, since adjusted benefit reserves are always net level. Where—as is usually the case with stock companies—a significant proportion of a company's statutory reserves is valued on a preliminary term or modified preliminary term basis, the comparison should still be made, but a good deal of judgment will

be required in interpreting the results of the comparison.*

Table 7–10 summarizes Crazy Quilt's model statutory reserves and adjusted benefit reserves on all ordinary business as of December 31, 1971. All statutory reserves are net level; Crazy Quilt computes statutory reserves on both the net level and preliminary term (or modified preliminary term, if applicable) bases; however, the Company uses a mixture of reserve bases in its Convention Statement, as would most stock companies.** The statutory mortality and interest bases are shown in Table 7–10. A summary of

*For example, the extent of distortion caused by using preliminary term or modified preliminary term reserves differs by type of business and age of the business. Also, a comparison covering several years will provide more insight into the relationship between adjusted and statutory reserves than a comparison for, say, one year.

**However, as discussed in Chapter 26, Crazy Quilt strengthened reserves in 1969 in connection with a Section 818(c) election.

Table 7–10.

SUMMARY OF ORDINARY LIFE AND ANNUITY NET LEVEL STATUTORY RESERVES AND ADJUSTED
BENEFIT RESERVES FOR CRAZY QUILT LIFE AT DECEMBER 31, 1971 (000 Omitted)

Plan and Ratebook	Era	Statutory Reserve Basis Mortality	Interest	In Force	December 31, 1971 Statutory Reserves	Adjusted Benefit Reserves
Par whole life	41–47	AE	3.0%	$ 7,711	$ 3,360	$ 3,607
	48–51	41 CSO	2.5	13,708	5,292	5,664
	52–61	41 CSO	2.5	52,950	13,212	13,895
	62–64	58 CSO	2.5	50,325	6,587	7,110
	65–69	58 CSO	2.5	171,825	11,187	12,070
	70–71	58 CSO	2.5	132,645	2,645	2,590
				429,164	42,283	44,936
Whole life	41–47	AE	3.0	21,736	8,938	9,662
	48–51	41 CSO	2.5	36,370	13,629	13,367
	52–56	41 CSO	2.5	99,044	30,583	30,067
	57–61	41 CSO	2.5	103,362	21,836	21,872
	62–67	58 CSO	3.0	615,430	62,940	64,463
	68–69	58 CSO	3.0	391,324	19,805	18,319
	70–71	58 CSO	3.0	591,925	12,613	10,091
				1,859,191	170,344	167,841
20-pay life	41–47	AE	3.0	28,825	17,479	17,454
	48–51	41 CSO	2.5	22,259	13,256	12,011
	52–56	41 CSO	2.5	31,268	15,830	14,333
	57–61	41 CSO	2.5	25,980	8,901	7,973
	62–67	58 CSO	3.0	93,597	13,076	12,589
	68–69	58 CSO	3.0	64,303	4,244	3,596
	70–71	58 CSO	3.0	111,167	2,894	2,134
				377,399	75,680	70,090
20-year endowment	48–61	41 CSO	2.5	36,674	27,930	27,976
5-year R & C term	41–47	AE	3.0	258	3	19
	48–51	41 CSO	2.5	3,560	37	323
	52–56	41 CSO	2.5	14,699	140	1,078
	57–61	41 CSO	2.5	16,285	118	719
	62–64	58 CSO	3.0	32,904	102	785
	65–67	58 CSO	3.0	79,600	198	1,348
	68–69	58 CSO	3.0	95,160	224	919
	70–71	58 CSO	3.0	156,476	320	524
				398,942	1,142	5,715
25-year decreasing term	57–61	41 CSO	2.5	14,470	72	220
	62–69	58 CSO	3.0	529,476	3,655	5,163
	70–71	58 CSO	3.0	472,005	1,451	1,141
				1,015,951	5,178	6,524
TOTAL ORDINARY LIFE BASIC PLANS					322,557	323,082
Miscellaneous *	Various	Various	Various	—	17,257	16,757
TOTAL ORDINARY LIFE				$4,117,321	$339,814	$339,839
Single-premium annuities	52–56	37SA(1S)	2.0		$ 2,557	$ 2,171
	57–61	37SA(1S)	2.5		5,679	5,063
	62–67	37SA(1S)	3.0		29,444	26,301
	68–69	A49(10P)	3.5		21,035	18,071
	70–71	A49(10P)	3.5		29,065	24,281
TOTAL ANNUITY					$ 87,780	$ 75,887

* Waiver of premium, accidental death, supplementary contracts involving life contingencies, deficiency reserves (statutory only), and other.

assumptions underlying the adjusted benefit reserves is shown in Table 7–1.

Some unusual relationships are apparent from Table 7–10. They will be explored in the chapters that follow.

Disclosure

The life insurance audit guide provides that "the methods employed and the assumptions used in calculating policy reserves should be disclosed in the financial statements." [18] The guide then suggests that for each material line of business, a tabular presentation of the components of the reserves should be shown, presumably in a note to the statements. The tabular presentation suggested by the guide would show insurance in force, reserve amount, issue years, interest rates, mortality assumptions, and withdrawal assumptions.

For all but the smallest companies the extent of disclosure suggested by the guide would probably be impractical. Table 7–1 reports the essential assumptions for Crazy Quilt Life's ordinary and annuity lines of business, except that amounts of insurance in force and reserves are not shown. Similar disclosure would theoretically have to be made for Crazy Quilt's other significant adjusted lines, industrial and health. The volume of disclosure would be so great as to raise the question of what the reader of the financial statements could do with it.

Crazy Quilt is, of course, a fairly simple company. Larger and more complex companies would require correspondingly larger and more complex exhibits. For consolidated groups the exhibits could run to many pages.*

It is important to appreciate the reason for disclosing reserve assumptions. The reason is to render the statements more informative. It is questionable whether reams of detail will in fact make the statements more informative. A reader wants to know something about the company's assumptions in order to form a judgment as to the relative degree of conservatism inherent in the reserve assumptions, to determine the general effect on the financial statements of the assumptions, and to compare the assumptions with those of other companies (although, to the extent that the underwriting practices, etc., of other companies differ, such comparisons are likely to be misleading). It would appear that a well-written narrative would adequately serve the reader's needs.

*One large consolidated group estimates that 40 pages of six-point type would be required to make the suggested disclosure. Its entire annual report was smaller than that.

A company can make the details available to those who request them, just as some companies provide lists of securities holdings to those who request them. To require publication, in the annual report, of an exhibit of adjusted policy reserves where such an exhibit would be very lengthy would seem to be carrying the principle of disclosure too far and may possibly frustrate the objectives of disclosure by presenting more detail than can reasonably be analyzed.

Further, as suggested in subsequent chapters, some assumptions—particularly mortality and withdrawal—defy meaningful descriptions, especially when presented in tabular form. In general, however, interest assumptions are of such significance that they should be described in detail.

Appropriate disclosure for Crazy Quilt Life's ordinary life line of business might take the following form:

ACCOUNTING POLICY NOTE

Liabilities for future policy benefits have been computed by the net level premium method based upon estimates of investment yield, mortality, and withdrawals applicable at the time of issue. Dividends on participating policies have been provided for ratably based on expected dividend scales.

OTHER NOTE

The principal assumptions employed in calculating benefit reserve liabilities are summarized as follows:

Mortality. The 1930–1939 Select and Ultimate Table, the 1946–1949 Select and Ultimate Basic Table, and the 1950–1954 Select and Ultimate Basic Table (slightly modified) have generally been used for issues of 1941–1951, 1952–1956, and 1957–1971, respectively. Reserves on term insurance include provision for extra mortality on renewal and conversion, as applicable.

Withdrawals. Withdrawal assumptions are based primarily on the Company's experience. In general, such assumptions are, in the aggregate, similar to the Linton B Table.

Interest. Interest assumptions for nonparticipating products are generally as follows: Issues of 1941–1947, 2.75%; 1948–1951, 3%; 1952–1956, 3.25%; 1957–1961, 4% graded to 3% in 20 years; 1962–1967, 4.5% graded to 3% in 25 years; 1968–1969, 5.5% graded to 3.5% in 25 years; and 1970–1971, 6.5% graded to 3.5% in 30 years. For participating products level interest assumptions related to the assumptions underlying the dividend scales are used.

Dividends. Dividends are provided for on the basis of dividend scales illustrated at the time of issue. In all cases, variances from the assumptions are recognized in the periods in which such variances occur. All assumptions are deemed to provide adequately for the risks of adverse deviations.

8 Mortality and Withdrawals

Two of the three basic assumptions entering into the calculation of adjusted benefit reserves are mortality and withdrawals. They can have significant effects on the level of reserves and the incidence of reserve changes and must be therefore chosen with care. It is not necessarily true that the interest assumption is so significant as to diminish the importance of the mortality and withdrawal assumptions. Mortality and withdrawals have their own personalities and cannot be shrugged off on the basis that interest is what counts most.

Mortality and withdrawals are discussed in isolation in this chapter. It should be borne in mind that mortality, withdrawals, and all the other assumptions interact, and the combined effect of all the assumptions is what really counts. Further, this discussion is limited to benefit reserves. Mortality and withdrawal assumptions also affect acquisition costs, sometimes dramatically. This is discussed in Chapter 16.

Mortality

Mortality tables are definitely not the province of accountants, few of whom, for example, would know how to fill in "intervening issue ages . . . by interpolation, using an osculatory formula based on a third-degree polynomial." [1]

So few accountants would be in a position to judge the propriety of the mortality assumption used in calculating a given set of adjusted reserves.

Nevertheless, the life insurance audit guide sets forth a few guidelines for mortality assumptions and, qualified or not to pass on the assumptions, accountants must somehow be able to come to a conclusion as to whether such assumptions are, or are not, appropriate in a given case. Usually they would rely on the judgment of qualified actuaries in coming to a conclusion. But "reliance" should be reasonably well-informed reliance, not blind reliance.

The material that follows is designed to inform accountants in a general way about mortality tables, mortality assumptions, and the effect of mortality assumptions on adjusted benefit reserves. The discussion makes no pretense of being "actuarially sound", so to speak.

Audit Guide Provisions as to Mortality

The life insurance audit guide's basic provisions about mortality are contained in a single paragraph:

The mortality assumption to be used in determining annual reserve additions [for long-term life insurance contracts] . . . should be based on realistic estimates of expected mortality. As in the case of other estimates, provisions for adverse deviations should be included. For any blocks of business which are subject to little or no underwriting selection, the use of ultimate-only or aggregate mortality tables will be appropriate. Where there is adequate medical underwriting, a select table should be used. [2]

How to reconcile "realistic estimates" with the requirement to provide for adverse deviation is not entirely clear, but the duality seems consistent with the guide's requirement that adjusted reserve assumptions should be "reasonably and realistically conservative." Adverse deviation is discussed in Chapter 6 and, as it relates specifically to the mortality assumption, later in this chapter.

Other statements about mortality in the audit guide are in the nature of supplemental commentary on the basic guideline quoted above.

Principal Mortality Tables

Table 8–1 * summarizes some of the principal published mortality tables dating from 1783 to the present day. With the exception of the Northampton, Carlisle, and 1959–61 U.S. Life tables (which are essentially based on combined insured and uninsured lives), all of the life insurance tables are based on insured lives while the annuity tables are based on annuitant mortality, which differs considerably from mortality of insured persons.

The life insurance tables are either aggregate tables (i.e., based on the experience of all insured lives) or ultimate tables (i.e., based on experience following the assumed period of select experience; for example, the 1958 CSO table excludes experience during the first five years after issue during which time the effect of underwriting is deemed to lessen the experienced death rate). Some of the tables are for males only, some are for females only, and some report combined experience.

Many of the mortality tables listed in Table 8–1 have in the past been required, or are currently required, to be used for purposes of statutory reserve valuations. For ordinary life insurance, for example, statutory requirements have been as follows:

Table	Issue Years
Actuaries'	To 1900
American Experience	1901–1947**
1941 CSO	1948–1965
1958 CSO	1966–Present

As respects annuities and supplementary contracts involving life contingencies, statutory requirements have varied. Generally the 1937 Standard Annuity table has represented the minimum standard; in practice, the four most recent tables are frequently found in use today.

The mortality tables summarized in Table 8–1 include, of course, death from all causes. For purposes of calculating statutory reserves on the additional ac-

cidental death benefit, tables of death by accidental means must be used in conjunction with the basic tables. The minimum statutory requirements for valuing the accidental death benefit from 1948–1965 was the 1926–33 Inter-Company Double Indemnity Mortality Table; from 1966 to the present the minimum standard has been the 1959 Accidental Death Benefits Table. Table 8–2 illustrates accidental death rates for these two tables.

An analysis carried out three years ago of the 1968 Convention Statements of 159 life insurance companies (141 stock and 18 mutual) as part of the Ernst & Ernst Life Insurance Accounting Research Project included an analysis of life insurance and annuity reserves by mortality table. The 159 companies represented, in 1968, about 75 percent of the industry in terms of assets and insurance in force. The analysis is summarized in Table 8–3.

Experience Tables

When the life insurance audit guide refers to "realistic estimates of expected mortality", it refers to estimates appropriate in the circumstances. "Appropriate circumstances" can cover a wide range. Thus an established company might assume for purposes of calculating adjusted reserves on new issues "its own [mortality] experience, if such experience is credible or, if appropriate, data from recently published tables," while for older issues the company should generally use "the company's experience or published experience used in the gross premium calculations." [3] For a new company, "an accepted published table [may be acceptable] if it is representative of the company's experience and underwriting practices," but "in some cases, the auditor may only be satisfied with the use of [statutory] tables or other more conservative tables." [4]

"Experience" is the central concept in the audit guide's provisions as to mortality. Experience should always be the starting point for constructing a mortality table for use in calculating adjusted reserves, whether the experience be the company's own experience or the experience of the industry or some representative sample thereof.

"Experience" is not limited to observed historical phenomena. A mortality table as used for purposes of calculating adjusted reserves is a representation of death rates that are occurring at the time of the study underlying the table *plus* a judgment that the rates will continue to be experienced in the future. Thus an "experience" table of mortality has reference to the

---

*Table 8–1 is based on Principal Mortality Tables Old and New, an excellent booklet published by Nelson and Warren, Inc., Consulting Actuaries.

**Some states permitted optional use of the American Men table during a part of this time period.

Table 8–1.

SOME IMPORTANT MORTALITY TABLES

Table	Approximate Year of Publication	Experience Years	Source of Data	Rounded Death Rate Per 1000 Individuals at Age								
				15	25	35	45	55	65	75	85	95
LIFE INSURANCE												
Northampton	1783	46 years	English parish	9.2	15.8	18.7	24.0	33.5	49.0	96.2	220.4	750.0
Carlisle	1815	1779–1787	Two Scottish parishes	6.2	7.3	10.3	14.8	17.9	41.1	95.5	175.3	233.3
Actuaries'	1843	Prior to 1838	English insurance experience	6.9	7.8	9.3	12.2	21.7	44.1	95.6	205.1	584.3
American Experience	1868	1843–1858	Mutual Life of N.Y.	7.6	8.1	9.0	11.2	18.6	40.1	94.4	235.6	1000.0
Standard Industrial	1906	1896–1905	Metropolitan Life	3.6	9.5	13.0	17.4	28.5	56.1	123.0	272.3	533.3
American Men	1918	1900–1915	59 companies	3.5	4.3	4.8	7.9	17.5	40.7	91.9	197.1	387.8
1941 Standard Industrial	1941	1930–1939	Metropolitan Life	2.9	4.7	6.6	12.3	24.8	53.3	106.3	221.8	442.0
Commissioners 1941 Standard Ordinary	1941	1930–1940	Large companies	2.2	2.9	4.6	8.6	18.0	39.6	88.6	194.1	396.2
Commissioners 1958 Standard Ordinary	1960	1950–1954	15 large companies	1.5	1.9	2.5	5.4	13.0	31.8	73.4	161.1	351.2
Commissioners 1960 Standard Group	1960	1950–1958	Intercompany studies	1.7	2.3	2.9	6.2	14.9	34.0	77.0	169.2	368.8
Commissioners 1961 Standard Industrial	1961	1954–1958	18 Large companies	1.5	2.2	3.3	7.3	15.7	33.9	75.6	172.9	393.0
1955–60 Basic	1962	1955–1960	16 large companies	.6	1.0	1.3	3.7	10.7	27.5	62.7	147.7	335.0
1959–61 U.S. Life	1962	1959–1961	U.S. population (1960 census)									
White males				.9	1.6	2.1	5.6	14.8	33.9	70.7	160.4	314.2
White females				.4	.7	1.2	3.0	6.9	17.4	47.4	136.3	314.2
Non-white males				1.2	3.2	5.1	10.4	22.7	43.7	66.7	122.8	314.2
Non-white females				.6	1.7	3.7	7.7	17.3	30.7	51.3	102.1	314.2

ANNUITIES

McClintock's Annuitants	1899	Prior to 1892	15 large companies	7.7	8.2	9.4	12.5	20.1	39.1	85.2	191.5	407.2
Combined Annuity	1928	various	Special construction	1.7	2.2	3.1	6.9	15.5	34.3	75.1	160.3	323.6
1937 Standard Annuity	1937	various	Special construction	1.3	1.6	3.0	6.4	13.6	28.9	60.5	124.8	248.1
a–1949:	1949	various	Special construction									
Males				.5	.8	1.4	3.6	10.6	23.1	54.5	134.2	316.8
Females				.3	.5	.9	2.0	4.7	12.4	35.8	104.8	288.2
1951 Group Annuity (male):	1951	various	Special construction									
Without projection				.5	.8	1.4	3.6	10.4	24.4	62.4	146.9	268.0
Projected 1965				.4	.6	1.2	3.0	8.8	20.5	54.2	140.2	268.0
1955 American Annuitants (male)	1955	1948–1953	Special construction	.5	.7	1.3	3.0	7.1	20.2	50.4	115.0	244.0

Table 8–2.

SAMPLE ACCIDENTAL DEATH RATES PER 1,000 INSURED LIVES FROM TWO WIDELY-USED TABLES

Age	1959 Table	1926–33 Table	Age	1959 Table	1926–33 Table	Age	1959 Table	1926–33 Table
1	.551	—	27	.424	.473	42	.405	.637
5	.339	.800	28	.409	.449	43	.413	.649
10	.303	.662	29	.400	.439	44	.422	.660
15	.476	.882	30	.394	.438	45	.431	.675
16	.637	.854	31	.390	.447	50	.465	.873
17	.723	.827	32	.387	.464	55	.514	1.115
18	.751	.801	33	.386	.481	60	.624	1.378
19	.758	.776	34	.386	.494	65	.809	1.720
20	.748	.752	35	.386	.502	70	1.065	2.053
21	.720	.728	36	.387	.511	75	1.710	2.801
22	.675	.697	37	.389	.523	80	3.277	4.519
23	.612	.654	38	.391	.544	85	5.419	6.926
24	.546	.605	39	.393	.571	90	8.022	11.344
25	.490	.555	40	.395	.598	95	11.495	15.265
26	.448	.509	41	.399	.621	99	15.009	15.820

past and the future, between which the present is merely a fragile link. Obviously the longer the curve of experienced mortality fits the curve of the mortality table being used, the more credible the table becomes—but only in the absence of information that changes one's outlook for the future. In any event, the important thing to appreciate is that an experience table of mortality is a projection of future experience based on (1) observations of past experience and (2) an assumption that the future will remain stable in terms of the factors causing death.

An experience table may be modified to anticipate future changes, such as annuity tables have been modified to reflect anticipated improvements in mortality. An experience table may also be effectively modified by holding fast to historical death rates and not projecting any reduction in such rates even when there is some evidence that reductions are likely to occur. In both cases experience is being tempered by a degree of conservatism deemed appropriate in the circumstances.

Larger, well-established companies generally develop their own mortality tables, or compare their own experience with a published experience table and express their own experience in terms of a modification of the published table—for example, 95 percent of the 1955–60 table for ages through 24, 100 percent for ages 25–39, and 105 percent for ages 40 and above.

Newer companies usually use published tables exclusively, or published tables modified by consulting actuaries on a judgment basis to recognize characteristics peculiar to the company.

In all cases, actuarial judgment of the highest order is needed to translate into a single table all of the factors likely to affect mortality for a particular company—the type of business being sold, characteristics of the market, underwriting policies, and so on.

The 1941 CSO table, the 1958 CSO table, the 1955–60 Basic Ultimate Combined table, the 1955–60 Basic Select and Ultimate Combined table for ages 30, 35, and 40, and Crazy Quilt Life's three sets of ratebook assumptions for standard issues to males at ages 25, 35, and 45 during the Company's 31-year history are summarized in Table 8–4. Crazy Quilt used three different experience tables for its assumptions: 1930–39 experience for issues of 1941–1947; 1946–49 experience, applied retroactively for issues of 1948–1956; and 1950–54 experience (which was the foundation for the 1958 CSO table) for issues of 1957–1971, with a slight modification for issues prior to 1970. Select tables were used in all cases, with a three-year select period in the early years of issue, a five-year select period in the middle years, and a 15-year select period in the later years.

While the 1955–60 table was slightly more up-to-date than the 1950–54 table, Crazy Quilt elected to continue using the 1950–54 table because of its slightly conservative edge over the 1955–60 table.

Similar information for annuities is shown in Table 8–5.

Effect on Reserves

The mortality assumption can have a relatively significant effect on valuation premiums and reserves.

Table 8–3.

STATUTORY RESERVES CLASSIFIED BY MORTALITY TABLE FOR 141 STOCK COMPANIES AND 18 MUTUAL COMPANIES IN 1968

Line of Business And Mortality Basis	*Reserves As Percentage Of Total Reserves for Line of Business*			
	Stock Companies		*Mutual Companies*	
	Ordinary, Industrial, And Group	*Ordinary Only*	*Ordinary, Industrial, And Group*	*Ordinary Only*
Life insurance:				
American Experience	22%	25%	23%	26%
American Men	3	2	7	8
Standard Industrial	2		8	
1941 SI	8		3	
1941 CSO	49	56	44	50
1958 CSO	15	16	10	11
Other and unclassified	1	1	5	5
	100%	100%	100%	100%
Annuities:				
1937 SA	11%	37%	11%	22%
A–49	3	15	9	53
1951 GA	71	2	71	4
1955 AA	1	8	1	8
Other and unclassified	14	38	8	13
	100%	100%	100%	100%
Supplementary contracts:				
1937 SA	24%	22%	30%	30%
A–49	43	51	29	30
1951 GA			3	
1955 AA	10	12	19	20
Other and unclassified	23	15	19	20
	100%	100%	100%	100%
Accidental death:				
1926 Inter-company	74%	78%	69%	71%
1959 ADB	10	15	9	10
Company experience	9		1	1
Other and unclassified	7	7	21	18
	100%	100%	100%	100%

Table 8–6 shows the effect of various mortality assumptions on benefit valuation premiums for selected 1971 issues of Crazy Quilt Life. Table 8–7 shows the effect on the reserves.

Using the 1955–60 Basic Select and Ultimate table as a frame of reference, the tables indicate that a 10 percent loading of the table produces modest (1 percent to 3 percent) margins in the reserves on permanent business and fairly sizeable margins in the term reserves. In fact, the term reserves increase almost in proportion to the percentage loading. A 50 percent loading increases the permanent reserves on the order of 10 percent or less, but again, in the case of the term reserves the increase is more nearly proportional to the percentage loading.

It should be noted that the Crazy Quilt Life ratebook assumptions for term plans include provisions for adverse mortality on renewal and/or conversion, as applicable. These provisions result in very high reserve levels in Crazy Quilt's case. Term renewals and term conversions are discussed later in this chapter.

Effect on Profits

Another useful method of evaluating the significance of the mortality assumption is to examine the relationships among profits, premiums, and death claims. Table 8–8 shows such values, expressed in amounts per $1,000 of original issue, for several key plans and issue years for Crazy Quilt Life. The values

Table 8-4.

SAMPLE ASSUMED DEATHS PER 1,000 INDIVIDUALS INSURED

| | Published Tables | | | | | | Crazy Quilt's Select and Ultimate Ordinary Ratebook Assumptions for Males | | | | | | | | |
| | Ultimate Combined | | 1955–60 | 1955–60 Select Basic Combined | | | 1957–1971 Issues: 1950–54 Experience * | | | 1948–1956 Issues: 1946–49 Experience ** | | | 1941–1947 Issues: 1930–39 Experience | | |
Age	1941 CSO	1958 CSO	Basic	Age 30	Age 35	Age 40	Age 25	Age 35	Age 45	Age 25	Age 35	Age 45	Age 25	Age 35	Age 45
25	2.88	1.93	1.00				.59			.79			1.40		
26	2.99	1.96	1.02				.69			.91			1.71		
27	3.11	1.99	1.04				.80			1.00			1.96		
28	3.25	2.03	1.05				.83			1.07			2.12		
29	3.40	2.08	1.05				.84			1.16			2.17		
30	3.56	2.13	1.06	.55			.85			1.31			2.23		
31	3.73	2.19	1.07	.67			.88			1.38			2.30		
32	3.92	2.25	1.10	.84			.94			1.46			2.39		
33	4.12	2.32	1.16	.89			1.03			1.54			2.50		
34	4.35	2.40	1.22	.95			1.13			1.62			2.63		
35	4.59	2.51	1.31	1.03	.76		1.24	.77		1.72	.92		2.79	1.85	
36	4.86	2.64	1.42	1.17	.95		1.44	.96		1.83	1.15		2.98	2.44	
37	5.15	2.80	1.53	1.35	1.20		1.60	1.22		1.96	1.33		3.20	2.99	
38	5.46	3.01	1.68	1.57	1.38		1.74	1.39		2.12	1.65		3.45	3.45	
39	5.81	3.25	1.85	1.79	1.57		1.92	1.58		2.32	2.01		3.73	3.73	
40	6.18	3.53	2.07	2.05	1.78	1.22	2.12	1.80		2.56	2.56		4.04	4.04	
41	6.59	3.84	2.33	2.32	2.06	1.63	2.36	2.06		2.85	2.85		4.39	4.39	
42	7.03	4.17	2.62	2.62	2.35	2.02	2.66	2.36		3.19	3.19		4.78	4.78	
43	7.51	4.53	2.95	2.95	2.70	2.37	3.02	2.71		3.58	3.58		5.21	5.21	
44	8.04	4.92	3.31	3.34	3.11	2.64	3.45	3.13		4.02	4.02		5.69	5.69	
45	8.61	5.35	3.73	3.73	3.56	3.08	3.96	3.56	1.88	4.50	4.50	2.20	6.22	6.22	4.07
46	9.23	5.83	4.22	4.22	4.05	3.56	4.51	4.13	2.57	5.02	5.02	2.95	6.80	6.80	5.53
47	9.91	6.36	4.74	4.74	4.58	4.01	5.09	4.72	3.23	5.57	5.57	3.84	7.44	7.44	6.94
48	10.64	6.95	5.31	5.31	5.25	4.51	5.71	5.44	3.86	6.18	6.18	4.90	8.15	8.15	8.15
49	11.45	7.60	5.96	5.96	5.89	5.10	6.34	6.17	4.41	6.84	6.84	6.12	8.93	8.93	8.93
50	12.32	8.32	6.61	6.61	6.61	5.79	6.94	6.94	5.07	7.57	7.57	7.57	9.79	9.79	9.79

51	13.27	9.11	7.29	7.29	6.63	7.29	7.56	7.56	5.78	8.39	8.39	8.39	10.73	10.73	10.73	10.73
52	14.30	9.96	8.02	8.02	7.58	8.02	8.32	8.32	6.44	9.29	9.29	9.29	11.76	11.76	11.76	11.76
53	15.43	10.89	8.82	8.82	8.58	8.82	9.20	9.20	7.06	10.31	10.31	10.31	12.88	12.88	12.88	12.88
54	16.65	11.90	9.69	9.69	9.54	9.69	10.09	10.09	7.86	11.44	11.44	11.44	14.09	14.09	14.09	14.09
55	17.98	13.00	10.66	10.66	10.66	10.66	11.00	11.00	8.92	12.71	12.71	12.71	15.40	15.40	15.40	15.40
56	19.43	14.21	11.73	11.73	11.73	11.73	12.06	12.06	10.47	14.12	14.12	14.12	16.81	16.81	16.81	16.81
57	21.00	15.54	12.91	12.91	12.91	12.91	13.26	13.26	12.29	15.67	15.67	15.67	18.33	18.33	18.33	18.33
58	22.71	17.00	14.24	14.24	14.24	14.24	14.60	14.60	14.06	17.35	17.35	17.35	19.98	19.98	19.98	19.98
59	24.57	18.59	15.71	15.71	15.71	15.71	16.06	16.06	15.91	19.15	19.15	19.15	21.77	21.77	21.77	21.77
60	26.59	20.34	17.31	17.31	17.31	17.31	17.69	17.69	17.69	21.05	21.05	21.05	23.71	23.71	23.71	23.71
65	39.64	31.75	27.52	27.52	27.52	27.52	27.99	27.99	27.99	32.10	32.10	32.10	36.11	36.11	36.11	36.11
70	59.30	49.79	42.47	42.47	42.47	42.47	42.90	42.90	42.90	47.14	47.14	47.14	54.15	54.15	54.15	54.15
75	88.64	73.37	62.73	62.73	62.73	62.73	63.36	63.36	63.36	70.45	70.45	70.45	81.09	81.09	81.09	81.09
80	131.85	109.98	96.72	96.72	96.72	96.72	97.68	97.68	97.68	105.45	105.45	105.45	122.16	122.16	122.16	122.16
85	194.13	161.14	147.69	147.69	147.69	147.69	149.17	149.17	149.17	161.68	161.68	161.68	177.05	177.05	177.05	177.05
90	280.99	228.14	227.38	227.38	227.38	227.38	229.66	229.66	229.66	224.66	224.66	224.66	265.61	265.61	265.61	265.61

* Slightly modified for issues of certain plans.
** Retroactively applied for reserve purposes; slightly different than ratebook assumptions.

Table 8-5.

SAMPLE ANNUITY MORTALITY RATES PER 1,000 ANNUITANTS

Age	1937 Standard Annuity	a-1949 (Males)	1951 GA Projected	1955 American Annuitants	Crazy Quilt Life Ratebook Assumptions for Males Age 65		
					1962-1971 Issues	1957-1961 Issues	1952-56 Issues
30	2.07	1.004	.831	.893			
35	2.98	1.391	1.152	1.273			
40	4.36	2.025	1.677	1.925			
45	6.36	3.625	3.002	2.975			
50	9.29	6.557	5.430	4.550			
55	13.55	10.565	8.751	7.073			
60	19.75	15.662	13.043	12.027			
65	28.75	23.066	20.475	20.192	13.84	17.30	23.07
66	30.99	25.030	22.802	22.256	15.02	20.02	25.03
67	33.39	27.193	25.250	24.491	17.68	24.47	27.19
68	35.98	29.577	27.660	26.911	22.18	28.10	29.58
69	38.76	32.202	30.140	29.531	28.98	31.24	32.20
70	41.76	35.092	32.957	32.367	35.09	35.09	35.09
71	44.98	38.272	36.468	35.436	38.27	38.27	38.27
72	48.44	41.771	40.379	38.756	41.77	41.77	41.77
73	52.17	45.620	44.612	42.346	45.62	45.62	45.62
74	56.17	49.852	49.236	46.226	49.85	49.85	49.85
75	60.46	54.501	54.233	50.417	54.50	54.50	54.50
76	65.08	59.609	59.942	54.941	59.61	59.61	59.61
77	70.03	65.216	66.508	59.821	65.22	65.22	65.22
78	75.35	71.368	73.892	65.081	71.37	71.37	71.37
79	81.05	78.113	82.045	70.747	78.11	78.11	78.11
80	87.16	85.503	90.763	76.847	85.50	85.50	85.50
81	93.71	93.593	99.923	83.411	93.59	93.59	93.59
82	100.72	102.443	109.476	90.471	102.44	102.44	102.44
83	108.23	112.113	119.356	98.061	112.11	112.13	112.13
84	116.26	122.669	129.594	106.217	122.67	122.67	122.67
85	124.84	134.178	140.151	114.977	134.18	134.18	134.18
90	177.14	208.485	200.594	169.202	208.49	208.49	208.49
95	248.06	316.834	268.025	243.947	316.83	316.83	316.83
100	362.12	463.415	365.462	342.402	463.42	463.42	463.42
105	610.44	638.956	537.605	466.881	638.96	638.96	638.96
109	1,000.00	1,000.000	870.434	587.551	1,000.00	1,000.00	1,000.00
110	—	—	999.999	624.586	—	—	—
114	—	—	—	1,000.000	—	—	—

shown are composites, i.e., composites of all issue ages weighted for the distribution among the various ages. Two sets of values are shown: present values (at the assumed interest rate) under original assumptions, i.e., assumptions used for rate-testing purposes; and present values (at the actual portfolio interest rates) under actual experience through 1971 and experience projected beyond 1971 based on the most current available information.

Table 8-8 is subject to varying interpretations, partly because of the intricate interrelationships among premiums, profits, interest, and mortality.

However, the information seems to suggest that ratebook assumptions for mortality on older blocks of business were adequate, i.e., were implicitly loaded with margins for conservatism. For newer issues the risks inherent in the mortality table are, of course, greater; for example, as respects the 5-year term plan, mortality at 115 percent of expected would consume all of the projected profits on 1970 issues. On the other hand, if the risk of adverse deviation were greatest some years after issue, a somewhat greater percentage of adversity would be tolerable because the present value of such adverse deviation would be

Table 8–6.

EFFECT OF VARYING MORTALITY RATES* ON BENEFIT RESERVES VALUATION PREMIUMS FOR 1971
ISSUES OF SELECTED PLANS AND AGES

Plan	Age	1955–60 Basic Select and Ultimate			58 CSO	Crazy Quilt Ratebook Assumptions
		100%	*110%*	*150%*		
Whole life	10	$ 4.22	$ 4.33	$ 4.77	$ 5.04	$ 4.22
	35	11.11	11.49	12.90	12.61	11.11
	60	33.30	34.95	41.13	44.31	33.30
20-pay life	10	7.12	7.23	7.67	8.06	7.08
	35	16.03	16.35	17.59	17.61	16.16
5-year R&C term	35	1.98	2.16	2.89	3.26	2.37
25-year decreasing term	35	3.72	3.89	4.55	5.03	3.72

* All other assumptions held constant.

less. However, a significant proportion of total expected profits would have been recognized, and while the present value of profits at issue might not fall below zero, the pattern of reported profits could well be positive in the early years and negative in the later durations.

The analysis of mortality, and an evaluation of the suitability of a provision for adverse deviation, is an extremely complex process which only an actuary is capable of carrying out. The accountant's responsibility is to see that the actuary's evaluation is oriented to financial reporting considerations, and it would not be improper for the accountant to inquire as to the relationships among mortality, the present value of profits, and the possible patterns of profits associated with the proposed provision for adverse deviation.

Provisions for Adverse Deviation

Any given mortality table based on the experience of several insurance companies represents the *aggregate* experience of the companies. The actual experience of the individual companies contributing to such a study will usually vary considerably. The so-called law of large numbers can only be depended on when dealing with large numbers. When the country's smallest life insurance company bases its mortality assumption on, say, the 1955–60 table, it is merely hoping for the best; it has no assurance that its own experience will even approximate the tabular pattern. When the country's largest company adopts a table, it has more confidence that its own experience will fit the indicated curve of mortality, but even the largest

company's exposure base may be somewhat limited in relation to the universe underlying the table. So it, too, hopes for the best.

Companies can take steps to limit the degree of adverse variability from the predicted curve of mortality. High underwriting standards help. Reinsurance provides some degree of protection. Stop-loss reinsurance generally limits losses to a given amount or a given percentage of expected mortality. When all is said and done, however, every company is exposed to some degree of the risk of adverse deviation.

There are, of course, forces operating in the opposite direction, too. Tables used for life insurance usually do not project improvements in mortality. Strict underwriting will improve the chances that mortality will turn out to be favorable in relation to the assumptions. Adverse deviation is a probability, but so is favorable deviation. The mortality table itself might be viewed as a kind of "balance" between the probability of adverse deviation on the one hand and favorable deviation on the other.

What constitutes a "suitable" provision for adverse deviation is ultimately a matter for the actuary's judgment. In terms of accounting principles, only the broadest of guidelines can be offered.

Older blocks of business. In general, mortality tables appropriate at the time of issue should generally be used for purposes of calculating adjusted reserves on older blocks of business. The tables were used in a period of improving mortality, which means that margins were inherent in the tables. Some tables, such as the statutory tables, provide for intentional additional margins. Use of statutory tables should be

Table 8-7.

EFFECT OF VARYING MORTALITY RATES* ON BENEFIT RESERVE FACTORS AT SELECTED DURATIONS
FOR 1971 ISSUES OF SELECTED PLANS AND AGES

Plan	Age	Duration	1955–60 Basic Select and Ultimate 100%	110%	150%	58 CSO	Crazy Quilt Ratebook Assumptions
Whole life	10	1	$ 4.19	$ 4.29	$ 4.67	$ 4.58	$ 4.19
		2	9.68	9.89	10.70	10.02	9.68
		3	15.40	15.74	16.97	15.71	15.40
		5	27.72	28.29	30.42	27.98	27.72
		7	40.36	41.17	44.21	40.60	40.36
		10	60.89	62.09	66.54	61.15	60.89
		15	99.38	101.27	108.18	100.56	99.38
		20	145.01	147.73	157.63	147.47	145.01
		30	258.73	263.73	282.49	262.54	258.57
		40	386.50	394.10	421.56	391.53	386.50
	35	1	11.07	11.42	12.72	11.73	11.07
		2	24.89	25.62	28.40	25.35	24.89
		3	38.61	39.72	43.92	38.99	38.61
		5	65.89	67.75	74.75	66.20	65.89
		7	94.86	97.49	107.34	94.98	94.86
		10	142.62	146.46	160.81	142.36	142.62
		15	230.19	235.97	257.30	230.49	230.19
		20	324.43	331.71	358.33	326.95	324.43
		30	516.25	525.01	556.40	523.39	516.25
		40	674.15	682.60	712.23	681.96	674.15
	60	1	31.44	32.84	38.07	35.60	31.44
		2	64.29	66.97	76.79	65.64	64.29
		3	94.90	98.69	112.45	94.56	94.90
		5	153.73	159.30	179.18	152.37	153.73
		7	215.28	222.69	248.81	210.16	215.28
		10	313.59	323.89	359.81	296.69	313.60
		15	463.07	475.99	520.56	433.71	463.08
		20	585.41	597.90	640.86	562.42	585.44
		30	780.48	789.44	820.94	761.58	780.83
20-pay life	35	1	16.15	16.45	17.56	16.90	16.29
		2	37.07	37.71	40.08	37.76	37.37
		3	56.55	57.51	61.09	57.29	57.04
		5	96.48	98.09	104.06	97.49	97.36
		7	139.29	141.61	150.22	140.58	139.82
		10	209.90	213.44	226.47	211.82	209.42
		15	342.46	348.13	368.77	347.59	341.24
		20	494.47	502.24	530.37	506.27	493.98
		30	652.81	660.54	687.99	664.33	652.85
		40	766.82	773.91	798.49	776.56	766.04
5-year R & C term	35	1	1.65	1.80	2.39	2.07	2.05
		2	3.25	3.53	4.67	3.13	4.19
		3	4.86	5.29	6.97	4.22	6.44
		5	8.00	8.68	11.38	6.13	11.10
		7	13.59	14.73	19.20	10.12	18.99
		10	18.63	20.14	26.04	12.95	26.59
		15	40.39	43.48	55.42	28.20	58.81
		20	66.66	71.49	90.13	48.88	101.80
		30	68.45	75.18	101.64	49.78	116.07
		35	19.69	21.70	29.83	22.94	29.83
25-year decreasing term	35	1	1.31	1.44	1.95	1.75	1.31
		2	2.40	2.64	3.57	2.41	2.40
		3	3.43	3.76	5.10	3.08	3.43
		5	5.34	5.85	7.91	4.35	5.34
		7	7.39	8.09	10.92	5.55	7.39
		10	9.17	10.05	13.54	6.24	9.17
		15	9.14	10.01	13.45	5.41	9.14
		20	6.06	6.66	9.04	3.10	6.06
		25	1.69	1.86	2.54	1.95	1.69

* All other assumptions held constant.

challenged. For example, the 1941 CSO table represents experience of 1930–1940, and that table was generally used for purposes of statutory valuations through 1965 (although some companies adopted the 1958 CSO table prior to the mandatory date). Experience during, say, 1955–1960 was significantly more favorable than is indicated by the 1941 CSO table and is expected to remain significantly more favorable in the future. So use of the 1941 CSO table for issues after 1950 should be challenged.

In short, provisions for adverse deviation on older blocks of business should be reasonable. Use of 200 percent of expected would probably be unreasonable. Use of 50 percent of expected would probably be unreasonable, too. Use of 90 percent, 100 percent, 110 percent, or some value that lies within a fairly narrow interval might be reasonable. The assumption used should not attempt to provide for calamity or solvency; it should represent an estimate of future mortality appropriate at the time of issue modified to reflect the degree of prudence that should always be associated with long-term accounting estimates.

In Crazy Quilt's case, tables used for rate-testing purposes were deemed to provide adequately for adverse deviation on older blocks of business.

Newer blocks of business. It is well-known that there has been no dramatic improvement in mortality for many years. Nor would it be prudent to assume improvement in the future with respect to insured lives.* This is another way of saying that one cannot assume that tables based on recent experience contain implicit margins such as would be the case if the mortality rate were to continue to decrease.

So consideration should normally be given to providing additional margins with respect to assumed mortality on recent issues if the underlying table is of recent vintage. It is, of course, not possible to generalize about how much of a margin is warranted.

It should not automatically be assumed that use of the statutory tables—which are already loaded—would necessarily be appropriate. A comparison of 1958 CSO mortality (reflecting 1950–54 experience with an additional margin for adverse experience) with mortality rates shown in the 1955–60 table (reflecting 1955–60 experience with no additional margins) indicates that 1958 CSO mortality, while satisfying statutory requirements for safety, may be unduly conservative for purposes of adjusted reserves (all rates are ultimate):

Age	1958 CSO Death Rate Per 1,000 Insureds	1955–60 Death Rate Per 1,000 Insureds	1958 CSO As % of 1955–60
15	1.5	.6	250%
25	1.9	1.0	190
35	2.5	1.3	192
45	5.4	3.7	146
55	13.0	10.7	122
65	31.8	27.5	116
75	73.4	62.7	117
85	161.1	147.7	109
95	351.2	335.0	105

For a large company whose experience more closely parallels 1955–60 experience, or for a newer company whose losses are limited by an irrevocable stop-loss agreement* to, say, 110 percent of expected mortality under the 1955–60 table, or for any company whose underwriting standards are significantly more strict than the average, use of the 1958 CSO table would probably not be appropriate for new issues.

On the other hand, for a company whose experience has deviated significantly from recent industry experience, or a newer company with little experience or a company with liberal underwriting standards, use of the 1958 CSO table or some variation thereof may be appropriate.

In any event, the table that is finally chosen should be a table that over the long term gives reasonable assurance of producing a ratio of actual to expected mortality that is slightly less than 100 percent in the case of life insurance and slightly more than 100 percent in the case of annuities.

Effect of exposure base. Adverse deviation is regarded in this book as an aggregative concept, which means simply that it has reference to an entire book of business, not a single policy or even a sizeable cohort of policies within a book of business.

That means among other things that the larger the book of business in force, the more likely it is that mortality experience will tend toward the predicted curve of mortality.**

The larger the book of business, then, the more confidence a company will have that its mortality experience will approximate assumed. And the more confidence a company has about that, the less the required margin for conservatism.

---

*This is hypothetical, since stop-loss contracts are always terminable before the end of the mortality table. Further, effective stop-loss coverages are very rare.

**A *likely tendency* is all there is. The experience of even the largest companies can deviate significantly from expected mortality.

---

*The reverse would be true for annuitant mortality.

Table 8–8.

PRESENT VALUES AT ISSUE PER $1,000 ORIGINALLY ISSUED OF PROFITS, PREMIUMS, AND MORTALITY

Plan	Sample Issue Year	Composite Present Values Under Original Rate Test Projections				Composite Present Values Recreating Experience To 1971 and Revising Projections Beyond 1971 Based on Most Current Data			
				Mortality				*Mortality*	
		Profits	*Premiums*	*Amount*	*% of Premiums*	*Profits*	*Premiums*	*Amount*	*% of Premiums*
Par whole life	1945	$ 7.48	$290.40	$ 89.28	31%	$48.16	$334.13	$69.12	21%
	1950	9.64	286.76	68.13	24	29.83	317.63	56.63	18
	1955	13.27	322.34	106.86	33	23.98	242.02	45.00	19
	1960	8.33	286.96	89.36	41	19.49	208.45	35.49	17
	1965	1.19	217.32	53.36	24	8.31	211.65	48.94	23
	1970	2.46	188.69	40.85	22	(7.29)	197.33	47.51	24
Whole life	1945	8.02	238.14	92.28	39	52.36	243.06	62.17	26
	1950	17.04	220.85	69.25	31	45.62	222.35	51.47	23
	1955	11.73	232.55	76.32	33	58.55	244.03	64.00	26
	1960	9.71	233.29	86.72	37	21.87	159.03	40.50	25
	1965	10.45	213.91	84.09	39	28.53	189.69	61.03	32
	1970	12.12	169.04	60.53	36	16.22	174.40	61.11	35
20-pay life	1945	5.53	261.31	86.43	33	52.92	263.97	50.52	19
	1950	12.37	248.49	65.56	26	51.18	250.23	43.93	18
	1955	3.66	233.44	61.95	26	48.28	229.63	39.13	17
	1960	4.56	225.08	54.85	24	34.38	203.40	36.23	18
	1965	4.49	182.73	46.71	26	23.54	166.78	32.41	19
	1970	17.13	160.66	33.84	21	20.87	161.11	32.48	20
20-year endowment	1945	9.93	501.94	71.06	14	42.99	440.46	39.82	9
	1950	7.97	465.87	54.98	12	43.35	402.96	39.55	10
	1955	9.48	475.92	61.27	13	62.52	393.50	39.20	10
	1960	9.48	475.92	61.27	13	63.24	378.24	36.73	10
5-year R&C term	1945	7.14	50.56	21.48	42	16.19	49.18	10.83	22
	1950	14.83	57.54	20.43	36	20.70	60.22	16.00	27
	1955	12.77	56.42	21.83	39	17.71	55.79	15.62	28
	1960	8.87	46.37	17.72	38	6.44	32.98	9.40	29
	1965	3.67	42.79	21.17	49	4.58	40.12	17.38	43
	1970	3.03	38.00	17.79	47	2.72	39.11	18.55	47
25-year decreasing term	1960	14.95	55.96	21.56	39	9.72	38.87	12.54	32
	1965	9.81	45.05	17.81	40	9.18	41.52	14.41	35
	1970	10.23	41.28	14.17	34	10.22	42.62	14.76	35

The question naturally arises as to whether a company should be given advance credit for increasing production in making its provision for adverse deviation in the mortality assumption. In principle, there is no reason why not. Thus, there is no theoretical objection to grading the provision for adverse deviation to a series of provisions that would be appropriate at various time intervals for the then-expected volume of insurance in force, projected using conservative assumptions. Just as a mortality assumption will usually recognize early mortality savings resulting from the underwriting process, so should it recognize that the exposure base will be growing in the future. To do otherwise would seem to conflict, at least partially, with the going-concern assumption.

As a practical matter, advance recognition is *always* given for an increasing exposure base. There is no way a company in its first few years of operation could have any confidence that its aggregate mortality, measured purely in terms of the volume of business in force, would follow any curve at all; mortality on a tiny book of business is more akin to gambling than to insurance.*

Effect of reinsurance. Standard ceded reinsurance arrangements ostensibly wouldn't have much, if

---

*As will be seen in Chapter 24, advance recognition of an increasing exposure base would also normally be given in providing for maintenance and overhead in a test for loss recognition.

any, effect on a company's mortality assumption. Reinsurance which limits a company's loss to its stated retention protects surplus, but it generally has no impact on the pattern of mortality applicable to the retained portion (unless the reinsurance arrangement is biased in favor of one of the parties). However, under the theory that the provision for adverse deviation should take aggregate exposures into consideration, then reinsurance will have an effect on the provision. Assuming zero retention, mortality would of course be zero and no provision for adverse deviation would be needed. As retention increases, so does the risk of adverse deviation. At some point the aggregate retained amount could become sufficiently large to warrant a reduction in the provision per unit of insurance in force, but until that point is reached, the provision for adverse deviation will tend to vary with the retention limit.

Another View of Adverse Deviation*

The foregoing comments adopt the view that the provision for adverse deviation should consider the aggregate risk "portfolio" of the insurance company and that the larger and more stable the portfolio, the smaller will be the provision for adverse deviation per unit of insurance in force. This general approach appears to be consistent with the concept of adverse deviation as a margin for conservatism, as propounded in Chapter 6.

An alternative view of adverse deviation would hold that the provision is directly related to the policies themselves and does not depend on characteristics of the rest of the portfolio. According to this view, the same type of insurance written under similar conditions with similar underwriting would have essentially the same mortality assumption whether the business is written in a large company or a small company. The aggregate provision for adverse deviation would increase proportionally as the business in force increases. This view appears to be closely allied to the pure release-from-risk theory.

Some believe that if two companies are exactly the same in every way except that one is 10 times as large as the other, then the larger company should report 10 times the income of the smaller company in each accounting period. Under the alternative view of adverse deviation, it would. Under the view of the provision for adverse deviation as a margin for con-

servatism that should take into account the size of the exposure base, it wouldn't. The larger company would probably report more than 10 times the income of the smaller company in the early durations and less than 10 times in the later durations.*

This book argues for consistent use of the first view of the provision for adverse deviation for reasons explained in Chapter 6. At the present time, however, both approaches are being used and both are presumably acceptable.

Term Renewal Mortality

Many term insurance policies are renewable at the option of the insured on the expiry date. In some cases it can be demonstrated that there is selection against the insurance company at the time of renewal —that those in poor health will have a greater tendency to renew than those in good health. In such cases mortality subsequent to renewal is higher than normal. When term renewal mortality is expected to be higher than normal, the mortality assumption used for purposes of calculating the adjusted reserves should reflect the higher level. Sometimes there is some question over the extent to which extra mortality on renewal is actually experienced; frequently the statistics necessary to decide the question one way or another for a particular company are not available. In cases in which statistics are lacking and there is some question as to whether extra mortality will be experienced, the question should be resolved by being conservative. In other words, in the absence of compelling evidence to the contrary, extra mortality on renewal should be assumed. The modifications to be made to recognize extra mortality should be based on the company's experience, if the experience data are available; if not, the modification should be based on the most relevant external data.

Under certain limited circumstances there may be no practical need to provide for extra mortality. For example, if the renewal period is of very short duration and the slope of the mortality curve is not steep during the period, the incidence of extra mortality might reasonably correspond to the incidence of extra gross premiums available to cover it.

Normally, however, theory and prudence would call for anticipating the extra mortality in calculating adjusted reserves.

---

*This discussion is based on comments by Richard S. Robertson, FSA, of the Lincoln National Life Insurance Company in a letter dated November 5, 1973.

*Ultimately, of course, the larger company will report total earnings for all years equal to 10 times the total earnings reported by the smaller company. The provision for adverse deviation only affects the incidence of reported earnings.

Crazy Quilt Life offers a five-year renewable and convertible term policy and, for ratemaking purposes, assumes mortality on renewal at a scale that eventually reaches 125 percent of standard mortality. This is discussed at some length in Chapter 3.

Crazy Quilt carried this assumption into its adjusted reserves. The effect on the reserves was dramatic. A comparison of reserves calculated using standard 1955–60 mortality (which approximates Crazy Quilt's standard mortality assumption) with reserves calculated using Crazy's Quilt's ratebook assumptions is shown in Table 8–7 and may be summarized as follows:

Adjusted Benefit
Reserve Per $1,000
For Issue Age 35

Duration	Standard Mortality	Ratebook Assumptions
1	$ 1.65	$ 2.05
2	3.25	4.19
3	4.86	6.44
5	8.00	11.10
7	13.59	18.99
10	18.63	26.59
15	40.39	58.81
20	66.66	101.80
30	58.45	116.07
35	19.69	29.83

The effect is further dramatized by comparing net level statutory reserves with adjusted reserves for the various ratebook eras as of December 31, 1971:

		Benefit Reserves (000)	
Ratebook Era	In Force (000,000)	Statutory Net Level	Adjusted
1941–47	$ 1	$ 3	$ 19
1948–51	4	37	323
1952–56	14	140	1,078
1957–61	16	118	719
1962–64	33	102	785
1965–67	80	198	1,348
1968–69	95	224	919
1970–71	156	320	524
	$399	$1,142	$5,715

It should be noted that the adjusted reserves also provide for the cost of conversion (discussed below), which generally has the effect of further increasing the level of the reserves.

The "When Paid" Assumption

Normally, for purposes of calculating adjusted reserves mortality should be distributed to the portion of the policy year in which it occurs. When deaths are assumed to occur at the end of the year, an additional reserve for immediate payment of claims, computed using assumptions that would have been appropriate to the underlying plan, should be provided for.

A reserve for non-deduction of deferred fractional premiums is usually necessary when the company in fact does not deduct deferred fractional premiums and reserve calculations are based on the assumption of receipt of a full annual premium without diminution for modes other than annual.

Reserve calculation techniques are discussed further in Chapter 12.

Settlement Options

Death claims are payable in the form of a lump sum or various settlement options mandated by the policyholder before his death or chosen by the beneficiary at the time of the insured's death.

Sometimes it is known in advance that the cost of a particular option differs from the amount nominally payable at death.

Suppose, for example, that while the face amount insured is $1,000, it is estimated that settlements will be distributed among the following options, each of which has a somewhat different cost:

Option	Percentage Settled	Cost of Settlement	Weighted Average Settlement Cost
Lump sum	50%	$1,000	$500
Held at interest	15	900	135
Certain installments	20	850	170
Life income	15	800	120
	100%		$925

Some would argue that the benefit that should be provided for is $925 in this case, not $1,000.

Except for special beneficiary provisions requested by the policyholder, the choice of a settlement option is at the discretion of the beneficiary. A new contract arises in respect of a beneficiary's choice, and settlement options should be accounted for as new contracts. For the sake of consistency, special beneficiary provisions should be treated the same way.

At such time as the proceeds are applied to purchase one of the options, the appropriate deposit liability or reserve should be established. In the case of amounts held at interest and amounts payable in certain installments, the proceeds should be credited directly to a liability account. In the case of supplementary contracts involving life contingencies, the proceeds should be recorded as revenue and a reserve should be established based on the then-current assumptions, just as if a new contract had been sold.*

Miscellaneous Ordinary Benefits and Coverages

Mortality and other aspects of reserving for accidental death benefits, supplementary contracts involving life contingencies, substandard business, and other miscellaneous benefits and coverages are discussed in Chapter 11.

Disclosure

The life insurance audit guide suggests that the mortality table used for each significant block of business should be disclosed in a note to the financial statements.[5] A method of making such disclosure for Crazy Quilt Life's ordinary business is discussed in Chapter 7.

It is often difficult to describe a mortality table. If the table is based on the company's own experience, it is helpful to say so, but it would be more helpful to describe the relationship, if any, between the table used and commonly-used published tables, for example: "Assumed mortality is equal to approximately 105 percent of mortality according to the 1955–60 Basic Table."

As a practical matter, there is a limit on the extent to which information on mortality can be disclosed in a simple note to the financial statements, and there is a limit on the extent to which the reader can evaluate the significance of a mortality assumption. As a practical matter, then, disclosure should be limited to a general description of the mortality basis.

When there are significant amounts of renewable term business and the company provides for extra mortality on renewal, the fact should preferably be disclosed. Otherwise the reader is entitled to believe that the indicated tables were used without modification for such special conditions.

Term Conversions

Just as there may tend to be some degree of selec-

tion against the company at the time of renewal, so might there be some degree of adverse selection at the time of conversion. A 10-year nonrenewable term policy that is convertible at any time into a permanent policy invites adverse selection.

Opinions differ as to whether term conversion reserves are really needed, particularly where a company encourages conversion.* Furthermore, statistics on the subject are scanty. Nevertheless, there is sufficient evidence ** that adverse selection occurs at the time of conversion to warrant careful consideration by any company writing significant amounts of convertible term business. Doubt should generally be resolved by providing for extra mortality.

Calculating the Cost of Conversion

Extra mortality on term conversions is measured by comparing experience under standard policies with experience under converted policies. If at the time of issuing the converted policy the present value of mortality on converted policies is $100 per $1,000 and the present value of mortality on standard policies is $50 per 1,000, then the present value of extra mortality is $50 per $1,000 converted.

However, if acquisition costs for a standard policy are $50 per $1,000 but only $25 for a converted policy (because there is no underwriting and, in addition, conversion may involve less marketing effort and expense), then conversion results in saving $25 by comparison with the sale of a standard policy.

It is tempting to conclude in this case that the cost of conversion at the time of conversion is $25—extra mortality of $50 less expense savings of $25.

Suppose, however, that the present value of profits on standard policies is $25. Should the cost of conversion be further reduced by the $25 profit, thus producing zero cost? The effect of doing this would be to produce a zero profit on the converted policy. Viewed another way, profits on the term policy *and* the converted policy would be recognized during the premium-paying period of the term policy.

That would constitute a violation of the matching

---

*For supplementary contracts with life contingencies whose guaranteed payments are based on an obsolete mortality table, this procedure could result in a loss at the time of the beneficiary's election.

*Of course, the degree of "encouragement" is subject to change from year to year; it cannot be deemed a constant.

**For example, one large company that writes substantial amounts of convertible term insurance determined after 20 years of study that there was indeed extra mortality on converted policies, and the additional reserves produced by this assumption were material.

principle; costs would not be charged to expense in proportion to the recognition of premium revenue.

Therefore the cost of conversion should preferably be computed as the difference between the present value of profits on a standard policy at the moment of issue and the present value of profits on a converted policy at the moment of conversion, for the same attained age. This will produce a "normal" profit on the converted policy.

Alternatively, the term and converted policies could be treated as a continuum with a variable premium. This would appear to be less practicable than accounting for the contracts separately.

In either case it is necessary to estimate the distribution of converted policies among the various plans and weight the cost of conversion accordingly.

The cost of conversion is treated as an additional benefit for purposes of calculating reserves for the underlying term policy. The amount of the benefit in any year is equal to the cost of conversion per unit converted multiplied by the percentage expected to convert in the given year. The cost of conversion is thus accrued systematically in the form of a component of the reserve on the converted term policy. This is the pre-conversion reserve.

When the term policy is converted the conversion reserve is released. In theory, the reserve on the converted policy at duration zero should include the reserve thus released. This is the post-conversion reserve; it should be run off in proportion to the run-off of differential experience under the converted policy.

To the extent that the actual percentage converting differs from the percentage expected to convert, there will be a gain or loss at the time of conversion.

To the extent that assumed experience under the converted policy differs from the experience assumed for purposes of calculating the cost of conversion, there will also be a gain or loss at the time of conversion attributable to such difference; the gain or loss would be measured by the difference between the cost of conversion reserve component released in respect of the term policy and the cost of conversion reserve component established at duration zero in respect of the converted policy. Since conversion may occur many years after issue of the term plan, the cost of conversion as calculated at the time of conversion (i.e., the cost of conversion calculated for use in reserving for convertible term plans then being issued) will reflect then-current assumptions. It is appropriate to establish the post-conversion reserve on the basis of the revised assumptions if the contracts

are accounted for as separate phenomena. When the contracts are accounted for as a continuum, it would be appropriate to retain the initial assumptions. As suggested previously, treating the contracts as a continuum involves such complexity as to rule it out as a viable alternative for most companies.*

Operation of the Conversion Mechanism

Crazy Quilt Life computed an estimated cost of conversion for all of its convertible term plans; the cost was equal to the difference between the present value of profits on standard plans and the present value of profits on converted plans. The cost was used in rate tests and was carried into Crazy Quilt's calculations of adjusted reserves.

For convertible term issues to males age 45 in 1956, for example, the cost of conversion per $1,000 converted at age 60 was computed as $51.49, as follows:

Present value per $1,000 of profits for issue age 60 on:	
Standard policies	$ 8.46
Converted policies	(43.03)
	$ 51.49

This net cost was comprised of the following elements:

	Present Value Per $1,000 Issued		
	Standard Policy	Converted Policy	Net
Premiums	$ 528.66	$ 531.42	$ 2.76
Deaths	(285.92)	(349.58)	(63.66)
Surrender values	(90.33)	(85.31)	5.02
First-year expenses	(95.04)	(91.94)	3.10
Renewal expenses	(48.91)	(47.62)	1.29
	$ 8.46	$ (43.03)	$(51.49)

Note that the cost of conversion recognizes differentials from all sources (including differences in withdrawal rates; converted policies are typically more persistent than standard policies).

The rate test for 1956 issues at age 45 assumed that 30 percent of those persisting at age 60—that is,

---

*The method of accounting for the cost of conversion described in this chapter is only one of several possible approaches. Any of the various approaches might be considered acceptable. The important thing, it would seem, is to develop an approach that is logical and reasonable and does justice to the concepts of matching costs with premium revenues while providing for adverse deviation.

in the 16th year after issue—would convert to a permanent plan. The 16th-year cost of conversion included in the rate was computed as follows:

Percentage of original insureds persisting prior to conversion at 16th duration	11.20%
Percentage converting at 16th duration	30.00%
Percentage of original insureds converting at 16th duration	3.36%
Cost of conversion per $1,000 converted at age 60	$51.49
Rate test cost of conversion in 16th duration per unit issued	$ 1.73

This cost was treated as a benefit payable in the 16th year in calculating reserves on 1956 issues at age 45 of the underlying term plan.

It can be seen that if the effective actual conversion rate differs from assumed, a gain or loss at the time of conversion will result. Such gain or loss would be preceded by other gains or losses to the extent of any deviations in persistency, since the cost of conversion is effectively reserved for by applying fixed factors to the amount of insurance in force.

Switching now to 1971, the outlook on term conversions had changed. Instead of a cost of conversion of $51.49 per $1,000 converted, as computed in 1956, Crazy Quilt projected the cost of conversion at age 60 as $87.79 in 1971, as follows:

	Present Value Per $1,000 Issued		
	Standard Policy	Converted Policy	Net
Premiums	$ 422.93	$ 434.65	$ 11.72
Deaths	(222.60)	(337.17)	(114.57)
Surrender values	(47.37)	(38.74)	8.63
First-year expenses	(85.75)	(80.25)	5.50
Renewal expenses	(40.52)	(39.59)	.93
	$ 26.69	$ (61.10)	$ (87.79)

And the adjusted reserve on the converted plan was increased by $87.79 at the moment of issue. The effect was to recognize an additional loss on conversion of $36.30:

Amount per $1,000 provided for on converted plan	$87.79
Amount per $1,000 released from term reserves	51.49
	$36.30

The $87.79 accrued in the adjusted reserve on the converted plan represents the post-conversion reserve; it runs off as the experience differences emerge, and a normal profit will be produced on the converted plan.

The pattern of deviations from expected values defies analysis in the case of a convertible term policy, as is probably apparent.

The cost of conversion reserve component, with respect to both the pre-conversion and post-conversion reserves, could be segregated into expense and benefit elements for purposes of balance sheet and income statement classifications. This would have very little effect and, in view of the difficulty of making such segregations, the practice should be discouraged. The net cost of conversion is best regarded as a benefit transaction.

The cost of conversion is typically innocuous during the early years of a convertible policy's life, and it may even be positive at the younger ages. The cost usually becomes quite significant for conversions that take place at the older ages.

Effect on Reserves

Provision for the cost of conversion can produce sizeable increases in the level of reserves on convertible term business, particularly at the later durations. In Crazy Quilt Life's case, for example, the use of select and ultimate mortality tables plus provision for the cost of conversion produced reserves on the Company's 25-year convertible decreasing term plan that were 26 percent greater than statutory at December 31, 1971:

Ratebook Era	In Force (000,000)	Net Level Statutory Reserve (000)	Adjusted Benefit Reserve (000)
1957–61	$ 14	$ 72	$ 220
1962–69	530	3,655	5,163
1970–71	472	1,451	1,141
	$1,016	$5,178	$6,524

For the converted plans the effect can also be significant, as is apparent from a comparison of reserve factors per $1,000 for issues at age 60 of whole life policies sold standard and issued in connection with a conversion:

Year	Standard Plan	Converted Plan
1	$ 31.44	$116.44
2	64.29	144.32
3	94.90	171.29
5	153.73	223.72
7	215.28	275.72
10	313.60	354.02
15	463.08	481.56
20	585.44	601.45
25	690.77	703.37
30	780.83	791.29
35	864.09	879.97
40	982.95	982.95

Combined Renewal and Conversion

Some term plans are renewable *or* convertible at the option of the policyholder. It is frequently argued —with considerable logic—that so long as a contract is renewable, adverse selection will take place on renewals but mortality on conversions that occur during the renewal periods will be standard. The reasoning is that those in poor health have no incentive to convert to a higher-premium permanent plan so long as they can renew their policies at the cheaper term rates, and that adverse selection on conversions is limited to conversions occurring after the renewal right has expired.

The treatment of conversion costs depends in part on the nature of the underlying statistics. In Crazy Quilt's case, for example, conversion mortality was studied in terms of *all* conversions; information was not available on the difference between (1) mortality on policies converted during the period of the renewal privilege and (2) mortality on policies converted in periods when the renewal privilege was not operative. To be consistent with the underlying data, Crazy Quilt provided for the cost of conversion without regard for whether the policy was renewable at the time of conversion. The effect was to spread the cost of conversion over all convertible term policies.

This procedure should be monitored when the mix of business as between renewable and convertible policies and convertible-only policies is changing materially, since the base from which the underlying statistics derive may begin to differ significantly from the base to which they are applied.

Separate Conversion Reserves

The preceding discussion assumes that (1) the pre-conversion reserve is accumulated as part of the reserve on the basic term plan and (2) the post-conversion reserve is established, and runs off, as part of the reserve on the basic converted plan.

Such refinement would be difficult to implement in practice. As respects the pre-conversion reserve, it may be desirable to group all term plans—convertible or not—into one model. In that case, it would be desirable to ignore the cost of conversion in calculating the basic reserves simply because it is not applicable to all the plans included in the model.

As respects the post-conversion reserve, each converted plan (or models of converted plans) will require two reserve calculations, one for standard policies and one for converted policies, if the conversion reserves are to be carried as part of the basic reserves. In other words, the amount of valuation work is approximately double.

Other practical difficulties could be cited, but the point is that it will often be desirable to make a separate calculation of the conversion reserves, and there should be no objection to separately-calculated amounts.

Group Conversions

The cost of a group conversion is charged (1) to the group itself if the case is experience-rated or (2) to the group line of business as a whole if the case is not experience-rated. In the former case the charge is offset by a reduction in the experience rating refund reserve if the reserve is positive. In the latter case, and in retention cases in which the experience rating reserve is negative, the charge is effectively made to income.

If the charges are treated as income to the ordinary line of business and no reserve is set up, then (1) when the charge has been made to a positive experience rating account, the effect is a net credit to income and future extra mortality is simply absorbed as it occurs; and (2) when the charge has been made to a negative experience rating account or to the group line as a whole, the effect on income is zero and future extra mortality is absorbed as it occurs. In the former case, income is credited currently and future income is understated. In the latter case, prior profits may be regarded as having been overstated to the extent of the cost of conversion computed as of the date of conversion. However, as a practical matter, because group contracts are typically renewable yearly, the cost of conversion can be regarded as being applicable to the current year.

In all cases in which term conversions are significant, post-conversion reserves should be established and should be run off in proportion to the emerging difference between experience on standard policies and experience on converted policies.

Philosophies differ among companies as to what the cost of conversion should cover. Further, competitive considerations tend to limit the amount of the charge to an experience rating account. So the cost of conversion may not produce a normal profit on the converted policy; the profit on the converted policy is probably less than normal in most cases.

But the actual charge made should be presumed to be rational. For example, the company obtains something in return for any reduction in what would be an "appropriate" cost of conversion, namely, continued good will of its group contract-holders as well as new ordinary volume that might not otherwise be sold.

Therefore, subject only to tests of loss recognition, the conversion reserve can logically be established in an amount equivalent to the charge to the group line of business. If a company wishes to establish a reserve on a basis that will produce a normal profit on the converted plan, on the theory that any difference between the reserve and the group charge is properly chargeable (or creditable) to group operations in the year of conversion—in other words, on the theory that all of the benefits of the cost differential accrue immediately to the group department—that practice would also be acceptable.

Disclosure

When there is a material volume of convertible term business in force and provisions for the cost of conversion produce, or are believed to produce, a material impact on the reserves, the fact that the company reserves for the cost of conversion should preferably be disclosed in notes to the financial statements.

Withdrawals

Selection of a scale of withdrawals for purposes of calculating adjusted reserves is one of the more challenging aspects of a conversion to generally accepted accounting principles. The law of large numbers applies, but very imperfectly by comparison with the mortality assumption. Withdrawals are affected by agent quality, underwriting, conservation efforts, advertising, characteristics of the insureds, premium levels, cash value scales, dividend scales (in the case of participating insurance), inflation, interest rates, the general state of the economy, and other factors.

So the assumed withdrawal rate is somewhat in the nature of an educated guess. Risks of deviation from expected withdrawal rates can be quantified, but the interval of the estimate is necessarily very wide.

Audit Guide Provisions

The life insurance audit guide notes that reserves computed without regard for withdrawals could produce adjusted benefit reserves that are "less than expected nonforfeiture benefits." [6] This is acceptable

so long as provision is made for such nonforfeiture benefits, which means that nonforfeiture benefits weighted for the probability of surrender should be treated as benefits in calculating the reserves.

The guide also notes that an assumption for withdrawals is necessary regardless of whether or not a policy provides cash values because withdrawals affect anticipated valuation premiums and death benefits and therefore the level of the adjusted reserve.

The guide permits reserves to be less than cash values "since, on a going concern basis, it is unrealistic to assume that all policies will be surrendered for cash." [7]

For established companies, the guide suggests that "the company's actual withdrawal experience" should generally form the basis for the withdrawal assumption, modified if necessary for "significant changes in underwriting practices which might affect the validity of historical data." Further, established companies "should use published withdrawal tables . . . only if the results produced by the use of such tables are comparable with the company's actual withdrawal experience." [8]

For newer companies, "industry data or data for companies similar to" the company under consideration should be used; published tables might be used "if such tables are conservative and produce results which are not more favorable than industry experience or the company's experience to date." [9]

The audit guide suggests that assumed withdrawal rates should be fairly refined:

Withdrawal rates used in computing reserves in conformity with generally accepted accounting principles should vary by plan, age, mode of premium payment, duration, and other factors. If composite rates are used, they should be representative of the company's actual mix of business . . . provision for the risk of adverse deviation . . . should be included. [10]

Withdrawal Tables

A withdrawal table is an expression of expected voluntary terminations. Large companies will typically use representations of past experience in constructing a table of withdrawal rates. Newer companies will typically use available industry data, published tables, or adaptations of the withdrawal rates experienced by similar companies for similar products.

Interestingly, it is not unusual to prepare rate tests using two or more withdrawal assumptions while holding the other assumptions—mortality, interest, and expenses—constant. This is done because of the uncertainty associated with the withdrawal assumption. A company generally wants to know how it will fare under various patterns of withdrawals. Initial acquisition costs are the same regardless of the withdrawal rate; obviously there is some point at which margins available to cover such costs are inadequate. A company needs to know its "break-even withdrawal rate", so to speak, to evaluate the risks involved in selling the product.

Adjusted reserves must be computed using a single scale of withdrawals. In the reserving process, there is no counterpart to multiple rate tests. Any errors can only be corrected later, when much of the damage has been done.

As will be seen later in this chapter, the answer to the problem of uncertainty is not to use an extremely conservative withdrawal table.

Table 8–9 shows several "published" withdrawal tables and Crazy Quilt Life's withdrawal assumptions for selected 1971 plans and issue ages.

The published tables do not differentiate by plan or age. They reflect observed withdrawal patterns but no claim is made that they are necessarily appropriate for any given company. They represent a starting point.

Crazy Quilt's assumptions differentiate by plan and age and are based on experience in the immediately preceding ratebook era, with respect to assumed rates in the early years; and a judgmental modification of experience in earlier ratebook eras, with respect to assumed rates in the later years. It will be observed that Crazy Quilt increases assumed withdrawal rates for permanent plans in the extreme durations, on the basis that older insureds tend to withdraw as the need for insurance lessens or the cash value begins to approximate the face amount. No adjustment was made, however, to later withdrawals for decreasing term insurance or 5-year renewable term policies. In the former case it was determined that "freezing" the face amount at a fixed amount after the 20th duration would eliminate lapses attributable to having negligible coverage for a level premium; and the nature of decreasing term was to reduce the face amount as the need for insurance grew less, so the withdrawal problem associated with reduced need was avoided. In the latter case, it was felt that substantially all of the withdrawals by reason of reduced need would take place on the renewal dates, and non-renewals were recognized in the table in each renewal year.

In practice it may not be necessary to vary lapse rates by plan and age, but use of a single table or a

relatively few tables should be monitored constantly. Ideally, actual insurance in force and assumed insurance in force for each major plan and year of issue should be compared annually to see that experience substantially conforms with the assumptions. When it doesn't, new assumptions should be refined. Whenever the deviations are severe enough to trigger the recalculation of acquisition cost factors, as discussed in Chapter 16, the benefit reserve factors should also be recalculated. This is discussed further below.

Nonforfeiture Benefits

The audit guide requires that nonforfeiture benefits be provided for in calculating adjusted reserves. If all nonforfeiture benefits were payable in the form of cash values, the provision would be easy. For any given policy, the value of the nonforfeiture benefit for any year would be the probability of withdrawal in that year, expressed as a percentage of individuals originally insured, multiplied by the cash value. For example, if the percentage of original insureds persisting prior to, say, the 20th year's withdrawals is 30 percent, the withdrawal rate for the year is assumed to be 5 percent, and the cash value is $500, then the assumed benefit provided for is $7.50 (30% × 5% × $500). This assumed benefit, computed for each year, is simply treated as a cash outflow in calculating the reserve factors.

It was pointed out earlier in this chapter that various settlement options can operate to change the true cost of death claims. The same thing is true of nonforfeiture options. Suppose the estimated cost of the reduced paid-up option is 80 percent of the cash value; the estimated cost of the extended term option is 60 percent of the cash value; nonforfeiture options in a given year are expected to be distributed 50 percent to surrenders and 25 percent each to reduced paid-up and extended term; and the cash value is $500. In that event the real surrender cost is $425:

Option	Equivalent Cost	Distribution Of Options	Weighted Surrender Cost
Surrender	$500	50%	$250
Reduced paid-up	400	25	100
Extended term	300	25	75
		100%	$425

The principal argument against recognizing differential settlement option costs is that settlement options should be viewed as new contracts with beneficiaries,

Table 8–9.

SELECTED WITHDRAWAL TABLES

Year	Linton			Moorhead			Selected Crazy Quilt Life 1971 Issues						
							Whole Life		20-Pay Life		25-Year Decreasing Term		5-Year R&C
	A	B	C	R	S	T	Age 25	Age 45	Age 25	Age 45	Age 25	Age 45	Term, Age 35
1	10.0%	20.0%	30.0%	7.00%	12.50%	20.00%	20%	14%	25%	20%	25%	15%	20%
2	6.0	12.0	18.0	5.00	10.00	20.00	7	7	8	4	15	10	14
3	5.0	10.0	15.0	3.50	4.50	7.00	4	4	4	4	12	9	10
4	4.4	8.8	13.2	3.00	3.50	4.50	4	3	4	4	10	8	10
5	4.0	8.0	12.0	2.75	3.00	4.00	4	3	4	4	8	6	12
6	3.6	7.2	10.8	2.50	2.75	3.50	3	3	4	4	8	6	6
7	3.2	6.4	9.6	2.25	2.60	3.00	3	3	4	4	7	5	5
8	2.9	5.8	8.7	2.00	2.50	3.00	3	3	4	4	7	4	5
9	2.7	5.4	8.1	1.80	2.45	3.00	3	2	4	4	6	4	5
10	2.5	5.0	7.5	1.70	2.40	3.00	3	2	4	4	5	3	15
11	2.4	4.8	7.2	1.60	2.35	3.00	2	2	4	4	4	3	8
12	2.3	4.6	6.9	1.55	2.30	3.00	2	2	4	3	4	3	8
13	2.2	4.4	6.6	1.50	2.25	3.00	2	2	4	3	4	3	8
14	2.1	4.2	6.3	1.45	2.20	3.00	2	2	4	3	4	3	7
15	2.0	4.0	6.0	1.40	2.15	3.00	2	2	3	3	4	3	15
16	2.0	4.0	6.0	1.35	2.10	3.00	2	2	3	3	4	3	4
17	2.0	4.0	6.0	1.30	2.05	3.00	2	2	3	3	4	3	3
18	2.0	4.0	6.0	1.25	2.00	3.00	2	2	2	2	4	3	2
19	2.0	4.0	6.0	1.20	1.90	3.00	2	2	2	2	4	3	2
20	2.0	4.0	6.0	1.15	1.80	3.00	2	2	2	2	4	3	15
21	2.0	4.0	6.0	1.10	1.70	3.00	2	3	2	2	4	3	3
22	2.0	4.0	6.0	1.05	1.60	3.00	2	3	2	2	4	3	2
23	2.0	4.0	6.0	1.00	1.50	3.00	2	4	2	3	4	3	2
24	2.0	4.0	6.0	1.00	1.50	3.00	2	4	2	3	4	3	2
25	2.0	4.0	6.0	1.00	1.50	3.00	2	6	2	5			15
26	2.0	4.0	6.0	1.00	1.54	3.04	2	6	2	5			2
27	2.0	4.0	6.0	1.06	1.74	3.24	2	6	2	6			2
28	2.0	4.0	6.0	1.11	1.93	3.43	2	7	2	6			2
29	2.0	4.0	6.0	1.16	2.12	3.62	2	8	2	6			2
30	2.0	4.0	6.0	1.21	2.30	3.84	2	9	2	6			15
35	2.0	4.0	6.0	(Not published beyond			3	11	3	11			
40	2.0	4.0	6.0	30th year)			4	16	5	16			
45	2.0	4.0	6.0				6	23	7	23			
50	2.0	4.0	6.0				9	31	9	31			
55	2.0	4.0	6.0				11	40	11	40			
60	2.0	4.0	6.0				16		16				
65	2.0	4.0	6.0				23		23				
70	2.0	4.0	6.0				31		31				
75	2.0	4.0	6.0				40		40				

Note—Percentages are expressed in relation to amounts in force at the beginning of the year

even when amounts are guaranteed under the original contracts. The exercise of a nonforfeiture option, however, is a feature of the original contract with the original policyholder, and it may be viewed as a part of the contract for accounting purposes. There should be no fundamental objection to weighting the surrender cost for the differential costs of the various nonforfeiture options so long as statistics are available to support the indicated differentials.

As a practical matter, statistics are seldom adequate to support differential costs, and in any event a company might let cash values serve as an approximation of the true settlement costs. To the extent that the cash value is higher than the weighted cost, use of

Table 8–10.

EFFECT OF VARYING WITHDRAWAL RATES* ON BENEFIT RESERVE VALUATION PREMIUMS FOR 1971
ISSUES OF SELECTED PLANS AND AGES

Plan	Age	Zero Withdrawals	Linton A	Linton B	Linton C	Crazy Quilt Ratebook Assumptions
Whole life	10	$ 4.48	$ 4.34	$ 4.02	$ 3.57	$ 4.22
	35	11.47	11.16	10.63	9.88	11.11
	60	34.31	33.37	32.24	30.86	33.30
20-pay life	10	6.92	7.54	7.55	7.16	7.08
	35	15.62	16.16	16.15	15.66	16.16
5-year R&C term	35	3.78	3.25	2.73	2.25	2.37
25-year decreasing term	35	1.89	1.73	1.57	1.42	3.72

* All other assumptions held constant.

the cash value might be viewed as a provision for adverse deviation. This was Crazy Quilt Life's approach.

Crazy Quilt did, however, modify the indicated cash values to recognize certain cost differentials in the case of the industrial line of business. This is discussed in Chapter 18.

Effect on Reserves

Table 8–10 shows the effect of various withdrawal assumptions on benefit valuation premiums for selected 1971 plans and ages for Crazy Quilt Life. Generally, as the withdrawal rate increases the valuation premium decreases.

Reserves are another matter. Table 8–11 shows the effect on the reserves. In the case of the permanent plans the level of the reserve after the first few years *increases* as the withdrawal rate increases. This is due mainly to the influence of cash values. In the case of the term plans the level of the reserve *decreases* as the withdrawal rate increases, except at the later durations.

It is very difficult to generalize about the effect of withdrawals. Table 8–11 suggests that tests should be made to support any inference about the effect of a particular withdrawal table whenever the table is selected to achieve a desired effect.

Effect on Profits

Some notion of the overall impact of withdrawals can be obtained from inspection of Table 8–12, which shows the effect on the present value of profits of various modifications of withdrawal assumptions for

age-35 issues of Crazy Quilt Life's principal plans. The percentage effect on profit is sometimes proportional to the percentage modifications; in other cases it is wildly disproportionate. Table 8–12 is further evidence that the effect of withdrawals can be severe and relatively unpredictable.

Provisions for Adverse Deviation

While the life insurance audit guide specifies that withdrawal assumptions should include provision for adverse deviation, this should be interpreted as requiring realism in the withdrawal assumption.

As Table 8–11 indicates, the use of a conservative assumption can tend to lower the level of reserves, in which case the objective of conservatism is frustrated. And as Chapter 16 indicates, a withdrawal table that is too conservative can play havoc with unamortized acquisition costs.

So the answer to the problem of uncertainty in the case of the withdrawal assumption is to use as realistic a withdrawal table as possible and, essentially, to hope for the best. Because the factors are applied to insurance in force, errors will be self-correcting to a certain extent.

When experience departs from the assumptions sufficiently to require a recalculation of acquisition cost factors, as required by the audit guide and as discussed in Chapter 16, the benefit reserve factors should also be recalculated. In other words, if experience warrants recalculation of one set of factors, the other set should also be recalculated. To do otherwise is to split the personality of the contracts being accounted for, and there is no logic sufficient to justify such schizophrenia.

Table 8–11.

EFFECT OF VARYING WITHDRAWAL RATES* ON BENEFIT RESERVE FACTORS AT SELECTED DURATIONS FOR 1971 ISSUES OF SELECTED PLANS AND AGES

Plan	Age	Duration	Zero With-drawals	Linton A	Linton B	Linton C	Crazy Quilt Ratebook Assumptions
Whole life	10	1	$ 4.46	$ 4.31	$ 3.98	$ 3.51	$ 4.19
		2	9.02	9.21	9.05	8.60	9.08
		3	13.85	14.52	14.69	14.42	15.40
		5	24.30	26.36	27.71	28.40	27.72
		7	35.64	38.88	41.35	43.04	40.36
		10	54.66	59.16	62.81	65.57	60.89
		15	91.42	97.28	102.21	106.13	99.38
		20	136.27	142.73	148.21	152.57	145.01
		30	249.11	255.88	261.83	266.59	258.57
		40	376.74	383.28	389.52	394.84	386.50
5-year R&C term	35	1	11.45	11.12	10.58	9.80	11.07
		2	23.15	23.76	24.08	24.06	24.89
		3	35.41	37.11	38.53	39.56	38.61
		5	61.79	64.88	67.81	70.38	65.89
		7	90.38	94.32	98.29	102.02	94.86
		10	137.87	142.35	147.12	151.85	142.62
		15	225.60	230.13	235.29	240.67	230.19
		20	320.76	324.61	329.32	334.43	324.43
		30	514.83	517.21	520.63	524.69	516.25
		40	675.45	676.58	678.72	681.61	674.15
25-year decreasing term	60	1	32.48	31.51	30.34	28.91	31.44
		2	62.97	63.80	64.62	65.35	64.29
		3	92.92	94.42	96.04	97.70	94.90
		5	152.20	154.13	156.46	159.09	153.73
		7	214.54	216.26	218.58	221.45	215.28
		10	314.06	315.16	316.99	319.53	313.60
		15	465.81	466.60	468.15	470.47	463.08
		20	592.94	593.20	594.17	595.89	585.44
		30	798.45	798.14	798.23	798.79	780.83
		40	982.95	982.95	982.95	982.95	982.95

Plan	Age	Duration	Zero With-drawals	Linton A	Linton B	Linton C	Crazy Quilt Ratebook Assumptions
20-pay life	35	1	$ 15.73	$ 16.28	$ 16.28	$ 15.77	$ 16.29
		2	31.97	35.01	37.36	39.10	37.37
		3	49.10	53.93	57.94	61.25	57.04
		5	86.18	93.66	100.19	105.95	97.36
		7	125.94	135.29	143.67	151.32	139.82
		10	192.60	203.94	214.12	223.57	209.42
		15	321.86	335.12	346.56	356.90	341.24
		20	473.51	487.03	497.47	505.73	493.98
		30	634.20	641.25	646.87	651.41	652.85
		40	752.59	756.06	759.04	761.62	766.04
5-year R&C term	35	1	3.50	2.96	2.42	1.92	2.05
		2	6.74	5.92	5.05	4.18	4.19
		3	9.96	8.92	7.74	6.52	6.44
		5	16.42	15.17	13.57	11.79	11.10
		7	26.38	25.04	23.08	20.68	18.99
		10	37.66	36.69	34.74	31.98	26.59
		15	64.96	65.41	64.05	61.02	58.81
		20	100.18	104.19	105.55	104.13	101.80
		30	90.35	102.67	113.29	121.22	116.07
		35	29.83	29.83	29.83	29.83	29.83
25-year decreasing term	35	1	1.56	1.40	1.23	1.07	1.31
		2	2.75	2.53	2.29	2.05	2.40
		3	3.83	3.57	3.27	2.97	3.43
		5	5.73	5.45	5.11	4.73	5.34
		7	7.61	7.42	7.14	6.77	7.39
		10	9.06	9.04	8.89	8.64	9.17
		15	8.72	9.02	9.20	9.25	9.14
		20	5.46	5.87	6.21	6.47	6.06
		25	1.69	1.69	1.69	1.69	1.69

* All other assumptions held constant.

Table 8–12.

SOME COMPARATIVE PRESENT VALUES TAKING INTO ACCOUNT MODIFIED WITHDRAWAL ESTIMATES

| | | Present Value of Profits at Issue Per $1,000 Issued at Age 35 Discounted at Assumed Investment Earnings Rate | | | Original Profit as Percentage of Modified Profit |
| | | | Modified Withdrawals | | |
Plan	Ratebook Era	Original Withdrawals	Percentage Modification	Amount	
Par whole life	41–47	$ 7.43	150%	$ 6.25	119%
	48–51	9.26	50	14.88	62
	52–61	7.54	300	(6.41)	–
	62–64	7.94	200	(4.33)	–
	65–69	6.88	150	.02	–
	70–71	9.19	50	20.34	45
Non-par whole life	41–47	12.37	200	2.12	583
	48–51	21.25	175	6.18	344
	52–56	15.71	150	5.73	274
	57–61	13.51	125	9.53	142
	62–67	15.28	110	13.45	114
	68–69	9.53	90	11.13	86
	70–71	13.60	75	18.65	73
Non-par 20-pay life	41–47	11.68	200	4.56	256
	48–51	21.74	150	10.12	215
	52–56	12.00	150	3.55	338
	57–61	10.82	150	1.45	746
	62–67	12.51	50	24.30	51
	68–69	22.29	50	40.06	56
	70–71	25.39	50	43.68	58
Non-par 5-year R & C term	41–47	9.05	150	4.64	195
	48–51	15.17	75	19.23	79
	52–56	13.49	200	4.20	321
	57–61	8.94	175	3.74	239
	62–64	8.23	150	4.63	178
	65–67	3.33	125	2.74	122
	68–69	1.74	110	1.68	104
	70–71	2.89	90	3.05	95
Non-par 25-year decreasing term	57–61	15.49	150	11.02	141
	62–69	10.61	200	3.79	280
	70–71	10.64	75	12.87	83

The "When Terminated" Assumption

Assumptions as to when withdrawals take place during the year can have a significant effect on the reserves. The "when terminated" assumption is an important consideration in choosing a reserve calculation technique. Reserve calculation techniques and the "when terminated" assumption are discussed in Chapter 12.

Term Renewals

When a renewable term contract is treated as a continuum—that is, when all of the renewal periods are linked together and the series of renewal periods is treated as a single period with a variable premium—it is necessary to estimate the proportion of insureds that renew their contracts at each renewal date.

In Crazy Quilt Life's case, for example, the estimated rate of nonrenewal on the five-year renewable term contract was made a part of the withdrawal table for purposes of calculating adjusted reserves. Thus the withdrawal rate for each fifth year reflected the proportion of policyholders that did not renew. The effect on the withdrawal table is indicated in the last column of Table 8–9.

Term Conversions

As indicated earlier in this chapter, if the cost of

conversion is to be recognized in the adjusted reserve, it is necessary to estimate the proportion of insureds that will convert to permanent plans. The expected conversion rate is usually introduced by means of a supplementary withdrawal table.

Table 8–9 does not reflect the assumed conversion rates for Crazy Quilt Life's convertible term plans; the rates were introduced by means of a separate table. Assumed conversion rates for term plans issued at age 25 may be summarized as follows:

| | *Percentage Converting During Period* | |
Age Bracket	5-Year Term	25-Year Decreasing Term
26–30	5%	5%
31–35	8	8
36–40	10	10
41–45	12	5
46–50	15	–
51–60	30	–

Disclosure

As in the case of the mortality assumption, it is often difficult to describe a withdrawal assumption, particularly when the tables are based on company experience or other sources of information that are not common knowledge. In such cases it would be helpful to describe the relationship, if any, of the withdrawal tables as a whole to published tables if the overall assumption is determinable and if such disclosure would not be misleading, such as, for example, where the company's mix of business has been changing significantly.

Mortality Fluctuation Reserves

Suppose that information was available with respect to a given company to demonstrate that while actual mortality may deviate from expected mortality randomly within an interval of plus or minus $1,000,000 from the dollar amount of expected mortality, there is a 95 percent probability that deviations outside this band will offset over the long term. Would the company be justified in holding the dollar amounts of deviations outside the band in suspense in the form of a mortality fluctuation reserve?

The most compelling argument in favor of a mortality fluctuation reserve is that it seeks to implement the matching concept. Deviations for which there is a suitably high—say 95 percent—probability of offset are smoothed out in such a way as to match the incidence of premium revenues. Deviations for which there is little or no probability of offset are charged or credited to operations as they appear; there is no basis for matching them with anything other than the period in which they occur.

A mortality fluctuation reserve may be viewed as a method of reapportioning actual mortality so that it better fits the curve of expected mortality. It may also be viewed as a means of reapportioning *expected* mortality so as to fit more precisely the curve of actual mortality.

It is, in effect, a means of restating the adopted mortality table. There should be no fundamental objection to using a modified mortality table if it more closely parallels a company's mortality experience. Inasmuch as it would be permissible to do this by modifying the table directly, it follows that another method of accomplishing the same thing should be acceptable.

However, the extent that a mortality fluctuation reserve is basically a means of reapportioning actual mortality to accounting periods other than the periods in which it occurs, such reapportionment may be viewed as a violation of the life insurance audit guide, which generally provides that deviations from original estimates are to be recognized as they occur.

Some believe that a mortality fluctuation reserve opens the door to manipulation of earnings, on the basis that the reserve can never operate with the degree of impartiality necessary to eliminate the potential for abuse.

Some also question whether statistical validity for such a reserve is possible to attain.

At the present time, there is little agreement on whether mortality fluctuation reserves are in conformity with generally accepted accounting principles. A few companies provide such reserves; most do not. Until the issue is resolved, those companies that utilize mortality fluctuation reserves should disclose the fact in notes to the financial statements. The amount of the reserve and the changes therein should also be disclosed if the amounts are material.

Arguments for and against the reserve are presented in Appendix D, which contains papers on the subject presented in 1974 to the Financial Accounting Standards Board by two major life insurance companies, each of which holds a different viewpoint on the matter.

9

Investment Yields

Everyone talks about interest rates but no one seems to do anything about them. Interest rates dart to and fro, responding to political developments, expansion or contraction of the money supply, expectations about inflation, stock prices, the balance of payments, and no one knows how many other things. Almost everyone attempts sooner or later to predict what interest rates are going to do, and one often hears very learned discourses on what interest rates are going to do; but in the final analysis no one really knows what they are going to do. Neither economists nor actuaries nor accountants nor bankers nor presidents have proven themselves particularly prescient with regard to interest rates. Interest rates are ever quicksilvery.

This, then, is the environment within which a life insurance company must select interest assumptions for rate-testing purposes and for purposes of calculating adjusted reserves. Interest rates must be predicted for decades into the future even when there is little certainty about their behavior six months hence. And the consequences of error can be severe.

Interest Assumptions in General

A few general statements can be made about interest assumptions. First, interest assumptions must be made; the task cannot be avoided. Second, the interest assumption has a very significant effect on benefit reserves. Third, interest-bearing liabilities such as reserves are the alter-egos of interest-bearing assets and valuation principles should be consistent between the two. Fourth, interest is a function of cash flows, new money rates, asset maturities, and other factors,

and all such factors must be taken into account in choosing an interest assumption. Fifth, predictions of future interest rates are made in an atmosphere of great uncertainty, and provision for adverse deviation is a matter of common sense. And sixth, any inflationary bias in the interest assumptions has implications for some other assumptions.

Audit Guide Provisions

"Interest" is defined in the life insurance audit guide as

. . . an expression of the composite yield rate assumed on the funds invested or to be invested to provide for the future benefits and expenses . . . the yield rate includes dividends, rental income and interest . . . net of investment expenses.[1]

Thus "interest" includes interest, dividends, and rents but it excludes capital gains (which are discussed later in this chapter). While the assumed rate is, according to the guide, supposed to cover *future* benefits and expenses, it should be noted that one effect of amortizing acquisition costs with interest, as apparently encouraged by the guide (and as discussed in Chapter 16), is to provide an interest return on *past* expenses.

The audit guide recognizes the difficulty of predicting future interest rates:

The selection of . . . an interest assumption is a subjective judgment which must be made by the company in light of the long-term nature of life insurance, the contractual obligations under life insurance policies, and the inherent inability to forecast the future with certainty.[2]

Table 9–1.

EFFECT OF VARYING INTEREST RATES* ON BENEFIT RESERVE VALUATION PREMIUMS FOR 1971 ISSUES
OF SELECTED PLANS AND ISSUES—PER $1,000

Interest Rate	Par Whole Life, Age 35	Non-Par Whole Life			20-Pay Life		5-Year R & C Term, Age 35 **	25-Year Decreasing Term, Age 35
		Age 10	Age 35	Age 60	Age 10	Age 35		
8%	$13.30	$ 2.31	$ 7.60	$28.93	$ 4.34	$11.29	$2.07	$1.55
7	14.60	2.66	8.54	30.61	4.89	12.62	2.18	1.59
6	16.13	3.13	9.65	32.47	5.63	14.23	2.30	1.64
5 1/2	16.99	3.42	10.28	33.48	6.10	15.18	2.37	1.67
5	17.92	3.75	10.97	34.53	6.64	16.22	2.44	1.69
4 1/2	18.94	4.14	11.72	35.64	7.29	17.39	2.51	1.72
4	20.04	4.59	12.54	36.81	8.06	18.70	2.59	1.74
9 graded to 4 1/2 in 25 years	15.63	3.32	9.39	30.13	5.59	13.52	2.17	1.56
7 graded to 4 1/2 in 25 years at .5% each 5 years	16.88	3.63	10.26	32.27	6.21	14.93	2.30	1.62
7 graded to 4 1/2 in 25 years at .1% each year	17.17	3.70	10.47	32.66	6.35	15.26	2.33	1.63
Crazy Quilt ratebook assumptions	16.13	4.22	11.11	33.30	7.08	16.16	2.37	1.65
Zero interest	32.86	12.20	22.38	48.57	25.15	32.75	3.35	1.99

* All other assumptions held constant
** Initial 5-year period.

Notwithstanding the fact that selection of an interest assumption is a "subjective judgment," the guide provides some fairly objective guidelines for choosing an assumption. First, the assumption for a given block of new business should be consistent with "actual yields, trends in yields, portfolio mix and maturities, and a company's overall investment experience generally," and the assumption "should include provision for the risk of adverse deviation." [3]

The guide also indicates that the assumption *"generally . . . should be based on the estimate of future interest expected at the time that the policies are issued."* [4] (Emphasis supplied.) This does not necessarily refer to ratebook assumptions, which are used only "as a part of the test of reasonableness of interest rates and yields experienced at the time the policies were issued." [5] It refers to what would have been a "reasonable and conservative" [6] assumption in the circumstances. Ratebook assumptions must be second-guessed, particularly if they do not provide for adverse deviation.

Other guidelines for choosing an interest assumption include the nature of the contract (for immediate annuities, "little provision for adverse deviation . . . is needed . . . since all of the consideration is invested immediately at a known rate of interest when the reserve is set up and the flow of investment cash can be matched very closely to the flow of benefits" [7]), new-money rates, portfolio rates, and depth of investment experience (for a company "not having sufficient experience . . . the average rate on long-term U.S. Government bonds, or some similar high-quality investment," could be substituted for the company's new-money rates and the industry portfolio rate could be substituted for the company's portfolio rates, for those years in which the company had no experience but for which information is needed to fashion a trend line against which interest assumptions can be measured [8]).

Nature of Interest

With one simple sentence in the section entitled "Recognition of Costs" the life insurance audit guide establishes that assumed interest is something other than a revenue item:

Annual charges for costs in conformity with generally accepted accounting principles should be determined using methods which include assumptions for *interest,* mor-

Table 9–2.

EFFECT OF VARYING INTEREST RATES* ON BENEFIT RESERVE FACTORS AT SELECTED DURATIONS FOR 1971 ISSUES OF SELECTED PLANS AND AGES

Plan	Age	Dura-tion	8%	7%	6%	5-1/2%	5%	4-1/2%	4%	9% Graded to 4-1/2%	7% Graded to 4-1/2% .5% Each 5 Years	7% Graded to 4-1/2% .1% a Year	Crazy Quilt Ratebook Assump-tions	Zero Interest
Par	35	1	$ 12.89	$ 14.17	$ 15.68	$ 16.52	$ 17.44	$ 18.43	$ 19.50	$ 15.39	$ 16.53	$ 16.83	$ 15.68	$ 31.93
whole		2	26.28	28.99	32.15	33.92	35.84	37.91	40.16	32.03	34.22	34.87	32.15	65.86
life		3	39.33	43.43	48.19	50.86	53.75	56.86	60.22	48.77	51.75	52.71	48.19	98.34
		5	65.90	72.63	80.41	84.74	89.41	94.43	99.83	84.17	87.76	89.10	80.41	159.89
		7	93.73	102.93	113.49	119.36	125.65	132.39	139.62	121.59	125.09	127.05	113.49	218.48
		10	137.30	150.00	164.46	172.43	180.94	190.02	199.70	182.95	184.31	186.50	164.46	302.32
		15	212.95	230.72	250.67	261.54	273.06	285.24	298.12	290.86	286.00	288.28	250.67	428.46
		20	290.32	311.87	335.72	348.57	362.07	376.23	391.07	396.68	385.74	386.96	335.73	534.69
		30	453.19	478.57	505.85	520.22	535.00	550.40	566.20	574.32	565.27	563.18	505.83	626.72
		40	618.16	640.25	663.30	675.16	687.23	699.50	711.94	714.19	708.63	707.35	663.30	814.43
Whole	10	1	2.23	2.59	3.05	3.34	3.67	4.06	4.51	3.29	3.58	3.66	4.19	12.04
life		2	5.09	5.90	6.97	7.63	8.39	9.28	10.31	7.67	8.26	8.44	9.68	27.25
		3	8.10	9.36	11.02	12.05	13.23	14.60	16.19	12.34	13.17	13.44	15.40	42.09
		5	14.48	16.66	19.52	21.28	23.30	25.65	28.36	22.69	23.72	24.12	27.72	71.57
		7	20.70	23.82	27.90	30.40	33.28	36.59	40.42	33.46	34.47	35.06	40.36	100.11
		10	30.04	34.68	40.70	44.38	48.60	53.43	58.98	51.41	51.77	52.46	60.89	142.68
		15	46.22	53.75	63.42	69.25	75.88	83.41	91.96	85.48	83.48	84.57	99.38	213.51
		20	67.22	77.93	71.42	99.45	108.48	118.64	130.05	126.04	122.22	122.57	145.01	282.30
		30	130.10	148.13	169.97	182.56	196.42	211.65	228.36	221.96	218.11	217.16	258.57	424.90
		40	229.10	254.01	282.90	299.02	316.34	334.94	354.86	343.64	340.39	339.59	386.50	562.13
	35	1	7.50	8.94	9.54	10.17	10.85	11.60	12.41	9.41	10.22	10.44	11.07	22.00
		2	16.81	18.87	21.30	22.68	24.18	25.81	27.58	21.33	22.98	23.47	24.89	48.29
		3	26.04	29.17	32.86	34.94	37.19	39.64	42.29	33.43	35.69	36.43	38.61	73.02
		5	44.15	49.30	55.31	58.69	62.34	66.28	70.54	58.20	61.01	62.06	65.89	118.73
		7	63.77	70.88	79.11	83.71	88.66	93.98	99.71	85.16	88.03	89.56	94.86	163.18
		10	96.19	106.16	117.61	123.95	130.74	138.00	145.76	131.22	132.79	134.57	142.62	229.05
		15	157.54	171.94	188.17	197.04	206.44	216.40	226.94	218.06	215.39	217.36	230.19	334.37
		20	228.23	246.14	265.96	276.64	287.86	299.62	311.95	312.03	304.90	306.17	324.43	431.51
		30	397.57	418.18	440.27	451.89	463.89	476.27	489.03	490.87	485.43	484.11	516.25	520.39
		40	571.82	590.97	611.01	621.34	631.89	642.63	653.55	651.82	648.40	647.56	674.15	745.58
	60	1	27.10	28.72	30.51	31.47	32.48	33.59	34.65	28.48	30.44	30.85	31.44	45.78
		2	55.08	58.41	62.07	64.03	66.08	68.24	70.50	58.49	62.25	63.12	64.29	92.90
		3	80.83	85.74	91.12	94.00	97.01	100.16	103.46	86.75	91.88	93.17	94.90	135.86
		5	129.91	137.61	145.99	150.45	155.10	159.95	165.01	142.51	148.96	150.66	153.73	213.73
		7	182.23	192.42	203.44	209.28	215.35	221.65	228.19	201.93	208.97	211.51	215.28	289.99
		10	266.86	280.05	294.17	301.58	309.25	317.17	325.35	300.31	305.43	308.24	313.60	400.41
		15	400.76	416.35	432.77	441.29	450.02	458.96	468.10	454.86	453.50	456.55	463.08	548.50
		20	517.64	532.99	548.90	557.06	565.35	573.77	582.31	583.46	576.07	578.48	585.44	654.48
		30	725.73	736.27	746.99	752.41	757.86	763.35	768.86	772.86	769.16	768.49	780.30	813.58
		40	962.25	966.74	971.29	973.59	975.90	978.23	980.58	978.23	978.23	978.23	982.95	1,000.00
20-pay	10	1	4.32	4.87	5.61	6.07	6.62	7.26	8.03	5.65	6.23	6.38	7.11	24.97
life		2	10.51	11.84	13.60	14.70	16.00	17.53	19.37	13.92	15.22	15.58	17.36	59.40
		3	17.89	20.05	22.92	24.72	26.84	29.34	32.33	23.87	25.83	26.40	29.40	97.17
		5	29.71	33.43	38.39	41.51	45.17	49.50	54.67	41.69	44.38	45.26	50.83	165.04
		7	40.55	45.97	53.20	57.74	63.07	69.37	76.87	59.79	62.96	64.28	72.70	234.44
		10	56.45	64.56	75.36	82.11	90.04	99.38	110.44	89.26	92.23	93.92	107.50	336.86
		15	84.40	97.64	115.11	125.97	138.61	153.41	170.81	145.08	146.63	148.85	172.93	509.15
		20	119.09	138.18	163.04	178.31	195.95	216.42	240.27	210.30	210.79	212.96	249.90	679.67
		30	176.51	201.91	233.66	252.52	273.79	297.84	325.10	297.84	297.84	297.84	355.25	748.24
		40	268.18	299.28	336.34	357.54	380.82	406.42	434.62	406.42	406.42	406.42	465.76	805.41

Continued

Table 9–2. Continued

Plan	Age	Dura-tion	8%	7%	6%	5-1/2%	5%	4-1/2%	4%	9% Graded to 4-1/2%	7% Graded to 4-1/2% .5% Each 5 Years	7% Graded to 4-1/2% .1% a Year	Crazy Quilt Ratebook Assumptions	Zero Interest
20-pay	35	1	11.34	12.66	14.26	15.20	16.24	17.39	18.69	13.72	15.05	15.40	16.29	36.91
life		2	26.04	28.98	32.56	34.65	39.96	39.53	42.39	31.81	34.59	35.37	37.37	82.49
		3	39.36	43.84	49.27	52.43	55.92	59.81	64.14	48.86	52.77	53.95	57.04	124.19
		5	66.54	73.94	82.88	88.06	93.79	100.14	107.18	84.90	90.14	91.87	97.36	203.56
		7	94.52	105.00	117.62	124.90	132.94	141.82	151.66	123.30	129.43	132.01	139.82	284.18
		10	138.67	154.12	172.61	183.23	194.89	207.74	221.91	187.92	193.70	197.05	209.42	408.15
		15	223.69	247.89	276.45	292.65	310.32	329.63	350.76	312.95	315.96	320.45	341.24	616.89
		20	332.14	364.61	402.30	423.44	446.31	471.10	498.00	458.17	459.26	463.75	493.98	823.93
		30	493.15	522.48	555.09	572.77	591.46	611.24	632.20	611.24	611.24	611.24	652.85	855.31
		40	638.52	663.21	689.80	703.87	718.50	733.72	749.55	733.72	733.72	733.72	766.04	903.18
5-year	35	1	1.75	1.86	1.98	2.64	2.11	2.18	2.25	1.86	1.98	2.01	2.05	2.96
R & C		2	3.52	3.75	4.00	4.14	4.28	4.43	4.59	3.80	4.04	4.10	4.19	6.09
term		3	5.36	5.71	6.10	6.31	6.53	6.76	7.00	5.87	6.21	6.30	6.44	9.27
		5	9.13	9.73	10.38	10.73	11.09	11.47	11.86	10.27	10.71	10.84	11.10	15.46
		7	15.64	16.61	17.66	18.21	18.78	19.38	19.99	17.82	18.37	18.60	18.99	25.45
		10	21.81	23.06	24.41	25.11	25.83	26.57	27.33	25.49	25.77	26.03	26.59	33.74
		15	48.68	51.02	53.45	54.69	55.94	57.20	58.46	58.13	57.31	57.72	58.81	67.89
		20	88.06	90.78	93.47	94.78	96.06	97.30	98.49	103.03	100.07	100.32	101.80	105.27
		30	110.72	110.75	110.46	110.18	109.81	109.33	108.74	118.71	115.07	114.37	116.07	99.43
		35	29.20	29.34	29.48	29.55	29.02	29.69	29.76	29.69	29.69	29.69	29.83	30.35
25-year	35	1	1.21	1.25	1.30	1.32	1.34	1.37	1.39	1.23	1.29	1.30	1.31	1.61
decreasing		2	2.21	2.29	2.38	2.42	2.47	2.51	2.56	2.26	2.36	2.38	2.40	2.97
term		3	3.14	3.26	3.38	3.44	3.51	3.57	3.64	3.23	3.37	3.40	3.43	4.21
		5	4.85	5.02	5.20	5.29	5.39	5.48	5.58	5.09	5.24	5.28	5.34	6.36
		7	6.75	6.96	7.18	7.28	7.39	7.50	7.62	7.13	7.27	7.32	7.39	8.49
		10	8.45	8.66	8.86	8.96	9.06	9.16	9.26	9.04	9.07	9.10	9.17	9.96
		15	8.62	8.72	8.80	8.84	8.88	8.91	8.94	9.28	9.10	9.11	9.14	9.03
		20	5.87	5.86	5.84	5.83	5.81	5.79	5.77	6.31	6.07	6.06	6.06	5.47

* All other assumptions held constant.

tality, withdrawals, expenses, and other benefits.[9] (Emphasis supplied.)

Thus the guide establishes that interest is to be considered a negative cost, not revenue, and proceeds to discuss interest as it relates to and affects the matching of costs with premium revenues.

This general concept extends only to interest required to support the reserves. Interest on capital, which is not discussed in the guide, apparently retains the character of revenue.

Significance of the Interest Assumption

Valuation premiums usually vary inversely with the interest assumption. As the assumed interest rate rises, the valuation premium falls. This is clear from Table 9–1. Valuation premiums corresponding to seven level

interest assumptions are shown. So is the valuation premium associated with an interest assumption of zero, also shown in Table 9–1 as a curiosity item.

The effect of interest is most pronounced with respect to permanent insurance, as one might expect. Thus the 4 percent valuation premium for the whole life policy issued at age 35 is 65 percent higher than the 8 percent valuation premium. For the 25-year decreasing term plan, the difference is only 12 percent.

Table 9–1 also demonstrates one other interesting aspect of the interest assumption. Grading of the interest rate has a pronounced effect on the valuation premium. Thus, for example, grading from 7 percent to 4 1/2 percent over 25 years produces a valuation premium comparable to a 5 1/2 percent valuation premium for the whole life plan issued at age 35. Crazy Quilt Life's ratebook assumption—6 1/2 percent graded to 3 1/2 percent over 30 years—produces a valuation premium slightly greater than the 5 percent valuation premium on that plan.

The level of the valuation premium is no predictor of the level of the reserves. Reserve factors calculated at 12 different interest rates are shown in Table 9–2. While Crazy Quilt's whole life (age 35) valuation premium was just slightly higher (1.3 percent) than the 5 percent valuation premium, the reserves eventually become significantly higher—for example, 13% in the 20th year. Perhaps 13 percent doesn't seem like very much, but it is equal to $36.57 per $1,000, and if there were, say, $100 million of insurance in force at the 20th duration, the difference is $3,657,000. If there were $1 billion of insurance in force, the difference would be $36 million. For companies with several billions of insurance in force, the effect on aggregate reserves of one interest assumption vs. another can be staggering.

Nor is the *change* in reserves anything to sneeze at. The difference between the first-year whole life (age 35) reserve at 4 percent and 6 percent is $2.87. Assuming sale of $100 million in new business, the effect on income is $287,000, a tidy sum indeed. Assuming an average gross premium of $18 per $1,000, the difference is equal to 16 percent of first-year premiums—a percentage greater than most companies can expect to earn in terms of *total* pre-tax profits on ordinary business.

The significance of the interest assumption to reserves, reported profits, and the integrity of the financial statements cannot be denied, particularly where permanent insurance is involved. The assumption must be chosen with great care.

Influences on the Interest Assumption

Choice of an interest assumption is a "subjective judgment" that is influenced strongly by a welter of facts and feelings. The mental pattern formed by all of the influences on the assumption may differ significantly depending on the background and biases of the individual who finally chooses the assumption, and hence no two people, working independently, are likely to choose precisely the same assumption for a given company.

The various influences on choice of an interest assumption should at least narrow the range within which subjective judgment must be brought to bear. Some of the factors that tend to confine the extremes of an interest assumption to a reasonable interval are as follows.

New money rates. Yields obtained on new investments provide a starting point for the interest assumption. Typically the new money rate effective at the time that business is sold will operate as the upper limit on the assumed rate, on the basis that while the new money rate is known it is likely to be transitory, and prudence would suggest that improvement in the rate should not be projected (unless it is unusually low and evidence that it will rise is compelling). The considerations involved are somewhat similar to the considerations involved in using a current mortality table for life reserves but not projecting any further improvement in mortality even though it is quite possible that mortality will improve.

There are cases, however, both in ratemaking and in computing adjusted reserves, in which the assumed interest rate has been scaled *upward* from the new money rate to a projected peak in the interest cycle, and then downward from there. This approach has been used occasionally with respect mainly to issues of the 1960s when interest rates were rising quite rapidly.

Portfolio rates. Average yields also tend to influence the interest assumption, usually somewhat indirectly. If a company's average yield has lagged behind the industry's, the company usually would tend to be somewhat more conservative in choosing an interest assumption than if the company's rate has exceeded the industry's. Some companies may wish to use the portfolio rate as a starting point for its interest assumptions—i.e., to limit the assumption to the portfolio rate—partly for the sake of expediency and partly for the sake of conservatism. Use of a portfolio rate avoids some of the problems associated with "tagging" assets and liabilities, which is sometimes required when new money rates are used. Since in recent years portfolio rates have lagged behind new money rates, use of a portfolio rate will tend to be conservative, at least in the early years of a block of business.

Statutory rates. Statutory interest assumptions may influence the adjusted reserve assumption indirectly. Some companies grade to statutory rates on the basis that such rates represent prudent long-term assumptions. While statutory assumptions are solvency-oriented, nevertheless a great deal of thought and history lie behind them, which lends them a fair degree of credibility for purposes of any long-range projections.

Type of business. A company whose business consists entirely of term insurance might tend to be fairly casual in selecting an interest assumption because of the relative insensitivity of reserves on such business to the assumed interest rate. The net result of being "casual" about the interest assumption could be a high rate, a low rate, or a middle-of-the-road rate; if the assumption is seen to have little effect on the reserves, the final choice of a rate may be quite arbitrary.

A company whose business consists almost entirely of single-premium business may tend to set its assumption close to the rate prevailing when the single premiums are invested. But consideration has to be given to the rate at which interest income will be reinvested, the rates at which reinvestment of principal will take place, and the possibility of capital losses on forced early disposal of the investments.

A company whose business consists primarily of participating business may tend to select a rate that approximates the rate implicit in the dividend scale, on the basis that any change in the rate will be offset by changes in the dividend scale.

Other examples of the influence of type of business on the interest assumption could be cited, but the main point to be made is that interest assumptions for a given type of business should vary somewhat with the incidence of cash flows associated with the given type.

Nature of obligations. It is no accident that some 80 percent of life insurance industry invested assets are in fixed-income securities. Obligations under life insurance contracts are largely fixed-benefit obligations. It would never do to fund such benefits wholly with volatile investment media such as stocks. Thus interest assumptions are usually based on the returns associated with fixed-income securities. Such returns are usually somewhat more dependable than returns on equities, and the price that is paid for dependability is a lower expected return.

Stage in the interest cycle. While opinions differ as to what period of time and range of rates constitute an interest "cycle", there can be little difference of opinion as to when rates are historically "low" and when they are historically "high". A rate of, say, 2 1/2 percent would be historically low; a rate of, say, 12 percent would be historically high. A company choosing its assumption when rates are historically low would not use an interest assumption that is, or becomes, even lower. Similarly, a company choosing its assumption when rates are historically high would not—hopefully—assume that rates are going to remain stratospheric forever. Thus one's perception of the stage of the interest cycle will tend to influence the interest assumption.

Asset-liability relationships. The relationship between asset maturities and the projected stream of benefit and expense payments will tend to influence the interest assumption. Obviously the valuation of assets at an amount that produces the yield rate assumed for purposes of calculating adjusted reserves assumes that the principal will be available when needed. Any forced liquidation of assets to meet maturing obligations would result in realizing market values, not book values, while the value of the obligations that are being met would not change in any way. To the extent that asset maturities and liabilities maturities are discernibly out of phase, the interest assumption might tend to reflect the dangers (or opportunities) associated with such a condition—in other words, to provide for possible capital gains or losses.

Ratebook assumptions. Assuming the ratebook interest assumption was rationally determined, it obviously will influence the interest assumption chosen for purposes of calculating adjusted reserves. Assuming that the ratebook assumption is believed to give proper effect to all the relevant facts and circumstances, it might be used without modification.

Expenses and taxes. Investment expenses will always affect the assumed interest rate, which is stated net of expenses. Thus a company's practices in allocating expenses to the investment function will have a direct impact on the assumed interest rate. Federal income taxes on Phase I income may also affect the interest rate to the extent that the company regards such taxes as a tax on investment income rather than as a tax on profits.

Provision for Adverse Deviation

It is doubtful that adverse deviation can be provided for very scientifically where the interest assumption is concerned. When all is said and done, what really counts is the estimate of prevailing interest rates far into the future, and no frequency distribution can do justice to the uncertainties involved in forecasting such long-term rates. Eventually, and presumably after much agonizing, the selection of an interest rate is, as the audit guide points out, a "subjective judgment."

Prudence and the concept of reasonable conservatism do suggest a few basic guidelines for providing for adverse deviation. First, as certainty diminishes, the assumed rate should grade down. Second, no one should be so foolhardy as to project the very high rates of 1973 far into the future; even if 1973 rates provide the starting point, assumed rates should grade down to something lower than today's rates—quite significantly lower for nonparticipating business.

It is reasonable and proper to assume a moderate or even a fairly low interest rate in the future. In the circumstances, nothing else is really defensible. No one knows what interest rates are going to be ten, 20, 30, or 40 years from now, and it seems distinctly imprudent to suppose that they are going to be high. The consequences of error are simply too great.

So assumptions about distant interest rates should be conservative. The assumption should be set at a level which is very unlikely to exceed the actual rate. That does not imply an absurdly low rate, merely a *prudent* rate. Various techniques can be used to help in the struggle to be prudent; some of the techniques are discussed later in this chapter.

To the extent that actual interest rates exceed assumed, "excess interest" will be recognized as income in the future. Excess interest results from a degree of conservatism appropriate in the circumstances, and while some may find excess interest to be an intellectually unsatisfying phenomenon, it is part of a rational and reasonable accounting process and is therefore eminently defensible.

Inflation and the Interest Assumption

The life insurance audit guide makes two teasing references to inflation:

Renewal expense assumptions should take into account the possible effect of inflation.[9]

Any anticipated effect of economic conditions on the interest assumption should be similarly considered for expense assumptions.[10]

What the audit guide is suggesting is that interest rates should perhaps be viewed as consisting of two components—a "pure" rate of interest, usually taken to be on the order of 3–4 percent; and a "premium" representing the lender's expectation of, and demand to be compensated for, inflation during the term of the loan. Thus, if the rate of inflation is 5 percent and this rate is expected to obtain for ten years, the interest rate on a ten-year loan would, by this reasoning, be 8 or 9 percent.

If the interest assumption contains an implicit premium for inflation, then the audit guide is suggesting that to the extent that future expenses are subject to inflationary pressures, such inflation should be reserved for.

On the other hand, if the interest assumption is non-inflationary, it follows that future inflation in expenses can be ignored, on the basis that any such inflation will be offset by higher interest rates. (However, this is true principally of permanent insurance. In the case of term insurance the reserves are often too low to provide sufficient excess interest to offset inflation.)

The notion that there is a relationship between interest rates and the rate of inflation has its proponents and its opponents, but where the reserve interest assumption is concerned it is wise to side with the proponents, if only because the result of doing so is to be a little more conservative. It doesn't take a great deal of bravery to guess that inflation will continue far into the future, but it takes a great deal of bravery to formalize the guess in the interest assumption.

Inflation is discussed further in Chapter 17.

Elements of the Interest Assumption

Ignoring capital gains for the time being—in other words, assuming that the investments to be considered in selecting an interest assumption are fixed-income senior securities that will be held to maturity—then the interest assumption can be viewed as consisting of four elements: gross investment income, investment expenses, income taxes on investment income, and the method used to translate the net result into a percentage equivalent.

Gross Investment Income

Gross investment income consists of interest received or accruable on bonds, mortgage loans, policy loans, collateral loans, savings accounts, certificates of deposit, accounts receivable, and similar items; dividends received or accruable on common and preferred stocks; rents on real estate held for investment; royalties; and any other receipts, other than capital gains, attributable to the company's investment function.

Asset allocations. The life insurance audit guide implies that all invested assets and the yields thereon should be considered together in deriving an interest assumption.

However, it would also be acceptable to allocate assets, and the related items of investment income, between (1) interest-bearing liabilities and (2) capital and surplus.

Generally, fixed-income investments—mainly bonds, mortgage loans, and policy loans—are sufficient in amount to cover reserve liabilities. This is usually

Table 9–3.

SUMMARY OF DISTRIBUTION OF INSURANCE INDUSTRY ASSETS AND LIABILITIES, 1920–1972

| | Distribution of Assets | | | |
| | Invested Assets | | | Reserves as % of Total Assets * |
Year	Fixed Income Securities	Real Estate, Stocks, and Other	Other Assets	
1920	90.2%	3.3%	6.5%	86.6%
1925	91.7	3.0	5.3	86.0
1930	89.1	5.7	5.2	85.7
1935	81.6	11.1	7.3	87.9
1940	85.0	8.7	6.3	88.4
1945	92.0	4.1	3.9	86.3
1950	90.4	5.5	4.1	85.8
1955	89.0	6.9	4.1	83.3
1960	88.3	7.3	4.4	82.4
1965	86.8	8.7	4.5	80.3
1970	84.3	10.4	5.3	80.8
1972	80.3	14.2	5.5	80.0

* Excluding dividends, dividend accumulations, and miscellaneous policyholder obligations.

true of statutory liabilities; it would usually be true of adjusted liabilities; and it would probably always be true of adjusted liabilities net of unamortized acquisition costs.

Table 9–3 shows certain industry relationships between assets and liabilities, both measured on a statutory basis, for the period 1920–1972. The percentage of assets allocated to traditional fixed-income investments has ranged between 81.6 percent and 92.0 percent for the period; reserves have ranged from 80.3 percent to 88.4 percent of total assets. The correlation is no accident, of course, since investment in fixed-income securities is only logical considering the nature of a life insurance company's obligations.* Furthermore, state laws are such as to require the bulk of a company's reserves to be invested in fixed-income securities.** Investments in real estate, stocks, and other relatively volatile investment media have been limited for the most part to surplus funds.

The logic of relating fixed-income securities to reserves extends also to adjusted reserves. The adjustment process does not change the nature of the life insurance obligation.

Assignment of fixed-income securities to the reserves has a number of practical advantages. Investment income is a little easier to measure and tends to be more stable than, say, real estate income. Some of

*This logic does not necessarily apply to variable products, which are discussed in Chapter 21.

**It is not the reserves that are invested, of course, but assets equal to the reserves.

the complications caused by capital gains (particularly unrealized capital gains) are avoided. Some of the possibly knotty problems discussed below are avoided.

Asset allocation of the type discussed here is optional, not mandatory. A company can, if it wishes, consider all assets as relating without substantial distinction to all liabilities and capital accounts. In that case, composite yields would be used as the interest assumption.

Other aspects of asset allocation are discussed later in this chapter.

Convertible bonds. The difference between interest rates on nonconvertible bonds and convertible bonds represents a kind of premium paid (equal to the interest foregone) to acquire the potential for capital gains on the equity securities to which the convertible bonds may be converted. Some believe that this difference should be recognized in some fashion—perhaps by crediting interest income for the difference and treating the offset as a deferred charge chargeable eventually against any capital gains on the bonds themselves (whose prices tend to fluctuate with the prices of the related stocks) or, after conversion, on the equity securities.

The convertible bond problem is one aspect of the overall problem of accounting for capital gains and losses, which is discussed later in this chapter. Under existing rules, any such adjustment of the indicated yield on convertible bonds would be improper.

Self-rent. One of the peculiarities of insurance accounting is that insurance companies charge themselves rent on premises owned and occupied by the company.

One result of this practice is that the effect on the overall yield can influence the adjusted reserve interest assumption in the case of companies that base their assumptions on overall yields. Ideally the self-rent, related expenses, and the investment base should be eliminated from the calculation of yields when the effect on the yield of self-rent is material, or the rents are not "fair", or the effect is otherwise distortive. Usually, however, the effect of self-rent is negligible.

Another possible result is the deferral of intra-company profits to the extent that self-rent is capitalized as part of deferred acquisition costs. If material, of course, any such intra-company profits should be eliminated in "consolidating" the insurance function and the investment function.

Principal office deduction. Some companies are permitted by state law to deduct property taxes on the home office from premium taxes under certain conditions.

The principal office deduction results in an "understatement" of insurance expenses to the extent of property taxes paid.

Where a company follows the practice of charging itself rent, and such self-rent enters into the calculation of the yield rate, the company should generally credit investment income for the amount of the principal office deduction. This procedure simply recognizes that one of the advantages of owning a home office building is the availability of the deduction, and the savings in premium taxes is in the nature of investment income.

Investments in subsidiaries and affiliates. Companies that do not allocate fixed-income assets to the reserves for purposes of calculating yields must deal with the problem of undistributed earnings of subsidiaries and 20-to-50 percent owned affiliates.

Should the equity in undistributed earnings of subsidiaries be reckoned as part of the interest assumption?

There is no easy answer to this question. The life insurance audit guide refers only to dividends received in its discussion of the interest assumption; no clue is offered as to whether the equity in undistributed earnings is to be included in the calculation of yield.

The recognition of equity in the undistributed earnings of a subsidiary or affiliate is in the nature of an anticipation of future dividend distributions or future capital gains. Increases in the carrying value of the investment by reason of recognizing the equity in undistributed earnings is akin to increases in market values of equity securities. Unrealized capital gains cannot under existing rules be counted as part of investment income. Under present rules, then, the evidence is on the side of excluding the equity in undistributed earnings from the calculation of yield.

Special considerations apply to a life insurance subsidiary whose assumptions are "consolidated" with those of the parent for purposes of calculating adjusted reserves. Such special considerations are discussed in Chapter 27.

Miscellaneous income. Sometimes it is difficult to classify a particular item of income as investment income; for example, rental of idle computer time. A practical rule to follow is to classify a particular item of income as investment or insurance on the basis of its principal function. In the case of the computer rental income the computer's principal function is to serve the insurance operation, and the rental income should preferably be regarded as insurance income. Another practical rule to follow is to treat an item of income as insurance income if the asset base to which the income relates is not readily determinable. In the case of the computer rental income it would be very difficult to apportion the investment in the computer between the rental income and the insurance operation and thus to translate the rental income into a percentage yield.

Investment Expenses

The life insurance audit guide provides that the interest assumption used for purposes of calculating adjusted reserves should be "net of investment expenses."

It goes without saying that allocations of expense to the investment function should be fair and reasonable. Allocations that are based on considerations that essentially lie outside the realm of adjusted reserves —such as the desire to maximize tax deductions— should be carefully reviewed to ensure that the allocations are appropriate. In particular, allocations of general administrative overhead should be severely limited.

Exclusion of any items of investment income from the yield calculation, such as income on real estate and equity investments, would require exclusion of any related expenses, of course.

Investment expenses are discussed further in Chapter 17.

Taxes on Investment Income*

The life insurance audit guide provides that a company taxed solely on taxable investment income and expecting beyond a reasonable doubt to be so taxed indefinitely need not provide deferred taxes on Phase II timing differences resulting from the conversion to generally accepted accounting principles because there will be no tax effect when such timing differences reverse. A company taxed on taxable investment income plus one-half of the excess of gain from operations over taxable investment income, and expecting to be so taxed indefinitely, must effectively tax-effect one-half of the Phase II timing differences. And a company taxed purely on gain from operations, and expecting to be so taxed indefinitely, must tax-effect 100 percent of the Phase II timing differences.

The only Phase I timing differences that would be tax-effected would be differences in items of investment income or expense attributable to differences in methods of accounting for such items. For example, depreciation computed on a straight-line basis for financial statement purposes and on an accelerated basis for tax purposes would give rise to a timing difference that would usually require a provision for deferred taxes if the timing difference is material.

Timing differences and deferred taxes are discussed in Chapter 26. The important thing at this point is to recognize that taxable investment income as such is not subject to deferred tax accounting. The level of the reserves will be different as between the tax return and the adjusted financial statements, thus creating a difference between the policyholders' share of investment income calculated on the basis of reserves reported for tax purposes and the indicated policyholders' share calculated on the basis of adjusted reserves. Any such difference is regarded as a permanent difference so far as deferred taxes are concerned:

While the inclusion of adjustments to life insurance reserves and deferral and amortization of acquisition costs resulting from the adoption of generally accepted accounting principles in a hypothetical tax return would indirectly affect taxable investment income, such effect is a permanent difference. These items affect only total assets or aggregate reserves, which amounts will, for income

*This material is based on concepts developed by John M. Bragg (Vice President and Chief Actuary, Life Insurance Company of Georgia) and James C. H. Anderson (Director, Tillinghast & Company, Inc.). Portions of the discussion are adapted with permission from the October 1973 issue of Emphasis, *published by Tillinghast & Company.*

tax purposes, always be greater or less than comparable amounts for accounting purposes. Accordingly, amounts of such differences do not reverse in subsequent periods.[11]

In essence, deferred tax accounting is limited to (1) amounts associated with differences in calculating items of investment income and expense and (2) Phase II timing differences, principally the adjustments for acquisition costs and reserves. The amount of the deduction for the policyholders' share of investment income is regarded as fixed, i.e., the same for tax purposes and financial statement purposes.

This means that taxable investment income is taxed as it is reported on the tax return. The tax is reported as an expense in the financial statements in the same amount and for the same period as the tax return amount, irrespective of its relationship to pre-tax income reported in the financial statements.

Recognition of investment income. In converting to adjusted reserves, the reserves are calculated in such a manner as to match benefits and expenses with premium revenue. Thus, if experience is equivalent to the reserve assumptions, the recognition of earnings will be proportional to the recognition of premium revenues. The effect of providing for adverse deviation is to modify the degree of proportionality, but proportionality remains the central tendency of the process.

The forces at work might be illustrated as follows:

Year	Gross Premiums	Interest	Deaths	Change in Reserve	Pre-Tax Earnings
1	$100	$ 8	$ 10	$ 88	$10
2	100	16	20	86	10
3	100	24	50	64	10
4	100	28	150	(32)	10
5	100	24	320	(206)	10
	$500	$100	$550	$ –	$50
Average	$100	$ 20	$110		$10

It is apparent that the reserve operates in such a manner as to level out total charges at $90 a year, which is equal to average deaths ($110) less average interest ($20), thus producing level earnings of $10 a year. In other words, the effect of the reserve is to level out all items of expense including interest, which is treated as a *negative expense,* not a revenue item.

The reserve can therefore be ignored and average expenses can simply be matched with level gross premiums:

147

| Year | Gross Premiums | Average Expense | | | Pre-Tax Earnings |
		Deaths	Interest	Net	
1	$100	$110	$ 20	$ 90	$10
2	100	110	20	90	10
3	100	110	20	90	10
4	100	110	20	90	10
5	100	110	20	90	10
	$500	$550	$100	$450	$50

Viewed another way, profits equal the difference between the gross premium and the valuation premium. The latter is the mechanism by which expenses are averaged. In the above case, the valuation premium is $90.

Assume now that taxes are paid on taxable investment income at a rate that works out to 50 percent of interest earned (in other words, assume for purposes of illustration that the policyholders' share is zero). Taxes paid would be as follows:

Year	Interest	Taxes
1	$ 8	$ 4
2	16	8
3	24	12
4	28	14
5	24	12
	$100	$50

While investment income has been reported as earned for tax purposes, it has effectively been leveled out for book purposes:

Year	Book	Tax	Book-Tax Difference
1	$ 20	$ 8	$12
2	20	16	4
3	20	24	(4)
4	20	28	(8)
5	20	24	(4)
	$100	$100	$ –

Thus after-tax earnings would be reported in the following pattern:

Year	Pre-Tax Book Earnings	Taxes Paid	After-Tax Book Earnings
1	$10	$ 4	$ 6
2	10	8	2
3	10	12	(2)
4	10	14	(4)
5	10	12	(2)
	$50	$50	$ –

If the company were taxed purely on Phase II income this difference would be tax-effected in calculating the gain from operations because (1) the change in reserves is taken into account in calculating the gain and (2) the difference between tax reserves and book reserves is treated as a timing difference.

In Phase I, however, the difference would not be tax-effected. In terms of the Phase I calculation viewed in isolation, this would seem to be proper. Actual investment income is always the same for book or tax purposes (absent such items as differences in depreciation, amortization of bond discount, etc.). The policyholders' share would be a more or less constant percentage of actual. Required interest on adjusted reserves might differ, but so long as the book reserves and tax reserves never cross, the difference is permanent in substantially all cases.

But it is not correct to view the Phase I calculation in isolation. The Phase I calculation involves treating investment income as revenue. For book purposes it is being treated as a level negative expense; where it shows up in the tax return is beside the point in the context of the financial statements. Because of this, the difference between the *increasing interest income* reported on the tax return and the *level negative expense* effectively reported in the financial statements might be viewed as a timing difference that should be tax-effected.

However, timing differences for deferred tax purposes usually relate to income that is taxed as such. Taxable investment income may bear no relationship to gain from operations, but it may be taxable anyway. The tax on taxable investment income is in the nature of a "gross receipts tax" similar, for example, to a premium tax. In other words, the tax on investment income could be viewed as an investment expense to be accounted for as such.

Computing tax expense. Taxes on investment income can be estimated in advance and translated into a reduction of the assumed interest rate.

For a company that expects to be taxed indefinitely on taxable investment income less $250,000 (hereinafter designated as "T"), the tax might be estimated according to the following form:

Let a = the pre-tax adjusted reserve interest assumption.

Let b = the statutory reserve interest assumption.

Let c = the tax rate.

Let d = the after-tax adjusted reserve interest assumption.

Then $d = a - [(1 - c)(a - a[1 - 10(a - b)])]$.

Thus, if the statutory reserve assumption is 3 percent, the pre-tax adjusted reserve assumption is 8 percent, and the tax rate is 50 percent, the approximate after-tax interest rate is 6 percent:

$$d = .08 - [(1-.5)(.08-.08[1-10(.08-.03)])]$$
$$d = .08 - .5 \times (.08 - .04)$$
$$d = .08 - .02 = .06 \text{ or } 6\%.$$

It is important to appreciate that this calculation is an *approximation*. The foregoing calculation assumes that an 8 percent reserve will be held, whereas the after-tax equivalent assumes a 6 percent reserve will be held. A 6 percent reserve is higher than an 8 percent reserve and thus earns more interest. The true after-tax equivalent would have to be calculated by an algebraic process that recognizes that interest earned on the reserve is the amount that will be taxed, while the tax itself is reflected in the interest rate that is used to obtain the *level* of the reserve. In the illustration above the true after-tax rate would be slightly greater than 6 percent.

For a company that expects to be taxed indefinitely on taxable investment income plus one-half of the excess of gain from operations (hereinafter designated as "G") over taxable investment income, the tax might be estimated according to the following form:

$$.08-d = 1/2(1-.5)(.08-.08[1-10(.08-.03)])$$
$$+ 1/2(1-.5)(.08-d)$$
$$.08-d = .25 \times .04 + .25 \times (.08-d)$$
$$.08-d = .01 + .02 - .25d$$
$$-d = -.05 - .25d$$
$$.75d = .05$$
$$d = .0667 \text{ or } 6.67\%.$$

And if all else stays the same except the pre-tax adjusted reserve interest assumption is 7 percent, the approximate after-tax interest rate is 6.07 percent:

$$.07-d = 1/2(1-.5)(.07-.07[1-10(.07-.03)])$$
$$+ 1/2(1-.5)(.07-d)$$
$$.07-d = .25 \times .028 + .25 \times (.07-d)$$
$$.07-d = .007 + .0175 - .25d$$
$$-d = -.0455 - .25d$$
$$.75d = .0455$$
$$d = .06067 \text{ or } 6.07\%.$$

As in the case of the company taxed only on T, the foregoing is an approximation. The true after-tax rate would be computed by an algebraic process that takes into account the level of the reserve assumed to be earning interest.

Approximate equivalent after-tax interest rates for several different pre-tax assumptions where statutory and tax-basis reserves are based on 3 percent are as follows:*

Pre-Tax Adjusted Reserve Interest Assumption	Equivalent After-Tax Interest Rate	
	Company Taxed on T	Company Taxed on 1/2 (G + T)
3%	3.0%	3.0%
4	3.8	3.9
5	4.5	4.7
6	5.1	5.4
7	5.6	6.1
8	6.0	6.7
9	6.3	7.2
10	6.5	7.7
11	6.6	8.1
12	6.6	8.4
13	6.5	8.7

Companies taxed entirely on gain from operations—i.e., G is less than T—do not pay a tax on investment income. Any excess of assumed interest over the policyholders' share is absorbed in the change in adjusted reserves.

However, a situation in which G is less than T is usually temporary. Thus, even for companies currently being taxed solely on G, the assumed interest rate should be net of taxes that will be payable in the company's ultimate tax posture.

Where there is any substantive doubt as to the company's ultimate tax posture, the tax posture assumed for purposes of computing equivalent after-tax interest assumptions should be that which gives the most conservative result—i.e., an assumption that T alone will be subject to tax. Otherwise a future revaluation may be necessary. (However, the effect of such revaluation could be offset in part or in whole by the deferred tax adjustments caused by a change in facts and circumstances. This is discussed further in Chapter 26.)

Where a company's assumed pre-tax interest rate is appropriately conservative, it may not be necessary to provide explicitly for taxes on T. This is a judgment that must be made based on the spread between the assumed rate and the equivalent after-tax rate. That spread represents, in effect, a reduction in the provision for adverse deviation. If the implicit provision for adverse deviation is felt to be adequate after "grossing

*Reprinted with minor modifications from the October 1973 issue of *Emphasis* published by Tillinghast & Company, Inc.

up" the interest assumption, no tax adjustment would seem to be called for.

Illustrations and additional commentary on the impact of taxes on interest assumptions, adjusted reserves, and associated profits will be found in Appendix B.

Yield Calculation

The statutory basis for calculating yield percentages is essentially to divide investment income by the mean of cash and invested assets for the year. This produces a valid result when cash flow from operations is evenly distributed throughout the year and funds are invested immediately.

When yield rates are being calculated in connection with a conversion to generally accepted accounting principles, it may be appropriate to modify the traditional methods of calculating yields to adjust for

▸ Uneven cash flows.
▸ Temporary yield-reducing conditions such as construction in progress.
▸ Income, expense, and asset adjustment of the type described earlier in this chapter.
▸ Adjustments called for by generally accepted accounting principles, such as amortization of mortgage commitment fees. (According to the life insurance audit guide, "normal fees should be recognized as income over the commitment period and excess fees should be recognized as an adjustment to the effective interest rate over the period of the mortgage loans." [12])

The objective of refining yield calculations is to portray a time series of interest rates that is as representative and accurate as possible. The interest assumption is influenced by the time series. So the effect of refining the yield calculation, while important, is indirect.

The relationship of indicated yields to capital gains and losses is discussed later in this chapter.

Selecting Interest Assumptions

While the choice of an interest assumption is a "subjective judgment," as the audit guide says, the judgment should represent something more than a mere opinion or a fervent wish. The judgment should be informed, conservative, and supportable.

Influence of Trends

An analysis of interest trends is indispensable to selecting an interest assumption. It's indispensability does not lie in projecting the trend, but in (1) establishing where a company's interest rates are in relation to where they have been, (2) determining an appropriate initial rate, and (3) providing a frame of reference for a prudent estimate of future rates. In addition, for older blocks of business a trend analysis will generally suggest the range of interest rates that would have been appropriate at the time of issue.

Crazy Quilt Life began its analysis of interest rate trends by graphing insurance industry interest rates. The graph is shown in Table 9–4. The industry's interest rate history, which covered a much greater time period than Crazy Quilt's term of existence, provided perspective necessary to evaluate Crazy Quilt's past, present, and probable future experience.

Crazy Quilt next arrayed its own history of interest rates. The array is shown in Table 9–5 and includes for Crazy Quilt's 31-year history:

▸ Coverage of statutory reserves (net of deferred and uncollected premiums) and other interest-bearing liabilities by fixed-income investments (bonds, mortgages, and policy loans),
▸ Gross new money rates on bonds, mortgages, and the entire portfolio (the policy loan rate has held constant at 5 percent over the period),
▸ New money rates net of expenses for the portfolio,
▸ Portfolio average rates net of expenses,
▸ Industry portfolio average rates net of expenses, and
▸ Adjusted reserve interest assumptions.

The adjusted reserve assumptions also represent ratebook assumptions, which were regarded as providing adequately for adverse deviation.

The Company found that its assumptions on older blocks of business were proven reasonable by historical development. The rates chosen were close to the earned rates at the time of choice. In the earlier years, when rates were rising, the Company held to level assumptions because the trend of increases was not yet fixed and assumption of an increasing rate was not justified; however, rates were sufficiently low in terms of the industry's interest rate history that the assumption of a decreasing rate was also not justified.

As time progressed and interest rates continued rising Crazy Quilt raised its assumed beginning rate to coincide with the rates then being earned. But Crazy Quilt was not willing to assume that rates would continue increasing, nor was it willing even to assume that rates would hold constant. Assuming there is such a thing as a long-term interest rate cycle, the Company perceived that its rates were climbing

Table 9–4.

INSURANCE INDUSTRY AVERAGE INTEREST RATES, 1930–1971

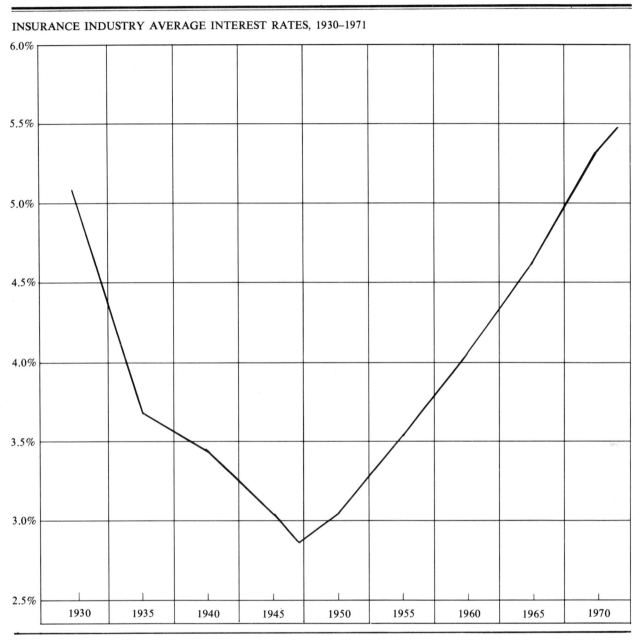

to a peak in the cycle. There was no way to know if rates would keep increasing, level off or begin falling, but in the absence of relative certainty the Company felt it was mandatory to assume that rates would begin falling. And so interest rates on non-par products were graded systematically to a conservative long-term assumption. The grading pattern took into account the lag between new-money rates and average rates, as will be described later in this chapter. The long-term

assumption reflected, in essence, Crazy Quilt's estimate of the pure rate of interest (that is, excluding inflation) without considering catastrophic events, such as wars, that can have dramatic effects on interest rates. Crazy Quilt recognized that no interest assumption, including statutory assumptions, can feasibly furnish protection against cataclysms. So the ultimate rate represented a conservative estimate about the future, but it did not provide for maximum adversity.

151

Table 9–5.

SUMMARY OF INTEREST RATES

Year	Coverage of Statutory Interest-Bearing Liabilities by Fixed-Income Investments	Gross New Money Rates — Bonds*	Gross New Money Rates — Mortgages	Gross New Money Rates — Total Portfolio	Portfolio New Money Rates Net of Investment Expenses**	Portfolio Average Rates Net of Investment Expenses**	Industry Portfolio Average Rates Net of Investment Expenses	Non-Par Products — Beginning Rate	Non-Par Products — Ending Rate	Non-Par Products — Grading Period in Years	Level Rate for Par Products	Level Rate for Single-Premium Products	Rate for Experience-Rated Group Products
1941	227%	2.95%		2.95%	2.85%	2.85%	3.42%						
1942	183	2.80		2.80	2.70	2.80	3.44						
1943	159	2.70	4.80%	3.23	3.02	2.91	3.33						
1944	141	2.70	4.70	3.32	3.83	2.98	3.23	2.75%	2.75%	—	3.50%		
1945	137	2.65	4.70	4.25	3.29	2.97	3.11						
1946	136	2.55	4.50	3.61	2.96	3.00	2.93						
1947	133	2.53	4.40	3.20	2.97	2.97	2.88					3.50%	
1948	132	2.71	4.50	3.39	3.02	3.02	2.96						
1949	130	2.62	4.60	3.53	3.25	3.06	3.06	3.00	3.00	—	3.50		
1950	122	2.57	4.60	3.81	3.40	3.15	3.13						
1951	117	2.82	4.70	3.56	3.26	3.23	3.18						
1952	115	2.93	4.80	3.70	3.34	3.29	3.28						
1953	113	3.18	4.90	3.95	3.61	3.38	3.36						
1954	111	2.80	5.00	3.76	3.39	3.40	3.46						
1955	107	3.03	4.90	3.93	3.55	3.47	3.51	3.25	3.00	10	3.50		
1956	104	3.33	4.90	4.14	3.75	3.56	3.63						
1957	100	3.96	5.80	4.76	4.34	3.76	3.75						
1958	100	3.74	5.70	4.73	4.33	3.87	3.85						
1959	101	4.37	6.10	5.01	4.66	4.08	3.96	4.00	3.00	20			
1960	100	4.37	6.30	5.05	4.72	4.26	4.11						
1961	101	4.41	6.10	4.96	4.63	4.38	4.22						
1962	102	4.26	6.00	4.84	4.52	4.45	4.34						
1963	104	4.22	5.90	4.81	4.48	4.49	4.45	4.50	3.00	30	4.50		
1964	108	4.37	6.00	4.95	4.64	4.56	4.53						
1965	108	4.43	5.80	4.87	4.57	4.61	4.61					4.50	
1966	106	5.08	6.00	5.38	5.05	4.77	4.73				5.00		
1967	104	5.43	6.50	5.62	5.31	4.97	4.82						
1968	104	6.08	7.00	6.04	5.72	5.25	4.95	5.50	3.50	30			
1969	102	6.98	7.50	6.97	6.68	5.65	5.12					5.50	
1970	101	7.38	7.50	7.25	6.96	5.98	5.30	6.50	3.50	30	6.00		
1971	102	7.09	7.50	6.82	6.54	6.04	5.44					6.00	

Adjusted Reserve Assumptions. The Rate for Experience-Rated Group Products is marked "Special and Negotiated."

* Combined U. S. Government, municipals, and corporates.

** On a calendar-year basis. Expressed on a policy-year basis, the rates would differ slightly.

While fixed-income investments were found to cover interest-bearing liabilities, it was decided to use over-all rates for purposes of the adjusted reserve assumptions because the tolerances were close and to allow for future changes in the mix of investments. In addition, the over-all rate was relatively conservative in relation to rates on fixed-income investments because the indicated yields on stocks and real estate were lower than on fixed-income investments; such conservatism was considered desirable.

With regard to the coverage of interest-bearing liabilities by fixed-income securities, it was recognized that adjusted reserves, net of acquisition costs, were significantly less than statutory, so the tolerances would be greater with respect to the adjusted reserves. But statutory reserves were used in testing coverage because the statutory measure represented a better measure of *safety*. The effect was to introduce still another conservative bias into the evaluation process. Also, as a practical matter, adjusted reserve amounts were not known at the time of making the evaluation.

Crazy Quilt distinguished between non-par products and par products in choosing its interest assumption, and made a further distinction between single-premium and level-premium non-par products. The reasons for making these distinctions are discussed later in this chapter.

Interest Models

Crazy Quilt also tested its assumptions for recent issues by the use of "interest models" in which

▸ Future new money rates, graded to a conservative estimate, were projected for each major type of investment,

▸ Operating cash flows (including interest on *statutory* reserves) were projected,

▸ Maturities and reinvestments of invested assets were projected, and

▸ The mix of new investments was projected.

The net result was to produce a weighted average interest rate for each year that each block of new business was expected to persist. The models thus gave effect to the actual current and estimated future mix of investments; expected interest rates on new investments and reinvestments; expected asset rollover; and projected cash flow from premiums, interest, claims, surrenders, and expenses. Inherent in the calculations was a determination of the extent to which asset maturities and liability maturities matched up. Where they didn't, capital gains and losses were estimated based on the then-current level of assumed interest rates vs. the average period to maturity and average interest rates on assets assumed to be liquidated.

The interest models were very complex, and as is the case with all such projections, the results were suspect. But not as suspect as a mere guess. The models provided necessary additional support for the Company's interest assumptions.

Taxes on Investment Income

Crazy Quilt Life reviewed the net effect of its interest assumptions and determined that the rates were sufficiently conservative to allow for any taxes on taxable investment income. This was true notwithstanding the grading patterns; overall, the Company's average assumed yields were about 4 percent and were not expected to exceed 4 1/2 percent in the forseeable future.

Plan Differentiation

Crazy Quilt Life found it necessary to make certain distinctions among plans or lines of business in selecting its interest assumptions. One set of assumptions was clearly not appropriate for all of Crazy Quilt's products.

Nonparticipating products. All nonparticipating individual life and health insurance products were considered together in choosing the main set of interest assumptions—ordinary life, industrial life, and long-term individual health coverages. All such products were deemed to share the same basic characteristics—long contract terms, continuous premiums, and uncertainty about interest rates at which premiums to be received in the distant future would be invested.

So interest rates for nonparticipating products issued after 1951, when interest rates were on the rise, graded to conservative ultimate rates, as indicated in Table 9–5 and as discussed previously. The grading pattern is detailed in Table 9–6.

The grading increments were chosen largely as a matter of convenience. It would have been possible, of course, to grade rates more gradually, for example, .1 percent a year; but the effect of more refined grading was minimal (see Table 9–2 for an example) and since the assumptions represented assumptions in any event, it was decided that no useful purpose would be served by refining the grading procedure.

During the 1960s interest rates were rising rapidly enough to support a pattern of *increasing* interest

Table 9–6.

DETAILS OF GRADING PATTERN FOR INTEREST ASSUMPTIONS ON NONPARTICIPATING PRODUCTS

Ratebook Era*	1–5	6–10	11–15	16–20	21–25	26–30	31 on
1941–1947	2.75%	2.75%	2.75%	2.75%	2.75%	2.75%	2.75%
1948–1951	3.00	3.00	3.00	3.00	3.00	3.00	3.00
1952–1956	3.25	3.25	3.00	3.00	3.00	3.00	3.00
1957–1961	4.00	3.75	3.50	3.25	3.00	3.00	3.00
1962–1967	4.50	4.25	4.00	3.75	3.50	3.25	3.00
1968–1969	5.50	5.00	4.50	4.25	4.00	3.75	3.50
1970–1971	6.50	6.00	5.50	5.00	4.50	4.00	3.50

*Interim partial ratebook revisions were assigned the interest assumption then prevailing for the major ratebook era.

rate assumptions for a few years, followed by a gradual grading downward to a conservative ultimate rate. In examining this possibility Crazy Quilt found that the effect of a modestly increasing rate in the early years was negligible, and that locking in the relatively realistic initial rate for a few years adequately recognized the then-prevailing level of earned interest rates.

The reasons for grading interest rates on nonparticipating products may be summarized as follows: net future cash inflows will be invested at rates that become increasingly less certain as time passes, and uncertainty demands a fair degree of conservatism. There are no dividends available to absorb declines in interest earnings; interest "losses" must be borne by available profit margins, which may not be adequate for the purpose because of the material effect of interest. Surplus is also available to absorb such declines, but that is another way of saying that surplus is available to absorb future *losses,* and every reasonable measure should be taken to avoid such losses, which may be viewed as being a result of being insufficiently conservative.

Limited-payment life business that was in the paid-up period was reserved for at the interest rate applicable to nonparticipating products of the given issue year. Thus, for example, reserves on 20-pay life business issued in 1971 were assumed to earn interest at 4.5 percent for Years 21 to 25, 4 percent for Years 26 to 30, and 3 1/2 percent thereafter. In theory a slightly different rate could have been justified, but that would have required identifying specific assets associated with paid-up business 20 years hence and matching future asset maturities with future liability maturities, all of which would have affected what was left to cover premium-paying policies; and it was decided that it was impracticable to make such refinements in estimates of what the situation would be in 20 years. Since none of the Company's basic

permanent life insurance plans had a premium-paying period of less than 20 years, this procedure was adopted for all limited-payment life insurance plans.

With respect to reduced paid-up insurance the same procedure was followed, partly because the points in time at which the nonforfeiture option was selected were scattered throughout the premium-paying period and partly because reduced paid-up reserves were not material.

And as for paid-up dividend additions, which in Crazy Quilt's case were nonparticipating, a single interest assumption (4 percent) was used as a matter of convenience. (Paid-up additions are discussed further in Chapters 10 and 11.)

Special considerations applicable to paid-up industrial business are discussed in Chapter 18.

Participating business. Because dividend scales on Crazy Quilt's participating business assumed a level interest rate, a level interest rate was also used for purposes of calculating reserves when the dividends were provided for, as benefits, in the reserves themselves. This had no impact on the nonparticipating assumptions; use of a level rate in the case of participating business is essentially equivalent to the use of a graded rate on nonparticipating business. This is discussed further in Chapter 10.

Assumed interest rates for participating business are shown in Table 9–5.

Single-premium annuities. Considerations for single-premium annuities are received in a lump sum that can be invested immediately at a known rate of return. Crazy Quilt's investments in respect of single-premium annuity business were made with an eye toward matching (1) asset maturities and (2) annuity payments net of interest earnings, thus substantially eliminating investment risk. So Crazy Quilt calculated adjusted reserves on such business using a level interest assumption approximately equivalent to

Table 9–7.

INCREASE IN POLICY LOANS AS PERCENTAGE OF INCREASE IN TOTAL ASSETS, 1967–1971*

| | *Increase in Policy Loans as Percentage of Increase in Total Assets* | | | | |
	1967	*1968*	*1969*	*1970*	*1971*
Mutual companies:					
6 diversified	5.7%	7.0%	17.5%	15.9%	4.5%
12 ordinary	25.1	31.9	97.5	63.5	14.8
18 total	11.6	14.8	39.7	30.4	13.2
Stock companies:					
13 diversified	4.4	5.9	18.7	13.9	2.2
8 ordinary	9.3	13.3	40.4	26.8	6.7
21 total	5.2	7.1	22.5	16.4	2.9
Balance of industry	6.9	8.4	17.4	13.8	7.2
Total industry	9.1%	11.5%	29.4%	22.3%	6.7%

*Adapted from "Life Insurance Industry Policy Loans" by Frederick V. Hill, published in October 1973 by Cyrus J. Lawrence, Inc. of New York.

the yield rate on the assets in which the annuity considerations were invested.

This procedure necessitated segregating assets applicable to the annuity business and separately accounting for such assets and the related investment income. The assets and investment income were eliminated from the interest models for other products and thus did not affect the assumptions developed for those products. This is essential since the relatively high yields on the annuity assets is needed to support the annuity reserves and can never become available for other products.

Assumed interest rates for single-premium annuities are shown in Table 9–5.

Certain group contracts. As discussed in Chapter 20, Crazy Quilt also allocated certain assets and investment income to certain group contracts where interest rates on policyholder funds were negotiated. The principles involved in making the allocations were basically the same as the principles employed with respect to single-premium annuities.

Dividend accumulations, etc. No special recognition was given to dividend accumulations, supplementary contracts not involving life contingencies, and similar deposit-type items. Current rates paid or credited on such items were less than rates being earned. The guaranteed rates, wherever applicable, were no greater than the assumed ultimate rates on nonparticipating business, and any actual decrease in interest rates would have resulted in corresponding reductions in the current payment rate. Further, interest-bearing assets covered all interest-bearing liabilities including

deposit-type items. So deposit-type items did not affect the interest assumptions for insurance products.

Interest on modified coinsurance reserves. Crazy Quilt's modified coinsurance reserves were immaterial and no special recognition was given to interest (5 percent) on such reserves.

Where modified coinsurance reserves are material, the interest rate on such reserves is fixed by contract, the period to recapture is generally subject to a minimum number of years, the ceding company cannot voluntarily pay back the reserves, and the contract rate exceeds the interest rate assumption at any time during the period to recapture, consideration should be given to adjusting the interest deemed available to cover retained business to recognize the fact that the interest differential paid to the reinsurer will not be available.

Reinsurance is discussed further in Chapter 22.

Policy Loans

When a life insurance company's portfolio of insurance in force is heavily concentrated in permanent ordinary products, special consideration must be given to the effect of the policy loan interest rate.

The investment problem posed by the policy loan privilege is fairly simple: in periods of tight credit or high interest rates, people tend to take out policy loans. As respects tight credit, the reason that policy loans come under pressure is that money from other sources is not readily available. As respects high interest rates, the more sophisticated policyholders tend to borrow cash values at relatively low interest rates and invest them at higher rates.

The impact of tight money and high interest rates on policy loan activity is suggested by Table 9–7, which traces increases in policy loans as a percentage of the increases in total assets for the period 1967–1971 for (1) 18 mutual companies, of which six are "diversified", i.e., are active in all lines of life insurance, and 12 are oriented primarily to permanent individual insurance, (2) 21 stock companies, of which 13 are "diversified" and eight are oriented primarily to individual ordinary insurance, (3) the balance of the life insurance industry, and (4) the total industry. The 18 mutual companies and 21 stock companies together represent about 75 percent of the industry in terms of assets. The 1969–1970 period represents a period of high interest rates and very tight money. The impact on companies heavily committed to individual ordinary insurance is readily apparent from Table 9–7.

To the extent that (1) high interest rates on bonds and mortgages are expected, (2) the expected high rates are higher than the policy loan rate, and (3) the high rates are carried into the interest assumption, then the interest assumption should also recognize the likely proportion of assets flowing into policy loans as a result of such high rates and, consequently, the reduction in yields resulting from the phenomenon.

It should also be mentioned that a policy loan is frequently the forerunner to a lapse. Hence the interest assumption may have an effect on the withdrawal assumption.

Capital Gains and Losses

While normally considered to be distinct from investment income, capital gains and losses really represent an element of investment yield. For example, capital gains and losses on bonds are typically related to changes in the market rate of interest. Capital gains and losses on equity securities may reflect the retention of earnings that could have been distributed as dividends but that were profitably reinvested.

The ultimate measure of yield on an investment is a combination of dividends, interest, etc., received plus the yield equivalent of capital gains and losses. If a particular investment in a common stock yields 4 percent in dividends and is sold after, say, 10 years for an amount that is equivalent to the original

cost compounded over the 10 years at 6 percent, the total yield on the investment is 10 percent.

Generally, however, a company cannot properly recognize capital gains and losses in establishing its adjusted reserve interest assumption, partly because they are considered too unpredictable to formalize in the interest assumption but mainly because existing accounting rules applicable to capital gains and losses operate to prevent the matching of revenue and expense.

Audit Guide Provisions

The life insurance audit guide notes that for all but securities brokers and dealers and investment companies, "carrying bonds at amortized cost has been considered a generally accepted practice." [13] Thus amortized cost is, by extension, the appropriate valuation basis for bonds owned by an insurance company. Underlying this general principle is the assumption that the bonds will be held to maturity and that the par value of the bonds will eventually be realized.

As respects mortgage loans, policy loans, collateral loans, and similar assets, the audit guide is silent. Valuing such investments at the unpaid principal balance is the usual method of accounting followed in other industries, and that method is also appropriate for life insurance companies. Again, underlying this principle is the premise that the principal amount will eventually be realized.

The audit guide is also silent about the valuation of real estate, but again, real estate, owned and occupied or acquired for investment, is usually valued at cost less allowances for depreciation in most other industries, and this method is also appropriate for life insurance companies.

As for common and preferred stocks, the audit guide sanctions any of four methods of valuing such investments and/or reporting related capital gains:

1. They may be carried at market with realized gains and losses reported in the income statement and unrealized gains and losses reported as a surplus entry.

2. They may be carried at market with realized and unrealized gains and losses reported in a separate statement of investment gains and losses.

3. They may be carried at market with realized and unrealized gains and losses reported as a surplus entry.

4. They may be carried at cost with realized gains and losses reported in the income statement.

Convertible bonds, which assume some of the

characteristics of equity securities, are presumably to be accounted for as bonds, i.e., at amortized cost.

The Problem with Capital Gains and Losses

Companies that rarely report capital gains and losses and that never expect to report material amounts of capital gains and losses will, for all practical purposes, recognize all of their investment income in the form of interest, dividends, rents, and other "normal" items of investment income. So long as their reserve interest assumptions are based on such normal items of investment income, investment income reported in the income statement is properly matched against required interest on the reserves, which is also reported in the income statement as a part of the increase in reserves.

For all other companies, however, capital gains and losses can introduce distortions into the income statement. The distortions are of several types; they are best described by example.

Situation A. The company reports realized and unrealized gains in the surplus account or in a separate statement of capital gains and losses. Its adjusted reserve interest assumption includes provision for capital gains and losses. Thus the capital gain and loss component of required interest is charged to income while the gains and losses themselves escape the income statement. The result is a mismatching of income and expense.

Situation B. The company reports realized and unrealized gains in the surplus account. Its adjusted reserve interest assumption is based only on "normal" items of investment income. But the company's investment in equity securities is very high—25 percent of invested assets. Its assumed interest rate is artificially low because yields on stocks are low. The company is heavily penalized; its operating income is significantly reduced by reason of the artificially low interest assumption.

Situation C. Same as Situation B, except the company reports realized capital gains as part of net income. However, the gains fluctuate violently depending on the decision whether to sell or hold, and analysts assign low credibility to capital gains anyway. The company gains no advantage, and matching is no better.

Situation D. The company explicitly provides for possible capital losses as part of its provision for adverse deviation. The result is somewhat the same as Situation B.

Situation E. The company turns over its entire portfolio of low-yielding bonds in a period of high interest rates, absorbing an enormous capital loss in the process. The capital loss is charged to surplus. The company retains its locked-in interest assumptions which were based in part on its history of low yields. As time progresses the capital loss originally charged to surplus is recouped through higher interest earnings that also exceed required interest and flow to net income. In addition, the new level of yields is used indirectly to support a higher interest assumption on new business. Although no economic advantage has been gained by the company's action—it has merely traded a current capital loss for future interest income—it has obtained a significant income statement advantage.

Lack of a Solution

There is at present no solution to the problems listed above (and, indeed, many more similar problems), except for Situation E which is discussed below. Nor will there be a solution ". . . until such time as generally accepted accounting principles for investments are more clearly defined by an authoritative opinion of the Accounting Principles Board or its successor" [14] [i.e., the Financial Accounting Standards Board].

Until such time as it is possible to report capital gains and losses on a yield-equivalent basis, companies should generally base their adjusted reserve interest assumptions purely on "normal" items of investment income.

Revaluations

However, where a wholesale liquidation of bonds or other fixed-income securities produces effects such as those described in Situation E above, reserves should be revalued to reflect the assumption that the new effective interest rate was applicable all along, i.e., with respect to the past *and*—to the extent that the "roll-forward" can be predicted—with respect to the future. This seems to represent a departure from the lock-in principle, but it actually doesn't. All it does is reproduce the effect that *should* be obtained by use of the lock-in principle. As indicated in Chapter 6, the lock-in principle is based in part on the relationship between assets and liabilities. When that relationship is disturbed by reason of a significant change in the valuation of assets, proper application of the lock-in principle requires that the liabilities be revalued in such a way as to restore the relationship.

The effect of the revaluation should be reflected in the same account as the related capital gain or loss.

Gains and Losses on Other Than Stocks and Bonds

The intent of the life insurance audit guide appears to be to permit recognition in the surplus account of realized and unrealized gains and losses on stocks and realized gains and losses on bonds, in both cases with respect to securities of companies which the insurance company does not control directly or indirectly.

Realized gains and losses (including *provisions* for losses) on every other type of investment should be reported in the income statement.

Securities Valuation Reserve

The life insurance audit guide states that "The Mandatory Securities Valuation Reserve is not a valuation reserve, but is an appropriation of surplus which should be included in the equity section of the balance sheet." [15]

Provisions for anticipated losses on specific securities would be charged to the account in which realized capital gains and losses would be entered. The resulting credit would be applied as a valuation allowance, i.e., deducted from the related asset.

Disclosure

The life insurance audit guide requires that interest assumptions for major blocks of business and years of issue be disclosed. A "major block of business" should be interpreted to include a plan of insurance within a line of business that is specially treated, as for example Crazy Quilt Life's participating business and single-premium annuities.

Because of possible misunderstanding, provision for Phase I taxes in the interest assumption should not be disclosed. The interest rates should be judged on their own merits.

The audit guide requires that capital gains, however accounted for, should be reported net of applicable taxes and should be "prominently displayed," with net unrealized gains, if any, reported in "a separate stockholders' equity account." Further, "when realized gains are excluded from the income statement, the last item in that statement should be designated as 'income, excluding realized investment gains or losses'." [16]

Disclosure of investment income and expenses is discussed in Chapter 5. Disclosure of reserve assumptions in general is discussed and illustrated in Chapter 7. Other matters of presentation and disclosure are discussed in Chapter 29.

10

Dividends

Mortality, withdrawals, nonforfeiture benefits, and interest are the main elements of an adjusted benefit reserve, but not the only ones. Policyholder dividends may be viewed as another element of an adjusted reserve for a participating policy, another type of benefit for which provision must be made in calculating the reserves.

It must be pointed out right at the start, however, that viewing dividends as a "benefit" represents only one way of thinking about them. They may also be thought of as a kind of profit-sharing device, or as a device for implementing release-from-risk concepts.

This chapter deals only with certain aspects of accounting for participating business sold by stock companies. Participating business sold by mutual companies, and the methods of accounting for it, are beyond the scope of this chapter.

Basics of the Par Adjustment

The life insurance audit guide distinguishes between two basic types of stock companies that sell participating business:

1. Those companies for which there are no restrictions on the earnings of participating policies which can inure to the benefit of shareholders, and

2. Those companies for which there are limitations on the amount of earnings on participating business that can inure to the benefit of shareholders.

Type 2 companies are discussed in Chapter 25. This chapter is concerned with Type 1 companies.

With respect to Type 1 companies, the audit guide provides that

For those companies for which there are no earnings restrictions and who use dividend scales that may be unrelated to actual earnings, the specified policy dividends (based upon dividends anticipated or intended in determining gross premiums or as shown by published dividend projections at the date policies are issued) should be provided for ratably over the premium-paying period. The specified dividend may be considered as a planned contractual benefit in computing reserves.[1]

And that is basically all the audit guide says about Type 1 companies.

"No Earnings Restrictions"

A Type 1 company is defined as one for which there are "no earnings restrictions." In fact, however, many state regulatory authorities review dividend scales to ensure that they remain equitable. A company that might otherwise never revise its dividend scales would likely do so because of regulatory pressures, implicit or explicit, when earnings attributable to participating business depart significantly from earnings effectively paid out through the dividend mechanism. In such cases, regulatory pressure or voluntary action may be thought of as constituting a "restriction" on earnings on participating business.

So the "no earnings restrictions" guideline should not be read literally. It refers to companies that are not subject to *formal* restrictions on earnings—i.e., to companies that are not Type 2 companies.

"Scales Unrelated to Actual Earnings"

The audit guide defines a Type 1 company as a company for which there are no earnings restrictions *and* "who use dividend scales that may be unrelated to actual earnings." This seems to establish a twofold test to qualify as a Type 1 company.

All dividend scales relate in some fashion to "actual earnings"; an initial scale relates to then-current earnings patterns and later revisions are designed to maintain a reasonable relationship between dividends and "actual earnings". If "unrelated to actual earnings" were read literally, it is doubtful that *any* company would qualify as a Type 1 company.

This guideline is designed to exclude from Type 1 classification those companies which pay out as dividends, or set aside for future dividends, a predetermined portion of actual participating earnings, whether required by statute to do so or not. Earnings on participating business under these circumstances are restricted, and a company subject to such restrictions is a Type 2 company.

"Specified Policy Dividends"

The general requirement that dividends illustrated at the time of issuing the policy be provided for ratably over the premium-paying period is an attempt to be consistent with the lock-in rule. Dividends are thus seen to be in the nature of an assumption made at the time of issue. Inherent in this view of dividends is the notion that later changes in the dividend scale should be recognized only as the differences between the revised scale and the initial scale actually materialize.

"Provided for Ratably"

Since benefits and expenses are provided for ratably over the premium-paying period, the life insurance audit guide also requires that dividends be provided for ratably over the premium-paying period. Otherwise pre-dividend profits would tend to be level while the curve of the dividend scale was sharply rising; excess profits would be recognized in the early years and reduced profits (and perhaps losses) in the later years.

The ratable recognition requirement means, in effect, that a valuation premium for the dividend must be calculated and a dividend "reserve" must be held equal to the difference between the present value of future dividends and the present value of future dividend valuation premiums, all calculated on the

basis of assumptions and dividend scales applicable at the time of issue.*

"Planned Contractual Benefit"

The life insurance audit guide provides that the initial dividend scale *may* be considered as a planned contractual benefit in calculating adjusted reserves. While the guide is permissive on the matter, possible alternative treatments are not discussed. Presumably any alternative, including separate calculation of the dividend "reserve", would be acceptable so long as the result is a ratable provision for dividends.

Significance of Dividends

The significance of dividends to policyholders may be suggested by examining a condensed summary of operations for the life insurance industry. Such a statement, for 1972, is shown in Table 10–1.

The statement shows that $4.3 billion in dividends to policyholders were incurred in 1972. This represents over 7 percent of revenue from all sources. The bulk of the dividends—87 percent—was incurred by mutual companies, as might be expected. Even for stock companies taken as a whole, however, dividends were not insignificant. They equalled over 22 percent of stock company statutory gain from operations before dividends and federal income taxes in 1972.

A 1968 study** of 141 stock companies, generally the country's largest, showed that 72 percent of such companies had participating insurance in force in 1968. Participating business represented more than 20 percent of ordinary insurance in force for 38 percent of the companies.

Dividends are therefore significant to the stock company segment of the life insurance industry.

Dividend Scales and Adjusted Reserves

While it is dangerous to generalize about a product as complicated as participating insurance, the theory underlying the product may perhaps be summarized as follows:

*Obvious problems arise where the dividend assumptions differ from the valuation assumptions, as they would for example in the case of mutual companies. This subject is beyond the scope of this chapter.

**The study was undertaken in connection with the Ernst & Ernst Life Insurance Accounting Research Project. Results were summarized in *Natural Reserves and Life Insurance Accounting,* an interim report on the Project published in August 1970.

Table 10–1.

CONDENSED LIFE INSURANCE INDUSTRY STATUTORY SUMMARY OF OPERATIONS FOR 1972*

| | Millions of Dollars | | | % of Total | |
	Mutual Companies	Stock Companies	Total Industry	Mutuals	Stocks
Revenue:					
Premiums:					
Ordinary life:					
First-year	$ 1,167	$ 1,029	$ 2,196	53%	47%
Single	836	252	1,088	77	23
Renewal	9,140	5,278	14,418	63	37
Total ordinary life	11,143	6,559	17,702	63	37
Individual annuity	656	803	1,459	45	55
Industrial	462	881	1,343	34	66
Individual health	1,081	2,646	3,727	29	71
Group:					
Life	2,743	2,891	5,634	49	51
Health	4,227	6,363	10,590	40	60
Annuity	2,611	1,433	4,044	65	35
Total premiums	22,923	21,576	44,499	51	49
Net investment income	8,116	4,011	12,127	67	33
Other	1,652	570	2,222	74	26
Total revenue	32,691	26,157	58,848	56	44
Benefits and expenses:					
Benefits paid or reserved for	22,408	17,562	39,970	56	44
Commissions	1,465	2,563	4,028	36	64
General insurance expenses	2,917	2,830	5,747	51	49
Taxes, licenses, and fees	487	509	996	49	51
Other expenses	169	248	417	41	59
Total benefits and expenses	27,446	23,712	51,158	54	46
Gain before dividends and federal income taxes	5,245	2,445	7,690	68	32
Dividends to policyholders	3,723	545	4,268	87	13
Gain before federal income taxes	1,522	1,900	3,422	45	55
Federal income taxes	1,035	499	1,534	68	32
NET GAIN FROM OPERATIONS	$ 487	$ 1,401	$ 1,888	26%	74%

*Source: Institute of Life Insurance.

1. Policyholders are expected to bear most of the risk of adverse deviation in mortality, interest, and expense. To ensure that they do, gross premiums are set at a high enough level to provide for the greatest degree of adversity that can reasonably be expected to occur, come what may.

2. In return for bearing this risk, policyholders also stand to reap the rewards of favorable experience.

3. Dividend scales are designed to implement the foregoing concepts by returning to policyholders the difference between assumed and actual experience in proportion to their contributions to such difference. The result, theoretically, is "insurance at cost".

4. Each class of policyholders—where "class" is defined roughly as a group of policyholders with sufficiently similar characteristics that the group can be considered homogeneous for all practical purposes —should be self-supporting. Otherwise the insurance at cost concept would not be equitably implemented; some classes would benefit to the detriment of others.

In the case of a stock company, some portion of earnings on participating business is usually credited to stockholders (1) for bearing the ultimate risk, (2) for financing sales, and (3) for providing a mechanism for administering the business.

Dividend Assumptions

Construction of a dividend scale by a stock company (but not necessarily a mutual company) might be viewed as beginning with two sets of assumptions:

1. Adverse experience assumptions, usually considered to be adequately represented by statutory reserve assumptions for interest and mortality.

2. Current experience assumptions. The current experience assumptions represent approximations of current average interest earnings (usually net of Phase I taxes) and current *ultimate* mortality rates (selection savings are usually not directly recognized in the dividend scale but are, instead, used to offset heavy first-year expenses).

The differences between the two sets of assumptions produce the mortality and interest contributions to the dividend. The "loading contribution" (discussed later) then becomes a balancing item, introduced in such a manner as to produce a reasonable dividend scale.

The foregoing describes, in somewhat oversimplified terms, the "classic" contribution system for determining dividends.

Mortality and interest. Development of the mortality and interest components of a dividend scale can be illustrated rather simply. Assume, for purposes of discussion, a 5-year endowment issued at age 60 for which the statutory valuation basis is 1958 CSO, 2 1/2 percent, net level. Valuation premium would be $194.92; reserves would be as follows:

Year	Initial Reserve	Terminal Reserve
1	$194.92	$ 183.19
2	378.11	373.63
3	568.55	572.37
4	767.29	780.65
5	975.57	1,000.00

Now assume a dividend experience assumption of 4 percent interest and Table X_{18} mortality.* The mortality and interest components of the initial dividend scale—i.e., the scale in effect when the policy is sold—would be calculated as shown in Table 10–2.

Assuming that 4 percent interest and X_{18} mortality are actually experienced, the effect of the dividend

*Table X_{18}, covering 1950–54 experience of 15 large companies, was based on standard medically examined lives for the sixth through 15th policy years and all standard lives, medical and non-medical, thereafter. The first five policy years were excluded. Table X_{18} grew into Table X_{17}, which developed in turn into the 1958 CSO Table.

scale would be to very nearly pay out 100 percent of earnings. A five-year income statement in which (1) the valuation premium is considered the same as the gross premium and (2) the dividend experience assumptions are actually realized, is also shown in Table 10–2. (Details of Table 10–2 are shown in Table 10–3.)

It will be observed that there is a slight profit remaining in each year. This is due to the fact that the dividend scales contemplate payments to all who begin the policy year whereas dividends are actually paid to those who survive to the end of the policy year. (In addition, there are some rounding differences.)

If reserves were calculated (1) assuming 4 percent interest and X_{18} mortality and (2) assuming the indicated dividend payouts, the valuation premium would be $194.70 (of which $9.04 relates to the dividends) and the terminal reserves would be as follows:

Year	Mortality, Endowment, and Interest Component	Dividend Component	Total	Statutory Terminal Reserve
1	$ 178.67	$4.39	$ 183.06	$ 183.19
2	366.71	6.73	373.44	373.63
3	565.29	6.86	572.15	572.37
4	775.81	4.66	780.47	780.65
5	1,000.00*	–0–	1,000.00	1,000.00

*Just prior to endowment.

It will be readily apparent that the adjusted terminal reserve is very close to the statutory terminal reserve. This will almost always be the case when the dividend assumptions and the reserve assumptions are the same.

Use of the $194.70 adjusted valuation premium as premium income would produce a zero profit in each year. Profits would emerge to the extent of the difference between the statutory valuation premium and the adjusted valuation premium.

Details of the adjusted reserve calculations are shown in Table 10–3.

Loading. Calculating the mortality and interest components in the manner described in the preceding section gives reasonable assurance that the contributions from these sources are equitably distributed (assuming, of course, that the experience rates used in the dividend scale are very close to actual experience).

In addition to mortality and interest, the dividend must also take into account contributions from loading, i.e., (1) the difference between the valuation pre-

Table 10–2.

CALCULATION OF INTEREST AND MORTALITY COMPONENTS OF DIVIDEND SCALE

	Year 1	Year 2	Year 3	Year 4	Year 5
Interest component:					
Initial reserve	$ 194.92	$ 378.11	$ 568.55	$ 767.29	$ 975.57
Excess interest:					
Experience rate	.040	.040	.040	.040	.040
Valuation rate	.025	.025	.025	.025	.025
Difference	× .015	× .015	× .015	× .015	× .015
	$ 2.92	$ 5.67	$ 8.53	$ 11.51	$ 14.63
Mortality component:					
Face amount	$1,000.00	$1,000.00	$1,000.00	$1,000.00	$1,000.00
Terminal reserve	183.19	373.63	572.37	780.65	1,000.00
Net amount at risk	$ 816.81	$ 626.37	$ 427.63	$ 219.35	$ –0–
Mortality savings:					
1958 CSO rates	.02034	.02224	.02431	.02657	.02904
X_{18} rates	.01757	.01928	.02112	.02310	.02525
Difference	×.00277	×.00296	×.00319	×.00347	×.00379
	$ 2.26	$ 1.85	$ 1.36	$ .76	$ –0–
Combined interest and mortality components	$ 5.18	$ 7.52	$ 9.89	$ 12.27	$ 14.63
Income statements:					
Beginning survivorship	1.000	.982	.963	.943	.921
Ending survivorship	.982	.963	.943	.921	.898
Valuation premiums	$ 194.92	$ 191.49	$ 187.80	$ 183.84	$ 179.59
Interest	7.80	14.86	21.91	28.95	35.95
	202.72	206.35	209.71	212.79	215.54
Deaths	17.57	18.94	20.35	21.79	23.26
Endowment					898.09
Reserve increase	179.97	180.02	179.84	179.42	(719.25)
Dividends	5.09	7.24	9.33	11.30	13.14
	202.63	206.20	209.52	212.51	215.24
BALANCE *	$ .09	$ .15	$ .19	$ .28	$ .30

*The indicated "balance" might be paid to policyholders in the form of a mortuary dividend.

mium and the gross premium, less (2) experience expense rates. This would be very simple if expenses were uniform. Suppose the gross premium for the 5-year endowment described earlier were $200.00. Loading would therefore be $5.08 ($200.00 − $194.92). If actual expenses (incurred at the beginning of the year) were $4.00, and in the absence of any other considerations, the contribution from loading would be $1.12 each year ($1.08 improved with interest of 4 percent for one year).

But expenses are not incurred uniformly, of course. Suppose all expenses of $17.84* are incurred at issue.

*The amount of $17.84 is the actuarial equivalent (X_{18} mortality, 4 percent interest) of a series of five annual amounts of $4.00.

Unless the expenses are amortized, the dividend scale would look most strange:

Year	Mortality and Interest	Loading*	Net
1	$ 5.18	$(13.06)	$(7.88)
2	7.52	5.28	12.80
3	9.89	5.28	15.17
4	12.27	5.28	17.55
5	14.63	5.28	19.91

How the excess expenses are amortized through the dividend scale is partly a matter of judgment. If amortized over two years, the result would be a steeply increasing dividend scale. If amortized over the entire

*Improved at 4 percent interest for one year in each case.

Table 10–3.

DETAILS OF ADJUSTED RESERVE CALCULATION WHERE DIVIDENDS ARE TREATED AS BENEFITS

Decrements:

Year	Beginning Survivors	X_{18} Death Rate	Deaths	Ending Survivors
1	1.00000	.01757	.01757	.98243
2	.98243	.01928	.01894	.96349
3	.96349	.02112	.02035	.94314
4	.94314	.02310	.02179	.92135
5	.92135	.02525	.02326	.89809

Present values:

Year	$1 Due at Beginning of Year Discounted at 4%	Present Value at 4% of Death and Endowment Benefits	Present Value at 4% of Dividends
1	$1.000	$ 16.894	$ 4.894
2	.945	17.511	6.694
3	.891	18.091	8.294
4	.838	18.626	9.659
5	.788	757.285	10.800
	$4.462	$828.407	$40.341
Annuity		$ 4.462	$ 4.462
Level premium		$185.66	$ 9.04

Reserves:

Year	Ending Fund		Units in Force	Reserve Per Unit	
	Deaths and Endowment Benefits	Dividends		Deaths and Endowment Benefits	Dividends
1	$175.53	$4.31	.98243	$178.67	$4.39
2	353.32	6.48	.96349	366.71	6.73
3	533.15	6.47	.94314	365.29	6.86
4	714.79	4.29	.92135	775.81	4.66
5	–0–	–0–	–0–	—	—

Income statements:

	Year 1	Year 2	Year 3	Year 4	Year 5
Valuation premiums	$194.70	$191.28	$187.59	$183.62	$179.39
Interest	7.80	14.86	21.91	28.94	36.02
	202.50	206.14	209.50	212.56	215.41
Deaths	17.57	18.94	20.35	21.79	23.26
Endowment					898.09
Reserve increase	179.84	179.96	179.82	179.47	(719.09)
Dividends	5.09	7.24	9.33	11.30	13.15
	202.50	206.14	209.50	212.56	215.41
	$ –0–	$ –0–	$ –0–	$ –0–	$ –0–

then all other events affecting the class of policy-five years, the result would be a more gradual increase in dividends.

The loading factor must do more than smooth out expenses. Thus far in the illustration, withdrawals have not been taken into account in any way, nor have select mortality savings, nor profits. Assuming once again that the interest and ultimate mortality assumptions used for dividend purposes are close to actual,

holders must be reflected in the loading factor. The loading factor, then, becomes the agent for producing a reasonable dividend scale. (Alternatively, a company might produce a reasonable scale by a percentage adjustment of the entire dividend without regard to the individual components.)

Companies often develop the loading factor by means of a profit test of some sort. Suppose, for example, that rate-test assumptions for the 5-year

Table 10–4.

ASSET SHARES BEFORE LOADING CONTRIBUTION, LOADING CONTRIBUTION, AND ASSET SHARES AFTER LOADING CONTRIBUTION

Decrements:

Year	Beginning Survivors	Deaths Rate	Deaths Number	Balance Before Withdrawals	Withdrawals Rate	Withdrawals Number	Ending Survivors
1	1.00000	.00879	.00879	.99121	.20	.19824	.79297
2	.79297	.01476	.01170	.78127	.05	.03906	.74221
3	.74221	.02112	.01567	.72654	.05	.03633	.69021
4	.69021	.02310	.01594	.67427	.05	.03371	.64056
5	.64056	.02525	.01617	.62439	(Endowment)		-0-

Benefits and expenses:

Year	Deaths	Surrenders and Endowment	Expenses *	Mortality and Interest Components of Dividends	Profit Objective *	Total
1	$ 8.79	$ -0-	$92.00	$4.11	$11.50	$116.40
2	11.70	9.77	9.12	5.58	9.12	45.29
3	15.67	18.16	8.54	6.83	8.54	57.74
4	15.94	26.33	7.94	7.86	7.94	66.01
5	16.17	624.39	7.37	9.13	7.37	664.43

* Incurred at beginning of year.

Asset share before loading contribution:

Year	Beginning Fund	Premiums	Interest	Benefits and Expenses	Ending Fund	Units in Force	Adjusted Asset Share**
1	$ -0-	$230.00	$ 5.06	$116.40	$118.66	.79297	$149.64
2	118.66	182.38	11.31	45.29	267.06	.74221	359.82
3	267.06	170.71	16.83	57.74	396.86	.69021	574.98
4	396.86	158.74	21.54	66.01	511.13	.64056	797.94
5	511.13	147.33	25.75	664.43	19.78	.62439 *	31.68

* Just prior to endowment. ** After deduction of profit objective.

Loading contribution:

Year	Asset Share Before Loading Contribution	Terminal Reserve	Asset Share Surplus	Change in Asset Share Surplus	Loading Contribution
1	$149.64	$183.19	$(33.55)	$(33.55)	$ (5.18)
2	359.82	373.63	(13.81)	19.74	(3.76)
3	574.98	572.37	2.61	16.42	5.00
4	797.94	780.65	17.29	14.68	14.00
5	31.68	-0-	31.68	14.39	23.49

Asset share after loading contribution:

Year	Ending Fund Before Loading Contribution	Loading Contribution Rate	Loading Contribution Amount	Cumulative at 4%	Ending Fund After Loading Contribution	Units In Force	Asset Share
1	$118.66	$ (5.18)	$ (4.11)	$ (4.11)	$122.77	.79297	$154.83
2	267.06	(3.76)	(2.79)	(7.06)	274.12	.74221	369.33
3	396.86	5.00	3.45	(3.89)	400.75	.69021	580.62
4	511.12	14.00	8.96	4.91	506.22	.64056	790.28
5	19.78	23.49	14.67	19.78	-0-	-0-	-0-

endowment are a gross premium of $230,* 4 percent interest, X_{18} mortality, selection savings of 50 percent in the first year and 25 percent in the second, withdrawals of 20 percent in the first year and 5 percent thereafter, expenses equal to 20 percent of premiums in the first year and 5 percent thereafter, a profit objective of 5 percent of premiums per year, and cash values as follows:

End of Year	Cash Value
1	$ –0–
2	250
3	500
4	781
5	1,000

Asset shares before the loading contribution are shown in Table 10–4. The loading contribution is distributed in such a way as (1) to produce a sharply increasing dividend scale and (2) to distribute all surplus. The final dividend scale appears as follows:

Year	Mortality	Interest	Loading	Total
1	$2.26	$ 2.92	$(5.18)	$ –0–
2	1.85	5.67	(3.76)	3.76
3	1.36	8.53	5.00	14.89
4	.76	11.51	14.00	26.27
5	–0–	14.63	23.49	38.12

Adjusted Reserves

Earlier it was noted that if adjusted reserves are computed based on the same interest and mortality assumptions as those underlying the dividend scales, the dividend is provided for as a benefit, and the dividend formula uses statutory reserves as a base, the adjusted reserves are very nearly the same as statutory reserves.

The small difference is accounted for primarily by the difference in the survivorship functions.

When withdrawals, nonforfeiture benefits, and expenses are introduced into the calculation of reserves, and the entire dividend including the loading element is treated as a benefit, the relationship between statutory and adjusted no longer holds up. Adjusted reserves that provide for all these elements are shown in Table 10–5, along with statutory and adjusted income statements.**

*The difficulty of marketing a 5-year $1,000 endowment for $230 a year is hereby acknowledged.

**With regard to the income statements shown in Table 10–5, interest is calculated on assets equal to the reserves being held. Since statutory reserves must be held in any event, adjusted income would be increased by interest on the excess of statutory over adjusted reserves.

The adjusted benefit reserves are substantially higher than statutory at all durations, due primarily to the influence of withdrawals. Use of adjusted reserves results in adjusted gain equal to 4.9 percent of premiums, which is within a whisker of the targeted profit of 5 percent.*

Changes in the Scale

A change in the dividend scale accompanying a change in experience may result in a minor effect on income. For example, if the earned interest rate increases and the dividend scale is changed immediately to reflect the change, excess interest earned is offset, to a large degree, by the additional dividend.

The offset is not 100 percent, however, because of differences between the assumed level of reserves and the actual level of reserves. For example, the formula for calculating the interest contribution to the dividend is the difference between the experience rate of interest and the statutory valuation rate multiplied by the initial reserve, and any difference between aggregate reserves calculated using statutory decrements and aggregate reserves that reflect actual decrements will result in an aggregate difference between interest earned and interest distributed through the dividend scale. For this reason, significant changes in dividend scales are often tested by means of another projection, and the loading contribution might also be changed as a result of the change in some other factor.

With respect to the 5-year endowment discussed in the preceding pages, the effect of a shift in the interest rate from 4 percent to 7 percent in the third year, with a concomitant revision of the interest component of the dividend scale (but no other revisions in the scale) is shown in Table 10–6. Note that the result of the revisions is to pay out less than 100 percent of the excess interest earned on the statutory reserve. A distributive rate of about 8.25 percent would be needed to pay out all of the excess interest. Normally such an adjustment would be made in the loading contribution (although it could also be made by adjusting the distributive interest rate.)

Interest earned on the adjusted reserve is, of course, less than on the statutory reserve because the adjusted reserve, net of unamortized acquisition costs, is less than the statutory reserve.

Nature of a Change in Dividend Scale

Revision of a dividend scale by a Type 1 company

*The minor difference is accounted for by some calculation technicalities.

Table 10–5.

RESERVES AND INCOME STATEMENTS FOR PARTICIPATING 5-YEAR ENDOWMENT

	Year 1	Year 2	Year 3	Year 4	Year 5
Reserves:					
Statutory	$183.19	$373.63	$572.37	$780.65	$ -0-
Adjusted:					
Benefits:					
All except dividends	$214.88	$401.26	$592.43	$790.96	$ -0-
Dividends	16.57	28.70	31.32	22.98	-0-
Total benefits	231.45	429.96	623.75	813.94	-0-
Expenses:					
Acquisition	(76.27)	(59.92)	(42.02)	(22.36)	-0-
Maintenance	-0-	-0-	-0-	-0-	-0-
Total expenses	(76.27)	(59.92)	(42.02)	(22.36)	-0-
Total adjusted	$155.18	$370.04	$581.73	$791.58	$ -0-
Statutory income statement:					
Gross premiums	$230.00	$182.38	$170.71	$158.75	$147.33
Interest on reserve	7.80	14.86	21.91	28.95	35.95
	237.80	197.24	192.62	187.70	183.28
Deaths paid	8.79	11.70	15.67	15.94	16.17
Surrenders paid		9.77	18.16	26.33	
Endowment paid					624.39
Dividends paid		2.79	10.28	16.83	23.80
Change in reserves	145.26	132.05	117.75	104.99	(500.05)
Expenses paid	92.00	9.12	8.54	7.94	7.37
	246.05	165.43	170.40	172.03	171.68
Statutory gain	$ (8.25)	$ 31.81	$ 22.22	$ 15.67	$ 11.60
Adjusted income statement:					
Gross premiums	$230.00	$182.38	$170.71	$158.75	$147.33
Interest on reserve	5.07	11.50	17.14	21.78	24.53
	235.07	193.88	187.85	180.53	171.86
Benefits:					
Deaths paid	8.79	11.70	15.67	15.94	16.17
Surrenders paid		9.77	18.16	26.33	
Endowment paid					624.39
Change in reserve	170.39	127.43	111.08	97.76	(506.66)
	179.18	148.90	144.91	140.03	133.90
Dividends:					
Paid		2.79	10.28	16.83	23.80
Change in reserve	13.14	8.16	.32	(6.90)	(14.72)
	13.14	10.95	10.60	9.93	9.08
Expenses:					
Paid	92.00	9.12	8.54	7.94	7.37
Change in reserves	(60.48)	16.01	15.47	14.68	14.32
	31.52	25.13	24.01	22.62	21.69
Total benefits and expenses	223.84	184.98	179.52	172.58	164.67
Adjusted gain	$ 11.23	$ 8.90	$ 8.33	$ 7.95	$ 7.19

is in the nature of a management decision that is accounted for after the decision is made.

So long as scales are changed as revisions in actual experience occur, the changes result in approximately matching the dividend revisions with the underlying earnings pattern.

Where scales perenially lag the experience pattern, the company effectively absorbs the differential during the period between revisions in the scale. The difference is permanent and should generally be taken into income. This would be the case, for example, where the company earns 5 percent while the dividend

Table 10–6.

DIVIDEND SCALE REVISION AND EFFECT ON INCOME

Scale revision to recognize 7% interest in Years *3–5:*

	Year 3	Year 4	Year 5
Initial reserve	$568.55	$767.29	$975.57
Additional interest dividend:			
New experience rate	7%	7%	7%
Old experience rate	4	4	4
	X 3%	X 3%	X 3%
Addition to scale	$ 17.06	$ 23.02	$ 29.27
Additional dividends paid:			
Dividend rate	$ 17.06	$ 23.02	$ 29.27
Survivors at time of payment	X .69021	X .64056	X .62439
Dividends paid on block of business	$ 11.77	$ 14.75	$ 18.28

Income statements:

	Year 1	Year 2	Year 3	Year 4	Year 5
Statutory:					
Table 10–5	$(8.25)	$31.81	$22.22	$15.67	$11.60
Additional interest on reserves:					
Earned			16.43	21.71	26.96
Distributed			(11.77)	(14.75)	(18.28)
	$(8.25)	$31.81	$26.88	$22.63	$20.28
Adjusted:					
Table 10–5	$11.23	$ 8.90	$ 8.33	$ 7.95	$ 7.19
Additional interest on reserve:					
Earned			12.86	16.34	18.40
Distributed			(11.77)	(14.75)	(18.28)
	$11.23	$ 8.90	$ 9.42	$ 9.54	$ 7.31

scale pays 4 percent; earns 6 percent after the company revises the scale to pay 5 percent; and so on.

Where scales are revised some time after experience emerges in a manner that results in retroactive recognition of experience during the period between revisions, then consideration should be given to providing for anticipated future dividend changes. For example, if a company earns 6 percent for five years while paying 5 percent, and then, in the sixth year, revises the scale so as to pay out 6 percent currently *plus* an apportionment of excess interest earned but not distributed in the preceding five years, and the company's intent is known in advance, sound accounting would call for reserving for the excess interest earned during the five-year period that is expected to be paid out subsequently.

Revising Reserves for Revised Dividend Scales

The life insurance audit guide provides that dividend scales applicable to the year of issue should be provided for in calculating adjusted reserves; future revisions would therefore be reflected as they occur.

Sometimes information on original scales is not readily available; or revised scales are stored in machine-readable form while original scales are not, which would make it much more convenient to include current scales in the reserves. Thus the question arises as to whether it might be appropriate to provide for dividends at the current scale rather than the original scale.

The answer is a qualified "maybe." Revised scales can sometimes stand in for original scales if the

Table 10–7.

EFFECT OF RECALCULATING RESERVES TO GIVE EFFECT TO DIVIDEND SCALE REVISIONS

Adjusted valuation premiums and adjusted benefit reserves:

	4%	*Adjusted Benefit Reserves and Dividends Based on* 4% Yrs. 1–2, 7% Yrs. 3–5	7%
Valuation premiums	$184.92	$183.60	$183.02
Reserves—Year 1	$231.45	$229.71	$230.02
—Year 2	429.96	426.55	428.15
—Year 3	623.75	621.09	622.26
—Year 4	813.94	812.77	813.15
—Year 5	-0-	-0-	-0-

Income patterns:

	Year 1	Year 2	Year 3	Year 4	Year 5
Original scale locked in— from Table 10–6	$11.23	$8.90	$9.42	$9.54	$7.31
Reserves and dividend "benefits" based on 4% for Years 1–2 and 7% for Years 3–5	$12.56	$9.95	$8.48	$8.26	$8.31
Reserves and dividend "benefits" based on 7% throughout	$12.29	$9.00	$8.91	$8.86	$8.55

reserve assumptions are consistent with the dividend assumptions. For example, in the case of the switch in interest rates from 4 percent to 7 percent in the third year of the 5-year endowment, recalculated reserves are very close to the initial reserves.

Table 10–7 shows the reserves and income produced by various approaches—lock-in of the original scale, recalculation based on 4 percent interest for Years 1 and 2 and 7 percent for Years 3 to 5, and recalculation based on 7 percent level. The benefit reserves are virtually the same in all cases. Assuming that Year 3 is the year of conversion, use of the revised scales would not seem to do violence to the intent of the audit guide in this case.

As a general rule, recalculation should yield about the same result as not recalculating where the profit objective is held more or less constant *and* the scale is revised at about the same time as the conditions causing the revision to occur *and* the payout is proportioned to the additional earnings. Where the profit objective is changed or the scale is revised before or after the conditions causing the revision to occur, but the revision is designed to anticipate or make up for

such lags, recalculation can produce a significantly different result.

In any event, the effect of using current scales, with corresponding changes in the underlying reserve assumptions, as an approximation of locking in original scales should be tested before the approach is actually used.

Use of Statutory Reserves

While statutory net level reserves and adjusted benefit reserves were not close together in the case of the 5-year endowment, they often are in the case of long-term business. When this is the case, adjustment of participating business might be effected by deferring and amortizing acquisition costs while holding statutory net level reserves.

The relationship between adjusted benefit reserves and statutory net level reserves for participating business is discussed and illustrated in Chapter 11.

Recoverability and Loss Recognition

Participating business sometimes requires special

treatment in testing recoverability and loss recognition. This is because the dividend can be cut, thereby shielding the company from losses on the business. Whether the company would in fact cut the scale in the face of competitive pressures is a key question to be resolved when there is a recoverability problem or a loss situation.

Recoverability and loss recognition are discussed in Chapter 24.

Adjusted Benefit Reserves

The distinguishing characteristics of benefit reserves for participating business are (1) recognition of expected dividends as "benefits" and (2) the need to establish a consistent relationship between certain reserve assumptions and the related dividend assumptions.

Dividend "Benefits"

It is tempting to conclude that the manner in which dividends are calculated is irrelevant so far as adjusted reserves are concerned. It would appear that all that is necessary is to introduce the published or illustrated dividend scale as a "planned contractual benefit," as the life insurance audit guide suggests, and proceed to calculate the benefit reserves just as if the business were non-participating.

The first part of the above formula is correct. Dividends should be introduced into the reserves as a "benefit". The second part, however, is not correct. Nonparticipating assumptions are not necessarily appropriate for participating business. If, for example, the current nonparticipating interest assumption is 4 percent but the current dividend assumption is 6 percent,* use of a non-participating interest assumption would produce insufficient interest income to pay the interest component of the dividend. Thus the valuation premium would have to be greater to pay the difference, the reserves would usually be higher than necessary, and a profit test would probably indicate a loss.

Perhaps the best way to discuss the development of adjusted reserve assumptions for participating business is to review a case study—in this case, Crazy

---

*All that is necessary with respect to a dividend scale is that *current* experience be illustrated, whether or not current experience is an appropriate long-term assumption for non-participating business.

Quilt Life's 1966–1969 issues of participating whole life.

The first 40 years of the dividend scale (male age 35) used for this period is illustrated in Tables 10–8 and 10–9. Table 10–8 shows the development of the mortality and interest contributions to the dividend based on experience rates of X_{18} and 4 percent, respectively, and valuation rates of 1958 CSO and 2 1/2 percent. Table 10–9 shows the loading contribution and the total dividend.

With respect to the loading contribution, the annual gross premium (exclusive of policy fee) for the policy whose dividend is illustrated in Tables 10–8 and 10–9 is $21.85. The statutory net level valuation premium is $17.67. The difference, $4.18, represents loading available for expenses. This amount, less expenses deemed chargeable for dividend purposes, produces the loading contribution to the dividend.

In Crazy Quilt's case, "expenses deemed chargeable for dividend purposes are the sum of two items: a percentage of gross premium and a constant per $1,000. Expense charges are smoothed by formula. They are designed to (1) amortize acquisition costs over 20 years, (2) reflect select mortality savings, (3) give credit for the policy fee, (4) smooth out renewal expenses, (5) recognize the effect of withdrawals, and (6) produce a reasonable profit to shareholders. In other words, the loading contribution is a balancing item that produces the dividend scale that profit tests show to be reasonable.

Profit Tests

Having established a dividend scale, Crazy Quilt made one final profit test to check the reasonableness of the scale. Nonparticipating select and ultimate mortality rates and historical withdrawal rates for participating whole life business were used in making the profit test. Expenses used in the profit study were those determined by functional cost analysis. The interest rate used was 5 percent rather than the 4 percent used in the dividend scale; the latter rate was chosen so as to give assurance of a constantly increasing dividend even under conditions of moderate adversity. But 5 percent was determined to be an appropriate after-tax assumption for testing purposes.

Crazy Quilt's profit test took the same form as tests of nonparticipating products, except that profits were discounted at the investment earnings rate. The reason: Crazy Quilt's profit objective for participating business differed from the objective for nonparticipating business (12 percent) because of the difference in the degree of risk assumed. Crazy Quilt's general

Table 10–8.

MORTALITY AND INTEREST CONTRIBUTIONS TO DIVIDENDS FOR 1966 ISSUES OF PAR WHOLE LIFE—MALE AGE 35

Year	(1) Terminal Reserve	(2) Net Amount at Risk— $1,000 – (1)	(3) 1958 CSO Mortality	(4) X_{18} Mortality	(5) Mortality Margin (3) – (4)	(6) Mortality Contribution (2) X (5)	(7) Initial Reserve	(8) Interest Contribution 1.5% * X (7)
1	$ 15.64	$984.36	.00251	.00141	.00110	$1.08	$ 17.67	$ .27
2	31.59	968.41	.00264	.00153	.00111	1.07	33.28	.50
3	47.83	952.17	.00280	.00168	.00112	1.07	49.26	.74
4	64.32	935.68	.00301	.00187	.00114	1.07	65.50	.98
5	81.05	918.85	.00325	.00210	.00115	1.06	81.99	1.23
6	98.01	901.99	.00353	.00236	.00117	1.06	98.72	1.48
7	115.17	884.83	.00384	.00264	.00120	1.06	115.68	1.74
8	132.55	867.45	.00417	.00295	.00122	1.06	132.84	1.99
9	150.12	849.88	.00453	.00328	.00125	1.06	150.22	2.25
10	167.90	832.10	.00492	.00363	.00129	1.07	167.79	2.52
11	185.85	814.15	.00535	.00402	.00133	1.08	185.57	2.78
12	203.97	796.03	.00583	.00445	.00138	1.10	203.52	3.05
13	222.24	777.76	.00636	.00492	.00144	1.12	221.64	3.32
14	240.63	759.37	.00695	.00546	.00149	1.13	239.91	3.60
15	259.12	740.88	.00760	.00606	.00154	1.14	258.30	3.87
16	277.71	722.29	.00832	.00672	.00160	1.16	276.79	4.15
17	296.35	703.65	.00911	.00745	.00166	1.17	295.38	4.43
18	315.05	684.95	.00996	.00821	.00175	1.20	314.02	4.71
19	333.79	666.21	.01089	.00902	.00187	1.25	332.72	4.99
20	352.54	647.46	.01190	.00992	.00198	1.28	351.46	5.27
21	371.29	628.71	.01300	.01091	.00209	1.31	370.21	5.55
22	390.02	609.98	.01421	.01201	.00220	1.34	388.96	5.83
23	408.69	591.31	.01554	.01322	.00232	1.37	407.69	6.12
24	427.29	572.71	.01700	.01455	.00245	1.40	426.36	6.40
25	445.78	554.22	.01859	.01599	.00260	1.44	444.96	6.67
26	464.14	535.86	.02034	.01757	.00277	1.48	463.45	6.95
27	482.34	517.66	.02223	.01928	.00295	1.53	481.81	7.23
28	500.37	499.63	.02431	.02112	.00319	1.59	500.01	7.50
29	518.19	481.81	.02657	.02310	.00347	1.67	518.04	7.77
30	535.77	464.23	.02904	.02525	.00379	1.76	535.86	8.04
31	553.09	446.91	.03175	.02761	.00414	1.85	553.44	8.30
32	570.10	429.90	.03474	.03021	.00453	1.95	570.76	8.56
33	586.74	413.26	.03804	.03308	.00496	2.05	587.77	8.82
34	602.97	397.03	.04168	.03624	.00544	2.16	604.41	9.07
35	618.77	381.23	.04561	.03966	.00595	2.27	620.64	9.31
36	634.14	365.86	.04979	.04330	.00649	2.37	636.44	9.55
37	649.10	350.90	.05415	.04709	.00706	2.48	651.81	9.78
38	663.72	336.28	.05865	.05100	.00765	2.57	666.77	10.00
39	678.06	321.94	.06326	.05501	.00825	2.66	681.39	10.22
40	692.16	307.84	.06812	.05923	.00889	2.74	695.73	10.44

* Experience rate, 4%, less statutory rate, 2–1/2%.

profit objective for participating business was 10 percent of profits before dividends.

The profit test is summarized in Table 10–10. Crazy Quilt didn't quite make its 10 percent profit objective but felt that 9.4 percent—the percentage of pre-

dividend profits remaining for shareholders—was close enough.

Reserve Assumptions

Crazy Quilt used the profit test assumptions in cal-

Table 10–9.

LOADING CONTRIBUTION TO DIVIDENDS AND RESULTING DIVIDEND SCALE FOR 1966 ISSUES OF PAR WHOLE LIFE—MALE AGE 35

Year	(1) Formula Percentage	(2) Percentage Amount (1) × $21.85	(3) Formula Constant	(4) Expense Charge (2) + (3)	(5) Loading Contribution $4.18 − (4)	(6) Mortality Contribution (Table 10–8)	(7) Interest Contribution (Table 10–8)	(8) Total Dividend (5) + (6) + (7)
1	11.59%	$2.53	$1.91	$4.44	$ (.26)	$1.08	$ .27	$ 1.09
2	11.27	2.46	1.77	4.23	(.05)	1.07	.50	1.52
3	10.94	2.39	1.63	4.02	.16	1.07	.74	1.97
4	10.60	2.32	1.48	3.80	.38	1.07	.98	2.43
5	10.26	2.24	1.33	3.57	.61	1.06	1.23	2.90
6	9.91	2.17	1.18	3.35	.83	1.06	1.48	3.37
7	9.55	2.09	1.02	3.11	1.07	1.06	1.74	3.87
8	9.18	2.01	.86	2.87	1.31	1.06	1.99	4.36
9	8.80	1.92	.70	2.62	1.56	1.06	2.25	4.87
10	8.42	1.84	.53	2.37	1.81	1.07	2.52	5.40
11	8.02	1.75	.35	2.10	2.08	1.08	2.78	5.94
12	7.61	1.66	.18	1.84	2.34	1.10	3.05	6.49
13	7.20	1.57	(.01)	1.56	2.62	1.12	3.32	7.06
14	6.77	1.48	(.20)	1.28	2.90	1.13	3.60	7.63
15	6.33	1.38	(.39)	.99	3.19	1.14	3.87	8.20
16	5.87	1.28	(.59)	.69	3.49	1.16	4.15	8.80
17	5.40	1.18	(.79)	.39	3.79	1.17	4.43	9.39
18	4.92	1.08	(1.00)	.08	4.10	1.20	4.71	10.01
19	4.42	.97	(1.22)	(.25)	4.43	1.25	4.99	10.67
20	3.90	.85	(1.45)	(.60)	4.78	1.28	5.27	11.33
21	3.87	.85	(1.49)	(.64)	4.82	1.31	5.55	11.68
22	3.84	.84	(1.52)	(.68)	4.86	1.34	5.83	12.03
23	3.81	.83	(1.56)	(.73)	4.91	1.37	6.12	12.40
24	3.78	.83	(1.59)	(.76)	4.94	1.40	6.40	12.74
25	3.76	.82	(1.63)	(.81)	4.99	1.44	6.67	13.10
26	3.73	.82	(1.67)	(.85)	5.03	1.48	6.95	13.46
27	3.70	.81	(1.70)	(.89)	5.07	1.53	7.23	13.83
28	3.67	.80	(1.74)	(.94)	5.12	1.59	7.50	14.21
29	3.64	.80	(1.77)	(.97)	5.15	1.67	7.77	14.59
30	3.62	.79	(1.80)	(1.01)	5.19	1.76	8.04	14.99
31	3.59	.78	(1.84)	(1.06)	5.24	1.85	8.30	15.39
32	3.56	.78	(1.87)	(1.09)	5.27	1.95	8.56	15.78
33	3.54	.77	(1.90)	(1.13)	5.31	2.05	8.82	16.18
34	3.51	.77	(1.93)	(1.16)	5.34	2.16	9.07	16.57
35	3.49	.76	(1.96)	(1.20)	5.38	2.27	9.31	16.96
36	3.47	.76	(1.99)	(1.23)	5.41	2.37	9.55	17.33
37	3.44	.75	(2.02)	(1.27)	5.45	2.48	9.78	17.71
38	3.42	.75	(2.05)	(1.30)	5.48	2.57	10.00	18.05
39	3.40	.74	(2.08)	(1.34)	5.52	2.66	10.22	18.40
40	3.38	.74	(2.11)	(1.37)	5.55	2.74	10.44	18.73

culating adjusted benefit reserves. (Acquisition costs were redefined for accounting purposes to meet the variability and attribution criteria described in Chapter 14.*)

*It could be argued that acquisition costs could be deferred up to the amount provided for by the dividend scale. Crazy Quilt decided that this approach would be inconsistent with the audit guide.

Thus, except for the interest assumption, participating business was reserved for just as if it were nonparticipating business, except that dividends were introduced as "benefits". And of course, withdrawal scales associated with the participating product were used.*

*In Crazy Quilt's case, withdrawal rates were lower on participating business than on nonparticipating business.

Table 10–10.

SUMMARY OF PROFIT TEST PER $1,000 ORIGINALLY ISSUED FOR 1966 ISSUES OF PARTICIPATING WHOLE LIFE—MALE AGE 35

	Present Value at 5%	*Level Annual Equivalent*
Premiums	$282.41	$24.66
Deaths	77.34	6.75
Surrenders	57.43	5.02
Expenses:		
Acquisition	38.55	3.37
Maintenance	35.99	3.14
	209.31	18.28
Profits before dividends	73.10	6.38
Dividends at illustrated scale	66.23	5.78
PROJECTED STOCKHOLDER PROFITS	$ 6.87	$ .60
Projected stockholder profits as percentage of profits before dividends	9.4%	

Provisions for Adverse Deviation

A dividend scale may be viewed as a means of providing for adverse deviation. Premiums are set high enough to cover extremely adverse experience and amounts not needed are returned to policyholders only as the risk of adverse deviation passes.

Inasmuch as the dividend scale serves as a buffer for adversity, it normally should not be necessary to provide for adverse deviation in calculating reserves for participating business when dividends are provided for as a benefit.

However, the logic of this approach should always be challenged. For example, if nonparticipating assumptions were experienced with respect to participating business it would probably be necessary to reduce dividends. The effect could be a serious increase in terminations, which could very well reduce the margins of the business and perhaps produce losses in later years. Consideration should be given to providing for some degree of adverse deviation above and beyond that provided by the dividend scale in reserving for participating business in circumstances such as these.

Adjusted Reserves

Statutory net level reserves, aggregate cash values, and adjusted benefit reserves for Crazy Quilt's participating business at December 31, 1971, and the 1971 changes in these items, are shown in Table 10–11. Adjusted benefit reserves are 106 percent of statutory, although the change in reserves is only 102 percent greater.

The interesting thing is that the adjusted benefit reserves are so close to statutory net level. This will often be the case where the dividend scale operates to distribute the bulk of the difference between experience and the statutory valuation assumptions.

Separating the Dividend Component

The life insurance audit guide indicates that

. . . it may be necessary to identify the amount of dividends [provided for in the reserves] in order to calculate deferred income taxes in those cases where there is a question as to whether the dividend provision in the reserves, together with dividends declared or paid, may exceed the amount of dividends otherwise deductible for federal income tax purposes in the "with and without" calculations.[2]

It would be possible to separate the benefit reserve into two components, dividends and everything else, and thus determine the provision for dividends included in the reserve increase for the year. Reference to Table 10-5, for example, will indicate that the adjusted benefit reserve for the 5-year endowment discussed previously in this chapter consists of the following elements:

	Reserve per $1,000		
End of Year	*Dividends*	*All Other Benefits*	*Total*
1	$16.57	$214.88	$231.45
2	28.70	401.26	429.96
3	31.32	592.43	623.75
4	22.98	790.96	813.94
5	–0–	–0–	–0–

Table 10–11.

RESERVES ON PARTICIPATING BUSINESS (000 OMITTED)

	Insurance in Force	Net Level Statutory Reserves	Cash Values	Adjusted Benefit Reserves
Level of reserves at December 31, 1971:				
1941–47 issues	$ 7,711	$ 3,360	$ 3,353	$ 3,607
1948–51 issues	13,708	5,292	5,156	5,664
1952–61 issues	52,950	13,212	12,843	13,895
1962–64 issues	50,325	6,587	6,561	7,110
1965–69 issues	171,825	11,187	11,033	12,070
1970–71 issues	132,645	2,645	1,785	2,590
	$429,164	$42,283	$40,731	$44,936
1971 change in reserves:				
1941–47 issues		$ (118)	$ (116)	$ (145)
1948–51 issues		(78)	(67)	(122)
1952–61 issues		231	310	226
1962–64 issues		545	558	554
1965–69 issues		1,956	2,146	2,073
1970–71 issues		1,681	1,371	1,693
		$4,217	$4,202	$4,279

And changes in the reserves per $1,000 originally issued include amounts that are, in effect, provisions for dividends above and beyond amounts actually paid:

	Increase in Reserves		
Year	Dividends	All Other Benefits	Total
1	$ 13.14	$ 170.39	$ 183.53
2	8.16	127.43	135.59
3	.32	111.08	111.40
4	(6.90)	97.76	90.86
5	(14.72)	(506.66)	(521.38)

In many cases it would not be necessary to separate the dividend component of the reserves, for example, in those cases in which special deductions can be fully utilized. The various deferred tax situations, and their effect on the dividend deduction, are discussed in Chapter 26.

In those cases in which it is necessary to remove the dividend component from the reserve increase for the year, the question arises as to how to calculate the dividend component.

It is possible, of course, to calculate separate reserves for the dividend component, or to calculate benefit reserves without regard for dividends and deduct them from reserves calculated with dividends included to determine the portion applicable to dividends. The mechanics are fairly simple.

The theory, though, is a little more difficult. When the dividend is removed from the adjusted benefit reserve, the provision for adverse deviation is also removed. What is left is a pro forma nonparticipating reserve calculated on the basis of participating assumptions.

Suppose the participating interest assumption is 6 percent and the non-par interest assumption is 4 percent. So long as the reserve is calculated with the dividend included, the dividend uses up most of the excess interest, and any reduction in interest rates would be presumed to be accompanied by a corresponding reduction in dividends, thus keeping everything more or less the same.

When the dividend is removed, however, the reserves are now calculated on the basis of 6 percent without having the dividend available in the reserve to use up the interest. In other words, the reserves are now nonparticipating reserves calculated on a basis that is considered inappropriate for nonparticipating reserves.

A dividend "benefit" is not independent of the underlying reserve assumptions. Elimination of the dividend from the reserve calculation destroys the relationship between the two. The amount taken to be the increase in reserves computed without regard for dividends should be the reserves calculated as if the business were nonparticipating. This means using nonparticipating interest assumptions and mortality assumptions in making the calculations. Withdrawals might also be modified to provide for adverse deviation, although the particular withdrawal pattern associated with the business might also be viewed as an inherent characteristic of the business and hence not subject to modification. Nonforfeiture values should not be changed.

Crazy Quilt Life calculated reserves excluding the dividend component by using nonparticipating assumptions. The results were as follows:

		000			
		Reserves, 12-31-71		1971 Reserve Change	
Ratebook Era	In Force 12-31-71 (000,000)	Including Dividends	Excluding Dividends	Including Dividends	Excluding Dividends
1941–47	$ 8	$ 3,607	$ 3,612	$ (145)	$ (138)
1948–51	14	5,664	5,201	(122)	(81)
1952–61	53	13,895	12,748	226	216
1962–64	50	7,110	6,068	554	510
1965–69	172	12,070	10,285	2,073	1,811
1970–71	133	2,590	1,989	1,693	1,300
	$430	$44,936	$39,903	$4,279	$3,618

Had nonparticipating assumptions not been used, reserves excluding dividends would have been about $36 million at December 31, 1971, and the related 1971 change in reserves would have been about $3.3 million.

Dividend Liabilities

In treating dividends as a benefit in calculating adjusted benefit reserves, an assumption must be made as to when dividends are paid. It may or may not be necessary to hold a separate dividend liability in conjunction with the adjusted benefit reserves.

Some thought must also be given to the various dividend options and how they should be accounted for.

Dividends Payable

Under statutory accounting practices many companies establish, as a liability at December 31, the dividends estimated to be payable on the next policy anniversary (which is to say in the next calendar year).

This practice generally results in some degree of overstatement. On average, six months' excess interest on the initial reserve would be unearned at December 31. Similarly, about half of the year's mortality savings would not yet be earned. And while all of the loading would have been received on annual-premium cases, this would not be true of modes for which premiums are deferred at December 31. Dividends will be paid only on those policies that persist into the next policy year. Finally, the dividend liability itself will not be discharged until six months after year-end, on the average, and the present value at December 31 is something less than the amount payable in the next calendar year.

Some companies discount the liability for persistency and interest. Others set up half of the annual dividend on the assumption that half is earned on December 31.

Where dividends are provided for in calculating adjusted reserves, the basis of accounting for dividends changes somewhat. A portion of the valuation premium is designed to fund the payment of dividends. Dividends "accrue" in the reserve. Annual dividends are "released" from the reserves according to an assumption about when they are paid.

Beginning-of-year assumption. One possible assumption about the incidence of dividends is that they are paid at the beginning of the policy year. Under this approach the present value of the dividend payable one year hence is released from the reserve on the anniversary date.

Suppose, for example, the year-end dividend to persisting policyholders is $3.76, 74.221 percent of the amounts originally insured persist, and the assumed interest rate is 4 percent. The present value at the beginning of the year of the dividend payable at the end of the year is $3.76 x .74221 x .96154 or $2.68.

The $2.68 would therefore be released from the reserve July 1. But it has not yet been paid as of December 31. A liability of $2.73 ($2.68 plus one-half year's interest) should therefore be set up at December 31.

The dividend released from the reserve is an *assumed* dividend. Actual may, of course, differ from assumed. The statutory liability for dividends payable in the following calendar year would be based on actual dividends and would effectively include assumed dividends plus variances from assumed. The statutory liability, discounted for interest and persistency, would therefore be a good approximation of the liability that should be held in conjunction with adjusted reserves.

However, care should be taken that the difference between actual and assumed is not too great. That's because the difference between the two represents amounts not contemplated in the dividends provided for in the reserves. Where the amount not funded by valuation premiums is material, consideration should be given to adjusting for portions unearned. For example, assume the current dividend scale calls for a dividend of $4.76 instead of the $3.76 originally illustrated and reserved for, and assume that the $1.00 difference represents excess interest, of which 50 percent will be earned in the next calendar year. The appropriate dividend liability would be $3.10, computed as follows:

Assumed		$ 3.76
Extra	$1.00	
Less 50% unearned	.50	.50
		$ 4.26
Year-end persistency		× .74221
Discount for 6 months' interest		× .98019
		$ 3.10

Crazy Quilt Life uses the beginning-of-the-year assumption and carries a dividend liability equal to the statutory amount for dividends payable in the following calendar year, which in Crazy Quilt's case are discounted for interest (at the portfolio *earned* rate) and persistency. No adjustment is made for unearned portions of the difference between actual and assumed dividends on the basis of materiality.

End-of-year assumption. If dividends are assumed to be payable at the end of the policy year, then the adjusted reserves at December 31 include the present value of assumed dividends payable in the next calendar year and no liability need be held for such amounts.

However, an estimate should be made of the earned difference between assumed and actual dividends, since the reserves would not include such amounts. This could, of course, be very difficult unless assumed dividends, in the aggregate, are known or can be estimated.

Interpolated terminals. When reserves are based in interpolating between terminal reserves, as discussed in Chapter 12, neither terminal reserve would include the current year's dividend, and hence a dividend liability would be required. Alternatively, the current year's terminal reserve might be modified

Dividend Options

Dividends might be paid in cash, applied to pay premiums, left on deposit, used to purchase one-year

to add back the current dividend before interpolating. term insurance, or used to purchase paid-up additions.

Where the costs of the various options differ, it would be possible to value dividends based on the weighted average cost of all the options, in a manner similar to reserving for the weighted average cost of nonforfeiture options. For example, a dividend might be applied to purchase nonparticipating paid-up additions whose reserve at the time of purchase is less than the amount of the dividend. This difference could be anticipated. However, it seems equally appropriate—and much more practical—to value dividends at their stated amount and recognize any differentials when dividends are applied.

Cash. No particular problems arise when dividends are paid in cash. Dividends paid would be charged and cash would be credited.

Premiums. When dividends are applied to pay premiums, dividends paid would be charged and renewal premiums would be credited.

Deposits. When dividends are left on deposit, the amount deposited should be recorded by a credit to a liability account, not as revenue. Interest on accumulations and accumulation surrenders should likewise be recorded by direct entries in the liability account.

Term. Dividends applied to purchase one-year term insurance should be recorded as single premiums. Usually the statutory reserve or one-half the single premium would provide an adequate measure of the reserve.

Reduced paid-up. Dividends may be applied to purchase an amount of paid-up insurance corresponding to the equivalent statutory net single premium. An adjusted reserve would usually differ somewhat from the statutory reserve in these circumstances, and a gain or loss (usually a gain) would be recognized equal to the difference between the net single premium and the adjusted valuation single premium (or, viewed another way, equal to the difference between the dividend applied and the reserve initially established).

Sometimes companies provide more insurance than a net single statutory premium will buy, in recognition of the conservatism of the statutory assumptions. This would tend to reduce the indicated gain.

Paid-up business, including paid-up additions, can present some difficult practical problems of valuation. Such problems are discussed in Chapter 11.

Coupons and Pure Endowments

Coupons and pure endowments "should also be provided for ratably, as opposed to being recognized only as such benefits become payable or mature." [3] Thus such benefits should be programmed into the calculation of adjusted reserves.

Coupon accumulations should be accounted for in a manner similar to the method of accounting for dividend accumulations.

Paid-Up Additions

The paid-up additions dividend option gives rise to reserves on paid-up business. Frequently such reserves are not material in relation to total reserves, and on this basis many companies will choose to hold statutory reserves on paid-up additions as an approximation of adjusted reserves.

However, reserves on paid-up business are often very responsive to changes in interest assumptions, and the effect of not adjusting the reserves should always be investigated. Crazy Quilt Life, for example, chose to adjust reserves on paid-up additions:

	000		
Year	*Pair-Up Additions In Force*	*Statutory Reserves*	*Adjusted Reserves*
1950	$ 271	$ 129	$ 114
1955	1,038	504	437
1960	2,201	1,098	951
1965	3,669	1,875	1,471
1970	5,556	2,893	2,128
1971	6,029	3,147	2,295

Disclosure

The life insurance audit guide requires that "the relative amount of participating business in force, the method of accounting for dividends and the amounts thereof should be disclosed in a note" [4] to the financial statements.

For a Type 1 company, the guide suggests that the following type of disclosure might be appropriate:

NOTE TO FINANCIAL STATEMENTS
Participating business approximates 10 percent of the Company's ordinary life insurance in force. Dividends to policyholders are determined annually by the Board of Directors.
Where dividends to policyholders are not separately captioned in the income statement, the amount for the year should be set forth in the note, perhaps as follows:

NOTE TO FINANCIAL STATEMENTS
. . . Dividends to policyholders ($1,438,000 and $1,319,000 in 1971 and 1970 respectively) are determined annually by the Board of Directors.

Where dividends for lines of business other than ordinary are material, the note should be modified to disclose the facts for each line of business for which participating business is a significant portion.

Experience rating refunds are usually quite different from dividends and should generally not be reported as such. (Experience rating refunds are discussed in Chapter 20.)

It is not entirely clear how the guide proposes that "the method of accounting for dividends" be disclosed for a Type 1 company. The illustrative note contained in the audit guide suggests that it may be sufficient to state that "Amounts allocable to participating policyholders are based on . . . published dividend projections* or expected dividend scales." [5] But that does not indicate what is meant by "allocable"; it could refer to amounts allocated by the Board of Directors, in which case the disclosure is somewhat in conflict with the disclosure that dividends are "determined" by the Board.

The method of accounting for dividends is really a matter for the accounting policies note and could be disclosed in the note setting forth adjusted reserve assumptions, as follows:

ACCOUNTING POLICIES NOTE:
Liabilities for future policy benefits have been computed by the net level premium method based upon estimated future investment yields, mortality, and withdrawals applicable at the time of issue. Dividends have been provided for ratably based on expected dividend scales.

It would be misleading for a Type 1 company to disclose the portion of the reserves represented by dividends, and even when such a calculation has been made the amounts should not be disclosed.

*Use of the term "projections" may be inappropriate, inasmuch as statutes prohibit "projections" but permit "illustrations" based on current experience. "Illustrations" would be a more suitable term.

11

Reserve Grading and Other Compromises

Most companies will want to make numerous compromises with theory in calculating adjusted benefit reserves. Among the most common "compromises" are reserve grading, the treatment of paid-up business, and the treatment of supplemental benefits and miscellaneous minor coverages.

It goes without saying that any such compromises should be well-disciplined—i.e., should not produce a financial statement result, individually or in the aggregate, that differs significantly from the result of not compromising at all.

Reserve Grading

For various reasons companies will often want to grade adjusted benefit reserves into statutory reserves after a period of time. Reserve grading can have significant effects on the income statement depending on methods used to effect the grading, the plan, the grading period, and the relationship between adjusted reserve assumptions and statutory assumptions.

Reasons for Grading

When a company decides to grade adjusted reserves into statutory reserves, it will generally do so to simplify or limit the work required to convert to generally accepted accounting principles. A secondary reason might be the wish to provide an extra measure of conservatism in the reserving process.

Factor calculations. Reserve grading eases the burden of calculating adjusted reserve factors somewhat. For example, if adjusted reserves are graded to statutory in 20 years, adjusted reserve factors need

be calculated for only 19 durations (if adjusted reserves are graded to statutory mean reserves in the 20th year) or 20 durations (if adjusted reserves are graded to statutory terminal reserves in the 20th year). Thus there is a savings in computer time required to calculate factors. There is also some savings in storage costs, since fewer factors have to be stored. And since fewer factors must be applied to insurance in force, there is a savings in computer time required to produce an adjusted reserve valuation.

Perhaps more important, the number of years for which adjusted reserve assumptions are required are limited to the grading period. Again assuming that the grading period is 20 years, it is only necessary to develop assumptions for mortality, withdrawals, cash values, dividends, and interest for 19 or 20 years.

Records maintenance. If adjusted reserves are graded to statutory, the grading period defines the period during which separate records must be maintained for insurance in force subject to reserve adjustments. This is a major consideration, since it is usually necessary to model insurance in force (as discussed in Chapter 28) and revalidate the model more or less continuously.

Thus, for example, a company adjusting in 1973 and reporting only 1973 earnings need only develop adjusted valuation data for issues subsequent to 1953 or 1954 (again depending on whether adjusted reserves are graded to mean or terminal statutory reserves) if the grading period is 20 years.

Remote historical data. Generally the more remote the issue year for which adjusted reserves must be calculated, the more difficult it is to determine the appropriate adjusted reserve assumptions. Typically information on ratebook assumptions and other fac-

178

tors affecting the selection of adjusted reserve assumptions is incomplete and inadequate. Reserve grading reduces the scope of this problem by shortening the period for which prior years' data must be accumulated.

Other simplifications. Deferred and uncollected and unearned premiums required in connection with an intermediate, mean, or mid-terminal adjusted reserve calculation (discussed in Chapter 12) must also be adjusted to a basis consistent with adjusted reserves. Reserve grading helps to limit the extent of such adjustments.

Where records of timing differences by issue year must be maintained in connection with the gross change method of calculating deferred taxes (discussed in Chapter 26), the necessary records can become quite voluminous. Reserve grading reduces the volume of records and calculations required to implement the gross change method.

There may be still other advantages of reserve grading, but those cited above suggest the very substantial savings in effort that are sometimes possible by grading.

Conservatism. A company may wish to grade adjusted reserves to statutory for the sake of conservatism. Obviously this is achieved only if the ungraded adjusted reserve is less than statutory at the end of the grading period.

Conservatism must be examined from two points of view, the balance sheet and the income statement. Balance sheet conservatism might be accompanied by a liberal income statement effect under certain circumstances, and vice-versa.

Generally companies that grade for the sake of conservatism have balance sheet conservatism in mind.

Audit Guide Provisions

The life insurance audit guide never refers to reserve grading. This is because there is no theoretical justification for grading. Grading is undertaken for purely practical reasons. Since there is no theoretical justification for doing it, grading must produce a financial statement result that is not materially different from the result of not grading. Stated somewhat differently, grading is acceptable only if it results in a good approximation of the level of adjusted reserves and the pattern of adjusted reserve accumulation.

Mechanics of Grading

Before discussing the effects of reserve grading and suggesting some general guidelines for deciding when to grade and when not to grade, a brief discussion of the *mechanics* of grading is necessary.

Maturing for the statutory reserve. The process of grading adjusted reserves to statutory involves treating the policy being adjusted as an endowment maturing at the end of the grading period. The endowment "benefit" is equal to the statutory reserve.

Thus the policy being adjusted can be said to mature for the statutory reserve at the end of the grading period.

To illustrate, assume a 10-year $1,000 endowment with zero mortality and zero withdrawals for which

▸ Statutory net level 3 percent reserves are held;
▸ The adjusted reserve interest assumption is 7 percent; and
▸ It is decided to grade to the terminal statutory reserve at the end of the fifth year.

For purposes of this illustration, assume that the policy year and the calendar year coincide.

Valuation premiums for the statutory reserves and the *ungraded* adjusted reserves would be $84.69 and $67.64, respectively, computed as follows:

	Statutory	Ungraded Adjusted
10th-year endowment	$ 1,000	$ 1,000
Amount of a $1 annuity due for 10 periods at:		
3%	$11.8078	
7%		$14.7836
Valuation premium	$84.69	$67.64

And statutory reserves and ungraded adjusted terminal reserves would be as follows:

Year	Statutory Reserve Level	Statutory Reserve Increase	Ungraded Adjusted Reserve Level	Ungraded Adjusted Reserve Increase
1	$ 87.23	$ 87.23	$ 72.37	$ 72.37
2	177.08	89.85	149.81	77.44
3	269.62	92.54	232.67	82.86
4	364.94	95.32	321.33	88.66
5	463.12	98.18	416.20	94.87
6	564.24	101.12	517.71	101.51
7	668.40	104.16	626.32	108.61
8	775.68	107.28	742.54	116.22
9	886.18	110.50	866.89	124.35
10	1,000.00	113.82	1,000.00	133.11
		$1,000.00		$1,000.00

Note that the statutory reserve is $463.12 at the end of the fifth year while the ungraded adjusted reserve is $416.20, a difference of $46.92.

To grade to the statutory reserve it is necessary that the adjusted reserve accumulate at 7 percent interest to $463.12 by the end of the fifth year. The valuation premium required to accomplish this is $75.26, computed as follows:

5th-year endowment for statutory reserve	$463.12
Amount of annuity due of $1 for 5 periods at 7%	$6.1533
Valuation premium	$75.26

So adjusted reserve factors are calculated for five years (1) using a valuation premium of $75.26 and (2) assuming an endowment benefit at the end of the fifth year of $463.12, the statutory reserve. The graded adjusted reserves accumulate in the following pattern for five years:

Year	Reserve Level	Reserve Increase
1	$ 80.53	$ 80.53
2	166.70	86.17
3	258.90	92.20
4	357.55	98.65
5	463.12	105.57
		$463.12

Thereafter the statutory valuation premium, $84.69, is used and the reserves follow the same pattern as the statutory reserves (because they *are* the statutory reserves).

The effect of grading in the fashion illustrated is to provide systematically each year for a portion of the total difference between the ungraded adjusted reserve and the statutory reserve at the end of the grading period. In the case of the illustration, this difference is $46.92, and the portion of the adjusted valuation premium used to fund it is $7.62:

Difference between ungraded adjusted reserve and statutory reserve at end of 5th year	$46.92
Amount of an annuity due of $1 for 5 periods at 7%	$6.1533
Valuation premium component	$7.62

This component $7.62, when added to the valuation premium for the ungraded adjusted reserve, $67.64, yields the valuation premium for the graded adjusted reserve, $75.26. And the differences in reserve increases represent the accumulation of the additional valuation premium component, $7.62, at 7 percent:

	Increase in		Difference —Annuity of $7.62
Year	Graded Adjusted Reserve	Ungraded Adjusted Reserve	Compounded at 7%
1	$ 80.53	$ 72.37	$ 8.16
2	86.17	77.44	8.73
3	92.20	82.86	9.34
4	98.65	88.66	9.99
5	105.57	94.87	10.70
	$463.12	$416.20	$46.92

The amount thus charged to income during the first five years "reverses" during the next five years, during which time statutory reserves are held:

Year	Ungraded Adjusted Reserve	Statutory Reserve	Difference
6	$101.51	$101.12	$ .39
7	108.61	104.16	4.45
8	116.22	107.28	8.94
9	124.35	110.50	13.85
10	133.11	113.82	19.29
	$583.80	$536.88	$46.92

Note that the pattern of reversal is not "smooth", but that the reversals are heavily weighted at the later durations.

Switching to statutory assumptions. It is tempting to conclude that the effect of grading the adjusted reserve to the statutory reserve is the same as switching the adjusted reserve assumptions to the statutory reserve assumptions at the end of the grading period. Under this reasoning, the adjusted reserves calculated using an interest assumption of 7 percent for the first five years and 3 percent thereafter should produce adjusted reserves equal to statutory at the end of the grading period.

Such is not the case. The adjusted reserves are calculated using one valuation premium, while the graded reserves are in effect calculated using two valuation premiums—adjusted during the grading period and statutory thereafter.

In the case of the 10-year endowment discussed earlier, for example, the valuation premiums for the graded reserves were as follows:

First five years (adjusted)	$75.26
Second five years (statutory)	84.69

But if adjusted reserves were calculated assuming 7 percent interest for the first five years and 3 percent thereafter, the valuation premium would be $79.36:

10-year endowment	$1,000.00
Amount of an annuity due of $1 for 10 periods at 7% for the first 5 periods and 3% for the second 5 periods	$ 12.6016
Valuation premium	$79.36

At the end of the fifth year the present value of future benefits at 3 percent is $862.61:

Endowment 5 years hence	$1,000.00
Present value of $1 due 5 years hence at 3%	.86261
Present value of benefits	$ 862.61

But the valuation premiums differ, and hence the present value at 3 percent of future valuation premiums also differs:

	Statutory	Adjusted
Valuation premium	$ 84.69	$ 79.36
Present value of $1 annuity due at 3% for 5 periods	4.7171	4.7171
Present value of future valuation premiums	$399.49	$374.32

Thus the reserves at the end of the fifth year must also differ:

	Statutory	Adjusted
Present value of future benefits	$862.61	$862.61
Present value of future valuation premiums	399.49	374.32
Reserve at end of 5th year	$463.12	$488.29

The differences may be observed by comparing reserves and reserve increases for the graded reserves and the reserves calculated on the basis of assuming a switch to statutory assumptions at the end of the fifth year:

	Reserve Level		Reserve Increase	
Year	Graded	Switched	Graded	Switched
1	$ 80.53	$ 84.91	$ 80.53	$ 84.91
2	166.70	175.76	86.17	90.85
3	258.90	272.97	92.20	97.21
4	357.55	376.99	98.65	104.02
5	463.12	488.29	105.57	111.30
6	564.24	584.67	101.12	96.38
7	668.40	683.95	104.16	99.28
8	775.78	786.20	107.28	102.25
9	886.18	891.52	110.50	105.32
10	1,000.00	1,000.00	113.82	108.48

All of the various reserves calculated for the 10-year endowment are summarized in Table 11–1.

Influence of decrements. It should be recognized that decrements in insurance in force, such as mortality and withdrawals, operate to reduce the "endowment" benefit at the end of the grading period. The effect generally is to reduce the provision for the "endowment" during the grading period, since premiums during the grading period are received from a greater number of policyholders than are persisting at the time of the "endowment".

This phenomenon may be illustrated very simply. Assume a $1,000 10-year term contract with zero interest and zero withdrawals and deaths of 100 percent at the end of the tenth year. The valuation premium would be $100 and $100 would be received every year. By the end of the fifth year, $500 would have been received. If the difference between the adjusted reserve and the statutory reserve were $100 at the end of the fifth year, the valuation premium would be increased to $120 during the first five years to provide for the extra reserve.

Now assume that withdrawals occur at the rate of 10 percent of the original issues each year. The number of policyholders persisting to the end of the fifth year (and into the sixth) would thus be 50 percent. So the reserve difference that must be provided for is $50, 50 percent of the per-unit difference. But this is funded by $400 in valuation premiums ($100 + $90 + $80 + $70 +$60), which represents 73 percent of total premiums ($400 + $50 + $40 + $30 + $10). So the valuation premium has to be increased by only $12.50 instead of $20:

Year	Persisting	Additional Valuation Premium	Provision for Endowment
1	100%	$12.50	$12.50
2	90	12.50	11.25
3	80	12.50	10.00
4	70	12.50	8.75
5	60	12.50	7.50
			$50.00

To illustrate further, assume a 10-year term contract for $1,000 where the death rate is 1 percent in the first year, 2 percent in the second, and so on, increasing 1 percent a year to 10 percent in the tenth year. The mortality assumption is the same for statutory reserves and adjusted reserves. Assume withdrawals at 10 percent per year of those persisting into the year; the withdrawal assumption is applicable, of course, only to the adjusted reserves. Finally, assume a statutory interest assumption of 3 percent and an adjusted reserve assumption of 7 percent.

181

Table 11–1.

ILLUSTRATIVE RESERVE GRADING PATTERNS FOR 10-YEAR $1,000 ENDOWMENT (INTEREST ONLY; ZERO MORTALITY AND WITHDRAWALS)

Year	Statutory (3%)	7%	7% Switching to 3%	7% Graded to Statutory
Valuation premiums:				
Years 1–5	$ 84.69	$ 67.64	$ 79.36	$ 75.26
Years 6–10	84.69	67.64	79.36	84.69
Reserves:				
Year 1	87.23	72.37	84.91	80.53
2	177.08	149.81	175.76	166.70
3	269.62	232.67	272.97	258.90
4	364.94	321.33	376.99	357.55
5	463.12	416.20	488.29	463.12
6	564.24	517.71	584.67	564.24
7	668.40	626.32	683.95	668.40
8	775.68	742.54	786.20	775.68
9	886.18	866.89	891.52	886.18
10	1,000.00	1,000.00	1,000.00	1,000.00
Change in reserves:				
Year 1	87.23	72.37	84.91	80.53
2	89.85	77.44	90.85	86.17
3	92.54	82.86	97.21	92.20
4	95.32	88.66	104.02	98.65
5	98.18	94.87	111.30	105.57
6	101.12	101.51	96.38	101.12
7	104.16	108.61	99.28	104.16
8	107.28	116.22	102.25	107.28
9	110.50	124.35	105.32	110.50
10	113.82	133.11	108.48	113.82

The reserves that would be produced by these assumptions are shown in Table 11–2. "Aggregate reserves" and "change in aggregate reserves" are computed based on the assumptions that $1,000 of insurance has been issued and that actual experience is the same as the adjusted reserve assumptions. Where applicable, adjusted reserves are graded to statutory at the end of the fifth year.

Comparison of Column (2) with Column (4) will indicate that as withdrawals are introduced, the effect is to reduce the early reserve changes and increase the later ones during the period of reserve accumulation. The same pattern occurs during the period of reserve liquidation. A comparison of Columns (3) and (5) indicates the same pattern during the accumulation period. (Thereafter, of course, the patterns are the same since the adjusted reserves have been replaced by statutory.)

Reference to Table 11–1 will show that increases in the graded adjusted reserves are consistently higher during the grading period than increases in ungraded adjusted reserves. As Table 11–2 suggests, however, an unchanging relationship cannot be assumed. Thus, while the net result of grading may be to produce a higher reserve than adjusted at the end of the grading period, the effect on the income statement is not necessarily to produce greater reserve increases than adjusted. Where grading is concerned, untested assumptions about the effect on the income statement are dangerous.

Effects of Grading

Crazy Quilt Life was lucky enough to have the capability to calculate adjusted reserves in all sorts of ways, and among other things the Company tested grading patterns to a fare-thee-well.

Effects on factors: high interest rates. At one point in the process of converting to generally accepted accounting principles Crazy Quilt Life considered the use of an interest assumption of a level 5 percent for adjusted reserves on nonparticipating issues

Table 11–2.

COMPARISON OF EFFECT OF VARIOUS RESERVE GRADING PATTERNS ON RESERVE FACTORS FOR 10-YEAR TERM POLICY

	Statutory (1)	Adjusted— Ignoring Withdrawals		Adjusted— Recognizing Withdrawals	
		Ungraded (2)	Graded (3)	Ungraded (4)	Graded (5)
Valuation premiums:					
Years 1–5	$ 47.21	$ 42.73	$ 43.30	$ 35.92	$ 36.63
Years 6–10	47.21	42.73	47.21	35.92	47.21
Reserve factors:					
Year 1	39.02	36.08	37.00	31.91	32.76
2	70.03	65.44	66.74	59.36	61.27
3	93.66	88.50	90.55	81.82	85.04
4	110.10	105.23	108.16	100.20	105.07
5	118.13	114.23	118.13	111.18	118.13
6	116.84	114.34	116.84	116.08	116.84
7	105.81	104.83	105.81	110.78	105.81
8	84.36	84.67	84.36	92.12	84.36
9	50.18	51.04	50.18	56.33	50.18
10	-0-	-0-	-0-	-0-	-0-
Aggregate reserves:					
Year 1	34.77	32.15	32.97	28.43	28.19
2	55.04	51.43	52.46	46.66	48.16
3	64.25	60.71	62.12	56.13	58.34
4	65.29	62.40	64.14	59.42	62.31
5	59.89	57.91	59.89	56.37	59.89
6	50.12	49.05	50.12	49.80	50.12
7	37.99	37.63	37.99	39.77	37.99
8	25.05	25.15	25.05	27.36	25.05
9	12.19	12.40	12.19	13.69	12.19
10	-0-	-0-	-0-	-0-	-0-
Change in aggregate reserves:					
Year 1	34.77	32.15	32.97	28.43	28.19
2	20.27	19.28	19.49	18.23	19.97
3	9.21	9.28	9.66	9.47	10.18
4	1.04	1.69	2.02	3.29	3.97
5	(5.40)	(4.49)	(4.25)	(3.05)	(2.42)
6	(9.77)	(8.86)	(9.77)	(6.57)	(9.77)
7	(12.13)	(11.42)	(12.13)	(10.03)	(12.13)
8	(12.94)	(12.48)	(12.94)	(12.41)	(12.94)
9	(12.86)	(12.75)	(12.86)	(13.67)	(12.86)
10	(12.19)	(12.40)	(12.19)	(13.69)	(12.19)

of 1970–1971. As explained in Chapter 9, the Company finally settled on 6 1/2 percent graded to 3 1/2 percent in 30 years.

In studying the 5 percent rate Crazy Quilt experimented with grading to statutory in 30 years and 40 years and also with switching to statutory interest (3 percent), mortality (1958 CSO), and withdrawal (zero, of course) assumptions in the 30th and 40th years, always comparing the result with the reserves produced by not grading.

In the case of the 5 percent reserves, 30 and 40 years were chosen to test grading because the difference between the tentative 5 percent adjusted reserve interest assumption and the 3 percent statutory reserve interest assumption was quite significant. It was felt that, particularly in the case of permanent insurance, anything less would produce a sizeable difference.

Samples of the adjusted benefit reserve factors for Crazy Quilt's whole life and 20-pay life plans are shown in Table 11–3. The table suggests what may be obvious: when assumed interest rates are relatively high, the grading period should be relatively long. A

Table 11–3.

COMPARISON OF EFFECT OF VARIOUS RESERVE GRADING PATTERNS ON 5% ADJUSTED RESERVE
FACTORS* FOR SELECTED ORDINARY LIFE PLANS

	Whole Life—Age 35					20-Pay Life—Age 35				
		Graded to Statutory Reserve in		Switched to Statutory Assumptions in			Graded to Statutory Reserve in		Switched to Statutory Assumptions in	
	Not					Not				
Duration	Graded	30 Years	40 Years	30th Year	40th Year	Graded	30 Years	40 Years	30th Year	40th Year
1	$ 10.85	$ 11.20	$ 10.92	$ 11.60	$ 10.98	$ 16.24	$ 16.87	$ 16.33	$ 16.94	$ 16.35
2	$ 24.18	24.96	24.32	25.88	24.46	36.96	38.42	37.18	38.57	37.21
3	37.19	38.42	37.40	39.87	37.64	55.92	58.22	56.26	58.47	56.32
4	49.60	51.27	49.88	53.25	50.20	74.62	77.76	75.09	78.10	75.16
5	62.34	64.48	62.70	67.04	63.11	93.79	97.86	94.40	98.30	94.50
6	75.31	77.96	75.76	81.11	76.27	113.24	118.34	114.00	118.88	114.12
7	88.66	91.84	89.20	95.63	89.81	132.94	139.16	133.86	139.82	134.01
8	102.34	106.10	102.98	110.58	103.70	153.11	160.57	154.22	161.36	154.40
9	116.38	120.76	117.13	125.98	117.96	173.77	182.58	175.08	183.52	175.29
10	130.74	135.78	131.60	141.78	132.56	194.89	205.19	196.42	206.30	196.66
11	145.40	151.17	146.38	158.03	147.48	216.53	228.47	218.30	229.74	218.59
12	160.33	166.88	161.44	174.66	162.70	238.68	252.42	240.71	253.88	241.04
13	175.51	182.89	176.76	191.68	178.17	261.91	277.48	264.22	279.15	264.59
14	190.88	199.18	192.30	209.04	193.88	285.78	303.36	288.38	305.24	288.80
15	206.44	215.72	208.02	226.76	209.78	310.32	330.08	313.24	332.20	313.72
16	222.17	232.52	223.93	244.83	225.90	335.54	357.70	338.82	360.08	339.35
17	238.17	249.68	240.12	263.38	242.32	361.46	386.26	365.12	388.90	365.72
18	254.48	267.25	256.64	282.46	259.08	388.12	415.79	392.20	418.76	392.86
19	271.04	285.18	273.44	302.03	276.14	416.70	447.24	421.21	450.51	421.94
20	287.86	303.49	290.50	322.12	293.48	446.31	479.98	451.27	483.58	452.08
21	304.96	322.23	307.88	342.82	311.18	460.26	496.70	465.64	500.61	466.50
22	322.37	341.43	325.59	364.14	329.23	474.55	514.05	480.36	518.28	481.32
23	340.06	361.09	343.62	386.15	347.62	489.16	532.01	495.46	536.60	496.49
24	358.02	381.20	361.94	408.84	366.36	504.08	550.64	510.92	555.62	512.04
25	375.69	401.52	380.04	432.31	384.97	519.33	570.02	526.82	575.45	528.03
26	393.53	422.30	398.38	456.62	403.87	533.80	589.65	542.09	595.63	543.42
27	411.49	443.56	416.88	481.82	423.00	548.55	610.13	557.68	616.72	559.15
28	428.95	465.10	435.02	508.24	441.92	563.59	631.61	573.66	638.88	575.28
29	446.39	487.18	453.23	535.88	461.02	577.92	653.98	589.16	662.13	590.98
30	463.89	509.98	471.60	565.00	480.41	591.46	677.60	604.18	686.82	606.24
31	481.56	533.08	490.28	589.24	500.24	605.21	695.33	619.64	705.75	621.97
32	498.85	550.40	508.82	604.98	520.22	618.17	706.43	634.72	717.02	637.41
33	516.24	567.42	527.65	620.44	540.74	631.20	717.35	650.27	728.10	653.38
34	533.14	584.09	546.38	635.58	561.58	644.30	728.04	666.33	738.96	669.92
35	550.04	600.36	565.44	650.37	583.16	657.44	738.48	682.98	749.55	687.16
36	566.86	616.22	584.82	664.78	605.54	669.78	748.65	699.82	759.88	704.73
37	583.13	631.70	604.38	678.84	628.93	682.16	758.57	717.64	769.94	723.44
38	599.53	646.82	624.75	692.58	653.94	694.65	768.27	736.71	779.79	743.61
39	615.64	661.66	646.02	706.06	681.23	706.46	777.79	757.08	789.45	765.40
40	631.89	676.26	668.62	719.32	711.26	718.50	787.15	779.72	798.96	789.78
45	708.81	744.99	744.99	781.76	784.99	775.92	831.23	831.23	843.70	843.70
50	778.25	802.11	802.11	833.66	836.12	825.60	867.87	867.87	880.88	880.88
60	893.49	900.93	900.93	923.44	924.58	910.40	931.25	931.25	945.21	945.21

* Adjusted assumptions are Crazy Quilt ratebook assumptions for mortality, withdrawals, and nonforfeiture benefits and 5% interest.

Table 11–4.

COMPARISON OF EFFECT OF VARIOUS GRADING PATTERNS ON 6% ADJUSTED RESERVE FACTORS FOR SINGLE-PREMIUM IMMEDIATE ANNUITIES

| | | | Adjusted | |
| | | | Graded to Statutory in | |
Duration	Statutory	Not Graded	20 Years	30 Years
1	$1,340.67	$1,120.65	$1,124.96	$1,120.70
2	1,294.70	1,080.79	1,085.43	1,080.85
3	1,248.63	1,040.01	1,045.02	1,040.08
4	1,202.58	999.88	1,005.29	999.95
5	1,156.59	962.29	968.17	962.36
6	1,110.80	927.98	934.42	928.06
7	1,065.24	895.12	902.21	895.21
8	1,020.04	862.17	869.99	862.27
9	975.27	829.18	837.86	829.29
10	931.03	796.24	805.89	796.36
12	844.48	730.77	742.91	730.92
15	720.65	634.71	652.60	634.94
17	643.07	572.93	596.96	573.25
20	535.50	484.96	525.19	485.49
22	470.30	430.10	470.30	430.88
25	383.13	354.28	383.13	355.90
27	332.36	308.38	332.36	311.27
30	266.74	246.68	266.74	255.07

grading period of 40 years seems to produce acceptable results, although the differences between grading and not grading become more significant at the later durations.

Switching to statutory assumptions at the end of the 30th and 40th years, respectively, produces reserves that are consistently higher than the comparable graded reserves. Switching at the 40th year produces a relatively minor additional distortion however.

Table 11–3 does suggest that when assumed interest rates are high, adjusted reserves on permanent plans should probably not be graded unless grading is regarded as being in the nature of a provision for adverse deviation. Even if grading is undertaken for that purpose, the propriety of the provision must be demonstrated.

While Crazy Quilt did not use a 5 percent interest assumption for nonparticipating ordinary issues of 1970–71, the Company did use high rates—6 percent —for nonparticipating single-premium annuities, for reasons described in Chapter 9. Because of the advanced average age of annuitants—65—and because the reserves were at their highest levels in the early durations, the Company tested the ungraded adjusted reserves against reserves graded to statutory in 20 years and 30 years. The results are shown in Table 11–4.

As Table 11–4 shows, a 30-year grading period produces, for all practical purposes, the same results as not grading. Even a 20-year grading period does not produce the distortion that one would expect, although the difference approaches 10 percent at the later durations.

For this type of business the grading period can usually be somewhat shorter for a given interest assumption than could be justified for level-premium plans with a comparable interest assumption.

Effects on factors: low interest rates. Inasmuch as Crazy Quilt rejected the use of a 5 percent interest assumption for nonparticipating issues of 1970–1971 and chose, instead, 6 1/2 percent graded to 3 1/2 percent over 30 years, the Company next compared ungraded factors with factors that graded to statutory in 20 years and 30 years. It was felt that since the ultimate adjusted reserve interest assumption was relatively close to statutory, a shorter grading period might be feasible.

Sample comparative factors for the whole life and 20-pay life plans are shown in Table 11–5. Either the 20-year or 30-year grading period seems to produce results that approximate the result of not grading in the case of the whole life plan.

For the 20-pay life plan, a 20-year grading period does not produce acceptable results, and even 30-

Table 11–5.

COMPARISON OF EFFECT OF VARIOUS RESERVE GRADING PATTERNS ON CRAZY QUILT LIFE ADJUSTED
RESERVE FACTORS FOR SELECTED 1970–1971 ORDINARY LIFE ISSUES

WHOLE LIFE:

Age	Duration	Statutory Net Level	Not Graded	Adjusted Graded to Statutory in 20 Years	Adjusted Graded to Statutory in 30 Years
25	1	$ 10.49	$ 7.22	$ 7.29	$ 7.19
	2	20.34	16.41	16.57	16.34
	3	30.47	25.54	25.78	25.43
	5	51.61	44.53	44.96	44.32
	7	73.93	65.10	65.77	64.78
	10	109.75	99.56	100.65	99.04
	12	135.20	124.49	125.91	123.82
	15	175.52	165.46	167.45	164.51
	17	203.65	194.53	196.96	193.37
	20	247.53	241.39	244.61	239.85
	22	277.85	273.19	277.85	271.35
	25	324.66	322.91	324.66	320.55
	27	356.57	355.75	356.57	352.98
	30	405.16	406.21	405.16	402.71
35	1	15.29	11.07	11.17	11.04
	2	29.77	24.88	25.12	24.82
	3	44.57	38.61	38.98	38.50
	5	75.09	65.89	66.56	65.70
	7	106.70	94.86	95.86	94.58
	10	156.03	142.61	144.23	142.16
	12	190.10	176.38	178.49	175.79
	15	242.73	230.18	233.19	229.34
	17	278.59	266.75	270.47	265.71
	20	333.21	324.42	329.46	323.01
	22	369.97	362.94	369.97	361.24
	25	425.17	422.35	425.17	420.08
	27	461.68	460.36	461.68	457.60
	30	515.51	516.25	515.51	512.38
45	1	22.45	16.90	16.97	16.86
	2	42.78	36.39	36.55	36.31
	3	63.36	55.41	55.67	55.28
	5	105.15	93.52	93.99	93.28
	7	147.66	133.10	133.81	132.73
	10	212.39	197.36	198.53	196.75
	12	255.97	242.00	243.54	241.20
	15	321.39	309.62	311.85	308.46
	17	364.67	353.53	356.34	352.07
	20	428.46	419.69	423.63	417.64
	22	469.82	462.22	469.82	459.65
	25	529.03	525.84	529.03	522.05
	27	566.18	565.10	566.18	559.96
	30	618.99	623.13	618.99	614.55

20-PAY LIFE:

Age	Duration	Statutory Net Level	Not Graded	Adjusted Graded to Statutory in 20 Years	Adjusted Graded to Statutory in 30 Years
25	1	$ 17.90	$ 11.73	$ 12.93	$ 12.08
	2	35.40	27.96	30.85	28.78
	3	53.42	42.86	47.40	44.16
	5	91.12	72.98	81.11	75.30
	7	131.09	105.26	117.72	108.83
	10	195.61	158.93	179.74	164.88
	12	241.82	197.63	225.38	205.56
	15	316.05	261.01	301.99	272.72
	17	368.88	306.40	357.23	320.93
	20	453.51	381.20	448.80	400.52
	22	475.36	409.26	475.36	431.47
	25	509.11	453.55	509.11	480.90
	27	532.11	482.06	532.11	513.35
	30	567.14	525.14	567.14	563.99
35	1	23.36	16.28	17.46	16.48
	2	46.17	37.37	40.12	37.84
	3	69.58	57.04	61.41	57.78
	5	118.18	97.36	105.25	98.70
	7	169.16	139.82	151.98	141.88
	10	250.25	209.41	229.88	212.89
	12	307.59	259.09	286.54	263.76
	15	398.89	341.24	380.99	348.00
	17	463.57	399.01	448.79	407.47
	20	567.14	493.98	561.30	505.43
	22	590.72	526.60	590.72	539.94
	25	626.12	577.13	626.12	594.00
	27	649.54	607.88	649.54	628.02
	30	684.06	652.84	684.06	680.24
45	1	30.33	22.57	23.59	22.66
	2	58.82	50.60	52.99	50.81
	3	87.86	75.50	79.17	75.82
	5	147.58	127.97	134.69	128.55
	7	209.53	181.37	191.85	182.28
	10	306.86	267.18	285.10	268.73
	12	375.03	327.87	352.20	329.98
	15	483.02	427.30	463.34	430.41
	17	559.66	497.09	543.11	501.07
	20	684.06	612.43	676.98	618.01
	22	706.43	645.95	706.43	652.68
	25	738.48	695.52	738.48	704.78
	27	758.57	723.34	758.57	735.49
	30	787.15	763.28	787.15	782.65

year grading results in moderate distortions (2–4 percent) at the middle and later durations, particularly for the younger ages.

Effect on factors: participating business. As mentioned in Chapter 9 and as further discussed in Chapter 10, Crazy Quilt Life used a level 6 percent adjusted reserve interest assumption for participating business. But when a high adjusted reserve interest rate is used in conjunction with a dividend scale that incorporates a high distributive interest rate and divi-

Table 11–6.

COMPARISON OF EFFECT OF VARIOUS RESERVE GRADING PATTERNS ON CRAZY QUILT LIFE ADJUSTED
RESERVE FACTORS FOR 1970–1971 ISSUES OF PARTICIPATING WHOLE LIFE

Age	Duration	*Not Graded*	*Graded to Statutory in*	
			20 Years	30 Years
25	1	$ 10.79	$ 10.94	$ 10.93
	2	23.18	23.52	23.49
	3	34.73	35.29	35.24
	5	57.85	58.89	58.79
	7	81.83	83.45	83.29
	10	119.37	122.13	121.87
	12	145.16	148.93	148.58
	15	184.73	190.46	189.91
	17	211.69	219.02	218.33
	20	252.43	262.79	261.81
	22	280.05	299.30	291.63
	25	322.79	347.57	338.14
	27	352.13	380.19	370.63
	30	397.35	429.49	421.85
35	1	15.67	15.87	15.80
	2	32.14	32.57	32.43
	3	48.19	48.87	48.64
	5	80.40	81.62	81.21
	7	113.49	115.32	114.70
	10	164.45	167.43	166.42
	12	198.96	202.87	201.55
	15	250.66	256.33	254.41
	17	284.83	291.95	289.54
	20	335.71	345.61	342.26
	22	369.85	389.49	377.95
	25	421.42	445.37	432.76
	27	455.62	482.08	469.92
	30	505.85	535.82	526.29
45	1	22.47	22.52	22.50
	2	44.98	45.09	45.05
	3	67.02	67.19	67.13
	5	110.83	111.15	111.03
	7	155.10	155.59	155.41
	10	222.59	223.40	223.10
	12	267.84	268.92	268.52
	15	332.99	334.61	334.01
	17	374.42	376.54	375.75
	20	433.35	436.49	435.32
	22	471.37	486.21	473.93
	25	527.02	545.43	530.84
	27	562.41	582.39	567.56
	30	614.28	634.65	622.71

dends are treated as benefits, the effect of a high
adjusted reserve interest assumption is offset to a
significant degree.

In these circumstances participating business can
usually be regarded as being in the nature of nonparticipating insurance for which relatively low adjusted reserve interest assumptions are used.

Table 11–6 shows various grading patterns for
1970–1971 issues of Crazy Quilt Life's participating
whole life plan.

Here there is not too great a difference between
20-year grading and 30-year grading. The difference between ungraded and graded reserves is considerably less than one would expect with a 6 percent

Table 11–7.

COMPARISON OF EFFECT OF VARIOUS RESERVE GRADING PATTERNS ON CRAZY QUILT LIFE ADJUSTED
RESERVE FACTORS FOR 1970–1971 TERM ISSUES

	Duration	Not Graded	Graded to Statutory in	
			20 Years	30 Years
5-year R & C term, age 35	1	$ 1.11	$ .69	$ .90
	2	2.29	1.25	1.77
	3	3.29	1.66	2.48
	5	5.47	2.43	3.97
	7	9.42	3.84	6.66
	10	15.09	5.15	10.19
	12	23.74	7.01	15.48
	15	33.50	6.77	20.31
	17	50.41	7.43	29.20
	20	59.29	2.21	31.12
	22	86.06	4.42	40.69
	25	89.91	3.69	31.64
	27	129.02	6.96	32.81
	30	128.99	5.78	7.48
25-year decreasing term, age 35	1	1.60	1.25	
	2	2.97	2.28	
	3	4.21	3.23	
	5	6.36	4.95	
	7	8.49	6.75	
				NOT APPLICABLE
	10	9.95	8.10	
	12	10.78	8.79	
	15	9.02	6.95	
	17	8.15	5.41	
	20	5.46	1.72	
	22	4.40	2.30	
	25	1.72	1.92	

interest assumption, particularly in the earlier durations. At the later durations the differences widen, particularly for the younger ages.

Effect on factors: term business. The interest assumption has a relatively modest effect on term insurance reserves. Typically mortality and withdrawal assumptions are more important.

Mortality and withdrawal assumptions can have a drastic effect on term reserves. The effect on adjusted reserves of term renewal mortality and term conversions is discussed in Chapter 8. As the chapter indicates, adjusted term reserves can be significantly higher than statutory. Where this is the case, grading to statutory may be viewed as unconservative. It may be necessary to use a fairly long grading period for term reserves under these circumstances.

Table 11–7 shows various grading patterns for 1970–1971 issues of Crazy Quilt Life's term plans. It is obviously impracticable to attempt any sort of grading for the 5-year term plan, since the statutory and adjusted reserving bases are so different. If term renewal mortality and conversion costs were separately reserved for, then grading would probably be feasible.

For the 25-year decreasing term plan, the reserves are again calculated on significantly different bases. The adjusted reserves provide for the cost of conversion; the statutory reserves don't. Thus the indicated differences are significant. And again, if conversion costs were separately reserved for, grading would probably be feasible.

Effect on factors: issues of prior years. As might be expected, reserve grading is especially useful with respect to older blocks of business. Reserve interest rate assumptions were typically quite low, thus bearing a closer relationship to statutory; much of the business is gone, thus reducing the absolute amount of the differences between adjusted and statutory; and much time has passed, thus narrowing the difference, in most cases, between statutory and adjusted in any event.

Table 11–8 shows sample factors for various plans of various prior issue years for Crazy Quilt Life.

Effect on blocks of business. Examination of reserve factors to determine the effect of grading adjusted reserves to statutory is ultimately unsatisfying. Somehow the effects must be translated into the effect on the financial statements as a whole.

One way to do this is to model insurance in force and apply the various factors to the model to produce the approximate effect of various grading patterns. Crazy Quilt went one step further than this. The Company calculated reserve factors for all its plans and made several different valuations of insurance in force. The various reserves at December 31, 1971, and the 1971 changes in the reserves are summarized in Tables 11–9 and 11–10.

Inspection of Tables 11–9 and 11–10 will suggest that it doesn't seem to matter much what Crazy Quilt does with respect to adjusted reserves on ordinary life plans:

	Level of Adjusted Reserves, 12-31-71	1971 Adjusted Reserve Increase
Not graded	$323,082,000	$24,611,000
Graded to statutory in:		
20 years	322,516,000	24,885,000
30 years	323,240,000	24,625,000

However, Crazy Quilt realized that the proximity of amounts produced by the various reserve bases could be the result of Crazy Quilt's size, mix of business, and volume, all measured at one point in time. So the Company decided to refine its analysis to show 1971 amounts applicable to issues of selected issue years. The figures are summarized in Table 11–11.

The Company observed a mixed pattern in reviewing Table 11–11 that suggested that further investigation was necessary. It was felt that bulk testing in terms of a single year's reserve changes was not sufficient.

So the Company next calculated the various reserves for several years surrounding its conversion year, 1971. This was done for (1) all ordinary life issues of selected issue years, shown in Table 11–12; and (2) selected issues of all issue years, shown in Table 11–13.

As shown in Table 11–12, reserve changes on the book of business as a whole were very similar regardless of whether the reserves were graded or not.

The maximum difference for issues of all years was on the order of 1 percent in each of the years from 1968 to 1971. But there were some fairly sizeable differences for certain years of issue; reserve changes in 1971 for issues of 1950, for example, varied as much as 14 percent. Further, as Table 11–13 shows, there were some significant differences for some plans.

Crazy Quilt decided to make one more test of the various reserves—project reserve changes for several years for business in force at the end of 1971; in other words, treat business in force at December 31, 1971 as a closed block of business and see what would happen to the reserves for the next few years. The closed block could thus be regarded as one "layer" of Crazy Quilt's financial statements, the second "layer" being new issues in subsequent years that could be dealt with more or less independently. The result of the projection is shown in Table 11–14.

Crazy Quilt observed from this projection that differences became quite sizeable in some years. For example, the projected change in reserves for 20-pay life business in 1979 was about 19 percent greater when reserves were graded to statutory in 20 years and 12 percent greater using a 30-year grading period. The expected differences in the increase in term reserves continued throughout the 10-year period.

Overall, Crazy Quilt could have justified grading, but the Company decided that the additional precision of *not* grading outweighed the advantages of grading. Thus adjusted benefit reserves were calculated for the full terms of the contracts.

Grading Guidelines

It is difficult to generalize about anything in the life insurance business, let alone reserve grading. Nevertheless, available evidence seems to suggest a few basic guidelines for grading, subject always to the qualification that the effects of grading—on the balance sheet and the income statement—should not be very much different from the effects of not grading.

Nonparticipating permanent. For issues of recent years, a grading period of less than 30 years would seem inappropriate for most of the standard forms of nonparticipating permanent insurance.

Where the ultimate assumed interest rate is fairly high, a grading period of 35 to 40 years should be considered.

Where cash values are high and the assumed lapse rate is fairly high, it would sometimes be possible to shorten the grading period, even where interest rates are relatively high.

Table 11–8.

COMPARISON OF EFFECT OF VARIOUS RESERVE GRADING PATTERNS ON CRAZY QUILT LIFE ADJUSTED RESERVE FACTORS FOR SELECTED ISSUES OF PRIOR YEARS

Plan	Duration	1950 Issues			1955 Issues			1960 Issues (1962 for Par Whole Life)			1965 Issues		
		Not Graded	Graded to Statutory in 20 Years	Graded to Statutory in 30 Years	Not Graded	Graded to Statutory in 20 Years	Graded to Statutory in 30 Years	Not Graded	Graded to Statutory in 20 Years	Graded to Statutory in 30 Years	Not Graded	Graded to Statutory in 20 Years	Graded to Statutory in 30 Years
Par whole life, age 35	1	$ 21.25	$ 20.31	$ 21.07	$ 8.36	$ 7.80	$ 8.07	$ 8.04	$ 7.77	$ 7.98	$ 7.71	$ 7.57	$ 7.72
	2	44.55	42.42	44.14	18.46	17.17	17.78	17.91	17.28	17.77	17.77	16.96	17.30
	3	67.96	64.58	67.31	28.70	26.66	27.63	26.71	25.70	26.48	25.78	25.27	25.82
	5	112.38	106.19	111.19	49.20	45.47	47.25	43.93	42.04	43.50	42.39	41.44	42.47
	7	155.26	145.75	153.44	69.74	64.03	66.74	61.48	58.57	60.82	59.32	57.83	59.44
	10	216.65	201.13	213.67	101.50	92.19	96.62	88.58	83.74	87.48	85.38	82.89	85.59
	15	309.00	280.19	303.46	157.47	139.75	148.18	135.92	126.40	133.76	130.63	125.65	131.05
	20	399.17	349.66	389.65	215.79	186.28	200.31	185.09	168.67	181.37	177.24	168.49	177.97
	25	485.13	448.00	468.74	276.76	247.00	253.06	236.91	227.00	231.00	227.31	226.92	228.49
	30	566.90	541.00	536.69	341.21	310.00	307.46	294.14	289.00	285.39	283.22	288.88	285.01
Whole life, age 35	1	5.82	5.86	5.90	6.04	6.20	6.17	5.43	5.39	5.49	5.09	4.85	4.93
	2	13.39	13.48	13.59	14.25	14.64	14.58	12.82	12.72	12.94	11.67	11.11	11.29
	3	21.63	21.78	21.96	23.56	24.21	24.11	20.86	20.70	21.07	18.40	17.52	17.80
	5	38.36	38.64	38.96	41.20	42.37	42.19	37.54	37.25	37.92	32.55	30.95	31.46
	7	55.17	55.59	56.08	58.65	60.43	60.15	53.42	52.98	53.98	46.93	44.54	45.30
	10	80.86	81.55	82.35	84.61	87.43	86.99	77.88	77.19	78.74	69.74	65.97	67.18
	15	127.70	129.05	130.58	129.64	134.68	133.90	121.05	119.87	122.54	111.90	105.22	107.36
	20	178.66	180.82	183.27	178.59	186.73	185.46	168.50	166.74	170.73	159.93	149.66	152.94
	25	232.61	241.00	239.70	232.35	247.00	247.97	220.28	223.00	223.44	214.47	203.00	204.31
	30	292.62	305.00	303.28	292.18	310.00	308.21	278.17	284.00	282.54	274.78	262.00	260.57
20-pay life, age 35	1	12.90	14.00	13.51	12.79	13.88	13.39	11.67	13.15	12.57	8.94	9.32	9.04
	2	30.21	32.81	31.64	29.99	32.57	31.41	28.27	31.89	30.46	21.64	22.60	21.91
	3	48.21	52.47	50.56	47.93	52.16	50.26	45.70	51.78	49.38	36.26	37.86	36.70
	5	81.50	89.30	85.79	81.22	88.98	85.49	76.74	87.84	83.45	62.23	65.17	63.04
	7	114.26	125.94	120.69	114.18	125.84	120.60	107.88	124.85	118.14	88.69	93.22	89.94
	10	164.86	183.36	175.05	165.48	184.05	175.71	155.77	182.78	172.11	129.81	137.08	131.81
	15	254.56	288.94	273.49	255.06	289.50	274.03	240.90	288.64	269.78	204.98	218.04	208.58
	20	352.74	408.29	383.33	352.74	408.29	383.33	334.42	407.73	378.77	290.37	310.78	295.99
	25	391.01	452.00	434.81	391.01	452.00	434.81	375.82	452.00	433.11	338.83	354.19	346.26
	30	433.30	498.00	496.18	433.30	498.00	496.18	422.06	498.00	496.13	391.01	401.60	400.75
5-year R & C term, age 35	1	1.16	.88	1.04	1.26	.90	1.09	1.11	.78	.96	1.29	.85	1.07
	2	2.20	1.53	1.92	2.44	1.58	2.05	2.25	1.45	1.89	2.70	1.62	2.16
	3	3.07	2.01	2.63	3.42	2.08	2.81	3.23	1.99	2.67	3.94	2.26	3.10
	5	4.64	2.78	3.87	5.34	2.93	4.25	5.25	3.02	4.24	6.56	3.51	5.05
	7	9.50	5.43	7.82	10.53	5.31	8.16	10.32	5.47	8.13	11.51	5.61	8.58
	10	12.80	6.04	10.01	14.84	6.13	10.89	14.91	6.77	11.24	17.29	7.15	12.26
	15	27.07	8.74	19.51	31.73	8.67	21.26	30.86	9.02	20.99	35.48	9.99	22.83
	20	49.79	3.49	30.68	59.25	3.56	33.97	56.54	3.54	32.60	58.25	3.39	31.03
	25	80.08	6.00	34.38	87.21	6.00	35.17	82.07	6.00	33.19	87.03	3.69	31.03
	30	108.76	8.00	8.52	112.20	8.00	8.52	103.63	8.00	7.38	120.13	5.78	7.37

Table 11–9.

COMPARATIVE STATUTORY AND ADJUSTED BENEFIT RESERVES AT DECEMBER 31, 1971 (000 Omitted)

Plan and Rate Book Era	Insurance in Force	Statutory Reserves Net Level	Statutory Reserves Modified	Next Terminal Cash Value	Adjusted Benefit Reserves Not Graded	Graded to Statutory in 20 Years	Graded to Statutory in 30 Years
Par whole life							
41–47	$ 7,711	$ 3,360*	$ 3,310	$ 3,353	$ 3,607	$ 3,360	$ 3,446
48–51	13,708	5,292	5,164*	5,156	5,664	5,164	5,501
52–61	52,950	13,212*	12,227	12,843	13,895	13,294	13,633
62–64	50,325	6,587	6,144*	6,561	7,110	6,926	7,080
65–69	171,825	11,187*	9,067	11,033	12,070	11,955	12,090
70–71	132,645	2,645*	956	1,785	2,590	2,616	2,614
Whole life							
41–47	21,671	8,905*	8,771	8,889	9,628	8,905	9,114
48–51	35,845	13,388	13,061*	13,048	13,129	13,061	13,155
52–56	95,643	29,316*	28,332	28,857	28,794	29,121	29,050
57–61	98,721	20,564*	19,413	19,204	20,569	20,465	20,629
62–67	585,216	58,651	53,014*	46,705	59,904	58,891	59,335
68–69	370,456	18,295*	13,553	9,163	16,806	17,111	16,812
70–71	566,836	11,775*	4,327	1,360	9,295	9,349	9,271
20-pay life							
41–47	28,825	17,479*	17,479	17,630	17,454	17,479	17,468
48–51	22,259	13,256	13,256*	13,377	12,011	13,256	12,628
52–56	31,268	15,830*	15,739	15,830	14,333	15,811	14,970
57–61	25,980	8,901*	8,634	8,636	7,973	8,827	8,352
62–67	93,597	13,076	11,786*	11,268	12,589	13,025	12,662
68–69	64,303	4,244*	3,195	2,704	3,596	3,934	3,685
70–71	111,167	2,894*	965	514	2,134	2,324	2,185
20-year endowment							
48–51	36,674	27,930	27,677*	27,847	27,976	27,976	27,976
5-year R & C term							
41–47	258	3*	3		19	3	14
48–51	3,560	37*	32		323	37	267
52–56	14,699	140*	120		1,078	376	951
57–61	16,285	118*	105		719	480	684
62–64	32,904	102*	96		785	586	755
65–67	79,600	198*	171		1,348	1,075	1,295
68–69	95,160	224	209*		919	771	893
70–71	156,476	320*	262		524	437	509
25-year convertible decreasing term							
57–61	14,470	72*	69		220	234	220
62–69	529,476	3,655*	3,108		5,163	4,929	5,163
70–71	472,005	1,451	964*		1,141	1,099	1,141
Conversion whole life (5 YT)							
41–47	65	33*	32	33	34	33	33
48–51	525	241	235*	233	238	235	238
52–56	3,401	1,267*	1,223	1,243	1,273	1,266	1,275
57–61	4,641	1,272*	1,204	1,201	1,303	1,284	1,301
62–67	23,812	3,485	3,157*	2,976	3,697	3,652	3,682
68–69	10,990	818*	612	528	872	875	871
70–71	11,035	382*	165	98	399	399	398

Continued

Table 11–9. Continued

Plan and Rate Book Era	Insurance in Force	Statutory Reserves		Next Terminal Cash Value	Adjusted Benefit Reserves		
		Net Level	Modified		Not Graded	Graded to Statutory in	
						20 Years	30 Years
Conversion whole life (25 YT)							
62–67	6,402	804	710*	658	862	851	858
68–69	9,878	692*	512	434	641	647	640
70–71	14,054	456*	187	103	397	397	396
TOTAL ORDINARY	$4,117,321	$322,557	$289,246	$273,270	$323,082	$322,516	$323,240

*Actually used by Crazy Quilt prior to 1969 reserve strengthening.

Table 11–10.

CHANGES IN COMPARATIVE STATUTORY AND ADJUSTED BENEFIT RESERVES IN 1971 (000 Omitted)

Plan and Ratebook Era	Statutory Reserves		Next Terminal Cash Value	Adjusted Benefit Reserves		
	Net Level	Modified		Not Graded	Graded to Statutory in	
					20 Years	30 Years
Par whole life						
41–47	$ 117	$ 111	$ 116	$ 145	$ 117	$ 150
48–51	78	68	67	122	53	130
52–61	(231)	(261)	(310)	(226)	(190)	(210)
62–64	(545)	(602)	(558)	(554)	(532)	(551)
65–69	(1,956)	(2,118)	(2,146)	(2,073)	(2,049)	(2,076)
70–71	(1,681)	(863)	(1,371)	(1,693)	(1,711)	(1,709)
Whole life						
41–47	264	249	261	319	264	336
48–51	200	177	169	210	149	209
52–56	(474)	(554)	(672)	(441)	(466)	(460)
57–61	(840)	(916)	(1,055)	(822)	(815)	(826)
62–67	(7,036)	(7,584)	(8,240)	(7,103)	(6,958)	(7,022)
68–69	(4,474)	(4,855)	(4,851)	(4,328)	(4,411)	(4,330)
70–71	(7,384)	(3,829)	(1,286)	(6,119)	(6,155)	(6,103)
20-pay life						
41–47	501	501	506	499	501	496
48–51	211	211	215	158	198	135
52–56	(546)	(598)	(633)	(433)	(524)	(473)
57–61	(446)	(490)	(504)	(385)	(454)	(415)
62–67	(1,531)	(1,673)	(1,762)	(1,448)	(1,509)	(1,459)
68–69	(986)	(1,135)	(1,244)	(863)	(951)	(886)
70–71	(1,766)	(900)	(502)	(1,384)	(1,508)	(1,418)
20-year endowment						
48–61	4,799	4,721	4,729	4,818	4,818	4,818
5-year R & C term						
41–47	1	1		5	1	6
48–51	4	5		19	5	24
52–56	10	11		98	130	103
57–61	10	10		40	48	41
62–64	13	6		(4)	14	(2)
65–67	10	18		(120)	(74)	(110)
68–69	25	11		(186)	(148)	(179)
70–71	(162)	(139)		(329)	(271)	(319)

Continued

Table 11–10. Continued

Plan and Ratebook Era	Statutory Reserves		Next Terminal Cash Value	Adjusted Benefit Reserves		
	Net Level	Modified		Not Graded	Graded to Statutory in	
					20 Years	30 Years
25 year decreasing term						
57–61	12	9		23	22	23
62–69	(101)	(182)		(412)	(371)	(411)
70–71	(817)	(583)		(708)	(680)	(708)
Conversion whole life (5 YT)						
41–47	1	2	1	1	1	2
48–51	10	10	10	11	9	11
52–56	1	(3)	(7)	3	4	3
57–61	(38)	(42)	(48)	(35)	(33)	(34)
62–67	(439)	(467)	(479)	(427)	(420)	(425)
68–69	(214)	(225)	(234)	(205)	(206)	(205)
70–71	(226)	(144)	(96)	(229)	(229)	(228)
Conversion whole life (25 YT)						
62–67	(121)	(127)	(131)	(121)	(118)	(120)
68–69	(188)	(196)	(204)	(185)	(187)	(185)
70–71	(281)	(165)	(103)	(249)	(249)	(248)
TOTAL ORDINARY	$(26,216)	$(22,530)	$(20,362)	$(24,611)	$(24,885)	$(24,625)
Single-premium annuities:						
52–56	$ 415			$ 721	$ 708	$ 720
57–61	632			1,171	1,154	1,169
62–67	2,206	NOT	NOT	4,119	4,068	4,116
68–69	1,189	APPLICABLE	APPLICABLE	2,179	2,170	2,179
70–71	(14,900)			(11,193)	(11,253)	(11,195)
TOTAL ANNUITY	$(10,458)			$ (3,003)	$ (3,153)	$ (3,011)

For issues of prior years, a shorter grading period—perhaps 15 or 20 years—may be appropriate.

Participating permanent. Because of the effect of the dividend "benefit", it should be possible to grade adjusted reserves for participating permanent insurance to statutory in a somewhat shorter period than comparable nonparticipating permanent.

Term. Absent renewal and conversion privileges, adjusted reserves on longer-duration term business can usually be graded to statutory in 20 years or less. This could also hold true for renewable and convertible business for which renewal and conversion are separately reserved for.

For short-duration term business, such as 10-year term, grading would seem to avail little.

Annuities. Reserves for single-premium immediate annuities, or reserves on deferred annuities which have entered into the liquidation period, can sometimes be graded to statutory in a period shorter than the period required for life insurance.

Reserves on installment annuities should be treated in a manner similar to reserves on level-premium life insurance during the accumulation period.

Older blocks of business. It should generally be feasible to grade reserves for older blocks of business to statutory in a relatively shorter period than reserves on recent issues for which guidelines are suggested above.

Relationship to Statutory Reserve Method

Adjusted benefit reserves are calculated on the net level method. Most stock companies employ modified reserves for statutory purposes. Considerable care must be taken when adjusted reserves are graded to modified statutory reserves, unless the modified statutory reserves are themselves graded to net level by the end of the adjusted reserve grading period.

When the grading period is suitably long—say 30 years—the modified and net level statutory reserves may be close enough that the error introduced by grading to modified reserves is negligible. For

Table 11–11.

1971 RESERVES AND RESERVE CHANGES FOR DIFFERENT GRADING PATTERNS FOR SELECTED ISSUES OF SELECTED YEARS (000 Omitted)

| | Units of Insurance | | Level of Adjusted Reserves At December 31, 1971 | | | 1971 Change in Adjusted Reserves | | |
| | Originally Issued | In Force 12–31–71 | Not Graded | Graded to Statutory in | | Not Graded | Graded to Statutory in | |
				20 Years	30 Years		20 Years	30 Years
1945 issues:								
Par whole life	$ 5,850	$ 1,289	$ 607	$ 566	$ 580	$ (22)	$ (18)	$ (26)
Whole life	19,500	3,838	1,710	1,584	1,622	(57)	(45)	(59)
20-pay life	19,500	5,077	3,073	3,078	3,075	(89)	(87)	(89)
5-year R & C term	11,050	36	3	2	2	nil	nil	nil
1950 issues:								
Par whole life	11,990	3,721	1,513	1,376	1,470	(35)	(21)	(38)
Whole life	34,880	9,547	3,452	3,432	3,459	(49)	(39)	(49)
20-pay life	18,530	5,804	3,113	3,438	3,239	(37)	(52)	(61)
5-year R & C term	23,980	962	89	11	74	(4)	2	(5)
1955 issues:								
Par whole life	12,700	4,338	1,234	1,185	1,214	(102)	(97)	(99)
Whole life	43,180	20,416	5,885	5,916	5,903	138	143	142
20-pay life	16,510	6,006	2,560	2,813	2,669	78	92	84
5-year R & C term	43,180	3,198	243	102	217	(10)	(16)	(11)
Single-premium annuity	1,780	787	506	558	510	(83)	(81)	(83)
1960 issues:								
Par whole life	17,050	7,039	1,365	1,307	1,340	22	18	21
Whole life	57,350	22,482	4,427	4,404	4,439	198	196	198
20-pay life	12,400	5,327	1,511	1,668	1,581	81	95	87
5-year R & C term	40,300	3,478	146	102	139	(4)	(5)	(5)
25-year decreasing term	21,700	6,345	60	64	60	36	39	36
Single-premium annuity	2,172	1,456	1,201	1,252	1,204	(135)	(133)	(136)
1965 issues:								
Par whole life	36,090	22,993	3,161	2,436	2,464	958	255	257
Whole life	160,400	104,645	10,811	10,630	10,710	1,234	1,210	1,221
20-pay life	32,080	16,666	2,262	2,340	2,273	258	268	257
5-year R & C term	52,130	19,201	409	316	391	26	14	24
25-year decreasing term	120,300	55,942	618	586	618	7	3	7
Single-premium annuity	5,625	4,823	4,707	4,809	4,713	(375)	(370)	(375)
1970 issues:								
Par whole life	68,310	55,749	1,469	1,485	1,484	804	813	812
Whole life	296,010	241,401	5,801	5,835	5,786	2,715	2,542	2,618
20-pay life	60,720	44,397	1,310	1,427	1,350	560	612	584
5-year R & C term	83,490	64,682	309	255	300	114	90	110
25-year decreasing term	250,470	204,278	657	631	657	225	213	225
Single-premium annuity	10,640	10,414	11,255	11,304	11,256	(586)	(582)	(585)

Crazy Quilt Life's whole life plan, for example, comparative reserve factors (1958 CSO, 3 percent) are as follows:

		20th Year	30th Year	40th Year
Age 25	Net level	$247.53	$405.16	$567.35
	Modified	240.30	399.47	563.25
Age 35	Net level	333.21	515.51	676.26
	Modified	323.74	508.69	671.77
Age 45	Net level	428.46	618.99	768.15
	Modified	416.98	611.43	763.67

And for Crazy Quilt's entire portfolio of whole life business, the differences between net level and modified for older blocks of business are relatively small at December 31, 1971:

| Ratebook Era | In Force (000,000) | 000 | | Net Level as % of Modified |
		Net Level	Modified	
1941–47	$22	$ 8,905	$ 8,771	101.5%
1948–51	36	13,388	13,061	102.5
1952–56	96	29,316	28,332	103.5

Table 11–12.

RESERVE CHANGES FOR DIFFERENT GRADING PATTERNS FOR ALL ORDINARY LIFE ISSUES OF SELECTED YEARS (000 Omitted)

		Level of Reserves			Change in Reserves		
		Not Graded	Graded to Statutory in		Not Graded	Graded to Statutory in	
			20 Years	30 Years		20 Years	30 Years
All 1945 issues	1968	$ 5,859	$ 5,645	$ 5,756	$ (124)	$ (109)	$ (129)
	1969	5,726	5,527	5,619	(133)	(118)	(137)
	1970	5,562	5,379	5,450	(164)	(148)	(169)
	1971	5,395	5,227	5,279	(167)	(152)	(171)
	1972	5,219	5,065	5,099	(176)	(162)	(180)
All 1950 issues	1968	14,103	14,108	14,196	105	107	111
	1969	14,140	14,148	14,240	37	40	44
	1970*	8,362	8,436	8,465	(5,778)	(5,712)	(5,775)
	1971	8,239	8,327	8,345	(123)	(109)	(120)
	1972	8,100	8,202	8,209	(139)	(125)	(136)
All 1955 issues	1968	12,539	12,613	12,623	473	481	480
	1969	12,960	13,044	13,052	421	431	429
	1970	13,270	13,374	13,369	310	330	317
	1971	13,561	13,675	13,668	291	301	299
	1972	13,757	13,881	13,872	196	206	204
All 1960 issues	1968	7,915	7,927	7,950	563	567	567
	1969	8,442	8,458	8,481	527	531	531
	1970	8,895	8,920	8,939	453	462	458
	1971	9,327	9,357	9,375	432	437	436
	1972	9,711	9,746	9,763	384	389	388
All 1965 issues	1968	11,325	11,169	11,264	2,394	2,328	2,380
	1969	13,588	13,394	13,512	2,263	2,225	2,248
	1970	15,536	15,309	15,445	1,948	1,915	1,933
	1971	17,418	17,154	17,312	1,882	1,845	1,867
	1972	19,196	18,894	19,075	1,778	1,740	1,763
All 1970 issues	1970	5,768	5,817	5,780	5,768	5,817	5,780
	1971	10,222	10,307	10,243	4,454	4,490	4,463
	1972	14,305	14,426	14,334	4,083	4,119	4,091
Issues of all years	1968	257,884	256,639	258,028	17,096	17,189	17,084
	1969	276,782	275,712	276,923	18,898	19,073	18,895
	1970	298,471	297,631	298,615	21,689	21,919	21,692
	1971	323,084	322,513	323,242	24,613	24,882	24,627
	1972	344,215	343,898	344,390	21,131	21,385	21,148

* Maturity year for 20-year endowments issued in 1950.

Grading to modified might sometimes be justified on the basis that the difference between statutory net level and modified at the end of the grading period approximates the difference between adjusted net level and statutory net level.

When adjusted reserves are graded to statutory, consideration should be given to the effect of the method used to amortize acquisition costs. If acquisition costs are amortized over the entire premium-paying period of the business, then the result of grading benefit reserves to modified might be viewed as a double deferral of acquisition costs to the extent of the difference between net level and modified. Amortization of acquisition costs over the grading period might provide additional support for grading to modified reserves, since the result is to continue amortization through the reserve mechanism. However, this is technically a violation of the audit guide's requirement that unamortized acquisition costs be stated separately in the financial statements.

Where the modified statutory reserve is deemed to be a good approximation of the net level adjusted reserve, then no particular consideration needs to be given to the relationship between the reserve grading

Table 11–13.

RESERVES AND RESERVE CHANGES FOR DIFFERENT GRADING PATTERNS FOR SELECTED ISSUES OF ALL YEARS (000 Omitted)

| | | In Force at End of Year | Level of Adjusted Reserves at End of Year | | | Change in Adjusted Reserves During Year | | |
| | | | Not Graded | Graded to Statutory in | | Not Graded | Graded to Statutory in | |
				20 Years	30 Years		20 Years	30 Years
Par whole life–	1968	$ 299,257	$ 33,380	$ 31,759	$ 32,875	$ 3,029	$ 2,982	$ 2,999
issues of all years	1969	338,153	36,821	35,168	36,286	3,441	3,409	3,411
	1970	381,754	40,657	39,004	40,098	3,836	3,835	3,813
	1971	429,164	44,935	43,314	44,364	4,278	4,311	4,265
	1972	398,308	48,615	47,022	48,032	3,679	3,708	3,668
Whole life–	1968	1,180,583	108,873	107,414	108,360	12,919	12,913	12,843
issues of all years	1969	1,358,865	123,491	122,084	122,904	14,618	14,670	14,544
	1970	1,558,106	139,841	138,510	139,170	16,350	16,426	16,266
	1971	1,774,397	158,126	156,903	157,367	18,285	18,393	18,197
	1972	1,652,478	174,754	173,645	173,914	16,628	16,742	16,547
20-pay life–	1968	280,741	59,241	62,728	60,644	3,170	3,480	3,291
issues of all years	1969	309,649	62,627	66,447	64,182	3,386	3,719	3,518
	1970	342,157	66,230	70,410	67,930	3,603	3,963	3,748
	1971	377,401	70,092	74,655	71,950	3,862	4,245	4,020
	1972	342,469	73,346	78,247	75,357	3,254	3,592	3,407
20-year endowment–	1968	60,715	42,485	42,485	42,485	(4,062)	(4,062)	(4,062)
issues of all years	1969	52,056	37,561	37,561	37,561	(4,924)	(4,924)	(4,924)
	1970	44,130	32,794	32,794	32,794	(4,767)	(4,767)	(4,767)
	1971	36,676	27,975	27,976	27,976	(4,818)	(4,818)	(4,818)
	1972	29,874	23,333	23,333	23,333	(4,643)	(4,643)	(4,643)
5-year R & C term–	1968	304,160	4,584	3,089	4,334	258	135	234
issues of all years	1969	327,692	4,889	3,264	4,613	305	175	279
	1970	360,074	5,240	3,470	4,932	351	206	319
	1971	398,937	5,715	3,765	5,369	475	295	437
	1972	341,293	6,015	3,910	5,632	300	145	263
25-year decreasing	1968	659,295	3,503	3,403	3,503	818	785	818
term–issue of	1969	799,795	4,438	4,296	4,403	935	893	935
all years	1970	951,704	5,428	5,233	5,428	990	937	990
	1971	1,120,588	6,523	6,261	6,523	1,095	1,028	1,095
	1972	992,379	7,146	6,820	7,146	623	559	623
Single-premium	1968		52,683	53,670	52,742	6,523	6,593	6,526
annuity–issues of	1969		59,931	60,994	59,993	7,248	7,324	7,251
all years	1970		67,580	68,731	67,644	7,649	7,737	7,651
	1971		75,887	77,135	75,955	8,307	8,404	8,311
	1972		70,586	71,883	70,656	(5,301)	(5,252)	(5,299)

method and the method of amortizing acquisition costs.

Amortization of acquisition costs is discussed further in Chapter 16.

Disclosure

Reserve grading is of sufficient important to warrant disclosure, preferably in an accounting policies note. A suitable note might be as follows:

ACCOUNTING POLICIES NOTE

Liabilities for future policy benefits have been computed by the net level premium method based upon estimated future investment yields, mortality, and withdrawals applicable at the time of issues. Such liabilities grade into the statutory net level reserves in 30 years for permanent insurance and 20 years for term insurance.

The note in which reserve assumptions are detailed should also make reference to grading. Otherwise the indicated assumptions could be misunderstood. For example, a 5 percent interest assumption takes on

Table 11–14.

PROJECTION OF RESERVE CHANGES FOR DIFFERENT GRADING PATTERNS FOR BUSINESS IN FORCE AT DECEMBER 31, 1971 (000 Omitted)

	In Force 12–31–71	Level of Reserves 12–31–71	Projected Reserve Changes								
			1972	1973	1974	1975	1976	1977	1978	1979	1980
Par whole life:	$429,164										
Not graded		$ 44,935	$ 3,679	$ 3,251	$ 2,889	$ 2,555	$ 2,257	$ 1,952	$ 1,660	$ 1,377	$ 1,103
Graded in 20 years		43,314	3,708	3,281	2,919	2,583	2,283	1,976	1,687	1,407	1,136
Graded in 30 years		44,364	3,668	3,243	2,884	2,556	2,264	1,966	1,684	1,410	1,144
Whole life:	1,774,397										
Not graded		158,126	16,628	15,509	14,525	13,640	12,847	12,042	11,269	10,534	9,772
Graded in 20 years		156,903	16,742	15,624	14,637	13,747	12,942	12,119	11,348	10,610	9,850
Graded in 30 years		157,366	16,547	15,433	14,457	13,583	12,803	12,012	11,247	10,509	9,744
20-pay life:	377,401										
Not graded		70,092	3,255	2,856	2,484	2,152	1,826	1,548	1,278	1,037	793
Graded in 20 years		74,655	3,592	3,163	2,766	2,412	2,065	1,771	1,485	1,229	970
Graded in 30 years		71,950	3,407	3,008	2,637	2,305	1,979	1,702	1,422	1,164	902
5-year R&C term:	398,937										
Not graded		5,715	299	176	77	30	(5)	(42)	(81)	(110)	(125)
Graded in 20 years		3,765	145	46	(30)	(55)	(68)	(95)	(133)	(161)	(185)
Graded in 30 years		5,369	263	140	42	(3)	(38)	(73)	(112)	(139)	(153)
25-year decreasing term:	1,120,588										
Not graded		6,523	623	411	183	3	(124)	(185)	(250)	(328)	(426)
Graded in 30 years		6,261	559	348	120	(59)	(186)	(246)	(311)	(387)	(483)
Graded in 30 years		– – – – – – – – – – – – NOT APPLICABLE – – – – – – – – – – – – –									
All ordinary plans*:	4,117,321										
Not graded		323,082	21,133	19,167	17,295	16,338	15,625	13,993	12,556	11,246	9,930
Graded in 20 years		322,516	21,382	19,420	17,541	16,579	15,853	14,196	12,760	11,427	10,094
Graded in 30 years		323,240	21,150	19,195	17,335	16,396	15,702	14,093	12,676	11,346	10,016
Single-premium annuities:	75,652										
Not graded		75,887	5,301	(5,208)	(5,111)	(4,983)	(4,831)	(4,651)	(4,465)	(4,257)	(4,039)
Graded in 20 years		77,135	5,252	(5,167)	(5,074)	(4,952)	(4,807)	(4,631)	(4,447)	(4,244)	(4,028)
Graded in 30 years		75,955	5,299	(5,205)	(5,107)	(4,981)	(4,828)	(4,648)	(4,461)	(4,254)	(4,035)

* Including 3 plans not detailed in the table.

a somewhat different character when reserves are graded. One good way to disclose grading is to add a column headed "Matures for Statutory Reserve in" to the tabular presentation of assumptions, and list number of years (0, 20, 30, 20 to 30, etc.) corresponding to each item in the table.

Paid-Up Business

Adjusted reserves on limited-payment life business are usually calculated for all durations including those extending beyond the premium-paying period. Thus no distinction would usually be made between pre-mium-paying policies and policies that have achieved paid-up status through the normal operation of the contract.

For reduced paid-up insurance arising under the nonforfeiture privilege, and for paid-up additions arising from the dividend option, however, separate calculation of adjusted reserves could be a herculean task for which the reward is miniscule. The valuation cells are usually small and numerous; much of the business dates back to remote antiquity; and frequently all the information necessary to calculate adjusted reserves by traditional techniques just isn't available. For example, it isn't necessary to know the issue age or issue year for paid-up business. The attained age, the plan, and the mortality and interest standards are all that must be known to calculate the statutory reserve. Thus a company may have had no need to maintain records of issue years and ages, which are necessary for purposes of calculating adjusted reserves.

Therefore approximation techniques will be necessary in some cases. Such techniques should be employed with great care.

Averaging

One method of approximation is to

▸ Identify an approximate issue era by valuation basis;

▸ Compute the average reserve per unit of insurance for each significant plan group* associated with the valuation basis;

▸ Find the reserve factor that most closely corresponds to the computed average in the published tables for the related valuation basis, which will indicate the average age;

▸ Calculate an adjusted reserve factor for the indicated age using assumptions appropriate to the issue era; and

▸ Apply the adjusted reserve factors thus computed to units of insurance to obtain adjusted reserves.

Substituted Statutory Basis

Another method of approximation is to use, for each major block of business, a uniform statutory valuation basis (say, for example, 1958 CSO and 3 1/2 percent) that reasonably reproduces the effect of using adjusted reserve factors. This is a difficult procedure, since it is necessary to *weight* the distribution of reserve factors to find a weighted average factor to compare with published statutory factors.

Single Valuation Basis

Still another method is to use a single set of adjusted reserve factors for each major plan but without distinguishing issue years, using assumptions that are weighted for issues over the years. This too is a difficult procedure, but it may be practical to use when issue ages are known or can reasonably be estimated.

*"Significant plan groups" are discussed in Chapter 28.

This was the method used by Crazy Quilt Life for paid-up additions, all of which are nonparticipating.

Statutory

Where the reserves are minor in amount, and particularly where the bulk of the reserves relate to older issues, it may be practical to use statutory reserves, which Crazy Quilt did for reduced paid-up and extended term insurance for the ordinary line.

Supplemental Benefits

There are various supplemental benefits sold in connection with basic plans that are usually relatively minor in the premium volume they produce. It is often the case that a company will not want to adjust reserves for such supplemental benefits on grounds that any such adjustment would be immaterial.

Materiality or immateriality must of course always be demonstrated in deciding whether or not to adjust any block of business. Further, while a given adjustment might be shown to be immaterial, all such items should be aggregated in evaluating materiality.*

Waiver of Premium

The waiver of premium benefit is one likely candidate for non-adjustment, first because the premiums and reserves on such business are relatively minor and second because adjusted reserves are often quite close to statutory.

A comparison of statutory net level reserves (1952 Disability Study—Period 2, 1958 CSO, 3 percent) and adjusted benefit reserves for a waiver of premium benefit is shown in Table 11–15. The plan illustrated is waiver for life, disability before 60, premiums to 60, issue age 35 (male), and the adjusted reserve assumptions are as follows:

Claim costs—1952 Disability Study—Period 2 with interest at 3 percent; select effect at 70 percent, 80 percent, 90 percent, and 101 percent in Years 1, 2, 3, and 4 on, respectively.

Mortality—1950–54 select.

Interest—5 percent graded to 3 percent in 20 years.

*This seems obvious, but individual adjustments are sometimes evaluated over a long period of time and the aggregate effect of not adjusting various blocks of business is not perceived until very late in the conversion process.

Table 11–15.

STATUTORY AND ADJUSTED RESERVES FOR TWO SUPPLEMENTAL BENEFIT COVERAGES*

Duration	Waiver		Accidental Death	
	Statutory	*Adjusted*	*Statutory*	*Adjusted*
1	$ 1.52	$ 1.29	$ 3.00	$ 2.05
2	2.83	2.59	4.10	2.82
3	4.16	3.86	5.20	3.60
4	5.49	5.10	6.30	4.40
5	6.83	6.35	7.50	5.23
6	8.17	7.59	8.60	6.08
7	9.50	8.85	9.80	6.95
8	10.82	10.14	11.00	7.83
9	12.12	11.46	12.10	8.70
10	13.40	12.80	13.20	9.54
11	14.65	14.12	14.30	10.35
12	15.86	15.42	15.30	11.10
13	17.01	16.69	16.20	11.83
14	18.06	17.92	17.10	12.54
15	19.00	19.06	18.00	13.27
16	19.76	20.02	18.90	14.00
17	20.29	20.73	19.80	14.72
18	20.50	21.13	20.70	15.44
19	20.30	21.12	21.50	16.16
20	19.58	20.57	22.30	16.86
21	18.20	19.28	23.00	17.49
22	15.96	17.02	23.60	17.99
23	12.83	13.77	24.10	18.40
24	8.78	9.46	24.40	18.68
25	3.69	3.91	24.50	18.81
26			24.40	18.79
27			24.00	18.58
28			23.30	18.13
29			22.30	17.39
30			20.80	16.32
31			18.90	14.84
32			16.40	12.93
33			13.30	10.52
34			9.50	7.53
35			4.90	3.87

* Information furnished by Milliman & Robertson, Inc.

Withdrawals—18 percent in Year 1, 6 percent in Year 2, 3 percent in Years 3 and 4, and 2 percent thereafter.

While adjusted lags statutory in the early years and exceeds statutory in the later years, the two sets of reserves are close enough that, considering the volumes involved, the reserves might well not be adjusted in this case. The company might hold statutory net level reserves and defer and amortize acquisition costs. This is what Crazy Quilt Life did.

In the past a few companies have provided statu-tory reserves for the waiver of premium benefit equal to one-half of the annual gross premium, and some have suggested that this practice might be appropriate for purposes of adjusted reserves. The practice should be discouraged because the unearned premium may bear no resemblance to a statutory reserve because of the nature of the business. In one significant test, for example, one-half the unearned premium averaged $16 per unit of insurance, while the statutory reserve—which may be presumed to be close to the adjusted reserve—averaged $36 per unit.

Disabled lives reserves are sometimes fairly significant, and interest can be a relatively important factor with respect to such reserves. Where the level of the reserves is sizeable, consideration should be given to adjusting them.

Crazy Quilt Life used statutory reserves as a stand-in for adjusted for both active lives and disabled lives reserves, based on tests and the immateriality of the reserves.

Accidental Death

Statutory net level reserves for the accidental death benefit are often higher than adjusted reserves. As an example, Table 11-15 shows a comparison of statutory net level reserves (1959 Accidental Death Benefits Table, 1958 CSO mortality, 3 percent) with benefit adjusted reserves for a $10,000 accidental death benefit (issue age 35, male, premiums and benefit to age 70). Adjusted reserve assumptions are the same as for the waiver benefit for interest and withdrawals; the mortality assumption is the 1950–54 Basic Select Table; accidental death assumption is the graduated 1951 to 1956 Accidental Death Claim Rates.*

Where statutory is close to adjusted or is somewhat more conservative, it will often be feasible to hold statutory reserves and defer and amortize acquisition costs. This is what Crazy Quilt did.

Substandard

For most companies substandard business is a small percentage of their total business, and extra premiums on such business are minor. So are the reserves. For

*The 1959 Table is the same table loaded 30 percent, subject to a minimum and a maximum addition.

such companies it will usually be feasible to carry statutory reserves (often half the annual gross extra premium) and defer and amortize acquisition costs.

Specialists in substandard business should, of course, calculate adjusted reserves on such business or test the business sufficiently to determine that adjustment would have a negligible effect.

Miscellaneous Coverages

Reserves for guaranteed insurability, payor death benefits, and other such coverages are usually quite minor and statutory reserves (together with deferral and amortization of acquisition costs) will often be an acceptable approximation of adjusted reserves for all practical purposes.

Supplementary Contracts

Supplementary contracts not involving life contingencies are deposits and no adjustment should be made.

Supplementary contracts involving life contingencies are similar to annuities and adjustment should be made if the volume of such contracts is material. Often the relative immateriality of supplementary contracts involving life contingencies, together with an assumption that conservative interest rates provide in effect for needed adverse deviation with respect to the mortality assumption, make it feasible to carry the reserves on a statutory basis.

12 Calculation Techniques

The life insurance audit guide does not offer any guidelines on how to calculate adjusted reserves. That matter is left purely to the judgment of actuaries, and properly so.

Nevertheless, a few general comments about calculation techniques need to be made. There are various methods of calculating reserves, and some methods are better than others. Choice of a method will be influenced by a number of considerations, most of them practical. It is important to understand the circumstances under which practicality can lead to a distorted result.

Incidence Assumptions

Deaths don't just "happen"; they happen at a point in time. So do withdrawals. So, for that matter, do dividend payments, term conversions, and premium receipts.

It is often useful to assume that a policy is dated July 1, that a full annual premium is received at the beginning of the policy year, and that deaths occur at the end of the year. Making such "incidence assumptions" simplifies the calculation of reserves.

But premiums are received, death claims are paid, and withdrawals often occur more or less continuously. So while assuming otherwise may simplify the calculation of reserves, it also results in reserves that do not accurately reflect the incidence of events.

Nature of the Incidence Problem

A reserve may be viewed as a fund accumulated in such a fashion as to anticipate benefits as they actually occur. Naturally the pattern of accumulation must be defined in advance.

Valuation premiums and interest are added to the fund; benefits are deducted from the fund. Each assumed fund transaction is supposed to be accompanied by an actual transaction which offsets it. If everything occurs as planned, profits emerge to the extent of the difference between the gross premium and the valuation premium. If the timing differs as between actual events and assumed events, profits are affected. For example, if mortality actually occurs on December 31 but is assumed to occur on June 30 (the end of the policy year), actual mortality is charged to profits in one calendar year and the offset, assumed mortality, is "released" from the reserve and hence credited to income in another calendar year.

Furthermore, the death and withdrawal assumptions represent assumed decreases in insurance in force. Reserve factors are calculated in such a way as to require an assumption as to how much insurance will be in force at any point in time. Application of the factors to assumed insurance in force thus produces the planned aggregate reserve fund.

Suppose, for instance, that assumed deaths are 10 percent, assumed withdrawals are 11 percent, decrements are assumed to occur at the end of the year, the policy anniversary date is July 1, the valuation premium is $200 per $1,000, and interest and cash values are zero. The reserve for the first year would be calculated as follows:

July 1, 19–1: valuation premium received	$ 200
December 31, 19–1 reserve fund	200
June 30, 19–2: deaths paid	(100)
June 30, 19–2 reserve fund	$ 100

Reserve factors are calculated by the percentage of insureds assumed to persist at each point in time, thus:

	Reserve Fund	Assumed to Persist	Reserve Factor
December 31, 19–1	$200	100%	$200
June 30, 19–2	100	80%	125

If the persistency assumption is correct, the correct reserve fund is obtained by applying the factors to insurance in force:

	Insurance in Force	Reserve Factor Per $1,000	Reserve Fund
December 31, 19–1	$1,000	$200	$200
June 30, 19–2	800	125	100

If, however, decrements occur evenly throughout the year—i.e., half in the first half of the policy year and half in the second half of the policy year—several things happen. First, the assumed and actual reserve funds differ at interim points in time:

	Actual	Assumed	Difference
July 1—premiums	$200	$ 200	$–0–
December 31—deaths	(50)	–0–	(50)
December 30—deaths	150	200	(50)
June 30—deaths	(50)	(100)	50
June 30—fund	$100	$ 100	$–0–

And second, the actual and assumed insurance in force differ, with the result that the mid-policy year actual fund produced by the valuation process differs from assumed:

	Actual	Assumed	Difference
In force December 31, 19–1	$900	$1,000	$100
Precalculated factor	200	200	–0–
December 31, 19–1 fund	180	200	20
In force June 30, 19–2	$800	$ 800	$–0–
Precalculated factor	125	125	–0–
June 30, 19–2 fund	100	100	–0–

The effect on profits may be summarized as follows:

	Actual	Assumed	Increase (Decrease) Profits
19–1 mortality	$ (50)	$ –0–	$(50)
19–1 reserve increase	(180)	(200)	20
19–1 total	$(230)	$(200)	$(30)
19–2 mortality	$ (50)	$(100)	$ 50
19–2 reserve decrease	80	100	(20)
19–2 total	$ 30	$ –0–	$ 30

The $30 distortion in the first calendar year is thus offset in the second. But the distortions continue, in amounts that vary with the difference between actual and assumed, to the next calendar year valuation, and the one after that, and so on.

In the above example the $30 distortion may be analyzed into two components (analysis is approximate and ignores certain minor factors):

Actual less assumed mortality		$(50)
Difference between actual and assumed persistency	10%	
Reserve factor	$200	20
		$(30)

Thus the incidence assumption involves a highly complex and interactive process. The foregoing example is simplified; in practice, interest, cash values, premiums, and all elements entering into a reserve calculation would affect the variance between actual and assumed.

Policy Anniversary

It is fairly typical to assume, for purposes of calculating reserves, that the average policy anniversary is July 1.

The July 1 assumption involves several other assumptions where adjusted reserves are concerned: that anniversaries are distributed evenly throughout the year, that the mix of plans and ages is constant at each anniversary, and that the distribution of premium modes is constant.

When one or more of these assumptions are not valid in all material respects, consideration should be given to modifying reserve calculation techniques to recognize more precisely the distribution of anniversaries. Usually the problem has possible significance only for young, rapidly-growing companies where the distribution of new business varies considerably by month.

The discussion that follows assumes that a July 1 anniversary assumption is valid.

Mortality

Assuming death benefits are paid evenly thoughout the policy year means, in effect, that for policies with an average issue date of July 1, half of a policy year's deaths are paid from July 1 to December 31 and half from January 1 to June 30.

It might, of course, involve more work to distribute deaths by *day,* so approximation of the stream of benefit payments would be appropriate. For example, it might be assumed that half the death claims are payable at the beginning of the policy year and half at the end (the assumption used by Crazy Quilt Life); or half at the end of the first quarter and half at the end of the third; and so on.

Withdrawals

The assumed incidence of withdrawals typically has the most significant impact on reserves, particularly in the early years. As in the case of death claims, withdrawals can be allocated between the first half of the policy year and the second half. This can be done, for example, by assuming a portion of the year's withdrawals occur at the beginning of the policy year and a portion at the end. The effect is that the policyholders assumed to withdraw at the beginning of the year pay no premiums for the year.

The allocation of withdrawals within policy years is partly a function of the premium mode. Monthly mode policies tend to lapse more rapidly, for example, than annual modes. Thus, instead of allocating withdrawals evenly between the two half-years, the weighting of the year's withdrawals for monthly modes might be, for example, 60 percent to the first half year and 40 percent to the second. Annual-mode policies are usually assumed to withdraw at the end of the policy year, i.e., the 13th-month premium is not paid, so withdrawals need not be allocated.

In practice, a single withdrawal assumption that recognizes the distribution of modes would usually be used. A composite withdrawal rate might be developed somewhat as follows:

Mode	Percentage of Volume	Total First-Year Withdrawals	Weighted First-Year Withdrawals	Proportion Occurring in First Half Year	Composite Withdrawals	
					First Half Year	Balance— Second Half Year
Monthly	40%	20%	8.0%	60%	4.80%	3.20%
Quarterly	20	18	3.6	40	1.44	2.16
Semi-annual	20	16	3.2	25	.80	2.40
Annual	20	14	2.8	–0–	–0–	2.80
	100%		17.6%		7.04%	10.56%

This might be translated into an over-all withdrawal assumption of 7 percent at the beginning of the policy year and 11 percent at the end.

Nonforfeiture Benefits

Nonforfeiture benefits, if any, would usually be assumed to be payable at the time of withdrawal. In the case of annual-premium business for which withdrawals are assumed to occur at the end of the policy year, for example, the assumed nonforfeiture benefit would be the terminal cash value (or, to the extent that differential costs of the various nonforfeiture options are recognized, the weighted average of the various nonforfeiture costs measured as of the end of the policy year).

Where withdrawals are assumed to occur at the beginning of the policy year, the nonforfeiture benefit assumed to be payable would be the previous year's terminal cash value (or its weighted average equivalent).

And where withdrawals are assumed to occur at interim points during the policy year (such as at the end of each quarter or in mid-year), the nonforfeiture benefit assumed to be payable would usually be the interpolated value, i.e., a straight-line apportionment of the difference between two terminal values to the period of time from the previous terminal value to the assumed time of withdrawal.

Dividends

As mentioned in Chapter 10, dividends that are accounted for as benefits in calculating adjusted reserves can be assumed to be paid at the beginning of the policy year or at the end. When dividends are assumed to be payable at the beginning of the year but are actually payable at the end, a separate liability must be held equal to the present value at December 31 of dividends payable in the following calendar year.

When dividends are assumed to be payable at the end of the policy year, no such liability need be held, since at mid-year the dividend liability is included in the benefit reserve liability.

Conversions

Costs of conversion are assumed to be incurred at the time of conversion, and conversions are usually assumed to occur on the policy anniversary.

Valuation Premiums

The incidence of valuation premiums is a function of the withdrawal assumption (as well as the mode assumption and reserve calculation method). If a portion of the year's withdrawals is assumed to occur at the beginning of the policy year, for example, obviously premiums will not be paid by those withdrawing. Thus the valuation premiums assumed to be received may vary from year to year.

Fractional Premiums

Where an annual-premium assumption is used it is necessary to recognize loss or refund of fractional premiums upon death. This could be accomplished by estimating the amount of such loss or refund for each year and allocating it to the periods in which death is assumed to occur. It would also be feasible to hold a separate reserve similar to the statutory reserve for non-deduction of deferred fractional premiums.

Interest

The incidence of assumed interest is a function of the assumed incidence of all the elements making up the reserve fund. If, for example, only half the valuation premium is assumed to be received at the beginning of the year, interest in the first half year will be earned only on half the valuation premium (adjusted for interest lost on benefits assumed to be paid).

Usually assumed interest rates are expressed on an annual basis. When compounding occurs more often than annually, it is necessary to translate annual rates into semi-annual equivalents. For example, the semi-annual equivalent of a 6 percent annual rate is 2.95630 percent, and a fund of $1 compounds to $1.06 over two six-month periods as follows:

$$
\begin{array}{r}
\$1.0295630 \\
\times \quad 1.0295630 \\
\hline
\$1.0600000 \\
\end{array}
$$

Thus the net cash transactions assumed to occur at the beginning of the policy year would be improved at 2.95630 percent interest to December 31.

Expenses

Assumptions as to the incidence of expenses usually follow the assumptions to which they relate. Non-percentage acquisition costs are usually assumed to occur at issue. Percentage expenses—acquisition and maintenance—are usually assumed to occur as premiums are assumed to be received. Per-policy and per-unit expenses are usually assumed to occur at the beginning of the policy year; although they could, of course, be distributed to two half-years, the effect of doing so would usually be negligible. If settlement processing costs are expressed on a per-event basis, they would usually be assumed to occur when the event itself is assumed to occur.

The assumed incidence of expenses has a significant effect on deferred and uncollected premiums, which are discussed in Chapter 23.

Intermediate Reserves

An intermediate reserve is calculated in such a way as to provide a fund which, when supplemented by the valuation premium, will accumulate to a fund sufficient to cover (1) the next terminal reserve plus (2) benefits occurring from the valuation date to the next anniversary.

Reserve Accumulation

The calculation of an intermediate reserve can be illustrated by accumulating a fund for an annual premium policy dated July 1 for 18 months and deriving reserve factors at various points in time. The assumptions are as follows:

Valuation premium	$8.61
Death rate (evenly distributed and occurring prior to withdrawals):	
First policy year	.00077
Second policy year	.00096
Withdrawals (occurring at end of year):	
First policy year	50%
Second policy year	10%
Interest	6%
Terminal cash value:	
First policy year	–0–
Second policy year	$10

The intermediate reserve "fund", and the related reserve factors, would develop through the first two policy years as shown in Table 12–1.

Table 12–1.

ACCUMULATION OF BENEFIT RESERVE FUND PER $1,000 ISSUED AND CALCULATION OF INTERMEDIATE BENEFIT RESERVE FACTORS THROUGH SECOND POLICY YEAR FOR ANNUAL-PREMIUM CASE

Date	Policy Year	Calendar Year		Fund Transactions	Units in Force	Reserve Factor Per Unit
7–1	1	1	Valuation premium ($8.61x1.000000)	$ 8.610	1.000000	
7–1	1	1	Deaths (50% x.00077x$1,000.00)	(.385)	(.000385)	
7–1	1	1	Balance	8.225	.999615	
12–31	1	1	Interest at .0295638	.243	—	
12–31	1	1	Balance	8.468	.999615	$ 8.47
6–30	1	2	Interest at .0295638	.250	—	
6–30	1	2	Deaths (50% x.00077x$1,000.00)	(.385)	(.000385)	
6–30	1	2	Balance before withdrawals	8.333	.999230	
6–30	1	2	Withdrawals (50% x.999230)*	–0–	(.499615)	
6–30	1	2	Balance	8.333	.499615	$16.68
7–1	2	2	Valuation premium ($8.61x.499615)	4.302	—	
7–1	2	2	Deaths (50% x.00096x$499.62)	(.240)	(.000240)	
7–1	2	2	Balance	12.395	.499375	
12–31	2	2	Interest at .0295638	.366	—	
12–31	2	2	Balance	12.761	.499375	$25.55
6–30	2	3	Interest at .0295638	.377	—	
6–30	2	3	Deaths (50% x.00096x$499.62)	(.240)	(.000240)	
6–30	2	3	Balance before withdrawals	12.898	.499135	
6–30	2	3	Withdrawals (10% x.499135x$10)	(.499)	(.049914)	
6–30	2	3	Balance	$12.399	.449221	$27.60

*No surrender values available in the first year.

Mean of Beginning and Ending Reserves

The intermediate reserve can be closely approximated by taking the mean of the "beginning reserve" and the "ending reserve". The beginning reserve is the reserve after any beginning-of-the-year decrements except deaths; the ending reserve is the reserve prior to the year's withdrawals and conversions (if any) but after the year's deaths. The reserves shown in Table 12–1 would be calculated using the beginning and ending reserve approach as follows:

	First Year	Second Year
Beginning reserve:		
$8.61 ÷ 1.000000	$ 8.61	
[$8.33 + $4.30] ÷ .499615		$25.29
Ending reserve		
$8.33 ÷ .999230	8.34	
$12.90 ÷ .499135		25.84
Total	$16.95	$51.12
Mean	$ 8.47	$25.56

The principal advantage of calculating beginning and ending reserves in the manner illustrated is that they can be used (1) to recognize skewness in the distributions of policy anniversaries and (2) for purposes of interim valuations, in both cases by *interpolating* between the beginning and ending funds.

For example, if the case illustrated in Table 12–1 were dated November 1, the December 31 reserve could be calculated as $8.61, the beginning reserve, plus one-sixth of the difference between that amount and the ending reserve, $8.34. Thus the December 31 reserve would be $8.61 plus one-sixth of ($8.34 − $8.61), or $8.56.

Similarly, if the case were dated January 1 and were valued on September 30 for an interim statement, the September 30 reserve would be $8.61 plus three-fourths of the difference (which is a negative $.27), or $8.41.

The effect of this procedure is to make a further allocation of death claims and other benefits to interim accounting periods. With respect to the November 1 policy that is valued on December 31, for example, the indicated reserve, $8.56, could be accumulated as follows:

Valuation premium	$8.61
1/6 of the year's deaths	
(1/6 × [$.385 + $.385])	(.13)
1/6 of the year's interest	
(1/6 × [$.243 + $.250])	.08
	$8.56

And as for the January 1 policy that is valued on September 30, the indicated reserve, $8.41, could be accumulated as follows:

Valuation premium	$8.61
75% of the year's deaths	
(75% × [$.385 + $.385])	(.57)
75% of the year's interest	
(75% × [$.243 + $.250])	.37
	$8.41

Thus the use of beginning and ending reserves facilitates approximation of true intermediate reserves at various points in time. (Problems arise when withdrawals are allocated between half-years on annual-premium cases, but such problems are beyond the scope of this chapter.)

Deferred and Uncollected Premiums

When intermediate reserves are calculated on the basis of assuming receipt of a full annual premium, it is necessary to take into account any portion of the premium that has not been received.

For example, the annual premium on the policy for which reserves are calculated in Table 12–1 is $8.61. If this were a semi-annual case, the second installment of the premium would be deferred at December 31 (and due on January 1), assuming it is not paid in advance of the due date.

The fact that the premium has not been collected would be compensated for by recording, as an offset to the reserve, a deferred premium of $4.30. To be fully consistent with the operation of the reserve, interest of $.13 (2.95638% x $4.30) should also be recorded as an offset to the reserve. But this is often ignored on the basis that premiums other than annual are "loaded" to compensate for the loss of interest, and the "loading" is taken into income when the premiums are received.

Uncollected premiums would be accounted for in much the same manner as deferred premiums.

Deferred and uncollected premiums are discussed at some length in Chapter 23.

Continuous-Premium Intermediate Reserves

It is also possible to calculate intermediate reserves that recognize modes other than annual and withdrawals that occur other than at the end of the year.

This could be accomplished by projecting monthly lapses (and surrender benefits) and monthly valuation premiums, applying the death rate uniformly across the year, and accumulating everything at interest, month by month; but the work involved in doing this would be prohibitive.

The effect of a month-by-month accumulation may be approximated by allocating part of the year's withdrawals to the beginning of the policy year and part to the end. The allocation is a function of mode and lapse rates by mode. The allocation should be made in such a way that the units in force at the beginning of the year, less the withdrawals allocated to the beginning of year, approximate the average exposure for the year.

Table 12–2 shows the result of allocating the year's withdrawals 60 percent to the beginning of the year and 40 percent to the end. The units in force remaining at the beginning of the first year, 70 percent (after withdrawals allocated to the beginning of the year), represents average exposures from July 1 to June 30. The valuation premium assumed to be received is immediately reduced to 70 percent of the annual valuation premium.

In calculating intermediate reserves by using the mean of the beginning and ending reserves, it is necessary to calculate the beginning reserve *before* receipt of the valuation premium for continuous-premium cases. Thus the intermediate reserves for the policy shown in Table 12–2 would be calculated as follows:

	First Year	Second Year
Beginning reserve:		
No reserve	$ –0–	
$5.833 ÷ .469493		$12.42
Ending reserve:		
$5.833 ÷ .699461	8.34	
$9.999 ÷ .469043		21.32
Total	$8.34	$33.74
Mean	$4.17	$16.87

If the reserves are calculated in this manner it is not necessary to record deferred premiums. The

Table 12–2.

ACCUMULATION OF BENEFIT RESERVE FUND PER $1,000 ISSUED AND CALCULATION OF INTERMEDIATE BENEFIT RESERVE FACTORS THROUGH SECOND POLICY YEAR FOR MONTHLY-PREMIUM CASE

Date		Fund Transactions	Units in Force	Reserve Factor Per Unit
7–1	Issues		1.000000	
7–1	Withdrawals (60%x50%)		(.300000)	
7–1	Balance		.700000	
7–1	Valuation premium (.700000x$8.61)	$6.027	—	
7–1	Deaths (50%x.00077x$700)	(.270)	(.000270)	
7–1	Balance	5.757	.699730	
12–31	Interest at .0295638	.170	—	
12–31	Balance	5.927	.699730	$ 8.47
6–30	Interest at .0295638	.176	—	
6–30	Deaths (50%x.00077x$700.00)	(.270)	(.000269)	
6–30	Balance	5.833	.699461	
6–30	Withdrawals (40%x50%)*	–0–	(.200000)	
6–30	Balance	5.833	.499461	$11.68
7–1	Withdrawals (60%x10%x.499461)	–0–	(.029968)	
7–1	Balance	5.833	.469493	
7–1	Valuation premium (.469493x$8.61)	4.044	—	
7–1	Deaths (50%x.00096x$469.49)	(.225)	(.000225)	
7–1	Balance	9.652	.469268	
12–31	Interest at .0295638	.285	—	
12–31	Balance	9.937	.469268	$21.16
6–30	Interest at .0295638	.294	—	
6–30	Deaths (50%x.00096x$469.49)	(.225)	(.000225)	
6–30	Balance	10.006	.469043	
6–30	Withdrawals (40%x10%x.499461x$10)	(.200)	(.019978)	
6–30	Balance	$9.806	.449065	$21.82

*No surrender values available in the first year.

calculation adjusts for the fact that the full year's premium has not been collected. In the illustrated case, the reserve can be accumulated as follows:

First year:
1/2 of valuation premium (50% × $6.027)		$ 3.02
1/2 of year's deaths (50% × [$.270 + $.269])		(.27)
1/2 of year's interest (50% × [$.170 + $.175])		.17
		$ 2.92
Units in force		.699730
Reserve per unit		$ 4.17

Second year:
Beginning fund		$ 5.83
1/2 of valuation premium (50% × $4.042)		2.02
1/2 of year's death claims (50% × [$.225 + $.225])		(.23)
1/2 of year's interest (50% × [$.280 + $.294])		.29
		$ 7.91
Units in force		.469268
Reserve per unit		$16.87

Uncollected premiums would also not have to be recorded if the reserve were interpolated to the paid-to date. Further, non-deduction of deferred fractional premiums is automatically taken into account by reducing the assumed premium income.

The continuous-premium beginning and ending reserves can be interpolated to yield interim valuation data or to recognize policy anniversary in the same fashion as the annual-premium reserve.

In practice, withdrawal allocations would normally be expressed in the form of composites, discussed earlier in this chapter. Reserve factors would be the same for all cases regardless of mode, but the modal distribution (and the related assumptions as to premiums received) would be reflected in the aggregate. Deferred premiums would be unnecessary if the reserves were interpolated to the paid-to date. Obviously this procedure must be carried out with great care, and the mix of modes and distribution of lapses must be monitored constantly to ensure that the reserve assumptions continue to be valid.

Similarity to Means and Mid-Terminals

Calculating intermediate reserves by taking the mean of beginning and ending reserves using the annual-premium assumption is similar in some respects to the traditional mean reserve calculation. Calculating intermediate reserves by taking the mean of beginning and ending reserves using the continuous-premium assumption is somewhat similar to the traditional calculation of mid-terminal reserves.

That doesn't mean, however, that intermediate reserves are the same as means or mid-terminals, as the case may be, for reasons discussed below.

Mean Reserves

The methods of calculating intermediate reserves described previously recognize the incidence of terminations. Terminations can have a very significant effect on reserves, particularly in the early years.

Reference to Table 12–1 will indicate that the first-year and second-year intermediate reserves are $8.47 and $25.55, respectively. A traditional mean reserve calculation would result in reserves of $12.65 and $26.45, respectively:

	First Year	Second Year
Prior terminal reserve	$ –0–	$16.68
Valuation premium	8.61	8.61
Initial reserve	8.61	25.29
Current terminal reserve	16.68	27.60
Total	$25.29	$52.89
Mean	$12.65	$26.45

The first-year intermediate reserve, $8.47, is only 67 percent of the first-year mean reserve, $12.65. The difference, $4.18, would represent an overstatement of the reserve if the mean reserve method were used. Assuming $1 billion of insurance in force was issued and $999,615,000 is in force December 31, the result of using mean reserves would be to overstate the benefit reserve liability by $4,178,391 (999,615 × $4.18).

Although the difference between mean and intermediate reserves will never disappear entirely, it usually diminishes with the passage of time as withdrawals diminish and cash values approach the reserves. In the second year, for example, the intermediate reserve is 97 percent of the mean reserve.

The difference between the intermediate and mean reserves reflects mainly the different recognition accorded to withdrawals. Where withdrawals are assumed to occur at the end of the year, the traditional mean reserve calculation actually allocates half of them to the first half of the year by dividing everything by 2. Thus the $4.18 first-year difference calculated above can be explained in large measure by multiplying half of the first-year withdrawals, 24.98 percent (50% × .499615), by the first-year terminal reserve, 16.68; the $.90 second-year difference is largely explained by multiplying half of the second-year withdrawals, 2.5 percent (50% × .049914), by the total of the valuation premium, $8.61, and the second-year terminal reserve, $27.60.

For various reasons, some companies will want to calculate adjusted reserves using traditional mean reserve techniques. Whether the error introduced by the mean reserve process is tolerable is a matter of individual judgment. As a general rule, the mean reserve error is greatest for companies (1) which are fairly new and growing rapidly, (2) whose in-force volume is heavily weighted by recent issues, and (3) whose reserves are based on the annual-mode assumptions.

Mid-Terminal Reserves

Mid-terminal reserves are very similar to mean reserves. A comparison of mean and mid-terminal reserves for the annual-premium case illustrated in Table 12–1 will demonstrate this:

	Mean	Mid-Terminal
Prior terminal reserve	$ –0–	$ –0–
Valuation premium	8.61	
Initial reserve	8.61	
Current terminal reserve	16.68	16.68
Total	$25.29	$16.68
Mean reserve	$12.65	
Mid-terminal reserve		$ 8.34
Unearned premium		4.31
Mid-terminal valuation amount		$12.65

Thus traditionally-calculated mid-terminal reserves suffer from the same deficiencies, relative to intermediate reserves, as mean reserves, and the decision to use them should be based on whether the resulting distortions are material.

Traditionally-calculated terminal reserves can be interpolated to interim valuation dates in much the same manner as continuous-premium intermediate reserves. Traditional mid-terminal techniques, however, are based on the assumption of a continuous distribution of decrements, so it would be necessary to record an unearned premium liability for premiums paid beyond the valuation date. Unless reserves are interpolated to the paid-to date rather than the valuation date, it would also be necessary to record uncollected premiums.

Expense Reserves

Although expenses are discussed in detail in Part III, the calculation of expense reserve factors deserves some attention in this chapter because the calculation of such factors is in all material respects the same as the calculation of benefit factors.

Assumed Incidence of Expenses

In calculating expense factors by the intermediate reserve approach, it is fairly typical to assume the following distribution of expenses:

Percentage acquisition costs—when premiums are received.

Non-percentage acquisition costs—at Duration 0, i.e., before any premium is received.

Percentage maintenance expenses—when premiums are received.

Non-percentage maintenance expenses—at the beginning of the policy year where the annual-premium assumption is used, and uniformly throughout the policy year (e.g., half at the beginning and half at the end) where the continuous-premium assumption is used.

Claim handling—when deaths are assumed to occur.

Surrender handling—when surrender values are assumed to be paid.

Annual-Premium Case Intermediate Reserves

Table 12–3 shows the development of intermediate expense reserve factors for an annual premium case where

The gross premium is $18,
The valuation premium is $9.03,
Percentage acquisition costs are 122 percent,
Non-percentage acquisition costs are $5.50 per $1,000,

Percentage maintenance expenses are 7 percent,
Non-percentage maintenance expenses are $.85 per $1,000,
Death claim handling expenses are $5 per $1,000 claim,
Surrender handling expenses are $2 per surrender, and
Withdrawal and mortality rates and the interest rate are as indicated in Table 12–1.

A comparison of intermediate and traditional mean reserves highlights the distortion introduced by the mean reserve approach:

	First Year	Second Year
Intermediate	$(19.86)	$(35.00)
Mean:		
Prior terminal reserve	$ –0–	$(40.91)
Valuation premium	9.03	9.03
Initial reserve	9.03	(31.88)
Current terminal reserve	(40.91)	(40.29)
Total	$(31.88)	$(72.17)
Mean	$(15.94)	$(36.09)
Intermediate as a % of mean	125%	97%

The distortion in this case is considerably lessened because of the very high first-year lapse rate (50 percent). If 75 percent persisted to the second year, then—ignoring certain minor complexities—the first-year terminal reserve would be $20.44 ÷ .75 or $(27.25) and the mean reserve would be $(9.11), or a mere 45 percent of the intermediate reserve.

The distortion can be mitigated somewhat by modifying the traditional mean reserve calculation to deduct beginning-of-the-year expenses in calculating the initial reserve; this is discussed further in Chapter 23. In this case, though, the modification would increase the distortion:

	First Year
Prior terminal reserve	$ –0–
Valuation premium	9.03
Initial expenses	(28.31)
Modified initital reserve	(19.28)
Current terminal reserve	(40.91)
Total	$(60.19)
Mean	$(30.10)
Intermediate as a % of mean	66%

Thus traditional mean reserves should rarely be used for expenses.

Intermediate expense reserves can also be approximated by use of the beginning and ending reserves as

Table 12–3.

ACCUMULATION OF EXPENSE RESERVE FUND PER $1,000 ISSUED AND CALCULATION OF INTERMEDIATE EXPENSE RESERVE FACTORS THROUGH SECOND POLICY YEAR ANNUAL-PREMIUM CASE

Date		Fund Transactions	Units in Force	Reserve Factor Per Unit
7–1	Issues	—	1.000000	
	Duration 0 expenses:			
7–1	Acquisition (1.000000x$5.50)	$ (5.50)	—	
7–1	Maintenance (1.000000x$ .85	(.85)	—	
7–1	Valuation premium	9.03	—	
	Duration 1 expenses:			
7–1	Acquisition (115%x$18x1.000000)	(20.70)	—	
7–1	Maintenance (7%x$18x1.000000)	(1.26)	—	
7–1	Death claim handling ($5x.00077x50%x1.000000)	nil	—	
7–1	Deaths (50%x.00077x1.000000	—	(.000385)	
7–1	Balance	(19.28)	.999615	
12–31	Interest at .0295638	(.57)	—	
12–31	Balance	(19.85)	.999615	$(19.86)
6–30	Interest at .0295638	(.59)	—	
6–30	Deaths (50%x.00077x.999615)	—	(.000385)	
6–30	Death claim handling ($5x.00077x50%x.999615)	nil	—	
6–30	Balance before withdrawals	(20.44)	.999230	
6–30	Withdrawals (50%x.999230)*	—	(.499615)	
6–30	Balance	(20.44)	.499615	$(40.91)
7–1	Valuation premium ($9.03x.499615)	4.51	—	
	Duration 2 expenses:			
7–1	Percentage (7%x$18x.499615)	(.63)	—	
7–1	Non-percentage ($ .85x.499615)	(.42)	—	
7–1	Death claim handling ($5x.00096x.499615)	nil	—	
7–1	Deaths (50%x.00096x.499615)	—	(.000240)	
7–1	Balance	(16.98)	.499375	
12–31	Interest at .0295638	(.50)	—	
12–31	Balance	(17.48)	.499375	$(35.00)
6–30	Interest at .0295638	(.52)	—	
6–30	Deaths (50%x.00096x.499375)	—	(.000240)	
6–30	Death claim handling ($5x.00096x50%x.499375)	nil	—	
6–30	Balance before withdrawals	(18.00)	.499135	
6–30	Withdrawals (10%x.499135)	—	(.049914)	
6–30	Surrender handling expense ($2.00x.049914)	(.10)	—	
6–30	Balance	$(18.10)	.449221	$(40.29)

*No surrender available in the first year.

described earlier in this chapter in connection with benefit reserves, except that initial expenses must be deducted in calculating the beginning reserve:

	First Year	Second Year
Beginning reserve:		
$(19.28) ÷ 1.000000	$(19.28)	
$(16.98) ÷ .499615		$(33.99)
Ending reserve:		
$(20.44) ÷ .999230	(20.46)	
$(18.00) ÷ .499135		(36.06)
Total	$(39.74)	$(70.05)
Mean	$(19.87)	$(35.03)

Continuous-Premium Cases

Calculation of the intermediate expense reserves on continuous-premium cases would follow the same pattern as calculation of continuous-premium intermediate benefit reserves. Recognition of the proper incidence of expense is critical.

The beginning and ending intermediate reserves would generally be calculated in the same fashion as has been described previously for continuous-premium intermediate benefit reserves, except that expenses deemed to occur at the beginning of the year would be deducted from the beginning reserve.

SUPPLEMENT TO CHAPTER 12
RESERVE FORMULAS*

Intermediate reserve definitions and formulas
and the definitions and formulas used
by Crazy Quilt Life are set forth here.

Decrement Rates:

Annual premiums: The mortality rate for policy year t is applied to the number of lives beginning the policy year to determine the number of deaths, which are assumed to occur evenly throughout the year. The withdrawal rate is applied to the number of lives surviving the year; all withdrawals occur at the end of the year. Likewise, the conversion rate is applied to the number of lives surviving to the end of the year, and all conversions occur at the end of the year. The formula for the number of lives beginning year $t + 1$ is

$$1_{[x]+t} = 1_{[x]+t-1}(1 - q_{[x]+t-1})(1 - w_{[x]+t-1} - (wc)_{[x]+t-1})$$

Non-annual premiums: The major difference between the non-annual and annual premium modes is in the treatment of withdrawals. To simulate the true incidence of withdrawals, a portion of the withdrawals for a policy year are assumed to occur at the beginning of the year and the remainder at the end. The portion allocated to the beginning of the year is a function of the mode distribution and the expected lapse experience by mode, and is determined in such a way that the lives beginning the year, less the withdrawals allocated to the beginning of the year, approximate the average exposure during the year.

The withdrawals allocated to the beginning of policy year t are assumed to occur immediately—they pay no premium for year t, are not exposed to death for year t, and receive the cash value (if any) payable at the end of year $t-1$. Hence, the withdrawal rate is adjusted for the end of year $t-1$ to include those withdrawals at the beginning of year t by calculating a table of allocated withdrawal rates ($w'_{[x]+t-1}$). These rates are applied to the number of lives surviving each policy year and are a combination of the withdrawals assumed to occur at the end of year $t-1$ and those assumed to occur at the beginning of year t (except the withdrawal rate for $t=0$ is the portion of the first year's withdrawals allocated to the beginning of the year). The formula for the number of lives beginning year $t+1$ is

$$1_{[x]+t} = 1_{[x]+t-1}(1 - q_{[x]+t-1})(1 - w'_{[x]+t-1} - (wc)_{[x]+t-1})$$

and the formula for the number of lives beginning policy year 1 is

$$1_{[x]} = (1 - w'_{[x]-1})$$

In practice, the withdrawal allocation factor is determined by weighting the annual and non-annual premiums.

Benefits:

Death benefits are paid as deaths occur, i.e., evenly throughout the year. The only exception is the payment of a dividend in the year of death, which is paid in the middle of the policy year (the discounted value of this benefit is assumed to be paid at the beginning of the policy year). The formula for the death benefits of year t, as of the beginning of year t, is

$$1_{[x]+t-1} \cdot q_{[x]+t-1}\left[\frac{td}{t\delta}\left(_{t-1}TD_x + _tI_x\right) + _tv^{1/2} \cdot h \cdot _tD_x\right]$$

where the approximation $\dfrac{td}{t\delta} = \dfrac{1 + _tv}{2}$ is used.

*Provided by Milliman & Robertson, Inc.

Surrender benefits are paid at the time of withdrawal, i.e., at the end of each policy year. The formula for the surrender benefits payable in year t, as of the beginning of year t, is

$$1_{[x]+t-1}(1 - q_{[x]+t-1})w'_{[x]+t-1}(_tTD_x + _tCV_x)_tv$$

Conversion costs are incurred on those policies converting at the end of the policy year. The formula for the conversion costs incurred in year t, as of the beginning of year t, is

$$1_{[x]+t-1}(1 - q_{[x]+t-1})(wc)_{[x]+t-1}\frac{_tI_x \cdot O_{[x]+t-1}}{1000} \cdot {}_tv$$

Coupons are paid to all those beginning the policy year. The formula for the coupons paid in year t, as of the beginning of year t, is

$$1_{[x]+t-1} \cdot {}_tK_x$$

Dividends are paid to all those who survive the policy year, except that to receive a first-year dividend the policyholder must pay the premium for the second policy year. The discounted value of the dividend payable at the end of year t is paid at the beginning of year t. This assumption makes it necessary to establish an additional liability for the current policy year dividends that will be paid in the next calendar year. The formula for the dividends payable in year t, as of the beginning of year t, is

$$1_{[x]+t-1}(1 - q_{[x]+t-1})_tD_x \cdot {}_tv$$

except in year 1 it is

$$1_{[x]+1} \cdot {}_1D_x \cdot {}_1v$$

The premium adjustment factor adjusts gross premium income for interest lost on deferred premiums and loss or refund of premiums due to death. It is treated as a benefit payable evenly throughout the policy year. The value of this benefit for policy year t, as of the beginning of the policy year, is

$$1_{[x]+t-1}\left(_tP_x + \frac{F}{A_x}\right)(1 + a)(b \cdot {}_td + c \cdot q_{[x]+t-1})$$

Expenses:

Claims handling expenses are assumed to be paid evenly throughout the policy year on the year's death claims.

Surrender handling expenses are assumed to be paid on policy anniversaries at the time the corresponding surrender value is paid.

Acquisition expenses, i.e., those input at t = 0, are incurred on every policy issued, in contrast to t = 1 expenses, which are incurred only on policies entering the first policy year. They are assumed to be paid at issue.

Expense component 3 percentage, per policy, and per unit expenses for t = 1 or more are assumed to occur at the beginning of each policy year.

The distribution of expense component 1 and 2 percentage, per policy, and per unit expenses for t = 1 or more depends upon whether annual or continuous premium reserves are calculated. For the annual premium reserves, the expenses occur at the beginning of each policy year; for the continuous premium reserves, they occur evenly throughout each policy year.

Reserve Factors:

Beginning reserve—annual premium case: The beginning benefit reserve for policy year t equals the present value, at the beginning of policy year t, of the benefits for years t and on, less the value of the coupon and annual dividend payable at the beginning of year t, less the present value of the benefit premiums payable in years t + 1, and on. Thus, the reserve assumes the benefit premium for policy year t has been received and assumes that the coupons and dividends for policy year t have already been paid. The beginning expense reserve for policy year t equals the present value, at the beginning of year t, of the expenses for years t and on, less the percentage, per policy, and per unit expenses payable at the beginning of year t, less the present value of the expense premiums payable in years t + 1 and on. Thus the reserve assumes the expense premium for policy year t has been received and the percentage, per policy, and per unit expenses for policy year t have already been incurred.

Beginning reserve—continuous premium case: The two difference between the valuation reserves for this case and the annual premium case are that the premiums for year t are assumed to have not yet been received, and component 1 and 2 expenses for year t (other than acquisition) are not deducted from the expense reserve.

Ending reserve—annual and continuous premium cases: The ending benefit reserve is the present value, at the end of policy year t but before the year's withdrawals or conversions have occurred, of the benefits payable in years t + 1, and on, plus the withdrawal benefits and conversion costs payable at the end of year t, less the present value of benefit premiums for years t + 1, and on. Thus, the reserve is valued before the year's conversions and withdrawals are assumed to have been paid. The ending expense reserve is the present value, at the end of policy year t but before the year's withdrawals or conversions have occurred, of the expenses payable in year t + 1, and on, plus the surrender handling expenses paid at the end of year t, less the present value of expense premiums for years t + 1, and on. Thus, the reserve is valued before the year's conversions and withdrawals are assumed to have occurred.

Intermediate reserves: The intermediate reserves are the mean of the beginning and ending reserves for all cases.

Definitions and Formulas:

x	is the age at issue
t	is the policy year or the calendar year, as appropriate to the function. Calendar year t is the one during which policy year t begins. (An exception exists where t is assigned the value 0; $t = 0$ does not designate a year, but rather the moment at which the policy is issued.)
m	is the insurance period
n	is the premium paying period
$q'_{[x]+t-1}$	is the unscaled rate of death during the tth policy year
s_t	is the mortality scaling factor for policy year t
$q_{[x]+t-1}$	is the scaled rate of death during the tth policy year $q_{[x]+t-1} = s_t \cdot q'_{[x]+t-1}$ but $q_{[x]+t-1} \ngtr 1.000$
$w_{[x]+t-1}$	is the rate of withdrawal at duration t; that is, at the end of the tth policy year
	Where $t = 0$, $w_{[x]-1}$ is the proportion of $1_{[x]-1}$ assumed to withdraw at the beginning of the first policy year
	A specified proportion of the voluntary terminations of any policy year is assumed to occur at the beginning of that year, and the balance at its end. This simulates the true termination pattern, wherein terminations are distributed irregularly through the year
$(wc)_{[x]+t-1}$	is the rate of conversion at the end of tth policy year (term plans)
$1_{[x]+t-1}$	is the number entering the tth policy year, after deducting the portion of that policy year's withdrawals assumed to occur at its beginning. It is, therefore, the average exposure during policy year t before deducting deaths
	Where $t = 0$, $1_{[x]-1}$ is the number issued, always 1.00000
$d_{[x]+t-1}$	is the number dying in the tth policy year $= 1_{[x]+t-1} \cdot q_{[x]+t-1}$

213

$W_{[x]+t-1}$ is the number withdrawing at the end of the tth policy year $= (1_{[x]+t-1} - d_{[x]+t-1})w_{[x]+t-1}$

$(WC)_{[x]+t-1}$ is the number converting at the end of the tth policy year $= (1_{[x]+t-1} - d_{[x]+t-1})(wc)_{[x]+t-1}$

$1_{[x]+t}$ $= 1_{[x]+t-1} - d_{[x]+t-1} - W_{[x]+t-1} - (WC)_{[x]+t-1}$

$_tP_x$ is the gross annual premium for age x for the plan of insurance, payable at the beginning of the tth policy year

F is the annual policy fee

$PREMIUM$ $= (1_{[x]+t-1})(_tP_x + \dfrac{F}{A_x})(1+a)[1 - b(_td) - c(q_{[x]+t-1})]$

The following expense related items are used in the calculation of expense component 1 reserves:

$_cE_t^{\%}$ is the percentage of PREMIUM required to cover commissions for policy year t

$_aE_t^{\%}$ is the percentage of PREMIUM covering such other agency expenses as are a function of premium income.

$_aE_t$ is the allowance for such other agency expenses as are a function of the number of policies issued or renewed at the beginning of policy year t

$_ae_t$ is the allowance for such other agency expenses as are a function of the number of units issued or renewed at the beginning of policy year t

$_dE$ is the claims handling expense per claim

$_sE$ is the expense of handling surrenders, per policy surrendered

The following expense related input items are used in the calculation of expense component 2 reserves:

$_0\hat{E}_t^{\%}$ is the percentage of PREMIUM covering such expenses (other than agency expenses) as are a function of premium income

$_0E_t$ is the allowance for such expenses (other than agency expenses) as are a function of the number of policies issued or renewed at the beginning of policy year t

$_0e_t$ is the allowance for such expenses (other than agency expenses) as are a function of the number of units issued or renewed at the beginning of policy year t

The following expense related input items are issued in the calculation of expense component 3 reserves:

$_0E'_t{}^{\%}$ is the percentage of PREMIUM covering such expenses (other than agency expenses) as are a function of premium income

$_0E'_t$ is the allowance for such expenses as are a function of the number of policies issued or renewed at the beginning of policy year t

$_0e'_t$ is the allowance for such expenses as are a function of the number of units issued or renewed at the beginning of policy year t

$_dE'$ is the claims handling expense per claim

$_sE'$ is the expense of handling surrenders per policy surrendered

$0_{[x]+t-1}$	is the conversion cost per $1,000 converted at the end of policy year t
$_ti$	is the assumed net investment earnings rate during the tth policy year
$_tv$	$= \dfrac{1}{1 + {}_ti}$
$_td$	$= {}_ti \cdot {}_tv$
$_tK_x$	is the coupon due at the beginning of policy year t, per unit
$_tD_x$	is the dividend payable at the end of policy year t, per unit
h	is a factor related to payment of dividend in the year of death h = 0, .5, or 1.0, according to provision for payment of no dividend, a pro rata dividend, or the full year's dividend
$_tTD_x$	is the termination dividend per unit, payable at the end of policy year t on policies terminating
$_tCV_x$	is the cash value at the end of policy year t, per unit
$_tI_x$	is the average death benefit during policy year t, per unit
A_x	is the average policy size, in number of units
a	is a function of the distribution of business by mode of premium payment and the factors for extra premiums for mode of payment. It is the proportion of one annual premium to be received as additional premium income due to fractional mode loadings.

If the respective proportions of annual, semiannual, quarterly, monthly and automatic monthly business are p_a, p_s, p_q, p_m, p_{am}, respectively,

where $p_a + p_s + p_q + p_m + p_{am} = 1.0$

and if the rates by which annual premiums are increased for fractional payments are, respectively, r_s, r_q, r_m, and r_{am}:

$a = p_s r_s + p_q r_q + p_m r_m + p_{am} r_{am}$

b	represents interest lost on deferred premiums and is a function of the distribution by mode of premium payment. It equals the proportion of an annual premium that is, on the average, in a deferred status $b = 1/4 p_s + 3/8 p_q + 11/24 p_m + 11/24 p_{am}$
c	represents the loss of premium through death c = 0 if deferred installments are collected upon death c = b if there is no refund of premium on death c = .4583 if there is refund of premium from the end of the month of death c = .5000 if there is refund of premium from the date of death
$_tP_x^{E(1)}$	is the expense valuation premium for policy year t for expense component 1
$_tP_x^{B}$	is the benefit valuation premium for policy year t
$_tP_x^{G}$	is the total valuation premium for policy year t
$_tI_x^{E(1)}$	is the initial expense reserve for policy year t for expense component i

$_t I_x^B$ is the initial benefit reserve for policy year t

$_t F_x^{E(i)}$ is the ending expense reserve for policy year t for expense component i

$_t F_x^B$ is the ending benefit reserve for policy year t

$_t \overline{V}_x^{E(i)}$ is the intermediate expense reserve for policy year t for expense component i

$_t \overline{V}_x^B$ is the intermediate benefit reserve for policy year t

$_t \overline{V}_x^G$ is the total intermediate reserve for policy year t

$^a f_t$ is the allocation factor for policy year t

for $t = 0$ $w_{[x]-1} = {}^a f_1 \cdot \overset{u}{w}_{[x]} + \overset{u}{w}_{[x]-1}$

for $t > 0$ $w_{[x]+t-1} = 1 - \dfrac{(1 - \overset{u}{w}_{[x]+t-1})\ (1 - {}^a f_{t+1} \cdot \overset{u}{w}_{[x]+t})}{1 - {}^a f_t \cdot \overset{u}{w}_{[x]+t-1}}$

where $\overset{u}{w}_{[x]+t-1}$ is the unallocated withdrawal rate.

For simplification of later formulas, expenses and benefits are adjusted to a per unit basis using the following approach.

$_t E_x^1$ the present value at the beginning of policy year t of the expenses incurred in policy year t for expense component 1

$$= ({}_c E_t^{\%} + {}_a E_t^{\%})({}_t P_x + \frac{F}{A_x})(1 + a)(1 - b \cdot {}_t d - c \cdot q_{[x]+t-1})$$

$$+ {}_a e_t + \frac{{}_a E_t}{A_x} + \frac{{}_d E}{A_x} \cdot q_{[x]+t-1} \cdot \frac{(1 + {}_t v)}{2}$$

$$+ \frac{{}_s E}{A_x} \cdot {}_t v \cdot w_{[x]+t-1} \cdot (1 - q_{[x]+t-1})*$$

$_t E_x^2$ the present value at the beginning of policy year t of the expenses incurred in policy year t for expense component 2

$$= {}_o E_t^{\%} ({}_t P_x + \frac{F}{A_x})(1 + a)(1 - b \cdot {}_t d - c \cdot q_{[x]+t-1}) + {}_o e_t + \frac{{}_o E_t}{A_x}$$

$_t E_x^3$ the present value at the beginning of policy year t of the expenses incurred at the beginning of policy year t for expense component 3

$$= {}_o E'^{\%}_t ({}_t P_x + \frac{F}{A_x})(1 + a)(1 - b \cdot {}_t d - c \cdot q_{[x]+t-1}) + {}_o e'_t + \frac{{}_o E'_t}{A_x}$$

$$+ \frac{{}_d E'}{A_x} \cdot q_{[x]+t-1} \cdot \frac{(1 + {}_t v)}{2} + \frac{{}_s E'}{A_x} \cdot {}_t v \cdot w_{[x]+t-1} \cdot (1 - q_{[x]+t-1})*$$

*include this term only if $_t CV_x > 0$

$_tB_x$ — the present value at the beginning of policy year t of the benefits in policy year t

$$= (_tP_x + \frac{F}{A_x})(1 + a)(b \cdot _td + c \cdot q_{[x]+t-1})$$

$$+ q_{[x]+t-1} [\frac{(1 + _tv)}{2} (_{t-1}TD_x + _tI_x) + (_tv^{1/2} \cdot h \cdot _tD_x)*]$$

$$+ (1 - q_{[x]+t-1})** _tD_x \cdot _tv$$

$$+ (_tTD_x + _tCV_x) \cdot _tv \cdot \overset{***}{w_{[x]+t-1}} \cdot (1 - q_{[x]+t-1})$$

$$+ \frac{_tI_x \cdot 0_{[x]+t-1}}{1000} \cdot wc_{[x]+t-1} \cdot _tv \cdot (1 - q_{[x]+t-1}) + _tK_x$$

*omit in policy year t = 1

**replace $(1 - q_{[x]+t-1})$ by $\frac{1_{[x]+1}}{1_{[x]}}$ in policy year 1 (t = 1)

***in policy year t = m, $w_{[x]+t-1}$ is forced to $(1 - wc_{[x]+t-1})$

$\overset{G}{\ddot{a}_{x:n|}}$ — is the present value at issue of future gross premiums divided by the gross premium for policy year one

$$= \sum_{t=1}^{n} \left[\frac{_tP_x + \frac{F}{A_x}}{_1P_x + \frac{F}{A_x}} \cdot 1_{[x]+t-1} \cdot \prod_{k=1}^{t-1} {}_kV \right]$$

note: $\prod_{k=1}^{0} {}_kV = 1$

$\overset{B}{_sA_x}$ — is the present value at the beginning of policy year s, per unit in force at the beginning of policy year s, of the future benefits payable

$$= \frac{1}{1_{[x]+s-1}} \sum_{t=s}^{m} {}_tB_x 1_{[x]+t-1} \prod_{k=s}^{t-1} {}_kV$$

note: $\prod_{k=s}^{s-1} {}_kV = 1$ and $_0v = 1$ and $_sA_x^B = 0$ if s > m

$\overset{E(i)}{_sA_x}$ — is the present value at the beginning of policy year s, per unit in force at the beginning of policy year s, of the future expenses

$$= \frac{1}{1_{[x]+s-1}} \sum_{t=s}^{m} {}_tE_x^{(i)} 1_{[x]+t-1} \prod_{k=s}^{t-1} {}_kV$$

note: $\prod_{k=s}^{s-1} {}_kV = 1$ and $_0v = 1$ and $_sA_x = 0$ if s > m

$\overset{P(i)}{_sA_x}$ — is the present value at the beginning of policy year s, per unit in force at the beginning of policy year s, of the future premiums

$$= \frac{1}{1_{[x]+s-1}} \sum_{t=s}^{m} {}_tP_x^{(i)} 1_{[x]+t-1} \prod_{k=s}^{t-1} {}_kV$$

note: $\prod_{k=s}^{s-1} {}_kV = 1$ and $_0v = 1$ and $_sA_x^B = 0$ if s > m

217

$_tP_x^{E(i)}$ is the expense valuation premium for policy year t and equals

$$\frac{\left(_tP_x + \dfrac{F}{A_x}\right) _0A_x^{E(i)}}{\left(_1P_x + \dfrac{F}{A_x}\right) \ddot{a}_{x:\overline{n}|}^{G}} \quad \text{where } i = 1, 2, \text{ or } 3$$

$_tP_x^{B}$ is the benefit valuation premium for policy year t and equals

$$\frac{\left(_tP_x + \dfrac{F}{A_x}\right) _0A_x^{B}}{\left(_1P_x + \dfrac{F}{A_x}\right) \ddot{a}_{x:\overline{n}|}^{G}}$$

$_tP_x^{G}$ is the total valuation premium and equals

$$_tP_x^{B} + {}_tP_x^{E1} + {}_tP_x^{E2} + {}_tP_x^{E3}$$

$_tI_x^{E1}$ is the beginning expense reserve for component 1 for policy year t

$$= {}_tA_x^{E1} - {}_tA_x^{PE1} + \left\{ P_t^{E1} - {}_ae_t - \frac{_aE_t}{A_x} \right.$$
$$\left. - ({}_cE_t^{\%} + {}_aE_t^{\%})\left(_tP_x + \frac{F}{A_x}\right)(1 + a)(1 - b \cdot {}_td - c \cdot q_{[x]+t-1}) \right\}^*$$

*include this term only if annual premium assumption

$_tF_x^{E1}$ is the ending expense reserve for component 1 for policy year t

$$= \left\{ _{t+1}A_x^{E1} - {}_{t+1}A_x^{PE1} \right\}(1 - w_{[x]+t} - wc_{[x]+t-1})$$
$$+ \frac{_sE}{A_x} \cdot w_{[x]+t-1} *$$

*include this term only if $_tCV_x > 0$

$_tI_x^{E2}$ is the beginning expense reserve for component 2 for policy year t

$$= {}_tA_x^{E2} - {}_tA_x^{PE2} + \left\{ _tP_x^{E2} - {}_0e_t - \frac{_0E_t}{A_x} \right.$$
$$\left. - {}_0E_t^{\%}\left(_tP_x + \frac{F}{A}\right)(1 + a)(1 - b \cdot {}_td - c \cdot q_{[x]+t-1}) \right\}^*$$

*include this term only if annual premium assumption

$_tF_x^{E2}$ is the ending expense reserve for component 2 for policy year t

$$= \left\{ _{t+1}A_x^{E2} - {}_{t+1}A_x^{PE2} \right\}(1 - w_{[x]+t-1} - wc_{[x]+t-1})$$

$_tI_x^{E3}$ is the beginning expense reserve for component 3 for policy year t

$$= {}_tA_x^{E3} - {}_tA_x^{PE3} + \left\{ _tP_x^{E3} \right\}^* - {}_0e'_t - \frac{_0E'_t}{A_x}$$

$$- {}_0E'^{\%}_t \left({}_tP_x + \frac{F}{A_x} \right)(1 - b \cdot {}_td - c \cdot q_{[x]+t-1})$$

*include only for annual premium assumption

${}_tF^{E3}_x$ is the ending expense reserve for component 3 for policy year t

$$= \left\{ {}_{t+1}A^{E3}_x - {}_{t+1}A^{PE3}_x \right\}(1 - w_{[x]+t-1} - wc_{[x]+t-1})$$

$$+ \frac{{}_sE'}{A_x} \cdot w^{*}_{[x]+t-1}$$

*include this term only if ${}_tCV_x > 0$

${}_tI^B_x$ is the beginning benefit reserve for policy year t

$$= {}_tA^B_x - {}_tA^{PB}_x - {}_tK_x$$

$$- {}_tD_x \left\{ (1 - q_{[x]+t-1}) \cdot {}_tv + h \cdot q_{[x]+t-1} \cdot {}_tv^{1/2} \right\}^{*} + {}_tP^{B}_x{}^{**}$$

*for t = 1 replace this term by $\frac{1_{[x]+1}}{1_x} \cdot {}_1v$

**include only for annual premium assumption

is the ending benefit reserve for policy year t

${}_tF^B_x$

$$= \left\{ {}_{t+1}A^B_x - {}_{t+1}A^{PB}_x \right\}(1 - w_{[x]+t-1} - wc_{[x]+t-1})$$

$$+ ({}_tCV_x + {}_tTD_x)w_{[x]+t-1} + \frac{{}_tI_xO_{[x]+t-1}}{1000} \cdot wc_{[x]+t-1}$$

${}_t\overline{V}^{(f)}_x$ is the intermediate reserve for policy year t

$$= 1/2({}_tI^{(f)}_x + {}_tF^{(f)}_x)$$

${}_tI_x$ total beginning reserve for policy year t

$$= {}_tI^{E1}_x + {}_tI^{E2}_x + {}_tI^{E3}_x + {}_tI^B_x$$

${}_tF_x$ total ending reserve for policy year t

$$= {}_tF^{E1}_x + {}_tF^{E2}_x + {}_tF^{E3}_x + {}_tF^B_x$$

total intermediate reserve for policy year t

${}_t\overline{V}_x$

$$= {}_t\overline{V}^{E1}_x + {}_t\overline{V}^{E2}_x + {}_t\overline{V}^{E3}_x + {}_t\overline{V}^B_x$$

Crazy Quilt Life Formulas:

Definitions and Formulas:

x is the age at issue.

t	is the policy year or the calendar year, as appropriate to the function. Calendar year *t* is the one during which policy year t begins. (An exception exists where t is assigned the value 0. t = 0 does not designate a year, but rather the moment at which the policy is issued.)
m	is the insurance period.
n	is the premium paying period.
$q_{[x]+t-1}$	is the rate of death during the tth policy year.
$w_{[x]+t-1}$	is the rate of withdrawal at duration t—that is, at the end of the tth policy year.
	Where t = 0, $w_{[x]-1}$ is the proportion of $1_{[x]-1}$ assumed to withdraw at the beginning of the first policy year.
	A specified proportion of the voluntary terminations of any policy year will be assumed to occur at the beginning of that year, and the balance at its end. This simulates the true termination pattern, wherein terminations are distributed irregularly through the year.
$(wc)_{[x]+t-1}$	is the rate of conversion at the end of tth policy year (term plans).
$1_{[x]+t-1}$	is the number entering the tth policy year, after deducting the portion of that policy year's withdrawals assumed to occur at its beginning. It is, therefore, the average exposure during policy year t before deducting deaths.
	Where t = 0, $1_{[x]-1}$ is the number issued, always 1.00000.
$d_{[x]+t-1}$	is the number dying in the tth policy year $= 1_{[x]t+1} \cdot q_{[x]+t-1}$
$W_{[x]+t-1}$	is the number withdrawing at the end of the tth policy year $= (1_{[x]+t-1} - d_{[x]+t-1})w_{[x]+t-1}$
$(WC)_{[x]+t-1}$	is the number converting at the end of the tth policy year $= (1_{[x]+t-1} - d_{[x]+t-1})(wc)_{[x]+t-1}$
$1_{[x]+t}$	$= 1_{[x]+t-1} - d_{[x]+t-1} - W_{[x]+t-1} - (WC)_{[x]+t-1}$
$1_{[x]+t-.5}$	is the number surviving at the end of calendar year t $= 1_{[x]+t-1}(1 - \frac{1}{2}q_{[x]+t-1})$
$_tP_x$	is the gross annual premium for age x for the plan of insurance, payable at the beginning of the tth policy year.
F	is the annual policy fee.
PREMIUM	$= (1_{[x]+t-1})(_tP_x + \frac{F}{A})(1 + a)\ [1 - b(_td) - c(q_{[x]+t-1})]$
$_cE_t^{\%}$	is the percentage of PREMIUM required to cover commissions for policy year t.
$_aE_t^{\%}$	is the percentage of PREMIUM covering such other agency expenses as are a function of premium income.
$_aE_t$	is the allowance for such other agency expenses as are a function of the number of policies issued or renewed at the beginning of policy year t.
$_ae_t$	is the allowance for such other agency expenses as are a function of the number of units issued or renewed at the beginning of policy year t.
$_oE_t^{\%}$	is the percentage of PREMIUM covering such expenses (other than agency expenses) as are a function of premium income.

$_oE_t$	is the allowance for such expenses (other than agency expenses) as are a function of the number of policies issued or renewed at the beginning of policy year t.
$_oe_t$	is the allowance for such expenses (other than agency expenses) as are a function of the number of units issued or renewed at the beginning of policy year t.
$_dE$	is the claims handling expense per claim.
$_sE$	is the expense of handling surrenders, per policy surrendered.
$O_{[x]+t-1}$	is the conversion cost per \$1,000 converted at the end of policy year t.
$_ti$	is the assumed net investment earnings rate during the tth policy year.
$_tv$	$= \dfrac{1}{1 + {}_ti}$
$_td$	$= {}_ti \cdot {}_tv$
$_tK_x$	is the coupon due at the beginning of policy year t, per unit.
$_tD_x$	is the dividend payable at the end of policy year t, per unit.
h	is a factor related to payment of dividend in the year of death. h = 0, .5, or 1.0, according to provision for payment of no dividend, a pro rata dividend, or the full year's dividend.
$_tTD_x$	is the termination dividend per unit, payable at the end of policy year t on policies terminating.
$_tCV_x$	is the cash value at the end of policy year t, per unit.
$_tI_x$	is the average death benefit during policy year t, per unit.
A_x	is the average policy size, in number of units.
a	is a function of the distribution of business by mode of premium payment and the factors for extra premiums for mode of payment. It is the proportion of one annual premium to be received as additional premium income due to fractional mode loadings.
	If the respective proportions of annual, semiannual, quarterly, monthly and automatic monthly business are p_a, p_s, p_q, p_m and p_{am}, respectively
	where $p_a + p_s + p_q + p_m + p_{am} = 1.0$,
	and if the rates by which annual premiums are increased for fractional payments are, respectively, r_s, r_q, r_m, and r_{am}:
	$a = p_s r_s + p_q r_q + p_m r_m + p_{am} r_{am}.$
b	represents interest lost on deferred premiums and is a function of the distribution by mode of premium payment. It equals the proportion of one annual premium that is, on the average, in a deferred status.
	$b = 1/4 p_s + 3/8 p_q + 11/24 p_m + 11/24 p_{am}$
c	represents the loss of premium through death.
	c = 0 if deferred installments are collected upon death.
	c = b if there is no refund of premium on death.
	c = .4583 if there is refund of premium from the end of the month of death.

$c = .5000$ if there is refund of premium from the date of death.

$_tP_x^E$ expense valuation premium for policy year t.

$_tP_x^B$ benefit valuation premium for policy year t.

$_tP_x^N$ total valuation premium for policy year t.

$_t\overline{V}_x^E$ intermediate adjusted expense reserve at end of calendar year t.

$_t\overline{V}_x^B$ intermediate adjusted benefit reserve adjusted at end of calendar year t.

$_t\overline{V}_x^N$ total intermediate adjusted reserve at end of calendar year t.

A table of allocation factors may be applied to the withdrawal rates to more closely approximate withdrawal experience. The factors are used to allocate a portion of the input withdrawal rate for a policy year to the beginning of that year by adding that portion into the previous year's rate.

^af_t is the allocation factor for policy year t.

for $t = 0$ $w_{[x]-1} = {}^af_1\overset{u}{w}_{[x]} + \overset{u}{w}_{[x]-1}$

for $t > 0$ $w_{[x]+t-1} = \dfrac{1 - (1 - \overset{u}{w}_{[x]+t-1})(1 - {}^af_{t+1} \cdot \overset{u}{w}_{[x]+t})}{1 - {}^af_t \cdot \overset{u}{w}_{[x]+t-1}}$

Where $\overset{u}{w}_{[x]+t-1}$ is the unallocated input withdrawal rate.

For simplification of later formulas, expenses and benefits are adjusted to a per unit basis using the following approach.

$_tE_x$ expense incurred during calendar year t per unit beginning calendar year t.

for $t = 1$:

$$(1 - w_{[x]-1})\left[({}_c\overset{\%}{E}_1 + {}_a\overset{\%}{E}_1 + {}_o\overset{\%}{E}_1)\left({}_1P_x + \frac{F}{A_x}\right)(1 + a)(1 - b \cdot {}_1d - c \cdot q_{[x]})\right.$$

$$\left. + {}_oe_1 + \frac{{}_oE_1}{A_x} + {}_ae_1 + \frac{{}_aE_1}{A_x} + \frac{{}_dE'_x}{2A_x} \cdot q_{[x]}\right] + \left[{}_oe_o + \frac{{}_oE_o}{A_x} + {}_ae_o + \frac{{}_aE_o}{A_x}\right]$$

for $1 < t \leq m$:

$$\frac{{}_{t-1}v^{1/2}(1 - w_{[x]+t-2} - (wc)_{[x]+t-2})(1 - q_{[x]+t-2})}{1 - \frac{1}{2}q_{[x]+t-2}}\left[({}_c\overset{\%}{E}_t + {}_a\overset{\%}{E}_t + {}_o\overset{\%}{E}_t)\right.$$

$$\left({}_tP_x + \frac{F}{A_x}\right)(1 + a)(1 - b \cdot {}_td - c \cdot q_{[x]+t-1}) + {}_ae_t + {}_oe_t + \frac{{}_aE_t + {}_oE_t}{A_x}$$

$$+ \frac{{}_dE_x}{2A_x}\left(q_{[x]+t-1} + \frac{q_{[x]+t-2}}{(1 - q_{[x]+t-2})(1 - w_{[x]+t-2} - (wc)_{[x]+t-2})}\right.$$

$$\left.\left. + \frac{{}_sE_x^*}{A_x}\left(\frac{w_{[x]+t-2}}{1 - w_{[x]+t-2} - (wc)_{[x]+t-2}}\right)\right]$$

for $t = m + 1$:

$$\frac{_m v^{1/2}}{1 - \frac{1}{2} q_{[x]+m-1}} \left[\frac{_d E_x}{2 A_x} q_{[x]+m-1} + \overset{*}{\frac{_s E_x}{A_x}} (1 - q_{[x]+m-1}) w_{[x]+m-1} \right]$$

*Include only when $_{t-1} CV_x \neq 0$

$_t B_x$ benefits incurred during calendar year t per unit beginning calendar year t.

for $t = 1$:

$$(1 - w_{[x]-1}) \left[\frac{1}{2} \cdot {_1}I_x q_{[x]} + {_1}K_x + \left({_1}P_x + \frac{F}{A_x} \right) (1 + a)(b \cdot {_1}d + c \cdot q_{[x]}) \right.$$
$$\left. + {_1}D_x \cdot {_1}v (1 - q_{[x]})(1 - w_{[x]} - (wc)_{[x]}) \right]$$

for $1 < t \leq m$:

$$\frac{_{t-1} v^{1/2}(1 - q_{[x]+t-2})(1 - w_{[x]+t-2} - (wc)_{[x]+t-2})}{\left(1 - \frac{1}{2} q_{[x]+t-2} \right)} \left[{_t}K_x + \left({_t}P_x + \frac{F}{A_x} \right) \right.$$

$$(1 + a)(b \cdot {_t}d + c \cdot q_{[x]+t-1})$$

$$+ q_{[x]+t-1} \left(\frac{1}{2} {_t}I_x + \frac{_{t-1}TD_x}{2} + {_t}D_x \cdot h \cdot {_t}v^{1/2} \right)$$

$$\left. + (1 - q_{[x]+t-1}) \cdot {_t}D_x \cdot {_t}v \right]$$

$$+ \frac{_{t-1}v^{1/2}(1 - q_{[x]+t-2})}{\left(1 - \frac{1}{2} q_{[x]+t-2} \right)} \left[{_{t-1}}TD_x w_{[x]+t-2} + {_{t-1}}CV_x \cdot w_{[x]+t-2} \right.$$

$$\left. + \frac{_{t-1}I_x}{1000} O_{[x]+t-2}(wc)_{[x]+t-2} \right] + \frac{_{t-1}v^{1/2} q_{[x]+t-2}}{1 - \frac{1}{2} q_{[x]+t-2}} \left(\frac{_{t-1}TD_x}{2} + \frac{1}{2} {_{t-1}}I_x \right)$$

for $t = m + 1$:

$$\frac{_m v^{1/2}(1 - q_{[x]+m-1})}{1 - \frac{1}{2} q_{[x]+m-1}} \left[{_m}TD_x w_{[x]+m-1} + {_m}CV_x \cdot w_{[x]+m-1} \right.$$

$$\left. + \frac{_m I_x}{1000} O_{[x]+m-1}(wc)_{[x]+m-1} \right] + \frac{_m v^{1/2} q_{[x]+m-1}}{1 - \frac{1}{2} q_{[x]+m-1}} \left(\frac{_m TD_x}{2} + \frac{1}{2} {_m}I_x \right)$$

$\underset{\ddot{a}_{x:\overline{n}|}}{^N}$ is the present value at issue of future gross premiums divided by the gross premium for policy year one and equals

$$= \sum_{t=1}^{n} \left[\frac{_t P_x + \frac{F}{A_x}}{_1 P_x + \frac{F}{A_x}} \cdot 1_{[x]+t-1} \cdot \prod_{k=1}^{t-1} k_v \right]$$

note: $\prod_{k=1}^{0} {_k}v = 1$

A_x^E is the present value at issue of future expenses and equals

$$_1E_x + \sum_{t=2}^{m+1} \left[(1 + {}_{t-1}i)^{1/2} 1_{[x]+t-3/2} \cdot {}_tE_x \cdot \mathop{\pi}_{k=1}^{t-1} {}_kV \right]$$

A_x^B is the present value at issue of future benefits and equals

$$_1B_x + \sum_{t=2}^{m+1} \left[(1 + {}_{t-1}i)^{1/2} 1_{[x]+t-3/2} \cdot {}_tB_x \cdot \mathop{\pi}_{k=1}^{t-1} {}_kV \right]$$

Reserve Factors:

Year t   is the calendar year in which policy year t begins

$_tP_x^E$ is the expense valuation premium for policy year t and equals

$$\frac{\left({}_tP_x + \dfrac{F}{A_x} \right) A_x^E}{\left({}_1P_x + \dfrac{F}{A_x} \right) \ddot{a}_{x:n}^N}$$

$_tP_n^B$ is the benefit valuation premium for policy year t and equals

$$\frac{\left({}_tP_x + \dfrac{F}{A_x} \right) A_x^B}{\left({}_1P_x + \dfrac{F}{A_x} \right) \ddot{a}_{x:n}^N}$$

$_tP_n^N$ is the total valuation premium and equals

$$_tP_x^E + {}_tP_x^B$$

$_t\bar{V}_x^E$ is the adjusted expense reserve at the end of the tth calendar year and equals

$$\frac{1}{1_{[x]+t-1/2}} \left[\sum_{s=t+1}^{m} \mathop{\pi}_{k=t+1}^{s-1} {}_kV \; (1_{[x]+s-3/2} \cdot {}_sE_x - {}_tv^{1/2} \, 1_{[x]+s-1} \cdot {}_sP_x^E) \right]$$

$_t\bar{V}_x^B$ is the adjusted benefit reserve at the end of the tth calendar year and equals

$$\frac{1}{1_{[x]+t-1/2}} \left[\sum_{s=t+1}^{m} \mathop{\pi}_{k=t+1}^{s-1} {}_kV \; (1_{[x]+s-3/2} \cdot {}_sB_x - {}_tv^{1/2} \cdot 1_{[x]+s-1} \cdot {}_sP_t^B) \right]$$

$_t\bar{V}_x^N$ is the total adjusted reserve and equals

$$_t\bar{V}_x^E + {}_t\bar{B}_x^B$$

Note: Crazy Quilt Life employed two expense components. Expense reserves were divided as follows:

$$_tE_x^1 \text{ included } {}_cE_t^\%, \; {}_aE_t^\%, \; {}_ae_t, \; {}_dE, \text{ and } {}_sE$$

$$_tE_x^2 \text{ included } {}_oE_t^\%, \; {}_oe_t, \text{ and } {}_oE_t$$

Part III

Expenses

13

Life Insurance Company Cost Accounting

The term "cost accounting" is usually associated with manufacturing activities. This is because two of the prime purposes of cost accounting historically have been inventory valuation and income determination. Another vital purpose of cost accounting is to facilitate planning and control. Planning and control are not unique to the manufacturing enterprise, but because many of the cost concepts used in planning and controlling operations derive from concepts of product costing, cost accounting for planning and control purposes is also typically associated with a manufacturing milieu.

Life insurance companies may readily be viewed as manufacturers. But the product they manufacture is intangible. Direct materials are negligible. Labor and overhead are everything, but it is very difficult to distinguish between direct labor and indirect labor, "factory burden" and selling and administrative overhead, "producing departments" and service departments. Also, final determination of the cost of the product depends to an extraordinary degree on events that occur in the future—the distant future. It is clear that a life insurance company bears slight resemblance to the typical manufacturer.

Furthermore, life insurance companies have never had to worry about inventory valuation in the traditional sense of that term. Under statutory accounting rules all expenses are charged to operations as incurred and the "inventory" of insurance in force is treated as a liability, to be valued in accordance with prescribed rules.

As a result, the purposes of cost accounting in the life insurance industry have historically been limited to planning and control, pricing, and the maintenance of equity among policyholders (particularly in the case of participating business). Inasmuch as the costing process has not entered directly into income determination, it has perhaps been subject to less discipline than cost accounting in the manufacturing industries. Consequently cost accounting systems in the life insurance industry range across the entire spectrum of quality—from excellent to good to terrible to non-existent.

Adoption of generally accepted accounting principles by a life insurance company introduces a new dimension into life insurance cost accounting. The costing process *does* enter directly into the determination of income under generally accepted accounting principles. In terms of its effect on financial statements presented on a generally accepted basis, cost accounting is every bit as significant in a life insurance environment as it is in a manufacturing environment.

Terminology

For purposes of this chapter and all of Part III, the terms "cost" and "expense" refer to operating expenses, i.e., non-benefit costs. Benefit costs are discussed in Part II.

A "cost" represents an outlay made, a benefit foregone, or a liability incurred to acquire something of value. An "expense" is an expired cost, i.e., one having no future utility. All costs have some future utility, even if only for an instant; they are frequently charged off immediately largely as a matter of convenience. The terms "cost" and "expense" are frequently used interchangeably, mainly because of custom, and they are so used in this chapter. Thus, for example, the Convention Statement refers to "general insurance expenses", whereas from the standpoint of generally accepted accounting principles, some portion of "general insurance expenses" represents acquisition costs having future utility; such costs may be deferred and expensed in periods subsequent to the period in which they are incurred.

Confusion over the meanings of the terms "cost" and "expense" is hereby acknowledged, and the failure of this book to resolve such confusion is also hereby acknowledged. Hopefully the reader will grasp the specific meaning of either term from the context in which it is used.

Terms that are peculiar to cost accounting in general or life insurance accounting in particular are generally described in some manner in the text.

Basic Cost Accounting Concepts

It is all well and good to say that cost accounting is "significant" to financial statements prepared in conformity with generally accepted accounting principles, but that doesn't explain what cost accounting is supposed to accomplish, what costs are relevant to the financial statements, and how costs should be calculated.

To be sure, these questions have been answered before. Many life insurance companies utilize some form of cost accounting. As mentioned above, however, income determination has not been one of the objectives of life insurance cost accounting historically. It is therefore necessary to examine some basic cost accounting concepts—which embrace the objective of income determination—and attempt to apply them in a life insurance environment.

The Costing Object

What is the product to which the life insurance cost accountant should seek to assign costs?

That's not a whimsical question. In manufacturing cost accounting the principal object for cost-finding is the manufactured product, pure and simple. In life insurance, the costing object isn't so readily apparent.

The life insurance "product" has been defined as assumption of the risk of adverse deviation. But this product isn't the sort of thing a cost can be attached to. The release from risk concept implies a stream of profits, a convergence of revenue and expense into an expression of services rendered. Recognition of revenue and expense is based, at least in theory, on a pre-existing notion of the pattern in which risk is released.

If each element of adverse deviation could be quantified precisely and reliably, and if all such quantities could be expressed in common units, then it might be possible to assign a cost to each unit. Suppose, for example, that a given year's new business could be expressed in terms of 1,000,000 equivalent units of adverse deviation, and that $1,000,000 was spent to acquire the business. Each unit of adverse deviation would bear a cost of $1.00, and $1.00 would be charged to expense each time the company was released from one unit of adverse deviation.

But adverse deviation cannot be quantified precisely and reliably, at least at this point in time, nor does there seem to be a practical way to express adverse deviation in common units. Anything is possible, of course; but with the present state of the art, attempting to assign costs to units of adverse deviation would probably be an exercise in futility.

There is also the question of what to do if provisions for adverse deviation do not use up the entire gross premium. If the valuation premium is less than the gross premium, the balance is pure profit loading. In such a case, some costs would have to be assigned to something other than units of adverse deviation. It is difficult to imagine what that something would be. Whatever it is, it too would apparently have to be expressed in the same language as the units of adverse deviation.

The foregoing discussion is based on viewing adverse deviation as the principal product a life insurance company has to offer. There is another view of adverse deviation that must be accorded recognition because of its popularity, and that is the view that adverse deviation is not a product but a margin for conservatism introduced more or less deliberately into the process of recognizing revenue and expense.* Under this point of view, assumption of the risk of adverse deviation is not itself a product but is rather a consequence of having sold another product, namely, insurance coverage—the policy itself.

Whatever one's view of adverse deviation—as a product or as a consequence—for cost accounting purposes the basic object of costing is the insurance coverage itself. Theory may or may not support this conclusion, depending on one's own concept of adverse deviation. In practical terms, however, there seems to be little choice.

---

*See Chapter 6 for an extended discussion of the alternative views of adverse deviation.

So the costing object might be described as a unit of insurance coverage. A unit of insurance coverage might be expressed in many ways, just as manufactured products can often be expressed in many ways (pounds, tons, gallons, cans, etc.). Regardless of the manner of expression, however, units of insurance coverage always have four characteristics that are fundamental in process cost accounting:

▶ The units are measurable,
▶ They can be expressed in common or equivalent units,
▶ The flow of units can be traced through their life-cycle, and
▶ Costs can logically be associated with the units.

The Flow of Costing Objects

In this discussion the costing object—that is, the unit of insurance coverage—will be represented by an individual insurance policy. A policy is perhaps the most complete expression of the costing object, comprehending thousands of dollars of face amount, hundreds of dollars of premiums, etc.

In addition, the discussion will assume that all insurance policies are exactly the same—same plan, same sex, same age, same face amount, same premium, same everything. Therefore the policies are freely convertible into other equivalent units. Complications that arise when a mix of products is sold will be dealt with in later discussions.

Insurance policies progress through many developmental, sales, production, and maintenance operations. Each operation involves incurring a cost of some kind. Before considering the extent to which such costs "attach" to the policies, it would be well to trace an insurance policy through its life-cycle.

Development. An insurance product is born with an idea. The idea may involve little more than copying someone else's policy form, or it may involve extensive market research and design of a unique new policy form.

Once the product has been designed it must be priced and tested to ensure that it yields a reasonable profit. A rate book (which is really a high-powered pricing manual) must be prepared and forms must be printed. At this point the product is ready to be sold.

But it can't be sold without one additional developmental operation. For a branch office or general agency company, a sales force must be recruited and trained to sell the product; for a brokerage company, brokerage recruiters have to be recruited and trained in techniques of soliciting brokerage business; and other similar capabilities must be acquired.

Many specialized functions in the home office and the field are brought to bear in the development process. Actuaries are involved in product design, pricing, and testing; the data processing department is involved in testing; marketing men are involved in market research and product design; the print shop is involved in printing rate books and policy forms; agency administrators are involved in recruiting and training; various field and home office service personnel provide support; and the president and his staff are actively involved in stimulating and monitoring the entire process.

Production. The term "production" is used here to denote the sale, underwriting, and issuance of an insurance policy after the development process is complete. In the manufacturing sense, "production" refers to the process by which goods are made ready for sale or delivery pursuant to a sales contract or similar document. In the insurance sense, "production" has a somewhat different meaning, encompassing the selling and distribution effort and all of the services incident to delivering the policy to the buyer. The significance of this concept of "production" to life insurance cost accounting is discussed later in this chapter.

Once a sales force has been recruited and trained and the necessary insurance products are available for sale, the selling effort begins. Operating from general agencies, branch offices, and occasionally from behind a desk, agents solicit business from the public. In the usual case the "closing ratio"—the percentage of solicitations that wind up in a sale—is something less than 100 percent (quite often *significantly* less than 100 percent). In the course of soliciting business the agent is supervised by a general agent or branch manager.

In the mail order business the agent's efforts are replaced by a barrage of mailings based on a customer list that is believed to contain names of individuals who are pre-disposed to buy insurance; or by "piggy-back" advertising with some other medium (such as credit card statements); or by inserts in newspapers; or by other methods.

Once a prospect applies for insurance the underwriting process begins. Actually, it begins before the application; to the extent that an agent screens his prospects in any way, he is doing some underwriting. The agent also performs some underwriting chores in helping the prospect fill out the application, for example, by seeing to it that essential information is provided. If the agent is qualified to write non-medical business, his participation in the underwriting process can be quite significant.

The application is then normally forwarded to the issue department, which establishes a file and a control over the application and any premium received with it. The application proceeds to the underwriting department, which reviews it in terms of the company's underwriting policies and procedures. The medical department may be consulted. Eventually the underwriter decides whether to accept the risk and, if so, on what terms. The underwriting department may also make any necessary reinsurance arrangements at this point. If the application is declined, the policyholder is notified, usually through the agent, and any premium advances are returned to him. If the application is accepted, the policy form is prepared by the issue department and is delivered to the policyholder, again usually through the agent. At this point the policyholder may decide not to take the policy. If the policyholder accepts the policy, the issue department processes the basic records that have hitherto been held in a pending file. Valuation and other records are created, the initial premium is credited to income, and the policy is "in force". Commissions are credited to the agent.

This is essentially the end of the production process, except for one thing. The agent may not be able to live on his commission income in the early months or years of his career. So the company may "finance" him for a while—that is, provide compensation beyond the amount earned in the form of commissions. Whether such financing is a developmental activity or a production activity is not entirely clear. This will be explored at length in Chapter 14.

Maintenance. Once the policy is in force it must be maintained. Maintenance includes premium collection, commission processing, policy changes, correspondence with policyholders, processing policy loans, processing surrenders, processing death claims, processing matured endowments, paying dividends (if the policy is participating), and making periodic valuations. Many departments will be involved in such activities, including the cashier, the accounting department, the agency department, the claims department, policyholders' service, data processing, the actuarial department, and field offices. The maintenance process continues as long as the policy is in force.

Where there is an optional mode of settlement, the maintenance process might continue for many years after the death of the policyholder. But the arrangement with the beneficiary may be viewed as a new undertaking, and it is so regarded here.

Service. Development, production, and maintenance may be regarded as operations more or less directly related to the sale and servicing of insurance policies. There are usually several departments that provide services to departments involved in development, production, and maintenance—for example, office services and mailroom services. Service departments also provide services to administrative and investment departments that are not related directly to the sale and servicing of insurance policies.

Administration. There are many departmental or sub-departmental operations that are in the nature of general corporate support functions—long-range planning, general legal work, general ledger accounting and statement preparation, internal auditing, general management, etc. Such operations are not directly related to the sale and servicing of insurance policies. They are not unique to the life insurance business. They represent corporate overhead which almost every type of organization must bear.

Investment. Investment departments are generally not directly related to the sale and servicing of insurance policies except to the exetnt that they supply information on interest rates required for purposes of pricing and profit-testing. The function of an investment department is to invest the funds generated by the insurance operation and reinvest the funds generated by the investment operation.

Classification of Costs

While it may be true, as Gertrude Stein once argued, that a rose is a rose is a rose, it does not necessarily follow that a cost is a cost is a cost. Notwithstanding Ms. Stein's general theory of fixity, the same cost can be classified many different ways, and each classification tends to change its nature somewhat.

Before attempting to deal with life insurance cost accounting techniques, perhaps it would be well to review some of the major classifications of life insurance company costs, namely

▶ Departmental and cost center classifications,
▶ Natural classifications,
▶ Functional classifications, and
▶ Variability classifications.

Departmental costs. A life insurance company may be viewed as an integrated series of departments, each of which has its own set of costs. And most life insurance companies of any maturity are organized into more or less formal departments to which expenses are charged.

The reasons for departmentalization are manifold, but generally the reasons have not included the need to account for product costs for financial statement purposes. Departmentalization has been prompted primarily by the need to establish responsibility and accountability and to delineate the boundaries of management activities.

As a general rule, company-wide expense budgets are translated into departmental budgets, sometimes with a distinction between controllable and non-controllable expenses, and actual departmental expenses are continually compared with budgeted expenses to highlight problem areas.* This is perhaps the principal reason for accumulating costs by department.

Another reason of considerable significance is to facilitate pricing and profit-testing. Actuaries must work with functional costs in setting or testing prices, and—as will be seen—departmentalization is usually necessary to compute reliable functional costs.

Cost centers. It is an easy step from the concept of departmentalization to the concept of a cost center. "A cost center is the smallest unit of activity or area of responsibility for which costs are accumulated." [1] An entire department may constitute a cost center, or the department may consist of numerous sub-departments or separate cost centers.

The advantage of the cost center concept is its flexibility. While departments usually consist of cost centers, there is no necessary reason for a cost center to bear a direct relationship to a department. The purpose of departmentalization might be to facilitate

*The general reader may be interested to know that there are three basic methods of setting budgets: from the top down, from the bottom up, and from the seat of the pants. Under the top-down approach, a company-wide profit plan (fixed or flexible) is the key to virtually all departmental activity, and budgets are designed to serve the objectives quantified by top management. Under the bottom-up approach, which is fairly typical of companies that operate without profit plans, departments pretty much set their own budgets, perhaps having to parry the challenges of top management in the process. The trouble is that the challenges of top management generally lack a solid frame of reference unless they are based on a quantifiable company-wide profit objective. Under the seat-of-the-pants approach, budgets are not used but department heads are called on the carpet based on management's intuition that expenses are out of line. This tends to strain employee relations, as might be obvious. While the bottom-up and seat-of-the-pants approaches leave something to be desired, some budget is better than no budget at all, which is the method used by all too many companies.

control; the purpose of establishing cost centers might be to facilitate the calculation of unit costs; and the same pool of costs may be treated differently depending on the objective. For example, all underwriting expenses might be charged to one department for control purposes; the department head is held responsible for substantially all underwriting expenses. For cost accounting purposes, however, it may be desirable to segregate expenses of medicals and inspection reports to determine separate unit costs for those items. In that case, medicals and inspections might be treated as a separate cost center.

Natural classifications. Costs can also be classified by their nature—salaries, rent, etc. The general expense exhibit contained in the Convention Statement is essentially an exhibit of general expenses classified by nature. The general expense exhibit might be viewed as a "consolidated" statement of the expenses of cost centers where cost center expenses are accumulated by natural classification.

Functional classifications. Costs can be classified by the function to which they apply. A functional cost is the cost of performing a specified operation regardless of how many departments or cost centers participate in the operation and regardless of how many natural classifications of expense are involved. For example, the issuance of a policy may involve several departments—treasurer's, accounting, data processing, agency, issue processing, and office services—and determination of the functional cost of issuing a policy would involve tracing the applicable expenses across departmental lines.

Variability classifications. A given cost can also be classified according to its variability with some measure of activity. Costs might be variable, semi-variable, or fixed.

Determination of the variability of a given cost is frequently a difficult problem. Commissions are generally fully variable with premiums—no premiums, no commissions. Underwriting expenses are usually semi-variable. The president's salary is usually fixed.

Many believe that virtually all costs are variable. In the case of underwriting expenses, for example, they point out that no underwriting department would be needed if no new business were sold. Therefore, they say, underwriting expenses can readily be deemed to vary with production.

This ignores the concept of the "relevant range" [2] of activity, which may be broadly defined as the range of activity within which operations are most likely to fall under reasonable operating condition. Viewed another way, the chance that operations will fall outside the relevant range is so remote that cost behavior applicable to operations outside the relevant range should be disregarded.

Summary. The perfect cost accounting system would classify a given cost according to all its characteristics, perhaps as follows:

Department
    Cost center within department
        Natural classification within cost center
            Function within natural classification
                Variability within function

A salary of, say, $100 might then be classified as follows:

Department A:	
Cost center A:	
Salaries:	
Function A:	
Variable	$ 10
Semi-variable	10
Fixed	10
Function B:	45
(Etc.)	
Cost center B:	25
(Etc.)	
	$100

This procedure would permit practically any type of cost analysis that might be desired.

In practice, of course, cost accounting systems are rarely so refined. The formal system is usually restricted to classifying expenses by natural classification and cost center. Variability and functional costs are usually determined by *ex post facto* analysis.

Unit Costs

The "unit cost" of a product is determined by dividing the total costs applicable to the units produced by the number of units produced.

In a continuous mass-production operation such as a life insurance company, unit costs are most readily computed using process-costing techniques, under which

. . . costs are accumulated by departments (sometimes called *operations* or *processes*). These departmental costs are applied to relatively great numbers of units which pass through the department. The center of attention is the total department costs for a given time period in relation to the units processed. Accumulated department costs are divided by quantities produced during a given period in order to get unit costs.[3]

Life Insurance Functional Costs

As mentioned earlier in this chapter, many life insurance companies utilize some form of cost accounting. Others use estimates and approximations to develop the types of information that a formal cost accounting system would produce.

Still others ignore cost accounting completely and choose to fly blind, as it were. Perhaps the generous cash flow generated by a life insurance operation has permitted some degree of laxity in the areas of cost control and pricing. Perhaps the conservatism of statutory accounting has tended to inhibit the development of techniques of cost control. Readers may recall the late 1950s and early 1960s, when statutory losses were ignored, earnings were "adjusted" by rule-of-thumb methods, and a life insurance company could do no wrong. That was hardly an ideal climate for effective cost control. And habits formed in that heady era have been slow to die.

Whatever the present situation for any particular company, it is fair to say that some form of cost accounting is going to be required for every company that seeks to conform with the provisions of the life insurance audit guide, which specifies that "Unit costs per policy or per thousand should be developed, based on cost studies." [4]

Nature of Functional Costs

Most large companies and many smaller ones have developed techniques for computing functional costs, and the concept of a "functional cost" provides a good starting point for discussing the type of cost accounting that is appropriate for purposes of implementing the life insurance audit guide.

A functional cost is, quite simply, the unit cost of performing a designated function. The Life Office Management Association defines functional costs as follows:

Functional costs combine the individual costs of a series of operations that have a designated purpose. These accumulated costs ignore departmental lines and the usual account classifications, and instead gather together from all sources direct and indirect costs . . . Costs defined in a functional sense relate to the dollar value of an employee's time, plus the cost of supplies, equipment, or anything that helps to achieve an objective.[5]

The LOMA Functional Cost Program

During the 1950s the Life Office Management Association sponsored a functional cost program for member companies. The LOMA program sought to improve cost accounting methods, standardize cost accounting to the extent possible, and provide a framework for inter-company comparisons of costs by the participating companies. The objectives of the program were manifold. Perhaps one of the most important objectives was cost control; it was believed that inter-company comparisons would result in continual pressure to equal or exceed the results of the low-cost companies, or at least determine the reasons why a particular functional cost was high in relation to that of reasonably comparable companies. Also, companies learned techniques through the LOMA program that they used internally to measure performance, set prices, validate budgets, and improve planning. The LOMA program recognized, in effect, that knowledge must precede action.

Only a handful of companies participated in the program in the 1950s. By 1974 over 130 companies were participating. It is generally believed that "it takes about three years before the figures and comparisons produced have been refined enough to use with some degree of reliability in determining the company's standing in relation to other companies." [6] Most of the companies participating in 1974 had already endured the three-year apprenticeship and had achieved the status of veteran participants.

LOMA functions. The LOMA program involves the assignment of costs to lines of business and to "functions" within the line of business. LOMA recommends segregation by the following lines of business: [7]

Ordinary
Individual health
Group (including wholesale)
Debit life
Debit health
Investment
Service
General overhead
Other

LOMA has defined basic functions for ordinary life, individual health, debit life, debit health, and investment. Thus far it has not proved feasible to develop inter-company data on group lines, probably because of the enormous variety in group products and methods of group operations and the related cost patterns (if indeed there are any patterns). Service and general overhead are treated as "lines of business" because it is felt that allocation of these types of costs to lines of business would be arbitrary and of limited utility.

While there is theoretically some degree of flexibility in the definition of a "function", the LOMA Inter-company Cost Comparison Analyses Program (as it is formally called) specifies the functions for which costs are to be accumulated. For the ordinary life line of business the functions, which currently number 13, are as follows: [8]

Initial expenses:
    Selling
    Selection
    Issue
Direct maintenance:
    Premium collection
    Commission processing
    Death claims
    Surrenders
    Matured endowments
    Policy changes
    All other direct maintenance
General maintenance:
    Actuarial and other research
    Electronic planning and conversion
    All other general maintenance

Periodically (or, for some companies, on a continuing basis) a selected function is studied in depth by some participants. A depth study of the selling function, for example, would involve determining and analyzing several sub-functions of the selling function: sales production, agent recruiting, agent training, agency administration, agents' club meetings, home office and regional supervision, field management training, and all other.

LOMA coverage. The LOMA functional cost program generally focuses on general expenses, i.e., those reported in Exhibit 5 of the Convention Statement. There are certain required adjustments of Exhibit 5 data designed to improve comparability among companies. Commissions are included in the debit analysis, mainly because of the integral relationship between commissions reported in Exhibit 1 and general expenses reported in Exhibit 5 for that line of business. Commissions and taxes are, at the date of this writing, being considered for inclusion in the ordinary life analysis.

LOMA techniques. The LOMA functional cost program involves the accumulation or allocation of costs (a) by line of business, (b) by function within

Table 13–1.

SCHEMATIC FLOW OF FUNCTIONAL COST DATA AND DERIVATION OF A FUNCTIONAL COST

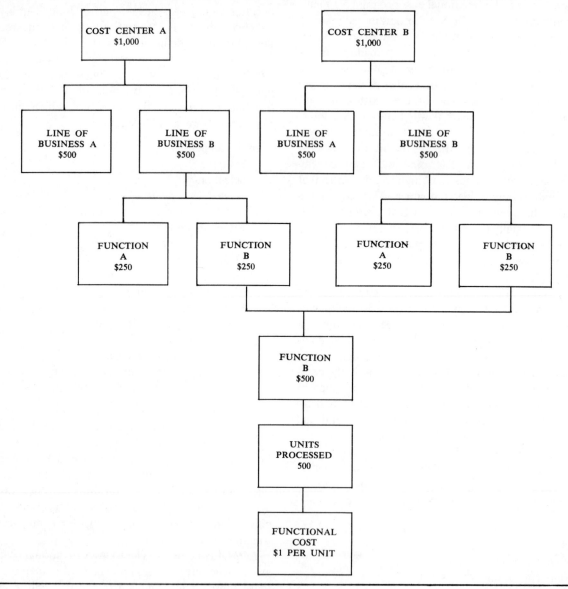

line, and sometimes (c) by sub-function within function.

Sometimes a cost center and a function are identical. In that case, all that is necessary to derive a functional cost is to divide the cost center's expenses by the units processed.

Usually, though, several cost centers contribute to a function. In that case, the costs of several departments attributable to a particular function must be added up to derive the desired functional cost.

Also, many cost centers perform more than one function for more than one line of business. In such cases it is necessary to distribute cost center expenses among several lines of business and several functions within each line. Costs attributable to a specific function are accumulated from the various cost centers to derive the final functional cost. Table 13–1 illustrates the flow of data and the derivation of a functional cost where there are two cost centers, each of which operates for the benefit of two lines of business, each of which involves two functions.

It will be obvious by now that the LOMA program

Table 13–2.

CONDENSED SUMMARY OF 1971 EXPENSE DATA FOR CRAZY QUILT LIFE BASED ON STATUTORY CLASSIFICATIONS OF EXPENSE (000 Omitted)

	Commissions (Exhibit 1)				General Insurance Expenses (Exhibit 5)	Taxes, Licenses, and Fees (Exhibit 6)	Other Items	Total	Total Classified By Company as	
	First Year	Single	Renewal	Total					Acquisition Costs	Maintenance Expenses
Ordinary life basic plans:										
Participating	$ 1,017	$ -0-	$ 254	$ 1,271	$ 2,626	$ 301	$ -0-	$ 4,198	$ 3,106	$ 1,092
Non-participating	7,186		1,562	8,748	15,707	1,800	25**	26,280	20,577	5,703
TOTAL ORDINARY LIFE BASIC	8,203	-0-	1,816	10,019	18,333	2,101	25	30,478	23,683	6,795
Ordinary life supplemental benefits:										
Total and permanent disability	122		50	172	115	25		312	111	201
Additional accidental death	81		33	114	77	16		207	74	133
Supplementary contracts					6			6		6
TOTAL ORDINARY	8,406	-0-	1,899	10,305	18,531*	2,142	25	31,003	23,868	7,135
Individual annuities:										
Fixed		528		528	538	325		1,391	923	468
Variable	1,699		157	1,856	809	34		2,699	1,754	945
TOTAL INDIVIDUAL ANNUITY	1,699	528	157	2,384	1,347*	359	-0-	4,090	2,677	1,413
Individual health:										
Cancellable		448		448	560	22		1,030	452	578
Guaranteed renewable	2,036		1,018	3,054	2,188	263		5,505	4,317	1,188
TOTAL INDIVIDUAL HEALTH	2,036	448	1,018	3,502	2,748*	285	-0-	6,535	4,769	1,766
Industrial	749		520	1,269	1,459*	150	-0-	2,878	1,539	1,339
Group:										
Life	33		153	186	373	138		697	124	573
Health	128		405	533	558	162		1,253	132	1,121
Annuity			1	1	17	4		22		22
Group Credit:										
Life		566		566	161	62		789	767	22
Health		508		508	198	64		770	712	58
TOTAL GROUP	161	1,074	559	1,794	1,307*	430	-0-	3,531	1,735	1,796
Investment					1,133*	327	437***	1,897		1,897
	$13,051	$2,050	$4,153	$19,254	$26,525	$3,693	$462	$49,934	$34,588	$15,346

* These totals trace to Table 13–3.

** Interest on modified coinsurance reserves (separate line on page 4 of Convention Statement).

*** Depreciation (Exhibit 2 of Convention Statement).

involves extensive allocations of costs. Salaries, which generally represent about half of a life insurance company's general expenses, are generally allocated to lines and functions by time studies or time estimates. Non-salary expenses are distributed directly, if possible, or (as is more typical) in proportion to various bases such as salaries. Service department expenses are usually apportioned to "operating" departments on some rational basis; alternatively, service department expenses may themselves be functionalized.

Crazy Quilt Life. Crazy Quilt Life has for ten years participated in LOMA's Inter-company Cost

Table 13–3.

SUMMARY OF 1971 GENERAL EXPENSES OF CRAZY QUILT LIFE IN THE LOMA FORMAT (000 Omitted)

LOMA Category	Convention Statement Classifications	Service and General Overhead	LOMA Classifications
Ordinary	$18,531	$(3,676)	$14,855
Individual health	2,748	(467)	2,281
Group	1,307	(221)	1,086
Debit life	1,459	(248)	1,211
Investment	1,133	(193)	940
Service		2,824	2,824
General overhead		2,210	2,210
Other	1,347*	(229)	1,118
TOTAL	$ 26,525	$ -0-	$26,525

* Represents general expenses allocated to individual fixed and variable annuities, which were eliminated from analysis of ordinary life functional costs (their usual treatment) because of their distortive effect.

Comparison Analyses Program. As soon as the 1971 Convention Statement was filed, Crazy Quilt's accountants began compiling 1971 functional cost data.

Much of the work had already been done. During the year, many expense items directly associated with a given line of business and function had been coded to indicate such line and function, and this information was stored in suitable form on magnetic tape. In addition, interdepartmental charges for service department costs were made monthly, generally based on usage statistics. Finally, work-measurement techniques were employed throughout the year to determine the effort being devoted to each line and function by each cost center that was responsible for more than one function.

Much of this information was used to allocate expenses to lines of business, as required for Convention Statement purposes. Allocation of all of Crazy Quilt's expenses ($50 million) to the various lines of business is shown in Table 13–2. Crazy Quilt maintains a somewhat more refined breakdown of lines of business than is required by the Convention Statement, and the degree of refinement is indicated in Table 13–2. The breakdowns shown in the Table are readily summarized into the standard Convention Statement breakdowns.

The functional cost analysis focused on general insurance expenses (Exhibit 5 of the Convention Statement), which in Crazy Quilt's case aggregated $26,525,000 in 1971. Crazy Quilt made no adjustments of Exhibit 5 totals for functional cost purposes. The preliminary allocations to lines of business had essentially already been made. However, the LOMA program treats service and general overhead as separate categories of expense, whereas for Convention Statement purposes such expenses must be allocated to lines of business.

Therefore service (covering personnel operations and general services) and general overhead (covering general management, general legal operations, general planning, public relations, etc.) were "backed out" of the Convention Statement line-of-business classifications for functional cost purposes.

The summary of general expenses in the LOMA format is shown in Table 13–3.

The $14,855,000 in individual ordinary expenses were then analyzed in terms of the detailed functions set forth in the LOMA reporting forms.[8] The analysis involved

▶ Sorting expenses that had been charged (coded) directly to a function to obtain a report of direct costs by function,

▶ Allocating cost center salaries of individuals who performed more than one function to the various functions based on time studies, and

▶ Allocating non-salary cost center expenses not directly identifiable with particular functions on the basis of usage statistics or other similar techniques where possible, and on the basis of cost center salaries charged to each function where direct attribution was not feasible.

The net result of the process was to develop total costs allocable to each of the 13 functions defined by LOMA. The functional allocations, and the related unit costs, are shown in Table 13–4.

LOMA gathers together the same functional cost data for all participating companies and publishes the data (however, distribution is limited to participating companies). Crazy Quilt selected eight other companies similar in size and mix of business for purposes of comparing costs. The comparison is also shown in Table 13–4.

Other cost studies. Crazy Quilt also participated in other functional cost comparisons, namely investment, individual health, and debit life. In addition, Crazy Quilt participated in a depth study of the ordinary life selling function.

Although group functional costs do not enter into the LOMA program, Crazy Quilt compiled group functional costs for internal purposes. Furthermore, Crazy Quilt used modified work-measurement techniques to measure the distribution of time of all commissioned field men.

In short, Crazy Quilt had a complete cost system, which was to prove invaluable in making the conversion to generally accepted accounting principles.

Actuarial Approaches to Cost Accounting

LOMA functional costs are expressed in terms of mutually exclusive unit costs. Thus, for example, Crazy Quilt's 1971 selling expenses are shown in Table 13–4 to be 79 percent of first-year premiums, *or* $138 per policy issued, *or* $10.80 per $1,000 of new business issued. In addition, the somewhat vague categories of services and general overhead are essentially eliminated from functional analysis under the LOMA program.

The reason is that the program is designed to facilitate comparisons—from year to year and with other companies—and hence cost control, and to accomplish this it is necessary to use relatively standard measurements of unit costs.

LOMA functional costs generally cannot be used as inputs to the ratemaking process without modification. As John C. Fraser points out in the *Study Notes* for Part 7 of the Actuarial Examinations,

. . . Functional unit costs developed by the cost accountant are intended to serve a quite different purpose than the unit costs developed by the actuary for use in determining premium rates and asset shares and the units used should reflect this difference.[9]

In essence, the actuary has two primary objectives when he introduces functional costs into the ratemaking process: (1) That the unit costs he uses will, when multiplied by the related volumes, reasonably reproduce total company expenses, and (2) that the allocation of expenses to individual policies is equitable.

With regard to reproducing total expenses, it must be recognized that the actuary is normally working with selected plan-year-age combinations, and he needs assurance that the model he is working with will come close to reproducing all expenses, including service and general overhead. In theory, this could be accomplished by using LOMA unit costs and "loading" them for expenses that were excluded from analysis.

However, this would create a dilemma. For example, Crazy Quilt's selection expense as reported for purposes of the LOMA functional cost program was $26.70 per policy issued, $2.10 per $1,000 of new business, or 15 percent of first-year premiums. When "loaded" for service and general overhead of about 20 percent, such costs become $32.05, $2.50, and 18 percent, respectively.

Any one of these measures could be inequitable if applied across-the-board. Compare, for example, a $5,000 permanent policy issued nonmedically with a $100,000 term policy issued medically. Obviously the selection cost per policy is not the same. Nor would the use of an amount per $1,000 be appropriate; a certain base level of cost is incurred regardless of the size of the policy, and a purely variable measure would not recognize this fact. In other words, the $5,000 policy would be benefited to the detriment of the $100,000 policy. The same objection applies to use of the percentage measure, with the additional problem that premium rates differ as between term and permanent coverages.

Thus, the need to reasonably reproduce total company expenses by the use of unit costs—which need could be satisfied by using fixed measurements of functional costs—is significantly affected by the need to apportion costs equitably to individual policies. To the extent that the premium rates or dividend scale for an individual policy is directly affected by the expenses deemed allocable to that policy, the importance of equitable expense allocation is obvious.

Cost allocation techniques. For ratemaking purposes the actuary will normally attempt to relate the total costs of a particular function to more than one basis. Sometimes this will be done more or less scientifically, i.e., by examining trend data, making scatter diagrams, etc. Sometimes it is done purely on the basis of logic; for example, it is typical to assess policy issue costs on a per-policy basis since the effort required to issue a policy—and hence the expense of issuing a policy—tend to be the same regardless of

Table 13–4.

CRAZY QUILT LIFE'S 1971 FUNCTIONAL COSTS AND COMPARATIVE FUNCTIONAL COSTS OF SELECTED COMPANIES

	Total Costs (000)	Measurement Units	Crazy Quilt Functional Cost	Comparative 1971 Functional Costs of Company							
				A	B	C	D	E	F	G	H
Initial Expenses:											
Selling:	$ 9,192										
$1,000's of new business (000)		851,145	$ 10.80	$ 12.40	$ 15.20	$ 9.10	$ 10.70	$ 7.05	$ 15.10	$ 7.90	$ 10.20
No. of policies issued		66,606	138.00	160.00	230.00	130.00	280.00	95.00	195.00	102.00	145.00
First-year premiums (000)		11,624	79%	73%	89%	38%	56%	43%	79%	41%	63%
Selection:	1,727										
$1,000's of new business (000)		851,145	2.10	2.50	1.80	1.60	2.30	2.85	2.85	2.25	2.95
No. of policies issued		66,606	26.70	32.70	32.50	35.00	42.30	29.70	37.60	28.50	43.05
First-year premiums (000)		11,624	15%	14%	13%	7%	8%	13%	12%	11%	16%
Issue:	597										
$1,000's of new business (000)		851,145	.72	.55	1.10	.70	.40	1.20	.90	.85	.90
No. of policies issued		66,606	9.25	7.00	17.00	10.40	10.30	16.10	11.40	10.90	13.00
First-year premiums (000)		11,624	5%	3%	7%	3%	2%	8%	5%	4%	6%
	11,516										
Direct maintenance:											
Premium collection:	902										
No. of premiums collected		2,000,112	.45	.30	.40	.29	.50	.45	.60	.40	.70
$1,000's of in-force (000)		3,874,270	.23	.25	.15	.28	.15	.35	.25	.20	.30
No. of policies in force		372,022	2.40	1.60	1.65	1.80	2.10	2.10	2.10	1.50	2.30
Commission processing:	232										
No. of premiums collected		2,000,112	.12	.06	.17	.03	.35	.10	.10	.10	.10
$1,000's of in-force (000)		3,874,270	.06	.05	.06	.03	.10	.07	.05	.05	.05
No. of policies in force		372,022	.62	.30	.75	.20	1.40	.50	.40	.40	.40
Death claim processing:	116										
No. of death claims		5,088	22.80	17.00	73.00	34.40	67.30	28.35	19.70	28.00	35.05
$1,000's of in-force (000)		3,874,270	.03	.02	.01	.05	.03	.04	.03	.04	.05
No. of policies in force		372,022	.31	.15	.17	.30	.35	.25	.20	.27	.33
Surrender processing:	78										
No. of surrenders		8,966	8.70	6.50	8.70	7.00	11.25	6.10	7.10	10.65	12.55
$1,000's of in-force (000)		3,874,270	.02	.04	.01	.02	.01	.02	.02	.03	.04
No. of policies in force		372,022	.21	.24	.11	.12	.20	.10	.12	.17	.25
Matured endowment processings:	39										
No. of maturities		2,287	17.05	18.50	—	16.60	6.35	4.10	18.15	15.00	37.70
$1,000's of in-force (000)		3,874,270	.01	.02	—	.01	.01	.01	.01	.01	.02
No. of policies in force		372,022	.10	.10	—	.07	.01	.02	.07	.06	.15

Policy changes:	387									
$1,000's of in-force (000)		3,874,270	.10	.10	.15	.05	.05	.07	.05	.13
No. of policies in force		372,022	1.05	.60	1.30	.95	.45	.30	.40	.35	.90
Other direct maintenance:	775									
$1,000's of in-force (000)		3,874,270	.20	.20	.07	.10	.10	.15	.30	.20	.30
No. of policies in force		372,022	2.08	1.15	.80	.90	1.25	.95	1.70	1.45	2.05
General maintenance:	810									
$1,000's of in-force (000)		3,874,270	.21	.20	.20	.10	.30	.25	.15	.25	.20
No. of policies in force		372,022	2.18	1.10	2.40	1.15	4.15	1.55	.90	1.65	1.60
Total premiums (000)		67,299	1.2%	1.2%	.8%	.5%	1.3%	1.2%	.6%	1.1%	1.0%
	$14,855									

Table 13–5.

SUMMARY OF CRAZY QUILT LIFE'S 1971 FUNCTIONAL ACQUISITION COSTS IN FORMAT USED FOR RATEMAKING

Category	Measurement Units	Unit Costs — Commissions or Equivalent*	Unit Costs — Other Selling	Unit Costs — Selection	Unit Costs — Issue	Extended Costs (000) — Commissions or Equivalent*	Extended Costs (000) — Other Selling	Extended Costs (000) — Selection	Extended Costs (000) — Issue	Extended Costs (000) — Total
Par whole life	First-year premiums (000) $ 1,589	73.0%	59.0%			$1,160	$ 937			$ 2,097
	Policies issued 10,325		$16.05	$12.45	$12.85		166	$ 128	$133	427
	New business (000) $ 75,141		$ 2.70	$ 1.65			203	124		327
Non-par whole life	First-year premiums (000) $ 5,893	83.0%	64.3%			4,892	3,790			8,682
	Policies issued 34,288		$16.05	$12.45	$11.25		550	427	386	1,363
	New business (000) 325,611		$ 2.70	$ 1.65			879	537		1,416
20-pay life	First-year premiums (000) $ 1,548	67.5%	52.5%			1,045	813			1,858
	Policies issued 8,501		$15.75	$12.20	$11.00		134	104	94	332
	New business (000) $ 66,792		$ 2.65	$ 1.60			177	107		284
5-year renewable and convertible term	First-year premiums (000) $ 523	62.5%	42.8%			327	224			551
	Policies issued 3,663		$16.05	$12.45	$10.20		59	46	37	142
	New business (000) $ 91,839		$ 1.65	$ 1.10			151	101		252
25-year decreasing convertible term	First-year premiums (000) $ 1,760	76.5%	42.8%			1,347	730			2,077
	Policies issued 9,366		$16.05	$12.45	$10.20		149	117	96	362
	New business (000) $280,170		$ 1.65	$ 1.10			457	308		765
Conversion whole life (from 5-year term)	First-year conversion premiums (000) $ 133	83.0%	64.3%			110	86			196
	Policies converted 212		$16.05		$11.25		3		2	5
	Amounts converted (000) $ 4,835		$ 2.70				13			13
Conversion whole life (from 25-year decreasing term)	First-year conversion premiums (000) $ 178	83.0%	64.3%			148	115			263
	Policies converted 251		$16.05		$11.25		4		3	7
	Amounts converted (000) $ 6,757		$ 2.70				18			18
						$9,029	$9,659	$1,999	$750	$21,437

* Includes certain noncommission expenses to producers that are reported in Exhibit 5. Crazy Quilt reduces the first-year commissions for commissions payable at the ultimate rate; such ultimate commissions are then treated for ratemaking purposes as renewal expenses incurred in all years including the first year. This is a refinement rarely encountered in practice. Renewal expenses are not shown in this table.

the size of the policy. And sometimes the basis is chosen arbitrarily, either to give effect to the company's philosophy (for example, assessing relatively more expenses on a per-policy basis to favor the larger policies, i.e., be more competitive in the market for larger policies) or because the time or information needed for extensive refined analysis just isn't available.

As a general rule, the actuary will seek to develop "normal" expense rates that operate to smooth fluctuations in actual expenses. For example, Fraser discusses "certain 'one-shot' expenses that perhaps should not be considered a normal cost of doing business . . . for example, when a company is engaged in a changeover to a new electronics system and is incurring the expenses of operating the existing system as well as the expenses of planning and testing the new system." [10] Fraser adds, "There is no reason why the expense results of several years may not be combined to yield asset share expense units." [11]

In addition, new companies typically do not have the volume to support competitive expense rates, so the rates actually used will be based on a "normal" level of operations that will not be achieved for some time to come, perhaps years. The result is some amount of expenses that is not absorbed by the existing volume of business. The amount of such unabsorbed expenses usually decreases with the passage of time.

Crazy Quilt Life. As Table 13–4 indicates, Crazy Quilt's "initial" expenses, based on the LOMA functional cost analysis, were $11,516,000 in 1971. Starting with this amount, Crazy Quilt's actuaries added a proportionate share of service and general overhead and taxes, licenses, and fees, all of which were excluded from the LOMA analysis. In addition, commission rates based on agents' contracts were taken into account. The net result may be summarized as follows:

	LOMA Totals	Allocated Service, General Overhead and Taxes	First-Year Commissions In Excess of Ultimate Rates	Revised Totals
Selling Expenses:				
Commissions			$7,855	$ 7,855
Other	$ 9,192	$1,641		10,833
	9,192	1,641	7,855	18,688
Selection expenses	1,727	272		1,999
Issue expenses	597	153		750
	$11,516	$2,066	$7,855	$21,437

Similar procedures were used to recast other LOMA functional costs into a format appropriate for ratemaking purposes.

Crazy Quilt's actuaries next examined each category of functional costs to establish logical relationships between costs and volume. It was necessary also to recognize differences among products. For example, issue expenses were related to the number of policies issued. But the raw per-policy expenses were further weighted to recognize that a little more expense is incurred in respect of permanent insurance than term insurance (putting cash values on tape, recording dividend options, etc.).

The final result of the analysis is summarized in Table 13–5, which shows unit acquisition costs developed for ratemaking purposes. Table 13–5 also shows an extension of unit acquisition costs to the previously-determined control totals. This gave assurance that the expense rates would reproduce total company expenses at the current volume level. Again, similar procedures were used for the other functional costs.

It should be recognized that Crazy Quilt's techniques are unique to Crazy Quilt and do not represent a "typical" method of analysis, nor are the resulting expense rates "typical". As Fraser points out, "There is probably no area as subjective as the area of expense analysis." [12]

Cost Accounting and Income Determination

That a life insurance company can be viewed as a "manufacturer" was suggested earlier in this chapter. This view of a life insurance company certainly facilitates the problem of accounting for product costs. All that is needed is to identify the operating departments, tally up their costs (including apportionments of the costs incurred by service departments), and divide the total by the units processed to obtain product costs.

But this is only half of the problem of accounting for product costs. The other half is the nature of the costs. The vast bulk of a life insurance company's expenses is represented by selling and administrative expenses. Such expenses are usually written off as incurred by a manufacturing or merchandising company.

The standard accounting treatment of selling and administrative expenses is a convention which through long usage has come to be "generally accepted". This convention has some very practical considerations behind it. It is usually extremely difficult to determine the future utility of a selling or administrative expense, so immediate write-off is warranted on grounds of expediency. More importantly, the selling and administrative expense incurred during a period tends to be accompanied by sales in that period; revenues and product costs are recorded at the time of sale; and the net result is a reasonable matching of revenue and expense.

Of course, when the manufacturer sells his product to a merchandiser at a price that covers the manufacturer's selling and administrative expenses, the merchandiser carries the full cost of the product in inventory; in that case the manufacturer's selling and administrative expenses are effectively carried in the merchandiser's inventory. In the case of inter-company sales for inventory, only the profits are eliminated in consolidation; selling and administrative expenses of the manufacturing subsidiary are included in the transfer price and are inventoried by the merchandising subsidiary.

In short, selling and administrative expenses are generally charged to expense as incurred *unless* they clearly "attach" to a product having future utility.

Custom has also been modified in other cases in which the customary treatment is unduly distortive. For example, finance companies typically recognize a disproportionate share of the loan discount in the month in which the loan is placed to cover the costs of placing it; the same result would be obtained by deferring and amortizing such costs in proportion to the normal pattern of discount amortization. Lease commissions are usually deferred and amortized against lease revenues. A construction company that works on, say, one five-year contract and uses the completed-contract method of reporting construction profits (this is admittedly very rare) will usually defer administrative expenses incurred during the five-year period. Research and development costs, which may consist entirely of non-manufacturing salaries and other "soft" costs, are sometimes deferred.

In other words, the customary treatment of selling and administrative expenses works only so long as the underlying revenue pattern is also customary. Absent a logical relationship between the recognition of revenue and the recognition of expense, dogged adherence to the customary treatment of selling and administrative expense flies in the face of common sense, not to mention rational accounting.

There should be little controversy over the principle that a life insurance company should account for selling and administrative expenses in a manner that makes sense for a life insurance company, irrespective of whether the method would be appropriate for a manufacturer or merchandiser.

Functional Costs and Inventoriable Costs

It is tempting to conclude that life insurance functional costs—either the LOMA variety or the actuarial variety—can be used without modification for accounting purposes. This is not the case:

Some eminent consultants and writers . . . seem instinctively preoccupied with "functional" costing—the classification of costs by function . . . The objective is meritorious, but the approach taken is often downright misleading. Many proponents of functional costing are grimly determined to slap a unit cost on nearly every activity without bothering to distinguish between variable and fixed behavior patterns . . . Cost studies too often seem primarily concerned with finding the cost of processing an order, of posting an invoice, of making a salesman's call. This attempt often entails making some flimsy assumptions as to what costs should be pertinent and what unit should be used at the base. Cost analysis in marketing is sometimes too much concerned with dividing total costs by units to get a magic unit cost for the wrong purpose.[13]

The author of this passage was writing about planning and control, not income determination; and he most assuredly was not writing about life insurance functional costs. But his words have a certain relevance to the problem of giving appropriate recognition to functional costs in the financial statements. The LOMA program and the actuary's approach each has its purpose, but in each case the purpose is "wrong" in terms of the financial statements.

This is because, as far as the financial statements are concerned, the purpose of cost accounting is to determine *product cost*. As the author quoted above points out, only costs that "can be looked upon as 'attaching' or 'clinging' to units produced . . . are classified as *inventoriable costs,* also commonly called *product costs.*"[14] The fact that it is usually quite difficult to separate inventoriable costs from period costs in a life insurance environment does not alter the fact that such a separation must be made. A line must be drawn between selling and administrative expenses that (1) are directly attributable, and hence may be deemed to "attach", to the life insurance product, and (2) are fundamentally no different than the selling and administrative expenses of any other kind of business, and hence should be written off.

Drawing that line will present the life insurance cost accountant with one of his most challenging tasks. His task will be all the more difficult because of management's habit of thinking about functional costs in their traditional non-accounting context.

14

Composition of Acquisition Costs

☙ "Acquisition expenses" [1] (or "acquisition costs", as they are generally called in this chapter) is a label which has come to mean different things to different people. In insurance literature it is typically a catchall for expenses of varying types which are deemed allocable to first-year business for ratemaking purposes. In accounting, the term refers to those expenses which are deemed capitalizable under generally accepted accounting principles. This difference in meanings has been the source of much friendly dispute between accountants and life insurance executives. The dispute is partly semantogenic, but there are, in fact, a few fundamental conceptual differences that deserve brief further examination.

Actuaries differ in their philosophies as to which items of expense constitute "acquisition costs". As pointed out in Chapter 13, cost allocation for pricing purposes is a subjective process. Thus one company assumes *all* overhead expenses are acquisition costs; another company assumes two-thirds are acquisition costs; another assumes one-half; and so on.

In general, the greater the proportion of expenses regarded as acquisition costs, the more conservative the pricing procedure. This is because the apparent first-year surplus strain is greater. The greater the surplus strain, the longer it takes to recoup it. So there is a tendency to recoup the additional strain faster by increasing premiums or adjusting the incidence of cash values or dividends. There are severe limits, competitive and otherwise, on the extent to which premiums can be increased or early cash values or dividends can be revised downward, however, so the practical effect of front-ending acquisition costs is, in most cases, to present a somewhat bleak picture of projected experience. This in turn tends to focus attention on those

products which minimize surplus strain or return the highest yield on the investment of surplus.

If actuarial assumptions as to what items of expense constitute acquisition costs were carried directly into the accounting process, then the most conservative pricing procedures would result in the most liberal accounting practices. The amounts deferred as acquisition costs would vary directly with the actuary's assumptions, which, as suggested above, differ among actuaries and among companies. In other words, there would be very little discipline over the methods used to account for acquisition costs.

Hence the life insurance audit guide specifies that, irrespective of a company's particular philosophy, acquisition costs must meet a two-fold test to qualify for deferral: They must "both vary with, and be primarily related to, the production of new business." [2]

Variability and Attribution

"Variability" is itself a variable concept; one man's notion of variability is often another man's notion of fixedness. In a similar vein, "attribution"—the process of assigning a relationship between one thing and another—often depends on the subtlety (perhaps the ingenuity) of one's insights.

Certainly in accounting there are endless arguments over whether X varies with Y and whether A begets B. Variability and attribution are particularly difficult problems in life insurance accounting, and the life insurance audit guide is not particularly helpful in providing guidelines for determining whether a particular cost item varies with production or is primarily related to production. In essence, the guide states the principle and leaves the details of implementation to the judgment of professionals. This is, of course, the way it has to be.

Variability

The problem of determining whether a given cost varies with the production of new business is largely a matter of defining the *degree* of variability required to do justice to the concept. As mentioned in Chapter 13, all costs are variable when viewed from the perspective of a company's entire lifetime. Furthermore, elimination of a given activity would also eliminate most or all of the costs associated with the activity. But financial statements must be prepared more frequently than once in a lifetime, and it is not reasonable to base one's decision about variability on an assumption about what would happen if a company simply went out of business.

So determining the existence of a variable relationship between acquisition costs and production is a practical problem that should be resolved using old-fashioned common-sense accounting methodology.

Cost-volume relationships. Table 14–1 shows, in graphical form, six general types of relationships between costs and volume, progressing from the most variable (Graph No. 1) to the least variable (Graph No. 6). Usually no distinction is made between "semi-variable" and "semi-fixed" costs, but such a distinction is made in Table 14–1.

Measurement bases. It is important to appreciate that variability will differ according to the base used to measure production. For example, commissions would usually be perfectly linear with respect to premiums, but may be only essentially linear with respect to face amounts. Suppose underwriting and issue were farmed out for a fixed fee per policy and per $1,000 of face amount; in that event those costs would be perfectly variable (1) with the number of policies issued, with respect to the per-policy portion of the cost, and (2) with face amounts issued, with respect to the per-$1,000 portion of the cost. Yet such underwriting and issue costs might bear only an essentially linear relationship to premiums.

No one measurement base is supreme. In manufacturing accounting, production costs are usually plotted against units produced, not selling prices, to determine variability. In life insurance accounting, "units produced" might be expressed in the form of premiums, number of policies, face amount of insurance issued, or "units" of insurance issued. Any one of these bases, or in fact a combination, might be appropriate for purposes of measuring variability.

Perfectly linear relationships. In those cases in which a cost item varies directly with production, there is no question that it is variable, and no further discussion is needed.

Essentially linear relationships. A cost may stray more or less randomly from the curve of production while retaining a tendency to adhere to the curve. Such fluctuations are neither extreme nor of long duration. In that case, the cost may be regarded as bearing an essentially linear relationship to production.

Step-cost relationships. Sometimes a given outlay will cover a range of production. Above the range another outlay is required and, when the range of production associated with the second outlay is exceeded, still another outlay is required, and so on. These circumstances would indicate a step-cost relationship. One characteristic of a step-cost relationship is an unavoidable period of under-utilization of capacity until the top of the range is reached. Nevertheless, the central tendency of the cost curve is to follow the curve of production.

Semi-variable relationships. When a cost departs significantly from the curve of production but moves grudgingly in the same direction, it may be regarded as semi-variable. It would not be unusual for the cost curve and the production curve to cross at some point. The principal difference between a semi-variable and a semi-fixed relationship is the frequency with which the level of cost changes relative to the level of production.

Semi-fixed relationships. When a cost changes very infrequently in relation to the curve of production, it may be regarded as semi-fixed.

Fixed relationships. And finally, when a cost is completely unresponsive to the level of production, it may be regarded as fixed.

Effect of inflation. In measuring variability it is generally appropriate to measure production and costs in constant units. Thus the effect, if any, of inflation would be eliminated in making the analysis. For example, if a president's salary is raised 5 percent a year to compensate for inflation, while the number of policies sold increases 5 percent a year, the president's salary should not be regarded as varying with the number of policies sold.

Satisfying the audit guide's criterion. The life insurance audit guide simply specifies that, to qualify for deferral, an acquisition cost must "vary with" production. What qualifies as "variable" is obviously a matter of judgment.

There is probably little dispute over the proposition that costs which bear a perfectly linear or essentially

Table 14–1.

VARIOUS COST/VOLUME RELATIONSHIPS

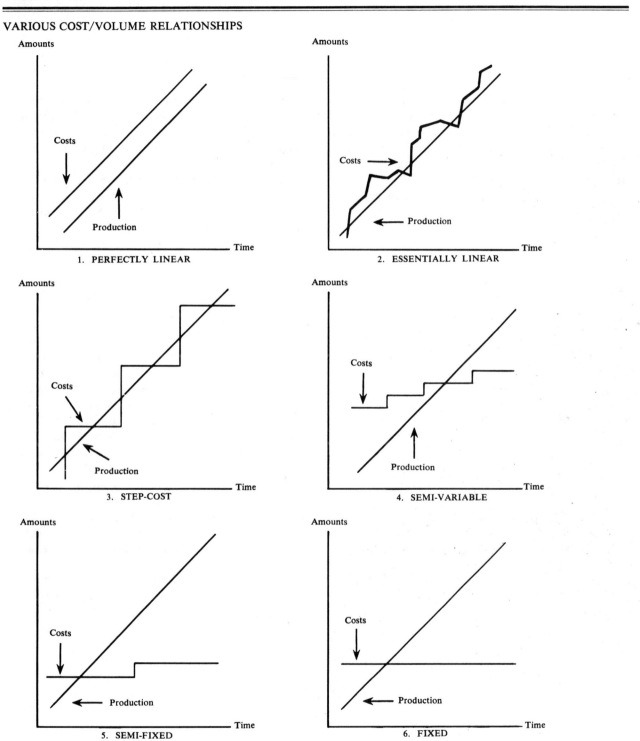

linear relationship to production qualify under the variability criterion.

Step-cost relationships should also qualify, as a general rule, so long as the range of production covered by the cost is not unreasonably wide.

Semi-variable costs (at least as they are defined herein) would rarely qualify under the guide's criterion, unless the attribution criteria are satisfied in so positive and convincing a manner that one is forced to conclude that the cost under consideration is an acquisition cost. In that case the variability criterion would be stretched to the limit to accommodate common sense.

Semi-fixed and fixed costs would never qualify under any reasonable concept of variability.

Attribution

A cost can properly be regarded as primarily relating to production only to the extent that

▸ There exists a *cause-and-effect* relationship between the cost and production,
▸ The cost can *logically* be attributed to production or vice-versa,
▸ The relationship is readily *demonstrable,*
▸ The relationship exists for the *accounting period* under study, and
▸ There exists some form of *precedence* for attributing the cost to production.

These conditions might for convenience be referred to as "tests" of causality, logic, demonstrability, finitude, and precedence, respectively.

These are fairly severe tests, but it is very important to apply them in determining whether the relationship between costs and production is sufficient to warrant deferring the costs as acquisition costs. The alternative is a lack of discipline over the deferral process, and that alternative is not acceptable.

Causality.   If an expenditure does not result in production, the causality test is not satisfied and the cost cannot properly be regarded as relating to production. The cost need not necessarily precede production to qualify; the true test of causality is whether production at the current level of volume would be impossible if the cost were not incurred. Thus selling, underwriting and issue costs would clearly qualify. "Production" in a life insurance company refers to paid-for business placed on the books, and selling, underwriting, and issue are all necessary to get the business on the books.

Logic.   If a cost cannot logically be associated with production—using "logic" as a synonym for common sense—then it cannot be deemed to relate primarily to production. For example, audit fees, while perhaps a necessary evil, cannot logically be associated with production.

Demonstrability.   If the relationship between a cost and production is not clearly demonstrable, a relationship cannot be deemed to exist. Expenditures for public relations might be regarded as bearing a causal relationship with the current level of production, but the relationship can rarely, if ever, be demonstrated.

Finitude.   The relationship between a cost and production must be measurable in terms of a single accounting period (i.e., year). A computer might be purchased primarily to facilitate the production process, but the cost of the computer is not applicable to the production of a single year.

The life insurance audit guide does not state explicitly that an acquisition cost must relate to production of the year in which it is incurred, but this condition is implicit in the guide's discussion of acquisition costs. In Appendix B of the guide, for example, reference is made to "aggregate acquisition costs for each year's block of business." [3] In its main discussion of acquisition costs, the guide indicates that "In many instances, commissions and other acquisition expenses will exceed related premiums during the initial year that policies are in force." [4] Variability is measured by comparing costs and production over a time series comprised of individual accounting periods.

Precedence.   The president of a life insurance company may spend a significant portion of his time on the selling function, and his compensation might conceivably vary with production. But there is little precedence for regarding a president's salary as an inventoriable cost.

In the process manufacturing industries, for example, some presidents spend considerable time on production matters, but presidents' salaries are rarely, if ever, capitalized in inventory. The president is seen to be primarily an administrative officer whose salary is a period expense.

The life insurance audit guide specifies that precedence should govern the treatment of certain types of expenses, such as policy maintenance and general overhead. "As in the case of other business enterprises," says the guide, "such expenses should be charged to operations in the period incurred." [5]

The relationship between a life insurance company and "other business enterprises" is sometimes a bit tenuous, mainly because of the unique nature of the life insurance business. So the precedence criterion must be applied with some care. Nevertheless, the criterion must be applied, and even if all of the other tests are satisfied, a cost cannot be regarded as primarily related to production if the imputation of such a relationship would clearly violate precedence.

Applicability of Process Costing Concepts

In Chapter 13 it was suggested that the life insurance production process includes selling, selection, and issue activities. It follows that costs clearly associated with those activities are potentially deferrable as acquisition costs.

Determining what costs are "clearly" associated with selling, selection and issue activities is not always easy. Regardless of available "tests", "guidelines", and "precedents", some degree of subjectivity will almost always be involved in deciding on what costs are properly associated with production activities.

Nevertheless, certain basic principles of process costing applied in the manufacturing industries can also be applied in the life insurance industry. Once a life insurance company's production departments are identified—and this is not always a simple task, particularly with respect to the selling function—then production costs can be viewed as consisting of (1) expenses chargeable directly to those departments plus (2) apportionments of the expenses of departments which render direct support to operating departments. "Operating departments" include production departments as well as non-production departments.

Defining deferrable costs in terms of the costs of production departments is, however, merely a starting point in the process of analyzing acquisition costs. To qualify for deferral, such costs must meet the tests of variability and attribution irrespective of whether they are classified as "production costs".

LOMA Suggestions

In February 1973, soon after the life insurance audit guide was published, the Life Office Management Association published a special release entitled *Acquisition Expenses for GAAP Reporting*. The purpose of the release was to provide specific suggestions for implementing the principles of deferral set forth in the guide. The release drew heavily on functional cost concepts and procedures. For example, costs are discussed in terms of their classifications within the

LOMA selling depth study; individual components of each depth study classification are analyzed in terms of the extent to which the component meets the criterion of variability.

The LOMA release, while not "official", is extremely helpful in deciding what items of cost qualify for deferral. Its influence on the discussion that follows is hereby acknowledged.

Selling Costs

A life insurance sales organization usually perceives itself as an integrated operation. And so it should. Recruiting, training, agent financing, agent conventions, agency administration, supervision—all are geared to the production of new business.

But not every dollar spent on the selling effort is born equal. Some of the money spent on selling results directly in new business. Some of the money is spent in the expectation of new business sometime in the future.

One might view an agency organization as being subdivided into three organizations—one concerned with agency development, one concerned with production, and one concerned with overall agency administration. Agency development encompasses most of the activities undertaken to prepare an agent to sell insurance successfully. Production encompasses the actual selling activity. And agency administration encompasses various supporting activities such as contract administration.

It is admittedly difficult to segregate these three basic functions of a life insurance sales organization, but the segregation must be made. In general, only costs associated directly with production are deferrable as acquisition costs. This chapter deals primarily with such costs. Agency development costs may or may not be deferrable; such costs present unusual problems that are discussed in Chapter 17. Agency administration is in the nature of administrative overhead and would normally not be deferred in any event; such costs are discussed later in this chapter and in Chapter 17.

First-Year Commissions and Commission Equivalents

Types of sales organizations and methods of compensating agents vary widely in the life insurance industry, to the point where the number of possible combinations of organization and compensation methods is virtually without limit. Thus one finds managing general agents; personal-producing general agents;

branch managers; brokers; and commissions, salaries, bonuses and allowances of every description.

Therefore it is necessary to think in terms of commissions and commission "equivalents", i.e., payments in the nature of commissions. Commissions and commission equivalents that relate to identifiable units of production qualify for deferral as acquisition costs.

Commissions to selling agents. A first-year commission to a selling agent, sub-agent, or broker based on his production would normally qualify for deferral as an acquisition cost. So would production bonuses that are based on defined levels of production.

Certain commissions paid to producers in subsequent years would generally also qualify for deferral; this is discussed later in this chapter.

Commissions paid to agents who actually write the business clearly vary with and are primarily related to the production of new business. Such costs generally meet all of the attribution tests.

Company practices vary with respect to the payment of commissions on policies having a payment mode other than annual. Sometimes a company will record an annualized commission in the form of an agent's balance and credit commissions to the balance only as they are earned, i.e., as premiums are received. In other cases the full annualized commission is immediately charged to expense; memorandum accounts are maintained to keep track of the advance.

When policies lapse before the first year has expired the unearned portion of the annualized commission is usually charged back to the agent in some manner. Companies using the agent's balance method will, of course, make no further credits to the agent's account; it is up to the agent to pay off the balance.* Companies using the immediate charge-off method will usually credit commission expense only as future payments to agents are reduced by the amount charged back to them or, in the case of terminated agents having insufficient commission credits to offset the amounts advanced, as amounts are paid back to the company. In the event a balance proves uncollectible, the company using the immediate charge-off method will usually make no further entries; the uncollectible balance is in effect left in the account for commission expense.**

Recording the annualized commission as an agent's

balance is perhaps the more precise approach, but the method of recording the commission has no particular significance in terms of accounting for deferred acquisition costs. Under the agent's balance approach the amount deferred is a function of cash premiums; under the immediate charge-off method the amount deferred is a function of annualized premiums. The mechanics of deferral are such that, all other things being equal, either approach would have the same effect on income, as shown in Table 14–2. The commissions vary with new business in either case. Under the agent's balance approach, commissions would vary with cash premiums; under the immediate charge-off approach, commissions would vary with annualized premiums, volume, or number of policies issued.

One cautionary note. When a company uses the immediate charge-off approach and significant amounts of unearned commissions are not recovered, the result is to overstate commission expense unless the uncollectible amount is transferred to the account for agents' balances charged off. Technically this compromises the condition of variability since the cost will vary with persistency of the business, persistency of the agent, productivity of the agent, solvency of the agent, and other such factors. In other words, at some point the commission would not vary with production. When the amounts involved are material, the uncollectible portions of annualized commissions should not be treated as deferrable commissions.

Salaries to selling agents. Some life insurance companies employ salaried agents. This is frequently the case, for example, in an insurance sales counter operation in a retail store. Other companies combine salaries and commissions, or establish a floor on commissions which effectively constitutes a salary.

It is important to distinguish between agent financing and compensation for production. For example, if an agent's compensation is based on commissions subject to a floor of, say, $800 a month, and his commission income does not exceed $800 for a year, then a significant portion of his income during the first year is clearly in the nature of financing. That is, the company is willing to carry the agent until he is sufficiently mature to produce enough business to pay his way. Financing is a development cost that generally does not qualify for deferral as an acquisition cost.

When financing is a significant element in agents' compensation, then the financing payments should be split between compensation for production and development costs. One way to make the split would be to

---

*Of course, agents don't always pay off their balances and sometimes balances are "forgiven" by companies. In either case, the result is a writeoff of the balance. Writeoffs of agents' balances are discussed later in this chapter.

**However, a few companies make a bookkeeping transfer of the uncollectible amount from the commission account to the account for agents' balances charged off.

Table 14–2.

EFFECT OF ANNUALIZED COMMISSION ON DEFERRED ACQUISITION COSTS UNDER (1) AGENT'S BALANCE APPROACH AND (2) IMMEDIATE CHARGE-OFF APPROACH

	Agent's Balance Approach			Immediate Charge-Off Approach	
	Agent's Balance	Commission Expense	Deferred Acquisition Costs	Commission Expense	Deferred Acquisition Costs
Annual premium—$200					
Premium collected during year—$100					
Commission rate—50%					
Annualized commission	$100			$100	
Commission earned during year	(50)	$50			
Amount deferred		(50)	$50	(100)	$100
Effect on income before amortization		$-0-		$ -0-	
Assets before amortization	$ 50		$50		$100

Note—Amortization charged to expense would be the same under either approach. If first-year amortization is 10 percent, for example, the amount charged to expense would be 10% X $50 or $5 under the agent's balance approach; under the immediate charge-off approach, the amount charged to expense would be 10% X $100 X 50% or $5. In the latter formula the 50% adjusts for the proportion of the first-year premium actually received; this is not necessary in the former formula since the 50% adjustment is implicit in the agent's balance approach. Amortization is discussed in Chapter 16.

allocate an amount based on the normal commission rate to acquisition costs and the balance to development costs.

When an agent achieves a level of production sufficient to produce commissions in an amount that equals or exceeds his base salary, occasional dips beneath the floor may be regarded as minor deviations from the commission pattern. Such deviations may safely be ignored, as a general rule. The principle of essential linearity would apply in such cases.

When an agent is compensated entirely by salary, then his compensation would tend to follow a step-cost pattern in relation to production. That's because one agent can handle only so much new business; when his limit is reached, another agent must be added. It would appear that his salary can be regarded as varying with production. However, salaries to an agent during his training period—that is, prior to the time that he is fully prepared to sell new business—should be regarded as financing, i.e., as a development cost.

It must be borne in mind that compensation systems vary so greatly that it is impossible to frame rules or procedures that will be applicable in every case. The important thing is to recognize that some portion of the agent's compensation is a reward for current production and some portion represents a sincere hope, expressed in dollars, that the agent will eventually produce business at a level sufficient to make him self-sustaining. The portion that represents a reward for production is an acquisition cost; the rest is a development cost.

Commissions to general agents. General agents often receive several different types of commissions. Personal-producing general agents receive writing agents' commissions on business produced by them; such commissions generally do not differ from the commissions to selling agents discussed above. In addition, general agents normally receive overrides for the production of sub-agents in their employ, in recognition of the fact that general agents hire, stimulate, supervise, and otherwise are responsible for the achievements of the sub-agents. Such overrides are also deferrable. Finally, a general agent typically receives production bonuses based on defined production quotas for his entire agency. Such production bonuses are essentially of the same nature as production bonuses paid to writing agents and would also qualify for deferral.

General agents also receive a myriad of special "allowances" that are sometimes paid in the form of commissions. Such payments might include recruiting allowances, training allowances, and office expense allowances. Recruiting and training allowances are basically development costs and should be so regarded for accounting purposes.

Office expense allowances are designed to assist the agent in covering his administrative overhead.* If material, they should be analyzed in terms of the administrative functions which they are supposed to cover, preferably by an analysis of agency activity. Some portion of an agency's office expenses is attributable to supporting the development function; some portion to supporting the direct production function; some portion to policy maintenance (e.g., collecting premiums, administering policy loan transactions following up on lapse notices, etc.); and some portion to general agency overhead. Only the portion of office expense allowances associated with the direct production function should be deferred as acquisition costs,** and then only if it passes the variability test.

Sometimes a general agent is paid one all-inclusive commission designed to cover various agency activities. Such a commission would usually be paid at a constant rate and would therefore be perfectly variable with premiums. However, amounts paid in excess of the amount that would normally be paid for direct production would not necessarily be primarily related to production. Suppose, for example, that a general agent is paid a first-year commission of 130 percent, that the going rate for sub-agents is 70 percent, that the going rate for overrides is 15 percent, and that an appropriate average rate for production bonuses for the agency's volume of production is 10 percent. This would suggest that the commission applicable to production is on the order of 95 percent and that the balance, 35 percent, represents payments for activities not directly related to production. Obviously, this is not a foregone conclusion; a higher rate may be justified on the basis that the agency sells particularly high-profit products, or that persistency of the business written by the agent is superior.*** But unusually high commissions to general agents should

be challenged; they should not be deferred unless they meet the tests of attribution.

Salaries to branch managers. A salaried branch manager is much the same as a general agent. In fact, in recent years the distinction between branch offices and general agencies has become blurred. In any event, salaries to branch managers tend to serve the same purposes as overrides, production bonuses, and recruiting and training allowances paid to general agents.*

The portion of a branch manager's compensation that is substantially equivalent to overrides and production bonuses paid to a general agent should generally be treated as a commission equivalent. Ideally the branch manager's compensation should be allocated based on analysis of his activities. The attribution criteria are readily satisfied, but it may be a bit difficult to meet the variability criterion (although it would seem to stand to reason that the greater the level of production, the greater the proportion of the manager's time devoted to production and hence the greater the cost associated with the direct production activity).

One possible method of approximating the proportion of a branch manager's salary allocable to production is to impute an amount equal to the rate (covering overrides and, if applicable, production bonuses) that would be paid a general agent doing the same volume of the same type of business in the same locale. Absent any identifiable tangible advantages of a branch-office form of organization—demonstrated better persistency would probably qualify as a "tangible" identifiable advantage; greater control over the sales function would not—it is reasonable to assume that a company is not willing to pay more for supervision by a branch manager than by a general agent. So the imputation of an override in these circumstances would be logical.

Salaries to assistant managers. The duties of assistant branch managers vary considerably from company to company. Sometimes the assistant manager's function is an extension of the manager's function; they both do essentially the same thing. Sometimes an assistant manager supervises production while the manager devotes his efforts to recruiting and training. And sometimes an assistant manager is primarily an

---

*Sometimes a company will pay some portion of a general agent's office expenses directly and account for such payments in the same manner as expenses incurred in the home office are accounted for.

**The Life Insurance Agency Management Association has developed an "Agency Activity Analysis" program designed to facilitate the task of determining the distribution of an agency's efforts.

***However, favorable persistency is usually rewarded by a bonus *after* the superior persistency is made manifest.

*Sometimes branch managers are compensated on the basis of a combination of salaries and commissions. Amounts payable in the form of commissions should generally be analyzed in the same manner as commissions to general agents, keeping in mind the nature and effect of the total compensation package.

observer of the manager's activities; in that case, the assistant manager's role is limited to training for a manager's role, possibly in another branch office.

Once again, only the portion of the assistant manager's salary attributable to direct production should be regarded as a deferrable acquisition cost. As a practical matter, all managers and assistant managers may be considered together in allocating managers' salaries to production. This unitary approach permits analysis of managerial activities taken as a whole and avoids the necessity of analyzing and accounting for the details of each man's activities and the associated costs. However, where salaries vary significantly, a weighting factor should be introduced to recognize the fact that a given time distribution will not produce the same dollar distribution.

Branch office expenses. While a general agent may be compensated in whole or in part for his office expenses by lump-sum office allowances, companies invariably pay branch office expenses directly.* The principles applied in analyzing such expenses would be the same as the principles applied to analyze office expense allowances paid to general agents. The portion of such expenses allocable to direct production would generally be deferrable if it qualifies under the variability test.

Agents' Stock Options

Some companies have had, or still have, stock option plans for agents. Under such plans options to purchase stock are granted provisionally based on production, but the right to exercise the options usually does not vest absolutely until a persistency requirement —for example, three years—is met with respect to the business for which the options are granted.

Some of the plans have provided for option prices significantly less than market at the time of grant. Frequently such plans have been accompanied by commission scales that are somewhat lower than normal, on the basis that the agent is being compensated in the form of stock.

Under generally accepted accounting principles the difference between the fair market value and the option price, measured on the date of the grant, is accounted for as compensation. Compensation ex-

pense is charged and capital is credited for the amount of such difference.

Should stock option costs be treated as acquisition costs subject to deferral? The question is of more than academic interest. In recent years stock options have tended to be relatively ineffective because of the condition of the stock market, and some of the plans have been terminated. In years past, however—primarily in the 1960s—stock option costs for some companies ran into the millions of dollars. To establish such stock option costs as acquisition costs retroactively has significant implications for financial statements prepared today.

Some believe that stock option costs represent acquisition costs. They point to the fact that commissions are typically lower when stock options are granted. In their view, the company conserves cash, but that's all; the cost of a stock option is a cost notwithstanding the fact that cash is not expended.

Most agents' stock option programs have been initiated at the inception of the company. One of the overriding considerations underlying such programs has been the development of an agency force. Stock options presented an opportunity to attract agents from established companies without the expenditure of cash. Not only were cash incentives unnecessary, the company found that the value of the options was so high— particularly in the market for life insurance stocks in the early 1960s—they were able to pay a somewhat lower rate of commissions than would otherwise be necessary. Finally, since there is no impact on total statutory capital and surplus as a result of issuing stock options, the entire program could be carried out without impacting statutory capital. In a very real sense, existing stockholders directly bore the cost of stock options.

Many if not most stock option plans were terminated or radically changed when the desired number of producing agents was attained. Companies retaining option plans began to offer options at market. Most also increased their commission scales.

It is clear that in these circumstances stock option costs represented a device for building an agency plant. The costs were therefore developmental in character. They should therefore be considered primarily as development costs, not acquisition costs, when the circumstances are similar to those described.

Furthermore, option costs would usually not vary with production. They would tend to vary instead with the stock market. One company, for example, reported unit stock option costs approximately as follows for a period of years:

---

*Alternatively, a branch office may maintain its own bank account and pay its own expenses, submitting accounting data to the home office periodically for recording in the company's books. The practical effect is the same.

Table 14–3.

ILLUSTRATION OF EFFECT OF "LEVELING" ALL COMMISSIONS

PREMIUMS AND COMMISSIONS:

| Year | Mortality and Lapse | Surviving and Persisting | Premiums | | Commissions | |
			Amount	% of Total	Rate	Amount
1	15%	100.0%	$100.00	14.67%	100%	$100.00
2	10	85.0	85.00	12.47	20	17.00
3	8	76.5	76.50	11.22	10	7.65
4	7	70.4	70.40	10.33	5	3.52
5	6	65.5	65.50	9.61	5	3.28
6	5	61.6	61.60	9.04	5	3.08
7	4	59.1	59.10	8.67	5	2.96
8	4	56.7	56.70	8.32	5	2.84
9	4	54.5	54.50	8.00	5	2.73
10	4	52.3	52.30	7.67	5	2.62
			$681.60	100.00%		$145.68

Total commissions as a percentage of total premiums   21.37%

WRITEOFF OF COMMISSIONS:

| | Ignoring Renewal-Year Commissions | | | | Including Renewal-Year Commissions | |
Year	Percentage of Total Premiums Collected	Amortization of First-Year Commissions	Renewal Commissions Incurred	Total Expense	Premiums Collected	21.37% Thereof
1	14.67%	$ 14.67	$ -0-	$ 14.67	$100.00	$ 21.37
2	12.47	12.47	17.00	29.47	85.00	18.17
3	11.22	11.22	7.65	18.87	76.50	16.35
4	10.33	10.33	3.52	13.85	70.40	15.05
5	9.61	9.61	3.28	12.89	65.50	14.00
6	9.04	9.04	3.08	12.12	61.60	13.16
7	8.67	8.67	2.96	11.63	59.10	12.63
8	8.32	8.32	2.84	11.16	56.70	12.12
9	8.00	8.00	2.73	10.73	54.50	11.65
10	7.67	7.67	2.62	10.29	52.30	11.18
	100.00%	$100.00	$45.68	$145.68	$681.60	$145.68

| | Option Costs | | |
Year	Per $1,000 of New Business	Per Policy Issued	As a Percentage of First-Year Premiums
1	$ 5.90	$260	60%
2	10.60	410	100
3	3.50	160	40
4	2.50	130	25
5	.40	20	5

The pattern does not indicate variability by any stretch of the imagination.

Option costs might be regarded as acquisition costs only to the extent of the *lesser* of (a) stock option costs for the period or (b) the aggregate difference for the period between commissions actually paid and commissions that would have been paid at a normal rate. Any excess of actual stock option costs over (b) should be treated as development costs.

Renewal-Year Commissions and Commission Equivalents

A first-year commission is only the first in a series of commission payments that may stretch out over many years, possibly to the end of the premium-paying period. Questions arise as to (1) whether any portion of commissions and commission equivalents payable in the second and subsequent years should be regarded as acquisition costs, (2) what effect agent terminations and vesting provisions have on the treatment of renewal-year commissions, and (3) what impact renewal-year commissions have on the amount deferred in the first year.

Renewal-year commissions. The life insurance audit guide provides that deferred acquisition costs "should include renewal commissions based on a descending commission scale even though such expenses are incurred subsequent to issue." [6] The theory under-

Table 14–4.

ILLUSTRATION OF EFFECT OF ACCRUING ALL FUTURE COMMISSIONS AT TIME OF SALE

PROGRESSION OF ASSET:

Year	Initial Accrual	Percentage of Total Premiums Collected	Expense— Amortization of Initial Accrual	Ending Asset
1	$145.68	14.67%	$ 21.37	$124.31
2		12.47	18.17	106.14
3		11.22	16.35	89.79
4		10.33	15.05	74.74
5		9.61	14.00	60.74
6		9.04	13.16	47.58
7		8.67	12.63	34.95
8		8.32	12.12	22.83
9		8.00	11.65	11.18
10		7.67	11.18	-0-
		100.00%	$145.68	

PROGRESSION OF LIABILITY:

Year	Initial Accrual	Commissions Paid	Ending Liability	Ending Net Asset
1	$145.68	$100.00	$45.68	$78.63
2		17.00	28.68	77.46
3		7.65	21.03	68.76
4		3.52	17.51	57.23
5		3.28	14.23	46.51
6		3.08	11.15	36.43
7		2.96	8.19	26.76
8		2.84	5.35	17.48
9		2.73	2.62	8.56
10		2.62	-0-	-0-
		$145.68		

lying this provision may be explained from two points of view.

First, premiums are recognized as revenue as they are received. Generally premiums are level. To implement the matching concept, policy-related expenses which are not proportional to premiums should be "leveled", that is, recognized in a pattern that is proportional to the recognition of revenue. The leveling point of view is illustrated in Table 14–3. Total commissions in all years are $145.68; total premiums in all years are $681.60; the ratio of total commissions to total premiums is 21.37 percent. To level the commission expense it is necessary to write off commissions equal to 21.37 percent of premiums received in each year. The effect of ignoring renewal-year com-

missions and writing off only first-year commissions is also shown in Table 14–3. It will be observed that total expense is significantly disproportionate to premiums if first-year commissions are amortized without regard for renewal-year commissions.

Secondly, renewal-year commissions may be viewed as accruing at the time of sale. There is, in effect, an asset and a liability, equal in amount, at the moment of issue. The asset is amortized against premium revenue; payments of renewal-year commissions are applied to reduce the liability. This point of view is illustrated in Table 14–4. The initial accrual for all commissions, $145.68, is amortized over the premium-paying period in proportion to the percentage of total premiums collected each year. The initial liability for all commissions, also $145.68, is reduced as payments are actually made. The "ending net asset" in Table 14–4 is simply the unamortized commission balance less the ending liability. Note that the ending net asset in Year 1 is $78.63. Reference to Table 14–3 will indicate that the ending Year 1 asset if renewal-year commissions are ignored is $85.33 ($100, first-year commissions incurred, less amortization of $14.67). This indicates that in Year 1, ignoring renewal-year acquisition costs is less conservative than recognizing them. In the following years the reverse will be true.

Thus renewal-year commissions should always be accounted for if renewal-year commission rates are anything but level or substantially level.

Level renewal commissions. When commission rates in subsequent years are incurred at a commission rate that does not change, or the rate changes nominally, it would be appropriate to ignore them. However, in such cases the first-year rate should be reduced for the rate applicable to subsequent years.

For example, if $100 in premiums are collected in the first year and $100 in commissions are incurred, the first-year commission rate is 100 percent. If commissions of 5 percent are payable in all renewal years, only 95 percent (or $95) should be deferred. This is to allow for the fact that 5 percent is, in effect, a maintenance expense that is incurred in every year including the first. It should be treated the same as a premium tax would be treated. Only the portion of the commission that is not incurred proportionally with the receipt of premiums should be deferred.

Agent terminations and vesting. Expected agent termination rates and vesting provision should be taken into account in determining whether renewal-year commissions are, in fact, incurred at a level rate.

The effect of agent terminations and vesting is best suggested by an illustration. Assume that, for a given company, the renewal commission rate is 20 percent in all years subsequent to the first year and

▸ Half the business is produced by agents whose contracts do not provide for vesting at all ("Class A" agents),
▸ One-fourth of the business is produced by agents whose contracts provide for vesting only if the agent survives five years with the company ("Class B" agents), and
▸ One-fourth of the business is produced by brokers whose contracts provide for unconditional vesting ("Class C" agents).

Now assume that experience indicates that 50 percent of the "Class A" agents will terminate in the fifth year and the remaining 50 percent in the tenth year, and that 50 percent of the "Class B" agents will survive five years. The effective renewal-year commission rate is not 20 percent in all years, but instead changes dramatically as a function of agent terminations, as shown in Table 14–5. It will be noted that the effect of vesting provisions and agent terminations is to produce a rather sharply descending effective commission rate.

Usually vesting provisions are known but agent termination rates can only be predicted. For mature companies such predictions are often quite accurate. For newer companies, or companies whose agency plant is rapidly changing character, it may be very difficult to predict the pattern of agent terminations. Where this is the case, it may be prudent to assume that all agents will survive. This is generally the more conservative approach.

Renewal-year commission equivalents. A portion of a branch manager's salary can usually be associated with renewal-year business. He is, in effect, receiving a renewal-year override in the form of salary. Such "overrides", which will probably have to be imputed based on the general agents' override rate, should be regarded as renewal commissions.

Persistency bonuses. Persistency bonuses should be treated as nonlevel commissions and, if material, should be accounted for as a part of acquisition costs, first-year or renewal depending on when the bonus accrues.

Sales Support

Commissions and commission equivalents represent a major part of total selling costs, but so-called "sales support"—agent financing, agency administration, advertising, sales analysis, agents' conventions, etc.— also requires very sizeable expenditures. For example, it would not be unusual for sales support to amount to 50 percent of commissions and commission equivalents (as it does in the case of Crazy Quilt Life).

Home office agency administration. Home office agency administration includes home office senior marketing executives, work on agents' licenses and contracts, processing of agents' complaints, and the like. Generally agency administration costs would fail the test of variability, and such costs would also fail most of the attribution tests. Agency administration is overhead and should be accounted for as such.

Field clerical. Most branch offices employ clerical

Table 14–5.

ILLUSTRATION OF EFFECT OF AGENT TERMINATION AND VESTING PROVISIONS ON EFFECTIVE RENEWAL COMMISSION RATE

	Class A Agents	Class B Agents	Class C Agents	Effective Commission Rate
Years 1–5:				
Contract rate	20.0%	20.0%	20.0%	
Proportion being paid	x100.0	x100.0	x100.0	
Proportion of total business produced	x 50.0	x 25.0	x 25.0	
Weighted rate	10.0%	5.0%	5.0%	20.0%
Years 6–10:				
Contract rate	20.0%	20.0%	20.0%	
Proportion being paid	x 50.0	x 50.0	x100.0	
Proportion of total business produced	x 50.0	x 25.0	x 25.0	
Weighted rate	5.0%	2.5%	5.0%	12.5%
Years 11 on:				
Contract rate	20.0%	20.0%	20.0%	
Proportion being paid	x -0-	x 50.0	x100.0	
Proportion of total business produced	x 50.0	x 25.0	x 25.0	
Weighted rate	-0-%	2.5%	5.0%	7.5%

workers whose responsibilities typically include administrative duties (correspondence, telephone, etc.), policyholder service (providing assistance to policyholders in applying for policy loans, etc.), and new business (preparing applications for transmittal to the home office, etc.). New business functions may properly be regarded as deferrable acquisition costs. Costs associated with administrative duties could be allocated between acquisition costs and other costs on an appropriate basis; for example, the salary of a manager's secretary might be allocated to acquisition costs in proportion to the percentage of the manager's salary so allocated. In general, field clerical and related expenses should be analyzed into the same elements as office expense allowances paid to general agents, and only the portion associated with the direct production function should be deferred as acquisition costs, assuming, of course, that the variability test is satisfied.

Recruiting. As indicated earlier in this chapter, recruiting is a development cost that would not qualify for deferral as an acquisition cost. Such costs would rarely be associated with the production of a single year. Recruiting costs would include the portion of managers' salaries associated with the time spent on recruiting, implicit or explicit recruiting allowances to general agents, travel expenses incurred in recruiting, advertising for agents, the cost of operating a home office recruiting unit, and so forth. Development costs, including recruiting, are discussed in Chapter 17.

Training. Agent training has the same characteristics as recruiting. It is designed to bring an agent up to the point at which he can sell effectively for the company. It is therefore a development cost that generally is not associated with the production of a given year. Training costs tend to ebb and flow with recruiting costs, since new agents must usually be trained. Training costs would include such items as salaries to branch managers associated with the time he spends on training, training allowances to general agents, training materials, maintenance of training facilities such as classrooms, the cost of operating a home office training department, CLU reimbursements, and so on. The cost of training established agents differs somewhat from the cost of training new agents in that the objective of such training is to make an effective agent more effective, to update or refine his skills; but it is still training, the cost of which is shouldered in the hope that the agent will in fact become more productive in the current and future years. So training would normally fail the variability or attribution tests or both.

Financing. Financing was discussed earlier in this chapter. As a general rule only that portion of financing that can be associated with specific units of production, whether by imputation of a normal commission or otherwise, should be deferred as acquisition costs.

Agents' balances written off usually represent financing gone awry, but not always. Sometimes, for example, an uncollectible sub-agent's balance which technically is the responsibility of the general agent is "forgiven" to retain the good will of the general agent. Whatever the case, agents' balances written off should never be regarded as an acquisition cost. It is often argued that the amount written off is merely a cost of developing agents—that some agents succeed and some fail, and the cost of uncollectible agents' balances is properly associated with the successes and hence should qualify for deferral. Nevertheless, even if the argument has merit, agents' balances written off is a financing cost, and financing costs are development costs, not acquisition costs.

Field supervision. In addition to branch managers companies often have regional supervisors who oversee the efforts of agents within a given geographical area. The portion of a regional supervisor's compensation associated with the time devoted to actual supervision of established producing agents may generally be regarded as an acquisition cost if it meets the variability criterion.

Companies that actively solicit brokerage business will usually have salaried marketing personnel to recruit brokers and maintain sound relationships with them. Brokers are established producers, and the efforts of a brokerage administrator can usually be traced to specific volumes of production. The cost of such brokerage support should usually qualify for deferral as acquisition costs.

Other agency support. The cost of an agents' convention can sometimes be regarded as a deferrable acquisition cost. That is because agents usually must meet production quotas to qualify to attend such conventions; hence they are in the nature of production bonuses.

Product advertising would usually not be deferrable; except for mail order companies (discussed below), it is virtually impossible to establish a causal relationship between product advertising and production.

Market research is either an administrative cost or a development cost, depending in part on the nature of the research and in part on one's point of view. In either case, the costs associated with market research activity would not be deferrable as acquisition costs.

A home office conservation unit usually has two functions—attempting to assign responsibility for, or otherwise conserve, orphaned business; and devising programs to maintain or improve persistency. The cost of such an operation should be treated as overhead. This may seem inconsistent with the treatment accorded persistency bonuses to agents, but persistency bonuses are paid only to the extent that persistency is specifically identifiable, and hence the cost qualifies as a renewal-year acquisition cost. Home office conservation efforts are not disciplined by such impartial criteria, and the costs can rarely be traced to specific units of production. Usually they would fail the tests of variability and demonstrability.

It is not possible to suggest all of the possible agency support activities that would be encountered in practice. Determining whether a given agency support cost meets the tests of variability and attribution is often very difficult, but difficult or not, the determination must be made for any portion of such costs to qualify for deferral as acquisition costs.

Mail Order Solicitation Costs

Companies operating on the mail order plan are very different. They have no agents. Instead of "hard" dollars paid to agents, their acquisition costs consist of advertising, postage, printing, and other relatively "soft" costs that would for the most part be expensed as period costs by a company operating on the general agency or branch office plan. Sometimes their first-year expenses seem disproportionately high in relation to first-year premiums.

First-year costs. Some observers of mail order companies have expressed surprise—even dismay—at the level of first-year costs. By comparison with companies operating on the general agency or branch office plans the costs simply seem out of line. Where an agency operation might defer costs equal to, say, 130 percent of first-year premiums, a mail order company might defer costs equal to, say, 200 percent.*

These observers frequently overlook two significant facts in comparing a mail order company with a company that sells through agents:

▸ The mail order company pays no renewal commissions. Therefore, the proper way to compare the cost of a mail order sale with the cost of an agent sale is to measure the mail order company's first-year costs against the present value of first-year costs plus all renewal commissions paid by a company that sells through agents. Table 14–6 portrays a computation of such a present value. If the facts shown in Table 14–6 applied in the circumstances, a mail order company could defer about 183 per-

*The percentages given are, of course, hypothetical.

Table 14–6.

ILLUSTRATIVE COMPUTATION OF PRESENT VALUE OF FIRST-YEAR ACQUISITION COSTS AND
RENEWAL-YEAR COMMISSIONS

Year	Mortality and Lapse	Surviving and Persisting	First-Year Acquisition Costs and Renewal-Year Commissions	5% Discount	Present Value at 5% of First-Year Acquisition Costs and Renewal Year Commissions
1	15%	100.0%	130.0%	1.000	130.0%
2	10	85.0	17.5	.952	14.2
3	8	76.5	12.5	.907	8.7
4	7	70.4	7.5	.864	4.6
5	6	65.5	7.5	.823	4.1
6	5	61.6	7.5	.784	3.5
7	4	59.1	7.5	.746	3.3
8	4	56.7	7.5	.711	3.0
9	4	54.5	7.5	.677	2.8
10	4	52.3	7.5	.645	2.5
11	4	50.2	5.0	.614	1.5
12	5	48.1	5.0	.585	1.4
13	5	45.7	5.0	.557	1.3
14	5	43.4	5.0	.530	1.2
15	5	41.2	5.0	.505	1.0
					183.1%

cent of first-year premiums (as compared with deferral of 130 percent by the company that sells through agents) and still maintain actuarial equivalency with the company that sells through agents.

▶ While a mail order company often seeks to market its product to a group of people known to need or desire the type of product being offered, the fact is that the initial mailing is a kind of sorting process. There will be many people in the group who will not take the insurance. The response rate—the percentage of favorable responses that a particular mailing draws—might be, say, one in 1,000. In other words, each 1,000 mailings results in a single application for insurance. The group that responds constitutes, in effect, a preselected group of people who are known to buy insurance through the mail. Future mailings for additional products may be expected to draw a better response. If the response rate on a subsequent mailing increases to, say, five per 1,000 mailings, unit acquisition costs would decrease dramatically—80 percent in this case, all other things being equal. The high initial costs might be viewed in part as an investment in business to be obtained subsequently.

Whether in fact first-year mail-order costs will turn out to be the actuarial equivalent of the cost of an agency sale, or whether in fact the expectation of higher response rates on additional mailings will be realized, depend to a large degree on future events. Inspection of Table 14–6 will indicate, for example, that the equivalency suffers as the lapse rate increases.

Nevertheless, these two considerations suggest why mail order companies are willing to spend substantial sums to acquire business. Much of the business, it should be pointed out, is of a type that could not economically be marketed by agents.

Deferrable marketing costs. As a general rule, costs of soliciting business that are traceable to specific volumes of production are deferrable. While response rates and hence cost-volume relationships may vary from campaign to campaign, costs incurred with respect to any given campaign vary with the results of that campaign by definition, and the costs also meet the tests of attribution.

Solicitation costs qualifying for deferral would include the following:

For mail campaigns:
   A customer list purchased for one-time use in the specific campaign

257

Copy design
Paper
Printing
Postage (outgoing and franchise returns)
Distribution (i.e., stuffing and handling the mailing)
For media campaigns:
Copy design
Media liaison (i.e., arranging for the advertisements)
Advertising space
Postage (franchise returns)
For "piggyback" mail campaigns:
Specific costs of "piggyback" rights
Copy design
Paper
Printing
Postage (outgoing, to the extent of any incremental costs, plus franchise returns)
Distribution (i.e., stuffing and otherwise participating in the mailing)

Other approaches will be found in practice. For example, brochures advertising insurance might be placed in grocery bags in supermarkets, or pads of applications might be hung in a bus or subway in conjunction with an advertising panel. Usually the pattern of costs will fit one or a combination of the patterns set forth.

The costs may be incurred in the form of purchased outside services or the operation of internal departments. For example, printing could be performed by an outside printer or the company's own print shop. The cost should be measured by invoiced costs or departmental costs, as applicable. Where a department performs the function, unit costs should generally be based on normal capacity to eliminate the possibility of deferring what are, in effect, fixed costs. In other words, the cost per unit of effort for a particular type of operation should be relatively constant from campaign to campaign.

The costs must be identifiable in terms of specific campaigns to meet the attribution tests. Thus, for example, general product advertising would not qualify for deferral for a mail order company any more than for a company operating on the general agency or branch office plan.

Costs associated with general marketing management, market research, response evaluation, and the like should not be regarded as deferrable.

The processing of applications after they have been received in the mail marks the beginning of the selection process. Usually a company offers to send a policy for inspection by the policyholder, during which time the policyholder is covered. For this interim coverage a nominal premium is usually paid. Only a certain percentage of the policyholders "convert" to regular coverage by paying the first regular premium. The non-converted policies are similar to not-taken policies in a company operating on the general agency or branch office plan. Costs incurred during the trial period could be regarded as selling costs, but they should as a practical matter be treated as issue costs, similar to the treatment usually accorded such costs by companies that sell through agents.

Effect of "load" potential. Some believe that the expected results of future "loads"—i.e., additional sales to existing policyholders—should be taken into account in deferring mail order solicitation costs. This could be done in two ways:

▶ By amortizing initial costs in a manner that anticipates future premiums on future sales net of the reduced level of acquisition costs to be amortized against such future premiums.
▶ By holding some portion of the initial cost in suspense and allocating it to "loads" as the "loads" materialize, presumably on the basis of some "normal" cost computed with regard for the entire volume of business, present and future, expected to flow from the initial campaign.

In either case, a portion of the initial acquisition cost is regarded as development cost, buried in unamortized acquisition costs in the first instance and separately captioned in the second. Presumably recoverability would be tested in terms of margins on future business as well as business already sold; to do otherwise would be grossly inconsistent.

This procedure involves too much conjecture. While a mail order company might be evaluated partly in terms of "load" potential, such potential is theoretical until it is realized. It isn't known with sufficient certainty whether a given group will respond as expected or whether the product offered will capture their fancy. For example, because an individual buys a health policy through the mail doesn't mean he will buy a life insurance policy. To anticipate that he will is one thing, but to formalize the anticipation in the accounting process is quite another. Anticipation for accounting purposes would seem to violate the requirement that adverse deviation be provided for. A reasonable application of the concept of adverse deviation would require that existing business support costs already incurred.

The fact is that mail order companies have an inherent initial accounting advantage over other companies already. To the extent that (1) costs are traceable to specific campaigns, (2) the costs can therefore be deferred as acquisition costs, (3) the business produced will support the costs incurred, and (4) the company expects a future benefit with respect to future new business in the form of reduced acquisition costs on such business, the mail order company is deferring an element of cost that could be regarded as a development cost (i.e., the excess of the initial unit costs over the average unit costs for all business to be placed with the initial group of policyholders). Such excess cost will operate to reduce reported margins on existing business, but margins on future business from the same policyholders will be higher (assuming, of course, that such future business materializes). To go beyond the initial advantage seems somewhat unfair.

Selection Costs

Costs of underwriting a policy generally vary with production in a step-cost relationship, and such costs typically meet all of the attribution criteria. An underwriting department is a relatively straightforward example of a "production" department.

Selection costs qualifying for deferral would usually include salaries of underwriters involved directly in the underwriting process, salaries of supervisory-level personnel whose responsibility is limited to direct supervision of underwriters, salaries of clerical support of the underwriting function, expenses of medical examinations and inspection reports, MIB fees, and the portion of a medical department's costs that relate to effort devoted solely to underwriting consultation. Costs incurred for printing of underwriting forms, telephone calls by underwriters, etc., would also normally qualify.

Such costs would be deferrable whether incurred in the home office or in regional or branch offices. In the case of branch offices in which a certain amount of underwriting is done, the employees performing the underwriting function typically have other duties; there is no separate underwriting department whose costs are readily identifiable. In such cases it will be necessary to allocate the portion of the branch office cost that relates to the time devoted to underwriting functions.

The senior underwriting executive should generally be regarded as general management; his salary and the salaries of his secretaries and assistants should not be deferred. Nor should any costs associated with medical, statistical, or other research.

Selection costs should be allocated to paid-for policies, without reduction for declinations and policies not taken. The fundamental role of an underwriting operation is to measure risk and ensure the integrity of the pool of insureds, and the pool of insureds represents the appropriate basis for allocating costs to units of production.

Selection costs are usually not incurred in respect of term renewals or term conversions. In the case of term conversions, such savings are usually offset against extra mortality costs in computing the cost of conversion for reserving purposes. The imputed savings are, in effect, capitalized in the form of a reduced provision for future extra mortality. At the time of conversion the "savings" are released as the reserve is released, and the reserve on the converted policy picks up the full mortality provision. To illustrate, assume that the savings in selection costs are $4 and the extra mortality is $10, and that at the time of conversion the related portion of the term reserve is $6. As the term policy goes out of force the $6 reserve is released, the reserve on the converted policy is $10, and the net effect on operations is a $4 charge. In theory, the $4 charge should be capitalized, since in this case the purpose of the provision for the cost of conversion is to produce a normal profit on the converted policy (as discussed in Chapter 8). In practice, this is rarely done. When term conversions are material, however, consideration should be given to offsetting the savings against the mortality charge at the time of conversion and amortizing the offset.

Issue Costs

Costs associated with issuing a policy—policy forms, policy preparation costs, premium calculations (whether manual or automated), setting up all of the records initially, control and suspense procedures pending delivery, and the cost of delivery itself—are properly deferrable as acquisition costs.

Branch offices frequently perform fairly significant issue functions; the portion of the branch office cost associated with such functions would usually qualify for deferral if it meets the variability test.

Costs of issuing term renewals and term conversions are also properly deferrable. Term renewal issue costs are properly anticipated from the moment of original issue, after the fashion of anticipating renewal commissions that exceed the ultimate rate. Term conversion issue costs are effectively anticipated through the mechanism of the cost of conversion provision where cost of conversion is based on the difference between profits on a standard policy and profits on the converted policy. So deferral of the costs would be consistent with the reserving procedure.

Indirect Costs

The life insurance audit guide makes only one direct statement about indirect costs:

The inclusion of any indirect expenses in acquisition expenses requires judgment on the part of both the company and the auditor with overriding considerations being those of reasonable conservatism, consistency, and recoverability.[7]

It goes without saying that any deferred acquisition costs, direct or indirect, must meet the test of recoverability. The need for consistency is also unquestioned; auditors, for example, must indicate in their opinions on financial statements not only that the statements have (or have not) been prepared in conformity with generally accepted accounting principles but also that such principles have (or have not) been applied consistently in the current and preceding years.

The real challenge in implementing the audit guide's provisions as to indirect costs is to define "reasonable conservatism". First, however, a word about what an "indirect cost" is.

Nature of Indirect Costs

In the manufacturing industries it is generally quite easy to distinguish between direct and indirect costs. Direct costs are materials and labor applied directly to the manufacture of a product. Such costs are "obviously related to and expediently traceable to" [8] the product. Indirect costs are "all factory costs other than direct material and direct labor: for example, supplies, indirect labor, heat, light, property taxes, repairs, depreciation on plant and equipment, and insurance." [9]

In the life insurance business the distinction is not so easily made. A commission to a sub-agent is a direct cost, "obviously related to and expediently traceable to" units of new business; so is the cost of a medical examination or inspection report. Thereafter the distinction blurs. Is a branch manager's salary a direct cost or an indirect cost? How about the cost of

the space he occupies? Is a pro rata charge from a data processing department to the issue department for setting up initial policy records a direct cost? Suppose the data processing charge includes a provision for covering a pro rata share of the data processing department's overhead?

The problem of distinguishing between direct and indirect costs is further complicated by the necessity to classify costs by function; functionalization is needed to identify the types of costs that relate to production. Determining the cost of a "function" involves measuring inputs from many departments, some of which may perform numerous operations having nothing to do with new business. The need to allocate a homogenous pool of costs between new business functions and other functions immediately raises the question of whether a cost that has to be allocated is direct.

Some believe that if a given cost varies with production it is automatically a direct cost. However, that is not necessarily the case. The data processing charge to the issue department is a good example of a variable cost that is not direct. Data processing will usually base its charges on work performed; thus the charge to the issue department will always vary with production. But the costs of the data processing department itself will not vary much. It is an ongoing operation with heavy fixed costs which themselves will not vary with production.

A direct cost should be viewed as a cost that by its nature varies with and is "obviously related to and expediently traceable to" units of new business. This would usually include commissions to sub-agents, production overrides, production and persistency bonuses, salaries of full-time underwriters, costs of medical examinations and inspection reports, printed forms used in the selling, selection, and issue processes, and salaries of personnel working exclusively on issuing policies. In the case of mail order companies direct costs would include solicitation costs (discussed earlier in this chapter) plus the underwriting and issue costs outlined above.

All other costs, and particularly costs requiring allocation between new business and other functions, should be regarded as indirect costs unless it can clearly be demonstrated that the cost is as readily traceable to new business as the items listed above.

Allocating Indirect Costs to New Business Functions

For purposes of discussing the assignment of indirect costs to new business functions it is useful to think of selling, selection, and issue departments as operating departments. Direct costs within those departments are assignable to new business. This leaves two types of indirect costs to consider: (1) indirect costs incurred within the departments themselves, and (2) costs incurred in other departments that provide services to the operating departments.

Intra-departmental costs that would generally qualify for allocation to new business functions would include the costs of supervision of and direct support for those functions whose costs are assignable to new business as direct costs. This would usually include, for example, such portion of a branch manager's salary as relates to the time he spends on supervision of agents' selling efforts, as well as a pro rata share of the cost of the space he occupies, secretarial assistance, and miscellaneous items such as telephone costs. It would generally include the cost of the space occupied by underwriters and issue personnel, clerical assistance rendered to such personnel, and miscellaneous costs such as telephone expense and postage.

Inter-departmental charges that would generally qualify for allocation to new business functions would include reasonable charges, predicated on actual work performed and priced on the basis of normal capacity, of the data processing department, office services (reproduction, mail room, printing, file service, and the like), and the accounting and policyholder service departments (but only to the extent that those departments perform services that could be performed directly by the operating departments).

Fringe benefits applicable to direct and indirect compensation deferred as acquisition costs should also be deferred.

"Reasonable Conservatism"

The procedures suggested above for accounting for indirect costs would seem to do justice to the audit guide's criterion of "reasonable conservatism". The procedure involves allocating to new business functions only those indirect costs that can logically and equitably be deemed to be related primarily to the production of new business. Variability must still be demonstrated; however, in the case of interdepartmental charges, variability would normally be achieved by basing the charges on unit costs computed on the basis of normal capacity. It isn't necessary that

the costs of service departments themselves vary with new business.

The suggested procedure applies some of the principles of manufacturing cost accounting—particularly process costing—to the problem of accounting for acquisition costs. In the manufacturing industries, the methods of accounting for indirect production costs have become fairly standardized through experience and custom. Thus factory burden is allocated to production. In the life insurance business "factory burden" is often not distinguishable from maintenance or overhead and there is very little custom available for guidance. So the determination of what indirect costs properly relate to production in the life insurance business is necessarily somewhat arbitrary. The alternative is to expense all indirect costs, but that is equally as arbitrary and seems somewhat inequitable.

The suggested procedure provides for a fair degree of conservatism and discipline in defining indirect costs that would qualify as acquisition costs. To go beyond the suggested procedure would seem to go beyond the boundaries of "reasonable conservatism", and would inevitably lead to deferring costs that are more properly regarded as maintenance or overhead. Maintenance and overhead, in the guide's words, "should be charged to operations in the period incurred." [10]

Latitude Allowed by the Audit Guide

The life insurance audit guide allows a measure of latitude in deferring indirect costs. The language of the guide is such as to discourage deferral of indirect costs, but deferral is in fact permitted. Thus the guide implicitly permits (1) no deferral at all or (2) a reasonably conservative deferral.

This latitude unfortunately introduces a measure of non-uniformity into the financial statements in an area in which reasonable uniformity could have been achieved. The guide preferably should have specified that indirect costs be included or excluded, but not both. Certainly a manufacturing company ordinarily does not have a similar choice in costing its inventory.

Hopefully practice will evolve toward a reasonably conservative deferral of indirect costs that are logically associated with new business functions. Non-deferral would seem to be unduly conservative.

15 Deferral of Acquisition Costs

It is all well and good to philosophize over the proper composition of deferrable acquisition costs, as was done in Chapter 14; but eventually the difficult task of accumulating costs and actually making the deferral must be undertaken.

The task can usually be divided into five sub-tasks:

▶ *Cost analysis,* to determine the costs that apply to each line of business and, within each line, the costs that will be considered for deferral.

▶ *Cost accumulation,* to assemble the costs that are to be deferred in a format that will facilitate subsequent analysis of and accounting for such costs.

▶ *Allocation* of deferrable costs to plans or blocks of business.

▶ *Comparison* of actual acquisition costs and assumed acquisition costs, to test reasonableness and recoverability.

▶ *Final expression* of deferrable acquisition costs in a format that is compatible with the company's method of amortization.

While the sub-tasks are listed separately above, and are discussed separately below, in practice many of them would be carried out more or less simultaneously. For example, it would be logical to analyze costs and accumulate them at the same time.

Cost Analysis

Cost analysis consists of (1) determining costs allocable to each line of business, (2) determining costs associated with new business functions, (3) segregating costs that meet the attribution criteria, and (4) testing such segregated costs for variability.

Line-of-Business Allocations

All companies must allocate expenses to the various lines of business for purposes of the statutory statements. The degree of refinement in such allocations varies considerably. Normally items of expense that apply to a specific line of business are charged to that line of business, but the accuracy with which even direct charges are classified depends in part on the company's method of coding expenses. Indirect charges, overhead items, etc., are usually allocated to lines of business based on premiums, salaries, or other apportionment bases.

Companies that have functional cost programs must allocate most expenses to the various lines of business in order to compute functional costs for a particular line. This is obvious; one cannot calculate functional costs for, say, the ordinary line without knowing the aggregate expenses that apply to the ordinary line. Some companies make many of the line-of-business allocations on the basis of studies undertaken to derive functional costs. Other companies allocate expenses by line by a combination of techniques and *then* functionalize them.

However the allocation is made, it should be rational and accurate. This is particularly important as regards those items of expense that may wind up being deferred as acquisition costs. Thus allocations of expenses that can reasonably be associated with selling, selection, and issue functions should be made with considerable care.

Crazy Quilt Life, of course, participates in the LOMA functional cost program and hence allocates most of its expenses to the various lines of business in connection with that program. Crazy Quilt's line-

Table 15–1.

SUMMARY OF EXPENSE ALLOCATED TO ORDINARY LIFE LINES OF BUSINESS IN CRAZY QUILT'S 1971 CONVENTION STATEMENT (000 Omitted)

	Ordinary Life Basic Plans	*Total and Permanent Disability*	*Additional Accidental Death*	*Supplementary Contracts*	*Total*
Commissions:					
First-year	$ 8,203	$122	$ 81		$ 8,406
Renewal	1,816	50	33		1,899
TOTAL COMMISSIONS	10,019	172	114		10,305
General expenses	18,333	115	77	$6	18,531
Taxes, licenses, fees	2,101	25	16		2,142
Interest on modified coinsurance reserve transfers	25				25
TOTAL EXPENSES	30,478	312	207	6	31,003
Reinsurance items:					
Renewal coinsurance and modified coinsurance reimbursements	48				48
Interest on modified coinsurance reserve transfers	(25)				(25)
DIRECT EXPENSES	$30,501	$312	$207	$6	$31,026

of-business allocations were discussed in Chapter 13 and are summarized in Table 13–2. Reference to Table 13–2 will indicate that costs allocated to the ordinary line of business (exclusive of costs applicable to individual annuities, which were segregated for special treatment) aggregated $31,003,000.

Table 15–1 re-summarizes expenses charged to the ordinary line of business and, in addition, adjusts for certain coinsurance items in order to derive total *direct* costs, which is what Crazy Quilt is concerned with at this point.

New Business Functional Costs

After distributing costs by line of business it is necessary to segregate them between costs associated with new business functions—selling, selection, and issue —and costs associated with maintenance and overhead.

First-year commissions. First-year commissions reported in the Convention Statement represent commissions incurred in the first policy year.

The portion of first-year commissions that is truly associated with the production function is the excess of the amount of commissions paid over the amount of commissions that would have been paid if the ultimate commission rate had been in effect. In other words, commissions at the ultimate rate are maintenance expenses payable in every year including the first.

By reference to production records and commission scales, Crazy Quilt was able to determine the approximate ultimate rates for 1971 production. How this is done, and the types of decisions it involves, are discussed later in this chapter. For the moment it is only necessary to understand that it was done by Crazy Quilt in determining commissions that might qualify as acquisition costs. The result of the analysis is summarized in Table 15–2.

Table 15–2 also segregates commissions among commissions to sub-agents, overrides, and production bonuses for ordinary life basic plans. Crazy Quilt maintains separate ledger accounts for these items. As the footnote to Table 15–2 indicates, allocations of commissions to supplemental benefits are based on average rates for all ordinary life business taken as a whole; Crazy Quilt does not account separately for commissions applicable to supplemental benefits.

Table 15–2.

SUMMARY OF FIRST-YEAR COMMISSIONS IN EXCESS OF COMMISSIONS PAYABLE AT "ULTIMATE" RATE
(000 Omitted)

	First Year Commissions	Commissions At Ultimate Rates	Acquisition Cost Commissions
Ordinary life basic plans:			
Commissions to sub-agents	$7,165	$270	$6,895
Overrides	784	78	706
Production bonuses	254		254
	8,203	348	7,855
Total and permanent disability*	122	11	111
Additional accidental death*	81	7	74
Supplementary contracts	–0–	–0–	–0–
	$8,406	$366	$8,040

*Commissions have been allocated to these lines of business based on average rates for commissions to sub-agents, overrides, and production bonuses. The individual amounts shown for such items under "ordinary life basic plans" have been reduced for allocations to the supplemental benefits. As is true of most companies, Crazy Quilt does not maintain separate ledger accounts for commissions on supplemental benefit premiums.

General insurance expenses. A company that has an on-going functional cost program will already have a segregation of general insurance expenses by function. Crazy Quilt, for example, participates in the LOMA functional cost program; and the $18,531,000 of ordinary general insurance expenses were already functionalized as shown in Table 13–4. New business functional costs are reconciled with the line-of-business total in Table 15–3.

Several assumptions had to be made at this point about the nature of costs associated with supplemental benefits and supplementary contracts. Crazy Quilt made the following assumptions:

▸ The only acquisition costs deemed to be applicable to supplemental benefits (such as waiver of

premium and accidental death) were commissions. The underlying policy was assumed to bear all other acquisition costs. This is a reasonable assumption because the effort required to add a rider or supplemental benefit to a basic plan is usually nominal, and the associated cost can ususally be presumed to be nominal.

▸ For all practical purposes, the premium-paying period for a supplemental benefit coincides with the premium-paying period of the underlying policy. Of course, the waiver benefit usually terminates at age 65 regardless of the term of the underlying policy. In Crazy Quilt's case, however, the average age at issue is about 35; it was recognized that even with respect to whole life business there would be a relatively small percentage of insurance orig-

Table 15–3.

RECONCILIATION OF NEW BUSINESS FUNCTIONAL COSTS WITH TOTAL OF GENERAL INSURANCE EXPENSES FOR ORDINARY LINE OF BUSINESS (000 Omitted)

Functionalized initial expenses:	
Selling	$ 9,192
Selection	1,727
Issue	597
	11,516
Functionalized maintenance expenses	3,339
TOTAL FUNCTIONALIZED COSTS	14,855
Service and overhead not functionalized	3,676
GENERAL INSURANCE EXPENSES FOR ORDINARY LINE	$18,531

Table 15–4.

1971 COMMISSIONS AND COMMISSION EQUIVALENTS DEEMED TO RELATE PRIMARILY TO PRODUCTION (000 Omitted)

	Total
Ordinary life basic plans:	
Commissions to sub-agents	$6,895
Overrides to general agents	706
Amounts paid in lieu of overrides to branch managers	864
Production bonuses to general agents	254
Production bonuses to branch managers	310
	9,029
Total and permanent disability	111
Additional accidental death	74
	$9,214

inally issued still in force at age 65; and any non-commission acquisition costs applicable to the waiver benefit that remained unamortized at age 65 because of having assigned them to the basic plans would be negligible indeed.

▸ Supplementary contracts usually do not give rise to acquisition costs of any consequence. There is a nominal cost involved in setting up records for, and issuing, a supplementary contract, but such costs are almost always immaterial. There is no underwriting effort and no selling effort. In any event, in Crazy Quilt's case supplementary contracts were issued and administered by the policyholders' service department, and any costs associated therewith were effectively functionalized as maintenance costs. So the costs identified as "initial" costs

under the LOMA program already excluded costs applicable to supplementary contracts.

So the total amount of LOMA "initial" expenses—$11,516,000—was regarded as being applicable to basic ordinary life plans issued by Crazy Quilt Life.

Meeting the Attribution Criteria

Functional costs provide a good starting point for determining what costs meet the attribution criteria—that is, what costs are "primarily related to" production.

But conventionally calculated functional costs are *only* a starting point. It would rarely be appropriate to treat functional costs, as conventionally defined, as acquisition costs without modification.

Table 15–5.

DETAILS OF SELLING FUNCTIONAL COSTS (000 Omitted)

	Salaries	*Other*	*Total*
Sales production	$2,038	$1,433	$3,471
Agent recruiting	426	669	1,095
Agent training	771	745	1,516
Administration of agents' activities	360	283	643
Agents' club meetings	134	742	876
Home office and regional supervision	427	525	952
Field management training	299	142	441
All other	119	79	198
	$4,574	$4,618	$9,192

Table 15–6.

DETAILS OF ADJUSTMENTS REQUIRED TO DERIVE 1971 DEFERRABLE SALES SUPPORT COSTS (000 Omitted)

| | *Total* | *Commission Equivalents* | *Reductions for* | | *Deferrable Acquisition Costs* |
			Development	*Overhead*	
Sales production	$ 3,471	$ 1,638	$ 127	$102	$1,604
Recruiting	1,095		1,062	33	
Training	1,516		1,469	47	
Administration	643		625	18	
Agents' meetings	876		123	27	726
Home office and regional supervision	952		138	30	784
Field management training	441		101	12	328
All other	198		191	7	
Total per functional cost analysis	9,192	1,638	3,836	276	3,442
Additional overhead allocated for rate-test purposes	1,641		1,176	465	
Reclassification of certain commission equivalents	(1,174)	(1,638)	289		175
Total per actuarial analysis (Table 13–5)	$ 9,659	$ –0–	$5,301	$741	$3,617

The reason is that conventional functional costs normally include items of cost that are not primarily related to production, that do not vary with production, or that *neither* relate to nor vary with production.

Commissions and commission equivalents. As suggested in Chapter 14, commissions may vary with production but it cannot be taken for granted that they primarily relate to production. To the extent that commissions include amounts properly associated with financing, recruiting, training, office allowances, and the like, such amounts should be excluded in determining what portion of commissions relates primarily to the production of new business.

In Crazy Quilt's case, analysis indicated that commissions related purely to production. Financing payments were recorded as agents' balances; entries to the commission account were limited to commissions earned. Office allowances to general agents were made in the form of direct payments of specified office expenses. Recruiting and training allowances were clearly identified as such and were charged to Exhibit 5 accounts (i.e., to general insurance expenses).

Therefore, total commissions to sub-agents, over-rides to general agents, and production bonuses—reduced by the equivalent of commissions at the ultimate rate—were regarded as deferrable acquisition costs.

In addition, because 55 percent of Crazy Quilt's new business was produced by branch offices headed by salaried managers, a portion of the managers' salaries was regarded as equivalent to general agents' overrides. Crazy Quilt had, in connection with its functional cost program, analyzed the activities of branch managers and found that $960,000 in salaries to branch managers was properly allocable to 1971 production. However, such salaries had to be reduced by the equivalent of a "renewal" salary, which is the salary equivalent of commissions payable at an ultimate rate. Crazy Quilt did this by imputing an ultimate rate equal to the ultimate rate associated with general agency business and applying such imputed rate to first-year premiums produced by branch offices. The reduction resulting from this calculation amounted to $96,000; hence deferrable branch manager salaries totaled $864,000 ($960,000, total salaries allocable to new business, less $96,000, the imputed

Table 15–7.

SUMMARY OF 1971 COSTS DEEMED TO RELATE PRIMARILY TO PRODUCTION—ORDINARY LIFE BASIC PLANS (000 Omitted)

Commissions and commission equivalents:	
Commissions to sub-agents	$ 6,895
Overrides to general agents	706
Amounts paid in lieu of overrides to branch managers	864
Production bonuses to general agents	254
Production bonuses to branch managers	310
	9.029
Sales support:	
Amount computed to be deferrable per Table 15–6	3,442
Adjustment for payroll taxes at 6% of salaries including branch manager salaries classified as commission equivalents*	175
	3,617
Selection:	
Functional cost total	1,727
Adjustment for payroll taxes at 6% of salaries included in functional cost total	52
	1,779
Issue:	
Functional cost total	597
Adjustment for payroll taxes at 6% of salaries included in functional cost total	18
	615
TOTAL DEFERRABLE COSTS	$15,040

*Crazy Quilt does not pay payroll taxes on its agents' earnings.

renewal portion). To this was added $310,000 in production bonuses paid to branch managers.

Total commissions and commission equivalents deemed to be primarily related to 1971 production for Crazy Quilt are summarized in Table 15–4. Since commissions on supplemental benefits were allocated to total and permanent disability and additional accidental death based on average rates, no adjustment was needed in respect of commission equivalents.

Sales support. As Table 15–3 indicates, Crazy Quilt calculated that selling expenses other than commissions totaled $9,192,000.

However, $1,270,000 of this amount had been treated as commission equivalents, i.e., $960,000 in branch managers' salaries allocable to first-year business (of which $96,000 was eliminated as being equivalent to renewal commissions) and $310,000 in production bonuses to branch managers. This left $7,922,000 to account for.

Because Crazy Quilt annually conducts selling depth studies that segregate selling costs by several sub-functions, analysis of the elements of the $7,922,000 was fairly straightforward. The sub-functions and related costs are shown in Table 15–5. Selling sub-

functions that were deemed to be primarily related to the production of new business were sales production, agents' conventions, and regional supervision; derivation of the related deferrable costs is shown in Table 15–6.

Selection and issue. Selection and issue functional costs of $1,727,000 and $597,000, respectively, were considered fully deferrable. No part of the salary and related costs of the executive vice presidents in charge of those functions was charged to the functions. However, salaries of executives directly involved with the functions were regarded as deferrable on the basis that their efforts were entirely related to the production of new business.

Indirect costs. Crzay Quilt's new business functional costs included pro-rations of the costs of service departments, principally data processing, office services, policyholder service, and—to a very limited extent—actuarial and accounting services peculiar to the production process. Review indicated that the allocation process resulted in fair apportionments of such costs to the production operations whose direct costs were primarily related to production, and that transfer prices were based on standard costs that approximated actual costs under conditions of normal capacity.

As respects clerical salaries, rent, telephone, and similar expenses incurred by the producing departments, review indicated that such expenses were fairly determined, either by direct charges or by rational allocation based on space, usage, etc. In other words, direct costs identified as acquisition costs were deemed to bear their fair share of intra-departmental overhead.

Crazy Quilt's functional costs excluded taxes, licenses, and fees. Most such items are either maintenance expenses (e.g., premium taxes) or investment expenses (e.g., real estate taxes). However, payroll taxes are in the nature of additional payroll costs. Such costs are not included in functional costs, at least in Crazy Quilt's case. Analysis indicated that payroll taxes averaged 6 percent of salaries. So acquisition costs were increased to the extent of 6 percent of salaries included in functional costs.

Certain other fringe benefits, such as pension costs, had already been allocated to functions, and no adjustment was necessary. Additional employee welfare, such as cost of the company's cafeteria operation, as well as the costs of the personnel department, were treated as overhead and not functionalized, and this practice was followed for purposes of computing deferrable costs.

A summary of 1971 costs deemed to relate primarily to production is shown in Table 15–7.

Variability Tests

The life insurance audit guide provides that actual acquisition costs should be deferred. It also provides that only those costs which vary with production should be deferred. Obviously levels of cost change as commission scales change, mix of business and average size of policies change, and so on.

A central problem in testing variability of acquisition costs is determining the time periods within which variability should be measured. The problem is best illustrated by a simple example. Suppose a commission scale for the first ten years of a company's existence calls for 50 percent in the first year, 40 percent in the second year, and nothing thereafter. In the second ten years of the company's existence the scale changes to 75 percent in the first year and nothing thereafter. Obviously first-year commissions will vary directly with premiums during the first ten years, considered in isolation, and also during the second ten years, again considered in isolation. Viewing the 20 years as a whole, however, commissions would apparently not be variable unless commissions were expressed in the form of actuarial equivalents rather than in the form of first-year commissions incurred.

Another central problem relates to the production measure with which a given cost is compared. One might compare selection costs with in-force volume sold, but the variable relationship between selection costs and new business volume will be affected by the fact that some portion of selection costs varies with policies issued, not volume.

Finally, inasmuch as the audit guide requires that actual acquisition costs be deferred, inflation—which may disturb a relationship which would be fully variable in terms of constant dollars—should be considered. Variability during the time period under study should theoretically be measured in constant dollars, so inflation should be adjusted for—subjectively or otherwise—when examining historical data in connection with an evaluation of variability.

Thus keen judgment must be used in evaluating variability. Changes in operations, product characteristics, and the economic environment must always be taken into account. It will be the rare case in which operations or products never change, and it will also be the rare case in which unit costs do not also change.

Table 15–8 shows Crazy Quilt Life's initial variability test. It will be observed that unit costs change markedly over Crazy Quilt's 31-year existence. But cost-volume relationships are relatively constant during each ratebook era.

As regards commissions and commission equivalents, commission structures were usually changed only when products and product prices were changed.

As for sales support, inflation was a major factor in the increase in such costs, and the relationship of such costs to premiums was further affected by the long-term trend toward term insurance. Thus, while sales support expressed as a percentage of premiums rose from 16 percent in 1941 to 31 percent in 1971, sales support per $1,000 decreased from $5.32 in 1941 to $4.25 in 1971.

Selection costs per $1,000 decreased from 1941 to 1971 in spite of inflation because of a constant increase in average policy size.

Issue costs per policy increased from 1941 to 1971 partly because of inflation but mainly because of the increase in average policy size. Issue costs per $1,000 decreased from $1.88 in 1941 to $.72 in 1971.

These are examples of the methods used by Crazy Quilt to analyze the data. In effect, Crazy Quilt looked at each cost-volume relationship from several points of view. Eventually the company was

Table 15–8.

COSTS PRIMARILY RELATED TO PRODUCTION AND NEW BUSINESS VOLUME FOR ORDINARY LIFE BASIC PLANS, 1941–1971

Rate Book Era	Year	Costs Primarily Related to Production (000)					Production			Commissions, Etc., as Percentage of Premiums	Sales Support As Percentage of Premiums	Selection Costs Per $1,000	Issue Costs Per Policy
		Commissions and Equivalents	Sales Support	Selection	Issue	Total	Volume (000,000)	Premiums (000)	Policies				
1	1941	$ 500	$ 133	$ 79	$ 47	$ 759	$ 25	$ 844	9,197	59%	16%	$3.16	$5.11
	1942	686	181	109	64	1,040	35	1,150	12,552	60	16	2.11	5.10
	1943	898	238	143	84	1,363	47	1,503	16,416	60	16	3.04	5.12
	1944	1,068	282	170	100	1,620	56	1,784	19,500	60	16	3.03	5.13
	1945	1,321	346	203	116	1,986	71	2,194	22,742	60	16	2.85	5.10
	1946	1,541	397	223	124	2,285	83	2,562	24,301	60	15	2.69	5.10
	1947	1,682	435	244	138	2,499	92	2,797	26,435	60	16	2.65	5.22
2	1948	1,687	589	256	134	2,666	90	2,627	19,857	64	22	2.84	6.74
	1949	1,878	654	283	148	2,963	100	2,923	21,922	64	22	2.83	6.75
	1950	1,977	681	295	151	3,104	109	3,046	22,671	65	22	2.71	6.66
	1951	2,106	721	314	159	3,300	120	3,226	23,975	65	22	2.62	6.63
3	1952	1,999	831	324	156	3,310	128	3,212	20,406	62	26	2.53	7.64
	1953	2,039	847	331	157	3,374	134	3,246	20,625	63	26	2.47	7.61
	1954	2,005	835	328	155	3,323	135	3,184	20,312	63	26	2.43	7.63
	1955	1,833	764	302	141	3,040	128	2,884	18,487	64	27	2.36	7.63
	1956	1,587	663	264	121	2,635	116	2,477	15,937	64	27	2.28	7.59
4	1957	1,445	633	261	116	2,455	116	2,255	14,617	64	28	2.25	7.94
	1958	1,535	674	283	124	2,616	126	2,382	15,620	64	28	2.25	7.94
	1959	1,631	719	306	133	2,789	140	2,514	16,740	65	29	2.19	7.95
	1960	1,809	797	340	145	3,091	156	1,762	18,318	66	29	2.18	7.92
	1961	2,049	901	387	164	3,502	180	3,100	20,661	66	29	2.15	7.94
5	1962	2,493	1,002	459	176	4,130	216	3,245	20,340	77	31	2.13	8.65
	1963	3,275	1,307	588	224	5,394	283	4,245	25,921	77	31	2.08	8.64
	1964	3,926	1,560	701	265	6,452	340	5,069	30,542	78	31	2.06	8.68
	1965	4,557	1,829	833	311	7,530	407	5,922	35,832	77	31	2.05	8.68
	1966	5,321	2,132	971	361	8,785	476	6,909	41,489	77	31	2.04	8.70
	1967	6,122	2,452	1,115	413	10,102	548	7,948	47,419	77	31	2.03	8.71
6	1968	6,316	2,603	1,230	432	10,581	615	8,477	48,492	75	31	2.00	8.91
	1969	7,085	2,915	1,375	482	11,857	689	9,498	54,121	75	31	2.00	8.91
	1970	8,279	3,312	1,611	560	13,762	774	10,652	60,594	78	31	2.08	9.24
	1971	9,029	3,617	1,779	615	15,040	851	11,625	66,598	78	31	2.09	9.23

satisfied that, in all material respects, costs deemed to qualify for deferral varied with production.

In theory, each major category of cost should be segregated into three components—the portion that relates to volumes issued, the portion that relates to the number of policies issued, and the portion that relates to premiums—and variability should be evaluated separately with respect to each component. In practice, the data are rarely available to do this, and pragmatic approaches to measuring variability, such as those used by Crazy Quilt, will usually be necessary.

Renewal-Year Acquisition Costs

First-year acquisition costs are by far the most significant element of the acquisition cost deferral, but in many cases there are certain acquisition costs arising in renewal years that also need to be considered. Such items might include renewal-year commissions and commission equivalents in excess of ultimate levels of expense, costs incurred at the time of a term renewal, and costs incurred at the time of a term conversion.

Table 15–9.

RENEWAL-YEAR ACQUISITION COST COMMISSIONS AND COMMISSION EQUIVALENTS INCURRED IN 1971

Effective Rate	Products	Issue Year	Duration	Premiums Received (000)	Acquisition Costs Incurred (000)
2.0%	Limited-payment life, decreasing term	1970	2	$2,348	$ 47
5.5%	Par whole life, whole life, limited-payment life, decreasing term	1962	10	1,688	93
		1963	9	2,313	127
		1964	8	2,897	159
		1965	7	2,993	165
		1966	6	3,653	201
		1967	5	4,448	244
8.0%	Decreasing term	1968	4	796	64
10.5%	Decreasing term	1969	3	1,008	106
15.5%	All except limited-payment life and decreasing term	1970	2	6,031	935

DEFERRABLE RENEWAL-YEAR COMMISSIONS AND
COMMISSION EQUIVALENTS $2,141

Commissions and Commission Equivalents

As discussed in Chapter 14, the life insurance audit guide provides that renewal commissions in excess of the ultimate rate should be regarded as acquisition costs.

Normally it is virtually impossible to determine the annual amount of such excess because a life insurance company's accounting system just isn't that refined. The amounts can be approximated by analysis, but such analysis is extremely complex.

Take, for example, Crazy Quilt Life.

Determination of renewal-year acquisition costs incurred in 1971 involved (1) analyzing agents' contracts to determine the years and products for which excesses were payable, (2) determining the effective rates of such excesses, (3) analyzing premiums by issue year, product, and applicable rate, and (4) extending such premiums by the effective rates.

In Crazy Quilt's case, effective rates were determined by tallying up sub-agent commissions and overrides (with an imputed override equal to the general agent's override in the case of branch office business) and deducting ultimate rates assuming full vesting and no agent terminations. This latter policy was adopted in the interests of conservatism as well as practicality. Thus the amount computed as available for deferral was a conservative approximation.

Analysis of premiums by issue year and product was, of course, difficult. Once this was done, the various groupings of premiums were readily extended by the corresponding effective rates to obtain estimated renewal-year acquisition cost commissions and commission equivalents. The process is summarized in Table 15–9.

The total deferrable renewal-year commissions and commission equivalents are $2,141,000. Yet renewal commissions shown in the Convention Statement are only $1,816,000 (see Table 15–1). The two amounts may be reconciled as follows:

	000
Renewal-year commissions per books	$1,816
Coinsurance ceded commissions (see Table 15–1)	48
First-year commissions at ultimate rate (see Table 15–2)	348
Branch manager salaries—portion in the nature of renewal overrides	368
Branch manager salaries—portion allocated to first year but equivalent to amounts payable at ultimate rates	96
Adjusted total	2,676
Deferrable	2,141
BALANCE	$ 535

Table 15–10.

RENEWAL-YEAR ACQUISITION COSTS INCURRED 1941–1971 (000 Omitted)

| Year | Renewal-Year Acquisition Commissions and Commission Equivalents | Term Renewal Acquisition Costs | | | |
		Commissions and Commission Equivalents	Sales Support	Issue	Total
1941	$ –	$ –	$ –	$ –	$ –
1942					
1943					
1944					
1945					
1946	1	1	–	–	1
1947	1	2	–	–	2
1948	2	2	–	–	2
1949	186	2	1	–	3
1950	323	2	1	1	4
1951	438	2	1	1	4
1952	535	3	2	1	6
1953	375	4	3	2	9
1954	296	5	3	2	10
1955	253	7	4	2	13
1956	245	8	4	3	15
1957	337	10	5	3	18
1958	193	14	6	3	23
1959	142	15	7	4	26
1960	90	15	8	4	27
1961	35	15	6	3	24
1962	26	12	5	3	20
1963	407	13	5	3	21
1964	767	13	5	3	21
1965	1,125	13	6	3	22
1966	1,375	13	6	3	22
1967	1,672	12	5	3	20
1968	2,021	13	6	3	22
1969	1,721	13	5	3	21
1970	1,578	15	7	4	26
1971	2,141	40	20	10	70

The "balance", $535,000, consists primarily of commissions paid at ultimate rates—"service fees", for the most part.

Crazy Quilt performed the same type of analysis of renewal-year acquisition cost commissions and commission equivalents for each year since 1941. The result is summarized in Table 15–10.

Term Renewals

Expenses of issuing term renewals were treated as renewal expenses by Crazy Quilt Life. Commissions on renewals were recorded in the renewal commission accounts; other costs were functionalized as maintenance expenses.

It is important to adopt a consistent attitude toward term renewals. Crazy Quilt treats renewable term business as a continuum; the various renewal periods are considered to comprise a single contract life. Other companies treat each renewal as a new contract. Regardless of how the associated expenses are classified, acquisition costs incurred at the time of renewal should be deferred and amortized if they are material.

Inasmuch as Crazy Quilt treats commissions on term renewals as renewal commissions and functionalizes other costs as "policy changes" (a mainte-

Table 15–11.

COMPARISON OF ACTUAL VS. ESTIMATED DEFERRALS OF COMMISSIONS AND COMMISSION EQUIVALENTS
(000 Omitted)

ESTIMATED DEFERRALS

Year	Total Premiums*	Adjusted Renewal Commissions and Commission Equivalents*	Average Rate*	First-Year Premiums	Computed Deduction	First-Year Commissions and Commission Equivalents	Deferrable Commissions and Commission Equivalents
1945	$ 6,127	$ 441	7.2%	$ 2,195	$ 158	$1,483	$1,325
1950	15,147	842	5.6	3,047	171	2,098	1,927
1955	22,876	1,284	5.6	2,885	162	2,031	1,869
1960	26,418	1,499	5.7	2,762	157	1,991	1,834
1965	35,804	1,414	4.0	5,922	237	4,706	4,469
1966	39,590	1,478	3.7	6,909	256	5,494	5,238
1967	44,041	1,566	3.6	7,948	286	6,320	6,034
1968	48,674	1,982	4.1	8,477	348	6,799	6,451
1969	53,979	2,389	4.4	9,498	418	7,624	7,206
1970	60,078	2,505	4.2	10,652	447	8,602	7,826
1971	66,722	2,676	4.0	11,626	465	9,377	8,912

COMPARISON OF ACTUAL DEFERRAL WITH ESTIMATED DEFERRALS

Year	Deferrable per Tables 15–8 and 5–10				Deferrable as Computed Above	
	First-Year	Renewal	Term Renewals	Total	Ignoring Renewals	Deducting Average Renewals
1945	$1,321	$ -0-	$-0-	$ 1,321	$1,483	$1,325
1950	1,977	323	2	2,302	2,098	1,927
1955	1,833	253	7	2,093	2,031	1,869
1960	1,809	90	15	1,914	1,991	1,834
1965	4,557	1,125	13	5,695	4,706	4,469
1966	5,321	1,375	13	6,709	5,494	5,238
1967	6,122	1,672	12	7,806	6,320	6,034
1968	6,316	2,021	13	8,350	6,799	6,451
1969	7,085	1,721	13	8,819	7,624	7,206
1970	8,279	1,578	15	9,872	8,273	7,826
1971	9,029	2,141	40	11,210	9,377	8,912

* Usually this calculation would be made by dividing renewal commissions by renewal premiums, adjusting the former quantity by any renewal commission equivalents paid in the form of salaries. This is simply a somewhat refined version of the usual procedure.

nance function) under their functional cost program, it was necessary to estimate term renewal acquisition costs that were effectively buried in renewal commissions and maintenance costs. The estimate was made by reference to renewal data, renewal premiums paid in the year of renewal, commission rates applicable to renewals, and a study of relative sales and issue effort. Estimated term renewal acquisition costs incurred are summarized in Table 15–10.

Term Conversions

Term conversions are accounted for as new issues by Crazy Quilt, and all first-year commissions and selling and issue functional costs are included in the appropriate classifications of acquisition costs.

Where this is not the case—where, in other words, such costs are treated as maintenance costs—they should, if material, be determined by the type of analysis described above for term renewals.

Approximation Techniques

Some believe that renewal-year acquisition cost commissions and commission equivalents can be ignored if first-year commissions are reduced by commissions computed at the average effective renewal rate.

Where commission scales are graded, this approach would generally not be acceptable unless the second year rate is very close to the ultimate rate—that is, unless the ultimate rate is, for all practical purposes, attained in the second year.

The effect of reducing deferrable commissions for commissions computed at an average rate is difficult to generalize about. The average would always be higher than the ultimate rate if there is any grading at all. This results in deferring less in the first year than would be deferred if the first-year deferral were reduced by commissions computed at the ultimate rate. So the balance sheet effect would be to understate deferred acquisition costs. The income statement effect would depend on the rate of growth in new business and the constancy of the commission scales. Assuming the scales do not change and production is increasing, the income statement effect would generally be an overstatement of expense.

Others have proposed that the effect of renewal-year acquisition costs might be taken into account by completely ignoring renewal-year commissions and commission equivalents. Under this approach first-year commissions would be deferred in total, i.e., without reduction for commissions and commission equivalents at an ultimate rate or an average rate. The idea behind the approach is to recognize acquisition costs on issues of *prior* years by overdeferring costs on issues of the *current* year. Two wrongs do not always add up to a right, and any such proposal should be very carefully investigated before it is used.

The effect on Crazy Quilt Life of using the average-rate approach and the no-reduction approach is shown in Table 15–11, as is a comparison between estimated deferrals and actual deferrals. It will be observed that the amounts deferred by the approximation techniques eventually become significantly less than amounts that should actually be deferred. This is particularly striking in view of the fact that Crazy Quilt's commission scales are not particularly "steep". Of course, amortization would tend toward equalizing expenses charged to income; the more or less that is deferred, the more or less that is amortized. But the degree of offset should be ascertained, not assumed.

All things considered, a company's method of deferral should take renewal-year acquisition costs into account explicitly.

As may be obvious by now, determining the amount of renewal-year acquisition costs is extremely difficult at best and impossible at the worst. Fortunately there are various techniques available to more closely approximate such amounts. Where factors are used to account for acquisition costs, the factors can be so constructed as to provide for renewal year acquisition costs automatically. Where worksheets are used to account for acquisition costs, amortization tables can be modified to take renewal-year acquisition costs into account. (Amortization is discussed in Chapter 16.)

Cost Accumulation

Most of the work involved in accumulating cost data is a natural adjunct to cost analysis. In Crazy Quilt's case, for example, all of the acquisition costs that varied with and were primarily related to production were accumulated during the analysis process described in the preceding section.

Relationship to Income Statement Format

Consideration should be given to financial statement format well in advance of accumulating cost data. It will be noted that the method used by Crazy Quilt results in merging several different types of costs—commissions, salaries, taxes, and other expenses—into essentially a single expression of "acquisition costs". That's because Crazy Quilt has already decided to report the adjustment for acquisition costs in a single line in the income statement. If, however, it is considered desirable to state individual items in the income statement net of deferral and amortization, then of course it is necessary to accumulate cost data in several different categories, one for each category of expense shown in the income statement. It would also be necessary to amortize each such category of cost separately.

There are three basic problems—one theoretical, two practical—in attempting to segregate acquisition costs by income statement category.

On a theoretical level, it is questionable whether individual expense items should be stated net of amortization. Consider the following presentation:

	Incurred	Deferred	Amortized	Reported
Benefits:				
Claims	$1,000			$1,000
Change in				
reserves	500			500
Expenses:				
Commissions	200	$100	$50	150
Salaries	200	100	50	150
Taxes	50	25	15	40
Other	200	100	50	150

Expenses incurred is important information; but the information is not available in the above presentation. Instead natural categories of expense are being reported net of *functional* adjustments. This would seem to be similar to mixing apples and oranges. Further, the treatment of expenses is inconsistent with the treatment of claims, which are reported on an incurred basis with the implicit corresponding reduction in reserves reported in a separate account. To be internally consistent, the income statement should show the change in "expense reserves" as a separate line item, which was the practice followed by Crazy Quilt.

On a more practical level, it is difficult—and may be impossible—to restate the various expense items later if a modification of income statement details is desired. Suppose that in the above example the company decides to split salaries and other expenses between field and home office. It would be difficult to do this, to say the least. For all practical purposes the company is locked into its initial decision about income statement details. This leaves very little room for flexibility in the future.

Another practical consideration is the volume of calculations that must be made to implement the item-by-item approach. In the above illustration four items of expense detail are shown in the income statement. This would require four times as many schedules or sets of factors as the single-line adjustment approach. Considering the questionable nature of the result of the item-by-item approach, it would seem that the work required to implement it is not really very worthwhile.

Estimates for Prior Years

Crazy Quilt Life is unusual in having adequate historical information, dating back to inception in 1941, on which to base its calculations of deferrable acquisition costs. Few companies have adequate data for more than a few recent years. In those circumstances,

acquisition costs incurred in prior years can only be estimated.

Techniques used to estimate acquisition costs will differ according to information available for those prior years. The more common techniques would include the following:

1. Where deferrable amounts are limited to commissions and medical expenses, the necessary information is available from Convention Statement accounts. The only estimates that would usually be required would be adjustments for branch office commission equivalents.

2. Where departmental cost data are available, estimates might be made based on applying percentages to the costs of certain departments. For example, if cost analysis for, say, the most recent five years indicates that 90 percent of underwriting department costs have been deferrable during those five years, and if operations have been relatively stable in prior years, then 90 percent of underwriting department costs might be considered deferrable for prior years.

3. Where departmental cost data are not available, index numbers representing relationships between costs deferred during the period when cost data are available and Convention Statement data during the same period might be applied to Convention Statement data of prior periods.

Obviously such estimates must be made with considerable care. Changes in operations should be taken into account even if the effect of such changes must be determined subjectively.

A variation of the third method described above is illustrated for Crazy Quilt Life in Table 15–12. The table assumes that only five years (1967–1971) of detailed cost data are available. Ratios developed using actual cost data are then projected backward in time, modified wherever necessary to accord recognition to significant changes in operations. Estimated deferrals for 1966, 1965, 1960, 1955, and 1950 are also illustrated.

While the technique illustrated in Table 15–12 is complex, it is generally self-explanatory, with two exceptions: Ultimate commission rates and equivalent branch office override rates were modified subjectively based on a study of agent contracts for the prior years for which deferrable costs were to be estimated, and the proportion of business written by branch offices had to be determined for each year because the proportion changed over the years. Otherwise, ratios or indices developed during the 1967–1971 period were used without modification for prior years,

Table 15–12.

DEVELOPMENT OF ESTIMATED DEFERRABLE FIRST-YEAR COSTS FOR PRIOR YEARS (000 Omitted)

DEVELOPMENT OF RATIO DATA BASED ON AVAILABLE ACTUAL INFORMATION:

	Source	1971	1970	1969	1968	1967
(1) First-year premiums	Exhibit 1	$11,626	$10,652	$ 9,498	$ 8,477	$ 7,948
(2) Percentage of business produced by branch offices	Co. records	55%	50%	45%	45%	40%
(3) Premiums estimated written by branch offices	(1) × (2)	6,394	5,326	4,274	3,815	3,179
(4) Branch office first-year equivalents	Available data	1,270	1,057	842	755	588
(5) Branch office rate	(4) ÷ (3)	20%	20%	20%	20%	19%
(6) First-year commissions	Exhibit 1	8,203	7,624	6,874	6,130	5,773
(7) First-year commissions and equivalents	(4) + (6)	9,473	8,681	7,716	6,885	6,361
Reduction for ultimate rates:						
(8) Agents	Available data	348	323	534	483	198
(9) Branch managers	Available data	96	79	97	87	41
(10) Total	(8) + (9)	444	402	631	570	239
(11) Percent of premiums	(10) ÷ (1)	4%	4%	7%	7%	3%
Exhibit 5 and 6 expenses allocated to ordinary:						
(12) Medicals and inspections	P. 5 of C/S	776	710	634	565	530
All other:						
(13) Total	P. 5 of C/S	$19,671	17,390	15,381	14,238	12,697
(14) Less first-year branch office commission equivalents	(4)	1,270	1,057	842	755	588
(15) Less premium taxes	2% × premiums	1,334	1,201	1,080	973	881
(16) Net	(13)−(14)−(15)	17,067	15,132	13,459	12,510	11,228
(17) Amount deferred net of medicals and inspections	Available data	5,235	4,773	4,138	3,700	3,450
(18) Amount deferred as a percentage of net Exhibit 5 and 6 expenses	(17) ÷ (16)	31%	32%	31%	30%	31%

DEVELOPMENT OF ESTIMATES OF PRIOR-YEAR AMOUNTS USING AVAILABLE DATA AND PROJECTIONS OF RATIOS:

		1966	1965	1960	1955	1950
(1) First-year premiums	Exhibit 1	$ 6,909	$ 5,922	$ 2,762	$ 2,885	$ 3,047
(2) Percentage of business produced by branch offices	Co. records	40%	40%	35%	25%	15%
(3) Premiums estimated written by branch offices	(1) × (2)	2,764	2,369	967	721	457
(4) Branch office rate	Est. Projection	17%	17%	13%	12%	12%
(5) Branch office first-year equivalents	(3) × (4)	470	403	126	87	55
(6) First-year commissions	Exhibit 1	5,018	4,293	1,870	1,941	2,037
(7) First-year commissions and equivalents	(5) + (6)	5,488	4,696	1,996	2,028	2,092
(8) Ultimate rate	Est. Projection	4%	4%	5%	5%	6%
(9) Ultimate amount	(1) × (8)	276	237	138	144	183
(10) Estimated deferrable commissions and equivalents	(7) − (9)	5,212	4,459	1,858	1,884	1,909
(11) Medicals and inspections	P. 5 of C/S	461	359	184	192	203
(12) Exhibit 5 and 6 expenses less medicals and inspections	P. 5 of C/S	11,067	9,276	4,342	4,029	3,468
(13) Premium taxes	2% × premiums	792	716	528	458	303
(14) Branch office equivalents	(5)	470	403	126	87	55
(15) Net Exhibit 5 and 6 expenses	(12)−(13)−(14)	9,805	8,157	3,688	3,484	3,110
(16) Deferral percentage	Est. projection	30%	30%	30%	30%	30%
(17) Estimated deferral of Exhibit 5 and 6 expenses	(15) × (16)	2,942	2,447	1,106	1,045	933
(18) Total estimated deferral	(10)+(11)+(17)	8,615	7,265	3,148	3,121	3,045

on the basis that methods of operation had not changed substantially.

The deferrable amounts estimated in Table 15–12 compare favorably with actual deferrable amounts (see Table 15–8):

		000	
Year	Estimated	Actual	% Estimated To Actual
1966	$8,615	$8,785	98%
1965	7,301	7,500	97
1960	3,148	3,091	102
1955	3,121	3,040	103
1950	2,990	3,104	96

The effect of errors is further mitigated by amortization from the date incurred to the date that adjusted statements are first prepared. This is discussed further in Chapter 16.

Allocations to Blocks of Business

Crazy Quilt Life determined that $15,040,000 was deferrable in 1971 as first-year acquisition costs for the ordinary line of business (basic plans only*). The next step was to allocate such costs to various blocks of business as strongly suggested by the life insurance audit guide:

After determining whether an acquisition expense is to be deferred, it is *usually necessary* to allocate such expenses . . . by type of business (e.g., permanent and term) or by some other classification in order to associate them with the related premium revenue.[1] [Emphasis supplied.]

The need to allocate acquisition costs by type of business is based primarily on the need to amortize acquisition costs in proportion to the receipt of premium revenue. The subject of amortization is dealt with at length in Chapter 16. The present discussion is concerned only with organizing acquisition costs in such a manner as to facilitate the amortization process.

Reasons for Allocation

If a company issued only one plan of insurance at one issue age, allocation of acquisition costs to "type

*In addition, as indicated in Table 15–2, commissions on the waiver of premium and additional accidental death benefits of $111,000 and $74,000, respectively, were considered deferrable.

of business" would not be necessary. In these circumstances there would only be one type of business, and the aggregate amount of acquisition costs—the acquisition cost "pool"—would apply to it.

Assume, however, that the company issues two plans—five-year term and single-premium life—for which premiums are received as follows:

Year	Term	Single-Premium	Total
1	$100	$340	$440
2	80		80
3	70		70
4	60		60
5	50		50

Now assume that the only acquisition costs incurred are commissions of $150, of which $100 relates to the term business and $50 to the single-premium business. Amortization should be as follows:

	Term Plan			Amortization of Acquisition Costs on	
	Premiums Received		Amortization of Acquisition Costs	Single-Premium Plan	Total Amortization
Year	Amount	% of Total			
1	$100	28%	$ 28	$50	$ 78
2	80	22	22		22
3	70	19	19		19
4	60	17	17		17
5	50	14	14		14
	360	100%	$100	$50	$150

If the acquisition costs were not so allocated but instead were amortized in bulk, amortization would be as follows:

	Premiums		
Year	Amount	% of Total	Amortization
1	$440	63%	$ 95
2	80	11	16
3	70	10	15
4	60	9	14
5	50	7	10
	$700	100%	$150

Thus, failure to allocate costs between the two plans would result in a material distortion of the amortization pattern in this case. Only if acquisition costs apply pro rata to premiums would it be appropriate to account for them in bulk.

Another reason for allocating acquisition costs by type of business is to provide for unexpected deviations in termination rates. Suppose that there are two plans involved, a five-year endowment and a five-year term plan, for which insurance in force and premiums based on *assumed* terminations are as follows:

	Beginning In Force			Premiums		
Year	Endow-ment	Term	Total	Endow-ment	Term	Total
1	$1,000	$1,000	$2,000	$ 50	$10	$ 60
2	800	800	1,600	40	8	48
3	700	700	1,400	35	7	42
4	600	600	1,200	30	6	36
5	500	500	1,000	25	5	30
				$180	$36	$216

Now assume that acquisition costs are incurred at the rate of 100 percent of first-year premiums—$60 in total—and that they are amortized in proportion to premiums assumed to be received:

	Pre-miums Received as %	Amortization			Unamortized Balance		
Year	of Total	Endow-ment	Term	Total	Endow-ment	Term	Total
1	28%	$14	$3	$17	$36	$7	$43
2	22	11	2	13	25	5	30
3	19	10	1	12	15	3	18
4	17	8	2	10	7	1	8
5	14	7	1	8	-0-	-0-	-0-

The unamortized balance may be translated into factors as follows:

	Endowment			Term		
Year	Ending In Force	Unamor-tized	Factor Per $1,000	Ending In Force	Unamor-tized	Factor Per $1,000
1	$800	$36	$45	$800	$7	$9
2	700	25	36	700	5	7
3	600	15	25	600	3	5
4	500	7	14	500	1	2
5	-0-	-0-	—	-0-	-0-	—

If all of the term business were to terminate in the second year, then the applicable unamortized acquisition costs—$7—would be charged to expense. Amortization would be as follows:

	Ending In Force		Factor Per $1,000		Total	
Year	Endow-ment	Term	Endow-ment	Term	Unamor-tized	Amor-tization
1	$800	$800	$45	$9	$43	$17
2	700	-0-	36	7	25	18
3	600	-0-	25	5	15	10
4	500	-0-	14	2	7	8
5	-0-	-0-	—	—	-0-	7

If the segregation is not made, but acquisition costs are adjusted for deviations in terminations, the practical effect is as follows:

Year	Assumed Com-bined Ending In Force	Com-bined Unamor-tized	Com-bined Factor Per $1,000	Actual Com-bined Ending In Force	Com-bined Factor Per $1,000	Com-bined Unamor-tized	Com-bined Amor-tization
1	$1,600	$43	$27	$1,600	$27	$43	$17
2	1,400	30	21	700	21	15	28
3	1,200	18	15	600	15	9	6
4	1,000	8	8	500	8	4	5
5	-0-	-0-	—	-0-	—	-0-	4

Thus deviations in termination experience are less distortive when acquisition costs have been allocated among plans.*

Finally, the accuracy of tests of recoverability are dependent in part on the accuracy with which costs have been allocated. Suppose there are two plans, A and B, with the following characteristics:

Plan	Premium	Future Profits	Acquisition Costs
A	$100	$50	$175
B	100	25	25

Suppose now that acquisition costs are simply allocated to the two plans equally, i.e., $100 per plan. In testing recoverability, Plan A will show an apparent $125 profit, while Plan B will show an apparent $50 *loss*. Assuming for the moment that each plan represents a major block of business for which losses, if any, would be recognized, an artificial loss of $50 would be recorded for Plan B simply because of inaccuracy in allocating acquisition costs.**

So the reasons for allocating costs to blocks of business may be summarized as follows:

1. To facilitate rational amortization.
2. To facilitate the proper recognition of deviations in termination experience.
3. To facilitate the proper application of principles of loss recognition.

---

*Deviations in termination experience and the effect on acquisition cost factors and unamortized balances is a complex subject that is explored in Chapter 16.

**Loss recognition and the blocks of business for which losses, if any, should be recognized are discussed in Chapter 24.

Allocation Principles

One can easily be carried away by allocation. Extensive studies could be made to develop bases for apportioning acquisition costs to individual policies. Such a study would be an exercise in futility. A very substantial proportion of total costs would wind up being allocated to policies in a very subjective and arbitrary manner, and the apparent precision of the result would mask the frailty that is inevitable in this type of activity.

On the other hand, one can also throw up one's hands and decide that, if subjectivity and arbitrariness are inevitable, it would be useless to do any allocating at all.

The allocation problem is best approached in an atmosphere of moderation. Extensive allocation is useless; no allocation is unacceptable; some allocation is necessary.

Where acquisition cost factors are used, allocations must be made with respect to each plan, year, and age. This is the technique that Crazy Quilt used and it is discussed later in this chapter. Even when allocations are this refined, however, a great deal of bulk allocating will normally be done before the costs are expressed in terms of plan-year-age factors.

In general, allocation should be limited to blocks of business that combine plans with similar characteristics. If a company's business is substantially all permanent business, of which whole life is predominant, allocation may not be necessary. If a company's business is partly permanent and partly term, and a single product is predominant in each case, a two-way allocation may be all that is necessary.

Where a company has significant amounts of different types of business, allocations should, as a minimum, be made for each major type of business. Crazy Quilt, for example, allocated costs to the following classes of business:

	1971 Volume (000,000)
Participating whole life	$ 75
Whole life	337
Limited-payment life	67
Level term	92
Decreasing term	280
	$851

Participating business was segregated for special treat-ment because Crazy Quilt is subject to a limitation on the stockholder charge against participating earnings; hence earnings had to be calculated separately for participating business, as discussed in Chapter 25. Long-term endowments (e.g., endowment at 85) and long-term limited-payment life contracts (e.g., life paid up at 85) were combined with whole life. Limited-payment policies of relatively short duration (e.g., 20-pay life) and short-term endowments (e.g., 20-year endowment) were considered as another class of business. All level term plans were regarded as another class of business; most such plans were renewable, which tended to equate their premium-paying periods. Finally, decreasing term plans were segregated as a class of business because of the very large average size.

The extent of cost allocation would normally be influenced by the procedures adopted for modeling insurance in force.* There should be some consistency between classes of business identified for purposes of allocating costs and classes of business identified for purposes of computing reserves. Many of the considerations involved in constructing a reserve model —especially premium-paying period and persistency— are also involved in determining what groupings of business are necessary for purposes of allocating costs.

Riders

A rider that extends substantially over the life of the underlying contract can logically be treated as part of the contract for purposes of cost allocation. A rider whose term is very limited in relation to the premium-paying period of the basic contract should normally be treated as if it were a separate contract.

Where acquisition costs are accounted for by means of factors, riders create special problems. Usually riders would be segregated in a listing of insurance in force. Factors must be separately applied to the underlying plan and the rider. It is relatively easy to determine commissions applicable to each (because the premiums and commission rates are known), but there is some question about what to do with noncommission acquisition costs.

In many cases it might be appropriate to assign noncommission acquisition costs to the underlying plans where the premium-paying period of the rider

---

*Reserve models are discussed in Chapter 28.

essentially coincides with that of the basic contract. While some additional sales, selection, and issue effort is usually devoted to the rider, little is lost by deferring and amortizing acquisition costs in terms of the basic contract.*

Where the rider period is significantly shorter than the premium-paying period of the underlying contract and the volume of such riders is material, noncommission acquisition costs should be apportioned between the two.

Allocation Techniques

Allocation is an art, not a science, and there are no firm rules on how to do it. About the only guideline that has to be followed consistently is that the allocations must be rational.

Bulk allocation. Table 15–13 illustrates a simple allocation of costs between permanent and term plans for Crazy Quilt Life. This is, perhaps, the crudest type of allocation that would still be acceptable.

One allocation base was chosen for each type of acquisition costs. It was felt that premiums were the best basis for allocating selling costs, volume for allocating selection costs, and policy count for allocating issue costs. Of course, these costs respond to more than one base, and if sufficient information is available, costs might be segregated in terms of the several bases and allocated accordingly. For example, if it is determined that selection costs are 40 percent a function of policy count and 60 percent a function of volume, $712,000 of such costs (40% × $1,779,000) would be apportioned on the basis of policies issued and the remainder, $1,067,000, on the basis of volume.**

In addition, weights could be assigned to recognize disproportionate conditions. Suppose, for example, the effort per $1,000 required to underwrite a permanent policy is twice as great as the effort per $1,000 required to underwrite a term policy simply because of the very large average size of the term policies. This condition could be recognized in the allocation process somewhat as follows:

---

*However, in testing recoverability of acquisition costs, recognition should be accorded margins on the entire contract including the rider.

**The result would be to allocate $1,173,000 to permanent and $606,000 to term instead of the $1,001,000 and $778,000, respectively, shown in Table 15–13.

	Total	Permanent	Term
Volume issued (000,000)	$ 851	$ 479	$372
Relative weight	—	2	1
Adjusted volume (000,000)	1,330	958	372
Ratio	100%	72%	28%
Costs allocated (000)	1,779	1,281	498

Allocation by block. The allocation process illustrated in Table 15–13 and discussed above could be extended to more blocks of business. The general approach would be the same, but it would tend to be progressively more refined as the number of blocks to which costs are allocated increases.

Allocation by plan. The ultimate allocation process would result in allocating acquisition costs to each plan and issue age. It would probably be unusual to recognize different issue ages in making such allocations; as suggested earlier, that degree of refinement is surely an exercise in futility.

But it would not be unusual to allocate acquisition costs by plan of insurance. In fact, that type of allocation is required if the factor method is used to account for acquisition costs.

Allocation of acquisition costs to plans of insurance means essentially that actuarial techniques of introducing acquisition costs into rate tests must be used for accounting purposes. The costs must be expressed in such a way that they can be translated into a single unit cost per unit of insurance, i.e., an acquisition cost factor.

The allocation process is considerably simplified if (1) the company has rate test data available and (2) the method of assessing acquisition costs for rate test purposes is reasonable. All that is necessary is to adjust the ratebook assumptions for the portion of such assumptions that is not deferrable.

Reference to Table 13–5 will show Crazy Quilt Life's 1971 ratebook assumptions for acquisition costs. It will be observed that the assumptions reproduce actual acquisition costs as the *Company* defines them for rate-testing purposes. The Company's definition of acquisition costs includes development costs and apportionments of general overhead. The Company's definition results in aggregate acquisition costs of $21,437,000.

Acquisition costs considered deferrable, however, aggregate $15,040,000 (see Table 15–8). The difference, $6,397,000, represents development costs and overhead not considered deferrable for accounting purposes.

By organizing the data appropriately, adjustment factors can be developed that, when applied to rate

Table 15–13.

ALLOCATION OF 1971 ACQUISITION COSTS BETWEEN PERMANENT AND TERM, IN BULK (000 Omitted)

	Total	Permanent	Term
Selling costs:			
First-year premiums (000)	$11,625	$ 9,342	$ 2,283
Ratio	100%	80.36%	19.64%
Costs allocated (000)			
Commissions and commission equivalents	$ 9,029	$ 7,256	$ 1,773
Sales support	3,617	2,907	710
Total	12,646	10,163	2.483
Selection costs:			
Volume issued (000,000)	851	479	372
Ratio	100%	56.29%	43.71%
Costs allocated (000)	1,779	1,001	778
Issue costs:			
Policies issued	66,516	53.487	13,029
Ratio	100%	80.41%	19.59%
Costs allocated (000)	615	495	120
Total costs allocated (000)	$15,040	$11,659	$ 3,381

test assumptions, will produce factors that properly reflect expenses considered deferrable.

Table 15–14 illustrates the development of percentages that must be applied to rate test assumptions to defer the appropriate amount of acquisition costs. As Table 15–14 indicates, accounting adjustments result in reducing rate test assumptions for sales support costs by 72 percent, selection costs by 11 percent, and issue costs by 18 percent.

It was decided to modify individual rate test assumptions pro rata for the computed percentage adjustments. This approach simply recognized that development and overhead were prorated to the assumptions from a large, amorphous pool of costs in the first place.* The modification is illustrated in Table 15–15, and the result—reproducing 1971 acquisition costs considered to be deferrable—is summarized in Table 15–16.

The factors shown in Table 15–16 were then used for developing acquisition cost reserve factors for Crazy Quilt Life's ordinary life basic plans.

Rate test assumptions could also be used to weight actual acquisition costs when it is necessary to allocate acquisition costs by plan or block of business in connection with the worksheet approach. Again, how-

* It is important to appreciate that costs should be "removed" on a basis consistent with the manner in which they were added in the first place.

ever, use of rate test assumptions for weighting purposes relies on the reasonableness of the rate test assumptions. If the assumptions are not reasonable, it would normally be necessary to start from scratch.

Joint Costs

In allocating acquisition costs to plans or blocks of business it is desirable to identify as many direct costs as possible and charge such costs directly to the relevant plans or blocks.

Some costs are very direct. For example, commissions can usually be associated directly with specific plans. Other costs are virtually direct and can be treated as direct costs for all practical purposes. An example would be costs of medical examinations and inspection reports.

Inevitably, however, there remains a pool of costs not identified with particular plans. Such a pool of costs may be viewed as contributing to the production of an assortment of products. Such costs may be regarded as joint costs similar in all material respects to joint costs encountered in many manufacturing operations (for example, petroleum refining in which one process creates a number of products).

Manufacturing joint costs are usually allocated to products on the basis of relative sales value. Thus, if two products, X and Y, are produced for a total joint

Table 15–14.

COMPUTATION OF PERCENTAGES TO BE APPLIED TO RATEBOOK ACQUISITION COST FACTORS TO DERIVE DEFERRABLE ACQUISITION COST FACTORS (000 Omitted)

	Commissions and Commission Equivalents	*Sales Support*	*Selection*	*Issue*
Expenses reproduced by factors developed for rate-testing purposes (see Table 13–5)	$9,029	$9,659	$1,999	$750
Expenses computed to be deferrable	9,029	3,617	1,779	615
Indicated adjustment	$ -0-	$6,042	$ 220	$135
Adjustment attributable to:				
Development costs:				
"Direct"		$4,401	$ -0-	$ -0-
Allocated overhead		900		
Total		5,301		
Overhead on remainder		741	220	135
		$6,042	$ 220	$135
Indicated percentage adjustments:				
Development		55%	–%	–%
Overhead		17	11	18
Total		72%	11%	18%

cost of $100, and the selling price of X is $150 while the selling price of Y is $50, then $75 of the joint cost would be allocated to X and $25 to Y.

"Sales value" measured in terms of selling prices has little relevance in a life insurance environment. Consider, for example, the situation in which the two products produced from a single pool of costs are a whole life policy and a single-premium policy. What are the relative sales values of the two products? Not first-year premiums, certainly; using first-year premiums would result in allocating too much cost to the single-premium plan. All renewal premiums on the whole life plan would get a free ride, so to speak.

There are three general methods that might be appropriate for allocating joint costs: relative effort, present value of premiums, and present value of profits.

Relative effort. Crazy Quilt allocated costs to individual products based on an evaluation of relative effort. This is implicit in basing the allocation on rate test assumptions that are themselves based on an evaluation of relative effort. There is nothing wrong with this approach so long as the evaluation is reasonable— that is, so long as it results in a fair determination of effort.

Present value of premiums. Use of the present value of premiums to allocate joint costs seems substantially similar to use of the relative sales value method of allocating manufacturing joint costs. But this approach is fallacious. The present value of premiums does not recognize differences in "gross margins", i.e., margins that are available to absorb acquisition costs. This is fundamentally different from the manufacturing situation, in which the allocation is made to value inventory and hence to *determine* gross margins.

Present value of profits. The most sophisticated— and perhaps the most accurate—method of allocating joint costs to various products would be based on the relative present values of profits computed without regard for the joint costs to be allocated.

The advantage of this technique will be apparent from two examples. Suppose the products produced are a whole life plan and a single premium plan which have the following characteristics:

	Whole Life	*Single Premium*
First year premium	$ 100	$1,000
Present value of premiums	1,000	1,000
Present value of profits computed without regard for joint costs	300	100

Table 15–15.

ADJUSTMENT OF RATEBOOK NONACQUISITION COST FACTORS TO OBTAIN 1971 DEFERRABLE ACQUISITION COST FACTORS

Plan and Allocation Basis	Rate Book Assumption*	Percentage Reductions for Development	Overhead	Deferrable Unit Cost
Par whole life:				
Selling:				
First-year premiums	59.0%	32.5%	4.5%	22.0%
Policies issued	$16.05	$ 8.83	$1.23	$ 5.99
New Business	$ 2.70	$ 1.49	$ .21	$ 1.10
Selection:				
Policies issued	$12.45		$1.37	$11.08
New business	$ 1.65		$ .18	$ 1.47
Issue–policies issued	$12.85		$2.31	$10.54
Non-par whole life:				
Selling:				
First-year premiums	64.3%	35.4%	4.9%	24.0%
Policies issued	$16.05	$ 8.83	$1.23	$ 5.99
New business	$ 2.70	$ 1.49	$ .21	$ 1.00
Selection:				
Policies issued	$12.45		$1.37	$11.08
New business	$ 1.65		$ .18	$ 1.47
			$2.03	$ 9.22
20-pay life				
Selling:				
First-year premiums	52.5%	28.4%	5.0%	19.1%
Policies issued	$15.75	$ 8.51	$1.23	$ 6.01
New business	$ 2.65	$ 1.43	$ .21	$ 1.01
Selection:				
Policies issued	$12.20		$1.34	$10.86
New business	$ 1.60		$ .18	$ 1.42
Issue–policies issued	$11.00		$1.98	$ 9.02
5-year renewable and convertible term:				
Selling:				
First-year premiums	42.8%	23.5%	3.3%	16.0%
Policies issued	$16.05	$ 8.83	$1.23	$ 5.99
New business	$ 1.65	$ .91	$ .13	$ .61
Selection:				
Policies issued	$12.45		$1.37	$11.06
New business	$ 1.10		$ .12	$ .98
Issue–policies issued	$10.20		$1.84	$ 8.36
25-year convertible decreasing term:				
Selling:				
First-year premiums	42.8%	23.5%	3.3%	16.0%
Policies issued	$16.05	$ 8.83	$1.23	$ 5.99
New business	$ 1.65	$ .91	$ .13	$ .61
Selection:				
Policies issued	$12.45		$1.37	$11.08
New business	$ 1.10		$ .12	$ .98
Issue–policies issued	$10.20		$1.84	$ 8.36

continued

Table 15–15. Continued

Plan and Allocation Basis	Rate Book Assumption*	Percentage Reductions for		Deferrable Unit Cost
		Development	Overhead	
Conversion whole life (from 5-year term):				
Selling:				
First-year premiums	64.3%	35.4%	4.9%	24.0%
Policies issued	$16.05	$ 8.83	$1.23	$ 5.99
New business	$ 2.70	$ 1.49	$ .21	$ 1.00
Issue–policies issued	$11.25		$2.03	$ 9.22
Conversion whole life (from 25-year decreasing term):				
Selling:				
First-year premiums	64.3%	35.4%	4.9%	24.0%
Policies issued	$16.05	$ 8.83	$1.23	$ 5.99
New business	$ 2.70	$ 1.49	$ .21	$ 1.00
Issue–policies issued	$11.25		$2.03	$ 9.22

* See Table 13–5.

Suppose that the joint costs to be allocated are $300. Allocation on the basis of the present value of premiums would result in reporting a loss of $50 on the single-premium plan. This loss would effectively be recouped over the premium-paying period of the whole life plan.

Now suppose that the present value of future profits are zero for the whole life plan and $400 for the single-premium plan. Allocation of any amount of acquisition costs to the whole life plan would result in an immediate reported gain followed by annual losses. It would obviously be improper to allocate costs based on the present value of future premiums in these circumstances.

It would be possible to obscure an abusive situation by the broadness of a loss recognition test. This is discussed further in Chapter 24. The point to be made here is that if a recoverability test is conducted in terms of aggregates, then careful attention should be paid to the method by which joint costs are allocated to different products.

Comparisons With Assumed

The life insurance audit guide provides that acquisition costs considered for deferral "should be measured against the expense assumptions used in setting premiums as a test of the reasonableness of allocations" [2] of such costs to plans or blocks of business. This assumes, of course, that the assumptions themselves represent reasonable allocations.

Comparison of actual and assumed for purposes of testing reasonableness was implicit in the manner in which Crazy Quilt's acquisition cost factors were developed. Where acquisition costs are accounted for by the worksheet method, it would usually be necessary to translate bulk amounts into factors to compare them with assumed expenses or, alternatively, to extend assumed factors by volumes issued for comparison with the bulk amounts to be deferred. Since normally the amounts deferred exclude development and overhead while the assumptions usually include such items, the main purpose of the comparison is to test the reasonableness of the distribution of acquisition costs to the various plans or blocks of business, not the amount of acquisition costs deferred.

The audit guide also provides that

Actual acquisition expenses, as distinguished from those assumed, should be used in the calculations as long as it can be shown that gross premiums charged are sufficient to cover the actual expense. However, as a practical matter, most actuarial techniques require the use of estimates to calculate the amounts to be deferred. Such estimates are made before the costs are actually incurred. As in the case of variances from standard costs in other businesses, it may not be necessary to adjust such estimates to actual if they do not vary significantly from actual acquisition expenses. [3]

A comparison of actual and assumed costs would normally be made by "grossing up" the factors to reproduce total expenses assumed to have been in-

Table 15–16.

SUMMARY OF 1971 ACQUISITION COSTS AFTER ALLOCATION OF FACTORS TO INDIVIDUAL PLANS

	Measurement Units	Commissions and Commission Equivalents		Deferrable Noncommission Costs		Total Deferred Costs (000)
		Unit Cost	*Amount (000)*	*Unit Cost*	*Amount (000)*	
Par whole life:						
Selling:						
First-year premiums (000)	$ 1,589	73.0%	$1,160	22.0%	$ 342	$ 1,502
Policies issued	10,325			$ 5.99	62	62
New business (000)	$75,141			$ 1.10	83	83
Selection:						
Policies issued	10,325			$11.08	114	114
New business (000)	$75,141			$ 1.47	110	110
Issue-policies issued	$10,325			$10.54	109	109
Non-par whole life:						
Selling:						
First-year premiums (000)	$ 5,893	83.0%	4,892	24.0%	1,420	6,312
Policies issued	34,288			$ 5.99	205	205
New business (000)	$325,611			$ 1.00	326	326
Issue–policies issued	34,288			$ 9.22	316	316
20-pay life:						
Selling:						
First-year premiums (000)	$ 1,548	67.5%	1,045	19.1%	296	1,341
Policies issued	8,501			$ 6.01	51	51
New business (000)	$66,792			$ 1.01	68	68
Selection:						
Policies issued	8,501			$10.86	92	92
New business (000)	$66,792			$ 1.42	95	95
Issue—policies issued	8,501			$ 9.02	77	77
5-year renewable and convertible term:						
Selling:						
First-year premiums (000)	$ 523	62.5%	327	16.0%	84	411
Policies issued	3,663			$ 5.99	22	22
New business (000)	$91,839			$ .61	56	56
Selection:						
Policies issued	$ 3,663			$11.08	40	40
New business (000)	91,839			$ .98	90	90
Issue–policies issued	3,663			$ 8.36	31	31
25-year convertible decreasing term:						
Selling:						
First-year premiums (000)	$ 1,760	76.5%	$1,347	16.0%	276	1,623
Policies issued	9,366			$ 5.99	56	56
New business (000)	$280,170			$ .61	168	168
Selection:						
Policies issued	9,366			$11.08	104	104
New business (000)	$280,170			$ .98	274	274
Issue–policies issued	9,366			$ 8.36	78	78
Conversion whole life (from 5-year term):						
Selling:						
First-year premiums (000)	$ 133	83.0%	110	24.0%	32	142
Policies issued	212			$ 5.99	1	1
New business	$ 4,835			$ 1.00	5	5
Issue–policies issued	212			$ 9.22	2	2

continued

Table 15–16. Continued

	Measurement Units	Commissions and Commission Equivalents		Deferrable Noncommission Costs		Total Deferred Costs (000)
		Unit Cost	Amount (000)	Unit Cost	Amount (000)	
Conversion whole life (from 25-year decreasing term):						
Selling:						
First-year premiums (000)	$ 178	83.0%	148	24.0%	43	191
Policies issued	251			$ 5.99	2	2
New business (000)	$ 6,757			$ 1.00	7	7
Issue–policies issued	251			$ 9.22	2	2
All other items					872	872
			$9,029		$6.011	$15,040

curred and comparing the total with expenses actually incurred.

Unless the cost factors inputted into the reserve calculation program are known, such a comparison may not be possible. In that case it would be necessary to "gross up" expenses by working backward from year-end balances of deferred costs. For example, if all that is available with respect to acquisition costs of a given year is a year-end unamortized balance of $900 and it is known, or can be estimated, that 10 percent of costs incurred are amortized in the first year, then the approximate incurred amount of $1,000 can be readily computed. Obviously there are dangers inherent in approximation methods such as these, and it would be preferable to retain sufficient information to reproduce costs using original inputs.

Where it is found that actual acquisition costs differ significantly from those assumed, it could be very awkward to recalculate factors. In these circumstances, adjustment could be made in bulk and a separate schedule maintained of such adjustments. For example, if assumed acquisition costs are $1,000 and actual are $900, and the unamortized balance (using the assumptions) at the end of the year is $800, the unamortized balance could be reduced by 10 percent, or $80. If at the end of the next year the unamortized balance is $700, it could be reduced by $70. And so on. The effect would be to adjust each year's unamortized balance and each year's amortization for the amount originally over-deferred or under-deferred.

It should be noted, however, that this technique

assumes that (1) the difference applies pro rata to the various plans or blocks and (2) that there are no renewal-year acquisition costs.

If the difference does not apply pro rata but is weighted differently for different blocks of business, the difference must be allocated to such different lines of business and each line should be separately adjusted each year.

If there are renewal-year acquisition costs, such costs will destroy the relationship between unamortized balances and amounts originally incurred. For example, if the unamortized balance is $900, of which $100 represents renewal-year acquisition costs for which adjustment is not required, and the original difference was 10 percent, application of the 10 percent adjustment to the unamortized balance would result in an erroneous adjustment of $10 in the unamortized balance of renewal-year acquisition costs.

In these circumstances it may be most expedient to maintain separate factors—and hence separate unamortized balances—for first-year acquisition costs and renewal-year acquisition costs. This assumes, of course, that factors for renewal-year costs reasonably reproduce actual renewal-year costs and that the adjustment problem is limited to first-year costs. As a practical matter, renewal-year costs are usually sufficiently small, and are sufficiently predictable, to eliminate the problem of having to adjust renewal-year costs.

In any event, it would probably be rare for a company to account for actual renewal-year costs, simply because the information is usually not available to do so. This suggests that the initial estimate of renewal-year costs should be made with as much care as possible.

Final Expression of Acquisition Costs

Table 15–16, discussed previously, represents the final expression of first-year acquisition costs applicable to Crazy Quilt Life's 1971 new business. Total ordinary acquisition costs for the year may be summarized as follows:

	000
Basic plans:	
First-year	$15,040
Renewal:	
Commissions	2,141
Term renewals	70
Supplemental benefits:	
Total and permanent disability	111
Additional accidental death	74
	$17,436

Crazy Quilt formatted its acquisition costs for basic plans in such a manner as to facilitate the development of factors. Deferrals of costs for supplemental benefits were limited to first-year commissions in excess of the average ultimate rate; renewal-year acquisition costs were ignored (except to the extent recognized in the ultimate rate) on grounds of immateriality; and the costs were formatted in such a manner as to amortize them in an approximate sum-of-the-years'-premiums pattern by the worksheet technique. Illustrations of factors, worksheets, amortization, and unamortized balances are included in Chapter 16, as is a discussion of the advantages and disadvantages of the worksheet and factor approaches.

Crazy Quilt deferred no acquisition costs in respect of individual fixed annuities because all of Crazy Quilt's fixed annuities are single-premium. Acquisition costs of $923,000 deemed applicable to individual fixed annuities were expensed in 1971. If Crazy Quilt had issued installment annuities, the method of deferring acquisition costs would have been substantially the same as the method employed for ordinary life business. (Of course, the problem of allocating costs between single-premium business and installment-premium business would have been a complicating factor.)

Individual variable annuities are discussed in Chapter 21.

Disclosure

The composition of deferred acquisition costs will vary from company to company. Because of this, the composition of acquisition costs for each significant line of business should be described in some detail in notes to the financial statements.

In addition, the nature and extent of renewal-year acquisition costs, if any, should be disclosed if such costs are material. Such disclosure is necessary to permit reasonable comparisons among companies.

Finally, while not required by the audit guide, the *amount* of acquisition costs deferred during the accounting period should be disclosed. It may also be appropriate to disclose the relationship between acquisition costs and some volume base, such as first-year premiums; however, any such disclosure must be made with considerable care so as not to be misleading. For example, it would be misleading to disclose that acquisition costs deferred amounted to 75 percent of first-year premiums if second-year commissions of 50 percent are going to be paid. It may, however, be appropriate to make this type of disclosure if the second-year arrangement is also disclosed.

Appropriate disclosure for Crazy Quilt Life (assuming that the only line of business is ordinary), ignoring disclosure of amortization methods and amounts (discussed in Chapter 16), might be as follows for 1971:

ACCOUNTING POLICIES NOTE:

The Company defers certain costs that vary with and are primarily related to the production of new business. Such costs include excess first-year and renewal commissions and payments in the nature of commissions, certain sales support costs, and costs of underwriting and issue.

OTHER NOTE:

Policy acquisition costs of $17,436,000 have been deferred during the period, of which $15,225,000 (128% of first-year premiums) relates to 1971 new business and $2,211,-000 relates to business produced in prior years.

16 Amortization of Acquisition Costs

꿩 Deferred acquisition costs, says the life insurance audit guide, should be "charged against income in proportion to premium revenues recognized." [1] This provision is, of course, designed to implement the matching principle.

Nature of Amortization

Depreciation and amortization are usually viewed as being designed to accomplish a rational and systematic allocation of costs to accounting periods. What is "rational and systematic" is often a matter of judgment.

Rational and Systematic Allocation

While what is rational and systematic may be a matter of judgment, there are some common-sense guidelines that are normally applied in establishing a policy for depreciating tangible assets or amortizing intangible assets.

In theory, the only reason for deferring a cost is that revenues attributable to the expenditure will be recognized in years subsequent to the year of expenditure. Thus the cost has "future utility" and is carried forward.

It follows, then, that the apportionment of the cost to accounting periods should be proportional to the revenue that is associated with it.

Sometimes it is not possible to identify precisely the revenue that is generated by a particular expenditure. This is often true, for example, of a machine that is used for, say, one of hundreds of operations required to manufacture a product. In these circum-

stances practical methods of depreciation are used. Straight-line depreciation is an example of a practical method that seeks to *approximate* proportionality to the associated revenue stream.

Where the related revenue stream can be identified and quantified with reasonable precision, then depreciation charges are usually modified to distribute the cost more directly to such revenue. The units-of-production method of depreciation is an example of a method designed to accomplish a better matching.

The same general considerations apply to amortization of intangibles.

The important thing to note is that the principal purpose of depreciation and amortization is to match costs and revenues. This is the primary criterion of deciding what is "rational and systematic".*

Depreciation and amortization involve certain assumptions and estimates about the future. All such assumptions and estimates relate to the stream of future revenues (or possibly, under certain circumstances, future cost savings). When circumstances indicate that the assumptions and estimates were materially incorrect, adjustments are made immediately. Thus obsolescence of a machine means that future revenue that can be attributed to the machine will be negligible or nonexistent, in which case the remaining book value is written off. Or it may become apparent that the useful life of the machine may be much longer or shorter than the life originally estimated, which means that revenue will be generated by use of the machine for a longer or shorter period. In that case, depreciation of the remaining book value would

*This is not intended to be an all-inclusive discussion of depreciation and amortization, which is a very complex subject indeed.

be modified so as to recognize the longer or shorter useful life.

It is significant that when depreciation or amortization are modified owing to a change in estimates about the future, adjustment is normally not made for depreciation taken in prior years. Suppose, for example, that $10,000 is spent on a machine with an expected life of 10 years and that it is depreciated on a straight-line basis. Now suppose that five years later it becomes apparent that the useful life is 20 years. This means that only $2,500 should have been amortized to date. But $5,000 has been amortized. The $2,500 excess is not reversed. Instead the then-remaining book value, $5,000, is spread over the then-remaining useful life, 15 years. Instead of recording depreciation of $1,000 a year, the annual charge will be $333.

The reverse situation is less clear-cut. If, for example, the originally estimated life was 20 years and five years later it becomes evident that the life is only going to be 10 years, then only $2,500 would have been depreciated with $7,500 remaining to be depreciated over five years, or $1,500 a year. If it were determinable that the attributable revenue amounts to only $1,200 a year, then failure to adjust accumulated depreciation immediately would result in deferring losses of $1,500 ($7,500, book value of machine, less five years of revenue at $1,200 a year, or $6,000). Judgment would call for an additional writeoff of $1,500 in the year of discovery under these circumstances.

Matching Premiums and Acquisition Costs

Inasmuch as the pattern of future premium revenues can reasonably be anticipated, it follows that a systematic and rational allocation of deferred acquisition costs to accounting periods should recognize the distinctive pattern of such revenues.

It is known with reasonable certainty that premium revenues on, say, a block of 10-pay life policies will be recognized as revenue over 10 years in a declining pattern, even though the block of business may persist for 50 years. Thus acquisition costs should be amortized in a declining pattern over 10 years.

It certainly would not be rational to amortize the costs straight-line over 50 years, the life of the block of business. This may be rational for a building for which the length and curve of the expected future revenue stream are simply not reasonably determinable, but there is no justification for using the method when the length and curve of the revenue stream *are* reasonably determinable.

Thus it is that the audit guide states that

Some [amortization] techniques will tend to produce unacceptable results. For example, amortization of costs on the basis of "average policy life" involving a straight-line chargeoff of a fixed sum per policy per year plus an immediate charge-off of the unamortized amounts attributable to terminated policies, will not result in a reasonable association of expenses with related revenues.[2]

Sum-of-the-Years'-Premiums Method

To be consistent with the matching concept, acquisition costs should be amortized in proportion to premiums received.* In theory, this procedure requires estimation of all premiums to be received with respect to a block of business and the incidence of such receipts; acquisition costs would then be amortized annually in an amount which, expressed as a percentage of total acquisition costs originally deferred, is equal to premiums received in that year expressed as a percentage of premiums expected to be received in all years.

While not separately stated, an amortization period and an amortization method are inherent in the procedure described in the preceding paragraph. The period is the premium-paying period; the method is the "sum-of-the-years'-premiums" method. It should be noted that the sum-of-the-years'-premiums method bears no *necessary* relationship to any particular table of terminations by death and withdrawal.

As a practical matter, any period and method which result in a pattern of amortization approximately the same as the pattern of premium receipts would be satisfactory. For example, it would rarely be necessary to extend the amortization period to the end of the premium-paying period in the case of whole-life contracts because the amounts involved after, say, 30 to 40 years would be immaterial.

In principle, amortization should be adjusted periodically as actual termination experience develops, if such experience is materially different from that assumed. Such an adjustment represents, in effect, a change in the estimate of total premiums to be collected and should normally be accounted for as a change in estimate, i.e., currently and/or prospectively.

*No distinction is made here between premiums recognized on a cash basis and premiums recognized on a "when due" basis. This distinction is discussed in Chapter 5.

Interest on Acquisition Costs

The life insurance audit guide states that "To be fully consistent with actuarial concepts, the rate of amortization [of acquisition costs] should give effect not only to estimated persistency, but to the interest assumed in benefit reserve calculations." [3] Use of the term "should" rather than "may" seems to imply that the guide *requires* interest to be taken into account in amortizing acquisition cost. But the recognition of interest is permissive, not mandatory. The basic principle set forth by the guide is simply that acquisition costs "should be charged against income in proportion to premium revenues recognized." Proportionality can be achieved without taking interest into account, and in fact Appendix B of the guide illustrates one method that does not recognize interest, thus presumably establishing that the no-interest method is acceptable.

The rate of amortization should give effect to interest to be fully consistent with actuarial concepts, but that assumes that one wishes to be fully consistent with such concepts in the first place. That's the basic decision that has to be made.

Arguments for Recognizing Interest

The rationale for recognizing interest in the amortization process may be expressed from two points of view: what might be called the "effective charge to policyholders" point of view, and what might be referred to as the "opportunity cost" point of view. In addition, there are some indirect precedents in accounting for recognizing interest.

Effective charge to policyholders. The policyholder is effectively charged interest on acquisition costs because of the manner in which premiums are calculated. A premium is the actuarial equivalent of benefits, expenses, and profits, and an "actuarial equivalent" always involves the recognition of interest.

Thus, amortization of acquisition costs with interest results in a better matching of revenue and expense. Premium revenue recognized during a period is designed to provide for costs net of interest. So the costs themselves should be adjusted for interest in matching them up with premiums.

Opportunity cost. Acquisition costs represent sums of money that could have been otherwise invested. Instead they were invested in new business. Amortization of acquisition costs with interest is a method of recognizing opportunity cost.

This view is not without its precedence in account-

ing. The annuity method of depreciation applies the theory that an opportunity rate of interest on the investment in fixed assets should be included in the cost of production.

Discounting. Long-term accounts and notes receivable and payable that do not provide for interest should normally be discounted at a rate of interest appropriate in the circumstances, according to Accounting Principles Board Opinion No. 21, "Interest on Receivables and Payables".

To the extent that acquisition costs may be viewed as being in the nature of long-term receivables from policyholders payable from portions of the gross premiums, they represent the present value of a series of future payments. Thus they should be improved with interest as the payments are received.

Arguments Against Recognizing Interest

At least two arguments against recognizing interest in the amortization process can also be marshalled: precedence in accounting and the fallacies in the opportunity cost concept.

Precedence in accounting. Depreciation or amortization with interest is very rare in accounting. Acquisition costs represent intangible assets, not receivables (because there is no enforceable claim on policyholders). Because amortization of intangibles rarely contemplates interest, no effect should be given to interest in amortizing acquisition costs.

Fallacies in the opportunity cost concept. The proper measure of opportunity cost is not necessarily the assumed interest rate. The assumed interest rate is based on a portfolio of securities whose investment qualities are partly governed by law. The securities are largely high-quality fixed-debt securities designed to cover a guaranteed set of benefits. This rate has no particular relevance to the rate of interest required to compensate for the returns foregone on funds invested in new life insurance production. Suppose the company's required rate of return on such investments is 12 percent, as discussed and illustrated in Chapter 4. The real opportunity cost is considered to be 12 percent, not 5 or 6 percent or whatever happens to be the long-term reserve interest rate assumption.

Opportunity cost is properly measured in the form of profits as they arise, not in terms of *imputing* such a cost.

A Matter of Choice

The question of whether to amortize acquisition costs with interest or without could be argued indefinitely. Ultimately, however, the decision is a matter of personal preference.

Effect of Interest

The effect of interest on acquisition costs often is not as great as one might believe.

Assume that $1,000 in acquisition costs is expended, that the reserve interest rate is 6 percent, that mortality and withdrawal are zero, and that the contract is a 5-year endowment with an annual premium of $1,000.

Ignoring interest would therefore result in amortization of $200 a year. Expressed another way, $200 of the $1,000 annual premium is used to reduce the balance of acquisition costs.

Recognizing interest involves recognizing the time value of the $1,000 investment. The $1,000 is the present value, at 6 percent, of five payments of $223.96. Thus, $223.96 of the $1,000 annual premium is used to pay interest on the balance of acquisition costs *and* reduce the balance. The effect is the same as amortizing a $1,000 mortgage loan at 6 percent interest with a level payment. Amortization would be as follows:

Year	Beginning Balance	"Payment" at Beginning of Year	Interest at 6%	Ending Balance	Amortization
1	$1,000.00	$223.96	$46.56	$822.60	$ 177.40
2	822.60	223.96	35.92	634.56	188.04
3	634.56	223.96	24.64	435.24	199.32
4	435.24	223.96	12.68	223.96	211.28
5	223.96	223.96	—0—	—0—	223.96
					$1,000.00

The difference is on the order of 11 percent in the first year and 12 percent in the fifth year, with a lesser difference in between.

Now assume that persistency is 80 percent, 70 percent, 60 percent, and 50 percent. Amortization without interest would be as follows:

Year	Amount	% of Total	Amortization
1	$1,000	27.778%	$ 277.78
2	800	22.222	222.22
3	700	19.444	194.44
4	600	16.667	166.67
5	500	13.889	138.89
	$3,600	100.000%	$1,000.00

Amortization reflects an annuity that recognizes terminations but not interest.

Amortization with interest would require the calculation of an annuity that recognizes terminations *and* interest, as follows:

Year	Percentage Persisting at Beginning of Year	6% Interest Discount	Present Value of $1.00
1	1.00	1.0000	$1.0000
2	.80	.9434	.7547
3	.70	.8900	.6230
4	.60	.8396	.5038
5	.50	.7920	.3960
			$3.2775

So the annuity required to amortize the $1,000 with interest is $305.11 ($1,000 ÷ $3.2775) and amortization would proceed as follows:

Year	Beginning Balance	"Payment" % Persisting	"Payment" Amount	Interest at 6%	Ending Balance	Amortization
1	$1,000.00	100%	$305.11	$41.69	$736.58	$ 263.42
2	736.58	80	244.09	29.55	522.04	214.54
3	522.04	70	213.58	18.51	326.97	195.07
4	326.97	60	183.07	8.63	152.53	174.44
5	152.53	50	152.53	—0—	—0—	152.53
						$1,000.00

The differences are as follows:

Year	Amortization without Interest	Amortization with Interest	Difference
1	$277.78	$263.42	5%
2	222.22	214.54	4
3	194.44	195.07	Nil
4	166.67	174.44	5
5	138.89	152.53	10

The differences are further affected by whether interest rates are graded, the length of the contract period, the mid-year assumption (the above illustrations are on a policy-year basis), the persistency pattern, and the influence of renewal-year acquisition costs.

Table 16–1 may offer some perspective on the effects of different interest rates on acquisition costs. Acquisition cost factors calculated using various interest rates (all other assumptions have been held constant) are shown for selected 1971 issues of Crazy Quilt Life. Note particularly that the use of a level interest assumption—at any level—does not significantly affect the acquisition cost factors. Use of a graded interest assumption tends to affect the factors more significantly, particularly in the later durations.

Table 16–1.

COMPARATIVE ACQUISITION COST FACTORS FOR 1971 ISSUES—SELECTED PLANS (AGE 35), DURATIONS AND INTEREST RATES*

Plan	Duration	8%	7%	6%	5-1/2%	5%	4-1/2%	4%	9% Graded to 4-1/2%**	7% Graded to 4-1/2%*** Graded .5% Each 5 Years	7% Graded to 4-1/2%*** Graded .1% a Year	Crazy Quilt Ratebook Assumptions****
Whole life	1	$30.58	$30.80	$31.02	$31.13	$31.24	$31.34	$31.45	$30.81	$31.05	$31.11	$31.17
	2	38.02	38.31	38.59	38.73	38.86	38.99	39.12	38.78	38.88	39.01	39.05
	3	40.96	41.27	41.55	41.69	41.82	41.95	42.07	42.35	42.17	42.33	42.36
	5	42.62	42.89	43.13	43.24	43.33	43.42	43.49	45.43	44.51	44.58	44.70
	7	43.16	43.37	43.53	43.60	43.64	43.67	43.68	47.04	45.49	45.59	45.66
	10	44.31	44.38	44.38	44.35	44.30	44.23	44.13	49.85	47.22	47.22	47.35
	15	41.30	41.07	40.75	40.55	40.22	40.05	39.75	48.47	44.52	44.39	44.51
	20	37.20	36.71	36.10	35.76	35.37	34.96	34.51	44.53	40.09	39.81	39.99
	30	26.70	25.94	25.09	24.62	24.14	23.62	23.08	30.83	27.69	27.28	27.82
	40	17.69	16.96	16.17	15.75	15.32	14.87	14.42	19.41	17.43	17.18	17.26
20-pay life	1	36.26	36.43	36.60	36.68	36.75	36.83	36.90	36.29	36.54	36.60	36.62
	2	43.15	43.29	43.41	43.47	43.52	43.56	43.60	43.48	43.54	43.65	43.60
	3	44.27	44.23	44.36	44.37	44.37	44.36	44.34	44.97	44.72	44.85	44.74
	5	42.49	42.37	42.21	42.11	42.00	41.88	41.75	44.01	43.08	43.09	43.00
	7	40.30	40.00	39.65	39.45	39.24	39.02	38.78	42.20	40.80	40.81	40.62
	10	35.98	35.42	34.81	34.48	34.14	33.78	33.41	38.25	36.24	36.15	35.93
	15	23.33	22.58	21.79	21.39	20.98	20.57	20.15	24.75	22.87	22.72	22.46
5-year R & C term	1	7.69	7.74	7.79	7.82	7.85	7.87	7.90	7.73	7.79	7.81	7.82
	2	8.65	8.72	8.79	8.82	8.85	8.89	8.92	8.80	8.83	8.87	8.87
	3	9.14	9.22	9.29	9.33	9.37	9.40	9.44	9.42	9.41	9.45	9.45
	5	9.37	9.46	9.54	9.59	9.63	9.67	9.71	9.99	9.84	9.86	9.89
	7	12.93	13.03	13.13	13.18	13.22	13.26	13.30	14.01	13.65	13.70	13.73
	10	11.65	11.75	11.84	11.88	11.92	11.95	11.97	13.26	12.64	12.66	12.71
	15	18.84	18.92	18.96	18.96	18.95	18.92	18.87	22.39	20.73	20.73	20.80
	20	27.29	27.04	26.70	26.50	26.27	26.02	25.74	32.45	29.46	29.33	29.34
	30	34.30	32.99	31.59	30.84	30.08	29.28	28.47	37.34	33.85	33.45	33.42
25-year decreasing term	1	8.60	8.64	8.69	8.71	8.73	8.75	8.77	8.61	8.68	8.69	8.70
	2	9.42	9.46	9.51	9.53	9.55	9.57	9.59	9.51	9.54	9.56	9.56
	3	9.69	9.73	9.77	9.79	9.80	9.82	9.83	9.86	9.84	9.88	9.87
	5	9.72	9.75	9.77	9.78	9.78	9.79	9.79	10.13	9.97	9.99	9.99
	7	10.11	10.11	10.09	10.08	10.07	10.06	10.04	10.68	10.40	10.42	10.39
	10	9.25	9.20	9.15	9.11	9.08	9.03	8.99	10.00	9.56	9.55	9.53
	15	7.71	7.59	7.46	7.38	7.31	7.23	7.14	8.47	7.90	7.87	7.83
	20	5.80	5.62	5.42	5.32	5.22	5.11	5.00	6.26	5.73	5.70	5.63

* All other assumptions are held constant.
** Graded .5% each 5 years to ultimate rate.
*** Graded over 25 years.
**** 6.5% graded to 3.5% (.5% each 5 years) in 30 years.

A somewhat more cosmic view of the relative effects of interest is available from Table 16–2, which shows unamortized balances of acquisition costs, computed with and without interest, on Crazy Quilt's entire line of basic ordinary plans as of December 31, 1971, and December 31, 1970, classified by ratebook era. The 1971 change in acquisition costs on both bases is also shown.

Normally the question of amortizing with or without interest must be dealt with only when the work-sheet technique of accounting for acquisition costs is used. This is discussed later in this chapter. When the factor approach (also discussed later in this chapter) is used, interest is automatically taken into account in the course of calculating the factors. There is no decision to make about interest in the latter case.

Table 16–2.

SUMMARY OF ACQUISITION COSTS AFTER AMORTIZING WITH AND WITHOUT INTEREST (000 Omitted)

| Ratebook Era | Unamortized Balance at End of Year | | | | 1971 Change | |
| | 1971 | | 1970 | | | |
	With Interest	Without Interest	With Interest	Without Interest	With Interest	Without Interest
41–47	$ 596	$ 535	$ 653	$ 591	$ (57)	$ (56)
48–61	518	454	672	592	(154)	(138)
48–51	1,751	1,651	1,897	1,798	(146)	(147)
52–56	2,986	2,717	3,284	2,999	(298)	(282)
52–61	1,442	1,348	1,536	1,446	(94)	(98)
57–61	3,737	3,307	4,056	3,631	(319)	(324)
62–69	6,147	6,172	6,473	6,550	(326)	(378)
62–67	25,746	24,997	26,276	25,794	(530)	(797)
62–64	2,304	2,337	2,383	2,432	(79)	(95)
65–69	4,935	4,989	5,170	5,254	(235)	(265)
65–67	701	709	721	733	(20)	(24)
68–69	13,291	13,181	13,898	13,977	(607)	(796)
70–71	25,413	26,285	12,114	12,567	13,299	13,718
	$89,567	$88,682	$79,133	$78,364	$10,434	$10,318

Persistency Adjustments

Under the sum-of-the-years'-premiums method of amortizing acquisition costs, premium revenue is projected based on assumptions about future terminations and acquisition costs are amortized annually in proportion to the ratio that each year's premiums bears to the total of such premiums in all years. In the case of five-year endowment discussed previously, premiums and amortization were projected as follows:

Projected Premiums

Year	Amount	% of Total	Amortization Schedule
1	$1,000	27.778%	$ 277.78
2	800	22.222	222.22
3	700	19.444	194.44
4	600	16.667	166.67
5	500	13.889	138.89
	$3,600	100.000%	$1,000.00

Actual persistency will almost always differ from assumed persistency. Suppose, for instance, that actual persistency and actual premiums are as follows:

| Year | Actual Percentage Persisting at Beginning of Year | Actual Premiums Received | |
		Amount	% of Total
1	100%	$1,000	31.250%
2	70	700	21.875
3	60	600	18.750
4	50	500	15.625
5	40	400	12.500
		$3,200	100.000%

Viewed in retrospect, then, amortization based on assumed persistency differed from amortization that should have been taken based on actual persistency as follows (amounts have been rounded):

| Year | Assumed | | Actual | |
	Amortization	Unamortized Balance	Amortization	Unamortized Balance
1	$ 278	$722	$ 313	$687
2	222	500	219	468
3	194	306	187	281
4	167	139	156	125
5	139	–0–	125	–0–
	$1,000		$1,000	

Should amortization be adjusted for such deviations in persistency? If so, how?

Audit Guide Requirements

The life insurance audit guide points out that where the factor method of accounting for acquisition cost is used, "some degree of self-correction" is provided:

If persistency is higher or lower than assumed, the unamortized cost factors . . . are multiplied by higher or lower in-force amounts. Thus, the [factor] method tends to provide some degree of self-correction in that it causes the rate of amortization to increase or decrease as actual persistency is higher or lower than initially estimated.[4]

The guide also notes that the worksheet method

. . . could be modified so that annual or periodic adjustments could be made to give effect to actual terminations.

293

Because of the volume of schedules that would be required, this technique may be impractical.[5]

The guide thus effectively indicates a preference for the factor method without, however, mandating it. The guide also suggests that adjustments should be made for deviations from assumed, but again without mandating it. The only "mandate" is:

If actual experience differs significantly from that assumed, the factors should be recomputed.[6]

Where this leaves the worksheet method is not entirely clear, since the "mandate" has reference to the factor method. Logic would suggest, however, that if deviations in persistency are sufficient to require the recomputation of factors, they would also be sufficient to warrant the redetermination of a worksheet amortization table.

Adjustments Without Recalculation

As the audit guide points out, use of the factor method results in "some degree of self-correction" for deviations in terminations.

To continue the example of the 5-year endowment, factors (expressed as an amount per $1,000 of acquisition costs incurred*) would be as follows (ignoring interest):

Year	Percentage Assumed To Persist at End of Year (1)	Projected Unamortized Balance (2)	Factor (2)÷(1)
1	80%	$722	$903
2	70	500	714
3	60	306	510
4	50	139	278
5	-0-	-0-	-0-

If persistency proceeds as expected, the natural result of applying the factors is as follows:

Year	Percentage Persisting at End of Year	Factor	Unamortized Balance	Amortization
1	80%	$903	$722	$ 278
2	70	714	500	222
3	60	510	306	194
4	50	278	139	167
5	-0-	-0-	-0-	139
				$1,000

*Factors would, of course, be expressed as an amount per unit of insurance, but no violation is done by using another index.

If persistency deviates as illustrated earlier, the result of applying the same factors to a different inforce amount is as follows:

Year	Actual Percentage Persisting at End of Year	Original Factors	Unamortized Balance	Amortization
1	70%	$903	$632	$ 368
2	60	714	428	204
3	50	510	255	173
4	40	278	111	144
5	-0-	-0-	-0-	111
				$1,000

The original factors were based on an assumption that 80 percent would persist at the beginning of the second year. Only 70 percent persisted. The result is to amortize the amount associated with the original persistency assumption, $278, plus the entire unamortized balance applicable to the excess terminations, $90 ($903, the factor, times the difference in persistency, 80 percent less 70 percent or 10 percent). Each year thereafter the unamortized balance differs by the cumulative persistency difference times the factor.

Projected amortization, actual amortization using original factors, and amortization that would have been taken under conditions of perfect clairvoyance are as follows:

Year	Expected Original Amortization	Actual Amortization Using Original Factors	"Experience Pattern" of Amortization
1	$ 278	$ 368	$ 313
2	222	204	219
3	194	173	187
4	167	144	156
5	139	111	125
	$1,000	$1,000	$1,000

If persistency were better than the original assumptions, the various amortization patterns would appear somewhat as follows:

Year	Persistency Assumed	Persistency Actual	Expected Original Amortization	Actual Amortization Using Original Factors	"Experience Pattern" of Amortization
1	80%	90%	$ 278	$ 187	$ 257
2	70	80	222	242	229
3	60	70	194	214	200
4	50	60	167	190	171
5	40	50	139	167	143
			$1,000	$1,000	$1,000

The first-year "correction" is almost always the most significant. In fact, the first-year "correction" is usually an over-correction because (1) the first-year lapse rate is usually the highest, and deviations tend to be quite high, and (2) the unamortized balance being adjusted upward or downward is at its maximum in the first year.

Where the worksheet method is used, it is necessary to translate bulk amounts of acquisition costs into factors in order to make the types of adjustments that are automatically made under the factor approach. This is discussed later in this chapter.

Adjustments with Recalculation

The audit guide provides that "If actual experience differs significantly from that assumed, the factors should be recalculated."

In essence, what this means is that the acquisition cost factors should be recalculated so as to give effect to (1) termination experience to date and (2) any indicated revisions in termination assumptions with respect to future years, and that such revised factors would be used (1) in the year in which the factors are recalculated and (2) in all subsequent years (absent, of course, still another revision).

This would have the effect of allocating the change in estimates to current and future years in a pattern which differs somewhat from the pattern associated with the continued use of original factors.

To continue the previous example, suppose that while the original assumption for first-year terminations was 20 percent the actual lapses are 35 percent and it is decided to revise the assumptions as follows:

	Percentage Persisting at Beginning of Year	
Year	*Original Assumptions*	*Revised Assumptions*
1	100%	100%
2	80	65
3	70	55
4	60	45
5	50	35

The associated factors for $1,000 in acquisition costs would be as follows:

Year	*Original Assumptions*	*Revised Assumptions*
1	$903	$1,026
2	714	818
3	510	593
4	278	334
5	–0–	–0–

Finally, amortization and unamortized balances would be as follows:

Year	Percentage Persisting at End of Year	Original Factors Amortization	Original Factors Unamortized Balance	Revised Factors Amortization	Revised Factors Unamortized Balance
1	65%	$ 413	$587	$ 333	$667
2	55	194	393	217	450
3	45	163	230	183	267
4	35	133	97	150	117
5	–0–	97	–0–	117	–0–
		$1,000		$1,000	

If actual terminations deviated significantly from assumed terminations in subsequent years, the entire process might have to be repeated. The objective of recalculation of factors is to apportion amortization among accounting periods based on the best information possible. Actual termination experience can never be forecast with perfect accuracy; regardless of how refined one attempts to be, there is no way to know the exact pattern of premium receipts until the contracts terminate. Thus any amortization method—use of original assumptions, use of original factors and actual in-force, and use of revised factors and actual in-force—is an approximation.

Guidelines for Persistency Adjustments

Every effort should be made to forecast terminations accurately, particularly with respect to the earlier years. Provisions for adverse deviation should be made primarily for the later years; termination assumptions for the early years should be as realistic as possible.

Where the worksheet method is used, periodic comparisons of actual and assumed insurance in force should be made for each major class of business for each issue year. If actual is significantly different from assumed, adjustment should be made based on an approximation of factors that would have been appropriate for the original assumptions. (This is further discussed later in this chapter.)

Where the factor method is used, adjustment for termination deviations will be automatic.

Where termination experience differs so radically from assumed that continued use of the original factors would materially affect income, assets, and/or surplus relative to the effect of recalculation, then the factors should be recalculated. In the case of the worksheet approach, amortization tables should be recast. The cumulative effect of recalculation would be charged or credited to income in the year of recalculation.

Recalculation should be undertaken only in extreme

situations. As discussed in Chapter 8, where the facts warrant recalculation of expense factors or a recasting of worksheet amortization tables, benefit reserve factors should also be recalculated to give effect to the revised termination assumptions.

Conflict with Lock-in

The audit guide indicates that reserve assumptions should normally be locked in and that "variances from original estimates [should be] recognized in the accounting periods in which such variances occur." [7]

The lock-in provision extends to termination assumptions. Yet, where acquisition costs are concerned, factors should be recalculated "if actual [termination] experience differs significantly from that assumed."

At first blush the recalculation provision appears to be direct conflict with the lock-in requirement. For reasons explained in Chapter 6, however, hindsight should be applied in developing persistency assumptions in a conversion to generally accepted accounting principles. An extension of this reasoning would suggest that persistency assumptions should be revised *whenever* experience proves that the original assumptions were radically in error.*

Thus the recalculation provision is reasonably consistent with the lock-in requirement.

Conflict with Release-from-Risk Concept

Recalculation of expense factors involves a violation of the pure release-from-risk concept of provisions for adverse deviation. As discussed and illustrated in Chapter 6, the fact that a provision for adverse deviation could result in deferring acquisition costs in an amount greater than what was incurred would not be objectionable if the risk of adverse deviation were so defined as to produce such a result.

Under the principle that a provision for adverse deviation primarily represents a margin for conservatism, however, there is no conflict. Recalculation amounts to an adjustment of the margin for conservatism appropriate in the circumstances.

Worksheet Methods

There are two basic methods of amortizing acquisi-

*However, the reasoning does not apply to the interest and mortality assumptions, for reasons that are also discussed in Chapter 6.

tion costs: the worksheet method and the factor method.

Both methods attempt to do the same thing, of course, which is to amortize acquisition costs over the premium-paying period in proportion to premium revenues recognized.

Neither method is really "superior". Use of a particular method is a matter of personal preference.

The worksheet method is discussed in this section.

Advantages and Disadvantages

There are, of course, numerous advantages and disadvantages associated with the worksheet approach. Advantages vis-à-vis the factor approach can be summarized as follows:

1. A worksheet is simple to set up initially and may be simpler to maintain thereafter.
2. A worksheet is readily understood by non-actuaries.
3. It is generally not necessary to worry about deferred and uncollected premium adjustments.
4. The method more readily accommodates a division of labor between actuarial personnel and accounting personnel.
5. The worksheet method generally reduces the extent of allocation of costs to plans or blocks of business.

On the other hand, the advantages of the factor method are the disadvantages of the worksheet method:

1. Persistency adjustments—i.e., adjustment for deviations of actual terminations from assumed—are difficult to make.
2. There is probably a greater probability of error using the worksheet approach.
3. Interest is difficult to take into account.
4. Renewal-year acquisition costs are more difficult to take into account.
5. Worksheets inevitably result in less refinement in allocation of costs to plans.

Amortization without Interest

Amortization of first-year acquisition costs without interest is fairly straightforward. It involves

▸ Developing a projection of gross premiums for each year of issue for each block of business for which costs are going to be separately accounted for;
▸ Computing the percentage which the premiums to

Table 16–3.

DEVELOPMENT OF AMORTIZATION TABLE FOR FIRST-YEAR ACQUISITION COSTS FOR 1971 ISSUES OF 20-PAY LIFE—EXCLUDING INTEREST

Year	Percent Expected to Persist	Sum-of-the Years' Percentages	Projected Gross Premiums* Amount (000)	% of Total	Acquisition Costs (000) ($1,724,000 Incurred) Amortization	Unamortized End of Year	Projected In-Force— $60,720,000 Production (000)	Unamortized Acquisition Costs Per $1,000 Projected In-Force
1971	.99966	.0985	$ 1,410	.0955	$ 165	$1,559	$60,699	$26
1972	.75514	.0744	1,077	.0729	126	1,433	45,852	31
1973	.67569	.0666	977	.0662	114	1,319	41,027	32
1974	.63733	.0628	927	.0628	108	1,211	38,699	31
1975	.60469	.0596	883	.0598	103	1,108	36,717	30
1976	.57371	.0565	841	.0570	98	1,010	34,836	29
1977	.54698	.0539	803	.0544	94	916	33,212	28
1978	.52269	.0515	767	.0519	89	827	31,737	26
1979	.49938	.0492	733	.0496	86	741	30,322	24
1980	.47702	.0470	701	.0475	82	659	28,965	23
1981	.45664	.0450	670	.0454	78	581	27,727	21
1982	.43702	.0431	641	.0434	75	506	26,536	19
1983	.41959	.0414	616	.0417	72	434	25,478	17
1984	.40273	.0397	591	.0400	69	365	24,454	15
1985	.38731	.0382	568	.0385	66	299	23,517	13
1986	.37400	.0369	548	.0371	64	235	22,709	10
1987	.36098	.0356	529	.0358	62	173	21,919	8
1988	.34826	.0343	509	.0344	59	114	21,146	5
1989	.33847	.0333	495	.0335	58	56	20,552	3
1990	.32956	.0325	482	.0326	56	-0-	20,011	-0-
	10.14685	1.0000	$14,768	1.0000	$1,724			

* Assuming annual mode.

be received in each year bear to the total of projected premiums; and

▶ Applying the percentages thus derived to first-year acquisition costs incurred.

Table 16–3 illustrates the development of an amortization table to be used in connection with the worksheet method for acquisition costs applicable to Crazy Quilt Life's 1971 issues of 20-pay life business, of which $60,720,000 in face amount was sold. Table 16–3 assumes that all of the business is annual-premium business.

Certain characteristics of Table 16–3 deserve comment. The 20-pay life policy extends coverage for the whole of life, but the premium-paying period is only 20 years. Therefore, acquisition costs must be written off over 20 years.

The percentage of insureds expecting to persist is simply a composite (i.e., for all ages combined) expression of persistency data; it represents expected persistency for each issue age weighted by the dis-

tribution of issues among the various ages. An example of weighting will be found in Table 16–8.

The sum-of-the-years'-percentages are, in effect, the sum-of-the-years'-digits where "digits" are the respective percentages expected to persist for the first 20 years.

Projected gross premiums are just that—a composite of total premiums expected to be received over the 20-year premium-paying period on the $60,720,000 of business sold. The percentage which each year's premiums bears to the total of all years' premiums is the sum-of-the-years'-premiums percentage that are applied to total acquisition costs (in this case, $1,724,000) to amortize them in proportion to premiums.

It will be observed that the sum-of-the-years' percentages and the sum-of-the-years'-premiums percentages are very nearly the same. In fact, the main reason they differ is that persistency and premiums differ by age, and the "runoff" of premiums is not perfectly proportional to the "runoff" of insurance in

Table 16–4.

DEVELOPMENT OF AMORTIZATION TABLE FOR FIRST-YEAR ACQUISITION COSTS FOR 1971 ISSUES OF 20-PAY LIFE—RECOGNIZING INTEREST AT 5% (000 Omitted from Amounts)

Year	Projected Gross Premiums	Present Value of Projected Gross Premiums		Unamortized Acquisition Costs				Amortization	
		5% Discount Factor	Amount	"Payment"— 16.5% of Projected Gross Premiums	Balance after "Payment"	5% Interest on Balance	Ending Balance	Amount	% of Total
1971	$ 1,410	1.0000	$ 1,410	$ 233	$1,491	$ 75	$1,566	$ 158	.092
1972	1,077	.9524	1,026	178	1,388	69	1,457	109	.063
1973	977	.9070	886	161	1,296	65	1,361	96	.056
1974	927	.8638	801	153	1,208	60	1,268	93	.054
1975	883	.8227	726	146	1,122	56	1,178	90	.052
1976	841	.7835	659	139	1,039	52	1,091	87	.050
1977	803	.7462	599	132	959	48	1,007	84	.049
1978	767	.7107	545	127	880	44	924	83	.048
1979	733	.6768	496	121	803	40	843	81	.047
1980	701	.6446	452	116	727	36	763	80	.046
1981	670	.6139	411	110	653	33	686	77	.045
1982	641	.5847	375	106	580	29	609	77	.045
1983	616	.5568	343	102	507	25	532	77	.045
1984	591	.5303	313	97	435	22	457	74	.043
1985	568	.5051	287	94	363	18	381	76	.044
1986	548	.4810	264	90	291	16	307	74	.043
1987	529	.4581	242	87	219	12	232	75	.044
1988	509	.4363	222	84	146	8	156	76	.044
1989	495	.4155	206	82	71	5	79	77	.045
1990	482	.3957	191	79	–0–	–0–	–0–	79	.045
	$14,768		$10,454	$2,437		$713		$1,724	1.000

Acquisition costs $ 1,724

Acquisition costs as percentage of present value of premiums   16.5%

---

force.* But the fact that the two quantities approximate each other is important, for reasons which will become clear momentarily.

If 1971 issues of 20-pay life business were the only business ever issued by Crazy Quilt Life, then amortization charged to expense in each of the 20 years would be as shown in the "amortization" column. The amount actually charged to expense in any given year would be the aggregate of the amounts shown in the "amortization" column for that year for *all* such worksheets.

In developing a worksheet of the type shown in Table 16–3, it is possible to compute prospectively

an unamortized acquisition cost factor per $1,000 expected to remain in force at the end of each year. Projected in-force in Table 16–3 is simply the percent expected to persist multiplied by new business volume. In 1980, for example, the percent expected to persist is .47702; this percentage multiplied by 1971 new business, $60,720,000, yields the projected in-force, $28,965,000. The projected unamortized balance of acquisition costs, $659,000, needs only to be divided by the projected in-force to obtain the related 1980 factor, $22.75, which in Table 16–3 is rounded to $23.

(The factors can also be computed without developing a projected in-force volume. For instance, the 1980 factor can be computed by dividing the unamortized balance, $659,000, by the volume issued, $60,720,000, which yields $10.85 per $1,000; this amount divided by the percentage expected to persist, .47702, yields the desired quantity, $22.75.)

*In addition, the persistency percentages shown in Table 16–3 represent percentages persisting on annual mode business at the end of the calendar year, i.e., after mortality but before withdrawal. A better correlation would be obtained by using persistency percentages applicable to the beginning of the policy year, i.e., *before* mortality.

Table 16–5.

SUMMARY OF EFFECT OF INTEREST ON AMORTIZATION OF FIRST-YEAR ACQUISITION COSTS ON 1971 ISSUES OF 20-PAY LIFE

Year	Rate of Amortization		Percentage of Total Unamortized		Unamortized Per $1,000 In Force	
	Without Interest	*With Interest*	*Without Interest*	*With Interest*	*Without Interest*	*With Interest*
1971	.096	.092	.904	.908	$26	$26
1972	.073	.063	.831	.845	31	32
1973	.066	.056	.765	.787	32	33
1974	.063	.054	.702	.735	31	33
1975	.060	.052	.643	.683	30	32
1976	.057	.050	.586	.633	29	31
1977	.054	.049	.531	.584	28	30
1978	.052	.048	.480	.536	26	29
1979	.050	.047	.430	.489	24	28
1980	.048	.046	.382	.443	23	26
1981	.045	.045	.337	.398	21	25
1982	.043	.045	.294	.353	19	23
1983	.042	.045	.252	.308	17	21
1984	.040	.043	.212	.265	15	19
1985	.039	.044	.173	.221	13	16
1986	.037	.043	.136	.178	10	14
1987	.036	.044	.100	.134	8	11
1988	.034	.044	.066	.090	5	7
1989	.033	.045	.032	.045	3	4
1990	.032	.045	–0–	–0–	–0–	–0–

The factors are important if persistency adjustments without recalculation are to be made. Suppose, for example, that actual in-force and projected in-force are as follows:

	000	
Year	*Projected In-Force*	*Actual In-Force*
1	$60,699	$60,500
2	45,852	45,300
3	41,027	40,000

The factors could be applied to actual in-force whenever the actual in-force is deemed to differ significantly from assumed. If this were judged to be the case in the third year, for example, third-year amortization would be $153,000 rather than the $114,000 originally projected:

In force (000)	$40,000
Factor per $1,000	32
Revised unamortized (000)	1,280
Prior unamortized (000)	1,433
Amortization (000)	153

Of course, these adjustments could also be made every year regardless of materiality. The effect would be to very nearly approximate the effect of using the factor method.

Of course it is necessary to keep track of actual persistency by year of issue to make the type of adjustment illustrated above.

Amortization with Interest

Table 16–4 shows the development of an amortization table which includes interest, at 5 percent, on unamortized acquisition costs.

To recognize interest on acquisition costs it is necessary to compute the present value of future gross premiums (at 5 percent, in this case) and establish the percentage relationship between the present value of acquisition costs (which, in this case, is the same as the amount incurred, $1,724,000, because the costs are incurred immediately) and the present value of premiums. This percentage represents the portion of each year's gross premiums required to amortize "principal", $1,724,000, with interest at 5 percent.

As Table 16–4 indicates, the acquisition cost "principal" is reduced in the same manner as a mortgage loan. The change in the ending balance of unamortized acquisition costs represents annual amortization. The interest itself would never show up in the statements unless one wished to reclassify it between accounts in the income statement, which seems unnecessary.

Table 16–5 summarizes various significant items relating to amortization with and without interest. It can be seen that the effect of interest is relatively innocuous in this case.

Illustrations of acquisition costs amortized with and without interest for Crazy Quilt Life's entire book of business are shown in Tables 16–2, 16–13, and 16–14.

Renewal-Year Acquisition Costs

Assume that commissions subsequent to the first year are payable as follows:

Year	Commission Rate
2	20%
3	15
4–10	10
11 on	5

It is apparent that the "ultimate" commission rate is 5 percent and that renewal-year acquisition costs amount to 15 percent in the second year, 10 percent in the third, and 5 percent in the fourth through tenth years. How can such expenses be accommodated in an amortization table?

Even if the expenses were segregated in some manner (which is very difficult to do in terms of most life insurance accounting systems) and deferred and amortized over the remaining premium-paying period, this would give an improper result. A part of the second year's acquisition costs actually applies against premiums received in the first year; part of the third year's acquisition costs applies against premiums received in the first and second years; and so on. *All* acquisition costs should be matched against *all* premiums.

There are probably only four practical alternatives for dealing with renewal-year acquisition costs:

1. Ignore them.
2. Include them in an "average" ultimate rate.
3. Account for them separately.
4. Modify the amortization table to give effect to them.

The first two alternatives should normally be rejected (for reasons discussed in Chapter 15) unless renewal-year acquisition costs are immaterial. The third alternative is feasible, but it is not very practical;

the volume of amortization tables would double (assuming all blocks of business for which amortization tables have been prepared are affected). The fourth alternative is usually the most satisfactory from a practical standpoint, because it *combines* what would otherwise be two separate sets of calculations.

The method by which an acquisition cost amortization table is "modified" to recognize renewal-year acquisition costs is illustrated in Table 16–6. Renewal-year acquisition costs are projected and both actual first-year acquisition costs and projected renewal-year acquisition costs are amortized by the sum-of-the-years'-premiums method. The indicated amortization amounts are then *reduced* by projected renewal-year acquisition costs in the year of their expected occurrence.

The modified amortization amounts are then divided by first-year acquisition costs to obtain the annual amortization percentages, and these percentages are applied to first-year acquisition costs to obtain annual amortization net of renewal-year acquisition costs.

The practical advantages of this approach are obvious.

Note that first-year amortization giving effect to renewal-year acquisition costs is 12.6 percent, whereas first-year amortization ignoring renewal-year acquisition costs is 9.6 percent. The difference is due to the fact that a portion of the renewal-year acquisition costs is amortized in the first year even though such costs have not yet been incurred. Viewed another way, a liability for renewal-year acquisition cost accrues in the first year. Thus it is less conservative in the first year to ignore renewal-year acquisition costs. Thereafter the reverse is true as renewal-year amounts are effectively deferred through the operation of the modified amortization table.

Interest on acquisition costs can also be recognized using the worksheet method when it is necessary to give effect to renewal-year acquisition costs. The method of doing this is illustrated in Table 16–7.

All of the projected unamortized balances can be translated into factors per $1,000 to make the types of persistency adjustments discussed earlier.

It will be observed that recognition of renewal-year acquisition costs results in mixing asset and liability elements. For example, reference to Table 16–3 will indicate that the unamortized balance at the end of the first year is $1,559,000 when renewal-year acquistion costs are ignored. Reference to Table 16–6 will indicate that the unamortized balance is $1,506,-000 (total incurred, $1,724,000, less amortization of $218,000). So the unamortized balance produced by

Table 16–6.

MODIFICATION OF AMORTIZATION TABLE TO RECOGNIZE PROJECTED RENEWAL-YEAR ACQUISITION COSTS—EXCLUDING INTEREST (000 Omitted from Amounts)

Year	Amortization of First-Year Acquisition Costs	Renewal-Year Acquisition Costs			Sum-of-the-Years' Premiums Percentage	Amortization of First-Year and Projected Renewal Acquisition Costs	Amortization Net of Projected Renewal-Year Acquisition Costs	
		Projected Gross Premiums	Excess Commission Rate	Projected Excess Commissions			Amount	% of First-Year Cost
1971	$ 165				.096	$ 218	$ 218	.126
1972	126	$1,077	15%	$162	.073	165	3	.002
1973	114	977	10	98	.066	150	52	.030
1974	108	927	5	46	.063	143	97	.056
1975	103	883	5	44	.060	136	92	.053
1976	98	841	5	42	.057	129	87	.050
1977	94	803	5	40	.054	122	82	.048
1978	89	767	5	38	.052	118	80	.046
1979	86	733	5	37	.050	113	76	.044
1980	82	701	5	35	.048	109	74	.043
1981	78				.045	102	102	.059
1982	75				.043	97	97	.056
1983	72				.042	95	95	.055
1984	69				.040	91	91	.053
1985	66				.039	88	88	.051
1986	64				.037	84	84	.049
1987	62				.036	82	82	.048
1988	59				.034	77	77	.045
1989	58				.033	75	75	.044
1990	56				.032	72	72	.042
	$1,724			$542	1.000	$2,266	$1,724	1.000

use of Table 16–6 is net of a liability for renewal-year acquisition costs of $53,000 ($1,559,000 − $1,506,-000).

It would be possible to account separately for the asset and liability elements, but the results are not worth the effort. It is better to classify unamortized balances as assets or liabilities based on whether the *net* amount is positive or negative. (Asset and liability elements of unamortized acquisition costs are discussed in Chapter 17.)

The question arises as to what to do if actual renewal-year acquisition costs differ significantly from assumed. There's no easy answer to this question. It would rarely be *known* if actual differs materially from assumed, simply because renewal-year acquisition costs are not usually accounted for separately. The most practical answer is to double-check the method of recognizing agents' contract rates in the first place, and monitor the contracts to make certain there are no retroactive rate adjustments (which would be rare).

Caution is advisable, however, in giving effect to vesting provisions. If full vesting is assumed, then to the extent that commissions do not vest and agents terminate before ultimate rates are reached, renewal-year acquisition costs that have never been incurred will wind up being deferred. When renewal-year acquisition costs are material, such costs should be weighted for non-vesting, and agent terminations should be monitored.

Calendar-Year Adjustments

All of the illustrations thus far have been based on annual-mode business and a policy-year progression.

Only two types of adjustments would be required to recognize a calendar-year basis:

1. Where acquisition costs are being amortized with interest, only a half-year's interest would be taken in the first year. Similar half-year adjustments would be made with respect to renewal-year acquisition costs, if applicable.

2. Usually actual acquisition costs are deferred. A

Table 16–7.

MODIFICATION OF AMORTIZATION TABLE TO RECOGNIZE PROJECTED RENEWAL-YEAR ACQUISITION COSTS—RECOGNIZING INTEREST AT 5% (000 Omitted from Amounts)

Year	Actual First-Year and Projected Renewal Acquisition Costs	Present Value of Acquisition Costs 5% Discount Factor	Present Value of Acquisition Costs Amount	Total Unamortized Acquisition Costs "Payment"—20.86% of Projected Gross Premiums	Total Unamortized Acquisition Costs Balance after "Payment"	5% Interest on Balance	Ending Balance	Amortization	Amortization Net of Present Value of Projected Renewal-Year Acquisition Costs Amount	Amortization Net of Present Value of Projected Renewal-Year Acquisition Costs % of First-Year Costs
1971	$1,724	1.0000	$1,724	$ 294	$1,887*	$ 94	$1,981	$ 200	$ 200	.116
1972	162	.9524	154	225	1,756	88	1,844	137	(17)	(.010)
1973	98	.9070	89	204	1,640	82	1,722	122	33	.019
1974	46	.8638	40	193	1,529	76	1,605	117	77	.045
1975	44	.8227	36	184	1,421	71	1,492	113	77	.045
1976	42	.7835	33	175	1,317	66	1,383	109	76	.044
1977	40	.7462	30	168	1,215	61	1,276	107	77	.045
1978	38	.7107	27	160	1,116	56	1,172	104	77	.045
1979	37	.6768	25	153	1,019	51	1,070	102	77	.045
1980	35	.6446	23	146	924	46	970	100	77	.045
1981				140	830	42	872	98	98	.057
1982				134	738	37	775	97	97	.056
1983				129	646	32	678	97	97	.056
1984				123	555	28	583	95	95	.055
1985				119	464	23	487	96	96	.055
1986				114	373	19	392	95	95	.055
1987				110	282	14	296	96	96	.055
1988				106	190	10	200	96	96	.055
1989				103	97	4	101	99	99	.058
1990				101	–0–	–0–	–0–	101	101	.059
	$2,266		$2,181	$3,081		$900		$2,181	$1,724	1.000

Present value of premiums $10,454

Present value of acquisition costs as percentage of present value of premiums 20.86%

*The beginning balance was $2,181,000.

full policy year's percentage expenses should normally be amortized in the first year, for reasons explained in Chapter 23. However, in theory only a half-year's amortization should be recognized in the first year for non-percentage expenses, for reasons that are also explained in Chapter 23. But this adjustment would rarely be material except for companies (such as mail-order companies) whose acquisition costs are primarily non-percentage costs incurred at the time of writing the business.

Usually there are no deferred and uncollected premium adjustments for acquisition costs when the worksheet method is used.

Estimates for Prior Years

Inevitably the question arises as to what to do about amortization tables for prior years. Usually the information is not available to construct amortization tables for prior years using the techniques illustrated in this chapter. Even when the data are available, most companies do not want to duplicate the excruciating process described herein with respect to issues of all prior years. It's too much work, and in view of the fact that unamortized balances today on deferrals of prior years are relatively small (particularly for the earliest years), the result is usually not deemed sufficient to justify the effort.

So there will usually be a strong desire to lump together acquisition costs for prior years in the broadest classifications feasible and to develop amortization tables to match.

Aggregations and estimates of deferrals are discussed in Chapter 15. Whatever decision is made with re-

Table 16–8.

DEVELOPMENT OF ESTIMATED AMORTIZATION RATES FOR ISSUES OF 1955

	55	56	57	58	59	60	61	62	63	64	65	66	67	68	69	70	71	Etc.
Approximate sum-of-the-years' percentages:																		
Par whole life	.08	.06	.06	.05	.05	.05	.04	.04	.04	.04	.03	.03	.03	.03	.03	.03	.03	
Whole life	.06	.04	.04	.04	.04	.04	.04	.03	.03	.03	.03	.03	.03	.03	.03	.03	.03	
Limited-pay life	.10	.07	.07	.06	.06	.06	.05	.05	.05	.05	.05	.04	.04	.04	.04	.04	.04	
Short-term endowments	.10	.08	.07	.06	.06	.06	.05	.05	.05	.05	.05	.04	.04	.04	.04	.04	.04	
Level term	.14	.11	.10	.09	.08	.06	.06	.05	.05	.04	.03	.03	.02	.02	.02	.01	.01	
Weighted distribution of issues:																		
Par whole life	.10																	
Whole life	.35																	
Limited-pay life	.13	(ALL YEARS ARE WEIGHTED BY THE SAME DISTRIBUTION PERCENTAGE)																
Short-term endowments	.09																	
Level term	.33																	
Composite sum-of-the-years' percentages:																		
Par whole life	.01	.01	.01	.01	.01	.01	.01	--	--	--	--	--	--	--	--	--	--	
Whole life	.02	.01	.01	.01	.01	.01	.01	.01	.01	.01	.01	.01	.01	.01	.01	.01	.01	
Limited-pay life	.01	.01	.01	.01	.01	.01	.01	.01	.01	.01	.01	.01	.01	.01	.01	.01	.01	
Short-term endowments	.01	.01	.01	.01	.01	.01	.01	.01	.01	.01	.01	--	--	--	--	--	--	
Level term	.05	.03	.03	.03	.03	.02	.02	.02	.02	.01	.01	.01	.01	.01	.01	--	--	
	.10	.07	.07	.07	.07	.06	.06	.05	.05	.04	.04	.03	.03	.03	.03	.02	.02	
Cumulative composite	.10	.17	.24	.31	.38	.44	.50	.55	.60	.64	.68	.71	.74	.77	.80	.82	.84	
100%—cumulative composite	.90	.83	.76	.69	.62	.56	.50	.45	.40	.36	.32	.29	.26	.23	.20	.18	.16	

spect to aggregating will affect amounts deferred and amounts amortized, since the amortization table must be a composite table for all the classes of business covered by the aggregate.

Perhaps the best method of developing composite amortization tables is to construct a "model" of sum-of-the-years' percentages for each major class of business and weight the percentages by the distribution of issues. The result would be a weighted composite sum-of-the-years' percentages table that can be used as a stand-in for the composite sum-of-the-years'-premiums percentages. This process is illustrated in Table 16–8 for Crazy Quilt Life's 1955 issues. While one year's issues are covered by Table 16–8, in practice it could be used for the issues of several years so long as the distribution of issues does not change radically during the period.

The composite rates would then be applied to estimated acquisition costs incurred to obtain annual amortization amounts, or unamortized balances for each relevant year-end could be developed by applying the unamortized percentage ("100%—cumulative composite" in Table 16–8) to the estimated amounts incurred.

The percentages developed in Table 16–8 do not contemplate interest or renewal-year acquisition costs, but those items could be taken into account by working directly with the cumulative composite percentages.

It is, of course, difficult to make persistency adjustments when composites are used. Composite actual insurance in force can be compared with assumed, and adjustments can be made using composite factors per $1,000. This is probably the only feasible thing to do where composites are concerned. There is a danger that the mix of actual terminations departs dramatically from the mix of assumed terminations, which—as discussed in Chapter 15—can create errors, but this can only be overcome by periodically comparing assumed in-force with actual in-force for each plan group included in the composite and then, if adjustment is indicated for a particular plan, allocating unamortized costs among plans (perhaps more or less subjectively) and making the indicated adjustment.

303

Table 16–9.

SUMMARY WORKSHEET FOR UNAMORTIZED ACQUISITION COSTS—RECOGNIZING INTEREST AND RENEWAL-YEAR ACQUISITION COSTS (000 Omitted)

| Year | First-Year Acquisition Costs Incurred | Unamortized Acquisition Costs | | | | | |
| | | 1969 | | 1970 | | 1971 | |
		%	Amount	%	Amount	%	Amount
1941	$ 759	4%	$ 27	3%	$ 25	3%	$ 22
1942	1,040	4	45	4	41	3	36
1943	1,363	5	67	4	61	4	55
1944	1,620	5	89	5	81	4	73
1945	1,986	6	125	6	114	5	103
1946	2,285	7	163	6	148	6	136
1947	2,499	8	201	7	184	7	168
1948*	2,666	14	377	13	347	12	317
1949	2,963	16	469	14	431	13	396
1950	3,103	18	551	16	515	15	474
1951	3,300	22	724	18	606	17	567
1952	3,310	22	746	20	650	17	554
1953	3,373	26	890	23	789	20	693
1954	3,323	30	989	27	891	24	793
1955	3,040	33	1,015	31	931	28	843
1956	2,635	37	979	34	899	32	835
1957	2,455	33	812	30	739	27	667
1958	2,616	36	941	33	862	30	787
1959	2,789	40	1,103	36	1,018	34	936
1960	3,091	43	1,331	40	1,240	37	1,146
1961	3,501	47	1,638	44	1,528	41	1,429
1962*	4,130	79	3,276	77	3,199	76	3,126
1963	5,394	82	4,409	80	4,300	78	4,199
1964	6,452	84	5,440	82	5,302	80	5,172
1965	7,530	86.	6,456	83	6,257	81	6,087
1966	8,785	89	7,791	86	7,543	84	7,366
1967	10,102	91	9,179	89	8,972	86	8,687
1968	10,581	88	9,313	84	8,902	80	8,502
1969	11,857	91	10,815	88	10,444	84	9,986
1970	13,762			88	12,114	88	12,175
1971	15,040					88	13,237
			$69,961		$79,133		$89,567
Net increase					$ 9,207		$10,434

*Significant change in renewal-year commission pattern.

Summary Worksheet

Table 16–9 shows a summary worksheet for acquisition costs for Crazy Quilt Life at the end of 1969, 1970, and 1971. Only first-year acquisition costs incurred are shown, but the unamortized balances reflect interest, renewal-year acquisition costs, and annual persistency adjustments using the simulated factor method previously described.

Acquisition Cost Factors

Crazy Quilt Life elected to use acquisition cost factors to amortize acquisition costs. The advantages of the factor method were the disadvantages of the worksheet method and vice-versa, and Crazy Quilt discovered three more advantages of the factor method that tilted management in its favor:

▸ Valuation premiums were a natural product of the process, and recoverability was therefore easier to test.

▸ While the initial work was greater than the worksheet method, thereafter the necessary work was much less.

▶ Integrating the accounting process—i.e., making projections and calculating factors in a uniform manner—yielded much data in a form suitable for certain additional management information that is discussed in Chapter 31.

Use of the factor method involved assignment of costs to individual plans and ages; computation of acquisition cost valuation premiums; calculation of acquisition cost factors; and application of acquisition cost factors to insurance in force.

Assignment of Costs

As discussed in Chapter 15, Crazy Quilt assigned costs to each major plan group. Plan groups were developed by a modeling process described in Chapter 28.

The only expenses deemed to vary by age were percentage expenses. They were automatically allocated to the various ages in the proper amount because the percentages were applied to gross premiums, and gross premiums varied by age.

Valuation Premiums

Acquisition cost valuation premiums were computed in the manner described in Chapter 7. The present value of a $1 annuity was computed using the basic reserve assumptions for mortality, withdrawals and interest. The present value of first-year and renewal-year acquisition costs was computed. The latter was divided by the former to obtain the valuation premiums.

Suitable modifications of this procedure were made in the case of variable-premium plans, as is also described in Chapter 7.

Calculation of Factors

Factors were also calculated in the manner described in Chapter 7. Valuation premiums and acquisition costs per $1,000 were accumulated at interest; the "fund" thus calculated as of the end of each calendar year was divided by the percentage of policyholders then assumed to persist to derive factors per $1,000.

Application of Factors

The factors were then applied to appropriate groupings of insurance in force to obtain unamortized balances of acquisition costs.

Special Problems with Factors

As discussed in Chapter 12, certain calculation techniques create distortions, which may be material, relative to the intermediate or "fund" method that Crazy Quilt uses. Those distortions apply also to acquisition costs. The subject of alternative calculation techniques as they affect the calculation of acquisition cost factors is further discussed in Chapter 23.

If the factor calculation method assumes receipt of a full annual premium and payment of all expenses on the policy anniversary, significant adjustments must be made to deferred and uncollected premiums and the portion of acquisition costs that has not yet been paid must be eliminated by adjustment. This is also discussed further in Chapter 23.

If the factor calculation method distributes premiums and expenses to the calendar year of incidence, there may be no deferred premium adjustments. Distributions to calendar year of incidence are discussed further in Chapter 18.

The use of mid-terminal acquisition cost factors is discussed in Chapters 18, 19, and 23.

Effect of Withdrawals and Mortality

As noted in Chapter 8, significant variations in withdrawal and mortality assumptions frequently do not have a material effect on benefit reserve factors.

In the case of acquisition cost factors, significant variations (particularly with respect to the withdrawal assumption) typically do have a material effect. This is suggested by Tables 16–10 and 16–11, which show the effect on acquisition cost factors of varying the withdrawal and mortality assumptions.

Table 16–10 shows the effect of assuming zero withdrawals (hence the only decrement assumed is mortality), as well as Linton A withdrawals, Linton B withdrawals, Linton C withdrawals, and Crazy Quilt Life's ratebook assumptions, all of which are discussed in Chapter 8. The differentials are most pronounced at the later durations.

Consider, for example, whole life at the twentieth duration. Assuming $100 million of insurance in force, the indicated unamortized balances of acquisition costs are as follows:

Linton A	—	$4,462,000
Linton B	—	5,253,000
Linton C	—	6,043,000

If Linton C withdrawals were assumed but Linton B were experienced, acquisition costs on $100 million

Table 16–10.

EFFECT OF VARYING WITHDRAWAL RATES* ON ACQUISITION COST FACTORS AT SELECTED DURATIONS FOR 1971 ISSUES (AGE 35) OF SELECTED PLANS

Plan	Duration	Zero Withdrawals	Linton A	Linton B	Linton C	Crazy Quilt Ratebook Assumptions
Whole life	1	$32.70	$31.32	$29.56	$27.39	$31.17
	2	34.92	35.79	36.30	36.45	39.05
	3	36.36	38.34	39.97	41.20	42.36
	5	38.12	41.79	45.19	48.20	44.70
	7	39.37	44.37	49.22	53.82	45.66
	10	41.49	47.76	54.06	60.24	47.35
	15	39.64	47.03	54.58	62.13	44.51
	20	36.89	44.62	52.53	60.43	39.99
	30	28.90	36.53	44.57	52.76	27.82
	40	19.41	25.68	32.60	39.95	17.26
20-pay life	1	38.77	37.36	35.53	33.19	36.62
	2	38.28	39.80	41.05	41.92	43.60
	3	37.18	40.10	42.85	45.29	44.74
	5	34.77	39.54	44.45	49.29	43.00
	7	31.84	37.76	44.17	50.88	40.62
	10	26.68	33.06	40.34	48.38	35.93
	15	15.32	20.05	25.81	32.59	22.46
5-year R & C term	1	8.65	8.39	8.00	7.49	7.82
	2	8.51	8.95	9.30	9.53	8.87
	3	8.36	9.17	9.91	10.51	9.45
	5	8.04	9.42	10.77	12.02	9.89
	7	10.70	12.79	14.97	17.11	13.73
	10	10.00	12.76	15.78	18.87	12.71
	15	12.51	16.75	21.64	26.89	20.80
	20	15.33	21.43	28.83	37.19	29.34
	30	13.71	20.93	30.66	42.88	33.42
25-year decreasing term	1	9.29	8.93	8.48	7.90	8.70
	2	9.14	9.47	9.72	9.89	9.56
	3	8.88	9.52	10.10	10.61	9.87
	5	8.30	9.34	10.36	11.33	9.99
	7	8.09	9.47	10.91	12.37	10.39
	10	6.94	8.41	10.01	11.69	9.53
	15	5.45	6.90	8.57	10.39	7.83
	20	3.66	4.86	6.30	7.97	5.63

*All other assumptions held constant.

of insurance in force would be overstated by $790,000, or 15 percent of the correct amount. This gives further evidence of the importance of using unadulterated realistic withdrawal assumptions.

As Table 16–11 indicates, the effect of mortality is relatively inconsequential by comparison with the effect of withdrawals. This indicates that the effect of the mortality assumption on the level of acquisition costs need be given little if any consideration.

Minor Lines of Business

It would not be unusual for a company to use fac-

tors for its major classes of business and worksheets for its minor lines or classes.

That's what Crazy Quilt Life did. Factors were developed for all of the basic plans, while worksheets were used for waiver of premium and additional accidental death. As discussed in Chapter 15, deferrals were limited to the excess of first-year commissions over renewals computed at the average renewal rate.

Acquisition costs incurred in 1971 were $111,000 for the waiver benefit and $74,000 for additional accidental death. Amortization in 1971 was $60,000 and $40,000, respectively, and unamortized balances at

Table 16–11.

EFFECT OF VARYING MORTALITY RATES* ON ACQUISITION COST FACTORS AT SELECTED DURATIONS
FOR 1971 ISSUES (AGE 35) OF SELECTED PLANS

| Plan | Duration | 1955–60 Basic Select and Ultimate | | | 58 CSO | Crazy Quilt Ratebook Assumptions |
		100%	110%	150%		
Whole life	1	$31.17	$31.15	$31.00	$31.12	$31.17
	2	39.05	39.00	38.68	38.97	39.05
	3	42.36	42.29	41.92	42.27	42.36
	5	44.70	44.59	43.99	44.59	44.70
	7	45.66	45.50	44.64	45.54	45.66
	10	47.35	47.12	45.84	47.23	47.35
	15	44.51	44.17	42.91	44.37	44.51
	20	39.99	39.57	38.03	39.74	39.99
	30	27.82	27.34	25.61	27.37	27.82
	40	17.26	16.83	15.31	16.84	17.26
20-pay life	1	36.63	36.62	36.60	36.60	36.62
	2	43.62	43.61	43.56	43.60	43.60
	3	44.77	44.75	44.69	44.76	44.74
	5	43.05	43.03	42.94	43.07	43.00
	7	40.65	40.63	40.52	40.71	40.62
	10	35.92	35.89	35.77	36.04	35.93
	15	22.43	22.42	22.38	22.59	22.46
5-year R & C term	1	7.83	7.83	7.81	7.82	7.82
	2	8.90	8.89	8.86	8.89	8.87
	3	9.50	9.49	9.44	9.48	9.45
	5	9.99	9.96	9.87	9.96	9.89
	7	13.89	13.85	13.69	13.85	13.73
	10	12.97	12.91	12.66	12.93	12.71
	15	21.49	21.34	20.74	21.42	20.80
	20	30.67	30.43	29.49	30.58	29.34
	30	34.53	34.35	33.63	34.61	33.42
25-year decreasing term	1	8.70	8.70	8.69	8.69	8.70
	2	9.56	9.56	9.54	9.55	9.56
	3	9.87	9.86	9.84	9.86	9.87
	5	9.99	9.98	9.94	9.98	9.99
	7	10.39	10.38	10.33	10.39	10.39
	10	9.53	9.51	9.45	9.54	9.53
	15	7.83	7.81	7.74	7.85	7.83
	20	5.63	5.62	5.60	5.66	5.63

*All other assumptions held constant.

December 31 were $560,000 and $373,000, respectively.

Individual Fixed Annuities

As mentioned in Chapter 15, all of Crazy Quilt Life's individual annuities are single-premium, so allocable acquisition costs are expensed immediately. There is, of course, no amortization.

Arbitrary Grading

It will often be considered desirable to amortize acquisition costs over a period that is shorter than the premium-paying period. Reasons for such arbitrary grading might include the following:

▶ Simplicity. Particularly when worksheets are used, arbitrary grading tends to limit the number of years over which a given year's acquisition costs must be accounted for.

▶ Conservatism. Obviously the faster something is written off, the more conservative the financial statements. This would always be true of the balance sheet and would usually, but not always, be true of the income statement.

Table 16–12.

PERCENTAGES OF FIRST-YEAR ACQUISITION COSTS REMAINING UNAMORTIZED FOR SELECTED PLANS, YEARS OF ISSUE, AND DURATIONS—IGNORING INTEREST

Issue Year	Duration	Par Whole Life	Whole Life	20-pay Life	20-Year Endowment	5-Year R & C Term	25-Year Decreasing Term
1945	10	52%	51%	38%	34%	18%	
	15	36	35	17	14	8	
	20	23	23	–	–	3	
	25	15	15	–	–	1	NOT
	30	9	9	–	–	nil	ISSUED
	35	4	5	–	–	nil	
	40	2	3	–	–	–	
1950	10	53	52	38	38	36	
	15	36	36	17	17	20	
	20	24	24	–	–	11	NOT
	25	15	15	–	–	6	ISSUED
	30	9	9	–	–	3	
	35	5	5	–	–	1	
	40	2	3	–	–	–	
1955	10	51	58	38	38	36	
	15	35	43	17	17	20	
	20	24	30	–	–	11	NOT
	25	15	20	–	–	7	ISSUED
	30	9	13	–	–	3	
	35	5	8	–	–	1	
	40	2	4	–	–	–	
1960	10	52	52	39	38	24	35%
	15	36	36	18	17	12	19
	20	25	24	–	–	5	8
	25	16	15	–	–	2	–
	30	10	9	–	–	nil	–
	35	6	5	–	–	nil	–
	40	3	3	–	–	–	–
1965	10	59	61	39		47	38
	15	44	45	18		31	20
	20	33	32	–	NOT	22	8
	25	23	22	–	ISSUED	11	–
	30	16	14	–		6	–
	35	10	9	–		2	–
	40	6	5	–		2	–
1970	10	59	60	39		47	38
	15	45	45	18	NOT	33	21
	20	33	32	–	ISSUED	22	8
	25	24	22	–		11	–
	30	16	14	–		6	–
	35	11	8	–		3	–
	40	6	5	–		2	–

▶ Reduction in the number of prior years for which acquisition costs must be estimated. For example, if the grading period is 20 years and the first year being reported on is 1970, acquisition costs need only be estimated for years subsequent to 1949. As-suming a company is, say, 50 years old, the savings in effort is substantial.

General Guidelines

The life insurance audit guide is silent on the matter

of arbitrary grading, but notes simply that acquisition costs should be amortized over the premium-paying period.

It follows, then, that the effect of arbitrary grading must reasonably approximate the effect of not grading. Stated another way, the difference between grading or not grading must not be material. Assuming that the effect of grading is not material to assets or capital, materiality in relation to the income statement must also be considered. In other words, the effect of grading should be "modeled" such that the year-to-year effect can be approximated.

Table 16-12 shows some percentages of acquisition costs unamortized for various plans, issue ages, and durations for Crazy Quilt Life, where amortization is based on the full premium-paying period. A few generalizations about grading in Crazy Quilt Life's case can be made based on Table 16-12.

It would be inappropriate to grade whole-life acquisition costs to zero in less than 30 years, and 35 years would be preferable. Acquisition costs on 20-pay life business should not be graded. For term business 20 or 25 years is the minimum acceptable grading period, depending on the withdrawal pattern which, as indicated by Table 16-2, has varied significantly among ratebook eras.

Relationship to Reserve Grading

In theory, there is no relationship between reserve grading (discussed in Chapter 11) and arbitrary grading of acquisition costs. There is no reason why reserves could not be graded to statutory over one period (or not graded at all) and acquisition costs over another period (or not graded at all).

Caution should be exercised, however, when reserves are graded to a statutory *modified* reserve. Unless acquisition costs are graded to zero over the same period, or some adjustment is made for the unamortized preliminary term allowance, the result could be a double deferral of acquisition costs to the extent of the allowance.

Some Comparisons

Table 16-13 summarizes unamortized balances of acquisition costs as of December 31, 1971, for all of Crazy Quilt's ordinary life basic plans, classified by ratebook era. Table 16-14 shows the changes during 1971. The tables illustrate the effects of using 13 different methods of amortization. The statutory pre-

liminary term allowance—i.e., the difference between net level and modified reserves for all of Crazy Quilt's business—is shown for comparative purposes. The tables represent the calculation of about 100,000 acquisition cost factors.

As for balances of unamortized acquisition costs, Table 16-13 indicates that, in Crazy Quilt's case, it doesn't much matter whether acquisition costs are amortized with or without interest; the aggregate balances are within 1 percent of each other. However, ignoring renewal-year acquisition costs would result in a significant error ($7 million, or about 8 percent of the balance). Grading over 20 years would simply not be proper in Crazy Quilt's case. Grading over 30 years would yield a balance about $4 million (4 percent) less than the theoretically correct amount; this is probably the minimum acceptable cutoff point overall. Failure to adjust amortization for deviations in termination experience would not introduce a material balance sheet distortion in Crazy Quilt's case.

However, the differences differ by plan and ratebook era, and the aggregate results for Crazy Quilt will not necessarily imply anything with respect to a company with a different mix of business, a different historical pattern, and radically different assumptions.

One interesting piece of information yielded by Table 16-13 is the aggregate preliminary term allowance, $33,311,000. This is the difference between net level and modified statutory reserves and represents the unamortized balance of the maximum first-year expense allowances permitted under the law. It will be observed that the aggregate allowance is equal to only 37 percent of the theoretically proper amount, $89,567,000.

Inspection of Table 16-14 will indicate that many of the same conclusions apply to the income statement effects of the various approaches.

Disclosure

The life insurance audit guide requires that "unamortized acquisition costs . . . be presented in the balance sheet as a deferred charge." The guide further provides that the method of amortizing acquisition costs, and the amount of amortization charged to income for the period, should be disclosed.[8]

Suitable disclosure would include comments on whether acquisition costs are amortized with interest or not and whether an arbitrary grading period (or periods) is used. Unless the methods used are sub-

Table 16–13.

SUMMARY OF UNAMORTIZED BALANCES OF ACQUISITION COSTS AT DECEMBER 31, 1971 USING VARIOUS AMORTIZATION TECHNIQUES

(000 Omitted)

Plan and Rate Book Era	Insurance in Force (000)	Statutory Preliminary Term Allowance	Amortization Adjusted for Deviations in Termination Experience							Amortization Based on Original Assumptions as to Termination Experience—Not Adjusted for Deviations					
			Full-Term Writeoff		Full-Term Writeoff Without Interest; Acquisition Costs Subsequent to First-Year Excluded	20-Year Writeoff		30-Year Writeoff		Full-Term Writeoff		20-Year Writeoff		30-Year Writeoff	
			With Interest	Without Interest		With Interest	Without Interest	With Interest	Without Interest	With Interest	Without Interest	With Interest	Without Interest	With Interest	Without Interest
Par whole life															
41–47	$ 8	$ 50	$ 144	$ 124	$ 124	$ -0-	$ -0-	$ 52	$ 40	$ 103	$ 89	$ -0-	$ -0-	$ 38	$ 30
48–51	14	128	514	478	340	-0-	-0-	339	289	393	365	-0-	-0-	262	223
52–61	53	985	1,442	1,348	1,348	625	539	1,188	1,048	1,827	1,703	778	669	1,504	1,324
62–64	50	443	1,951	1,986	1,469	1,486	1,392	1,807	1,754	1,942	1,978	1,479	1,385	1,799	1,746
65–69	172	2,120	4,935	4,989	4,918	4,442	4,280	4,782	4,700	4,933	4,987	4,441	4,279	4,781	4,699
70–71	133	1,689	3,363	3,547	3,475	3,250	3,336	3,330	3,461	3,363	3,547	3,250	3,336	3,330	3,461
Whole life															
41–47	22	134	446	405	405	-0-	-0-	148	121	338	307	-0-	-0-	112	92
48–51	36	327	1,145	1,085	806	-0-	-0-	729	635	910	861	-0-	-0-	582	506
52–56	96	984	2,407	2,191	2,191	556	463	1,925	1,661	1,775	1,617	409	340	1,411	1,217
57–61	99	1,151	2,693	2,383	2,383	1,634	1,382	2,385	2,055	3,759	3,330	2,245	1,898	3,305	2,847
62–67	585	5,637	21,198	20,647	16,564	17,232	16,261	20,030	19,207	21,141	20,593	17,184	16,216	19,975	19,154
68–69	370	4,742	10,116	10,036	9,910	9,384	9,121	9,903	9,730	10,117	10,036	9,384	9,121	9,904	9,731
70–71	567	7,488	13,885	14,375	14,116	13,350	13,636	13,730	14,132	13,884	14,374	13,349	13,636	13,730	14,131
20-pay life															
41–47	29	-0-	-0-	-0-	-0-	-0-	-0-	-0-	-0-	-0-	-0-	-0-	-0-	-0-	-0-
48–51	22	-0-	-0-	-0-	-0-	-0-	-0-	-0-	-0-	-0-	-0-	-0-	-0-	-0-	-0-
52–56	31	91	209	174	174	209	174	209	174	187	156	187	156	187	156
57–61	26	267	557	477	477	557	477	557	477	569	487	569	487	569	487
62–67	94	1,290	3,475	3,138	2,740	3,475	3,318	3,475	3,318	3,632	3,469	3,632	3,469	3,632	3,469
68–69	64	1,049	1,879	1,847	1,822	1,879	1,847	1,879	1,847	1,965	1,931	1,965	1,931	1,965	1,931
70–71	111	1,929	2,740	2,790	2,775	2,740	2,790	2,740	2,790	2,777	2,827	2,777	2,827	2,777	2,827
20-year endowment															
48–61	37	253	518	454	454	518	454	518	454	544	478	544	478	544	478
5-year R & C term															
41–47	1	-0-	5	5	5	-0-	-0-	3	3	5	5	-0-	-0-	3	3
48–51	3	5	78	75	74	-0-	-0-	64	59	54	52	-0-	-0-	47	43
52–56	14	20	296	285	290	104	94	263	245	268	256	96	86	244	227
57–61	16	13	224	217	225	157	143	214	203	409	396	279	255	390	370
62–64	33	6	353	351	390	292	275	344	337	389	386	324	305	379	371
65–67	80	27	701	709	768	623	607	687	686	694	702	618	602	680	679
68–69	95	15	687	705	782	649	647	681	692	688	705	649	647	681	692
70–71	156	58	1,011	1,046	1,088	989	1,011	1,007	1,038	1,011	1,046	989	1,011	1,007	1,038

Amortization of Acquisition Costs

25-year decreasing term															
57–61	14	3	166	146	146	132	115	166	146	254	223	202	175	254	223
62–69	529	547	6,147	6,172	5,325	5,743	5,694	6,147	6,172	6,183	6,207	5,776	5,725	6,183	6,207
70–71	472	487	3,675	3,772	3,753	3,631	3,708	3,675	3,772	3,683	3,780	3,639	3,717	3,683	3,780
Conversion whole life (5YT)															
41–47	nil	1	1	1	1	-0-	-0-	1	1	1	1	-0-	-0-	1	1
48–51	1	6	14	13	9	-0-	-0-	11	10	11	10	-0-	-0-	9	7
52–56	3	44	74	67	67	24	20	66	57	46	41	15	13	41	36
57–61	5	68	97	84	84	66	55	92	78	125	108	85	71	119	101
62–67	24	328	849	814	610	746	700	832	793	874	752	689	647	769	733
68–69	11	206	321	312	307	308	297	319	309	302	293	290	279	300	291
70–71	11	217	333	340	329	324	329	331	338	333	340	324	329	331	338
Conversion whole life (25 YDT)															
62–67	6	94	224	218	169	202	192	221	213	207	201	186	177	204	196
68–69	10	180	288	281	276	277	267	286	278	271	263	260	250	269	261
70–71	14	269	406	415	403	396	401	404	413	406	415	396	401	404	413
	$4,117	$33,351	$89,567	$88,502	$81,592	$76,000	$74,025	$85,540	$83,736	$90,373	$89,317	$77,010	$74,918	$86,405	$84,519

Table 16–14.

DECREASES AND (INCREASES) IN UNAMORTIZED BALANCES OF ACQUISITION COSTS IN 1971 USING VARIOUS AMORTIZATION TECHNIQUES (000 Omitted)

Plan and Ratebook Era	Statutory Preliminary Term Allowance	Amortization Adjusted for Deviations in Termination Experience							Amortization Based on Original Assumptions as to Termination Experience–Not Adjusted for Deviations					
		Full-Term Writeoff		Full-Term Writeoff Without Interest; Acquisition Costs Subsequent to First Year Excluded	20-Year Writeoff		30-Year Writeoff		Full-Term Writeoff		20-Year Writeoff		30-Year Writeoff	
		With Interest	Without Interest		With Interest	Without Interest	With Interest	Without Interest	With Interest	Without Interest	With Interest	Without Interest	With Interest	Without Interest
Par whole life														
41–47	$ 6	$ 13	$ 14	$ 14	$ -0-	$ -0-	$ 18	$ 15	$ 11	$ 11	$ -0-	$ -0-	$ 13	$ 10
48–51	10	45	45	32	-0-	-0-	54	50	36	36	-0-	-0-	42	39
52–61	30	94	98	98	143	130	110	111	102	108	173	157	123	126
62–64	57	33	46	80	87	101	50	67	36	49	89	103	52	70
65–69	162	235	265	261	336	396	266	319	236	267	336	397	266	319
70–71	(818)	(1,788)	(1,891)	(1,779)	(1,752)	(1,766)	(1,766)	(1,834)	(1,788)	(1,891)	(1,713)	(1,752)	(1,766)	(1,834)
Whole life														
41–47	15	43	41	41	-0-	-0-	52	45	34	33	-0-	-0-	40	34
48–51	23	95	96	70	-0-	-0-	115	108	82	82	-0-	-0-	96	91
52–56	80	150	149	149	281	240	185	178	141	138	215	183	161	153
57–61	76	184	193	192	256	242	205	208	193	211	317	301	230	241
62–67	548	309	527	853	878	1,073	476	705	332	549	897	1,090	498	726
68–69	381	363	506	499	564	739	422	583	362	506	565	738	421	582
70–71	(3,555)	(7,403)	(7,641)	(7,235)	(7,049)	(7,154)	(7,300)	(7,481)	(7,403)	(7,639)	(7,048)	(7,155)	(7,301)	(7,480)
20-pay life														
41–47	-0-	-0-	-0-	-0-	-0-	-0-	-0-	-0-	-0-	-0-	-0-	-0-	-0-	-0-
48–51	-0-	-0-	-0-	-0-	-0-	-0-	-0-	-0-	-0-	-0-	-0-	-0-	-0-	-0-
52–56	52	115	99	99	115	99	115	99	104	90	104	104	104	89
57–61	44	80	76	76	80	76	80	76	84	80	83	80	83	79
62–67	142	200	239	274	200	239	200	239	220	260	219	260	220	260
68–69	149	153	185	182	153	185	153	185	137	172	138	172	137	172
70–71	(866)	(1,384)	(1,399)	(1,381)	(1,384)	(1,399)	(1,384)	(1,399)	(1,420)	(1,435)	(1,421)	(1,435)	(1,421)	(1,435)
20-year endowment														
48–61	78	154	138	138	154	138	154	138	170	152	170	152	170	152
5-year R & C term														
41–47	-0-	1	1	1	-0-	-0-	1	1	1	1	-0-	-0-	2	1
48–51	(1)	4	4	7	-0-	-0-	5	5	5	4	-0-	-0-	5	5
52–56	(1)	27	28	34	36	32	28	29	27	27	34	31	29	28
57–61	-0-	28	28	34	30	29	28	28	37	38	45	43	38	39
62–64	7	46	49	40	51	53	46	49	51	54	57	59	52	55
65–67	(8)	20	24	46	33	38	21	27	35	39	46	51	37	42
68–69	14	75	79	61	85	93	76	83	74	79	85	93	76	83
70–71	(23)	(507)	(523)	(550)	(492)	(500)	(504)	(518)	(507)	(523)	(492)	(500)	(504)	(518)

25-year decreasing term														
57–61	3	18	19	19	21	19	18	19	24	25	28	28	24	25
62–69	81	326	378	501	395	450	326	378	356	408	423	479	356	408
70–71	(234)	(1,875)	(1,917)	(1,896)	(1,845)	(1,875)	(1,875)	(1,917)	(1,883)	(1,925)	(1,854)	(1,884)	(1,883)	(1,925)
Conversion whole life (5YT)														
41–47	(1)	-0-	-0-	-0-	-0-	-0-	-0-	-0-	-0-	-0-	-0-	-0-	-0-	-0-
48–51	-0-	2	2	1	-0-	-0-	2	1	2	(2)	-0-	-0-	1	2
52–56	4	6	6	6	10	9	7	7	5	5	7	5	5	5
57–61	4	9	8	8	11	10	9	9						
62–67	28	16	25	41	32	40	19	28	19	26	33	40	21	28
68–69	11	9	14	14	13	19	10	15	13	19	17	23	14	19
70–71	(82)	(146)	(148)	(131)	(140)	(141)	(145)	(147)	(146)	(148)	(140)	(141)	(145)	(147)
Conversion whole life (25YT)														
62–67	6	5	6	11	8	10	4	7	5	7	9	11	5	8
68–69	8	7	12	12	10	15	8	13	11	17	15	20	12	17
70–71	(116)	(196)	(199)	(180)	(189)	(190)	(194)	(197)	(196)	(198)	(189)	(190)	(194)	(197)
	$(3,686)	$(10,434)	$(10,318)	$(9,258)	$(8,869)	$(8,550)	$(9,905)	$(9,668)	$(10,388)	$(10,258)	$(8,739)	$(8,440)	$(9,871)	$(9,617)

313

stantially the same for all lines of business, methods and amounts applicable to each major line of business should be disclosed.

Disclosure of the amount of amortization charged to income during the year may be difficult when the amount of renewal-year acquisition costs incurred is not determinable. In that case, the amount reported as being deferred would represent first-year acquisition costs only, and the amount shown for amortization, being a reconciling amount, would be net of renewal-year acquisition costs. Where this is the case, it would be preferable to state that "Amortization charged to income for the year, net of provisions for renewal-year acquisition costs, was $XXXXX" rather than simply to state, as the guide suggests, that "Amortization charged to income for the year . . . amounted to $XXXXX." [9]

Disclosure of amortization for Crazy Quilt Life's ordinary line of business might take the following form (disclosure of amounts deferred is discussed in Chapter 15):

ACCOUNTING POLICIES NOTE:

Acquisition costs are amortized with interest over the premium-paying period in proportion to the estimated recognition of premium revenues. Mortality, withdrawal, and interest assumptions used for amortization purposes are identical to those used in providing for policy reserves.

OTHER NOTE:

Amortization of policy acquisition costs charged to income for the year was $6,817,000.

17 Development, Maintenance, and Other Costs

Acquisition costs are by far the most significant and complex types of operating costs that must be dealt with in preparing a life insurance company's financial statements on the basis of generally accepted accounting principles, but there are several other types of costs that must also be accounted for: development costs, maintenance and settlement costs, investment expenses, and general overhead.

Development Costs

The life insurance audit guide makes two references to development costs:

Cost studies should . . . isolate developmental and other similar expenses so that a determination can be made as to whether any of such costs should be deferred.[1] If an expenditure has substantial future utility, and is clearly associated with and recoverable from future revenue, it may be considered for separate deferral in line with practices followed in other industries. An example of such an expenditure might be computer systems costs. If separately deferred, the expense should be amortized in a systematic and rational manner.[2]

Interestingly, earlier versions of the guide referred specifically to such development costs as agency-building, ratebook development, development of lines of business, and computer systems.[3] The final edition of the guide was much less specific, apparently at the behest of the SEC, which did not want to encourage deferrals by making such specific references.

Nature of Development Costs

A development cost may be defined roughly as a cost incurred in the expectation that profits attributable to the expenditure will be realized in future years. The expenditure does not immediately result in a stream of income. Thus development costs are fundamentally different from acquisition costs, which result in an identifiable block of insurance in force that begins generating revenues and profits immediately. Any benefits associated with development costs lie in the future. Development costs are essentially speculative in nature. Acquisition costs are collaterized, as it were, by insurance already in force. Development costs represent a hope about the future.

Types of Development Costs

Development costs might be classified as follows. The list does not purport to be all-inclusive:

▶ Agency development (costs of recruiting, training, and financing agents to bring them to the point at which they are self-sustaining producers; costs of establishing branch offices).
▶ Ratebook development.
▶ Development of a new line of business.
▶ Development of a specialized market.
▶ Administrative systems, such as significant new computer software development.

Some Arguments for Deferral

According to Accounting Research Study No. 7,

A great deal of the essence of accrual accounting is to be found in the proper matching of revenues realized with their related costs, and the pattern of assignment of costs and expenses to periods must be coordinated with policies and circumstances controlling the realization of revenues.[4]

Inasmuch as revenues attributable to development costs are expected to be recognized in future periods, many believe that development costs should be deferred and amortized to income in such future periods.

Because of the extremely long operating cycle of a life insurance company, some believe that the distinction between costs which are directly related to revenue of the current period and costs which are not so related is artificial.

Development costs are incurred for one purpose only: to produce new business or, in the case of systems development, to effect cost savings. Failure to defer and amortize such costs fails to recognize their purpose.

Some Arguments Against Deferral

While it may be true that revenues or cost savings are expected to accrue in future periods as a result of a development cost incurred in the current period, many believe that this expectancy is not susceptible to quantification with the degree of objectivity that should govern deferrals. As Accounting Research Study No. 7 points out,

To the extent that the rate of asset expiration is either erratic or unpredictable, reliable measurement is tempered or replaced by judgment as a basis by which cost is allocated between expenses and assets. Substantial uncertainty as to whether benefits may reasonably be expected to be realized in the future are resolved by charging the costs against current revenue.[5]

A long operating cycle is not peculiar to the life insurance industry. Manufacturing, particularly by high-technology industries, now involves a very long operating cycle. Thus, the period of time required for research, design, testing, manufacturing, training, marketing, negotiating contracts, and finally selling a product may be a decade or more in the case of highly sophisticated equipment. Revenue may continue to be realized long after the period of maximum development effort. In the usual case—and especially with respect to training and marketing—the cost of such effort is expensed in the period in which it is incurred. Precedence is therefore on the side of expensing development costs as incurred.

The matching principle is not limited to matching revenue and expense. Costs not directly identifiable with specific revenues are usually "matched" with the period in which they are incurred. Some believe that the period expense concept applies to development costs.

Research and development costs almost always apply to new product development. The fact that research and development costs are sometimes capitalized in other industries lends partial support to deferrals of the costs of ratebook development and costs associated with entering new lines of business, but it has no relevance to costs of agency development.*

APB Opinion No. 17

Development costs are generally identifiable as such, and Accounting Principles Board Opinion No. 17 ("Intangible Assets") applies to "identifiable intangible assets." [6]

But according to Opinion No. 17, mere identifiability is not sufficient to qualify an intangible cost for deferral:

Costs of developing, maintaining, or restoring intangible assets which are not specifically identifiable, have indeterminate lives, *or* are inherent in a continuing business and related to an enterprise as a whole . . should be deducted from income when incurred.[7] [Emphasis supplied.]

Assuming that development costs meet the test of identifiability, they (1) generally do not have a determinable life and (2) often are inherent in a continuing business and are related to the enterprise as a whole.

1. They do not have a determinable life. Development costs incurred in Year 1 may or may not benefit operations in Year 5, 10, 20, and so on. Any such benefit (and its expected life) simply cannot be measured with the objectivity with which the benefit of direct acquisition costs can be measured.

2. Some development costs are inherent in a continuing life insurance operation and they are related to the enterprise as a whole. For example, a company would not long sell insurance without continually developing new agents. Agent turnover is a continuing fact of existence for a life insurance company. The replacement of terminating business with enough additional new business for growth is the lifeblood of a life insurance company.

It is clear that the weight of evidence is on the side of charging development costs to expense as they are incurred, and that those companies that defer such

---

*At the time of this writing, it appears that the Financial Accounting Standards Board will soon issue pronouncements prohibiting the deferral of research and development costs, deferral of pre-operating costs; etc. Such pronouncements may have implications for the treatment of life insurance development costs.

costs must bear the burden of demonstrating conclusively that deferral is proper—that the expenditure has "substantial future utility and is clearly associated with and recoverable from future revenue."

Agency Development

Agency development costs include principally the costs of recruiting, training, and financing agents and, for branch office companies, the costs of physically establishing new branches.

Sometimes it can be demonstrated that there is a very rapid "turnaround time" for agency development costs—that is, the time required for recruiting, training and financing is highly compressed, production attributable to such efforts begins almost immediately, and the pattern is repeated every year. In that case it may be possible to demonstrate conclusively that agency development costs vary with and are primarily related to production and they might be accounted for as acquisition costs. It would be the rare case in which agency development costs would follow this pattern.

Well-established companies that have a long and successful history of agency development can sometimes justify deferral of agency development costs. A successful past is taken as the prelude to a successful future. There is little question that uncertainty about the future is diminished somewhat by past success. But the assumption that historical patterns will be carried forward into future years must be severely challenged. The life insurance environment is changing, perhaps to a greater degree than ever before, and there are new pressures on the agency method of selling. So the future should be regarded with healthy skepticism so far as agency development costs are concerned, even for established companies. Such companies must also demonstrate that the types of costs they propose to defer are "in line with practices followed in other industries."

Smaller or newer companies will generally have a very difficult time demonstrating that agency development costs have future utility.

Companies that charge agency development costs to income as incurred should consider disclosing the amount of such costs charged to expense for the period. This type of disclosure could be made in notes to the financial statements or in a supplemental text in the annual report. The disclosure would be more meaningful if accompanied by supplemental disclosure of agents recruited, agents terminated, agents surviving, and the like. Such information lends perspective to the financial statements; the financial statements themselves cannot be expected to bear the full burden of financial public relations. Disclosures of this type have been rare in the past, possibly because statutory statements did not provide a meaningful starting point for such disclosures. Generally accepted accounting principles do provide a meaningful starting point.

If a company chooses to defer agency development costs, they should be amortized in proportion to expected production. For example, if an expenditure of $1,000,000 in Year 1 is expected to result in level amounts of business for 10 years, then the cost should be amortized straight-line over ten years. Usually it will not be possible to predict the production pattern, and an arbitrary amortization pattern might be used. For example, if the agency plant turns over every ten years, on average, and production for a given group of agents tends to diminish because of terminations, agency development costs might be amortized by the declining-balance method over ten years.

The question sometimes arises as to whether development costs incurred in excess of a "normal" level of such costs should be deferred, on the theory that the excess represents expenditures for development above and beyond the level that is "inherent in a continuing business and related to an enterprise as a whole." It would appear that this position is tenable so long as the policy is consistently applied.

The question also sometimes arises as to whether amortization of agency development costs should be considered an acquisition cost in the year of amortization. For example, if the $1,000,000 expenditure discussed above does in fact result in level amounts of new business for 10 years and if the cost is amortized at the rate of $100,000 a year, should the $100,000 of amortization be treated as an acquisition cost to be deferred and amortized over the premium-paying period? This is sometimes referred to as the "double deferral" method—development costs are deferred until business is produced and are then re-deferred as acquisition costs applicable to such new business.

The double-deferral approach might have some merit if production for each year could be forecast with reasonable accuracy. This is usually not the case. So it may be questioned whether the double-deferral approach represents rational and systematic amortization, as required by the audit guide. To the extent that actual production differs from anticipated production, hindsight will demonstrate that the amounts amortized did not vary with production. Hindsight should preferably be translated into foresight, which means essentially that the double-deferral approach should rarely, if ever, be used.

Recoverability of deferred agency development costs must be evaluated in terms of profits on business not yet produced. This is, of course, fundamentally different from measuring future profits on business in force. With respect to business in force, the volume of new business is known, premium rates are known, and the amount of first-year acquisition costs is known. None of these facts is known with respect to future new business. These additional uncertainties, combined with the uncertainties inherent in forecasting future profits for an *existing* block of business (all of which uncertainties apply also to forecasting future profits on future new business) combine to make the problem of testing recoverability of agency development costs a very difficult problem indeed. It will require a stout heart to quantify future margins available to absorb deferred agency development costs.

Crazy Quilt Life expenses agency development costs as incurred.

Ratebook Development

A ratebook costs something to produce. In-house actuarial effort and computer time are usually required in copious quantities; consulting actuaries are often engaged to develop a ratebook; and printing expenses can be sizeable.

Where ratebooks are produced frequently, as in Crazy Quilt's case, they are in the nature of continuing overhead and should preferably be expensed as incurred (Crazy Quilt's practice).

Where ratebooks are produced infrequently—say every ten years—it may be appropriate to defer the related costs and amortize them over the period during which the ratebook is expected to be effective. If the ratebook is printed fairly frequently, it may be appropriate to defer only non-printing costs. Any indirect costs allocated to ratebook development should be limited to supporting costs directly associated with allocable salaries, etc.

It is difficult to find precedence for deferring the costs of producing a price list, which is essentially what a ratebook is; so ratebook development costs should be deferred only in unusual cases.

Costs of Developing a New Line of Business

It is not at all unusual for a life insurance company to start a new line of business from time to time. In the 1950s, for example, many companies entered the group business. In the 1960s some companies that traditionally wrote only ordinary life insurance entered the individual health business. A significant number of companies entered the variable annuity business in the late 1960s. Currently there is a fair amount of effort being devoted to variable life insurance.

A "new line of business" does not refer to a new plan in an existing line of business nor to novel combinations or variations of existing plans. It refers to a line of business that differs substantively from lines of business sold in the past.

The costs of entering a new line of business sometime can be very substantial. For example, Crazy Quilt Life began business in 1941 selling ordinary and industrial products, and the initial costs of investigating markets, doing the necessary legal work, etc., were significant. However, such costs were in the nature of organizational costs or start-up costs and were expensed. Thereafter, Crazy Quilt added several lines of business at considerable cost, as follows:

	Development Costs (000)
1952—Individual annuities	$ 85,000
1955—Group insurance	Not segregated
1960—Individual medical expense	80,000
1963—Individual disability income	420,000
1968—Variable annuities	655,000

Crazy Quilt Life also charged these costs (which exclude any agency development costs) to expense as incurred. Should they be deferred, and if so, under what circumstances?

Market research, legal fees, and the like incidental to operating an insurance business are normally charged to expense as incurred. In the case of entering new lines of business, however, the costs tend to be large and non-recurring. They tend, in other words, to represent an activity (1) that is not a part of normal operations and (2) that is designed to produce new sources of revenue in the future.

In theory, then, when the various conditions indicated above are met, the costs could be deferred and amortized over a period of time reasonable in the circumstances. What would be a "reasonable" period is a matter of judgment, but a degree of arbitrariness is tolerable:

An apparently unlimited useful life may in fact be indefinite and benefits cannot be reasonably predicted . . . a reasonable estimate of the useful life may often be based on upper and lower limits even though a fixed existence is not determinable.[8]

Table 17–1.

SUMMARY OF DEVELOPMENT COSTS* APPLICABLE TO ORDINARY LINE OF BUSINESS, 1941–1971
(000 Omitted)

Year	Ordinary Agency Development	Ordinary Ratebooks	New Lines of Ordinary Business	Ordinary Specialized Markets**	Major Administrative Systems***	Total
1941	$ 180	$ 32	$422		$ 27	$ 661
1942	328					328
1943	430					430
1944	511					511
1945	625					625
1946	718					718
1947	785					785
1948	758	52				810
1949	900					900
1950	723				221	944
1951	1,005					1,005
1952	937	64	75			1,076
1953	1,021					1,021
1954	1,006					1,006
1955	420				501	921
1956	799					799
1957	433	128		$ 201		762
1958	813					813
1959	867					867
1960	731				230	961
1961	1,087					1,087
1962	1,245	72				1,317
1963	1,275			445		1,720
1964	2,015	41				2,056
1965	2,404	33				2,437
1966	1,025				1,817	2,842
1967	3,231	37				3,268
1968	2,219	190		1,273		3,682
1969	3,100				1,023	4,123
1970	4,683	172				4,855
1971	5,302					5,302
	$41,576	$821	$497	$1,919	$3,819	$48,632

* Including pro-rations of overhead.

** 1957—business life insurance; 1963—mass merchandising; 1968—mass merchandising in connection with contacts obtained through variable annuity program.

*** Ordinary systems plus allocable share of generalized systems.

That is all well and good, but the real problem to be faced is a determination of the probable success of the line of business. Some companies that entered the variable annuity business in the 1960s wish now that they had not done so; margins are so thin in some cases that the prospects of recovering the investment in the business are very gloomy.

Making the necessary determinations involves considerations that are not particularly unique to the life insurance business. Probably the only guideline that can be given is this: When the probability of a future lump-sum writeoff appears negligible based on all the available facts and circumstances, including the success that other companies have had with the same type of business, deferral might be appropriate.

Development of Specialized Markets

Sometimes entry into a new market occasions significant expenditures for travel, legal work, etc. An example might be the entry of a United States company into the Canadian, European, South American, or Far Eastern markets.

The considerations involved in deciding whether to defer such costs are much the same as the considerations involved in deciding whether to defer costs of developing new lines of business. The company's success in similar prior ventures might provide some comfort with respect to new ventures. When all is said and done, however, deferral depends on a subjective evaluation of the probability of success in the new market.

Administrative Systems

The costs of developing new administrative systems (such as "computer systems costs" cited as an example in the life insurance audit guide) should be dealt with in the same manner as they are dealt with in other industries.*

Summary

The appropriate attitude to take toward development costs of all types is to operate on the assumption that it is best to charge them to expense as incurred, and to place the burden of proof of doing otherwise on those who would do otherwise.

As a matter of possible interest, Table 17–1 summarizes development costs applicable to Crazy Quilt Life's ordinary line of business for the company's 31-year history. Had such costs been deferred, the unamortized balance at December 31, 1971 would have been about $30 million, equivalent to 33 percent of total unamortized ordinary life acquisition costs of $90 million.

Disclosure

Because of their nature, each category of deferred development costs should be separately captioned as such in the balance sheet. The company's policy with respect to such deferrals, the method of amortization, the amount deferred and the amount amortized during the period should be described in notes to the financial statements. Companies that charge agency development costs to income as incurred should preferably

---

*This is not to imply that the manner in which such costs are dealt with in other industries is uniform or based on commonly-applied principles. The only point made here is that the degree of agonizing over such costs is no greater or no less in the case of a life insurance company than in the case of a noninsurance entity.

make a positive disclosure of the fact in notes to the financial statements, together with an indication of the amount charged to income during the period if such amount is reasonably determinable.

Appropriate disclosure for Crazy Quilt Life's ordinary line of business might be as follows:

ACCOUNTING POLICIES NOTE:

> The Company charges development costs to income as incurred.

OTHER NOTE:

> Development costs charged to income for the period, all of which related to agency development, aggregated approximately $5,302,000.

Maintenance and Settlement Costs

The life insurance audit guide provides that

> Non-level expenses, such as termination or settlement expenses, and expenses after the premium-paying period must be provided [for] during the premium-paying period . . . A portion of a . . . company's expenses, such as policy maintenance and general overhead, . . . should be charged to operations in the period incurred . . . level renewal expenses in the premium-paying period do not require a reserve to be provided, but the expense portion of the gross premium must be adequate to cover such expenses.[9]

There are some conflicts and possible misinterpretations inherent in the audit guide's provisions that need to be resolved before the provisions can be discussed.

First, the guide provides that non level expenses, such as settlement costs and expenses occurring after the premium-paying period, must be reserved for. Some companies treat settlement costs as essentially level, i.e., as so much per policy or so much per $1,000 per year.

If this is the company's approach, then the guide should not be taken to mean that the company's approach is wrong. The guide does not have the authority to force revisions in proven and accepted methods of accounting for such costs.

Second, in stating that certain expenses *must* be provided for, the guide should always be interpreted as referring to material amounts. Where the reserves produced by providing for such expenses are negligible, it is not necessary to reserve for them.

Third, "level" should be interpreted to refer to a more or less constant percentage of premiums. A level expense of, say, $50 a policy will not necessarily be a constant percentage of premiums for a given block of business. In theory, the only expenses that would never give rise to a reserve would be expenses that are a constant percentage of premiums.

And fourth, the guide states that "policy maintenance and general overhead" should be charged to operations in the period incurred and that "therefore level renewal expenses in the premium-paying period do not require a reserve to be provided." Apparently the guide regards maintenance and overhead as "level renewal expenses." Whether reserved for or not, such expenses must be considered in testing the adequacy of valuation premiums. However, as discussed below and in Chapter 24, while maintenance expenses should always be considered in testing the adequacy of valuation premiums, general overhead should be considered only under very unusual circumstances.

Nature of Maintenance and Settlement Costs

Reference to Table 13–4 will indicate all of the maintenance and settlement functions so defined for purposes of the LOMA functional cost program as carried out by Crazy Quilt Life. The functions represent policy-related administrative activity. *Policy-related* is the key to defining maintenance and settlement functions and hence to determining maintenance and settlement costs.

Maintenance costs may be defined as commissions and commission equivalents at ultimate rates, premium taxes, costs associated with premium collection and the processing of commissions, costs of policy changes, other direct maintenance (such as the costs of dividend calculations and payments, policyholders' service, etc.), and general maintenance (such as the maintenance of valuation data).

Settlement costs may be defined as the costs of investigating and processing death claims, processing surrenders, and processing maturities.

Relationship to Cost Accounting

LOMA functional cost determinations or their equivalent, adjusted to include premium taxes, ultimate commissions, and any fringe benefits exluded from the functional cost calculations but properly associated with the salary components of functional costs, provide a good measure of functional costs for accounting purposes. Appropriate allocations of indirect costs should be included in calculations of maintenance and settlement costs. However, general corporate overhead—salaries of top-level executives and their staffs, planning departments, general legal activities, general accounting and budgeting, corporate-image advertising, and the like—should not be treated as maintenance costs. They are not policy-related costs.

Reasons for Reserving

There are three basic reasons for recognizing maintenance and settlement costs in calculating valuation premiums and reserves:

▸ To test the adequacy of valuation premiums. The gross premium must be adequate to cover all policy-related costs.

▸ To effect a better matching of premium revenues and maintenance and settlement costs. To the extent that such costs are not incurred in a pattern equivalent to a constant percentage of premiums, use of a reserve effectively accomplishes equivalency.

▸ To provide for certain liabilities. If it costs $50 to investigate and process a $10,000 death claim, the real cost of the claim from the company's point of view is $10,050. Use of a maintenance and settlement cost reserve would provide for the $50.

Calculating Reserves

Maintenance and settlement cost reserves are calculated in exactly the same manner as benefit reserves, except that maintenance and settlement costs are substituted for benefits and a "maintenance and settlement cost valuation premium" is substituted for the benefit valuation premium.

When Reserves are Needed

A glance at Table 17–2 will suggest when maintenance and settlement cost reserves are needed—and when they're not needed. Table 17–2 shows such rserves for Crazy Quilt Life in 1971.

In general, the reserves are needed only when a company has a significant volume of limited-payment life business in force. Analysis of Table 17–2 will indicate, for example, that limited-payment life business, which constitutes less than 10 percent of ordinary insurance in force, produces 72 percent of total maintenance and settlement cost reserves applicable to ordinary life business and 73 percent of the increase in such reserves in 1971. The reserves on the limited-payment life business average $2.66 per $1,000 at December 31,1971.

Because the 20-year endowment business is getting

Table 17–2.

MAINTENANCE AND SETTLEMENT COST RESERVES FOR ORDINARY PLANS

Plan	Ratebook Era	Insurance In Force, 12–31–71 (000,000)	Maintenance And Settlement Cost Reserves, 12–31–71 (000)	1971 Change (000)
LIFE INSURANCE				
Par whole life	41–47	$ 8	$ 16	$ nil
	48–51	14	16	nil
	52–61	53	24	1
	62–64	50	(3)	1
	65–69	172	(16)	(4)
	70–71	133	9	nil
		430	46	(2)
Whole life	41–47	22	39	nil
	48–51	36	37	nil
	52–56	100	78	1
	57–61	103	57	3
	62–67	615	170	9
	68–69	391	68	3
	70–71	591	55	34
		1,858	504	50
20-pay life	41–47	29	377	(15)
	48–51	22	219	(8)
	52–56	31	331	20
	57–61	26	170	14
	62–67	94	235	29
	68–69	64	51	8
	70–71	111	36	23
		377	1,419	71
20-year endowment	48–61	37	115	(20)
5-year R & C term	41–47	1	(1)	nil
	48–51	4	(11)	1
	52–56	15	(34)	3
	57–61	16	(19)	1
	62–64	33	(21)	(1)
	65–67	80	(28)	(3)
	68–69	95	(16)	(4)
	70–71	156	(8)	(5)
		400	(138)	(8)
25-year decreasing term	57–61	14	3	nil
	62–69	529	25	3
	70–71	472	4	3
		1,015	32	6
		$4,117	$1,978	$ 97
ANNUITIES (All single-premium)	52–56		63	$ (9)
	57–61		116	(14)
	62–67		488	(39)
	68–69		296	(18)
	70–71		360	183
			$1,323	$103

close to maturity, reserves on that business—representing mainly the cost of processing maturities—are also fairly high.

As might be expected, the expense reserves for single-premium annuities are also quite high.

Table 17–2 also indicates that maintenance and settlement cost reserves are not always positive. Reserves on the 5-year term plan are uniformly nega-

Table 17–3.

EFFECT OF VARYING INTEREST RATES* ON MAINTENANCE AND SETTLEMENT COST RESERVE FACTORS AT SELECTED DURATIONS FOR 1971 ISSUES (AGE 35) OF SELECTED PLANS

Plan	Duration	8%	7%	6%	5 1/2%	5%	4 1/2%	4%	9% graded to 4 1/2%**	7% graded to 4 ½%**	Crazy Quilt Ratebook Assumptions**	Zero Interest
Whole life	1	$ .05	$ .06	$ .06	$ .06	$ .06	$ .06	$ .07	$ .06	$ .06	$ .06	$ .09
	2	.12	.13	.13	.13	.14	.14	.15	.13	.14	.14	.20
	3	.07	.08	.08	.09	.09	.10	.11	.09	.09	.10	.18
	5	.08	.09	.11	.12	.13	.14	.15	.12	.13	.14	.27
	7	.13	.15	.17	.18	.19	.21	.22	.19	.19	.21	.39
	10	.22	.24	.27	.29	.31	.33	.35	.31	.31	.34	.58
	20	.60	.65	.70	.73	.52	.80	.83	.83	.81	.87	1.18
	30	1.10	1.16	1.23	1.26	1.29	1.33	1.36	1.37	1.35	1.44	1.69
	40	1.58	1.64	1.69	1.72	1.75	1.78	1.81	1.81	1.80	1.87	2.07
20-pay life	1	.11	.12	.14	.15	.16	.17	.18	.13	.15	.16	.51
	2	.26	.29	.32	.34	.36	.38	.41	.32	.34	.36	1.20
	3	.29	.32	.37	.40	.43	.46	.50	.37	.40	.44	1.65
	5	.46	.52	.61	.65	.70	.76	.82	.62	.67	.73	2.68
	7	.67	.77	.89	.95	1.03	1.11	1.19	.92	.98	1.07	3.80
	10	1.10	1.25	1.42	1.52	1.63	1.75	1.87	1.53	1.60	1.73	5.66
	15	2.24	2.48	2.75	2.90	3.06	3.23	3.42	3.03	3.07	3.28	9.35
	20	4.21	4.49	4.81	4.99	5.17	5.38	5.59	5.24	5.25	5.51	13.21
	30	3.54	3.71	3.90	4.01	4.11	4.23	4.35	4.23	4.23	4.46	10.11
	40	3.12	3.23	3.34	3.40	3.47	3.53	3.60	3.53	3.53	3.67	7.07
5-year R&C term	1	(.03)	(.04)	(.04)	(.04)	(.04)	(.04)	(.05)	(.03)	(.04)	(.03)	(.06)
	2	(.08)	(.08)	(.09)	(.09)	(.10)	(.10)	(.10)	(.08)	(.09)	(.07)	(.14)
	3	(.13)	(.14)	(.15)	(.16)	(.16)	(.17)	(.17)	(.14)	(.15)	(.11)	(.23)
	5	(.27)	(.28)	(.30)	(.31)	(.32)	(.32)	(.33)	(.29)	(.31)	(.21)	(.42)
	7	(.41)	(.44)	(.46)	(.48)	(.49)	(.51)	(.52)	(.47)	(.48)	(.38)	(.65)
	10	(.60)	(.03)	(.66)	(.68)	(.70)	(.71)	(.73)	(.69)	(.70)	(.67)	(.88)
	15	(1.26)	(1.31)	(1.37)	(1.39)	(1.42)	(1.45)	(1.48)	(1.48)	(1.46)	(1.58)	(1.67)
	20	(2.08)	(2.13)	(2.19)	(2.21)	(2.24)	(2.26)	(2.29)	(2.42)	(2.34)	(2.63)	(2.40)
	30	(3.07)	(3.06)	(3.04)	(3.03)	(3.02)	(3.00)	(2.98)	(3.24)	(3.14)	(5.55)	(2.70)
Single-premium annuity***	1										18.99	26.97
	2										18.30	25.57
	3										17.59	24.20
	5										16.24	21.68
	7										15.07	19.56
	10										13.97	16.63
	15										10.61	12.36
	20										8.07	8.88
	30										4.07	4.10

*All other assumptions held constant
**Graded in 5-year increments over 25 years (30 years in the case of the ratebook assumptions)
***Age 65

tive, i.e., a "deferred charge", in Crazy Quilt's case. The reserve is simply a suspense account, as it were, for costs that are not proportional to premiums, and the sign of the factor depends on the incidence of expense vis-a-vis the incidence of valuation premiums.

Practical Approaches

Some companies regard the cost of processing a death claim as the principal non-level cost and provide for such cost by increasing the indicated benefit. In other words, the benefit reserve includes provision for death claim settlement costs and other maintenance and settlement costs not reserved for. For contracts whose premium-paying period substantially coincides with the contract term, this reduces even further the already immaterial effect of omitting the reserves.

Table 17–4.

EFFECT OF VARYING WITHDRAWAL RATES ON MAINTENANCE COST RESERVE FACTORS AT SELECTED
DURATIONS FOR 1971 ISSUES (AGE 35) OF SELECTED PLANS*

Plan	Duration	Zero Withdrawals	Linton A	Linton B	Linton C	Crazy Quilt Ratebook Assumptions
Whole life	1	$ .04	$ .07	$ .11	$ .15	$ .06
	2	.09	.15	.25	.37	.14
	3	.13	.14	.19	.27	.10
	5	.23	.15	.12	.14	.14
	7	.33	.18	.09	.06	.21
	10	.51	.28	.12	.03	.34
	15	.83	.52	.29	.14	.59
	20	1.18	.83	.55	.35	.87
	30	1.89	1.51	1.18	.93	1.44
	40	2.48	2.16	1.86	1.60	1.87
20-pay life	1	.21	.17	.17	.18	.16
	2	.43	.38	.39	.45	.36
	3	.67	.50	.43	.43	.44
	5	1.19	.83	.60	.48	.73
	7	1.77	1.24	.88	.64	1.07
	10	2.77	2.02	1.48	1.08	1.73
	15	4.83	3.79	3.00	2.41	3.28
	20	7.48	6.28	5.40	4.75	5.51
	30	6.65	5.82	5.33	4.65	4.46
	40	5.49	5.01	4.60	4.26	3.67
5-year R&C term	1	(.08)	(.07)	(.05)	(.04)	(.03)
	2	(.17)	(.14)	(.12)	(.09)	(.07)
	3	(.26)	(.23)	(.20)	(.16)	(.11)
	5	(.46)	(.43)	(.39)	(.34)	(.21)
	7	(.70)	(.66)	(.61)	(.55)	(.38)
	10	(1.02)	(1.00)	(.95)	(1.13)	(.67)
	15	(1.66)	(1.68)	(1.65)	(1.58)	(1.58)
	20	(2.35)	(2.46)	(2.51)	(2.48)	(2.63)
	30	(2.54)	(2.86)	(3.13)	(3.33)	(5.55)

*All other assumptions held constant.

This shortcut does not help much in the case of limited-pay business, for obvious reasons.

It is possible to reduce the assumed interest rate slightly below the rate that would otherwise be assumed to provide, in effect, an extra margin in the benefit reserves to cover maintenance and settlement costs. Because the incidence of the effect on the benefit reserves may not coincide even approximately with the incidence of maintenance and settlement costs, this particular shortcut method should be used with great care and only after suitable testing.

Effect of Interest

As might be expected, interest affects maintenance and settlement cost reserves in much the same man-ner as it affects benefit reserves. Table 17–3 illustrates some maintenance and expense reserve factors using varying interest assumptions for selected 1971 issues of Crazy Quilt Life.

Effect of Withdrawals

While a more conservative withdrawal rate will often increase benefit reserves, depending on the level of the cash values, conservative rates will generally reduce the level of the maintenance and settlement cost reserve, simply because there are fewer policies for which maintenance and settlement costs will be incurred. This is illustrated in Table 17–4.

The same general effect would usually be produced by the mortality assumption.

Effect of Grading

When benefit reserves are graded into statutory reserves (as discussed in Chapter 11) or acquisition costs are graded to zero over an arbitrary period, it is usually considered desirable, as a practical matter, to grade maintenance and settlement cost reserves to zero. For example, if benefit reserves are graded to statutory in 30 years and acquisition costs are graded to zero in 30 years, it is obviously desirable to be rid of any maintenance and settlement cost reserves by the 30th year.

In theory, benefit reserves are graded to statutory because statutory is an acceptable approximation of adjusted by the end of the grading period. Similarly, acquisition costs are graded to zero because the un-amortized balances at the end of the grading period would be immaterial. So there is no theoretical justification for doing away with maintenance and settlement cost reserves at the end of the grading period if they are considered necessary in the first place.

However, it would appear that dogged adherence to principle would frustrate the objectives of grading. In such circumstances every effort should be made to demonstrate that statutory reserves provide a margin adequate to cover maintenance and settlement costs.

Effect of Inflation

The life insurance audit guide provides that "renewal expense assumptions should take into account the possible effect of inflation." [10]

The guide also suggests that "any anticipated effect of economic conditions on the interest assumptions should be similarly considered for expense assumptions." [11] This appears to infer that if an "inflationary" interest rate is assumed (as discussed in Chapter 9), an "inflationary" maintenance and settlement cost assumption should be used.

Usually unit maintenance and settlement costs would be determined based on functional cost studies. Such cost studies reflect unit costs at the price level prevailing at the time the costs are incurred.

Assuming an inflationary economic environment, certain unit costs will tend to rise with the passage of time. Commissions will not increase, since they are fixed by contract. Premium taxes could increase, but any such increase is usually not anticipated on the basis that the increase would be nominal due partly to political factors and partly to the fact that this would be unfair to an industry that charges premiums, fixed by contract, that were calculated on the assumption of a constant premium tax rate.*

So inflation would tend to apply to maintenance and settlement costs other than commissions and premium taxes.

Some companies claim that increasing efficiency will offset the effects of inflation on renewal and maintenance costs. This is not demonstrable with respect to the future. Significant savings have been achieved through automation in past years, but such savings cannot be projected indefinitely. Indeed, some believe that savings from automation have reached their limit.

Some companies claim also that increasing volume will tend to reduce unit costs. This is possible, but demonstration would be very difficult. Past savings in maintenance costs, *exclusive* of any savings from automation, would have to be demonstrated, and the sources of such savings would have to be identified, in order to make a rational assumption about the effect of increasing volume in the future. In the absence of reasonable proof, it should generally be assumed that future maintenance and settlement costs, measured in constant dollars, will remain fixed.**

So if any one of a given company's assumptions reflects, or tends to reflect, an inflationary bias, inflation should generally be recognized in providing for maintenance and settlement costs.

The likeliest candidate for an inflationary bias is, of course, the interest assumption. Admittedly there are conflicts of opinion over the extent to which interest rates reflect inflationary expectations (or inflation itself), but in accounting, such conflicts should normally be resolved by reference to the doctrine of conservatism.

In short, a company's interest assumption should be separated into two components, "pure" interest and the rate of inflation, and the implicit rate of inflation should be applied to maintenance and settlement cost assumptions.

The effect of doing this is suggested by Table 17–5. The "pure" rate of interest is taken to be 4 percent, and the interest assumption is taken to be 7 percent. The difference, 3 percent, is the implicit rate of inflation. Non-percentage maintenance and settlement costs are shown at several durations (1) at the current price level and (2) at a price level compounded for inflation at 3 percent a year.

*A life insurance company executive who read this chapter stated, in regard to this sentence, "Dubious, but a nice try."

**An exception would be appropriate in the case of new companies. The exception is discussed in Chapter 24.

Table 17–5.

EFFECT OF INFLATION ON MAINTENANCE AND SETTLEMENT COSTS ON 1971 ISSUES (AGE 35) OF 20-PAY LIFE

| Duration | Projected Non-Percentage Maintenance and Settlement Costs per $1,000 | |
	At Current Price Level	Assuming Annual 3% Inflation
1	$ .35	$ .35
2	.36	.37
3	.46	.49
5	.44	.50
7	.40	.48
10	.39	.51
15	.40	.61
20	.38	.67
25	.70	1.42
30	.77	1.81
35	.81	2.21
40	.87	2.76
45	.91	3.34
50	1.05	4.47

Table 17–5 is based on maintenance and settlement costs for a 20-pay life policy. The more limited the premium-paying period in relation to the term of the contract, the more significant inflation reserves will tend to be. The same principles would, however, apply to a whole-life policy or any other type of policy whose premium-paying period and contract term coincide. While maintenance and settlement cost reserves might be negligible when based on current dollars, they may be material when based on inflated dollars.

Relationship to Recoverability Tests

Whether reserved for or not, maintenance and settlement costs should be recognized in making tests of the recoverability of acquisition costs and in calculating the present value of losses in a deficiency situation. These subjects are discussed in detail in Chapter 24.

"Single-Reserve" Factors

A maintenance and settlement cost reserve is usually a liability (although, as some of the tables indicate, the reserve is not always positive). Crazy Quilt Life reports aggregate maintenance and settlement cost reserves as liabilities in its adjusted balance sheet.

Some companies prefer to calculate one set of factors for all expenses—first-year acquisition costs, renewal-year acquisition costs, and maintenance and settlement costs. A factor thus becomes an amount with asset and liability elements, and the amount shown for unamortized acquisition costs will be the net of aggregate asset and liability elements.

There should be no objection to reporting "net" unamortized acquisition costs unless maintenance and settlement cost reserves are very significant.

Some single-reserve factors for selected Crazy Quilt Life 1971 plans are shown in Table 17–6.

Disclosure

There would normally be a presumption that maintenance and settlement costs are charged to expense as incurred in the absence of evidence to the contrary.

When maintenance and settlement costs are reserved for, this fact should be spelled out in an accounting policies note.

When the costs are not identifiable, as for example when single-reserve factors are used, it would be appropriate to state that acquisition costs net of provisions for maintenance and settlement costs have been deferred.

Table 17–6.

ELEMENTS OF SINGLE-RESERVE FACTORS FOR SELECTED 1971 PLANS (AGE 35) AT SELECTED DURATIONS

Plan	Duration	Acquisition Cost Factor*	Maintenance And Settlement Cost Factor	Single Factor
Whole life	1	$21.96	$ .06	$21.90
	2	28.12	.14	27.98
	3	30.88	.10	30.78
	5	33.02	.14	32.88
	7	34.09	.21	33.88
	10	36.00	.34	35.66
	15	33.85	.59	33.26
	20	30.41	.87	29.54
	30	21.15	1.44	19.71
20-pay life	1	26.06	.16	25.90
	2	31.18	.36	30.82
	3	31.99	.44	31.55
	5	30.75	.73	30.02
	7	29.05	1.07	27.98
	10	25.69	1.73	23.96
	15	16.06	3.28	12.78
	20		5.51	(5.51)
	30		4.46	(4.46)
5-year R&C term	1	5.48	(.04)	5.52
	2	6.23	(.09)	6.32
	3	6.65	(.16)	6.81
	5	7.01	(.31)	7.32
	7	9.59	(.50)	10.09
	10	8.93	(.72)	9.65
	15	14.52	(1.49)	16.01
	20	20.42	(2.38)	22.80
	30	23.16	(3.16)	26.32
25-year decreasing term	1	6.33	-0-	6.33
	2	6.98	.01	6.97
	3	7.21	.01	7.20
	5	7.29	.02	7.27
	7	7.59	.03	7.56
	10	6.96	.05	6.91
	15	5.72	.07	5.65
	20	4.11	.07	4.04

*As adjusted for accounting purposes.

Appropriate disclosure for Crazy Quilt Life—assuming that only the ordinary line is being reported on—might be as follows:

ACCOUNTING POLICIES NOTE:

Maintenance and settlement costs are provided for ratably over the premium-paying period.

In Crazy Quilt's case, maintenance and settlement cost reserves are separately captioned in the balance sheet and the change therein is separately captioned in the income statement, so no further disclosure would be necessary.

Investment Expenses

The life insurance audit guide states that the assumed interest rate "should be net of investment expenses." [12]

Since investment expenses reduce investment income dollar-for-dollar and therefore affect yields directly, it is necessary to give brief consideration to what principles should govern the allocation of expenses to the investment function.

Nature of Investment Expenses

Investment expenses are expenses associated with acquiring, servicing, and disposing of investments.

They may also be viewed from a functional cost point of view: Investment expenses represent costs attributable to investment functions as determined by functional cost analysis.

Crazy Quilt Life allocated expenses to the investment function based on the results of the LOMA functional cost program. Functional costs by category of investment for Crazy Quilt may be determined by comparing gross yields with net yields in Tables 2–7 and 2–8.

Reasonableness

Because investment expenses affect yield rates, which in turn affect reserve interest assumptions, which in turn have a "multiplier" effect because of compounding, it goes without saying that allocations of expenses to the investment function should be reasonable.

The principles employed in making the allocations should be essentially similar to principles employed in allocating expenses to lines of business. Allocations should be based on time studies (such as those that usually underlie functional cost calculations) and apportionments of indirect costs should be restricted

to "service department" costs as described in Chapter 14.

General corporate overhead should not be allocated to the investment function.

Disclosure

Disclosure of investment expenses is discussed in Chapter 5.

Overhead

Overhead is represented by the expenses that are left over after segregating acquisition costs, development cost, maintenance and settlement costs, and investment expenses. It would also include any of the above items that were not so segregated as a matter of convenience. (For example, development costs might not be segregated if the company's policy is to charge them to expense as incurred.)

More positively, overhead would generally include top-level management salaries, bonuses, and support expenses; public relations; general legal activities; general accounting (to the extent of effort related to preparation of financial statements, posting of general ledgers, and similar general activities); and all other non-policy-related costs.

Such costs are not unique to life insurance companies and should be accounted for in a manner that is consistent with practices in other industries. That means they should be treated as period expenses.

Certain aspects of overhead in relation to tests of recoverability and loss recognition procedures are discussed in Chapter 24.

❧ Part IV

Other Lines
of Business

18

Industrial Insurance

The production of industrial insurance—i.e., small policies for which premiums are collected weekly at the policyholder's home—has been declining for many years, and so has industrial insurance in force. Reasons include increasing affluence of the market for which the industrial product was designed and the constantly increasing costs of servicing small weekly-premium policies. Some companies have ceased selling industrial business and are letting existing business run off.

But the apparent decline of industrial business is somewhat misleading. The industrial market still exists and still produces a significant volume of business, but the business increasingly consists of regular home office-billed ordinary policies or "monthly debit ordinary" policies, i.e., larger policies for which premiums continue to be collected at the policyholder's home but monthly rather than weekly. Ordinary policies, whether billed or monthly debit, are usually classified as ordinary business for purposes of industry statistics. Some companies classify debit policies as "industrial" or ordinary on the basis of size—for example, policies under $1,000 might be classified as "industrial" while larger policies are classified as "ordinary".

So the apparent decline does not mean the industrial market itself is vanishing. It means, at least in part, that the market is changing. Indeed, some believe the industrial market represents unparalleled opportunity: its constituents are becoming more affluent and sophisticated and are thus able to afford and appreciate a broader and more complex range of products, yet the traditional advantage of continuing close personal contact with the policyholder has been retained. As one senior executive of a well-known and successful combination company put it,

The debit system is here to stay. It is effective. It puts the salesman face to face with the buyer. Its future is perhaps as bright, if not brighter, than ever before in its history. This, I believe, is true because this vast well-organized sales organization will, in the future, be marketing on the same face to face basis to a purchaser with considerably more affluence and ability to pay for more of the product.

This chapter discusses and illustrates weekly premium business. Regular ordinary business marketed by combination agents and monthly debit ordinary are not specifically discussed.

Products and Marketing

Conceptually, industrial insurance products are no different than ordinary life products, and combination agents are fundamentally no different than ordinary agents. In practice, however, the differences are often quite significant.

Marketing

The combination agent usually sees the industrial policyholder every week or every other week either at the policyholder's home or at some mutually convenient location, for purposes of collecting the weekly premium and often for the purpose of exhorting the policyholder to keep his policy in force. At the same time the agent prospects for new business in his territory.

The agent is supported by a formidable district office system staffed by superintendents, managers, assistant managers, and clerical staff. District office

331

Table 18–1.

SUMMARY OF PRINCIPAL PROVISIONS OF COMBINATION AGENTS' CONTRACTS, 1941–1971

Contract Period	Contract Highlights
1941–1942	Collection commission of 15% of premiums collected plus sales commission equal to the first 15 weeks of new premiums collected; no further chargebacks for lapses after the 15th week.
1943–1947	Same as 1941–1942 plus conservation commission equal to 10 times the net increase in the debit; conservation commission limited to a maximum of $10 a week.
1948–1952	Advance for first 13 weeks of employment; thereafter, collection commission of 12 1/2% of premiums collected (subject to a minimum of $27 a week) plus sales commission of 45% of annualized new premium less first-year lapses plus conservation commissions on a sliding scale of $3 to $9 a week depending on size of debit and relationship of lapse rates on agent's debit to company-wide lapse rates, all credited to a sales "core" and paid in 13 weekly installments in the quarter following the quarter in which earned.
1953–1956	Same as 1948–1952 contract, except sales commission raised to 55%.
1957–1959	Same as 1953–1956 contract, except sales commission raised to 57 1/2%.
1960–1964	Same as 1957–1959 contract, except minimum collection commission raised to $42 a week.
1965–1969	Salary of $75 a week for first 5 weeks of employment, plus a training allowance of $20 per week beginning in the first week of employment and, after 5 weeks, decreasing $1 a week to zero in the 24th week; after 5 weeks, collection commission of 12 1/2% of weekly premiums in force subject to a minimum of $45 a week plus sales commission of 57 1/2% of annualized new premium less first-year lapses plus "debit allowance" of $5 a week plus conservation commission on a sliding scale of $30 to $3 a week depending on size of debit and lapse rates of the debit in relation to company-wide rates plus, after 3 years, a "career bonus" of from $1 to $10 a week, all credited to a sales "core" and paid in 13 weekly installments in the quarter following the quarter in which earned.
1970–1971	Same as 1965–1969 contract, except salary raised to $80 a week for first 5 weeks of employment and "debit allowance" raised to $10 a week.

personnel recruit, train, and supervise agents. They also perform significant accounting and administrative functions.

The combination agent is usually paid three separate commissions or commission equivalents—a collection commission, a first-year sales commission on new business, and a conservation commission. This basic compensation scheme may be supplemented by temporary financing payments, production bonuses, and other allowances and benefits. Often the agent's compensation is credited to a "memorandum" account and paid out to him in installments to help stabilize his income.

Historically, compensation systems for combination agents have been quite complicated because of the collection system, the need to provide special incentives for conservation in the case of debit business, and other factors. In recent years debit compensation patterns have tended toward equality with compensation on ordinary business.

Crazy Quilt Life's combination agents' contracts for the period of 1941–1971, patterned after those of a large combination company, are summarized in Table 18–1 and will suggest the elements of compensation typically associated with debit business.

Underwriting

Because of the small average size of industrial policies, little underwriting is done in the home office. Medicals are usually required only for applicants above a certain age or for applicants for whom a cursory home office inspection of the application indicates a medical is necessary. Thus combination companies rely on agents to do a fair amount of underwriting. One combination company's agent manual, for example, tells its combination agents:

Do not write applications on: persons not seen by you; persons of immoral or intemperate habits; persons using a crutch; idiots; morons; midgets; inmates of charitable institutions; persons totally blind; persons deaf and dumb; racers; muckers; steeplejacks; jockeys; wrestlers; paratroopers; persons in illegal occupations; or anyone in any way connected with the submarine service or diving.

Products

Industrial insurance is issued in several different plans, but the most popular plans have been life paid-up at 65, 70, or 75, 20-pay life, and 20-year endowment. The economics of the industrial policy are such that a high premium (such as the level of premiums associated with the indicated plans) is needed. Further, the industrial market has traditionally favored cash value insurance; for many policyholders, the cash values represent their only savings.

Crazy Quilt Life's most popular industrial policy is a nonparticipating 20-pay life policy.

Industrial policies are sometimes sold in premium units (although this practice is less frequent than it used to be). In Crazy Quilt's case, for instance, $1.00 a week will buy $900 of 20-pay life insurance at age 35, 75 cents will buy $900 at age 20; 55 cents will buy $900 at age 5. Usually industrial insurance is written on the lives of all members of a family. In Crazy Quilt's case, a weekly premium of $3.00 will buy $900 of insurance on two 35-year-old parents and two five-year-old children.

Nonforfeiture benefits are provided, but usually the policyholder cannot take out loans, at least for a considerable period of time after issue, partly because the size of the loan available under a small policy does not justify the processing expense involved.

Usually certain supplemental benefits are automatically included in the premium. In Crazy Quilt's case, accidental death, dismemberment, loss of sight, waiver of premium for defined disabilities (mainly dismemberment or loss of sight), and an extra benefit for death on a common carrier are provided automatically. Other supplemental benefits—guaranteed insurability, full waiver of premium, return of premiums, etc.—are also usually available optionally.

Weekly premium policies often permit attained-age conversion to any plan of monthly premium industrial insurance, and some companies permit the exchange of an industrial policy for an ordinary life policy of not less that the minimum amount written on the ordinary plan.

Pricing

The pricing of industrial products is very similar to the pricing of ordinary products. There are, however, several considerations unique to industrial insurance that need to be taken explicitly into account.

Mortality. Large combination companies typically use their own experience in projecting industrial mortality. Since there is little underwriting, the effect of selection may be ignored or the select period may be very short. Usually mortality improvements are not projected, although there have been dramatic improvements in industrial mortality in this century, particularly in recent years, as is suggested by comparative mortality rates for the three statutory tables:

Age Last Birthday	Death Rate Per 1,000 Insureds		
	1906 SI	1941 SI	1961 CSI
5	7.20	3.29	1.37
20	7.56	4.13	2.04
35	13.22	6.91	3.58
50	22.77	18.77	11.62
65	60.53	57.21	36.81
80	199.02	165.40	124.21

Comparisons between industrial mortality and ordinary mortality are difficult because of the significantly greater proportion of industrial business written on female lives and because there are no significant studies of mortality by sex in the case of industrial business. Nevertheless, it is apparent that the gap between industrial mortality and ordinary mortality is diminishing.

Mortality rates assumed for price testing purposes by Crazy Quilt Life for its various industrial rate-book eras are shown in Table 18–2. Crazy Quilt used a four-year select period.

Withdrawals. Lapse rates on industrial policies are usually quite high by comparison with ordinary. First-year lapse rates of 50 percent or more are sometimes encountered. Table 18–3 shows Crazy Quilt Life's assumed withdrawal rates for its various issue eras. These withdrawal rates (which should not be considered as representative), in conjunction with mortality, give rise to the following persistency patterns:

End of Calendar Year	Percentage of Original Issue Still in Force		
	Issue Age 5	Issue Age 20	Issue Age 35
1	63.1%	59.8%	66.4%
5	24.3	17.6	29.0
10	17.1	10.7	20.8
15	13.4	8.1	16.6
20	10.8	6.5	13.6
25	8.8	5.4	11.0
30	7.1	4.5	9.0
40	4.7	3.2	5.5
50	3.2	2.2	1.7

Table 18–2.

ASSUMED INDUSTRIAL MORTALITY—DEATHS PER 1,000 INSURED

Select: Issue Age	Year	Industrial Business— Crazy Quilt Life Assumed Mortality			
		1941–1947	*1948–1952*	*1953–1964*	*1965–1971*
5	1	1.68	1.24	.81	.63
	2	1.43	1.06	.69	.54
	3	1.28	.94	.60	.47
	4	1.14	.84	.54	.42
	5	1.03	.77	.50	.39
20	1	1.91	1.58	1.25	1.00
	2	2.05	1.68	1.31	1.05
	3	2.17	1.77	1.36	1.09
	4	2.29	1.84	1.39	1.11
	5	2.39	1.92	1.40	1.12
35	1	4.11	3.18	2.25	1.78
	2	4.30	3.37	2.45	1.94
	3	4.53	3.60	2.68	2.12
	4	4.81	3.87	2.94	2.33
	5	5.09	4.18	3.26	2.58

Ultimate: Attained Age					
10		1.03	.77	.50	.39
15		.99	.85	.70	.55
20		1.75	1.46	1.18	.94
25		2.39	1.92	1.40	1.12
30		3.06	2.31	1.57	1.24
35		3.87	2.98	2.08	1.65
40		5.09	4.18	3.26	2.58
45		7.42	6.31	5.20	4.28
50		11.64	9.83	8.02	6.89
55		16.37	14.43	12.49	10.72
60		23.66	21.36	19.07	16.38
65		35.17	32.09	29.02	24.93
70		57.36	51.23	45.10	37.55
75		85.50	76.30	67.10	55.85
80		128.46	114.32	100.18	84.02
85		191.86	170.94	150.01	127.58
90		282.16	249.98	217.80	187.33

Interest. The considerations involved in selecting interest assumptions are basically the same as for ordinary life. To the extent that industrial life business is more heavily concentrated in limited-payment business, there may be a little more confidence in interest assumptions.

Crazy Quilt Life's industrial assumptions for its various industrial ratebook eras were consistent with nonparticipating ordinary assumptions:

Issue Years	Interest Assumption
1941–1947	2.75% level
1948–1952	3% level
1953–1964	3.25% grading to 3% in 10 years
1965–1969	4.5% grading to 3% in 30 years
1970–1971	6.5% grading to 3.5% in 30 years

Nonforfeiture costs. It is fairly common for all types of business to assume that the cash value measures the cost of the nonforfeiture option, whether the option taken is cash surrender, reduced paid-up, or extended insurance.

The automatic nonforfeiture option in the case of industrial insurance is usually extended insurance. Some companies have found that mortality on extended insurance has been more favorable than normal mortality. Crazy Quilt Life, for example, found that mortality savings on extended term insurance, weighted by the proportion of nonforfeiture options going into extended term, affected nonforfeiture costs for the first 20 years, most significantly in the early years and diminishing as the years went by.

Table 18–3.

ASSUMED INDUSTRIAL WITHDRAWAL RATES, 1948–1971*

| Year | Issue Age | | |
	5	20	35
1	55.0%	60.0%	50.0%
2	27.5	35.0	25.0
3	13.5	17.5	12.0
4	10.0	13.0	8.0
5	8.5	11.0	7.0
6	10.0	13.0	8.5
7	6.0	10.0	7.0
8	5.5	8.0	5.0
9	5.5	7.0	4.5
10	5.0	6.5	4.0
11	5.0	6.0	4.0
12	5.0	5.5	4.0
13	4.5	5.0	4.0
14	4.5	4.5	4.0
15	4.0	4.0	3.0
20	4.0	3.5	3.0
25	4.0	3.0	2.0
30	4.0	3.0	1.5
35	3.5	2.0	1.0
40	3.5	1.5	2.0
45	3.0	1.0	2.0
50	3.0	1.0	4.0
55	2.0	2.0	6.0
60	1.5	2.0	15.0
70	1.0	6.0	—
80	4.0	25.0	—
90	15.0	—	—

*Expected withdrawals for 1941–1947 were somewhat lower. These withdrawal rates should not be considered representative of the industry.

Cash values, and the assumed weighted cost of non-forfeiture benefits for 1970–1971 issues, are shown in Table 18–4.

Supplementary benefits. The cost of supplementary benefits included automatically with an industrial policy is usually nominal, and it would not be unusual to assume a constant annual cost per $1,000. This was Crazy Quilt's practice; studies indicated that the cost of automatic supplemental benefits was adequately provided for by assuming a constant cost of 60 cents per $1,000 per year.

Expenses. As might be expected from the earlier discussion about compensation schemes for combination agents and the large and complex district office system, expense assumptions for industrial business are complicated to develop. They are also very important because of the high level of expenses and the consequences of high lapse rates.

Crazy Quilt Life participates with several other combination companies in a special industrial insurance functional cost program conducted for combination companies by the Life Office Management Association. Functional costs derived for purposes of the LOMA program were translated into formats suitable for rate-testing. Crazy Quilt Life's expense assumptions for 1970–1971 issues of industrial 20-pay life are summarized in Table 18–5.

Average size. Assumed average policy sizes for Crazy Quilt Life's industrial policies, required to make expense allocations, were as follows for the various ratebooks:

| Issues of | Issue Age | | |
	5	20	35
1941–1947	$250	$300	$250
1948–1952	350	450	325
1953–1964	500	600	500
1965–1971	700	800	700

Price test. Crazy Quilt Life's price tests for industrial insurance were carried out in the same manner as for ordinary insurance. The results for the 1970–

Table 18–4.

CASH VALUES AND ASSUMED WEIGHTED COST OF NONFORFEITURE BENEFITS FOR 1970–1971 ISSUES OF INDUSTRIAL 20–PAY LIFE—PER $1,000 OF INSURANCE

	Issue Age 5		Issue Age 20		Issue Age 35	
Year	Cash Value	Weighted Cost	Cash Value	Weighted Cost	Cash Value	Weighted Cost
1	$–0–	$–0–	$–0–	$–0–	$–0–	$–0–
2	–0–	–0–	4	2	14	7
3	10	5	22	11	39	20
4	23	12	41	21	66	33
5	36	18	60	30	93	47
6	51	26	80	40	120	60
7	65	34	100	52	148	77
8	80	44	121	67	177	97
9	95	55	142	82	207	120
10	111	69	165	102	237	147
11	127	84	187	123	268	177
12	144	101	211	148	299	209
13	161	119	235	174	331	245
14	178	139	260	203	364	284
15	196	161	285	234	398	326
16	215	185	312	268	433	372
17	234	211	339	305	469	422
18	253	238	366	344	506	476
19	273	268	395	387	544	533
20	294	294	424	424	583	583

1971 ratebook edition of industrial 20-pay life issued at age 20 may be summarized as follows:

	Present Value at Issue per $1,000 Issued
Gross premiums ($42.90 per year per $1,000)	$84.66
Benefits and expenses	76.99
Profits	$ 7.67

The gross premium, $42.90 per year per $1,000, is a translation of weekly premium units into an expression of premiums comparable to the basis used for ordinary life. The average premium unit is 66 cents and the average size, as indicated previously, is $800; this is translated into an annual premium equivalent as follows:

Weekly premium	$ .66
Number of weeks in year	52
Annualized premium	$34.32
Average size	$800
Equivalent annual premium per $1,000	$42.90

Equivalent annual age-35 premiums for the industrial 20-pay life plan by Crazy Quilt were as follows for the various ratebook eras:

Issues of	Premium
1941–1947	$51.64
1948–1951	52.32
1952–1956	52.32
1957–1961	52.32
1962–1964	52.32
1965–1967	51.32
1968–1969	51.32
1970–1971	59.15

The sharp increase in industrial rates in 1970 was the direct result of higher servicing costs. Combination agents and support personnel were being paid more; security had become an expensive problem (to the extent that armed guards had to accompany debit agents into some areas); and the long period of offsetting inflation with automation in the home office had ended.

Benefit Reserves

Calculation of adjusted benefit reserves for industrial business involves the same general procedures as the calculation of benefit reserves for ordinary business: assumptions must be chosen, calculation techniques must be selected, and miscellaneous practical problems–such as whether to grade reserves to statu-

Table 18–5.

EXPENSE ASSUMPTIONS FOR 1970–1971 ISSUES OF INDUSTRIAL 20–PAY LIFE

	Duration 0 or 1	Duration 2–20	Duration 21 on*
Percentage expenses:			
First-year production commission	55%	—%	—
First-year production override	10	—	—
Collection commission	15	15	—
Average conservation commission	—	2	—
Average conservation override	—	2	—
Miscellaneous agent benefits	—	5	—
Agency supervision	35	—	—
Agent financing and training	10	—	—
Premium taxes	2	2	—
Total	127%	26%	
Per-policy expenses:			
Agency support	$5.75	$__	$__
Selection	1.50	—	—
Issue	1.00	—	—
Maintenance	1.10	1.10	.60
	$9.35	$1.10	$ .60
Per-occurrence expenses:			
Death claims	$5.00	$5.00	$5.00
Surrenders		2.50	2.50

*Premium-paying period ends in 20th year.

tory and what to do about paid-up business—must be dealt with.

Assumptions

The various assumptions discussed earlier in this chapter in connection with pricing industrial products will usually form the basis for adjusted benefit reserves on such business. Considerations involved in providing for adverse deviation with respect to industrial insurance assumptions are basically the same as for ordinary business, except that somewhat more attention must usually be paid to lapse rates in the case of industrial insurance.

In Crazy Quilt Life's case, assumptions used for pricing purposes were deemed suitable for adjusted reserve purposes. Mortality assumptions were considered to provide inherently for adverse deviation because of long-term mortality improvements which were not projected in the tables used. Assumptions as to future withdrawals were quite conservative to begin with. Nonforfeiture values were set equal to cash values except for 1970–1971 ratebook issues, for which weighted nonforfeiture costs—supported by

adequate experience studies—were used. Interest assumptions were consistent with ordinary assumptions. Automatic supplemental benefits were assumed to be incurred at the rate of 60 cents per $1,000 per year. A summary of industrial adjusted reserve assumptions is shown in Table 18–6.

Differential Nonforfeiture Costs

The treatment of "savings" under the extended insurance option, recognized in calculating adjusted reserves for 1970–1971 issues, required some special thought. Normally a reserve calculation assumes the cash value cost is incurred on termination and the cash value measures the net single premium for any nonforfeiture option other than cash surrender. To the extent that the extended insurance option is taken and it has a lower cost than the cash value, then one of two things happen:

1. If the reserve on the extended insurance does not recognize the "savings", the "savings" on the option are recognized over time, as the option runs off.

2. If the reserve on the extended insurance recog-

Table 18–6.

SUMMARY OF INDUSTRIAL ADJUSTED RESERVE ASSUMPTIONS

	Ratebook Era				
	1941–1947	1948–1952	1953–1964	1965–1969	1970–1971
Mortality:					
Metropolitan Life, 1936–1940	x				
Metropolitan Life, 1936–1940 (Modified)		x			
Metropolitan Life, 1946–1950			x		
1954–1958 Basic				x	x
Withdrawals (at age 20):					
40% first year, 15% second year, 10% third year, grading to 1% in 45th year	x				
60% first year, 35% second year, 17 1/2% third year, grading to 1% in 50th year		x	x	x	x
Nonforfeiture costs:					
Cash value	x	x	x	x	
Cost weighted for distribution of nonforfeiture options					x
Interest:					
2.75% level	x				
3% level		x			
3 1/4% to 3% in 10 years			x		
4 1/2% to 3% in 30 years				x	
6 1/2% to 3 1/2% in 30 years					x
Automatic supplemental benefits— 60 cents per $1,000 per year	x	x	x	x	x

nizes the "savings", then the "savings"—equal to the difference between the cash value and the extended insurance reserve—are recognized as such immediately; there is no future gain or loss.

Provision in the basic reserve for the "savings" results in spreading it over the premium-paying period. So long as the reserve on the extended insurance reflects the "savings", there is no gain or loss at the time the option is effected or afterward. If, however, the reserve on the extended insurance does not recognize the "savings", then there is a charge to operations at the time of effecting the option equal to the then present value of the savings; this charge is reversed over time. If, say, statutory reserves on extended insurance are held for convenience, then theoretically the charge to operations should be deferred and spread out over the period of time that the "savings" are being realized, i.e., as the option runs off.

Studies indicated the "savings" to run off at approximately the following rate:

Year 1	6 %
2	13
3	12½
4	12½
5	12½
6	12½
7	12½
8	12½
9	6

Calculation Techniques

Adjusted reserves on industrial business can be calculated by the mid-terminal technique (the usual statutory method), the mean reserve technique, or the intermediate reserve technique. Where the mid-terminal technique is used, it is necessary to tabulate uncollected and unearned premiums (the latter might

Table 18–7.

STATUTORY RESERVES AND ADJUSTED BENEFIT RESERVES PER $1,000 IN FORCE FOR INDUSTRIAL 20–PAY LIFE POLICIES—1970–1971 ISSUES

	Age 5		Age 20		Age 35	
Year	Statutory Net Level*	Adjusted**	Statutory Net Level*	Adjusted**	Statutory Net Level*	Adjusted**
1	$ 5.86	$ 3.23	$ 8.92	$ 4.45	$ 13.00	$ 7.67
2	17.86	11.55	24.92	16.70	36.00	26.53
3	28.86	21.84	41.92	32.33	60.00	47.53
4	40.86	31.48	58.92	46.21	85.00	67.15
5	52.86	41.42	75.92	60.37	110.00	87.32
6	65.86	52.32	94.92	76.00	136.00	109.03
7	78.86	63.69	112.92	93.09	162.00	132.47
8	91.86	75.09	132.92	110.40	189.00	156.35
9	105.86	87.13	151.92	128.10	216.00	180.70
10	119.86	99.82	172.92	146.63	244.00	205.98
11	134.86	112.79	193.92	165.48	273.00	231.73
12	149.86	126.05	215.92	184.53	302.00	257.96
13	164.86	139.71	237.92	204.00	332.00	285.17
14	180.86	153.78	260.92	223.93	363.00	313.29
15	196.86	168.24	283.92	244.28	395.00	342.07
16	213.86	182.65	307.92	264.55	427.00	370.69
17	230.86	196.92	332.92	284.57	460.00	399.10
18	248.86	211.39	357.92	304.80	495.00	428.06
19	266.86	226.06	384.92	325.16	530.00	457.50
20	285.86	240.82	410.92	345.62	566.00	487.38
25	329.75	286.30	470.75	409.05	634.75	567.03
30	372.75	331.30	523.75	469.02	690.75	636.99
35	419.75	374.87	578.75	523.70	743.75	695.90
40	470.75	422.14	634.75	580.36	792.00	753.40
45	523.75	472.21	690.75	638.40	837.00	806.41
50	578.75	525.44	743.75	695.90	875.00	852.52
55	634.75	580.66	792.00	753.40	905.00	890.86
60	690.75	637.83	837.00	806.41	937.00	931.35

*Including unearned weekly net premium to 20th duration and increment of $.75 for supplemental benefits to expiry date (attained age 70).

**Intermediate reserve method with premium receipts apportioned to each six-month period.

be taken as one-half of a weekly net premium). Where mean reserves are used, deferred and uncollected premiums must be tabulated.

Use of the traditional mid-terminal or mean reserve technique can produce fairly significant distortions in the case of industrial business because of the lapse pattern. For weekly premium business, the year's lapses tend to be heavily skewed toward the first six months of the policy year. This follows from the weekly mode; all other things being equal, the more frequent the mode the heavier the lapses. The problem is, of course, greatest in the first year, when lapses tend to be the greatest.

Crazy Quilt Life used the intermediate reserve technique, but avoided the need for setting up either deferred or unearned premiums by providing for the

incidence of premiums assumed to be received throughout the year. Based on month-by-month studies of experience, Crazy Quilt assumed for reserve calculation purposes that, in the first policy year, two-thirds of the premiums were received at the beginning of the first six months and one-third at the end of the second six months; after the first year, the year's premiums were assumed to be received 50 percent in each six months.*

The result was to produce a different valuation premium for each year in the premium-paying period, representing the amount of the valuation premium

* It should be re-emphasized that while this approach was deemed appropriate for Crazy Quilt, it would not necessarily be appropriate for any other company. *Proper* recognition of the skew of premium receipts is very important.

assumed to be received in that year. The benefit premiums for 1970–1971 issues of industrial 20-pay life (age 20), for example, were as follows:

Calendar Year	Benefit Premium	Calendar Year	Benefit Premium
1	$5.10	11	$8.58
2	9.92	12	8.56
3	9.94	13	8.53
4	9.06	14	8.50
5	8.87	15	8.48
6	8.87	16	8.47
7	8.85	17	8.47
8	8.72	18	8.48
9	8.64	19	8.48
10	8.60	20	8.46
		21	4.30

Calculation of intermediate reserves was thereafter fairly straightforward, being a simple accumulation of valuation premiums and assumed experience. The first-year factor of $4.45, for example, was calculated as follows:

	Reserve	Units in Force
Issued 7–1		1.00000
Assumed lapses—60% x .67		(.40200)
Adjusted initial in-force		.59800
Valuation premium— $5.10 x .59800	$3.06	
Deaths— $1.00 x 50% x .59800	(.30)	(.00030)
Supplemental benefits— $.60 x 50% x .59800	(.18)	
Balance 7–1	2.58	
Interest at 3.2%	.08	
Balance 12–31	$2.66	.59770
Reserve per unit 12–31— $2.66 ÷ .59770	$4.45	

Adjusted reserve factors are illustrated in Table 18–7 for 1970–1971 issues. Statutory reserves are shown for comparative purposes. Due mainly to the effect of interest rates on high-reserve plans like 20-pay life, the differences are quite significant at almost all durations.

Grading

Inspection of Table 18–7 will probably suggest the obvious: adjusted reserves on industrial business should not be graded to statutory without extensive testing.

Table 18–8 shows industrial 20-pay life reserve factors (for various ages and durations) for two common

grading plans—20 years (modified to 21 years because of the effect on the 21st year of allocating premiums to half-years) and 30 years. While the distortions are not too severe in the early durations, they gradually become quite serious, particularly when 20-year grading is employed.

The effect on reserve levels and changes of grading for large blocks of this type of business—Crazy Quilt's, in this case—is shown in Table 18–9.

Paid-up Business

Paid-up business is usually a major part of a combination company's business in force, due mainly to the disproportionate share of limited-payment life plans usually associated with industrial business and to the sizeable proportion of terminated business that converts to reduced paid-up.

Often data on issue age, issue year, etc. are not readily available for paid-up business; only attained age and valuation basis is needed, for instance, to obtain statutory reserves.

Thus shortcut methods are often needed to deal with paid-up business. Some shortcuts are discussed in Chapter 11.

Paid-up reserves should not be carried on the statutory basis without careful analysis of the effect of not adjusting because of the impact on such reserves of even minor adjustments of the assumed interest rate.

Expenses

Expenses associated with industrial insurance have several unique characteristics, and dealing with them in the accounting process requires a fair degree of ingenuity.

Accounting Records

Usually a combination agent sells ordinary and industrial insurance and perhaps other products. A company may or may not keep track of the components of agent compensation by product. Or the company may keep track of them until they are channeled into the "sales core", after which identification is lost. Yet payments out of the sales core are recorded as expense.

Suppose, for example, that in a given calendar quarter the agent earns $1,300, comprised as follows:

	Production Commission	Collection Commission	Renewals	Conservation Commission	Total
Industrial life	$350	$100		$ 50	$ 500
Industrial health	100	50		50	200
Debit ordinary	100	50		50	200
Regular ordinary	100		$100		200
Individual health	150		50		200
	$800	$200	$150	$150	$1,300

However, no payments are made in the quarter the compensation is earned. Instead a memorandum record of the $1,300 is maintained and it is paid out to the agent in the ensuing quarter at the rate of $100 a week. The $100 a week in cash outlays is recorded as an expense.

The company may or may not keep a supplemental record of the components of the $1,300 that were credited to the agent in the memorandum record. Assume that it does. Identification of the elements of each $100 payment would usually be lost in any event. Yet the actual payments are recorded as

Table 18–8.

VARIOUS GRADING PATTERNS FOR ADJUSTED BENEFIT RESERVES FOR INDUSTRIAL 20–PAY LIFE FACTORS—1970–1971 ISSUES—PER $1,000 IN FORCE

	Issue Age 5			Issue Age 20			Issue Age 35		
		Graded to Statutory in			Graded to Statutory in			Graded to Statutory in	
Year	Ungraded	21 Years	30 Years	Ungraded	21 Years	30 Years	Ungraded	21 Years	30 Years
1	$ 3.23	$ 3.55	$ 3.37	$ 4.45	$ 4.83	$ 4.59	$ 7.67	$ 8.25	$ 7.85
2	11.55	12.71	12.03	16.70	18.18	17.28	26.53	28.58	27.16
3	21.84	24.02	22.74	32.33	35.28	33.48	47.53	51.36	48.70
4	31.48	34.69	32.81	46.21	50.61	47.93	67.15	72.75	68.87
5	41.42	45.75	43.21	60.37	66.38	62.72	87.32	94.81	89.62
6	52.32	57.94	54.65	76.00	83.92	79.09	109.03	118.70	112.00
7	63.69	70.74	66.61	93.09	103.27	97.06	132.47	144.65	136.21
8	75.09	83.56	78.60	110.40	122.94	115.30	156.35	171.16	160.90
9	87.13	97.19	91.29	128.10	143.14	133.98	180.70	198.26	186.10
10	99.82	111.62	104.71	146.63	164.38	153.57	205.98	226.50	212.28
11	112.79	126.47	118.46	165.48	186.17	173.56	231.73	255.44	239.01
12	126.05	141.80	132.58	184.53	208.38	193.85	257.96	285.16	266.32
13	139.71	157.72	147.17	204.00	231.23	214.64	285.17	316.23	294.71
14	153.78	174.23	162.25	223.93	254.77	235.98	313.29	348.64	324.15
15	168.24	191.34	177.81	244.28	278.96	257.83	342.07	381.98	354.33
16	182.65	208.53	193.37	264.55	303.27	279.68	370.69	415.31	384.40
17	196.92	225.79	208.88	284.57	327.63	301.39	399.10	448.78	414.36
18	211.39	243.54	224.71	304.80	352.62	323.48	428.06	483.31	445.03
19	226.06	261.80	240.86	325.16	378.22	345.89	457.50	518.88	476.36
20	240.82	280.50	257.26	345.62	404.27	368.53	487.38	555.51	508.31
21	252.07	295.69	270.14	361.40	425.57	386.47	509.22	584.13	532.23
22	260.03	305.75	279.72	372.68	439.75	399.90	523.04	600.75	548.13
23	268.39	313.75	289.84	384.34	449.75	413.92	537.19	611.75	564.59
24	277.14	321.75	300.52	396.42	459.75	428.57	551.73	622.75	581.68
25	286.30	329.75	311.79	409.05	470.75	443.93	567.03	634.75	599.65
26	295.29	337.75	323.00	421.30	480.75	458.95	581.73	645.75	617.04
27	303.82	345.75	333.88	432.84	491.75	473.41	595.24	656.75	633.42
28	312.64	354.75	345.25	444.64	501.75	488.37	608.93	667.75	650.28
29	321.81	363.75	357.19	456.69	512.75	503.87	622.80	679.75	667.66
30	331.30	372.75	369.69	469.02	523.75	519.94	636.99	690.75	685.65
31	340.32	381.75	381.75	480.51	534.75	534.75	650.09	701.75	701.75

Table 18–9.

EFFECT OF GRADING ON ADJUSTED BENEFIT RESERVE LEVELS AND CHANGES IN SELECTED FINANCIAL REPORTING YEARS—INDUSTRIAL 20–PAY LIFE (000 Omitted)

	Face Amount Issued Through 1971	In Force 12–31–71	Adjusted Benefit Reserves				Projected			
			1968	1969	1970	1971	1972	1973	1974	1980
Issues prior to 1964:	$454,285	$34,147								
Ungraded:										
Level			$17,216	$17,598	$17,910	$18,159*	$18,351	$18,475	$18,543	$17,947
Change			485	382	312	249	192	124	68	(210)
Graded in 20 years:										
Level			17,842	18,271	18,625	18,915	19,141	19,297	19,362	18,870
Change			512	429	354	290	226	156	65	(211)
Graded in 30 years:										
Level			17,520	17,926	18,261	18,536	18,751	18,899	18,992	18,541
Change			488	406	335	275	215	148	93	(222)
Issues 1965–1969:	162,900	60,477								
Ungraded:										
Level			1,217	1,790	2,318	2,766*	3,163	3,529	3,873	5,565
Change			476	573	528	448	397	366	344	236
Graded in 20 years:										
Level			1,253	1,845	2,390	2,854	3,267	3,648	4,039	5,788
Change			490	592	545	464	413	381	391	253
Graded in 30 years:										
Level			1,228	1,808	2,341	2,793	3,196	3,567	3,915	5,635
Change			481	580	533	452	403	371	348	244
Issues 1970–1971:	71,850	36,670								
Ungraded:										
Level					109	352*	591	787	958	1,779
Change					109	243	239	196	171	127
Graded in 20 years:										
Level					119	382	643	858	1,047	1,976
Change					119	263	261	215	189	145
Graded in 30 years:										
Level					113	363	610	813	991	1,851
Change					113	250	247	203	178	134

*Total reserves at December 31, 1971: $21,277,000.

expense. In these circumstances, agent compensation recorded as expense on the books would not be segregated by line of business or by first year and renewal.

Thus special studies are often needed to make the necessary allocations of compensation payments to combination agents. If the company keeps a breakdown of the elements of compensation going into the memorandum account, the applicable percentages can be used to apportion the recorded expense. The process can get quite complicated because of payment limits, chargebacks for lapses, and the like; but complicated or not, reasonably accurate allocations are needed for accounting purposes.

The "Times" System

Often a portion of a combination agent's compensation is based on a multiple of the net increase in his debit, i.e., the collections for which he is responsible. For example, suppose the agent's debit increases from $450 to $500. He might be paid a production commission or a conservation commission or both based on the $50 increase in his debit. His commission would be reckoned as a certain multiple of the increase—for example, 10 times the increase.

The "times" system has certain implications for accounting purposes that need some elaboration.

For purposes of discussion, assume that 36.4 times the increase in the weekly debit is provisionally credited to the agent as his selling commission. This is equivalent to 70 percent of the annualized first-year premium (that is, 36.4 divided by 52). Assuming no terminations, the net effect would be the same as paying a 70 percent first-year commission. Thus, if 1,000 policies were sold in the first week for $20 per policy per year ($.38461 per week), the net increase in the agent's debit would be 1,000 x $.38461 or $384.61, and his commission credit would be $384.61 x 36.4 or $14,000.

Assume now that five policies lapse in the second week and that he sells no more policies. The net decrease in his debit is 5 x $.38461 or $1.92, and he is charged back $1.92 x 36.4 or $69.89 in commissions. But the company would have received $1.92 in premiums in the first week. The effective commission rate on premiums collected is something less than 70 percent at this point.

Now continue the process to the end of the first year, assuming no further sales and terminations according to the following pattern:

Week 1	–0–%
Weeks 2–6	.5
Weeks 7–43	1.0
Weeks 44–52	.5

It will be found that the effective first-year termination rate is 35.6 percent—that 644 policies persist to the end of the year. The net increase in the debit for the year is 644 x $.38461 or $247.69, and the agent's net commission credits are $247.69 x 36.4, or $9,016. This total may be anaylzed as follows:

Provisional commission credits—	
1,000 x $.38461 x 36.4	$14,000
Chargebacks—356 x $.38461 x 36.4	(4,984)
Net credit	$ 9,016

Assume a 30 percent termination rate in the second year; this is equivalent to 19.3 percent of the original issue of 1,000 policies. Thus, 193 policies terminate in the second year. The agent is charged back for 193 x $.38461 x 36.4 or $2,702, reducing the aggregate net credit to $9,016 minus $2,702 or $6,314.

It can be seen that if this process continues, zero commissions will have been paid simply because all policies must terminate eventually.

Thus, the "times" method in this case is essentially a financing device. The advances are really agents' balances. In theory, the "recoverability" of such advances from agents should be evaluated on the basis that they are receivables. Balances due from terminating agents would be written off (presumably against an allowance for uncollectible agents' accounts) when they terminate.

The difficulty of charging back advances results in spreading out the advances. In the case illustrated above, if the entire multiple were paid to the agent in the week of sale and the agent disappeared as soon as he received payment, the company would lose $14,000. Thus, the advances are usually credited to a memorandum "sales core" and paid out over time.

Even though the "times" method may be viewed as a financing device, it is proper to regard some portion of the financing as commissions for accounting purposes. This is because it is known that a substantial portion of the advances will never be charged back to agents. In practice, the "times" method is both a financing method and a compensation system.

Assume that the historical pattern indicates that 50 percent of the advance will not be collected. Technically, advances should be allocated 50 percent to agents' balances and 50 percent to commissions.

The question now arises as to the disposition of net payments under a "times" system in any given year. Such net payments represent advances in respect of new business less chargebacks applicable to terminations of policies issued in all prior years plus chargebacks which cannot be made because some agents have terminated.

Consider the following pattern of advances to an agent who terminates during year 2:

	New Business Advances	Theoretical Chargebacks	Actual Chargebacks	Net Payments
Year 1	$1,000	$ 400	$400	$600
Year 2	400	300	300	100
Year 3		400	–0–	–0–
Year 4		300	–0–	–0–
All years	$1,400	$1,400	$700	$700

Table 18–10.

CALCULATION OF 1971 DEFERRABLE ACQUISITION COSTS FOR INDUSTRIAL LINE OF BUSINESS

	Related to Premiums	*Related to Policies*	*Total*
1971 acquisition costs incurred (000):			
Production commissions	$ 332		$ 332
Overrides	64		64
Agency support	262	$ 310	572
Selection		78	78
Issue		52	52
	658	440	1,098
Less:			
Development	(105)	(124)	(229)
Overhead	(28)	(32)	(60)
Deferrable	$ 525	$ 284	$ 809
1971 deferrable unit costs:			
Units produced	$583,000	$49,150	
Deferrable per unit	90%	$ 5.78	

The effective overall commission rate is 50 percent of the rate used for purposes of making advances. Theoretically, in Year 1 $500 of the $600 advanced should be recorded as commissions and $100 should be set up as an agent's balance; in Year 2 $200 should be recorded as commissions and $100 should be credited to the agent's balance. The net effect in either case is to record as expense the net amount paid to the agent.

As indicated previously, "times" advances are often credited to a memorandum "sales core" which forms the basis for actual payments. Suppose that 8 percent of the "sales core" balance is paid out weekly. Assuming sale of a policy in the first week which has a $1.00 weekly premium, assuming no further transactions, and assuming a multiple of 35, the operation of the "sales core" system may be illustrated as follows:

	Memo Sales Core	*Expensed in Statutory Statement— Represents Net Payments*
Sale—$1.00 x 35	$35.00	
Week 1 payment—8%	(2.80)	$2.80
	32.20	
Week 2 payment—8%	(2.58)	2.58
	29.62	
Week 3 payment—8%	(2.37)	2.37
	27.25	
Week 4 payment—8%	(2.18)	2.18
	25.07	
	(et cetera)	

It can be seen that the statutory statement departs from the accrual basis. Technically the entire advance should be accrued and accounted for. The entries would be as follows:

At time of sale:		
Commission expense	$35.00	
Commission payable		$35.00
Week 1 payment:		
Commissions payable	2.80	
Cash		2.80
Week 2 payment:		
Commissions payable	2.58	
Cash		2.58

In theory, then, the "sales core" should be recorded. Allocations of net payments between commission expense and agents' balances would be made on the accrual basis.

Deferral of Acquisition Costs

The principles of variability and attribution apply to deferrable acquisition costs on industrial business. In general, the following expenses would qualify for deferral:

Production commissions
Conservation commissions
Production bonuses
Override on production commissions, conservation commissions, and production bonuses
That portion of district office expenses allocable to production supervision
Home office selection and issue expenses

Table 18–11.

SELECTED ACQUISITION COST VALUATION PREMIUM AND FACTORS FOR 1971 ISSUES OF INDUSTRIAL 20–PAY LIFE—PER $1,000 IN FORCE

	Issue Age 5		Issue Age 20		Issue Age 35	
	Valuation	*Acquisition Cost*	*Valuation*	*Acquisition Cost*	*Valuation*	*Acquisition Cost*
Year	*Premium*	*Factor**	*Premium*	*Factor**	*Premium*	*Factor**
1	$ 5.61	$25.86	$ 8.57	$28.13	$ 7.64	$37.13
2	10.70	53.19	16.65	64.64	14.70	79.39
3	10.63	61.46	16.69	78.85	14.63	90.21
4	9.96	64.05	15.21	83.79	13.78	92.95
5	9.81	65.12	14.89	86.24	13.57	93.29
6	9.80	66.14	14.88	88.83	13.59	93.68
7	9.74	66.32	14.85	91.38	13.60	94.01
8	9.62	64.72	14.63	91.58	13.47	92.54
9	9.60	62.74	14.51	90.15	13.37	89.59
10	9.59	60.37	14.44	87.75	13.33	85.85
11	9.57	57.40	14.40	84.32	13.31	81.28
12	9.58	53.95	14.36	79.76	13.32	76.06
13	9.57	49.97	14.32	74.23	13.31	70.34
14	9.55	45.44	14.27	67.68	13.31	64.05
15	9.54	40.31	14.23	60.07	13.28	56.81
16	9.53	34.47	14.21	51.39	13.24	48.47
17	9.52	27.98	14.22	41.73	13.24	39.26
18	9.53	20.87	14.23	31.14	13.25	29.23
19	9.53	13.08	14.23	19.54	13.25	18.30
20	9.53	4.55	14.20	6.79	13.25	6.36
21	4.86	–0–	7.22	–0–	6.76	–0–

*Negative (i.e., an "asset") in all durations

The types of expenses qualifying for deferral on industrial are the same in all material respects as those deferrable on ordinary business. Because turnover of combination agents is typically very high, recruiting and training is a continual process. It may well be that the relationship between recruiting and training and production is sufficiently direct and timely as to qualify such expenses as acquisition costs; but the burden of proof for demonstrating this beyond a reasonable doubt is, of course, on the company.

"Times" payments and "sales cores". Usually a company will want to defer net payments under the "times" system for the sake of simplicity. So long as it can be demonstrated that deferral of net payments does not materially distort the balance sheet and income statement, there should be no objection to this.

Generally, recognition of a "sales core" will tend to produce an asset that is substantially offset by a corresponding liability. The income and surplus effect would usually be nominal. In such cases the distortion of the financial statements is limited to total assets and total liabilities. It is to be expected that such distortions will not be material in most cases.

It is, of course, necessary to allocate net payments between first year and renewal and among lines of business. While payments must be allocated in some fashion to lines of business for statutory purposes, many companies do not segregate first-year from renewal payments, particularly for the industrial line. In such cases it will be necessary to make the segregation for deferral purposes, presumably by analyzing inputs into the "sales core" and activity within the "sales core" prior to the commencement of installment payments to the agent.

Allocations to valuation cells. Where the factor method of accounting for acquisition costs is used, acquisition costs must be allocated to valuation cells. The considerations involved in making such allocations are described in Chapter 16.

Special attention must be paid to the incidence of expense assumed for purposes of calculating factors. The assumption that the year's expenses are incurred at the moment of issue is of course erroneous. Where premiums are allocated to half-years in connection with an intermediate reserve calculation, generally the assumed incidence of expenses will present no problem

Table 18–12.

INDUSTRIAL ACQUISITION COSTS DEFERRED AND AMORTIZED, 1941–1971 (000 Omitted)

Issue Year	Acquisition Costs Incurred				Unamortized (with Interest) at December 31				Unamortized Without Interest, 1972 (Projected)**
	In Issue Year	In Following Year*	Total In Issue Year	Total In Both Years	1969	1970	1971	1972 (Projected)	
1941	$ 143	$ 44	$ 143	$ 187					
1942	191	58	235	249					
1943	240	73	298	313					
1944	276	84	349	360					
1945	288	97	372	385					
1946	302	101	399	403					
1947	311	103	412	414					
1948	335	113	438	448					
1949	347	116	460	463					
1950	353	118	469	471	$ 8				
1951	361	122	479	483	23	$ 8			
1952	365	123	487	488	40	24	$ 8		
1953	412	170	535	582	60	42	25	$ 8	$ 7
1954	400	171	570	571	79	60	42	25	21
1955	391	167	562	558	95	77	59	42	35
1956	380	162	547	542	111	93	75	57	49
1957	355	163	517	518	130	112	94	76	66
1958	363	167	526	530	153	133	114	95	84
1959	373	172	540	545	178	157	137	118	105
1960	388	179	560	567	207	185	164	143	129
1961	387	188	566	575	242	218	195	172	157
1962	411	199	599	610	283	256	231	206	191
1963	462	224	661	686	349	318	288	259	244
1964	493	239	717	732	409	373	339	307	293
1965	562	257	801	819	478	437	400	365	347
1966	593	270	850	863	549	502	459	420	405
1967	617	282	887	899	627	572	523	478	468
1968	635	290	917	925	719	646	589	539	535
1969	654	298	944	952	568	740	665	606	610
1970	810	383	1,108	1,193		673	889	801	822
1971	809	385	1,192	1,194			676	893	925
TOTAL	$13,007	$5,518			$5,308	$5,626	$5,972	$5,610	$5,493
CHANGE					$ 228	$ 318	$ 344	$ (362)	$ (391)

*Representing percentage acquisition costs incurred when a portion of first-policy year premiums are received in the second calendar year.

**Shown for comparative purposes.

so long as it rides along with the assumed receipt of premiums. Where mean or mid-terminal reserves are used, or intermediate reserves assume receipt of a full annual premium, special adjustments are required to calculate factors. The considerations involved are set forth in Chapter 23.

Crazy Quilt Life. The development of deferrable acquisition costs for Crazy Quilt Life's industrial line was substantially the same as for ordinary life acquisition costs. Starting with LOMA functional costs, development and overhead costs were identified and eliminated. Actuarial unit costs used for pricing purposes, which had been developed by additional analysis of the LOMA functional costs, were then adjusted for pro rata shares of development and overhead. Factors were then calculated. The process is sum-

Table 18–13.

MAINTENANCE AND SETTLEMENT RESERVES ON INDUSTRIAL 20–PAY LIFE

Maintenance and settlement expense reserves per $1,000—1970–1971 Issues:

Year	Issue Age 5	Issue Age 20	Issue Age 35
1	$ (.42)	$ (.26)	$ (.40)
5	.93	.23	.36
10	2.87	1.91	2.44
15	6.28	5.31	6.06
20	11.47	10.54	11.45
25	12.92	11.95	12.72
30	13.32	12.17	12.42
35	13.51	12.04	11.43
40	13.50	11.59	10.31
50	13.42	10.00	8.49
60	12.58	8.19	6.83

Aggregate maintenance and settlement expense reserves (000):

	In Force 12–31–71	Reserves 1969	Reserves 1970	Reserves 1971
Issues of 1945:	$ 1,310			
Level		$ 35	$ 34	$ 32
Change		(2)	(1)	(2)
Issues of 1955:	2,363			
Level		27	29	31
Change		2	2	2
Issues of 1965:	5,941			
Level		7	8	10
Change		2	1	2
Issues of all years:	131,294			
Level		634	662	689
Change		30	28	27

marized with respect to 1971 issues of weekly premium business in Table 18–10. Crazy Quilt considered conservation commissions to be incurred levelly; acquisition cost commissions were limited to production commissions and overrides.

Amortization of Acquisition Costs

Many combination companies will probably want to use worksheets to amortize acquisition costs on the industrial line, mainly because factor calculations can become quite complicated.

Worksheet methods discussed in Chapter 16 are applicable also to acquisition costs on industrial business.

Because of the high lapse rate on industrial business, and because of the high proportion of limited-pay business typically associated with the industrial line, it would usually be feasible to use arbitrary cutoffs for

amortization of industrial acquisition costs. It should rarely be necessary to amortize such costs beyond 20 years.

True to form, Crazy Quilt Life ignored simplicity and chose to calculate factors. Selected valuation premiums and factors for the 20-pay life plan are shown in Table 18–11. Total acquisition costs deferred and amortized, and related unamortized balances, are shown in Table 18–12.

Maintenance and Settlement Expenses

Industrial insurance is typically of the limited-payment variety, and, as discussed in Chapter 17, limited-payment business inevitably gives rise to fairly sizable reserves for maintenance and settlement expenses. Unless there are obvious offsetting factors, such as ultra-conservative interest assumptions, maintenance and settlement expense reserves should usually be provided on such business.

In Crazy Quilt's case, valuation premiums for maintenance and settlement expenses average over 70 percent of acquisition cost valuation premiums. Reserve factors at selected durations, and the level of and change in aggregate maintenance and settlement reserves for several years, are shown in Table 18–13.

Disclosure

Disclosure for the industrial line of business should generally follow the pattern of disclosure for ordinary business. Where industrial business is material, as it usually is for combination companies, disclosure of reserve assumptions and amounts and acquisition cost amounts should preferably be made separately.

19

Individual
Health Insurance

The varieties of individual health insurance policy forms are virtually without limit. There are hospital, surgical, and medical expense policies; comprehensive and major medical policies; accident policies; supplemental hospitalization policies; dental policies; disability income policies; and others.

For purposes of discussing generally accepted accounting principles adjustments, however, individual health policies may be classified three ways:

▶ Commercial forms
▶ Noncancellable business
▶ Guaranteed renewable business

In addition, because of their unique nature, return-of-premium policies might be classified as a fourth category of individual health policies even though they are typically written in conjunction with noncancellable or guaranteed renewable business.

Commercial Forms

Commercial forms of individual health insurance may be defined as individual policies of health insurance for which the insurance company reserves the right to change the premium, cancel the policy, or renew the policy. In many respects the business is comparable to standard cancellable casualty coverages offered by property-liability companies and indeed, many property-liability companies do offer health insurance.*

*Not only commercial individual forms but also individual noncancellable and guaranteed renewable business, credit health insurance, and group health insurance.

Revenue

The life insurance audit guide provides that, where health insurance policies "which are expected to be in force for a reasonable period of time *and* for which elements of expense *or* benefit costs are not level," premiums should be recognized as revenue "over the premium-paying period," i.e., when due (emphasis supplied). "For other kinds of health insurance, gross premiums should be recognized as revenues on a pro rata basis over the period covered by the premium." [1]

Commercial forms of health insurance are, by their nature, short-term contracts since they may be cancelled by the company. Since policies are cancellable and premiums are adjustable, it is normally presumed that benefits will be more or less "level". In fact, of course, benefits are not level; they fluctuate, sometimes wildly, but cancellations and premium adjustments are theoretically available to produce the desired constancy from year to year. Where expenses are relatively level, a commercial form would generally meet the criterion for recognizing gross premiums as revenue on an earned basis, i.e., pro rata over the period covered by the premium. The active life reserve at any point in time would be the unearned gross premium. This is the property-liability approach to revenue recognition.

Some companies, however, pay heaped commissions on commercial policies. There may, in addition, be more sales support expense and underwriting and issue costs in the initial year than in renewal years. Thus expenses would not be "level". Cancellable or not, the company obviously expects some of the policies to remain in force for "a reasonable period of time." Since the guide appears to require only that the contract be expected to remain in force for a reasonable period of time and that benefits *or* expenses be non-level to qualify for recognition of premiums as revenue when due, some believe that the circumstances described in this paragraph would warrant recognition of premiums as revenue when due.

Nevertheless, the nature of commercial health insurance is such that pro data gross unearned premiums should be held in respect of active lives in all cases and acquisition costs should be amortized to income in proportion to premiums earned.

Composition of Acquisition Costs

As a matter of principle, commercial health acquisition costs qualifying for deferral would include commissions, premium taxes, and such items of general expenses—sales support, underwriting, and issue—as may be related primarily to production. The costs deferred should meet the audit guide's general criteria of variability and attribution.

Some believe that deferrals should be limited to commissions and premium taxes. Some believe deferrals should include commissions, premium taxes, and 50 percent of general expenses exclusive of claims handling costs. And some believe deferrals should include commissions, premium taxes, and *all* general expenses except claims handling and servicing costs. These are rules of thumb; one of them—commissions, premium taxes, and 50 percent of general expenses other than loss adjustment expenses—is widely used in the property-liability industry. Used or not, a rule of thumb is a rule of thumb. The method used should be based on reasonable cost accounting determinations.

Casualty Approach

Where acquisition costs are deemed to be incurred more or less uniformly in proportion to premiums written, all that is necessary to adjust commercial health acquisition costs is to calculate the "equity" in the unearned premium reserve. This might be accomplished as follows:

Acquisition costs	$ 300
Premiums written	$1,000
Ratio	30%
Unearned premium reserve	$ 500
Equity in unearned premium reserve	$ 150

The equity in the unearned premium reserve would be reported as deferred acquisition costs in the balance

sheet; the change in such equity would be reflected as an adjustment of the income statement.

The amount deferrable is subject to a loss ratio limitation. Suppose, for example, that the commercial health loss ratio is 70 percent, that this loss ratio is expected to be constant in the foreseeable future, that claims handling costs 5 percent, and that 5 percent of premiums is deemed to be needed to cover other servicing costs. In that event, the deferrable equity in unearned premiums is 20 percent, not 30 percent:

Base	100%
Less:	
Anticipated loss ratio	70
Claims handling expense	5
Servicing costs	5
	80
Deferral percentage	20%

When there is good evidence that an apparent loss ratio limitation is temporary, it generally should not be projected to the period in which unearned premiums will be earned. The anticipated loss ratio for subsequent periods is the ratio to be taken into account for purposes of calculating loss ratio limitations. Obviously a fair degree of judgment is needed in determining whether deferrals must be limited because of future loss ratios.

It should be noted that averaging techniques are frequently employed to develop deferral percentages and loss ratio limitation percentages. For example, five years of acquisition cost and premiums written data might be used to obtain the former, and five years of losses incurred and premiums earned data to obtain the latter; however, it is always important to adjust loss ratio averages to reflect emerging or anticipated trends. Averaging is used mainly to eliminate the influence of random fluctuations.

Crazy Quilt Life

Crazy Quilt Life limited acquisition cost deferrals on commercial health business to commissions and premium taxes, on the basis that other expenses that would qualify for deferral were nominal. Underwriting was slight, sales support was nominal (because the business was marketed through ordinary life agents whose principal function was to write the business if requested by an ordinary life policyholder or prospect rather than to promote the business aggressively as an independent product), and issue costs were negligible.

A summary of commercial health experience on a

Table 19–1.

SUMMARY OF EXPERIENCE OF COMMERCIAL HEALTH LINES FOR CRAZY QUILT LIFE, 1960–1971 (000 Omitted)

	1960	1961	1962	1963	1964	1965	1966	1967	1968	1969	1970	1971
Premiums written	$3,299	$3,276	$3,432	$3,134	$2,994	$2,570	$2,422	$2,914	$2,719	$2,658	$3,273	$2,241
Unearned premiums:												
Ending	990	983	1,030	940	898	874	751	729	653	638	1,080	695
Beginning	—0—	(990)	(983)	(1,030)	(940)	(898)	(874)	(751)	(729)	(653)	(638)	(1,080)
Change	990	(7)	47	(90)	(42)	(24)	(123)	(22)	(76)	(15)	442	(385)
Premiums earned	2,309	3,283	3,385	3,224	3,036	2,594	2,545	2,936	2,795	2,673	2,831	2,626
Losses:												
Paid	508	812	911	1,142	1,050	1,407	985	1,091	1,558	1,778	1,524	2,099
Ending reserve	508	911	1,489	1,733	2,049	1,809	2,198	2,810	3,041	2,947	3,320	2,849
Beginning reserve	—0—	(508)	(911)	(1,489)	(1,733)	(2,049)	(1,809)	(2,198)	(2,810)	(3,041)	(2,947)	(3,320)
Incurred	1,016	1,215	1,489	1,386	1,366	1,167	1,374	1,703	1,789	1,684	1,897	1,628
	1,293	2,068	1,896	1,838	1,670	1,427	1,171	1,233	1,006	989	934	998
Expenses:												
Commissions (20%)	660	655	686	627	599	514	484	583	544	532	655	448
Premium Taxes (2%)	66	66	69	63	60	51	48	58	54	53	65	45
Other	621	762	784	749	675	603	593	476	538	485	593	537
	1,347	1,483	1,539	1,439	1,334	1,168	1,125	1,117	1,136	1,070	1,313	1,030
Statutory gain (loss)	(54)	585	357	399	336	259	46	116	(130)	(81)	(379)	(32)
Equity in unearned premiums at 22%:												
Ending	218	216	227	207	198	192	165	160	144	140	238	153
Beginning	—0—	(218)	(216)	(227)	(207)	(198)	(192)	(165)	(160)	(144)	(140)	(238)
Change	218	(2)	11	(20)	(9)	(6)	(27)	(5)	(16)	(4)	98	(85)
Adjusted gain (loss)	$164	$583	$368	$379	$327	$253	$19	$111	$(146)	$(85)	$(281)	$(117)

statutory and an adjusted basis from 1960 (the year Crazy Quilt got into the business at a cost of $80,000, which was expensed) to 1971 is shown in Table 19–1.

In 1968, when losses on the business were first experienced, the current pattern of losses was not projected into the next calendar year. This rationale was used in 1968–1971 to justify non-recognition of loss ratio limitations. Hindsight demonstrated that the rationale was not sound. But it must be remembered that the loss ratio limitation test contemplates the future. In view of Crazy Quilt's history, there was little to justify the assumption of chronic losses. By 1971 a new pattern had emerged, and in 1972 Crazy Quilt decided to apply the loss ratio limitation test in terms of five years of experience.

"Heaped" Acquisition Costs

Where acquisition costs are "heaped" in the year of original issue—in other words, where acquisition costs are not proportional to premiums written—it is necessary to account for the first-year excess separately.

For example, if acquisition costs are equal to 60 percent of premiums written in the year of original issue and 20 percent in renewal years,

▶ The normal 20 percent should be accounted for by the traditional method, i.e., deferring the equity in the unearned, and

▶ The excess 40 percent should be amortized in proportion to the sum-of-the-years' *earned* premiums with or without interest.

The equity in unearned premiums would rarely be calculated using an interest factor because of the quick turn-around time for unearned premiums—usually less than one year. Use of an interest factor might be appropriate with respect to first-year excess costs amortized over a reasonably long period.

Typically there is considerable uncertainty as to the termination patterns that can be anticipated for commercial health business. In such cases a conservative method and period of amortization would be appropriate—e.g., over five years by the sum-of-the-years'-digits method.

Where acquisition costs—mainly commissions—are at varying percentages in renewal years, the incidence of renewal-year acquisition costs can be taken into account by modifying the amortization table along the lines suggested in Chapter 16.

Property-Liability Practice

Deferral of the equity in the unearned premium reserve is common in the property-liability business, and the methods of calculating and deferring such equity described in this section are reasonably consistent with property-liability practice.

With respect to changes in unearned premium reserves, property-liability companies record such changes as revenue adjustments while life insurance companies record them as reserve increases, i.e., an expense.

Because commercial health revenues are defined as *earned* premiums, property-liability practice should preferably be followed by life insurance companies.

Claim Reserves

The statutory method of estimating or calculating reserves for outstanding losses would also be used for purposes of adjusted statements.

It may in certain circumstances be appropriate to discount certain long-term claim reserves. This matter is discussed further in the next section.

Disclosure

Where commercial health insurance is a material line of business, the fact that premiums are recognized as revenue when earned should be disclosed in the accounting policies note. The method of deferring and amortizing acquisition costs should also be described and relevant amounts should be disclosed. Where deferrals are limited to equity in the unearned premium reserve, it should only be necessary to disclose the net increase or decrease in such equity, not the separate elements of gross deferrals and gross amortization.

Noncancellable Business

The distinguishing characteristic of noncancellable health insurance is that the premium is fixed for the term of the contract and the company cannot cancel the contract. In general, noncancellable coverages are limited pretty much to disability income or similar coverages. The risks associated with noncancellable coverage of medical expense, hospital and surgical expense, etc., are typically deemed to be too great to cover at a reasonable premium.

In all material respects, the basic concept of noncancellable health insurance is the same as for life insurance. A level premium is charged for an increasing claim cost; rates of disability, like rates of

Table 19–2.

PRICING ASSUMPTIONS FOR NONCANCELLABLE DISABILITY INCOME POLICY TO AGE 65 ISSUED TO MALE AGE 45—2–YEAR SICKNESS, LIFETIME ACCIDENT, 30–DAY ELIMINATION—1963 AND 1970 RATEBOOKS

	1963 Ratebook	*1970 Ratebook*
Morbidity	1926 Class (3) modified	1969 special study

Selection factor

	Year							*Year*						
	1	*2*	*3*	*4*	*5*	*6 on*		*1*	*2*	*3*	*4*	*5*	*6*	*7*
	.80	.90	.95	1.00	1.05	1.10		.70	.80	.90	1.00	1.10	1.15	1.20

Mortality	1955–60 Select and Ultimate		1955–60 Select and Ultimate		

Total terminations

	Year					*Year*			
	1	*2*	*3*	*4 on*		*1*	*2*	*3*	*4 on*
	30%	15%	10%	8%		25%	12%	8%	7%

Insurance unit	$100 monthly income	$100 monthly income
Average policy size	2 units	3 units
Mode	Annual	Annual
Interest	Ordinary life assumptions (4.5% graded)	Ordinary life assumptions (6.5% graded)
Statutory reserves	1926 Class (3), 3%, 1–year P.T.	1964 CDT, 3%, 1–year P.T.
Claims handling expense	5% of incurred claims	5% of incurred claims

Other expenses:

	Year					*Year*					
	0	*1*	*2–10*	*11 on*		*0*	*1*	*2*	*3*	*4–10*	*11 on*
Percentage:											
Commissions		50%	12.5%	3%			60%	20%	15%	10%	3%
Agency support		25%					30%				
Premium taxes		2%	2%	2%			2%	2%	2%	2%	2%
Per policy	$50.00	$5.00	$5.00	$5.00		$61.50	$6.50	$6.50	$6.50	$6.50	$6.50
Per unit	1.00					2.00					
Contingency and profit	10% of premiums					10% of premiums					

death, generally increase with age. Acquisition costs typically follow the same pattern as for life insurance. So do maintenance expenses, except that the cost of handling claims, which in the extreme case may require literally hundreds of monthly payments and frequent investigations as to the degree of the insured's disability, is usually much higher.

Pricing

The methods used to price disability income insurance are somewhat similar to the methods used to price life insurance, but the assumptions required to do the job are often more complex. An example will suggest the elements that must be taken into consideration.

Crazy Quilt Life began offering individual noncancellable disability income policies in 1963. The 1963 ratebook was used until 1970, at which time a new ratebook was issued. The most popular policy was one which had a two-year sickness benefit, a lifetime accident benefit, and a 30-day elimination period. The assumptions used to price the policy for each ratebook are summarized in Table 19–2.

For profit-testing purposes, the morbidity assumptions were translated into assumed "claim costs" per $100 of monthly income (the unit of insurance) for each of the benefits offered under the contract. The claim costs for various attained ages are shown in

Table 19–3.

DISABILITY INCOME CLAIM COST ASSUMPTIONS ASSOCIATED WITH 1969 MORBIDITY STUDY

Male Attained Age	Ultimate Claim Costs Per Unit of $100 Monthly Income			Selection Factors for Issue Age			Select and Ultimate Claim Costs Per Unit of $100 Monthly Income for Issue Age		
	2–Year Sickness	Lifetime Accident	Total	25	35	45	25	35	45
25	$ 4.51	$ 2.43	$ 6.94	.7			$ 4.86		
26	4.70	2.45	7.15	.8			5.72		
27	4.89	2.47	7.36	.9			6.62		
28	5.09	2.49	7.58	1.0			7.58		
29	5.30	2.51	7.81	1.1			8.59		
30	5.51	2.55	8.06	1.15			9.27		
31	5.73	2.58	8.31	1.2			9.97		
32	5.96	2.60	8.56	1.2			10.27		
33	6.20	2.64	8.84	1.2			10.61		
34	6.45	2.68	9.13	1.2			10.96		
35	6.72	2.73	9.45	1.2	.7		11.34	$ 6.62	
36	6.99	2.77	9.76	1.2	.3		11.71	7.81	
37	7.29	2.83	10.12	1.2	.9		12.14	9.11	
38	7.61	2.92	10.53	1.2	1.0		12.64	10.53	
39	7.97	3.02	10.99	1.2	1.1		13.19	12.09	
40	8.35	3.15	11.50	1.2	1.15		13.80	13.23	
41	8.76	3.35	12.11	1.2	1.2		14.53	14.53	
42	9.21	3.59	12.80	1.2	1.2		15.36	15.36	
43	9.72	3.87	13.59	1.2	1.2		16.31	16.31	
44	10.29	4.16	14.45	1.2	1.2		17.34	17.34	
45	10.94	4.48	15.42	1.2	1.2	.7	18.50	18.50	$10.79
46	11.69	4.81	16.50	1.2	1.2	.8	19.80	19.80	13.20
47	12.52	5.16	17.68	1.2	1.2	.9	21.22	21.22	15.91
48	13.43	5.52	18.95	1.2	1.2	1.0	22.74	22.74	18.95
49	14.44	5.89	20.33	1.2	1.2	1.1	24.40	24.40	22.30
50	15.55	6.27	21.82	1.2	1.2	1.15	26.18	26.18	25.13
51	16.76	6.64	23.40	1.2	1.2	1.2	28.08	28.08	28.08
52	18.07	7.03	25.10	1.2	1.2	1.2	30.12	30.12	30.12
53	19.50	7.43	26.93	1.2	1.2	1.2	32.32	32.32	32.32
54	21.05	7.82	28.87	1.2	1.2	1.2	34.64	34.64	34.64
55	22.74	8.16	30.90	1.2	1.2	1.2	37.08	37.08	37.08
56	24.57	8.58	33.15	1.2	1.2	1.2	39.78	39.78	39.78
57	26.56	8.95	35.51	1.2	1.2	1.2	42.61	42.61	42.61
58	28.70	9.31	38.01	1.2	1.2	1.2	45.61	45.61	45.61
59	30.98	9.66	40.64	1.2	1.2	1.2	48.77	48.77	48.77
60	33.44	9.99	43.43	1.2	1.2	1.2	52.12	52.12	52.12
61	36.18	10.29	46.47	1.2	1.2	1.2	55.76	55.76	55.76
62	38.91	10.56	49.47	1.2	1.2	1.2	59.36	59.36	59.36
63	34.01	11.69	45.70	1.2	1.2	1.2	54.84	54.84	54.84
64	30.39	12.60	42.99	1.2	1.2	1.2	51.59	51.59	51.59

Table 19–3. Also shown are the selection factors and the claim cost assumptions for three issue ages.

Note that both components of the claim cost—sickness and accident—increase over time, quite sharply at the later durations. It is intuitively obvious that this claim pattern, together with a level premium, will produce sizeable reserves.

The profit test for the policy issued to males age 45 is shown in Table 19–4. In this case it is assumed that the premium has already been calculated or otherwise

Table 19–4.

PROFIT PROJECTION FOR DISABILITY INCOME POLICY ISSUED TO MALE AGE 45—1970 RATEBOOK—PER UNIT OF $100 MONTHLY INCOME ISSUED

Year	Units In Force at End of Year	Statutory Mid-Terminal Reserve* Per Unit In Force	Statutory Mid-Terminal Reserve* Per Unit Issued	Premiums Received	Unearned Premiums Change	Unearned Premiums Ending Reserve	Premiums Earned	Expenses Incurred	Claims Incurred	Claims Paid	Claims Ending Liability
1	1.000			$ 51.30	$25.65	$25.65	$ 25.65	$ 72.13	$ 5.40	$ 2.00	$ 3.40
2	.750	$ 9.00	$ 6.75	38.47	(6.42)	19.23	44.89	10.61	10.35	6.75	7.00
3	.660	25.00	16.50	33.86	(2.31)	16.92	36.17	7.69	10.20	8.08	9.12
4	.607	42.00	25.50	31.15	1.35)	15.57	32.50	5.60	11.00	9.07	11.05
5	.565	57.00	32.19	28.97	1.09)	14.48	30.06	5.31	12.07	10.68	12.44
6	.525	71.00	37.29	26.94	(1.01)	13.47	27.95	5.02	12.90	12.07	13.27
7	.488	85.00	41.51	25.06	(.94)	12.53	26.00	4.73	13.45	12.65	14.07
8	.454	97.00	44.06	23.30	(.88)	11.65	24.18	4.46	13.70	13.13	14.64
9	.422	107.00	45.20	21.67	(.82)	10.83	22.49	4.20	13.67	13.41	14.90
10	.393	115.00	45.18	20.15	(.76)	10.07	20.91	3.95	13.63	13.54	14.99
11	.365	121.00	44.21	18.74	(.71)	9.36	19.45	2.41	13.58	13.59	14.98
12	.340	125.00	42.47	17.43	(.64)	8.72	18.07	2.28	13.53	13.58	14.93
13	.316	126.00	39.82	16.21	(.61)	8.11	16.82	2.17	13.49	13.54	14.88
14	.294	122.00	35.85	15.08	(.56)	7.55	15.64	2.06	13.43	13.49	14.82
15	.273	115.00	31.43	14.02	(.53)	7.02	14.55	1.96	13.37	13.43	14.76
16	.254	103.00	26.18	13.04	(.49)	6.53	13.53	1.87	13.29	13.36	14.69
17	.236	87.00	20.57	12.13	(.47)	6.06	12.60	1.78	13.21	13.29	14.61
18	.220	65.00	14.29	11.28	(.42)	5.64	11.70	1.70	13.12	13.21	14.52
19	.204	39.00	7.97	10.49	(.39)	5.25	10.88	1.57	12.13	12.70	13.95
20	.190	13.00	2.47	9.75	(.37)	4.88	10.12	1.43	10.51	11.65	12.81
21	–	–0–	–0–	–0–	(4.88)	–0–	4.88	.25	4.90	8.48	9.23
Totals				$439.04	$ –0–	$ –0–	$439.04	$143.18	$250.93	$241.70	$ 9.23
Present value at moment of issue							$295.78	$120.96	$144.91		
Present value of profits at moment of issue								$ 29.91			

*One-year preliminary term.

selected and is being subjected to its final test. The present values (at the assumed interest rate) of the significant components of the study are summarized at the bottom of Table 19–4. However calculated, it is clear that the profit objective of 10 percent has been achieved:

	Gross	Present Value
Premiums earned	$439.04	$295.78
Expenses incurred	143.18	120.96
Claims incurred	250.93	144.91
	394.11	265.87
Profit	$ 44.93	$ 29.91
Profit as % of premiums	10.2%	10.1%

Note that *earned* premiums are regarded as revenue for purposes of the profit test and that *earned* premiums are discounted to a present value. This is because unearned gross premiums are held in conjunction with mid-terminal reserves for statutory purposes. Note also that claims *incurred* are discounted in the profit test; the test distinguishes between claims paid and claims incurred. This is rarely done in the case of life insurance, but the length of time during which a disability income claim is outstanding makes it desirable to take this step in the case of disability income insurance.

Interest on the mid-terminal reserve and changes in the mid-terminal reserve are not shown in Table 19–4. The present values of these items would offset, just as they do in life insurance. But there are two other sources of interest that are not offset: interest on the unearned premium reserve and interest on the claim reserve. These represent additional sources of profit

Table 19–5.

PRE-TAX IMPACT ON STATUTORY SUMMARY OF OPERATIONS OF DISABILITY INCOME POLICY ISSUED TO MALE AGE 45—1970 RATEBOOK—PER UNIT OF $100 MONTHLY INCOME ISSUED

Year	Premiums Earned	Unearned Premiums	Interest on Mid-Terminal Reserve	Claim Reserve	Increase in Mid-Terminal Reserve	Claims Incurred	Expenses Incurred	Pre-Tax Profit
1	$25.65	$ .80	$–0–	$ .11	$ –0–	$ 5.40	$72.13	$(50.97)
2	44.89	1.42	.21	.33	6.75	10.35	10.61	19.14
3	36.17	1.14	.73	.51	9.75	10.20	7.69	10.91
4	32.50	1.02	1.32	.63	9.00	11.00	5.60	9.87
5	30.06	.95	1.82	.74	6.69	12.07	5.31	9.50
6	27.95	.85	2.22	.78	5.10	12.90	5.02	8.78
7	26.00	.76	2.30	.80	4.23	13.45	4.73	7.45
8	24.18	.70	2.51	.84	2.54	13.70	4.46	7.53
9	22.49	.66	2.62	.86	1.14	13.67	4.20	7.62
10	20.91	.61	2.64	.87	(.02)	13.63	3.95	7.47
11	19.45	.55	2.40	.84	(.97)	13.58	2.41	8.22
12	18.07	.48	2.33	.80	(1.74)	13.53	2.28	7.61
13	16.82	.45	2.21	.80	(2.66)	13.49	2.17	7.28
14	15.64	.42	2.04	.80	(3.96)	13.43	2.06	7.37
15	14.55	.39	1.80	.79	(4.42)	13.37	1.96	6.62
16	13.53	.35	1.41	.75	(5.25)	13.29	1.87	6.13
17	12.60	.31	1.14	.71	(5.61)	13.21	1.78	5.38
18	11.70	.29	.85	.71	(6.28)	13.12	1.70	5.01
19	10.88	.27	.55	.69	(6.32)	12.13	1.57	5.01
20	10.12	.25	.26	.65	(5.50)	10.51	1.43	4.84
21	4.88	.12	.05	.52	(2.47)	4.90	.25	2.89

which are not shown in Table 19–4. Over the 20-year period, interest of $27.32 would be received on assets equal to the two reserves, the present value of which would be $16.94. This raises the effective profit percentage to 15.7 percent:

Present value of profits without regard for interest on unearned premiums and claim reserves	$ 29.91
Present value of interest on unearned premiums and claim reserves	16.94
	$ 46.55
Present value of gross premiums	$295.78
Revised profit ratio	15.7%

The projected impact on statutory profits is shown in Table 19–5. Note that even with the use of one-year preliminary term reserves, the statutory surplus strain is quite severe.

Revenue

Noncancellable health insurance coverages "are expected to be in force for a reasonable period of time and . . . elements of expense or benefit costs are not level." [2] Thus such coverages fulfill the criteria of the life insurance audit guide for recognizing premiums as revenue when due.

There is, however, one method of calculating adjusted reserves that involves holding unearned gross premiums and which consequently defers recognition of the difference between the unearned gross premium and the unearned valuation premium. The practical effect is to report revenue and profits in proportion to premiums earned. While technically a violation of the "when due" provision, some believe that the approach is justified (1) because it corresponds to the method used for statutory purposes, which establishes a kind of "tradition" for revenue recognition on health contracts; (2) because it is easier than changing revenue recognition methods, i.e., is more practical; and (3) because it is more conservative. The implications and results of using the gross unearned premium approach are discussed later in this chapter.

Benefit Reserve Assumptions

For long-term health insurance contracts, "reserves should be provided on the same principle as the reserves used for ordinary life insurance," says the life insurance audit guide. "Such reserves represent the present value of future costs less the present value of expected future valuation premiums, calculated using actuarial assumptions which, as for life insurance, make reasonable provision for the risks of adverse deviation." [3]

There are few reliable guidelines that can be offered for health insurance assumptions. The volatility of health insurance claims, the influence of economic conditions on claim patterns, and the many variations in coverage make it very difficult to generalize.

Morbidity. The life insurance audit guide suggests that "the morbidity and lapse risks will likely be more significant [than the interest risk] in an accident and health contract." [4]

The morbidity assumption is indeed significant. Health insurance is similar to term life insurance; thus a sizeable portion of the premium is required to pay claim costs since there are no nonforfeiture benefits.*

The audit guide suggests that claim cost assumptions

. . . should be based on realistic estimates of expected claim cost experience at the time premiums are established, or revised [applicable only to cancellable or guaranteed renewable business], or policies are issued. Consideration should be given to the level and incidence of claims for various types of coverage . . . and for such other factors as occupational class, waiting period, sex, age, and benefit period. Where company experience is unavailable or inadequate, an appropriate basis for claim cost assumptions would be industry experience adjusted for expected experience for a specific coverage. [5]

Provision for adverse deviation with respect to the claim cost assumption would usually be made by applying percentages to experience tables unless the tables are deemed to be inherently conservative. It will be noted from Table 19–3, for example, that Crazy Quilt Life loaded the experience table 20 percent at the later durations for the 1970 ratebook; the same morbidity assumptions were used for purposes of calculating adjusted reserves.

Studies of actual morbidity experience of the individual company should be made frequently to support continued use of a morbidity assumption.

The notion that claim cost assumptions have a dramatic impact on benefit reserves has a solid basis in fact. The effect can be proportional, as is suggested

*There is, however, a form of health insurance that provides for a return of premiums, similar to a cash value, under certain circumstances. Return-of-premium business is discussed later in this chapter.

by Table 19–6, which shows adjusted reserves for Crazy Quilt's disability income policy using various claim cost assumptions. It will be noted that an increase of 50 percent in assumed claim costs results in raising the level of the reserves by an approximately equivalent percentage.

The other point to be made from Table 19–6 is that the *slope* of morbidity costs has a significant impact on the reserves. Claim costs under the 1964 CDT table are higher than under the 1969 study, yet the reserves are lower until the 18th year. This is attributable to the steeper slope of claim costs under the 1969 study.

Terminations. In calculating statutory reserves, the only source of terminations that is usually given effect is mortality. In profit-testing and calculating adjusted reserves for health business, mortality and voluntary terminations are sometimes combined into one expression of total terminations. This was Crazy Quilt's practice (see Table 19–2).

The life insurance audit guide notes that "Lapse rates will have a material effect on the level of the reserves . . . It should be noted that for coverages which have increasing claim costs, it is not conservative to assume high lapse rates in renewal years." [6] Implicit in this statement is a view of the provision for adverse deviation as a means of introducing additional conservatism. The statement appears to suggest that the purpose of the provision, at least as it relates to the health insurance lapse assumption, is to raise the level of the reserve.

Interest. The life insurance audit guide states that, although the interest assumption for health insurance may be less significant than for life insurance, the interest assumption should be adjusted "to a more appropriate rate" when such an adjustment "would have a material effect on the financial statements." [7]

It should not automatically be assumed that interest has little effect. Interest is earned not only on the adjusted reserve but also on unearned premiums, if any, and claim reserves, if any. This is discussed further below. The important point is to appreciate that the effect of the interest assumption on the reserves must be tested before coming to a conclusion.

Mid-terminal adjusted benefit reserves, computed with and without interest for three issue ages for the 1970 ratebook version of Crazy Quilt Life's noncancellable disability income policy, are shown in Table 19–7. It will be noted that the longer the term of the contract, the more significant the interest assumption becomes.

Other assumptions. Inherent in the claim cost

Table 19–6.

DISABILITY INCOME RESERVES FOR MALE AGE 35 UNDER 3 DIFFERENT CLAIM COST ASSUMPTIONS—ALL OTHER ASSUMPTIONS HELD CONSTANT

Year	Annual Claim Costs Per $100 of Monthly Income		Reserve Per Unit of $100 Monthly Income when Claim Cost Assumption is based on		
	1964 CDT (3%)*	1969 Study**	1964 CDT (3%)	1969 Study	150% of 1969 Study
1	$14.18	$ 6.62	$ 2.50	$ 3.77	$ 5.64
2	14.64	7.81	9.82	14.43	21.57
3	15.18	9.11	17.45	24.65	36.84
4	15.80	10.53	25.21	34.23	51.14
5	16.49	12.09	33.17	43.15	64.45
6	17.25	13.23	41.57	51.91	77.54
7	18.17	14.53	50.33	60.59	90.51
8	19.20	15.36	59.62	69.52	103.87
9	20.39	16.31	69.40	78.95	117.96
10	21.68	17.34	79.67	88.84	132.73
11	23.13	18.50	90.11	98.82	147.64
12	24.75	19.80	100.57	108.68	162.40
13	26.52	21.22	111.26	118.61	177.26
14	28.43	22.74	122.17	128.52	192.09
15	30.50	24.40	133.30	138.29	206.69
16	32.73	26.18	144.15	147.30	220.16
17	35.10	28.08	154.40	155.21	232.02
18	37.65	30.12	164.14	162.26	242.58
19	40.40	32.32	172.96	168.17	251.43
20	43.30	34.64	180.47	172.62	258.10
21	46.35	37.08	185.69	174.75	261.29
22	49.73	39.78	187.93	173.94	260.11
23	53.27	42.61	187.07	170.23	254.57
24	57.02	45.61	182.44	163.05	243.84
25	60.96	48.77	173.38	151.77	226.99
26	65.15	52.12	158.40	135.19	202.17
27	69.71	55.76	136.06	112.27	167.90
28	74.21	59.36	105.14	82.68	123.64
29	68.55	54.84	64.22	49.68	74.28
30	64.49	51.59	20.36	16.55	24.77

*Ultimate
**Select and ultimate

assumption is an assumption about sex, occupational class, elimination period, etc. If each policy in force is valued, then of course the "assumptions" about these items match precisely the characteristics of the policy.

When the business is modeled, however, it is usually necessary to make assumptions about the average elimination period, occupational class, sex, etc. in order to make manageable the number of cells which must be valued. Modeling techniques, including techniques which might be used for health insurance, are discussed in Chapter 28.

As will be seen, it may be necessary to make an assumption as to the level of claim reserves.

Benefit Reserve Calculations

The methods of calculating adjusted benefit reserves for noncancellable health insurance coverages are substantially similar to methods used in calculating adjusted life insurance reserves. Benefits are projected based on the underlying assumptions; the present value of such benefits is calculated; and the present value of benefits is translated into a valuation pre-

Table 19-7.

NET LEVEL ADJUSTED MID-TERMINAL BENEFIT RESERVES COMPUTED WITH AND WITHOUT INTEREST*
—NONCANCELLABLE DISABILITY INCOME POLICY—1970 RATEBOOK

	Reserve Factor Per Unit of $100 Monthly Income					
	Age 25		Age 35		Age 45	
Duration	With Interest	Without Interest	With Interest	Without Interest	With Interest	Without Interest
Valuation premium	$ 8.05	$ 12.46	$ 12.66	$ 18.56	$ 22.20	$ 29.32
Reserves:						
1	$ 2.18	$ 3.80	$ 3.77	$ 5.97	$ 6.82	$ 9.26
2	8.78	15.05	14.42	22.43	24.56	32.76
3	15.43	25.94	24.65	37.43	40.82	53.09
4	21.31	35.23	34.23	50.85	55.28	70.18
5	26.86	43.79	43.15	62.87	68.10	84.51
6	31.71	51.29	51.91	74.51	79.40	96.73
7	36.46	58.72	60.59	85.90	89.13	106.90
8	41.45	66.27	69.52	97.15	97.73	115.21
9	46.89	74.15	78.95	108.46	105.48	121.96
10	52.83	82.35	88.84	119.72	112.08	126.86
11	59.11	90.88	98.81	130.82	116.82	129.67
12	65.71	99.77	108.67	141.60	119.16	130.03
13	72.87	109.00	118.61	151.91	119.04	127.55
14	80.63	118.56	128.50	161.58	115.99	121.86
15	88.99	128.41	138.29	170.43	109.45	112.54
16	97.69	138.50	147.29	178.26	98.35	99.16
17	106.62	148.78	155.21	184.86	81.79	81.15
18	116.02	159.14	162.25	189.97	59.45	58.02
19	125.85	169.47	168.16	193.33	34.73	33.47
20	136.06	179.67	172.62	194.61	11.02	11.13
21	146.18	189.62	174.74	193.53		
22	155.93	199.15	173.94	189.68		
23	165.65	208.10	170.22	182.61		
24	175.19	216.19	163.04	171.88		
25	184.42	223.54	151.77	157.02		
26	192.60	229.62	135.18	137.47		
27	199.36	234.32	112.26	112.58		
28	205.00	237.37	82.67	81.75		
29	209.23	238.48	49.66	48.53		
30	211.70	237.33	16.55	16.52		
31	211.43	233.60				
32	207.79	226.87				
33	200.88	216.67				
34	190.13	202.54				
35	174.90	183.98				
40	19.13	19.57				

*6.5% graded to 3.5% over 30 years in .5% increments each 5 years.

mium that bears a constant percentage relationship to the gross premium. Reserves are simply the difference between the present value of future benefits and the present value of future valuation premiums.

Reserves may be calcuated by the mean reserve approach (in which case deferred premiums must be set up, or the reserve itself must recognize the mode) or the mid-terminal approach (in which case unearned premiums must be recorded). In either case, the calculation may be refined to recognize the true distribution of claims, lapses, etc.

Table 19-8 summarizes the calculation of valua-

Table 19–8.

SUMMARY OF CALCULATION OF BENEFIT VALUATION PREMIUMS ON TWO BASES—NONCANCELLABLE DISABILITY INCOME POLICY ISSUED TO MALE AGE 45—1970 RATEBOOK

	Basis 1—Valuation Premium Recognized when Earned		Basis 2—Valuation Premium Recognized when Received	
	Gross Amount	Present Value	Gross Amount	Present Value
Projected gross premiums	$439.04	$295.78	$439.04	$304.58
Projected benefits:				
Claims incurred	250.93	144.91	250.93	144.91
Less interest on:				
Gross unearned premiums	12.79	8.82	—	—
Claim reserve	14.53	8.12	14.53	8.12
	27.32	16.94	14.53	8.12
Net benefit cost	$223.61	$127.97	$236.40	$136.79
Ratio of net benefit cost to projected gross premiums		.4327		.4491
Valuation premium—ratio x gross ($51.30)		$ 22.20		$ 23.04
Alternative approach:				
Present value of projected net benefits		$127.97		$136.79
Present value of $1 annuity for:				
Premium-earning period		$ 5.764		
Premium-paying period				$ 5.937
Valuation premium		$ 22.20		$ 23.04

tion premiums by two methods for the disability income policy for which the profit test is shown in Table 19–4. Basis 1 assumes the valuation premium is received as the gross premium is earned. Basis 2 assumes the valuation premium is received when the gross premium is received. In both cases an annual mode is assumed.

Since recognition of valuation premiums on an earned basis results in constant deferral of recognition of half the valuation premium by comparison with the cash basis, the present value of earned gross premiums is inevitably less than the present value of cash premiums received. However, the difference is largely offset by interest on the unearned gross premium reserve. In the Basis 1 calculation, interest on the unearned gross premium reserve is applied to reduce benefit costs. In theory, interest on the unearned gross premium reserve could be allocated among benefits, acquisition costs, and maintenance costs (if reserved for); however, application of such interest to projected benefit costs is a practical approach.

Note that the Basis 1 calculation assumes unearned *gross* premiums are held. If unearned valuation pre-

miums are assumed to be held for purposes of the adjusted reserve calculation, the indicated interest on the unearned premium reserve would be less.

Interest on the unearned premium reserve disappears, of course, when reserves are calculated on Basis 2. There is no unearned premium reserve so far as the Basis 2 calculation is concerned.

Inspection of Table 19–4 will indicate that incurred claims are projected. Thus the claim liability is also projected. This is a refinement of the typical life insurance calculation, in which claims are assumed to be paid in cash. The refinement is designed to recognize that health claim liabilities—particularly in the case of disability income business—are typically on the books a good deal longer than liabilities for incurred death claims.

Since incurred claims, not cash claims, were projected, it is necessary to consider interest on the claim liability. Such interest has been recognized as a reduction in benefit cost on both calculation bases.

The effect of introducing interest on unearned premiums and claim liabilities is to level out these elements of cost by incorporating them in the valuation premium. Recognition of such interest in the reserve

Table 19–9.

CALCULATION OF FIRST TWO BENEFIT RESERVE FACTORS ON TWO BASES—NONCANCELLABLE
DISABILITY INCOME POLICY ISSUED TO MALE AGE 45—1970 RATEBOOK

		Basis 1—Reserves Calculated on Earned Premium Basis	Basis 2—Reserves Calculated on Cash Premium Basis
FIRST YEAR			
7–1	Valuation premium received	$ 22.20	$ 23.04
7–1	Unearned (50% x $22.20)	(11.10)	
7–1	Valuation premium earned	11.10	
7–1	Claims incurred (50% x $10.79)	(5.40)	(5.40)
7–1	Balance	5.70	17.64
12–31	Interest on fund at 3.2%*	.19	.56
12–31	Interest on unearned gross premium (3.2% x $25.65)	.82	
12–31	Interest on claim reserve (3.2% x $3.40)	.11	.11
12–31	Balance	$ 6.82	$ 18.31
12–31	Units in force	1.000	1.000
12–31	Reserve per unit of $100 monthly income	$ 6.82	$ 18.31
SECOND YEAR			
1–1	Balance	$ 6.82	$ 18.31
6–30	Interest on fund at 3.2%	.22	.59
6–30	Valuation premium earned (50% x $22.20)	11.10	
6–30	Claims incurred (50% x $10.79)	(5.40)	(5.40)
6–30	Interest on unearned gross premium (3.2% x $25.65)	.82	
6–30	Interest on claim reserve (3.2% x $3.40)	.11	.11
6–30	Balance	13.67	13.61
7–1	Valuation premium received (75% x $22.20; 75% x $23.04)	16.65	17.28
7–1	Unearned (50% x $16.65)	(8.33)	
7–1	Claims incurred (50% x 75% x $13.20)	(4.95)	(4.95)
7–1	Balance	17.04	25.94
12–31	Interest on fund at 3.2%	.54	.83
12–31	Interest on unearned gross premium (3.2% x $19.24)	.62	
12–31	Interest on claim reserve (3.2% x $7.00)	.22	.22
12–31	Balance	$ 18.42	$ 26.99
12–31	Units in force	.750	.750
12–31	Reserve per unit of $100 monthly income	$ 24.56	$ 35.98

*3.2% is the semi-annual compound equivalent of an annual rate of 6.5%.

calculation is certainly not mandatory. It should be noted that the interest is inherently taken into account when (1) cash premiums define the incidence of valuation premiums and (2) cash claims are projected. When the cash basis is modified, it is desirable to recognize the effect of the modification.

Basis 1 and Basis 2 reserves for the first two calendar years are calculated in detail in Table 19–9. The two reserves may be reconciled as follows:

	Year 1	Year 2
Basis 1 reserve	$ 6.82	$24.56
Unearned valuation premium—50% of $22.20	11.10	11.10
	17.92	35.66
Other items	.39	.32
Basis 2 reserve	$18.31	$35.98

The "other items" include interest on the unearned valuation premium ($.36 in both years) and other

Table 19–10.

SELECTED RESERVE GRADING PATTERNS FOR NONCANCELLABLE DISABILITY INCOME POLICY

		Reserve Factor Per Unit of $100 Monthly Income				
		Male Age 25			Male Age 35*	
		Ungraded Adjusted Reserves	Adjusted Reserves Graded to Statutory** in		Ungraded Adjusted Reserves	Adjusted Reserves Graded to Statutory*** in 20 Years
Ratebook	Year		20 Years	30 Years		
1963	1	$ 2.59	$ 2.94	$ 2.61	$ 4.45	$ 4.44
	2	9.67	11.01	9.75	16.68	16.63
	3	16.14	18.53	16.28	27.97	27.90
	4	22.18	25.68	22.40	38.54	38.45
	5	27.85	32.53	28.13	48.46	48.32
	6	33.38	39.40	33.74	58.16	57.99
	7	38.97	46.51	39.42	67.85	67.64
	8	44.96	54.22	45.51	77.98	77.73
	9	51.40	62.62	52.09	88.59	88.29
	10	58.35	71.77	59.16	99.71	99.38
	11	65.75	81.64	66.70	111.21	110.80
	12	73.53	92.18	74.63	122.75	122.27
	13	81.75	103.53	83.03	134.15	133.58
	14	90.43	115.75	91.90	145.33	144.70
	15	99.59	128.94	101.31	156.17	155.45
	20	150.59	208.71	153.95	195.02	193.63
	25	204.26	261.90	210.53	174.58	162.08
	30	235.39	261.92	246.83	19.31	15.46
	35	199.69	195.03	195.03	—	—
	40	22.21	18.82	18.82	—	—
1970	1	2.18	2.50	2.23	3.77	3.87
	2	8.78	10.12	8.97	14.42	14.82
	3	15.43	17.92	15.77	24.65	25.37
	4	21.31	25.00	21.82	34.23	35.29
	5	26.86	31.90	27.57	43.15	44.58
	6	31.71	38.20	32.62	51.91	53.78
	7	36.46	44.59	37.59	60.59	62.97
	8	41.45	51.47	42.83	69.52	72.47
	9	46.89	59.11	48.59	78.95	82.57
	10	52.83	67.57	54.88	88.84	93.24
	11	59.11	76.70	61.54	98.81	104.07
	12	65.71	86.56	68.61	108.67	114.90
	13	72.87	97.46	76.31	118.61	125.99
	14	80.63	109.49	84.66	128.50	137.20
	15	88.99	122.74	93.70	138.29	148.48
	20	136.06	206.02	145.89	172.62	193.85
	25	184.42	253.00	203.75	151.77	166.00
	30	211.70	259.00	248.08	16.55	18.00
	35	174.90	198.00	198.00	—	—
	40	19.13	21.00	21.00	—	—

*Since the policies expire at age 65, 30-year grading at age 35 and 20- and 30-year grading at age 45 are the same as full-term.
**One-year preliminary term, 1926 Class (3), 3%
***One-year preliminary term, 1964 CDT, 3%

relatively minor interest differences.

The Basis 1 reserve is the one that will probably be used in most cases. This is because the necessary unearned gross premium calculations have usually already been made for statutory purposes. Use of the

Basis 1 reserve therefore eliminates the need to tabulate deferred premiums or otherwise provide for modes other than annual.

The Basis 1 reserve presented here assumes that an unearned valuation premium, not an unearned gross

Table 19–11.

RATIOS OF ADJUSTED BENEFIT RESERVES TO STATUTORY NET LEVEL RESERVES FOR 3 DISABILITY
INCOME PLANS OF A MAJOR COMPANY

	Duration				
	1	5	10	15	20
Plan 1:					
Age 25	12%	16%	16%	19%	24%
35	24	34	40	49	58
45	34	52	60	67	70
55	33	54	51	—	—
Plan 2:					
Age 25	Nil	21	22	27	33
35	9	44	54	67	80
45	19	66	81	93	100
55	18	69	80	—	—
Plan 3:					
Age 25	16	36	33	34	39
35	26	53	61	75	91
45	38	83	97	106	113
55	39	84	93	—	—

premium, is held. Use of the unearned valuation premium results in releasing profits on the unearned premiums. The question of whether to hold unearned gross or unearned valuation premiums is discussed later in this chapter.

Grading to Statutory

It will often be considered desirable to grade adjusted health insurance reserves to statutory for the reasons set forth in Chapter 11, which deals with grading for ordinary life.

The assumed interest rate generally does not have the impact on health insurance reserves that it has on life insurance reserves (particularly reserves on permanent insurance). The lapse and morbidity assumptions have a very significant effect. Further, the relationship between adjusted reserves and statutory reserves is quite age-sensitive for certain forms of health insurance.

Table 19–10 shows the relationship between ungraded adjusted reserves and adjusted reserves graded to statutory in 20 and 30 years for Crazy Quilt Life's noncancellable disability income policy at selected ages and durations. The statutory reserve is the one-year preliminary term mid-terminal reserve, in recognition of the fact that many, if not most, stock companies use some form of modified reserve method (typically one- or two-year preliminary term) for long-term health insurance coverages. The adjusted

reserve is based on the earned valuation premium approach, which is desirable if reserves are to be graded to statutory mid-terminals.

It will be noted that 20-year grading does not appear to be acceptable at age 25; the distortions are significant. This is because the contract has 40 years to run at age 25. Thirty-year grading produces a much better pattern. For age 35, 20-year grading might be considered acceptable, due in large measure to the fact that the contract has only 30 years to run. Whether it is acceptable to grade to statutory in 20 years overall would in this case depend to a significant degree upon the mix of ages.

The sometimes unusual relationship of adjusted reserves to statutory is further underscored by tests made by a major company, which are summarized in Table 19–11. It is obvious that for Crazy Quilt Life and the company represented in Table 19–11, grading should be undertaken only after careful consideration and extensive testing.

Reserve Behavior

The behavior of various types of reserves for Crazy Quilt's noncancellable disability income insurance issued from 1963 (year of commencement of the business) to 1971 is shown in Table 19–12.

Reserve Set A shows statutory one-year preliminary term mid-terminal reserves. Reserve Set B shows adjusted net level mid-terminal reserves. Reserve Sets

C and D show adjusted mid-terminal reserves graded to statutory in 20 and 30 years respectively.

Reserve Set E shows gross unearned premiums held for statutory purposes. Aggregate statutory active life reserves are the sum of Reserve Sets A (mid-terminal additional reserves) and E (unearned gross premiums).*

Reserve Set F represents unearned adjusted benefit valuation premiums, computed by multiplying the ratio of valuation premiums to gross premiums by gross unearned premiums. In 1971, for example, unearned adjusted valuation premiums, $1,832,000, were computed as follows:

Ratio of adjusted benefit valuation premiums to gross premiums**	37.8%
Unearned gross premiums (000)	$4,851
Unearned valuation premiums (000)	$1,832

The sum of Reserve Sets B and F represent so-called "Basis 1" reserves, which are shown as Reserve Set G. Reserve Set H represents "Basis 2" reserves, i.e., reserves calculated on the basis of assuming receipt of the annual valuation premium; in other words, the reserves are comparable to mean or intermediate reserves as they would be calculated for ordinary life insurance. As was suggested earlier, Basis 1 and Basis 2 reserves are very much the same, as inspection of Reserve Sets G and H will confirm.

Reserve Set I, adjusted mid-terminal reserves computed with a zero interest assumption, are presented partly for their curiosity value. In addition, comparison of Reserve Set I with Reserve Set B demonstrates that the effect of interest on reserves of this type can have a fairly significant effect.

Claim Liabilities

Some liabilities for health insurance claims incurred are based on disabled lives tables and an assumed interest rate. In theroy there is no reason why claim liabilities cannot be adjusted to give effect to more realistic assumptions where appropriate. As a practical matter, however, the effect of such adjust-

*It should be noted that for statutory purposes some companies hold the greater of (1) unearned gross premiums or (2) additional reserves plus unearned net premiums. Sometimes the total of (2) is reported in two pieces—the equivalent of unearned gross premiums, and the difference between the total and such unearned gross premium amount.

**Methods of deriving this ratio are discussed later in this chapter.

ments are usually quite minor and are often not made.

Crazy Quilt retained the statutory basis (various tables and 3 percent interest) for health claim liabilities provided for by the use of factors.

Composition of Acquisition Costs

Acquisition costs for noncancellable health insurance normally follow the same general pattern as acquisition costs on life insurance. Commissions are quite high in the first year, additional sales support expense is incurred, and there are the usual selection and issue costs.

Usually it is necessary to functionalize health insurance expenses to determine acquisition costs. The Life Office Management Association sponsors a health insurance functional cost program for member companies that write significant amounts of individual health insurance. The approach used is essentially the same as the approach used for ordinary life functional costs.

Crazy Quilt Life participates in the LOMA health functional cost program. Unit costs determined by functional cost analysis are translated into the actuarial format for rate-testing purposes. A summary of the translated first-year functional costs is shown in Table 19–13. Also shown in Table 19–13 are the eliminations of development and overhead required to obtain deferrable unit costs.

In addition, because of Crazy Quilt's commission structure, acquisition costs equal to commissions incurred in excess of commissions that would have been incurred at the ultimate renewal rate (3 percent) were also incurred in renewal years, as follows (new annualized premiums and first-year deferrable costs are also shown for comparative purposes):

	000		
	New Annualized Premiums	Acquisition Costs	
		First-Year	Renewal
1963	$ 790	$ 743	$–0–
1964	1,086	1,022	49
1965	1,382	1,301	108
1966	1,679	1,581	178
1967	2,271	2,138	257
1968	2,567	2,416	364
1969	2,863	2,694	477
1970	2,453	2,499	616
1971	2,453	2,500	818

It can be seen that renewal-year acquisition costs rapidly became significant; such costs in 1971 were equal to 33 percent of first-year acquisition costs

Table 19–12.

BENEFIT AND RELATED RESERVES ON VARIOUS BASES FOR NONCANCELLABLE DISABILITY INCOME
INSURANCE ISSUED 1963–1971

Reserve Set	1963	1964	1965	1966	1967	1968	1969	1970	1971
Volume (units of $100 monthly income):									
Issued	16,000	22,000	28,000	34,000	46,000	52,000	58,000	64,000	64,000
Terminated	–0–	5,640	9,593	13,442	17,382	23,545	28,417	33,137	34,678
In force	16,000	32,360	50,767	71,325	99,943	128,398	157,981	188,844	218,166
A. Statutory mid-terminal reserves (000):									
Level	$ –0–	$ 78	$ 301	$ 684	$ 1,242	$ 2,020	$ 3,038	$ 4,291	$ 5,802
Change	–0–	78	223	383	558	778	1,018	1,253	1,511
B. Ungraded adjusted mid-terminal reserves ("Basis 1" reserves) (000):									
Level	73	282	628	1,119	1,790	2,658	3,714	4,917	6,276
Change	73	209	346	491	671	868	1,056	1,203	1,359
C. Graded to statutory in 20 years:									
Level	75	288	641	1,143	1,828	2,716	3,796	5,033	6,438
Change	75	213	353	502	685	888	1,080	1,237	1,405
D. Graded to statutory in 30 years:									
Level	73	282	628	1,120	1,792	2,661	3,719	4,925	6,287
Change	73	209	346	492	672	869	1,058	1,206	1,362
E. Unearned gross premiums (000):									
Level	395	802	1,260	1,774	2,488	3,200	3,942	4,363	4,851
Change	395	407	458	514	714	712	742	421	488
F. Unearned benefit valuation premiums (000):									
Level	155	315	495	697	978	1,258	1,549	1,671	1,832
Change	155	160	180	202	281	280	291	122	161
G. Ungraded adjusted mid-terminal reserves ("Basis 1" reserves) plus unearned benefit valuation premiums (000):									
Level	228	597	1,123	1,816	2,768	3,916	5,263	6,588	8,108
Change	228	369	526	693	952	1,148	1,347	1,325	1,520
H. Ungraded intermediate adjusted reserves ("Basis 2" reserves) (000):									
Level	233	606	1,137	1,836	2,749	3,950	5,303	6,637	8,164
Change	233	373	531	699	913	1,201	1,353	1,334	1,527
I. Adjusted mid-terminal reserves without interest (000):									
Level	102	388	856	1,519	2,423	3,550	4,928	6,529	8,361
Change	102	286	468	663	904	1,127	1,378	1,601	1,832

Table 19–13.

1971 NONCANCELLABLE HEALTH INSURANCE FIRST-YEAR FUNCTIONAL COSTS IN ACTUARIAL FORMAT AND ADJUSTMENTS REQUIRED TO OBTAIN DEFERRABLE AMOUNTS

	Commissions	Other Selling	Selection	Issue	Total
Total 1971 first-year costs per functional cost analysis (000):					
Related to premiums	$1,398*	$ 785			$ 2,183
Related to policies		720	$ 269	$ 192	1,181
Related to volume			135		135
Total	$1,398	$ 1,505	$ 404	$ 192	$ 3,499
Units of measure:					
First-year premiums (000)	$2,453	$ 2,453			$ 2,453
Policies issued		18,286	18,286	18,286	18,286
Volume issued (units of $100 monthly income)			64,000		64,000
Functional costs used in ratemaking:					
Percentage	57%*	32%			89%
Per policy		$ 39.40	$ 14.70	$ 10.50	$ 64.60
Per unit			$ 2.10		$ 2.10
Eliminations for accounting purposes:					
Development:					
Percentage		16%			16%
Per policy		$ 20.65			$ 20.65
Overhead:					
Percentage		2.7%			2.7%
Per policy		$ 3.19	$ 2.24	$ 2.30	$ 7.73
Per unit			$ .32		$ .32
Deferrable unit costs:					
Percentage	57%	13.3%			70.3%
Per policy		$ 15.56	$ 12.46	$ 8.20	$ 36.22
Per unit			$ 1.78		$ 1.78
Total 1971 deferrable costs (000):					
Related to premiums	$1,398*	$ 326			$ 1,724
Related to policies		285	$ 228	$ 149	662
Related to volume			114		114
Total	$1,398	$ 611	$ 342	$ 149	$ 2,500

*Net of ultimate renewal commissions at a rate of 3%.

incurred in 1971. Therefore Crazy Quilt decided to defer and amortize both first-year and renewal acquisition costs.

Deferral and Amortization

The mechanics of deferring and amortizing health insurance acquisition costs are essentially the same as for life insurance. Either the factor or the worksheet method can be used; amortization can be with or without interest; renewal-year acquisition costs can be accommodated directly (by incorporating them in factors or separately accounting for them) or indirectly (by modifying amortization tables to give recognition to them). As a practical matter, separately accounting for renewal-year acquisition costs—i.e., segregating them in each renewal year and amortizing them separately—is so difficult (because the data are normally not available) as to fail to qualify as an alternative.

Table 19–14.

COMPUTATION OF ACQUISITION COST VALUATION PREMIUMS AND FIRST TWO RESERVE FACTORS ON TWO BASES FOR DISABILITY INCOME POLICY ISSUED TO MALE AGE 45—1970 RATEBOOK

		Basis 1— Earned Premiums	Basis 2— Cash Premiums
Valuation premiums:			
Present value of acquisition costs:			
First-year		$ 49.91	$ 49.91
Renewal		18.49	18.49
Total		$ 68.40	$ 68.40
Present value of $1 annuity (see Table 19–8) for:			
Premium-earning period		$5.764	
Premium-paying period			$5.937
Valuation premium		$ 11.86	$ 11.52
Acquisition cost reserve factors:			
Year 1:			
7–1	Valuation premium received	$ 11.86	$ 11.52
7–1	Unearned	(5.93)	
7–1	Expenses paid	(49.91)	(49.91)
7–1	Balance	(43.98)	(38.39)
12–31	Interest at 3.2%	(1.41)	(1.23)
12–31	Balance	$ (45.39)	$ (39.62)
12–31	Units in force	1.000	1.000
12–31	Reserve per unit	$ (45.39)	$ (39.62)
Year 2:			
1–1	Balance	$ (45.39)	$ (39.62)
6–30	Interest at 3.2%	(1.45)	(1.27)
6–30	Valuation premium earned	5.93	
7–1	Valuation premium received (75%)	8.90	8.64
7–1	Unearned	(4.45)	
7–1	Expenses paid	(6.54)	(6.54)
7–1	Balance	(43.00)	(38.79)
12–31	Interest at 3.2%	(1.38)	(1.24)
12–31	Balance	$ (44.38)	$ (40.03)
12–31	Units in force	.750	.750
12–31	Reserve per unit	$ (59.17)	$ (53.37)

Reconciliation of reserve factors:	Year 1	Year 2
Basis 1 reserve factor	$(45.39)	$(59.17)
Unearned valuation premium	5.93	5.93
Interest differences	(.16)	(.13)
Basis 2 reserve factor	$(39.62)	$(53.37)

Table 19–14 shows the calculation of "Basis 1" and "Basis 2" acquisition cost factors for a disability income policy issued to a male age 45. First-year acquisition costs of $49.91 may be reconciled to the unit costs shown in Table 19–13 as follows:

Gross premium per unit	$51.30	
Times applicable percentage	70.3%	$36.06
Per policy cost	$36.22	
Divided by average size ($300) in units of $100 monthly income	3	12.07
Per unit cost		1.78
Total		$49.91

Renewal-year acquisition costs represent renewal-year commissions in excess of commissions payable at the ultimate rate, discounted to the moment of issue at the assumed interest rate.

Note that the Basis 1 reserve calculation produces a higher value for unamortized acquisition costs than the Basis 2 calculation. The difference is largely offset by the unearned premium liability that must be carried when Basis 1 reserves are used. The acquisition cost reserve factors are reconciled at the bottom of Table 19–14.

The factor approach illustrated in Table 19–14

Table 19–15.

SUMMARY WORKSHEET FOR AMORTIZING FIRST-YEAR AND RENEWAL ACQUISITION COSTS WITH INTEREST IN TERMS OF PERCENTAGES APPLIED TO FIRST-YEAR COSTS—NONCANCELLABLE DISABILITY INCOME ISSUES, 1963–1971

	1963	1964	1965	1966	1967	1968	1969	1970	1971
Acquisition costs incurred (000):									
First year	$ 743	$ 1,022	$ 1,301	$ 1,581	$ 2,138	$ 2,416	$ 2,694	$ 2,499	$ 2,500
Renewal	–0–	49	108	178	257	364	477	616	818
Total	$ 743	1,071	$ 1,409	$ 1,759	$ 2,395	$ 2,780	$ 3,171	$ 3,115	$ 3,318
Unamortized as % of first year acquisition costs:									
1963	85.8%	74.3%	67.7%	62.3%	57.9%	54.5%	51.7%	49.1%	47.1%
1964		85.7	74.2	67.6	62.2	57.7	54.5	51.7	49.1
1965			85.8	74.2	67.6	62.3	57.7	54.4	51.7
1966				85.7	74.1	67.5	62.2	57.7	54.5
1967					85.7	74.2	67.5	62.3	57.8
1968						85.8	74.2	67.6	62.3
1969							85.9	74.2	67.6
1970								82.1	81.4
1971									82.0
Unamortized balances (000):									
1963	$ 638	$ 552	$ 503	$ 463	$ 430	$ 405	$ 384	$ 365	$ 350
1964		876	758	691	636	590	557	528	502
1965			1,116	965	879	810	751	708	672
1966				1,355	1,172	1,067	984	912	861
1967					1,832	1,586	1,444	1,332	1,235
1968						2,074	1,792	1,633	1,505
1969							2,313	1,999	1,822
1970								2,052	2,035
1971									2,049
Total	$ 638	$ 1,428	$ 2,377	$ 3,474	$ 4,949	$ 6,532	$ 8,225	$ 9,529	$ 11,031
Increase	$ 638	$ 790	$ 949	$ 1,097	$ 1,475	$ 1,583	$ 1,693	$ 1,304	$ 1,502

provides naturally for renewal-year acquisition costs. When the worksheet method is used, it is necessary to build a provision for renewal-year acquisition costs into the amortization table. A method of doing this is described in Chapter 16. A summary worksheet for amortizing first-year and renewal acquisition costs on Crazy Quilt Life's noncancellable disability income business is shown in Table 19–15. The amortization percentages are relatively constant until 1970, when a new commission scale was adopted.

Arbitrary Amortization Cutoff

It is typically feasible to amortize health insurance acquisition costs over a period shorter than the premium-paying period because of higher persistency and a limiting age (e.g., age 65).

Sum-of-the-years' premium percentages for Crazy

Quilt Life's noncancellable disability income business are shown on both the cash premium basis and the earned premium basis in Table 19–16. It will be noted that a 20- or 25-year cutoff could be made with little effect on the financial statements.

A comparison of unamortized acquisition costs (assuming in all cases that separate unearned premiums are held) for all of Crazy Quilt's issues of noncancellable disability income insurance issued from 1963 to 1971 is shown in Table 19–17. Table 19–17 also gives some indication of the effect on the pool of acquisition costs of amortizing with and without interest and of ignoring renewal-year acquisition costs.

Maintenance Costs

While maintenance and settlement costs for ordinary life insurance are often not reserved for on the

Table 19–16.

SUM-OF-THE-YEARS' PREMIUMS AMORTIZATION RATES FOR DISABILITY INCOME POLICY COMPOSITE ON CASH PREMIUM BASIS AND EARNED PREMIUM BASIS

	Cash Premium Basis		Earned Premium Basis	
	Amortization	*Unamortized*	*Amortization*	*Unamortized*
1	12.2%	87.8%	6.1%	93.9%
2	8.6	79.2	10.4	83.5
3	7.3	71.9	8.0	75.5
4	6.6	65.3	7.0	68.5
5	6.1	59.2	6.3	62.2
6	5.6	53.6	5.8	56.4
7	5.2	48.4	5.4	51.0
8	4.8	43.6	5.0	46.0
9	4.4	39.2	4.6	41.4
10	4.1	35.1	4.3	37.1
11	3.8	31.3	3.9	33.2
12	3.5	27.8	3.6	29.6
13	3.2	24.6	3.4	26.2
14	3.0	21.6	3.1	23.1
15	2.8	18.8	2.9	20.2
16	2.5	16.3	2.6	17.6
17	2.4	13.9	2.4	15.2
18	2.2	11.7	2.3	12.9
19	2.0	9.7	2.1	10.8
20	1.9	7.8	1.9	8.9
21	1.0	6.8	1.4	7.5
22	.9	5.9	1.0	6.5
23	.8	5.1	.9	5.6
24	.8	4.3	.9	4.7
25	.7	3.6	.8	3.9
26	.7	2.9	.8	3.1
27	.6	2.3	.7	2.4
28	.6	1.7	.6	1.8
29	.5	1.2	.5	1.3
30	.5	.7	.5	.8
31	.1	.6	.1	.7
32	.1	.5	.1	.6
33	.1	.4	.1	.5
34	.1	.3	.1	.4
35	.1	.2	.1	.3
36	.1	.1	.1	.2
37	.1	Nil	.1	.1
38	Nil	Nil	.1	Nil
39	Nil	Nil	Nil	Nil
40	Nil	–0–	Nil	Nil
41	–0–		Nil	–0–
	100.0%		100.0%	

basis of immateriality, in the case of health insurance claims handling expense—and thus total maintenance expense—can be significant. Health insurance claims handling expenses are similar to loss adjustment expenses in the property-liability business.

Crazy Quilt Life's functional cost system had disclosed that for the Company's noncancellable disability income business, claims handling expenses average 5 percent of incurred claims and other maintenance expenses (except renewal commissions and premium

Table 19–17.

COMPARATIVE UNAMORTIZED ACQUISITION COSTS FOR NONCANCELLABLE DISABILITY INCOME
INSURANCE ISSUED 1963–1971—ASSUMING UNEARNED PREMIUMS ARE HELD (000 Omitted)

	1963	1964	1965	1966	1967	1968	1969	1970	1971
Amortized with interest:									
Ungraded:									
Level	$727	$1,609	$2,661	$3,875	$5,513	$7,255	$9,117	$10,553	$12,181
Change	727	882	1,052	1,214	1,638	1,742	1,862	1,436	1,628
Graded to zero in:									
20 years:									
Level	722	1,592	2,622	3,804	5,397	7,079	8,863	10,209	11,745
Change	722	870	1,030	1,182	1,593	1,682	1,784	1,346	1,536
30 years:									
Level	726	1,607	2,657	3,868	5,502	7,239	9,094	10,522	12,152
Change	726	881	1,050	1,211	1,634	1,737	1,855	1,428	1,630
Amortized without interest:									
Ungraded:									
Level	732	1,627	2,694	3,924	5,581	7,343	9,224	10,6o2	12,343
Change	732	895	1,067	1,230	1,657	1,762	1,881	1,458	1,661
Graded to zero in:									
20 years:									
Level	726	1,602	2,638	3,823	5,417	7,096	8,873	10,210	11,731
Change	726	876	1,036	1;185	1,594	1,679	1,777	1,337	1,521
30 years:									
Level	731	1,624	2,688	3,913	5,563	7,316	9,185	10,630	12,276
Change	731	893	1,064	1,225	1,650	1,753	1,869	1,445	1,646
Amortized without interest - ungraded - ignoring renewal-year acquisition costs:									
Level	752	1,655	2,715	3,916	5,526	7,204	8,961	10,233	11,456
Change	752	903	1,060	1,201	1,610	1,678	1,757	1,272	1,223

taxes) average $6.50 per policy. The $6.50 translates into a per-unit cost of $2.17, based on an assumed average size of $300 of monthly income insured.

Renewal commissions (at the ultimate rate of 3 percent) and premium taxes (2 percent) are incurred as a level percentage of premiums received.

The net effect of claims handling and normal maintenance expenses is shown in Table 19–18. Constant percentage expenses have no effect on the reserves and are not shown in Table 19–18. In this case the normal maintenance, $2.17 a year, is also a constant percentage of the gross premium and has no effect on the reserves. The reserves—which eventually become sizeable—are thus solely for claims handling expenses.

When benefit reserves and/or acquisition costs are graded, it is usually desirable to grade maintenance expense reserves to zero over a corresponding period.

The effect of doing this can be somewhat unusual, as Table 19–19 suggests. Table 19–19 shows maintenance expense reserve factors and total maintenance expense reserves for Crazy Quilt Life during the years 1963–1971. Note that grading produces lower reserves —or, rather, higher negative reserves—in this case. This is to be expected, since the reserve otherwise required at the end of the grading period is amortized over the grading period.

The maintenance expense reserves in Table 19–19 are negative at many durations because the reserves are based on a mid-terminal approach. Unearned premiums are carried separately; the maintenance expense component of such unearned premiums, together with the reserves shown in Table 19–19, produce total reserves that are substantially equivalent to the reserves shown in Table 19–18.

Table 19–18.

UNIT CLAIMS HANDLING AND MAINTENANCE EXPENSES AND RELATED MAINTENANCE EXPENSE
RESERVES FOR NONCANCELLABLE DISABILITY INCOME POLICY

Year	Male Age 25				Male Age 45			
	Expenses Per Unit in Force			*Reserve Per Unit in Force***	*Expenses Per Unit in Force*			*Reserve Per Unit in Force***
	Claims Handling	*Normal Maintenance**	*Total*		*Claims Handling*	*Normal Maintenance**	*Total*	
1	$ .12	$2.17	$2.29	$ .35	$ .27	$2.17	$2.44	$ .98
2	.33	2.17	2.50	.70	.69	2.17	2.86	1.94
3	.34	2.17	2.51	1.06	.77	2.17	2.94	2.81
4	.38	2.17	2.55	1.37	.91	2.17	3.08	3.58
5	.42	2.17	2.59	1.65	1.14	2.17	3.31	4.25
6	.47	2.17	2.64	1.89	1.28	2.17	3.45	4.85
7	.50	2.17	2.67	2.14	1.40	2.17	3.57	5.37
8	.53	2.17	2.70	2.39	1.51	2.17	3.68	5.82
9	.54	2.17	2.71	2.67	1.62	2.17	3.79	6.22
10	.56	2.17	2.73	2.98	1.73	2.17	3.90	6.57
11	.58	2.17	2.75	3.30	1.86	2.17	4.03	6.81
12	.60	2.17	2.77	3.64	1.99	2.17	4.16	6.94
13	.62	2.17	2.79	4.01	2.14	2.17	4.31	6.94
14	.65	2.17	2.82	4.40	2.28	2.17	4.45	6.77
15	.67	2.17	2.84	4.83	2.45	2.17	4.62	6.42
20	.88	2.17	3.05	7.25	2.58	2.17	4.75	1.26***
25	1.22	2.17	3.39	9.73				
30	1.75	2.17	3.92	11.14				
35	2.44	2.17	4.61	9.28				
40	2.82	2.17	4.99	1.27***				

*Excluding renewal commissions and premium taxes.
**Basis 2, i.e., no separate unearned premium reserve held.
***Reserves for 41st year expenses and 21st year expenses, respectively.

Unearned Premiums

It is probably fair to assume that most companies
will calculate mid-terminal adjusted reserves* and
hold unearned premium reserves, mainly because this
is the way computer programs and record-keeping is
geared (to accommodate statutory requirements).
Few companies will calculate "Basis 2" reserves as
Crazy Quilt did—eliminating unearned premiums and
using either (1) an annual premium assumption together with deferred premiums or, less likely, (2) a
reserve that adjusts for the proportion of the annual
premium received by the valuation date. (Crazy
Quilt had no problem, since all of its disability income
business was on the annual mode.)

Table 19–20 compares the two basic approaches
in considerable detail. Note that the mid-terminal

*Actually, it is necessary to modify the traditional calcula-
tion where acquisition costs are concerned; this is discussed
in Chapter 23. Also, the mid-terminal approach can be refined to take into account the distribution of lapses and other
events, thus producing what might be called an "intermediate
mid-terminal reserve".

approach produces almost the same reserve as the
intermediate approach when unearned valuation premiums are carried. When unearned gross premiums
are carried, the result is of course to produce a larger
liability.

Should a company using the mid-terminal approach
hold unearned gross premiums or unearned valuation
premiums? The only justification for holding unearned
gross premiums are (1) balance sheet conservatism,
(2) immateriality, and (3) practicality. It is not
sufficient to hold unearned gross premiums just because that happens to be statutory practice.

What is involved, quite simply, is the deferral of
profit. In Crazy Quilt's case, the deferral would have
amounted to over $1.2 million by December 31, 1971,
if the Company had set up unearned gross premium
reserves. The effect on income would have been a
reduction in excess of $120,000. Table 19–21 shows
the effect of holding unearned gross premiums instead
of unearned valuation premiums.

It may, of course, be difficult to determine valuation premiums. While the life insurance line may be so

Table 19–19.

MAINTENANCE EXPENSE RESERVES FOR NONCANCELLABLE DISABILITY INCOME POLICY UNDER SELECTED GRADING PATTERNS (ASSUMING SEPARATE UNEARNED PREMIUMS ARE HELD)*

Maintenance Expense Reserve Per Unit of $100 Monthly Income in Force—
1970 Ratebook

| Year | Male Age 25 | | | Male Age 35 | | |
| | | Graded to Zero in | | | Graded to Zero in | |
	Ungraded	*20 Years*	*30 Years*	*Ungraded*	*20 Years*	*30 Years*
1	$(1.72)	$(1.75)	$(1.74)	$(1.80)	$(1.85)	
2	(1.38)	(1.51)	(1.44)	(1.24)	(1.41)	
3	(1.04)	(1.29)	(1.14)	(.71)	(1.03)	
4	(.75)	(1.12)	(.91)	(.23)	(.69)	
5	(.49)	(.99)	(.70)	.22	(.41)	
6	(.26)	(.90)	(.53)	.66	(.16)	
7	(.02)	(.83)	(.37)	1.11	.08	SAME
8	.22	(.78)	(.21)	1.56	.28	AS
9	.48	(.73)	(.03)	2.03	.47	UNGRADED
10	.77	(.70)	.15	2.52	.63	
11	1.08	(.68)	.33	3.03	.76	
12	1.40	(.67)	.53	3.53	.84	
13	1.76	(.68)	.73	4.04	.86	
14	2.14	(.73)	.93	4.54	.80	
15	2.55	(.80)	1.13	5.03	.65	
20	4.91	(2.05)	1.96	6.77	(2.32)	
25	7.36		1.59	5.72		
30	8.77		(2.07)	(1.11)		
35	7.01					
40	(.83)					

Total Maintenance Expense Reserves for Issues 1963–1971 (000 Omitted)

| Year | Ungraded | | Graded to Zero in | | | |
| | | | 20 Years | | 30 Years | |
	Level	*Change*	*Level*	*Change*	*Level*	*Change*
1963	$ (36)	$(36)	$ (37)	$(37)	$ (36)	$(36)
1964	(66)	(30)	(68)	(31)	(66)	(30)
1965	(94)	(28)	(99)	(31)	(94)	(94)
1966	(119)	(25)	(130)	(31)	(121)	(27)
1967	(156)	(37)	(173)	(43)	(158)	(37)
1968	(182)	(26)	(208)	(35)	(186)	(28)
1969	(201)	(19)	(239)	(31)	(207)	(21)
1970	(188)	13	(240)	(1)	(195)	12
1971	(171)*	17	(239)	1	181	14

*Assuming separate unearned premiums are not held, the reserve at December 31, 1971 would be a positive $432,000.

significant as to warrant tabulating annualized valuation premiums to obtain the ratio to gross,* the size of the health line—and its complexity—may not warrant it.

One simple approach to estimating the necessary ratios is detailed in Table 19–22. The method involves making a mini-model of health insurance in force. Premium elements are weighted and the resulting ratios are applied to unearned gross premiums to produce the corresponding unearned valuation premiums.

*This subject is discussed at greater length in Chapter 23.

Unearned valuation premium components should be applied to the reserves to which they relate. For example, Crazy Quilt's unearned valuation premiums (assuming for the moment that Crazy Quilt uses mid-terminal reserves) at December 31, 1971 may be summarized as follows:

	000
Benefits	$1,832
Acquisition costs	1,183
Maintenance expenses	616
Total	$3,631

Table 19-20.

COMPARISON OF INTERMEDIATE AND MID-TERMINAL RESERVES PER UNIT OF $100 MONTHLY INCOME FOR NONCANCELLABLE DISABILITY INCOME POLICY—1970 RATEBOOK

| | | Intermediate Approach - Adjusted Reserve Computed Assuming Receipt of Total Valuation Premium | | | | Mid-Terminal Approach - Adjusted Reserve Computed Assuming Receipt of Earned Valuation Premium | | | | | Total Effective Reserve | |
| | | Adjusted Reserve | | | | Adjusted Mid-Terminal Reserve | | | | | Holding Net Unearned Premium | Holding Gross Unearned Premium |
Age	Duration	Benefits	Acquisition Costs	Maintenance Expenses	Total	Benefits	Acquisition Costs	Maintenance Expenses	Total	Unearned Premium		
25	1	$ 6.50	$-26.98	$ .35	$-20.13	$ 2.18	$-31.42	$-1.72	$-30.96		$-20.24	$-15.91
	2	13.02	-40.33	.70	-26.61	8.78	-44.80	-1.38	-37.40		-26.68	-22.35
	3	19.58	-48.26	1.06	-27.62	15.43	-52.77	-1.04	-38.38		-27.66	-23.33
	4	25.38	-51.42	1.37	-24.67	21.31	-55.97	- .75	-35.41		-24.69	-20.36
	5	30.83	-53.87	1.65	-21.39	26.86	-58.46	- .49	-32.09	Annual:	-21.37	-17.04
	6	35.60	-55.25	1.89	-17.76	31.71	-59.87	- .26	-28.42	Gross $30.10	-17.70	-13.37
	7	40.30	-56.70	2.14	-14.26	36.46	-61.34	- .02	-24.90	Valuation 21.44	-14.18	- 9.85
	8	45.22	-58.36	2.39	-10.75	41.45	-63.03	.22	-21.36	Loading $ 8.66	-10.64	- 6.31
	9	50.59	-60.28	2.67	- 7.02	46.89	-64.98	.48	-17.61		- 6.89	- 2.56
	10	56.44	-62.49	2.98	- 3.07	52.83	-67.23	.77	-13.63	Unearned - 50%:	- 2.91	1.42
	15	92.25	-63.15	4.83	33.93	88.99	-68.04	2.55	23.50	Gross $15.05	34.22	38.55
	20	139.00	-62.33	7.25	83.92	136.06	-67.35	4.91	73.62	Valuation 10.72	84.34	88.67
	25	187.19	-58.66	9.73	138.26	184.42	-63.76	7.36	128.02	Loading $ 4.33	138.74	143.07
	30	214.50	-49.86	11.14	175.78	211 70	-54.94	8.77	165.53		176.25	180.58
	35	178.19	-32.14	9.28	155.33	174.90	-37.02	7.01	144.89		155.61	159.94
	40	23.36	-0-	1.27	24.63	19.13	- 4.49	- .83	13.81		24.53	29.19
35	1	10.42	-31.20	.55	-20.23	3.77	-35.88	-1.80	-33.91		-20.35	-15.61
	2	21.00	-44.22	1.13	-22.09	14.42	-48.94	-1.24	-35.76		-22.20	-17.46
	3	31.14	-50.29	1.67	-17.48	24.65	-55.03	- .71	-31.09		-17.53	-12.79
	4	40.62	-52.49	2.17	- 9.70	34.23	-57.27	- .23	-23.27	Annual:	- 9.71	- 4.97
	5	49.45	-53.75	2.63	- 1.67	43.15	-58.56	.22	-15.19	Gross $36.60	- 1.63	3.11
	6	58.15	-55.08	3.09	6.16	51.91	-59.92	.66	- 7.35	Valuation 27.13	6.21	10.95
	7	66.77	-56.46	3.55	13.86	60.59	-61.33	1.11	.37	Loading $ 9.47	13.93	18.67
	8	75.65	-58.05	4.02	21.62	69.52	-62.94	1.56	8.14		21.70	26.44
	9	85.02	-59.89	4.50	29.63	78.95	-64.81	2.03	16.17	Unearned - 50%:	29.73	34.47
	10	94.83	-62.01	5.01	37.83	88.84	-66.96	2.52	24.40	Gross $18.30	37.96	42.70
	15	144.01	-58.87	7.57	92.71	138.29	-63.94	5.03	79.38	Valuation 13.56	92.97	97.71
	20	178.23	-50.73	9.34	136.84	172.62	-55.85	6.77	123.54	Loading $ 4.74	137.10	141.84
	25	157.59	-33.45	8.26	132.40	151.77	-38.48	5.72	119.01		132.57	137.31
	30	23.14	-0-	1.26	24.40	16.55	- 4.72	-1.11	10.72		24.28	29.02
45	1	18.31	-39.62	.98	-20.33	6.82	-45.39	-2.00	-40.57		-20.47	-14.92
	2	35.98	-53.37	1.94	-15.45	24.56	-59.17	-1.06	-35.67	Annual:	-15.57	-10.02
	3	52.16	-59.06	2.81	- 4.09	40.82	-64.88	- .20	-24.26	Gross $51.30	- 4.16	1.39
	4	66.53	-60.18	3.58	9.93	55.28	-66.04	.55	-10.21	Valuation 40.20	9.89	15.44
	5	79.26	-60.73	4.25	22.78	68.10	-66.62	1.21	2.69	Loading $11.10	22.79	28.34
	6	90.50	-61.21	4.85	34.14	79.40	-67.14	1.79	14.05		34.15	39.70
	7	100.21	-61.60	5.37	43.98	89.13	-67.54	2.30	23.89	Unearned - 50%:	43.99	49.54
	8	108.78	-62.05	5.82	52.55	97.73	-68.00	2.74	32.47	Gross $25.65	52.57	58.12
	9	116.49	-62.56	6.22	60.15	105.48	-68.53	3.13	40.08	Valuation 20.10	60.18	65.73
	10	123.05	-63.14	6.57	66.48	112.08	-69.13	3.47	46.42	Loading $ 5.55	66.52	72.07
	15	120.44	-41.53	6.42	85.33	109.45	-47.52	3.32	65.25		85.35	90.90
	20	22.52	-0-	1.26	23.78	11.02	- 5.79	-1.73	3.50		23.60	29.15

The $1,832,000 in benefit premiums and $616,000 in maintenance expense premiums should be applied to increase the benefit reserve and maintenance expense reserve, respectively; while the $1,183,000 in acquisition cost premiums should be applied to reduce unamortized acquisition costs. Corresponding treatment should be accorded the related income statement amounts.

Table 19–21.

UNEARNED GROSS PREMIUMS AND UNEARNED VALUATION PREMIUMS FOR NONCANCELLABLE
DISABILITY INCOME BUSINESS, 1963–1971 (000 Omitted)

Year	Unearned Gross Premiums	Unearned Valuation Premiums				Loading	Increase in Loading
		Benefits	Acquisition Costs	Maintenance Costs	Total		
1963	$ 395	$ 155	$ 91	$ 49	$ 295	$ 100	$100
1964	802	315	185	99	599	203	103
1965	1,260	495	290	156	941	319	116
1966	1,774	697	408	220	1,325	449	130
1967	2,488	978	572	308	1,858	630	181
1968	3,200	1,258	736	397	2,391	809	179
1969	3,942	1,549	907	489	2,945	997	188
1970	4,363	1,671	1,043	550	3,264	1,099	102
1971	4,851	1,832	1,183	616	3,631	1,220	121

Uncollected Premiums

For statutory purposes, health insurance premiums due but unpaid as of December 31 are recorded as an asset. Any related percentage expenses—typically commissions and premium taxes—are usually set up as a liability or deducted from the asset. The treatment is basically the same as the treatment of uncollected life premiums.

Part of the uncollected premiums are unearned. That is, unearned premiums include (1) amounts paid for a period that extends beyond year-end, and (2) amounts due and uncollected as of December 31 whose period extends beyond year-end.

Assuming a company follows the cash basis of revenue recognition, uncollected premiums should be converted into uncollected *valuation* premium components and such components should be applied as adjustments of the adjusted reserves.

There are certain circumstances under which it is necessary to distinguish between unearned premiums that have been received in cash as opposed to those that have merely been recorded as due. In other words, it may be necessary to determine the proportion of uncollected premiums unearned as of December 31.

Those companies that record gross uncollected premiums as an asset should, of course, provide an allowance for uncollectible profit margins. Where unearned gross premiums are held, all that's required is an allowance for profit margins on uncollected premiums applicable to the period prior to December 31. Where unearned valuation premiums are held, an allowance is needed with respect to profit margins on all uncollected premiums. Any expenses that will

be incurred when uncollected gross premiums are collected should be accrued.

It may be necessary to accrue expenses on uncollected gross premiums even where uncollected valuation premiums are held, depending on what assumption has been made about the incidence of expenses. This subject is discussed further in Chapter 23.

Statutory as an Approximation

Many companies feel that modified statutory reserves provide a suitable approximation of adjusted amounts, and argue that no adjustment is necessary for long-term health insurance.

One-year preliminary term statutory reserves and net mid-terminal adjusted reserves (i.e., the net of *all* reserve elements including acquisition costs), ignoring unearned premiums in both cases, for Crazy Quilt Life's disability income business were as follows from 1963–1971:

Year	Annualized Gross Premiums	Statutory Reserves	Net Adjusted Reserves
1963	$ 790	$ –0–	$ (689)
1964	1,603	78	(1,393)
1965	2,521	301	(2,127)
1966	3,548	684	(2,875)
1967	4,976	1,243	(3,879)
1968	6,401	2,020	(4,778)
1969	7,884	3,038	(5,604)
1970	8,726	4,291	(5,823)
1971	9,702	5,802	(6,087)

Thus, even ignoring unearned premiums (which would widen the disparity to the extent of the loading),

Table 19–22.

ESTIMATION OF UNEARNED VALUATION PREMIUMS FOR NONCANCELLABLE DISABILITY INCOME
BUSINESS AT DECEMBER 31, 1971

	Gross Premium	Valuation Premium		
		Benefits	Acquisition Costs	Maintenance Expenses
1963 RATEBOOK				
Unweighted premiums:				
Age 25	$38.60	$12.99	$ 9.29	$5.24
Age 35	47.70	18.39	10.91	6.00
Age 45	65.30	28.78	14.57	7.47
Distribution of issues:				
Age 25	——————————— 30% ———————————			
Age 35	——————————— 45% ———————————			
Age 45	——————————— 25% ———————————			
Weighted premiums:				
Age 25	$11.58	$ 3.90	$ 2.79	$1.57
Age 35	21.47	8.28	4.91	2.70
Age 45	16.32	7.20	3.64	1.87
Total	$49.37	$19.38	$11.34	$6.14
Ratio to gross		.393	.230	.124
Unearned 1963 ratebook premiums, 12–31–71 (000)	$2,760	$1,085	$635	$342
1970 RATEBOOK				
Unweighted premiums:				
Age 25	$30.10	$ 8.05	$ 9.13	$4.26
Age 35	36.60	12.66	9.63	4.84
Age 45	51.30	22.20	11.86	6.14
Distribution of issues:	——————— Same as 1963 Ratebook ———————			
Weighted premiums:				
Age 25	$ 9.03	$ 2.42	$ 2.74	$1.28
Age 35	16.47	5.70	4.33	2.18
Age 45	12.82	5.55	2.97	1.54
Total	$38.32	$13.67	$10.04	$5.00
Ratio to gross		.357	.262	.131
Unearned 1970 ratebook premiums, 12–31–71 (000)	$2,091	$ 747	$ 548	$274
UNEARNED PREMIUMS (000)	$4,851	$1,832	$1,183	$616

the difference between statutory and adjusted at December 31, 1971 was almost $12 million on annualized premium of less than $10 million. Use of a two-year preliminary term method would narrow the gap somewhat, but certainly not by enough to make a difference. Obviously assumptions about the relationship between statutory and adjusted should be made with care.

Disclosure

Where noncancellable business is material it should be treated as a separate line of business for disclosure purposes. The revenue recognition method, the reserving method, and the composition of acquisition costs, as well as the amortization method, should be specifically described in the accounting policies note. Morbidity, termination, and interest assumptions should be set forth along with related reserve amounts (unearned premiums could be shown separately if the segregation among components is not practicable). Acquisition costs deferred and amortized during the period should be disclosed.

Guaranteed Renewable Business

The distinguishing characteristic of guaranteed renewable health insurance, as compared with noncancellable business, is that while renewability is guaranteed by the company, premium rates are not guaranteed. Premiums may be revised upward or downward, although it may be fair to say that downward revisions are probably quite rare.

While noncancellable coverages are usually limited to disability income business, many companies offer on a guaranteed renewable basis, not only disability income policies but a wide assortment of medical expense policies—guaranteed renewable major medical insurance is a popular product, for example.

Guaranteed renewable business is usually reserved for in basically the same manner as noncancellable business. Some believe that because the company has the right to raise premiums, provisions for adverse deviations need not be made. Others believe that rate increases are accompanied by increased withdrawals of healthy lives and that anti-selection largely offsets the increases; those who believe this argue that provisions for adverse deviation for guaranteed renewable business should be fully as stringent as for noncancellable business.

It does appear that adjusted reserves on guaranteed renewable business should be calculated as if the business were noncancellable, on the assumption that any future rate increases will be offset by increases in claims and incremental expenses.

When rates are significantly increased, it is usually necessary to revise assumptions for the future to give effect to increased claim costs, increased expenses, and poorer persistency. The existing reserve would not be changed; only future additions to the reserves would be modified. Such a prospective revision does not violate the lock-in concept. Guaranteed renewability is the key "lock-in" feature; all else rides along with it. Thus guaranteed renewable business may be viewed as noncancellable business with an open-ended possibility of future revision of reserve assumptions.

Collectively renewable business usually shares in the characteristics of cancellable and guaranteed renewable business. The reserve method to be used will depend on which of the characteristics are predominant.

Return-of-Premium Business

In recent years, return-of-premium disability income insurance has proven to be a very popular product. Some smaller companies have specialized in the product, which has found a ready market, particularly among professionals.

Return-of-premium health insurance introduces an additional dimension of risk that may or may not be adequately provided for under existing statutory practices.

Product Design

The return-of-premium benefit may be viewed as a rider attached to a basic guaranteed renewable or noncancellable disability income policy which provides that upon death or at a specified maturity date, premiums paid less benefits paid will be returned to the policyholder. The benefit may in fact be sold as a rider or it may be incorporated into the basic product. For purposes of discussion, the return-of-premium benefit will be treated as a separate rider.

There are several variations of the return-of-premium benefit. For example, under one plan, any excess of gross premiums over benefits at age 65 is returned to the policyholder; upon surrender prior to maturity, the excess is reduced by a surrender charge. Under another plan, the excess of premiums over claims is returned each ten years so long as claims do not exceed a specified percentage of premiums; if the percentage is exceeded, nothing is returned.

This is a species of cash value health insurance designed to encourage persistency, discourage questionable claims, and improve marketability of the disability income product.

Risk

Absent the return-of-premium rider, the underlying disability income policy would operate like any disability income policy. However, to the extent that the rider operates to hold down claims and improve persistency, profitability of the pure disability income portion of the contract may be improved. In terms of adjusted reserves, presence of the rider may affect termination and claim cost assumptions.

However, as persistency and claim experience improve, the return-of-premium benefit becomes correspondingly more expensive, simply because more money will be returned to policyholders.

At this point in time little experience has developed with respect to the actual costs of the return-of-premium benefit under varying economic conditions and for varying occupational classes, issue ages, and so on. Thus the potential cost of the return-of-premium rider represents a significant, relatively unspecifiable risk.

Acquisition and Other Costs

Acquisition and other costs present no particular problems in the case of return-of-premium business. They would be deferred and amortized or reserved for, as the case may be, in a manner similar to methods used for regular disability income insurance.

Liabilities for Incurred Claims

Similarly, incurred claims would be valued in basically the same manner as for regular disability income insurance.

Active Life Reserves

Active life reserves are another matter. As indicated previously, reserves for the disability income benefit will be affected by any modification in assumptions as to claim cost and persistency caused by the return-of-premium feature. So, of course, will reserves for the return-of-premium feature.

The issues involved can best be highlighted by a simple example. Assume a block of noncancellable disability income policies with return-of-premium riders are issued to males age 45, that the policies carry an annual gross premium of $100 per unit of insurance, and that at age 65 the excess of premiums over claims is returned to the policyholder, with no nonforfeiture benefits in the interim.

Assume now the following pattern of assumptions and experience:

	Actual— Pure Disability Income Policies	Return-of-Premium Policies	
		Assumed	Actual
Developed loss ratios:			
Policies persisting to age 65	60%	40%	20%
Policies terminating prematurely	40	60	80
Terminations and deaths:			
Year 1	25%	10	5
Years 2–10	5	5	3
Years 11–15	4	4	2
Years 16–19	3	3	1
Year 20	3	0	0
Interest (for simplicity)	Zero	Zero	Zero
Present value of zero-interest annuity of $1 for 20 years	$10.55	$12.47	$15.28

Percentage of original issues in force at age 65	33%	42%	63%

Thus the *assumed* profit (ignoring expenses and taxes) on the return-of-premium policy per unit issues would be $289:

Gross premium per unit	$100
Present value of annuity	$12.47
Gross premiums	$1,247
Claims:	
On persisting policies (42% x $1,247 x 40%)	210
On terminating policies (58% x $1,247 x 60%)	434
Return of premium (42% x $1,247 − $210)	314
Total benefits	958
Margin before expenses and taxes	$ 289

However, the *actual* profit before expenses and taxes would develop to $113, or 39 percent of assumed:

Gross premium per unit	$100
Present value of annuity	$15.28
Gross premiums	$1,528
Claims:	
On persisting policies (63% x $1,528 x 20%)	193
On terminating policies (37% x $1,528 x 80%)	452
Return of premium (63% x $1,528 − $193)	770
Total benefits	1,415
Margin before expenses and taxes	$ 113

Thus the cost of the return-of-premium policy may be radically altered by the withdrawal pattern and the claim cost and the effect of those elements on the return-of-premium benefit.

Unless the reserving mechanism is appropriately sensitive to developing experience, early profits on the disability portion of the policy could easily become losses later on the return-of-premium benefit.

Active life reserves for return-of-premium disability income business should therefore be conservative. It would appear appropriate to set the gross premium equal to the valuation premium in the absence of clear evidence that a lesser valuation premium is required. Further, because of the nature of the coverage, reserves for the return-of-premium benefit should be updated periodically (ideally, on an annual basis) to reflect claims actually paid, since the return-of-premium benefit is a function of claim payments.

It should be recognized that the example given ignores interest, expenses, interim non-forfeiture values, and other complicating factors. In practice, reserving for return-of-premium business is possibly

377

more complex, and involves a greater degree of judgment, than most other forms of business.

Disclosure

Return-of-premium business should be treated as a separate line of business for disclosure purposes when the volume of such business is material. Methods of recognizing revenues and costs should be described in the accounting policies note, reserve assumptions and related amounts should be set forth, and acquisition costs deferred and amortized should be disclosed.

20

Credit and Group Insurance

Long-term individual coverages present most of the more difficult problems in converting a life insurance company's financial statements to a generally accepted accounting principles basis. But the "mass" coverages —credit and group insurance—present unique problems of their own.

It is generally necessary to adjust credit business. It is usually unnecessary to adjust group term life and health insurance. Group annuities will sometime require adjustment.

Group permanent business is substantially similar to corresponding individual coverages and is not discussed in this chapter.

Credit Insurance

Credit insurance is possibly the fastest-growing segment of the life insurance business. There was $4 billion in credit life insurance in force in 1950; in 1972 the total approximated $130 billion. In 1950 credit life accounted for just over 1 percent of all life insurance in force; in 1972 it represented about 7 percent of the total. Credit disability insurance has also grown very rapidly. About 14 percent of the business is classified as "individual" and the balance is classified as "group". In practice, there is generally no substantive difference between the classifications.

Until the late 1960s credit insurance was quite profitable. It was unregulated; direct competition for customers (i.e., borrowers) was virtually nonexistent; low loss ratios were quite common. There was, however, intense competition for sales outlets, and commissions (or "experience rating refunds", which are basically equivalent to commissions) were high.

The California Insurance Department began regulating credit insurance in the late 1960s. Citing "reverse competition", the Department established prima facie "fair" rates and made rate deviations very difficult to obtain. Other states followed suit. Today, a majority of jurisdictions establish maximum rates or set minimum loss ratios.

Many of the small companies established to cash in on the credit insurance bonanza have fallen on hard times. Even many of the larger companies, with a significantly larger revenue base over which to spread overhead, now find it difficult to make money on credit insurance. Just as the regulations tightened in the late 1960s, recession set in and disability income loss ratios rose. It is clear that, as a general proposition, credit insurance is no longer a source of "easy" profits nor is it likely to be so in the foreseeable future.

Types of Business

Credit insurance is usually classified by type of lender and underlying transaction. For example, California regulations establish five general classes of business:

Class 1—personal property broker (UCC definition); industrial loan company.

Class 2—bank: home improvement loans; bank: mobile home loans; mobile home dealer; home improvement dealer (including swimming pools).

Class 3—personal property broker: loans secured by real estate; industrial loan company: loans secured by real estate; land development companies: loans secured by real estate; mortgage loan companies specializing in second deeds of trust.

Class 4—bank: agricultural loans; production credit association.

Class 5—bank: other; savings and loan associations; finance companies: installment sales; automobile dealer; motorcycle dealer; truck and trailer dealer; equipment leasing dealer; furniture and appliance dealer; jewelry dealer; education loan business; securities margin loan business; credit unions; boat dealer.

The California regulations promulgate rates (or detailed computation guidelines) for each class of business.

Credit insurance may also be classified by form of premium payment and commission arrangement:

1. Single-premium (lump sum collected at beginning of contract term):

a. Commissions payable immediately; commissions applicable to refunds charged back when refunds are made. Typical example: auto dealers.

b. Administrative fee payable in advance and "experience rating refunds" payable annually (or more often) on an earned-premium basis. The combined effective rate is about the same as the going commission rate. Typical example: banks, which are prohibited from receiving "commissions" as such.

2. Outstanding-balance (premiums collected monthly based on the in-force balance). Commissions and commission equivalents are typically paid on an earned-premium basis.

Reinsurance arrangements in the credit insurance business defy classification. Major lenders sometimes set up captive companies, typically with minimum capital, and arrange for business to be written through a larger company (or companies) and reinsured with the captive. The captive pays the larger company an allowance which really constitutes a fee for using the larger company's licenses, etc.

Statutory Reserves

The typical statutory minimum for life insurance reserves is some percentage (for example, 130 percent) of the 1958 CSO (for individual policies) or 1960 CSG (for group policies) mortality table, with 3 1/2 percent interest. Since there is little if any practical difference between group and individual policies, this distinction is regarded by most actuaries as artificial.

For credit disability insurance, the minimum may be a reserve based on, for example, 130 percent of the 1964 Commissioner's Disability Table with 3 1/2

percent interest; however, the total reserve typically cannot be less than the pro rata gross unearned premium reserve. With respect to level insured amounts, this means a true pro rata unearned premium; with respect to decreasing amounts, this means a Rule-of-78 unearned premium. In the usual case the unearned premium reserve is higher, and apparently most companies use it.

Refunds (payable upon early retirement of the underlying debt) under single-premium business are made on the basis of Rule-of-78 or full pro rata unearned premiums, depending on whether the sum insured is decreasing or level.

Benefit Patterns

For various reasons, credit life coverages generally appear to operate like casualty coverages. Monthly benefit cost per unit of insurance tends to be constant for contracts of relatively short duration. Benefits therefore conform reasonably with the "earned premium" pattern (Rule-of-78 for decreasing coverages and full pro rata for level coverages).

Credit disability coverages typically do not follow this pattern; monthly benefit cost per unit of insurance is *not* constant. Benefits therefore do not necessarily conform with the "earned premium" pattern.

The implications are that Rule-of-78 or pro rata unearned premium reserves are generally adequate for decreasing term and level term credit life insurance, respectively, but not for credit disability insurance.

Rule-of-78, full pro rata, and "true" unearned premium reserves for three companies for declining-balance credit disability insurance were as follows at one recent year-end:

	000		
	Company A	Company B	Company C
Rule of 78 reserve	$1,082	$1,032	$146
Full pro rata reserve	1,586	1,446	189
"True" reserve	1,404	1,293	175

As will be seen, the pattern of benefits is extremely important in selecting a method for recognizing revenue. It is difficult to generalize about what patterns are "appropriate". There is a general consensus that the Rule-of-78 is typically proper for credit life insurance. There is less agreement about credit health; company experience appears to vary considerably. Thus some companies have in fact experienced a Rule-of-78 pattern for health claims, while others have

Table 20–1.

COMPARISON OF EXPOSURES (MEASURED BY OUTSTANDING LOAN BALANCE) WITH RULE-OF-78 AND MODIFIED PRO RATA EARNED PREMIUM PATTERNS

Month	Balance of $1,000 Loan Amortizable with Interest at 8% Amount	%	Balance of $1,000 Loan Amortizable with Interest at 18% Amount	%	Rule-of-78 Pattern	Modified Pro-Rata Pattern*
1	$ 961	8.1%	$ 965	7.9%	8.0%	6.0%
2	923	7.8	930	7.6	7.7	6.0
3	884	7.5	894	7.3	7.3	5.7
4	844	7.2	857	7.0	7.0	5.7
5	805	6.8	820	6.7	6.7	5.3
6	765	6.5	782	6.4	6.3	5.3
7	725	6.1	744	6.1	6.0	5.0
8	684	5.8	706	5.8	5.7	5.0
9	644	5.5	666	5.5	5.3	4.7
10	603	5.1	626	5.1	5.0	4.7
11	561	4.7	586	4.8	4.7	4.3
12	520	4.3	545	4.5	4.3	4.3
13	478	4.1	503	4.1	4.0	4.0
14	436	3.7	460	3.7	3.7	4.0
15	394	3.3	417	3.4	3.3	3.7
16	351	3.0	374	3.1	3.0	3.7
17	308	2.6	329	2.7	2.7	3.3
18	265	2.2	285	2.3	2.3	3.3
19	222	1.9	239	2.0	2.0	3.0
20	178	1.5	193	1.6	1.7	3.0
21	134	1.1	145	1.2	1.3	2.7
22	90	.8	98	.8	1.0	2.7
23	45	.4	49	.4	.7	2.3
24	–0–	–0–	–0–	–0–	.3	2.3
	$11,820	100.0%	$12,213	100.0%	100 %	100 %

*As used here, the mean of Rule-of-78 and full pro-rata.

experienced a "modified pro rata" pattern—i.e., benefits that create a pattern somewhere between full pro rata and Rule-of-78. The pattern adopted for purposes of implementing the life insurance audit guide should be based on a careful study of experience. Where experience is lacking, conservatism is warranted. Generally, this would mean assuming a modified pro rata pattern for health claims.

Audit Guide Provisions

The life insurance audit guide provides that gross premiums on credit life insurance should be recognized "in proportion to the amounts of insurance in force." [1] For level term insurance, this means a straight pro rata recognition of premiums. For decreasing term insurance, this means recognition of premiums on a Rule-of-78 basis.

Premiums on credit health insurance should be recognized "in reasonable relationship to the anticipated claims." [2] This means that premiums would be recognized in any accounting period in an amount which, expressed as a ratio of total premiums expected to be earned in all periods, is equal to the ratio of claims incurred during the period to total claims expected to be incurred in all periods.

If premiums are recognized as revenues in the manner described, then reserves are in effect equal to unearned premiums, i.e., the portion of premiums received that has not yet been recognized as revenue.

Because this treatment of reserves could have adverse tax consequences, the guide provides an alternative: actuarially-computed reserves may be provided and "additional reserves" may be carried so that the combined total "approximates the amount of premium revenues which would be deferred" [3] under the recommended unearned premium approach.

Acquisition costs, says the guide, "should be amor-

Table 20–2.

SUMMARY OF ASSUMED CREDIT INSURANCE EXPERIENCE EXPRESSED IN TERMS OF $1,000 OF SINGLE PREMIUM ORIGINALLY ISSUED—AGGREGATES FOR 24-MONTH CONTRACTS—AUTO DEALER/PERSONAL PROPERTY BROKER TYPE BUSINESS

	Life		Health	
	Amount	*%*	*Amount*	*%*
Premiums written	$1000.00		$1000.00	
Refunds at 1% a month (Rule-of-78 basis)	72.53		72.53	
Premiums earned	927.47	100.0%	927.47	100.0%
Claims	417.21	45.0	482.13	52.0
Acquisition costs:				
Commissions	370.95	40.0	370.95	40.0
Taxes	18.66	2.0	18.66	2.0
Solicitation	25.00	2.7	25.00	2.7
Net acquisition costs	414.61	44.7	414.61	44.7
Total direct expense	831.82	89.7	896.74	96.7
Underwriting profit before maintenance expenses	95.65	10.3	30.73	3.3
Maintenance expenses	10.62	1.1	32.05	3.5
Underwriting profit (loss)	85.03	9.2%	(1.32)	(.2)%
Interest on assets at 5.5%	27.23		25.18	
Reported profit	$ 112.26		$ 23.86	
Computation of equity in unearned premium reserve:				
Premiums written	$1000.00		$1000.00	
Commissions - 40%	$ 400.00		$ 400.00	
Taxes - 2%	20.00		20.00	
Solicitation	25.00		25.00	
	$ 445.00		$ 445.00	
Equity as computed at time of issue	44.5%		44.5%	

tized in proportion to the amount of premium revenue recognized in each accounting period." [4]

Table 20–1 suggests why the Rule-of-78 produces a good approximation of "amounts of insurance in force." Monthly outstanding balances of an amortizable $1,000 loan—one at 8 percent interest and the other at 18 percent—are shown, as are the percentages of the monthly balances to the total of all such balances. The percentages might be referred to as "sum-of-the-months'-outstanding-balances" percentages. The outstanding balances measure insurance exposures. Assuming a constant mortality rate per unit of insurance in force—usually a reasonable assumption for relatively short-term credit life insurance where turnover of insureds is such as to produce a stable average age—then the Rule-of-78 percentages match quite closely the sum-of-the-months'-outstanding-balances percentages, and recognition of premiums in a Rule-of-78 pattern will usually reasonably match the pattern of death claims.

Table 20–1 also shows the "modified pro rata" percentages considered appropriate—for purposes of illustration—for credit health insurance. Use of the Rule-of-78 to recognize premium revenues would result in premature recognition of income, since claims are postponed relative to the Rule-of-78 pattern.

Long-Term Business

The audit guide provisions discussed above apply to "short-term" contracts. In Chapter 5, "short-term" contracts were defined as those (1) of less than five years' duration and (2) whose slope of mortality or morbidity is relatively smooth.

Where those conditions are not present—for example, in the case of long-term mobile home credit insurance—the contracts should be accounted for in a manner similar to the accounting for other types of long-term contracts.

Table 20–3.

CREDIT LIFE CASH TRANSACTIONS AND STATUTORY PRE-TAX EARNINGS PER $1,000 OF SINGLE PREMIUM ORIGINALLY ISSUED—AUTO DEALER/PERSONAL PROPERTY BROKER TYPE BUSINESS

Month	Premiums Received	Interest on Assets	Rule-of-78 Refunds	Benefits	Commis-sions	Premium Taxes	Adminis-trative Expenses	Cash Flow	Change in Statutory Reserve*	Statutory Pre-Tax Net Income
1	$1,000.00	$ 2.40	$ 9.20	$ 36.00	$396.32	$19.81	$25.50	$515.57	$(728.64)	$(213.07)
2		2.23	8.34	34.15	(3.34)	(.16)	.49	(37.25)	67.40	30.15
3		2.07	7.54	32.34	(3.02)	(.14)	.49	(35.14)	63.54	28.40
4		1.91	6.79	30.56	(2.72)	(.13)	.48	(33.07)	59.77	26.70
5		1.77	6.08	28.81	(2.43)	(.12)	.48	(31.05)	56.10	25.05
6		1.64	5.42	27.10	(2.17)	(.10)	.47	(29.08)	52.52	23.44
7		1.51	4.80	25.41	(1.92)	(.09)	.47	(27.16)	49.03	21.87
8		1.38	4.22	23.76	(1.69)	(.08)	.46	(25.29)	45.63	20.34
9		1.28	3.69	22.14	(1.48)	(.07)	.46	(23.46)	42.32	18.86
10		1.17	3.19	20.55	(1.28)	(.06)	.45	(21.68)	39.10	17.42
11		1.08	2.74	18.99	(1.10)	(.05)	.45	(19.95)	35.96	16.01
12		.99	2.32	17.45	(.93)	(.04)	.44	(18.25)	32.90	14.65
13		.92	1.95	15.95	(.78)	(.03)	.44	(16.61)	29.93	13.32
14		.84	1.60	14.47	(.64)	(.03)	.43	(14.99)	27.02	12.03
15		.79	1.30	13.03	(.52)	(.02)	.43	(13.43)	24.21	10.78
16		.73	1.03	11.61	(.41)	(.02)	.43	(11.91)	21.47	9.56
17		.67	.79	10.21	(.32)	(.01)	.42	(10.42)	18.80	8.38
18		.64	.59	8.85	(.24)	Nil	.42	(8.98)	16.21	7.23
19		.59	.41	7.51	(.17)	Nil	.41	(7.57)	13.68	6.11
20		.56	.27	6.19	(.11)	Nil	.41	(6.20)	11.24	5.04
21		.54	.16	4.90	(.06)	Nil	.40	(4.86)	8.85	3.99
22		.52	.08	3.64	(.03)	Nil	.40	(3.57)	6.55	2.98
23		.50	.02	2.40	(.01)	Nil	.40	(2.31)	4.29	1.98
24		.50	–0–	1.19	–0–	–0–	.39	(1.08)	2.12	1.04
	$1,000.00	$27.23	$72.53	$417.21	$370.95	$18.66	$35.62	$112.26	$ –0–	$ 112.26

*Approximation of 130% of 1958 CSO, 3 percent, net level.

Single-Premium Non-Bank Business

Table 20–2 summarizes assumed experience per $1,000 of single premiums originally written for 24-month decreasing-balance auto dealer/personal property broker type business.

Life. Table 20–3 summarizes assumed 24-month cash flows and statutory pre-tax income per $1,000 of single credit life insurance premiums written. Death claims are assumed to occur in a Rule-of-78 pattern, namely, 24/300 in the first month, 23/300 in the second month, etc. All values are adjusted for decreases in insurance in force owing to deaths and refunds. Note the familiar statutory pattern—a first-month loss followed by gains. This pattern would of course be modified if modified reserves were used (net level reserves are used in Table 20–3).

The result of adjusting to the audit guide's recom-mended method of accounting for short-term single-premium credit life insurance is shown in Table 20–4. Interest and maintenance expenses have been excluded from the calculation to highlight the "casualty" approach called for by the guide. The indicated under-writing income, $95.65, can be traced to Table 20–2 and thus reconciled with total pre-tax income, including interest and maintenance expenses, of $112.26 shown in Tables 20–2 and 20–3.

Health. Table 20–5 summarizes assumed 24-month cash flows and statutory pre-tax income per $1,000 of single credit health insurance premiums written. Disability claims are assumed to occur in a pattern midway between a Rule-of-78 pattern and a full pro rata pattern. It will be observed that losses are reported in the last few months. This is a result of recognizing premium revenues too rapidly in relation to the claim pattern.

Table 20–4.

PURE CASUALTY APPROACH—CREDIT LIFE BUSINESS—AUTO DEALER/PERSONAL PROPERTY TYPE—PER $1,000 SINGLE PREMIUM ORIGINALLY ISSUED

Month	Cash Flow, Excluding Interest and Maintenance Expenses	Rule-of-78 Unearned Premium Reserve Level	Change	Equity in Unearned Premium Reserve Level	Change	Direct Underwriting Income
1	$513.67	$910.80	$910.80	$405.31	$405.31	$ 8.18
2	(38.99)	826.55	(84.25)	367.81	(37.50)	7.76
3	(36.72)	747.13	(79.42)	332.47	(35.34)	7.36
4	(34.50)	672.42	(74.71)	299.23	(33.24)	6.97
5	(32.34)	602.29	(70.13)	268.02	(31.21)	6.58
6	(30.25)	536.64	(65.65)	238.80	(29.22)	6.18
7	(28.20)	475.35	(61.29)	211.53	(27.27)	5.82
8	(26.21)	418.31	(57.04)	186.15	(25.38)	5.45
9	(24.28)	365.41	(52.90)	162.61	(23.54)	5.08
10	(22.40)	316.53	(48.88)	140.86	(21.75)	4.73
11	(20.58)	271.56	(44.97)	120.84	(20.02)	4.37
12	(18.80)	230.46	(41.10)	102.55	(18.29)	4.01
13	(17.09)	193.05	(37.41)	85.91	(16.64)	3.68
14	(15.40)	159.27	(33.78)	70.88	(15.03)	3.35
15	(13.79)	129.01	(30.26)	57.41	(13.47)	3.00
16	(12.21)	102.17	(26.84)	45.47	(11.94)	2.69
17	(10.67)	78.67	(23.50)	35.01	(10.46)	2.37
18	(9.20)	58.42	(20.25)	26.00	(9.01)	2.04
19	(7.75)	41.31	(17.11)	18.38	(7.62)	1.74
20	(6.35)	27.26	(14.05)	12.13	(6.25)	1.45
21	(5.00)	16.19	(11.07)	7.20	(4.93)	1.14
22	(3.69)	8.02	(8.17)	3.57	(3.63)	.85
23	(2.41)	2.65	(5.37)	1.18	(2.39)	.57
24	(1.19)	–0–	(2.65)	–0–	(1.18)	.28
	$ 95.65					$95.65

The "casualty" approach suggested by the life insurance audit guide is illustrated in Table 20–6. Again, interest and maintenance expenses have been eliminated. Two adjustment methods are shown: Rule-of-78 and "modified pro rata"; the latter is what is intended by the audit guide when it calls for recognition of premium revenues "in reasonable relationship to the anticipated claims" which, in this case, follow a pattern which falls midway between Rule-of-78 and full pro rata.

Interest. Careful review of Tables 20–6 and 20–2 will indicate an "underwriting loss" on the credit health business:

Direct underwriting income per Table 20–6	$30.73
Maintenance expenses per Table 20–2	32.05
Underwriting loss	$(1.32)

In property-liability accounting such a "loss" would normally result in reducing the equity in the unearned premium reserve to an amount designed to produce a break-even. This is discussed at greater length in Chapter 24.

However, interest of $25.18 on assets—primarily assets supporting the unearned premium reserve—is also available to meet claims and expenses. Such interest is generally quite significant in the case of single-premium business of even short duration, and it should always be taken into account in evaluating the profitability of the business.

In fact, when interest is material, consideration should be given to including it in the revenue base against which acquisition costs are amortized. Since interest on single-premium business is most significant in the early months, when unearned premiums are highest, the result would be to accelerate amortization.

Table 20–5.

CREDIT HEALTH CASH TRANSACTIONS AND STATUTORY PRE-TAX EARNINGS PER $1,000 OF SINGLE PREMIUM ORIGINALLY ISSUED—AUTO DEALER/PERSONAL PROPERTY BROKER TYPE BUSINESS

Month	Premiums Received	Interest on Assets	Rule-of-78 Refunds	Claims	Commissions	Premium Taxes	Administrative Expenses	Cash Flow	Change in Statutory Reserve*	Statutory Income
1	$1,000.00	$ 2.40	$ 9.20	$ 31.79	$396.32	$19.81	$26.50	$518.78	$(910.80)	$(392.02)
2		2.25	8.34	31.47	(3.34)	(.16)	1.48	(35.54)	84.25	48.71
3		2.10	7.54	29.43	(3.02)	(.14)	1.47	(33.18)	79.42	46.24
4		1.94	6.79	29.13	(2.72)	(.13)	1.45	(32.58)	74.71	42.13
5		1.80	6.08	27.14	(2.43)	(.12)	1.44	(30.31)	70.13	39.82
6		1.67	5.42	26.87	(2.17)	(.10)	1.42	(29.77)	65.65	35.88
7		1.55	4.80	24.94	(1.92)	(.09)	1.41	(27.59)	61.29	33.70
8		1.40	4.22	24.69	(1.69)	(.08)	1.39	(27.13)	57.04	29.91
9		1.29	3.69	22.81	(1.48)	(.07)	1.38	(25.04)	52.90	27.86
10		1.19	3.19	22.59	(1.28)	(.06)	1.37	(24.62)	48.88	24.26
11		1.07	2.74	20.76	(1.10)	(.05)	1.35	(22.63)	44.97	22.34
12		.98	2.32	20.55	(.93)	(.04)	1.34	(22.26)	41.10	18.84
13		.88	1.95	18.78	(.78)	(.03)	1.32	(20.36)	37.41	17.05
14		.78	1.60	18.59	(.64)	(.03)	1.31	(20.05)	33.78	13.73
15		.71	1.30	16.88	(.52)	(.02)	1.30	(18.23)	30.26	12.03
16		.63	1.03	16.71	(.41)	(.02)	1.29	(17.97)	26.84	8.87
17		.53	.79	15.03	(.32)	(.01)	1.27	(16.23)	23.50	7.27
18		.48	.59	14.88	(.24)	Nil	1.26	(16.01)	20.25	4.24
19		.40	.41	13.26	(.17)	Nil	1.25	(14.35)	17.11	2.76
20		.34	.27	13.13	(.11)	Nil	1.23	(14.18)	14.05	(.13)
21		.27	.16	11.55	(.06)	Nil	1.22	(12.60)	11.07	(1.53)
22		.23	.08	11.44	(.03)	Nil	1.21	(12.47)	8.17	(4.30)
23		.16	.02	9.90	(.01)	Nil	1.20	(10.95)	5.32	(5.58)
24		.13	–0–	9.81	–0–	–0–	1.19	(10.87)	2.65	(8.22)
	$1,000.00	$25.18	$72.53	$482.13	$370.95	$18.66	$57.05	$ 23.86	$ –0–	$ 23.86

*Rule-of-78 unearned premium.

Single-Premium Bank-Type Business

Table 20–7 summarizes assumed experience per $1,000 of single premiums originally written for 24-month decreasing-balance bank type business. The principal difference between auto dealer/personal property broker type business and bank-type business is that commissions are paid at the time that premiums are written in the former case while in the latter case—since banks are usually prohibited from accepting commissions—an "administrative fee" is typically paid when the premiums are written and "experience rating refunds" are usually paid annually on an earned-premium basis.

Life. Table 20–8 summarizes assumed 24-month cash flows and statutory pre-tax income per $1,000 of single credit life insurance premiums written. Deaths are assumed to occur in a Rule-of-78 pattern. All values are adjusted for decreases in insurance in force due to deaths and refunds.

Because there are no commissions in the first month a sizeable first-month statutory profit is reported. This profit would be greater still if modified reserves were used.

The result of adjusting to the audit guide's recommended method is shown in Table 20–9. Once again, interest and maintenance expenses have been eliminated from the tabulation to show the results on a "casualty" basis. The effect of the adjustment process is to "smooth" profits; they are reported in a pattern approximately corresponding to the Rule-of-78 earned premium pattern.

Health. Table 20–10 shows assumed 24-month cash flows and statutory pre-tax income per $1,000 of single credit health insurance premiums written. Again, disability claims are assumed to occur in a pattern midway between a Rule-of-78 pattern and a full pro rata pattern.

Table 20–6.

PURE CASUALTY APPROACH—CREDIT HEALTH BUSINESS—AUTO DEALER/PERSONAL PROPERTY BROKER TYPE—PER $1,000 SINGLE PREMIUM ORIGINALLY ISSUED

Month	Cash Flow, Excluding Interest and Maintenance Expenses	Rule-of-78				Modified Pro-Rata				Direct Underwriting Income	
		Unearned Premium Reserve		Equity in Unearned Premium Reserve		Unearned Premium Reserve		Equity in Unearned Premium Reserve			Modified
		Level	Change	Level	Change	Level	Change	Level	Change	Rule-of-78	Pro Rata
1	$517.88	$910.80	$910.80	$405.31	$405.31	$930.60	$930.60	$414.12	$414.12	$12.39	$ 1.40
2	(36.31)	826.55	(84.25)	367.81	(37.50)	862.49	(68.11)	383.81	(30.31)	10.44	1.49
3	(33.81)	747.13	(79.42)	332.47	(35.34)	798.88	(63.61)	355.50	(28.31)	10.27	1.49
4	(33.07)	672.42	(74.71)	299.23	(33.24)	736.45	(62.43)	327.72	(27.78)	8.40	1.58
5	(30.67)	602.29	(70.13)	268.02	(31.21)	678.37	(58.08)	301.87	(25.85)	8.25	1.56
6	(30.02)	536.64	(65.65)	238.80	(29.22)	621.38	(56.99)	276.51	(25.36)	6.41	1.61
7	(27.73)	475.35	(61.29)	211.53	(27.27)	568.56	(52.82)	253.01	(23.50)	6.29	1.59
8	(27.14)	418.31	(57.04)	186.15	(25.38)	516.74	(51.82)	229.95	(23.06)	4.52	1.62
9	(24.95)	365.41	(52.90)	162.61	(23.54)	468.94	(47.80)	208.68	(21.27)	4.41	1.58
10	(24.44)	316.53	(48.88)	140.86	(21.75)	422.04	(46.90)	187.81	(20.87)	2.69	1.59
11	(22.35)	271.56	(44.97)	120.84	(20.02)	379.02	(43.02)	168.66	(19.15)	2.60	1.52
12	(21.90)	230.46	(41.10)	102.55	(18.29)	336.83	(42.19)	149.89	(18.77)	.91	1.52
13	(19.92)	193.05	(37.41)	85.91	(16.64)	298.36	(38.47)	132.77	(17.12)	.85	1.43
14	(19.52)	159.27	(33.78)	70.88	(15.03)	260.62	(37.74)	115.98	(16.79)	(.77)	1.43
15	(17.64)	129.01	(30.26)	57.41	(13.47)	226.48	(34.14)	100.78	(15.20)	(.85)	1.30
16	(17.31)	102.17	(26.84)	45.47	(11.94)	192.99	(33.49)	85.88	(14.90)	(2.41)	1.28
17	(15.49)	78.67	(23.50)	35.01	(10.46)	162.97	(30.02)	72.52	(13.36)	(2.45)	1.17
18	(15.23)	58.42	(20.25)	26.00	(9.01)	133.52	(29.45)	59.42	(13.10)	(3.99)	1.12
19	(13.50)	41.31	(17.11)	18.38	(7.62)	107.40	(26.12)	47.79	(11.63)	(4.01)	.99
20	(13.29)	27.26	(14.05)	12.13	(6.25)	81.79	(25.61)	36.40	(11.39)	(5.49)	.93
21	(11.65)	16.19	(11.07)	7.20	(4.93)	59.38	(22.41)	26.42	(9.98)	(5.51)	.78
22	(11.49)	8.02	(8.17)	3.57	(3.63)	37.40	(21.98)	16.64	(9.78)	(6.95)	.71
23	(9.91)	2.65	(5.37)	1.18	(2.39)	18.51	(18.89)	8.24	(8.40)	(6.93)	.58
24	(9.81)	–0–	(2.65)	–0–	(1.18)	–0–	(18.51)	–0–	(8.24)	(8.34)	.46
	$30.73									$30.73	$30.73

In this case, a statutory loss is reported in the first month, gains are reported in the ensuing 14 months, and losses are reported in the last nine months.

Table 20–11 shows two sets of adjusted figures—Rule-of-78 and "modified pro rata". Under the latter approach, premiums are taken into income in a pattern that corresponds to the claim pattern *and* experience rating refunds, which are paid on a Rule-of-78 earned premium basis, are accrued on a modified pro rata basis. The effect is readily apparent from inspection of the last two columns in Table 20–11.

Coinsurance

The foregoing discussions and illustrations deal with direct business. As indicated previously, complex reinsurance arrangements are common to the credit insurance business.

Tables 20–12 and 20–13 reflect highly condensed summaries of two common forms of coinsurance agreements, in both cases with respect to auto dealer type business:

1. Life—Full coinsurance, except that expenses (including non-percentage expenses) are represented by a percentage reinsurance expense allowance.

2. Disability—Settlements are made on a Rule-of-78 earned premium basis.

In these illustrations, which adopt the ceding company's point of view, the reinsurance expense allowance is 50 percent, which is designed to cover commissions (40 percent) and all other expenses (10 percent). Any profit would come from the 10 percent.

It will be noted that significant distortions arise when the Rule-of-78 method is used for credit disa-

Table 20–7.

SUMMARY OF ASSUMED CREDIT INSURANCE EXPERIENCE—EXPRESSED IN TERMS OF $1,000 OF SINGLE
PREMIUM ORIGINALLY ISSUED—AGGREGATES FOR 24-MONTH CONTRACTS—BANK TYPE BUSINESS

	Life		Health	
	Amount	*%*	*Amount*	*%*
Premiums written	$1000.00		$1000.00	
Refunds at 1% a month				
(Rule-of-78 basis)	72.53		72.53	
Premiums earned	927.47	100.0%	927.47	100.0%
Claims	417.21	45.0	482.13	52.0
Acquisition costs:				
Administrative fees	46.36	5.0	46.36	5.0
Taxes	18.66	2.0	18.66	2.0
Solicitation	25.00	2.7	25.00	2.7
Net acquisition costs	90.02	9.7	90.02	9.7
Experience rating refunds				
(Rule-of-78 basis)	324.57	35.0	324.57	35.0
Total direct expense	831.80	89.7	896.72	96.7
Underwriting profit before				
maintenance expenses	95.67	10.3	30.75	3.3
Maintenance expenses	10.62	1.1	32.05	3.5
Underwriting profit (loss)	85.05	9.2%	(1.30)	(.2)%
Interest on assets at 5.5%	49.61		47.56	
Reported profit	$ 134.66		$ 46.26	
Computation of equity in				
unearned premium reserve:				
Premiums written	$1000.00		$1000.00	
Administrative fees -5%	$ 50.00		$ 50.00	
Taxes -2%	20.00		20.00	
Solicitation	25.00		25.00	
	$ 95.00		$ 95.00	
Equity as computed at				
time of issue	9.5%		9.5%	

bility reinsurance and that highly intricate calculations must be made to accommodate the modified pro rata approach.

Level Term Business

Credit insurance on debt not subject to repayment in installments is essentially level term insurance.

In the case of life insurance, premiums would normally be recognized as revenue in level monthly amounts.

In the case of health insurance, premiums might be recognized in a pattern that *increases* from month to month if claims follow the pattern assumed in the previous illustrations.

The various adjustments described previously would also apply to level term business. The result would tend to be a level recognition of profit in the case of

life insurance and a level to increasing recognition of profit in the case of health insurance.

Outstanding Balance Business

Outstanding balance credit insurance operates in much the same fashion as group insurance. Premiums are paid monthly on the basis of exposures then in force. Percentage expenses are usually paid as premiums are received. There may be some initial acquisition costs involved in soliciting, and setting up records for, new business; such costs might qualify for deferral and amortization. Experience rating refunds may be accruable.

In the case of credit health insurance, the effect of the outstanding balance method may be to pay premiums on a Rule-of-78 basis (for declining-balance business) or a pro rata basis (for level-amount busi-

Table 20–8.

CREDIT LIFE CASH TRANSACTIONS AND STATUTORY PRE-TAX INCOME PER $1,000 OF SINGLE PREMIUM ORIGINALLY ISSUED—BANK TYPE BUSINESS

Month	Premiums Received	Interest on Assets	Rule-of-78 Refunds	Claims	Administrative Fees	Experience Refunds	Premium Taxes	Administrative Expenses	Cash Flow	Change in		Statutory Pre-Tax Income
										ERR Liability*	Statutory Reserve**	
1	$1,000.00	$ 3.96	$ 9.20	$ 36.00	$49.54		$19.81	$25.50	$ 863.91	$(28.00)	$(728.64)	$107.27
2		3.78	8.34	34.15	(.42)		(.16)	.49	(38.62)	(26.56)	67.40	2.22
3		3.62	7.54	32.34	(.38)		(.14)	.49	(36.23)	(25.16)	63.54	2.15
4		3.46	6.79	30.56	(.34)		(.13)	.48	(33.90)	(23.76)	59.77	2.11
5		3.31	6.08	28.81	(.30)		(.12)	.48	(31.64)	(22.42)	56.10	2.04
6		3.19	5.42	27.10	(.27)		(.10)	.47	(29.43)	(21.08)	52.52	2.01
7		3.05	4.80	25.41	(.24)		(.09)	.47	(27.30)	(19.77)	49.03	1.96
8		2.92	4.22	23.76	(.21)		(.08)	.46	(25.23)	(18.49)	45.63	1.91
9		2.83	3.69	22.14	(.18)		(.07)	.46	(23.21)	(17.22)	42.32	1.89
10		2.71	3.19	20.55	(.16)		(.06)	.45	(21.26)	(15.99)	39.10	1.85
11		2.63	2.74	18.99	(.14)		(.05)	.45	(19.36)	(14.78)	35.96	1.82
12		1.42	2.32	17.45	(.12)	$246.80	(.04)	.44	(265.43)	233.23	32.90	.70
13		1.36	1.95	15.95	(.10)		(.03)	.44	(16.85)	(12.40)	29.93	.68
14		1.27	1.60	14.47	(.08)		(.03)	.43	(15.12)	(11.25)	27.02	.65
15		1.22	1.30	13.03	(.07)		(.02)	.43	(13.45)	(10.14)	24.21	.62
16		1.17	1.03	11.61	(.05)		(.02)	.43	(11.83)	(9.03)	21.47	.61
17		1.11	.79	10.21	(.04)		(.01)	.42	(10.26)	(7.95)	18.80	.59
18		1.08	.59	8.85	(.04)		Nil	.42	(8.74)	(6.88)	16.21	.59
19		1.03	.41	7.51	(.02)		Nil	.41	(7.28)	(5.85)	13.68	.55
20		1.01	.27	6.19	(.01)		Nil	.41	(5.85)	(4.82)	11.24	.57
21		.97	.16	4.90	(.01)		Nil	.40	(4.48)	(3.82)	8.85	.55
22		.97	.08	3.64	Nil		Nil	.40	(3.15)	(2.83)	6.55	.57
23		.95	.02	2.40	Nil		Nil	.40	(1.87)	(1.87)	4.29	.55
24		.59	–0–	1.19	–0–	77.77	–0–	.39	(78.76)	76.84	2.12	.20
	$1,000.00	$49.61	$72.53	$417.21	$46.36	$324.57	$18.66	$35.62	$ 134.66	$ –0–	$ –0–	$134.66

*Experience rating refund liability accrued on Rule-of-78 earned premium basis.
**Approximation of 130% of 1958 CSO, 3%, net level.

ness). But claims may follow another pattern. Where this is the case, consideration should be given to reserving some portion of the early monthly premiums for later release into income.

Adverse Deviation

It is very difficult to generalize about provisions for adverse deviation in the case of credit insurance. About all that can be said is that assumed mortality and morbidity should be "loaded" to the extent feasible. As a general rule, the margins available for such "loadings" are very thin, and it would not be unusual to be forced to adhere to best estimates.

However, mortality and morbidity assumptions should be challenged in the light of relevant industry experience and common sense. For example, owners of less expensive cars tend to be somewhat younger than buyers of luxury cars, and some believe they tend also to be less settled in their occupations. This suggests in turn that owners of less expensive cars may be more prone to press for disability claims in a recessionary economy. A company specializing in credit life and health insurance on buyers of low-cost automobiles might well take such factors into account in providing for adverse deviation.

Crazy Quilt Life

Tables 20–14 and 20–15 summarize, in casualty insurance format, Crazy Quilt Life's credit insurance experience for its two principal classes of business, auto dealer/personal property broker type business and bank type business, from 1968—when Crazy Quilt first entered the credit insurance business —to 1971.

Table 20–9.

PURE CASUALTY APPROACH—CREDIT LIFE BUSINESS—BANK TYPE—PER $1,000 SINGLE PREMIUM ORIGINALLY ISSUED

Month	Cash Flow, Excluding Interest and Maintenance Expenses	Rule-of-78						Underwriting Income
		Experience Rating Refund Liability		Unearned Premium Reserve		Equity in Unearned Premium Reserve		
		Level	Change	Level	Change	Level	Change	
1	$860.45	$ 28.00	$ 28.00	$910.80	$910.80	$86.53	$86.53	$ 8.18
2	(41.91)	54.56	26.56	826.55	(84.25)	78.52	(8.01)	7.77
3	(39.36)	79.72	25.16	747.13	(79.42)	70.98	(7.54)	7.36
4	(36.88)	103.48	23.76	672.42	(74.71)	63.88	(7.10)	6.97
5	(34.47)	125.90	22.42	602.29	(70.13)	57.22	(6.66)	6.58
6	(32.15)	146.98	21.08	536.64	(65.65)	50.98	(6.24)	6.18
7	(29.88)	166.75	19.77	475.35	(61.29)	45.16	(5.82)	5.82
8	(27.69)	185.24	18.49	418.31	(57.04)	39.74	(5.42)	5.44
9	(25.58)	202.46	17.22	365.41	(52.90)	34.71	(5.03)	5.07
10	(23.52)	218.45	15.99	316.53	(48.88)	30.07	(4.64)	4.73
11	(21.54)	233.23	14.78	271.56	(44.97)	25.80	(4.27)	4.38
12	(266.41)	–0–	(233.23)	230.46	(41.10)	21.89	(3.91)	4.01
13	(17.77)	12.40	12.40	193.05	(37.41)	18.34	(3.55)	3.69
14	(15.96)	23.65	11.25	159.27	(33.78)	15.13	(3.21)	3.36
15	(14.24)	33.79	10.14	129.01	(30.26)	12.26	(2.87)	3.01
16	(12.57)	42.82	9.03	102.17	(26.84)	9.71	(2.55)	2.69
17	(10.95)	50.77	7.95	78.67	(23.50)	7.47	(2.24)	2.36
18	(9.40)	57.65	6.88	58.42	(20.25)	5.55	(1.92)	2.05
19	(7.90)	63.50	5.85	41.31	(17.11)	3.92	(1.63)	1.73
20	(6.45)	68.32	4.82	27.26	(14.05)	2.59	(1.33)	1.45
21	(5.05)	72.14	3.82	16.19	(11.07)	1.54	(1.05)	1.15
22	(3.72)	74.97	2.83	8.02	(8.17)	.76	(.78)	.84
23	(2.42)	76.84	1.87	2.65	(5.37)	.25	(.51)	.57
24	(78.96)	–0–	(76.84)	–0–	(2.65)	–0–	(.25)	.28
	$ 95.67							$95.67

Adjusted reserves on life insurance are Rule-of-78 unearned premiums, and for health insurance, modified pro rata unearned premiums. Acquisition cost deferrals and, where applicable, experience rating refund accruals have been adjusted to bases that conform with the methods of recognizing premium revenues.

It is interesting to note that the adjustments result in a reduction of income relative to statutory in the case of bank type business.

Crazy Quilt's credit health experience deteriorated in 1970, a year in which the economy slumped. As the tables indicate, Crazy Quilt's credit insurance margins are relatively thin and quite volatile, particularly margins on credit health.

Income Statement Classifications

The question arises as to whether to reflect changes in unearned premium* reserves in the premium account (i.e., as a revenue item) or in the reserve increase account (i.e., as an expense item).

Where credit insurance is incidental to the company's business, increases in unearned premiums should preferably be recorded in the reserve increase account to retain intra-statement consistency.

Where credit insurance accounts for substantially

*This encompasses those situations in which actuarial reserves are provided and sufficient "additional reserves" are provided to bring total reserves up to the equivalent of unearned premium reserves.

Table 20–10.

CREDIT HEALTH CASH TRANSACTIONS AND STATUTORY PRE-TAX INCOME—PER $1,000 OF SINGLE PREMIUM ORIGINALLY ISSUED—BANK TYPE BUSINESS

Month	Premiums Received	Interest on Assets	Rule-of-78 Refunds	Claims	Adminis-trative Fees	Experience Refunds	Premium Taxes	Adminis-trative Expenses	Cash Flow	Change in ERR Liability*	Change in Statutory Reserve**	Statutory Pre-Tax Income
1	$1,000.00	$ 3.96	$ 9.20	$ 31.79	$49.54		$19.81	$26.50	$ 867.12	$(28.00)	$(910.80)	$(71.68)
2		3.80	8.34	31.47	(.42)		(.16)	1.48	(36.91)	(26.56)	84.25	20.78
3		3.65	7.54	29.43	(.38)		(.14)	1.47	(34.27)	(25.16)	79.42	19.99
4		3.49	6.79	29.13	(.34)		(.13)	1.45	(33.41)	(23.76)	74.71	17.54
5		335	6.08	27.14	(.30)		(.12)	1.44	(30.89)	(22.42)	70.13	16.82
6		3.21	5.42	26.87	(.27)		(.10)	1.42	(30.13)	(21.08)	65.65	14.44
7		3.08	4.80	24.94	(.24)		(.09)	1.41	(27.74)	(19.77)	61.29	13.78
8		2.95	4.22	24.69	(.21)		(.08)	1.39	(27.06)	(18.49)	57.04	11.49
9		2.84	3.69	22.81	(.18)		(.07)	1.38	(24.79)	(17.22)	52.90	10.89
10		2.74	3.19	22.59	(.16)		(.06)	1.37	(24.19)	(15.99)	48.88	8.70
11		2.62	2.74	20.76	(.14)		(.05)	1.35	(22.04)	(14.78)	44.97	8.15
12		1.40	2.32	20.55	(.12)	$246.80	(.04)	1.34	(269.45)	233.23	41.10	4.88
13		1.32	1.95	18.78	(.10)		(.03)	1.32	(20.60)	(12.40)	37.41	4.41
14		1.21	1.60	18.59	(.08)		(.03)	1.31	(20.18)	(11.25)	33.78	2.35
15		1.14	1.30	16.88	(.07)		(.02)	1.30	(18.25)	(10.14)	30.26	1.87
16		1.07	1.03	16.71	(.05)		(.02)	1.29	(17.89)	(9.03)	26.84	(.08)
17		.98	.79	15.03	(.04)		(.01)	1.27	(16.06)	(7.95)	23.50	(.51)
18		.90	.59	14.88	(.04)		Nil	1.26	(15.79)	(6.88)	20.25	(2.42)
19		.85	.41	13.26	(.02)		Nil	1.25	(14.05)	(5.85)	17.11	(2.79)
20		.78	.27	13.13	(.01)		Nil	1.23	(13.84)	(4.82)	14.05	(4.61)
21		.72	.16	11.55	(.01)		Nil	1.22	(12.20)	(3.82)	11.07	(4.95)
22		.67	.08	11.44	Nil		Nil	1.21	(12.06)	(2.83)	8.17	(6.72)
23		.61	.02	9.90	Nil		Nil	1.20	(10.51)	(1.87)	5.37	(7.01)
24		.22	-0-	9.81	-0-	77.77	-0-	1.19	(88.55)	76.84	2.65	(9.06)
	$1,000.00	$47.56	$72.53	$482.13	$46.36	$324.57	$18.66	$57.05	$ 46.26	$ -0-	$ -0-	$ 46.26

*Experience rating refund liability accrued on Rule-of-78 basis.
**Rule-of-78 unearned premiums.

all the company's business, it would appear that either treatment would be appropriate. Since the business is being accounted for in a manner similar to the accounting for property-liability insurance, precedence would appear to be on the side of reporting premiums on an "earned" basis, i.e., recording changes in unearned premiums in the premium account.

Where property-liability and life insurance company financial statements are consolidated and both types of companies write credit health insurance, the treatment of changes in the unearned premium reserve should be consistent. The method to be used should be a function, at least in part, of the relative significance of property-liability premiums to consolidated premiums.

Disclosure

Generally, credit life and health insurance accounting practices would not warrant disclosures beyond those appropriate for any line of business. Where the volume of credit insurance is significant, accounting policies applicable to credit insurance should be described in the accounting policies note and acquisition cost details should be included in the note that sets forth amounts deferred and amortized during the period. Instead of describing mortality, interest, and withdrawal bases it would normally be appropriate to limit the description of the reserve bases to "Rule-of-78 unearned premiums", "modified pro rata unearned premiums", and similar descriptions.

Table 20–11.

PURE CASUALTY APPROACH—CREDIT HEALTH BUSINESS—BANK TYPE—PER $1,000 SINGLE PREMIUM ORIGINALLY ISSUED

Month	Cash Flow, Excluding Interest and Maintenance Expenses	Rule-of-78 Experience Rating Refund Liability Level	Change	Unearned Premium Reserve Level	Change	Equity in Unearned Premium Reserve Level	Change	Modified Pro-Rata Experience Rating Refund Liability Level	Change	Unearned Premium Reserve Level	Change	Equity in Unearned Premium Reserve Level	Change	Underwriting Income Rule-of-78	Modified Pro-Rata
1	$864.66	$ 28.00	$ 28.00	$910.80	$910.80	$86.53	$86.53	$ 21.06	$ 21.06	$930.60	$930.60	$88.41	$88.41	$12.39	$ 1.41
2	(39.23)	54.56	26.56	826.55	(84.25)	78.52	(8.01)	41.97	20.91	862.49	(68.11)	81.94	(6.47)	10.45	1.50
3	(36.45)	79.72	25.16	747.13	(79.42)	70.98	(7.54)	61.58	19.61	798.88	(63.61)	75.89	(6.05)	10.27	1.50
4	(35.45)	103.48	23.76	672.42	(74.71)	63.88	(7.10)	81.04	19.46	736.45	(62.43)	69.96	(5.93)	8.40	1.59
5	(32.80)	125.90	22.42	602.29	(70.13)	57.22	(6.66)	99.24	18.20	678.37	(58.08)	64.45	(5.51)	8.25	1.57
6	(31.92)	146.98	21.08	536.64	(65.65)	50.98	(6.24)	117.29	18.05	621.38	(56.99)	59.03	(5.42)	6.41	1.60
7	(29.41)	166.75	19.77	475.35	(61.29)	45.16	(5.82)	134.10	16.81	568.56	(52.82)	54.01	(5.02)	6.29	1.58
8	(28.62)	185.24	18.49	418.31	(57.04)	39.74	(5.42)	150.76	16.66	516.74	(51.82)	49.09	(4.92)	4.51	1.62
9	(26.25)	202.46	17.22	365.41	(52.90)	34.71	(5.03)	166.20	15.44	468.94	(47.80)	44.55	(4.54)	4.40	1.57
10	(25.56)	218.45	15.99	316.53	(48.88)	30.07	(4.64)	181.50	15.30	422.04	(46.90)	40.09	(4.46)	2.69	1.58
11	(23.31)	233.23	14.78	271.56	(44.97)	25.80	(4.27)	195.60	14.10	379.02	(43.02)	36.01	(4.08)	2.61	1.53
12	(269.51)	-0-	(233.23)	230.46	(41.10)	21.89	(3.91)	(37.25)	(232.85)	336.83	(42.19)	32.00	(4.01)	.91	1.52
13	(20.60)	12.40	12.40	193.05	(37.41)	18.34	(3.55)	(24.47)	12.78	298.36	(38.47)	28.34	(3.66)	.86	1.43
14	(20.08)	23.65	11.25	159.27	(33.78)	15.13	(3.21)	(11.82)	12.65	260.62	(37.74)	24.76	(3.58)	(.76)	1.43
15	(18.09)	33.79	10.14	129.01	(30.26)	12.26	(2.87)	(.33)	11.49	226.48	(34.14)	21.52	(3.24)	(.84)	1.32
16	(17.67)	42.82	9.03	102.17	(26.84)	9.71	(2.55)	11.03	11.36	192.99	(33.49)	18.33	(3.19)	(2.41)	1.27
17	(15.77)	50.77	7.95	78.67	(23.50)	7.47	(2.24)	21.26	10.23	162.97	(30.02)	15.48	(2.85)	(2.46)	1.17
18	(15.43)	57.65	6.88	58.42	(20.25)	5.55	(1.92)	31.36	10.10	133.52	(29.45)	12.68	(2.80)	(3.98)	1.12
19	(13.65)	63.50	5.85	41.31	(17.11)	3.92	(1.63)	40.36	9.00	107.40	(26.12)	10.20	(2.48)	(4.02)	.99
20	(13.39)	68.32	4.82	27.26	(14.05)	2.59	(1.33)	49.23	8.87	81.79	(25.61)	7.77	(2.43)	(5.49)	.92
21	(11.70)	72.14	3.82	16.19	(11.07)	1.54	(1.05)	57.02	7.79	59.38	(22.41)	5.64	(2.13)	(5.50)	.79
22	(11.52)	74.97	2.83	8.02	(8.17)	.76	(.78)	64.69	7.67	37.40	(21.98)	3.55	(2.09)	(6.96)	.70
23	(9.92)	76.84	1.87	2.65	(5.37)	.25	(.51)	71.29	6.60	18.51	(18.89)	1.76	(1.79)	(6.93)	.58
24	(87.58)	-0-	(76.84)	-0-	(2.65)	-0-	(.25)	-0-	(71.29)	-0-	(18.51)	-0-	(1.76)	(8.34)	.46
	$ 30.75													$30.75	$30.75

Table 20–12.

COINSURANCE CEDED—CREDIT HEALTH—AUTO DEALER/PERSONAL PROPERTY BROKER TYPE BUSINESS—
PER $1,000 OF PREMIUM ORIGINALLY CEDED

| | | | | | | | | Change in Modified Pro-Rata Reserve | | Decrease (Increase) in Reported Net Income | |
Month	Premiums Paid	Interest Foregone	Refunds Reimbursed	Claims Reimbursed	Allowances Received	Net Cash Outflow (Inflow)	Rule-of-78 Reserve	Unearned Premium Adjustment	Allowance Adjustment	Rule-of-78*	Modified Pro-Rata
1	$ 89.20	$.08	$ 9.20	$ 31.79	$ 40.00	$ 8.29		$ 19.80	$(9.90)	$ 8.29	$ (1.61)
2	84.25	.13	8.34	31.47	37.94	6.63		16.14	(8.07)	6.63	(1.44)
3	79.42	.16	7.54	29.42	35.93	6.69		15.81	(7.90)	6.69	(1.22)
4	74.71	.20	6.79	29.13	33.96	5.03		12.28	(6.14)	5.03	(1.11)
5	70.13	.19	6.08	27.14	32.01/	5.09		12.05	(6.03)	5.09	(.93)
6	65.65	.22	5.42	26.87	30.11	3.47		8.66	(4.33)	3.47	(.86)
7	61.29	.23	4.80	24.94	28.24	3.54	NO	8.47	(4.23)	3.54	(.70)
8	57.04	.23	4.22	24.69	26.40	1.96	RE-	5.22	(2.61)	1.96	(.65)
9	52.90	.24	3.69	22.81	24.60	2.04	SERVE;	5.10	(2.55)	2.04	(.51)
10	48.88	.23	3.19	22.59	22.83	.50	PRE-	1.98	(.99)	.50	(.49)
11	44.97	.22	2.74	20.76	21.10	.59	MIUMS	1.95	(.98)	.59	(.38)
12	41.10	.26	2.32	20.55	19.40	(.91)	AND	(1.09)	.55	(.91)	(.37)
13	37.41	.21	1.95	18.78	17.72	(.83)	COMMIS-	(1.06)	.53	(.83)	(.30)
14	33.78	.22	1.60	18.59	16.09	(2.28)	SIONS	(3.96)	1.98	(2.28)	(.30)
15	30.26	.19	1.30	16.87	14.47	(2.19)	PAID ON	(3.88)	1.94	(2.19)	(.25)
16	26.84	.17	1.03	16.71	12.89	(3.62)	RULE-	(6.65)	3.33	(3.62)	(.30)
17	23.50	.15	.79	15.03	11.35	(3.52)	OF-78	(6.52)	3.26	(3.52)	(.26)
18	20.25	.15	.59	14.88	9.83	(4.90)	BASIS	(9.20)	4.60	(4.90)	(.30)
19	17.11	.10	.41	13.26	8.34	(4.80)		(9.01)	4.50	(4.80)	(.29)
20	14.05	.08	.27	13.13	6.88	(6.15)		(11.56)	5.78	(6.15)	(.37)
21	11.07	.04	.16	11.55	5.45	(6.05)		(11.34)	5.67	(6.05)	(.38)
22	8.17	.03	.08	11.44	4.04	(7.36)		(13.81)	6.90	(7.36)	(.45)
23	5.37	(.01)	.02	9.90	2.67	(7.23)		(13.52)	6.76	(7.23)	(.47)
24	2.65	(.05)	–0–	9.81	1.32	(8.53)		(15.86)	7.93	(8.53)	(.60)
	$1,000.00	$3.67	$72.53	$482.11	$463.57	$(14.54)				$(14.54)	$(14.54)

*Same as statutory.

Group Term Life and Health Insurance

It appears to be commonly accepted that it is not necessary to "adjust" group term life and health insurance for one or all of the following reasons:

1. The adjustments would be immaterial; statutory is an acceptable approximation of adjusted.
2. Allocation of acquisition costs would be arbitrary in the extreme because of the nature of group expenses.
3. As for experience-rated cases, most of any adjustments would have to be reserved for in the form of a deferred experience rating refund liability.
4. Group business is too volatile to justify adjustment.

Some of the reasons are somewhat contradictory.

For example, some recognition must be accorded to expenses—including the amount and incidence of acquisition costs—in establishing retention formulas for experience-rated business; arbitrary or not, some degree of rationality must be presumed. And just as some adjustments might wind up being deferred as an experience rating refund liability, those same liabilities serve to cushion the volatility of group experience.

As a general proposition, it is probably safe to say that adjustments for group term life and health insurance will rarely be made. But such a decision should be based not on glib assumptions but on analysis of prevailing facts and circumstances. Group insurance is one of the more creative lines of business; every company operates somewhat differently. Different types of operations require different types of accounting approaches.

Table 20–13.

COINSURANCE CEDED—CREDIT HEALTH—AUTO DEALER/PERSONAL PROPERTY BROKER TYPE BUSINESS— PER $1,000 SINGLE PREMIUM ORIGINALLY CEDED

Month	Premiums Paid	Interest Foregone	Refunds Reimbursed	Claims Reimbursed	Allowances Received	Net Cash Outflow (Inflow)	Statutory Reserve	Change in Rule-of-78 Reserve — Unearned Premium	Acquisition Costs	Decrease (Increase) in Reported Net Income — Statutory	Rule-of-78
1	$1,000.00	$ 2.16	$ 9.20	$ 36.00	$495.40	$461.56	$728.64	$910.80	$(457.00)	$(267.08)	$ 7.76
2		2.00	8.34	34.15	(4.17)	(36.32)	(67.40)	(84.25)	41.00	31.08	6.93
3		1.83	7.54	32.34	(3.77)	(34.28)	(63.54)	(79.42)	39.00	29.26	6.14
4		1.69	6.79	30.56	(3.39)	(32.27)	(59.77)	(74.71)	36.50	27.50	5.94
5		1.54	6.08	28.81	(3.04)	(30.31)	(56.10)	(70.13)	34.50	25.79	5.32
6		1.41	5.42	27.10	(2.71)	(28.40)	(52.52)	(65.65)	32.50	24.12	4.75
7		1.28	4.80	25.41	(2.40)	(26.53)	(49.03)	(61.29)	30.50	22.50	4.26
8		1.17	4.22	23.76	(2.11)	(24.70)	(45.63)	(57.04)	28.50	20.93	3.84
9		1.07	3.69	22.14	(1.84)	(22.92)	(42.32)	(52.90)	26.50	19.40	3.48
10		.97	3.19	20.55	(1.59)	(21.18)	(39.10)	(48.88)	24.50	17.92	3.20
11		.87	2.74	18.99	(1.37)	(19.49)	(35.96)	(44.97)	22.50	16.47	2.98
12		.78	2.32	17.45	(1.16)	(17.83)	(32.90)	(41.10)	21.00	15.07	2.27
13		.72	1.95	15.95	(.97)	(16.21)	(29.93)	(37.41)	19.00	13.72	2.20
14		.63	1.60	14.47	(.80)	(14.64)	(27.02)	(33.78)	17.50	12.38	1.64
15		.59	1.30	13.03	(.65)	(13.09)	(24.21)	(30.26)	15.50	11.12	1.67
16		.53	1.03	11.61	(.51)	(11.60)	(21.47)	(26.84)	14.00	9.87	1.24
17		.47	.79	10.21	(.39)	(10.14)	(18.80)	(23.50)	12.00	8.66	1.36
18		.45	.59	8.85	(.29)	(8.70)	(16.21)	(20.25)	10.50	7.51	1.05
19		.40	.41	7.51	(.20)	(7.32)	(13.68)	(17.11)	9.00	6.36	.79
20		.37	.27	6.19	(.13)	(5.96)	(11.24)	(14.05)	7.50	5.28	.59
21		.33	.16	4.90	(.08)	(4.65)	(8.85)	(11.07)	6.00	4.20	.42
22		.33	.08	3.64	(.04)	(3.35)	(6.55)	(8.17)	4.50	3.20	.32
23		.31	.02	2.40	(.01)	(2.10)	(4.29)	(5.37)	3.00	2.19	.27
24		.31	–0–	1.19	–0–	(.88)	(2.12)	(2.65)	1.50	1.24	.27
	$1,000.00	$22.21	$72.53	$417.21	$463.78	$ 68.69				$ 68.69	$68.69

Group Products

Group products include a seemingly endless array of coverages. One company's group underwriting manual, for example, lists 20 major classifications of coverage, with innumerable sub-classifications and variations within the 20 major classifications. They can be categorized as follows:

Term life
Paid-up life
Accidental death and dismemberment
Accident and sickness
Long-term disability
Hospital expense
Surgical expense
Medical expense
Major medical expense
Comprehensive medical expense
Dental expense
Group permanent

Various supplemental benefits, such as the waiver of premium benefit, extended coverage, and a total disability benefit are also available. Many coverages can be converted to individual plans upon withdrawal from the group.

Group Pricing

Group rate manuals are developed based on an extensive analysis of risks—risks associated with the type of group insured, the size of the group, the type of industry represented by the group, geographical location, and other factors.

For smaller groups whose experience is pooled, rates are usually not retroactively adjustable; adjustments are typically prospective. For larger groups subject to experience rating, rates may be effectively adjusted through the experience rating process described below.

Group insurance pricing is not unlike property-liability pricing. The insurance company hopes its

Table 20–14.

SUMMARY OF CRAZY QUILT LIFE'S CREDIT INSURANCE UNDERWRITING EXPERIENCE FOR AUTO DEALER/
PERSONAL PROPERTY BROKER TYPE BUSINESS, 1968–1971 (000 Omitted)

	Life				*Health*			
	1968	1969	1970	1971	1968	1969	1970	1971
Statutory:								
Revenues:								
Premiums:								
Written	$ 500	$ 700	$1,000	$1,500	$ 500	$ 700	$1,000	$1,500
Ceded			(300)				(139)	(143)
Net	500	700	700	1,500	500	700	861	1,357
Coinsurance fees			29	(1)			13	13
TOTAL REVENUES	500	700	729	1,499	500	700	874	1,370
Benefits and expenses:								
Refunds	22	44	51	86	22	44	51	86
Claims	89	256	301	412	75	217	340	478
Commissions	191	262	260	566	191	262	324	508
Taxes	10	13	19	28	10	13	19	28
Solicitation	13	17	25	38	13	17	25	38
Maintenance	1	5	8	11	4	14	24	34
	326	597	664	1,141	315	567	783	1,172
Income before reserve changes	174	103	65	358	185	133	91	198
Change in benefit reserves	(215)	(109)	(9)	(343)	(268)	(136)	(173)	(286)
UNDERWRITING INCOME	$ (41)	$ (6)	$ 56	$ 15	$ (83)	$ (3)	$ (82)	$ (88)
Adjusted:								
Income before reserve changes	$ 174	$ 103	$ 65	$ 358	$ 185	$ 133	$ 91	$ 198
Changes in:								
Benefit reserves	(268)	(136)	(12)	(429)	(311)	(191)	(188)	(354)
Unamortized acquisition costs	119	61	29	170	138	85	92	156
UNDERWRITING INCOME	$ 25	$ 28	$ 82	$ 99	$ 12	$ 27	$ (5)	$ –0–
Adjusted underwriting income as percentage of premiums earned:								
Net premiums written	$ 500	$ 700	$ 700	$1,500	$ 500	$ 700	$ 861	$1,357
Refunds	(22)	(44)	(51)	(86)	(22)	(44)	(51)	(86)
Change in reserves	(268)	(136)	(12)	(429)	(311)	(191)	(188)	(354)
Net premiums earned	$ 210	$ 520	$ 637	$ 985	$ 167	$ 465	$ 622	$ 917
Underwriting income:								
Amount	$ 25	$ 28	$ 82	$ 99	$ 12	$ 27	$ (5)	$ –0–
Percentage of premiums earned	12%	5%	13%	10%	7%	6%	(1)%	–0–%

rates will prove to be adequate and that any deficiency will be covered by future rate increases or the experience rating process. In periods of rising frequency and/or severity, rates seem at times to lag perpetually behind experience, particularly in the health lines. Many companies suffered severe losses in the late 1960s and early 1970s as competition drove rates down while inflation and other adverse developments drove claims up.* Recently the major carriers have been less impressed with volume and more impressed with profits; "shopping" group insurance has become less rewarding; companies have been monitoring the

*One group insurance specialist put it this way in an interview in early 1971: "Group insurance is only for the stout of heart and surplus."

business closely and demanding higher rates; and the sometimes enormous losses of recent years appear to have been stemmed by many companies.

Experience Rating

Experience rating, limited typically to groups large enough to produce credible experience, usually involves the maintenance of an "account" with each policyholder. The account, usually divided between life and health, is credited with premiums (and sometimes interest) and is charged with claims paid, increases in claim liabilities, increases in various special reserves ("contingency" reserves, "credibility" reserves, "stabilization" reserves, and similar items which are designed as a hedge against adversity and as a source of invest-

Table 20–15.

SUMMARY OF CRAZY QUILT LIFE'S CREDIT INSURANCE EXPERIENCE FOR BANK TYPE BUSINESS, 1968–1971
(000 Omitted)

	Life				Health			
	1968	*1969*	*1970*	*1971*	*1968*	*1969*	*1970*	*1971*
Statutory:								
Premiums written	$ 500	$ 700	$1,000	$1,500	$ 500	$ 700	$1,000	$1,500
Benefits and expenses								
Refunds	22	44	64	94	22	44	64	94
Claims	84	221	342	474	76	198	355	523
Experience refunds		123	212	301		123	212	301
Administrative fees	24	33	47	70	24	33	47	70
Taxes	10	13	19	28	10	13	19	28
Solicitation	13	17	25	38	13	17	25	38
Maintenance	1	5	8	11	4	14	24	34
	154	456	717	1,016	149	442	746	1,088
Income before reserve changes	346	244	283	484	351	258	254	412
Changes in:								
Benefit reserves	(215)	(109)	(138)	(229)	(268)	(136)	(173)	(286)
ERR liability	(68)	(54)	(51)	(84)	(68)	(54)	(51)	(84)
UNDERWRITING INCOME	$ 63	$ 81	$ 94	$ 171	$ 15	$ 68	$ 30	$ 42
Adjusted:								
Income before reserve changes	$ 346	$ 244	$ 283	$ 484	$ 351	$ 258	$ 254	$ 412
Changes in:								
Benefit reserves	(268)	(136)	(173)	(286)	(311)	(191)	(213)	(351)
ERR liability	(68)	(54)	(51)	(84)	(58)	(34)	(32)	(61)
Unamortized acquisition costs	25	13	16	27	30	18	20	33
UNDERWRITING INCOME	$ 35	$ 67	$ 75	$ 141	$ 12	$ 51	$ 29	$ 33
Adjusted underwriting income as percentage of premiums earned:								
Premiums written	$ 500	$ 700	$1,000	$1,500	$ 500	$ 700	$1,000	$1,500
Refunds	(22)	(44)	(64)	(94)	(22)	(44)	(64)	(94)
Change in reserves	(268)	(136)	(173)	(286)	(311)	(191)	(213)	(351)
Premiums earned	$ 210	$ 520	$ 763	$1,120	$ 167	$ 465	$ 723	$1,055
Underwriting income:								
Amount	35	67	75	141	12	51	29	33
Percentage of premiums earned	17%	13%	10%	13%	7%	11%	4%	3%

ment income), and a "retention" charge to cover commissions, premium taxes, administrative expenses, risk, and profit. Any balance remaining in the experience rating account is either paid back to the policyholder or is held on deposit at interest. Any amounts held on deposit are usually available to buffer losses, if any.

When separate experience rating accounts are maintained for life and health coverages, it is typical for a surplus on one to be used to offset a deficit on the other. When this is the case, the accounting distinction between life and health is somewhat artificial. Life and health coverages are often sold as a package, and many companies evaluate group operations in terms of combined results.

Cost Accounting

For various reasons, group insurance expenses are very difficult to account for. Few companies are able to develop expense formulas that will reproduce company expenses. Intercompany comparisons, such as those made for ordinary and industrial life and individual health lines under the LOMA program (see Chapter 13), have not been successful when attempted because of the great variety in group operations.

Nevertheless, as discussed below, some form of cost accounting is needed for purposes of ratemaking and experience rating. To the extent that such cost accounting can be demonstrated to be reasonable and fairly reliable, it could serve as a basis for the deferral of acquisition costs.

Table 20–16.

DETAILS OF EXPERIENCE RATING FOR RETENTION CASE NO. 1, 1965–1971

	1965 Experience Rating Refund	1965 Operating Statement	1966 Experience Rating Refund	1966 Operating Statement	1967 Experience Rating Refund	1967 Operating Statement	1968 Experience Rating Refund	1968 Operating Statement	1969 Experience Rating Refund	1969 Operating Statement	1970 Experience Rating Refund	1970 Operating Statement	1971 Experience Rating Refund	1971 Operating Statement
LIFE:														
Balance forward	$ -0-		$ 104,058		$ 472,345		$ 1,005,625		$ 1,510,924		$ 1,842,077		$ 2,546,538	
Premiums	1,012,237	$1,012,237	1,028,398	$1,028,398	1,877,736	$1,877,736	2,690,702	$2,690,702	2,901,840	$2,901,840	3,078,524	$3,078,524	3,169,274	$3,169,274
Claims	(906,885)	(906,885)	(655,657)	(655,657)	(1,349,169)	(1,349,169)	(2,174,020)	(2,174,020)	(2,479,315)	(2,479,315)	(2,447,868)	(2,447,868)	(3,217,882)	(3,217,882)
Retention	(40,894)	-0-	(32,395)	-0-	(61,590)	-0-	(94,713)	-0-	(128,841)	-0-	(123,450)	-0-	(160,649)	-0-
Transfer from health	37,050	-0-	13,911	-0-	29,045	-0-	16,069	-0-	(51,683)	-0-	74,449	-0-	28,704	-0-
Interest on fund	2,550	-0-	14,030	-0-	37,258	-0-	67,261	-0-	89,152	-0-	122,806	-0-	152,538	-0-
Net	104,058	(104,058)	368,287	(368,287)	533,280	(533,280)	505,299	(505,299)	331,153	(331,153)	(704,461)	704,461	(28,015)	28,015
Ending ERR liability	$ 104,058		$ 472,345		$1,005,625		$1,510,924		$1,842,077		$2,546,538		$2,518,523	
Expenses:														
Commissions		(4,049)		(2,140)		(3,005)		(4,279)		(4,613)		(4,586)		(5,030)
Acquisition		(43,915)		(-0-)		(12,000)		(-0-)		(-0-)		(7,344)		(-0-)
Claims		(4,534)		(3,278)		(4,047)		(8,072)		(7,438)		(7,344)		(12,872)
General Administrative		(7,895)		(5,350)		(7,810)		(8,185)		(8,765)		(16,945)		(20,290)
Taxes		(16,196)		(16,412)		(31,298)		(53,135)		(66,559)		(62,651)		(83,635)
Operating income before investment income and federal income taxes		(75,295)		(22,726)		(62,873)		(62,288)		3,997		(165,331)		(142,420)
Investment income		8,000		21,000		49,000		93,000		141,000		201,000		247,000
Statutory gain from operations before Federal income taxes		(67,295)		(1,726)		(13,873)		30,712		144,997		35,669		104,580
Acquisition costs deferred		32,295				12,000								
Acquisition costs amortized		(6,459)		(6,459)		(8,859)		(8,859)		(8,859)		(2,400)		(2,400)
Adjusted net income before Federal income taxes		$ (41,459)		$ (8,185)		$ (10,732)		$ 21,853		$ 136,138		$ 33,269		$ 102,180
Acquisition costs:														
Prior balance		$		$ 25,836		$ 19,377		$ 22,518		$ 13,659		$ 4,800		$ 2,400
Deferral		32,295				12,000								
Amortization		(6,459)		(6,459)		(8,859)		(8,859)		(8,859)		(2,400)		(2,400)
Ending balance		$ 25,836		$ 19,377		$ 22,518		$ 13,659		$ 4,800		$ 2,400		$ -0-
HEALTH:														
Balance forward	$ -0-		$ -0-		$ -0-		$ -0-		$ -0-		$ -0-		$ -0-	
Premiums	58,529	$ 58,529	58,023	$ 58,023	85,239	$ 85,239	122,679	$ 122,679	128,190	$ 128,190	133,782	$ 133,782	137,436	$ 137,436
Claims	(19,114)	(19,114)	(42,284)	(42,284)	(53,398)	(53,398)	(102,291)	(102,291)	(174,181)	(174,181)	(53,969)	(53,969)	(101,958)	(101,958)
Retention	(2,365)	-0-	(1,828)	-0-	(2,796)	-0-	(4,319)	-0-	(5,692)	-0-	(5,364)	-0-	(6,774)	-0-
Transfer to life	(37,050)	-0-	(13,911)	-0-	(29,045)	-0-	(16,069)	-0-	51,683	-0-	(74,449)	-0-	(28,704)	-0-
Net	$ -0-	-0-	$ -0-	-0-	$ -0-	-0-	$ -0-	-0-	$ -0-	-0-	$ -0-	-0-	$ -0-	-0-
Ending ERR liability	$ -0-		$ -0-		$ -0-		$ -0-		$ -0-		$ -0-		$ -0-	
Expenses:														
Commissions		(234)		(122)		(136)		(196)		(205)		(200)		(220)
Acquisition		(2,455)		(-0-)		(-0-)		(-0-)		(-0-)		(-0-)		(-0-)
Claims		(478)		(1,057)		(534)		(1,023)		(1,742)		(540)		(1,122)
General administrative		(695)		(550)		(850)		(850)		(850)		(1,185)		(1,195)
Taxes		(936)		(928)		(1,415)		(2,417)		(2,935)		(2,716)		(3,436)
Operating income before investment income and Federal income taxes		34,617		13,082		28,906		15,902		(51,723)		75,172		29,505
Investment income		-0-		-0-		-0-		-0-		1,000		1,000		1,000
Statutory gain from operations before Federal income taxes		34,617		13,082		28,906		15,902		(50,723)		76,172		30,505
Acquisition costs deferred		2,455												
Acquisition costs amortized		(491)		(491)		(491)		(491)		(491)				
Adjusted net income before Federal income taxes		$ 36,581		$ 12,591		$ 28,415		$ 15,411		$ (51,214)		$ 76,172		$ 30,505
Acquisition costs:														
Prior balance		$		$ 1,964		$ 1,473		$ 982		$ 491		$		$
Deferral		2,455												
Amortization		(491)		(491)		(491)		(491)		(491)				
Ending balance		$ 1,964		$ 1,473		$ 982		$ 491		$ -0-		$		$

Reserves

Statutory reserves for group term life insurance are usually carried on the basis of unearned premiums, although recently several companies have switched to mean reserves because of tax advantages.

Statutory reserves for group health insurance also take the form of unearned premium reserves.

Since active life reserves are for very short periods of time, discounting is often ignored. Longer-term obligations—for example, disabled lives reserves for the waiver of premium benefit, total and permanent disability benefits provided in connection with life insurance,* and long-term disability benefits—are usually provided for on an actuarial basis with interest rates in the range of 2 1/2 to 3 1/2 percent.

The statutory basis of reserving for active life reserves will usually be suitable for adjusted statements, too. As for longer-term obligations, it may be appropriate to use more realistic assumptions if the amounts involved are sizeable. However, as will be discussed below, reserve adjustments on experience-rated cases that are not in a deficit position would usually result in an equal and offsetting entry in the experience rating refund liability. When most of the indicated adjustments would be so treated, it seems unnecessary to make them.

Retention Business

Perhaps the best way to discuss retention business is to examine the workings of a couple of retention cases and analyze their accounting implications.

Crazy Quilt Life entered the group business in a small way in 1956, writing some experience-rated business for some medium-sized groups. In 1961 Crazy Quilt entered the "baby group" field and during the 1960s began to take on larger retention cases.

Case No. 1. Crazy Quilt issued a group policy to a large manufacturing company in 1965; the case persisted to 1971. Most of the coverage was life insurance; the policyholder carried its health insurance with Blue Cross. The only health insurance carried with Crazy Quilt was accidental death and dismemberment insurance.

Since the contract was dated January 1 and premiums were payable monthly, Crazy Quilt carried no unearned premiums at year-end. There were, of course, claim liabilities and claim reserves at year-end.

*Total and permanent disability reserves are often provided for on the basis of a percentage—e.g., 75 percent—of the face amount.

The policyholder agreed to leave all experience rating refunds on deposit at interest with Crazy Quilt.

The experience rating account with the policyholder showed the following transactions in 1965, the first year of the contract (which coincided with the calendar year):

| | 000 | | |
	Life	Health	Total
Premiums earned	$1,012	$ 58	$1,070
Interest credited on experience rating fund	3	–0–	3
Claims incurred	(907)	(19)	(926)
Retention	(41)	(2)	(43)
Balance before transfer	67	37	104
Transfer	37	(37)	–0–
Balance after transfer	$ 104	$–0–	$ 104

Claims incurred included a provision for outstanding claims and incurred but not reported claims of $279,000. Interest on the experience rating fund was credited quarterly on the fund. No interest was paid on claim liabilities or other noncash charges.

Retention was based on an agreement with the policyholder, who was charged for the following items:

Commissions	$ 4,283
Premium taxes	17,132
Operating expenses	11,778
Risk charge	5,889
Profit	4,177
	$43,259

Commissions and premium taxes were actual amounts. Operating expenses were based on a formula that included provision for amortization of acquisition costs over five years; the expense formula was negotiated but was based generally on an analysis of actual expenses. The risk charge was a normal one for a case of this size; it, plus the profit charge, represented in effect Crazy Quilt's "fee" for assuming risk and administering the coverage.

The retention charges of $43,000 did not, however, precisely correspond with actual costs allocable to the contract, which were $81,000, as follows:

| | 000 | | |
	Life	Health	Total
Commissions	$ 4	$nil	$ 4*
Acquisition costs	44	2	46
Claims processing	4	1	5
General administrative	8	1	9
Premium taxes	16	1	17*
	$76	$5	$81

*Same as amount included in retention charge.

Table 20–17.

DETAILS OF EXPERIENCE RATING FOR RETENTION CASE NO. 2 FOR SELECTED YEARS

	Experience Rating Fund			Effect on Statutory Summary of Operations*			Combined Statutory Liabilities			Combined Adjusted Income* if Acquisition Costs and Deficits are Deferred
	Life	Health	Combined	Life	Health	Combined	Claim Liability	Contingency Reserve	Experience Rating Refunds	
1956 (initial year):										
Beginning balance	$ -0-	$ -0-	$ -0-				$ -0-	$ -0-	$ -0-	
Premiums	3,837	19,050	22,887	$ 3,837	$ 19,050	$ 22,887				$ 22,887
Claims - paid	-0-	(8,208)	(8,208)	-0-	(8,208)	(8,208)				(8,208)
- change in liability	-0-	(3,508)	(3,508)	-0-	(3,508)	(3,508)	3,508			(3,508)
Change in contingency reserve	(1,919)	-0-	(1,919)	(1,919)	-0-	(1,919)		1,919		(1,919)
Retention	(1,019)	(5,058)	(6,077)							
Experience refunds paid	(899)	(2,276)	(3,175)	(899)	(2,276)	(3,175)				(3,175)
Expenses				(3,412)	(11,030)	(14,442)				(7,794)
Net change in fund	-0-	-0-	-0-	$ (2,393)	$ (5,972)	$ (8,365)				
Ending balance	$ -0-	$ -0-	$ -0-				$ 3,508	$ 1,919	$ -0-	$ (1,717)
1964 (deficit):										
Beginning balance	$ -0-	$ (9,303)	$ (9,303)				$ 39,947	$ -0-	$ -0-	
Premiums	17,816	135,733	153,549	$ 17,816	$ 135,733	$ 153,549				$ 153,549
Claims - paid	(11,524)	(136,964)	(148,488)	(11,524)	(136,964)	(148,488)				(148,488)
- change in liability	-0-	(4,415)	(4,415)	-0-	(4,415)	(4,415)	4,415			(4,415)
Retention	(2,138)	(16,288)	(18,426)							
Transfer	(4,154)	4,154	-0-							
Expenses				(2,033)	(12,368)	(14,401)				(14,401)
Net change in fund	-0-	(17,780)	(17,780)	$ 4,259	$ (18,014)	$ (13,755)				17,780
Ending balance	$ -0-	$ (27,083)	$ (27,083)				$ 44,362	$ -0-	$ -0-	$ 4,025
1966 (recovery of deficit):										
Beginning balance	$ -0-	$ (27,072)	$ (27,072)				$ 49,112	$ -0-	$ -0-	
Premiums	26,316	272,486	298,802	$ 26,316	$ 272,486	$ 298,802				$ 298,802
Claims - paid	(5,947)	(196,762)	(202,709)	(5,947)	(196,762)	(202,709)				(202,709)
- change in liability	3,325	(14,267)	(10,942)	3,325	(14,267)	(10,942)	10,942			(10,942)
Retention	(2,179)	(22,562)	(24,741)							
Expenses				(2,304)	(18,967)	(21,271)				(21,271)
Net change in fund	21,515	38,895	60,410	(21,515)	(11,823)	(33,338)			33,338	(60,410)
Ending balance	$ 21,515	$ 11,823	$ 33,338	$ (125)	$ 30,667	$ 30,542	$ 60,054	$ -0-	$ 33,338	$ 3,470

1971 (stable surplus):

Beginning balance	$ 47,500	$ 23,750	$ 71,250				$293,669	$ –0–	$ 71,250
Premiums	148,102	1,174,919	1,323,021	$ 148,102	$1,174,919	$1,323,021			1,323,021
Claims – paid	(52,910)	(996,111)	(1,049,021)	(52,910)	(996,111)	(1,049,021)			(1,049,021)
– change in liability							(7,719)		
Retention	44,769	(37,050)	7,719	44,769	(37,050)	7,719			7,719
Interest on fund balance	(8,279)	(65,677)	(73,956)						
Experience refunds paid	2,137	1,069	3,206	(133,819)	(77,150)	(210,969)			(210,969)
Expenses	(133,819)	(77,150)	(210,969)	(6,420)	(42,225)	(48,645)			(48,645)
Net change in fund	–0–	–0–	–0–	(278)	22,383	22,105		–0–	22,105
Ending balance	$ 47,500	$ 23,750	$ 71,250			$ 22,105	$285,950	$ –0–	$ 22,105

*Before allocation of investment income and taxes.

Thus there was an unfavorable variance between actual expenses and retention charges. The reason is that the retention charge was negotiated, and Crazy Quilt was unable to charge the experience rating fund with the full amount of allocable expenses for competitive reasons. Among other things, acquisition costs were amortized for purposes of calculating retentions over a five-year period. As one might expect, retention charges soon recovered acquisition costs and produced a favorable balance:

Year	Retention Charges	Actual Expenses	Excess or (Deficiency)
1965	$ 43	$ 81	$(38)
1966	34	29	5
1967	64	60	4
1968	99	78	21
1969	134	93	41
1970	129	96	33
1971	167	128	39

The excess of retention charges over actual expenses, plus investment income earned in excess of interest credited to the experience rating account, were the principal sources of pre-tax profits on the contract.

If a statutory summary of operations were to be made up for the case in 1965, it would appear as follows:

	000		
	Life	Health	Total
Premiums	$1,012	$ 58	$1,070
Investment income	8	nil	8
Claims	(907)	(19)	(926)
Increase in experience rating refund liability	(104)	–0–	(104)
Expenses	(76)	(5)	(81)
Pre-tax statutory gain or (loss)	$ (67)	$ 34	$ (33)

This can be reconciled with the net change in the experience rating refund liability as follows:

	000		
	Life	Health	Total
Pre-tax statutory gain or (loss)	$(67)	$ 34	$(33)
Excess of expenses incurred over retention charged	35	3	38
Excess of interest earned over interest credited	(5)	nil	(5)
Transfer	37	(37)	–0–
Increase in experience rating refund liability	104	–0–	104
	$104	$–0–	$104

It was mentioned that Crazy Quilt's practice is to amortize acquisition costs over a five-year period for purposes of calculating retentions. The company's definition of acquisition costs differed, of course, from the accounting definition of acquisition costs:

	Life	Health
Company definition:		
Per life cost at $1.00	$19,000	
Per contract cost	300	$1,300
Additional coverage cost	50	50
	19,350	1,350
25% credit for 2 coverages	(4,840)	(325)
Fixed cost	350	350
Sales overhead	29,055	430
	43,915	2,455
Accounting definition:		
Non-deferrable development and overhead	11,620	—
	$32,295	$2,455

Crazy Quilt decided to defer and amortize the $34,750 in acquisition costs straight-line over a five-year period to achieve a better matching of retention income and related expenses. The straight-line method and five-year period were chosen because they reasonably related to the patterns assumed for purposes of retention charges.

In 1967 an additional $12,000 in acquisition costs were deferred and amortized because of the addition of a new plant by the policyholder and a resulting bulge in costs to enroll the new employees, set up records, etc.

Crazy Quilt's decision to defer and amortize acquisition costs was made only after a great deal of soul-searching. The issues involved are discusssed later in this chapter.

A reconciliation of the experience rating refund account and statutory and adjusted operating statements for Case No. 1 for the years 1965–1971 is shown in Table 20–16.

Case No. 2. Case No. 2, a combined life-health retention case written in 1956 and persisting to 1971, provided initially that experience rating refunds should be paid as they accrue. Thus Crazy Quilt was not sheltered against adverse experience by retaining experience rating refunds. Instead, the Company set up "contingency reserves" in the early years. As time progressed, however, experience proved to be favorable, and eventually the contingency reserves were eliminated.

In 1963, however, experience deteriorated, and the case developed a deficit. Not until 1966 were rates

Table 20–18.

SUMMARY OF EXPERIENCE ON GROUP RETENTION BUSINESS, 1962–1971 (000 Omitted)

Year	Premiums	Investment Income	Benefits	Expenses	Provision for Experience Rating Refunds	Statutory Pre-Tax	Acquisition Cost Adjustments	Adjusted Pre-Tax
Life:								
1962	$ 15	$Nil	$ 8	$ 1	$(11)	$ 17	$ –0–	$ 17
1963	15	1	2	2	11	1	–0–	1
1964	17	1	11	2	4	1	–0–	1
1965	1,032	9	918	77	72	(26)	26	–0–
1966	1,097	22	704	38	368	9	(2)	7
1967	1,961	52	1,366	62	562	23	(1)	22
1968	2,831	96	2,231	81	562	53	(10)	43
1969	3,034	146	2,554	94	430	102	(11)	91
1970	3,229	208	2,534	97	687	119	(2)	117
1971	3,361	253	3,255	135	86	138	1	139
Health:								
1962	94	1	96	9	8	(18)	–0–	(18)
1963	120	1	120	12	(11)	–0–	–0–	–0–
1964	135	2	141	12	(4)	(12)	–0–	(12)
1965	236	2	183	20	32	3	2	5
1966	436	2	339	37	31	31	4	35
1967	608	8	453	29	113	21	(2)	19
1968	952	13	797	47	92	29	(2)	27
1969	1,007	17	982	47	(41)	36	(3)	33
1970	1,038	20	874	39	102	43	–0–	43
1971	1,857	27	1,690	107	96	(9)	10	1
Combined:								
1962	109	1	104	10	7	(1)	–0–	(1)
1963	135	2	122	14	–0–	1	–0–	1
1964	152	3	152	14	–0–	(11)	–0–	(11)
1965	1,268	11	1,101	97	104	(23)	28	5
1966	1,533	24	1,043	75	399	40	2	42
1967	2,569	60	1,819	91	675	44	(3)	41
1968	3,783	109	3,028	128	654	82	(12)	70
1969	4,041	163	3,536	141	389	138	(14)	124
1970	4,267	228	3,408	136	789	162	(2)	160
1971	5,218	280	4,945	242	182	129	11	140

raised sufficiently to cover the deficit. Thereafter a balance (on which Crazy Quilt paid interest) was retained in the experience rating refund account to cover possible future adverse experience.

The experience rating refund account, and the effect of the case on the summary of operations, are shown in Table 20–17 for four years:

  1956, the initial year
  1964, during which time the case was producing deficits,
  1966, the year in which the accumulated deficit was recovered, and
  1971, a year during which a positive balance was retained in the experience rating refund account.

The interesting question that Case No. 2 raises is what to do with deficits. For purposes of statutory accounting, deficits are ignored, i.e., are effectively charged to operations as they occur. The effect on the statements can be dramatic, since any recovery of a deficit is taken into income in the year of recovery.

Should deficits be deferred for purposes of the adjusted statements? In general, the answer is no. A group policyholder can always terminate his contract, and many do when rates are raised. There is rarely, if ever, any certainty about recovering a deficit. It is the rare case in which a deficit should be deferred. Crazy Quilt's policy was not to defer them.

Acquisition costs. There are five basic criteria that should be satisfied to justify the deferral of acquisition costs on retention business:

Table 20–19.

SUMMARY OF CRAZY QUILT LIFE'S POOLED GROUP EXPERIENCE, 1961–1971 (000 Omitted)											
	1961	1962	1963	1964	1965	1966	1967	1968	1969	1970	1971
Statutory:											
Life:											
Premiums:											
First year	$ 933	$ 285	$ 373	$ 388	$ 461	$ 666	$ 560	$ 254	$ 266	$ 489	$ 325
Renewal		700	739	840	921	1,037	1,277	1,378	1,254	1,140	1,481
Total	933	985	1,112	1,228	1,382	1,703	1,837	1,632	1,520	1,629	1,806
Benefits and expenses:											
Claims incurred	569	552	667	663	788	1,056	1,102	947	836	863	1,120
Commissions	93	99	111	123	138	170	184	163	152	163	181
Premium taxes	19	20	22	25	28	34	37	33	30	33	36
Administrative:											
Acquisition	315	216	130	144	137	220	144	63	65	110	118
Maintenance	109	130	154	148	275	236	221	211	210	213	126
	1,105	1,017	1,084	1,103	1,366	1,716	1,688	1,417	1,293	1,382	1,581
UNDERWRITING INCOME	$ (172)	$ (32)	$ 28	$ 125	$ 16	$ (13)	$ 149	$ 215	$ 227	$ 247	$ 225
Health:											
Premiums:											
First year	$3,124	$ 955	$1,250	$1,316	$1,543	$2,233	$1,782	$ 918	$ 990	$1,070	$1,280
Renewal		2,343	2,474	2,793	3,082	3,469	4,277	4,544	4,079	3,815	4,052
Total	3,124	3,298	3,724	4,109	4,625	5,702	6,059	5,462	5,069	4,885	5,332
Benefits and expenses:											
Claims incurred	2,352	2,275	2,815	2,966	3,537	4,572	4,425	4,161	3,723	3,560	4,140
Commissions	312	330	372	411	463	570	606	546	509	489	533
Premium taxes	62	66	74	82	93	114	121	109	102	98	107
Administrative expenses:											
Acquisition	315	90	130	190	156	200	164	84	86	88	113
Maintenance	242	266	305	335	381	452	472	406	382	359	392
	3,283	3,027	3,696	3,984	4,630	5,908	5,788	5,306	4,802	4,594	5,285
UNDERWRITING INCOME	$ (159)	$ 271	$ 28	$ 125	$ (5)	$ (206)	$ 271	$ 156	$ 267	$ 291	$ 47
Adjusted:											
Life:											
Statutory underwriting income	$ (172)	$ (32)	$ 28	$ 155	$ 16	$ (13)	$ 149	$ 215	$ 227	$ 247	$ 125
Acquisition costs:											
Deferred	315	216	130	114	137	220	144	63	65	110	118
Amortized	(104)	(156)	(165)	(157)	(152)	(164)	(158)	(129)	(106)	(100)	(100)
ADJUSTED UNDERWRITING INCOME	$ 39	$ 28	$ (7)	$ 112	$ 1	$ 43	$ 135	$ 149	$ 186	$ 257	$ 143
Health:											
Statutory underwriting income	$ (159)	$ 271	$ 28	$ 125	$ (5)	$ (206)	$ 271	$ 156	$ 285	$ 291	$ 47
Acquisition costs:											
Deferred	315	90	130	190	156	200	164	84	86	88	113
Amortized	(104)	(115)	(131)	(157)	(162)	(169)	(173)	(146)	(121)	(104)	(101)
ADJUSTED UNDERWRITING INCOME	$ 52	$ 246	$ 27	$ 158	$ (11)	$ (175)	$ 262	$ 94	$ 250	$ 275	$ 59

Table 20–20.

DEFERRAL AND AMORTIZATION (5-YEAR SUM-OF-THE-YEARS'-DIGITS) OF ACQUISITION COSTS FOR POOLED GROUP INSURANCE, 1961–1971

Year	Costs Incurred	Unamortized at End of Year										
		1961	1962	1963	1964	1965	1966	1967	1968	1969	1970	1971
LIFE:												
1961	$315,000	$211,050	$126,000	$ 63,000	$ 22,050							
1962	216,000		144,720	86,400	43,200	$ 15,120						
1963	129,500			86,765	51,800	25,900	$ 9,065					
1964	114,000				76,380	45,600	22,800	$ 7,980				
1965	136,500					91,455	54,600	27,300	$ 9,555			
1966	220,000						147,400	88,000	44,000	$ 15,400		
1967	143,500							96,145	57,400	28,700	$ 10,045	
1968	63,000								42,210	25,200	12,600	$ 4,410
1969	64,500									43,215	25,800	12,900
1970	110,000										73,700	44,000
1971	117,500											78,725
UNAMORTIZED, END OF YEAR		211,050	270,720	236,165	193,430	178,075	233,865	219,425	153,165	112,515	122,145	140,035
NET CHANGE		$211,050	$ 59,670	$(34,555)	$(42,735)	$(15,355)	$ 55,790	$(14,440)	$(66,260)	$(40,650)	$ 9,630	$ 17,890
HEALTH:												
1961	$315,000	$211,050	$126,000	$63,000	$ 22,050							
1962	90,000		60,300	36,000	18,000	$ 6,300						
1963	129,500			86,765	51,800	25,900	$ 9,065					
1964	190,000				127,300	76,000	38,000	$ 13,300				
1965	156,000					104,520	62,400	31,200	$ 10,920			
1966	200,000						134,000	80,000	40,000	$ 14,000		
1967	164,000							109,880	65,600	32,800	$ 11,480	
1968	84,000								56,280	33,600	16,800	$ 5,880
1969	86,000									57,620	34,400	17,200
1970	88,000										58,960	35,200
1971	112,500											75,375
UNAMORTIZED, END OF YEAR		211,050	186,300	185,765	219,150	212,720	243,465	234,380	172,800	138,020	121,640	133,655
NET CHANGE		$211,050	$(24,750)	$ (535)	$ 33,385	$ (6,430)	$ 30,745	$ (9,085)	$(61,580)	$(34,780)	$(16,380)	$ 12,015

1. The costs must be reasonably determinable.

2. The portion recovered by the first-year retention charged must be reasonably determinable, since such portion should not be deferred.

3. The effective period of amortization through the retention mechanism should be reasonably determinable, since this would normally define the period of amortization for accounting purposes.

4. There must be reasonable assurance as to profitability of the contract.

5. There must be reasonable assurance as to persistency of the contract.

Given a sufficient volume of retention business of similar characteristics, averages and aggregates could be used in making these determinations.

Reserves. Reserve adjustments would normally be expected to be nominal. When a case is in a surplus (or zero surplus) position, any reserve adjustment would likely wind up being held as a deferred experience rating refund liability. When a case is in deficit, any such adjustment would impact the operating statement directly.

Deficits. As discussed above, deficits should not be deferred unless recovery is certain. (Retrospective premiums should of course be recorded where applicable.) When deficits are deferred in material amounts, the relevant amounts should be disclosed in notes to the financial statements.

Materiality. In many cases, adjustments in respect of retention business will not be material. In Crazy Quilt's case, for example, it didn't much matter whether acquisition costs were deferred or not, as is suggested by the summary of retention business shown in Table 20–18.

Table 20–21.

POLICYHOLDER MEMORANDUM ACCOUNTS FOR IMMEDIATE PARTICIPATION GUARANTEE GROUP ANNUITY CASE AND RELATED FINANCIAL STATEMENT EFFECTS IN 1971

	Policyholder Accounts		
	Annuity Accumulation Fund	Retired Lives Fund	Financial Statements
Deposits	$ 228,310		$ 228,310
Annuity premiums		$ 420,562	420,562
Interest credits on liabilities held	66,190	50,670	
Annuity benefits		(86,088)	(86,088)
Withdrawals:			
To purchase annuities	(420,562)		(420,562)
Transfers to separate accounts	(205,856)		(205,856)
Other	(49,180)		(49,180)
Expense, risk, and profit charges	(10,646)	(2,946)	
Balance before reserve increases		382,198	
Increases in:			
Retired lives reserve		(358,828)	(358,828)
Contingency reserve		(18,696)	(18,696)
Balance before experience rating refund		4,674	
Experience rating refund paid		(4,674)	(4,674)
Experience rating refund balance		$ –0–	
Net change in accumulation fund	(391,744)		391,744
Beginning balance	1,577,514		
Ending balance	$1,185,770		
Investment income earned			115,012
Expenses			(10,174)
Pre-tax operating statement results			$ 1,570
Statement liabilities:			
	Beginning	Changes	Ending
Annuity accumulation funds	$1,577,514	$(391,744)	$1,185,770
Retired lives reserve	361,250	358,828	720,078
Contingency reserve	(1,924)	18,696	16,772
	$1,936,840	$ (14,220)	$1,922,620

Pooled Business

Crazy Quilt entered the "baby group" business in 1961, and volume grew somewhat erratically to $7 million in premiums in 1971.

Such business is usually treated as a pool and is not subject to experience rating. Rate changes are usually prospective.

Pooled group business is short-term business within the definitions provided in the life insurance audit guide. When acquisition costs are determinable, persistency of the pooled business is demonstrable, and profitability of the business is highly probable, acquisition costs might qualify for deferral. Crazy Quilt Life deferred and amortized the costs over a five-year period using the sum-of-the-years' digits method, which was a conservative representation of persistency of pooled business.

A summary of pooled group experience for the years 1961–1971 is shown in Table 20–19, and a schedule of deferrals and amortization of pooled group acquisition costs is shown in Table 20–20.

Group Annuities

There are many types of group annuity arrangements; some—for larger policyholders—are custom-made. All tend to be fairly complicated. Two types sold by Crazy Quilt Life—an immediate participation guarantee case and a deposit administration case, both with experience rating—are summarized in Tables 20–21 and 20–22, respectively.

For experience-rated group annuity business, the relationship between acquisition costs and retention charges should be investigated to determine whether

Table 20–22.

POLICYHOLDER MEMORANDUM ACCOUNTS FOR DEPOSIT ADMINISTRATION GROUP ANNUITY CASE AND
RELATED FINANCIAL STATEMENT EFFECTS IN 1971

	Policyholder Accounts	*Financial Statements*
Deposit administration fund:		
Beginning fund	$1,447,724	
Deposits	235,424	
Interest credits on deposit administration fund	74,682	
Annuity purchases	(239,810)	
Withdrawals and transfers	(64,384)	
Ending fund	$1,453,636	
Change in ending fund:		
Active lives reserve	$ 5,766	
Contingency reserve	146	$ (146)
	$ 5,912	
Experience rating account:		
Deposits	$ 235,424	235,424
Interest credits on all liabilities held	114,960	
Annuity premiums	239,810	239,810
Annuity purchases	(239,810)	(239,810)
Withdrawals and transfers	(64,384)	(64,384)
Annuity benefits paid	(63,788)	(63,788)
Change in active lives reserve	(5,766)	(5,766)
Change in retired lives reserve	(187,112)	(187,112)
Change in contingency reserves	(8,532)	(8,532)
Expense, risk, and profit charges	(15,570)	
Balance	5,232	
Experience rating refund paid	(5,232)	(5,232)
	$ –0–	
Reconciliation to summary of operations (pre-tax):		
Investment income		119,368
Expenses		(11,580)
		$ 8,252

Statement liabilities:	*Beginning*	*Additions*	*Ending*
Deposit administration fund:			
Active lives reserve	$1,393,030	$ 5,766	$1,398,796
Experience rating liability	54,694	146	54,840
Retired lives reserve	566,992	187,112	754,104
Contingency reserve	35,704	8,532	44,236
	$2,050,420	$201,556	$2,251,976

acquisition costs might possibly qualify for deferral. The criteria to be satisfied in making such deferrals are substantially similar to those applicable to group life and health insurance.

It was suggested earlier in this chapter that reserve adjustments on experience-rated business will often result in an equivalent increase in the experience rating refund liability. This is also true of experience-rated group annuity business.

It was also suggested earlier that deficits on experi-

ence-rated business should not be deferred. In the case of group annuity business, however, there is one type of deficit which would be eminently deferrable, and that is the deficit that arises as a result of statutory limitations on assumptions used to value reserves on retired lives.

Surplus strain from writing, say, single-premium group annuities can be severe. When the retired lives experience is part of the experience rating process, the result of the surplus strain is typically an indicated experience rating deficit. When this occurs, and the deficit is traceable to an unduly conservative valuation basis, the deficit should be deferred. It normally should not be necessary to revalue the reserves themselves. It goes without saying that the amount deferred should not exceed the difference between statutory reserves and adjusted reserves computed using reasonable assumptions.

When the retired lives experience is not experience-rated, the reserves should be adjusted in basically the same manner as reserves on individual annuities.

21

Variable Products

The life insurance audit guide is relatively silent about the accounting treatment of variable products. The guide limits itself to a few paragraphs about variable annuities.

In addition to variable annuities, "variable products" include variable life—which, although untested, may capture a large share of the market in the years ahead; certain unit-linked coverages sold in some foreign countries, including Britain and Canada; and certain index-linked inflation-protected products sold or under development in the United States and elsewhere. Each of these products presents unique accounting problems.

Variable Annuities

Variable annuities were first offered to the public by a few companies in the late 1950s. They became popular on a grand scale in the late 1960s, when legislation was passed which was designed to encourage development of pension plans for self-employed persons and certain other professions. The variable annuity product was well-suited for this market.

Until the advent of variable life insurance, which as of this writing was still in the development stage, variable annuities constituted the principal variable product (excluding mutual funds) offered by U. S. life insurance companies.

Product Design

While the mechanics of the variable annuity product are quite complicated, the concept underlying the prod-

uct is fairly simple. Contract-holders make periodic payments to the sponsoring insurance company. The company deducts sales and administrative charges specified in the prospectus. The balance is translated into "units" of credit and the related cash is allocated to a separate account—i.e., segregated from other company assets—which is invested largely in common stocks. The value of the separate account at any point in time is allocated to contract-holders based on their units of credit. The value of each unit times the units of credit equals the contract-holder's equity in the separate account. Viewed another way, the value of the units is the amount available to the contract-holder at any time. (There may, however, be a nominal surrender charge at the time of surrender.) In the event of death during the accumulation period, the contract-holder sometimes receives the greater of stipulated payments made or the value of the units.

At the time of retirement, the contract-holder's equity may be applied to purchase of a fixed annuity, in which case the greater the value of his equity the larger the annuity payments; or the annuity payments themselves may be so many units per period, with the amount of the payment fluctuating with the value of the units.

The insurance company levies a specified annual charge on the separate account for investment management services and also levies a charge for mortality and expense risks. With respect to the mortality risk, the company assumes the risk that annuitant mortality will be less than the rates assumed. With respect to the expense risk, the company assumes the risk that sales, administrative, and investment expenses will exceed the specified charges therefor.

Statutory Reserves

The costs of the risks assumed by the insurance company are very difficult to measure. For example, assumption of the risk that the rates of annuitant mortality will be less than the assumed rates is no different, fundamentally, from assumptions made in the case of fixed annuities. But in the case of fixed annuities the payments that would be made are known. In the case of variable annuities, the payments that would be made would be a function of the value of the units, which is not determinable.

As for benefits payable on early death, the company bears the risk that the sum of stipulated payments made will be greater than the value of the units. The probable spread between the two values may not be reasonably determinable.

Some companies believe these risks are negligible and provide no reserves for them; the only reserves held in such cases are equal to the value of the separate account. Other companies are holding as a reserve the accumulated charges to contract-holders until such time as it is possible to measure the risk with sufficient accuracy. And other companies have made various assumptions, admittedly without the benefit of historical development, and have calculated reserves "scientifically".*

Operation of a Separate Account

Crazy Quilt Life began selling individual variable annuities in 1968. Development expenses of $655,000 were incurred (in 1968 and 1969) to get into the business. By 1971 the separate account had grown to $29,771,000. The progression of the separate account from 1968 to 1971 is shown in Table 21–1.

Table 21–1 also shows the impact of Crazy Quilt's variable annuity operation on the Company's general accounts. Income consisted of the various deductions from stipulated payments and charges against the separate account. Expenses consisted of commissions, general expenses, and development costs. The net effect on Crazy Quilt's statutory summary of operations was, to say the least, severe.**

Revenue

The life insurance audit guide provides that variable

*Maryland regulatory authories require a reserve for the guarantees to be carried by any company doing business in Maryland.

**The indicated excess of general account disbursements over general account income is without regard for interest on the net cash outflow.

annuity revenues consist of "deductions from considerations or sales charges and asset charges or management fees." [1] It is against these fees that costs should be matched, i.e., the fees constitute "revenue".

Thus stipulated payments under variable annuity contracts should preferably not be reported as revenue. They should preferably be accounted for as direct additions to the separate account.

Sales and other charges deducted from stipulated payments are usually based on a constant percentage of such payments. In Crazy Quilt Life's case, for example, sales charges are fixed at 6.5 percent and administrative charges at 2 percent (with a few deviations from this scale for certain products).

Investment management charges and mortality and expense risk charges are usually levied against the value of the separate account based on a fixed schedule of percentages applied to such value. In Crazy Quilt's case, investment management fees average about .25 percent and mortality and expense risk charges about .75 percent of the value of the separate account.

Deferral of Acquisition Costs

It is not unusual for a life insurance company to pay non-level commissions on variable annuity sales. In Crazy Quilt's case—which is patterned after a company that does a significant volume of variable annuity business—first-year commissions average about 14 percent of first-year stipulated payments. In addition, there are certain issue and other costs related to the variable annuity sales, which in Crazy Quilt's case average about 6 percent. Renewal commissions (payable through the tenth year) and maintenance expenses (exclusive of general overhead allocations) average about 2.75 percent and 1 percent, respectively.

Thus, while Crazy Quilt collects a level amount for sales and administrative charges of about 8.5 percent, its related first-year costs are about 20 percent and renewal expenses are about 3.75 percent. Obviously the first-year excess cost, 16.25 percent, must be recognized from future excess deductions from stipulated payments, 4.75 percent.

In short, it is necessary to defer excess first-year costs that vary with and are primarily related to production and amortize them against the anticipated revenue stream. The "anticipated revenue stream" consists of sales and administrative charges deducted from stipulated payments. (The life insurance audit guide also provides that asset charges can also be used in part to cover amortization under certain circum-

Table 21–1.

OPERATION OF CRAZY QUILT LIFE'S VARIABLE ANNUITY SEPARATE ACCOUNT, 1968–1971*

	Separate Account				General Account			
	1968	1969	1970	1971	1968	1969	1970	1971
Gross stipulated payments:								
First year	$1,009,234	$5,732,000	$ 7,364,000	$ 8,576,522				
Renewal		533,556	3,762,040	5,697,512				
	1,009,234	6,265,556	11,126,040	14,274,034				
Deductions from stipulated payments:								
Selling charge	64,672	419,854	730,778	924,958	$ 64,672	$ 419,854	$ 730,778	$ 924,958
Administrative charge	18,738	124,538	211,814	276,512	18,738	124,538	211,814	276,512
	83,410	544,392	942,592	1,201,470				
NET STIPULATED PAYMENTS	925,824	5,721,164	10,183,448	13,072,564				
Investment income	4,028	140,904	511,150	719,352				
Realized capital gains		(12,114)	(253,572)	286,960				
Unrealized capital gains	(924)	(273,102)	694,820	1,080,650				
Withdrawals	(2,076)	(164,716)	(596,902)	(1,762,372)				
Annuity payments	(638)	(2,376)	(2,472)	(6,104)				
Investment management charge	(364)	(9,340)	(35,398)	(73,586)	364	9,340	35,398	73,586
Mortality and expense risk charge	(2,086)	(34,104)	(109,630)	(227,890)	2,086	34,104	109,630	227,890
	(2,060)	(354,848)	207,996	17,010				
CHANGE IN SEPARATE ACCOUNT	923,764	5,366,316	10,391,444	13,089,574				
Separate account at beginning of year	–0–	923,764	6,290,080	16,681,524				
SEPARATE ACCOUNT AT END OF YEAR	$ 923,764	$6,290,080	$16,681,524	$29,771,098				
GENERAL ACCOUNT INCOME					85,860	587,836	1,087,620	1,502,946
General account disbursements:								
Commissions:								
First year					225,654	1,103,834	1,355,226	1,698,858
Renewal						19,848	118,160	157,228
					225,654	1,123,682	1,473,386	1,856,086
Variable administrative expense:								
First year					65,208	327,380	392,941	506,776
Renewal						4,778	32,165	49,660
					65,208	332,158	425,106	556,436
General overhead					201,182	217,670	257,699	286,793
Development costs					430,000	225,000	–0–	–0–
					922,044	1,898,510	2,156,191	2,699,315
EXCESS OF GENERAL ACCOUNT DISBURSEMENTS OVER GENERAL ACCOUNT INCOME					$836,184	$1,310,674	$1,068,571	$1,196,369

*Gains and losses from mortality, which were nominal in the first few years, are ignored in this tabulation.

stances; this subject is discussed later in this chapter.) Deferrable costs were defined as first-year costs in excess of normal renewal costs. The principal component of the deferral was commissions, as might be expected. In Crazy Quilt's case, commissions represented about 75 percent of all costs deferred, the balance being certain sales support and issue expenses. The definition of variable annuity acquisition costs followed the definition of acquisition costs on regular life insurance, by and large, except there were no selection costs.

Amortization of Acquisition Costs

Crazy Quilt found it very difficult to develop an amortization table. For one thing, the Company had no history of terminations. For another, a contract-holder can change (or stop) the amount of his stipulated payment at will. And finally, Crazy Quilt pays commissions on two bases, generally at the option of the agent:

▸ First-year commissions are computed and paid on the basis of *annualized* first-year stipulated payments. Renewal commissions are paid as payments are received.

▸ First-year commissions and renewal commissions are paid as payments are received.

The impact of these factors on the period and method of amortization can best be appreciated by a fairly detailed analysis of the variable annuity mechanism as it operates in Crazy Quilt's case.

"First-Year" vs. "Renewal"

The distinction between first-year and renewal stipulated payments is artificial in view of the fact that the contract-holder may change his payments (or terminate) at any time without prejudice to his rights. There is, for example, no loss on surrender such as would be occasioned on surrender of a life insurance policy. Also, the concepts of paid-to dates and policy years are not really applicable to variable annuity contracts.

Crazy Quilt therefore defined "first-year" and "renewal" in terms of 10 years (the total number of years during which commissions are paid) together with the *amount agreed in advance* to be paid by the contract-holder in the first year.*

Thus, for example, if a contract-holder agrees to pay $100 a month, commissionable first-year payments are held to be $1,200. If the contract-holder pays in $1,200 in, say, six months, the renewal period runs for nine years and six months.

Commissions on ordinary life insurance sales are frequently annualized and are advanced to agents. The advance is regarded as such and is usually treated as a receivable, reduced by the application of commission earnings credited to the agent as premiums are received.

Annualized commissions on variable annuity business are typically not treated as advances. Thus, such commissions are treated as expense when paid. If the Company does not receive, in the first year, the amount upon which the annualized commissions are based, the difference *may* be charged back to the salesman. Each such situation requires a decision by management; *there is no automatic chargeback,* at least in Crazy Quilt's case.

Assume stipulated payments of $100 a month and first year and renewal commission rates of 15 percent and 3 percent, respectively. A commission of $180 is paid to the salesman upon receipt of the first stipulated payment of $100.

▸ If the contract-holder pays $1,200 in, say, four months, the $180 commission has been "covered." All further stipulated payments are commissionable at the 3% rate.

▸ If the contract-holder pays $100 a month for six months and then pays $50 in the seventh and subsequent months, obviously the first-year annualized premium is $900, not $1,200, and the proper first-year commission is $135, not $180. In this case, management must decide whether to charge the difference, $45, to the agent. In this case, the chargeback would probably be made. If the difference were immaterial, the chargeback would probably not be made. However, no additional commissions would be paid to the agent until the $1,200 is received—in 18 months, if the contract-holder in this example continues paying $50 a month. The renewal rates would apply to all payments received for the duration of the ten-year period—in this case, eight years and six months.

Commissions paid as stipulated payments are received present no particular problem. All payments received in the first year are commissionable at the first-year rate; payments received for the next nine years are commissionable at the renewal rate.

A contract-holder may change the amount of his stipulated payment at any time. If the change is a decrease, no special problems arise except in connection with annualized commissions as noted above. If the payment is an increase, the increase is subject to first-year commissions *if* the change in payments is accompanied by an amended application. In other words, first-year commissions are paid on the increase if the agent originated the increase.

If the agent is on an annualized commission basis, all monies received subsequent to the increase are applied to reduce the annual commission paid. Thus,

*This procedure is not typical. Most companies pay a first-year commission on all first-year payments received regardless of the contract-holder's undertaking.

Table 21–2.

DEFERRAL AND AMORTIZATION OF VARIABLE ANNUITY ACQUISITION COSTS

	First Year Stipulated Payments	Expenses Incurred and Unamortized	Normal Renewals	Deferrable Excess	Sum-of-the-Years'-Digits Amortization			
					1968	1969	1970	1971
1968 Level commissions	$ 576,778	$ 90,262	$ 17,304	$ 72,958	$13,278	$ 11,966	$ 10,580	$ 9,266
Annualized commissions	432,456	135,392	12,974	122,418	11,140	21,178	18,914	16,650
Administrative expense		65,208	8,432	56,776	5,167	9,823	8,772	7,721
	$1,009,234	290,862	$ 38,710	$ 252,152				
Normal renewals					38,710			
Total amortization		(68,295)			$68,295			
Unamortized balance		222,567						
1969 Level commissions	$3,275,838	441,534	$ 98,276	$ 343,258		62,472	56,294	49,772
Annualized commissions	2,456,162	662,300	73,684	588,616		53,564	101,830	90,940
Administrative expense		327,380	51,264	276,116		25,127	47,769	42,660
	$5,732,000	1,431,214	$223,224	$1,207,990				
Normal renewals						223,224		
Total amortization		(407,354)				$407,354		
Unamortized balance		1,246,427						
1970 Level commissions	$4,208,526	542,090	$126,256	$ 415,834			75,682	68,196
Annualized commissions	3,155,474	813,136	94,664	718,472			65,380	124,294
Administrative expense		392,941	63,151	329,790			30,011	57,054
	$7,364,000	1,748,167	$284,071	$1,464,096				
Normal renewals							284,071	
Total amortization		(699,303)					$699,303	
Unamortized balance		2,295,291						
1971 Level commissions	$4,901,482	679,544	$147,044	$ 532,500				96,916
Annualized commissions	3,675,040	1,019,314	110,252	909,062				82,724
Administrative expense		506,776	74,770	432,006				39,313
	$8,576,522	2,205,634	$332,066	$1,873,568				
Normal renewals								332,066
Total amortization		(1,017,572)						$1,017,572
Unamortized balance		$3,483,353						

Summary of recorded gain or loss from sales and administrative loading:

					1968	1969	1970	1971
Sales fees received					$64,672	$419,854	$730,778	$ 924,958
Administrative fees received					18,738	124,538	211,814	276,512
					83,410	544,392	942,592	1,201,470
Amortization, as above					68,295	407,354	699,303	1,017,572
Renewal commissions					–0–	19,848	118,160	157,228
Renewal administrative expenses					–0–	4,778	32,165	49,660
					68,295	431,980	849,628	1,224,460
					$15,115	$112,412	$ 92,964	$ (22,990)

for example, if a contract-holder has been paying $100 a month and raises his payment to $150 in the second year due to an agent's efforts, the agent is paid an annualized commission based on $600 (the additional payment, $50, times 12 months.) The first four $150 payments received in the second year ($600 in all) are not commissionable. Renewal rates would apply to all payments after the fourth year.

Amortization period. To determine the average life of variable annuity contracts, Crazy Quilt computed the expected lives of the contracts in force (weighted by annualized stipulated payments) assuming retirement at age 65 and no voluntary terminations. This produced an indicated average life (assuming no terminations) of 18 years. To allow for the effect of terminations, Crazy Quilt arbitrarily reduced the expected life to 10 years.*

Amortization method. Crazy Quilt adopted the sum-of-the-years'-digits method of amortization until such time as experience would indicate the true persistency pattern. "Persistency" does not mean the same as it does for life insurance policies; a decrease in a stipulated payment (even to zero) does not affect rights accrued under the contract but may be regarded as a "termination" for purposes of accounting for acquisition costs.

It was felt that the 10-year sum-of-the-years'-digits method which resulted in amortizing 73 percent of the cost in five years, was appropriately conservative in the circumstances.

Amortization results. All acquisition costs other than annualized commissions were amortized in the 10-year sum-of-the-years'-digits pattern. Annualized commissions were amortized on the basis of 20 six-month periods, also in the sum-of-the-digits form; only the first six-month amount was amortized in the first year since, on average, about half the stipulated payments to which the commissions applied were received in the first year.

The net result of the amortization process for the years 1968–1971 is shown in Table 21–2. It will be observed that by 1971 the Company was experiencing a "loss from loading". As it turned out, this was due to deteriorating persistency due to stock market conditions. In 1972 Crazy Quilt was obliged to strengthen its amortization table to amortize 30 percent in the first year. Rates in subsequent years were adjusted accordingly.

It goes without saying that variable annuity persistency must be carefully monitored. Even in 1974 it is a relatively new product.

Other Revenue Sources for Matching Purposes

The life insurance audit guide provides that if deductions from stipulated payments "are insufficient to recover commissions and other acquisition costs, it may be appropriate to match certain acquisition costs against a portion of asset charges if there is sufficient margin in future asset charges." [2] That's a big "if". As the guide also points out, "asset charges are intended to cover investment management, certain administrative expenses, [and] mortality and expense risks." [3] Such charges should be used to absorb amortization of acquisition costs only as a last resort.*

General Overhead

So long as all contract-related acquisition and maintenance expenses are covered by revenue sources, general overhead allocated as a matter of administrative practice to the variable annuity line of business need not be specifically provided for. Indicated future losses attributable to such overhead should not be recognized.**

Development Costs

Many companies incurred substantial development costs in creating a variable annuity operation. In Crazy Quilt's case, such costs aggregated $655,000 and were expensed in view of the uncertainties associated with the product. This is a good rule to follow in the case of variable annuities.

Reserves

In view of the differences of opinion as to the need for reserves for mortality and expense guarantees, there should be no presumption that the practices adopted for statutory purposes are inappropriate for purposes of adjusted statements unless no reserves are carried. In that case the burden of proof for not reserving for such risks is on the company.

Separate account contingency reserves should normally be reported as appropriated surplus unless there is every reason to believe that such reserves will inure directly to the benefit of contract-holders.

Separate Account Surplus

Often separate account assets and liabilities are equal. Other times the separate account may show a

---

*It should be noted that the amortization procedure described here was used in the absence of adequate statistical data. Actuaries would seriously question the conceptual propriety of the procedure.

*Some believe that the audit guide errs in striving to separate the purposes of the various deductions and asset charges, which is not done with respect to other life insurance products.

**Principles of loss recognition are discussed in detail in Chapter 24.

surplus attributable to "seed money" invested by the company at the inception of the account, retention of asset charges or other amounts owed to the company in the separate account, or other factors. Such surplus should be reported as company surplus.

Presentation and Disclosure

Some believe that the assets and liabilities of a separate account should be "consolidated" with the insurance company's general accounts. Others believe that a separate account has an independent existence and should not be reported in the insurance company's balance sheet at all.

Because of the special nature of a separate account, its assets and liabilities should not be "consolidated" with those of the insurance company. Because the separate account is under the insurance company's control to a significant degree and participates in the insurance company's agency operation and risk-bearing function it should not be omitted from the balance sheet.

Existing practice of showing the assets and liabilities of the separate account as one-line items in the balance sheet should, therefore, be retained.

Disclosure of the variable annuity deferral and amortization policies as well as relevant amounts should be made along the lines of disclosures made for acquisition costs on regular life insurance.

Variable Life Insurance

Variable life insurance is an insurance contract in which death benefits and other values may vary, reflecting the investment experience of a separate account. Certain regulatory requirements as of the date of this writing provide that a variable life contract must, among other things,

▶ Provide life insurance for the whole of life,
▶ Provide that the insurance company will assume mortality and expense risks,
▶ Guarantee that the death benefit will be no less than the initial sum insured, and
▶ Provide that gross premiums shall be level.

Thus the variable life contract must be basically and predominantly a life insurance contract providing protection against death.

Variable life is seen by its advocates as a means of recapturing some of the savings dollars lost in the post-World War II era to other savings media. Returns on fixed-dollar policies are limited by the restrictions placed by state laws on general account investments. Variable life insurance will involve separate accounts whose investments will not be subject to such restrictions. It is expected that a large portion of separate accounts will be invested in equities; however, it should be noted that there is nothing conceptually incorrect about having no equity investments in a separate account.

The discussion that follows should be regarded as tentative in every respect. The discussion concerns a product about which there has been much controversy. As of the date of this writing, the regulatory status of variable life is such that one cannot be certain whether the variable life product will ever become a reality and, if it does, what form it will take. The purpose of the discussion that follows is merely to highlight some of the accounting issues that may have to be dealt with if the product eventually emerges.

Some of the discussion may, however, prove useful with respect to variable products now being sold in countries other than the United States.

Product Design

All variable life product designs proposed thus far operate by a common "excess interest" mechanism. At any point in time the assets of the separate account are supporting certain contract liabilities, usually (but not necessarily) the policy reserves. These liabilities require a fixed assumed valuation rate of interest to grow according to the valuation assumptions. However, the separate account will be earning some actual rate of return; the excess or deficit of the actual rate of return over the required valuation rate of return is used to cause the face amount of the policy to vary

▶ By using the excess interest to purchase positive or negative premium-paying variable life additions,
▶ By using the excess interest to purchase positive or negative paid-up whole life additions, or
▶ By using a portion of the excess interest to purchase term insurance and a portion to purchase paid-up additions.

Unlike the cash value of a fixed policy, the cash value of a variable life policy can decrease as duration increases. Thus it is likely that policy loans equal to 100 percent of the cash value will not be permitted. Policy loans will likely have some of the characteristics of stock market margin loans.

By its nature, a variable life product is participating to the extent of excess interest. In addition, the product can be modified to provide dividends of the usual type incorporating gains from mortality, from loading, and perhaps from separate account expense and risk charges. Contracts limited to separate account excess interest participation are usually called nonparticipating; contracts that provide additionally for a regular scale of dividends are called participating.

Pricing

Indications are that variable life contracts will call for level premiums.

Regulations permitting, premiums for variable life contracts may be determined with a fair degree of flexibility. The main consideration is that premiums, asset charges, expense and benefit features interrelate to produce reasonable margins.

General Account vs. Separate Account

In general, variable life gross premiums are received in the company's general accounts, just like premiums on regular business. A specified portion of the premiums is allocated to the separate accounts; the balance is retained by the company. Separate account asset growth or shrinkage will depend on after-tax investment earnings of the separate account assets. Separate account assets are used to fund reserves that in turn reflect the company's mortality and cash value obligations. If the separate account assets drop below the level necessary to support policy liabilities, the company must make up the difference from its own surplus. Generally the absolute amount of the cash value is not subject to a floor, so one of the company's principal risks is the possibility that separate account earnings will not be sufficient to pay the minimum sum insured. This risk is funded by a general account reserve. The company also bears the risk that actual mortality and expenses will exceed those assumed.

The company levies charges on the separate account, based on a specified percentage of the asset value at periodic measurement dates, designed to compensate for investment management and assumption of the mortality and expense risks. It should be recognized that, in theory, there is no compelling reason for the company to levy charges against the separate account. The portion of the gross premium allocated to the separate account could be adjusted to produce the necessary additional income. But linking a portion of the company's income to the growth of the separate account makes the company a kind of partner with the policyholder, which is generally very desirable

where relatively risky investments are concerned.

Thus the company's sources of income are loadings (i.e., the difference between the gross premiums and the amounts allocated to the separate account), asset charges, and any gains on mortality and lapse. From this income the company must pay commissions and administrative expenses, costs of managing the separate account's investments, benefits, and any dividends. The company must also allocate amounts to build contingency reserves to fund the contract guarantees.

The relationship between the separate account and the company's general accounts for one relatively complex participating variable life product is represented in Table 21–3.

Revenue

Earlier in this chapter it was suggested that variable annuity stipulated payments do not constitute "revenue"—that revenue from variable annuity business is limited to deductions from stipulated payments (for sales and administrative charges) and periodic assessments against the separate account (for investment management and carrying the mortality and expense risks).

Variable life insurance appears to involve some of the same characteristics. "Premiums" might be viewed as similar to stipulated payments from which the company deducts a loading equal to the difference between gross premiums received and amounts transferred to the separate account. Periodic assessments against the separate account are substantially the same in concept as those which are assessed against variable annuity separate accounts.

There are, however, some significant differences between variable annuity stipulated payments and variable life premiums. Stipulated payments are basically discretionary deposits that can be changed at will by the contract-holder. This is not true of variable life premiums, which have essentially the same character as premiums on fixed benefit contracts. Further, the variable life contract operates in much the same manner as a fixed life contract except that the policyholder bears a larger part of the investment risk (and consequently stands to reap greater rewards).

Thus variable life gross premiums should preferably be regarded as revenue against which benefits and expenses should be matched.

Variable Life Valuation

Conceptually separate account assets should equal

Table 21–3.

SCHEMATIC REPRESENTATION OF VARIABLE LIFE TRANSACTIONS IN GENERAL ACCOUNT AND SEPARATE ACCOUNT

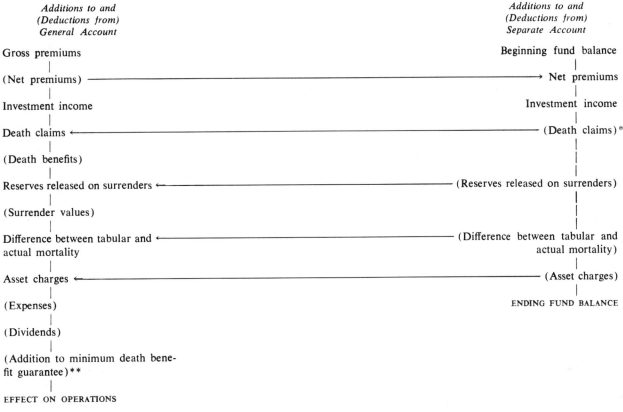

*It is practical to view this as a transfer of tabular mortality, pure and simple.
**Assumes that the minimum death benefit guarantee reserve is separately maintained.

separate account liabilities, although in practice the separate account may be allowed to retain a part of the surplus allocable to the company.

Generally, then, variable life valuation (for purposes of adjusted financial statements) would be limited to expected transactions in the general account. What are these transactions and how should they be valued?

The transactions occurring in the general account may be classified into five general types:

1. Gross premiums received
2. Amounts transferred to the separate account
3. Amounts received from the separate account
4. Payments to policyholders
5. Expenses

The elements to be valued include all of the indicated transactions except gross premiums. (Gross premiums would of course be taken into account in making tests of recoverability.) Valuation of each element would take into account interest expected to be earned on general account assets generated by variable life transactions and expected rates of mortality and withdrawal.

Amounts transferred to separate account. Transfers to the separate account should be regarded as disbursements for the purpose of calculating adjusted general account reserves.

Amounts received from separate account. Asset charges and amounts made available for benefit payments should be regarded as negative disbursements for the purpose of calculating adjusted general account reserves.

Payments to policyholders. Amounts paid from the general account for death claims, surrenders, and dividends should be regarded as disbursements.

Expenses. Commissions, sales support, underwriting, issue, maintenance, and settlement expenses disbursed from the general account should be regarded as items to be deferred and amortized or reserved for, as applicable.

Assumptions

The assumptions required to calculate adjusted reserves for variable life business include all of the assumptions required to value fixed policies plus a few additional items of considerable complexity.

Mortality. The selection of a mortality assumption involves basically the same considerations as selection of a mortality assumption for fixed policies.

Withdrawal. The same goes for the withdrawal assumption. The problem of forecasting termination behavior under varying stock market conditions may tend to complicate selection of a table, but so does the problem of fluctuating interest rates complicate the selection of a table for fixed policies. Were absolute amounts of cash values subject to a floor, the withdrawal assumption would assume enormous importance.*

General account interest. Selection of a general account interest assumption involves the same considerations as selection of an interest assumption for fixed policies.

Transfers to separate account. The portion of the gross premium to be transferred to the general account is usually specified.

Separate account investment earnings rate. The growth in the separate account will have a material influence on asset charges receivable by the general account. As will be seen, it generally will also affect death claim costs and dividends. Selection of a long-term investment earnings rate that encompasses interest, dividends, and other items of "normal" investment yield, as well as realized and unrealized capital gains and losses, is perhaps the most difficult of all the assumptions. But an assumption must be made.

Taxes. The separate account investment earnings rate assumption must be net of taxes. Thus an assumption about tax rates must be made. (As of the date of this writing, the method of taxing variable life and capital gains had not been determined.)

Dividends. A dividend assumption that relates to all the other assumptions must be made where the product is participating.

Acquisition costs. The determination of acquisition costs is basically the same as determining such costs for fixed policies.

Maintenance and settlement expenses. This is also true of maintenance and settlement costs, except that the additional administrative burdens of variable life—periodic valuations, reports, etc.—need to be given special consideration.

Investment management expenses. Unless the assumption is made that asset charges for investment management will exactly offset the related expenses, an assumption must be made about the cost of managing the separate account.

Cost of minimum death benefit guarantee. Determination of an appropriate "risk premium" for the minimum death benefit guarantee, and the related reserves and release from risk under the guarantee, is a matter of extreme complexity. It is related to other assumptions about separate account investment earnings rates, mortality and dividends.

Other items. Depending on product design, other transfers between the separate account and general account may need to be valued.

Once the various assumptions have been made, adjusted reserves can be calculated by a method that is essentially the same as the method used to calculate adjusted reserves for fixed policies.

Impact of Assumptions

Assume for purposes of discussion a participating variable whole life contract issued to males age 35. The assumptions are as follows:

Gross premium	$23.72
General account interest	Zero %*
Separate account after-tax	
investment earnings rate:	
Test 1	1%
Test 2	4%
Test 3	7%
Mortality	Current fixed policy experience
Withdrawals	Current fixed policy experience
Net premium transfers	1958 CSO, 3%, net level
Cash values per $1,000	Minimum, 1958 CSO, 3%
Commissions and	
premium taxes	Current fixed policy experience
Other expenses	Special analysis
Dividends	Special scale
Present value at zero interest of $1 annuity	
for premium-paying period	$18.81

*Zero interest has been assumed for purposes of simplifying. As will be seen, the effect of interest on the adjusted reserves is relatively insignificant in this case.

---

*Cash values would usually be subject to a floor amount (or fixed amount) per $1,000 of insurance in force, but since the face amount varies, there is no absolute floor. Thus the face amount could, because of poor investment performance, drop to, say, $800. Only 80 percent of the cash value for $1,000 of original face amount would be available to the policyholder. However, $1,000 would still be payable on death under minimum death benefit guarantee provisions.

Table 21–4.

GENERAL ACCOUNT AND SEPARATE ACCOUNT TRANSACTIONS IN SELECTED YEARS FOR $100,000 ORIGINAL AMOUNT OF PARTICIPATING VARIABLE WHOLE LIFE INSURANCE ISSUED TO MALE AGE 35

General Account Transactions (Assuming Zero Interest) Where After-Tax Yield Rate Of Separate Account Is				*Separate Account Transactions Where After-Tax Yield Rate Is*		
1%	*4%*	*7%*		*7%*	*4%*	*1%*
			YEAR 1			
			Beginning balance	$ –0–	$ –0–	$ –0–
$ 2,372	$ 2,372	$ 2,372	Gross premiums			
(1,678)	(1,678)	(1,678)	Net premiums	1,678	1,678	1,678
–0–	–0–	–0–	Investment income	55	32	8
107	108	109	Face amount of death claims	(109)	(108)	(107)
(108)	(108)	(109)	Death benefits			
275	278	281	Reserves on withdrawals	(281)	(278)	(275)
–0–	–0–	–0–	Surrender benefits			
138	144	150	Excess tabular mortality	(150)	(144)	(138)
8	8	8	Asset charges	(8)	(8)	(8)
(2,223)	(2,223)	(2,223)	Expenses			
(1,109)	(1,099)	(1,090)	Balance before dividends	$ 1,185	$ 1,172	$ 1,158
–0–	–0–	–0–	Dividends			
$(1,109)	$(1,099)	$(1,090)	Effect on operations			
			YEAR 10			
			Beginning balance	$ 9,083	$ 8,012	$ 7,079
$ 1,331	$ 1,331	$ 1,331	Gross premiums			
(948)	(948)	(948)	Net premiums	948	948	948
–0–	–0–	–0–	Investment income	663	336	75
138	157	179	Face amount of death claims	(179)	(157)	(138)
(157)	(157)	(179)	Death benefits			
265	304	350	Reserves on withdrawals	(350)	(304)	(265)
(265)	(304)	(350)	Surrender benefits			
89	103	119	Excess tabular mortality	(119)	(103)	(89)
75	84	95	Asset charges	(95)	(84)	(75)
(220)	(220)	(220)	Expenses			
308	350	377	Balance before dividends	$ 9,951	$ 8,648	$ 7,535
(233)	(255)	(280)	Dividends			
$ 75	$ 95	$ 97	Effect on operations			
			YEAR 30			
			Beginning balance	$23,538	$15,105	$10,136
$ 702	$ 702	$ 702	Gross premiums			
(495)	(495)	(495)	Net premiums	495	495	495
–0–	–0–	–0–	Investment income	1,627	600	101
467	700	1,100	Face amount of death claims	(1,100)	(700)	(467)
(700)	(700)	(1,100)	Death benefits			
182	275	436	Reserves on withdrawals	(436)	(275)	(182)
(182)	(275)	(436)	Surrender benefits			
52	79	126	Excess tabular mortality	(126)	(79)	(52)
101	150	232	Asset charges	(232)	(150)	(101)
(110)	(110)	(110)	Expenses			
17	326	455	Balance before dividends	$23,766	$14,996	$ 9,930
(218)	(286)	(405)	Dividends			
$ (201)	$ 40	$ 50	Effect on operations			

Table 21–5.

GENERAL ACCOUNT TRANSACTIONS (ASSUMING ZERO GENERAL ACCOUNT INTEREST) UNDER VARYING SEPARATE ACCOUNT YIELD RATES—PER $1,000 INITIAL FACE AMOUNT OF VARIABLE WHOLE LIFE ISSUED TO MALE AGE 35

	Sum of General Account Transactions for All Years When After-Tax Yield Rate of Separate Account is		
	1%	*4%*	*7%*
Acquisition costs paid:			
Commissions:			
First year	$ 12.70	$ 12.70	$ 12.70
Renewal years	11.37	11.37	11.37
Other-first-year only:			
Sales support	4.40	4.40	4.40
Selection	2.16	2.16	2.16
Issue	.92	.92	.92
	31.55	31.55	31.55
Maintenance and settlement costs paid	44.00	44.00	44.00
Investment management:			
Expenses paid	13.43	13.43	13.43
Fees received from separate account	(9.52)	(13.43)	(20.66)
Net premiums transferred to separate account	315.60	315.60	315.60
Death benefits:			
Paid	314.39	314.39	571.20
Face amounts received from separate account	(196.13)	(314.39)	(571.20)
Surrender benefits:			
Paid	84.88	116.89	174.98
Reserves on withdrawals received from separate account	(88.33)	(120.36)	(178.45)
Excess of tabular over actual mortality received from separate account	(31.15)	(42.02)	(61.84)
Mortality and expense risk charges received from separate account	(28.57)	(40.29)	(61.99)
Dividends	112.72	136.48	180.40
	562.87	441.85	437.02
Indicated profit or (loss)	(116.70)	4.32	9.15
Gross premiums	$ 446.17	$ 446.17	$ 446.17

General account and separate account transactions for $100,000 of business are shown for selected years (the first, tenth, and 30th) in Table 21–4. Figures are shown for the three trial assumptions of after-tax investment earnings rates for the separate account.

Three matters are especially worthy of note:

▶ The general account surplus strain in Year 1 is similar to that which one would expect in the case of fixed policies.

▶ In the case of the 1 percent assumption, the difference between amounts made available for death claims from the separate account and the amounts required to be paid under the minimum death benefit guarantee eventually become very sizeable. See, for example, the 30th year.

▶ Maintenance of dividend scales would create significant losses in later years under the 1 percent assumption. But it would be possible to cut dividends. In the case of nonparticipating business this option, is of course, not available.

The various projected general account transactions under the three investment earnings rate assumptions per $1,000 of insurance originally issued are shown

Table 21–6.

GROSS PREMIUMS AND VALUATION PREMIUMS FOR $1,000 INITIAL AMOUNT VARIABLE LIFE INSURANCE ISSUED TO MALE AGE 35

| | Separate Account Assumed to Earn | | | | | |
| | 1% | | 4% | | 7% | |
	Present Value of Total	*Level Annual Equivalent*	*Present Value of Total*	*Level Annual Equivalent*	*Present Value of Total*	*Level Annual Equivalent*
GROSS PREMIUM	$446.17	$23.72	$446.17	$23.72	$ 446.17	$23.72
VALUATION PREMIUM:						
Acquisition costs:						
First-year	$ 20.18	$ 1.07	$ 20.18	$ 1.07	$ 20.18	$ 1.07
Renewal	11.37	.61	11.37	.61	11.37	.61
Total acquisition costs	31.55	1.68	31.55	1.68	31.55	1.68
Maintenance and settlement expenses	44.00	2.34	44.00	2.34	44.00	2.34
Benefits:						
Net premium transfers to separate account	315.60	16.78	315.60	16.78	315.60	16.78
Benefits less transfers from separate account	55.09	2.93	(85.78)	(4.56)	(127.30)	(6.77)
Cost of minimum death benefit guarantee	4.32	.23	4.32	.23	4.32	.23
	375.01	19.94	234.14	12.45	192.62	10.24
Dividends	112.72	5.99	136.48	7.25	180.40	9.59
Total benefits	487.73	25.93	370.62	19.70	373.02	19.83
TOTAL VALUATION PREMIUM	$563.28	$29.95	$446.17	$23.72	$ 448.57	$23.85

in Table 21–5. For the 1 percent assumption the net result—assuming dividend scales are maintained—is a loss of $116.70, representing mainly the cost of fulfilling the minimum death benefit guarantee. A 4 percent assumption produces close to a break-even situation; in fact, $4.32, the indicated margin, is considered to be the normal cost of furnishing the minimum death benefit guarantee, and so the 4 percent assumption may be considered the break-even assumption. From the point of view of the separate account, the 4 percent assumption is really a 3 percent assumption because asset charges amount to 1 percent. The 7 percent assumption produces a contribution to surplus.

The various patterns of benefits and expenses can readily be translated into valuation premiums. All that's needed in this case is to divide the various amounts in Table 21–5 by the present value of a zero-interest annuity of $1 for the premium-paying period, which is $18.81. This is done in Table 21–6. The only modification of the data in Table 21–5 made for purposes of calculating the valuation premiums are:

▶ To eliminate investment management fees and the related expenses, on the assumption the two will adequately match on a cash basis.
▶ To assess a uniform charge of $4.32 for the mini-

mum death benefit guarantee. This amount is deemed to be "paid out" to a special reserve held for the benefit of all blocks of business.

Thus, given an assumed investment earnings rate of 4 percent, the valuation premium equals the gross premium. Given an assumed investment earnings rate of 1 percent, a loss of $117.11 ($563.28 − $446.17) would need to be recognized.*

The reserves for the 4 percent assumption are shown in Table 21–7. These reserves would yield a margin of zero each year so long as actual experience follows the assumptions. In Year 1, for example, the adjusted income statement would report the components shown in Table 21–8.

Because the net premium transfers follow the pattern of general account valuation premiums, and because net recoveries from the separate account follow the pattern of benefit payments, the adjusted general account reserves are quite nominal in this case. Separate account reserves per unit in force are shown for comparative purposes in the last column of Table 21–7.

*Losses that became apparent after the year of issue would be measured in the same way; the indicated loss would be reduced by the net reserves then being held. Loss recognition is discussed in Chapter 24.

Table 21–7.

PROGRESSION OF GENERAL ACCOUNT RESERVES (ASSUMING ZERO INTEREST) FOR $1,000 VARIABLE WHOLE LIFE ISSUED TO MALE AGE 35

| Year | Units In Force At Beginning of Year | Acquisition Costs | | | Maintenance and Settlement Expenses | | | Benefits |
		Valuation Premiums Received	Costs Incurred	Ending Fund	Valuation Premiums Received	Costs Incurred	Ending Fund	Valuation Premiums Received
1	1.000	$1.68	$20.18	$ −18.50	$2.34	$2.03	$ .31	$19.70
2	.809	1.36	1.59	−18.73	1.89	1.74	.46	15.94
3	.768	1.29	1.06	−18.50	1.80	1.65	.61	15.13
4	.730	1.23	1.01	−18.28	1.71	1.57	.75	14.38
5	.695	1.17	.96	−18.07	1.63	1.50	.88	13.69
6	.664	1.12	.92	−17.87	1.55	1.43	1.00	13.08
7	.635	1.07	.88	−17.68	1.49	1.37	1.12	12.51
8	.608	1.02	.84	−17.50	1.42	1.31	1.23	11.98
9	.584	.98	.81	−17.33	1.37	1.26	1.34	11.50
10	.561	.94	.78	−17.17	1.31	1.21	1.44	11.05
11	.541	.91	.54	−16.80	1.27	1.17	1.54	10.66
12	.522	.88	.52	−16.44	1.22	1.13	1.63	10.28
13	.504	.85	.50	−16.09	1.18	1.09	1.72	9.93
14	.488	.82	.49	−15.76	1.14	1.06	1.80	9.61
15	.473	.80	.47	−15.43	1.11	1.03	1.88	9.32
16	.460	.77		−14.66	1.08	1.01	1.95	9.06
17	.446	.75		−13.91	1.04	.98	2.01	8.79
18	.434	.73		−13.18	1.01	.96	2.06	8.55
19	.422	.71		−12.47	.99	.93	2.12	8.31
20	.410	.69		−11.78	.96	.91	2.17	8.08
21	.398	.67		−11.11	.93	.89	2.21	7.84
22	.387	.65		−10.46	.91	.87	2.25	7.62
23	.376	.63		− 9.83	.88	.85	2.28	7.41
24	.365	.61		− 9.22	.85	.83	2.30	7.19
25	.354	.59		− 8.63	.83	.81	2.32	6.97
26	.343	.58		− 8.05	.80	.80	2.32	6.76
27	.331	.56		− 7.49	.78	.78	2.32	6.52
28	.320	.54		− 6.95	.75	.76	2.31	6.30
29	.308	.52		− 6.43	.72	.74	2.29	6.07
30	.296	.50		− 5.93	.69	.72	2.26	5.83
31	.284	.48		− 5.45	.66	.70	2.22	5.60
32	.271	.46		− 4.99	.63	.68	2.17	5.34
33	.259	.44		− 4.55	.61	.66	2.12	5.10
34	.246	.41		− 4.14	.57	.64	2.05	4.85
35	.233	.39		− 3.75	.55	.61	1.99	4.59
36	.220	.37		− 3.38	.51	.59	1.91	4.33
37	.207	.35		− 3.03	.48	.56	1.83	4.08
38	.194	.33		− 2.70	.45	.54	1.74	3.82
39	.181	.30		− 2.40	.42	.51	1.65	3.57
40	.169	.28		− 2.12	.39	.49	1.55	3.33
41	.156	.26		− 1.86	.37	.46	1.46	3.07
42	.144	.24		− 1.62	.34	.43	1.37	2.84
43	.132	.22		− 1.40	.31	.41	1.27	2.60
44	.120	.20		− 1.20	.28	.38	1.17	2.36
45	.108	.18		− 1.02	.25	.35	1.07	2.13
46	.098	.16		− .86	.23	.33	.97	1.93
47	.087	.15		− .71	.20	.30	.87	1.71
48	.077	.13		− .58	.18	.27	.78	1.52

Continued

Table 21–7. Continued

Benefits				Units	General Account Adjusted Reserves Per Unit In Force				Separate Account
Transfers to (from) Separate Account		Benefits		In Force		Maintenance			Reserve
Net Premiums	Net Recoveries	and Dividends	Ending Fund	at End of Year	Acquisition Costs	and Settlement Expenses	Benefits	Total	Per Unit In Force
$16.78	$ (5.36)	$ 1.31	$ 6.97	.809	$−22.87	$ .38	$ 8.62	$−13.87	$ 15.00
13.69	(3.46)	2.63	10.05	.786	−24.39	.60	13.09	−10.70	30.00
12.99	(3.99)	3.60	12.58	.730	−25.34	.84	17.23	− 7.27	45.00
12.35	(4.47)	4.48	14.60	.695	−26.30	1.08	21.01	− 4.21	61.00
11.76	(4.89)	5.25	16.17	.664	−27.21	1.32	24.35	− 1.54	77.00
11.23	(5.26)	5.77	17.51	.635	−28.14	1.57	27.57	1.00	93.00
10.74	(5.58)	6.25	18.61	.608	−29.08	1.84	30.61	3.37	110.00
10.29	(5.84)	6.62	19.52	.584	−29.97	2.11	33.42	5.56	126.00
9.87	(6.08)	6.97	20.26	.561	−30.89	2.39	36.11	7.61	143.00
9.49	(6.27)	7.29	20.80	.541	−31.74	2.66	38.45	9.37	160.00
9.14	(6.45)	7.56	21.21	.522	−32.18	2.95	40.63	11.40	178.00
8.82	(6.60)	7.82	21.45	.504	−32.62	3.23	42.56	13.17	196.00
8.52	(6.74)	8.01	21.59	.488	−32.95	3.52	44.24	14.81	213.00
8.25	(6.87)	8.24	21.58	.473	−33.32	3.81	45.62	16.11	231.00
7.99	(6.99)	8.45	21.45	.460	−33.54	4.09	46.63	17.18	250.00
7.75	(7.23)	8.81	21.18	.446	−32.87	4.37	47.49	18.99	268.00
7.53	(7.47)	9.12	20.79	.434	−32.05	4.63	47.90	20.48	287.00
7.31	(7.68)	9.40	20.31	.422	−31.23	4.88	48.13	21.78	305.00
7.10	(7.91)	9.68	19.75	.410	−30.41	5.17	48.17	22.93	324.00
6.90	(8.11)	9.95	19.09	.398	−29.60	5.45	47.96	23.81	343.00
6.71	(8.34)	10.05	18.51	.387	−28.71	5.71	47.83	24.83	361.00
6.52	(8.70)	10.32	17.99	.376	−27.82	5.98	47.85	26.01	380.00
6.33	(9.06)	10.56	17.57	.365	−26.93	6.25	48.14	27.46	399.00
6.14	(9.43)	10.82	17.23	.354	−26.05	6.50	48.67	29.12	418.00
5.95	(9.80)	11.10	16.95	.343	−25.16	6.76	49.42	31.02	437.00
5.76	(10.16)	11.38	16.73	.331	−24.32	7.01	50.54	33.23	455.00
5.56	(10.53)	11.69	16.53	.320	−23.41	7.25	51.66	35.50	474.00
5.36	(10.91)	12.00	16.38	.308	−22.57	7.50	53.18	38.11	492.00
5.16	(11.30)	12.35	16.24	.296	−21.72	7.74	54.86	40.88	511.00
4.95	(11.66)	12.68	16.10	.284	−20.88	7.96	56.69	43.77	529.00
4.74	(12.03)	13.15	15.84	.271	−20.11	8.19	58.45	46.53	547.00
4.53	(12.36)	13.54	15.47	.259	−19.27	8.38	59.73	48.84	564.00
4.31	(12.66)	13.92	15.00	.246	−18.50	8.62	60.98	51.10	582.00
4.09	(12.92)	14.23	14.45	.233	−17.77	8.80	62.02	53.05	598.00
3.87	(13.14)	14.47	13.84	.220	−17.05	9.05	62.91	54.91	615.00
3.65	(13.28)	14.65	13.15	.207	−16.33	9.23	63.53	56.43	631.00
3.43	(13.34)	14.71	12.43	.194	−15.62	9.43	64.07	57.88	647.00
3.20	(13.33)	14.70	11.68	.181	−14.92	9.61	64.53	59.22	662.00
2.99	(13.26)	14.61	10.91	.169	−14.20	9.76	64.56	60.12	677.00
2.77	(13.12)	14.46	10.13	.156	−13.59	9.94	64.94	61.29	692.00
2.56	(12.93)	14.25	9.32	.144	−12.92	10.14	64.72	61.94	706.00
2.35	(12.66)	13.94	8.53	.132	−12.27	10.38	64.62	62.73	721.00
2.14	(12.35)	13.60	7.74	.120	−11.67	10.33	64.50	63.16	735.00
1.95	(11.99)	13.68	6.46	.108	−11.11	10.83	59.82	59.54	748.00
1.76	(11.56)	12.70	5.69	.098	−10.41	10.92	58.06	58.57	761.00
1.57	(11.07)	12.13	4.99	.087	− 9.89	11.15	57.36	68.62	774.00
1.40	(10.53)	11.52	4.31	.077	− 9.22	11.30	55.97	58.05	785.00
1.24	(9.98)	10.91	3.60	.068	− 8.53	11.47	53.82	56.76	797.00

Continued

Table 21–7. Continued

| Year | Units In Force At Beginning of Year | Acquisition Costs | | | Maintenance and Settlement Expenses | | | Benefits |
		Valuation Premiums Received	Costs Incurred	Ending Fund	Valuation Premiums Received	Costs Incurred	Ending Fund	Valuation Premiums Received
49	.068	.11		− .47	.16	.25	.69	1.34
50	.059	.10		− .37	.14	.22	.61	1.16
51	.051	.09		− .28	.12	.20	.53	1.01
52	.043	.07		− .21	.10	.17	.46	.85
53	.037	.06		− .15	.09	.15	.40	.73
54	.030	.05		− .10	.07	.13	.34	.59
55	.025	.04		− .06	.06	.11	.29	.49
60	.007	nil		nil	.02	.05	.05	.14
65	.001	nil		–0–	nil	.02	–0–	.02

Under certain product designs it would be possible for adjusted benefit reserves to be negative for many durations. Presumably this would be offset by an overstatement of the separate account liability. Adjusted benefit reserves should preferably be combined with separate account liabilities for balance sheet purposes where this is the case.

Variable life valuation is on the frontier of generally accepted accounting principles for life insurance companies and will call for ingenious approaches by companies, actuaries, and accountants.

Presentation and Disclosure

The general format shown in Table 21–8 might be appropriate for presenting variable life transactions in the income statement, although some degree of combining of amounts might be desirable.

As far as the balance sheet is concerned, separate account assets and liabilities should generally be shown separately, as should material receivables from the separate account.

The accounting policies note should describe the methods used to account for variable life. Assumptions and amounts should be disclosed in a manner appropriate to a separate line of business.

Index-Linked Products

An index-linked life insurance product is designed such that the benefits vary not with a pool of investments but with an index of some sort—the Consumer Price Index, the Dow-Jones Industrial Average, or some other general index.

Thus the face amount payable on death (and hence the cash value, assuming a constant durational cash value per $1,000 of insurance) might be adjusted to compensate, for example, for increases in the Consumer Price Index since the date of purchase. The face amount therefore compounds at a rate roughly equivalent to the rate of inflation, subject usually to a maximum.

An index-linked policy might be considered to represent increasing protection for a level premium. It is necessary to project the behavior of the index, calculate the present value of the benefits that will be payable if the index behaves in the projected manner, calculate a valuation premium appropriate to such present value, and calculate reserves based on the valuation premium and the assumed pattern of benefits.

Presumably the interest assumption will bear some relationship to the index assumption. It seems unreasonable, for example, to assume 3 percent interest and 6 percent inflation in the Consumer Price Index.

Where benefits are linked to a stock average, it is theoretically possible to hedge risk by investing in the stocks making up the average, subject of course to legal restrictions on equity investments. Where this is done, separation of the index-linked business from all other business would be appropriate in developing interest assumptions. Where investments are in media

Table 21–7. Continued

Benefits				Units In Force at End of Year	General Account Adjusted Reserves Per Unit In Force				Separate Account Reserve Per Unit In Force
Transfers to (from) Separate Account		Benefits and Dividends	Ending Fund		Acquisition Costs	Maintenance and Settlement Expenses	Benefits	Total	
Net Premiums	Net Recoveries								
1.08	(9.34)	10.20	3.06	.059	− 7.97	11.70	51.86	55.59	808.00
.94	(8.66)	9.42	2.52	.051	− 7.25	11.96	49.41	54.12	818.00
.80	(7.93)	8.61	2.05	.043	− 6.51	12.33	47.67	53.49	829.00
.68	(7.18)	7.80	1.60	.037	− 5.67	12.43	43.24	50.00	839.00
.57	(6.43)	6.97	1.22	.030	− 5.00	13.33	40.67	49.00	848.00
.47	(5.69)	6.16	.87	.025	− 4.00	13.60	34.80	44.40	858.00
.39	(4.97)	5.37	.57	.020	− 3.00	14.50	28.50	40.00	868.00
.11	(2.08)	2.22	.10	.005	nil	10.00	20.00	30.00	920.00
.01	(.76)	.79	−0−	−0−	−	−	−	−	−

other than the stocks making up the index, there is a significant, relatively undeterminable risk that the underlying investments will not perform as well as the index. Fairly heavy provision for adverse deviation—preferably setting the gross premium equal to the valuation premium—would seem to be appropriate in such cases.

Where index-linked business is material, disclosure of methods, assumptions, and amounts should generally be made as if the business were a separate line.

Table 21–8.

FIRST YEAR ADJUSTED INCOME STATEMENT FOR $1,000 VARIABLE WHOLE LIFE ISSUED TO MALE 35

Gross premium		$ 23.72
Interest		−0−
Received from separate account:		
Face amounts of death claims		1.08
Reserves on withdrawals		2.78
Mortality and expense risk charges		.06
Excess of tabular over actual mortality		1.44
	TOTAL INCOME	29.08
Net premiums		16.78
Death claims		1.08
Surrenders		−0−
Dividends		−0−
Cost of minimum death benefit guarantee		.23
Acquisition costs		20.18
Maintenance and settlement expenses		2.03
	TOTAL OUTGO	40.30
	BALANCE BEFORE RESERVE CHANGES	(11.22)
Changes in:		
Benefit reserve		(6.97)
Acquisition cost reserves		18.50
Maintenance and settlement cost reserve		(.31)
	TOTAL RESERVE CHANGES	11.22
	PROFIT	$ −0−

22

Reinsurance

Adjustments for acquisition costs and reserves give rise to special problems where reinsurance is significant to the company making the adjustments. With respect to reinsurance ceded, there is an intimate relationship among adjustments on direct business, adjustments on the ceded portion, and provisions of the reinsurance treaty. With respect to reinsurance assumed, there is a complex relationship among the assuming company's assumptions and the provisions of the reinsurance treaty. Special reinsurance agreements can have a dramatic impact on financial statements.

Most of the discussion which follows adopts the ceding company's point of view. The assuming company's point of view, which in some respects is the reciprocal of the ceding company's point of view, is discussed under a separate caption toward the end of the chapter.

Reinsurance in General

Companies reinsure portions of life and health insurance risks with other companies for various reasons—to protect solvency, stabilize mortality, provide surplus relief, provide additional agency earnings on business that would otherwise be declined, obtain the advantages of the reinsurer's underwriting and administrative skills, limit investment and lapse risks, and so on.[1]

Reinsurance ceded is usually very significant for smaller companies and has a significant effect on profits. Reinsurance also has a signicant effect on the profits of those relatively few companies (mostly large ones) that specialize in reinsurance assumed.

Yearly Renewable Term

Yearly renewable term reinsurance (also called annual renewable term and risk premium reinsurance) involves the purchase, by the ceding company, of term insurance from the assuming company for the net amount at risk. The rates charged are those of the assuming company. The first-year rate may be a fraction of the renewal rate for the same age—in some cases the first-year premium is zero—to provide, in effect, an expense allowance to the ceding company.*

The cost of yearly renewable term reinsurance to the ceding company can be measured in much the same manner as profits on direct business. Reinsurance premiums, claims recoveries, and incremental costs of handling the cessions can be projected (using, of course, the mortality and withdrawal assumptions of the ceding company). For example, Crazy Quilt Life's YRT reinsurance on 1961 issues of whole life (male age 35) was projected as shown in Table 22–1 (cost of handling cessions was ignored by Crazy Quilt because such cost was included in expenses allocated to direct business).

Suppose now that Crazy Quilt provided for net reinsurance cost in profit-testing direct business. Assume that 10 percent of the business is reinsured, on average, and that the net amount at risk (face amount less the reserve) per $1,000 of direct business in the tenth year is $844. The net reinsurance cost in the tenth year, provided for as an expense in profit-testing direct business, would be $.14:

*In addition, the early rates may reflect select mortality savings.

424

Table 22–1.

PROJECTION OF NET YRT REINSURANCE COSTS PER $1,000 OF REINSURANCE CEDED

Year	Units in Force	YRT Premium Paid	Statutory Reserve Credit Interest On	Statutory Reserve Credit Increase In	Deaths Recovered	Net Reinsurance Cost Per Unit Issued	Net Reinsurance Cost Per Unit in Force
1	1.000	$1.71	$.02	$1.22	$ .38	$ .13	$ .13
2	.779	2.78	.04	(.22)	.74	2.31	2.97
3	.662	2.51	.04	(.10)	.75	1.90	2.87
4	.608	2.46	.04	(.01)	.78	1.72	2.83
5	.570	2.46	.04	.01	.81	1.67	2.93
6	.547	2.52	.04	.05	.86	1.65	3.02
7	.524	2.57	.04	.02	.93	1.67	3.19
8	.502	2.63	.04	.04	1.00	1.64	3.27
9	.485	2.72	.05	.05	1.08	1.63	3.36
10	.469	2.81	.05	.05	1.18	1.63	3.48
.	.	.	.	.	.	.	.
15	.394	3.38	.08	.08	1.77	1.62	4.11
.	.	.	.	.	.	.	.
20	.315	3.91	.10	.07	2.08	1.86	5.90
.	.	.	.	.	.	.	.
30	.151	4.05	.10	(.02)	1.91	2.26	14.97

10th-year net reinsurance cost per reinsurance unit in force	$3.48
Proportion reinsured	x 10%
Net amount at risk ÷ $1,000	x 84%
Percentage persisting into 10th year	x 47%
10th-year net reinsurance cost per $1,000 of direct business issued as it would appear in profit study	$ .14

The premiums, unearned gross premiums, and statutory mean reserves for the YRT reinsurance projected in Table 22–1 are shown in Table 22–2. It will be noted that unearned gross premiums exceed statutory mean reserves until the 25th year, after which statutory mean reserves—which are merely unearned net premiums in the case of annual renewable term insurance—exceed the unearned gross premiums until the later durations. This indicates that deficiency reserves (which should be nominal) will have to be set up at certain later durations by the assuming company.*

*However, it should be noted that YRT reinsurance agreements almost always reserve to the reinsurer the right to change the premium, at least to the extent of equaling the valuation premium, in order to avoid the necessity of setting up deficiency reserves.

Coinsurance

Coinsurance is basically a proportional sharing of premiums, claims, surrenders, and other benefits. However, certain benefits are subject to "convenience" adjustments. For example, "The complications that would attend reinsurer involvement in such things as paid-up dividend additions or settlement options are almost invariably avoided by providing that the ceding company shall accept a lump sum in payment for benefits under the life (but not disability) portion of the policy." [2]

While premiums, reserves, and benefits are shared proportionally, expense reimbursements by there reinsurer are subject to negotiation. The incidence of expense reimbursements may or may not bear a reasonable relationship to the amount and incidence of expenses actually paid by the ceding company.

In 1968 Crazy Quilt Life negotiated a coinsurance agreement with a major reinsurer. The proposal upon which the agreement was based is summarized in Table 22–3.

The first-year reinsurance allowances provided for under the proposal do not, of course, cover all direct

Table 22–2.

YRT REINSURANCE PREMIUMS, UNEARNED GROSS PREMIUMS, AND STATUTORY MEAN RESERVES PER $1,000 OF REINSURANCE IN FORCE

Year	YRT Premium Per $1,000	Unearned Gross Premium	Statutory Mean Reserve	Year	YRT Premium Per $1,000	Unearned Gross Premium	Statutory Mean Reserve
1	$ 1.71	$ .86	$1.22	21	$ 13.29	$ 6.65	$ 6.31
2	3.57	1.79	1.28	22	14.31	7.16	6.90
3	3.79	1.90	1.36	23	15.40	7.70	7.54
4	4.04	2.02	1.46	24	16.56	8.28	8.25
5	4.31	2.16	1.58	25	17.76	8.88	9.02
6	4.60	2.30	1.74	26	19.08	9.54	9.87
7	4.91	4.46	1.86	27	20.57	10.29	10.80
8	5.24	2.62	2.02	28	22.28	11.14	11.80
9	5.59	2.80	2.20	29	24.22	12.11	12.90
10	5.97	2.99	2.39	30	26.48	13.24	14.10
11	6.40	3.20	2.60	31	29.10	14.55	15.41
12	6.88	3.44	2.83	32	31.96	15.98	16.86
13	7.39	3.70	3.09	33	35.02	17.51	18.47
14	7.94	3.97	3.37	34	38.39	19.20	20.23
15	8.54	4.27	3.69	35	42.21	21.11	22.14
16	9.21	4.61	4.04	40	68.42	34.21	33.07
17	9.92	4.96	4.42	45	105.75	52.88	49.12
18	10.67	5.34	4.83	50	155.11	77.56	72.82
19	11.48	5.74	5.29	55	224.05	112.03	103.14
20	12.35	6.18	5.78	60	327.44	163.72	153.72

first-year expenses. Renewal-year allowances, together with policy fees and the effect of full vesting, are generally adequate to cover renewal-year expenses (i.e., commissions, premium taxes, and maintenance and settlement expenses). All other things being equal, and absent any refund provision, the cost of reinsurance in this case might be viewed as either (1) the excess of actual expenses over expenses reimbursed on the reinsured amounts, or (2) profits foregone on the reinsured business, or (3) the sum of (1) and (2).

A projection of coinsurance costs per $1,000 coinsured would look pretty much like a projection of profits on direct business per $1,000 issued, except that expenses used for projection purposes would give effect to the specific provisions of the reinsurance agreement.

Modified Coinsurance

Modified coinsurance might be viewed as being identical to coinsurance plus a "loan" from the assuming company to the ceding company of an amount equivalent to the statutory reserves on the business reinsured. The interest rate applicable to the "loan" might be fixed by the reinsurance agreement, it might

be based on a formula specified in the reinsurance agreement, it might be negotiated annually, or it might be equal to the ceding company's actual investment earnings rate.

The advantages of modified coinsurance are much the same as the advantages of coinsurance. In addition, the ceding company is able to include among its assets an amount equal to the reserves retained. Finally, the ceding company will often be able to earn investment income on such assets in excess of the interest paid to the assuming company.

Non-Proportional Reinsurance

Certain types of coverages similar in many respects to excess loss contracts found in the property-liability business are often encountered in the life insurance business.

Catastrophe reinsurance is designed to protect a company from catastrophic loss attributable to a single accidental event. For example, a company selling insurance in the college market is exposed to the risk that a group of insured students from a single campus will die together in a dormitory fire or in an automobile accident. Catastrophe reinsurance will

Table 22–3.

COINSURANCE PROPOSAL FOR CRAZY QUILT LIFE*

Reinsurance Premiums

The reinsurance premium will be the premium charged the insured, exclusive of the policy fee if any.

Reinsurance Allowances

Policy Year	Commission	Expense Allowance	Total Allowance
1	84.0%	11.0%	95.0%
2	9.5	5.5	15.0
3 on	9.5	.5	10.0

These allowances are fully vested.

Premium Tax

Crazy Quilt Life will be reimbursed for state premium taxes incurred on coinsurance premiums.

Recapture

After an increase in retention, recapture may be exercised according to the terms of the reinsurance treaty, subject to a time limit of 20 years.

*Developed for Crazy Quilt by The Lincoln National Life Insurance Company.

---

limit the company's exposure in such a situation to a defined amount.

Stop-loss reinsurance is available to limit a company's total loss for a period to a defined amount. For example, a small company whose exposure base is insufficient to have much confidence in the law of large numbers might buy coverage limiting its aggregate claims during a calendar year to, say, 110 percent of 1955–60 tabular mortality.

Recapture

When a company increases its retention limit it generally wants to "recapture" previously-ceded business in an amount sufficient to bring the retention limits applicable to the older business into line with the new retention limit.

In the case of yearly-renewable term business, recapture is effected simply by adjusting the net amount at risk on the anniversary date and paying YRT premiums on the new amounts. Of course, the ceding company must then carry the reserves on the recaptured business.

In the case of coinsurance, recapture is generally accomplished by surrendering the business for the cash values applicable to the portion recaptured. The ceding company must carry the reserves on the business. The difference between cash values received and reserves set up is charged to operations or surplus for statutory purposes.

The effect of recapturing modified coinsurance is approximately the same as coinsurance.

Reinsurance treaties usually specify a minimum period before recapture is permitted. This is designed to allow the assuming company to recover its investment in the business.

Table 22–4.

ILLUSTRATION OF YRT EXPERIENCE RATING CALCULATION FOR ONE YEAR

Premiums earned	$100,000
Claims incurred	(40,000)
Expense and risk charges at $1.00 per $1,000	(20,000)
Balance before application of loss carryforward	40,000
Net loss carryforward from prior two years	(20,000)
	20,000
50% retained by assuming company	(10,000)
EXPERIENCE REFUND	$ 10,000

Table 22–5.

ILLUSTRATION OF COINSURANCE EXPERIENCE RATING CALCULATION FOR ONE YEAR

Premiums	$500,000
Interest on:	
Life reserves	50,000
Contingency reserve	10,000
	560,000
Less:	
Claims incurred	100,000
Surrenders paid	50,000
Reinsurance allowance	125,000
Risk and profit charge at $1.00 per $1,000	25,000
Federal income taxes	25,000
Increase in reserves	135,000
	460,000
Balance	100,000
Allocation to contingency reserve	50,000
Balance	50,000
Reinsurer's share (50%)	25,000
EXPERIENCE REFUND	$ 25,000

Contingency reserve:

	Assuming Company's	Ceding Company's
Beginning balance	$125,000	$125,000
Addition for year	25,000	25,000
Ending balance	$150,000	$150,000

Recapture before the expiration of the minimum period can sometimes be negotiated. Early recapture may call for restitution to the assuming company of some portion of its unamortized investment in the business.

Experience Rating

Many reinsurance treaties provide for experience rating under which the ceding company shares in the profits on the reinsured business. Experience rating has become common for all forms of reinsurance. In the case of YRT reinsurance, many reinsurers offer the ceding company a choice of higher rates with experience refunding and lower rates without experience refunding.

A typical YRT refund formula might provide for returning to the ceding company one-half of the profits on the ceded business after deducting a charge by the reinsurer—say 10 percent of premiums—for risk and profit. Losses are not "shared" and there is typically a loss carryforward limitation, i.e., losses incurred in a given year serve to offset profits in future

years for a defined number (e.g., two) of years. The workings of a simple YRT refund formula are illustrated in Table 22–4.

A coinsurance experience rating formula typically requires the development of a summary of operations for the block of reinsured business. Usually there is an unlimited loss carryforward provision under coinsurance agreements because of the high initial acquisition costs.

The year's profit on the reinsured business, after deducting the reinsurer's charge for risk and profit, is divided equally between the assuming company and the ceding company. But "equal division" does not necessarily imply that 50 percent of the indicated gain from operations is paid to the ceding company. Usually 50 percent of the profit is allocated to a contingency reserve, and 50 percent of the amount remaining after the allocation is paid to the ceding company. Half the contingency reserve is maintained for the account of the ceding company; half is maintained for the account of the assuming company. Eventually the portion of the contingency reserve allocated to the ceding company will be paid to the ceding company or used to offset future losses. The assuming company reports the contingency reserve (usually including its own share, which it may label as a "reserve for stabilization of reinsurance experience") as a liability for statutory purposes. The ceding company takes credit for its share of the contingency reserve only when it is received in cash or, indirectly, when it is used to offset future losses.

The workings of a simple experience rating formula for coinsured business is illustrated in Table 22–5. A modified coinsurance formula would work in much the same manner, except that the increase in reserves would be replaced by the reserves actually returned in cash to the ceding company.

Special Reinsurance Agreements

The discussion thus far has dealt largely with "normal" reinsurance agreements, i.e., those designed to implement a company's retention policy. A normal reinsurance agreement might be defined as one which shifts economic risk to the reinsurer to a degree consistent with the ceding company's ability to carry risk itself. Such an agreement may furnish surplus relief, but not to such an extent as to give the ceding company a disproportionate front-ending of assets or income or both.

Special reinsurance agreements may be defined as those which either do not shift economic risk or which provide a disproportionate front-ending of assets or income or both to the ceding company.

Special reinsurance agreements are defined and discussed at length later in this chapter.

"Cost of Reinsurance"

Occasional reference was made in preceding pages to the "cost of reinsurance". In general, this term has been used to describe the difference between (1) financial results that would have been experienced if the business had not been reinsured and (2) the financial results experienced after taking reinsurance into account.

In terms of economic benefits and detriments, however, calculation of the "cost of reinsurance" is much more complicated than that. For example, to the extent that policies subject to reinsurance could not be written in the absence of a reinsurance agreement because the company's retention would be exceeded, it can be argued that there really is no reinsurance "cost"—that in fact the reinsurance arrangement produces a profit.

Exactly how a life insurance company views the "cost of reinsurance" may have little or no relationship to accounting notions of cost.

Accounting for Normal Agreements

The life insurance audit guide is silent on the accounting procedures to be followed with respect to normal reinsurance agreements. The guide limits its discussion to "special" reinsurance agreements, which are discussed later in this chapter.

The principal formal discussion of the accounting aspects of standard reinsurance agreements is to be found in "Recommendation No. 4" of the Committee on Financial Reporting Principles of the American Academy of Actuaries, which provides that

(1) When reserves are computed according to generally accepted accounting principles, the cost of reinsurance ceded must be taken into consideration. An equivalent alternative to recognizing the cost directly in the reserve calculation is to calculate the reserves without consideration of reinsurance and calculate an adjustment to this reserve for the ceded reinsurance. Although this adjustment is frequently referred to as a "reinsurance reserve credit", it is important to keep in mind that it is actually an adjustment of the basic reserve and has no special independent significance. In particular, there is no necessary relationship between the reinsurance reserve adjustment of the reinsured company and the reserve for the reinsurance accepted established by the reinsurer (except in the case of affiliated companies filing consolidated statements).

(2) The degree of materiality of reinsurance adjustments is such that most companies will be able to use simplified approaches without materially distorting their financial statements. For example, for YRT, most companies will find it convenient to calculate, as the reinsurance adjustment, the statutory reserve credit, the unearned reinsurance premium, or possibly no adjustment at all. For coinsurance, the adjustment to the benefit reserve would usually be proportional to the benefit reserve computed prior to adjustment for reinsurance and the expense reserve would need to be adjusted to reflect the amount and incidence of expenses reimbursed by the reinsurer. Although the theoretical adjustment for modified coinsurance can be very complicated, usually the same approach as for coinsurance will give satisfactory results except that the interest rate used should recognize the interest rate on which the mean reserve adjustment is calculated. Special consideration must be given to those reinsurance arrangements where the conditions of the reinsurance do not parallel those of the original policy.

(3) In determining the reinsurance cost, it is appropriate to take into consideration the expected value

of all transactions between the reinsurer and the reinsured including reinsurance premiums, claim reimbursements, experience refunds, and any other benefits or expenses reimbursed by the reinsurer. Because the reinsurance reserve adjustment relates to the reserves for the basic policy, it is important that the assumptions for the reinsurance adjustment be consistent with the original assumptions. When testing for recoverability of acquisition expenses or when testing for the necessity for reserve strengthening to recognize future losses, the expected cost of the reinsurance must be taken into consideration.[4]

There are several very significant points raised in the proposed "Recommendation No. 4" that will be explored in the pages that follow.

Treatment of Reinsurance "Cost"

Inherent in the American Academy's proposed "Recommendation No. 4" is the view of reinsurance as a cost to be taken into account in essentially the same manner as any benefit or expense. Thus reinsurance represents "an adjustment of the basic reserve and has no special independent significance." In other words, the cost of reinsurance should generally bear a constant percentage relationship to the direct gross premium; such cost becomes an element of the direct valuation premium just like direct claims, surrender values, etc.

In essence, then, reinsurance cost becomes a more or less constant percentage of the direct gross premium. Of course, the reinsurer may structure the agreement so as to produce profits in a completely different pattern.

The American Academy points out that while reinsurance can properly be taken into account directly in the calculation of the reserve on the underlying direct business, an "equivalent alternative" is to calculate the reserve credit separately. Separate calculation is what is most often done in practice, and that is the approach adopted for purposes of the discussion that follows.

Yearly Renewable Term

From the ceding company's point of view, statutory adjustments for yearly renewable term reinsurance ceded are usually fairly simple. In theory, each year's premium (which is normally paid on the annual mode) pays for one year of insurance—no more and no less—so the reserve credit to be taken is, again in theory, equal to the portion of the premium not yet absorbed by mortality costs. On the average, one-half

the premium would be unexpired at the end of the calendar year.

In the traditional statutory mean reserve calculation, the mean reserve credit for **YRT** reinsurance equals one-half of the net premium. This is because the terminal reserve is zero at the beginning and end of the policy year; the only quantity entering into the calculation is the net premium. For convenience, some companies use the unearned gross reinsurance premium as the reserve credit, which overstates it to the extent of the loading. Such overstatement is usually countenanced on grounds of materiality.

In adjusting YRT reinsurance reserves to a generally accepted accounting principles basis, in theory all future reinsurance gross premiums and claim recoveries per unit of underlying direct business issued should be projected, the present value should be computed, and the reinsurance valuation premium component should be expressed as a constant percentage of the gross premium on the underlying direct business.

For level-premium insurance, the present value of projected net reinsurance outlays would be divided by an annuity of $1 for the premium-paying period of the underlying direct business to obtain the valuation premium component for reinsurance cost. For variable-premium insurance, the present value of projected net reinsurance outlays would be divided by the present value of future direct gross premiums; the resulting percentage would be applied to the variable direct gross premium to obtain the variable valuation premium component. The reinsurance reserve credit would naturally derive from the operation of the valuation premium component and the stream of reinsurance outlays.

The net amount at risk for **YRT** reinsurance decreases over time. At the same time, the gross reinsurance premium per $1,000 of net amount at risk is increasing. In terms of each $1,000 of direct business in force, the net effect is to produce some degree of "smoothing" of reinsurance premiums, particularly in the earlier durations. Similarly, reinsurance mortality cost per $1,000 of net amount at risk is increasing, but the cost per $1,000 of direct business is smoothed out somewhat, again primarily in the earlier years. The forces at work are illustrated in Table 22–6.*

Assuming a level reinsurance premium and a level recovery of death claims, and assuming further that

---

*It will be noted from Table 22–6 that the spread between gross reinsurance premiums and mortality cost is greatest in the early years. This suggests that the bulk of the reinsurer's profits is realized in the early years.

Table 22–6.

NET AMOUNT AT RISK, GROSS REINSURANCE PREMIUMS, AND PROJECTED MORTALITY COSTS—YRT
REINSURANCE ON WHOLE LIFE POLICY ISSUED TO MALE AGE 35

| Duration | Underlying Direct Business in Force | Net Amount at Risk* | Gross Reinsurance Premium | | Projected Deaths** | |
			Per $1,000 Net Amount at Risk	Per $1,000 Direct Business in Force	Per $1,000 Net Amount at Risk	Per $1,000 Direct Business in Force
0	$1,000	$1,000	—	—	—	—
1	1,000	985	$ 1.71***	$ 1.68	$ .77	$ .76
2	1,000	969	3.57	3.46	.96	.93
3	1,000	954	3.79	3.62	1.22	1.16
4	1,000	938	4.04	3.79	1.39	1.30
5	1,000	921	4.31	3.97	1.58	1.46
10	1,000	837	5.97	5.00	3.13	2.62
15	1,000	747	8.54	6.38	6.17	4.61
20	1,000	655	12.35	8.09	10.09	6.61
30	1,000	472	26.48	12.50	25.83	12.19
40	1,000	309	68.42	21.14	58.16	17.97
50	1,000	186	155.11	28.85	135.00	25.11
60	1,000	100	327.44	32.74	302.02	30.20

*Net level, 1958 CSO, 3% reserves.

**1950–54 select and ultimate.

***First-year premium is 50% of rate manual premium.

mortality is distributed across the policy year, then the adjusted reinsurance ceded reserve credit would be approximately equal to one-half the projected death claim recoveries for the year. This may be rather simply illustrated as follows:

1. Assume the present value of a projection of reinsurance net costs as follows:

Reinsurance premiums ($20 a year level)	$200
Death claim recoveries ($16 a year level)	160
Net reinsurance cost	$ 40

2. Assume the present value of an annuity of $1 for the premium-paying period of the underlying direct level-premium policy equals — $ 10

3. Then the valuation premium component for reinsurance cost is — $ 4

4. The portion of the reserve on the direct policy applicable to reinsurance cost would progress as follows, ignoring interest:

Valuation premium received 7/1	$ 4
Reinsurance premium paid 7/1	(20)
Death claims recovered by 12/31	8
Reinsurance reserve credit included in reserve on underlying policy	$ 8

The "smoothing" tendency in the early years, the typically immaterial amounts associated with YRT

reinsurance reserves, and the fact that little YRT business remains in force at the later durations, are usually considered as justifying the use of either statutory reserves or unearned gross reinsurance premiums as the reserve credit for purposes of the adjusted statements.

Further Comments on YRT Reserves

However, the assumption that statutory approximates adjusted should not be taken as an article of faith. All articles of faith should be put to the test eventually, and the YRT/statutory convention is no exception.

If adjusted reserves for YRT reinsurance are computed as if YRT reinsurance were independent of the underlying business, then the reinsurance valuation premium will vary with the reinsurance gross premium, and reinsurance reserves (hence reinsurance costs) would be recognized as if reinsurance were a "negative" line of business, with no direct relationship to the underlying direct business. In Crazy Quilt Life's case, for example, valuation premiums per unit of reinsurance in force, computed on this basis, are as follows for issue age 35 at several durations:

Duration	Valuation Premium Per Unit	Reserve Per Unit
1	$ 1.15	$ .78
5	2.72	7.59
10	3.42	14.25
15	4.37	20.38
20	5.54	25.46
25	6.84	28.96
30	8.56	29.52
40	14.48	23.59
50	19.76	21.46
60	22.42	17.95

The net effect is to take reserve credits proportional to reinsurance premiums paid. The "loading", i.e., the reinsurer's profit (absent any refund features) is expensed in proportion to reinsurance premiums paid.

This, however, would be improper. Adjusted reserves on YRT reinsurance should be computed as if YRT reinsurance gross premiums net of claim recoveries represent a cost to be associated like any benefit with the underlying direct premiums; thus the reinsurance valuation premium is a constant percentage of the premium on the direct policy. For a whole life plan, Crazy Quilt's age 35 YRT reinsurance valuation premiums and reserves computed on this basis are as follows for several durations:

Duration	Valuation Premium Per Unit	Reserve Per Unit
1	$1.90	$ (.61)
2	1.90	(.14)
3	1.90	.51
4	1.90	1.22
5	1.90	1.96
10	1.90	3.98
15	1.90	6.09
20	1.90	8.04
25	1.90	8.83
30	1.90	6.40
40	1.90	(.70)
50	1.90	4.96
60	1.90	11.62

The differences in factors are summarized in Table 22–7. Statutory reserves are shown for comparison. The column headed "Adjusted Benefit Reserve Related to Direct Premiums" shows the theoretically correct reserve.

Table 22–8 summarizes the various types of reserves for all YRT reinsurance for Crazy Quilt Life. Note that in this case unearned gross valuation premiums represent a better approximation of the theoretically correct reserves than statutory reserves do.

Implicit Expense Allowances

Usually there is no stated expense allowance paid by the reinsurer to the ceding company in the case of YRT reinsurance. The coverage is often viewed as a purchase of insurance by the ceding company rather than as a sharing arrangement. However, there is often an *implicit* expense allowance in YRT premiums.

In Table 22–6, it was indicated that the first-year reinsurance premium was 50 percent of the normal premium. This constitutes an implicit expense allowance to the ceding company. Some reinsurers do not charge any premium in the first year; this concession is offset by higher premiums in subsequent years.

When YRT reinsurance reserves are adjusted, the projection of net reinsurance cost and the calculation of the reinsurance reserve credit take the difference in incidence into account, and the implicit first-year allowance is effectively amortized over the premium-paying period of the underlying direct policy. Opinion differs as to whether the implicit expense allowance should be separated and offset against direct acquisition costs or whether net reinsurance cost should be treated as equivalent to a benefit. Purists would probably use the former approach, but it may also be argued that net reinsurance cost is borne for the purpose of limiting benefit payments and that the net reserve credit is properly applied to the benefit reserve only (the approach used by Crazy Quilt Life). Both approaches have merit and there should be no objection to either treatment.

When YRT reinsurance reserves are not adjusted —that is, when statutory reserves are held to be an acceptable approximation of adjusted reserves—then implicit expense allowances must be handled separately. They can be calculated by "grossing up" first-year reinsurance premiums, deferring the difference between the grossed-up amount and the amount actually paid, and amortizing the difference by the sum-of-the-years'-premiums method:

First-year reinsurance premiums paid	$100,000
Percentage concession on first-year premiums	25%
Equivalent rate manual premiums	$133,333
Implicit aggregate expense allowance to be deferred and amortized	$ 33,333

Where the first-year premium is zero, it would be necessary to multiply the amounts ceded by the appropriate manual premium, which would probably have to be determined by estimation. Presumably an

Table 22–7.

YRT REINSURANCE RESERVE FACTORS ON 3 BASES—AGE 35

		Adjusted Benefit Reserve	
		---	---
Duration	Statutory Reserve	Related to Reinsurance Premiums	Related to Direct Premiums
1	$ 1.20	$ .78	$(.61)
2	1.24	2.46	(.14)
3	1.30	4.15	.51
4	1.37	5.85	1.22
5	1.46	7.59	1.96
6	1.57	9.09	2.51
7	1.65	10.38	2.88
8	1.76	11.68	3.24
9	1.88	12.96	3.60
10	2.00	14.25	3.98
15	2.76	20.38	6.09
20	3.79	25.46	8.04
25	5.07	28.96	8.83
30	6.66	29.52	6.40
35	8.57	27.32	2.53
40	10.22	23.59	(.70)

average premium would be used to reduce the work involved in calculating the amount.

YRT Refunds

As indicated earlier in this chapter, YRT reinsurance is very often subject to experience rating. The refund is typically equal to 50 percent of the profits of the account, where profits are calculated by deducting from reinsurance premiums the sum of claims, reinsurer's retention, and any loss carryforwards.

Where YRT reserves are adjusted, experience rating refunds may be anticipated. The refund is a natural outgrowth of the projections necessary to calculate the reserve; all that's needed is to take into account, in addition to premiums and claims, the reinsurer's retention. Thus, to carry further a previous illustration, refunds could be recognized according to the following form:

1. Present value of:

Reinsurance premiums	$200
Death claim recoveries	(160)
Reinsurer's retention at $1 per year per $1,000 net amount of risk	(20)
	$ 20
Refunds at 50%	$ 10

2. Net reinsurance cost:

Premiums paid	$200
Claims recovered	(160)
Refunds received	(10)
	$ 30

3. Present value of annuity of $1 for the underlying policy — $ 10

4. Valuation premium component for net reinsurance cost after refunds — $ 3

Comprised of:	
Premiums less claims	$ 4
Refunds	(1)
	$ 3

The reinsurance premium and claim data shown in Table 22–6 are recast in Table 22–9 to show net reinsurance cost after expected refunds at various durations. Assuming "net reinsurance cost after refund" is included as a cost in calculating reserves on the direct business, then the practical effect is to record an asset for expected refunds and to "release" this asset component as refunds are assumed to be received. At any point in time, the reserve will include the present value of refunds earned but not yet received. To the extent that refunds are paid in an amount or at a time other than the amount or the time assumed for reserve purposes, the variances will flow to income.

Note that the refund and the net reinsurance cost are quite level, particularly in the early years (except for the first year, which is affected by the implicit

Table 22–8.

SUMMARY OF YRT REINSURANCE CEDED TRANSACTIONS AND AGGREGATE YRT REINSURANCE CEDED
RESERVE OFFSETS ON 4 BASES (000 Omitted)

Year	Face Amount of YRT Reinsurance Ceded	Units of Original Cessions In Force	Face Amount of Ceded YRT Reinsurance In Force	YRT Reinsurance Ceded Premiums	Unearned Gross Premiums	Statutory Reserves	Adjusted Benefit Reserve Related to Reinsurance Premiums	Adjusted Benefit Reserve Related to Direct Premiums
1941	$ 938	$ 937	$ 923	$ 2	$ 1	$ 1	$ 1	$ (1)
1942	1,386	2,116	2,072	5	3	3	3	(1)
1943	1,806	3,505	3,416	9	5	4	7	(1)
1944	2,117	5,009	4,857	14	7	6	12	(1)
1945	2,665	6,885	6,644	20	10	8	20	1
1946	3,000	8,876	8,523	27	14	11	30	3
1947	3,305	10,969	10,477	34	17	14	43	5
1948	3,648	13,216	12,559	43	22	18	58	9
1949	3,947	15,570	14,717	52	26	21	76	13
1950	4,186	17,976	16,898	61	31	25	96	18
1951	4,443	20,465	19,131	72	36	29	119	24
1952	4,606	22,944	21,324	82	41	33	144	30
1953	4,828	25,491	23,553	94	47	38	171	38
1954	4,717	27,767	25,487	105	53	42	201	46
1955	4,462	29,699	27,055	116	58	47	232	55
1956	3,876	31,024	28,002	126	63	50	265	65
1957	3,857	32,412	29,000	135	68	54	297	75
1958	4,200	34,154	30,332	145	73	59	330	85
1959	4,471	36,060	31,811	156	78	64	364	95
1960	4,970	38,319	33,622	169	85	70	398	105
1961	5,637	41,032	35,862	182	91	76	434	114
1962	6,848	44,665	38,989	199	100	83	473	124
1963	8,525	49,526	43,293	219	110	93	515	135
1964	9,797	55,015	48,173	242	121	103	561	146
1965	11,228	61,278	53,768	269	135	115	612	158
1966	12,507	68,115	59,871	298	149	128	669	172
1967	13,680	75,414	66,366	330	165	141	732	187
1968	14,157	82,491	72,577	362	181	155	801	205
1969	14,962	89,820	78,972	396	198	169	875	224
1970	15,787	97,418	85,567	432	216	184	955	244
1971	16,281	104,935	92,016	469	235	200	1,039	266

expense allowance). Some believe that this condition justifies ignoring refunds in the reserve calculation and simply recording them as received. So long as refunds are paid annually, the only distortion of any consequence is the omission of refunds earned but not received as of December 31. After the first year, however, the lags overlap, thus reducing the effect to negligible proportions. Thus many believe that (1) YRT reserves can be held on a statutory basis, statutory being an acceptable approximation of adjusted; and (2) refunds can be recognized as received.

This approach may indeed be warranted on the basis of materiality, but it should always be tested. Among other things, reinsurers sometimes accelerate refunds for competitive reasons, in which case they are effectively paid before they are earned. Further, implicit first-year expense allowances are amortized very quickly for refund purposes, whereas they may be amortized over a considerable period of time by the ceding company; in that event, either amortization or recognition of the refund should be adjusted.

All of the foregoing comments assume that refunds are paid annually. Thus, for instance, the reserve "releases" the accrued refund component each year as the refunds are assumed to be paid. If there is any significant interruption of this payment pattern, it would generally be necessary to keep track of the refund component of the reserve and adjust it only as the related payments are made. This can become extremely complicated. The problem is probably most

Table 22–9

PROJECTED YRT CASH TRANSACTIONS INCLUDING ESTIMATED REFUNDS PER $1,000 OF DIRECT BUSINESS IN FORCE

Duration	Reinsured Net Amount at Risk*	Projected Gross Reinsurance Premium	Projected Death Claim Recoveries	Reinsurer's Retention at $1 Per $1,000 NAR	Projected Account Profitability	Expected Refund	Net Reinsurance Cost after Refund
1	$985	$ 1.68	$ .76	$.99	$(.07)		$ .92
2	969	3.46	.93	.97	1.49**	$ .75	1.78
3	954	3.62	1.16	.95	1.51	.76	1.70
4	938	3.79	1.30	.94	1.55	.78	1.71
5	921	3.97	1.46	.92	1.59	.80	1.71
10	837	5.00	2.62	.84	1.54	.77	1.61
15	747	6.38	4.61	.75	1.02	.51	1.26
20	655	8.09	6.61	.66	.92	.46	1.02
30	472	12.50	12.19	.47	(.16)	—	.31
40	309	21.14	17.97	.31	2.86	1.43	1.74
50	186	28.85	25.11	.19	3.55	1.78	1.96
60	100	32.74	30.20	.10	2.44	1.22	1.32

*Whole life, male age 35, net level 1958 CSO 3% reserves.
**After application of $.07 loss carryforward from Year 1.

common in the case of coinsurance and modified coinsurance experience rating. The procedures necessary to account for experience rating refunds when refund payments are unpredictable are discussed below under "Coinsurance Refunds".

The treatment of loss carryforwards on the books of the ceding company often presents a difficult problem. Assume, for purposes of discussion, that an experience rating account on the reinsurer's books shows the following (ignoring reinsurer's retention):

	Year 1	Year 2
Premiums	$ 100,000	$100,000
Claims	(120,000)	(60,000)
Loss carryforward		(20,000)
Loss carried forward	$ (20,000)	
Profit		$ 20,000
Refund to ceding company		$ 10,000

Viewed from the vantage point of hindsight, the ceding company had a "profit" on reinsurance transactions in Year 1 that was reversed in Year 2. Should the ceding company defer any part of the "profit" in Year 1?

The answer is yes if the ceding company has any reason to believe that the loss carryforward will be utilized. In this case, the ceding company should record a liability of $10,000 (profit-sharing percentage, 50 percent, times the loss, $20,000) at the end of Year 1. Only where it is known beyond a reasonable

doubt that the loss will not be applied in the future should the ceding company take the reinsurer's loss into income.

Occasionally a reinsurance arrangement might provide that a net loss will be recovered in the future by increasing reinsurance premiums. This is similar in some respects to a funding arrangement. In such cases the entire amount of the loss expected to be recovered by future premium increases should be recorded as a liability by the ceding company, to be reduced only as the related premium increases are paid.

One final word on YRT experience rating refunds. Sometimes the reinsurer reserves the right to modify the refund formula unilaterally. Where there is any evidence that the formula might be changed in such a manner as to reduce the refunds to the ceding company, any anticipation of refunds by the ceding company should be extremely conservative. Preferably, refunds should not be anticipated under such circumstances.

Coinsurance

Absent experience rating or recapture provisions, adjustments for coinsurance are generally quite straightforward. The benefit reserve credit is a simple proportionate share of the direct reserve. The coinsurance expense allowance would be accounted for in the same manner as direct expenses. Direct acquisition costs would be reduced by the amount of the reinsurance acquisition cost reimbursement and the net amount would be amortized. Level renewal expense reimbursements could be ignored; non-level reimbursements would, of course, give rise to a reserve.

Net coinsurance cash flows could, of course, be factored into the calculation of the related reserves on direct business. Normally, however, it will be more convenient to calculate coinsurance reserve and expense offsets separately.

In those cases in which the coinsurance allowance exceeds direct expenses, any such excess should normally be amortized. This is discussed further below under "Accounting for Special Agreements".

One of the complications of YRT reinsurance—i.e., non-level reinsurance costs and the need to translate them into a valuation premium that bears a constant percentage relationship to the gross premium on the underlying direct business—is avoided in the case of coinsurance, since the reinsurance transactions are proportional to the direct transactions.

Modified Coinsurance

The simplest way to view modified coinsurance is to view it as coinsurance coupled with a loan from the reinsurer in an amount equivalent to the statutory reserve. Under this view, a credit against the adjusted reserve would be taken just as if the agreement were a coinsurance agreement. Reinsurance expense allowances would be handled in the same manner as regular coinsurance expense allowances. And the ceding company would carry a liability equal to the "loan", i.e., the statutory reserve. Interest on the statutory reserve "loan" would be recognized as expense when it accrues. This might be referred to as the "coinsurance-with-loan" approach.

That's the simple way. The complicated way is to project reserve transfers and interest payments on the loaned reserves and bring those quantities into the calculation of reinsurance reserves. This might be referred to as the "full-calculation" approach. Complicated or not, this approach is most consistent with the American Academy's "Recommendation No. 4" which specifies that the "expected value of all transactions between the reinsurer and the reinsured" should be taken into account in determining the reinsurance cost that must be reserved for.

If the interest rate applicable to the statutory reserve "loan" is the same as the underlying assumed interest rate, either the coinsurance-with-loan approach or the full-calculation approach will produce the same financial statement result.

If, however, the interest rate applicable to the "loan" differs from the underlying assumed rate, the two approaches will produce different results. Under the coinsurance-with-loan approach, interest income on the statutory reserve is recognized as it is earned and the related interest expense is recognized as it accrues. Since the reserve increases with time, the differential interest income (assuming the earnings rate is higher than the payment rate, which is usually the case) will also increase with time. Under the full-calculation approach, however, this differential is leveled. Thus, the difference between the two approaches lies in the incidence of recognition of differential interest.

Since interest rates on reserves transferred under modified coinsurance agreements are specified in the treaty or negotiated, or are equal to the ceding company's net earned rates which will usually differ from the assumed rates, it would be rare for the payment rate to be exactly equal to the ceding company's underlying assumption. Usually the reserve payment rate is something less than the ceding company expects to earn; this constitutes the principal advantage of modified coinsurance to the ceding company. Thus there would usually be a difference between the coinsurance-with-loan approach and the full-calculation approach. In general, the coinsurance-with-loan approach is more conservative, since the recognition of larger interest differentials associated with the high level of statutory reserves in the later durations is deferred to such later durations.

If a ceding company views its modified coinsurance agreement as a financing arrangement under which the company borrows at one rate and earns another, higher rate, then use of the coinsurance-with-loan approach would be entirely proper even though reserve transfer transactions, and interest on reserves transferred, are not taken into account in calculating reserves. The reinsurer is conceived to be something other than a reinsurer so far as the "loan" agreement is concerned. In other words, the reinsurer is viewed as a lender with respect to the reserve transfers, and the transfers may properly be viewed as something other than reinsurance transactions.

If, however, a company views the modified coinsurance agreement as an integrated reinsurance agreement in which the reserve transfers have no independent significance, the full-calculation approach would be appropriate.

Thus, either approach should be acceptable in practice.

Unless there is a significant disparity between the direct assumed rate and the reserve transfer rate, the

Table 22–10.

EFFECT OF COINSURANCE VS. MODIFIED COINSURANCE FOR $10,000,000 WHOLE LIFE BUSINESS
REINSURED BY CRAZY QUILT LIFE IN 1968 AND 1969 (000 Omitted)

	1968	*1969*	*1970*	*1971*
Amounts reinsured	$10,000	$10,000	$ –0–	$ –0–
Coinsurance				
Premiums paid:				
First year	$ (165)	$ (165)	$ –0–	$ –0–
Renewal		(137)	(265)	(250)
	(165)	(302)	(265)	(250)
Expenses reimbursed:				
Acquisition	140	147	7	–0–
Maintenance	20	36	32	30
Benefits recovered:				
Deaths	5	16	24	27
Surrenders			3	8
	165	199	66	65
Cash outflow before interest	–0–	(103)	(199)	(185)
Interest at earned rates	–0–	(3)	12	(25)
Cash outflow after interest	–0–	(106)	(187)	(210)
Increase in statutory reserves	148	235	175	179
Increase (decrease) in income	$ 148	$ 129	$ (12)	$ (31)
Adjusted amounts:				
Cash outflow after interest	$ –0–	$ (106)	$(187)	$(210)
Change in unamortized acquisition costs	(130)	(130)	6	9
Change in adjusted benefit reserves	114	205	177	170
(Decrease) in income	$ (16)	$ (31)	$ (4)	$ (31)
Modified coinsurance:				
Cash outflow before interest and				
reserve transfers	$ –0–	$ (103)	$(199)	$(185)
Reserve transfers	148	235	175	179
Cash inflow (outflow) before interest	148	132	(24)	(6)
Interest:				
Earned	4	12	16	15
Paid to reinsurer		(7)	(17)	(25)
Increase (decrease) in income	$ 152	$ 137	$ (25)	$ (16)
Adjusted amounts:				
Increase (decrease) in income	$ 152	$ 137	$ (25)	$ (16)
Statutory reserve increases	(148)	(235)	(175)	(179)
Change in unamortized acquisition costs	(130)	(130)	6	9
Change in adjusted benefit reserves	114	205	117	170
(Decrease) in income	$ (12)	$ (23)	$ (77)	$ (16)

difference between the results produced by the two methods should be relatively minor.

All of the foregoing assumes, of course, that the reinsured business is pro rata with respect to all benefit elements except interest on the statutory reserves transferred. Whether under a coinsurance or a modified coinsurance agreement, any divergence of benefit elements would produce a reinsurance reserve that differs from the underlying reserve.*

*YRT reinsurance, in fact, is an illustration of a reinsurance arrangement under which the benefit elements diverge.

Under statutory accounting practices, reserve transfers are usually treated by the ceding company as revenue. However, such transfers do not constitute revenue within the accepted definition of the term. In adjusted statements, reserve transfers should be treated as direct deposits to a liability account.

The difference in treatment of coinsurance and modified coinsurance (without experience rating refund or recapture provisions) on both a statutory basis and an adjusted basis is summarized in Table 22–10 for $10,000,000 in whole life business reinsured by Crazy Quilt Life by each reinsurance method in 1968 and 1969. Note that the only difference, statutory or adjusted, is the effect of interest. Table 22–10 reflects the result of the coinsurance-with-loan approach for modified coinsurance. The full-calculation approach would yield a somewhat different answer. Since the rate paid on reserve transfers to the reinsurer, 4.5 percent, is less than the earned rate, the full-calculation approach would produce a lower decrease in adjusted income than the coinsurance-with-loan approach.

Coinsurance Refunds

As indicated earlier in this chapter, experience rating for coinsurance and modified coinsurance (hereinafter referred to as "coinsurance" without distinction) is based on a kind of accrual-basis statutory summary of operations for the business being experience-rated. Increases in statutory reserves, interest, coinsurance allowances incurred, reinsurer's expense and profit charges, and various other items are taken into account in the experience rating process.

Among other things, this means that the first-year statutory loss is reflected in the account. Primarily for this reason, there is usually an indefinite carryforward of losses under coinsurance refund formulas.

It also means that payment of a refund may be deferred to a distant year when the refund account turns positive. If an increasing level of new business is continually coinsured, the actual payment of refunds could be deferred indefinitely, since the experience rating account reflects composite results. In other words, statutory losses on new coinsurance could offset renewal profits for many years. An experience rating refund may be accumulating, but it may not see the light of day for decades. Even then only part of the refund may be liberated; the reinsurer usually keeps part of it in a contingency reserve.

All these factors make it quite difficult for the ceding company to account for experience rating refunds on coinsured business.

One possible way to approach the problem is to (1) calculate the level annual equivalent of expected refunds, (2) accumulate the resulting valuation premiums at interest, and (3) reduce the accumulation for the portion of refunds paid (*when* they are paid) that represent amounts expected to be paid. Obviously, it may be difficult to separate payments into the portion that assumed experience produced and the portion that variations from assumed experience produced. A variation of the approach is to adjust the accumula-

tion annually for variances from expected experience and reduce the accumulation for amounts actually paid. This latter approach has its difficulties, too, since it requires annual measurement of deviations from expected experience on an adjusted basis.

The calculation of a valuation premium for expected refunds is fairly simple. In Crazy Quilt Life's case, for instance, the level annual equivalent of refunds for 1969 issues of whole life (male age 35) would be as follows per $1,000:

Gross premium to reinsurer	$16.62
Valuation premium for reinsurance recoveries	15.12
	1.50
Reinsurer's expense charge at $1 per $1,000	1.00
Annual profit per $1,000	$ .50
Annual value of refund per $1,000 at 50%	$ .25

This $.25 amount might be referred to as the "refund premium".

It is also fairly simple to accumulate the refund premiums at interest. Assuming that the interest rate used is the same as that used for purposes of calculating adjusted reserves on the underlying business—i.e., 5.5 percent grading .25 percent each five years to an ultimate rate of 3.5 percent—then the $.25 refund premium per $1,000 issued would accumulate to $35.19 in 65 years.

The interrelationship between accumulated refund premiums and the experience rating account is suggested in Table 22–11. The table assumes issue of $100,000 of coinsured whole life business (1969 ratebook) for males age 35. The accumulation of the refund premium assumes no refunds are paid by the reinsurer during the life of the block of business. The experience rating account on the reinsurer's books—assuming the reinsurer's rate is the same as the ceding company's assumption—is also shown.

Note that the contingency reserve allocations (one-half of the refunds computed to be payable) accumulate ultimately to $1,759.77. Although not shown in Table 22–11, the refunds that would normally be payable (the half not allocated to the contingency reserve) would also accumulate to $1,759.77. Assuming both pieces of the refund—the contingency reserve and the accumulated annual refunds—were paid to the ceding company after the block of business has run off would be $1,759.77 plus $1,759.77, or $3,519.54. Except for a minor rounding error, this is equal to the accumulated refund premiums, $3,519.68. At the time the refunds are actually received by the ceding company, the receivable represented by the

Table 22–11.

ACCUMULATION OF REFUND PREMIUMS AND REINSURER'S EXPERIENCE RATING ACCOUNTS FOR $100,000
IN WHOLE LIFE COINSURANCE—MALE AGE 35—1968–69 RATEBOOK

Year	Accumulated Refund Premiums Assuming No Refunds Received	Statutory Gain	Expense Charge at $1.00 Per $1,000	Refund Account before Refund	Indicated Refund at 50%	Accumulated Contingency Reserve Allocations
			Reinsurer's Experience Rating Accounts			
1	$ 25.68	$(1,477.00)	$100.00	$(1,663.74)		
2	48.13	247.00	81.94	(1,581.11)		
3	70.33	214.00	76.13	(1,522.62)		
4	93.13	130.00	73.76	(1,537.54)		
5	116.60	155.00	71.44	(1,533.95)		
6	140.79	136.00	69.90	(1,544.91)		
7	165.71	134.00	68.34	(1,556.91)		
8	191.55	151.00	66.80	(1,550.03)		
9	218.34	169.00	65.27	(1,522.23)		
10	246.15	187.00	63.75	(1,472.43)		
11	274.72	193.00	62.25	(1,408.76)		
12	304.02	194.00	60.76	(1,339.30)		
13	334.40	209.00	59.28	(1,249.06)		
14	365.93	222.00	57.81	(1,139.11)		
15	398.66	234.00	56.34	(1,009.52)		
16	432.14	229.00	54.88	(875.08)		
17	466.33	222.00	53.42	(740.06)		
18	501.78	230.00	51.96	(588.72)		
19	538.54	239.00	50.51	(419.24)		
20	576.67	247.00	49.05	(231.80)		
21	615.50	235.00	47.59	(46.39)	$67.13	$ –0–
22	654.99	221.00	46.13	134.26	95.27	34.31
23	695.88	227.00	44.67	190.53	98.66	84.55
24	738.23	232.00	43.19	197.31	101.22	138.78
25	782.00	235.00	41.29	202.43	81.43	196.76
26	825.28	196.00	39.41	162.85	60.55	246.65
27	867.87	154.00	37.56	121.10	60.66	287.39
28	911.60	152.00	35.36	121.31	61.24	329.81
29	956.53	151.00	33.23	122.48	60.76	374.23
30	1,002.74	148.00	31.16	121.51	42.35	420.18
31	1,047.76	111.00	29.16	84.70	22.29	457.48
32	1,091.28	70.00	26.94	44.57	22.87	484.83
33	1,135.78	69.00	24.82	45.73	22.48	513.44
34	1,181.27	66.00	22.56	44.96	22.55	542.84
35	1,227.82	64.00	20.43	45.09	22.02	573.31
36	1,275.48	61.00	18.45	44.04	20.49	604.58
37	1,324.30	56.00	16.41	40.98	19.39	636.16
38	1,374.35	52.00	14.54	38.77	17.75	668.29
39	1,425.68	47.00	12.70	35.50	16.02	700.71
40	1,478.38	42.00	11.04	32.04	14.78	733.38
41	1,532.53	38.00	9.45	29.55	12.40	766.57
42	1,588.22	32.00	8.05	24.79	10.96	799.71
43	1,645.54	28.00	6.82	21.92	10.00	833.27
44	1,704.58	25.00	5.68	20.00	8.46	867.52
45	1,765.42	21.00	4.65	16.92	6.85	902.19
46	1,828.17	17.00	3.77	13.69	5.70	937.25
47	1,892.92	14.00	3.00	11.39	4.48	972.95
48	1,959.77	11.00	2.34	8.96	3.73	1,009.29
49	2,028.82	9.00	1.79	7.46	2.41	1,046.51
50	2,100.16	6.00	1.34	4.82		

Continued

Table 22–11. Continued

			Reinsurer's Experience Rating Accounts			
Year	Accumulated Refund Premiums Assuming No Refunds Received	Statutory Gain	Expense Charge at $1.00 Per $1,000	Refund Account before Refund	Indicated Refund at 50%	Accumulated Contingency Reserve Allocations
51	2,173.92	5.00	.98	4.16	2.08	1,084.36
52	2,250.18	3.00	.70	2.38	1.19	1,123.37
53	2,329.06	2.00	.49	1.56	.78	1,163.29
54	2,410.66	2.00	.33	1.73	.87	1,204.41
55	2,495.09	1.00	.21	.82	.41	1,247.00
56	2,582.45	1.00	.13	.90	.45	1,290.86
57	2,672.86	.41	.08	.33	.17	1,336.27
58	2,766.42	21	.05	.16	.08	1,383.13
59	2,863.25	Nil	Nil	Nil	Nil	1,431.58
60	2,963.47	Nil	Nil	Nil	Nil	1,481.68
61	3,067.19	Nil	Nil	Nil	Nil	1,533.54
62	3,174.55	Nil	Nil	Nil	Nil	1,587.21
63	3,285.65	Nil	Nil	Nil	Nil	1,642.77
64	3,400.65	Nil	Nil	Nil	Nil	1,700.26
65	3,519.68	Nil	Nil	Nil	Nil	1,759.77

accumulated refund premiums would be reversed to income.

Assuming that experience exactly follows the assumptions, any refund paid by the reinsurer would be applied to reduce the accumulated refund premiums balance. Suppose, for example, that one-half the refunds are payable as they appear in the experience rating account, with the other half being retained in a contingency reserve until the business runs off. The accumulated refund balance would be reduced for each such payment. At the end of the 65th year the accumulated refund balance would be $1,760, which would be the amount of the contingency reserve then payable to the ceding company by the reinsurer.

The question naturally arises as to what happens if actual refunds differ from expected refunds. Suppose, for example, the refund that develops in the 22nd year is $75.00, not $67.13, and the amount then payable is $37.50, not $33.57. Obviously actual experience underlying the refund has differed from expected experience. One approach is to record the difference at the time of payment. Thus $7.87 ($75.00 − $67.13) would be recorded as additional income at the time of payment. The conceptual entries would be as follows on the ceding company's books:

Cash	$37.50	
Reinsurance refunds		$37.50
To record refund received.		

Reinsurance refunds	33.57	
Accumulated refund premiums		33.57
To reduce accumulated refund premiums for expected portion of refunds received.		
Additional refunds receivable	3.94	
Reinsurance refunds		3.94
To increase refunds receivable for amounts earned in excess of expected and added to contingency reserves.		

The disadvantages of this approach are obvious. First, the variances are recorded as such when refunds are paid by the reinsurer rather than when they are earned. While a "variance" in this case could be so defined as to accommodate this treatment in terms of theory, it does not match the recording of the variances with the incidence of the underlying deviations giving rise to the refund differences.

Second it is necessary to keep track of expected refunds and correlate them with actual refunds. Given a single block of business like the one illustrated, this would be difficult. Given many years of issue, however, it may be impossible to relate a particular actual refund to discrete refund premium accumulations.

Therefore it may be preferable to compute actual adjusted refunds each year and carry, as a receivable, the accumulated actual adjusted refunds.

As indicated in Table 22–11, the first-year statutory

loss on the coinsured business is $1,477.00. The expected first-year adjusted gain is $150.00:

Gross premium per $1,000	$ 16.62
Valuation premium for reinsurance recoveries	15.12
Expected adjusted gain per $1,000	$ 1.50
Units of $1,000 issued	100
Expected adjusted gain	$150.00

The adjusted gain is the adjusted reinsurance cost to the ceding company before any refunds. The expected net cost after refunds would be $125.00.

Assume that first-year actual experience is the same as assumed.

Now consider the second year. The expected statutory gain is $247.00 and the expected adjusted gain is $123.00:

Units expected to persist into second year	$81,940
Expected adjusted gain per $1,000	$ 1.50
Expected adjusted gain	$123.00

Suppose that the actual adjusted gain is $133.00 and that $83,000 of face amount persists into the second year. The actual refund on an adjusted basis would be calculated as follows:

Actual adjusted gain	$133.00
Reinsurer's expense charge (83 x $1.00)	83.00
	$ 50.00
Actual adjusted refund (50%)	$ 25.00
Expected refund—	
($81,940 ÷ $1,000) x .25 x 100	20.49
Additional refund earned	$ 4.51

This additional amount, $4.51, could be added to the accumulated refund premiums balance to accumulate at interest. Actual refunds would then be applied in full against the accumulated refund premiums balance. There would be no need to apportion payments between expected refunds and variances from expected.

What interest rate should be used to calculate actual adjusted refunds and accumulate refund premiums and refund variances? If the ceding company's accounting basis were the same as the basis used for purposes of the reinsurer's experience rating account, then the rate or rates credited by the reinsurer would be used. That would produce a receivable on the ceding company's books exactly equal to the payable on the reinsurer's books.

However, the ceding company's accounting basis differs from that of the experience rating account. One is adjusted; the other is statutory. Thus the only practical approach is to use a conservative estimate of effective rates, presumably the same as the rates assumed on the underlying business. Periodic revaluations using a model office approach can be made to bring the refund accumulations into line with the rates actually used by the reinsurer.

Recapture

As indicated previously, reinsurance agreements commonly provide that after a specified number of years (the "minimum holding period") the ceding company may recapture amounts reinsured up to the ceding company's new retention limit. The minimum holding period is designed to permit the reinsurer to recoup its investment in the business and turn a reasonable profit.

The mechanics of recapture are generally quite simple. For YRT reinsurance, the ceding company simply stops paying premiums on the net amount at risk recaptured. For coinsurance and modified coinsurance, the ceding company usually surrenders the recaptured amount for the applicable cash surrender values.

If the reinsurance agreement permits recapture, should recapture be assumed for purposes of calculating the reinsurance reserve credit? There are three possibilities:

1. Weight the recapture provision by the probability of recapture and take it into account in calculating the reinsurance reserves.

2. Assume that recapture will occur and take it fully into account in calculating the reinsurance reserves.

3. Assume that recapture will not occur and ignore the possibility in calculating the reinsurance reserves.

Possibility No. 1 would not be proper for a ceding company. The probability of recapture means very little where only a handful of reinsurance agreements are in force. (However, as discussed later in this chapter, provision for the probability of recapture may well be appropriate for reinsurers in calculating reserves on reinsurance assumed.)

Thus, for all practical purposes, the choice for the ceding company is Possibility No. 2 (assume recapture) or Possibility No. 3 (don't assume recapture).

In general, the assumption that should be used is that which gives the most conservative answer. Consider, for example, Table 22–12, which shows the cash

Table 22–12.

COMPARISON OF CASH VALUES AVAILABLE ON SURRENDER AND RELATED REINSURANCE RESERVE
CREDITS—WHOLE LIFE, MALE AGE 35, 1968–69 RATEBOOK—PER $1,000 IN FORCE

Duration	Cash Value*	Adjusted Reserve		
		Expense	Benefit	Net
1	$ –0–	$13.06	$ 11.64	$ (1.42)
2	3.00	16.22	26.03	9.81
3	19.00	16.96	40.21	23.25
4	36.00	17.01	53.88	36.87
5	52.00	17.08	68.00	50.92
6	69.00	16.95	82.13	65.18
7	87.00	16.79	96.41	79.62
8	104.00	16.63	111.14	94.51
9	122.00	16.46	126.35	109.89
10	140.00	16.28	142.06	125.78
11	159.00	16.08	158.09	142.01
12	177.00	15.84	174.40	158.56
13	196.00	15.60	191.19	175.59
14	215.00	15.35	208.44	193.09
15	235.00	15.08	226.15	211.07
16	254.00	14.79	244.03	229.24
17	274.00	14.47	262.03	247.56
18	294.00	14.13	280.43	266.30
19	314.00	13.78	299.24	285.46
20	334.00	13.41	318.48	305.07
21	353.00	13.01	337.76	324.75
22	371.00	12.58	357.01	344.43
23	389.00	12.13	376.63	364.50
24	408.00	11.66	396.62	384.96
25	426.00	11.29	416.89	405.60
30	516.00	9.31	512.38	503.07
40	675.00	5.79	670.60	664.81
50	799.00	3.16	797.62	794.46

*Graded to net level statutory reserve (1958 CSO, 3%) at 20th duration and rounded up to next dollar.

values per $1,000 of insurance in force available on recapture at various durations and the related coinsurance reserve offsets. Note that after the fourth year the cash value exceeds the net reserve credit. If the minimum holding period is greater than four years (as it usually would be in the case of coinsurance), then the assumption of recapture would produce greater reserve credits. For example, if the minimum holding period is 10 years, assuming recapture at that time would produce a tenth-year net reserve offset of $140.00, which is greater than the net adjusted reserve (ignoring recapture) of $125.78. In this case recapture should not be assumed.

If, however, the net adjusted reserve at the end of the minimum holding period is *greater* than the cash value, then recapture should generally be assumed. Exactly how to provide for recapture will depend on a company's particular circumstances. If it is assumed

that all business coinsured will be recaptured, then the adjusted reserve would be graded to the cash value by the end of the minimum holding period. If it is assumed that only part of the business will be recaptured—in other words, if the new retention limits can be forecast with reasonable assurance—then the provision for recapture would be weighted by the proportion of business expected to be recaptured.

A gain or loss—usually a gain if the ceding company follows the most conservative approach—will usually arise upon recapture. Such gain or loss is measured by the difference between the surrender value received and the net adjusted reserve released. Table 22–12, for example, shows that the 20th year cash value is $334.00 and the 20th year net adjusted reserve is $305.07. Assuming recapture in the 20th year, there would be a gain of $28.93 ($334.00 – $305.07) per $1,000 recaptured. If the cash value were, say,

$280.00 and the ceding company did not assume recapture, there would be a loss of $25.07 ($305.07 − $280.00).

The gain or loss should preferably be amortized in proportion to the remaining direct premiums to be collected. However, if the recapture is based on new economic circumstances, amortization could justifiably be based on the pattern of profits produced by revised assumptions, which may depart from the pattern of premium receipts. The method used should be responsive to the underlying reasons for recapture, and the gain or loss should be amortized in such a manner as to match the emergence of increases or decreases in future profits resulting from the recapture.

Non-Proportional Reinsurance

Catastrophe, stop-loss, and similar types of reinsurance would normally not call for adjustment.

A possible exception would be an arrangement which constitutes, in effect, a funding arrangement. Liabilities should be established for current-period recoveries that are expected to be recouped by the reinsurer from future premium increases.

Other Lines of Business

Reinsurance on individual health insurance, individual annuities, group insurance, and credit insurance* has its unique characteristics in each case, but the principles of life reinsurance discussed in the preceding pages should generally be adaptable to such other lines of business.

Unauthorized Reinsurance

Statutory liabilites for unauthorized reinsurance should be eliminated from adjusted statements.

In those rare cases in which a reinsurer fails, of course, any reinsurance credits not expected to be recovered should be written off.

Disclosure

When the methods used to account for reinsurance ceded correspond in all material respects to the methods used for direct business, a simple statement to that effect should constitute adequate disclosure of the accounting methods employed.

*Credit coinsurance is briefly discussed in Chapter 20.

When the methods used to account for reinsurance ceded differ significantly from the methods used with respect to direct business, then a separate description of such methods should be provided in the accounting policies note and material balances should also be disclosed.

Accounting for Special Agreements

While normal reinsurance agreements are sometimes complex and frequently difficult to account for, they have one overwhelming virtue: they're what they seem to be.

Special reinsurance agreements may or may not be what they seem to be.

Audit Guide Provisions

As indicated earlier in this chapter, the life insurance audit guide does not deal with the usual forms of reinsurance but limits its provisions to the treatment of "special reinsurance agreements", which are described in the guide as large block agreements designed to provide surplus relief or tax benefits.

The guide states that where such special agreements do not truly shift economic risk, net credits or debits arising from the agreements should be treated as "a deferred credit or liability by the ceding company" and as "deferred charges or receivables" by the assuming company.[5]

As for special agreements that do result in shifting a "significant part of the economic risk from one company to another," then any gain or loss arising from the agreement can apparently be recognized:

Under generally accepted accounting principles for special reinsurance agreements which are constructed so as to shift a significant part of the economic risk from one company to another, that portion of the proceeds from the transaction which represents recovery of acquisition costs should be charged with the applicable unamortized acquisition costs. If the ceding company has agreed to do all the servicing of the business without adequate compensation, a liability should be provided for estimated future servicing costs under the agreement. Any gain or loss, if material, should be appropriately disclosed. The net cost to the assuming company should be treated as acquisition expense to be amortized over the premium-paying period on a basis consistent with that used for acquisition expense of other business.[6]

As will be seen, the conditions which must be satisfied to warrant the recording of a gain or loss are quite stringent.

Definition of a "Special Agreement"

"Special reinsurance agreements", while discussed in the life insurance audit guide, are not really defined by the guide. The guide indicates, however, that such agreements are "usually of the coinsurance type," are designed for the purpose "of increasing . . . statutory surplus position to meet minimum capital and/or surplus requirements or to avoid the loss of an operating loss carryforward for tax purposes," * and involve "a large block of business." [7]

Thus a "special agreement" might be defined in terms of the motives underlying the agreement and the size of the block of business involved. The motives must be somewhat special or unusual and the block of business must be quite substantial. In addition, one other characteristic of a special agreement is implicit in the guide's discussions: the financial effects of the agreement must be somewhat unusual.

Obviously judgments about motive, size, and financial effect will differ. A "motive" may represent a mixture of motives; thus surplus relief, an increase in reported income, and implementation of normal retention policy may all influence the negotiation of an agreement. What constitutes a "large" block of business will sometimes depend on subjective notions of materiality; maybe it's 5 percent of business written, or 10 percent, or 25 percent. And what represents an "unusual" financial effect may depend on what the individual doing the evaluating is used to; some may think a 150 percent first-year coinsurance allowance is unusual, others may not.

As a working principle, a "special agreement" might be defined as a coinsurance or modified coinsurance arrangement which has any of the following characteristics:

1. There is a limitation of the reinsurer's risk as to mortality, lapse, interest, or any other significant element.

2. The agreement provides for a disproportionate front-ending of expense allowances.

3. The agreement permits recapture at the ceding company's option (irrespective of a nominal minimum holding period) with or without provision for a penalty for early recapture.

4. The agreement constitutes an outright sale of the business with no possibility of recapture.

*Or, one might add, to increase reported income.

Limitation of Risk

Any limitation of the reinsurer's risk will tend to convert the reinsurance agreement into a special agreement. While the determination of whether a shift in economic risk has taken place is inevitably a matter of judgment, any provisions limiting the reinsurer's participation in mortality, lapse, interest, or any other significant contract characteristic should generally be interpreted to mean that a shift of risk has not occurred.

For example, assume that the reinsurer advances a very generous expense allowance—say 200 percent—in the first year but requires the ceding company to guarantee persistency. Such an arrangement may properly be viewed as a special agreement.

Or assume that the reinsurer's mortality risk is limited to a specified table*, or that the agreement requires the ceding company to guarantee the reinsurer's interest rate under a pure coinsurance agreement.** In either case, the arrangement might well be viewed as a special agreement.

In short, any limitation of risk should be presumed to create a special agreement in the absence of clear and convincing proof to the contrary.

Disproportionate Expense Allowances

Where expense allowances in the early years are unusually high—for example, in excess of 110 percent in the first year, or a pattern during the first few years which will obviously produce accounting profits for the ceding company—then the agreement should be regarded as a special agreement. In all cases except those in which the agreement constitutes an outright sale of the business (discussed below), the expense allowances should be deferred and amortized just as if the arrangement were a standard agreement. Under no circumstances should the amortization period be shorter than the minimum holding period.

Optional Recapture

Unless the agreement specifically prohibits recapture—forever or for a specified period of time—then recapture can be viewed to be at the ceding company's option, and the agreement should generally

*It should be noted that this could also occur with respect to a YRT arrangement, in which case the YRT arrangement might be viewed as a special agreement.

**Modified coinsurance agreements result in a transfer of the bulk of the investment risk to the ceding company, but this is accepted practice in the business which should not be construed as a limitation on the reinsurer's risk.

be viewed as a "warehousing" arrangement to be accounted for as a special agreement.

Outright Sale

Where the agreement absolutely prohibits recapture forever, and there is no possibility that the business will be returned to the ceding company, it would be appropriate to account for the business as if it were an installment sale, the revenue from which is represented by the coinsurance allowances received in cash. Applicable acquisition and maintenance costs should be matched against such allowances.

An equivalent outright sale should generally be considered to be the only type of special agreement that is "constructed so as to shift a significant part of the economic risk" to the reinsurer. And it is the only type that should qualify for any acceleration of profit recognition. All others should be accounted for in basically the same manner as standard agreements.

Disclosure

Needless to say, special reinsurance agreements can produce unusual effects in the financial statements. In all cases, the nature of the agreements, the methods used to account for the agreements, the effect on the balance sheet and statement of operations, and the probable future effects of the agreements should be disclosed.

Reinsurance Assumed

Up to this point the discussion has dealt largely with reinsurance ceded. It must be recognized that the assuming reinsurer will rarely calculate adjusted reserves on reinsurance assumed in a manner that corresponds to the calculations made by the ceding company.

The discussion that follows is oriented to the operations of large reinsurers. Companies that accept small amounts of reinsurance as an incidental marketing activity may use simpler approaches than those described below.

Yearly Renewable Term

Whereas the ceding company should, in theory, translate the cost of YRT reinsurance ceded into a constant percentage of gross premiums on the underlying direct business, the YRT reinsurance *is* direct business for the reinsurer.

YRT reinsurance premiums should be recognized as revenue in level amounts per $1,000 (or other unit) of original face amount and costs should be matched against revenues thus recognized. This is a departure from the general principle of recognizing premiums as revenue when received, but the departure is justified in the case of YRT reinsurance assumed since, from the reinsurer's standpoint, there is little real difference between YRT, coinsurance, and modified coinsurance. The indicated treatment of YRT reinsurance places it in the same accounting posture as coinsurance and modified coinsurance.

Implicit expense allowances should preferably be deferred and amortized in proportion to premium revenues. Such costs, incurred in the form of a rate reduction, vary with and are related to production; the same effect would be obtained by collecting the full premium and making a separate payment for the expense allowance. In addition, any internal acquisition costs that meet the tests of variability and attribution should also be deferred and amortized.

Adjusted benefit reserves should take into account

▶ Expected death claims,
▶ Expected experience rating refunds,
▶ Expected forgiveness of loss carryforwards,
▶ Interest,
▶ Lapses,
▶ Reductions in net amount at risk, and
▶ Probability of recapture.

With regard to the last item (probability of recapture), introduction of recapture as a decrement would be appropriate for a reinsurer with a large portfolio of reinsurance agreements and a historical pattern of recapture experience.

Where premium taxes are reimbursed and the revenue-recognition pattern differs from the incidence of cash premiums, such premium taxes should be reserved for. Similarly, internal maintenance and settlement expenses incurred in a pattern different from the revenue-recognition pattern should also be reserved for when they are significant.

Coinsurance and Modified Coinsurance

Expense and benefit reserve adjustments for coinsurance would take into account the same items as would be recognized in calculating expense and benefit reserve adjustments for YRT reinsurance plus surrender values paid. Usually there would be no forgiveness of loss carryforwards to deal with since such carryforwards are usually unlimited in the case of coinsurance contracts.

Modified coinsurance could be calculated using the coinsurance-with-loan approach, but it is preferable for an assuming reinsurer to use the full-calculation approach because the interest earned on reserve transfers is typically at a lower rate than the reinsurer could expect to earn if it retained the reserves. This fact might be ignored where the assumed rate is no greater than the reserve transfer rate, even though the actual rate is higher than the assumed rate.

Special Agreements

Most of the comments on special reinsurance agreements from the point of view of the ceding company also apply—in reverse—for the assuming company.

Contingency Reserves

Amounts held aside in "contingency reserves" for the account of ceding companies would be reported as liabilities by the assuming company, either in the form of a reserve provision (if expected refunds, including amounts allocated to contingency reserves, are taken into account in calculating reserves), a separate liability (if contingency reserves are separately accounted for), or a combination (if expected refunds, including contingency reserve amounts, are included in the reserves and variances from expected are separately accounted for).

Amounts held in contingency reserves for the account of the assuming company should normally not be recognized for purposes of the adjusted statements.

Disclosure

Inasmuch as reinsurance assumed is similar to direct business from the point of view of the assuming company, disclosure should generally follow the same pattern as disclosures appropriate for direct business. Of course, assumptions unique to reinsurance—such as the provision for recapture and the provision for expected experience rating refunds—should be appropriately described.

Part V

Special Problems

23

Deferred and Uncollected Premiums

Some accountants regard deferred and uncollected premiums as one of the great mysteries of the universe. Even actuaries are sometimes less than unambiguous in describing what deferred and uncollected premiums are all about.

Small wonder. The fundamental character of deferred and uncollected premiums is a matter of controversy: Asset or reserve offset? Revenue or correction of the increase in reserves? Further, there is a very sensitive and complex relationship between deferred and uncollected premiums and the assumptions underlying calculation of the reserves, and this relationship is not always fully appreciated. Finally, calculation of deferred and uncollected premiums—particularly the element of loading or cost of collection—is fraught with difficult theoretical and practical problems.

Nature of Ordinary Life Deferred and Uncollected Premiums

Deferred and Uncollected Premiums as an Asset

Some believe that deferred and uncollected premiums represent receivables. Under this reasoning, recognition of deferred and uncollected premiums is necessary to state revenue on an accrual basis.

Statutory accounting practices appear to support this view. The change in gross deferred and uncollected premiums is recorded in the premium account. Loading represents a provision for expenses to be incurred in collecting the premiums receivable. Deduction of loading from the premium receivable, rather than

inclusion of loading among the liabilities, could be regarded as one of the quirks of statutory accounting; some regard the practice as similar to deducting encumbrances on real estate from the related real estate asset.

Deferred and Uncollected Premiums as a Reserve Correction

Some believe that deferred and uncollected premiums simply correct an overstatement of the reserves. Mean reserves are calculated on the assumption that a full annual premium has been collected. If in fact a full annual premium has not been collected, then the reserves would be overstated if the premiums to be received through the next policy anniversary were not recognized.

Recording deferred and uncollected premiums net of loading in the balance sheet is consistent with this view. It is the net premium that is assumed to have been received for purposes of the reserve calculation. However, the amount should be treated as a reduction of reserves, not as an asset, to maintain such consistency. Nor is the recognition as revenue of the change in gross deferred and uncollected premiums (and the recognition as expense of the change in loading) consistent with the view of net deferred and uncollected premiums as a reserve correction; instead, the change in net deferred and uncollected premiums should be reflected in the "increase in reserves" account.

Statutory Accounting Tradition

The Convention Blank adopted in 1871 by the National Convention of Insurance Commissioners contained the following items among the assets: [1]

(a) Gross amount of premiums in process of
collection and transmission reported
to Insurance Department as being in
force December 31, 1871 $ xxx
(b) Gross amount of deferred premiums   xxx
(c) Total   xxx
(d) Amount deducted by the company to reduce
the [total gross amount] to the net values
charged against the policies on
account of those premiums   xxx
(e) Net amount $ xxx

It is apparent from Item (d) that deferred and uncollected premiums were viewed as corrections of the reserves. Technology was such in 1871 that it was essential to compute reserve factors (and hence the reserves themselves) which uniformly assumed the receipt of the annual gross premium.

However, there existed some ambivalence in the commissioners' thinking about deferred and uncollected premiums. Deferred premiums were "not to be entered until actually received; or, if entered, only the net amount (not the gross) treated as an asset and a corresponding liability to be created." [2] If the liability were calculated first, then the asset would surely follow. If the asset were calculated first, then the liability must follow. Ambivalent or not, the practical effect of the rules adopted in 1871 was to calculate reserves on the basis of net premiums received in cash as of the statement date.

In developing the modern form of the Convention Blank (which was adopted in 1951), the Joint Committee on Blanks of the American Life Convention and the Life Insurance Association of America advanced a new theory: that gross deferred and uncollected premiums represented accounts receivable in all material respects and should be reported gross among the assets, with the related cost of collection reported as a liability. The reserves would, of course, continue to be based on the assumption that a full annual net premium had been received. The result would have been to place a company "in approximately the same surplus position as it would be if the premium had been paid." [3]

The NAIC rejected this approach and continued the traditional treatment. In effect, then, deferred and uncollected premiums continue to be viewed as reserve adjustments, even though they are reported as assets.

There is no statutory requirement to compute mean reserves, i.e., reserves which assume the receipt of an annual net premium. But companies continue to do so, primarily for ordinary insurance, in part because this approach is traditional, in part because published tables of reserve factors use the mean reserve approach, and in part because the volume of reserve factors which recognize mode and paid-to date would be so great as to constitute an administrative problem of monstrous proportions.

Deferred and uncollected premiums typically represent a very minor proportion of total assets in the statutory balance sheet (about 2 percent, on the average). Their principal significance lies in the confusion that surrounds them. "There is probably no feature of the annual statement of a life insurance company which is quite as unintelligible to the typical layman as this particular asset item." [4]

Cost of Collection in Excess of Loading

Brief mention should be made here of "cost of collection on premiums and annuity considerations deferred and uncollected in excess of total loading thereon", a liability item in the statutory balance sheet. Net deferred and uncollected premiums represent valuation net premiums, and the difference between gross premiums and valuation net premiums is theoretically available for expenses. When expenses exceed the available loadings, a statutory accounting loss results. Any such excess applicable to gross deferred and uncollected premiums must be reported as a liability in the Convention Statement. Computation of the excess involves comparison of aggregate loadings (first year and renewal are combined) with estimated commissions, taxes, and other expenses directly related to, and contingent upon the receipt of, deferred and uncollected premiums. It should be noted that general overhead and other expenses that must also be covered by "loading" need not be considered in making the calculation.

Cost of collection in excess of loading is most peculiar. If a company chose to calculate reserves that recognize the premium mode and paid-to date, it would report no deferred and uncollected premiums and, hence, presumably would not have to calculate any cost of collection in excess of loading. Thus companies that use the mean reserve approach are penalized.

Provision for the cost of collection in excess of loading had reference only to the following calendar year, when the deferred and uncollected premiums (or, hopefully, most of them) are received in cash. (The liability is generally not discounted for the probability of non-receipt.) Further, the excess of loadings over

Table 23–1.

POSSIBLE INCONSISTENCIES IN RELATIONSHIPS AMONG GROSS PREMIUMS, NET PREMIUMS, DIRECT EXPENSES, AND DEFICIENCY RESERVES FOR 10-PAY LIFE POLICY*—SEMI-ANNUAL MODE

	Policy A	Policy B	Combined
Year 1:			
50% of annual premium received	$ 15	$ 10	$ 25
50% of annual premium deferred	15	10	25
Annual premium	$ 30	$ 20	$ 50
Effect of deferred premium and deficiency reserves at end of year 1:			
Deferred gross premium	$ 15	$ 10	$ 25
Net premium	10	15	25
Loading (loading deficiency)	5	(5)	–0–
Anticipated direct expenses	6	6	12
Net loss expected in Year 2	$ (1)	$ (11)	$ (12)
Recorded effect on surplus— increase (decrease):			
Loading	$ (5)	$ 5	$ –0–
Cost of collection in excess of loading	(1)	(11)	(12)
Deficiency reserves—18 semi-annual premiums X loading deficiency	–0–	(90)	(90)
	$ (6)	$ (96)	$(102)
Surplus (decrease) if the excess of loadings over expenses on other policies offsets the excess of expenses over loadings on these policies	$ (5)	$ (85)	$ (90)
Unrecognized losses:			
Future losses expected—19 semi-annual premiums	$(19)	$(209)	$(228)
Maximum recorded surplus decrease in respect of the 19 remaining premiums	6	96	102
Unrecognized losses**	$(13)	$(113)	$(126)

*Interest and survivorship are ignored in this illustration. The illustration assumes that net premiums are fully required to fund benefits and that direct expenses are level.

**Any expenses allocable to the policies but not directly related to collecting the premium would increase the losses.

expenses on some policies may be used to offset the excess of expenses over loadings on other policies. This is not entirely consistent with deficiency reserve requirements, under which (1) the deficiency reserves contemplate loading deficiencies for the entire premium-paying period but without regard for any cost of collection in excess of loading and (2) the deficiency reserves must be computed with respect to each individual policy—i.e., offsets are not permitted. Table 23–1 crudely illustrates some of the possible inconsistencies.

As a practical matter, it is rare for a relatively mature company to report cost of collection in excess of loading because aggregate renewal loadings are usually sufficiently greater than aggregate direct renewal expenses to offset the first-year excess. It is, however, fairly common for newer companies to report such an item.

Deferred and Uncollected Premiums in the Context of Adjusted Statements

For purposes of financial statements prepared in conformity with generally accepted accounting principles, deferred and uncollected premiums represent reserve adjustments, for several reasons:

Table 23–2.

STATUTORY DEFERRED AND UNCOLLECTED PREMIUMS AND COST OF COLLECTION IN EXCESS OF
LOADING THEREON AT DECEMBER 31, 1971 (000 Omitted)

	First Year	Renewal	Total
Deferred and uncollected premiums:			
Net annualized premiums in force	$ 2,533	$44,922	
Gross annualized premiums in force	$11,618	$54,529	
Ratio	21.8%	82.4 %	
Reciprocal ratio	78.2%	17.6 %	
Gross deferred and uncollected premiums	$ 2,744	$12,499	$15,243
Less loading (gross X reciprocal)	2,146	2,200	4,346
Net deferred and uncollected premiums	$ 598	$10,299	$10,897
Cost of collection in excess of loading:			
1971 direct commissions, per ledger	$ 8,203	$ 1,864	
1971 payments in lieu of commissions, per ledger	1,269	368	
1971 functional cost analysis:			
Premium collection	163	771	
Commission processing	47	220	
Total	$ 9,682	$ 3,223	
1971 direct premiums received, per ledger	$11,626	$55,096	
Ratio	83.3%	5.8 %	
Premium tax rate	2.0	2.0	
Cost of collection rate	85.3	7.8	
Loading rate	78.2	17.6	
Rate for cost of collection in excess of loading	7.1%	(9.8)%	
Gross deferred and uncollected premiums	$ 2,744	$12,499	
Cost of collection in excess of loading	$ 195	$(1,225)	$–0–

▸ Because a company has no enforceable claim on deferred and uncollected premiums, they are not receivables.

▸ Because they are not receivables, deferred and uncollected premiums do not represent realized revenue.

▸ From the installment sales point of view, the premiums are not "earned" until they are received.

▸ Since deferred and uncollected premiums are neither realized revenue nor earned revenue, they should not be recognized as revenue.

▸ The perfect reserve calculation would recognize the paid-to date of the policy. Such a reserve would eliminate the need for deferred and uncollected premiums. It follows that the treatment accorded deferred and uncollected premiums should look toward approximating the perfect reserve.

Thus, in terms of general-purpose financial statements, deferred and uncollected premiums should preferably be accounted for as if they were reserves. This means that the change in net deferred and uncollected premiums should be recorded in the "increase in reserves" account in the income statement and that aggregate net deferred and uncollected premiums should be deducted from related reserve items in the balance sheet. Under this approach premium revenue is not affected by deferred and uncollected premiums and the item "increase in loading on deferred and uncollected premiums" disappears from the income statement.

It is likely that companies will be loath to abandon the conventional treatment of deferred and uncollected premiums. As a general rule, deferred and uncollected premiums increase from year to year in proportion to the increase in premium income. All other things being equal, the conventional treatment results in reporting more premium revenue than would otherwise be the case (unless, of course, the company is not growing or there is a material change in the mode of payment).

The conventional approach can be used for general-purpose statements, but—as will be seen—the conventional approach can result in scattering distortions throughout the financial statements. Some of the distortions can be material, and if they are material, they should not be countenanced.

Premium revenue as traditionally reported is a hodge-podge of unrelated items and has little intrinsic or extrinsic significance. The reporting of premiums on an earned basis—i.e., premiums collected, literally or constructively—is internally consistent and represents the revenue base against which expenses are being matched. The revenue on this basis is therefore significant.

Calculation of Deferred and Uncollected Premiums

Relationship to Mean Reserves

Most companies compute mean reserves for ordinary life and annuity business. The general form for such a calculation is:

Prior terminal reserve	$1,000
Annual net premium	120
Initial reserve	$1,120
Current terminal reserve	$1,170
Mean of initial reserve and current terminal reserve	$1,145

Inasmuch as the calculation assumes the receipt of a full annual net premium, it can readily be seen that receipt of anything less will result in a distortion. For example, if in the case illustrated above the policy is dated July 1 and is on a monthly mode and, as of December 31, only five $10 net premiums have been received, the failure to provide deferred and uncollected net premiums would result in an unjustified charge to surplus of $70. Therefore, one uncollected net premium ($10) and six deferred net premiums ($60) would be recorded. The net result would approximate the calculation of the policy reserve as of the paid-to date of the policy.

Computing Statutory Deferred and Uncollected Net Premiums

As a general rule, deferred and uncollected gross premiums must be inventoried; there is typically no satisfactory method of estimating the amounts. Normally this is readily accomplished by reference to the paid-to date of the policy, the anniversary date, the mode, and the modal gross premium.

Practice varies with respect to computing net premiums. Traditionally net premiums have been estimated by computing the ratio between annual or annualized gross premiums and annual net premiums

(these values were typically carried in a valuation file) and applying the ratio to gross deferred and uncollected premiums to approximate net deferred and uncollected premiums. Inaccuracies arise where the distribution of business in the net-to-gross calculation differs from the distribution of business in the tabulation of deferred and uncollected gross premiums. Inaccuracies can also arise because of the "mode loading" on premiums other than annual, but this problem is readily solved by use of a composite mode loading adjustment factor.

In recent years, companies installing new computer systems have increasingly provided for seriatim (or essentially seriatim) calculation of deferred and uncollected net premiums by electronic means. Net premiums are carried in the master file or in a rate tape, as are gross premiums, modes, anniversary dates, and paid-to dates, and net deferred and uncollected premiums are computed automatically as part of the valuation process.

The traditional approach is used by Crazy Quilt Life. A summary calculation of deferred and uncollected statutory net premiums is shown in Table 23–2. Although Crazy Quilt reports no amount for cost of collection in excess of loading, the method of computing the amount is shown in Table 23–2 for illustrative purposes.

Computing Adjusted Deferred and Uncollected Valuation Premiums

The problem of calculating adjusted deferred and uncollected premiums—that is, deferred and uncollected valuation premiums that are used to correct adjusted reserves—is somewhat more complex than the problem of computing statutory deferred and uncollected premiums. In computing statutory deferred and uncollected premiums, only benefit premiums need be considered. In computing adjusted deferred and uncollected premiums, up to three valuation premiums must be considered:

▶ The benefit premium, to correct the adjusted benefit reserve;
▶ The acquisition cost premium, to correct the asset for deferred acquisition costs; and
▶ The maintenance expense premiums, to correct the reserve for maintenance expenses.

Stated simply, each of the three reserve calculations generally assumes receipt of the full annual valuation premium element, and where the full valuation pre-

Table 23–3.

DEFERRED AND UNCOLLECTED ADJUSTED RESERVE VALUATION PREMIUMS AT DECEMBER 31, 1971
(000 Omitted)

Adjusted valuation premiums in force:		
Benefits		$40,567
Acquisition costs:		
"Full"	$14,345	
Less development and overhead	3,449	
Modified	$10,896	10,896
Maintenance expenses		6,818
		$58,281
Gross premiums in force		$66,147
Ratio of adjusted valuation premiums in force to gross premiums in force:		
Benefits		61.3%
Acquisition costs:		
"Full"	21.7%	
Less development and overhead	5.2	
Modified	16.5%	16.5
Maintenance expenses		10.3
		88.1%
Gross deferred and uncollected premiums		$15,243
Adjusted deferred and uncollected valuation premiums:		
Benefits		$ 9,344
Acquisition costs:		
"Full"	$ 3,308	
Less development and overhead	793	
Modified	$ 2,515	2,515
Maintenance expenses		1,570
ADJUSTED DEFERRED AND UNCOLLECTED VALUATION PREMIUMS		$13,429

mium element has not been received, it must be recorded in the form of an adjustment for deferred and uncollected premiums.

Computation of adjusted deferred and uncollected valuation premiums as of December 31, 1971 for Crazy Quilt Life is illustrated in Table 23–3. Valuation premiums had to be computed to develop adjusted reserve factors for Crazy Quilt's book of business. The valuation premiums were expressed in terms of annual amounts. Gross premiums were tabulated in the form of annualized amounts. The resulting ratios were then applied to deferred and uncollected gross premiums to determine estimated adjusted deferred and uncollected valuation premiums.

Use of annualized gross premiums rather than annual gross premiums introduces mode loadings into the calculation of the ratio to be applied to gross deferred and uncollected premiums, and the resulting ratio is therefore somewhat more accurate than would be the case if annual gross premiums were used. However, the additional accuracy is only a matter of degree. There are never any annual premiums in a deferred state. Therefore, the mix of modes incorporated in the tabulation of gross deferred and uncollected premiums differs from the mix of modes incorporated in the tabulation of annualized gross premiums. Absolute accuracy would be obtained only by a seriatim calculation of the general form illustrated in Table 23–3.*

---

*All of Crazy Quilt's ordinary life business is annual business, and these deferred and uncollected premiums have been computed only for illustrative purposes. Because all business is on the same mode, the distribution of modes is the same in all cases. Therefore, the relationships between valuation premiums and gross premiums illustrated in Table 23–3 are "accurate".

Cost of Collection on Gross Deferred and Uncollected Premiums

Just as the calculation of a mean reserve factor normally assumes receipt of a full annual valuation premium, so it normally assumes payment of the full annual expense associated with the policy year. Some expenses are incurred only as premiums are received. When such expenses have not yet been paid, they must be accrued.

Progression of reserves through year-end. Table 23–4 shows (in rather crude fashion) the theoretical journal entries to be made for reserves, deferred and uncollected premiums, and certain costs of collection on deferred and uncollected premiums. Pro forma annualized amounts are shown for comparison.

Several significant assumptions underlie the information displayed in Table 23–4:

▸ It is assumed that non-percentage expenses are incurred on the anniversary date and that percentage expenses are incurred when premiums are received.

▸ Although no benefits are indicated to have been paid, it is assumed that benefits are distributed evenly throughout the year (zero, in this case).

▸ Interest is ignored. As will be seen later, interest can affect the calculations.

▸ It is assumed that reserve factors are calculated for all elements of the reserve—benefits, acquisition costs, and maintenance expenses. When this is not the case—when, for example, acquisition costs are accounted for manually—the computations shown in Table 23–4 would be modified. (This is also discussed later in this chapter.)

▸ It is also assumed that mean reserves are calculated which assume receipt of the full annual valuation premium.

▸ And finally, the reserve illustrated is based on a reserve "fund". To translate the accumulated reserve into a factor to be applied to insurance in force would of course involve dividing the fund by the percentage of policyholders persisting as of the calendar year-end.

It will quickly be noted that failure to provide for expenses to be incurred upon receipt of the deferred premiums would result in overstating income and surplus by $105. This means that a $95 loss ($105 less the correct amount of profit, $10, that should be recognized in the next calendar year) would be reported the next year.

Statement presentation. Table 23–5 illustrates

several income statement and balance sheet presentations for the information shown in Table 23–4. The traditional method of reporting deferred and uncollected premiums results in severe distortions in both the income statement and the balance sheet. The distortion is exaggerated, of course; in a real-company situation the distortion would be diluted considerably by the volume of business. In a small, rapidly-growing company, however, the distortion can be material.

If a company chooses to report the change in gross deferred and uncollected premiums in the premium account, some—but not all—of the distortion can be eliminated by proper classification of the expense accruals. This is illustrated in Table 23–5 under the heading "Modified Traditional Method". It would appear that the change in loading—which is all but meaningless—must be reported as an expense in this case.

The preferred method illustrated in Table 23–5 is far superior to either the traditional method or the modified traditional method because the preferred method is in no way distortive.

Crazy Quilt's Calculations of Cost of Collection

Crazy Quilt found the calculation of the cost of collection to be somewhat involved in practice. Fortunately Crazy Quilt's in-force tabulations provided most of the information necessary to make the calculations. Lacking that, some crude and possibly unreliable approximations would have been required.

First-year acquisition costs. In computing the first-year cost of collection, Crazy Quilt first had to resolve some difficult conceptual problems:

▸ What expenses would be incurred upon receipt of the deferred and uncollected premiums?

Certain expenses, such as selection and issue expenses, were clearly incurred at the time of issue and were in no way related to the receipt of subsequent premiums. Such expenses were not included in the cost of collection calculation.

Commissions and commission equivalents were clearly incurred in proportion to the receipt of premiums, so commissions to agents and in-lieu payments to branch managers were included in the calculation.

Agency support expenses required careful analysis. For ratemaking purposes the Company assumed that some of these expenses were incurred at the moment of issue and others were distributed more or less evenly across the first year. In the former case, the

Table 23–4.

ILLUSTRATION OF PREFERRED METHOD OF ACCOUNTING FOR FIRST-YEAR DEFERRED PREMIUM (IGNORING INTEREST)

Date	Pro-Forma Annualized — Journal Entries Dr.	Cr.	Effect on Income/Surplus	Assets	Liabilities	Actual Per Books — Journal Entries Dr.	Cr.	Income/Surplus	Assets	Liabilities	Reserve Buildup — Acquisition Costs	Benefits	Renewal Expenses	Total
7–1 Cash	$200			$200		$100			$100					
Benefit premium		$130	$130				$65	$65				$130		$130
Acquisition cost premium		30	30				15	15			$30			30
Renewal expense premium		20	20				10	10					$20	20
Profit loading		20	20				10	10						
Gross premium received														
7–1 Percentage acquisition costs (100%)	200		(200)			100		(100)			(200)			(200)
Non-percentage acquisition costs	100		(100)			100		(100)			(100)			(100)
Cash		300		(300)			200		(200)					
Acquisition costs paid														
7–1 Percentage maintenance expenses (5%)	10		(10)			5		(5)					(10)	(10)
Non-percentage maintenance expenses	5		(5)			5		(5)					(5)	(5)
Cash		15		(15)			10		(10)					
Maintenance expenses paid														
12–31 Benefits (change in benefit reserve)	130		(130)			130		(130)						
Expenses (change in maintenance expense reserve)	5		(5)			5		(5)						
Deferred acquisition costs	270			270		270			270					
Expenses (change in acquisition cost reserve)		270	270				270	270						
Benefit reserve		130			$130		130			$130		$130		
Maintenance expense reserve		5			5		5			5			$5	
Record reserve increase											$(270)			
PRELIMINARY STATUS AT 12–31	$920	$920	$ 20	$155	$135	715	715	25	160	135				$(135)

12–31 Benefit reserve	65				(65)
Deferred acquisition costs	15			15	
Maintenance expense reserve	10				(10)
Benefits (change in benefit reserve)		65	65		
Expenses (change in acquisition cost reserve)		15	15		
Expenses (change in maintenance expense reserve)		10	10		
Set up deferred premiums					
12–31 Expenses (change in acquisition cost reserve)	100	100	(100)		
Deferred acquisition costs				(100)	
Accrue percentage acquisition costs					
12–31 Expenses (change in maintenance expense reserve)	5	5	(5)		
Maintenance expense reserve		5			5
Accrue percentage maintenance expenses					
FINAL STATUS AT 12–31	$910	$910	$10	$75	$65

Table 23–5.

FINANCIAL STATEMENT EFFECTS OF ACCOUNTING FOR FIRST-YEAR DEFERRED PREMIUM (IGNORING INTEREST)

	Pro-Forma Annualized		Actual Per Books	
		Preferred Method	Traditional Method	Modified Traditional Method
Income Statement:				
Premium collected	$200	$100	$100	$100
Change in deferred gross premium			100	100
TOTAL REVENUE	200	100	200	200
Change in benefit reserve	130	130	130	130
Change in deferred benefit premium		(65)		
BENEFITS	130	65	130	130
Acquisition costs paid	300	200	200	200
Change in acquisition cost reserve	(270)	(270)	(270)	(270)
Change in deferred acquisition cost premium		(15)		
Accrual of acquisition costs in respect of gross premium deferred		100		100
ACQUISITION COSTS	30	15	(70)	30
Maintenance expenses paid	15	10	10	10
Change in maintenance expense reserve	5	5	5	5
Change in deferred maintenance expense premium		(10)		
Accrual of maintenance expenses in respect of gross premium deferred		5		5
MAINTENANCE EXPENSES	20	10	15	20
Change in loading and cost of collection in excess of loading on deferred premium	–0–	–0–	115	10
TOTAL DEDUCTIONS FROM REVENUE	180	90	190	190
PROFIT	$ 20	$ 10	$ 10	$ 10
Balance sheet:				
Assets:				
Cash	$(115)	$(110)	$(110)	$(110)
Deferred acquisition costs:				
Gross	270	270	270	270
Deferred premium element		15		
Expense accrual		(100)		(100)
	270	185	270	170
Deferred premium:				
Benefit element			65	65
Acquisition cost element			15	15
Maintenance expense element			10	10
	–0–	–0–	90	90
TOTAL ASSETS	$155	$75	$250	$150
Liabilities:				
Benefit reserve:				
Gross	$130	$130	$130	$130
Deferred premium element		(65)		
	130	65	130	130
Maintenance expense reserve:				
Gross	5	5	5	5
Deferred premium element		(10)		
Expense accrual		5		5
	5	–0–	5	10
Cost of collection in excess of loading			105	
Surplus	20	10	10	10
TOTAL LIABILITIES	$155	$75	$250	$150

Table 23–6.

CALCULATION OF ADJUSTED COST OF COLLECTION OF DEFERRED AND UNCOLLECTED GROSS PREMIUMS
AT DECEMBER 31, 1971 (000 Omitted)

		Premiums In Force	Deferral Percentage	Attributable Expenses	Base for Computing Cost of Collection	Cost of Collection Percentage	Related Gross Deferred and Uncollected Premiums	Provision for Cost of Collection
Acquisition costs:								
First-year:								
Par whole life		$ 1,588	95.0%	$ 1,509				
Whole life		6,254	107.0	6,633				
20-pay life		1,547	84.6	1,309				
5-year term		523	78.5	411				
25-year decreasing term		1,706	92.5	1,628				
		$11,618		$11,490	$11,618[1]	98.9%	$ 2,744[1]	$2,714
Renewal years—all plans:								
Duration	Commission Plan							
2	A	$ 7,745	15.5	$ 1,200				
2	B	2,347	2.0	47				
3	A	1,008	10.5	106				
4	A	795	8.0	64				
5–10	A	17,986	5.5	989				
		$29,881		$ 2,406	$54,529[2]	4.4%	$12,499[2]	549
Term Renewals:								
Duration								
6	First	$ 177	16.4	$ 29				
11	Second	49	16.4	8				
16	Third	68	16.5	11				
21	Fourth	25	16.4	4				
26	Fifth	2	16.4	Nil				
31	Sixth	Nil	16.5	Nil				
		$ 321		$ 52	$ 2,806[3]	1.9%	$ 64[3]	1
TOTAL ACQUISITION								3,264
Maintenance expenses:								
Commissions and commission equivalents at average ultimate rate						4.0%		
Premium taxes						2.0		
Handling						1.8		
						7.8%	$15,243 [4]	1,189
TOTAL COST OF COLLECTION								$4,453

(1) First-year premiums
(2) Renewal year premiums
(3) Term renewal premiums
(4) Total premiums

expenses were expressed as a flat amount per $1,000 or as a flat amount per policy; in the latter case, the expenses were expressed as a percentage of premiums.

Further investigation indicated that Crazy Quilt's allocation procedures were sound. While inevitably there was some degree of subjectivity involved in assigning agency support expenses to the various allocation bases, the evidence suggested that Crazy Quilt's methods were rational and systematic and, given consistent application, yielded reasonable results. Thus, for example, attendance at agents' conventions were based in part on first-year premiums collected; much supervisory effort was devoted to persistency; and so on. Therefore, Crazy Quilt's basic allocation method was deemed suitable for purposes of calculating the cost of collection percentage. In other words, the percentage included commissions plus other expenses that were expressed in terms of a percentage of premiums.*

▶ Should the cost of collection percentage be limited to items qualifying for deferral?

Crazy Quilt's ratemaking procedures involved the use of "conventional" expense rates, that is, expenses including full allocations of development and overhead. Development and overhead were excluded in computing deferred acquisition costs. In effect, development and overhead were deemed to be period expenses. Inasmuch as the Company did not take credit for them in computing deferred acquisition costs, they were not included in calculating the cost of collection. To do so would have been grossly unfair. So the calculation was limited to expenses expressed as a percentage of premiums that were considered deferrable.

Calculation of the first-year cost of collection percentage of 98.9 percent is illustrated in Table 23–6.

Renewal-year acquisition costs. Some of Crazy Quilt's plans carry a commission rate in certain renewal years that exceeds the ultimate rate. Such "renewal-year acquisition costs" are contemplated in the adjusted reserves. Therefore, it is necessary to accrue the corresponding cost of collection.

Crazy Quilt tabulated premiums in force by duration and plan and then further tabulated the amounts according to applicable renewal-year commission rates. The resulting calculation is shown in Table 23–6, as is calculation of the related cost of collection.

Term renewal acquisition costs. Certain percentage expenses are incurred upon renewal of renewable term plans. In Crazy Quilt's case acquisition commissions are not paid on renewal, so the deferral percentage is limited to certain agency support expenses.

Crazy Quilt tabulated premiums in force for policies that were in a renewal year. This was readily accomplished because premiums in force were tabulated by plan and duration. Applicable deferral percentages were determined by reference to other records. Calculation of the cost of collection is shown in Table 23–6.

Maintenance expenses. Crazy Quilt calculates maintenance expense reserves; the reserves assume that maintenance expenses for the year have been incurred. Maintenance expenses that are a function of premiums collected therefore had to be included in the calculation of the cost of collection.

Crazy Quilt's maintenance expense reserves include commissions at *ultimate* rates, premium taxes, regular policy maintenance, and expenses of settling death claims and processing surrenders. Effective ultimate commission rates were determinable by analysis and the premium tax rate, 2 percent, was known. Surrender and death claim processing costs were incurred in connection with the related surrenders and claims, which were appropriately distributed for purposes of calculating the reserves.

As for regular policy maintenance, for ratemaking purposes the Company assessed such expenses as a flat amount per policy. However, some expenses—for example, premium billing and collection and commission processing—are incurred as premiums are collected. Analysis of functional cost data indicated such items amounted to about 1.8 percent of premiums, and this rate was used in the cost of collection calculation.

The calculation of the maintenance expense portion of the cost of collection is shown in Table 23–6.

Other approaches. While perhaps going to unusual lengths in calculating the cost of collection, Crazy Quilt nevertheless used several approximation techniques. Ideally, gross deferred and uncollected premiums should be tabulated by plan and duration and the percentages should be applied individually.

But there is a point of diminishing returns in making calculations such as these, and more, rather than less, approximation will generally be encountered in practice. The relative immateriality of the amounts involved suggests that approximation is entirely warranted.

---

*Since a liability is in effect established for the cost of collection, this is also the most conservative approach.

Table 23–7.

ILLUSTRATION OF EFFECT OF AMORTIZATION IN RELATION TO ACQUISITION COSTS INCURRED AS A PERCENTAGE OF PREMIUMS

Annual premium	$ 200
Premiums received—50% of annual	$ 100
Percentage acquisition costs actually incurred at 100%	$ 100
Total premiums to be received over the life of the policy	$2,000
Premiums received during the period (half a policy year) as a percentage of the total $ 100 ÷ $2,000	5%
Amortization of acquisition costs incurred in proportion to premiums received—5% x $100	$ 5
Accrual of acquisition costs remaining to be incurred and allocable pro-rata to premiums received—$100 x 100% x 5%	$ 5
Total acquisition cost expense for the period	$ 10
Proof:	
Pro-forma acquisition costs	$ 200
Premiums received	$ 100
Total premiums to be received	$2,000
Premiums received as percentage of total premiums to be received	5%
Amortization—5% x $200	$ 10

Interest on the Cost of Collection Adjustment

When acquisition costs are amortized with interest, this means in effect that interest is accrued on all elements of the reserve, including expenses incurred. To be consistent with this approach, interest should also be accrued on the cost of collection adjustment.

For example, if the reserve calculation assumes that acquisition costs are incurred in the first month of the policy year (when premiums are assumed to be received), then the deferred acquisition cost asset is increased by imputed interest. This is apparent from the following illustration of the development of an acquisition cost reserve factor:

Acquisition costs incurred:	
Percentage	$ 80
Flat	30
Applicable valuation premium received	(10)
	100
Interest at 6% for 6 months	3
Reserve factor (assuming no survivorship adjustment)	$103

If half the premium is deferred, then $40 in percentage acquisition costs remain to be incurred. The reserve assumes that the expenses have in fact been incurred and "improves" them with interest. To put the cost of collection adjustment on the same basis—in other words, to make a corresponding reserve adjustment—the computed cost of collection should also be accumulated at interest using the interest rate inherent in the reserve calculation.

In Crazy Quilt's case the interest-adjusted cost of collection might be computed as follows (000 omitted from amounts):

	Unadjusted Amount	Annual Interest Rate	Interest-Adjusted Amount
First-year acquisition costs	$2,714	6.5% (1)	$2,802
Renewal-year acquisition costs	549	5.0% (2)	563
Term renewal acquisition costs	1	4.0% (2)	1
Maintenance expenses	1,189	4.0% (2)	1,212
	$4,453		$4,578

(1) First-year rate for new ratebook.
(2) Estimated average rate for the mix of years involved.

This is a very subtle adjustment, and it is doubtful that it would often be made in practice. In the first place, the absolute amounts involved are relatively immaterial. In the second place, the change in the amount (and hence the income statement effect) from year to year may be presumed to be nominal. Therefore the adjustment should be considered optional.

Some Other Considerations

Accounting Separately for Acquisition Costs

When acquisition costs are accounted for independently of the reserve—for example, manually—many of the problems associated with the cost of collection disappear. This is because there is no need to assume

461

Table 23–8.

RELATIONSHIP BETWEEN DEFERRED PREMIUMS TO BE PROVIDED WITH RESPECT TO MEAN RESERVES AND UNEARNED PREMIUMS TO BE PROVIDED WITH RESPECT TO MID-TERMINAL RESERVES

Anniversary Month	Mean Reserves Number of Deferred Premiums To be Recorded for Mode*				Mid-Terminal Reserves Proportion of Mode Premium To be Recorded as Unearned*			
	Monthly	Quarterly	Semi-Annual	Annual	Monthly	Quarterly	Semi-Annual	Annual
January	–0–	–0–	–0–	–0–	.50	.167	.083	.042
February	1	–0–	–0–	–0–	.50	.500	.250	.125
March	2	–0–	–0–	–0–	.50	.833	.417	.208
April	3	1	–0–	–0–	.50	.167	.583	.292
May	4	1	–0–	–0–	.50	.500	.750	.375
June	5	1	–0–	–0–	.50	.833	.917	.458
July	6	2	1	–0–	.50	.167	.083	.541
August	7	2	1	–0–	.50	.500	.250	.625
September	8	2	1	–0–	.50	.833	.417	.708
October	9	3	1	–0–	.50	.167	.583	.792
November	10	3	1	–0–	.50	.500	.750	.875
December	11	3	1	–0–	.50	.833	.917	.958

*To be adjusted to net premium equivalents in all cases. Unearned premium percentages assume that policy dates are evenly distributed throughout the month.

receipt of the full annual premium and payment of the full annual expense.

As a general rule, when acquisition costs are accounted for independently of the reserve, *actual* costs are deferred. There is no assumption that the full annual cost has been incurred. As a result, there is generally no need to accrue the cost of collection in respect of such costs.

Problems arise, however, in connection with the pattern of amortization.

Percentage expenses. Percentage expenses are incurred only as premiums are collected. In all such cases amortization should theoretically be based on the assumption that a full annual premium has been collected even when this is not the case. The reason is that proper allocation of expense requires (1) amortization of costs incurred plus (2) an accrual of expenses not yet incurred.

This is illustrated in Table 23–7. It can be seen that the amortization of acquisition costs actually incurred on the sum-of-the-years'-premiums method will result in deficient amortization unless an additional accrual is made. Such an accrual need not be made if the costs are amortized on a policy-year basis (10 percent, in this case).

The reason for this phenomenon may be explained in two ways:

▶ Over-amortization just offsets the under-accrual.
▶ With respect to the acquisition costs actually in-

curred, namely, half a year's acquisition costs, the total applicable annual premium revenue has been received, namely, half a year's premiums.

Non-percentage expenses. The foregoing reasoning does not hold up for non-percentage expenses. They are incurred at the point of issue; there are no more to be incurred. Therefore, costs actually incurred should be amortized on a calendar-year basis.

Mid-Terminal Reserves

The use of mid-terminal reserves would do away with deferred premiums, but would require that unearned premiums be recorded in some fashion. As compared with a mean reserve calculation, the calculation of a mid-terminal reserve would take the following form for an annual-mode policy dated July 1:

	Mean	Mid-Terminal
Prior terminal reserve	$1,000	$1,000
Annual net premium	120	
Initial reserve	$1,120	
Current terminal reserve	$1,170	$1,170
Mean	$1,145	$1,085
Unearned net premium		60
Statement reserve	$1,145	$1,145

If the policies were on any mode other than annual, then a deferred premium adjustment would reduce the

Table 23–9.

COMPARISON OF MEAN AND MID-TERMINAL CALCULATIONS OF THE ACQUISITION COST RESERVE*

	Mean Reserves		Mid-Terminal Reserves	
	Traditional Calculation	Modified Calculation	Traditional Calculation	Modified Calculation
Prior terminal reserve	$ –0–	$ –0–	$ –0–	$ –0–
Acquisition cost valuation premium	20	20		
Initial reserve	$ 20	20		
Acquisition costs incurred		(200)		(200)
Adjusted initial reserve		$(180)		
Adjusted prior terminal reserve				$(200)
Current terminal reserve	$(180)	$(180)	$(180)	$(180)
Mean reserve	$ (80)	$(180)		
Mid-terminal reserve			$ (90)	$(190)
Unearned acquisition cost valuation premium			10	10
Statement reserve	$ (80)	$(180)	$ (80)	$(180)

*Assuming an annual-premium case dated July 1.

effective mean reserve by $60 to $1,085. No unearned premium would be reported with respect to the mid-terminal reserve.

In practice, a company using mid-terminal reserves would normally assume that one-half of all modal premiums in force as of the valuation date are unearned and adjust gross amounts to net amounts using overall gross-to-net ratios. This assumes an even distribution of policy anniversaries throughout the year. The efficacy of this procedure can be determined by inspection of table 23–8. Obviously the procedure works only if the assumption of an even distribution of anniversary dates is warranted.*

A mid-terminal reserve calculation, like a mean reserve calculation, implicitly assumes an even distribution of deaths and terminations throughout the year. Any significant deviation from this assumption will result in reserve distortions. This is discussed at length in Chapter 12.

Unearned benefit valuation premiums. Assuming an even distribution of benefits throughout the year, no special problems arise in computing unearned benefit premiums. The computation would take the following general form:

---

*This is, of course, also true of the mean reserve calculation. Any serious skewness of business would distort the results whether mean reserves or mid-terminal reserves are calculated.

$$\frac{\text{Annual adjusted benefit valuation premiums in force}}{\text{Annualized gross premiums in force}} \times \frac{\text{Modal gross}}{\text{premiums in force}} \times 50\%$$

Unearned acquisition cost valuation premiums. As discussed elsewhere, the classical mean reserve calculation simply will not work in the case of acquisition cost reserves; adjustment must be made for acquisition costs. In effect, acquisition costs are treated the same as premiums in computing the initial reserve that enters into the mean reserve calculation. The valuation premium assumed to be received becomes a kind of "effective premium" assumed to be received.

The same is true of a mid-terminal reserve calculation. The need to make an adjustment in both cases is depicted in Table 23–9.

When the "adjusted prior terminal reserve" is based on the assumption that the full year's expenses have been incurred, but less than the full annual premium has been received, then the cost of collection must be accrued with respect to premiums remaining to be collected to complete the policy year.

Unearned maintenance expense premiums. When a company records maintenance expense reserves, percentage maintenance expenses applicable to gross premiums remaining to be received for the balance of the policy year must also be recorded as a liability if the reserve assumes that a full year's expenses have been incurred.

463

Uncollected premiums. Uncollected premiums may or may not need to be recorded in connection with a mid-terminal reserve calculation depending on the method used to calculate unearned premiums. If the calculation of unearned premiums recognizes the paid-to-date—this would be a fairly sophisticated refinement—then it would appear that uncollected premiums need not be recorded. Unearned premiums would be carried net of any uncollected premiums. For a given policy, it would be possible to provide a negative unearned premium using this approach in certain circumstances.

If the calculation of unearned premiums and mid-terminal reserves assumes that all policies are current—this seems to be implicit in taking unearned premiums as equal to half the modal premiums in force—then uncollected premiums should be recorded to adjust the reserve amounts to a paid-to basis.

Uncollected Group Premiums

Companies generally have an enforceable claim on uncollected group premiums. When this is the case, such premiums are in the nature of receivables and should be reported as assets. Of course, any related liabilities—such as premium taxes—should be recorded.

The "When Due" Provision

As indicated in Chapter 5, the life insurance audit guide permits premium revenue on long-term contracts to be recorded as such when due, and this is sometimes interpreted to mean that uncollected gross premiums may be carried as an asset even though the policyholder is under no obligation to pay the premium.

When a company elects to treat uncollected premiums as revenue, it must also record a liability for any costs to be incurred upon collecting the premiums receivable. In addition, it is necessary to provide for an allowance for uncollectible profit margins in recognition of the fact that not all premiums will be collected. In other words, the valuation premium portion of the uncollected gross premium is offset by related reserve increments. Expenses that must be covered by the uncollected premiums are offset by the above-mentioned liability. All that remains to reserve for is the profit that will not be realized.

24

Recoverability
and Loss
Recognition

From the moment of issue until the last policy terminates, the assets and liabilities associated with a block of insurance policies must be "sufficient". This means simply that when all the policy assets and liabilities are tabulated, the net amount must, at a minimum, be sufficient to cover all future net cash outflows associated with the block of business. The net amount can be more than sufficient, but it cannot be permitted to be less.

There are basically two types of sufficiency tests: tests made in the year of issue and tests made for the issues of all years. The former must be made every year; the latter would be made when there exists the possibility that overall experience for an entire block of business, without regard for issue year, might be more adverse than the original assumptions contemplate.

Audit Guide Provisions

The life insurance audit guide specifies in several places that gross premiums must be sufficient to "cover" acquisition costs:

Actual acquisition expenses . . . should be . . . [deferred] . . . as long as it can be shown that the gross premiums charged are sufficient to cover the actual expense.[1]
The expense portion of the gross premium must be adequate to cover . . . [level renewal] expenses as well as deferred costs.[2]
Only those acquisition costs which are recoverable should be deferred and amortized.[3]

The guide does not explicitly state that the test

of recoverability must be met with respect to each year's issues, but that is implicit in the context in which the matter is discussed. Furthermore, common sense dictates that each year's issues must stand on their own. Otherwise, a company could issue new business at a loss so long as prior issues, in the aggregate, are generating a profit. That practice would constitute a fraud on stockholders* and so would an accounting method that masked it. Except in very unusual circumstances discussed later in this chapter, any losses associated with a given year's issues should be recognized in the year of issue if the facts are then apparent.

"Recoverability" is something of a misnomer. It is convenient to examine unamortized acquisition costs in terms of their "recoverability" from future premiums. The fact is, though, that future premiums must cover a great deal more than amortization of acquisition costs. They must cover future benefits and future maintenance expenses, too. Recoverability refers to profitability; new issues must be profitable, or at least do no worse than break even, in the future. If one prefers to focus on acquisition costs, they should be thought of as being recoverable from future margins, not gross premiums. "Margin" here refers to what remains to absorb amortization after providing for everything else that the gross premium must cover.

The audit guide is somewhat more specific in its discussion of losses on business already in force:

It is anticipated that the original assumptions will con-

---

*It might also represent a fraud on policyholders if the rates discriminated unfairly against prior generations of policyholders.

tinue to be used . . . during the period in which reserves are accumulated . . . It is possible that actual experience . . . may be such as to indicate that accumulated reserves, together with the present value of future gross premiums, will not be sufficient (a) to cover the present value of future benefits and settlement and maintenance expenses and (b) to recover the unamortized portion of deferred acquisition expenses.[4]

A test for deficiency would usually be made by comparing (1) a gross premium reserve (i.e., the present value of future benefits and expenses less the present value of future gross premiums, computed so as to give effect to current best estimates as to mortality, interest, withdrawals, etc.) with (2) the net liabilities (i.e., benefit reserves plus maintenance expense reserves, if any, reduced by unamortized acquisition costs) carried on the books at the time of making the comparison. Any excess of (2) over (1) is ignored; any excess of (1) over (2) is recorded immediately as a loss.

Any loss required to be recognized in connection with issue-year tests would be computed in the same manner.

Issue-Year Recoverability Tests

Each year's issues must be tested to give every reasonable assurance that they will be profitable in future years, or at least that they will do no worse than break even.

To conduct such tests, it is necessary to determine

▶ What must be tested,
▶ What elements of income and outgo should enter into the test,
▶ What assumptions should be used in making the test,
▶ How to make the test,
▶ How to record a loss that appears as the result of the test, and
▶ What disclosures need to be made.

Test Frames

One of the central questions to be resolved in making an issue-year test is, What should be tested?

▶ A plan-year-age cell?
▶ A plan?
▶ A group of similar plans?
▶ A line of business?
▶ All lines of business together?

With respect to insurance already in force, the audit guide states that "a provision for reserve deficiency may be required only if the aggregate reserves on an *entire line of business* are deficient." [5] (Emphasis supplied.) With respect to issue-year tests, the guide offers no specific suggestions.

"Recommendation No. 1" of the American Academy of Actuaries (discussed in detail in Chapter 7) indicates that the tests should be made in terms of "an entire line of business or a major block of business." While "Recommendation No. 1" is not binding on accountants, it *is* binding on members of the American Academy of Actuaries. Since accountants must depend to a significant extent on the work of actuaries who will be guided by "Recommendation No. 1", and since in any event a good deal of thinking by well-informed actuaries lay behind "Recommendation No. 1", the provisions of "Recommendation No. 1" carry a good deal of authority.

Two of the possible testing frames can be dismissed immediately: (1) plan-year-age cells and (2) all lines of business together.

Testing individual plan-year-age cells is wholly impracticable, and there is some question as to whether it would be proper even if it were feasible to make such tests. Because of smoothing, grading, approximate expense allocations, and other pricing techniques, it is not unusual for a plan to produce indicated losses at some issue ages. Such losses are largely artificial, being the result of producing a schedule of rates that is reasonable and competitive. Some reallocation of expenses would often produce a profit on such plan-year-age cells, and it is difficult to quarrel with the allocation of joint costs on the basis of relative profitability of the individual cells (see Chapter 15). In the absence of very unusual circumstances, a deficiency should never be recognized with respect to an individual plan-year-age cell.

Combining all lines of business for purposes of the issue-year test would also be improper. For example, group or individual health insurance differ markedly in their basic characteristics from ordinary life, and the factors producing gains or losses are correspondingly different. Combining all lines of business for purposes of the test would be similar to deferring the recognition of losses of a grocery store because they will be offset by the future profits of a computer manufacturer that happens to be owned by the same parent.

That leaves a plan, a group of similar plans, or a line of business.

The inventory analogy. Testing the profitability of a block of life insurance policies is similar to testing inventories in applying the "lower-of-cost-or-market rule". In both cases the tests are designed to demonstrate realizability—of deferred acquisition costs, in the first instance; and of inventory carrying values, in the second instance. It is therefore instructive to consider briefly how the cost-or-market test is applied to inventories.

There are three ways to apply the cost-or-market test:

(1) By comparing the cost and market for each item in the inventory, and using the lower figure.

(2) By comparing the total cost and market for major inventory categories, and using the lower figure.

(3) By comparing the total cost and market for the entire inventory, and using the lower figure.[6]

If one views a plan as an "item", a group of similar plans as a "major category", and a line of business as "the entire inventory"; and if one further views the present value of future profits as "market" and recorded net policy assets or liabilities as "cost"; then one can approach the problem of making issue-year tests in much the same manner as making cost-or-market tests.

As a general proposition, it should be considered acceptable to make issue-year recoverability tests in terms of

Each plan issued during the year,
A group of similar plans issued during the year, or
All issues for the year for the line of business.

That does not mean, however, that the choice is entirely discretionary. Selection should be based on careful consideration of all relevant factors, some of which are discussed below.

Significance. An issue-year recoverability test should only be made with respect to a significant block of business. The smaller the block the less dependable are allocations of expenses, estimates of future mortality, etc. The block being tested should be of sufficient size that experience associated with the block can reasonably be forecast, which means that the law of large numbers must reasonably be applicable to the block.

Similarity of characteristics. The block of business being tested should share the same characteristics, broadly speaking. It would generally be inappropriate, for example, to combine single-premium permanent insurance with, say, five-year renewable term; or participating permanent with nonparticipating permanent; or untested new products of highly innovative design with established products. Interest assumptions, lapse patterns, and mortality patterns will often differ markedly among different classes of business. As regards participating business, it might be dangerous to lump such business together with nonparticipating business for testing purposes, since much of the "buffer" provided by a dividend scale is not available to apply to any deficiencies on nonparticipating business.

The similarity criterion extends beyond the type of business being tested. Marketing characteristics should also be similar. It would generally be inappropriate, for example, to combine mail order business with agency business, or college business with regular business. Each type of market has its own pattern of risks and rewards and a block of business associated with a particular market should stand on its own.

Relationship to other accounting policies. In deciding what blocks of business should be tested, consideration should be given to the definitions of blocks of business utilized in modeling, allocating acquisition costs, etc. Presumably groupings made for such other purposes were made for a reason, e.g., similarity of characteristics; and the degree of refinement used in testing should be reasonably consistent with the degree of refinement used for such other purposes.

Loss leaders. Although the practice is very infrequent, once in a while a company will market a plan that is known in advance to produce a loss. Typically the sale of such a plan is designed to accomplish some other objective, for example, to round out an agent's portfolio or otherwise accommodate agents in order to encourage the production of profitable business.

Where sale of a "loss leader" is accompanied by the sale of profitable business, and a reasonable correlation between the two is discernible, then the loss leader should generally be combined with the profitable business for purposes of testing recoverability. When such a correlation cannot be observed, and the "loss leader" accounts for a significant proportion of total sales, it should generally be tested separately.

When a "loss leader" is designed to accomplish an objective the benefits of which are deferred to another accounting period—for example, to become established in a new market—the "loss leader" should also be tested separately. Failure to recognize losses in such cases is tantamount to deferring development costs, and whether or not to recognize the loss should be based on the principles applicable to development costs.

Sometimes an inter-line "loss leader" will be encountered. For example, occasionally a company will offer unprofitable health insurance policies through its ordinary agents in order that the agents are not put in the position of having to refuse their life insurance clients when the clients request such coverage. When this is the case, and the life insurance profits are sufficient to cover the related health insurance losses, the losses should not be recognized.*

Test Elements

The various elements entering into a recoverability test include all of the benefits and most (but usually not all) of the expenses that the gross premium must cover.

Adverse deviation. In theory recoverability should be tested in terms of best estimates, i.e., without provision for adverse deviation. In practice, some degree of adverse deviation will often be introduced into the test to allow for error.

Gross premiums. The test should recognize all gross premiums, including premiums applicable to supplemental benefits and policy fees. Any loss of premium from non-deduction or refund provisions, as well as from modes other than annual,** should also be recognized in the test.

Average size. The test should generally recognize the average policy size. This is due to the fact that items expressed as so much per policy or as a percentage of premiums must usually be translated into a per-unit equivalent for testing purposes.

Decrements. Withdrawals, conversions, mortality, and any other sources of decreases in units of insurance in force must be taken into account in the test.

Benefits. All benefits—mortality, morbidity, coupons, nonforfeiture benefits, dividends, conversions, etc.—must be included in the test.

Care must be taken to ensure that benefits that are separately reserved for are included in the recoverability test. For example, certain supplemental benefits might be reserved for on the basis of unearned premiums applicable to the benefit.*** In general, such benefits and the related premiums should be included with the test of the basic plan.

First-year deferred acquisition costs. First-year acquisition costs actually deferred must be included in the recoverability test. Any "excess" acquisition costs—i.e., costs considered as acquisition costs by the

---

*For purposes of internal line-of-business reporting, consideration should be given to transferring the annual health insurance loss to the life insurance line of business.

**Which would often be taken into account in the assumed distribution of withdrawals.

***An example might be substandard extra reserves, or industrial insurance supplemental benefits treated for reserving purposes as an annual "coupon".

company but not qualifying for deferral under the

variability and attribution criteria (described in Chapter 14) and therefore charged to expense for accounting purposes—would of course be excluded.

Development costs. Development costs would not be considered in a recoverability test whether they are charged to expense or separately deferred. In the latter case, the future "utility" of deferred development costs would be tested separately according to principles outlined in Chapter 17.

Renewal-year acquisition costs. Estimated acquisition costs subsequent to the first year that are to be deferred must be included in the recoverability test.

Maintenance and settlement costs. Provision must be made for policy-related maintenance and settlement costs. Special considerations will usually apply to new companies, whose actual maintenance costs may temporarily be much greater than "normal". Such special considerations are discussed below.

Maintenance and settlement costs should generally be expressed in terms of amounts that exclude allocations of general overhead, or at least the portion of such costs representing general overhead should be determinable. Provisons for general overhead should under certain circumstances be separately examined, as discussed below.

General overhead. The treatment of general overhead in a recoverability test is a matter of some delicacy. Where the gross premium is sufficient to cover all of the various test elements including general overhead, no problem arises. Where the gross premium is not sufficient to cover everything, the question arises as to whether gross premiums on existing business should be required to bear the full burden of paying for future general overhead.

The problem can be highlighted by a simple example. Suppose that for a policy whose gross premium is a level $100, the best-estimate valuation premium is as follows:

	Best-Estimate Level Annual Equivalent
Benefits	$ 50
Acquisition costs deferred	30
Policy-related maintenance and settlement costs	15
General overhead allocated	10
	$105
Annuity required to obtain level annual equivalent	$10

It will be observed that the indicated gross premium

deficiency is $5 ($100, the gross premium, minus $105, the best-estimate valuation premium). Since the annuity is $10, the present value of all such deficiencies is $5 x 10 or $50. Should the indicated loss be recognized?

Generally the loss should not be recognized under these circumstances. General overhead in a life insurance company is fundamentally no different from general overhead in any other business; some part of it must be paid for from profits on future sales. If a manufacturer has a loss of, say, $500,000 and overhead is $1 million, the present value of future "excess overheads" is not recognized. It is assumed that the excess is temporary. Where the excess is not temporary but there is a serious fundamental weakness in markets or technology that is expected to persist, the deficiency still isn't recognized; instead, the going-concern assumption is called into question. One cannot assume a going concern and also assume indefinite future losses; the two assumptions are contradictory.

Therefore, where any apparent gross premium deficiency can be attributed to provisions for general overhead, the deficiency should not be recognized so long as the going-concern assumption is warranted, because inherent in the going-concern assumption is the assumption that the failure to cover general overhead is temporary.* Where the failure appears to be permanent, the problem should be dealt with as a going-concern problem, not as a loss-recognition problem.

New Companies

The problem of unabsorbed overhead is perhaps most noticeable in the case of new companies, and the point made in the preceding discussion is perhaps best illustrated in terms of the typical pattern for a new company. One new company, for example, analyzed its general overhead as follows for the first six years of its existence:

		000	
Year	Actual	Total per Pricing Assumptions	Excess of Actual over Assumed
1	$425	$ 75	$350
2	510	213	297
3	632	378	254
4	710	597	113
5	796	734	62
6	843	860	—

*In addition, to the extent that general overhead is "controllable", credit is usually given for the fact that the controllable portion can be eliminated or reduced if necessary.

The fallacy of assuming in any year up to the sixth that excess overhead will continue indefinitely is readily apparent from the above.

The same phenomenon is often experienced with respect to policy-related maintenance and settlement costs. Often a base processing capacity is acquired before the volume corresponding to the acquired capacity is achieved. In pricing or testing its products, the company must assume for competitive purposes that its unit maintenance costs will tend toward normality, i.e., toward industry averages. For a few years, of course, actual will typically exceed assumed. In testing recoverability, full recognition should be given to the probable effect of future production on unit maintenance and settlement costs.

Test Methods

Methods of testing recoverability are discussed and illustrated in Chapter 7. In general, a test would be made in one of two ways: (1) By comparing the valuation premium with the gross premium, or (2) by projecting expected results.

Valuation premium comparisons. Comparison of a valuation premium with the corresponding gross premium would usually involve the following steps:

1. First, the gross premium per unit of insurance must be calculated. This is usually straightforward, but not always. For example, it will usually be necessary to determine a value for the average policy fee per unit. Under certain circumstances it may be necessary to include an average value for supplemental benefits.

2. The effective valuation premium must be calculated. When the valuation premium is that amount required to support the adjusted reserve, it is necessary to add any items not reserved for but which must be covered by the gross premium, e.g., premium taxes.

3. If the valuation premium exceeds the gross, provisions for adverse deviation should be eliminated. If the valuation premium still exceeds the gross, excess maintenance and overhead should be adjusted. If the valuation premium *still* exceeds the gross, a loss is indicated and should generally be recognized.

Early attention should be given to the test frame, i.e., the plan, block, or line of business for which recoverability is to be tested. Then composite values giving effect to the distribution of new business among the various plans included in the test frame would be computed. Alternatively, comparisons for key plan-age combinations might be examined; if all tests are satisfactory, or if any individual deficiencies are negligible and are obviously more than offset by profits on other business included in the test frame, it would usually be unnecessary to compute composite values.

In addition to comparing gross premiums with valuation premiums, it is usually necessary to make certain projections to ensure that the profit pattern associated with the company's reserve assumptions is reasonable. Generally such projections should take the form of projecting income statements using best-estimate assumptions combined with adjusted reserves based on the reserve assumptions finally adopted. While the projections are not, strictly speaking, part of a test of recoverability, as a practical matter the projections will often be made at the same time as the recoverability tests are made. Projections to test reasonableness of the profit pattern are discussed in Chapter 7.

Projections. If the assumptions used in a projection are the same as those underlying the valuation premium, the values developed by a projection represent either (1) the present value of all future assumed experience discounted at the assumed investment earnings rate or (2) the accumulation of such experience at the assumed investment earnings rate, depending on how the projection is made.

Projections are discussed in some detail in Chapter 3, Chapter 7, and Appendix A.

Calculating a Deficiency

A deficiency would usually be calculated at the moment of issue in one of two ways for level-premium business:

1. The excess of the valuation premium, as adjusted for items discussed earlier, over the gross premium is multiplied by the appropriate present value of an annuity to yield the present value of all such future excesses. Such present value is the amount of the deficiency.

2. Future gross premiums, benefits, and expenses are projected, all amounts are discounted at the assumed investment earnings rate, and the difference between the present value of gross premiums and the present value of benefits and expenses measures the deficiency.

Where premiums are not level, the deficiency might be calculated by Method (2) or it might be calculated by determining the percentage relationship between the valuation premium and the gross premium, based on Method (1) calculations, and applying the percent-

age to the present value of gross premiums, based on Method (2) calculations.

The various methods might be crudely illustrated as follows:

Method (1):

Best-estimate valuation premium, adjusted to include or exclude items as appropriate	$30
Gross premium	25
Excess of valuation premium over gross premium	$ 5
Present value of annuity of $1 for premium-paying period	$10
Deficiency	$50

Method (2):

Present value of gross premiums	$250
Present value of:	
Benefits	150
Acquisition costs deferred	75
Maintenance and settlement costs	75
	300
Deficiency	$ 50

Combination method:

Excess of valuation premium over gross premium	$ 5
Gross premium	$ 25
Percentage	20%
Present value of gross premiums	$250
Deficiency	$ 50

Another variation is to compute the present value of profits without regard for acquisition costs and compare the result with the amount deferred; the difference measures the deficiency:

Present value of gross premiums	$250
Present value of:	
Benefits	150
Maintenance and settlement costs	75
	225
Remainder	$ 25
Acquisition costs deferred	$ 75
Deficiency	$ 50

All of the foregoing methods assume that the recoverability tests are made at the moment of issue. If the tests are made at the end of the first calendar year, all values would change slightly to recognize the timing difference. The amount of the deficiency calculated at the end of the year would ordinarily be somewhat less than the amount calculated at issue, since some portion of the deficiency would already have been recognized (namely, the deficiency on gross premiums already collected).

In practice, the test would usually be made at issue, a "reserve" for any deficiency would be set up—hypothetically—at the moment of issue, and reserve factors would operate to reduce the deficiency reserve by year-end in an amount equal to the portion of the deficiency recognized through the collection of premiums. The principles involved are much the same as the principles applied in calculating statutory deficiency reserves.

Recording a Deficiency

Once a deficiency is computed, there remains the question of what to do with it.

If all policy assets and liabilities were netted in a single amount, then the disposition of the deficiency would be automatic. The net amount would be adjusted by the amount of the deficiency. This is because the reserve is a gross premium reserve (see Appendix A), which represents the present value of all benefits and expenses reduced by the present value of all gross premiums.

However, the gross premium reserve is divided into two or three components for purposes of financial statement presentation—benefit reserves, unamortized acquisition costs, and possibly a reserve for maintenance and settlement costs. Which component should reflect the deficiency?

In the absence of a deficiency problem, unamortized acquisition costs represent an asset in the more or less conventional sense. That is, the deferred costs have future utility measured by future profits associated with the block of business.

The effect of recognizing a deficiency is to recognize that the "utility" of the asset is impaired to the extent of the deficiency. Recognition of a deficiency is tantamount to writing the asset down to net realizable value, where "net realizable value" is defined as the amount to be realized in the normal course of business.* So the deficiency should preferably be applied to reduce deferred acquisition costs, holding liability items unchanged.

An alternative approach is to establish a separate provision for losses and carry it as a liability, somewhat after the fashion of providing for losses on construction contracts. This approach has some practical disadvantages and results in further fragmentation of policy assets and liabilities, which some believe is undesirable.

*This may, and probably would, be greater than market value, i.e., that amount which would be realized in a *sale* of the business.

Special Problems

The procedures described above for testing recoverability and calculating and recording deficiencies apply generally to long-term life and health insurance coverages—nonparticipating ordinary and industrial life insurance, individual fixed annuities, and individual guaranteed renewable health insurance. Other types of business require different approaches.

Participating business. Except in very unusual cases, apparent deficiencies should not be recognized on participating business so long as the dividend scale is sufficient to absorb them. The company always has the option to reduce or eliminate dividends, and full recognition should generally be given to this option in testing recoverability. However, effect should also be given to the consequences of any indicated reduction in the dividend scale—for example, increased withdrawals.

Where a loss is indicated and the company plans to maintain the dividend scale in any event, the reason for maintaining the scale in the face of probable losses should be investigated. If, as is usually the case, the company is willing to bear the losses to maintain the goodwill of policyholders and agents, the loss should generally not be recognized. As the losses materialize—incrementally—they will presumably be accompanied by incremental gains attributable to the goodwill associated with the company's action. Only where there is evidence that the action does not give rise to tangible or intangible benefits should the loss be recognized.

However, when profits on participating business are restricted (a subject that is discussed in the next chapter), the stockholders' share of any losses should be recognized. This is further discussed later in this chapter.

Guaranteed renewable business. While guaranteed renewable business sometimes deteriorates to the point at which losses are a virtual certainty—this is discussed later in this chapter—at the time of issue there is a presumption that rate increases will be sufficient to absorb the effects of adverse experience. So it would be the rare situation in which losses are recognized in the year of issue on guaranteed renewable business.

If deterioration is so rapid that it becomes apparent by the end of the year of issue that prospective losses will not be recouped by future rate increases, then the loss should of course be recognized. Generally this would happen only when there has been an immediate and fundamental change in loss patterns, to the extent that initial assumptions are immediately invalidated and relevant experience indicates that rate increases will not be adequate to cover the short-fall.

Cancellable coverages. Cancellable coverages are somewhat in the nature of property-liability insurance, and there is little justification for recognizing losses beyond the date on which the coverage can be cancelled. To do otherwise is to assume that the company will renew loss business, which is not a very rational assumption.*

Deferred acquisition costs on coverages for which unearned premiums are held—for example, commercial health coverages and credit life and health insurance—would normally be subject to a loss ratio limitation test similar to that used in property-liability accounting. This assumes, of course, that acquisition costs are essentially proportional to premiums written. Deferral would be limited to that percentage of unearned premiums represented by 100 percent minus the sum of

▸ The loss ratio,
▸ The loss-adjustment (i.e., claims settlement) ratio, and
▸ An allowance for policy-related maintenance expense.

If the coverage is of relatively long duration—for example, five-year single-premium credit insurance—then credit should be taken for interest on funds held in respect of the block of business. This would usually have the effect of increasing the indicated margins available for amortization of acquisition costs and thus reducing the write-down.

When cancellable business is treated like long-term business—for example, when acquisition costs are front-ended and renewals must be assumed to support deferral and amortization beyond the renewal or cancellation date—then it would usually be necessary to compute the margins available to absorb amortization of acquisition costs. If it should appear that (1) the available margins at the existing premium level are inadequate and (2) future rate increases, if any, will be limited to amounts required to offset future adverse claims experience, then deferred acquisition costs should be written down to the estimated recoverable amounts.

Most of the deficiency problems associated with cancellable coverages are likely to be line-of-business

---

*Unless, as discussed earlier, there is a good and sufficient reason for issuing and renewing loss leaders, in which case the loss would probably not be recognized anyway.

problems rather than issue-year problems. Line-of-business problems are discussed below.

Practical Considerations

It should rarely be necessary to make exhaustive tests of recoverability. Generally spot checks should do. This is particularly true where a company has tested its premium rates in reasonable depth. Such tests provide a convenient means of testing recoverability. If, for example, the rate tests include all items which must be covered by the gross premiums, the assumptions underlying each item are reasonable and realistic, and acquisition costs assumed for purposes of the tests are no less than the amounts deferred, then the rate tests might be used to test recoverability without modification.

When acquisition costs have been conservatively defined for accounting purposes, recoverability will seldom be a problem. However, when acquisition costs are heavily concentrated in the first year and unit costs are relatively uncontrollable, recoverability should generally be tested in some detail. In the mail order business, for example, solicitation costs are relatively fixed, and a slight difference in the response rate can have a significant effect on unit costs. Recoverability tests are mandatory in those cases in which unit costs considered to qualify for deferral exceed the assumed amount.

Disclosure

A writedown of unamortized acquisition costs attributable to a failure to meet the test of recoverability is a significant event. It means that the block of business in respect of which the writedown is made is expected to produce zero profits in the future.

But readers of the financial statements expect insurance in force to produce profits in the future. The level of future profits is always fairly uncertain, of course; this uncertainty is a common business risk. Uncertainty about the level of future profits differs most substantially from a virtual certainty that profits will be zero. And when new business is valued on a basis designed to produce a break-even, the fact should be disclosed in a note to the financial statements. Such a note might read somewhat as follows:

Acquisition costs incurred on new business issued during the year aggregated $15 million; however, the amount deferred has been limited to $10 million, which represents the portion estimated to be recoverable from future revenues. The unrecoverable balance, $5 million, has been charged to expense. It is expected that new business issued during the year will not contribute to profits in future years.

Loss Recognition

In theory, recoverability tests are performed each year for the year's issues. The test is made once. If the year's issues pass the test, nothing further need be done. If they fail the test, acquisition costs are written down by the amount of any deficiency; thereafter the block of business is left to live out its life in the company of the issues of all years.* In effect, the year's issues are merged with all other business in force of the same kind. Gains or losses are reckoned with respect to the entire portfolio.

It is possible that at some future date portfolio experience will deteriorate to the point at which future losses are indicated. At that point, the present value of such future losses must be recognized immediately by a charge to operations.

Defining a "Line of Business"

The life insurance audit guide provides that "a provision for reserve deficiency *may* be required only if the aggregate reserves on an entire line of business are deficient." [7] (Emphasis supplied.)

The apparent permissiveness of the guide extends to the block of business for which a deficiency must be recorded. Recognition of a deficiency for an entire line of business is the minimum requirement. If a sizable block of business *within* a line of business is deficient, and if the block is clearly distinguishable from other blocks within the line, it would be entirely appropriate to recognize the deficiency attributable to that block. Examples might be:

▸ Deposit term insurance, for which persistency assumptions, used to justify very high first-year commissions, do not hold up.
▸ College business, for which persistency turns out to be disastrous.
▸ "Funeral insurance" sold at advanced ages where mortality is much worse than expected.
▸ Guaranteed renewable medical expense insurance, where claim frequency and/or severity are much

*Except that persistency must be monitored and amortization tables may need revision if actual persistency differs materially from assumed persistency. This is discussed in Chapter 16.

worse than expected and future rate increases are not expected to be adequate.

Many of the same principles applied to define a line of business for purposes of testing recoverability apply also to defining a line of business for purposes of loss recognition. As a general rule, however, the definition of a line of business should tend to be somewhat broader for purposes of loss recognition. The block of business for which a deficiency is calculated should be clearly distinguishable from other blocks within the line, the deterioration associated with the block should be clearly discernible, the losses expected to be produced by the block should be material in relation to annual income, and the present value of the losses should also be material in relation to income and surplus.

Indicators of a Deficiency

It is difficult to generalize about the conditions that could lead to a deficiency with respect to a line of business or a major block (or blocks) within a line. Typically a combination of adverse developments would be necessary to produce losses. Furthermore, the adversity would be measured against average reserve assumptions for issues of all years, and the average assumptions would include (1) the conservatism usually inherent in assumptions on older blocks of business as well as (2) deliberate provisions for adverse deviation. Obviously it would usually take a fairly drastic turn of events to produce aggregate losses.

Interest. Declining interest rates are probably the likeliest source of trouble for permanent life insurance. If the average assumed rate for a block of business is, say, 4 1/2 percent level and indications are that average earned rates will drop to 3 1/2 percent, a possible loss situation is indicated.

Withdrawals. Adverse persistency is another likely source of losses, particularly if acquisition costs are high and cash value scales are generous.

Mortality and morbidity. It is doubtful that mortality, in and of itself, would create a deficient situation for a block of life insurance policies unless there is a fundamental change in mortality patterns or monumental negligence in underwriting. Improving mortality could, of course, result in losses on annuities. Health insurance claim costs are sensitive to economic conditions, inflation, and other relatively unpredictable factors, and it is not unheard-of to develop perpetual losses in certain classes of business due to deteriorating claims experience.

Expenses. It would probably be very rare for maintenance expenses to rise to such an extent as to produce losses. However, even a slight increase in maintenance expenses attributable to inflation or declining volume could, in combination with other factors, contribute to a loss situation.

Economic conditions. General economic conditions may be such as to signal cause for alarm. A recession sometimes results in significant increases in disability claims, for example.

Combinations of factors. No one of the above factors may be sufficient to produce a deficiency, but a combination of factors may spell trouble. Recession, declining interest rates, and soaring withdrawals (which may be attributable to the other two factors) should prompt a close re-evaluation of reserve assumptions.

The life insurance audit guide states that

Gross premium reserves should be computed periodically for comparison with the actual reserves, and particularly when the company has experienced or anticipates adverse deviations from original assumptions that could materially affect the reserves.[8]

Because the calculation of gross premium reserves is so cumbersome and time-consuming, the guide's suggestion that the reserves should be computed periodically is perhaps a little harsh. They should be computed only when there is probable cause for concern.

Elements of a Deficiency Calculation

The life insurance audit guide indicates that a deficiency should be calculated in the following manner for a deficient block of business:

1. Calculate the present value of all future cash outflows for benefits, renewal-year acquisition costs not yet incurred, maintenance expenses, and settlement costs.

2. Calculate the present value of all future cash inflows from gross premiums.

3. Subtract (2) from (1). This is the gross premium reserve.

4. Tabulate the net policy assets or liabilities being held—benefit reserves plus maintenance expenses reserves (if any), less unamortized acquisition costs.

5. Compare (3) and (4). If (3) represents a larger liability (or a smaller asset) than (4), the difference is charged to expense immediately.

Assumptions used in calculating the gross premium

reserve should be best estimates; any intentional loading for adverse deviation would increase the amount of any indicated loss and would result in charging income currently for a loss some portion of which—to the extent of the intentional loading for adverse deviation—would reverse to income in future years. This would violate the audit guide, which states that "no charge should be made to record an indicated loss currently which will result in creating an apparent profit in the future."[9]

Thus the guide makes a distinction between new business assumptions—which are loaded for adverse deviation, which in turn results in reducing the level of current profits and increasing the level of profits in later years—and assumptions used for purposes of computing a deficiency, which are supposed to be best estimates.

The general methodology used in computing deficiencies is the same as that used in testing recoverability. It should be re-emphasized that general corporate overhead should *not* be allocated to a deficient block of business for purposes of computing a deficiency.

Recording a Deficiency

The life insurance audit guide indicates that a deficiency "should be recognized immediately by a charge to earnings to increase reserves and/or reduce deferred acquisition expense."[10]

This could pose difficult mechanical problems. The deficiency is calculated as a single amount, i.e., by computing a gross premium reserve. If it is considered desirable to segregate the reserve into several components, it will likewise be necessary to divide the gross premium into several components. It would probably be more practical to apply the deficiency first to reduce (or eliminate) unamortized acquisition costs and then, to the extent of any remaining deficiency, to increase the benefit reserves.

The loss should preferably be calculated as of the *beginning* of the year in which it first becomes apparent.

Special Problems

The foregoing discussion applies generally to all forms of long-term life and health insurance, and particularly nonparticipating ordinary and industrial life, individual annuities, noncancellable individual health insurance, and group permanent. Other lines of business have unique characteristics that must be taken into account in calculating deficiencies.

Participating business. Absent evidence to the contrary, it should be assumed that a company will reduce dividend scales to the extent necessary to absorb adverse experience. It would therefore be the rare case that future losses on participating insurance would be recognized. The principles involved are the same as those discussed above under the caption "Issue-Year Recoverability Tests".

However, when a company is limited in its "charge" against earnings on participating business to a percentage of pre-dividend earnings, the stockholders' percentage of any losses should be recognized. Suppose, for example, adjusted participating surplus without regard for dividends is $1 million and the stockholders' share, 10 percent, is $100,000, which has been taken into income over the years. Suppose now that reserves are strengthened in the amount of $600,-000 because of deteriorating experience. Adjusted participating surplus drops to $400,000, and the stockholders' share drops to $40,000. The difference between the original stockholders' share, $100,000, and the recomputed share, $40,000, or $60,000, should be recognized as a loss currently.

Restricted participating business is discussed in detail in Chapter 25.

Needless to say, in those very rare cases in which the present value of losses on participating business exceeds the present value of dividends, the loss should be recognized in full.

Commercial forms of health insurance. Projected losses on cancellable individual health insurance for which acquisition costs are deferred in the form of a computed equity in the unearned premium reserve would be accounted for through the operation of the loss-ratio limitation test common to property-liability insurance.

Projected losses on cancellable coverages accounted for as long-term business—i.e., those cases in which acquisition costs are "heaped" into the first year and renewals must be assumed in order to support deferral and amortization—would be recognized by writing down the unamortized amount to the margins projected to be available to absorb them. Interest should be taken into account in the projections when a fairly lengthy period of time is involved.

Guaranteed renewable health insurance. Recognition of losses on guaranteed renewable health insurance is an extremely complex matter. Sometimes losses are only temporary, and will continue only until the next rate increase. Sometimes losses are more or less perpetual because healthy lives terminate as rates are increased, leaving a diminishing number of increasingly impaired risks which produce losses that rate increases never seem to cover.

Where losses are expected to be temporary they should not be recognized in advance. Fluctuations in experience are normal for this type of business and it would be improper to charge income for a loss currently when the business is expected to produce profits over the long term.

Where losses are "perpetual", there are several possible approaches to computing the present value of the losses:

1. Treat the business as if it were noncancellable. Under this approach, it is assumed that future rate increases will be absorbed by future claim increases; the loss is measured in terms of the existing levels of premiums and claim costs. This approach results in "freezing" the lag in rate increases by assuming that all future rate increases apply to future additional claim costs. Also, even assuming the present value of future rate increases might equal the present value of additional claims, the incidence would not likely be the same, and profits would be distorted. This approach has very limited utility.

2. Revalue each time there is (a) a rate increase or (b) a change in outlook with respect to the benefit pattern. Conceivably the business might be revalued annually. This may well be the most practical approach.

3. Project future rate increases and future increases in claim costs and make one calculation covering the future in its entirety, revaluing only if experience completely invalidates the underlying assumptions. This is perhaps the purest approach, but it requires a great deal of insight, depending as it does on interpretations of historical patterns and judgments about the likely course of future rate increases, claim costs, and withdrawals.

There are no firm guidelines for calculating deficiencies on guaranteed renewable business. It is an area requiring the keenest of actuarial judgment.

Credit insurance. Acquisition costs on single-premium credit insurance are usually expressed in the form of a percentage of unearned premiums. In such cases, loss recognition would take the form of a write-down of unamortized costs to the amount indicated by a loss-ratio limitation test. When the coverage is for a long period of time and interest is a material factor—as it will often be in the case of single-premium business—the recorded loss should be reduced for expected investment income.

Losses on outstanding-balance credit insurance should be recognized to the extent of the period during which rates are guaranteed.

Any expected sharing of losses through experience rating should be recognized in calculating the loss to be recognized.

Group insurance. Losses on group insurance should only be recognized through the date as of which the coverage can be cancelled by the company, i.e., only to the extent of the rate guarantees. Pooled business should be treated as one line of business; retention business should be treated as another. Generally, life and health coverages should be considered together in making the calculation, since group coverages are usually sold as a "package" and are usually best viewed that way for accounting purposes. Group annuities should be considered a separate line of business.

Any provision for losses on experience-rated business should give full effect to available experience rating refund reserves* and retrospective premium provisions.

Recognition of deficiencies on group insurance will probably be very rare. Volatility of experience is usually a common characteristic of group insurance, and it would be highly unusual to have both (1) a credible trend and (2) a lengthy period of rate guarantees. Yet both conditions would ordinarily be necessary to justify the recognition of losses.

Disclosure

Recognition of a loss on a line of business is a significant event that requires adequate disclosure.

---

*However, refund reserves would have to be applied on a case-by-case basis in making the calculation since individual case surpluses are not available to offset individual case deficits.

"Adequate disclosure" consists, at a minimum, of (1) clearly displaying the amount of the loss, net of related tax effects, as a separate (but not extraordinary) item in the income statement and (2) describing in a note to the financial statements the line or block of business involved, the circumstances causing the loss, the general method of calculating the loss, and the estimated amount of the loss which would have been recognized during the year if the deficiency (measured as of the beginning of the year) had not been recognized. For example, disclosure might be somewhat as follows:

INCOME STATEMENT:

Income before provision for losses on certain health insurance policies	$20,000,000
Provision for losses on certain health insurance policies, less applicable taxes of $11,000,000	30,000,000
NET LOSS	$10,000,000

NOTE TO FINANCIAL STATEMENTS:

Because of continuing adverse claims experience on a significant closed block of individual guaranteed renewable major medical policies, and because it is evident that future rate increases will be inadequate to cover future claims, the Company has provided currently for the present value of estimated losses on such business. The provision was calculated as of the beginning of the current year. Had the provision not been made, it is estimated that "Income before provision for losses on certain health insurance policies" would have been reduced by approximately $3,000,000.

Any provision for losses made at the time of an initial conversion would generally be included in the initial surplus adjustment. Thus the provision would not be charged to income of any year.

However, the amount of the provision included in the initial surplus adjustment should be disclosed, and all other disclosures indicated above should also be made.

25

Restricted Participating Business

Stock companies selling participating business were classified in two ways in Chapter 10. A "Type 1" company was defined as a company for which there are no formal restrictions on the amount of earnings on participating policies which can be credited to the stockholders' account. A "Type 2" company was defined as a company for which there are formal restrictions on the amount of such earnings which can inure to the benefit of stockholders.

Type 1 companies are discussed in Chapter 10. Type 2 companies are discussed in this chapter.

As will be seen, restrictions on the earnings of participating business present the accountant with some of the most challenging problems in life insurance accounting.

Audit Guide Provisions

The life insurance audit guide provides that

For those companies for which there are limitations on the amounts of earnings which may inure to stockholders, the policyholders' share of earnings on such business which cannot be expected to inure to stockholders, should be excluded from stockholders' equity by a charge to operations and a credit to an appropriate liability account in a manner similar to the accounting for earnings applicable to minority interests. Dividends declared or paid should be charged to the liability account. Dividends declared or paid on such business, in excess of the liability account, should be charged to operations.[1]

Percentage Restrictions

Where restrictions are based on a percentage of

pre-dividend income, the guide indicates that pre-dividend income should be calculated on a generally accepted accounting principles basis and the percentage restriction should be applied to the adjusted amount. Suppose, for example, the restriction is 10 percent, statutory earnings allocable to participating business are $500,000 after dividends of $100,000, and generally accepted accounting principles adjustments are $900,000, as follows:

Increase in unamortized acquisition costs applicable to participating business	$500,000
Adjustment of policy reserves on participating business to recognize revised assumptions as to interest, mortality, withdrawals, and nonforfeiture benefits; dividends ignored	350,000
Realized capital gains (reported in income statement) allocable to participating business	50,000
Deferred taxes (zero because taxes are allocated to the participating line as if it were a separate company and the participating line is "Phase I")	–0–
	$900,000

Adjusted pre-dividend earnings would be $1,500,000 (statutory pre-dividend income, $600,000, plus adjustments of $900,000), and 90 percent of that amount, $1,350,000, would be charged to operations and recorded as a liability. Dividends paid, $100,000, would be charged to the liability.

Flat Amount Per $1,000

Where restrictions are based on a fixed amount per $1,000, such as 50 cents per thousand, the stockholders' share of earnings is fixed by law and timing differences do not affect the incidence of such share.

For example, if participating business in force is $500,-000,000 and the 50-cent rule applies, for the situation described previously the same amount of adjusted pre-dividend income, $1,500,000, would be reported, but $1,250,000 ($1,500,000 less 50 cents x 500,000 or $250,000) would be charged to operations and recorded as a liability. It should be noted that the pre-dividend adjustment in these circumstances does not affect the amount of net income, but it does affect individual items in the financial statements, and "the auditor must determine whether the adjustments to individual items within the financial statements are necessary for a fair presentation of financial position and results of operations." [2] Presumably the individual items will usually be materially affected and adjustment would be necessary for "fair presentation" in most cases.

Greater of Percentage or Amount

Where the restrictions are based on an alternative calculation, such as the greater of a percentage or a flat amount, the guide suggests that adjustment should generally be based on the calculation basis that will be applicable when the indicated "timing differences" reverse. In effect, "timing differences should be considered in the same manner as timing differences between financial statements and tax returns are considered in calculating provisions for deferred income taxes." [3] The audit guide is silent as to what to do when the calculation base shifts back and forth between the percentage and the flat amount.

100 Percent Restriction

Finally, where 100 percent of earnings on participating business is held to the credit of policyholders, 100 percent of the earnings would be deducted from the statement of operations. There is, of course, no effect on earnings applicable to shareholders where *all* of the earnings are restricted; materiality of the effect on individual financial statement items would dictate whether earnings would have to be adjusted. As a practical matter, very few companies would be subject to this provision of the audit guide, since most companies provide for a stockholder "charge" against earnings on participating business.

"Inure to Stockholders"

The guide thus provides that earnings on participating business that "cannot be expected to inure to stockholders" should be deducted in arriving at net income. "Inure to stockholders" is not defined by the guide and the phrase is subject to some degree of interpretation. "Inure" means, in essence, "to legally accrue", and whether such earnings accrue to stockholders, and when, are matters about which there are differences of opinion.

Comparison with Type 1 Company

It was suggested in Chapter 10 that dividend scales almost always operate to restrict the profits on participating business that inure to the benefit of shareholders in the case of Type 1 companies. To the extent that the fairness of a dividend scale is reviewed by regulatory authorities, it may be said that an informal regulatory restriction limits the shareholders' charge against such profits to a reasonable amount.

The essential difference between a Type 1 company and a Type 2 company lies in the *formality* of the restriction. For a Type 1 company the dividend scale may bear an erratic relationship to the pattern of earnings on participating business, and the only restriction on shareholders' access to such earnings is the dividend scale itself. For a Type 2 company the dividend scale might also bear an erractic relationship to earnings, but earnings above and beyond the sum of (1) dividends and (2) the stockholder charge must be segregated in the company's accounts. In the statutory statement, however, accumulated undistributed earnings allocable to participating policyholders is not reported as a liability. While separate accounts are maintained, participating surplus and stockholders' surplus are added together in making up the Convention Statement. Thus the restricted amounts are reported in a memorandum account. All of the company's surplus, from whatever source derived, is considered available to protect all the policyholders, whether participating or nonparticipating. The distinction between the interests of policyholders and the interests of stockholders is thus a very important one so far as the treatment of participating surplus is concerned.

Type of Restrictions

There are several types of restrictions on earnings on participating business. The life insurance audit guide refers to restrictions "imposed by law, charter, or contract" and to "self-imposed [restrictions] as demonstrated by company policy or practice." [4]

The guide also describes the usual forms of the restrictions: percentage, amount, and greater of percentage or amount.

Regulatory Restrictions

Several states have written restrictions into the law. For example, New York law provides for a limitation equal to the greater of 10 percent of participating profits (before dividends) or 50 cents per $1,000 on all participating business wherever written for companies licensed to do business in New York; the New York law thus has extraterritorial effect and is generally regarded as the nation's strictest law. Other states have laws restricting the stockholder charge against earnings applicable to business written in the particular state or to all participating business written by insurers domiciled in the particular state.

Statutory restrictions can therefore be classified in several ways, each of which has different implications for the financial statements:

▶ Restrictions on profits on participating business written within the state irrespective of the state of domicile;
▶ Restrictions on business wherever written for companies domiciled in the state; and
▶ Restrictions on business wherever written for companies licensed in the state irrespective of the state of domicile.

It should be noted that the various states have various means of implementing the restrictions. New York, Illinois, and New Jersey, for example, provide for the restrictions in the statutes. Wisconsin imposes the restrictions by regulation. Some states have adopted informal rules.

According to one study, states having restrictions of some type include Connecticut, the District of Columbia, Idaho, Illinois, Indiana, Iowa, Massachusetts, Nebraska, New Jersey, New Mexico, New York, and Wisconsin.*

Charter Restrictions

Occasionally a company's charter will specify restrictions on the stockholder charge against earnings

*For a thorough discussion of the background, nature, and reasons for the restrictions as well as an analysis of applicable state laws, see Joseph Belth, *Participating Life Insurance Sold by Stock Companies,* S. S. Huebner Foundation for Insurance Education, 1965.

on participating business. While a charter provision could be regarded as "self-imposed", the charter provision represents an undertaking by the company that has legal status unless the charter is changed.

Contractual Restrictions

It is very rare for life insurance policy provisions to commit a company to restricting the stockholder charge against earnings on participating business. Such provisions are most common in the case of "founders' policies", under which the policies—issued when a company was getting started in the life insurance business—provide that a certain fixed share of profits shall inure to the benefit of holders of the policies.

Self-Imposed Restrictions

Some companies restrict the stockholder charge against earnings on participating business by declaration of the board of directors. The restriction is therefore terminable at the option of the company.

Sometimes a company will impose restrictions on itself in order to accommodate the laws of various states. Suppose, for example, that a company domiciled in a non-restrictive state does business in several states that restrict the stockholder charge against earnings on participating business written in those states. In the absence of an overall restriction, a separate accounting would have to be made to each restrictive state for participating insurance held by residents of each such state. By adopting a company-wide restriction equivalent to the most stringent statutory restriction to which any part of the company's participating business is subject, the company avoids numerous separate calculations and filings, which is to say that it avoids a great deal of administrative inconvenience.

Interpreting the Restrictions

In determining how to account for restrictions on earnings associated with participating business it is first necessary to decide on what the restrictions mean—whether they have a practical restrictive effect on participating earnings inuring to the benefit of shareholders.

At first blush it would seem that the answer is obvious. A law is a law, a regulation is a regulation, a charter is a charter. But one is hard-pressed to find cases supporting a particular *interpretation* of the law.

In such an environment, varying interpretations are possible.

Apart from certain legal imponderables, there are some accounting imponderables that cloud the issue. What counts most in accounting for the restriction, ultimate ownership of surplus or the mere fact of a *current* restriction? Exactly what constitutes "inuring to the benefit of stockholders?"

Finally, a company's *intent* may have some bearing on how the participating restriction should be accounted for in some cases. Assuming that the effect of a particular law or regulation or charter provision is not clearly discernible, then a company's own interpretation of the law or regulation—i.e., whether it considers itself restricted or not—may determine how it accounts for the restriction.

A review of the New York law on the matter of restrictions on the stockholder charge against participating profits provides a convenient frame of reference for discussing the significance of the restrictions.

The New York Law

Section 216(6) of the New York Insurance Law provides that

. . . [N]o foreign . . . stock life company shall deliver or issue for delivery in this state any participating policy or contract unless it has a special permit from the superintendent to do so. Any such company authorized to do business in this state may apply to the superintendent for such a permit. Such application shall be in the form prescribed by the superintendent and shall contain such information as he may require. Such application shall contain or be accompanied by:

(a) . . .

(b) An agreement by such company, evidenced by a resolution of its board of directors or other appropriate body having power to bind such corporation and its stockholders, to the effect that, so long as any outstanding participating policies or contracts of such company are held by persons resident in the state of New York, no profits on participating policies and contracts in excess of the larger of (a) ten per cent of such profits, or (b) fifty cents per thousand dollars of participating life insurance other than group term insurance in force at the end of the year, shall inure to the benefit of the stockholders; and that the profits on its participating policies and annuity contracts shall be ascertained by allocating to such policies and annuity contracts specific items of gain, expense or loss attributable to such policies and contracts and an equitable proportion of the general gains or outlays of the company.

. . . In every annual statement made by such company to the superintendent after the issuance of such permit, and so long as its agreement pursuant to paragraph (b) above is in force, such company shall exhibit the amount of participating policyholders' surplus. Such participating policyholders' surplus shall be used only for the payment or apportionment of dividends to participating policyholders at least to the extent hereinbefore required, or for the purpose of making up any loss on the participating policies of such company. Nothing herein contained shall be deemed to give any class of policyholders priority with respect to the assets of any such company in liquidation. . . .

The term "profits on participating policies and contracts" is not defined in the New York Insurance Law. It has, however, historically been interpreted to refer to statutory participating profits before dividends to policyholders.

Section 207 of the New York Insurance Law establishes a maximum surplus limitation—the greater of (1) 10 percent of reserves on participating business or (2) $850,000—for domestic mutual companies and the participating branches of domestic stock companies. Although the law is applicable solely to domestic companies, the New York Insurance Department has consistently required substantial compliance by foreign insurers licensed to do business in New York.

Management Fee Concept

Some believe that the practical effect of the New York law is to divide a stock company selling participating business into two branches, one mutual and one stock, with stockholders having the equivalent of a management contract with the mutual branch. The fee for managing the mutual branch is set by statute at 50 cents per $1,000 or 10 percent of statutory pre-dividend profits, whichever is greater. Under this view the "fee" is not subject to adjustment since it is dictated by statute. In other words, stockholders' compensation is clearly defined for each accounting period.

The management fee concept, while appealing because of its simplicity, introduces some troublesome problems. If the mutual branch is a separate entity producing merely a management fee, then it is very similar to a separate account, and the assets, liabilities, surplus, income, and expense should be eliminated from the financial statements to be consistent with the concept. The financial statement effect would be limited to a one-line entry for the statutory management fee.

Because of the interrelationships between the two branches (they share the same administrative organization, investment department, and sales force), because stockholders assume the ultimate risk of failure of the participating branch, and because the accounts can be separated only by many arbitrary allocations, fair presentation would seem to demand that the accounts of the two branches be consolidated. Exclusion from income of all profits attributable to participating business but the statutory "management fee" would be possible, and it may be desirable if a company considers itself to be truly restricted to that amount forever.

Whether this approach fairly represents a fair measure of the stockholders' real interest in participating earnings depends in part on how one defines "real interest". It might be defined in terms of the ultimate ownership of surplus or in terms of the *current* restriction on distributions to shareholders.

Ultimate Ownership of Surplus

Case law—most of which has involved mutual companies—has generally established the principle that the interest of a policyholder (or a class of policyholders) in a life insurer's surplus is limited to amounts allocated for distributions to policyholders by company management, and management has considerable discretion in making such allocations, so long as they are made in good faith.*

New York law does not impair the discretionary authority of management. The law does not state that accumulated participating earnings in excess of accumulated stockholder charges must be paid to participating policyholders; it states only that no more than the computed stockholder charge can inure to the benefit of shareholders in any one year. "Inure to the benefit of shareholders" appears to refer to distributions to shareholders, in that the stockholder charge is actually transferred to nonparticipating surplus and is generally available, together with gains on nonparticipating business, for such distributions.

Some attorneys are of the opinion that upon the happening of any event causing the restrictions to become ineffective with respect to a given state, all

---

*See, for example, Greef v. Equitable Life Assurance Society, 1899, 160 N.Y.; *Fidelity & Casualty Company of New York v. Metropolitan Life Insurance Company,* 1964, 42 Misc. 2d.; *Rhine v. New York Life Insurance Company,* 1936 248 App. Div. 120, 289 N.Y.S.; *State ex rel National Life Association v. Matthews,* 58 Ohio State 1; and *State ex rel Ellis v. Union Central Life Insurance Company,* 84 Ohio State 459.

surplus applicable to participating policies held by residents of such state would cease to be subject to the restriction and would legally constitute surplus belonging to shareholders. Under this view, for example, a company licensed in New York might sell all participating business on residents of New York State to another company (or a subsidiary), in which case the extraterritorial effect of the New York law would no longer apply and—in the absence of restrictions imposed by other states—restrictions on the remaining participating surplus would disappear.*

Even in the absence of some event causing the restrictions to be ineffective, some believe that in a "runoff" of the restricted participating business, any remaining surplus would revert to shareholders. Unfortunately there are no cases demonstrating this conclusively one way or the other. Those who hold this view usually base it on (1) the thrust of case law, described earlier, concerning a policyholder's interest in surplus, (2) the inequitability of the "tontine" effect that it is assumed would accompany a runoff of the business, and (3) the ultimate inability of states to enforce a particular pattern of surplus distribution to policyholders resident in other states.**

Those who believe that the ultimate ownership of surplus resides in shareholders also believe—generally —that Type 2 companies should be treated essentially the same as Type 1 companies. They believe, in short, that the restrictions have little or no practical effect. They believe that advance recognition should be accorded to all the things that a company can do to remove the restrictions; that the ultimate significance of extraterritorial power is negligible; that the company's obligation to policyholders is limited to dividends declared; and that so long as dividend scales are equitable, the company has no further responsibility to policyholders under the law. They believe that if there are indeed any restrictions, they are limited to participating policies on residents of the restrictive states, and that any accounting recognition of restrictions should be limited to profits and surplus on participating business in force in such states.

Current Restrictions on Surplus

Some view participating policyholders' surplus as a permanent deferral of profits that may or may not be

---

*However, it should be noted that New York authorities would probably demand that an equitable allocation of surplus be made to any policies transferred in the manner described.

**In other words, the extraterritorial New York law would, under this view, have no effect on actual distributions of restricted surplus to other than New York policyholders.

claimed eventually by shareholders; because of the indefiniteness of time and amount of such claim, they hold that there is insufficient evidence for recording any such claim currently. They thus believe that the *current* restriction on the stockholder charge, not the ultimate ownership of surplus, is the significant consideration from an accounting point of view.

They believe further that any action to remove the restrictions is an economic event of the year in which such action is taken, and that advance recognition should not be accorded the mere possibility that action could be taken. As for the ultimate inability of a state—such as New York—to enforce rules relating to distributions to policyholders of other states, they argue that the surplus limitation rules operate to enforce such rules currently and that any future ineffectiveness of such rules is mere conjecture. They believe that the doctrine of conservatism requires recognition of the restrictions. In short, they believe that regulatory restrictions, whether extraterritorial or otherwise, have full force and effect until and unless events prove conclusively to the contrary.

The management fee concept is one variation of this point of view. Another variation would call for profits to be calculated as if the business were non-participating, with the statutory restrictions applied to the adjusted figures. Under this latter approach, the fact of the restriction is acknowledged, but (1) it is believed that the individual items in the financial statements should be consistently stated, and "consistency" is defined in terms of principles of nonparticipating business, and (2) with respect to percentage restrictions, it is believed that the timing of recognition of the stockholders' share should be based on non-participating rules, on the theory that a percentage of participating profits is no different, for all practical purposes, than total profits on a block of nonparticipating business equal in size to the applicable percentage of the block of participating business.

Company Intent

Given that the laws and regulations relating to restrictions on participating profits and surplus are subject to varying interpretations, it follows that it may be impossible to arrive at a definitive conclusion as to the effect of such laws and regulations. In this environment, a company's intent—i.e., its own view of the effect of the laws—is a significant element in deciding how to account for the restrictions. Indeed, some believe that intent should *determine* how to account for the restrictions.

If a company views itself as being restricted, and its policies and practices support this view, then for all practical purposes the company *is* restricted. So long as the company holds to this view the profits on participating business that inure to the benefit of shareholders will be limited in practice to the stockholder charge. Irrespective of the effect of the law, shareholders cannot look forward to anything more than the stockholder charge until such time as the company changes its intent, and then only to the extent that the law is accommodating.

If a company does not view itself as being restricted and is able—as it usually is—to summon legal opinions supporting this view, then it may be very difficult to marshal evidence sufficient to force the company to recognize the restrictions. The burden of proof is on the company and its counsel, of course, and counsel's opinion should preferably be reviewed by independent counsel who has expertise in the particular laws of the particular state involved.

Some believe that company intent has little relevance in accounting. But recognition of intent is often a way of recognizing economic substance. With respect to an investor's share of income of a foreign investee, for example, deferred taxes need not be provided where the investor's intent—as supported by its policies, practices, and plans—is to reinvest such earnings abroad indefinitely. In short, where future events with material financial impact are uncertain, all available evidence, including evidence of intent, should be used in deciding what provision to make currently for such future events.

Importance of the Interpretation

The method of accounting for restricted participating business depends essentially on the interpretation of the restriction, i.e., a determination as to whether the law, regulation, informal procedure, charter provision, or company policy has a practical restrictive effect on the stockholders' share of earnings and surplus on participating business. At present there seems to be no basis, short of an arbitrary rule of some sort, for interpreting the various laws, etc., the same way in every case. Thus one might find two stock companies that write participating business, both licensed in New York, accounting for the New York restrictions in two different ways.

The possible interpretations of New York law might be summarized as follows:

1. At the liberal extreme, a company might decide,

on the basis of legal opinion and its own intent, that the restrictions need not be recognized.

2. At the conservative extreme, a company might decide, based possibly on a conservative interpretation of the law and an analysis of its own intent, that the New York law applies to all participating business and that restrictions on aggregate participating surplus should be recognized.

3. And as a compromise, a company may decide, based on an analysis of its options as well as the opinion of counsel, that it is necessary to recognize only the restrictions on surplus allocable to participating insurance on residents of New York.

The foregoing list pretty well covers the range of possible interpretations (give or take a modification or two) of any of the various forms of restrictive situations. All three interpretations are likely to be found in practice.

Arriving at a viable interpretation of the restrictions is therefore the first order of business for a company subject to the restrictions. Accounting for the restrictions in a manner consistent with the interpretation is difficult, but not nearly as difficult as making the interpretation in the first place.

General Guidelines for Interpretations

It would seem appropriate to assume that state laws have a practical restrictive effect in the absence of conclusive evidence to the contrary. Thus the burden of proof should be on those who choose not to recognize the restrictions. This approach is in keeping with the doctrine of conservatism, under which uncertainties about the future are usually resolved in favor of the approach that produces the more conservative effect on the balance sheet and the current income statement.

Some believe that the uncertainties surrounding the par question are so great that when the amounts involved are material, the independent accountant should refuse to give an opinion on the financial statements whether or not the restrictions are recognized in whole or in part. This would seem to do a disservice to the life insurance industry and the accounting profession, and one hopes that this particular approach is not considered acceptable.

A company's interpretation of the restrictions should be based on the opinion of counsel with respect to the effect of the restrictions *on the particular company*. Counsel's opinion should generally look to the ultimate ownership of surplus, since the financial statements purport to represent the stockholders' equity in the increase in net economic resources of the corporation, and such measurement should not be unduly affected by current restrictions that do not have a substantive long-term effect.*

Counsel's opinion should also be supported by a declaration of the company's intent. But a mere declaration of intent is not sufficient; it should be supported in turn by past actions and future plans. Past actions and future plans must be interpreted as to their content and meaning, of course, and any such interpretation may be highly subjective. But there are few major accounting issues in which some degree of subjective business judgment is not necessary.

Some recognition might be accorded to methods by which a company might remove the restrictions. Such evidence would be supportive, not conclusive. This guideline has relevance primarily to extraterritorial laws. Even when a company decides that an extraterritorial law has no practical restrictive effect, restrictions applicable to business in force in the restrictive state should be recognized in the absence of compelling proof to the contrary.

Separation of Statutory Accounts

Recognition of restrictions on the stockholder charge against earnings on participating business requires, of course, that a separate accounting be made of such earnings. In effect, a company's accounts must be separated into two "branches", the participating branch and the nonparticipating branch. Where only part of a company's participating business is subject to restrictions—for example, in those cases in which only the participating business written in one state is affected—the separation would be made between the business so restricted and all other business.

General Approaches

The sale and servicing of ordinary insurance is a highly integrated operation, and a separation of accounts requires a significant degree of allocation and estimation. Various methods are used to make the separation. The methods are usually subject to the review and approval of regulatory authorities.

*Any excess of adjusted over statutory earnings on all types of business, participating or nonparticipating, is currently restricted, and if it is believed that current restrictions on participating earnings are the significant fact, then this principle should be applied consistently, in which case only statutory earnings would be reported.

Table 25–1.

SEPARATION OF STATUTORY BALANCE SHEET ACCOUNTS BETWEEN PAR AND NON-PAR BRANCHES AT DECEMBER 31, 1971 (000 Omitted)

	Par	Non-Par	Company Total
Admitted assets:			
Bonds	$ 18,644	$ 262,466	$ 281,110
Stocks	3,179	39,211	42,390
Mortgage loans	10,056	124,027	134,083
Policy loans	5,503	39,486	44,989
Real estate	885	10,917	11,802
Cash	420	5,180	5,600
Investment in subsidiary	–0–	3,243	3,243
Deferred and uncollected premiums	1,101	9,796	10,897
Other assets	125	1,545	1,670
Separate accounts	–0–	29,771	29,771
	$ 39,913	$ 525,642	$ 565,555
Reserves, liabilities, and capital:			
Policy reserves	$ 40,594	$ 414,793	$ 455,387
Claims	171	8,441	8,612
Dividends	1,399	–0–	1,399
Dividend accumulations	2,281	–0–	2,281
Other policyholder funds	122	7,307	7,429
Other liabilities	126	3,419	3,545
Mandatory securities valuation reserve	1,088	12,878	13,966
Separate accounts	–0–	29,771	29,771
Accumulated unpaid stockholder charges	1,625	(1,625)	–0–
	47,406	474,984	522,390
Capital:			
Common stock		27,721	27,721
Paid-in surplus		14,699	14,699
Unassigned surplus	(7,493)	8,238	745
	(7,493)	50,658	43,165
	$ 39,913	$ 525,642	$ 565,555
Ordinary insurance in force	$429,000	$3,688,000	$4,117,000

Generally, operating statement items are allocated between par and non-par accounts directly wherever feasible. Premiums, benefits, reserve increases, and commissions can usually be separated by appropriate coding of input. Investment income is usually allocated based on (1) assets, if assets are allocated between branches, or (2) liabilities, if assets are not so allocated. General insurance expenses not directly identifiable with either branch will usually be allocated on the basis of time studies, premium ratios, and similar methods.

Degrees of Separation

Some companies make completely separate sets of statements for the participating and nonparticipating branches. This necessitates allocations of assets,* liabilities, revenues, expenses, and surplus items.

Other companies maintain separate accounts only with respect to liabilities, revenues, expenses, and surplus items. In such cases proportionate totals of liabilities are generally used to allocate investment income between branches.

Where the amounts involved are small, such as cases in which the company's business in force in a restrictive state whose law does not have extraterritorial effect is minor in amount, income and surplus allocable to the participating branch might be estimated by highly approximate methods, assuming the state in question is satisfied by such an approximation.

*Assets might be allocated pro rata (except for policy loans, which are directly assignable), or certain distinctions might be made in assumed investment philosophies—for example, equity investments might, because of their risk characteristics, be allocated wholly to the nonparticipating branch.

Table 25–2.

SEPARATION OF STATUTORY OPERATING AND SURPLUS ACCOUNTS BETWEEN PAR AND NON-PAR
BRANCHES IN 1971 (000 Omitted)

	Par	Non-Par	Company Total
Operating statement:			
Premiums	$ 9,932	$109,678	$119,610
Proceeds left on deposit	331	686	1,017
Other revenue items		2,268	2,268
Net investment income	2,244	28,189	30,433
	12,507	140,821	153,328
Death and other benefits	3,125	51,907	55,032
Increase in reserves	3,576	33,036	36,612
Commissions, expenses, and taxes	4,198	44,038	48,236
	10,899	128,981	139,880
Gain before taxes and dividends	1,608	11,840	13,448
Federal income taxes	12	1,754	1,766
Gain before dividends	1,596	10,086	11,682
Dividends to policyholders	1,438		1,438
Net gain from operations	$ 158	$ 10,086	$ 10,244
Statement of unassigned surplus:			
Balance at January 1, 1971	$(7,389)	$ 14,987	$ 7,598
Additions (deductions):			
Net gain from operations	158	10,086	10,244
Net realized capital gains	19	244	263
Unrealized capital gains	239	2,945	3,184
Change in MSVR	(269)	(3,323)	(3,592)
Change in non-admitted assets	(37)	(453)	(490)
Change in liability for unauthorized reinsurance		115	115
Excess cost of subsidiary		(13,902)	(13,902)
Dividends to stockholders		(2,675)	(2,675)
Stockholder charge*	(214)	214	–0–
Net change	(104)	(6,749)	(6,853)
Balance at December 31, 1971	$(7,493)	$ 8,238	$ 745
*Computation of stockholder charge:			
(1) Gain before dividends			$ 1,596
(2) Net realized capital gains			19
(3) Total of (1) + (2)			1,615
(4) 10% of (3)			162
(5) Participating insurance in force			429,164
(6) $.50 x (5)			214
(7) Greater of (4) or (6)			$ 214

Crazy Quilt Life

For statutory purposes, Crazy Quilt Life maintains a full separation of accounts and limits the stockholder charge to the greater of (1) 10 percent of (a) pre-dividend statutory income plus (b) net realized capital gains, or (2) 50 cents per $1,000 of participating ordinary insurance in force at the end of the year.

Premiums, claims, commissions, and reserve increases are coded directly to the appropriate branch. All other revenue and expense items are allocated between branches on the basis of formulas approved by regulatory authorities.

Policy loans and deferred and uncollected premiums are coded directly to the appropriate branch. All other invested assets and cash are prorated based on the relationships of interest-bearing liabilities, which are associated directly with each branch. Miscellaneous liabilities are also allocated using various bases.

Federal income taxes are allocated based on two separate calculations, i.e., each branch is treated for

Table 25–3.

HISTORY OF THE STATUTORY STOCKHOLDER CHARGE LIMITATION, 1941–1971 (000 Omitted)

Year	*(1)* Participating Insurance in Force	*(2)* 50¢ per $1,000	*(3)* Par Gain from Operations Net	*(4)* Dividends	*(5)* Pre-Dividend	*(6)* Allocable Net Realized Capital Gains*	*(7)* Total [(5) + (6)]	*(8)* 10% x (7)	*(9)* Stockholder Charge— Greater of (2) or (8) 50¢ Rule	*(10)* 10% Rule	*(11)* Ending Par Surplus
1941	$ 1,999	$ 1	$ (54)	$ 2	$ (52)	$ –0–	$ (52)	$ (5)	$ 1		$ (55)
1942	4,493	2	(54)	7	(47)	–0–	(47)	(5)	2		(111)
1943	8,009	4	(62)	16	(46)	–0–	(46)	(5)	4		(177)
1944	12,030	6	(48)	27	(21)	–0–	(21)	(2)	6		(231)
1945	16,758	8	(27)	42	15	–0–	15	2	8		(267)
1946	22,802	11	(31)	66	35	–0–	35	4	11		(309)
1947	29,068	15	(2)	95	93	–0–	93	9	15		(326)
1948	35,742	18	90	117	207	–0–	207	21		$ 21	(257)
1949	44,004	22	24	159	183	–0–	183	18	22		(255)
1950	52,645	26	14	207	221	–0–	221	22	26		(267)
1951	61,851	31	18	263	281	–0–	281	28	31		(279)
1952	71,381	36	(220)	343	123	–0–	123	12	36		(535)
1953	80,955	40	(157)	384	227	–0–	227	23	40		(732)
1954	89,720	45	(104)	422	318	–0–	318	32	45		(881)
1955	95,604	48	5	465	470	–0–	470	47	48		(922)
1956	99,890	50	68	506	574	–0–	574	57		57	(912)
1957	104,011	52	113	545	658	–0–	658	66		66	(1,269)
1958	108,987	54	78	586	664	28	692	69		69	(1,263)
1959	116,227	58	46	628	674	(8)	666	67		67	(1,346)
1960	124,546	62	(128)	670	542	19	561	56	62		(1,584)
1961	134,535	67	(20)	714	694	29	723	72		72	(1,702)
1962	147,439	74	166	758	924	22	946	95		95	(1,678)
1963	163,723	82	48	805	853	52	905	91		91	(1,722)
1964	184,505	92	(108)	862	754	33	787	79	92		(1,960)
1965	206,478	103	(634)	909	275	33	308	31	103		(2,727)
1966	233,185	117	(684)	965	281	(158)	123	12	117		(3,634)
1967	264,436	132	(741)	1,033	292	90	382	38	132		(4,483)
1968	299,261	150	(791)	1,116	325	105	430	43	150		(5,479)
1969	338,150	169	(800)	1,214	414	106	520	52	169		(7,357)
1970	381,746	192	307	1,319	1,626	(11)	1,615	162	192		(7,389)
1971	429,164	214	158	1,438	1,596	19	1,615	162	214		(7,493)
		$1,981	$(3,530)	$16,683	$13,153	$ 359	$13,512	$1,353	$1,526	$538	

*Not allocated to par branch until 1958.

all practical purposes as a separate company, except that certain special deductions are apportioned between the two.

Crazy Quilt Life's separate balance sheet accounts at December 31, 1971 are shown in Table 25–1. The separate 1971 operating and surplus statements are shown in Table 25–2. The history of Crazy Quilt's par accounts is summarized in Table 25–3.

As Table 25–3 indicates, the par surplus account has always been in deficit. This is due to growth plus a relatively generous dividend policy. In effect, stockholders are financing the par deficit, which is collateralized, as it were, by future par profits, which in turn are collateralized by future participating "spreads", i.e., the difference between par premiums and non-par premiums for comparable products. The 1971 stockholder charge, $215,000, represents only 2.9 percent of the average par deficit, which means that stockholders are currently being "paid" less than 3 percent on the surplus they have provided to finance the participating branch. Obviously the stockholders must look to the future for an adequate return on their investment in participating business.

Analysis of the par deficit of $7,493,000 at De-

Table 25–4.

PROJECTION OF STATUTORY RESULTS FOR PARTICIPATING BUSINESS IN FORCE AT DECEMBER 31, 1971

Year	Projected Insurance in Force (000,000)	50¢ per $1,000	Statutory Pre-Tax Net Gain	Taxes at 48% of Taxable Investment Income Less $250,000*	Dividends (Current Scales)	Pre-Dividend Gain	Stockholder Charge— 10% of Pre-Dividend Gain	Gain Less Taxes and Stockholder Charge	Cumulative at Interest**
								Effect on Par Surplus	
1972	$398	$199	$2,213	$589	$1,444	$3,068	$307	$1,317	$(4,741)
1973	377	187	2,139	642	1,532	3,029	303	1,194	(3,634)
1974	359	180	2,139	694	1,612	3,057	306	1,139	(2,551)
1975	342	171	2,098	740	1,685	3,043	304	1,054	(1,523)
1976	327	164	1,754	709	1,767	2,812	281	764	(756)
1977	312	156	1,401	558	1,826	2,669	267	576	(160)
1978	298	149	1,319	581	1,878	2,616	262	476	350
1979	285	143	1,241	601	1,923	2,563	256	384	779
1980	272	136	1,194	618	1,962	2,538	254	322	1,156
1981	260	130	1,157	632	1,995	2,520	252	273	1,493
1982	248	124	1,070	643	2,022	2,449	245	182	1,747
1983	237	118	991	651	2,042	2,382	238	102	1,927
1984	226	113	924	657	2,054	2,321	232	35	2,044
1985	216	108	860	660	2,055	2,255	226	(26)	2,102
1986	207	204	800	662	2,048	2,186	219	(81)	2,107
1987	197	99	755	661	2,033	2,127	213	(119)	2,074
1988	189	95	721	660	2,009	2,070	207	(146)	2,013
1989	180	90	689	656	1,977	2,010	201	(168)	1,929
1990	172	86	668	650	1,938	1,956	196	(178)	1,833
1991	164	82	648	643	1,891	1,896	190	(185)	1,728
1992	157	79	634	634	1,843	1,843	184	(184)	1,621
1993	150	75	617	624	1,794	1,787	179	(186)	1,510
1994	143	72	599	612	1,743	1,730	173	(186)	1,396
1995	136	68	581	600	1,690	1,671	167	(186)	1,279
1996	130	65	563	585	1,582	1,560	156	(178)	1,168
1997	123	62	546	569	1,527	1,504	150	(173)	1,059
1998	117	59	530	552	1,471	1,449	145	(167)	954
1999	111	56	510	533	1,414	1,391	139	(162)	851
2000	105	53	494	514	1,355	1,335	134	(154)	754
2001	99	50	474	493	1,355	1,336	134	(153)	656
2002	93	47	456	471	1,295	1,280	128	(143)	566
2003	88	44	434	449	1,234	1,219	122	(137)	479
2004	82	41	414	425	1,172	1,161	116	(127)	400
2005	77	39	391	400	1,110	1,101	110	(119)	328
2006	72	36	370	375	1,047	1,042	104	(109)	264
2007	67	34	350	350	986	986	99	(99)	208
2008	62	31	330	324	926	932	93	(87)	163
2009	57	29	310	299	866	877	88	(77)	127
2010	53	27	291	274	808	825	82	(65)	102
2011	49	25	274	250	752	776	78	(54)	88
2012	45	23	256	225	698	729	73	(42)	85
2013	41	21	237	202	646	681	68	(33)	91
2014	38	19	219	178	596	637	64	(23)	108
2015	34	17	202	156	547	593	59	(13)	135
2016	31	16	185	133	501	553	55	(3)	172
2017	28	14	168	112	456	512	51	5	218
2018	25	13	152	91	414	475	47	14	275
2019	23	12	136	72	374	438	44	20	339
2020	20	10	121	53	337	405	40	28	412

Continued

Table 25–4. Continued

| | | | | Projected Financial Results (000) | | | | | |
| Year | Projected Insurance in Force (000,000) | 50¢ per $1,000 | Statutory Pre-Tax Net Gain | Taxes at 48% of Taxable Investment Income Less $250,000* | Dividends (Current Scales) | Pre-Dividend Gain | Stockholder Charge— 10% of Pre-Dividend Gain | Effect on Par Surplus | |
								Gain Less Taxes and Stockholder Charge	Cumulative at Interest**
2021	18	9	107	36	302	373	37	34	493
2022	16	8	95	20	270	345	35	40	582
2023	14	7	84	10	240	314	31	43	676
2024	12	6	74	9	213	278	28	37	766
2025	11	6	66	8	188	246	25	33	854
2026	10	5	59	8	167	218	22	29	940
2027	8	4	52	7	148	193	19	26	1,025
2028	7	4	46	7	130	169	17	22	1,108
2029	6	3	40	6	114	148	15	19	1,190
2030	6	3	35	6	100	129	13	16	1,271
2031	5	3	31	5	87	113	11	15	1,353
2032	4	2	26	5	76	97	10	11	1,432
2033	4	2	23	4	65	84	8	11	1,513
2034	3	2	20	4	56	72	7	9	1,594
2035	3	2	17	3	48	62	6	8	1,676
2036	2	1	15	3	41	53	5	7	1,759
2037	2	1	13	2	35	46	5	6	1,843
2038	2	1	11	2	29	38	4	5	1,928
2039	1	1	9	2	23	30	3	4	2,014
2040	1	1	7	2	19	24	2	3	2,101

*Except in years in which dividends are less than $250,000.

**Beginning modified operating deficit ($3,604,000) and annual gains (less taxes and stockholder charges) accumulated at 90% of net-of-tax interest rates (2.8% for first five years, 2.3% thereafter), reduced for interest-free stockholder charges of $1,625,000. See text.

cember 31, 1971 would indicate that it is comprised of the following elements:

		000
Accumulated net gain from operations:		
Gain after taxes but before dividends	$13,153	
Dividends	16,683	$(3,530)
Accumulated realized capital gains, net of taxes		359
Unrealized capital gains		14
Mandatory securities valuation reserve		(1,088)
Non-admitted assets		(482)
1969 reserve strengthening		(708)
Other items		6
Accumulated stockholder charges:		
50¢ rule	1,526	
10% rule	538	(2,064)
		$(7,493)

As mentioned in Chapter 10, Crazy Quilt sets its dividend scales in a manner designed to distribute 90 percent of pre-dividend income to policyholders, with the balance accruing to stockholders. As of December 31, 1971, the Company had distributed 127 percent of pre-dividend gain as dividends and has transferred 16 percent to stockholders because of the workings of the alternative stockholder charge calculation.

It will be noted from Table 25–3 that the normal mode for the stockholder charge is 50 cents per $1,000, which has been used 75 percent of the time since inception and in each of the last eight years.

Since 1958 Crazy Quilt has made an interest free "loan" to the participating branch for stockholder charges. Charges since 1958, $1,625,000, are carried as an account payable by the participating branch (and as an account receivable by the non-participating branch) at December 31, 1971.

Table 25–5.

CALCULATION OF STOCKHOLDERS' SHARE OF ADJUSTED PAR SURPLUS ON 2 BASES AT DECEMBER 31, 1971 (000 Omitted)

	Statutory	Adjusted Reserves Provide for Dividends	Adjusted Reserves Ignore Dividends
Statutory par deficit	$(7,493)		
Unrealized gains	(14)		
Mandatory securities valuation reserve	1,088		
Non-admitted assets	482		
Adjusted statutory par deficit	(5,937)		
Reverse statutory reserves	40,594		
Net assets before adjustments	$34,657	$ 34,657	$ 34,657
Adjustments:			
Unamortized acquisition costs		12,349	12,349
Benefit reserves		(44,936)	(39,903)
Maintenance expense reserves		(46)	(46)
Adjusted net assets		2,024	7,057
Elimination of 90%			6,351
Undistributed surplus to stockholders		$ 2,024	$ 706
Reconciliation of total contribution to stockholder surplus as shown in Table 25–7:			
Undistributed, per above		$ 2,024	$ 706
Distributions already made per Table 25–3:			
50¢ rule		1,526	1,526
10% rule		538	538
Adjustments, roundings, etc.		(16)	(209)
Total contribution to stockholder surplus per table 25–7		$ 4,072	$ 2,561

Accounting for the Restriction

Crazy Quilt Life decided that since its intent was to pay out 90 percent of participating profits in the form of dividends, leaving 10 percent for stockholders, it would recognize the statutory restrictions on participating profits.

To do this, Crazy Quilt had to make several crucial determinations:

▶ What stockholder charge mode the company was likely to experience in the future, 50 cents or 10 percent.

▶ Whether to exclude dividends from the adjusted reserves, and if so, how.

▶ If dividends were excluded from the adjusted reserves, what reserve assumptions to use.

Stockholder Charge Mode

Crazy Quilt recognized that in any "runoff" of participating business in force, statutory pre-dividend profits would be at such a level that the 10 percent rule would inevitably produce a larger stockholder charge than the 50 cent rule. To test this notion Crazy Quilt projected the statutory results of operations of business in force at December 31, 1971 and made several test calculations.

The projections and test calculations are summarized in Table 25–4.*

While the effect of new business was often to depress participating earnings to levels that brought the 50 cent rule into play, it was clear that in terms of a given block of business considered in isolation, the 10 percent rule would usually apply after the first year. Further, as mentioned previously, Crazy Quilt's dividend scales were set so as to pay out 90 percent of pre-dividend profits to policyholders. Thus Crazy Quilt viewed any 50 cent charges as temporary "advances"

*The data summarized in Table 25–4 represent an adaptation of facts applicable to a stock company subject to the 10 percent—50 cents limitation. Crazy Quilt's participating model is based on a real company situation.

to the extent of the excess over the 10 percent charge; it was felt that such "advances" would reverse later as the business ran off.

On the other hand, if Crazy Quilt's dividend scales were set to pay out everything but 50 cents per $1,000, just the reverse would be true.

Thus two of the key determinants of the stockholder charge mode to be assumed for adjustment are (1) the relationship of the dividend scale to pre-dividend profits and (2) the company's intentions with respect to adhering to its dividend objective.

Table 25–4 illustrates the fact that dividend scales are indeed set to pay out 90 percent of pre-dividend profits. Application of the 10 percent rule results in a par surplus of very meager proportions.

Several adjustments were made to the beginning par deficit for purposes of accumulating it, plus projected par profits, at interest. As Table 25–1 indicates, the par deficit at December 31, 1971, was $7,493,000. For purposes of the projection, this amount was adjusted to $5,229,000, of which $3,604,000 was accumulated at interest:

	000
Deficit per statement	$(7,493)
Reserve strengthening (projection made on basis of pre-strengthened reserves)	708
Unrealized gains	(14)
Mandatory securities valuation reserve	1,088
Non-admitted assets	482
Interest-free stockholder charges	1,625
Interest-bearing deficit	(3,604)
Interest-free stockholder charges	(1,625)
Total adjusted deficit	$(5,229)

In effect, Crazy Quilt ignored all future capital gains and such conditional items as the mandatory securities valuation reserve and non-admitted assets.

Since projected results included interest on reserves, par surplus was accumulated at the projected interest rates less taxes and the 10 percent stockholder charge. The small indicated accumulated surplus represented a safety margin considered appropriate in the circumstances.

One interesting by-product of the projection shown in Table 25–4 was a re-evaluation of the slope of dividend scales. It was noted that the scale produced negative results from 1985 to 2016, and that in some years taxes would slightly exceed the pre-tax gain from operations. The projection was the first time that Crazy Quilt had examined *all* of its participating business in terms of current assumptions and current dividend scales.

Treatment of Dividends

Because Crazy Quilt had determined that the proper stockholder charge mode was the 10 percent rule, and because dividend scales were set to pay out 90 percent of pre-dividend gains, Crazy Quilt pondered whether it was really necessary to compute reserves excluding dividends. So long as dividend scales were up-to-date, it was believed that the effect of treating dividends as a benefit would be to reserve for 90 percent of pre-dividend profits.

The problem was that dividend scales were not always up-to-date. Like most companies, Crazy Quilt did not revise its dividend scales every year. Dividend scales were revised when administratively convenient or when competitive forces demanded they be revised. Between revisions experience always differed somewhat from the assumptions underlying the dividend scales used during the interim period. At the time of revision Crazy Quilt would reflect experience during the interim period prospectively, i.e., the revised dividend scale would be adjusted to absorb any differences between actual and assumed since the last revision.

In view of this fact, Crazy Quilt decided that it would be appropriate to calculate reserves without regard for dividends and reserve 90 percent of the indicated surplus. The effect of doing this is shown in Table 25–5. As the table indicates, valuing the business as if Crazy Quilt were a Type 1 company would produce undistributed "free" par surplus of $2,024,-000. Recognition of the 90 percent restriction produces undistributed "free" surplus of $706,000. The difference, $1,318,000, largely represents par surplus that has not yet been distributed to policyholders but which Crazy Quilt intends to distribute to them eventually.

Reserve Assumptions

When dividends are ignored in computing adjusted reserves on participating business, the business is being treated essentially as if it were nonparticipating. Removal of the dividend removes a buffer for adverse experience. Thus, a level 6 percent interest assumption might be appropriate for participating business whose dividends can be adjusted if interest rates fall below 6 percent. But a level 6 percent would generally not be an appropriate rate for nonparticipating business for which there is no such buffer.

Any surplus produced by computing reserves without dividends is diluted to the extent of any applicable

Table 25–6.

ILLUSTRATIONS OF METHODS OF ACCOUNTING FOR VARIOUS TYPES OF RESTRICTIONS

ASSUMPTIONS

Participating insurance in force at year-end	$40,000
Statutory income applicable to participating business:	
Gain from operations before dividends and federal income taxes	$ 400
Dividends	(100)
Federal income taxes	(100)
Gain from operations	$ 200
Reserve increases:	
Statutory	$ 1,000
Adjusted—6%—dividend "benefit" included*	900
Adjusted—6%—dividend "benefit" excluded*	400
Adjusted—6 1/2% graded to 3 1/2%—dividend "benefit" excluded*	800
Deferred taxes	Zero

INCOME APPLICABLE TO SHAREHOLDERS

	Type 1 (No Restrictions)	50¢ Rule	Type 2 — 10% Rule — Approach A**	Type 2 — 10% Rule — Approach B***
Statutory income before dividends but after taxes	$ 300	$ 300	$ 300	$ 300
Statutory reserve increase	1,000	1,000	1,000	1,000
Adjusted reserve increase*	(900)	(900)****	(400)	(800)
Dividends	(100)	(100)****		
Income before restrictions	300	300	900	500
Elimination reducing reported income to amount equal to:				
Unrestricted income	–0–			
50¢ per $1,000		(280)		
10% of pre-dividend income			(810)	(450)
Income applicable to shareholders	$ 300	$ 20	$ 90	$ 50

*Net of acquisition cost adjustment.

**Reserves computed by excluding dividends but holding all other assumptions constant, including the interest assumption.

***Reserves computed by excluding dividends and modifying the interest assumption to the non-par rate.

****It should be noted that this treatment represents an interpretation of the format of the adjustments necessary to present individual income statement items "fairly".

---

percentage stockholder charge limitation. Suppose, for example, that participating reserves at 6 percent are $50 million with dividends included and $25 million with dividends excluded, and that the stockholder charge limitation is 10 percent. Of the difference of $25 million, $2.5 million will wind up in stockholders' surplus.

Now assume that the reserves computed without dividends would be $40 million if nonparticipating interest rates were used. This reduces the difference to $10 million and stockholders' surplus to 10 percent of that, or $1 million.

As a general rule, when dividends are removed from the benefit reserves, the business should be reserved for as if it were nonparticipating business. Inter-

est assumptions should be adjusted to conform to nonparticipating assumptions. Mortality and withdrawal assumptions generally would not be modified.

Table 25–6 illustrates the issues. Use of the 10 percent rule results in considerably different earnings figures depending on the method used to calculate the reserves. Approach A results in current income of $90 applicable to shareholders. Approach B results in $50. The latter amount is theoretically more correct, since the amount of the stockholders' share of 10 percent of pre-dividend profits on participating business should be limited to that amount which would be recognized as income if the business were nonparticipating.

Crazy Quilt Life calculated adjusted reserves with-

Table 25–7.

PAR NET GAIN AND SURPLUS COMPONENTS UNDER VARYING RESERVE APPROACHES, 1941–1971 (000 Omitted)

Year	Statutory Net Gain	Stockholder Charge	Cumulative Contribution to Surplus Policyholders	Stockholders	Adjusted Reserves Include Dividends Net Gain	Cumulative Net Gain	Adjusted Reserves Exclude Dividends Pre-Dividend Net Gain	10% to Stockholders Annual	Cumulative	90% to Policyholders	Dividends Paid	Ending Additional Par Liability
1941	(54)	$ 1	$ (55)	$ 1	$(13)	$ 13	$ (3)	$ —	$ —	$ (3)	$ 2	$ (5)
1942	(54)	2	(111)	3	(15)	(28)	9	1	1	8	7	(4)
1943	(62)	4	(177)	7	(19)	(47)	27	3	4	24	16	4
1944	(48)	6	(231)	13	(15)	(62)	56	6	10	50	27	27
1945	(27)	8	(266)	21	(3)	(65)	97	10	20	87	42	72
1946	(31)	11	(308)	32	-0-	(65)	140	14	34	126	66	132
1947	(2)	15	(325)	47	8	(57)	189	19	53	170	95	207
1948	90	21	(256)	68	(12)	(69)	223	22	75	201	117	291
1949	24	22	(254)	90	(18)	(87)	283	28	103	255	159	387
1950	14	26	(266)	116	(2)	(89)	367	37	140	330	207	510
1951	18	31	(279)	147	18	(71)	462	46	186	416	263	663
1952	(220)	36	(535)	183	53	(18)	534	53	239	481	343	801
1953	(157)	40	(732)	223	70	52	592	59	298	533	384	950
1954	(104)	45	(881)	268	96	148	649	65	363	584	422	1,112
1955	5	48	(924)	316	136	284	716	72	435	644	465	1,291
1956	68	57	(913)	373	168	452	773	77	512	696	506	1,481
1957	113	66	(866)	439	205	657	832	83	595	749	545	1,685
1958	78	69	(857)	508	231	888	887	89	684	798	586	1,897
1959	46	67	(878)	575	226	1,114	916	92	776	824	628	2,093
1960	(128)	62	(1,068)	637	110	1,224	838	84	860	754	670	2,177
1961	(20)	72	(1,160)	709	269	1,493	1,038	104	964	934	714	2,397
1962	166	95	(1,089)	804	189	1,682	1,028	103	1,067	925	758	2,564
1963	48	91	(1,132)	895	227	1,909	1,151	115	1,182	1,036	805	2,795
1964	(108)	92	(1,332)	987	169	2,078	1,201	120	1,302	1,081	862	3,014
1965	(634)	103	(2,069)	1,090	166	2,244	1,284	128	1,430	1,156	909	3,261
1966	(684)	117	(2,870)	1,207	(47)	2,390	1,176	118	1,548	1,058	965	3,354
1967	(741)	132	(3,743)	1,339	193	2,622	1,540	154	1,702	1,386	1,033	3,707
1968	(791)	150	(4,684)	1,489	232	2,925	1,720	172	1,874	1,548	1,116	4,139
1969	(800)	169	(5,653)	1,658	303	3,405	1,761	176	2,050	1,585	1,214	4,510
1970	307	192	(5,537)	1,849	480	4,072	2,344	234	2,284	2,110	1,319	5,301
1971	158	214	(5,594)	2,064	667	2,197	2,765	277	2,561	2,488	1,438	6,351

out dividends for purposes of acounting for the stockholder charge limitation, and used nonparticipating interest assumptions in doing so.

Table 25–7 traces income and surplus accounts from 1941 to 1971 under three different approaches—statutory, Type 1 adjusted, and Type 2 adjusted (i.e., computing reserves without regard for dividends and limiting reported earnings to 10 percent of the indicated result). As discussed previously, Crazy Quilt Life adopted the latter approach.

Cost Allocations

Expenses should be allocated to the participating branch according to practices adopted for statutory purposes. In other words, allocations should not be adjusted except for timing differences arising from practices peculiar to statutory accounting, such as the immediate writeoff of furniture and equipment.

Participating business should be treated as a separate line of business for purposes of calculating de-

Table 25–8.

ILLUSTRATION OF TIMING DIFFERENCE PROBLEMS CAUSED BY SHIFTING STOCKHOLDER CHARGE MODES

	Year 1	Year 2	Year 3	Year 4	Year 5	5-Year Total	Residual
Insurance in force	$30,000	$22,000	$14,000	$6,000	$ –0–	$ –0–	
Pre-dividend net income—statutory basis	60.00	90.00	100.00	125.00	125.00	$500.00	
Pre-dividend net income before stockholder charge— adjusted basis	100.00	100.00	100.00	100.00	100.00	500.00	
Stockholder charge patterns:							
Statutory	15.00	11.00	10.00	12.50	12.50	61.00	NA
Adjusted:							
10% mode assumed	10.00	10.00	10.00	10.00	10.00	50.00	$11.00
50¢ mode assumed	15.00	11.00	7.00	3.00	–0–	36.00	25.00
Greater of 10% or 50¢	15.00	11.00	10.00	10.00	10.00	56.00	5.00
"Management fee" approach	15.00	11.00	10.00	12.50	12.50	61.00	–0–

ferrable acquisition costs (and, where applicable, for purposes of calculating maintenance expense reserves). Calculation of deferrable amounts should be based on the principles set forth in Chapters 14 and 15.

Deferred Taxes

Deferred taxes should generally be provided on the basis used for statutory purposes. If taxes are allocated pro rata to lines of business, then the participating branch should share pro rata in total company deferred taxes. If taxes are based on an assumption that the participating branch is a separate company, then the separate-company approach should also be used in calculating deferred taxes on par adjustments.

In Crazy Quilt's case, taxes were calculated each year as if the participating branch were a separate company. As is typical for the participating line, each year the branch was in a "Phase I" position, i.e., taxes were based on taxable investment income less $250,000. Therefore no deferred taxes were provided on the par adjustments. Assumed interest rates were provided on the par adjustments. Assumed interest rates were, however, considered to be net of Phase I taxes, for reasons discussed in Chapter 9.

Proper allocation of deferred taxes to the participating branch is important when percentage stock-

holder charge limitations are recognized, since such taxes affect the base to which the percentage is applied.

Care must be taken to recognize the effect of any allocation of deferred taxes to the participating branch on deferred taxes calculated with respect to nonparticipating adjustments. (Deferred taxes are discussed further in Chapter 26.)

Shifting Stockholder Charge Modes

Crazy Quilt Life assumed that the dominant mode for the stockholder charge would be 10 percent. Implicit in this assumption was the further assumption that the workings of the dividend scale would eventually offset any differences created by use of the 50 cent mode in certain years.

This was all well and good for Crazy Quilt, but it doesn't answer the question of what to do when (1) the mode shifts from one mode to another and (2) there is no basis for assuming that any differences will be offset.

The potential problem created by shifting modes is illustrated in Table 25–8. Assumption of either of the two modes results in an unaccounted-for residual when the business has run off. Presumably the residual would be taken into income after the business has in fact run off. But it is difficult, if not impossible, to identify residuals in terms of individual blocks of business. As a practical matter, the residual is likely to remain unaccounted for as long as there is any participating business on the books.

The life insurance audit guide suggests that recognition of the restriction be based on an estimate of which calculation basis will be used when the indicated "timing differences" reverse, but the guide's suggestion will rarely be feasible in practice.

When the stockholder charge mode shifts erratically and there is no basis for assuming that a given mode will ultimately prevail, strong consideration should be given to translating the shifting modes into a *weighted average restriction,* either in terms of an amount or a percentage, whichever is dominant.

Alternatively, consideration might be given to using the management fee approach, i.e., limiting the reported stockholder charge to the statutory amount.

Testing the Method Adopted

Records should be kept which detail par contributions to stockholder surplus (1) on the statutory basis and (2) on an adjusted basis. As time passes the two amounts should tend to move closer together. Divergences should be analyzed. In Crazy Quilt's case, for example, the cumulative total of statutory-basis stockholder charges can be compared with the recorded stockholder equity in par surplus somewhat as follows:

Stockholder charges through 1971—statutory basis (Table 25–7)		$2,064
Excess of 50-cent charges over 10% charges:		
Total charges	$2,064	
10% of total pre-dividend income of $13,153	1,315	749
		1,315
Capital gains (Table 25–3)		359
		956
Difference		250
As adjusted (Table 25–5)		$ 706

Par Deficits

Occasionally participating surplus will be in a deficit position even after adjustment. This might happen, for example, where growth of the participating branch is rapid and expenses not qualifying for deferral are very significant.

The effect of a par deficit on the financial statements can be dramatic. Suppose adjusted amounts are as follows:

	Policyholder Account	Stockholder Account	Total
Beginning surplus	$(100)	$200	$100
Income	30	30	60
Ending surplus	$ (70)	$230	$160

If the par deficit is deemed to be recoverable, beginning surplus as reported in the financial statements will be $200, reported income will be $30, and ending surplus will be $230. If, on the other hand, the par deficit is not deemed to be recoverable, beginning financial statement surplus will be $100, reported income will be $60 (of which $30 represents a recovery of the deficit charged off previously), and ending surplus will be $160. In the latter case, the $30 recovery is in the nature of an extraordinary item, although it would probably not so qualify in the technical accounting sense. Because of its unusual nature, recovery of a par deficit that is reported as income should be clearly disclosed in the financial statements.

Now suppose adjusted amounts are as follows:

	Policyholder Account	Stockholder Account	Total
Beginning surplus	$(100)	$200	$100
Income	(30)	90	60
Ending surplus	$(130)	$290	$160

If the deficit is considered recoverable, financial statement beginning surplus will be $200, reported income will be $90, and ending surplus will be $290. If the deficit is not considered recoverable, reported beginning surplus will be $100, reported income will be $60 (of which $30 represent an addition to the par deficit absorbed by stockholders), and ending surplus will be $160. In this case the $30 charge is not in the nature of an extraordinary item, since the situation giving rise to it would usually be expected to continue (which is consistent with the assumption of non-recoverability).

In general, adjusted par deficits that result from accounting decisions—for example, a restrictive definition of acquisition costs and the use of nonparticipating interest assumptions in calculating reserves without dividends—should be considered recoverable and be treated as a deferred charge. Because of its special nature it would not be proper to classify such an item as an acquisition cost.

Deficits that result from some fundamental problem with the business should not be considered re-

Table 25–9.

MINORITY INTEREST METHOD OF RECOGNIZING PARTICIPATING POLICYHOLDERS' INTEREST IN INCOME FOR YEAR ENDED DECEMBER 31, 1971 (000 Omitted)

	Par		Non-Par—	Company Adjusted
	Statutory	*Adjusted*	*Adjusted*	*Total*
Revenues:				
Premiums	$ 9,932	$ 9,932	$107,300	$117,232
Proceeds left on deposit	331			
Other revenue items			1,510	1,510
Investment income	2,244	2,514	30,235	32,749
	12,507	12,446	139,045	151,491
Benefits:				
Death and other benefits	3,125	2,971	51,886	54,857
Dividends	1,438			
Increase in reserves	3,576	3,617	29,422	33,039
	8,139	6,588	81,308	87,896
	4,368	5,858	57,737	63,595
Expenses:				
Incurred:				
Insurance	4,198	4,198	43,839	48,037
Investment		270	1,627	1,897
Change in:				
Unamortized acquisition costs		(1,366)	(12,317)	(13,683)
Maintenance expense reserves		(2)	698	696
	4,198	3,100	33,847	36,947
Income before federal income taxes, realized capital gains, and participating policyholders' interest	170	2,758	23,890	26,648
Federal income taxes:				
Current	12	12	1,754	1,766
Deferred			5,233	5,233
	12	12	6,987	6,999
Income before realized capital gains and participating policyholders' interest	$ 158	2,746	16,903	19,649
Realized capital gains, less taxes of $90,000		19	244	263
Income before participating policyholders' interest		2,765	17,147	19,912
Participating policyholders' interest in income		2,488		2,488
NET INCOME		$ 277	$ 17,147	$ 17,424

coverable. Usually such deficits would be accompanied by future losses. Special considerations involved in recognizing future losses on participating business are discussed in Chapter 24.

Financial Statement Presentations

Recognition of restrictions on profits and surplus attributable to participating business is a complex matter, and so is the subject of presenting restricted amounts in the financial statements.

Income Statement

The life insurance audit guide specifies that the portion of pre-dividend earnings that cannot inure to stockholders should be accounted for "in a manner similar to the accounting for earnings applicable to minority interests." [5] This method is illustrated in Table 25–9. The last column in Table 25–9 represents amounts that would be reported to shareholders, and the approximate format in which they would be reported, using the minority interest method.

However, there is a fundamental difference between pre-dividend income on participating business and income that inures to the benefit of minority interests. In the former case, pre-dividend income is an artificial amount from the point of view of stockholders and has little relevance to the operation of the enterprise as a whole; most of such income is automatically spoken for by current dividend scales. In the latter case, income of the enterprise as a whole is a significant quantity which is not fettered by existing commitments similar to dividend scales, and it is proper to highlight income before minority interests.

Thus participating policyholders' interest in pre-dividend participating income should preferably be reported as a benefit. Income before participating policyholders' interest should not be highlighted in the manner shown in Table 25–9; to do so is somewhat misleading.

Participating policyholders' interest in pre-dividend participating income might be captioned "provision for policyholders' equity in participating earnings", or something similar, in the benefits section of the income statement. While the distinction between benefit reserves and what amounts to a provision for future dividends is somewhat tenuous because of the inter-relationship of reserve assumptions and dividend scales,* the nature of the provision is sufficiently unique to warrant separate disclosure.

Since the provision is in the nature of an increase in reserves, consistency would seem to suggest that dividends declared be shown as a benefit with the net increase in the liability for policyholders' equity reported as a separate item. This conforms to the treatment of death claims and the related reserve increase.

The life insurance audit guide indicates that dividends declared should be charged to the liability for policyholders' equity, so that alternative—while perhaps somewhat inconsistent with the treatment of

---

*Some believe, with good reason, that the increase in the liability for policyholders' equity and the increase in benefit reserves should be combined and no distinction should be made.

other items in the income statement—is also available. It should be noted that under this method, dividends as such are never reported in the income statement except to the extent that they exceed the liability for policyholders' equity.

Surplus Statement

Policyholders' interest in any surplus statement items must also be eliminated from the surplus statement. The most common example might be capital gains where a company chooses to report such gains in the surplus statement. Such items might be reported as follows:

Change in unrealized capital gains, less deferred
    federal income taxes of $90,000 and participating
    policyholders' interest of $19,000 $244,000

Balance Sheet

Accumulated participating earnings allocable to policyholders should be reported as a liability in the balance sheet, captioned as "policyholders' interest in accumulated participating earnings" or something similar.

Notes to Financial Statements

Where participating earnings are restricted, the company's method of accounting for the restriction should be described in the note setting forth accounting policies, as for example:

ACCOUNTING POLICIES NOTE
The Company records as a liability the interest of participating policyholders in earnings attributable to participating policies.

The nature of the restrictions and the amount of the restriction recognized during the year should also be set forth:

ACCOUNTING POLICIES NOTE (OR OTHER NOTE):
Under state law the portion of earnings attributable to participating policies that can inure to the benefit of shareholders is limited to the greater of 10 percent of such earnings before dividends or 50 cents per $1,000

of participating ordinary insurance in force at the end of the year. The Company accounts for such restriction by charging operations for an amount equal to 90 percent (the expected prevailing limitation) of earnings before dividends computed in accordance with generally accepted accounting principles.

If the amount charged to operations and the amount of the year-end liability are not clearly evident from the financial statements themselves, such amounts should be set forth in the note.

Other disclosures relating to dividends are discussed in Chapter 10.

26

Deferred Taxes*

The story is told of a company that decided to make the conversion to generally accepted accounting principles and assigned the acquisition cost work to company accountants, the benefit reserve work to company actuaries, and the deferred tax work to the tax staff. The three groups were in different parts of the building and never spoke to each other, going their separate ways. The accountants feverishly compiled the acquisition cost adjustments, the actuaries zealously computed the benefit reserve adjustments, and the tax staff cold-bloodedly calculated the deferred taxes. On the day the earnings were to be released to the press the three adjustments were finally brought together in one place. The acquisition cost adjustment resulted in a satisfying boost to income and the reserve adjustment resulted in a modest increase in earnings. But the deferred tax adjustment was exactly equal to the combined acquisition cost and reserve adjustments; the net effect on earnings was zero; and the company wound up reporting income that was $100,000 less than it would have reported on a statutory basis, the $100,000 being the costs incurred to convert to generally accepted accounting principles.

Deferred taxes aren't usually that bad, fortunately, but they often take a sizeable bite out of the pre-tax earnings adjustment. The interesting thing about deferred taxes is that the amount recorded in a given accounting period is, to an extraordinary degree, a matter of judgment. Regardless of the effort and agony devoted to the pre-tax adjustment, as much as 48 percent of it hangs upon a simple human judgment.

*This chapter is based primarily on GAAP *Deferred Taxes,* a book published by Ernst & Ernst in 1974, and *Federal Taxation of Life Insurance Companies,* an Ernst & Ernst training manual.

This chapter is devoted to a discussion of the facts, circumstances, conditions, and calculations that affect or give expression to that judgment.

Life Insurance Taxation

The story is also told of the life insurance company president who, when asked by a tax expert which phase his company was in, replied "Downhill!"

The complexities of life insurance taxation are such that the good president may be forgiven his minor lapse.

Brief History of Life Insurance Taxation

There are two great epochs in the history of life insurance taxation: the period prior to 1958, and 1958 to the present day. From the standpoint of deferred taxes the latter period is the most significant. But a brief history of both epochs is important to a full understanding of deferred tax accounting for a stock life insurance company.

Life insurance taxes prior to 1958. Life insurance company taxation has persisted in one form or another since the enactment of the 16th Amendment to the Constitution in 1913.

Between 1913 and 1921, life insurance companies were taxed under a total income concept. This scheme of taxation was found to be unsatisfactory since the overwhelming proportion of policies in force and being written during that period were participating policies sold by mutual companies. Deductions for policyholder dividends reduced taxable income of the industry to such an extent that tax revenues generated by the industry were deemed inadequate by Congress.

The Revenue Act of 1921 was an attempt to increase taxes paid by the industry. Under the 1921 law, only investment income, to the extent it was not required to support policy reserves, was taxed. This general scheme of taxation remained substantially intact from 1921 to 1957, although several temporary modifications of the 1921 law were made from time to time as taxable excess interest rose and fell with the general level of interest rates.

The 1959 Act. During the late 1950s Congress considered a number of basic changes in the nature of the life insurance industry which had taken place between 1921 and 1957. Stock life insurance companies had obtained an increased share of industry insurance in force and assets. This basic change introduced questions of equity as between mutual and stock companies. Also, group insurance, term insurance, credit insurance, and other types of coverages that generate relatively modest amounts of investment income were growing in importance.

With these considerations in mind, Congress enacted the Life Insurance Company Income Tax Act of 1959 ("the 1959 Act"). The 1959 Act made extensive and far-reaching changes in the life insurance company tax structure. The provisions for the 1959 Act formed the basis for taxing life insurance companies for 1958 and subsequent years. Some of the major features of the 1959 Act:

▶ It continued to tax investment income.

▶ It required each life insurance company to determine, based on its own experience, the portion of investment income deemed to be allocable to policyholders.

▶ It taxed underwriting income for the first time since 1921.

▶ It permitted special deductions for certain types of insurance policies written (nonparticipating policies, group life policies, and accident and health policies).

▶ It permitted companies which computed their reserves on a preliminary term basis for statutory purposes to recompute these reserves for tax purposes on a net level basis.

▶ It permitted a deferral of a portion of underwriting profits in recognition of the long-term nature of the life insurance business.

Phases of Taxation

The taxation of underwriting income under the 1959 Act resulted in a complicated classification scheme to differentiate investment and underwriting income. The Act established three "phases" of taxable income:

Phase I—Taxable investment income:

1. Investment income (interest, dividends, etc.)
2. Less—Investment expenses
3. Equals—Investment yield
4. Less—Investment yield allocable to policyholders
5. Equals—Investment yield allocable to company
6. Plus—Net long-term capital gains
7. Less—Small business deduction and company's share of exempt income
8. Equals—Taxable investment income

Phase II—Gain (or loss) from operations:

1. Investment yield (company's share)
2. Plus—Net long-term capital gains
3. Plus—Premiums and other income
4. Less—Death benefits, increase in reserves, other deductible expenses, small business deduction, company's share of exempt income, and operations loss deduction
5. Equals—Gain (or loss) from operations

Phase III—Distributions (or deemed distributions) to shareholders of that portion of income which had previously been untaxed.

Capital gains and losses of life insurance companies are generally subject to the same rules which are applied to all corporations, i.e., net long-term capital gains are included in taxable income and capital loss limitations and carryback/carryforward rules are applied in much the same manner.

Phases I and II. As previously stated, Congress believed that both investment income and underwriting income of a life insurance company should be subject to an income tax. However, while the determination of investment income did not pose insurmountable problems, Congress did conclude that a determination of true underwriting income for any given year was a difficult task because of the long-term nature of life insurance contracts. Congress decided that an equitable solution was to permit a company to postpone from taxation one-half of the Phase II income in excess of Phase I income. The effect is to postpone from tax a portion of the underwriting gain. (However, an underwriting loss is fully deductible from investment income.)

Thus, if taxable investment income (Phase I) is greater than the gain from operations (Phase II), the taxable income is the gain from operations. If the gain from operations (Phase II) is greater than taxable investment income (Phase I), the taxable in-

Table 26–1.

TAX CALCULATIONS UNDER THREE DIFFERENT SITUATIONS (000 Omitted)

	Company's Taxable Investment Income Exceeds Gain From Operations	Company's Taxable Investment Income is Less than Gain From Operations	Company Experiences a Loss From Operations
1. Taxable investment income	$100	$ 40	$ 40
2. Gain (Loss) from operations (including taxable investment income)	$ 40	$100	($100)
3. The smaller of line 1 or line 2	$ 40	$ 40	($100)
4. 50% of the excess (if any) of line 2 over line 1	None	$ 30	None
5. Life Insurance Company taxable income (line 3 plus line 4)	$ 40	$ 70	None
6. Amount of income which is postponed from taxation	None	$ 30	None
7. Operations loss which may serve to reduce taxes in another year	None	None	($100)

come is taxable investment income plus 50 percent of the excess of the gain from operations over taxable investment income.

The interplay of taxable investment income and gain from operations determines the amount of tax which is imposed under Phase I and Phase II. This concept is illustrated in Table 26-1, which displays the computational process for determining a life insurance company's taxable income under three different circumstances: when taxable investment income exceeds gain from operations, when gain from operations exceeds taxable investment income, and when there is a loss from operations.

Policyholder dividends and special deductions. Included in deductions when determining gain or loss from operations (Phase II income) are three classes of deductions which are subject to limitation. Listed in the order of their deductibility for tax return purposes, these special deductions are as follows:

1. A deduction for dividends to policyholders.
2. A deduction equal to 2 percent of premiums received for accident and health and group life contracts.
3. A deduction, related to certain nonparticipating contracts, equal to the greater of 10 percent of the increase in reserves pertaining to such contracts or 3 percent of premiums received on such contracts.

Although policyholder dividends are not "special" deductions, all three types of deductions are referred to hereinafter as "special deductions".

Congress believed that an unlimited deduction for policyholder dividends would result in a major part of the investment income of mutual life insurance companies escaping taxation. However, taking counter-arguments into consideration, Congress concluded that policyholder dividends should be allowed as offsets, to a limited extent, against taxable investment income (Phase I income). The deduction for accident and health and group life contracts was allowed to compensate for the concentration of risks. The deduction for nonparticipating insurance, excluding annuities, was provided in an effort to equalize the taxation of stock and mutual companies.

The maximum offset for these special deductions against taxable investment income is $250,000. Special deductions otherwise allowable are limited to $250,000 plus the excess of the gain from operations, before special deductions, over taxable investment income. Providing that the special deductions amount to at least $250,000, the result of the limitation is either (1) to fully tax investment income, less $250,000, or (2) to increase an underwriting loss by $250,000.

Table 26–2 illustrates the workings of the limitations under three different sets of circumstances.

Table 26–2.

ILLUSTRATION OF OPERATION OF LIMITS ON SPECIAL DEDUCTIONS UNDER THREE DIFFERENT SETS OF CIRCUMSTANCES (000 Omitted)

	Situation		
	1	*2*	*3*
1. Gain from operations, before special deductions	$4,000	$1,250	$5,000
2. Deduct taxable investment income	3,000	3,000	3,000
3. Excess of line 1 over line 2	1,000	–0–	2,000
4. Add statutory allowance	250	250	250
5. Maximum possible amount of special deductions (i.e., available special deductions)	$1,250	$ 250	$2,250
6. Computed special deductions:			
Policyholder dividends	$ 400	$ 400	$ 400
Accident and health and group	450	450	450
Non-par	600	600	600
	$1,450	$1,450	$1,450
7. Allowable amount of special deductions in determining gain from operations*	$1,250	$ 250	$1,450

*The amount of the special deductions which can be deducted cannot exceed the total available amount. Furthermore, unused special deductions are not allowed to be carried to any other year.

Phase III. A life insurance company is required to maintain two memorandum accounts for tax purposes; namely, a "Shareholders' Surplus Account" and a "Policyholders' Surplus Account". These accounts appear only on the tax form and are not included in the Convention Statement or in the company's books and records. A working knowledge of these two tax accounts is important to an understanding and comprehension of the 1959 Act.

The Shareholders' Surplus Account represents, in effect, income of the life insurance company that has been fully taxed. In addition, it includes certain amounts and items which a company is specifically permitted to include therein. The following reconciliation format presents the items that a life insurance company will generally add to or subtract from its Shareholders' Surplus Account annually (certain items encountered infrequently have been omitted):

Balance—End of preceding year

Additions:

Life insurance company taxable income (including excess of long-term capital gains over net short-term capital losses)

Interest income exempt from tax and dividends-received deduction

Small business deduction

Subtractions:

Tax incurred for the year on Phase I and Phase II income and tax incurred on long-term capital gains

Amounts distributed or deemed to be distributed to shareholders to the extent of the balance in this account

Balance—End of current year

The Policyholders' Surplus Account represents, in effect, income of the life insurance company that has not been subjected to federal income taxes. In other words, the Policyholders' Surplus Account includes those items on which a tax may ultimately become payable but on which a tax has been deferred indefinitely. The following reconciliation format presents the items that a life insurance company will generally add to or subtract from its Policyholders' Surplus Account annually (certain items encountered infrequently have been omitted):

501

Table 26–3.

CONDENSED 1971 TAX RETURN CALCULATIONS FOR CRAZY QUILT LIFE (000 Omitted)

Investment yield:

Dividends 100% exempt	$ 512
Dividends 85% exempt	1,517
Tax-exempt interest	286
Rent	1,311
Other items	28,704

Investment expenses:

Real estate	(301)
Depreciation	(437)
Other	(1,159)*
Per Convention Statement	30,433

Home office adjustments:

Rent	(319)
Real estate expense	81
Depreciation	118
Adjusted investment yield	$ 30,313

Assets:

Per Convention Statement	$565,555
Company-occupied real estate	(3,186)
Non-admitted assets	5,511
Separate accounts	(29,771)
Excess of fair market value over carrying value of:	
Subsidiary	9,137
Investment real estate	3,695
Net deferred and uncollected premiums	(10,897)
Loading on deferred and uncollected premiums	514
Tax basis - end of year	540,558
Tax basis - beginning of year	481,246
Tax basis - mean	$510,902

Earnings rates:

Current earnings rate	5.93%
Sum of preceding 4 years	20.99
	26.92%
Average for 5 years	5.38%
Lower of current or average	5.38%

Life insurance reserves:

Per Convention Statement	$442,311
818(c) adjustment	19,530
Deficiency reserves	(500)
Health insurance additional reserves	5,802
Group annuity pension reserves	(1,474)
Other	(10,897)
Tax basis - end of year	454,772
Tax basis - beginning of year	410,932
Tax basis - mean	$432,852

*Within limitation
**Excluding capital gains.

Pension reserves:

End of year (see above)	$ 1,474
Beginning of year	928
Mean	$ 1,201

Required interest on life reserves:

Assumed Rate	Mean of Reserves	Required Interest
2.00%	$ 2,764	$ 55
2.50	153,340	3,834
3.00	229,497	6,885
3.50	47,251	1,654
2.87%	$432,852	$ 12,428

Phase I policy requirement:

Mean of reserves	$432,852
100% + 10 x 2.87%	
- 10 x 5.38%	x 74.90%
Adjusted life reserves	$324,206
Adjusted reserves rate	x 5.38%
	$ 17,442
Interest on mean pension reserves ($1,201 x 5.93%)	71
Interest paid or credited on amounts on deposit, etc.	557
	$ 18,070

Phase I income:

Adjusted investment yield	$ 30,313
Policyholder share	18,070
Company share	$ 12,243
Company %	40.39%

Dividends 100% exempt $ 512		$ 207
Dividends 85% exempt 1,517	x 40.39%	613
Tax-exempt interest 286		116
Other items of yield 27,998		11,307
$30,313		12,243

100% dividend exclusion	(207)
85% dividend exclusion	(521)
Tax-exempt interest	(116)
Small business deduction	(25)
Taxable investment income	$ 11,374**

continued

Table 26–3. Continued

Phase II interest exclusions:			Alternative tax calculation:	
Required interest on life reserves as computed in Phase I		$12,428	Phase I income	$ 11,374
			Phase II income	3,693
			The lesser	3,693
Required interest on pension reserves ($1,201 x 3%)		36	50% of excess of II over I	–0–
Required interest on amounts on deposit		229	Taxable income	$ 3,693
Policyholder share		$12,693	Tax - 48% x $3,693 - $5,500	$ 1,766
Total investment yield		$30,313	Tax on capital gains - 30% x $300	90
Policyholder share		12,693	Phase III tax	–0–
Company share		$17,620	Total tax	$ 1,856
Company %		58.13%		

Company share of:			Shareholder surplus account:	
Dividends 100% exempt $ 512		$ 298	Balance at beginning of year	$ 19,225
Dividends 85% exempt 1,517		882	Taxable income	3,693
Tax-exempt interest 286		166	Realized capital gains	300
		1,346	Dividend exclusions, etc.	1,801
15% of share of dividends 85% exempt		132	Tax-exempt interest	286
			Small business deductions	25
Excludable from Phase II income		$ 1,214	Current taxes	(1,856)
			Dividends to shareholders	(2,400)
			Balance at end of year	$ 21,074

Phase II income:			Policyholder surplus account:	
Pre-tax gain from operations before taxes		$12,010	Balance at beginning of year	$ 10,302
Investment yield exclusion		(1,214)	50% of excess of Phase II income over Phase I income	–0–
Increase in loading		1,135	Special deductions	–0–
Increase in 818(c) adjustment		(9,265)	Other items	–0–
Amortization of reserve strengthening		(1,045)	Balance at end of year	$ 10,302
Home office rental expense		319		

Home office real estate and depreciation		(199)	Special calculation items:	
Dividends to policyholders		1,438	Capital gains	$ 393
Experience rating refunds		990	Appreciation prior to 1958	93
Decrease in deficiency reserves		(100)	Taxable	$ 300
Other items		(101)		
Small business deduction		(25)	818(c) adjustment:	
		3,943	Permanent in-force reserved for by CRVM method	$835,737
Special deductions		250	$21 per $1,000	$ 17,550
Gain from operations		$ 3,693**	2.1%	(368)
				$ 17,182

Special deduction limitation:				
Statutory amount		$ 250	Qualifying term in-force	$628,481
Phase II income before special deductions		3,943	$5 per $1,000	$ 2,360
Phase I income		11,374	.5%	(12)
Excess of II over I		–0–		$ 2,348
Maximum deduction		$ 250	Total adjustment	$ 19,530

503

Table 26–4.

SUMMARY TAX CALCULATIONS FOR CRAZY QUILT LIFE, 1958–1971 (000 Omitted) (Dollars unless otherwise indicated)

	1958	1959	1960	1961	1962	1963	1964	1965	1966	1967	1968	1969	1970	1971
Adjusted investment yield	$ 6,146	$ 7,155	$ 8,247	$ 9,322	$ 10,297	$ 11,221	$ 12,440	$ 13,827	$ 15,222	$ 17,091	$ 19,814	$ 23,133	$ 26,678	$ 30,313
Assets:														
End of year	172,669	189,496	209,124	229,382	247,530	266,976	297,912	320,409	340,849	373,315	413,924	443,047	481,246	540,558
Mean	162,615	181,083	199,310	219,253	238,456	257,253	282,444	309,087	330,629	357,082	393,620	428,486	462,147	510,902
Current earnings rate	3.78%	3.95%	4.14%	4.25%	4.32%	4.36%	4.40%	4.47%	4.60%	4.79%	5.03%	5.40%	5.77%	5.93%
Average earnings rate	3.52%	3.65%	3.80%	3.95%	4.09%	4.20%	4.29%	4.36%	4.43%	4.52%	4.66%	4.86%	5.12%	5.38%
Mean of life insurance reserves	141,117	156,253	171,714	186,894	200,667	214,191	229,256	246,639	265,969	287,964	314,500	345,261	361,269	432,852
Average interest rate assumed	2.69%	2.69%	2.67%	2.69%	2.68%	2.69%	2.70%	2.71%	2.72%	2.73%	2.76%	2.80%	3.07%	2.87%
Reserve adjustment factor	91.70%	90.40%	88.70%	87.40%	85.90%	84.90%	84.10%	83.50%	89.90%	82.10%	81.00%	79.20%	79.50%	74.90%
Adjusted life reserves	129,453	141,253	152,310	163,345	172,376	181,848	192,804	205,944	220,488	236,418	254,745	273,447	287,209	324,206
Interest at adjusted reserves rate	4,557	5,156	5,788	6,452	7,050	7,638	8,271	8,979	9,768	10,686	11,871	13,290	14,705	17,442
Other interest paid or credited	100	106	100	115	121	116	134	148	198	232	295	360	501	623
Phase I policyholder requirement	4,657	5,262	5,888	6,567	7,171	7,754	8,407	9,135	9,975	10,930	12,175	13,635	15,193	18,070
Company share	1,489	1,893	2,359	2,755	3,126	3,467	4,033	4,694	5,247	6,161	7,639	9,498	11,485	12,243
Exclusions from company share	94	121	150	178	197	211	234	250	277	363	421	539	673	689
Phase I income	1,395	1,772	2,209	2,577	2,929	3,256	3,799	4,444	4,970	5,798	7,218	8,959	10,812	11,374
Convention statement pre-tax gain from operations	3,527	4,193	4,352	4,961	7,234	5,296	5,506	4,398	3,988	5,028	1,020	3,242	11,813	12,010
Investment yield exclusions	(105)	(145)	(190)	(235)	(267)	(287)	(318)	(337)	(378)	(447)	(567)	(718)	(846)	(1,214)
818(c) adjustment													(10,265)	(9,265)
Amortization of reserve strengthening													(1,045)	(1,045)
Dividends and refunds	600	635	673	731	758	805	855	1,026	1,378	1,761	1,926	1,982	2,640	2,428
Other tax adjustments	175	77	276	176	(124)	(125)	(25)	(34)	(125)	(125)	(125)	(125)	(747)	1,029
Gain from operations before special deductions	4,197	4,760	5,111	5,633	7,601	5,689	6,018	5,053	4,863	6,217	2,254	4,381	1,532	3,943
Special deductions:														
Statutory amount	250	250	250	250	250	250	250	250	250	250	250	250	250	250
Excess of gain from operations before special deductions over Phase I income	2,802	2,988	2,902	3,056	4,672	2,433	2,219	609	–0–	419	–0–	–0–	–0–	–0–
Limitation	3,052	3,238	3,152	3,306	4,922	2,683	2,469	859	250	669	250	250	250	250
Policyholder dividends and experience refunds	600	635	673	731	758	805	855	1,026	1,378	1,761	1,926	1,982	2,640	2,428
Group life and A & H deduction (2% x premiums)	1	2	2	83	88	162	170	197	227	268	292	294	318	349

Non-par deduction:													
10% x increase in reserves	1,187	1,207	1,087	892	907	988	1,073	1,175	1,330	1,861	1,962	2,614	2,951
3% x premiums	743	763	1,010	837	888	956	1,041	1,144	1,264	1,379	1,511	1,681	1,863
The greater	1,187	1,207	1,087	892	907	988	1,073	1,175	1,330	1,861	1,962	2,614	2,951
Total special deductions	1,788	1,844	1,901	1,738	1,874	2,013	859	250	669	250	250	250	250
Gain from operations	2,409	2,916	3,732	5,863	3,815	4,005	4,194	4,613	5,548	2,004	4,131	1,282	3,693
Taxable income:													
Taxable investment income	1,395	1,772	2,577	2,929	3,256	3,799	4,444	4,970	5,798	7,218	8,959	10,812	11,374
Gain from operations	2,409	2,916	3,732	5,863	3,815	4,005	4,194	4,613	5,548	2,004	4,131	1,282	3,693
50% of excess of gain from operations over taxable investment income	507	572	578	1,467	280	103							
Total taxable income	1,902	2,344	3,155	4,396	3,536	3,902	4,194	4,613	5,548	2,004	4,131	1,282	3,693
Tax:													
On taxable income	984	1,214	1,635	2,280	1,833	1,944	2,007	2,208	2,657	1,050	2,175	624	1,766
On capital gains		9	58	78	138	142				114	451	(57)	90
Shareholders' surplus account	828	1,907	3,100	4,737	6,878	8,399	10,439	12,541	14,302	16,459	16,962	19,384	21,074
Policyholders' surplus account	—	1,781	3,511	5,258	7,705	9,061	10,302	10,302	10,302	10,302	10,302	10,302	10,302

Balance—End of preceding year

Additions:

50 percent of the amount by which the gain from operations exceeds taxable investment income

The deduction allowed for accident and health and group life insurance contracts

The deduction allowed for certain nonparticipating contracts

Subtractions:

Amounts distributed or deemed to be distributed to shareholders in excess of the balance in the Shareholders' Surplus Account

Tax imposed under Phase III

Amounts treated as a subtraction where the balance in the Shareholders' Surplus Account exceeds a limitation imposed by the Internal Revenue Code

Balance—End of current year

Net subtractions from the Policyholders' Surplus Account are added to the taxable income base as defined above in connection with the discussion of taxable investment income (Phase I income) and gain from operations (Phase II income). Since losses from operations do not offset the amount of the subtraction, a net subtraction from the Policyholders' Surplus Account may result in an income tax being incurred even though there was a loss from operations for the taxable year.

The conditions that will trigger a Phase III tax are as follows:

1. If distributions to shareholders are made in excess of the amount in the Shareholders' Surplus Account, a Phase III tax is incurred.

2. If the amount in the Policyholders' Surplus Account at the end of a year is in excess of a specified maximum, a Phase III tax is incurred.

3. If a company ceases to be a life insurance company (as defined by the tax code), a Phase III tax is incurred.

4. If voluntary transfers from the Policyholders' Surplus Account to the Shareholders' Surplus Account are made, a Phase III tax is incurred.

Section 818(c) election. A life insurance company has the option of making an election for tax purposes which is unique to the life insurance industry. This election relates to certain life and accident and health contracts and is generally referred to as the 818(c) election.

Without going into considerable detail and without describing all of the technicalities, the 818(c) election permits a life insurance company to revalue its Convention Statement insurance reserves (life reserves, as well as noncancellable and guaranteed renewable accident and health reserves) from a preliminary term basis to a net level basis. These recalculated reserves are frequently referred to as 818(c) reserves and derive their name from the Internal Revenue Code section which permits this revaluation of reserves.

There are two tax return effects involved with an 818(c) election. The combination of these two effects will generally result in a reduction of the current income tax expense. First, an 818(c) election results in an increase in the amount of the policyholders' share of investment yield because of the additional reserves; this additional amount reduces taxable investment income. Secondly, the 818(c) election results in an increase in reserves; this increase in reserves usually reduces taxable gain from operations.

Crazy Quilt Life

Table 26–3 summarizes Crazy Quilt Life's tax return for 1971. Table 26–4 summarizes basic information on Crazy Quilt Life's taxes from 1958 to 1971.

Notice that in 1971 Crazy Quilt Life strengthened its beginning reserves to net level in connection with an 818(c) election. The amount of the strengthening is being amortized for tax purposes over 10 years, as required by the tax law.

Table 26–4 indicates that Crazy Quilt's tax situation has varied considerably—from being taxed on taxable investment income only, to being taxed on taxable investment income plus one-half of the excess of gain from operations over taxable investment income, to being taxed only on gain from operations when the gain from operations was less than taxable investment income. The instability of Crazy Quilt's tax situation proved to have important implications for the Company's provisions for deferred taxes.

Principles of Deferred Tax Accounting

The life insurance audit guide states that "life insurance companies presenting financial statements in conformity with generally accepted accounting principles ... must follow Accounting Principles Board Opinions Nos. 11, 23, and 24." *[1]

*Opinion No. 24 deals with deferred taxes on undistributed earnings of subsidiaries when such earnings are recognized in the parent company's income statement. The Opinion is not discussed in this chapter.

Easier said than done. There is probably no problem of deferred tax accounting more difficult than the problem of accounting for a life insurance company's deferred taxes.

Accounting Principles Board Opinion No. 11

Accounting Principles Board Opinion No. 11, issued in 1967, indicates that

The principal problems in accounting for income taxes arise from the fact that some transactions affect the determination of net income for financial accounting purposes in one reporting period and the computation of taxable income and income taxes in a different reporting period. The amount of income taxes determined to be payable for a period does not, therefore, necessarily represent the appropriate income tax expense applicable to transactions recognized for financial accounting purposes in that period. A major problem is, therefore, the measurement of the tax effects of such transactions and the extent to which the tax effects should be included in income tax expense in the same periods in which the transactions affect pre-tax accounting income.[2]

The principal provisions of Opinion No. 11 may be summarized as follows:

1. Interperiod tax allocation is an integral part of the determination of net income.

2. Comprehensive interperiod tax allocation principles should be followed rather than partial interperiod tax allocation concepts.

3. Tax allocation should be based only on the tax effect of timing differences; accordingly, it is inappropriate to account for the tax effect of permanent differences as they do not affect other periods.

4. Tax allocation should be made under the deferred method rather than under the liability method or the net of tax method.

5. The tax effect of a timing difference should be measured by computing income taxes with and without the inclusion of the transaction creating the difference between financial statement pre-tax income and taxable income.

6. The measurement of the tax effect can be accomplished by either considering individual timing differences or by grouping similar timing differences.

7. The net change in deferred taxes for a period may be determined on either the gross change method or the net change method.

8. The tax effects of operations loss carrybacks should be allocated to the loss periods. The tax effects of operations loss carryforwards usually should not be recognized until the periods of realization.

Notwithstanding the peculiar nature of life insurance company taxation, life insurance companies are subject to the provisions of Opinion No. 11.

Timing Differences

Opinion No. 11 requires that the tax effects of "timing differences", i.e., those transactions which enter into the determination of financial statement pre-tax income either earlier or later than they become determinants of taxable income, should be recognized in the periods in which these differences between financial statement pre-tax income and taxable income arise and in the periods in which they reverse. Opinion No. 11 also recognizes that some differences are not merely timing differences but constitute permanent differences that do not affect other accounting periods and concludes that interperiod tax allocation is not necessary with respect to such permanent differences.

Opinion No. 11 distinguishes between timing differences and permanent differences as follows:

Timing differences: Differences between the periods in which transactions affect taxable income and the periods in which they enter into the determination of pre-tax accounting income. Timing differences originate in one period and reverse or "turn around" in one or more subsequent periods. Some timing differences reduce income taxes that would otherwise be payable currently; others increase income taxes that would otherwise be payable currently.
Permanent differences: Differences between taxable income and pre-tax accounting income arising from transactions that, under applicable tax laws and regulations, will not be offset by corresponding differences or "turn around" in other periods.[3]

The life insurance audit guide indicates that timing differences arise primarily with respect to Phase II income, i.e., the gain from operations. The most significant timing differences arise, of course, from the acquisition cost and benefit reserve adjustments.

With respect to Phase I income, the guide indicates that the only timing differences in Phase I are occasioned by reporting items of investment income on one basis for financial statement purposes and on another basis for tax purposes. Indicated differences in taxable investment income resulting from substituting adjusted reserves for tax-basis reserves in comput-

Table 26–5.

SIMPLIFIED EXAMPLE OF WITH-AND-WITHOUT CALCULATION OF DEFERRED TAXES (000 Omitted)

	Convention Statement	Tax Return Adjustments	Tax Return ("Without")	Conversion Adjustments	Adjusted Tax Return ("With")
PHASE I - TAXABLE INVESTMENT INCOME:					
Gross investment income	$18,230	$ 420	$18,650	$ (500)	$18,150
Investment expenses	(2,215)	(12)	(2,227)	12	(2,215)
Policyholders' requirements		(12,500)	(12,500)		(12,500)
Capital gains		34	34	80	114
Tax-exempt interest, etc.		(178)	(178)	15	(163)
	$16,015	$(12,236)	$ 3,779	$ (393)	$ 3,386
PHASE II - GAIN FROM OPERATIONS:					
Gross investment income	$18,230	$ 420	$18,650	$ (500)	$18,150
Investment expenses	(2,215)	(12)	(2,227)	12	(2,215)
Capital gains		34	34	80	114
Tax-exempt interest, etc.		(219)	(219)		(219)
Premiums	73,000		73,000		73,000
Benefits	(22,701)	(34)	(22,735)	34	(22,701)
Increase in reserves	(31,843)	(300)	(32,143)	2,000	(30,143)
Other deductions	(27,685)	(136)	(27,821)	5,073	(22,748)
Special deductions		(3,010)	(3,010)	(91)	(3,101)
	$ 6,786	$ (3,257)	$ 3,529	$6,608	$10,137
TAX CALCULATIONS:					
(1) Taxable investment income			$ 3,779		$ 3,386
(2) Gain from operations			$ 3,529		$10,137
(3) Lesser of taxable investment income or gain from operations			$ 3,529		$ 3,386
(4) 50% of excess of gain from operations over taxable investment income			–0–		3,375
(5) Net long-term capital gain			(34)		(114)
(6) Balance			3,495		6,647
(7) Surtax exemption			(25)		(25)
(8) Balance			$ 3,470		$ 6,622
Taxes:					
30% of line (3)			$ 10	$ 24	$ 34
22% of line (6)			769	693	1,462
26% of line (8)			902	820	1,722
			$ 1,681		$ 3,218
DEFERRED TAXES				$1,537	

ing the policyholders' share of investment income are regarded as permanent differences:

While the inclusion of adjustments to life insurance reserves and deferral and amortization of acquisition costs . . . in a hypothetical tax return would indirectly affect taxable investment income, such effect is a permanent difference.[4]

While the Phase I effect is a "permanent difference" for purposes of deferred tax calculations, it should be considered in choosing the adjusted reserve interest assumption. Taxes on investment income, and their effect on interest assumptions, are discussed in Chapter 9 and Appendix B.

Applying Opinion No. 11

To apply the deferred tax principles set forth in APB Opinion No. 11 to the adjusted financial statements of a life insurance company, it is necessary to

1. Identify the differences between financial statement pre-tax income and taxable income;
2. Classify the differences as timing differences or permanent differences;

Table 26–6.

ILLUSTRATIONS OF CATEGORIES OF TAXATION AS DEFINED BY THE LIFE INSURANCE AUDIT GUIDE (000 Omitted)

	Audit Guide Category				
	1	*2*	*3*	*4*	*5*
1. Phase I income—taxable investment income	$1,000	$1,000	$1,000	$1,000	$1,000
2. Gain from operations before special deductions	$1,500	$ 900	$ 900	$3,000	$2,100
3. Available special deductions	$1,200	$1,200	$ 200	$1,200	$1,200
4. Allowable special deductions	$ 750	$ 250	$ 200	$1,200	$1,200
5. Phase II income—gain from operations after special deductions (line 2 minus line 4)	$ 750	$ 650	$ 700	$1,800	$ 900
6. Taxable income	$ 750	$ 650	$ 700	$1,400	$ 900 ·

3. Determine an appropriate method of grouping timing differences;

4. Measure the tax effect of timing differences by making "with-and-without" calculations; and

5. Examine the tax effect tentatively calculated in the first four steps to ascertain whether such tax effect will reverse in the future so that a determination can be made as to the amount of deferred taxes to be provided.

The "with-and-without" calculation refers to a computational technique required by Opinion No. 11:

The tax effect of a timing difference should be measured by the differential between income taxes computed with and without inclusion of the transaction creating the difference between taxable income and pre-tax accounting income. The resulting income tax expense for the period includes the tax effects of transactions entering into the determination of results of operations for the period. The resulting deferred tax amounts reflect the tax effects which will reverse in future periods.[5]

Thus, in making a deferred tax calculation, to the extent that any timing differences exist between financial statement pre-tax income and taxable income reported in the tax return, financial statement income and deductions must be rearranged and classified in accordance with the requirements of the Internal Revenue Code as if that income was the actual taxable income. Because this rearrangement and classification may sometimes cause practical difficulties, some of which are not easily recognizable, the differences be-

tween financial statement income and actual taxable income must be carefully analyzed to determine their nature and tax effect.

A simple example of a "with-and-without" deferred tax calculation will be found in Table 26–5. A number of simplified procedures have been used for purposes of Table 26–5, so it should not be regarded as reflecting precisely the types of calculations that would be made in practice.

Categories of Tax Situations

The life insurance audit guide identifies five possible "categories" of tax situations in which a life insurance company might find itself:

1. Gain from operations before special deductions exceeds taxable investment income, available special deductions are greater than allowable, and the company's tax base effectively consists of taxable investment income minus $250,000.

2. Gain from operations before special deductions is less than taxable investment income (i.e., an underwriting loss has been incurred), available special deductions are greater than allowable, and the tax base effectively consists of gain from operations minus $250,000.

3. Gain from operations before special deductions is less than taxable investment income, available special deductions are less than allowable, and the tax base consists of gain from operations minus available special deductions. This is a variation of Category 2.

Table 26–7.

TAXABLE INCOME UNDER SEVERAL DIFFERENT SITUATIONS (000 Omitted)

	Situation					
	A	B	C	D	E	F
1. Phase I income—taxable investment income	$500	$500	$500	$500	$500	$ 500
2. Gain from operations before special deductions	$ –	$300	$600	$650	$900	$1,000
3. Available special deductions	$400	$400	$400	$400	$400	$ 400
4. Allowable special deductions	$250	$250	$350	$400	$400	$ 400
5. Phase II income—gain (loss) from operations after special deductions	($250)	$ 50	$250	$250	$500	$ 600
6. Audit guide category	2	2	1	1	4	4
7. Taxable income: Lesser of line 1 or line 5	($250)	$ 50	$250	$250	$500	$ 500
50% of the excess of line 5 over line 1	–	–	–	–	–	50
Taxable income	($250)	$ 50	$250	$250	$500	$ 550

4. Gain from operations before special deductions is greater than taxable investment income, available special deductions are fully allowable, and the tax base consists of taxable investment income plus 50 percent of the excess of gain from operations (after special deductions) over taxable investment income.

5. Gain from operations before special deductions is greater than taxable investment income, available special deductions exceed the difference between taxable investment income and gain from operations before special deductions but are fully allowable, and the tax base consists of the gain from operations less the special deductions. This is also a variation of Category 2.

The five categories are illustrated in Table 26–6, and further illustrations of the interplay of the Phase I and II elements of the tax law are contained in Table 26–7.

If Table 26–7 were considered to represent several different tax situations for one company, certain generalizations about the company's tax posture can be made. Assuming taxable investment income of $500,00 and available special deductions of $400,000, whenever its gain from operations, before special deductions (both before and after the change)—

▶ Is less than $500,000, or between $650,000 and

$900,000, taxable income will increase or decrease by the amount of any change in underwriting income or deductions (Phase II income).

▶ Is between $500,000 and $650,000, a change in underwriting income or deductions (Phase II income) will not affect taxable income.

▶ Is in excess of $900,000, the taxable income will be increased by one-half of the change.

If the gain from operations before special deductions in this illustration were assumed to be $400,000, the taxable income would be $150,000. An increase of $1,000,000 in underwriting income would result in the following effects on taxable income and tax expense:

	000			Tax as a Percentage of
	Increase in Underwriting Income	Increase in Taxable Income	Tax Expense-at 48%	Increase in Underwriting Income
First	$ 100	$100	$ 48	48.0%
Next	150	—	—	—
Next	250	250	120	48.0
Next	500	250	120	24.0
TOTAL	$1,000	$600	$288	28.8%

Thus the company's particular tax situation determines the amount of tax that it will pay. A company's expected *future* tax category will affect the amount of deferred taxes that it will provide.

Since Categories 3 and 5 are variations of Category 2, the only categories discussed hereafter are Categories 1, 2, and 4.

The Future-Category Assumption

The life insurance audit guide provides that

The differential tax effect tentatively determined in the "with-and-without" calculation must be further examined to determine whether such tax effect will reverse in the future. For example. . ., timing differences affecting only gain from operations may result in a current tax effect in such a "with-and-without" calculation which may not reverse in the future for companies who continue to be taxed on taxable investment income. Deferred taxes are not required to be provided for the current tax effect of timing differences if circumstances indicate that there will not be a reversal of such current tax effect in the future.[6]

The guide also states that

Deferred taxes need not be provided unless such taxes will reverse in the future, and a change in category of taxation resulting from the "with-and-without" calculation should not be recognized unless circumstances indicate that such change in category will result when the timing differences reverse. . . Where the reversal of tax effects cannot be reasonably determined, deferred income taxes should be provided based on the differential computed using a "with-and-without" calculation as if the company's tax return was filed on the basis on which financial statements were prepared, including any resulting change in phase of taxation.[7]

In other words, provisions for deferred taxes should be based on an assumption as to the category of taxation applicable at the time that timing differences reverse and hence the extent to which the indicated timing differences will actually be taxed. Where future uncertainties are such that it is impracticable to estimate the company's tax category at the time of reversal, deferred taxes are to be provided on the basis of the category of taxation indicated for the *adjusted* statements by the year's "with-and-without" calculation.

Determination of a company's likely future tax position is a perilous undertaking. A company may have been taxed in Category 1 ever since 1958, and there may be every reason to believe that it will continue to be so taxed. Thus no deferred taxes need be provided for Phase II timing differences. If, how-

ever, the company's category changes to, say, Category 4, 50 percent of the timing differences will be taxed. Viewed from the vantage point of hindsight, the failure to provide deferred taxes was based on an erroneous assumption about the future. For a large company, the error could amount to tens of millions (possibly *hundreds* of millions) of dollars, effectively representing overstatements of income of prior years.

On the other hand, provision for deferred taxes based on an assumption that a company would be in Category 4 at the time of reversal would result in the opposite error if the company actually winds up in Category 1. Deferred taxes provided in earlier years will prove to have been unnecessary; income of such prior years will effectively have been understated.

Table 26–8 illustrates the impact of the future-category assumption on deferred tax calculations under varying circumstances.

Determining a company's future tax category is a highly complex matter for which definitive guidelines cannot feasibly be formulated.* It will tax** the ingenuity of anyone who has to do it. The consequences of an erroneous determination can be severe.

Changes in Facts and Circumstances

When there is a change in the facts and circumstances on which the deferred tax provisions have been based, it may become apparent that either too much or too little deferred tax has been provided in prior years. The life insurance audit guide states that

If deferred taxes have not been provided on timing differences on the presumption that such timing differences will have no tax effects when they reverse and circumstances change so that it becomes apparent that tax effects will result, a company should accrue as an expense of the current period income taxes attributable to those timing differences; income tax expenses for such timing differences should not be accounted for as an extraordinary item. . . If deferred income taxes have been provided on timing differences and circumstances change so that it becomes apparent that the tax effects will differ from those originally expected, deferred income taxes previously accrued should be included in income only as the related timing differences reverse.[8]

Thus, where taxes have not been provided on timing differences and it is later found that provision

---

*However, discussion of various fact patterns and circumstances and their effect on the determination will be found in *Deferred Taxes and Appendix C,* mentioned previously.

**No pun is intended.

Table 26–8.

ILLUSTRATIONS OF IMPACT OF FUTURE-CATEGORY ASSUMPTION

	CATEGORY 1			CATEGORY 2			CATEGORY 4		
	Actual Tax Return	Difference	With GAAP Adjustments	Actual Tax Return	Difference	With GAAP Adjustments	Actual Tax Return	Difference	With GAAP Adjustments
Investment income:									
1. Investment yield	$12,000		$12,000	$12,000		$12,000	$12,000		$12,000
2. Deduct policyholders' share	8,975		8,975	8,975		8,975	8,975		8,975
3. Company's share of investment income	3,025		3,025	3,025		3,025	3,025		3,025
4. Small business deduction	25		25	25		25	25		25
5. TAXABLE INVESTMENT INCOME	$ 3,000	$ –0–	$ 3,000	$ 3,000	$ –0–	$ 3,000	$ 3,000	$ –0–	$ 3,000
Gain from operations:									
6. Investment yield	$12,000		$12,000	$12,000		$12,000	$12,000		$12,000
7. Deduct policyholders' share	7,000		7,000	7,000		7,000	7,000		7,000
8. Company's share of investment income	5,000		5,000	5,000		5,000	5,000		5,000
9. Gross premiums	50,000		50,000	50,000		50,000	51,000		51,000
10. Total	$55,000	$ –0–	$55,000	$55,000	$ –0–	$55,000	$56,000	$ –0–	$56,000
Deductions:									
11. Death benefits, etc.	$25,000		$25,000	$25,000		$25,000	$25,000		$25,000
12. Increase in reserves	8,000	$(1,000)	7,000	8,000	$(1,000)	7,000	8,000	$(1,000)	7,000
13. Small business deduction	25		25	25		25	25		25
14. Other deductions	17,975	(3,000)	14,975	20,725	(3,000)	17,725	17,975	(3,000)	14,975
15. Total	$51,000	$(4,000)	$47,000	$53,750	$(4,000)	$49,750	$51,000	$(4,000)	$47,000
16. Dividends to policyholders	$ 300	$ 90	$ 390	$ 250	$ 140	$ 390	$ 300	$ 90	$ 390
17. Accident and health, group life	50		50	–0–	50	50	50	–0–	50
18. Nonparticipating contracts	900	150	1,050	–0–	1,050	1,050	1,100	(50)	1,050
19. Total special deductions	$ 1,250	$ 240	$ 1,490	$ 250	$ 1,240	$ 1,490	$ 1,450	$ 40	$ 1,490
20. Total deductions	$52,250	$(3,760)	$48,490	$54,000	$(2,760)	$51,240	$52,450	$(3,960)	$48,490
21. GAIN FROM OPERATIONS	$ 2,750	$ 3,760	$ 6,510	$ 1,000	$ 2,760	$ 3,760	$ 3,550	$ 3,960	$ 7,510
Taxable income:									
1. Taxable investment income	$ 3,000		$ 3,000	$ 3,000		$ 3,000	$ 3,000		$ 3,000
2. Gain from operations	$ 2,750		$ 6,510	$ 1,000		$ 3,760	$ 3,550		$ 7,510
3. Smaller of line 1 or line 2	$ 2,750	$ 250	$ 3,000	$ 1,000	$ 2,000	$ 3,000	$ 3,000	$ –0–	$ 3,000
4. 50% of excess of line 2 over line 1	–0–	1,755	1,755	–0–	–0–	–0–	275	1,980	2,255
5. Amount subtracted from policyholders' surplus	–0–	–0–	–0–	–0–	–0–	–0–	–0–	–0–	–0–
6. TAXABLE INCOME (total of lines 3, 4, and 5)	$ 2,750	$ 2,005	$ 4,755	$ 1,000	$ 2,000	$ 3,000	$ 3,275	$ 1,980	$ 5,255
7. TAXABLE INCOME assuming circumstances indicate no deduction for unused and/or recalculated Special Deductions (this possibility is not considered to be realistic)			$ 4,875			$ 4,000			$ 5,275
8. TAXABLE INCOME assuming no change in category when timing difference reverse			$ 2,750			$ 3,000			$ 5,255
9. TAXABLE INCOME assuming Category 1 position at time of reversal of tax effects			$ 2,750			$ 2,750			$ 3,275

should have been made, the entire cumulative deferred tax is charged to income in the year in which the new facts first became apparent. If it is found that prior provisions have been excessive as a result of a change in circumstances, the excess is taken into income only as the underlying timing differences themselves reverse.

It may well be that a company that expects to remain in Category 1 indefinitely will want to provide for deferred taxes anyway, on the basis that it is better to be safe than sorry. The provision is a hedge against a future change in category. Any company that makes such a decision should make it consistently in all future years in the absence of compelling evidence that the decision is no longer warranted.

In situations in which a change in category is *anticipated*, this expected change should be taken into consideration when the deferred tax provision is made. For example, where a company in the current year is in either a Category 2 or Category 4 position but expects to reach a stable Category 1 position after three years, the reversal of timing differences need be tax effected only for those three subsequent years. In effect, the deferred tax provision for the current year need reflect only the tax effects of reversals of timing differences for the next three years.

Another example of a situation in which anticipated changes in category might be considered would be the situation in which a company has cyclical patterns of profits. For example, such a company may have had losses for three years on its group business which caused the company to be in an actual Category 1 position and, therefore, the company chooses not to provide for deferred taxes. Subsequently, the company may have taken corrective action in its group area which resulted in the company being in an actual Category 4 position in the fourth year. If this cyclical pattern has occurred with some regularity over a period of years and if the company could reasonably expect this same pattern of profits and losses to continue, the amount of the deferred tax credit to be established as of the beginning of the first year of the conversion to generally accepted accounting principles could probably reflect this situation. In other words, the amount of deferred tax that results from the "with-and-without" calculation could be reduced by roughly three-fourths, assuming a level rate of reversing timing differences. Refinements in such an approach could be made by projecting the pattern of the reversal of the timing differences.

Special Deductions

As previously indicated, the calculation of life insurance company taxable income includes an allowance for special deductions for policyholder dividends, accident and health and group life contracts, and nonparticipating contracts. The total allowable amount of these special deductions is subject to a statutory limitation. Both the amount of the special deductions available and the limitation itself may be affected by timing differences. This fact creates significant problems that must be considered in calculating deferred taxes.

Unused special deductions. Where special deductions are limited on the tax return, can the unused amount be applied against adjustments arising from the conversion to generally accepted accounting principles for purposes of calculating deferred taxes?

The following example will highlight the problem:

Special Deduction	Available Special Deductions	Allowable Special Deductions Category 1	Category 2	Category 4
Policyholder dividends	$ 300	$ 300	$ 250	$ 300
Accident and health and group life contracts	50	50	—	50
Nonparticipating contracts	1,100	900	—	1,100
Total	$1,450	$1,250	$ 250	$1,450
Unused special deductions		$ 200	$1,200	$ —

A company in Category 1 will usually have unused special deductions, sometimes large amounts and at other times small amounts. A company in Category 2 will usually have a severe limitation; therefore, the amount of unused special deduction will normally be relatively large. A company in Category 4 will always use all of the available special deductions computed on the return.

The question, then, involves the extent to which Category 1 and Category 2 companies can "use" their unused special deductions in calculating deferred taxes.

Recalculated special deductions. Even assuming that all of the special deductions calculated on the tax return are useable, what happens when substitution of adjusted amounts for tax return amounts produces an indicated change in the special deductions? For example:

1. Assume that the nonparticipating deduction is based on 10 percent of the increase in reserves. Substitution of adjusted reserves would produce a different amount for the special deduction. Should the different amount be used in the deferred tax calculation?

2. Assume that the change in reserves on participating business includes an implicit provision for dividends (where dividends are treated as benefits in calculating the reserves) of several million dollars. Should such implicit provision be treated as a special deduction in calculating deferred taxes?

Audit guide provisions. These are not easy questions and the life insurance audit guide does not furnish easy answers:

Although (1) certain special deductions never enter into the determination of pre-tax accounting income in any period and/or (2) the amount of dividends to policyholders and certain special deductions may be subject to limitation on the tax return so that unused deductions will not be available in subsequent periods, such deductions may be properly recomputed in the "with-and-without" calculation. For example, unused dividends to policyholders and special deductions may be used to offset timing differences which affect taxable income to the extent that the limitations on these deductions change when based on pre-tax accounting income, unless known or anticipated circumstances indicate that future taxable income resulting from such timing differences will not be offset by like deductions when they reverse. Similarly, in the case of provisions for dividends to policyholders which are timing differences themselves, statutory limitations should not be applied so as to eliminate their current tax effect unless circumstances indicate that such dividends will be limited when they reverse. Special deductions that are directly affected by timing differences should be recomputed in the "with-and-without" calculation unless circumstances indicate that future special deductions will not be directly affected by the timing differences when such differences reverse.[9]

Thus the audit guide indicates that unused and/or recalculated special deductions should be used in calculating deferred taxes unless it is reasonably clear from known or anticipated circumstances that special deductions of equal amount will not offset timing dif-

ferences when they reverse. Because of the difficulty in obtaining sound data concerning known or anticipated circumstances of a company's future condition, most companies will probably use their unused and/or recalculated special deductions (including policyholder dividends).

Category 1 companies have no need to be concerned with the problem of unused and/or recalculated special deductions where circumstances indicate that there will be no change in category when the timing differences reverse. Category 1 companies that are unable to determine that there will be no change in their category or, conversely, that have certain knowledge that there will be a change, must generally recalculate the special deductions and determine the limitation, if any, on the deductible amount of the unused and/or recalculated special deductions.

Category 2 companies would not have any reason to recalculate the special deductions since they would consistently be limited to the statutory amount of $250,000. However, if a change of category in the company's actual tax return was indicated, a recalculation of special deductions should generally be made and used.

If a company is in a Category 4 position, the adjustments caused by the conversion to generally accepted accounting principles would be expected to increase the gain from operations as that term is defined for income tax purposes. The "with-and-without" calculation for a Category 4 company would not be expected to result in a change in category for that year; however, consideration must be given to whether such a company will be a Category 4 company indefinitely. Also, since such a company would not be limited in the amount of deductible special deductions, there would be no unused special deductions. However, the amount of the special deductions would be recalculated if the adjustment to generally accepted accounting principles resulted in a changed amount of policyholder dividends (including provisions for future dividends included in benefit reserve calculations), since the provisions for policyholder dividends is itself a timing difference. Also, a Category 4 company would recompute the nonparticipating deduction where that deduction is based on the increase in reserves since the deduction would be directly affected by timing differences related to the nonparticipating reserves.

The dividend deduction. The life insurance audit guide states that

For purposes of computing deferred taxes, it will be necessary to identify the amounts of dividends to policyholders deducted in the financial statements even when they are considered as benefits in the reserving method.[10]

This means that if dividends are accounted for as benefits in calculating adjusted reserves, as discussed in Chapter 10, the increase in the portion of the reserves attributable to the dividend benefit should be segregated for inclusion among the recalculated special deductions in calculating deferred taxes. This recalculation could, of course, add millions of dollars to the special deductions.

Treatment of the portion of the reserve increase that represents a provision for dividends as a deduction for dividends means that it should be eliminated from the increase in reserves in computing adjusted Phase II income. Thus each dollar of additional special deductions is accompanied by a dollar increase in Phase II income before special deductions.

For Category 4 companies that are expected to remain in Category 4 and that can use all of their special deductions, including recalculated amounts, the effect on taxable income is nil, and so is the effect on deferred taxes. It seems unnecessary to segregate the dividend component of the reserves in these circumstances.

For Category 1 companies that are expected to remain in Category 1 the calculation also has no impact. Again it seems unnecessary to make the segregation.

For Category 2 companies that are expected to remain in Category 2, however, and whose special deductions are subject to limitations, the segregation could have dramatic effects. Phase II income increases by reason of excluding the portion of the reserve increase that represents a provision for dividends that may not be deductible as a special deduction. The result could well be a substantial increase in deferred taxes.

Companies would be well-advised to make the dividend recalculation with great care.

Operations Losses

A net operations loss is sustained by a life insurance company when its total allowable deductions exceed its total taxable income. When a company sustains an operations loss, certain tax benefits are usually available. The company can generally obtain a refund of taxes paid in prior profitable years (by carrying back the current loss to prior years and applying it as a reduction of previously reported taxable income) or because the company can generally reduce taxes that would otherwise be payable in the future (by carrying forward the current loss to future years and applying it as a reduction of the otherwise reportable taxable income).

The operations loss deduction is allowed life insurance companies in lieu of the net operating loss deduction available to other companies. The operations loss deduction allowable in any profitable year is the sum of the available operations loss amounts for all of the years which can be carried back or forward and offset against the otherwise taxable income of the profitable years. Generally, an operations loss may be carried back three years and carried forward five years. An operations loss is first carried back to the earliest year to which such loss may be carried. Any unabsorbed amount is then carried forward until fully absorbed or until the loss expires. As an equity measure for new life insurance companies, there is a tax provision for an eight-year carryforward of operations losses, providing the company qualifies as a new company in the year of the loss if that year begins not more than five years from the date that the company was authorized to do business as an insurance company.

When operations losses are carried back and/or forward, a company's taxable income must be recomputed for the years to which the carryback or carryover is applied. This recomputation involves recalculating the limitation on special deductions. Table 26–9 illustrates the interplay of the loss carryback and carryforward provisions.

Accounting for operations losses. Accounting Principles Board Opinion No. 11 provides that the tax benefit of a loss can be reflected in the financial statements for the loss year if the loss can be carried back to any of the three previous profitable years. Opinion No. 11 also provides that the potential tax carryforward benefit of a loss should generally not be recognized in the financial statements until the tax benefit is actually realized, except in unusual circumstances when realization is assured beyond any reasonable doubt at the time the loss carryforward arises.

Opinion No. 11 also recognizes there should be appropriate adjustments of deferred tax credits relating to unamortized timing differences when an operations loss is sustained for which there are prior years to which the loss carried back. Also, when such a situation exists and when the tax effect of a loss carryforward cannot be recognized in the loss period because realization cannot be assured beyond a reasonable doubt, the deferred tax balance should be

Table 26–9.

ILLUSTRATION OF OPERATIONS LOSS CARRYBACK AND CARRYFORWARD PROVISIONS (000 Omitted)

	1967	1968	1969	1970	1971	1972	1973
Tax return data (before giving effect to operations loss carrybacks and carryforwards):							
1. Taxable investment income	$300	$350	$300	$450	$500	$550	$600
2. Gain (loss) from operations, before operations loss deduction and special deductions	$700	$500	$300	$ 50	($100)	$200	$800
3. Available special deductions	$400	$500	$300	$400	$500	$500	$500
4. Allowable special deductions	$400	$400	$250	$250	$250	$250	$450
5. Gain (loss) from operations, before operations loss deduction	$300	$100	$ 50	($200)	($350)	($ 50)	$350
Recomputed gain (loss) from operations, after giving effect to the operations loss deduction:							
6. Line 2 above	$700	$500	$300	$ 50	($100)	$200	$800
7. Operations loss deduction application:							
1970	(200)			200			
1971		(250)	(50)		350		(50)
1972						50	(50)
8. Recomputed gain (loss) from operations, before special deductions	500	250	250	250	250	250	700
9. Allowable recomputed special deductions	(400)	(250)	(250)	(250)	(250)	(250)	(350)
10. Recomputed gain (loss) from operations, after giving effect to the operations loss deduction carrybacks and carryforwards	$100	$–0–	$–0–	$–0–	$–0–	$–0–	$350

reduced by the lower of (1) the tax effect of the loss carryforward or (2) the amortization of the deferred tax liability that would otherwise have occurred during the carryforward period.

Opinion No. 11 also indicates that, if the loss carryforward is realized in whole or in part in periods subsequent to the loss period, the reductions made to the deferred tax balance in the loss years should be reinstated (at the then current tax rates) on a cumulative basis as, and to the extent that, the tax benefit of the loss carryforward is realized.

To summarize, the computation of the operations loss tax benefit, if any, in a loss year is generally made in the following sequence:

Step 1. The carryback: Determine whether the company had profitable operations, for tax purposes, in any of the three previous years to which the current year's loss can be applied under the applicable provisions of the tax laws. Since there is reasonable assurance that taxes paid during the carryback period will be refunded currently, the refund would be recognized in the financial statements in the loss year. Also, deferred taxes provided in the prior years to which the operations loss is carried back are eliminated to the extent that the current financial statement loss offsets the financial statement income in the carryback period.

Step 2. The carryforward: If not all of the operations loss can be utilized by applying Step 1, determine whether sufficient justification exists to contend that a tax benefit relating to the current operations loss will be realized in the carryforward period.

Step 3. The existing deferred tax balance: If a loss carryforward still exists after applying Step 1, and Step 2 cannot be used, part or all of the tax effect of the loss carryforward may possibly still be recognized in the loss year by reducing or eliminating an existing deferred tax balance. For example, if a 1973 operations loss results in a carryback to years 1970, 1971, and 1972, and taxes provided in those years are "recouped" (i.e., taxes paid in those years are recovered and deferred taxes provided in those years are reversed), and there still remains a portion of the 1973 loss to be carried forward (assuming that there is no definite assurance of future realization of any tax benefit), such carryforward can possibly be recognized in 1973 by reducing the balance in the deferred tax account. The adjustment would be the lower of either the tax effect of the loss carryforward or the amortization of the deferred tax credit that would otherwise have occurred during the carryforward period.

In applying these three steps, the tax benefit to be reflected in the financial statements in the loss year is based on the financial statement pre-tax income (loss) rather than on the income (loss) determined for tax purposes.

Initial conversion. In the computation of deferred income taxes that are to be retroactively reflected in the initial conversion to generally accepted accounting principles, an analysis must be made of the company's financial statement *and* taxable income history since January 1, 1958, or date of organization, whichever is later. Deferred taxes will then be computed on the company's financial statement pre-tax income, taking into consideration the timing differences represented by the retroactive conversion adjustments and any other timing differences.

Such histories must identify the operations losses which were carried back or forward and utilized as offsets to taxable income as well as identifying those losses which expired and were never used. Obviously, those losses which expired for tax purposes cannot be used to offset financial statement pre-tax income since no tax benefit of those losses was ever realized.

Recognition of tax benefits of operations loss carryforwards. In retroactively computing deferred taxes during the initial conversion to generally accepted accounting principles, some practical and theoretical arguments suggest that the income tax effect of prior year losses, which were subsequently carried forward and offset against taxable income prior to the year of conversion, should be recognized in the loss years instead of in the year of actual realization. From an historical point of view, realization of the tax effect of loss is assured, i.e., the tax benefit of the loss was realized in specific subsequent years.

Under this approach the accounting for past transactions would be based upon facts and circumstances as known at the time of conversion to generally accepted accounting principles. Basing the accounting on the facts and circumstances as known at the time of conversion would generally assume that such retroactive accounting applications would be consistent with those expected to be utilized in the future.

However, in retroactively accounting for deferred taxes, if the tax effect of a loss carryforward is recognized in the loss year only because of the hindsight available at the time of conversion, such accounting could result in future inconsistencies. For example, an apparent inconsistency would result if a statement of operations is presented which includes a previous loss year where the tax benefit was recognized at that time (on the basis of hindsight) and the summary also includes a current loss year in which a loss has been sustained but for which the potential tax benefit to be derived therefrom cannot be recognized because the loss cannot be carried back and its future realization is uncertain. Another example of an apparent inconsistency resulting from the use of hindsight could occur if there is taxable income in the current year and if the tax benefit of a prior year loss is realized by reducing currently taxable income. In this situation, the tax benefit derived from the prior year loss should probably be recognized in the current year since the current year's income was the basis for assuring realization of the tax benefit.

In addition to hindsight, a life insurance company incurring an operations loss which is to be carried forward must also evaluate the loss in light of other accounting criteria. For example, if a company could establish that the operations loss resulted from the sale of a block of business or the abandonment of a major area of operation and if the company could determine that future taxable income would be virtually certain to be large enough to offset this operations loss, such factors might be considered sufficient to meet the criteria of Opinion No. 11 in permitting current recognition of the tax benefits where future realization is assured.

As previously indicated, under certain circumstances current recognition of the potential tax benefit of an operations loss carryforward may be appropriate in the year of the loss. Such recognition would be accounted for by reducing the deferred tax balance, if one exists. The adjustment should be the lower of (1) the tax effect of the financial statement loss carryforward, or (2) the amortization of the deferred tax balance that would otherwise have occurred during the carryforward period. For a life insurance company, limitation (2) will normally result in the lower adjustment.

The calculation of limitation (1) will normally not present any particular difficulty. However, the calculation of limitation (2) is somewhat more complex. In this calculation, the company must determine the timing differences which are expected to reverse during the carryforward period. The tax effects, if any, of these calculated or estimated timing difference reversals must be evaluated before recognition is given in the financial statements to any potential tax benefit.

Recently-organized growing companies will usually have operations losses for a number of years until their income from renewal business is sufficient to offset the losses normally sustained on first-year business. For this type of company, the adjustments made in the conversion process may well be sufficient to reduce and possibly eliminate these operations losses for financial statement purposes. Deferred taxes need not be provided when conversion adjustments are made if the timing differences do not result in financial statement pre-tax income. Thus, a portion or all of the tax effect of the operations losses of a company in this situation may effectively be recognized in the loss year. Stated differently, at any point in time, there is no deferred tax balance applicable to the unamortized

timing differences to the extent that these timing differences resulted in the elimination (or reduction) of both an operations loss and a financial statement pre-tax loss rather than an addition to financial statement pre-tax income.

When this type of situation exists, the company should disclose that the operations loss carryover available to reduce future income taxes has been recognized, in whole or in part, in the deferred tax calculation (even though no deferred tax provisions may have resulted therefrom).

Policyholders' Surplus

According to Accounting Principles Board Opinion No. 23, deferred taxes need not be provided on additions to the Policyholders' Surplus Account. Such additions are deemed to represent permanent differences—i.e., amounts from which taxes are sheltered indefinitely.

If anything happens to trigger a Phase III tax, or payment of a Phase III tax is imminent, then the tax is recognized as an expense (but not as an extraordinary item) in the period in which the facts become known.

Deferred Tax Calculations

After pondering categories of taxation, treatment of special deductions, and sundry other problems that often defy resolution, the time finally comes when deferred taxes must be calculated and recorded, for better or worse.

There are still two more decisions that have to be made before the calculations can be made: whether to group various timing differences together for purposes of calculating deferred taxes, and if so, how; and, assuming timing differences are grouped, whether to use the gross change or net change methods.

Grouping of Timing Differences

Accounting Principles Board Opinion No. 11 states that, for purposes of computing deferred taxes, timing differences may be considered individually or similar timing differences may be grouped. "Similar timing differences" refers to timing differences which arise from the same kinds of transactions.

Under the individual-transaction approach, deferred taxes are computed separately with respect to each transaction giving rise to a timing difference.

Thus, for example, if two sales of land are reported on the installment basis for tax purposes and on the completed-sale basis for financial statement purposes, deferred taxes would be computed separately for each sale.

Under the grouped-transaction approach, deferred taxes are computed with respect to the aggregate timing differences arising from a group of similar transactions. In the example cited above, deferred taxes would be computed on the combined total of the timing differences arising from the two sales. However, if in the above example there were other differences such as those relating to depreciation, a separate "with-and-without" calculation would be made under the grouped-transaction approach as described in Opinion No. 11.

Individual-transaction approach. While many types of timing differences may arise in any accounting period, the most significant differences will usually be those associated with acquisition cost and benefit reserve adjustments.

Some believe that the timing difference associated with each policy sold represents an individual-transaction timing difference. Others believe that each policy sold gives rise to two individual-transaction timing differences, the acquisition cost adjustment and the benefit reserve adjustment. Under these views, each individual policy timing difference (or differences) would be separately tax-effected.

This approach would result in a very large number of separate deferred tax calculations and seems to be completely impractical for use by life insurance companies.

Groups of similar transactions. What constitutes a "group of similar transactions"? Some would define a group of similar transactions in terms of a plan of insurance, a group of plans, a premium ratebook era, a line of business, or all the issues of all lines of business. However, the intent of Opinion No. 11 seems to be to group transactions by the nature of the timing differences, e.g., depreciation, installment sales, etc. Following that logic, a differentiation of timing differences by plan or line of business would appear inappropriate.

Thus, there are two related questions:

1. Should acquisition cost adjustments give rise to one group of similar timing differences and benefit reserve adjustments give rise to another separate group of timing differences?, or

2. Should acquisition cost and benefit reserve adjustments together represent one group of timing differences?

The life insurance audit guide provides that

. . . adjustments to reserves and the deferral and amortization of acquisition costs constitute similar timing differences which could be grouped. While reserves and deferred acquisition costs will be segregated in the balance sheet, their grouping for the purpose of determining pretax accounting income is justified because of their interrelationship and similar reversing characteristics. In addition, grouping of other timing differences may be most appropriate because separate treatment of individual timing differences can produce results which vary significantly from those that would result from the grouping of all timing differences. These different results are produced when the "with-and-without" calculation causes a change in category of taxation. When results are produced which vary significantly from the company's current tax status because of the method used or the grouping or separate treatment of timing differences, consideration must be given to the reversal of the tax effects calculated.[11]

The life insurance audit guide says only that the reserve and acquisition cost adjustments *could* be grouped together. While this statement apparently sanctions the use of either method, the guide appears to express a strong preference for the overall grouping of all timing differences when significant differences result due to a change in category of taxation. Thus, if separate "with-and-without" calculations of the adjustments for acquisition costs, benefit reserves, and other timing differences are to be made, it is necessary to determine the effects of the calculation method utilized on the deferred tax provision. In many cases, depending upon the deferred tax calculation method utilized, the results will vary significantly and a calculation using an "overall grouping of all timing differences" approach should probably be made. This single grouping approach is preferred because of the life insurance multiple-phase tax structure.

In summary, acquisition cost and reserve adjustments should be considered as a single group of similar timing differences and should be combined with all other timing differences in making one overall "with-and-without" tax calculation.

Other types of timing differences (including extraordinary items but excluding unrealized capital gains) should also be combined in one deferred tax calculation for the reasons cited above in connection with

Table 26–10.

COMPARISON OF NET CHANGE AND GROSS CHANGE METHOD FOR CRAZY QUILT LIFE (000 Omitted)

Year	Tax Phase	Current Taxes as Reported In Tax Return*	Deferred Taxes Net Change Method Income Statement Charge	Net Change Method Ending Balance Sheet Credit	Gross Change Method Income Statement Charge	Gross Change Method Ending Balance Sheet Credit
1958	I–II	$ 984	$ 316	$ 316	$ 759	$ 759
1959	I–II	1,214	340	656	727	1,486
1960	I–II	1,403	463	1,119	715	2,201
1961	I–II	1,635	592	1,711	844	3,045
1962	I–II	2,280	144	1,855	1,332	3,377
1963	I–II	1,833	707	2,562	893	4,270
1964	I–II	1,944	976	3,538	1,104	5,374
1965	I	2,007	1,029	4,567	1,127	6,501
1966	II	2,208	1,056	5,623	1,161	7,662
1967	I	2,657	1,358	6,981	1,506	9,168
1968	II	1,050	3,862	10,843	4,024	13,192
1969	II	2,175	4,039	14,882	3,963	17,155
1970	II	624	6,074	20,956	5,939	23,094
1971	II	1,766	5,937	26,893	5,233	28,327

*Excluding taxes on realized capital gains. See Table 26–4 for details of calculation.

the acquisition cost and reserve adjustments. Because of their nature, unrealized capital gains can logically be tax-effected separately at the capital gains rate in most cases, and the tax effect should be reflected in the financial statement in which changes in unrealized gains are reported. In other words, it is preferable to group all timing differences, excluding unrealized capital gains, in a given period, and a single deferred tax calculation should be made. The resulting deferred taxes can be apportioned to the respective groups of timing differences, if necessary.

Gross Change and Net Change Methods

Opinion No. 11 and the life insurance audit guide both state that either the gross change method or the net change method may be used for a group of similar timing differences. Under both the gross change method and the net change method, a tax effect is based on a differential calculation. The tax effect is the amount of tax measured by the differential between income taxes computed with and without inclusion of the transaction creating the difference between taxable income and financial statement pre-tax income. The essential difference between the two methods is that the gross change method separates originating timing differences and their tax effects from reversing timing differences and amortization of their tax effects while the net change method combines the net tax effect of originating and reversing timing differences.

Under the gross change method, tax effects of originating timing differences are calculated only at the time that timing differences originate. The amount of the tax effect is determined by a differential calculation on the amount of the gross timing difference originating during the current period. Tax rates in effect during the year of origination of timing differences are used. The deferred taxes are amortized as the related timing differences reverse using either the specific identification, first-in-first-out, or average rate methods. If, for a group of similar timing differences, the entire unamortized timing difference reverses to zero during a period, the entire related deferred tax credit should be amortized regardless of the amount of tax effect determined by the differential calculation.

Under the net change method, tax effects are calculated on the net of the originating timing differences and the reversing timing differences, i.e., the net change during the period in the remaining unamortized timing differences. The amount of the tax effect is determined by a differential calculation using current tax rates.

Table 26-11.

DEFERRED TAXES BY THE NET CHANGE METHOD FOR CRAZY QUILT LIFE, 1958–1971 (000 Omitted)

	1958	1959	1960	1961	1962	1963	1964	1965	1966	1967	1968	1969	1970	1971
Phase I income per tax return	$1,395	$1,772	$2,209	$2,577	$2,929	$3,256	$3,799	$4,444	$4,970	$5,798	$7,218	$8,959	$10,812	$11,374
Phase II income before special deductions per tax return	4,197	4,760	5,111	5,633	7,601	5,689	6,018	5,053	4,863	6,217	2,254	4,381	1,532	3,943
Net timing differences:														
Acquisition cost deferrals	753	739	1,093	1,545	1,473	3,498	4,942	6,264	7,619	9,059	9,372	10,080	12,221	14,093
Benefit reserves	590	709	837	889	(776)	(997)	(1,241)	(1,014)	(1,303)	(1,688)	3,231	3,939	(3,011)	(2,125)
Maintenance expense reserves	(129)	(138)	(151)	(157)	(148)	(178)	(206)	(234)	(260)	(289)	(748)	(681)	(321)	(319)
818(c) increase													10,265	9,265
Reserve strengthening amortization													1,045	1,045
Other						395	407	458	514	714	1,382	1,124	282	571
	1,214	1,310	1,779	2,277	549	2,718	3,902	5,474	6,570	7,796	13,237	14,462	20,481	22,530
Adjusted Phase II income before special deductions	5,411	6,070	6,890	7,910	8,150	8,407	9,920	10,527	11,433	14,013	15,491	18,843	22,013	26,473
Special deductions:														
Tax return amount	1,788	1,844	1,904	1,901	1,738	1,874	2,013	859	250	699	250	250	250	250
Excess utilized								1,437	2,530	2,358	3,829	3,988	5,322	5,478
Total	$1,788	$1,844	$1,904	$1,901	$1,738	$1,874	$2,013	$2,296	$2,780	$3,057	$4,079	$4,238	$5,572	$5,728
Adjusted Phase II income	$3,623	$4,226	$4,986	$6,009	$6,412	$6,533	$7,907	$8,231	$8,653	$10,956	$11,412	$14,605	$16,441	$20,745
Taxable income	$2,509	$2,999	$3,598	$4,293	$4,671	$4,895	$5,853	$6,338	$6,812	$8,377	$9,315	$11,782	$13,627	$16,060
Tax:														
At normal rates	$1,300	$1,554	$1,866	$2,227	$2,424	$2,540	$2,920	$3,036	$3,264	$4,015	$4,912	$6,214	$6,698	$7,703
Currently payable	984	1,214	1,403	1,635	2,280	1,833	1,944	2,007	2,208	2,657	1,050	2,175	624	1,766
Deferred	$316	$340	$463	$592	$144	$707	$976	$1,029	$1,056	$1,358	$3,862	$4,039	$6,074	$5,937
Ratio of deferred tax to net timing differences	26%	26%	26%	26%	26%	26%	25%	19%	16%	17%	29%	28%	30%	26%
Cumulative deferred taxes	$316	$656	$1,119	$1,711	$1,855	$2,562	$3,538	$4,567	$5,623	$6,981	$10,843	$14,882	$20,956	$26,893
Pre-1958 timing differences included in net timing differences	$(1,704)	$(1,482)	$(965)	$(941)	$(783)	$(657)	$(616)	$(525)	$(395)	$(559)	$(267)	$443	$244	$530
Tax applicable to pre-1958 timing differences included in deferred taxes:														
Annual	$(443)	$(385)	$(251)	$(245)	$(204)	$(171)	$(154)	$(100)	$(63)	$(95)	$(77)	$124	$73	$138
Cumulative	$(443)	$(828)	$(1,079)	$(1,324)	$(1,528)	$(1,699)	$(1,853)	$(1,953)	$(2,016)	$(2,111)	$(2,188)	$(2,064)	$(1,991)	$(1,853)

Table 26–12.

DEFERRED TAXES BY THE GROSS CHANGE METHOD FOR CRAZY QUILT LIFE, 1958–1971 (000 Omitted)

	1958	1959	1960	1961	1962	1963	1964	1965	1966	1967	1968	1969	1970	1971
Timing differences originating in:														
1958	$2,910	$2,466	$2,060	$1,819	$1,607	$1,505	$1,411	$1,313	$1,232	$1,141	$1,091	$1,023	$952	$884
1959		3,125	2,647	2,207	1,942	1,712	1,598	1,492	1,387	1,298	1,199	1,145	1,070	994
1960			3,717	2,960	2,478	2,185	1,932	1,798	1,684	1,566	1,467	1,360	1,295	1,211
1961				4,639	3,635	2,963	2,556	2,227	2,069	1,940	1,807	1,695	1,574	1,494
1962					3,243	3,106	2,915	2,760	2,582	2,503	2,483	2,442	2,436	2,370
1963						4,743	4,499	4,271	3,979	3,850	3,746	3,721	3,667	3,650
1964							5,736	5,461	5,210	4,995	4,734	4,597	4,575	4,511
1965								7,230	6,837	6,497	6,208	5,852	5,663	5,587
1966									8,425	7,984	7,589	7,252	6,849	6,636
1967										9,864	9,289	8,862	8,498	8,047
1968											15,404	13,537	12,697	12,097
1969												17,567	15,305	14,371
1970													24,383	24,796
1971														24,029
	$2,910	$5,591	$8,424	$11,625	$12,905	$16,214	$20,647	$26,552	$33,405	$41,638	$55,017	$69,053	$88,964	$110,677
Gross change items														
Originating	$2,910	$3,125	$3,717	$4,639	$3,243	$4,743	$5,736	$7,230	$8,425	$9,864	$15,404	$17,567	$24,383	$24,029
Reversing	-0-	(444)	(884)	(1,438)	(1,963)	(1,434)	(1,303)	(1,325)	(1,572)	(1,631)	(2,025)	(3,531)	(4,472)	(2,316)
Net change items	2,910	2,681	2,833	3,201	1,280	3,309	4,433	5,905	6,853	8,233	13,379	14,036	19,911	21,713
Reserve strengthening	8	111	(89)	17	52	66	85	94	112	122	125	(17)	306	148
Amortization of reserve strengthening												10,451	(1,025)	(906)
													1,045	1,045
	$2,918	$2,792	$2,744	$3,218	$1,332	$3,375	$4,518	$5,999	$6,965	$8,355	$13,504	$24,470	$20,237	$22,000
Phase I income per tax return	$1,395	$1,772	$2,209	$2,577	$2,929	$3,256	$3,799	$4,444	$4,970	$5,798	$7,218	$8,959	$10,812	$11,374
Phase II income before special deductions per tax return	$4,197	$4,760	$5,111	$5,633	$7,601	$5,689	$6,018	$5,053	$4,863	$6,217	$2,254	$4,381	$1,532	$3,943
Timing differences:														
Originating gross change items	2,910	3,125	3,717	4,639	3,243	4,743	5,736	7,230	8,425	9,864	15,404	17,567	24,383	24,029
Net change items	2,918	3,236	3,628	4,656	3,295	4,809	5,821	7,324	8,537	9,986	15,529	17,550	24,709	24,316
Adjusted Phase II income before special deductions	7,115	7,996	8,739	10,289	10,896	10,498	11,839	12,377	13,400	16,203	17,783	21,931	26,241	28,259
Special deductions	1,788	1,844	1,904	1,901	1,738	1,874	2,013	2,296	2,780	3,359	4,079	4,238	5,572	5,728
Adjusted Phase II income	$5,327	$6,152	$6,835	$8,388	$9,158	$8,624	$9,826	$10,081	$10,620	$12,844	$13,704	$17,693	$20,669	$22,531
Taxable income	$3,361	$3,962	$4,522	$5,483	$6,044	$5,940	$6,813	$7,263	$7,795	$9,472	$10,461	$13,326	$15,741	$16,953
Tax:														
At normal rates	$1,743	$2,055	$2,346	$2,846	$3,138	$3,084	$3,400	$3,480	$3,736	$4,541	$5,517	$7,029	$7,739	$8,131
Currently payable	984	1,214	1,403	1,635	2,280	1,833	1,944	2,007	2,208	2,657	1,050	2,175	624	1,766
Deferred	$759	$841	$943	$1,211	$858	$1,251	$1,456	$1,473	$1,528	$1,884	$4,467	$4,854	$7,115	$6,365

Deferred Taxes

Deferred on:														
Originating gross change items	$ 757	$ 812	$ 966	$ 1,207	$ 844	$ 1,234	$ 1,435	$ 1,454	$ 1,508	$ 1,861	$ 4,431	$ 4,849	$ 7,021	$ 6,300
Net change items	2	29	(23)	4	14	17	21	19	20	23	36	5	94	65
	$ 759	$ 841	$ 943	$ 1,211	$ 858	$ 1,251	$ 1,456	$ 1,473	$ 1,528	$ 1,884	$ 4,467	$ 4,854	$ 7,115	$ 6,365
Ratio of deferred tax to timing differences	26%	26%	26%	26%	26%	26%	25%	20%	18%	19%	29%	28%	29%	26%

Table 26–13.

AMORTIZATION OF ORIGINATING DEFERRED TAXES UNDER THE GROSS CHANGE METHOD (000 Omitted)

Year	Originating Deferred Taxes	1958 %	1958 Amount	1959 %	1959 Amount	1960 %	1960 Amount	1961 %	1961 Amount	1962 %	1962 Amount	1963 Unamortized %	1963 Unamortized Amount
1958	$ 757	100	$757	85	$ 643	71	$ 537	63	$ 477	55	$ 416	52	$ 394
1959	812			100	812	85	690	71	576	62	503	55	447
1960	966					100	966	80	773	67	647	59	570
1961	1,207							100	1,207	78	941	64	772
1962	844									100	844	96	810
1963	1,234											100	1,234
1964	1,435												
1965	1,454												
1966	1,508												
1967	1,861												
1968	4,431												
1969	4,849												
1970	7,021												
1971	6,300												
Total-gross change items			$757		$1,455		$2,193		$3,033		$3,351		$4,227
Annual change:													
Gross change items			$757		$ 698		$ 738		$ 840		$ 318		$ 876
Net change items			2		29		(23)		4		14		17
Total			$759		$ 727		$ 715		$ 844		$ 332		$ 893
Cumulative balance			$759		$1,486		$2,201		$3,045		$3,377		$4,270

Crazy Quilt Life

Crazy Quilt Life computed deferred taxes in two ways—by the net change method and by the gross change method. The results are summarized in Table 26–10. After inspecting the data and considering the facts and circumstances, Crazy Quilt selected the gross change method for financial reporting purposes. The reason was essentially because of the erratic movement of Crazy Quilt between phases of taxation. The Company wanted to be able to keep track of components of deferred taxes in order to have the capability of disposing of them properly irrespective of the phase in which the Company might be taxed.

Tables 26–11, –12, and –13, summarize Crazy Quilt's calculations on both bases. "With-and-without" calculations were made each year. Unused special deductions were applied in full on the basis that they would be available when timing differences reversed; however, they were limited to maximum amounts computed on a tax return basis since recomputation was believed to yield "phantom" deductions.

A comparison of the gross change and net change methods will indicate that the two methods often produce significantly different results. Gross changes shown in Table 26–12 are reconcilable to net changes shown in Table 26–11, as may be illustrated by the following reconciliation of 1971 figures:

	000
Gross change items (Table 26–12):	
Originating	$24,029
Reversing	(2,316)
Net change items	287
Pre-1958 differences	530
Net change (Table 26–11)	$22,530

A close study of Table 26–12 will indicate the types of records that must be maintained to implement the gross change method. The volume of such records can be substantial, particularly if the specific identification method is used.

Crazy Quilt's models were so constructed as to yield the necessary information on originating timing differences. Lacking this capability, the gross change method could not have been used.

Disclosure

There are at least seven types of disclosure that should be made with respect to reported income tax expense and tax liabilities and credits carried in the balance sheet:

▸ The company's deferred tax accounting policy.
▸ A distinction between taxes currently payable and deferred taxes.

balances															
1964		1965		1966		1967		1968		1969		1970		1971	
%	Amount	%	Amount	%	Amount	%	Amount	%	Amount	%	Amount	%	Amount	%	Amount
48	$ 363	45	$ 340	42	$ 318	39	$ 295	37	$ 280	35	$ 265	33	$ 250	30	$ 226
51	414	48	390	44	357	41	333	38	308	37	300	34	276	32	259
52	502	48	464	45	435	42	406	39	377	36	348	35	338	32	308
55	664	48	579	45	543	42	507	39	471	36	434	34	410	32	385
90	760	85	717	80	675	77	650	76	641	75	633	75	633	73	615
95	1,172	90	1,111	84	1,036	81	1,000	79	975	78	962	77	950	77	950
100	1,435	95	1,363	91	1,306	87	1,248	83	1,191	80	1,148	80	1,148	79	1,134
		100	1,454	95	1,381	90	1,309	86	1,250	81	1,178	78	1,134	77	1,120
				100	1,508	95	1,433	90	1,357	86	1,297	81	1,221	79	1,191
						100	1,861	94	1,749	90	1,675	86	1,600	81	1,507
								100	4,431	88	3,899	82	3,633	79	3,500
										100	4,849	87	4,219	82	3,976
												100	7,021	93	6,530
														100	6,300
	$5,310		$6,418		$7,559		$9,042		$13,030		$16,988		$22,833		$28,006
	$1,083		$1,108		$1,141		$1,483		$ 3,988		$ 3,958		$ 5,845		$ 5,168
	21		19		20		23		36		5		94		65
	$1,104		$1,127		$1,161		$1,506		$ 4,024		$ 3,963		$ 5,939		$ 5,233
	$5,374		$6,501		$7,662		$9,168		$13,192		$17,155		$23,094		$28,327

▸ An explanation of the reason why income tax expense is not proportional to reported pre-tax income.

▸ The nature and amount of the shareholders' and the policyholders' surplus tax account.

▸ Operation losses.

▸ Unused deductions and credits.

▸ Portion of retained earnings in excess of statutory surplus for which no tax is provided.

An appropriate accounting policy note for Crazy Quilt Life might be as follows:

ACCOUNTING POLICY NOTE:

The Company provides for deferred taxes by the gross change method on differences between reported pre-tax income and income as reported on the Company's federal income tax return when such differences are other than permanent. The provision is based on the assumption that the Company will be taxed on an amount equal to taxable investment income plus 50 percent of the excess over taxable investment income.

Distinction between current and deferred taxes can be made in the financial statements, as Crazy Quilt does, or in a note.

A reconciliation of the tax expense computed by applying normal rates to pre-tax accounting income with reported tax expense might take the following form for Crazy Quilt:

OTHER NOTE:

A reconciliation of federal income tax expense computed at normal rates with federal income tax as reported in the income statement is as follows:

Income tax at 48% of reported pre-tax income ($24,550,000) less surtax exemption	$11,778,000
One-half of excess of gain from operations over taxable investment income ($6,588,000) not taxable	(3,162,000)
Special deductions ($3,300,000) available for tax purposes	(1,584,000)
Company's share of tax-exempt investment income ($1,214,000)	(583,000)
Other items	(130,000)
Reported income tax expense	$ 6,999,000

It may be desirable or necessary to detail the components of deferred income tax expense, which for Crazy Quilt Life might take the following form:

525

OTHER NOTE:

Deferred income tax expense is comprised of the following components:

Acquisition cost, policy reserve, and other timing differences originating during the period ($24,029,000)	$5,767,000
Acquisition cost, policy reserve, and other timing differences reversing during the period ($2,316,000)	(534,000)
	$5,233,000

The disclosure of the balance of the policyholders' surplus tax account might take the following form:

OTHER NOTE:

At December 31, 1971, up to $4,945,000 (at current tax rates) would be required for possible federal income taxes which might become due, in whole or in part, in future years if any portion of $10,302,000 of the Company's gains from operations since January 1, 1959, presently included in retained earnings and identified as "Policyholders' Surplus" under the Life Insurance Company Income Tax Act of 1959 ("The Act"), becomes includable in taxable income by reason of distributions to shareholders in excess of the balance of "Shareholders' Surplus" ($21,074,000 at December 31, 1971) or by reason of exceeding a prescribed maximum for the "Policyholders' Surplus Account". Under existing circumstances the Company does not expect to pay any such taxable distributions or to exceed the prescribed maximum.

27

Business Combinations

The announcement of a business combination almost always stirs excitement. Security analysts wax enthusiastic; stock prices rise; and executives—at least some of them—happily survey the prospect of a larger sphere of influence and responsibility.

The announcement of a business combination also stirs feelings of dread in the hearts of accountants. Accounting for business combinations ranks high on the list of perplexing accounting problems. In the case of a business combination involving the merger or acquisition of a life insurance company, the problem can become so difficult as to defy satifactory resolution.

Poolings

"The pooling of interests method of accounting," says Opinion No. 16 of the Accounting Principles Board, "is intended to present as a single interest two or more common stockholder interests which were previously independent and the combined rights and risks represented by those interests." [1] Provided that a business combination meets the rather strict criteria for poolings set forth in Opinion No. 16, the accounts of the combining companies are essentially added together in preparing the financial statements of the combined enterprise. This is true regardless of whether the combined companies retain their separate identities, whether one company is the survivor, or whether a new company is formed to absorb the combining companies.

The principal problem in a pooling is the determination of whether the combination meets the criteria for a pooling in the first place. Once this determination is made, the accounting is relatively straightforward, because assets, liabilities, and retained earnings accounts are stated at their pre-combination amounts.

Poolings involving life insurance companies generally present no special accounting problems beyond those of a life insurance company operating independently, with one exception: the problem of conforming the accounting methods of the constituent companies where there are wide variations in such methods.

Consistency and Opinion No. 16

APB Opinion No. 16 states that the separate companies involved in a pooling "may have recorded assets and liabilities under differing methods of accounting and the amounts may be adjusted to the same basis of accounting if the change would otherwise have been appropriate for the separate company. A change in accounting method to conform the individual methods should be applied retroactively, and financial statements presented for prior periods should be restated." [2]

Opinion No. 16 provides that inconsistent methods *may* be conformed in a pooling, but it does not *require* that they be conformed. It further provides that the consistency adjustment should be made only where the adjustment could have been made in the absence of a pooling.

Poolings Involving Non-Life Insurance Companies

In a pooling involving a life insurance company (or companies) and a non-life insurance company (or companies), the identities of the life insurance constituents and the non-life insurance constituents would almost always be retained. A merger of more than one life insurance company involved in such a business combination would be possible, as would a merger of more than one non-life insurance company; but except in very unusual circumstances, none of the non-life insurance constituents would be merged with any of the life insurance constituents.

This means that the pooling of a life insurance company and a non-life insurance company will generally take the form of an acquisition or a consolidation effected by an exchange of voting common stock.

Acquisition—life insurance company is dominant. When a life insurance company acquires substantially all of the stock of a non-life insurance company, statutory accounting practices have generally required that the investment be carried on the basis of the life insurance company's equity in "net admitted assets" of the non-life insurance company.* Thus, the non-life insurance company's assets are adjusted for those amounts which the life insurance company would not be permitted to admit as assets if the life company owned the assets directly. Changes in the net admitted asset value of the subsidiary are recorded variously as unrealized capital gains or losses or as changes in non-admitted assets, flowing through the surplus account in either case.

When the life insurance company's statements are presented on the basis of generally accepted accounting principles, the investment account on the life insurance company's books should be restated to report the life company's equity in the net assets of the subsidiary stated on the basis of generally accepted accounting principles. In the year of the pooling the life insurance company's equity accounts would be increased by an amount equivalent to its share of the retained earnings of the subsidiary at the beginning of the reporting period. The life company's equity in the net earnings of the subsidiary for the period would be reported in the life company's income statement.

Sometimes the accounts of a non-life insurance subsidiary are not consolidated with those of a life insurance company; the life company's equity in the earnings of the non-life insurance company is some-times reported as dividend income, to the extent that the subsidiary pays dividends, and as a one-line entry in the income statement for the undistributed balance. Alternatively, equity in total net income of the subsidiary might be reported in a one-line entry, with dividends applied to reduce the investment account. The investment account represents the life insurance company's share of the net assets of the subsidiary.

In those few cases in which the financial statements are fully consolidated, the effect on reported net income and total equity is the same as if the equity method of accounting described above had been followed.

Occasionally the non-life insurance company will hold assets that the life insurance company also holds. This can create problems where the accepted valuation bases differ. For example, some believe that the proper basis for carrying investments in common stock is cost for a non-life insurance company, and market in the case of a life insurance company. Unless an existing difference in valuation methods is justifiable in terms of the underlying operations of the companies, it would seem that the valuation methods of the subsidiary should be consistent with those of the dominant life insurance company. However, Opinion No. 16 provides that a consistency adjustment has to be "appropriate for the separate company," and market is not an acceptable method of valuation for most types of noninsurance companies. Under these circumstances it appears that the valuation inconsistency must be retained after the pooling. If the resulting differences are material, the extent of the inconsistency and the reasons for it should be disclosed in notes to the financial statements.*

Acquisition—non-life insurance company is dominant. When a non-life insurance company, say a manufacturing company, acquires a life insurance company in a transaction accounted for as a pooling of interests, the life insurance company's accounts should be stated on the basis of generally accepted accounting principles for purposes of recording the pooling and equity in earnings of the life company.

The problem of consistent valuation of assets is most likely to arise when a non-life insurance company acquires a life insurance company. The valuation practices of the life insurance company should be conformed to those of the dominant non-life insurance

---

*However, as of this writing this practice is being reviewed by the Committee on Valuations of the National Association of Insurance Commissioners. It is possible that, for statutory purposes, valuation of investments in non-life insurance subsidiaries will approach consistency with generally accepted methods of valuing such investments.

*Others believe that cost is the appropriate basis of valuing common stocks in all cases. Under this approach there would be no inconsistency; stocks of both life insurance and non-life insurance constituents would be reported at cost.

company where there is no fundamental difference in operations to justify the difference in valuation practices. For example, the non-life insurance company may carry its temporary investments in marketable securities at cost. To the extent that the life insurance company's investments are also classified as "temporary"—common stocks come to mind most readily—then they should be valued on the same basis, because there is no *requirement* under generally accepted accounting principles that the life company value them at market for purposes of reporting as a separate entity.

Consolidation. A business combination effected in the form of a consolidation involves the exchange of shares of a new corporation for those of two or more existing corporations. In effect, the new corporation is a holding company, although it may conduct business of its own.

The basic problems involved in accounting for a consolidation involving a life insurance company and a non-life insurance company are essentially the same as accounting for an acquisition. However, it is quite possible that none of the constituent companies will be regarded as "dominant". In that case it may be difficult to choose a common valuation basis for assets that are common to the life insurance company and the non-life insurance company. In these circumstances it may be appropriate to retain the respective valuation bases and simply disclose the inconsistencies and the reasons for them.

Poolings Involving Life Insurance Companies Only

Superficially it would appear that poolings involving life insurance companies exclusively raise few, if any, problems of consistency. In fact, however, serious problems of consistency can arise, whether the accounts be stated on a statutory basis or a generally accepted accounting principles basis.

In the discussion which follows, it is assumed that the financial statements of the constituent life insurance companies are to be consolidated. Thus, the point of view adopted is that of an acquisition or a consolidation. Nevertheless, the discussion applies equally to those cases in which the statements are not consolidated and those in which the combination is effected in the form of a merger.

Consolidating statutory accounts. When all of the combining companies are rendering reports to shareholders on the statutory basis or substantially the

statutory basis,* adjustments required to conform the companies' accounting practices are generally minor. It might be desirable to capitalize furniture and equipment previously expensed by one of the companies but not the other; provide a full year's provision for dividends payable in the following calendar year where one of the companies has followed the practice of providing half that amount but the other has provided the full amount; and so on.

One inconsistency can be especially troublesome: differing reserve valuation methods. For example, where one company values new business on a preliminary term basis and the other on a net level basis, the resulting financial statements can be somewhat misleading. The net level company cannot "weaken" its reserves and the preliminary term company is generally loath to strengthen to net level. The net level company can switch to preliminary term methods after the combination is effected, but that doesn't do much for the statements presented in the first year of the combination—which are presented as if the companies were combined for the entire period—and for restated prior-years' statements presented for comparative purposes. Further, the switch only makes the companies consistent with respect to new business; inconsistency as to reserve changes and reserve levels remain with respect to older blocks of business.

Generally, disclosure is the only feasible alternative in this situation. Some believe that the label "statutory" embraces the entire range of valuation bases (including valuation methods) permitted by regulatory authorities, and that additional disclosure is not necessary. This position has little merit. Valuation methods have such material effect that the reader of the financial statements deserves to know something about them, including a description of their effect (perferably quantified) on net income. In this case it is not proper to dismiss the problem by citing "statutory practices".

As a practical matter, very few stock companies use net level methods for new business. In most cases,

*For purposes of this discussion, "substantially the statutory basis" refers to accounting for acquisition costs and reserves on the statutory basis. Adjustments to include realized capital gains in income, eliminate the mandatory securities valuation reserve, recognize non-admitted assets, record deferred taxes, reduce stocks to cost, etc. are, for purposes of this discussion, not sufficient to disqualify the financial statements from the "substantially statutory" classification. Nor, of course, is the mere act of consolidating the accounts, which also violates statutory rules.

therefore, valuation methods used by combining companies will be reasonably consistent.

Mortality tables are for the most part uniform among all companies because of statutory requirements. Statutory reserve interest rate assumptions can theoretically vary quite widely,* but generally the assumptions actually used fall within a fairly narrow range. Further, interest rate assumptions are frequently related to underlying contract characteristics. Inconsistencies in interest rate assumptions that are attributable to truly arbitrary choice and that also have profound effects on the financial statements are probably quite rare. Normally, therefore, inconsistencies in reserve valuation bases (other than inconsistencies in valuation methods) would not call for special treatment.

Consolidating adjusted accounts when one of the constituents has been reporting on a statutory basis. Consolidating the accounts of a company that has been reporting on a statutory basis with the accounts of a company that has been reporting on a generally accepted basis** would normally require that the statutory accounts be adjusted to conform to the adjusted accounts. This means that the same general accounting policies—composition of acquisition costs, general amortization method, etc.—should be applied in making the adjustment.

This assumes that the dominant company has already adjusted and that its practices will prevail. Where the dominant company has not yet adjusted, it may wish to follow a somewhat different adjustment policy than the less-dominant company. In that case, the accounts of the less-dominant company need generally not be brought into conformity with the accounting policies chosen to guide the adjustments of the dominant company, unless the two companies follow grossly inconsistent practices.

Consolidating adjusted accounts with adjusted accounts. Where the pooled life insurance companies both state their accounts on the basis of generally accepted accounting principles, but they follow different accounting policies, the accounting policies should

be conformed to one standard in all cases, notwithstanding the permissiveness of Opinion No. 16.

For example, one company may defer development costs while the other expenses such costs as incurred. Or, one company may be considerably more liberal in its definition of acquisition costs than the other. The accounts of all constituents should be adapted to one standard, preferably the most conservative.

There is another somewhat philosophical reason for conforming the methods. The adjusted statements purport to be in conformity with generally accepted accounting principles. The reader of such statements is entitled to expect the statements to be internally consistent. He should not be required to accept unreasonably inconsistent statements merely because Opinion No. 16, literally taken, appears on the surface to permit such inconsistency.

Generally, adjusted benefit reserves would not need to be restated to meet the consistency requirement. This is because the underlying assumptions generally may be presumed to be appropriate, and there is relatively less latitude for choice in calculation techniques. In other words, benefit reserves typically do not involve the range of choices among accounting alternatives that characterizes acquisition and development costs.*

Purchases

When a business combination does not qualify as a pooling, it must be accounted for as a purchase. In years past a business combination was accounted for as "part purchase, part pooling" when the combination had the attributes of both (for example, when both stock and cash were involved in the transaction), but in Opinion No. 16 the Accounting Principles Board mercifully did away with this particular form of schizophrenia. Now a business combination must be accounted for as either a pooling or a purchase, but not both.

In a pooling, the accounts of the parties to the pooling are carried forward in combination at their recorded historical amounts. In a purchase, one of the parties is deemed to be an acquirer and a new basis of accountability is created for the company acquired. In effect, the tangible and intangible assets and liabilities of the acquired company or companies are revalued at amounts which represent current fair values; the difference, if any, between the price paid

---

*A study of the 1968 Convention Statements of 141 stock companies whose shares are publicly traded indicated that average interest rate assumptions for ordinary life business ranged between 2.8 percent and 3.1 percent for 74 percent of the companies and between 2.5 percent and 3.2 percent for 96 percent of the companies.

**"Generally accepted" in this context refers to financial statements prepared on the basis of generally accepted accounting principles, which includes deferral and amortization of acquisition costs and appropriate restatement of benefit reserves.

*This is subject to challenge, of course, where the reserves of one of the constituents do not adequately contemplate the risk of future adversity. For example, a level interest rate of, say, 6½ percent does not articulate very well with a rate that grades, say, to 3½ or 4 percent.

and the restated net assets is generally regarded as goodwill.*

Purchases of Life Insurance Companies

Until 1972, if one life insurance company purchased another for cash, the acquiring company, for purposes of the statutory statements, had to record its investment at an amount equivalent to its share of the statutory net assets of the acquired company; any difference was charged to surplus. In 1972, the NAIC adopted new valuation procedures which permitted deferral and amortization over a limited period (generally 10 years) of the excess of cost over statutory net assets.

If the purchase is effected by stock, generally the capital stock account is credited with the par value of the stock given up to acquire the company; the difference between the statutory net assets of the acquired company and the par value of the stock issued by the acquiring company is credited to additional paid-in capital.

For purposes of financial statements to shareholders, the accounting treatment of purchase transactions has varied:

▸ Where the reporting entity is a life insurance company that owns another life insurance company acquired in a purchase transaction, and the statements of the acquiring company are presented on a statutory basis, the statutory method has usually been used, even when, as in some cases, the statements have been consolidated.

▸ Where the reporting entity is a holding company that owns a life insurance company acquired in a purchase transaction, and the statutory (or modified statutory**) method of accounting is followed with respect to the life insurance subsidiary, any cost in excess of statutory net assets has generally been reported as goodwill. With respect to purchase

---

*This is an oversimplification. If stock is exchanged for stock, and neither stock has a determinable fair value, then the assets and liabilities are valued and this valuation determines the acquisition price. Goodwill may not arise in this instance. In the usual case, however, the fair value of the stock is known, and it is the value of the stock that determines the purchase price; the difference between the price thus determined and the revalued net assets of the acquired company is generally presumed to represent goodwill.

**The "modified statutory method" refers to a method which is essentially statutory but may have been tempered for relatively minor items, such as reporting realized capital gains as part of net income.

transactions initiated prior to the effective date (November 1970) of Accounting Principles Board Opinion No. 17, such goodwill has typically not been amortized.*

▸ In a few cases the net assets as of the date of purchase of a life insurance subsidiary have been restated to reflect an adjustment for reserves and acquisition costs computed on the basis of assumptions appropriate at the purchase date (i.e., then-current assumptions), the principle being that computing reserves using current assumptions results in reporting policy assets and liabilities at fair value. In effect, goodwill has been adjusted retroactively. Any amount thus allocated to the reserves is effectively amortized through the reserve mechanism.

In terms of accounting theory, this latter practice is sounder than the other two. But even the latter practice fails to recognize fully one aspect of a purchase transaction that has implications for the financial statements: the fact that the acquiring company has invested in the future profits attributable to the subsidiary's book of insurance in force on the purchase date. Such profits have a limited term of existence, and they emerge on the books of the acquired company in a distinctive pattern. The investment in such profits represents an identifiable intangible asset that should be amortized in accordance with the pattern of the underlying earnings.

Crazy Quilt's Strategy for Acquisitions

In mid-1970 the management of Crazy Quilt Life decided to embark on a program of acquisitions. It was recognized that Crazy Quilt had gotten quite large and that the rate of internal growth would tend to decrease simply because of the size of the base from which such growth is measured. Further, it was becoming more difficult for Crazy Quilt's top management to maintain personal contact with the Company's growing agency force. Finally, the Company was becoming institutionalized despite having a decidedly anti-bureaucratic policy; more and more had to be accomplished through "accepted procedure", with the result that it was increasingly difficult to respond promptly to new ideas, new markets (particularly specialized markets), and new opportunities.

---

*For example, one 1970 annual report indicated that the parent company's "investment in its life insurance subsidiaries exceeded its equity in the [statutory] net assets of these subsidiaries by $27,204,522. This excess is attributable to intangibles with continuing value and is not being amortized."

Table 27–1.

EARNINGS, MARKET VALUES, AND ACQUISITION PRICE (AS OF JANUARY 1, 1971) OF McCABE LIFE

Earnings history:

Year	Total (000)		Per Share (1,000,000 Outstanding)	
	Statutory	*GAAP*	*Statutory*	*GAAP*
1967	$ 313	$ 482	$ .31	$ .48
1968	368	560	.37	.56
1969	434	687	.43	.69
1970	600	940	.60	.94

Market values:

Year	Year-End Market	Price-Earnings Ratio		Aggregate Market (000)
		Statutory	*GAAP*	
1967	$ 6.875	22.2	14.3	$ 6,875
1968	6.000	16.2	10.7	6,000
1969	7.625	17.7	11.1	7,625
1970	13.000	25.5	16.3	13,000

Acquisition price and premium (000):

Cash paid to certain McCabe shareholders	$ 5,000
Market value of Crazy Quilt stock paid to certain McCabe shareholders	12,145
Cost of 90% interest in McCabe	17,145
Market value of McCabe stock— 90% x $13,000	11,700
Premium (46.54%)	$ 5,445

The Company's management resolved to begin acquiring well-managed smaller companies which would be able to draw on Crazy Quilt's resources and range of administrative capabilities and share in the economies of scale, but which would retain an essentially independent mode of operation. A network of subsidiaries, each with its own decision-making top management, seemed preferable to a network of divisions headed by vice presidents. In short, Crazy Quilt intended to make sure that operating units retained their status and prestige. This seemed the best way to maintain the loyalty of agents and to promote prompt, effective top-level decision-making.

The Purchase of McCabe Life

In July 1970 Crazy Quilt opened negotiations with McCabe Life, a small ($35 million in assets) well-managed midwestern life insurance company specializing in ordinary life insurance. McCabe's field force operated primarily in rural areas, while Crazy Quilt's agents tended to be oriented to urban areas. McCabe's operations were obviously complementary to Crazy Quilt's.

The negotiations consumed many months. On De-cember 29, 1970, the companies reached agreement on the terms of the acquisition: Crazy Quilt would pay $19.05 per share for McCabe stock, which had a market value of $13 a share. This price represented a premium of 46.54 percent over the market value of McCabe stock.

In determing the price Crazy Quilt considered a number of factors. One was the trend of McCabe's adjusted earnings; McCabe's impact on Crazy Quilt's financial statements would be measured in terms of adjusted earnings, so Crazy Quilt was, in part, buying McCabe's adjusted earnings. The purchase price represented about 20 times McCabe's estimated 1971 adjusted earnings, which seemed a fair multiple in view of the rate of growth (15 percent compounded) of such earnings. Finally, the price appeared to result in some small advantage in terms of the market value of Crazy Quilt's stock, which was selling at 21 times adjusted earnings.

Crazy Quilt also reviewed McCabe from another point of view—McCabe's going-concern value. Estimates were made of the value of McCabe's insurance in force, the value of the company's agency plant, and the market value of McCabe's assets. These estimates also suggested a price of about $19 a share.

Table 27–2.

McCABE'S BALANCE SHEET AT DECEMBER 31, 1970 (000 Omitted)

	Statutory	GAAP
Assets		
Bonds at amortized cost (market, $14,038)	$15,359	$15,359
Common stocks (market, $2,370; cost, $1,968)	2,370	1,968
Mortgage loans at unamortized balances (market, $12,848)	13,524	13,524
Real estate at cost less accumulated depreciation of $930 (market, $1,330)	1,087	1,087
Policy loans at unamortized balances	1,461	1,461
Cash	325	325
	34,126	33,724
Deferred and uncollected premiums	860	
Accrued investment income	277	277
Other assets	159	159
Non-admitted assets		396
Deferred acquisition costs		7,913
	$35,422	$42,469
Equities		
Insurance reserves:		
Benefits	$30.386	$29,847
Renewal expenses		188
Claims and other policy liabilities	524	524
Federal income taxes:		
Current	52	52
Deferred		2,166
Other liabilities	218	218
Mandatory securities valuation reserve	932	
Liability for unauthorized reinsurance	120	
	32,232	32,995
Capital and surplus:		
Paid-in capital	1,000	1,000
Earned surplus	2,190	8,474
	3,190	9,474
	$35,422	$42,469

Crazy Quilt offered a choice of cash or Crazy Quilt stock for McCabe's shares. Crazy Quilt acquired 90 percent of McCabe's outstanding shares. Aggregate value of the transaction was $17,145,000, of which $5 million was paid in cash and the balance in Crazy Quilt stock. The purchase date was January 1, 1971.

Certain background information on McCabe Life, as well as details of the purchase, are given in Table 27–1. McCabe Life's balance sheets, statutory and adjusted as of December 31, 1970 (just prior to the purchase date), are shown in Table 27–2.

Crazy Quilt paid $17,145,000 for its 90 percent interest in McCabe. Crazy Quilt's accountants immediately set about allocating the purchase price to individual assets and liabilities, according to the principles set forth in Accounting Principles Board Opinion No. 16:

Acquiring assets in groups requires not only ascertaining the cost of the assets as a group but also allocating the cost to the individual assets which comprise the group. . . A portion of the total cost is . . . assigned to each individual asset acquired on the basis of its fair value. A difference between the sum of the assigned costs of the tangible and identifiable intangible assets acquired less liabilities assumed and the cost of the group is evidence of unspecified intangible values.[3]

The effort to allocate the purchase price was undertaken solely for the purpose of preparing financial statements based on generally accepted accounting principles. For purposes of the statutory statements, Crazy Quilt recorded its investment in McCabe at an amount ($2,871,000) equal to 90 percent of McCabe's statutory net worth, $3,190,000. The difference between 90 percent of McCabe's statutory net worth and

Table 27–3.

VALUATION OF INVESTMENTS OF McCABE LIFE AT JANUARY 1, 1971 (000 Omitted)

	Value	*Adjustment To Market*	*Other Adjustments*	*Purchase Valuation*
Bonds	$15,359	$(1,321)	$100*	$14,138
Stocks	1,968	402	(100)*	2,270
Mortgage loans	13,524	(676)		12,848
Real estate	1,087	243		1,330
Policy loans	1,461			1,461**
Total	$33,399	$(1,352)	$ –0–	$32,047

*Crazy Quilt expects to realize its gains on stocks (all long-term and all on property whose appreciation occurred after 1958) and will realize losses on bonds only to the extent of such gains. The adjustments indicated represent tax effects.

**Because there is no market for policy loans, and because of the relationship of policy loans, cash values, statutory reserves, and adjusted reserves (which assume surrenders at full cash value), policy loans were valued at book value.

the purchase price of $17,145,000, which difference was $14,274,000, was constructively charged to surplus for statutory purposes.

Purchase Valuations

In many respects, accounting for the purchase of a life insurance company is no different than accounting for the purchase of any other kind of company. Thus, invested assets are valued at market; liabilities are valued at their discounted present value.

In Crazy Quilt's case, market values were generally used to value McCabe's invested assets. Details of the valuation, which aggregated $32,047,000 (excluding cash of $325,000, which was of course taken at face value), are shown in Table 27–3. The mandatory securities valuation reserve was ignored for purposes of determining the portion of the purchase price allocable to McCabe's invested assets.

Non-admitted assets were valued at their estimated realizable value, $396,000. Accrued investment income and miscellaneous assets were valued at book value, which was regarded as substantially equivalent to fair value.

Policy and contract claims, taxes payable, accounts payable, and miscellaneous liabilities were valued at book value, which was regarded as substantially equivalent to fair value for these short-term items. The liability for unauthorized reinsurance was ignored in making the valuation.

Thus far the process of allocating the purchase price had been relatively straightforward. Crazy Quilt's accountants next considered how to value policy

reserves, insurance in force, and other identifiable intangible assets.

Valuation of Policy Reserves

McCabe Life was already using two bases of valuing policy reserve liabilities. For statutory purposes, statutory reserves were used. Statutory was also used for tax purposes; McCabe had not made the 818 (c) election. For purposes of reporting to existing shareholders, McCabe used adjusted reserves based on original assumptions.

For purposes of recording the purchase, however, it was clear that reserve liabilities would have to be revalued based on *current* assumptions. According to APB Opinion No. 16.

Accounts and notes payable, long-term debt, and other claims payable [should be valued] at present values of amounts to be paid determined at appropriate current interest rates.[4]

What are "current" assumptions for reserves on an existing block of insurance in force?

It is tempting to say that current assumptions represent assumptions that would be appropriate for new issues as of the purchase date (adjusted, of course, for the fact that all or part of the select period for mortality and the high-lapse period for withdrawals would have passed). But this is not sufficient. Assumptions appropriate to new issues refer to the future. Assumptions appropriate to an existing block of business refer to the past *and* the future. In other words, a beginning reserve must be computed for a purchased block of business. The beginning reserve enters directly into the calculation of the valuation premium, which is computed as follows (amounts are hypothetical):

Present value of future benefits using current assumptions	$1,000
Beginning reserve	(800)
Present value of future benefits to be provided for by future valuation premiums	$ 200
Present value of an annuity of $1 due for the remaining premium-paying period, using current assumptions	$ 5
Revised valuation premium	$ 40

Computation of the present value of future benefits is relatively straightforward. Benefits after the valuation date are projected using current estimates for mortality, withdrawal, and interest. Mortality and lapse rates would be those appropriate to current issues. The interest assumption would generally be based on the adjusted portfolio rate (after adjustment of the assets to market) graded downward to the interest rates assumed for purposes of computing reserves on the acquiring company's own current issues.

Computation of the revised valuation premium is also straightforward. The difference between the present value of future benefits and the beginning reserve is the amount that must be funded from future valuation premiums. This amount is translated into a level annual equivalent—the valuation premium—by dividing into it the present value of a $1 annuity due computed using the same assumptions as were used to compute the present value of future benefits.*

The real problem in this process is determining the beginning reserve on a purchased block of business. There are several possibilities; for example:

▶ Use statutory reserves.
▶ Use original-assumption adjusted reserves.
▶ Use recomputed adjusted reserves.

Statutory reserves represent a legal liability of the acquired company, and some would say that the fair value of a legal liability is its stated amount. This would seem to have no merit. If it did, then the same

*This assumes a level annual gross premium. If the gross premium varies, the valuation premium would be expressed as a constant percentage of the gross premium.

reasoning would apply to direct new issues, and there would be no grounds for adjusting reserves at all. Fair value is an economic concept, not a legal concept.

Original-assumption adjusted reserves would represent fair value only if hindsight justifies the underlying assumptions. For example, a 3 percent interest assumption may not represent a reasonable expression of fair value if actual interest rates have risen to, say, 6 percent. This is because reserves have accumulated at a rate of interest that, with hindsight, is known to have been inappropriate. Use of original-assumption reserves suffers from the same theoretical deficiencies as the use of statutory reserves. Neither necessarily represents an expression of "fair value".

This suggests that recomputed adjusted reserves should be used. That is all well and good as a concept; but what does it mean in practice?

Viewed retrospectively, a reserve is in large measure the result of accumulating *past* valuation premiums at interest (for purposes of this discussion, assumed charges against the reserve are ignored). Viewed prospectively, a reserve is that amount which, together with *future* valuation premiums and interest, will be sufficient to fund the payment of benefits. When a block of business is purchased, there are two series of valuation premiums—one in the past and one in the future—that converge in a single reserve calculation.

Here lies the crux of the difficult problem of recomputing adjusted reserves in a manner which recognizes assumptions that are current at the purchase date. Calculation of the future series of valuation premiums has reference to the reserve being held. The reserve being held has reference to the past series of valuation premiums. Put another way, the calculation of future valuation premiums depends upon the calculation of past valuation premiums.

This means that both series of valuation premiums must "articulate"—that is, must be based on the same rational framework of assumptions. Otherwise there is no way the reserve at the purchase date will be equivalent to fair value.

This, in turn, means that valuation premiums should be recomputed from the date of issue to reflect assumptions that are appropriate both before and after the date of purchase. For example, if issues of 1960 were valued on the basis of a level 4 percent assumption that was appropriate in terms of 1960 interest rates, the adjusted portfolio rate in 1970 is 6 percent, and the current practice with respect to new issues is to grade interest rates to 4 percent, assumptions used to recompute valuation premiums for purchased 1960

Table 27–4.

McCABE LIFE'S RESERVE LIABILITIES ON THREE BASES AS OF JANUARY 1, 1971 (OOO Omitted)

	Statutory— Mix of Net Level and CRVM	Adjusted—All Net Level	
		Original Assumptions	Revised Assumptions
Benefit reserves	$30,386	$29,847	$27,715
Deferred and uncollected premiums	(860)		
Renewal expense reserves		188	240
NET RESERVE AMOUNTS	$29,526	$30,035	$27,955
Difference between statutory and adjusted		$ 509	$(1,571)
Difference between (1) adjusted-original assumptions and (2) adjusted-revised assumptions			$(2,080)

issues should grade systematically upward from 4 percent in 1960 to 6 percent in 1970 and downward to 4 percent over a suitable period.

The net result is to allocate fair value elements between two series of valuation premiums and to give recognition to this allocation in the form of a single coordinated set of valuation premiums. In the example cited, the valuation premium would accumulate to reserves in 1970 that assume 6 percent interest, and future valuation premiums would accumulate by departing from reserves that assume 6 percent. In other words, both series of valuation premiums meet at a point that reasonably represents fair value whether viewed retrospectively or prospectively.

It should be noted that this rather painful exercise is necessitated by fragmenting the gross premium and segregating policy assets and liabilities. If the reserve were stated as a single amount and a gross premium valuation were employed, the painful exercise would not be necessary. This is discussed later in this chapter.

It should also be noted that original-assumption reserves may occasionally approximate the recomputed reserves due to the complex relationships among valuation premiums, present values, annuities, required interest, etc. It goes without saying that where this is the case, reserves should not be recomputed. One can envision the difficulty of maintaining four sets of reserves—statutory, tax, original assumptions

(where there is a minority interest), and revised assumptions.

Crazy Quilt Life recomputed McCabe's reserves along the lines described above. A single series of revised valuation premiums was computed by projecting experience from the dates of issue of the various blocks of business (1) to the purchase date, by tracing to the extent practicable actual experience as it had developed to that date, and (2) after the purchase date by making prudent estimates of future experience. As regards the interest assumption, the market rate of interest for McCabe's portfolio was simulated for each issue year and this rate was graded up to the market rate of interest on McCabe's revalued assets at the date of acquiring McCabe (January 1, 1971). The rate was graded down to Crazy Quilt's own ultimate rate on new issues for the period after January 1, 1971.

The relationships among the various bases of valuing McCabe's policy reserves are shown in Table 27–4. The reserves recomputed in the manner described above using revised assumptions, $27,955,000, were carried into the consolidated balance sheet at the purchase date.

Determination of Acquisition Cost

If Crazy Quilt had simply acquired a block of insurance in force instead of 90 percent of an entire company, the acquisition cost of the business would have been readily apparent. The entries to record the sale of a block of insurance in force would be as follows (amounts are hypothetical):

On seller's books:

Reserves (assumed by buyer)	$1,000	
Assets (transferred to buyer)		$ 800
Gain on sale of in-force		200

On buyer's books:

Assets (received from seller)	$ 800	
Consideration paid for in-force	200	
Reserves (assumed from seller)		$1,000

On the buyer's books, "consideration paid for in-force" would simply be the difference between assets received and liabilities assumed. In other words, determination of the acquisition cost of a purchased block of business is more or less automatic. The cost is attributable solely to the business acquired. What is the nature of the cost? Insurance in force has a market value that can be measured in terms of the stream of future earnings it produces. It is clearly a "specific identifiable intangible asset" within the meaning ascribed to that term by APB Opinion No. 17. So the cost of a block of insurance in force should be deferred and amortized in proportion to the revenue or profits attributable to the block.

In Crazy Quilt's case, of course, 90 percent of an entire company was acquired. So the portion of the purchase price allocable to McCabe's insurance in force had to be computed. The only question was *how* the value of McCabe's insurance in force should be computed.

APB Opinion No. 16. Accounting Principles Board Opinion No. 16 does not specify what procedure should be used to determine the acquisition cost of a block of insurance in force. The opinion does, however, provide valuation guidelines for various other tangible and intangible assets. The most relevant guideline is as follows:

Intangible assets which can be identified and named, including contracts, patents, franchises, customer and supplier lists, and favorable leases, [should be valued] at appraised values.[5]

What is the "appraised value" of insurance in force?

"Replacement cost" of deferred acquisition costs. One possible approach to determining an "appraised value" of insurance in force is to calculate the "depreciated replacement cost" of unamortized acquisi-

tion costs, after the fashion of valuing used property and equipment (see APB Opinion No. 16). The theory is that this is the amount that would have to be spent to acquire the business if the business were produced internally. This generally would involve the application of index numbers to unamortized acquisition cost balances by year of issue which take into account inflation, changes in cost structure, changes in cost allocation methods, changes in average size of policies issued, changes in interest rates (assuming acquisition costs are being amortized with interest), changes in persistency patterns, and so on. In McCabe's case, the value thus determined was $8,546,000, or $633,000 more than the amount ($7,913,000) reported for unamortized historical-cost acquisition costs in McCabe's adjusted balance sheet as of December 31, 1970 (see Table 27–2).

But reflection indicated this approach to be invalid. On the simplest level, there would be no way to produce business this year that is, say, 20 years old, so use of "replacement cost" of unamortized acquisition costs with respect to such business is somewhat illogical. On a deeper level, the "replacement cost" of unamortized acquisition costs is not what is being purchased. What is being purchased is a stream of future profits, and the current value of the profit stream bears no relationship, except coincidentally, to the "replacement cost" of unamortized acquisition costs.

Present value of future profits. Crazy Quilt's accountants therefore decided that the acquisition cost of McCabe's insurance in force would have to be determined by discounting future profits. How should this be done? To discover a clue, Crazy Quilt's accountants investigated the purchase negotiations in depth. All available documents were scrutinized and management personnel were interviewed at length. It was found that, while McCabe would be reporting on an adjusted basis for purposes of reports to shareholders, Crazy Quilt's management had looked to statutory earnings for valuation purposes, on the basis that it was statutory earnings that would be available for investment in new business or distribution to the parent company. Also, Crazy Quilt's management indicated that had a calculation actually been made—a precise calculation was not made prior to setting the purchase price—they would have used a discount rate of 12 percent, which expresses Crazy Quilt's general pre-tax profit objective for new business, and would have taken into account approximately 30 years of pre-tax earnings, after which present values taken at a 12 percent discount rate would generally be immaterial. In addition to expressing Crazy Quilt's profit objective, the 12 percent discount rate seemed appropriate in terms of the risk characteristics of the business.

This information provided a clue, but that's all. All that had really been accomplished was to resolve in principle that the portion of the purchase price to be allocated to McCabe's insurance in force would be computed by discounting future profits. Two critical questions loomed in the gathering murk:

▸ Which profits should be discounted?
▸ What discount rate should be used?

Which profits? While Crazy Quilt's management had statutory profits in mind when estimating the value of McCabe's insurance in force, consolidated results of operations would include McCabe's income on an *adjusted* basis. That is, income attributable to McCabe's insurance in force at the purchase date would reflect changes in reserve liabilities that had been calculated on the basis of present values appropriate at the purchase date, less amortization of the amount finally deemed to represent acquisition cost.

What Crazy Quilt's management had in mind was important, but it did not necessarily govern what should be done for accounting purposes. After all, the price paid for McCabe was also based, in part, on the basis of the relationship of the market value of McCabe's stock to McCabe's historical adjusted earnings (that is, earnings adjusted for reserves and acquisition costs computed on the basis of original assumptions). Further, McCabe would continue to report adjusted earnings to the minority interest on the basis of original-assumption reserves. There were therefore three different earnings patterns to consider: adjusted on the basis of original assumptions, adjusted on the basis of current assumptions, and statutory.

Profits adjusted on the basis of original assumptions. While original-assumption reserves would continue to be used in adjusted statements prepared for McCabe's minority interest, such reserves were essentially irrelevant to the purchase. A new basis of accountability arose at the time of the purchase; original-assumption reserves would not be used for purposes of consolidated reporting. The fact that McCabe's "historical" price-earnings ratio (where earnings reflected original-assumption reserves) was considered in evaluating the feasibility of the acquisition had no special significance. Both McCabe and Crazy Quilt were reporting on the original-assumption basis; it was the relationship of the multiples at the purchase date that was of significance. Assuming that Crazy Quilt's multiple held up, Mc-

Cabe's earnings *as reported in consolidation* would be valued at Crazy Quilt's multiple.

For purposes of valuing insurance in force, McCabe's profits adjusted on the basis of original assumptions were not given further consideration.

Profits adjusted on the basis of current assumptions. Because McCabe's results of operations would be reported in the consolidated statements on the basis of reserves adjusted to reflect current assumptions, it was tempting to conclude that profits adjusted on the basis of current assumptions should enter into the calculation of the value of insurance in force.

But such adjusted profits are not available for distribution to Crazy Quilt nor for reinvestment in new business. Assets equivalent to statutory reserves would have to be retained by McCabe, and the return on such assets would be limited to the investment earnings rate. It is fundamental to the concept of discounting future profits that such profits be available for reinvestment or distribution; otherwise nothing of substance is being discounted. Nothing discounted is still nothing.

Statutory profits. From Crazy Quilt's point of view, McCabe's statutory profits represent cash flow available for distribution to Crazy Quilt or reinvestment in new business, agency development, etc. In essence, McCabe can distribute or reinvest no more than statutory profits.*

McCabe's statutory profits represent cash flow to Crazy Quilt, and it is cash flow that should be discounted to arrive at a rational valuation. The principles involved are basically no different from the principles involved in valuing, say, an apartment house.

Thus, even though Crazy Quilt adjusted McCabe's

---

*Actually, McCabe could distribute or reinvest adjusted profits up to the point of zero statutory surplus, assuming regulatory authorities would countenance it. Such distributions might follow this general pattern:

	At Acquisition	Year 1	Year 2	Year 3
Statutory surplus	100	50	–0–	–0–
Adjusted surplus	200	200	200	250
Statutory profits		25	25	25
Adjusted profits		75	75	75
Distribution		75	75	25

Obviously there are limits on how long adjusted profits can be distributed. (Any invasion of adjusted surplus as it existed at the date of acquisition would represent a return of capital from an accounting viewpoint.)

Table 27–5.

COMPUTATION OF VALUE (AS OF JANUARY 1, 1971) OF McCABE LIFE'S INSURANCE IN FORCE

Year	Projected Statutory Profits (000)	12% Discount Factor	Present Value of Projected Statutory Profits (000)
1971	$ 1,929	.893	$ 1,723
1972	1,829	.797	1,458
1973	1,780	.712	1,267
1974	1,775	.636	1,129
1975	1,743	.567	988
1976	1,567	.507	794
1977	1,364	.452	617
1978	1,343	.404	543
1979	1,317	.361	475
1980	1,294	.322	417
1981	1,271	.287	365
1982	1,236	.257	318
1983	1,200	.229	275
1984	1,178	.205	241
1985	1,141	.183	209
1986	1,104	.163	180
1987	1,057	.146	154
1988	1,030	.130	134
1989	1,001	.116	116
1990	970	.104	101
1991	939	.093	87
1992	909	.083	75
1993	870	.074	64
1994	849	.066	56
1995	817	.059	48
1996	760	.053	40
1997	721	.047	34
1998	697	.042	29
1999	671	.037	25
2000	650	.033	21
	$35,012		$11,983

*Assumes profits are available for distribution, reinvestment, earnings per share calculations, etc. at the end of the year. The profits emerge *on the books* around the middle of the year, on the average.

reserves to a current-assumption basis, statutory profits, not adjusted profits, were discounted to determine the portion of the purchase price allocable to McCabe's insurance in force at the purchase date.

What discount rate? As indicated earlier in this chapter, Crazy Quilt's general profit objective for new business is a yield of 12 percent on surplus invested to acquire it. Among other things, that rate represents an informed evaluation of the risk associated with future statutory profits. In other words, the rate is rational. It was therefore used to discount McCabe's projected statutory profits to a present value. The calculation is shown in Table 27–5. The value assigned to McCabe's insurance in force was $11,983,000.

The discount rate is in part subjectively determined.

It depends on the type of business, the predictability of future profits (which is heavily influenced by past history), yield on alternative investments with comparable risk characteristics, and other factors. It might be lower or higher than the 12 percent used by Crazy Quilt. Determination of an appropriate discount rate will present accountants and actuaries who are involved in acquisition accounting with some challenging problems.

Reconciling adjusted reserves, statutory reserves, and the value assigned to insurance in force. The decision that statutory profits should be discounted to determine the cost to be allocated to McCabe's insurance in force was not the end of the story. Statutory profits involve increases and decreases in statutory

Table 27–6.

AMORTIZATION OF PRESENT VALUE OF FUTURE STATUTORY PROFITS OF McCABE'S LIFE INSURANCE IN FORCE AT JANUARY 1, 1971 (000 Omitted)

Year	Projected Profits	Amortization with Interest		Unamortized Balance	Amortization without Interest		Unamortized Balance
		Allocation of Projected Profits					
		12% Interest on Unamortized Balance	*Principal*		*Ratio of Projected Profits to Total*	*Amortization*	
Investment, 1–1–71				$11,983			$11,983
1971	$ 1,929	$1,438	$491	$11,492	5.5%	$659	$11,324
1972	1,829	1,379	450	11,042	5.2	623	10,701
1973	1,780	1,325	455	10,587	5.1	611	10,090
1974	1,775	1,270	505	10,082	5.1	611	9,479
1975	1,743	1,210	533	9,549	5.0	599	8,880
1976	1,567	1,146	421	9,128	4.5	539	8,341
1977	1,364	1,095	269	8,859	3.9	467	7,874
1978	1,343	1,063	280	8,579	3.8	455	7,419
1979	1,317	1,030	287	8,292	3.8	455	6,964
1980	1,294	995	299	7,993	3.7	443	6,521
1981	1,271	959	312	7,681	3.6	431	6,090
1982	1,236	922	314	7,367	3.5	419	5,671
1983	1,200	884	316	7,051	3.4	407	5,264
1984	1,178	846	332	6,719	3.4	407	4,857
1985	1,141	806	335	6,384	3.3	395	4,462
1986	1,104	766	338	6,046	3.2	383	4,079
1987	1,057	726	331	5,715	3.0	359	3,720
1988	1,030	686	344	5,371	2.9	348	3,372
1989	1,001	645	356	5,015	2.8	336	3,036
1990	970	602	368	4,647	2.8	336	2,700
1991	939	558	381	4,266	2.7	323	2,377
1992	909	512	397	3,869	2.6	312	2,065
1993	870	464	406	3,463	2.5	300	1,765
1994	849	416	433	3,030	2.4	287	1,478
1995	817	364	453	2,577	2.3	276	1,202
1996	760	309	451	2,126	2.2	264	938
1997	721	255	466	1,660	2.1	251	687
1998	697	199	498	1,162	2.0	240	447
1999	671	139	532	630	1.9	228	219
2000	650	20*	630*	–0–	1.8	219*	–0–
	$35,012				100.0%		

*Adjusted to compensate for rounding errors.

reserve liabilities, but reserve liabilities adjusted to reflect current assumptions were to be reported in the consolidated statements. It remained to reconcile statutory reserves, which lay behind the value of McCabe's insurance in force, with adjusted reserves.

A reserve at any point in time equals the present value of future benefits less the present value of future valuation premiums. In the case of statutory reserves, these present values are computed with reference to statutory requirements. In the case of adjusted reserves, they are computed with reference to a realistic (but conservative) projection of future experience.

In the case of Crazy Quilt's purchase of McCabe, it was agreed between the companies that the insurance in force could be sold by transferring the policy liabilities to a buyer along with assets having current value of $17,543,000. The value of assets to be transferred in this case was determined as the difference between the statutory policy reserves ($29,526,000) and the present value of future statutory profits ($11,983,000). The amount of assets required to be transferred with the policy obligations directly influences the value of the insurance in force.

The acquisition cost of McCabe's insurance in force is, then, the difference between the current value of assets acquired and liabilities assumed:

Policy liabilities as recorded	$27,955,000
Assets, at market	17,543,000
Acquisition cost	$10,412,000

This is also, in this case, the present value of future profits, as calculated, adjusted by the difference between statutory reserves and reserves to be recorded according to generally accepted accounting principles:

Present value of future profits		$11,983,000
Policy reserves:		
Statutory	$29,526,000	
Adjusted	27,955,000	1,571,000
		$10,412,000

Amortization of Acquisition Cost

If statutory reserves continued to be carried then acquisition cost could be amortized in proportion to expected future statutory profits. As indicated by Table 27–5, the present value of such future statutory profits is $11,983,000 in McCabe's case. Amortization of the $11,983,000, with and without interest, is shown in Table 27–6. It will be noted that amortization with 12 percent interest results in reporting, as profit, 12 percent of the declining balance of the investment, assuming that projected profits are actually earned in the projected pattern.

But Crazy Quilt has recomputed McCabe's reserves to a current-assumption basis and has thereby assigned a portion of acquisition cost to the reserves.

Acquisition cost, originally computed at $11,983,000, the present value of future statutory profits, is carried at $10,412,000; the difference, $1,571,000, represents the amount by which statutory reserves exceed current-assumption reserves at the date of acquisition.

What this means in essence is that a portion of future statutory profits has been capitalized at the interest rate assumption used for purposes of recomputing the reserves and will be amortized with interest at that same assumed rate through the operation of the reserve. The residual balance of the acquisition cost remains to be amortized in some rational and systematic fashion.

That's easier said than done. When acquisition cost is computed on the basis of holding one type of reserve, but another type of reserve is reported for statement purposes, the processes at work are very complex, and the procedures required to achieve a proper matching of revenue and expense are correspondingly complex.

What happens. The processes at work can best be explained by analyzing a simple illustration. Consider a nonparticipating ten-year pure endowment of $1,000 valued on the basis of 3 percent interest, zero mortality, and zero withdrawal. The net level premium required to fund such an endowment is $84.69. At the end of the eighth year the reserve on the business would be $775.68. The reserve would grow to $1,000 at the end of the tenth year—that is, at the time the policy endows—in the following manner:

Reserve at beginning of ninth year	$ 775,68
Net premium	84.69
Funds held one year	869.37
Interest at 3 percent	25.81
Reserve at end of ninth year	886.18
Net premium	84.69
Funds held one year	970.87
Interest at 3 percent	29.13
Endowment value	$1,000.00

Assume that the selling company, S, is charging $90 for this policy and that the interest rate actually being earned is 6 percent.

Company S then sells out to the buying company, B, at the beginning of the ninth year. Company B decides to value the business on the basis of the remaining two years of statutory profits discounted at 12 percent. The business is valued in the following manner:

	Projected	
	Year 9	Year 10
Gross premium	$ 90.00	$ 90.00
Interest on reserve:		
6% x $775.68	46.54	
6% x $886.18		53.17
Increase in reserve:		
$886.18—$775.68	(110.50)	
$1,000—$886.18		(113.82)
Endowment:		
Benefit paid $1,000.00		
Less decrease in reserve 1,000.00		
Statutory profits	$ 26.04	$ 29.35
12% discount factor	.893	.797
Present value*	$ 23.25	$ 23.39
		23.25
Amount paid for the business		$ 46.64

*Assumes profits are available at the end of the year.

Company B and Company S agree to transfer the business from S to B with transfer of assets currently valued at $729.04 ($775.68 less $46.64).

Company B proceeds to revalue the reserves to a 6 percent basis. The recomputed reserve is $750.91 and grows to the endowment value, $1,000, as follows:

Recomputed reserve at beginning of ninth year	$ 750.91
Recomputed net premium	71.57
Funds held one year	822.48
Interest at 6 percent	49.35
Recomputed reserve at end of ninth year	871.83
Net premium	71.57
Funds held one year	943.40
Interest at 6 percent	56.60
Endowment value	$1,000.00

Company B therefore has a residual acquisition cost of $21.87, as follows:

Policy liabilities assumed (as recomputed)	$750.91
Assets transferred (at market)	729.04
Acquisition cost	$ 21.87

Company B will show income before amortization on this business as follows:

	Statutory		Adjusted	
	Year 9	Year 10	Year 9	Year 10
Gross premium	$90.00	$90.00	$90.00	$90.00
Interest:				
On reserve	46.54	53.17	45.05	52.31
On excess of statutory over adjusted reserve			1.49	.86
Change in reserve	(110.50)	(113.82)	(120.92)	(128.17)
	$26.04	$29.35	$15.62	$15.00

The effect of the endorsement benefit, $1,000, at the end of Year 10 is cancelled by the release of the reserve of an equivalent amount.

If Company B continued to hold statutory reserves, the acquisition cost of $46.64 could be amortized "scientifically" against statutory profits, as follows:

Year	Beginning Balance of Acquisition Cost	Statutory Profits	12% Interest on Acquisition Cost	Amortization of Aquisition Cost	Ending Balance of Acquisition Cost
9	$46.64	$26.04	$5.60	$20.44	$26.20
10	26.20	29.35	3.15	26.20	–0–

But Company B is holding recomputed reserves and a residual acquisition cost of only $21.87. The amount capitalized in the reserve recomputation, $24.77, is effectively being amortized at 6 percent interest:

Year	Beginning Balance of Reserve Difference	Interest at 6%	Change in Reserve Difference	Total of Interest and Change in Reserve Difference
9	$24.77	$1.49	$10.42	$11.91
10	14.35	.86	14.35	15.21

The "total of interest and change in reserve difference" represents the gross amount of statutory profits discounted and capitalized at 6 percent in the form of the reserve recomputation. At 12 percent, these profits have a present value of $22.76, as follows:

Year	Gross Amount	12% Discount Factor	Present Value
9	$11.91	.893	$10.64
10	15.21	.797	12.12
			$22.76

Thus, the present value at 12 percent of the amount ($24.77) capitalized at 6 percent is $22.76. The difference between these two values, $2.01, really represents the present value, at 12 percent of interest on the reserve difference at 6 percent:

Year	6% Interest on Balance of Reserve Difference	12% Discount Factor	Present Value
9	$1.49	.893	$1.33
10	.86	.797	.68
			$2.01

"Scientific" amortization of the residual acquisition cost of $21.87 could be achieved by recomputing the residual as if the amount capitalized at 6 percent in the reserve were actually capitalized at 12 percent, as follows:

Residual acquisition cost		$21.87
Amount capitalized in reserve:		
At 6 percent	$24.77	
At 12 percent	22.76	2.01
Theoretical acquisition cost		$23.88

This amount, $23.88, can be amortized with interest at 12 percent by reducing statutory profits by the gross amounts capitalized in the reserve recomputation:

Year	Beginning Balance of Theoretical Acquisition Cost	Statutory Profits As Reported	Statutory Profits Equivalent Amount Capitalized In Reserve	Net	Interest at 12% on Acquisition Cost	Amortization of Acquisition Cost
9	$23.88	$26.04	$11.91	$14.13	$2.87	$11.26
10	12.62	29.35	15.21	14.14	1.52	12.62
						$23.88

All that's necessary now is to "back out" the $2.01 difference between residual acquisition cost and theoretical acquisition cost:

Year	Beginning Balance of $2.01 Difference	6% Interest On Reserve Difference	12% Interest on Balance of $2.01 Difference	Amortization of Difference
9	$2.01	$1.49	$.24	$1.25
10	.76	.86	.10	.76
				$2.01

The final amortization table can now be constructed:

Year	Theoretical Amortization	Amortization of $2.01 Difference	Adjusted Amortization
9	$11.26	$1.25	$10.01
10	12.62	.76	11.86
	$23.88	$2.01	$21.87

Applying this to reported adjusted profits yields the following result:

Year	Adjusted Profits Before Amortization	Amortization of Residual Acquisition Cost	Net Profits
9	$15.62	$10.01	$5.61
10	15.00	11.86	3.14

It will be found that this process yields the same result as carrying statutory reserves and amortizing the initial amount of acquisition cost, $46.64, at interest:

Year	Statutory Profits Before Amortization	Amortization of Acquisition Cost	Net Profits
9	$26.04	$20.44	$5.60*
10	29.35	26.20	3.15*

*Differs by $.01 due to roundings.

Thus it is possible to give effect to the "scientific" amortization schedule implicit in the purchase transaction even though reserves are recomputed.

Amortization with interest at the rate assumed for reserves. All of the foregoing is pretty heady stuff, and perhaps it is time to leap to a conclusion that is probably already painfully obvious: Few people will want to perform the excruciating calculations necessary to implement the "scientific" method of amortization. Nor is it necessary to use the "scientific" method. Discounting statutory profits at a risk discount rate is merely a method of computing a purchase price (and hence an acquisition cost); amortization of this cost for accounting purposes need not reconstruct the process used in arriving at the price.

Inasmuch as the portion of the purchase price capitalized in the reserve recomputation is amortized automatically, the only problem is how to amortize what's left over. Ideally, amortization of the residual should be consistent with the method of amortization implicit in the reserving process. This means amortizing the residual with interest assumed for reserving purposes, generally over the premium-paying period. To continue the example, the residual acquisition cost of $21.87 can be amortized with 6 percent interest over the premium-paying period as follows:

1. Compute the present value of gross premiums at 6 percent:

Year	Gross Premiums	6% Discount Factor	Present Value
9	$90.00	1.000	$ 90.00
10	90.00	.943	84.87
			$174.87

2. Compute the ratio of residual acquisition cost to the present value of gross premiums:

Residual acquisition cost	$ 21.87
Present value of gross premiums	$174.87
Ratio	12.51%

3. Compute the portion of the gross premium required to amortize the expense:

Gross premium	$ 90.00
Ratio from above	12.51%
Required amount	$11.26

4. Construct the amortization table:

Year	Beginning Unamortized Balance of Residual Acquisition Cost	Premium Received	Interest at 6% on Unamortized Balance of Residual Acquisition Cost	Amortization of Residual Acquisition Cost
9	$21.87	$11.26	$ .65	$10.61
10	11.25	11.26	—	11.26
				$21.87

Amortization without interest.   It is, of course, not mandatory to amortize an asset with interest. The residual acquisition cost could be amortized using the sum-of-the-years'-premium method, as follows for the example:

Year	Projected Gross Premiums	Percent of Total	Amortization of Residual Acquisition Cost
9	$ 90	50%	$10.94
10	90	50	10.93
	$180	100%	$21.87

Problems with adverse deviation.   It is entirely possible that the acquisition cost for a block of business will be based on "best estimates" as to interest, mortality, etc. If such best estimates were adhered to in recomputing reserves, there would be no particular problem in amortizing residual acquisition cost in proportion to the receipt of premiums.

However, it is likely that the recomputed reserves will provide for adverse deviation, which means that some of the profits will emerge in a manner that is "out of phase" with the receipt of premiums. In theory, profits, not premiums, are purchased in the acquisition of a block of business; and profits, not premiums, should constitute the base against which acquisition cost should be amortized.

However, the problem is really no different than the problem of pricing internally-generated new business on the basis of best estimates but accounting for such new business in a manner that provides for the risk of adverse deviation. Presumably the discount rates applied to a stream of "best estimate" profits allow for the possibility of adverse deviation, whether the frame of reference is a purchased block of business or an internally-generated block of business. So residual acquisition cost should generally be amortized against premiums.

However, this is subject to challenge where the introduction of provisions for adverse deviation, together with amortization of acquisition cost over the premium-paying period, produce apparent losses. In such cases the amortization pattern should be modified so as to allocate a portion of the acquisition cost to profits associated with release from the risk of adverse deviation. The portion so allocated would be equal to the present value of the apparent losses, provided of course that the computation of such present value is consistent with the principles of loss recognition.

Excess interest.   One of the reasons for computing a purchase price on the basis of discounted statutory profits is that assets equivalent to the statutory reserves are withheld from distribution and must be invested in relatively safe assets with relatively low yields. Thus, for example, investment income equal, say, to 6 percent of the reserves is discounted at a risk rate, say 12 percent.

It would be possible—and usually defensible—to amortize acquisition cost in relation to premiums and interest on the excess of the statutory reserve over the recomputed reserve. In the example used previously, this would be accomplished as follows:

1. Calculate excess interest:

| | Interest at 6% on | | | Present Value of Excess |
Year	Statutory Reserve	Adjusted Reserve	Excess	At 6%
9	$46.54	$45.05	$1.49	$1.41
10	53.17	52.31	.86	.76
				$2.17

2. Calculate the present value of premiums and excess interest:

Year	Premiums *	Excess Interest	Total	Present Value At 6%
9	$90.00	$1.49	$91.49	$ 86.28
10	90.00	.86	90.86	80.86
				$167.14

*Assumed for simplicity to be received at the end of the year.

3. Calculate the ratio of residual acquisition cost to the present value of premiums and excess interest:

Residual acquisition cost	$21.87
Present value of premiums and excess interest	$167.14
Ratio	13.08%

4. Compute the "payments" deemed to be received in each year:

Year	Premiums and Excess Interest Received	"Payment" —13.08%
9	$91.49	$11.97
10	90.86	11.88

5. Construct the amortization table:

Year	Beginning Balance of Residual Acquisition Cost	"Payment" Received	Interest At 6% on Balance of Residual Acquisition Cost	Amortization of Residual Acquisition Cost
9	$21.87	$11.97	$1.31	$10.66
10	11.21	11.88	.67	11.21
				$21.87

The question arises as to why it would be proper to do this for purchased business but not for business generated internally. One answer would be that in theory there is nothing wrong with doing it for business generated internally; the investment in the excess of statutory over adjusted reserves could be viewed as generating revenue available to absorb the amortization of acquisition costs.

A better answer, however, is that when a purchase price is determined by discounting statutory profits, a *specific* portion of the price is directly associated with interest on the excess reserves. This is not true of business generated internally; acquisition cost is equal to dollars paid out for commissions, underwriting, issue expenses, etc. Such an association could be imputed for business generated internally, of course; this would give some degree of accounting recognition to the internal rate of return on the investment of statutory surplus. But to the extent that interest on the excess reserves is specifically paid for, as it frequently is in a purchase transaction, there is a potential for relatively greater distortion in reported income if such interest is ignored in amortizing the purchase price.

Crazy Quilt. Crazy Quilt elected to amortize the residual acquisition cost ($10,412,000) of McCabe's insurance in force over 30 years in proportion to premiums and with interest at a level 4 percent, which was believed to be a reasonable approximation of the overall effective reserve rate during the period.

The mechanics of the process are set forth in Table 27–7.

Special Problems in Valuing Insurance in Force

Losses. It would be possible, though unlikely, that a gross premium valuation of a purchased block of business at the time of acquisition, employing loss recognition principles, would indicate a loss, even after substantially eliminating provisions for adverse deviation.

In general, such apparent loss should be considered to be a part of goodwill. Companies do not generally purchase losses, and in the absence of evidence of error or sheer ignorance or incompetence, rationality can be presumed.

Assuming there *is* evidence of error or sheer ignorance or incompetence, then the amount of the loss should be charged to income, presumably as an extraordinary item.

Negative acquisition cost. It would be possible for negative acquisition cost to arise in a purchase under certain circumstances.

Consider, for example, a paid-up endowment for $1,000 valued (for statutory reserve purposes) at 3 percent interest and zero mortality. In the year prior to maturity, the reserve on the endowment would be $970.87. If the earned interest rate is 6 percent, then the final year's profits would be reckoned as follows:

Table 27–7.

AMORTIZATION WITH 4% INTEREST OF RESIDUAL ACQUISITION COST OF McCABE'S LIFE INSURANCE IN FORCE (000 Omitted)

	Projected Gross Premiums	4% Discount Factor	Present Value of Projected Gross Premiums	18.12% of Projected Gross Premiums	4% Interest on Unamortized Balance	Amortization of "Principal"	Unamortized Balance of Residual Acquisition Cost
Investment, 1–1–71							$10,412
1971	$ 5,510	.962	$ 5,300	$ 998	$416	$ 582	$ 9,830
1972	5,224	.925	4,832	947	393	554	9,276
1973	5,084	.889	4,520	921	371	550	8,726
1974	5,069	.855	4,334	919	349	570	8,156
1975	4,978	.822	4,092	902	326	576	7,580
1976	4,475	.790	3,535	811	303	508	7,072
1977	3,895	.760	2,960	706	283	423	6,649
1978	3,835	.731	2,803	695	266	429	6,220
1979	3,761	.703	2,644	681	249	432	5,788
1980	3,695	.676	2,498	669	232	437	5,351
1981	3,630	.650	2,360	658	214	444	4,907
1982	3,530	.625	2,206	640	196	444	4,463
1983	3,327	.600	1,996	603	179	424	4,039
1984	3,164	.577	1,826	573	161	412	3,627
1985	2,959	.555	1,642	536	145	391	3,236
1986	2,753	.534	1,470	499	129	370	2,866
1987	2,519	.513	1,292	456	114	342	2,524
1988	2,341	.494	1,156	424	101	323	2,201
1989	2,159	.475	1,025	391	88	303	1,898
1990	1,870	.456	853	339	76	263	1,635
1991	1,682	.439	738	305	65	240	1,395
1992	1,496	.422	631	271	56	215	1,180
1993	1,385	.406	562	251	47	204	976
1994	1,325	.390	517	240	39	201	775
1995	1,133	.375	425	205	31	174	601
1996	971	.361	350	176	24	152	449
1997	859	.347	298	156	18	138	311
1998	690	.333	230	125	12	113	198
1999	616	.321	198	112	8	104	94
2000	556	.308	171	101	7	94	–0–
	$84,491			$15,310		$10,412	

Present value of projected gross premiums	$57,464
Residual acquisition cost	$10,412
Ratio of residual acquisition cost to projected gross premiums	18.12%

Interest on reserve		
(6% X $970.87)		$58.25
Increase in reserve		
($1,000—$970.87)		29.13
		29.12
Endowment benefit:		
Payment	$1,000	
Reserve released	1,000	–0–
Profit		$29.12

Now assume that a buyer pays $26.00 for the business, which represents the profits discounted at 12 percent, and also revalues the reserve to a 6 percent basis. The recomputed reserve would be $943.39, or $27.48 less than statutory reserve. This would produce a negative acquisition cost of $1.48:

	Asset	*Liability*
Statutory	$ 26.00	$970.87
Effect of recomputing reserve	(27.48)	(27.48)
Adjusted basis	$ (1.48)	$943.39

The negative acquisition cost arises because of the effect of discounting profits at one interest rate while discounting future benefits at another. Viewed another way, the negative acquisition cost arises simply because the buyer insists on a profit on the paid-up business. In the absence of a provision for adverse deviation, there are theoretically no future profits to be had on paid-up business simply because there are no future premiums to be had.

The negative acquisition cost cannot be taken into profit immediately; profits are not created by a purchase. Nor should the negative acquisition cost serve to reduce goodwill, because it is directly associated with a specifically identifiable intangible asset.

Instead, the negative acquisition cost should be amortized over the life of the business, preferably by increasing the reserve by a like amount. This could be accomplished by providing for a series of "endowments" (the present value of which is equal to the negative acquisition cost) which follow the pattern of (1) provisions for adverse deviation, to the extent of such provisions, and (2) changes in the difference between the statutory reserve and the recomputed reserve, to the extent of any amount remaining after offsetting provisions for adverse deviation.

Alternatively, negative acquisition cost could be separately amortized over the life of the business in some rational and systematic manner.

Implications of Not Assigning Part of the Purchase Price to Insurance in Force

Insurance in force is an identifiable intangible asset with a limited term of existence, and the cost of that asset should be amortized against related earnings over the period that those earnings will be generated. Failure to do so means inevitably that the earnings attributable to insurance in force is overstated. The overstatement can be material.

Some argue that, even assuming that some portion of the purchase price is allocable to insurance in force, any such value is not diminished with the passage of time, and it can therefore be treated the same as goodwill. This argument is without merit. The "asset" represented by insurance in force diminishes in value with the passage of time. The fact that new insurance replaces the old is tangential. Future profits on new issues cannot, under generally accepted accounting principles, be recognized. Future profits attributable to an indentifiable block of business in force can be recognized—and should be recognized—if they are embodied in an exchange transaction.

Restatement of reserves on the basis of current assumptions generally results in capitalizing a significant portion of the allocable purchase price. However, unless the adjusted reserves are substantially equivalent to gross premium reserves, there will generally be some positive amount associated with future profits. This positive amount should be amortized against the profits as they emerge.

Some believe that it would be proper, as a practical matter, to include any residual value of insurance in force with goodwill, to be amortized over, say, 40 years.* However, the rate of amortization applied to goodwill may not be appropriate with respect to the portion of goodwill representing the investment in insurance in force. For example, straight-line amortization over 40 years would result in an annual writeoff of 2 1/2 percent. In McCabe's case, amortization without interest would be 5.5 percent in the first year, decreasing to 1.8 percent in the thirtieth year (see Table 27–6). The difference in amortization occasioned by such differential rates of amortization can be material.

The pattern of amortizing goodwill could of course

---

*Accounting Principles Board Opinion No. 17 permits goodwill arising after November 1970 to be amortized over a reasonable period but no more than 40 years. "The straight line method of amortization . . . should be applied unless a company demonstrates that another systematic method is more appropriate." [6]

Table 27–8.

COMPUTATION OF VALUE OF McCABE LIFE'S AGENCY PLANT AT JANUARY 1, 1971

Valuation of production:

Year	Production (000,000)	Production Growth Rate	12% Present Value of Profits At Issue (000)			Mean Present Value Of Profits Per $1,000
			Statutory	Adjusted	Mean	
1967	$55	15%	$ 78	$316	$197	$3.58
1968	62	13	97	278	188	3.02
1969	69	11	110	304	207	3.00
1970	77	12	124	293	209	2.71
1971 estimated	85	10	142	315	229	2.69
5-year average						$3.00

Valuation of agency:

Year	Assumed Production Growth Rate	Estimated Production (000,000)	Estimated Present Value Of Profits ' At $3.00 Per $1,000 (000)	Discount		Discounted Value of Agency Plant (000)
				Rate	Factor*	
1971	10%	$ 85	$ 255	10%	.909	$ 232
1972	10	94	282	11	.812	229
1973	9	102	306	12	.712	218
1974	9	111	333	13	.613	204
1975	8	120	360	14	.519	187
1976	8	130	390	15	.432	168
1977	8	140	420	15	.376	158
1978	8	151	453	15	.327	148
1979	8	163	489	15	.284	139
1980	8	176	528	15	.247	130
1981	7	188	564	15	.215	121
1982	7	201	603	15	.186	112
1983	7	215	645	15	.162	105
1984	7	230	690	15	.141	97
1985	7	246	738	15	.123	91
1986	6	261	783	15	.107	84
1987	6	277	831	15	.093	77
1988	6	294	882	15	.081	71
1989	6	311	933	15	.070	65
1990	6	330	990	15	.061	60
1991	5	346	1,038	15	.053	55
1992	5	364	1,092	15	.046	50
1993	5	382	1,146	15	.040	46
1994	5	401	1,203	15	.035	42
1995	5.	421	1,263	15	.030	38
Rounding						23
						$2,950

*Ignores the fact that production occurs sometime before the end of the year, on the average. Partial offset was achieved by rounding up the value to $2,950,000.

be modified to recognize the pattern of amortization appropriate to the acquisition cost of insurance in force; it is not necessary to amortize goodwill on a straight-line basis. Even so, however, acquisition cost of insurance in force is not goodwill and should not be so labeled in the balance sheet.

Value of Agency Plant

After assigning a portion of the purchase price to McCabe's insurance in force, Crazy Quilt's accountants found that a value of $2,950,000 had been ascribed to McCabe's agency force. In this case the

Table 27–9.

ALLOCATION OF PURCHASE PRICE OF McCABE LIFE, COMPUTATION OF CHARGE TO CRAZY QUILT'S SURPLUS, AND RECORDING THE PURCHASE AS OF JANUARY 1, 1971 (000 Omitted)

	Statutory Balance Sheet	Purchase Valuation	Recording the Purchase for Purposes of GAAP Consolidation	
			Adjustments	Pro-Forma
Assets				
Bonds	$15,359	$14,138		$14,138
Common stocks	2,370	2,270		2,270
Mortgage loans	13,524	12,848		12,848
Real estate	1,087	1,330		1,330
Policy loans	1,461	1,461		1,461
Cash	325	325		325
	34,126	32,372		32,372
Deferred and uncollected premiums	860	860	$ (860)	
Accrued investment income	277	277		277
Other assets	159	159		159
Non-admitted assets		396		396
Value of insurance in force		11,983	(1,571)	10,412
Value of agency plant		2,950	(2,950)	
Unidentfied goodwill		1,233	2,950	4,183
	35,422	50,230		47,799
Equities				
Insurance reserves:				
Benefits	30,386	30,386	(2,671)	27,715
Renewal expenses			240	240
Claims and other policy liabilities	524	524		524
Federal income taxes	52	52		52
Other liabjlities	218	218		218
Mandatory securities valuation reserve	932			
Liability for unauthorized reinsurance	120			
	32,232	31,180		28,749
NET ASSETS	$ 3,190	$19,050	$ –0–	$19,050
90% INTEREST	$ 2,871	$17,145		$17,145
Cost in excess of statutory net assets, charged against Crazy Quilt's surplus for statutory purposes:				
Stockholder's investment—90% x $19,050		$17,145		
Statutory net assets—90% x $3,190		2,871		
Charge to surplus		$14,274		

calculation had actually been made by Crazy Quilt's management. Crazy Quilt had projected the future production of McCabe's agents and agents expected to be added to the sales force in the future. In other words, the agency plant's "momentum" was recognized in the calculation. Production was priced at $3.00 per $1,000, which was based on the average present value (discounted at 12 percent) at issue of McCabe's production for the most recent five years (including 1971 on an estimated basis). The extended values were then discounted at an interest rate in-creasing from 10 percent in the first year to 15 percent in the sixth and subsequent years. This discount rate series reflected the risk that expectations as to the agency plant's performance would not be fulfilled. The net result was to discount profits first by 12 percent, then again by 10 to 15 percent. The result was a conservative estimate of the value of the agency plant. Details of the calculation are shown in Table 27–8.

Crazy Quilt's accountants were concerned about what to do with the computed value of the agency plant. Should it be regarded as the cost of an identi-

Table 27–10.

RECORDING THE PURCHASE OF McCABE LIFE FOR CONSOLIDATION PURPOSES ON JANUARY 1, 1971 (000 Omitted)

	McCabe Life's Statutory Accounts	McCabe Life's GAAP Accounts	Consolidating Effect of Investment on Crazy Quilt's Books	Consolidating Adjustments and Eliminations Dr (Cr)	Pro-Forma Consolidated GAAP Accounts
Assets:					
Bonds	$15,359	$15,359		$ (1,221)	$14,138
Common stocks—McCabe	2,370	1,968		302	2,270
Common stocks—Crazy Quilt			$17,145	(17,145)	
Mortgage loans	13,524	13,524		(676)	12,848
Real estate	1,087	1,087		243	1,330
Policy loans	1,461	1,461			1,461
Cash	325	325			325
	34,126	33,724	17,145		32,372
Deferred and uncollected premiums	860				
Accrued investment income	277	277			277
Other assets	159	159			159
Non-admitted assets	396				396
Deferred acquisition costs		7,913		(7,913)	
Value of insurance in force				10,412	10,412
Goodwill				4,183	4,183
	35,422	42,469	17,145		47,799
Liabilities:					
Insurance reserves:					
Benefits	30,386	29,847		2,132	27,715
Renewal expenses		188		(52)	240
Claims and other policy liabilities	524	524			524
Federal income taxes:					
Current	52	52			52
Deferred		2,166		2,166	
Other liabilities	218	218			218
Mandatory securities valuation reserve	932				
Liability for unauthorized reinsurance	120				
Minority interest				(1,905)	1,905
	32,232	32,995	–0–		30,654
Capital and surplus:					
Paid-in capital	1,000	1,000	17,145	1,000	17,145
Earned surplus	2,180	8,474		8,474	
RECORDED NET ASSETS	$ 3,190	$ 9,474	$17,145	$ –0–	$17,145

fiable intangible asset, or should it be lumped together with the unidentifiable intangibles (i.e., goodwill)?

It was decided that the value of the agency plant was too ambiguous a quantity to be accounted for as a specifically identifiable intangible asset. Insurance in force represented a definable block of paying business, but the value of the agency plant was com-puted on the basis of highly speculative futures. The degree of uncertainty attending the estimate of the value of the agency plant was such as to constitute a substantive difference from the uncertainty associated with projecting future profits on insurance in force. Accordingly, the value of the agency plant was recorded as goodwill.

Table 27–11.

McCABE LIFE'S 1971 INCOME STATEMENTS SEGREGATED BETWEEN BUSINESS ACQUIRED IN PURCHASE AND NEW BUSINESS (000 Omitted)

	Pre-1971 Business		1971 Business Statutory (Principally CRVM Reserves)	Adjusted*	Pre-1971 Business and 1971 New Business Combined	
	Statutory	Adjusted			Statutory	Adjusted
Revenue:						
Premiums	$5,510	$5,510	$ 1,163	$ 1,163	$6,673	$ 6,673
Net investment income:						
On assets equal to book basis of reserves	1,746	1,212	6	(20)	1,752	1,192
On assets equal to additional reserves required to be held for statutory purposes		534		26		560
On other assets					399	399
Total net investment income	1,746	1,746	6	6	2,151	2,151
Total revenue	7,256	7,256	1,169	1,169	8,824	8,824
Benefits paid or provided:						
Death claims	1,098	1,098	45	45	1,143	1,143
Surrenders	1,404	1,404			1,404	1,404
Other	140	140			140	140
Change in benefit reserves	1,890	1,863	261	586	2,151	2,449
Total benefits paid or provided	4,532	4,505	306	631	4,838	5,136
Revenue less benefits	2,724	2,751	863	538	3,986	3,688
Insurance expenses:						
Commissions	508	508	947	947	1,455	1,455
General expenses	287	287	1,310	1,310	1,597	1,597
Change in acquisition cost reserves				(1,324)		(1,324)
Change in maintenance expense reserves		62		44		106
Total insurance expenses	795	857	2,257	977	3,052	1,834
Income before amortization, federal income taxes, and minority interest	1,929	1,894	(1,394)	(439)	934	1,854
Amortization of purchased insurance in force	–0–	582	–0–	–0–	–0–	582
Income before amortization of goodwill, federal income taxes, and minority interest	$1,929	$1,312	$(1,394)	$ (439)	934	1,272
Amortization of goodwill					–0–	104
Income before federal income taxes and minority interest					934	1,168
Provision for federal income taxes:						
Current					52	52
Deferred						82
					52	134
Net income before minority interest					882	1,034
Minority interest in net income					88	103
NET INCOME IN CONSOLIDATION					$ 794	$ 931

*Modified adjusted reserve basis. Development and overhead totaling $640,000, classified as acquisition costs by McCabe, were expensed for accounting purposes.

Goodwill

Crazy Quilt's auditors had now accounted for all but $1,233,000 of the purchase price. This was regarded as general goodwill, attributable primarily to the expertise of McCabe's management.

This amount, together with the value of the agency plant ($2,950,000), was recorded as purchased goodwill of $4,183,000.

Table 27–9 sets forth McCabe's statutory balance sheet, summarizes the allocation of the purchase price, and shows the method of recording the purchase used by Crazy Quilt's accountants.

McCabe's books were not affected by the purchase; all entries were made only in consolidation. Consolidating working papers, and pro forma consolidated accounts, are shown in Table 27–10.

Table 27–11 sets forth McCabe's 1971 income statements on several bases. The statements are segregated between pre-1971 business (i.e., the insurance in force at the date of purchase) and 1971 new business. The effect on the consolidated income statement is shown in the last column in Table 27–11.

Other Approaches

It should be recognized that the treatment of purchase transactions described in this chapter is only one of several different possible approaches. While the suggested method appears to be reasonably consistent with authoritative literature, other methods can also be regarded as being consistent with authoritative literature. At least nine different methods of accounting for purchased insurance in force have been identified thus far;* the differences among them run to the assumptions to be employed in calculating the reserves on the acquired business.

It remains to be seen whether one method will come to be used predominantly, or whether an official body prescribes the use of one method. Until such time as a method becomes generally accepted, the methods and assumptions used to account for purchased life insurance companies should be described in some detail in the financial statements.

Inter-Company Relationships

Accounting for New Business

In a business combination involving two or more life insurance companies which retain their separate identities, the question arises as to how new business reserve assumptions should be established. That is, should they be developed separately for each company?*

Obviously it is more convenient to use one set of assumptions across the board than to use separate assumptions for each company. Only one basic set of reserve factors needs to be developed. It is easier to make the valuations. In some cases all of the companies can be combined into one model and the adjustments to a generally accepted accounting principles basis can be made *en toto* on a consolidating worksheet.

Where the separate companies are really extensions of the parent's ego, this approach may be perfectly valid. For example, where assets are shifted among companies primarily for tax reasons, it makes little sense to look to individual company investment results to support a reserve interest rate assumption. It makes a great deal more sense to combine the investment results of the companies to support a "consolidated" interest rate assumption.

Similarly, items of expense can within limits be allocated among companies arbitrarily. A parent might, for example, perform underwriting chores for a subsidiary for the parent's incremental cost; the subsidiary's unit underwriting cost might be, say, half the parent's. It seems inappropriate to calculate acquisition costs separately for each company in this case.

On the other hand, where the constituent companies are ruggedly independent, calculating assumptions on a combined basis would normally not be appropriate. Where each company pursues its own investment program, for example, the interest rate assumption should be established in terms of each company's experience and prospects. Where each company controls its own agency operations and incurs its expenses in arm's-length transactions, expense factors should be computed separately for each company.

Criteria for independence. There are no stringent rules for gauging the independence of the members of a business combination for purposes of determining whether to use a common set of assumptions or to use a separate set for each company. The determination is based on the degree of independence, which can never be total, and is partly subjective.

However, when all transactions are at arm's length, when the parent's announced policy is that its subsidiaries shall operate autonomously, when all available evidence indicates that the subsidiaries do in fact operate autonomously, when operating management of the subsidiary differs from that of the parent, and

---

*The methods are described in a paper dated December 14, 1973, prepared by Gary Corbett for the Committee on Financial Reporting Principles of the American Academy of Actuaries.

*This problem, of course, does not arise in the case of a merger, because the assets and liabilities of the acquired company or companies are assumed by the acquiring company, and subsequent new business assumptions are necessarily homogeneous.

when the composition of the board of directors of the subsidiary substantially differs from that of the parent's board, independence can generally be presumed.

Separate statements of subsidiaries. When a common set of assumptions is used, problems arise if separate statements of subsidiaries must be presented. The problem is acute if such separate statements are part of a filing with the Securities and Exchange Commission in which an accountants' report must accompany each statement, or if separate statements are included in an annual report to shareholders.* Briefly stated, the problem is this: while a common set of assumptions may be entirely appropriate for consolidated statements, such assumptions may be entirely inappropriate for the separate statements of the constituents.

There is no easy answer; the problem is really the lack of independence of the subsidiary, and no method of developing assumptions will overcome the basic deficiency of the separate statements. (The deficiency, it might be noted, runs to the statutory statements, too.)

The most satisfactory solution seems to be to present the separate statements on either a statutory basis or an adjusted basis and explain their relationship to the consolidated statements. The fact is that the separate statements may not be particularly meaningful taken alone, and if this is the case, it should be clearly spelled out.

Sale of a subsidiary. Sale of a subsidiary will usually give rise to a gain or loss. When the subsidiary has been accounted for as a separate entity, and reserves have been calculated based on assumptions unique to the subsidiary, the carrying value of the subsidiary is the proper basis for recognizing gain or loss.

Some believe that when a common set of factors has been used, the carrying value of the subsidiary is not the proper basis for recognizing gain or loss. They believe that reserves should be restated to reflect the assumptions that would be appropriate for the subsidiary taken as a separate entity.

However, sale of the subsidiary may be viewed as (1) a sale of the specific assets held by the subsidiary and (2) a transfer of a pro rata share of the combined organization's liabilities. Under this view, the carrying value of the subsidiary is the proper one.

*Existence of a minority interest would generally preclude extensive inter-company dealings, particularly dealings that might be construed to be detrimental to the interests of the minority shareholders. Hence assumptions might be developed separately in such cases.

As a practical matter, restatement of the reserves and the resulting modification of recorded gain or loss would offset. So long as both items are reported in the same statement, there seems to be little reason to restate the reserves. There is some question as to whether a meaningful restatement could be made in any event.

When adjustments are made *en toto* for the combined organization—for example, when a single model is used to compute adjusted reserves for all subsidiaries—the adjustment must be allocated between the subsidiary being sold and the remaining subsidiaries for purposes of computing the gain or loss. Generally this will not prove to be particularly difficult, since each subsidiary's input to the model is usually identifiable. When this is not the case—when, for example, common valuation cells are combined—it may be necessary to develop a separate model of the subsidiary being sold, and use that model to compute gain or loss as well as to remove the subsidiary's insurance in force from the master model.

Inter-Company Profits

It sometimes happens that a parent or subsidiary performs services for other constituents of the business combination at a profit. For example, one company may perform underwriting and issue services for all companies, or lend agency support, for fees that include a profit margin.

To the extent that the costs of such services are capitalized as acquisition costs or development expenses, then inter-company profits are also being capitalized. Any such profits are in the nature of inter-company profits in fixed assets and should be dealt with accordingly.

20-to-50 Percent Equity Investments

Accounting Principles Board Opinion No. 18 requires that the equity method of accounting be used not only for investments in unconsolidated subsidiaries but also generally for an investment in 20 percent or more of the voting stock of any other investee. In the absence of evidence to the contrary, such an investment leads to a presumption that the investor "has the ability to exercise significant influence over an investee."[7] Under these circumstances the Board has concluded that the equity method is superior to the cost method or the market value method.

In recent years many insurance and non-insurance companies have taken sizable minority positions in the common stocks of life insurance companies; 20-to-50 percent investments in life companies are fairly common.

Application of Opinion No. 18 can create difficult problems for the investor where

▸ The life insurance investee reports on the statutory basis, the investor reports on a generally accepted basis, and the investor's equity in the earnings of the investee, is, or may be, material;

▸ There is a significant difference between cost of the investment and equity in underlying net assets of the investee; and/or

▸ The investor is another life insurance company whose accounts are adjusted to a generally accepted basis, and the investee also adjusts its accounts but uses a materially different method of doing so.

While a 20 percent or greater investment may lead to a presumption of influence, it could well be that such influence may not be sufficient to induce the investee to modify its accounting practices to suit the investor's convenience.

Reporting the Equity in Statutory Earnings

Although Opinion No. 18 is silent on the subject, there is a presumption that the equity method of accounting will be applied to an investee's net income determined in conformity with generally accepted accounting principles.

This may not be possible if the investee reports on a statutory basis and information is not available to convert the investee's accounts to a generally accepted basis. Normally information would be available for conversion of many statutory statement items, such as reclassification of various surplus entries. However, information would normally not be available with respect to reserve and acquisition cost adjustments, restrictions on participating profits, carrying values and net income effects of insurance subsidiaries, and the like.

Yet the investor's equity in such adjustments may be material to the investor's net income, assets, or net worth. Unfortunately it may not be possible to determine whether the adjustments are material or not; for example, the equity in reported statutory net income may not be material, but the equity in adjusted net income—assuming it could be computed—could very well turn out to be material. Educated guesses as to the range of the adjustment can be made, and may be appropriate in some cases. It is fair to say, however, that such guesses often fall wide of the mark.

When the effect is not known, or when there is reason to believe that the effect is material, the accountant has little choice but to issue a qualified opinion, a disclaimer, or, in the extreme case, an adverse opinion.

Such a state of affairs might, together with other information, indicate that the presumption of investor influence on the investee's affairs is not warranted. In that case the investor could perhaps revert to the cost basis of accounting for the investment, thereby solving the problem.

Cost in Excess of Book Value

An investor typically acquires a large minority interest in an investee by purchase on the open market or in negotiated transactions with holders of large blocks of the stock. In virtually every case the cost of the stock will differ from the related pro rata share of net assets; usually the cost will be greater.

Opinion No. 18 states that the difference should be allocated to specific accounts of the investee, if practicable; otherwise "the difference should be considered to be goodwill and amortized over a period not to exceed forty years." [8]

In the case of a life insurance investee it will rarely, if ever, be practicable to assign cost in excess of book value to specific accounts. Therefore the difference must be accounted for as goodwill.

However, consideration should be given to recognizing, even indirectly, that a portion of the excess cost is attributable to future profits on insurance in force at the date of purchase. Whether book value is stated on a statutory or generally accepted basis, subsequent earnings of the block of business in force on the purchase date typically follow a declining pattern. Absent this condition, it may be deemed appropriate to amortize goodwill on a straight-line basis. Recognizing the condition would generally call for amortizing goodwill by a modified declining-balance method.

Inconsistent Adjusted Accounts

Occasionally a life insurance company which reports on an adjusted basis will have an investment of 20 percent or greater in a life insurance investee which also reports on an adjusted basis which differs significantly from that of the investor.

Because the investor does not have majority control there can be no presumption that the investee's reports are prepared primarily for the benefit of the investor. Therefore, there can be no presumption of control over the investee's accounting practices, even if the investor's influence is sufficient for the investment to qualify for the equity method of accounting. There is no basis for conforming the investee's accounting practices to those of the investor.*

Where the investor's equity in the earnings and/or net assets of a life insurance investee (or investees) is material to the investor's financial statements, and the accounting policies of the investee or investees differ markedly from those of the investor, accounting policies followed by the investee or investees should preferably be described in notes to the financial statements, if the inconsistencies are such as to be themselves material in relation to the investor's financial statements.

Consolidation Policies

The life insurance audit guide suggests some broad guidelines for determining when consolidation of financial statements is appropriate. In general, the guide suggests that consolidation may be appropriate when the group is "engaged in diverse financial services." [9]

"Diverse financial services" has been interpreted quite broadly by many companies. In fact, some companies present consolidated statements that variously include life insurance, property-liability insurance, banking, savings and loan, general agencies, real estate, equities distribution, broadcasting and other entertainment forms, airlines, manufacturing, and other types of operations.

Subject to rules of the Securities and Exchange Commission, it would appear that consolidation would generally be appropriate to display the aggregate resources and liabilities, aggregate results of operations, and aggregate financial activities of a business enterprise. After all, management is responsible for the total operations, and to the extent that the financial statements purport to report on management's stewardship, presentation of anything less than consolidated statements would not fully reflect such stewardship.

Of course, as the guide suggests, "Consideration should be given to the presentation of separate financial statements of significant subsidiaries or operating groups" [10] when consolidated statements are presented.**

---

*As indicated earlier, when the investee is a subsidiary the accounting practices *should* be conformed with those of the parent.

**See Ernst & Ernst's *Financial Reporting Trends—Life Insurance Edition* for information on current consolidation policies and practices.

Stock Companies Controlled by Mutual Companies

Some mutual life insurance companies own or control stock life insurance subsidiaries. The life insurance audit guide applies to stock companies but not to mutual companies. How should a mutual company report its equity in a stock life insurance subsidiary?

Wholly-Owned Subsidiaries

If a mutual company owns 100 percent of a stock subsidiary, the subsidiary is in the nature of a branch of the mutual company and its accounts should be prepared on the same basis as is followed by the mutual company parent. Therefore the mutual company's equity in the stock company subsidiary would be stated on a basis that is consistent with the accounting principles applicable to the mutual company.

There is no reason why the financial statements of a stock life insurance subsidiary should not be consolidated with the financial statements of the controlling mutual company if there is no substantive difference between a branch and a subsidiary, but prevailing practice is to report the equity in the subsidiary as an investment and to report the change in the carrying value of the investment in the surplus account.

Interestingly, one mutual company with a material foreign branch was recently confronted with the prospect of having to convert the branch to a stock subsidiary because of certain requirements of the foreign government. Because the branch was so large the mutual company made plans to consolidate the statements of the two entities, and obtained the approval of the domiciliary state to issue consolidated statements. It turned out that it was not necessary to convert the branch to a subsidiary, so the plan was never carried out; but the event does suggest that such a consolidation is feasible and may sometimes be desirable.

Partially-Owned Subsidiaries

Some mutual companies own an interest in a stock life insurance subsidiary some of whose stock is publicly held. Often mutual companies currently own 100 percent of a stock company subsidiary or a downstream life insurance holding company but intend to distribute part of the stock to the public eventually.

When a portion of the subsidiary's stock is publicly-owned it would usually be necessary or desirable to prepare statements of the subsidiary that conform with generally accepted accounting principles. But the mutual company's interest in the subsidiary should continue to be reported on the basis of accounting principles applicable to the mutual company.

Disclosure

All pertinent details of an acquisition, whether effected by means of a pooling or purchase, should be described in notes to the financial statements in the year of acquisition, and principles of consolidation should be described every year. In Crazy Quilt's case, appropriate disclosure might be as follows:

ACCOUNTING POLICIES NOTE:

The accounts of the Company and its 90%-owned life insurance subsidiary, McCabe Life Insurance Company, are included in the accompanying consolidated financial statements. All significant inter-company accounts and transactions have been eliminated in consolidation. The excess of cost over net assets (measured at fair value) at the date of acquisition of McCabe Life Insurance Com-

pany is being amortized by the straight-line method over 40 years.

OTHER NOTE:

On January 1, 1971, the Company acquired 90% of the issued and outstanding common stock of McCabe Life Insurance Company for cash of $5,000,000 and stock having a fair market value of $12,145,000. The excess of cost over the fair value of net assets acquired, which excess was $4,183,000, is being amortized at the rate of $104,000 a year. Revenues and net income after minority interest applicable to McCabe Life Insurance Company in 1971 were $8,824,000 and $931,000, respectively.

The methods used to account for policy reserves and the acquisition cost assigned to purchased insurance in force, and relevant amounts, should be described in the notes which set forth the details of reserves and acquisition costs. Generally the methods used to account for purchased insurance in force differ significantly from methods used with respect to direct business, and it is preferable to treat purchased business as a separate line of business for disclosure purposes where the amounts are material.

28   Conversion Mechanics

Anyone who has endured the first 27 chapters of this book or who has actually participated in a conversion to generally accepted accounting principles will recognize the need to use all available means to ease the task of conversion, consistent of course with necessary standards of quality.

"Easing" the conversion may consist of doing less work or it may consist of doing more work. Properly administering a conversion means more work but fewer disasters. Reserve models mean less work. Techniques of recording adjustments suggested in this chapter do not seem to increase or reduce the time required for a conversion but assist in making sure that none of the adjustments is omitted through simple oversight.

Administering a Conversion

A conversion to generally accepted accounting principles involves, among other things, an enormous administrative effort. Proper administration will greatly improve the chances for a successful conversion. "Proper administration" consists primarily of organizing, planning, and documenting a conversion.

Organization of the Conversion Effort

The task of converting to generally accepted accounting principles is a difficult one; the effort required to do it is usually underestimated. As a result, the conversion effort is typically understaffed. Crises often develop at the last minute.

A company converting to generally accepted accounting principles should staff the effort adequately. In general, an adequate staffing effort requires:

- A top-level executive with overall policy responsibility;
- A conversion chairman;
- A supervisor of accounting applications, with appropriate staff support;
- A supervisor of actuarial applications, with appropriate staff support;
- A supervisor of data processing applications, unless data processing is comprehended under one of the functions listed above; and
- Coordinators for subsidiaries, if any.

Conversion Timetable

Work on an initial conversion to generally accepted accounting principles should begin at least six months prior to the date as of which the statements will be prepared. Larger, more complex companies should plan on devoting more time to the effort—perhaps as much as a year.

A target date should be established for each significant step in the conversion. The "critical path" should be well-defined.

Table 28–1 summarizes the timetable used by Crazy Quilt Life for its initial conversion.

Planning Meetings

The company should meet with its independent accountants and consulting actuaries at the earliest opportunity to

- Establish basic technical ground rules for the conversion,

Table 28–1

TIMETABLE FOR INITIAL CONVERSION TO GENERALLY ACCEPTED ACCOUNTING PRINCIPLES*

3–15	Complete preliminary summary of proposal and obtain concurrence of top management.
4–15	Meet with independent accountants and consulting actuaries to review preliminary summary and discuss basic principles and methods.
4–30	Obtain agreement on basic principles and methods among Company, independent accountant, and consulting actuary.
6–30	Complete first draft of detailed description of proposal, calculate test factors, and determine approximate effects of proposed assumptions and methods on financial statements of prior years and current year; estimate effects for the next five years.
7–31	Finalize detailed description of proposal.
8–15	Meet with independent accountants and consulting actuaries and obtain agreement on the detailed description of proposal.
8–31	Obtain approval of assumptions from the Board of Directors.
9–30	Complete factor calculations for all individual lines to be adjusted.
11–15	Prepare financial statements for all prior years.
12–15	Prepare all valuations for current year using projections of insurance in force from 11–30 to 12–31.
1–31	Prepare financial statements for current year.
2–5	Release earnings data to the press.
2–28	Publish annual report.

*Adapted by Crazy Quilt Life from a timetable used by an actual company of Crazy Quilt's size.

▶ Establish methods of communication among the three parties as the conversion progresses, and
▶ Establish general areas of responsibility for the consulting actuary.

Documentation

The company should document every significant aspect of the conversion as it proceeds. This is of extreme importance. A conversion is very complex. If an employee terminates and a substantial part of the background of the conversion effort terminates with him, the effect on the company can be disastrous.

In addition, with the passage of time it sometimes becomes difficult to recall why a particular decision was made. There are a great many decisions to make in connection with a conversion, and the consequences of each decision are material and will be of long duration. It follows that the company should be able to recall why the decisions were made, the facts underlying the decisions, and so on; and the company should not depend on frail memory for such recall.

Application of generally accepted accounting principles in the life insurance industry is in an evolutionary phase. Methods presently being used are experimental.

New concepts and techniques will be necessary to compare the company's existing practices with the suggested new practices. Such comparisons are very difficult to make if remembrance has faded.

Reserve Models

One might readily envision three sets of books for a life insurance company: one for statutory purposes, one for tax purposes, and one for external reporting purposes. If management chooses to implement the "value added" concept or other measurements of progress for internal use, as discussed in Chapter 31, the result could be *four* or more sets of books.

This would be an intolerable burden if precision were required in every case. Precision is, of course, required for purposes of the statutory statements. In the case of a company making the Section 818(c) election, net level reserves for tax purposes may be computed precisely or approximated using formulas prescribed by the Internal Revenue Code. And in the case of adjusted reserves, reserves will usually be estimated in some manner.

A General Approach

One valid method of estimating adjusted reserves is the use of a series of "reserve models". A model in this context refers to a simulation of a company's book of business for purposes of estimating reserves in a manner which will closely approximate the results which would be obtained by a precise valuation.

A reserve model bears a close relationship to a model office and can, in fact, serve as basic input for a model office simulation. A model office is designed to recreate a company's operations for purposes of analysis and projection; it is of special importance in assessing the probable financial effects of a given course of action.

There is no "right" way to build a reserve model. The construction of a reserve model involves artistry to an extraordinary degree. Such artistry should, of course, be informed artistry because judgment and experience are required at all stages of development of the model. Put another way, the individual who is responsible for creating a reserve model should preferably have experience in building models and validating them. Without exception the individual should have appropriate background and training in life insurance and actuarial science.

The purpose of the model should be clearly understood. For example, a model might be created with two objectives in mind: estimation of reserves and a projection of operations. To the extent that these objectives conflict, such conflicts must be reconciled.

Furthermore, concepts of consistency and materiality must be clearly defined and communicated. For example, it is not unusual for an actuary to judge the materiality of a reserve error in terms of the level of reserves. The accountant will also be interested in the reported change in reserves. Obviously notions of consistency and materiality may differ significantly depending on the frame of reference.

Recognizing that techniques of developing reserve models may differ greatly, it may be useful to summarize the steps which might be taken under one method of developing a model.

1. *Determine the purpose of the model.*
In this case it is assumed that the model is to be developed only for purposes of estimating adjusted reserves. There are no conflicts to resolve.

2. *Determine the periods for which adjusted reserves are required.*
This is an intricate problem. Adjusted reserves must be estimated as of two year-ends to produce the change in reserves for a given year. In this case it is assumed that the company decides to report on a generally accepted basis for the first time and that one year's operations will be reported. Problems of reporting more than one year are discussed later in this chapter.

3. *Determine the general ground rules for materiality and consistency.*
This was discussed earlier. In this case it is determined that the materiality of probable errors in the beginning reserves should be judged on the basis of the level of reserves, and that the consistency of calculation and the materiality of probable errors with respect to the ending reserves should be judged in terms of the change in reserves. Acceptable tolerances are not quantified in this simplified illustration; they may be in a real situation. But quantification of error tolerances will tend to complicate the model-building process significantly, and and it will probably be better to test the results after the fact. The point to be made here is that the concepts of materiality and consistency applicable in the circumstances should be clearly understood by all parties involved in developing the model at this point in time.

4. *Determine the format of information required to be generated.*
This is extremely important. If adjusted reserve information must be obtained by issue year, for example to implement the gross change method of accounting for deferred taxes, then the model should be so constructed as to yield the necessary information in the necessary format. It is usually difficult, and sometimes impossible, to derive the information by *ex post facto* analysis.

5. *Determine a timetable for the work.*
Beginning reserves in the year in which adjusted reserves are first calculated present no special time problems; the beginning reserve model may be developed during the year. Ending reserves are another matter. Ending reserves must relate to ending insurance in force, and ending insurance in force is not known until year-end. Considering the time pressures involved in putting together the Convention Statement and a report to shareholders, timing of year-end work is of critical importance. In this case it is assumed that insurance in force is available early in January and that electronic applications developed earlier will produce the reserve model quickly. This is explained a little later, as are some possible alternative techniques for "updating the reserve model." The point is that the

timetable and the techniques finally adopted are intimately related.

6. *Obtain basic data for developing beginning reserves.*

A detailed in-force listing is required. Ideally the listing should show plan, age, duration, annual or annualized premiums in force (or a tabulation of mode premiums in such form that they may be annualized), policy counts, units of measure, insurance in force, and statutory reserves.

"Plan", as used here, refers to each plan arising at the time of an effective rate change—i.e., a change in premiums and/or cash values. The reserve basis is not a factor in classifying plans. Participating insurance may require supplemental data (such as information on changes in dividend scales), but that is not considered here.

"Units of measure" refers to the units in terms of which insurance in force is measured. For example, a certain type of decreasing term policy might be represented by letting one "unit" equal $10 of monthly income or possibly $1,000 of initial face amount. Hence one unit might at some point in time be equal to a commuted value of monthly income payments of $1,500, $500, or any amount which is applicable at the time of valuation. Reserve factors are usually applied to the units; in other words, the reserve factors themselves take changes in insurance in force into account.

7. *Decide, by reviewing the data, what plans are necessary in the model to represent insurance in force.*

This is a critical step which is performed manually and the one which perhaps requires the most judgment. Insurance in force is summarized by plan and those plans are selected for the model which represent the bulk of insurance in force. In this case it is assumed that the plans selected must represent 85 percent of insurance in force. Normally it will be found that relatively few plans are necessary to accomplish this.

The number of plans selected will increase, of course, with the age of the company and the extent to which the company has sold "specialty" policies or other nonstandard forms in the past.

Insurance in force is only the first test of the plans selected for the model. The 15 percent proposed to be excluded from the *basic* model structure (the 15 percent are provided for later) would be reviewed carefully to ensure that there are no unusual con-

Table 28–2.

DIAGRAM OF A RESERVE MODEL

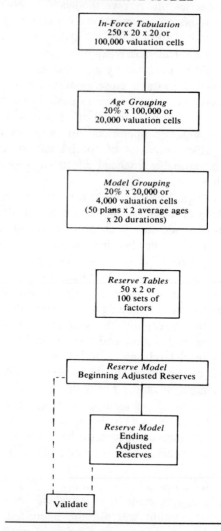

ditions requiring the inclusion of some of them. For example, unusually high premiums or reserves might require that one or more of the initial "discards" be included in the model.

It is obvious that great care must be exercised. The individual who selects the plans for the model must recognize situations which will disproportionately affect adjusted reserves irrespective of whether statutory reserves would be disproportionately affected. This may require some preliminary testing of some sort. In general, disproportionate effects should not be a problem. But the data must be scrutinized carefully at every point.

8. *Determine appropriate age groupings for each plan to be included in the model.*

Table 28–3.

VALIDATION OF A RESERVE MODEL FOR ORDINARY LIFE AS PERFORMED BY A MEDIUM-SIZED COMPANY IN CONNECTION WITH A 1973 CONVERSION (000 Omitted)

	1973	1972	1971
Statutory reserves:			
Convention Statement Exhibit 8, Part A, Ordinary	$328,277	$305,671	$284,630
Items not adjusted	11,202	10,718	10,923
Items adjusted	317,075	294,953	273,707
Model statutory reserves	314,580	292,338	270,916
Difference	2,495	2,615	2,791
Percentage difference	.8%	.9%	1.0%
Statutory reserve increase			
Convention Statement	22,122	21,246	
Model	22,242	21,422	
Difference	120	176	
Pre-tax statutory earnings	29,673	26,193	
Difference as percentage of earnings	.4%	.7%	
Net premiums in force			
Statutory valuation	42,566	41,082	39,359
Model	42,823	41,443	39,799
Difference	257	361	440
Percentage difference	.6%	.9%	1.1%

This step involves a review (generally accomplished manually) of the age distribution of each plan to be included in the model and selection of a "representative" age. Normally a quinquennial grouping would be appropriate—for example, ages 20–24 would be represented by age 22, ages 25–29 by age 27, etc. The middle range is valid only for a reasonably even distribution of ages; hence the plans must be scrutinized to seek out anomalous situations. The average statutory reserve might serve as a guideline for the average age selected, i.e., the average reserve per $1,000 for the grouping under study should correspond within a reasonable tolerance with the reserve per $1,000 for the representative age selected.

9. *Group all plans by representative age.*

Assuming all ages are represented in the detailed valuation, this step will reproduce insurance in force in a listing 10 percent the size of the full detailed listing (assuming a decennial grouping). All plans are grouped by age including those not provided for in the basic model. Plan and duration identification continue to be maintained.

It would rarely be feasible to perform this step manually except for small companies. Standard computer programs are available to accomplish this task.

10. *Assign minor plans to the major plans they best fit.*

The 15 percent of insurance in force representing plans not included in the basic model are now "merged" with the basic plans. This involves "assigning" the minor plans to the major plans they best correspond with. The assignment plan is essentially a manual process. The mechanics of merging plans can best be accomplished electronically for larger companies; standard computer programs are available to do this.

Assuming a company has 250 plans, of which 50 account for 85 percent of insurance in force, the remaining 200 plans (comprising 15 percent of insurance in force) are now expressed in terms of the 50 major plans. An additional reduction in details of approximately 80 percent is thus made. The total reduction of detail is therefore approximately 96 percent of the initial total (80 percent—representing the age averaging—plus 80 percent of the 20 percent remaining—representing the plan reduction). The model is 4 percent of the size of the full book of business.

Table 28-4.

RECONCILIATION OF STATUTORY AND ADJUSTED AMOUNTS FOR CRAZY QUILT LIFE AT DECEMBER 31, 1971 (000 Omitted)

Item	Table Reference*	Statutory Prior	Statutory Current	Adjusted Prior	Adjusted Current	Dr (Cr) Assets	(Dr) Cr Liabilities	(Dr) Cr Paid-in Capital	(Dr) Cr Beginning Retained Earnings	(Dr) Cr Retained Earnings Changes	(Dr) Cr Income
Statutory amounts	2–9, 2–10					$565,556	$522,390	$42,420	$ 7,599	$(6,854)	$10,244
1. Unrealized appreciation	2–12, 2–10	$ (2,996)	$ 188			(188)			2,996	(3,184)	
2. Realized capital gains	2–12								(263)		263
Non-admitted assets:											
3. Agents' balances	2–12			$ 4,519	$ 4,960	4,960			4,519	441	
4. Furniture and equipment	2–12			502	551	551			502	49	
5. Subsidiary	27–9, 27–10, 27–11				14,321	14,321			13,902		419
6. Stock dividend	2–2							2,714	(2,714)		
7. Mandatory securities Valuation reserve	2–12	10,374	13,966				(13,966)		10,374	3,592	
8. Unauthorized reinsurance	2–12	128	14				(14)		128	(114)	
Acquisition costs:											
9. Ordinary—basic plans	16–9			79,133	89,567	89,567			79,133		10,431
10. Accidental death	—			508	560	560			508		52
11. Waiver—active	—			339	373	373			339		34
12. Coinsurance	22–10			(252)	(242)	(242)			(252)		10
13. Modified coinsurance	22–10			(252)	(242)	(242)			(252)		10
14. Commercial health	19–1			238	153	153			238		(85)
15. Long-term health	19–15			9,529	11,031	11,031			9,529		1,502
16. Industrial	18–12			5,628	5,971	5,971			5,628		343
17. Variable annuities	21–2			2,295	3,483	3,483			2,295		1,188
18. Group life and health	20–18, 20–19			245	286	286			245		41
19. Credit life	20–14, 20–15			257	457	457			257		200
20. Credit health	2C–14, 20–15			429	641	641			429		212
21. Deferred and uncollected premiums	23–3			2,212	2,515	2,515			2,212		303
22. Cost of collection	23–6			(3,116)	(3,264)	(3,264)			(3,116)		(148)
23. Reserve transfers payable	22–10			558	737		737		(558)		(179)
Reserves:											
24. Ordinary—basic plans	7–10, 11–12	289,940	310,458	298,471	323,084		12,626		(8,531)		(4,095)
25. Paid-up additions	p. 283	2,893	3,147	2,128	2,295		(852)		765		87
26. YRT reinsurance	22–8	(185)	(201)	(245)	(266)		(65)		60		5
27. Coinsurance	22–10	(558)	(737)	(496)	(665)		72		(62)		(10)
28. Modified coinsurance	22–10			(496)	(665)		(665)		496		169
29. Accidental death	—	522	488	522	488						
30. Waiver—active	—	1,177	1,186	1,177	1,186						
31. Waiver—disabled	—	1,625	1,855	1,625	1,855						

		Table Reference*	Statutory Prior	Statutory Current	Adjusted Prior	Adjusted Current	Dr (Cr) Assets	(Dr) Cr Liabilities	(Dr) Cr Paid-in Capital	(Dr) Cr Beginning Retained Earnings	(Dr) Cr Retained Earnings Changes	(Dr) Cr Income
32.	Industrial	18–9	20,685	21,821	20,337	21,277		(544)		348		196
33.	Individual annuities	7–10, 11–12	77,321	87,779	67,580	75,887		(11,892)		9,741		2,151
34.	Supplementary contracts involving life contingencies	—	2,201	2,331	2,201	2,331						
35.	Group annuities—retired lives	20–21, 20–22	928	1,474	928	1,474						
36.	Credit life	20–14, 20–15	796	1,368	993	1,708		340		(197)		(143)
37.	Credit health	20–14, 20–15	1,156	1,728	1,403	2,107		379		(247)		(132)
	Guaranteed renewable and noncancelable health:											
38.	Unearned premiums	19–12	4,363	4,851	6,637	8,163		(4,851)		4,363		488
39.	Additional reserves	19–12	4,291	5,802				2,361		(2,346)		(15)
40.	Commercial health unearned premiums	19–1	1,080	695	1,080	695						(100)
41.	Deficiency reserves	—	600	500				(500)		600		391
42.	Miscellaneous	—	9,713	10,482	7,926	8,664		(2,178)		1,787		669
43.	Deferred and uncollected premiums	23–3			(8,675)	(9,344)		(9,344)		8,675		
44.	Deferred and uncollected gross	23–2	13,909	15,243			(15,243)			(13,909)		(1,334)
45.	Deferred and uncollected loading	23–2	4,147	4,346			4,346			4,147		199
	Maintenance and expense reserves:											
46.	Ordinary	17–2			1,881	1,977		1,977		(1,881)		(96)
47.	Guaranteed renewable and noncancellable health	19–19			350	432		432		(350)		(82)
48.	Industrial	18–13			663	689		689		(663)		(26)
49.	Individual annuities	17–2			1,221	1,324		1,324		(1,221)		(103)
50.	Deferred and uncollected premiums	23–3			(1,474)	(1,570)		(1,570)		1,474		96
51.	Cost of collection	23–6			1,081	1,189		1,189		(1,081)		(108)
52.	Deferred taxes	26–13			23,094	28,327		28,327		(23,094)		(5,233)
	Reclassifications:											
	Dividends left on deposit:											
53.	Revenue	—										(331)
54.	Reserve changes	—										331
	Supplementary contract deposits:											
55.	Revenue	—										(686)
56.	Reserve changes	—										686
	Group annuity deposits:											
57.	Revenue	—										(413)
58.	Reserve changes	—										413

continued

Table 28–4. Continued

	Table Reference*	Statutory Prior	Statutory Current	Adjusted Prior	Adjusted Current	Dr (Cr) Assets	(Dr) Cr Liabilities	(Dr) Cr Paid-in Capital	(Dr) Cr Beginning Retained Earnings	(Dr) Cr Retained Earnings Changes	(Dr) Cr Income
Changes in unearned premiums:											
Revenue											
59. Comercial health	—										385
60. Credit life	—										(715)
61. Credit health	—										(704)
62. Reserve changes	—										1,034
Reserve transfers:											
63. Revenue	—										(179)
64. Reserve changes	—										179
Investment expenses:											
65. Revenue	—										1,897
66. Expense	—										(1,897)
Other:											
67. Revenue	—										(174)
68. Benefits	—										174
Rounding	—					(1)			3		
69. Total income adjustments	—									7,570	7,570
Adjusted income	—										$17,814
70. Total retained earnings change	—										
Adjustments	—									19,279	
71. Adjusted retained earnings changes	—										
Total beginning retained earnings adjustments	—									$12,425	
Adjusted beginning retained earnings	—								94,036		
72. Total paid-in capital adjustments	—								$101,630		
Total paid-in capital adjustments	—							2,714			
73. Adjusted paid-in capital	—							$45,134			
Total liability adjustments	—						4,012				
Total liabilities	—						$526,402				
74. Total asset adjustments	—					120,035					
Total assets	—					$685,591					

*Amounts may differ slightly among schedules due to variations in rounding.

The model now consists of a relatively few plans stated at average ages for each duration.

11. *Test the model grouping.*

"Testing" the model at this stage will usually take several forms. First, statutory reserves would probably be computed for the plan-age-duration valuation cells in the model; the resulting aggregate reserves should reasonably approximate actual aggregate reserves as reflected in the basic detailed in-force tabulation. Second, annual premiums would probably be developed for the model valuation cells and the total thereof compared with total annual (or annualized) premiums reflected in the actual tabulation. Other tests would doubtless be performed.

Insurance in force and durations should generally be the same since they have been preserved throughout the process.

12. *Correct any errors.*

Little can be said about any errors appearing through testing the model. It is assumed here that no errors appeared. Suffice it to say that the testing must be carried out under a trained and watchful eye.

13. *Determine adjusted reserve assumptions for the plan-age combinations contained in the model grouping.*

Considerations involved in determining the various adjusted reserve assumptions are discussed in other chapters. In practice, most of the assumptions would be chosen before the modeling process is completed.

14. *Generate adjusted reserve factors for all durations for each plan-age combination.*

Development of reserve factors would usually be accomplished electronically. Standard programs are available to do it.

15. *Apply adjusted reserve factors to the model grouping.*

Again, this would normally be done electronically and, again, standard programs are available to do it. At this point, beginning adjusted reserves have been determined and the beginning reserve model is complete.

16. *Review the reserve model for reasonableness.*
This needs no discussion. A "reasonableness" review is not subject to precise definition. The review would generally be carried out by the individual responsible for constructing the model.

17. *Estimate ending adjusted reserves and review for reasonableness.*

This is an intricate matter that involves the continued integrity of the model, projections of insurance in force to year-end from some interim point when the time is not available to do the work after December 31, and so on. This is discussed later in this chapter.

The steps outlined above for creation of a reserve model are charted in Table 28–2 for a company with 250 plans, of which 50 plans comprise 85 percent of insurance in force; each plan has an average of 20 ages and 20 durations. Validation of a reserve model for ordinary life insurance, as performed by a medium-sized company in 1973, is shown in Table 28–3.

Health Insurance Models

Principles of modeling health insurance are basically the same as for life insurance, but implementation is frequently more complex. Groupings by ratebook era and age are reasonably straightforward. Groupings by plan, however, must take into account occupational classes (for disability income insurance), elimination and benefit period (for disability income insurance), inside limits and maximum benefits (for major medical and comprehensive), and miscellaneous policy characteristics. Because of the great variety of health policy forms, modeling can be a formidable task.

Subsidiaries

Whether or not subsidiaries should be lumped together in developing reserve models will depend on the operating characteristics of the subsidiaries. This subject is discussed in Chapter 27.

Recording Conversion Adjustments

It is axiomatic in statutory accounting that since financial statement items of material amount are not under ledger control, great care must be taken to ensure that all non-ledger items are included. The same thing applies to adjustments made in connection with a conversion.

Working Papers

Every separate component of a conversion should be documented in a separate file or working paper. The number of separate files will vary according to valuation systems, number of lines and business, age of the

Table 28–5.

CONDENSED STATUTORY AND ADJUSTED BALANCE SHEET FOR CRAZY QUILT LIFE AT DECEMBER 31, 1971 (000 Omitted)

	Statutory	Adjustments Table 28–4 Items	Adjustments Total Amount	Adjusted
ASSETS				
Bonds	$281,110			$281,110
Common stocks:				
Subsidiary	3,243	5	$ 14,321	17,564
Marketable	42,390	1	(188)	42,202
Mortgage loans	134,083			134,083
Investment real estate	8,616			8,616
Policy loans	44,989			44,989
Cash	5,600			5,600
Receivables:				
Agents' balances		3	4,960	4,960
Accrued investment income	970			970
Deferred policy acquisition costs		9–22	111,289	111,289
Property and equipment:				
Home office real estate	3,186			3,186
Furniture and equipment		4	551	551
Deferred and uncollected premiums	10,897	44–45	(10,897)	
Other assets	700			700
Separate accounts	29,771			29,771
	$565,555			$685,591
LIABILITIES AND CAPITAL				
Policy reserves	$455,387	24–43	(14,376)	$441,011
Claims	8,612			8,612
Dividends	1,399			1,399
Dividend accumulations	2,281			2,281
Supplementary contracts not involving life contingencies	1,628			1,628
Deposit administration funds	1,399			1,399
Annuity accumulation funds	1,186			1,186
Experience rating refunds	3,216			3,216
Reserve for maintenance and settlement expenses		46–51		4,041
Accounts payable	1,175			1,175
Miscellaneous liabilities	500			500
Federal income taxes:				
Current	1,856			1,856
Deferred		52	28,327	28,327
Separate accounts	29,771			29,771
Mandatory securities valuation reserve	13,966	7	(13,966)	
Reserve for unauthorized reinsurance	14	8	(14)	
TOTAL LIABILITIES	522,390			526,402
Common stock	27,721			27,721
Additional paid-in capital	14,699	5	2,714	17,413
Retained earnings	745*	70–71	113,310	114,055
	$565,555			$685,591

*As indicated elsewhere, Crazy Quilt's statutory surplus was voluntarily depleted by $24,000,000 in 1970 and 1971 by reserve strengthening and the acquisition of a subsidiary.

Table 28–6.

CONDENSED STATUTORY AND ADJUSTED STATEMENTS OF OPERATIONS AND RETAINED EARNINGS FOR YEAR ENDED DECEMBER 31, 1971 (000 Omitted)

	Statutory	Adjustments Table 28–4 Items	Adjustments Total Amount	Adjusted
Revenue:				
Premiums:				
Ordinary	$ 69,306	44	$ (1,334)	$ 67,972
Industrial	4,401			4,401
Individual annuities	15,078			15,078
Individual health	11,942	59	385	12,327
Group life and health	12,357			12,357
Group annuities	660			660
Credit life and health	5,856	60–61	(1,419)	4,437
Receipts—SCNILC	686	55	(686)	
Dividends left on deposit	331	53	(331)	
Reserve transfers	179	63	(179)	
Group annuity deposits	413	57	(413)	
Investment income	32,330	5	419	32,749
Investment expenses	(1,897)	65	1,897	
Management fees and other	1,684	67	(174)	1,510
TOTAL REVENUE	153,326			151,491
Benefits:				
Claims and other benefits	56,469	68	(174)	56,295
Change in reserves	36,611	23–43, 54, 56, 58, 62, 64	(2,125)	34,486
TOTAL BENEFITS	93,080			90,781
BALANCE	60,246			60,710
Expenses:				
Insurance expenses	48,037			48,037
Change in loading	199	45	(199)	
Change in deferred acquisition costs		9–22	(14,093)	(14,093)
Change in maintenance expense reserves		46–51	319	319
Investment expenses			1,897	1,897
TOTAL EXPENSES	48,236			36,160
BALANCE	12,010			24,550
Taxes:				
Current	1,766			1,766
Deferred		52	5,233	5,233
TOTAL TAXES	1,766			6,999
Income before realized capital gains	10,244			17,551
Realized capital gains		2	263	263
NET INCOME	10,244			17,814
Realized capital gains	263	2	(263)	
Change in unrealized capital gains	3,184	1	(3,184)	
Cost of subsidiary in excess of net assets acquired	(13,902)	5	13,902	
Change in non-admitted assets	(490)	3–4	490	
Change in mandatory securities valuation reserve	(3,592)	7	3,592	

continued

Table 28–6. Continued

| | Statutory | Adjustments | | Adjusted |
		Table 28–4 Items	Total Amount	
Change in reserve for unauthorized reinsurance	114	8	(114)	
Cash dividends	(2,400)			(2,400)
Stock dividends	(275)	6	(2,714)	(2,989)
TOTAL RETAINED EARNINGS CHANGES	(6,854)			12,425
Beginning retained earnings	7,599	71	94,031	101,630
ENDING RETAINED EARNINGS	$ 745			$114,055

company, complexity of the conversion, and other factors. Typically, a great many files will be needed.

Each file should contain a listing of all of the sources of input to the file. Sources might include computer print-outs, manually-prepared working papers, memoranda from specified departments, etc. The role of each input source should be described. And a carry-forward worksheet listing input sources and amounts (where applicable) should be maintained. The objectives of the carryforward are (1) to serve as a checklist of all items of information required to develop the particular conversion component and (2) to provide a convenient means of comparing each item from period to period to spot unusual or unexpected fluctuations.

In short, the systematic assembly procedures used to prepare a statutory statement are also needed to prepare an adjusted statement.

Reconciliations

Each input file may contain many items of information. Hopefully the file will be so designed as to ensure that all necessary information has been tabulated, submitted, and properly taken into account.

As a final check on the assembly process, statutory and adjusted figures should be reconciled according to a pre-determined format that takes all elements of the conversion into account in advance.

Table 28–4 shows the reconciliation for Crazy Quilt Life. The "table reference" might be viewed as file references—i.e., each "table reference" refers to the page in the book where the particular item will be found. The schedules and narrative associated with the item represent, in effect, a "file".

In addition, each account should be reconciled from statutory to adjusted. This can be readily accomplished by use of a trial balance in which the entries to each account are listed in advance. Tables 28–5 and 28–6 represent stylized trial balances. The "Table 28–4 items" are the reconciliation items affecting each account.

There are other ways to keep track of and record conversion adjustments. The important thing is to develop a systematic approach that provides an automatic check that all conversion components are recorded properly.

Part VI

Perspectives on GAAP

29 Financial Statements

Once the work of the conversion is done, it still remains to prepare the financial statements. It's a difficult and demanding job and an extremely important one, since the financial statements represent the means of communicating the results of a conversion and something about its quality.

Presentation Methods

Some states have historically required that published financial statements of domiciliary life insurance companies be in substantially the same form as the statutory statements. While it appears that most such states will relax this requirement—because of public pressure and because of the obvious discrimination in favor of holding companies, which have more flexibility in financial reporting—it could be that certain states will continue to enforce the requirement.

Also, in the rare case a company may as a matter of policy present its primary statements on a statutory basis notwithstanding the fact that regulatory authorities do not prohibit the publication of adjusted statements.

Thus the primary financial statements published by a stock life insurance company might be either adjusted or statutory depending on the circumstances.

Adjusted Primary Statements

"The preferable method of financial statement presentation," says the life insurance audit guide, ". . . is to present the . . . statements in conformity with generally accepted accounting principles." [1] In that case the statements stand on their own; there are no special problems.

However, as the guide points out, "it is desirable . . . to include a reconciliation of net income and stockholders' equity determined under generally accepted accounting principles with net gain from operations and capital and surplus determined under regulatory accounting practices." [2]

In some cases it may be necessary because of state regulations, or because of a company's policy, to present statutory statements as the primary statements. In that case, adjusted amounts might be presented in one of four ways:

▶ As separate statements, relegated to "secondary" status by emphasis and placement. The practical effect is the same as presenting adjusted primary statements with separate statutory statements.
▶ As a footnote reconciliation between statutory income and capital and adjusted income and capital.
▶ As a supplemental schedule, having the status of an additional statement, which reconciles statutory income and capital and adjusted income and capital.
▶ In the form of condensed adjusted statements shown in a note to the statutory statements.

Disclosure

The financial statements are presumed to contain all disclosures necessary for them to be not misleading.

In addition to the types of disclosures generally required (or considered desirable) for any commercial and industrial company, there are certain disclosures peculiar to life insurance company financial statements presented on a generally accepted basis. Some of the disclosures are required; some are desirable.

Required Disclosures

The audit guide states that matters "peculiar to life insurance company financial statements presented in conformity with generally accepted accounting principles" requiring disclosure in the statements include the following:

Disclosure of principles of recognition of premium revenues and related benefits and expenses.[3]

Nature of acquisition costs qualifying for deferral for each significant line of business.[4]

Method of amortizing deferred acquisition costs for each significant line of business.[5]

The amount of amortization of deferred acquisition costs charged to income for each significant line of business.[6]

Presentation of unamortized acquisition costs in the balance sheet as a deferred charge.[7]

Methods and assumptions employed in calculating adjusted benefit reserves for each significant line of business.[8]

The relative amount of participating business in force, the method of accounting for dividends to policyholders, and the amount of such dividends.[9]

Amount, if any, of adjusted earnings on participating business allocated to participating policyholders.[10]

The amount of statutory surplus, restrictions on shareholders' equity attributable to statutory requirements and any impairment of statutory solvency.[11]

The existence and effects on the financial statements of material reinsurance transactions.[12]

The basis of providing for current and deferred income taxes.[13]

Disclosures relating to the "policyholders' surplus account" as defined by the Life Insurance Company Income Tax Act of 1959.[14]

The amount of retained earnings in excess of statutory unassigned surplus upon which no current or deferred income tax provisions have been made and the reasons therefor.[15]

The amounts and expiration dates of any tax loss carryforwards.[16]

Any other pertinent details relating to income taxation and provisions for current and deferred income taxes.[17]

Prominent display of realized and unrealized investment gains or losses and related taxes.[18]

Segregation in stockholders' equity of any unrealized investment gains or losses net of related taxes.[19]

Description of the last item in the income statement as "income, excluding realized investment gains or losses,"

where realized gains or losses are not included in determining net income.[20]

Desirable Disclosures

While not necessarily required, the following disclosures may be considered desirable:

A reconciliation of statutory income and capital with adjusted income and capital.

Amount of acquisition costs deferred for each significant line of business.

Components of investment income.

The amount and significant components of investment expense.

The amount of self-charged rent.

Variations between generally accepted accounting principles and statutory accounting practices for the particular company.

Condensed statutory financial statements.

Treatment of development costs and the amount thereof.

Treatment of maintenance and settlement expenses.

There are, of course, other disclosures that may be required or desirable depending on the company. Further, the amount of detail that should be disclosed is largely a matter of judgment.

Numerous suggestions relating to disclosure matters are included throughout this book.

Annual Reports

The subject of annual reports—what information to include in them, how to present the information, how much financial information to provide, etc.— is so vast that it cannot feasibly be discussed in a few paragraphs. The form and content of life insurance annual reports are discussed and illustrated at length in the life insurance edition of *Financial Reporting Trends,* an annual publication of Ernst & Ernst.

Description of the Conversion

One general principle for life insurance annual reports that include adjusted financial statements should, however, be mentioned. The methods and assumptions used in converting the statements to a generally accepted accounting principles basis should be described in detail, particularly in the initial year of a conversion. The financial statements themselves will not ordinarily carry all of the information necessary to describe the conversion, so supplementary text would usually be needed to do the job.

The reason for providing a detailed description of the conversion is simply to permit security analysts and other knowledgeable readers of the financial statements to study the company's methods in some depth. For a period of time there is going to be some uncertainty about the conversion process and what it achieves; uncertainty about the degree of conservatism being used by a company; uncertainty over how to compare one company with another; and so on. While details of a company's conversion can always be misinterpreted, the alternative—suspicion—is worse than the possibility of misinterpretation.

Such a description, while it should be detailed in the initial conversion year, could be condensed in subsequent years; and eventually it could be discontinued.

Some companies may find it desirable to include a description of the conversion in a supplement to the annual report prepared for those who specifically request it.

Some companies prepare statistical supplements to the annual report for the use of security analysts and others who wish to study a company's operations in greater detail than the usual annual report permits. Statistical supplements are usually furnished only when specifically requested.

The types of information that might be presented in a statistical supplement are virtually without limit. Useful supplemental information relating to a conversion—in addition to the description of the conversion discussed previously—might include the following for several years:

Statutory and adjusted income statements by line of business, or a reconciliation of statutory and adjusted income by line of business.

First-year, single, and renewal premiums by line of business and related deferrals and amortizations of acquisition costs.

A detailed breakdown of adjusted reserves (and possibly changes therein) for each line of business showing issue years, types of business (e.g., permanent or term), adjusted reserve amounts, and assumptions. Where the net level method is used for statutory purposes, it would also be appropriate to show comparable statutory amounts.

Information concerning return on premiums and return on equity.

Additional details of the calculation of deferred income taxes.

Interim Statements

It's difficult enough to produce an annual statement on a generally accepted basis; interim state-

ments are in some respects even more difficult. Few companies will want—or be able—to mount a full-scale conversion at each quarterly reporting date. Estimates will have to be made, and estimates are inevitably dangerous.

If a company is equipped to produce adjusted reserve models as a by-product of the regular quarterly statutory valuation, interim statements will generally be much easier. But a significant degree of estimating will be necessary in any event.

The important thing, it would seem, is to plan well in advance for the types of information needed to prepare interim statements and the form which the information must take.

Provisions of APB Opinion No. 28

Accounting Principles Board Opinion No. 28—"Interim Financial Reporting"—is effective for interim periods included in fiscal years beginning after December 31, 1973. Thus life insurance companies that issue interim financial statements will generally use APB Opinion No. 28 guidelines beginning in 1974.

The key provisions of the Opinion as they affect life insurance companies may be summarized as follows:

▶ Each interim period should be viewed as an integral part of an annual period.[21]

▶ Revenue should be recognized during the interim period on the same basis as is followed for the full year.[22]

▶ Costs associated directly with revenue should be recognized in the same period as the related revenue.[23]

▶ Costs not directly associated with revenues may be either (1) charged against revenue in the interim periods as incurred, or (2) allocated among interim periods based on estimates of time expired, benefits received, or activity associated with the periods.[24]

▶ Income tax provisions should be based on the tax rate expected to be applicable for the entire year.[25]

▶ Extraordinary and infrequently occurring transactions should be included in full in the interim periods in which they occur.[26]

▶ Changes in accounting estimates should be accounted for in the interim periods in which they occur.[27]

▶ Fourth-quarter results should be separately disclosed even though the annual report embraces all interim periods.[28]

There are few hard and fast rules to guide the preparation of interim statements; the methods used will to an extraordinary degree reflect individual ingenuity.

Generally the most difficult matters to deal with are acquisition costs, development costs, benefit reserves, changes in estimates, capital gains, and federal income taxes, the "big ticket" items in most statements prepared in conformity with generally accepted accounting principles. A summary of some of the methods of dealing with these items that have been found to work for some companies may be helpful in gaining some insights into how to approach the interim statement problem.

Acquisition Costs

Accounting for acquisition costs for purposes of preparing interim statements might be approached in the following manner:

Acquisition costs incurred in years prior to the current one:

1. Determine by projection the approximate amount of prior-years' acquisition costs to be amortized (net of any renewal-year acquisition costs projected to be incurred) in the current year. This should be fairly simple in view of the work that must be done to determine unamortized balances as of the prior-year-end.
2. Determine by reference to historical patterns the proportion of premiums on prior years' issues expected to be received in each quarter and charge to expense a proportional share of the anticipated amortization for the year.
3. It is desirable to make the approximations in terms of as fine a breakdown of the business as available information permits.
4. Early-warning indicators that terminations are deviating significantly from assumed should be closely monitored so that amortization may be accelerated or reduced in response to such deviation.

Current-year acquisition costs:

1. Determine prior-year unit costs qualifying for deferral.
2. Make any changes in such unit costs as known changes in operations—e.g., a new agency contract—may make appropriate.
3. Apply the unit costs to units of new business.
4. Compare the total of the extended unit costs to actual acquisition costs incurred, if currently accounted for; otherwise compute ratios of totals to key statutory data and compare the ratios with corresponding ratios for the prior year. Investigate and explain any significant differences.

5. Determine the year's expected amortization rate, either by projection or by reference to the prior year, and apply it to the deferred amount. (Make sure to adjust if necessary for any excess amortization of nonpercentage expenses.)
6. Again, make the estimates in terms of as fine a breakdown of the business as available information permits and monitor persistency of new business so that estimated amortization rates may be adjusted if necessary.

Development Costs

Those companies that expense development costs as incurred might consider apportioning unusual amounts incurred in a particular interim period to the remaining interim periods or, if the amount to be incurred can be estimated in advance, to all interim periods in the year.

Changes in Estimates

Changes in estimates—such as revisions required to recognize losses or otherwise revalue reserves (for example, in connection with a rate increase on guaranteed renewable health insurance)—should be recognized in the accounts when the changes are made.

Benefit Reserves

Estimation of benefit reserves for purposes of interim statements is a tricky business indeed.

Where there is sufficient history and stability to develop reliable ratios between adjusted reserves and statutory reserves, statutory reserves for various blocks of business could be "ratioed" up or down to arrive at an estimation of adjusted reserves for both new business and prior years' issues.

Alternatively, reserve increases on prior years' issues might be projected by an extension of the model used in the prior year, and the increase apportioned based on the same techniques as are used for apportioning amortization of acquisition costs on prior years' issues. Issues of the current year might be valued by using interim models; only one duration would be required, and perhaps only one central issue age might be necessary if the distribution of issues is consistent with the prior year. If one assumed issue age is used, it should be validated by reference to the average statutory reserve per unit for the plan.

Capital Gains and Losses

Capital gains and losses often fluctuate wildly from year to year. From quarter to quarter the fluctuations are typically unbelievably violent, and some regard reported capital gains and losses during so short a period as being all but meaningless.

Should capital gains and losses be allocated to interim periods? While various techniques can be used to smooth out such gains over a calendar year, it is doubtful that certainty about gains and losses to be experienced in the balance of the year is sufficient to make the smoothing meaningful. Until such time as the Financial Accounting Standards Board prescribes another method which can be applied to capital gains and losses, they should be reported in the financial statements in the interim period in which they occur, distasteful as that might seem.

Income Taxes

Presumably the techniques of calculating deferred taxes were well-developed in prior years. Maintenance of a worksheet containing the key calculation items, with space for inserting quarterly and year-to-date amounts and for annualizing the year-to-date amounts, should make interim deferred tax calculations fairly straightforward.

Often it will be feasible to apply an effective tax rate, based on experience, directly to the total of the timing differences. Such rate may or may not be the same as the tax rate applied to current taxable income, depending on the company's expected future tax status.

The rate used for purposes of calculating taxes currently payable should take into account anticipated investment tax credits and other available tax planning techniques.

SEC Reporting

Financial statements prepared for purposes of inclusion in filings with the Securities and Exchange Commission are subject to Article 7A of Regulation S-X, which governs the form and content of life insurance company financial statements filed with the Commission.

Article 7A, as revised, requires the use of generally accepted accounting principles by stock life companies that file statements with the Commission beginning in 1974.

Article 7A generally requires the same types of disclosure as would be associated with good reporting in any event. Several schedules are required, however, that may demand special efforts to develop the necessary information, and conversion planning should take such requirements into account.

30

A Few Audit Considerations

Adjustments of financial statements of stock life insurance companies to conform with principles set forth in the life insurance audit guide creates some new and challenging problems for companies making the adjustments. The adjustments also create new and challenging problems for auditors and actuaries.

Independent Audits

There is probably little that can be done to make the audit of a conversion easy. It's a difficult job and will usually require that senior staff perform more of the work than is customary.

Established Companies

The vast bulk of this book has dealt with the considerations involved in converting an established company's financial statements to a generally accepted accounting principles basis. Those considerations, while discussed generally from the company's point of view, also represent matters to be considered by the auditor in his examination of the financial statements of an established company.

An "established" company, for audit guide purposes, is one whose experience is reliable. The passage of time and reliability of experience are not necessarily synonymous, but generally the older a company the more reliable its record of experience with respect to mortality, terminations, interest rates, expenses, etc. Crazy Quilt Life, for its foibles, clearly qualifies as an "established" company, for example.

New Companies

In discussing audit guidelines for a new life insurance company, the audit guide warns that

Because of the lack of reliable experience for a new company, the auditor will have difficulty in forming an opinion as to the reasonableness of assumptions to be used in calculating adjusted reserves and as to the related recoverability of acquisition costs to be deferred . . . the auditor will probably need to be more conservative than he would be with an established company.[2]

What is a "new" company? Is it a company that is one year old? Five years old? Ten years old? When does a company cease being "new" and join the cherished ranks of the "established"?

Since "reliable experience" is one of the principal criteria for judging whether a company is new or established, and since the period of time it requires to produce reliable experience is not predictable, there is no way to determine in advance when a company will become "established". A company that has been in business for many years, and is clearly "established", may change its marketing approach and methods of operation so dramatically that it is suddenly "new" again. On the other hand, a brand new company may acquire a seasoned and stable block of business that is so large in relation to its total volume that the new company is automatically "established".

Other factors to be evaluated in determining whether a company is new or established include its size, its growth rate, the type of business it sells, the markets in which it operates, its reinsurance program, its statutory surplus position, its profitability, its expense levels, its cash flow patterns, and management's experience and capability.

While evaluation of the degree to which a company meets the various criteria for it to be considered established is influenced by factual data, the determination is ultimately a matter of subjective judgment. At such time as the auditor is reasonably confident about the company's future prospects and its ability to realize its assumptions about interest, mortality, withdrawal, and maintenance and settlement expenses, the company is "established", but not before.

Assuming that a company is regarded as "new", the audit guide provides a few general guidelines for the auditor who must evaluate the company's acquisition cost deferrals and adjusted reserve assumptions.

Acquisition costs and withdrawals. Whether or not acquisition costs are recoverable depends in large measure on the size of the amount deferred and the course of future terminations. As for the amount deferred, the life insurance audit guide suggests that a conservative definition of acquisition costs is desirable for a new company:

For example, it may only be appropriate to defer the most directly variable expenses such as commissions and medical examination fees.[3]

As for terminations, the guide offers few suggestions except to use tables which are "conservative and produce results which are not more favorable than industry experience or the company's experience to date."[4] As a practical matter, termination patterns usually emerge fairly rapidly except where the product is novel, the market is new or unstable, or possible changes in economic or political conditions are likely to have a dramatic impact on the particular type of business sold by the company.

Interest. Even though a new company might have little in the way of interest rate histories, its current returns and maturities can be determined and compared with current assumptions used for the related liabilities. The problem of forecasting future interest rates is not much different from forecasting such rates for an established company. Assuming a new company has a positive cash flow, then, the interest assumption should not present too severe a problem. New company or established company, the assumption should be decently conservative.

Mortality. A new company has two problems in connection with its mortality assumption: its size, which affects the degree to which the law of large numbers will apply; and its experience, which affects the extent to which its underwriting practices are put to the test.

Appropriate reinsurance arrangements can be of great help in controlling the mortality risk. Underwriting practices can be evaluated in advance. The market in which the company operates will have some effect on the mortality risk.

In the absence of unusual conditions or circumstances, a new company's mortality assumptions should generally not be considered dubious merely because the company is small. The company is in business to assume the risk, and it seems inappropriate to challenge the presumption of the rationality of the company's basic undertaking.

Maintenance expenses. The new company has a special problem in regard to its assumptions about future maintenance expenses, which assumptions affect its recoverability tests. The considerations involved are discussed in Chapter 24.

Reasonableness Reviews

Regardless of how much detailed audit work is performed in connection with a conversion, and regardless of whether the company is new or established, it is essential for the auditor (and, as suggested later, for the actuary) to step back and contemplate the reasonableness of the results of the conversion. This is particularly important in the early years of reporting on the audit guide basis since there is no historical pattern of ratios, relationships to statutory amounts, etc. Even where several years have been restated and an apparent pattern has emerged, the pattern should be reviewed with some degree of skepticism since an error of material amount, if consistent over the restated period, may escape detection.

Methods of reviewing the reasonableness of the results of a conversion will differ, of course; there is no "one" way to do it. But the following suggestions may be indicative of the general type of review that should be made:

Results should be reviewed by line of business. It means little to combine the results of significantly different lines of business for purposes of reviewing reasonableness.

Adjusted income, before taxes and excluding interest on capital, expressed as a percentage of premiums, should be reconciled within a reasonable tolerance to profit margins indicated by key profit studies for each major line of business for which adjustments are made.

Unusual relationships between statutory and adjusted reserves, and the changes therein, for major blocks of business should be explained.

Unusual variations in indicated amortization of acquisition costs should be explained.

Comparisons of key ratios (e.g., pre-tax adjusted profits, excluding interest on mean adjusted capital, as a percentage of premiums and as a percentage of mean adjusted capital) with those of other companies of similar characteristics should be made and unusual differences should be investigated.

Participation of Actuaries

At one point in the development of the life insurance audit guide actuaries felt much maligned. An early draft of the guide referred to the auditor's expression of reliance on actuaries as "gratuitous". Actuaries took great umbrage at this, feeling that it reflected a low opinion of their work. Mercifully, the term was dropped from later versions of the audit guide.

Use of the term was misunderstood by actuaries. Such are the pitfalls of mere language. The fact is that the overriding importance of the actuary's role in the life insurance business in general, and conversion to generally accepted accounting principles in particular, has been well-recognized in all versions of the audit guide.

Audit Guide Provisions

The life insurance audit guide discusses the actuary's role in a conversion to generally accepted accounting principles in two contexts:

▶ His role in formulating the concepts and methods to be used in determining actuarial and actuarial-related items to be reported in the financial statements, and

▶ His role as an expert in providing the independent auditor with competent evidential matter with respect to actuarial and actuarial-related items reported in the financial statements.

The formulating role. The audit guide states that "the choice of actuarial assumptions and the disciplining of that choice are primary responsibilities of the actuarial profession." [5] The guide notes that the principles of the actuarial profession require that actuarial assumptions be "adequate and appropriate" and that methods employed by the actuary be "consistent with the sound principles established by precedents or common usage" within the actuarial profession.

Since the accounting principles described in the life insurance audit guide are quite new, there are few precedents and little common usage applicable specifically to the conversion process. Precedents and common usage come with the passage of time. However, the guide suggests that the general requirements that actuarial assumptions be " 'adequate and appropriate' is consistent with the concept, under generally accepted accounting principles, that actuarial assumptions be characterized by conservatism which is 'reasonable and realistic'." [6] In other words, while there are few specific guidelines available to the actuary, the broad concepts governing the work of the actuary are seen to be adequate to cover his responsibilities in a conversion. His only additional responsibility is to make sure that such concepts are implemented in such a manner as to give due recognition, as best he can, to the accounting criteria set forth in the audit guide.

Which raises an important point. The accounting criteria set forth in the audit guide are comprehensible only in terms of the traditions, objectives, and doctrines of financial accounting, many of which are not set forth clearly in written form. Indeed, a few of the traditions, objectives, and doctrines of financial accounting are subconscious. Who knows, for example, exactly what constitutes "fairness" in a set of financial statements? The accountant may know because of his training and background; but he may be hard-pressed to explain precisely what fairness consists of. His determination of fairness is a professional judgment, and the exercise of professional judgment involves factors which often cannot be explicated in highly specific terms.

Thus a key responsibility of the accountant is to interpret the objectives and criteria of the audit guide for the guidance of the actuary. The actuary who formulates the concepts and methods used in the conversion cannot be expected by himself to determine whether his concepts and methods are fully consistent with generally accepted accounting principles.

The evidential role. "The professional qualifications required of the independent auditor," says the audit guide, ". . . do not include those of a person trained for or qualified as an actuary. Therefore, auditors will need the advice of a qualified actuary* in such matters." [7]

Such advice represents evidential matter to be considered by the auditor in forming his opinion

---

*The audit guide states that "membership in the American Academy of Actuaries . . . is generally considered to be acceptable evidence of professional qualifications." Others believe that the actuary should be an FSA, should practice primarily in the life insurance area as opposed to the pension area, and should be familiar with and understand the details of the life insurance audit guide.

on the financial statements. "The auditor should utilize the expertise of an actuary in much the same manner as he uses the expertise of attorneys or those in other areas of specialization in forming a judgment in his own area of expertise, namely, expressing his opinion on the fairness with which overall financial position and results of operations are presented." [8] In other words, the auditor cannot abdicate his responsibility by blind reliance on the actuary.

The exact nature and extent of the auditor's true reliance on actuaries to provide competent evidential matter are not entirely clear. Notwithstanding the audit guide's suggestion that actuarial expertise should be used "in much the same manner" as the expertise of attorneys, mining engineers, appraisers, and other experts is used, the fact is that actuarial considerations are so material and so all-pervasive in a life insurance environment as to constitute a substantive difference from most other situations in which the auditor relies on experts for advice. In short, the auditor's implicit reliance on actuaries is probably greater than his reliance on other experts notwithstanding the notion that the actuary's advice is basically an additional element of evidence to be considered by the auditor. The actuary's advice and opinion do indeed constitute evidence, but it is evidence that the auditor cannot do without under any circumstances. The auditor's *de facto* reliance on the actuary's advice and opinion is inevitable, even though the *degree* of reliance will depend in part upon the training and experience of the auditor.

It is clear that the audit guide's characterization of the evidential nature of the actuary's advice and opinion has reference to the fact that actuaries are not auditors and that accountants therefore cannot rely on their work to the extent that they rely on the work and reports of other auditors:

Actuaries are not practicing auditors; they are not specifically trained in auditing procedures, nor are they governed by generally accepted auditing standards. Therefore, there is no justification for the auditor to omit all audit procedures or to perform only token procedures as to the reserves reviewed by the consulting actuary* unless the terms of the engagement contemplate a qualification or denial of opinion by the auditor.[9]

Thus the auditor is prohibited from formally expressing reliance on the actuary in his opinion on the financial statements. Unless the auditor himself is fully

*In context, "consulting actuary" as used in this passage appears to refer to an independent consulting actuary rather than one who is performing the functions that would otherwise be performed by an in-house actuary.

satisfied as to the propriety of the amounts at which actuarial items are stated, he normally would have to "disclaim any opinion as to the fairness of the financial statements taken as a whole." [10] What this means in essence is that the auditor must determine for himself that his *de facto* reliance on the actuary is warranted and not pass the consequences of reliance on to the reader of the financial statements.

Independent Actuaries

Determination of the auditor's degree of reliance on the actuary's advice and opinion will generally determine whether the expertise of a management actuary will suffice or whether the assistance of an independent consulting actuary is needed.*

An auditor who is sufficiently experienced in auditing life insurance reserves may be able to form an opinion by working with the qualified actuary who was responsible for calculating the reserves . . . In other cases the auditor may need to utilize the services of a qualified consulting actuary to assist him.[11]

While this passage does not refer to an *independent* consulting actuary, it is clear from context that the guide refers in the foregoing passage to a consulting actuary who is essentially independent of the actual calculation process. A consulting actuary or an employee of the company may be the actuary "who was responsible for calculating the reserves."

What constitutes "independence" of a consulting actuary? There is, of course, a temptation for auditors to define the actuary's independence in terms of standards of independence required for auditors by the ethics of the accounting profession and certain statutory and administrative criteria.

It is difficult to apply standards to a profession beyond those required by the profession itself. The actuarial profession does not, for example, prohibit consulting actuaries from owning the securities of their clients, although a few consulting firms do have such a rule. In general, actuaries have traditionally been advocates of their clients, much as attorneys are advocates. They have generally not been considered as having the responsibility to third parties that accountants have.

To the extent that a consulting actuary reviews

*The life insurance audit guide also states that reserve certifications by state insurance departments may also be sufficient under certain circumstances; however, such certifications would run to statutory reserves, not adjusted reserves, and are not relevant to this discussion.

the work and representations of management for purposes of lending additional integrity to the financial statements, he is inevitably assuming some degree of responsibility to third parties. This is true notwithstanding the fact that the auditor cannot formally express reliance on the actuary. As suggested previously, the accountant must inevitably rely in fact on the actuary's advice and opinion to some degree; and while there are good reasons for prohibiting a formal declaration of reliance, the substance of the situation is that the auditor does rely on the actuary with respect to extremely material components of the financial statements. It would appear that both the auditor and the actuary should respond appropriately to the substance of the situation.

Thus, an independent consulting actuary should challenge his standards of independence when he is called upon to assist an auditor in reviewing adjusted reserves and other actuarial items computed for purposes of preparing financial statements in conformity with generally accepted accounting principles.

In addition to ethical standards imposed by the actuarial profession, the consulting actuary should, with respect to a company for which he is assisting the auditor, generally attempt to follow a few additional guidelines for independence:

▸ Neither he nor any members of his firm should have a financial interest in, or be an officer or director of, the company.

▸ He should not have a direct family relationship with an officer or director of the company.

▸ He should be essentially independent of the conversion process, even though other members of his firm might participate significantly in the process.

These guidelines are basically voluntary. It appears, however, that these or similar guidelines would be appropriate for a consulting actuary who considers himself truly independent.

Coordination with Auditors

The life insurance audit guide suggests that where . . . independent actuaries (i.e., outside experts) are utilized in the process of reviewing amounts established for reserves, the auditor should plan his work with the consulting actuary to insure a coordinated program to achieve the objectives of the audit.[12]*

One method of developing a coordinated program between the auditor and the consulting actuary may be described as follows:

Initial Conversion	*Subsequent Conversions***
The auditor should determine the actuary's qualifications and independence.	The auditor should update his evaluation of the actuary's qualifications and independence.
The auditor should review any written material available from the consulting actuary with respect to standards and procedures for reviews of actuarial aspects of conversions.	The auditor should review any updates of such written material.
The company's preliminary proposal for the conversion should be jointly reviewed and an understanding of, and agreement on, the issues of theory and technique should be reached.	Preliminary proposals for handling new lines of business (e.g., variable life) and new problems (e.g., loss recognition situations) should be jointly reviewed and agreement reached on the broad issues.
Final details of the company's proposal should be jointly reviewed and agreement reached on theory and technique.	Same for new lines and problems.
The auditor should develop a tentative audit program for each area of the conversion which gives due regard to internal controls over the conversion process and which clearly sets forth the objectives of the program for each area, an outline of the responsibilities of each party, steps to be performed by the auditor, and steps to be performed by the actuary.	Same, incorporating any modifications appropriate to a subsequent audit.
The actuary should review his portion of the proposed audit program in detail and confer with the auditor to ensure there is a common understanding as to the objectives of the audit, adequacy of the program to attain the objectives, and respective responsibilities for carrying out the program.	Same.
Agreement should be reached	Same.

*The guide also states that "such coordinated review should enable the auditor to restrict the extent of his testing of reserve factors, in-force records, and clerical accuracy of listing from that which would otherwise be required absent the utilization of the consulting actuary." The testing of factors might be restricted as a result of the participation of consulting actuaries, but not the integrity of in-force records and clerical accuracy, neither of which requires actuarial expertise. In other words, reliance is not warranted in areas unequivocally within the auditor's competence.

**Assuming retention of the same consulting actuary.

Initial Conversion	*Subsequent Conversions***
on the general form and content of any letters of opinion, comfort, or assurance to be furnished by each party to the other.	
The audit program should be finalized in a form which details the steps to be performed by both the auditor and the actuary and establishes the relationships between the work of the two parties.	Same.
The audit and actuarial review work should be performed and each party should sign off the applicable steps listed in the audit program.	Same.
The auditor should furnish the actuary with any agreed-upon written or verbal assurances with respect to in-force records, clerical accuracy of listings, and any other items which enter into the actuary's work but for the propriety of which he relies on the auditor.	Same.
The actuary should furnish the auditor with any agreed-upon written opinions with respect to actuarial items.	Same.
Informal conferences to discuss problems and progress should be held by the auditor and actuary as the audit progresses.	Same.

It is difficult to generalize about the areas in which the expertise of independent actuaries might be utilized; this will depend on the characteristics of the company, its conversion methodology, and the training and experience of the auditor. Some of the areas in which assistance may be needed are as follows:

Propriety of actuarial assumptions, including adequacy of provisions for adverse deviation.
Propriety of the methods utilized to calculate reserve factors.
Propriety of the methods utilized to calculate deferred, uncollected, and unearned premiums.
Tests of factor calculations.
Propriety of amortization tables used in connection with the worksheet method of amortizing acquisition costs.
Propriety of the methods of allocating expenses to individual plans and ages for purposes of calculating expense factors.
Appropriateness of models.
Satisfaction as to recoverability.

Propriety of loss recognition calculations.
Effect of not adjusting certain reserves.
Satisfaction that all policy provisions are adequately reserved for.
Overall reasonableness of the results of the conversion.
Satisfaction as to the accuracy of statutory reserves and loading on statutory deferred and uncollected premiums.

With respect to this latter area—propriety of statutory reserves—some believe that since adjusted reserves are being reported on, statutory reserves can be given short shrift. However, it is necessary to know statutory surplus—hence statutory reserves—in order to determine and disclose restrictions on retained earnings. Also, disclosure of a reconciliation between statutory and adjusted amounts makes it imperative that statutory amounts be properly stated. Finally, in the extreme case it would be possible for a company to be insolvent on a statutory basis without this fact being apparent due to an error in the reserves, all the while reporting glowing adjusted earnings. Needless to say, such a situation is acutely embarrassing to all concerned.

One other matter relating to coordination of the efforts of actuaries and accountants deserves ventilation even though it is a bit sensitive. Some actuaries resent the fact that accountants are now concerned about matters which have historically been the exclusive domain of actuaries. Occasionally routine audit questions are taken to be personal insults. It is very important, therefore, that the auditor communicate clearly the objectives of an audit, the auditor's responsibilities, and the reasons for his investigative ways. Similarly, the actuary must realize that audit inquiries about actuarial matters are not intended to challenge the actuary in his own discipline but are merely routine questions required to be satisfactorily answered in the course of conducting an audit.

Actuaries' Letters

When an independent actuary assists independent accountants, it is usually considered desirable for the accountants to obtain a letter from the actuary setting forth the scope of the work performed and the actuary's opinion with respect to each significant area reviewed by him.

The life insurance audit guide provides that

The auditor should obtain a written opinion from the qualified actuary who calculated the reserves or who verified the reserves, the same as he would obtain letters from counsel on legal matters and other representations from management on various matters.[13]

There is usually a fundamental difference between a letter from the actuary who *calculated* the reserves and a letter from the actuary who *verified* the reserves. The calculating actuary represents management and his letter is in the nature of a management representation. The verifying actuary operates as an independent reviewer of the work of the calculating actuary and his letter is in the nature of a supporting independent opinion. If the verifying actuary is also a member of management or is a consulting actuary who performs duties in lieu of an in-house actuary, he too represents management and his letter is also a management representation.

An opinion from a management actuary is extremely important, since it provides evidence as to the discharge of management's responsibilities as well as adherence to guides to professional conduct for actuaries. But a letter from a management actuary should be distinguished from a letter from an independent actuary, just as a letter from a controller who happens to be a CPA—and thus is bound by the ethics of his profession—differs from the report of an independent accountant.

The letter from the calculating actuary should normally represent that the various actuarial items computed for use in the adjusted statements conform with generally accepted actuarial principles and with provisions of the life insurance audit guide.

The letter from an independent actuary should normally describe the scope of his examination, and his opinion with respect to each significant actuarial aspect of the conversion.

Actuaries' letters subsequent to the initial conversion might be considerably shorter, limited, for example, to factors for new plans, new assumptions, continued integrity of the model, new amortization tables, continued validation of persistency assumptions, new recoverability tests when called for, and overall reasonableness of indicated results of operations.

Citations of Actuary's Participation

The life insurance audit guide prohibits the expression of reliance on actuaries in the opinion paragraph of an accountants' report and indicates that

So that there may be no misunderstanding as to the significance of the use of actuaries insofar as it relates to the degree of responsibility being assumed by the auditor expressing an opinion on overall financial position and results of operations, it is considered preferable not to refer to the utilization of actuarial expertise in the scope

paragraph. Such disclosure of the use of actuaries may be interpreted as an indication that the auditor making such reference had performed a more thorough audit than an auditor not making such a reference, thereby implying an additional degree of assurance.[14]

The guide thus discourages any mention of the utilization of actuarial expertise anywhere in the accountants' report.

It should be pointed out that the accountants' report is the only item in an annual report or other documents that is the exclusive responsibility of the accountant. Everything else is the responsibility of management.

A review of the conversion process by independent consulting actuaries is clearly in the public interest, and so is disclosure of the fact that such a review has been made. It is clearly permissible for the company to mention the fact that a review was made in the annual report or other document. Such mention might take the form of discussion in the text, publication of the actuary's letter reporting the scope and results of his review, or a note to the financial statements which discloses that such a review was made.

Statements of the Actuarial Profession

The Society of Actuaries in 1973 released an opinion dealing with the actuary's responsibilities in connection with life insurance company financial statements prepared in conformity with generally accepted accounting principles, and the Committee on Financial Reporting Principles of the American Academy of Actuaries published a "Recommendation" dealing with actuaries' letters. Auditors should be familiar with these releases, which are reproduced in Appendix E.

Internal Audits

It is commonly thought that company accountants and actuaries and independent accountants and actuaries do all the work relating to a conversion. And so it often is. Internal auditors, by and large, have not participated in the conversion process except to the extent of providing temporary accounting assistance.

However, internal auditors do have an important role to play in the conversion process, and a role which moreover is consistent with the internal audit function.

Internal Controls and Procedures

One of the prime responsibilities of most internal audit departments is to monitor the effectiveness of, and compliance with, the system of internal controls and procedures.

Internal control over the conversion process is no less important than, say, internal control over the compilation of amounts to be included in the statutory statements. Internal control may even be more significant in the case of a conversion in view of the need to use numerous significant approximations—for example, reserve models.

Review of the organization established to make the conversion, checks and balances established to ensure that all elements of the conversion are accounted for, and systems and procedures adopted to produce the necessary information are all proper subjects for internal audit review.

Data Integrity

The information used in making a conversion is voluminous and complex. Functional costs, in-force data, historical investment earnings rates, persistency studies, mortality studies, and other data all impact on the conversion.

Tests of integrity of such data represent an appropriate internal audit function.

Cost Effectiveness

It is probably fair to say that some conversion systems were jerrybuilt. The difficulties and pressures of conversion were too severe for many companies to spend the time to take a systems approach to the conversion. Thus some models are maintained manually at enormous cost in time and effort; manually-prepared worksheets threaten to suffocate the accounting department; frantic searches for needed but virtually inaccessible information are undertaken.

Assuming that operating economies are within the domain of the particular internal audit department, reviews to determine better and more economical ways to accomplish the conversion constitute a proper function for internal auditors.

Liaison

Internal auditors can provide needed liaison between the company and its independent accountants with respect to a conversion and, assuming it is one of the internal audit department's responsibilities to assist the independent auditors, there is no reason why such assistance cannot be extended to the conversion process.

Other Possibilities

The foregoing are a few of the areas in which internal auditors have a role to play in a conversion. No doubt there are many others. Such work broadens the internal auditor's responsibilities and presents new and interesting challenges, and the company is bound to benefit.

Boards and Audit Committees

Some companies have felt that the conversion to generally accepted accounting principles is of such importance that either the audit committee or the board of directors has passed upon major policy matters related to the conversion. In such cases the board or audit committee has typically approved benefit reserve assumptions, the definition of acquisition costs, and possibly the company's position with respect to its future tax status for purposes of computing deferred taxes. Usually board or audit committee action is based on extensive discussions with top management, senior actuarial and accounting personnel, independent actuaries and accountants, and, in some cases, security analysts.

Because of the impact of a conversion on a company's financial statements and its image in the financial community, such participation by boards or audit committees is very desirable.

31

Using GAAP

In recent years financial statements have been directed increasingly toward "sophisticated" readers. This orientation is due in part to the significance of institutional investors, in part to recognition of the fact that few individual investors read financial statements, and in part to acknowledgement of the fact that, in any case, only the sophisticated reader can make his way through the thicket of modern financial accounting.

This is especially true of life insurance company financial statements. Traditionally the statements have been virtually incomprehensible. But investors—mainly institutional investors—have bought life insurance stocks anyway. They have necessarily relied very heavily on analysts who specialize in insurance stocks.

Security analysis is a somewhat subjective and quite mysterious process which does not readily lend itself to generalization. Nevertheless, it can fairly be said that the intelligent analyst seeks to understand the economy, the role and outlook of the particular industry within the economy, and the role and outlook of the particular company within the industry. In examining the role and outlook of the company, the analyst evaluates management, markets, investment practices, operating controls, and all those things that make an enterprise function; and he also attempts to evaluate the quality, level, and growth of earnings in order to understand the company's historical record and provide a basis for projecting earnings into the future.

For most industries net income of a particular company is a given quantity; the analyst can proceed immediately to evaluation of the figure. The insurance stock analyst, however, historically has had a somewhat more difficult chore: he has had to estimate the earnings figure, using a rule of thumb, before evaluating it. In addition to all the imponderables associated with evaluating earnings, the analyst—and the analyst's customer—have had to deal with the imponderables associated with *estimating* earnings.

The advent of generally accepted accounting principles for stock life insurance companies should make the analyst's job a little easier. Earnings are still heavily influenced by estimates, but the estimates are disciplined by the judgments of actuaries and accountants. One might argue that judgments differ and that reported earnings of a life insurance company remain obscure and undependable. But there are only two alternatives: hold to statutory practices or impose arbitrary rules. Statutory practices do not suit the needs of shareholders. Arbitrary rules simply are no substitute for professional judgment, with all due regard for the fallibility of judgment.

When all is said and done, the life insurance audit guide is a worthwhile first step to reasonably believable financial statements prepared from the investor's point of view. Implementation of the guide is unavoidably experimental at this point in time, and there is going to be some uncertainty about life insurance company financial statements for a while. Meantime the analyst can best serve his public by learning to work with GAAP earnings.

Evaluating GAAP Earnings

As indicated in the introduction to this chapter, security analysts are interested in evaluating the qual-

Table 31–1.

MINI-QUIZ FOR INSURANCE STOCK ANALYSTS

1. Which is generally the more conservative interest assumption for whole life insurance in terms of (a) the balance sheet and (b) the income statement, in both cases 10 years after the issue year?
   (1) 6 1/2% graded to 3 1/2% in 30 years
   (2) 4 1/2% level

2. As compared with the interest assumption, what relative effect does the mortality assumption have on reserves for permanent insurance?

3. As compared with the interest assumption, what relative effect does the morbidity assumption have on reserves for non-cancellable or guaranteed renewable disability income insurance?

4. What are the main arguments for and against mortality fluctuation reserves?

5. Under what circumstances can the assumption of heavy lapses result in unconservative reserves in terms of the balance sheet?

6. How does a 15% pre-tax profit return on ordinary life premiums, excluding interest on adjusted capital, compare with industry returns?

7. What characteristics of industrial insurance tend to make excess interest a more significant element of profits than for ordinary business?

8. What are the elements of a going-concern valuation?

9. How can a mail-order company sometimes afford to spend more in first-year acquisition costs than an agency company?

10. How should the purchase of a life insurance company be accounted for?

11. What is the effect of assuming that a company will always be taxed on taxable investment income (a) on the deferred tax provision and (b) on the reserve interest assumption?

12. How can capital losses be converted to long-term excess interest earnings without the losses ever being recognized in the income statement?

---

ity, level, and growth of earnings. There are three conditions precedent to such evaluation: a knowledgeable analyst, a reasonably coherent body of accounting principles and practices, and adequate disclosure.

Knowledgeable Analysts

Table 31-1 contains a "mini-quiz" for insurance stock analysts. The analyst who feels comfortable with most of the questions probably has sufficient technical background to evaluate a life insurance company's reported GAAP earnings. The analyst who cannot begin to answer most of the questions probably does not have sufficient background to evaluate a life insurance company's GAAP earnings.

There are few good sources of information on the subject of GAAP accounting at the present time, so the analyst's attempt to learn the subject is likely to be very frustrating. Nevertheless, the effort will be repaid handsomely, not only in an increased expertise in dealing with GAAP accounting but in an increased knowledge of the life insurance business as well.

Coherent Principles

Say what one will about the life insurance audit guide, the accounting principles and practices set forth in the guide are basically rational and coherent. The principles are designed to give a company credit for success and penalize it for failure, to subject accounting determinations to a degree of discipline, and to give effect to the conservatism necessarily associated with a long-term undertaking. The principles will, of course, be unevenly applied, and the results on occasion are going to be flawed. But the principles themselves are defensible.

Disclosure

It is impossible to evaluate reported earnings unless information is furnished about the major principles, practices, and assumptions utilized in the accounting process. This is true of the reported earnings of any company; it is especially true of life insurance earnings in the early years of implementing the life insurance audit guide.

This is because, while GAAP earnings may have a basic core of coherency, issues of credibility and comparability remain unresolved. It is disconcerting, for example, to read the 1972 annual reports of 30 companies and find 16 sets of interest assumptions

Table 31–2.

NEW BUSINESS INTEREST RATE ASSUMPTIONS FOR 30 COMPANIES IN 1972

6% level	6 1/2% graded to 4 1/2%
5 3/4% level	5 1/2% graded to 4 1/2%
6% graded to 5 1/2%	5% graded to 4 1/2%
5 1/2% level	4 1/4% level
7% graded to 5%	6% graded to 4%
6% graded to 5%	5% graded to 4%
5% level	4% level
7% graded to 4 1/2%	6 1/2% graded to 3 1/2%

for new business, ranging from 6 percent level to 6 1/2 percent graded to 3 1/2 percent (see Table 31–2). What is the analyst to make of such a situation?

One thing he can do is demand more information. A footnote may disclose that a company's interest assumptions "range from 6 1/2 percent to 2 1/2 percent depending on the issue year," but the analyst should know the relative volumes of reserves for each rate, and he should be able to get some idea of the effect of the company's array of interest assumptions on the financial statements this year and in the future.

To evaluate earnings intelligently the analyst needs to know, among other things,

▸ Adjustments for each major line of business,
▸ Interest assumptions and the corresponding issue years and reserve volumes,
▸ Deferral policy in considerable detail,
▸ Costs deferred, costs amortized, and first-year premiums for each major line of business,
▸ Treatment of renewal-year acquisition costs,
▸ Treatment of maintenance and settlement costs,
▸ Composition, treatment, and amount of development costs,
▸ General practices with respect to mortality and withdrawal assumptions,
▸ Information concerning special items such as mortality fluctuation reserves, participating restrictions, etc.,
▸ Details of the company's present tax posture, its expected future tax posture, and the methods used in providing for deferred taxes,
▸ The treatment of acquisitions and relevant amounts, and
▸ A detailed description of the GAAP conversion process.

In many (perhaps most) cases, such disclosures cannot feasibly be made in the compass of a formal financial statement; supplemental disclosure is usually necessary to do the job. Some companies provide the necessary information in some fashion; others do not. When the information is not furnished, the analyst should ask for it. When the request is denied, the analyst should find out why. There are few reasons adequate to justify non-disclosure of all pertinent details of a GAAP conversion.

Given adequate information, the informed analyst can make a reasonably dependable judgment about the composition and quality of earnings. Such a judgment is essential to analyzing and predicting the level and growth of earnings.

Some Approaches to Analysis

The life insurance audit guide has made it somewhat easier to perform certain types of basic financial analysis that are fairly commonplace for other forms of enterprise but which have rarely been used in the case of life insurance companies. These include line-of-business analysis, return on sales, and return on equity.

Line-of-Business Analysis

A complex life insurance company is similar in some respects to a multi-market industrial corporation. Each major line of business has its own characteristics and its own potential, and it is important to know the contribution of each such line to total profits.

Determining operating results by line of business is fraught with dangers for the unwary analyst. The allocation of investment income to lines of business may be arbitrary. The allocation of general expenses to lines of business may also be arbitrary. And there is the question of what to do about interest on capital

Table 31–3.

CRAZY QUILT LIFE'S 1971 ADJUSTED RESULTS BY LINE OF BUSINESS (000 Omitted)

	All Lines	Ordinary Partici-pating	Ordinary Non-Par-ticipating	Industrial	Individual Annuities	Variable Annuities	Individual Health	Group Life And Health	Group Annuities	Credit Life And Health
REVENUE										
Premiums:										
First-year	$ 17,507	$ 1,588	$10,300	$ 972			$ 2,452	$ 2,195		
Single	23,474		673		$15,078		2,626		$ 660	$4,437
Renewal	76,251	8,344	47,067	3,429			7,249	10,162		
	117,232	9,932	58,040	4,401	15,078		12,327	12,357	660	4,437
Management fees	1,502					$ 1,502				
Miscellaneous income	8		8							
Net investment income	30,852	2,493	19,448	1,400	5,596	(215)	1,075	559	260	236
	149,594	12,425	77,496	5,801	20,674	1,287	13,402	12,916	920	4,673
BENEFITS										
Claims and other benefits	56,295	4,562	24,517	1,031	7,847		3,766	10,391	1,165	3,016
Change in reserves	34,486	4,124	19,841	940	8,307		1,526		(252)	
	90,781	8,686	44,358	1,971	16,154	–0–	5,292	10,391	913	3,016
BALANCE	58,813	3,739	33,138	3,830	4,520	1,287	8,110	2,525	7	1,657
EXPENSES										
Expenses paid or accrued	48,037	4,198	26,805	2,877	1,389	2,700	6,534	1,953	21	1,560
Change in unamortized acquisition costs	(14,093)	(1,366)	(9,326)	(343)		(1,188)	(1,417)	(41)		(412)
Provision for future maintenance and settlement expenses	319	(1)	109	26	103		82			
	34,263	2,831	17,588	2,560	1,492	1,512	5,199	1,912	21	1,148
INCOME BEFORE INCOME TAXES AND REALIZED CAPITAL GAINS	24,550	908	15,550	1,270	3,028	(225)	2,911	613	(14)	509
INTEREST ON CAPITAL										
Interest on capital	8,848	717	5,583	398	1,601	(62)	310	159	71	71
LINE-OF-BUSINESS INCOME BEFORE INCOME TAXES AND REALIZED CAPITAL GAINS AND EXCLUDING INTEREST ON CAPITAL	$ 15,702	$ 191	$ 9,967	$ 872	$ 1,427	$ (163)	$ 2,601	$ 454	$ (85)	$ 438

INTEREST ON CAPITAL detail:

Net investment income	$ 30,852
Mean invested assets	÷ $505,362
Rate	= 6.1%
Mean GAAP capital	x $145,045
Interest on capital	= $ 8,848*

* Allocated to lines of business in proportion to total investment income allocated to each line.

and surplus, which must be eliminated if line-of-business results are to stand on their own.

Therefore line-of-business analysis should be undertaken with full knowledge of the limitations of this type of analysis. Limitations or not, however, the exercise is eminently worthwhile.

Perhaps a stylized example will suggest some approaches that might be useful. Table 31–3 shows Crazy Quilt Life's adjusted operating results, before taxes and capital gains, by line of business. The table is based on Convention Statement line-of-business breakdowns plus supplemental information from the Company about participating business and variable annuities. Revenue figures are from the Convention Statement, except that certain deposit-type items are eliminated against the corresponding reserve increases and except that unearned premium changes for commercial health and credit life and health coverages are applied to reduce premium revenue.

It so happens that Crazy Quilt Life allocates investment on line-of-business cash flows. Interest on corporate funds is allocated in proportion to direct line-of-business interest. General overhead is allocated to lines of business in proportion to "direct" expenses, where "direct" expenses are determined by functional cost analysis.

Table 31–3 reflects the distribution of GAAP adjustments by line of business. Interest on capital is eliminated by the same method as was used for allocation in the first place. No adjustment is made for general overhead; it is left where it is, i.e., allocated to lines of business. (Some analysts would prefer to eliminate such overhead from the analysis.)

The information shown in Table 31–3 can be analyzed in several ways.

Composition of earnings. The contribution to earnings by line can be displayed in amounts and percentages:

	Contribution To Earnings	
	Amount (000)	% of Total
Ordinary:		
Participating	$ 191	1.2%
Non-participating	9,967	63.5
Industrial	872	5.6
Individual annuities	1,427	9.1
Variable annuities	(163)	(1.0)
Individual health	2,601	16.6
Group life and health	454	2.9
Group annuities	(85)	(.5)
Credit life and health	438	2.8
Line-of-business results	15,702	100.0%
Interest on capital	8,848	
General overhead *	-0-	
Taxes	(6,999)	
Capital gains	263	
Net Income	$17,814	

*As indicated in the text, general overhead is allocated to lines of business in this example. Some may wish to treat such overhead as an item "below" the line-of-business results.

Such an analysis is useful in itself. Over time it can help identify trends, both good and bad, so long as the analysis is consistent from year to year. Within strict limits, the analysis can be used for inter-company comparisons.

Operating ratios. Line-of-business results as a percentage of premiums can be computed:

	Line-of-Business Results	Premiums or Other Revenues	%
Ordinary:			
Participating	$ 191	$ 9,932	2%
Non-participating	9,967	58,040	17
Industrial	872	4,401	20
Individual annuities	1,427	15,078	9
Variable annuities	(163)	1,502	(11)
Individual health	2,601	12,327	21
Group life and health	454	12,357	4
Group annuities	(85)	660	(13)
Credit life and health	438	4,437	10
	$15,702	$118,734	13%

Again, this type of analysis can be useful in a time series format and, again within strict limits, it can be used for inter-company analysis.

Operating ratios of the type described above are further discussed later in this chapter.

Internal relationships. The analysis is also useful for examining certain internal relationships. For example, benefits, reserve changes, and expenses may be expressed as a ratio for the non-par ordinary line of business as follows:

	Amount (000)	%
Line-of-business revenue	$77,496	
Interest on capital	5,583	
Adjusted revenue	71,913	100%
Benefits:		
Claims, etc.	24,517	34
Change in reserves	19,841	28
	44,358	62
Expenses:		
Paid or accrued	26,805	37
Adjustments	(9,217)	(13)
	17,588	24
Line-of-business income	$ 9,967	14%

Within limits—*always* within limits—this particular analysis can be used to spot fluctuations, a deteriorating situation, or an improving situation.

Return on Sales

Profits expressed as a percentage of sales has always been an important element of financial analysis for most companies. Profits as a percentage of premiums has rarely been used in analyzing life insurance company statements.

The life insurance audit guide calls for profits to be distributed over the life of the contract in proportion to insurance in force irrespective of the premium-

Table 31–4.

PRE-TAX GAAP OPERATING INCOME (EXCLUDING INTEREST ON CAPITAL) AS A PERCENTAGE OF PREMIUMS FOR 28 COMPANIES IN 1972

HEAVY DEBIT OPERATIONS:		HEAVY GROUP OPERATIONS:	
12%	1 company	5%	3 companies
14%	1 company	6%	1 company
18%	1 company	7%	1 company
HEAVY ORDINARY OPERATIONS:		HEAVY HEALTH OPERATIONS:	
0–5%	5 companies	12%	1 company
6–10%	6 companies	21%	2 companies
11–15%	4 companies	over 30%	2 companies

paying period. For various reasons which are beyond the scope of this chapter, it is nevertheless useful to examine profits as a percentage of premiums.

In discussing Table 31–3, "operating ratios"—line-of-business profits as a percentage of premiums—were calculated for each line of business. For the Company as a whole, the operating ratio may be summarized as follows:

Line-of-business profits	$ 15,702,000
Premiums, etc.	$118,734,000
Ratio	13%

Crazy Quilt might be regarded as a "heavy ordinary" company. It is interesting to compare Crazy Quilt's 13 percent operating ratio with 15 other companies heavily oriented to ordinary business, whose 1972 operating ratios were as follows:

1972 Operating Ratio	Number of Companies
0–5%	5
6–10	6
11–15	4

Thus Crazy Quilt ranks among the more profitable ordinary companies.

Table 31–4 shows 1972 operating ratios for 28 companies of varying orientations. A company's indicated operating ratio, when compared with those of other similar companies, serves as a useful frame of reference for analysis. Why is Crazy Quilt's ratio fairly high? Is it simply because the Company is successful? Is it because of liberal accounting? Is it because of too much conservatism in reserving for issues of prior years? There may be no absolute answer, but it's certainly helpful to have enough information to ask the questions.

Return on Equity

Crazy Quilt Life's pre-tax return on equity may be computed readily:

1971 earnings before taxes and capital gains	$ 24,550,000
Mean GAAP capital	$145,045,000
Return on equity	17%

Interestingly, Crazy Quilt's return on equity is comparable to the 1972 weighted average return on equity (16.4 percent) for 29 companies, details of which are shown in Table 31–5. Again, the comparison is useful as a frame of reference. While Crazy Quilt may not be setting the world on fire at 17 percent, nevertheless there is a certain comfort in the fact that the Company's indicated return on equity is neither extravagantly higher nor disastrously lower than comparable averages.*

Rules of Thumb

The 1972 annual report of a stock life insurance company (which shall go nameless) showed a sizeable GAAP loss. One would think it difficult to explain away a GAAP loss. But the president of this particular company did it very handily: "Our statement shows a loss on a GAAP basis," he said; "but if you take our increase in insurance in force and add $20 a thousand for permanent and . . ."

Rules of thumb are slow to die, and a few words about them are still appropriate.

*In examining Table 31–5, for example, one wonders how long competition, regulation, or accounting methods will tolerate returns of 30 to 40 percent.

Table 31–5.

PRE-TAX GAAP RETURN ON MEAN GAAP EQUITY FOR 29 COMPANIES IN 1972

Number of Companies	Indicated Return on Equity
1	40%
1	37
1	33
2	32
1	29
1	27
1	21
2	19
2	18
4	17
1	16
2	15
4	14
1	12
1	10
1	9
1	6
2	4
Mean	18.6%
Weighted average	16.4%

Dollars-Per-Thousand Method

The objective of adjusting statutory earnings by adding so many dollars per thousand of the increase in insurance in force is apparently to recognize the change in the present value of future statutory profits. This might be called the "value-added" approach to adjusted earnings—earnings for a period consist of reported earnings plus the present value of all future earnings to be derived from the net addition to the inventory of insurance in force.

The method is, of course, fraught with pitfalls. Calculation of the present value of future earnings depends on (1) a projection of future earnings and (2) a discount rate. Future earnings depend on (1) the reserve method used, (2) the level of gross premiums, (3) future experience as to interest, mortality, and lapse, and (4) the taxability of earnings. The appropriate discount rate depends on (1) inherent risk, (2) reserve method (since net level earnings are less "risky" than CRVM earnings), and (3) rates of return available on competitive investments.

The dollars-per-thousand method has generally been applied without regard for the variables described above. In short, it has been applied more or less indiscriminately.

That the dollars-per-thousand method can produce strange results under differing circumstances is suggested by Table 31–6. The table shows

▶ Pre-tax statutory income of Crazy Quilt Life's ordinary business on three reserve bases: mixed (i.e., a combination of net level and modified reserves), all net level, and all modified. (Crazy Quilt was so constructed that the ordinary line constitutes, in effect, a model company selling just ordinary business. The reserves were all calculated by means of rate tapes; no estimates are involved.)

▶ The increase in insurance in force, segregated between permanent and term.

▶ An "adjustment" equal to $20 per $1,000 of the increase in permanent insurance in force and $10 per $1,000 of the increase in term insurance in force.

▶ Statutory after the dollars-per-thousand adjustment, again on the three reserve bases.

▶ Actual GAAP, as calculated according to methods described in this book.

▶ Actual value added, computed by adding to statu-

Table 31–6.

COMPARATIVE PRE-TAX RESULTS FOR ORDINARY LIFE MODEL (000 Omitted)

Year	Statutory Income Mixed Model	Net Level Model	CRVM Model	Increase in In-Force (000) Permanent	Term	Dollars per Thousand* Adjustment	Adjusted Statutory Income After Dollars Per Thousand Adjustment Mixed	Net Level	CRVM	Actual GAAP	Value Added—Mixed Model Change in Present Value of Future Profits At 12%	Value Added
1941	$(1,189)	$(1,338)	$ (934)	$ 23	$ 2	$ 480	$(709)	$ (858)	$ (454)	$ (636)	$ 1,000	$ (189)
1942	(880)	(1,047)	(576)	26	4	560	(320)	(487)	(16)	(288)	1,261	381
1943	(930)	(1,135)	(573)	32	5	690	(240)	(445)	117	(286)	1,592	662
1944	(876)	(1,073)	(450)	37	6	800	(76)	(273)	350	(234)	1,810	934
1945	(891)	(1,095)	(347)	46	7	990	99	(105)	643	(140)	2,241	1,350
1946	(778)	(1,006)	(179)	51	8	1,100	322	94	921	(14)	2,631	1,853
1947	(541)	(731)	118	54	8	1,160	619	429	1,278	151	2,874	2,333
1948	732	(453)	460	45	9	990	1,722	537	1,450	313	1,234	1,966
1949	353	(734)	195	51	9	1,110	1,463	376	1,305	447	1,992	2,345
1950	292	(695)	185	51	13	1,150	1,442	455	1,335	684	2,516	2,808
1951	465	(473)	400	53	15	1,210	1,675	737	1,610	1,028	2,879	3,344
1952	(696)	(214)	595	51	19	1,210	514	996	1,805	1,336	4,185	3,489
1953	(128)	235	976	51	22	1,240	1,112	1,475	2,216	1,647	4,190	4,062
1954	451	787	1,403	47	21	1,150	1,601	2,388	2,553	2,056	4,249	4,700
1955	751	1,532	1,923	37	20	940	1,691	2,472	2,863	2,362	4,057	4,808
1956	1,720	2,496	2,640	25	16	660	2,380	3,156	3,300	2,908	3,689	5,409
1957	2,304	3,026	3,134	27	14	680	2,984	3,706	3,814	3,439	2,660	4,964
1958	2,685	3,429	3,579	23	22	680	3,365	4,109	4,259	3,895	2,671	5,356
1959	3,225	3,928	4,081	31	20	820	4,045	4,748	4,901	4,423	2,648	5,873
1960	3,268	4,152	4,445	42	22	1,060	4,328	5,212	5,505	4,889	2,859	6,127
1961	3,394	4,209	4,662	39	31	1,090	4,484	5,299	5,752	5,191	3,306	6,700
1962	5,489	4,290	4,673	62	34	1,580	7,069	5,870	6,253	5,520	2,177	7,666
1963	4,402	2,946	3,953	96	57	2,490	6,892	5,436	6,443	5,800	3,973	8,375
1964	3,575	2,077	3,413	120	71	3,110	6,685	5,187	6,523	5,938	5,353	8,928
1965	2,693	1,429	3,078	149	93	3,910	6,603	5,339	6,988	6,299	7,060	9,753
1966	2,535	985	2,969	176	109	4,610	7,145	5,595	7,579	6,848	8,353	10,888
1967	2,619	774	3,132	203	124	5,300	7,919	6,074	8,432	7,614	9,484	12,103
1968	(606)	1,359	3,901	222	136	5,800	5,194	7,159	9,701	8,730	12,274	11,668
1969	756	1,995	5,004	248	149	6,450	7,206	8,445	11,454	10,307	11,982	12,738
1970	1,282**	2,222	5,640	280	166	7,260	8,542	9,482	12,900	12,324	11,111	12,393
1971	1,638**	2,477	6,164	301	185	7,870	9,508	10,347	14,034	14,328	11,698	13,336

*$20 per $1,000 for permanent, $10 per $1,000 for term.

**Effect of 1970 reserve strengthening eliminated.

tory earnings (mixed reserve bases) the change in the present value of projected future statutory earnings accurately calculated by computer techniques using a discount rate of 12 percent.

The tremendous range of values produced by the various adjustment methods is dramatically illustrated in the table. In particular, the effect of reserve method on the indicated results of the dollars-per-thousand approach is worth special scrutiny. The figures simply confirm the obvious: No *uniform* dollars-per-thousand method can be relied upon.

AIFA Method

In November 1969 the Committee on Life Insurance Earnings Adjustments of the Association of Insurance and Financial Analysts, a group of New York security analysts, issued a report which pro-

Table 31–7.

COMPARISON OF 1972 GAAP AND AIFA EARNINGS FOR 31 COMPANIES**

Company	Earnings Per Share		GAAP as
	GAAP	AIFA	% of AIFA
1	$ 6.50	$ 6.41	101%
2	1.95	1.97	99
3	1.04	1.13	92
4	2.09*	2.17	96
5	1.34*	1.39	96
6	2.13	2.30	93
7	1.49*	2.84	52
8	2.70	2.75	98
9	1.36*	1.48	92
10	6.09	6.02	101
11	4.34*	4.75	91
12	4.43	4.69	94
13	1.05	1.79	59
14	1.67*	2.39	70
15	6.66*	7.83	85
16	4.21	4.06	104
17	1.86*	1.84	101
18	1.64*	2.05	80
19	3.51*	4.48	78
20	1.95*	1.76	111
21	4.72	4.79	99
22	3.27*	3.27	100
23	4.16*	3.96	105
24	3.27	2.91	112
25	3.78	3.81	99
26	2.97	3.22	92
27	3.17*	3.51	90
28	2.83*	3.79	75
29	1.52	2.39	64
30	2.04*	2.07	99
31	1.17*	2.45	48

* Substantially all life.

**Source: Best's Insurance Securities Research Service, Report of November 23, 1973.

posed a new method of adjusting earnings of life insurance companies (hereinafter referred to as the "AIFA method"). The AIFA method was a vast improvement over the welter of dollars-per-thousand methods. It achieved wide acceptance by the life insurance industry. AIFA method earnings were reported as supplemental information by a large minority of publicly-traded companies until the advent of the life insurance audit guide.

The method involved the deferral and amortization of specified acquisition costs, adjustment of reserve interest assumptions by use of the "Rule of 10", and recognition of deferred taxes at one-half the corporate rate.

The AIFA method depended on Convention Statement information, a practical necessity. The method also made no distinction for the reserve method used.

One would expect these deficiencies to prove fatal, but the fact is that the AIFA method did a pretty good job as Table 31–7 suggests. The table compares AIFA earnings and GAAP earnings for 31 companies in 1972. It appears that enough of the deficiencies of the AIFA approach offset to produce reasonably credible figures for many companies. But the differences are frequent enough, and severe enough, that the AIFA method, as good as it is, should be regarded with the same caution as the dollars-per-thousand approach.

Management Uses of GAAP

The principal purpose of GAAP is to provide a basis for reporting on the economic affairs of an enterprise to owners, creditors, and others. That's all well and good, but what can GAAP do for management?

The discussion that follows is intended to suggest a few of the ways that a GAAP conversion might be used to facilitate the management process. The creative manager will no doubt find many other useful by-products of the conversion.

Analyzing Business in Force

In the course of studying various blocks of business in connection with a GAAP conversion, some companies have developed new insights into their business. One company found, for instance, that a small and long-neglected block of participating business was producing sizeable losses. Dividend reductions were made immediately. Another company found that business sold to a specific specialized market was deteriorating rapidly; the company quit the market.

Perhaps companies should be expected to keep on top of these things with or without GAAP, but the fact is that the demands on management energies often limit the energy available for extensive ex-post-facto product analysis. GAAP simply makes analysis mandatory, and an alert management can derive much more benefit from analysis than an adjusted financial statement.

Earnings by Source

The types of studies that must be conducted to develop and validate GAAP reserve assumptions can be used to develop an analysis of earnings by source, perhaps in the following format:

Interest on capital and surplus	xxx
Built-in profit loading	xxx
Effect of variances from expected:	
Mortality	xxx
Persistency	xxx
Interest	xxx
Acquisition costs	xxx
Maintenance expenses	xxx
Total GAAP earnings	xxx

This type of analysis has always been controversial, and various somewhat arbitrary assumptions—such as whether deaths or terminations occur first—must be made.

Assuming, however, that the underlying GAAP reserve assumptions are rational, an analysis of earnings by source can have considerable value to an actuary and, by extension, to top management.

Corporate Models

In-force models developed for the purpose of calculating adjusted reserves can readily be utilized in corporate planning models. Getting existing in-force "on the model" has been one of the more difficult tasks in modeling; GAAP has forced companies to do the job, which is otherwise easily postponed.

Some thought should be given to the early stages of modeling to what breakdowns are needed for purposes of the corporate model—agency breakdowns, regional breakdowns, etc. Often the model structure deemed desirable for management purposes will be far more complex than what is needed for accounting purposes, and thought should be given to management needs well in advance of actually building the model.

Profit Planning

Everyone talks about profit planning, but very few do anything about it.

Nevertheless a few blithe spirits in the life insurance business have undertaken profit planning in earnest. Many profit plans have been developed in terms of statutory accounting. The ideal profit planning format would show both statutory and adjusted results. Both are needed and—assuming a respectably sophisticated model—both are readily obtainable.

Valuing Business in Force

GAAP reserve models can be used to value insurance in force periodically; all that is needed is to project future experience using current experience data and model in-force. Providing that statutory reserves can be accommodated in the model, best-estimate statutory earnings can be projected and discounted to obtain in-force values.

Such values are useful in and of themselves. GAAP is useful from a public reporting standpoint, but "value added"—i.e., the change in the value of insurance in force—is perhaps a better measurement from management's standpoint of how the company really did during a period, or across several periods.

The usefulness of such values in merger negotiations, defenses against takeovers, etc. is readily apparent.

Agency Evaluation

Assuming that model data and experience input are appropriately coded, the valuation of business in force can be broken down by agency, district, or other marketing unit. Value added by an individual marketing unit can be one valuable measure of the success of the unit's efforts for the year.

Incentive Compensation

There appears to be no real obstacle to measuring the performance of certain operating units in terms of GAAP and gearing executive compensation at least in part to GAAP results.

The feasibility of doing this is especially apparent with respect to top executives. It is doubtful that the life insurance industry has properly recognized top management performance—good or bad—in the past, perhaps because acceptable measures of performance have been lacking. GAAP results might well be regarded as one acceptable measure of performance.

Cost Accounting

The life insurance industry has done some remarkable things with functional costs. But it has not done a good job in identifying variable, semi-variable, and fixed costs.

Whether for "costing" a proposed new product, profit planning, flexible budgeting, responsibility accounting, or any other undertaking involving cost behavior, the industry could usefully adopt some of the conventions of industrial cost accounting, including clear differentiations among direct and indirect costs, fixed and variable costs, controllable and non-controllable costs.

The types of studies undertaken to identify those costs which "vary with and are primarily related to production" can, if carefully conducted, provide some of the basic information needed to modernize life insurance cost accounting.

Maximizing Returns from GAAP

The conversion to generally accepted accounting principles represents a major investment of time, talent, and money for any life insurance company. Top management has a right to expect appropriate returns from the investment. An adjusted financial statement, in and of itself, does not represent an appropriate return. Management should expect more, and should challenge the company's actuaries and accountants to extract every available management aid from the conversion process.

32 Whither GAAP?

The heat of the 1973 conversions had barely died down before the hue and cry began. Security analysts and a not inconsiderable number of company presidents claimed that the only effect GAAP had on the price of life stocks was to reduce the multiple; prices didn't budge. Professor Briloff wrote an article to "alert the reader regarding latent booby traps" in GAAP statements. An angry actuary with an ear for catchy phrases wrote that "GAAP should be scrapped." He complained it was too expensive, and had accomplished little except to enrich accountants and actuaries, himself included. Accountants and actuaries were so exhausted by the the traumas of 1973 that they didn't have the energy to count their riches and in fact would gladly have handed them back if only the agonies could have been reversed. Annual reports were published so late that some stockholders wondered if their companies were still in business. Accountants and actuaries could look forward to an unhappy year or two of wondering when an undetected error would surface. The field of life insurance financial reporting was littered with the debris of failed software systems, failed computer print-outs, and here and there a failed accountant and a failed actuary. For the life insurance industry and everyone associated with it, World War III would be anticlimactic.

With so auspicious a beginning, many people wonder what GAAP can possibly do for an encore.

Well, for one thing GAAP can grow up, given half a chance. Accounting principles need time to mature. They do not spring full-blown from the head of Zeus or an AICPA committee or anyone else. It took over a hundred years for statutory accounting to develop to its present state. GAAP deserves a little time too, albeit not a hundred years. "I will be the pattern of all patience," said King Lear at a difficult moment on the storm-toss'd heath. Admittedly he might have sung a different tune if he'd had GAAP to worry about, but in any event a little patience is a good thing. The nay-sayers are perhaps a little unfair to the babe in swaddling clothes. The alternatives to GAAP are not readily apparent. Certainly the critics have not offered any viable alternatives.

GAAP will probably take another quantum leap a few years hence. Being a product of plain old human beings (i.e., actuaries and accountants, notwithstanding the occasional question concerning the humanity of same), GAAP is eminently imperfect. With experience will come some perspective on what's good and what's bad about GAAP, which is to say what works and what doesn't. It's easy to guess in advance what may not work, but it's impossible to *know* in advance what *hasn't* worked, and that kind of knowledge is essential for the next step. The next step might be the use of gross premium valuations, or standard-profits per unit of insurance in force, or maybe even a return to statutory. Whatever form the quantum leap takes, it's bound to happen.

Finally, it is quite likely that GAAP will eventually creep into the regulatory process, either by influencing valuation procedures, by serving as one of the "early warning" indicators, or by some other means.

So GAAP's future looks possibly bright, possibly dim, but always interesting and inevitably controversial.

Appendixes

Appendix A

Present Values and Related Concepts

The inventor of the venerable proverb "A bird in the hand is worth two in the bush" probably didn't have interest rates in mind, but he was clearly speaking in terms of present values. Without appropriate qualification, however, the proverb must be regarded with suspicion. Whether or not a bird in the hand is worth two in the bush depends in part upon the prevailing interest rate.

Present values and related concepts of mathematics are second nature to actuaries, of course. Accountants have a passing acquaintance with such concepts too. But the complexities of actuarial science in a life insurance environment are such that a passing acquaintance sometimes is not enough.

This appendix is designed to describe and illustrate several fundamental actuarial concepts and techniques as they apply to life insurance accounting. Actuaries could well skip the material unless they'd like a few chuckles. Accountants and other non-actuaries may find the somewhat elementary material in this appendix to be helpful in interpreting the book.

A 20-year endowment insurance policy issued to a male age 25 in 1951 is used throughout the appendix for illustrative purposes. While the mortality table, interest rate, etc. are all outdated now, use of a 1951 issue has at least two advantages. First, experience assumed when the contract was issued can be compared with actual experience for the entire duration of the contract; all 20-year endowment policies issued in 1951 were out of force by the end of 1971. And second, level interest rates were typically given effect in rate calculations in 1951, whereas variable interest rates are typically used today; use of a level interest rate greatly simplifies the illustrations.

The assumptions underlying the illustrated policy are set forth in Table A–1.

The endowment policy illustrated in this appendix was issued by Crazy Quilt Life in 1951. Crazy Quilt Life is described in Chapter 5. All of the thousands of ordinary life model components that went into the development of Crazy Quilt were based on essentially the same techniques as are illustrated in this appendix.

The illustrations are always expressed in terms of one "unit" of insurance, which in this case is $1,000 of face amount. With a few obvious exceptions, the quantities shown can be expanded to represent any volume of insurance issued simply by multiplying each figure by the appropriate number of "units" issued.

Statutory Reserves

Statutory reserves are computed by selecting a mortality table, an interest rate, and a valuation method, computing reserve factors (or using standard published factors) that correspond to the parameters selected, and multiplying units in force by the factors. Limits or requirements for mortality table, interest rate, and valuation method are set forth in the Standard Valuation Law. The mortality table is specifically prescribed. Interest rates are subject to a maximum of 3 1/2 percent (3% in New York).*

---

*This does not necessarily mean that a company may choose *any* rate less than the maximum. Any company that selects a rate that is unreasonably low would probably be challenged by the state insurance department. This has happened in at least one case; the company was not permitted to use a rate which the insurance department found to be unreasonably low.

Table A–1.

SUMMARY OF ASSUMPTIONS UNDERLYING ILLUSTRATIONS OF PRESENT VALUES, ETC., FOR A 20-YEAR ENDOWMENT POLICY ISSUED TO A MALE AGE 25

Mortality:
Statutory reserves and cash values—1941 CSO Table
Premiums, projections, and natural reserves—1946–49 Basic Table (modified)

Interest:
Statutory reserves—2½%
Cash values—2½%
Premiums, projections, and natural reserves—3%

Withdrawals (premiums, projections, and natural reserves)—20% in Year 1, 9% in Year 2, 5% in Years 3–9, 4% thereafter.

Average size: $2,500

Gross premium per $1,000: $49.58

Expenses:
Commissions:

	Sub-Agent	General Agent
First year	45.0%	15.0%
Renewal	5.0%	2.5%

Additional first-year agency expense:
38.3% of premiums, plus $10.75 per policy, plus $2.15 per $1,000.

First-year selection expense:
$9.85 per policy, plus $2.15 per $1,000.

First-year issue expense—$8.95 per policy.

Premium taxes—2%

Annual maintenance—$4.90 per policy.

Cost of settling death claim—$21.25 per claim.

Cost of processing surrender—$12.75 per surrender.

Valuation methods are limited essentially to two basic methods (net level and CRVM) or interpolations between them. Notwithstanding these general provisions (and other restrictive provisions not discussed here), the possible combinations of table, rate, and method are numerous, and the combination chosen can have a material effect on the financial statements.

Net Level Premiums

A net level premium is computed by computing a net single premium and dividing the result by the appropriate annuity due of $1.

The procedure for calculating a net level premium for the endowment described earlier is illustrated in Table A–2. The calculation is fairly straightforward:

▶ The present value of expected future death claims is computed by multiplying the probability of death in each year by the face amount and discounting the result by the discount factor appropriate to the assumed interest rate. In the 19th year, for example, the calculation is:

(a)	Probability of death	.00751
(b)	Percentage of people originally insured expected to survive to the 19th year	.92204
(c)	Face amount of insurance	$1,000
(d)	Expected death claims (a X b X c)	$6.92
(e)	2 1/2% discount	.62553
(f)	Present value of expected death (d X e)	$4.33

▶ The present value of the endowment is computed by multiplying the percentage of people expected to survive through the 20th year by the face amount then payable and discounting the result for interest. Thus:

600

Table A–2.

CALCULATION OF STATUTORY NET PREMIUMS (1941 CSO, 2 1/2%) FOR A 20-YEAR ENDOWMENT POLICY ISSUED TO A MALE AGE 25

Policy Year	Attained Age	Probability Of Death— 1941 CSO	Survivors at Beginning Of Year	Expected Deaths	Discount at 2½%	Present Value of Expected Claims	Present Value of $1 Annuity Due*
1	25	.00288	1.00000	.00288	.97561	$ 2.81	$1.000
2	26	.00299	.99712	.00298	.95181	2.84	.973
3	27	.00311	.99414	.00309	.92860	2.87	.946
4	28	.00325	.99105	.00322	.90595	2.92	.920
5	29	.00340	.98783	.00336	.88385	2.97	.895
6	30	.00356	.98447	.00350	.86230	3.02	.870
7	31	.00373	.98097	.00366	.84127	3.08	.846
8	32	.00392	.97731	.00383	.82075	3.14	.822
9	33	.00412	.97348	.00401	.80073	3.21	.799
10	34	.00435	.96947	.00422	.78120	3.30	.776
11	35	.00459	.96525	.00443	.76214	3.38	.754
12	36	.00486	.96082	.00467	.74356	3.47	.732
13	37	.00515	.95615	.00492	.72542	3.57	.711
14	38	.00546	.95123	.00519	.70773	3.67	.690
15	39	.00581	.94604	.00550	.69047	3.80	.669
16	40	.00618	.94054	.00581	.67362	3.91	.649
17	41	.00659	.93473	.00616	.65720	4.05	.630
18	42	.00703	.92857	.00653	.64117	4.19	.610
19	43	.00751	.92204	.00692	.62553	4.33	.591
20	44	.00804	.91512	.00736	.61027	4.49	.572
20	44**	NA	.90776	NA	NA	NA	NA
Value of term insurance						$69.02	
20-year 2½% discount			.61027				
Face amount			$1,000				
Value of pure endowment			$ 553.98			553.98	
Net single premium						$623.00	
Present value of $1 annuity due						$ 15.455	$15.455
Net level premium						$ 40.31	

*Equal to survivors at beginning of year multiplied by the prior year's discount.
**Just prior to 45th birthday.

(a) Percentage of people originally insured expected to survive to the end of the 20th year   .90776
(b) Face amount of endowment $1,000
(c) Expected endowment payments (a X b) $907.76
(d) 2 1/2% discount   .61027
(e) Present value of expected endowment payments (c X d) $553.98

▶ The present value of a $1 annuity due is computed by multiplying the percentage of people surviving at the beginning of the year by the discount rate; the discount factor is always for a period that is one year less than is used for the benefit calculations. In the 20th year, for example, the present value of the $1 payment by survivors is computed as follows:

(a) Percentage of people expected to survive to end of 18th year and pay premiums in the 19th year   .92204
(b) Present value at 2 1/2% of $1 payable 18 years hence $.64117
(c) Present value of $1 due in 19th year (a X b) $.591

▶ The net single premium for the insurance and the endowment is divided by the present value of the $1 annuity due to determine the net level premium. Thus:

(a) Present value of expected death claims $69.02

Table A–3.

PROGRESSION OF A NET LEVEL STATUTORY RESERVE (1941 CSO, 2 1/2%) FOR A 20-YEAR ENDOWMENT POLICY ISSUED TO A MALE AGE 25

Policy Year	Attained Age	Fund at Beginning Of Year	Units in Force At Beginning Of Year	Net Level Premiums Received at Beginning of Year - Units X $40.31	Initial Fund	Interest At 2½%	Claims at End of Year	Terminal Fund	Units in Force at End of Year	Terminal Reserve per Unit In Force*
1	25	$ –0–	1.00000	$40.31	$ 40.31	$ 1.01	$2.88	$ 38.44	.99712	$ 38.55
2	26	38.44	.99712	40.19	78.63	1.97	2.98	77.62	.99414	78.08
3	27	77.62	.99414	40.07	117.69	2.94	3.09	117.54	.99105	118.60
4	28	117.54	.99105	39.95	157.49	3.94	3.22	158.21	.98783	160.16
5	29	158.21	.98783	39.82	198.03	4.95	3.36	199.69	.98447	202.84
6	30	199.62	.98447	39.68	239.30	5.98	3.50	241.78	.98097	246.47
7	31	241.78	.98097	39.54	281.32	7.03	3.66	284.69	.97731	291.30
8	32	284.69	.97731	39.40	324.09	8.10	3.83	328.36	.97348	337.31
9	33	328.36	.97348	39.24	367.60	9.19	4.01	372.78	.96947	384.52
10	34	372.78	.96947	39.08	411.86	10.30	4.22	417.94	.96525	432.99
11	35	417.94	.96525	38.91	456.85	11.42	4.43	463.84	.96082	482.75
12	36	463.84	.96082	38.73	502.57	12.56	4.67	510.46	.95615	533.87
13	37	510.46	.95615	38.54	549.00	13.73	4.92	557.81	.95123	586.41
14	38	557.81	.95123	38.34	596.15	14.90	5.19	605.86	.94604	640.62
15	39	605.86	.94604	38.13	643.99	16.10	5.50	654.59	.94054	695.97
16	40	654.59	.94054	37.91	692.50	17.31	5.81	704.00	.93473	753.16
17	41	704.00	.93473	37.68	741.68	18.54	6.16	754.06	.92857	812.07
18	42	754.06	.92857	37.43	791.49	19.79	6.53	804.75	.92204	872.79
19	43	804.75	.92204	37.17	841.92	21.05	6.92	856.05	.91512	935.45
20	44	856.05	.91512	36.89	892.94	22.32	7.36	907.90	.90776	1,000.15

*May be off by pennies due to rounding.

(b) Present value of expected endowment payment		$553.98
(c) Net single premium (a + b)		$623.00
(d) Present value of $1 annuity due		$15.455
(e) Net level premium (c ÷ d)		$40.31

Net Level Reserves

Terminal reserves. A reserve is usually defined as the present value of future benefits less the present value of future net premiums. This definition, while fairly uncomplicated, frequently leaves non-actuaries somewhat up in the air because it is difficult to visualize in concrete terms.

Most present value calculations can also be illustrated by an accumulation process, which is really the same thing from another point of view. An accumulation process is usually easier to understand, at least for non-actuaries.

Table A–3 shows the development of net level terminal reserves using the accumulation technique.

The process illustrated is implicit in the definition of a reserve.

The "terminal fund" at any point in time represents the amount needed which, together with future net premiums and interest, is exactly sufficient to fund future death claims and endowments. The "terminal fund" represents the fund per $1,000 originally issued. To find the factor to be applied to insurance in force at any point in time it is necessary to divide the fund by the percentage surviving at the end of the year. When applied to insurance in force, the statement result will be the "terminal fund."

Suppose, for example, that insurance in force at the end of the 15th year is $9,405,400. This amount multiplied by the reserve per $1,000, $695.97, would give an aggregate reserve of $6,545,876. Except for rounding this is equivalent to the "terminal fund" per unit, $654.59, multiplied by the units originally issued, which in this case would be $10,000 (that is, $10,000,000 in face amount of insurance).

Table A–4.

CALCULATION OF STATUTORY NET LEVEL MEAN RESERVE (1941 CSO, 2 1/2%) FOR A 20-YEAR ENDOWMENT POLICY ISSUED TO A MALE AGE 25

Calendar Year	Prior Terminal Reserve	Net Level Premium	Initial Reserve	Current Terminal Reserve	Mean of Initial Reserve And Current Terminal Reserve*	Mean Reserve— Rounded
1	$ –0–	$40.31	$ 40.31	$ 38.55	$ 39.43	$ 39
2	38.55	40.31	78.86	78.08	78.47	78
3	78.08	40.31	118.39	118.60	118.50	118
4	118.60	40.31	158.91	160.16	159.54	160
5	160.16	40.31	200.47	202.84	201.66	202
6	202.84	40.31	243.15	246.47	244.81	245
7	246.47	40.31	286.78	291.30	289.04	289
8	291.30	40.31	331.61	337.31	334.46	334
9	337.31	40.31	377.62	384.52	381.07	381
10	384.52	40.31	424.83	432.99	428.91	429
11	432.99	40.31	473.30	482.75	478.03	478
12	482.75	40.31	523.06	533.87	528.47	528
13	533.87	40.31	574.18	586.41	580.30	580
14	586.41	40.31	626.72	640.62	633.67	633
15	640.62	40.31	680.93	695.97	688.45	688
16	695.97	40.31	736.28	753.16	744.72	745
17	753.16	40.31	793.47	812.07	802.77	803
18	812.07	40.31	852.38	872.79	862.59	862
19	872.79	40.31	913.10	935.45	924.28	924
20	935.45	40.31	975.76	1,000.15	987.96	988

*May be off by pennies due to rounding.

Mean reserves. The terminal reserve represents the reserve at the end of the policy year. Since financial statements are prepared on a calendar year basis, it is necessary to adjust the reserves to such basis.

On the assumption that policy anniversaries are distributed evenly throughout the year, and hence carry an average anniversary date of July 1, reserves for financial statements prepared as of December 31 are generally computed as the mean of two terminal reserves plus half of the net premium deemed to be "unearned". The mean reserve factor can be calculated by taking the mean of the "initial fund" shown in Table A–3 (which is simply the prior terminal fund plus the current year's net premium) and the "terminal fund" and dividing the result by the percentage surviving at mid-policy year. This process is illustrated in Table A–4.

The mean reserve calculation illustrated in Table A–4 inherently assumes that the average policy anniversary date as weighted by reserve amounts is July 1, that interest is earned pro rata during the year, and that deaths occur at the end of the year. None of these conditions is absolutely true in reality. So the mean reserve is only an approximation of the amount needed at mid-year under the mortality and interest assumptions used.

Modified Reserves

Modified reserve systems were developed to afford companies some relief from the first-year surplus strain which invariably accompanies the sale of a life insurance policy.*

*However, there have been a few cases in which there was no such strain. For example, in the past some companies have paid level commissions or otherwise departed from normal expense patterns. When modified reserves were used in conjunction with such a practice, the result has been to report substantially greater profits.

Table A–5.

CALCULATION OF CRVM NET PREMIUMS (1941 CSO 2 1/2%) FOR A 20-YEAR ENDOWMENT POLICY ISSUED TO A MALE AGE 25

Expense allowance:		
Net level premium for 19-payment life policy issued at age 26		$ 25.71
Net single premium for 1-year term insurance issued at age 25 (cost of mortality, $2.88, times 2½% discount factor, .9751)		2.81
	SPECIAL FIRST-YEAR EXPENSE ALLOWANCE	$ 22.90
Modified premium:		
Net single premium (see Table A–2)		$623.00
Expense allowance		22.90
Adjusted net single premium		$645.90
Present value of $1 annuity due (see Table A–2)		$ 15.455
	MODIFIED PREMIUM	$ 41.79
First-year net premium:		
Modified premium		$ 41.79
Expense allowance ($25.71 – $2.81)		22.90
	FIRST-YEAR NET PREMIUM	$ 18.89
Renewal net premiums - equal to modified premium		$ 41.79
Alternative calculation of modified premium:		
Net level premium (see Table A–2)		$ 40.31
Expense allowance	$22.90	
Present value of $1 annuity due (see Table A–2)	$15.455	
Level annual equivalent of expense allowance	$ 1.48	1.48
	MODIFIED PREMIUM	$ 41.79

In essence, a modified reserve involves (1) a first-year net level premium that is reduced in order to provide a special first-year expense allowance in addition to normal level loading and (2) renewal net level premiums that are increased to amortize the special first-year expense allowance. Taken together, aggregate modified net premiums are the actuarial equivalent of aggregate net level premiums.

At one time the various states had their own standards for calculating modified reserves. Effective in 1948, however, the Commissioners Reserve Valuation Method became a part of the Standard Valuation Law. For policies issued in 1948 and thereafter, companies had a choice of the net level method, the Commissions Reserve Valuation Method, or any reasonable method in between (such as grading to net level over, say, 20 years).

Modified premiums. To determine the level modified premium that together with the expense allowance is the actuarial equivalent of the net level premium, it is necessary merely to add the first-year expense allowance to the net single premium for the plan under consideration and divide the result by the present value of a $1 annuity due for the plan under consideration. The expense allowance deducted in the first year is exactly equivalent to the present value of the annual series of differences between the modified premium and the net level premium. This process is illustrated in Table A–5 for the 20-year endowment policy.

Expense allowances are defined by regulatory authorities and are subject to a limitation, namely, that the allowance not be greater than the net level premium on a 20-pay life policy issued at an age one year older than the age of the insured, less the net single premium for a one-year term policy issued at the age of the insured. In the case of the 20-year endowment policy, the limitation applies.

Modified reserves. Progression of a CRVM reserve is illustrated in Table A–6. The technique of calculating the modified reserve factors is exactly the same as the technique of calculating net level reserve factors, except that modified premiums (reduced in the first year for the expense allowance) are substituted for net level premiums.

It will be readily apparent that the practical effect of the CRVM reserve is to amortize the expense allowance, $22.90, over the premium-paying period using the annuity method of amortization, where the annuity gives effect to mortality as well as interest.

Table A–6.

PROGRESSION OF A CRVM STATUTORY RESERVE (1941 CSO, 2 1/2%) FOR A 20-YEAR ENDOWMENT POLICY ISSUED TO A MALE AGE 25

Policy Year	Attained Age	Fund at Beginning Of Year	Units in Force at Beginning Of Year	Modified Premiums Received at Beginning Of Year*	Initial Fund	Interest At 2½%	Claims at End of Year	Terminal Fund	Units in Force at End of Year	Terminal Reserve	Mean Reserve— Rounded
1	25	$ –0–	1.00000	$18.89	$ 18.89	$ .47	$2.88	$ 16.48	.99712	$ 16.53	$ 18
2	26	16.48	.99712	41.67	58.15	1.45	2.98	56.62	.99414	56.95	58
3	27	56.61	.99414	41.55	98.16	2.45	3.09	97.52	.99105	98.40	99
4	28	97.52	.99105	41.42	138.94	3.47	3.22	139.19	.98783	140.90	141
5	29	139.19	.98783	41.28	180.47	4.51	3.36	181.62	.98447	184.48	184
6	30	181.62	.98447	41.14	222.76	5.57	3.50	224.83	.98097	229.17	228
7	31	224.83	.98097	40.99	265.82	6.65	3.66	268.81	.97731	275.03	273
8	32	268.81	.97731	40.84	309.65	7.74	3.83	313.56	.97348	322.08	319
9	33	313.56	.97348	40.68	354.24	8.86	4.01	359.09	.96947	370.36	367
10	34	359.09	.96947	40.51	399.60	9.99	4.22	405.37	.96525	419.93	416
11	35	405.37	.96525	40.34	445.71	11.14	4.43	452.42	.96082	470.83	466
12	36	452.42	.96082	40.15	492.57	12.31	4.67	500.21	.95615	523.11	518
13	37	500.21	.95615	39.96	540.17	13.50	4.92	548.75	.95123	576.84	571
14	38	548.75	.95123	39.75	588.50	14.71	5.19	598.02	.94604	632.08	625
15	39	598.02	.94604	39.54	637.56	15.94	5.50	648.00	.94054	688.91	681
16	40	648.00	.94054	39.31	687.31	17.18	5.81	698.68	.93473	747.40	739
17	41	698.68	.93473	39.06	737.74	18.44	6.16	750.02	.92857	807.64	798
18	42	750.02	.92857	38.80	788.82	19.72	6.53	802.01	.92204	869.75	860
19	43	802.01	.92204	38.53	840.54	21.01	6.92	854.63	.91512	933.82	923
20	44	854.63	.91512	38.24	892.87	22.32	7.36	907.83	.90776	1,000.00	988

*$18.89 in first year, $41.79 thereafter. See Table A–5.

Table A–7.

CALCULATION OF ADJUSTED PREMIUMS (1941 CSO, 2 1/2%) FOR A 20-YEAR ENDOWMENT POLICY ISSUED TO A MALE AGE 25

Maximum expense allowance:

2% of amount of insurance, $1,000	$ 20.00
40% of the lesser of $40.00 and the adjusted premium of $42.89*	16.00
25% of the lesser of $40.00 and the adjusted premium for a whole life policy issued at the same age (which is $15.78)	3.95
MAXIMUM EXPENSE ALLOWANCE	$ 39.95

Adjusted premium:

Net single premium for benefits (see Table A–2)	$623.00
Maximum expense allowance	39.95
Adjusted net single premium	$662.95
Present value of $1 annuity due (see Table A–2)	$ 15.455
ADJUSTED PREMIUM	$ 42.89

First-year adjusted premium:

Adjusted premium	$ 42.89
Expense allowance	39.95
FIRST-YEAR ADJUSTED PREMIUM	$ 2.94

Renewal adjusted premiums - same as adjusted premium	$ 42.89

*Note that the expense allowance is in part a function of the adjusted premium, which is in turn a function, in part, of the expense allowance. The calculation thus involves algebraic functions which are not illustrated here.

Table A–8.

PROGRESSION OF CASH VALUES (1941 CSO, 2 1/2%) FOR A 20-YEAR ENDOWMENT POLICY ISSUED TO A MALE AGE 25

Policy Year	Attained Age	Beginning Fund	Units in Force at Beginning Of Year	Adjusted Premium Received At Beginning Of Year*	Interest At 2½%	Claims at End of Year	Terminal Fund	Units in Force at End of Year	Cash Value	Cash Value— Rounded Up
1	25	$ –0–	1.00000	$ 2.94	$ .07	$2.88	$ .13	.99712	$ .13	$ 1
2	26	.13	.99712	42.77	1.07	2.98	40.99	.99414	41.23	42
3	27	40.99	.99414	42.64	2.09	3.09	82.63	.99105	83.38	84
4	28	82.63	.99105	42.51	3.13	3.22	125.05	.98783	126.59	127
5	29	125.05	.98783	42.37	4.19	3.36	168.25	.98447	170.90	171
6	30	168.25	.98447	42.22	5.26	3.50	212.23	.98097	216.35	217
7	31	212.23	.98097	42.07	6.36	3.66	257.00	.97731	262.97	263
8	32	257.00	.97731	41.92	7.47	3.83	302.56	.97348	301.80	302
9	33	302.56	.97348	41.75	8.61	4.01	348.91	.96947	359.90	360
10	34	348.91	.96947	41.58	9.76	4.22	396.03	.96525	410.29	411
11	35	396.03	.96525	41.40	10.94	4.43	443.94	.96082	462.04	463
12	36	443.94	.96082	41.21	12.13	4.67	492.61	.95615	515.20	516
13	37	492.61	.95615	41.01	13.34	4.92	542.04	.95123	569.83	570
14	38	542.04	.95123	40.80	14.57	5.19	592.22	.94604	626.00	626
15	39	592.22	.94604	40.52	15.82	5.50	643.06	.94054	683.71	684
16	40	643.06	.94054	40.34	17.09	5.81	694.68	.93473	743.19	744
17	41	694.68	.93473	40.09	18.37	6.16	746.98	.92857	804.44	805
18	42	746.98	.92857	39.83	19.67	6.53	799.95	.92204	867.59	868
19	43	799.95	.92204	39.55	20.99	6.92	853.57	.91512	932.74	933
20	44	853.57	.91512	39.25	22.32	7.36	907.78	.90776	1,000.00	1,000

*$2.94 in Year 1, $42.89 thereafter. See Table A–7.

Cash Values

Companies are free to adopt any basis for calculating cash values so long as they are not less than "minimum" cash values as defined in the Standard Nonforfeiture Law. The Standard Nonforfeiture Law provides currently that cash values shall not be less than the values derived by using (1) the 1958 CSO Table of Mortality (1941 CSO in 1951, the year of issue of the 20-year endowment policy illustrated in this appendix), (2) 3 1/2 percent interest, and (3) an expense allowance that is not greater than a defined maximum.* However, any combination of table, rate, and expense allowance can be used providing the result is a cash value scale that is greater than the minimum.**

*The maximum expense allowance used for calculating cash values is greater than that permitted for purposes of calculating modified reserves.

**In the case of participating insurance, there are some additional provisions applicable to the relationship between the cash value interest rate assumption and the reserve interest rate assumption. These additional provisions are quite complex and are beyond the scope of this appendix.

Calculation of a scale of cash values is very similar to calculation of modified reserves. In fact, given the same mortality and interest assumptions, the only difference between a modified reserve and cash value would be the unamortized portion of the difference in the expense allowance.

Adjusted Premiums

Adjusted premiums are to the cash value what modified premiums are to the CRVM reserve, and they are calculated in the same fashion.

Calculation of the adjusted premium for the 20-year endowment policy is illustrated in Table A–7. The general procedure is exactly the same as the general procedure used to calculate modified premiums, except that the adjusted premium is greater than the modified premium because there is a greater first-year expense allowance to be amortized.

The formula for calculating the expense allowance on the 20-year endowment policy indicates the statutory requirements for calculating maximum expense

Table A–9.

PATTERN OF ASSUMED DEATHS, SURRENDERS, AND MATURITIES FOR A 20-YEAR ENDOWMENT POLICY ISSUED TO A MALE AGE 25

Policy Year	Attained Age	Units In Force At Beginning Of Policy Year (July 1)	Deaths Assumed— 50% in First Half Of Policy Year		Units In Force At Middle Of Policy Year (December 31)	Deaths Assumed— 50% in Last Half Of Policy Year		Balance Before Surrenders	Surrenders Assumed At End of Policy Year (Failure to Pay Renewal Premium)		Units In Force At End Of Policy Year (June 30)
			Rate	Number		Rate	Number		Rate	Number	
1	25	1.000000*	.000395	.000395	.999605	.000395	.000395	.999210	.200000	.199842	.799368
2	26	.799368	.000455	.000364	.799004	.000455	.000364	.798640	.090000	.071873	.726762
3	27	.726762	.000500	.000363	.726399	.000500	.000363	.726036	.050000	.036302	.689734
4	28	.689734	.000535	.000369	.689365	.000535	.000369	.688996	.050000	.034450	.654546
5	29	.654546	.000580	.000380	.654166	.000580	.000379	.653787	.050000	.032689	.621098
6	30	.621098	.000655	.000407	.620691	.000655	.000406	.620285	.050000	.031014	.589271
7	31	.589271	.000690	.000407	.588864	.000690	.000406	.588458	.050000	.029423	.559035
8	32	.559035	.000730	.000408	.558627	.000730	.000408	.558219	.050000	.027911	.530308
9	33	.530308	.000770	.000408	.529900	.000770	.000408	.529492	.050000	.026475	.503017
10	34	.503017	.000810	.000407	.502610	.000810	.000407	.502203	.040000	.020088	.482115
11	35	.482115	.000860	.000415	.481700	.000860	.000414	.481286	.040000	.019251	.462035
12	36	.462035	.000915	.000423	.461612	.000915	.000422	.461190	.040000	.018448	.442742
13	37	.442742	.000980	.000434	.442308	.000980	.000433	.441875	.040000	.017675	.424200
14	38	.424200	.001060	.000450	.423750	.001060	.000449	.423301	.040000	.016932	.406369
15	39	.406369	.001160	.000471	.405898	.001160	.000471	.405427	.040000	.016217	.389210
16	40	.389210	.001280	.000498	.388712	.001280	.000498	.388214	.040000	.015529	.372685
17	41	.372685	.001425	.000531	.372154	.001425	.000530	.371624	.040000	.014865	.356759
18	42	.356759	.001595	.000569	.356190	.001595	.000568	.355622	.040000	.014225	.341397
19	43	.341397	.001790	.000611	.340786	.001790	.000610	.340176	.040000	.013607	.326569
20	44	.326569	.002010	.000656	.325913	.002010	.000655	.325258	1.000000**	.325258**	–0–

*Moment of issue.
**Endowment.

allowances. It will be noted that the cash value expense allowance is $39.95, while the CRVM expense allowance was $22.90.

Terminal Cash Values

Cash values are calculated in exactly the same manner as reserves, except that adjusted premiums are substituted for net premiums.

Calculation of terminal cash values for the 20-year endowment policy is illustrated in Table A–8. Terminal values are those applicable at the end of the policy year indicated. Mean values would have no particular significance in the case of cash values. If a policyholder surrenders his policy at any time other than the policy anniversary, an interpolated value will be paid to him.

The cash values shown in Table A–8 would be referred to as "minimum" cash values because the maximum expense allowance was used. However, use of the maximum interest rate of 3 1/2% would have resulted in a lower scale of values which could truly be called "minimum". As a general rule, companies tend to use the same interest rate for both cash values and reserves.

Gross Premiums

Reserves are calculated according to statutory guidelines. So, to a certain extent, are cash values.

Gross premiums are another matter. A company has a relatively free hand in calculating gross premiums so long as the result is reasonable, adequate, and not unfairly discriminatory.

A company may "scientifically" calculate gross premiums or it may simply lift a set of gross pre-

Table A–10.

PRESENT VALUE OF ASSUMED CASH FLOW FOR A 20-YEAR ENDOWMENT POLICY ISSUED TO A MALE AGE 25

Calendar Year	Attained Age	Gross Cash Flow in Middle of Year			Surrenders And Maturities	Cash Flow	3% Interest Discount	Present Value at Issue			Surrenders And Maturities	Cash Flow
		Premiums	Expenses	Deaths				Premiums	Expenses	Deaths		
1	25	$ 49.58	$ 66.96	$ .39		$ (17.77)	1.0000	$ 49.58	$ 66.96	$ .39		$ (17.77)
2	26	39.63	6.36	.76	$ .20	32.31	.9709	38.48	6.18	.74	$ .19	31.37
3	27	36.03	5.22	.73	3.02	27.06	.9426	33.96	4.92	.69	2.85	25.50
4	28	34.20	4.79	.73	3.05	25.63	.9151	31.30	4.38	.67	2.79	23.46
5	29	32.45	4.55	.75	4.38	22.77	.8885	28.83	4.04	.66	3.89	20.24
6	30	30.79	4.32	.79	5.59	20.09	.8626	26.56	3.73	.68	4.82	17.33
7	31	29.22	4.10	.81	6.73	17.58	.8375	24.47	3.43	.68	5.64	14.72
8	32	27.72	3.89	.81	7.74	15.28	.8131	22.54	3.16	.66	6.29	12.43
9	33	26.29	3.69	.82	8.68	13.10	.7894	20.75	2.91	.65	6.85	10.34
10	34	24.94	3.50	.82	9.53	11.09	.7664	19.12	2.68	.62	7.30	8.52
11	35	23.90	3.33	.82	8.26	11.49	.7440	17.78	2.47	.62	6.15	8.54
12	36	22.91	3.19	.84	8.91	9.97	.7224	16.55	2.30	.60	6.44	7.21
13	37	21.95	3.05	.86	9.52	8.52	.7014	15.40	2.14	.60	6.67	5.99
14	38	21.03	2.93	.88	10.07	7.15	.6810	14.32	2.00	.60	6.86	4.86
15	39	20.15	2.80	.92	10.60	5.83	.6611	13.32	1.85	.61	7.01	3.85
16	40	19.30	2.69	.97	11.09	4.55	.6419	12.39	1.73	.62	7.12	2.92
17	41	18.48	2.57	1.03	11.55	3.33	.6231	11.51	1.60	.65	7.20	2.06
18	42	17.69	2.46	1.10	11.97	2.16	.6050	10.70	1.49	.66	7.24	1.31
19	43	16.93	2.36	1.18	12.35	1.04	.5874	9.94	1.39	.69	7.25	.61
20	44	16.19	2.26	1.27	12.70	(.04)	.5703	9.24	1.29	.73	7.24	(.02)
21	44*	–0–	1.66	.66	325.25	(327.57)	.5537	–0–	.92	.36	180.09	(181.37)
		$529.38	$136.68	$17.94	$481.19	$(106.43)		$426.74	$121.57	$13.18	$289.89	$ 2.10

*Immediately prior to 45th birthday.

miums from a competitor's ratebook and test them.* In either case, a relatively sophisticated set of calculations underlies the scale that is finally adopted.

For purposes of this discussion it is assumed that the company starts with a rate of $49.58 per $1,000 for a 20-year endowment issued to a male age 25, and tests the rate.

Deaths and Terminations

In testing the proposed premium the company must decide what patterns of deaths and voluntary terminations are likely to be experienced.

Assume that a company decided that for 1951 issues the 1946–49 Basic Table, slightly modified, was representative of the death claims that could

*Admittedly some companies borrow rates without bothering to test them. This must be regarded as a dangerous practice, and it is not used as a model for the practices discussed in this appendix.

reasonably be expected. This table differed significantly from the 1941 CSO Table, particularly during the select period. It was assumed that death claims would occur in an even distribution throughout the year, or in the middle of the year on the average. Because the company wanted to test the premium on a calendar-year basis, it was decided to translate this mid-year assumption into an assumption that half of the deaths occur at the beginning of the year and half at the end.

In deciding on an assumption for voluntary terminations the company studied its own experience as well as the trend of experience and decided that an adaptation of the Linton B table was appropriate for the plan and issue age. Because an annual-premium case was being tested, it was assumed that surrenders and lapses would occur at the end of the policy year, i.e., at the time the renewal premium was due. Any other mode or distribution of modes would have resulted in a different assumption as to the timing of voluntary terminations.

The pattern of deaths and voluntary terminations is shown in Table A–9.

Other Assumptions

Assumptions as to expenses were developed by reference to commission scales and functional cost studies. They are summarized in Table A–1.

The assumption of a 3 percent interest rate was based on the facts and circumstances applicable in 1951. Interest rates were on the upswing after a precipitous decline during and after World War II, but there was no telling when the rise would peak out. The assumed rate seemed reasonable in the circumstances.

Projection of Cash Flow

Based on a given premium and carefully developed assumptions as to mortality, voluntary terminations, expenses, and interest, the next step was to project anticipated gross cash flows excluding interest. The result is shown in Table A–10. The gross cash flow for any year can be reconstructed from the information already given about premiums, cash values, expenses, deaths, and voluntary terminations. For example, gross cash flow in the fifth calendar year was computed as follows:

Premiums:		
Gross premium per $1,000		$49.58
Survivors persisting at beginning of fifth policy year		X .654546
Premiums received		$32.45
Expenses:		
Percentage—9.5% x $32.45		$ 3.08
Per policy:		
Per policy expense	$ 4.90	
Average size	$2,500	
Cost per $1,000	$ 1.96	
Percentage in force	× .654546	1.29
Death claim processing:		
Unit cost	$21.25	
Average size	$2,500	
Cost per $1,000	$ 8.50	
Deaths	× .000759	.01
Surrender processing:		
Unit cost	$12.75	
Average size	$2,500	
Cost per $1,000	$ 5.10	
Surrenders	× .032689	.17
		$ 4.55
Deaths—.000759 x $1,000		.75
Surrenders:		
Cash value per $1,000	$ 127	
Surrenders	.034450	$ 4.38

Having projected gross cash flows, present values of such cash flows (discounted at 3 percent, the assumed interest rate) were readily computed. The calculation of present values is also shown in Table A–10.

As Table A–10 indicates, the net result of the present value calculations was a positive value of $2.10. This means that the proposed premium is sufficient to cover benefits and expenses and yield a profit, the present value of which is $2.10.

Asset Shares

The final test of the proposed premium was to calculate expected asset shares at each calendar year-end. This calculation simply involved accumulating gross cash flows at the assumed interest rate and dividing the fund at the end of each year by the units then in force to yield the asset share, which is defined as the amount of accumulated assets per unit of insurance in force. The asset share was then compared with the mean reserve to indicate asset share surplus, which measured the strain on surplus.

The calculation of asset shares is shown in Table A–11. Asset share surplus at each duration is also shown. It will be noted that this policy does not produce a positive asset share surplus until the nineteenth year where net level reserves are used. This is not generally regarded as satisfactory. In this case, however, asset shares at older ages were more favorable. Because of competitive conditions, and because asset shares at older ages tended to offset the surplus strain shown for age 25, the premium was not modified.

It should be noted that the use of modified reserves would have increased asset share surplus (or at least reduced the deficit) at each duration.

Level Annual Equivalents

The company knew the amount of the level annual gross premium when it started the testing. Suppose the company wanted to know the level annual equivalent of all of the elements of the gross premium—benefits, expenses, and profits?

It would have to calculate an annuity due. It would calculate the annuity in much the same fashion as it would calculate the annuity required to compute statutory net level premiums with one important difference. While voluntary terminations are not taken into account in calculating statutory net premiums, they would be taken into account in computing the annuity in this case.

Table A–11.

ASSET SHARES FOR A 20-YEAR ENDOWMENT POLICY ISSUED TO A MALE AGE 25

Calendar Year	Attained Age	Beginning Fund (January 1)	6 Months Interest (June 30)	Mid-Year Cash Flow** (July 1)	Mid-Year Fund (July 1)	6 Months Interest (December 31)	Terminal Fund (December 31)	Units In Force (December 31)	Asset Share (December 31)	Mean Net Level Reserve (December 31)	Asset Share Surplus (December 31)
1	25	$ –0–	$ –0–	$ (17.77)	$(17.77)	$(.26)	$(18.03)	.99961	$ (18)	$ 39	$(57)
2	26	(18.03)	(.27)	32.31	14.01	.21	14.22	.79900	18	78	(60)
3	27	14.22	.21	27.06	41.49	.62	42.11	.72640	58	118	(60)
4	28	42.11	.63	25.63	68.37	1.02	69.39	.68937	101	160	(59)
5	29	69.39	1.03	22.77	93.19	1.39	94.58	.65417	145	202	(7)
6	30	94.58	1.41	20.09	116.08	1.73	117.81	.62069	190	245	(55)
7	31	117.81	1.75	17.58	137.14	2.04	139.18	.58886	236	289	(53)
8	32	139.18	2.07	15.28	156.53	2.33	158.86	.55863	284	334	(50)
9	33	158.86	2.36	13.10	174.32	2.60	176.92	.52990	334	381	(47)
10	34	176.92	2.63	11.09	190.64	2.84	193.48	.50261	385	429	(44)
11	35	193.48	2.88	11.49	207.85	3.09	210.94	.48170	438	478	(40)
12	36	210.94	3.14	9.97	224.05	3.34	227.39	.46161	493	528	(35)
13	37	227.39	3.39	8.52	239.30	3.56	242.86	.44231	549	580	(31)
14	38	242.86	3.62	7.15	253.63	3.78	257.41	.42375	607	633	(26)
15	39	257.41	3.83	5.83	267.07	3.98	271.05	.40589	668	688	(20)
16	40	271.05	4.04	4.55	279.64	4.16	283.80	.38871	730	745	(15)
17	41	283.80	4.22	3.33	291.35	4.34	295.69	.37215	795	803	(8)
18	42	295.69	4.40	2.16	302.25	4.50	306.75	.35618	861	862	(1)
19	43	306.75	4.57	1.04ˈ	312.36	4.65	317.01	.34078	930	924	6
20	44	317.01	4.72	(.04)	321.69	4.79	326.48	.32591	1,002	988	14
21	44*	326.48	4.86	(327.57)	3.77	.06	3.83	—	—	—	—

*Immediately prior to 45th birthday.
**See Table A–10.

Calculation of the annuity is shown in Table A–12. The column headed "percentage of people originally insured persisting at beginning of year" may be traced to Table A–9. It will be found that the discount for voluntary terminations is inherent in the calculations illustrated in Table A–12.

Computation of level annual equivalents is now very easy; the present values of assumed cash flows shown in Table A–10 are simply divided by the annuity of $8.608:

	Present Value Of Total (From Table A–10)	Present Value Of $1 Annuity Due (From Table A–12)	Level Annual Equivalent
Benefits:			
Death claims	$ 13.18	$8.608	$ 1.53
Surrenders	109.80	8.608	12.76
Maturities	180.09	8.608	20.92
	303.07		35.21
Expenses	121.57	8.608	14.12
	424.64		49.33
Profits	2.10	8.608	.25
Gross premiums	$426.74		$49.58

Further breakdowns could be made. For example, expenses can be separated into acquisition costs and maintenance expenses. Acquisition costs aggregate $60.29, the level annual equivalent of which is $7.00. The present value of maintenance expenses is $61.28, the level annual equivalent of which is $7.12.

Break-Even Premiums

Suppose the company did not start with a gross premium but instead computed the gross premium directly? In that case the company might calculate a break-even premium. Offhand it might appear that this would simply be the gross premium, $49.58, less the level annual equivalent of profits, $.25, or $49.33.

However, any change in the premium will result in a change in percentage expenses. The calculation of a break-even premium is therefore a little more complicated than at first appears.

The break-even premium is calculated by dividing the present value of benefits and expenses (less percentage expenses) by the present value of a $1

Table A–12.

CALCULATION OF $1 ANNUITY DUE THAT CONTEMPLATES DEATHS, SURRENDERS, AND INTEREST FOR A 20-YEAR ENDOWMENT POLICY ISSUED TO A MALE AGE 25

Policy Year	Attained Age	Percentage of People Originally Insured Persisting at Beginning Of Year*	3% Interest Discount	Present Value
1	25	1.000000	1.000000	$1.000
2	26	.799368	.970874	.776
3	27	.726762	.942596	.685
4	28	.689734	.915142	.631
5	29	.654546	.888487	.582
6	30	.621098	.862609	.536
7	31	.589271	.837484	.494
8	32	.559035	.813092	.454
9	33	.530308	.789409	.419
10	34	.503017	.766417	.386
11	35	.482115	.744094	.359
12	36	.462035	.722421	.334
13	37	.442742	.701380	.310
14	38	.424200	.680951	.289
15	39	.406369	.661118	.269
16	40	.389210	.641862	.250
17	41	.372685	.623167	.232
18	42	.356759	.605016	.216
19	43	.341397	.587395	.200
20	44	.326569	.570286	.186
				$8.608

*See Table A–9.

premium. The present value of benefits and expenses less percentage expenses is $339.08, computed as follows (see Tables A–1 and A–10 for underlying data):

Present value of benefits and expenses	$424.64
Less present value of percentage expenses:	
Year 1 only: $49.58 x 90.8%	(45.02)
All years: $426.74 x 9.5%	(40.54)
	$339.08

The present value of a $1 premium is $6.88, as shown in Table A–13. The break-even premium is therefore $339.08 divided by $6.88143, or $49.27. The reader is invited to substitute this value in place of the gross premium in the cash flow schedule and make the necessary calculations to prove that the break-even premium will indeed result in a present value of zero as well as an accumulation of zero.

Natural Reserves

If the level gross premium is deloaded of profit, the result is a level natural premium, which is the level annual equivalent of benefits and expenses assumed for purposes of calculating the gross premium. The natural premium for the 20-year endowment policy illustrated in this chapter is $49.33, computed by dividing the present value of benefits and expenses ($424.64) by the present value of a $1 annuity due ($8.61). (See Table A–10 and A–12 and the discussion associated with Table A–12 for supporting data.)

The natural premium is used in lieu of the gross premium in a fund accumulation from which natural reserves are derived. Assuming that experience actually follows the underlying assumption, profits will emerge each year equal to the difference between gross premiums received and natural premiums allocated to the reserve.

Table A–13.

PRESENT VALUE OF A $1 PREMIUM FOR A 20-YEAR ENDOWMENT POLICY ISSUED TO A MALE AGE 25

Policy Year	Attained Age	$1 x Percentage of People Originally Insured Paying Premiums*	Expenses		$1 Premium Less Percentage Expenses	3% Discount	Present Value
			Rate	Amount			
1	25	$1.000000	100.3%	$1.003000	$(.003000)	1.000000	$(.003000)
2	26	.799368	9.5	.075940	.723428	.970874	.702357
3	27	.726762	9.5	.069042	.657720	.942596	.619964
4	28	.689734	9.5	.065525	.624209	.915142	.571240
5	29	.654546	9.5	.062182	.592364	.888487	.526308
6	30	.621098	9.5	.059004	.562094	.862609	.484867
7	31	.589271	9.5	.055981	.533290	.837484	.446622
8	32	.559035	9.5	.053108	.505927	.813092	.411365
9	33	.530308	9.5	.050379	.479929	.789409	.378860
10	34	.503017	9.5	.047787	.455230	.766417	.348896
11	35	.482115	9.5	.045801	.436314	.744094	.324659
12	36	.462035	9.5	.043893	.418142	.722421	.302075
13	37	.442742	9.5	.042060	.400682	.701380	.281030
14	38	.424200	9.5	.040299	.383901	.680951	.261418
15	39	.406369	9.5	.038605	.367764	.661118	.243135
16	40	.389210	9.5	.036975	.352235	.641862	.226086
17	41	.372685	9.5	.035405	.337280	.623167	.210182
18	42	.356759	9.5	.033892	.322867	.605016	.195340
19	43	.341397	9.5	.032433	.308964	.587395	.181484
20	44	.326569	9.5	.031024	.295545	.570286	.168545
							$6.881433

*See Table A–9.

Progression of a natural reserve on a calendar-year basis (referred to as an intermediate natural reserve) is shown in Table A–14. It will be observed that there is no fundamental difference between techniques used to calculate natural reserves and techniques used to calculate statutory reserves, cash values, or other policy values. The difference is in the assumptions, the additional provision for terminations, and the degree of refinement or accuracy employed in the calculations.

Table A–14 represents the development of aggregate reserve factors, that is, benefits and expenses are combined to produce one set of reserve values. Any desired breakdowns of the reserve can be obtained by using exactly the same technique, but limiting the fund accumulation to the elements entering into the particular reserve component being calculated. Natural reserve factors are segregated into acquisition costs, maintenance expenses, and benefits in Table A–15.

Present Value of Book Profits

All of the preceding discussions deal with cash flows. Very often, however, it is desirable to compute the present value of profits. For example, it is book profits, not cash flows, that can be distributed to shareholders in the form of dividends or reinvested in new business, development of an agency plant, etc.

Book profits involve non-cash accruals, of course. In the case of a life insurance company, the principal policy-related non-cash accrual is the policy reserve.

Interest on Reserve

It is axiomatic that when reserves are set up on the books of a life insurance company, assets at least equivalent to the reserves must be set aside. Interest on such assets may conveniently be referred to as "interest on the reserve." This will always mean

Table A-14.

PROGRESSION OF AN INTERMEDIATE NATURAL RESERVE FOR A 20-YEAR ENDOWMENT POLICY ISSUED TO A MALE AGE 25

Calendar Year	Attained Age	Beginning Fund	6 Months Interest	Units in Force at Beginning of Policy Year*	Mid-Calendar Year Transactions				Fund at End of Calendar Year	Units in Force at End of Year	Intermediate Natural Reserve Per Unit In Force**
					Natural Premiums Received	Expenses, Deaths, Surrenders and Maturities	Mid-Year Fund	6 Months Interest			
1	25	$ —	$ —	1.000000	$49.33	$ 67.35	$(18.02)	$(.27)	$(18.29)	.999605	$(18.30)
2	26	(18.29)	(.27)	.799368	39.43	7.32	13.55	.20	13.75	.799004	17.22
3	27	13.75	.21	.726762	35.85	8.97	40.84	.61	41.45	.726399	57.08
4	28	41.45	.62	.689734	34.02	8.57	67.52	1.01	68.53	.689365	99.42
5	29	68.53	1.02	.654546	32.29	9.68	92.16	1.37	93.53	.654166	143.01
6	30	93.53	1.39	.621098	30.64	10.70	114.86	1.71	116.57	.620691	187.86
7	31	116.57	1.74	.589271	29.07	11.64	135.74	2.02	137.76	.588864	234.00
8	32	137.76	2.05	.559035	27.58	12.44	154.95	2.31	157.26	.558627	281.58
9	33	157.26	2.34	.530308	26.16	13.19	172.57	2.57	175.14	.529900	330.61
10	34	175.14	2.61	.503017	24.81	13.85	188.71	2.81	191.52	.502610	381.17
11	35	191.52	2.85	.482115	23.78	12.41	205.74	3.06	208.80	.481700	433.63
12	36	208.80	3.11	.462035	22.79	12.94	221.76	3.30	225.06	.461612	487.75
13	37	225.06	3.35	.442742	21.84	13.43	236.82	3.53	240.35	.442308	543.61
14	38	240.35	3.58	.424200	20.93	13.88	250.98	3.74	254.72	.423750	601.31
15	39	254.72	3.79	.406369	20.05	14.32	264.24	3.93	268.17	.405898	660.90
16	40	268.17	3.99	.389210	19.20	14.75	276.61	4.12	280.73	.388712	722.45
17	41	280.73	4.18	.372685	18.38	15.15	288.14	4.29	292.43	.372154	786.04
18	42	292.43	4.36	.356759	17.60	15.53	298.86	4.45	303.31	.356190	851.80
19	43	303.31	4.52	.341397	16.84	15.89	308.78	4.60	313.38	.340786	919.87
20	44	313.38	4.67	.326569	16.11	16.23	317.93	4.73	322.66	.325913	990.36
21	44***	322.66	4.91****	—	—	327.57*****	-0-	—	—	—	—

*See Table A-9.
**May be off by pennies due to rounding.
***Immediately prior to 45th birthday.
****$.11 added to offset accumulated rounding errors.
*****The policy matures at the end of the policy year. For convenience, this has been grouped with all transactions that take place at mid-year, whether occurring on June 30 or July 1.

Table A–15.

INTERMEDIATE NATURAL RESERVE FACTORS FOR A 20-YEAR ENDOWMENT POLICY ISSUED TO A MALE AGE 25

Calendar Year	Acquisition Cost Reserve	Maintenance Expense Reserve	Benefit Reserve	Total Reserve*
1	$(54.10)	$ .45	$ 35.35	$(18.30)
2	(62.60)	(.26)	80.08	17.22
3	(63.81)	(.36)	121.25	57.08
4	(62.14)	(.22)	161.78	99.42
5	(60.34)	(.06)	203.41	143.01
6	(58.39)	.10	246.15	187.86
7	(56.27)	.28	289.99	234.00
8	(53.99)	.48	335.08	281.58
9	(51.51)	.69	381.42	330.61
10	(48.82)	.92	429.07	381.17
11	(45.35)	1.21	477.76	433.63
12	(41.63)	1.53	527.84	487.75
13	(37.63)	1.87	579.37	543.61
14	(33.34)	2.23	632.42	601.31
15	(28.73)	2.62	687.01	660.90
16	(23.79)	3.04	743.20	722.45
17	(18.47)	3.49	801.02	786.04
18	(12.76)	3.97	860.60	851.80
19	(6.61)	4.48	922.00	919.87
20		5.03	985.33	990.36

*See Table A–14.

"interest on assets equivalent to the reserves being held."

Table A–16 shows interest, at 3 percent, earned on the natural reserve for the 20-year endowment policy. If reserves in any other amount were held—such as statutory reserves—reported interest earned would differ.

Given one amount for total assets, then interest earned by the company would always be the same regardless of the level of the reserves being held. Capital and surplus would be the balancing account. But this is more than a matter of form. Surplus is available for dividends, investment in new business, etc.; reserves, generally speaking, are not. That is why reserves are deemed to represent the amount of assets earning interest. Interest attributable to stockholder funds is not properly allocable to policies.

Book Profits Discounted at Assumed Investment Earnings Rate

If books profits are discounted at the interest rate assumed for projection purposes, the present value of

interest on the reserves is equal to the present value of changes in the reserve. They offset. In other words, the present value, at the time of issue, of future book profits is always exactly the same as the present value of future net cash flows. This phenomenon is explained by the interaction of the assumed interest rate and the discount rate (which are the same) and the fact that interest and discount are both computed with respect to a reserve, the increases and decreases in which always sum to zero eventually.

Table A–17 shows a comparison of the present value of expected net cash flows and the present value of expected book profits when a 3 percent interest assumption is used uniformly. It will be observed that the present value at the moment of issue is the same in both cases, $2.10.

Book Profits Discounted at a Risk Rate

An investor almost always weighs one investment proposal against another, and this is typically done by capitalizing profits at some interest rate, possibly

Table A-16.

INTEREST (AT 3%) ON NATURAL RESERVE AND RESERVE INCREASES FOR A 20-YEAR ENDOWMENT POLICY ISSUED TO A MALE AGE 25

Calendar Year	Attained Age	Units in Force	Intermediate Natural Reserve Per Unit	Intermediate Natural Reserve Per Unit Issued	Interest at 3% For 6 Months* On Beginning Reserve	On Ending Reserve	Total Interest
1	25	.99961	$(18.30)	$(18.29)	$ —	$(.27)	$(.27)
2	26	.79900	17.22	13.76	(.27)	.20	(.07)
3	27	.72640	57.08	41.46	.20	.61	.81
4	28	.68937	99.42	68.54	.61	1.01	1.62
5	29	.65417	143.01	93.55	1.02	1.37	2.39
6	30	.62069	187.86	116.60	1.39	1.71	3.10
7	31	.58886	234.00	137.79	1.74	2.02	3.76
8	32	.55863	281.58	157.30	2.05	2.31	4.36
9	33	.52990	330.61	175.19	2.34	2.57	4.91
10	34	.50261	381.17	191.58	2.61	2.81	5.42
11	35	.48170	433.63	208.88	2.86	3.06	5.92
12	36	.46161	487.75	225.15	3.11	3.30	6.41
13	37	.44231	543.61	240.44	3.35	3.53	6.88
14	38	.42375	601.31	254.80	3.58	3.74	7.32
15	39	.40589	660.90	268.26	3.79	3.94	7.73
16	40	.38871	722.45	280.82	3.99	4.12	8.11
17	41	.37215	786.04	292.52	4.18	4.29	8.47
18	42	.35618	851.80	303.40	4.36	4.45	8.81
19	43	.34078	919.87	313.47	4.52	4.60	9.12
20	44	.32591	990.36	322.76	4.67	4.73	9.40
21	44**	—	—	—	4.81	—	4.81

*Interest is deemed to be received semi-annually at a compounding rate of 1.489%, which is the equivalent of an annual rate of 3%. Interest received in the first six months (i.e., on the beginning reserve) is deemed to be received at mid-calendar year. Interest received in the second six months (i.e., on the ending reserve) is received at year-end; it is discounted at 1.489% (present value factor: .9851) to treat it as if it were also received at mid-year.

**Just prior to 45th birthday.

subjective, that reflects the investor's estimate of risk associated with the proposed investment. The true capitalization rate is not always apparent; obviously a stock that is selling at 100 times earnings does not mean that investors are willing to accept a 1 percent return. The price, at least in theory, is a function of expected future profits and an appropriate rate of return for the risk involved. The multiple of 100 might represent an expectation of future earnings which are vastly greater than the current level of earnings, discounted at, say, 12 percent.

When the discount rate differs from the interest rate assumption, the present value of book profits differs from the present value of cash flows. The reason is that investment earnings and the discount do not offset simply because they are not the same. The effect of applying a 12 percent discount rate to

cash flows and book profits on the 20-year endowment policy is illustrated in Table A–17.

When a risk discount rate is used, the reserve basis directly affects the present value of book profits. Natural reserves are used in Table A–17, and the result is that the present value of future profits discounted at 12 percent is positive. Using statutory net level reserves results in a loss of $21.21 on a present-value basis. This is illustrated in Table A–18. The present value of the first-year loss is so great that the present value of renewal profits is not sufficient to cover it. Where the first-year statutory loss represents an investment of capital and surplus, as it does, then the indicated negative value is highly significant. Stockholders must provide the $56.18 (i.e., the first-year statutory loss) needed to finance the sale of the policy. Their return is limited to book

Table A-17.

PRESENT VALUE AT 3% AND 12% OF BOOK PROFITS (USING NATURAL RESERVES) ON A 20-YEAR ENDOWMENT POLICY ISSUED TO A MALE AGE 25

Calendar Year	Attained Age	Gross Amounts				3% Discount Factor	3% Present Value at Issue				12% Discount Factor	12% Present Value at Issue			
		Cash Flow	Interest on Reserve	Increase in Reserve	Book Profits		Cash Flow	Interest on Reserve	Increase in Reserve	Book Profits		Cash Flow	Interest on Reserve	Increase in Reserve	Book Profits
1	25	$(17.77)	$ (.27)	$ (18.29)	$ .25	1.0000	$ (17.77)	$ (.27)	$(18.29)	$ .25	1.0000	$(17.77)	$ (.27)	$(18.29)	$ .25
2	26	32.31	(.07)	32.05	.19	.9709	31.37	(.07)	31.12	.18	.8929	28.85	(.06)	28.62	.17
3	27	27.06	.81	27.70	.18	.9426	25.50	.77	26.11	.16	.7972	21.58	.65	22.08	.15
4	28	25.63	1.62	27.07	.17	.9151	23.46	1.48	24.78	.16	.7118	18.24	1.15	19.27	.12
5	29	22.77	2.39	25.02	.16	.8885	20.24	2.13	22.22	.15	.6355	14.47	1.52	15.90	.09
6	30	20.09	3.10	23.05	.15	.8626	17.33	2.68	19.89	.12	.5674	11.40	1.76	13.08	.08
7	31	17.58	3.76	21.19	.14	.8375	14.72	3.14	17.74	.12	.5066	8.91	1.90	10.74	.07
8	32	15.28	4.36	19.50	.13	.8131	12.43	3.55	15.86	.12	.4523	6.91	1.97	8.82	.06
9	33	13.10	4.91	17.89	.13	.7894	10.34	3.88	14.12	.10	.4039	5.29	1.98	7.23	.04
10	34	11.09	5.42	16.39	.13	.7664	8.52	4.15	12.57	.10	.3606	4.00	1.95	5.91	.04
11	35	11.49	5.92	17.30	.12	.7440	8.54	4.40	12.87	.07	.3220	3.70	1.91	5.57	.04
12	36	9.97	6.41	16.27	.11	.7224	7.21	4.64	11.75	.10	.2875	2.87	1.84	4.68	.03
13	37	8.52	6.88	15.29	.11	.7014	5.99	4.82	10.73	.08	.2567	2.19	1.77	3.92	.04
14	38	7.15	7.32	14.36	.10	.6810	4.86	4.98	9.78	.06	.2292	1.64	1.68	3.29	.03
15	39	5.83	7.73	13.45	.10	.6611	3.85	5.11	8.89	.07	.2046	1.19	1.58	2.75	.02
16	40	4.55	8.11	12.57	.10	.6419	2.92	5.21	8.07	.06	.1827	.83	1.48	2.30	.01
17	41	3.33	8.47	11.70	.09	.6231	2.06	5.28	7.29	.05	.1631	.54	1.38	1.91	.01
18	42	2.16	8.81	10.87	.09	.6050	1.31	5.33	6.58	.06	.1456	.31	1.28	1.58	.01
19	43	1.04	9.12	10.08	.08	.5874	.61	5.35	5.92	.04	.1300	.14	1.19	1.31	.02
20	44	(.04)	9.40	9.29	.08	.5703	(.02)	5.37	5.30	.05	.1161	(.01)	.11	.11	(.01)
21	44*	(327.57)	4.81	(322.76)	—	.5537	(181.37)	2.66	(178.71)	-0-	.1037	(33.97)	(.50)	(33.47)	(1.00)
		$(106.43)**	$109.01***	$ (1) ***	$2.61		$2.10**	$74.59	$74.59	$2.10		$81.31	$26.27	$107.31	$ .27

*Just prior to 45th birthday.
**See Table A-10.
***See Table A-16.

Table A–18.

PRESENT VALUE AT 12% OF FUTURE BOOK PROFITS (USING STATUTORY NET LEVEL RESERVES) ON A 20-YEAR ENDOWMENT POLICY ISSUED TO A MALE AGE 25

Calendar Year	Attained Age	Gross Amounts				12% Discount Factor	12% Present Value at Issue			
		Cash Flow*	Interest on Reserve**	Increase in Reserve**	Book Profits		Cash Flow	Interest on Reserve	Increase in Reserve	Book Profits
1	25	$ (17.77)	$ .57	$ 38.98	$(56.18)	1.0000	$(17.77)	$ .57	$ 38.98	$(56.18)
2	26	32.31	1.49	23.34	10.46	.8929	28.85	1.33	20.84	9.34
3	27	27.06	2.19	23.40	5.85	.7972	21.58	1.75	18.65	4.68
4	28	25.63	2.90	24.58	3.95	.7118	18.24	2.06	17.50	2.80
5	29	22.77	3.58	21.84	4.51	.6355	14.47	2.28	13.88	2.87
6	30	20.09	4.20	19.93	4.36	.5674	11.40	2.38	11.31	2.47
7	31	17.58	4.76	18.11	4.23	.5066	8.91	2.41	9.17	2.15
8	32	15.28	5.27	16.40	4.15	.4523	6.91	2.38	7.42	1.87
9	33	13.10	5.74	15.31	3.53	.4039	5.29	2.32	6.18	1.43
10	34	11.09	6.17	13.73	3.53	.3606	4.00	2.22	4.95	1.27
11	35	11.49	6.59	14.63	3.45	.3220	3.70	2.12	4.71	1.11
12	36	9.97	7.01	13.48	3.50	.2875	2.87	2.02	3.88	1.01
13	37	8.52	7.39	12.81	3.10	.2567	2.19	1.90	3.29	.80
14	38	7.15	7.75	11.69	3.21	.2292	1.64	1.78	2.68	.74
15	39	5.83	8.09	11.02	2.90	.2046	1.19	1.66	2.25	.60
16	40	4.55	8.41	10.34	2.62	.1827	.83	1.54	1.89	.48
17	41	3.33	8.69	9.25	2.77	.1631	.54	1.42	1.51	.45
18	42	2.16	8.95	8.19	2.92	.1456	.31	1.30	1.19	.42
19	43	1.04	9.19	7.85	2.38	.1300	.14	1.19	1.02	.31
20	44	(.04)	9.41	7.12	2.25	.1161	(.01)	1.09	.83	.25
21	44***	(327.57)	4.79	(322.00)	(.78)	.1037	(33.97)	.50	(33.39)	(.08)
		$(106.43)	$123.14	$ –0–	$16.71		$81.31	$36.22	$138.74	$(21.21)

*See Table A–10.
**See Table A–4 for mean reserves (rounded figures have been used) and Table 4–16 for units in force and method of computing reserve increase and interest on reserve.
***Just prior to 45th birthday.

profits. If they require a 12 percent return on their money, then they will have to invest their funds elsewhere.

Value of Insurance in Force

The present value of unrecognized book profits at any point in time is one accepted method of determining the value of a block of insurance in force.

The method for determining the present value, at 3 percent, of insurance in force for the 20-year endowment policy is illustrated in Table A–19. At the moment of issue the present value of future book profits is $2.10 (see Table A–17). As time goes on profits are recognized which of course reduce the present value of future *unrecognized* profits. Interest on the unamortized balance of future profits must be

added at the rate used to discount the profits in the first place.

The price at which the business can be sold as of any given year-end—assuming the buyer uses a 3 percent discount rate—is expressed as a value per unit ($1,000 of face amount in this case) of insurance in force. Thus, the value of the business at the end of the tenth year is $1.70 per $1,000.

Usually a risk rate would be used to value insurance in force. The values derived using, say, 12 percent would of course differ from the values shown in Table A–19, but the technique used to calculate the value would be the same.

Gross Premium Reserves

Gross premium reserves are equivalent to the

Table A–19.

PROGRESSION OF PRESENT VALUE (AT 3%) OF FUTURE BOOK PROFITS (NATURAL RESERVE BASIS) ON A 20-YEAR ENDOWMENT POLICY ISSUED TO A MALE AGE 25

Calendar Year	Attained Age	Beginning In-Force Value	6 Months Interest	Profits Recognized	Balance	6 Months Interest	Ending In-Force Value	Units In Force	Present Value Per Unit In Force*
1	25	$2.10		$.25	$1.85	$.03	$1.88	.99961	$1.89
2	26	1.88	$.03	.19	1.72	.03	1.75	.79900	2.18
3	27	1.75	.03	.18	1.60	.02	1.62	.72640	2.23
4	28	1.62	.02	.17	1.47	.02	1.49	.68937	2.16
5	29	1.49	.02	.16	1.35	.02	1.37	.65417	2.10
6	30	1.37	.02	.15	1.24	.02	1.26	.62069	2.03
7	31	1.26	.02	.14	1.14	.02	1.16	.58886	1.96
8	32	1.16	.02	.13	1.05	.01	1.06	.55863	1.88
9	33	1.06	.01	.13	.94	.01	.95	.52990	1.80
10	34	.95	.02	.13	.84	.01	.85	.50261	1.70
11	35	.85	.01	.12	.74	.01	.75	.48170	1.58
12	36	.75	.01	.11	.65	.01	.66	.46161	1.45
13	37	.66	.01	.11	.56	.01	.57	.44231	1.31
14	38	.57	.01	.10	.48	.01	.49	.42375	1.16
15	39	.49	.01	.10	.40	.01	.41	.40589	1.00
16	40	.41	.01	.10	.32	.01	.33	.38871	.83
17	41	.33	.01	.09	.25	Nil	.25	.37215	.65
18	42	.25	Nil	.09	.16	Nil	.16	.35618	.44
19	43	.16	Nil	.08	.08	Nil	.08	.34078	.23
20	44	.08	Nil	.08	–0–	Nil	–0–	.32591	–0–

*May not compute precisely due to rounding.

natural reserve less the present value of future profits discounted at the assumed investment earnings rate. Gross premium reserve factors for the 20-year endowment policy are shown in Table A–20.

The effect of using gross premium reserves is to book a profit equal to the present value (using a discount rate equal to the assumed investment earnings rate) of all future net cash flows at the moment of issue. With respect to the 20-year endowment, this would be $2.10:

Cash flow (See Table A–10)	$(17.77)
Gross premium reserve (See Table A–20)	20.19
Interest on gross premium reserve (3% for 6 months)	(.30)
Profits in first calendar year	$ 2.12
Discount for 6 months interest at 3%	x .99
Profits recognized at issue	$ 2.10

Comparing Actual and Assumed

A company rarely has the opportunity to look back and see how its assumptions worked out over the life of a block of business. Periodic comparisons of actual experience and assumed experience can be made, but any such measurement is tainted, so to speak, by the fact that much of the future has yet to play its hand. Until the block of business runs off the books, any interim evaluations of experience are not conclusive as to the final result. As the time approaches that the policies finally terminate once and for all, of course, interim evaluations can be made with more and more confidence.

In the case of the 20-year endowment policy issued in 1951, all of the material presented thus far is based on "assumed" experience. By 1971 all of the policies issued in 1951 had matured and "actual" experience was known. It is worth comparing assumed experience and actual experience to see how hazardous assumptions can be.

"Assumed" experience was based on the best information available in 1951. "Actual" experience was based on a recreation of mortality, voluntary terminations, interest, and expenses. The recreation was based on taking full advantage of hindsight available in 1971. In other words, life insurance

Table A–20.

GROSS PREMIUM RESERVE FACTORS FOR A 20-YEAR ENDOWMENT POLICY ISSUED TO A MALE AGE 25

Calendar Year	Intermediate Natural Reserve Factor*	Present Value Per Unit In Force**	Gross Premium Reserve Factor
1	$(18.30)	$1.89	$(20.19)
2	17.22	2.18	15.04
3	57.08	2.23	54.85
4	99.42	2.16	97.26
5	143.01	2.10	140.91
6	187.86	2.03	185.83
7	234.00	1.96	232.04
8	281.58	1.88	280.00
9	330.61	1.80	328.81
10	381.17	1.70	379.47
11	433.63	1.58	432.05
12	487.75	1.45	486.30
13	543.61	1.31	542.30
14	601.31	1.16	600.15
15	660.90	1.00	659.90
16	722.45	.83	721.62
17	786.04	.65	785.39
18	851.80	.44	851.36
19	919.87	.23	919.64
20	990.36	–0–	990.36

*See Table A–14.
**See Table A–19.

industry experience over the past 20 years was adapted to the 20-year endowment policy.

The actual average size was $2,000 rather than the $2,500 assumed. Voluntary terminations were greater (for example, 25 percent in the first year versus an assumed 20 percent rate). Mortality was significantly better than assumed, as might be expected. Non-percentage expenses were higher than assumed, due in part to inflation and in part to the fact that the average size was only $2,000. Interest rates were dramatically greater, rising from 3.26 percent in 1951 to 6.1 percent in 1971.

The net result, expressed in the form of present values computed using the investment earnings rate, may be summarized as follows per $1,000 issued:

	Undiscounted Amounts		Present Value at Issue	
	Assumed	Actual	Assumed	Actual
Premiums	$529.38	$451.24	$426.74	$348.38
Deaths	17.94	11.53	13.18	7.62
Surrenders	155.94	112.33	109.80	77.06
Maturities	325.25	289.32	180.09	123.63
Acquisition costs	60.29	65.13	60.29	65.13
Maintenance expenses	76.39	70.28	61.28	53.14
			424.64	326.58
Profits			$ 2.10	$ 21.80

It will be recalled that the natural premium incorporating the original assumptions was $49.33. The "experience" premium (i.e., the level annual amount that, with hindsight, was just sufficient to pay benefits and expenses) turned out to be $46.46. The difference, $2.87, represents the level annual equivalent of the additional profits that emerged.

Experience is never equal to the underlying assumptions. In this case the assumptions proved to be conservative. It is critically important to note, however, that what finally eventuates can also be more adverse than the underlying assumptions. The "experience" premium could have been $2.87 more than the natural premium, not $2.87 less. This is a very real-world possibility with which insurance companies must deal.

Appendix B

Taxes on Investment Income

The concept that federal taxes on investment income represent a "gross receipts" tax—i.e., an investment expense—is discussed in Chapter 9.

The subject is extraordinarily complex. Following are some illustrations and commentary designed to assist in analyzing the issues and financial statement effects associated with the treatment of taxes on investment income as a type of investment expense.

Source Data for Illustrations

Table B–1 contains source data on (1) reserves and (2) interest for the illustrations that follow.

Company Taxed on T

Assume a 5-year endowment contract with a gross premium of $170, a pre-tax adjusted reserve interest assumption of 8 percent, and a statutory (and tax-basis) reserve assumption of 3 percent. Assume further that the company is taxed solely on taxable investment income minus $250,000 ("T").

Table B–2 illustrates the effect of using an 8 percent assumption for purposes of calculating the reserves. Line 12 of Table B–2 shows that an after-tax loss would be reported in Years 4 and 5 even though pre-tax income is level.

Table B–2 also illustrates the effect of using a 6 percent assumption. Line 24 shows a more level incidence of after-tax earnings. The reason after-tax earnings are not perfectly level is that the 6 percent reserve is only an approximation of the true effective rate, as discussed in Chapter 9. The effect of using an 8 percent reserve is to produce an effective after-tax rate of interest slightly higher than 6 percent:

Year	Initial 8% Adjusted Reserve	8% Interest	50% of T	Net-of-Tax Interest	Effective Rate
1	$157.83	$12.63	$ 2.66	$ 9.97	6.32%
2	328.29	26.26	5.70	20.56	6.26
3	512.38	40.99	9.19	31.80	6.21
4	711.20	56.90	13.15	43.75	6.15
5	925.93	74.07	17.61	56.46	6.10

This indicates that the proper after-tax interest rate used for purposes of calculating the adjusted reserves should be slightly higher than 6 percent.

Company Taxed on 1/2 (G+T)

The situation is slightly more complicated when a company is taxed on taxable investment income plus one-half of the excess of gain from operations over taxable investment income ("1/2 [G+T]").

Suppose statutory earnings form the basis for preparing the tax return and look like this:

Year	Gross Premiums	Interest at 8%	Change in 3% Reserve	Pre-Tax Earnings
1	$185.00	$ 14.63	$ 188.35	$ 11.28
2	185.00	29.70	194.01	20.69
3	185.00	45.22	199.83	30.39
4	185.00	61.20	205.82	40.38
5	185.00	77.67	211.99	50.68
	$925.00	$228.42	$1,000.00	$153.42

Assume that the reserve at the end of the fifth year, $1,000, is payable then as an endowment.

Taxable income is comprised of two elements, taxable investment income and gain from operations. Taxable investment income is computed as follows:

Year	Interest at 8%	Rule-of-10 Reserves	Policy-holders' Share	Taxable Investment Income
1	$ 14.63	$ 91.44	$ 7.31	$ 7.32
2	29.70	185.61	14.85	14.85
3	45.22	282.62	22.61	22.61
4	61.20	382.53	30.60	30.60
5	77.67	485.44	38.84	38.83
	$228.42		$114.21	$114.21

Gain from operations may be viewed for purposes of analysis as being comprised of the following elements:

Year	Gross Premiums	Valuation Premiums	Loading Gain	Interest at 8%	Required Interest on 3% Reserves	Interest Gain	Total Gain
1	$185.00	$182.87	$ 2.13	$ 14.63	$ 5.48	$ 9.15	$ 11.28
2	185.00	182.87	2.13	29.70	11.14	18.56	20.69
3	185.00	182.87	2.13	45.22	16.96	28.26	30.39
4	185.00	182.87	2.13	61.20	22.95	38.25	40.38
5	185.00	182.87	2.13	77.67	29.12	48.55	50.68
	$925.00	$914.35	$10.65	$228.42	$85.65	$142.77	$153.42

Taxes are therefore levied as follows:

Year	T	G Loading	Interest	(G+T)	½ (G+T)	Taxes at 50%
1	$ 7.32	$ 2.13	$ 9.15	$ 18.60	$ 9.30	$ 4.65
2	14.85	2.13	18.56	35.54	17.77	8.89
3	22.61	2.13	28.26	53.00	26.50	13.25
4	30.60	2.13	38.25	70.98	35.49	17.74
5	38.83	2.13	48.55	89.51	44.76	22.38
	$114.21	$10.65	$142.77	$267.63	$133.82	$66.91

Suppose now that the company uses 8 percent adjusted reserves. "Theoretical T" changes because interest is earned on assets equivalent to the adjusted reserve, which is less than the statutory reserve. "Theoretical T" and actual T may be reconciled as follows:

Year	8% Interest on Adjusted Reserve	Policy-holders' Share (No Change)	Theoretical T	8% Interest on Excess of Statutory Reserve over Adjusted Reserve	Tax Return T
1	$ 12.63	$ 7.31	$ 5.32	$ 2.00	$ 7.32
2	26.26	14.85	11.41	3.44	14.85
3	40.99	22.61	18.38	4.23	22.61
4	56.90	30.60	26.30	4.30	30.60
5	74.07	38.84	35.23	3.60	38.83
	$210.85	$114.21	$96.64	$17.57	$114.21

When adjusted reserves are used earnings are leveled, that is, expenses net of interest income are averaged out and all the gain is from loading (again absent any provisions for adverse deviation):

Year	Gross Premiums	Valuation Premiums	Loading Gain	Interest at 8%	Required Interest on 8% Reserves	Interest Gain	Total Gain
1	$185.00	$157.83	$ 27.17	$ 12.63	$ 12.63	$ —	$ 27.17
2	185.00	157.83	27.17	26.26	26.26	—	27.17
3	185.00	157.83	27.17	40.99	40.99	—	27.17
4	185.00	157.83	27.17	56.90	56.90	—	27.17
5	185.00	157.83	27.17	74.07	74.07	—	27.17
	$925.00	$789.15	$135.85	$210.85	$210.85	$ —	$135.85

The apparent tax base and taxes would be as follows:

Year	Theoretical T	Adjusted G	Adjusted (G+T)	½ Adjusted (G+T)	Taxes at 50%
1	$ 5.32	$ 27.17	$ 32.49	$ 16.25	$ 8.12
2	11.41	27.17	38.58	19.29	9.65
3	18.38	27.17	45.55	22.77	11.39
4	26.30	27.17	53.47	26.73	13.37
5	35.23	27.17	62.40	31.20	15.60
	$96.64	$135.85	$232.49	$116.24	$58.13

This may be reconciled with conventional deferred tax calculations as follows:

Year	Theoretical T	Theoretical Tax Return G*	Reserve Timing Difference	Adjusted (G+T)	½ Adjusted (G+T)	Taxes at 50%
1	$ 5.32	$ 9.28	$ 17.89	$ 32.49	$ 16.24	$ 8.12
2	11.41	17.25	9.92	38.58	19.29	9.65
3	18.38	26.16	1.01	45.55	22.78	11.39
4	26.30	36.08	(8.91)	53.47	26.74	13.37
5	35.23	47.08	(19.91)	62.40	31.20	15.60
	$96.64	$135.85	$ —	$232.49	$116.25	$58.13

* Actual tax return G reduced by interest on the excess of statutory reserves over adjusted reserves.

The effect of the conventional process may be summarized as follows:

Year	Pre-Tax Adjusted Income	Taxes, Including Deferred	After-Tax Adjusted Income
1	$ 27.17	$ 8.12	$19.05
2	27.17	9.65	17.52
3	27.17	11.39	15.78
4	27.17	13.37	13.80
5	27.17	15.60	11.57
	$135.85	$58.13	$77.72

Table B–1.

SOURCE DATA FOR ILLUSTRATIONS OF EFFECTS OF TAXES ON INVESTMENT INCOME

		Year 1	Year 2	Year 3	Year 4	Year 5	Total
	Statutory reserves and interest:						
(1)	Valuation premium—3%	$182.87	$182.87	$182.87	$182.87	$ 182.87	$ 914.35
(2)	Initial reserve	182.87	371.22	565.23	765.06	970.88	—
(3)	Terminal reserve	188.35	382.36	582.19	788.01	1,000.00	—
(4)	Change in terminal reserve	188.35	194.01	199.83	205.82	211.99	1,000.00
	Interest on initial reserve:						
(5)	3%	5.48	11.14	16.96	22.95	29.12	85.65
(6)	8%	14.63	29.70	45.22	61.20	77.67	228.42
	Tax-basis reserves and interest:						
(7)	Initial reserve	91.44	185.61	282.62	382.53	485.44	—
(8)	Policyholder share	7.31	14.85	22.61	30.60	38.84	114.21
(9)	Taxable investment income	7.32	14.85	22.61	30.60	38.83	114.21
(10)	Phase II required interest	9.15	18.56	28.26	38.25	48.55	142.77
	8% adjusted reserves:						
(11)	Valuation premium	157.83	157.83	157.83	157.83	157.83	789.15
(12)	Initial reserve	157.83	328.29	512.38	711.20	925.93	—
(13)	Terminal reserve	170.46	354.55	553.37	768.10	1,000.00	—
(14)	Change in terminal reserve	170.46	184.09	198.82	214.73	231.90	1,000.00
(15)	8% interest on initial reserve	12.63	26.26	40.99	56.90	74.07	210.85
	6% adjusted reserves:						
(16)	Valuation premium	167.36	167.36	167.36	167.36	167.36	836.80
(17)	Initial reserve	167.36	344.76	532.80	732.12	943.40	—
(18)	Terminal reserve	177.40	365.44	564.76	776.04	1,000.00	—
(19)	Change in terminal · reserve	177.40	188.04	199.32	211.28	223.96	1,000.00
	Interest on initial reserve:						
(20)	6%	10.04	20.68	31.96	43.92	56.60	163.20
(21)	8%	13.39	27.58	42.62	58.57	75.47	217.63
	6 2/3% adjusted reserves:						
(22)	Valuation premium	164.11	164.11	164.11	164.11	164.11	820.55
(23)	Initial reserve	164.11	339.16	525.88	725.05	937.50	—
(24)	Terminal reserve	175.05	361.77	560.94	773.39	1,000.00	—
(25)	Change in terminal reserve	175.05	186.72	199.17	212.45	226.61	1,000.00
	Interest on initial reserve:						
(26)	6 2/3%	10.94	22.61	35.06	48.34	62.50	179.45
(27)	8%	13.13	27.13	42.07	58.00	75.00	215.33
	Theoretical taxable investment income:						
(28)	On 8% reserves	5.32	11.41	18.38	26.30	35.23	96.64
(29)	On 6% reserves at 8% interest	6.08	12.73	20.01	27.97	36.63	103.42
(30)	On 6 2/3% reserves at 8% interest	5.82	12.28	19.46	27.40	36.16	101.12

Table B–2.

ILLUSTRATION OF EFFECT OF TAXES ON INVESTMENT INCOME ON RESERVES AND PROFITS WHERE COMPANY IS TAXED ON T

		Year 1	Year 2	Year 3	Year 4	Year 5	Total
	Statutory earnings:						
(1)	Premiums	$ 170.00	$ 170.00	$ 170.00	$ 170.00	$ 170.00	$ 850.00
(2)	Interest on reserve	14.63	29.70	45.22	61.20	77.67	228.42
(3)	Increase in reserve	(188.35)	(194.01)	(199.83)	(205.82)	(211.99)	(1,000.00)
(4)	Income before taxes	(3.72)	5.69	15.39	25.38	35.68	78.42
(5)	Taxes	3.66	7.42	11.31	15.30	19.42	57.11
(6)	Income	$ (7.38)	$ (1.73)	$ 4.08	$ 10.08	$ 16.26	$ 21.31
	Adjusted earnings 8% reserves:						
(7)	Premiums	$ 170.00	$ 170.00	$ 170.00	$ 170.00	$ 170.00	$ 850.00
(8)	Interest	12.63	26.26	40.99	56.90	74.07	210.85
(9)	Increase in reserve	(170.46)	(184.09)	(198.82)	(214.73)	(231.90)	(1,000.00)
(10)	Pure pre-tax adjusted earnings	12.17	12.17	12.17	12.17	12.17	60.85
(11)	Taxes	2.66	5.70	9.19	13.15	17.62	48.32
(12)	Pure after-tax adjusted earnings	9.51	6.47	2.98	(.98)	(5.45)	12.53
	Interest on excess statutory reserve:						
(13)	Gross	2.00	3.44	4.23	4.30	3.60	17.57
(14)	Taxes	1.00	1.72	2.12	2.15	1.80	8.79
(15)	Net	1.00	1.72	2.11	2.15	1.80	8.78
(16)	Income	$ 10.51	$ 8.19	$ 5.09	$ 1.17	$ (3.65)	$ 21.31
	Adjusted earnings 6% reserves:						
(17)	Premiums	$ 170.00	$ 170.00	$ 170.00	$ 170.00	$ 170.00	$ 850.00
	Interest						
(18)	On 8% reserve	12.63	26.26	40.99	56.90	74.07	210.85
(19)	On additional reserve	.76	1.32	1.63	1.67	1.40	6.78
	Increase in reserve:						
(20)	8% reserve	(170.46)	(184.09)	(198.82)	(214.73)	(231.90)	(1,000.00)
(21)	Additional reserve	(6.94)	(3.95)	(.50)	3.45	7.94	—
(22)	Pure pre-tax adjusted earnings	5.99	9.54	13.30	17.29	21.51	67.63
(23)	Taxes	3.04	6.37	10.00	13.98	18.32	51.71
(24)	Pure after-tax adjusted earnings	2.95	3.17	3.30	3.31	3.19	15.92
	Interest on excess statutory reserve:						
(25)	Gross	1.24	2.12	2.60	2.63	2.20	10.79
(26)	Taxes	.62	1.06	1.30	1.32	1.10	5.40
(27)	Net	.62	1.06	1.30	1.31	1.10	5.39
(28)	Income	$ 3.57	$ 4.23	$ 4.60	$ 4.62	$ 4.29	$ 21.31

If theoretical T is leveled out, a level tax expense results from using conventional deferred tax procedures:

Year	Level Theoretical T	Theoretical Tax Return G	Reserve Timing Difference	Adjusted (G+T)	½ Adjusted (G+T)	Taxes at 50%
1	$19.33	$ 9.28	$ 17.89	$ 46.50	$ 23.25	$11.63
2	19.33	17.25	9.92	46.50	23.25	11.62
3	19.33	26.16	1.01	46.50	23.25	11.63
4	19.33	36.08	(8.91)	46.50	23.25	11.62
5	19.32	47.08	(19.91)	46.49	23.25	11.63
	$96.64	$135.85	$ —	$232.49	$116.25	$58.13

Thus the tax expense would be level at $11.63, pretax earnings would be level at $27.17, and after-tax earnings would be level at $15.54.

The reported tax expense would, of course, be increased for taxes (at 25 percent, in this case) on interest on the excess of statutory over adjusted reserves.

Suppose now that 6 2/3 percent reserves are used even though the company expects to earn 8 percent. Theoretical T changes slightly because interest at 8 percent is being earned on a 6 2/3 percent reserve. The apparent tax base would be as follows:

Year	Gross Premiums	Valuation Premiums	Loading Gain	Interest at 8%	Required Interest on 6⅔% Reserves	Interest Gain	Total Gain
1	$185.00	$164.11	$ 20.89	$ 13.13	$ 10.94	$ 2.19	$ 23.08
2	185.00	164.11	20.89	27.13	22.61	4.52	25.41
3	185.00	164.11	20.89	42.07	35.06	7.01	27.90
4	185.00	164.11	20.89	58.00	48.34	9.66	30.55
5	185.00	164.11	20.89	75.00	62.50	12.50	33.39
	$925.00	$820.55	$104.45	$215.33	$179.45	$35.88	$140.33

Taxes would be calculated as follows:

Year	Theoretical T	Theoretical Tax Return G	Reserve Timing Difference	Adjusted (G+T)	½ Adjusted (G+T)	Taxes at 50%
1	$ 5.32	$ 9.78	$ 13.30	$ 28.40	$ 14.20	$ 7.10
2	11.41	18.13	7.29	36.83	18.42	9.21
3	18.38	27.24	.66	46.28	23.14	11.57
4	26.30	37.18	(6.63)	56.85	28.42	14.21
5	35.23	48.01	(14.62)	68.62	34.31	17.15
	$96.64	$140.34	$ —	$236.98	$118.49	$59.24

So adjusted income and taxes would line up as follows:

Year	Pre-Tax Adjusted Income	Taxes	After-Tax Adjusted Income
1	$ 23.08	$ 7.10	$15.98
2	25.41	9.21	16.20
3	27.90	11.57	16.33
4	30.55	14.21	16.34
5	33.39	17.15	16.24
	$140.33	$59.24	$81.09

As usual, taxes on the interest on the excess of statutory reserves over adjusted reserves would also be payable, in proportion to the amount of such interest.

After-tax income is not quite level because a 6 2/3 percent reserve is not precise, for reasons explained previously.

Company Taxed on G

As suggested earlier, no recognition need be given to taxes on investment income when a company is taxed solely on gain from operations because adjusted required interest absorbs assumed earned interest and all necessary adjustments are effected by means of the traditional deferred tax calculation. Table B–3 illustrates a situation in which the company is taxed on gain from operations ("G").

As also suggested earlier, a situation in which G is less than T should be viewed as temporary and normally should not be considered a permanent condition for purposes of computing taxes allocable to investment income.

Nontaxable Investment Income

Certain items of investment income are not taxed, for example tax-exempt interest.

Frequently such items are negligible and can be ignored in calculating the reduction in yield attributable to taxes on investment income.

When the items are material they should, of course, be taken into account in computing the tax rate. It is often difficult to forecast the proportion of investment income represented by such items. In such cases a very conservative assumption about the proportion exempt from tax would be in order.

Interest on Statutory Reserve

It could be argued that interest, net of taxes, on the excess of the adjusted reserve will always be available

Table B–3.

ILLUSTRATION OF EFFECT OF CONVENTIONAL DEFERRED TAX PROCEDURES WHEN COMPANY IS TAXED ON G

		Year 1	Year 2	Year 3	Year 4	Year 5	Total
	Statutory earnings:						
(1)	Premiums	$ 170.00	$ 170.00	$ 170.00	$ 170.00	$ 170.00	$ 850.00
(2)	Interest on reserve	14.63	29.70	45.22	61.20	77.67	228.42
(3)	Increase in reserve	(188.35)	(194.01)	(199.83)	(205.82)	(211.99)	(1,000.00)
(4)	Income before taxes	(3.72)	5.69	15.39	25.38	35.68	78.42
(5)	Taxes	(1.86)	2.85	7.69	12.69	17.84	39.21
(6)	Income	$ (1.86)	$ 2.84	$ 7.70	$ 12.69	$ 17.84	$ 39.21
	Tax calculation:						
(7)	Taxable investment income	$ 7.32	$ 14.85	$ 22.61	$ 30.60	$ 38.83	$ 114.21
(8)	Gain from operations	(3.72)	5.69	15.39	25.38	35.68	78.42
(9)	Taxes on lesser	(1.86)	2.84	7.70	12.69	17.84	39.21
	Adjusted earnings 8% reserves:						
(10)	Premiums	$ 170.00	$ 170.00	$ 170.00	$ 170.00	$ 170.00	$ 850.00
(11)	Interest on reserve	12.63	26.26	40.99	56.90	74.07	210.85
(12)	Change in reserve	(170.46)	(184.09)	(198.82)	(214.73)	(231.90)	(1,000.00)
(13)	Pure pre-tax adjusted earnings	12.17	12.17	12.17	12.17	12.17	60.85
(14)	Taxes, including deferred	6.08	6.09	6.08	6.09	6.08	30.42
(15)	Pure after-tax adjusted earnings	6.09	6.08	6.09	6.08	6.09	30.43
	Interest on excess statutory reserve:						
(16)	Gross	2.00	3.44	4.23	4.30	3.60	17.57
(17)	Taxes	1.00	1.72	2.12	2.15	1.80	8.79
(18)	Net	1.00	1.72	2.11	2.15	1.80	8.78
(19)	Income	$ 7.09	$ 7.80	$ 8.20	$ 8.23	$ 7.89	$ 39.21
	Deferred tax account:						
(20)	Timing differences	$ 17.89	$ 9.92	$ 1.01	$ (8.91)	$ (19.91)	$ —
(21)	Origination (amortization)	8.94	4.96	.51	(4.45)	(9.96)	—
(22)	Ending balance	8.94	13.90	14.41	9.96	—	—
	Tax expense:						
(23)	Current	$ (1.86)	$ 2.85	$ 7.69	$ 12.69	$ 17.84	$ 39.21
(24)	Deferred	8.94	4.96	.51	(4.45)	(9.96)	—
(25)	Total	$ 7.08	$ 7.81	$ 8.20	$ 8.24	$ 7.88	$ 39.21
	Reconciliation:						
(26)	Taxes on pure pre-tax adjusted earnings	$ 6.08	$ 6.09	$ 6.08	$ 6.09	$ 6.08	$ 30.42
(27)	Taxes on interest on excess reserve	1.00	1.72	2.12	2.15	1.80	8.79
(28)	Total, as above	$ 7.08	$ 7.81	$ 8.20	$ 8.24	$ 7.88	$ 39.21

to help pay taxes on interest on adjusted reserves, since assets equal to statutory reserves must always be held. Under this reasoning the taxes on investment income would be reduced by the net-of-tax interest on such excess reserve. In effect, interest on the excess reserve would be anticipated and "credited" to the indicated tax.

Since the excess of statutory reserves over adjusted reserves shows up as adjusted surplus, interest on such excess should be viewed as interest *revenue* on adjusted surplus. The adjusted reserves should stand on their own.

Discounting Future Tax Payments

Reducing the assumed interest rate for taxes on investment income effectively results in building a liability for future tax payments into the reserve. Such tax payments are discounted to a present value and translated into a level annual equivalent; and the related portion of the reserve is improved with interest.

This seems entirely proper if the taxes are viewed as being in the nature of investment expenses.

If the taxes thus reserved for are viewed as being a species of deferred taxes, then it appears that discounting runs counter to requirements of Accounting Principles Board Opinion No. 11, which provides that deferred taxes are not to be discounted. To do justice to the non-discounting requirement it would appear necessary to calculate a level equivalent with zero interest and *not* improve the liability with interest. But this would run counter to the basic notion of a Phase I tax, which is a tax on investment income. The assets generating investment income are themselves being improved with interest, and to ignore this fact would result in a gross mismatching of revenue and expense. Thus, discounting the liability appears fully consistent with the operation of the related assets and hence results in an appropriate expression of *current* tax benefits. In short, discounting in these circumstances appears to conform with APB Opinion No. 11.

Appendix C   Crazy Quilt Life

This appendix contains selected information on Crazy Quilt Life, the Ernst & Ernst model office, which was developed during the period 1969–1972.

The objective of the model office was to provide a reasonably credible laboratory for testing and evaluating various approaches to life insurance accounting. "Approaches" refers principally to reserve methods, which lie at the heart of the principal problems in life insurance accounting. "Reserve methods" is here used in the broad sense. The term refers to "expense reserves" as well as benefit reserves.

The model was built with a view toward simulating what could have happened to a given life insurance company over the period 1941–1971. In other words, one central objective of the model was credibility of its experience. The model was designed to be an entity unto itself, not a representation of the life insurance industry or of any specific company. To represent the life insurance industry by an accounting model would be patently impossible. To represent an existing company would be possible but flexibility would be greatly reduced. The approach adopted was essentially to simulate a company that was started from scratch.

Given a credible record of experience, then the model serves as an appropriate vehicle for testing reserve methods in a controlled but realistic environment. The model is ideal for testing various theoretical concepts and proposed practical approaches.

A full description of the model is beyond the scope of this appendix. However, the following general comments will be helpful in understanding how the model was developed.

Individual Lines

Models for the ordinary life, individual annuity, industrial, and guaranteed renewable disability income lines of business were so constructed that each age, plan, year of issue, rate book era, etc. constitutes a separate model. This facilitated analysis of the behavior of accounting data under conditions of growth, stability, and decline; for growing blocks of business and closed blocks of business; under conditions of good persistency and bad persistency; etc.

The model began business in 1941. That year was selected not because it was an especially propitious year in which to begin business, but (among other reasons) because the 30 years since 1941 have encompassed some radical changes in mortality, interest rates, mix of business, expenses, etc.

Premiums, dividends, and cash values were for the most part "stolen" from other companies' ratebooks. The premiums were tested and modified where necessary. In general, seven rate book "eras" were used from 1941 to 1971.

Interest rates were developed on an annual basis (and were varied by calendar year) by creating a portfolio of assets that followed fairly closely the industry's pattern of investment acquisitions. The gross interest rate was determined with respect to each category of investment by investigation of inter-test rate histories. (Investment expenses are discussed below.) Investment income was computed by the year-of-investment method, partly because it was necessary to know new-money rates for purposes of testing premiums, partly because the method was required to obtain internally consistent annual port-folio rates, and partly because interest credits to certain group reserves were based on the year-of-investment method.

Mortality and morbidity (select and ultimate) were determined primarily by reference to published tables applicable to the period during which the business was issued. Such rates were graded into updated tables over time. Mortality fluctuation was introduced by reference to published materials on the subject, with due regard for the volumes of insurance in force, that is, gross exposures.

Expenses (including investment expenses) were based on a study of functional costs of 80 companies in 1968, plus highly detailed examinations of the functional costs of several large companies whose characteristics were similar to those of the model. Expense rates were projected forward and backward based on available information on the relationship of functional costs in years other than 1968 to the 1968 functional costs. Information for the 1940s and 1950s was scanty, so expenses in those years were extended backward from the earliest available data based on judgment and a limited study of inflation (net of automation savings) in the life insurance business.

Volume was based on a defined initial volume compounded over the long term at 9 percent. However, a good deal of variation within this general pattern was introduced.

Mix of volume among plans and ages was based generally (but not entirely) on industry trends (particularly trends within the stock company segment of the industry), as were average policy sizes.

Generally, five issue ages—10, 25, 35, 45, and 60—were used. This range of ages was expanded or contracted as circumstances warranted.

Terminations were based roughly on the experience of some very large stock companies. However, terminations were often varied from the general experience pattern, generally for the worse. In any case, profits were calculated using a great number of termination alternatives while holding all other experience constant.

Thirty-six sets of reserve factors were calculated for each major individual line of business covered by the model, approximately 400,000 factors in all.

Reserve factors were calculated using "best estimates" tempered by (1) published information available at the time of developing rate books, (2) experience in preceding years, and (3) conservatism as to the future. Evaluation of and provision for future risk was an inherent part of rate-testing and reserve computation.

Present values of future profits were computed using a discount rate of 12 percent, which was deemed to represent a reasonable measure of the risk from the point of view of investors. Alternative present values using the investment yield rate were computed in many instances.

Models were created on two bases: "assumed" (i.e., an aggregate projection of assumptions underlying the premiums) and "actual" (i.e., an aggregation of experience as it actually developed based on application of all the criteria discussed previously).

A study of the Convention Statements of 160 companies representing some 70 percent of the industry in terms of assets and insurance in force was undertaken to furnish reasonableness guidelines for the model. In addition, available industry statistical information was used extensively.

Input for the model office was developed by the staff members of Ernst & Ernst and by Mrs. Beverly Rose, FSA. Advice and guidance was provided by numerous insurance company executives and by Milliman & Robertson, Inc. Major assistance was contributed by 13 large life insurance companies. Reserve factors, rate tests, and model office projections were prepared by M & R Services, Inc. Creation and operation of the model and its associated reserve systems has, to an extraordinary degree, involved the cooperative efforts of accountants, actuaries, systems analysts, programmers and, of course, a bevy of large computers.

It is felt that as much care as possible has gone into development of the models of individual lines and that the results are sufficiently credible to serve validly as a controlled environment for the testing of various accounting approaches. In several cases the model also provides a sound basis for generalization.

With that synoptic background, there follow 13 tables which summarize the various plans covered by the models for individual lines. Comments accompany each table.

In testing premiums and computing reserve factors for the model, it was necessary to project assumptions as to premium volume, investment income, death claims, surrenders, expenses, etc. Such projections become a kind of standard against which emerging actual experience can, within limits, be measured. Table C–1 compares, for combined ordinary life plans, (1) aggregate "assumed" experience, obtained by multiplying the rate-test assumptions by the volumes actually issued, with (2) aggregate actual experience through 1971. Only selected financial statement items are shown in Table C–1, and the information is highly condensed and summarized.

Projections of "actual" experience beyond 1971 are based on a "best estimate" of experience after that year in view of all relevant information available in that year.

It must be recognized that the items shown in Table C–1 are interrelated to a significant degree, as a result of which the information shown does not constitute a variance analysis.

On the other hand, the table is useful in identifying trends. It will be seen, for example, that assumed mortality exceeded actual mortality by 50 percent in 1950, 40 percent in 1960, 12 percent in 1970 and is projected to exceed actual by only 2 percent in 1980. This suggests—but does not prove—that mortality margins may be shrinking. The projection also suggests that surrenders are exceeding expectations (due in part, no doubt, to a flight of cash values to higher interest rates) and that actual acquisition costs are exceeding assumed despite frequent rate book revisions and despite the fact that the average size of new policies has been increasing. The reader may speculate further as to the significance of the information shown in Table C–1. The important point is that the data suggest, at least superficially, that risks beyond the risks quantified by "best estimates" are an inherent part of the life insurance business. Provision for such risks should, of course, be made in any reserve system which enters into the computation of net income. Put another way, reserve assumptions should be respectably conservative.

"Full adjusted reserves" refer to the *net* reserve—acquisition costs, benefits, and maintenance expenses. In this tabulation development costs and overhead are factored into acquisition costs.

Table C–2 reports additional pertinent comparisons of aggregate assumed and actual experience, again for all ordinary life plans combined. All profits are reported on a pre-tax basis in Table C–2 (as well as in subsequent tables). The present value of assumed future profits, computed prospectively at the time of introducing the policies and expressed for volumes actually issued, is shown on two discount bases, the assumed investment earnings rates (which vary by rate book era) and a risk rate, 12 percent. The present value of "actual" future profits, computed by looking back in 1971 and discounting experience through 1971 in *ex post facto* fashion while discounting post-1971 experience on a pro-

spective basis, is also shown; the discount rate used is 12 percent. It should be noted that present values are measured as of the end of the calendar year, with the result that the reserve basis directly affects the year-end present values. The higher the reserve, the greater the present value of unrecognized profits. (This is discussed in greater detail in the tables which follow.) In this case, full adjusted reserves (see the discussion applicable to Table C–1), the most liberal application of the adjusted reserve concept, have been used. Nevertheless, the present value of unrecognized profits accumulates to a substantial sum ($73 million in 1971). As time passes, however, the spread between the *increase* in present values and reported earnings diminishes, with the result that reported earnings become more closely allied to measures of economic progress.

The question naturally arises as to why a small loss is reported in 1941 when full adjusted reserves are being used. The answer is that experience—primarily expenses—was more adverse than expected.

The results shown in Table C–2 reflect direct business, i.e., without modification in respect to reinsurance ceded. Finally, each line or plan of business is regarded as self-sufficient.

All of the tables subsequent to Table C–2 deal entirely with "actual" experience.

Table C–3 reports selected information on actual experience for all ordinary life plans combined (supplementary benefits, supplementary contracts, and miscellaneous items are excluded). Earnings are shown as computed using three reserve bases: statutory, full adjusted (described in the discussion applicable to Table C–1), and modified adjusted (described below). The indicated pre-tax earnings are shown on two bases, namely, assuming (a) immediate distribution of profits and (b) retention of profits. Present values, computed at a 12 percent discount rate, are also shown for the three reserve bases. The relationship between the reserve basis and the present value of unrecognized profits is dramatically illustrated in Table C–3.

The irrational pattern of periodic statutory profits is due in part to changing reserve bases. In 1968, for example, Crazy Quilt made a wholesale shift from modified to net level reserves despite a healthy growth rate. The year 1963 marked a tremendous upsurge in new business, and even the use of modified statutory reserves at that time could not cope with the resulting drain.

Modified adjusted reserves are the same as full

Table C-1.

COMPARISON OF SELECTED AGGREGATE FINANCIAL STATEMENT ITEMS—"ASSUMED" VS. "ACTUAL" EXPERIENCE FOR ACTUAL PRODUCTION VOLUME—ALL ORDINARY LIFE PLANS COMBINED (000 Omitted)

ACTUAL RESULTS FOR BUSINESS PRODUCED THROUGH 1971

Year	Interest on Assets Equivalent to Full Adjusted Reserves		Death Claims		Maturities And Surrenders		Dividends		Acquisition Costs*		Maintenance Expenses		Increase in Full Adjusted Reserves	
	Assumed	Actual	Assumed	Actual	Assumed	Actual	Assumed	Actual	Assumed	Actual	Assumed	Actual	Assumed	Actual
1941	$ (4)	$ (4)	$ 30	$ 12			$ 3	$ 3	$ 1,012	$ 1,046	$ 96	$ 117	$ (323)	$ (323)
1942	(8)	(8)	106	55			7	8	1,387	1,432	216	253	74	71
1943	1	1	215	119			15	16	1,819	1,877	366	419	589	579
1944	27	28	360	170	$ 46	$ 37	25	27	2,163	2,231	539	609	1,246	1,244
1945	70	74	543	232	116	104	39	42	2,679	2,732	747	835	1,921	1,929
1946	135	144	766	358	215	205	59	65	3,126	3,142	981	1,083	2,782	2,797
1947	226	242	1,021	531	344	340	84	94	3,427	3,438	1,225	1,342	3,803	3,822
1948	342	371	1,246	714	512	520	101	115	3,591	3,663	1,373	1,476	4,700	4,720
1949	479	530	1,433	910	722	755	137	155	4,176	4,255	1,539	1,642	5,376	5,353
1950	640	719	1,631	1,076	1,045	1,129	179	202	4,512	4,586	1,715	1,818	6,170	6,033
1951	826	939	1,845	1,181	1,315	1,482	226	256	4,895	4,973	1,878	1,970	7,038	6,736
1952	1,038	1,190	2,093	1,310	1,632	1,848	298	334	5,001	5,100	2,148	2,203	7,906	7,478
1953	1,277	1,474	2,385	1,575	2,009	2,228	330	372	4,936	5,037	2,395	2,412	8,863	8,355
1954	1,547	1,792	2,710	1,898	2,443	2,653	364	409	4,785	4,890	2,614	2,586	9,708	9,160
1955	1,844	2,153	3,045	2,213	2,891	3,099	394	450	4,363	4,463	2,779	2,711	10,528	9,948
1956	2,166	2,586	3,378	2,541	3,352	3,548	422	489	3,808	3,902	2,887	2,782	11,133	10,540
1957	2,497	3,082	3,697	2,752	3,810	3,966	448	527	3,629	3,677	2,978	2,833	11,260	10,732
1958	2,828	3,624	4,018	2,860	4,257	4,370	476	566	3,856	3,868	3,092	2,925	11,152	10,799
1959	3,163	4,221	4,358	3,030	4,734	4,763	507	605	4,059	4,063	3,219	3,026	11,086	10,853
1960	3,502	4,843	4,711	3,374	5,206	5,142	540	644	4,447	4,432	3,375	3,150	10,988	10,813
1961	3,809	5,401	5,057	3,820	8,183	7,118	577	686	4,978	4,947	3,555	3,298	8,242	9,025
1962	4,052	5,863	5,416	4,211	9,298	7,853	614	727	5,729	5,817	3,552	3,250	7,213	8,362
1963	4,242	6,270	5,838	4,601	10,457	8,553	656	772	7,742	7,955	3,639	3,315	5,407	6,880
1964	4,398	6,645	6,322	5,119	11,426	9,124	706	826	9,545	9,787	3,766	3,441	4,371	6,302
1965	4,537	7,038	6,873	5,719	12,451	9,717	746	870	11,518	11,687	3,979	3,671	3,470	5,974
1966	4,673	7,525	7,501	6,487	13,526	10,398	798	922	13,508	13,686	4,245	3,968	2,958	6,011
1967	4,831	8,163	8,228	7,389	14,050	10,816	862	986	15,664	15,816	4,573	4,331	3,331	6,638
1968	5,027	8,952	9,104	8,238	12,832	12,355	942	1,062	16,877	17,114	5,243	5,028	6,165	6,748
1969	5,284	9,879	10,135	9,116	13,651	13,428	1,037	1,152	18,359	18,624	5,960	5,757	7,187	7,583
1970	5,567	10,929	11,331	10,151	13,580	13,583	1,139	1,248	20,709	21,253	6,440	6,250	8,721	8,926
1971	5,889	11,756	12,691	11,433	13,801	14,039	1,251	1,359	23,267	23,683	7,021	6,832	10,151	10,276

PROJECTION OF BUSINESS IN FORCE AT 1971 YEAR-END

Year														
1972	6,754	12,706	13,756	12,386	13,937	14,369	1,337	1,444	2,722	2,740	6,481	6,285	25,769	25,677
1973	8,067	14,090	14,460	12,892	13,964	14,517	1,426	1,532	1,974	1,985	6,093	5,903	24,070	23,823
1974	9,282	15,426	15,134	13,389	14,115	14,742	1,509	1,612	1,483	1,491	5,756	5,578	22,335	22,015
1975	10,403	16,681	15,611	13,872	13,667	14,325	1,587	1,685	1,168	1,180	5,443	5,273	21,391	21,043
1976	11,438	16,423	15,938	14,390	13,162	13,832	1,658	1,767	978	993	5,160	4,994	20,654	20,303
1977	12,398	15,932	16,299	14,976	13,571	14,316	1,723	1,826	667	677	4,915	4,751	19,210	18,788
1978	13,283	16,810	16,666	15,606	13,810	14,586	1,781	1,878	633	637	4,684	4,421	17,664	17,216
1979	14,083	17,615	17,026	16,251	13,899	14,723	1,833	1,923	586	588	4,466	4,093	16,284	15,762
1980	14,780	18,355	17,403	16,911	13,889	14,740	1,881	1,962	355	356	4,258	3,841	15,118	14,533

*Including, where applicable, acquisition costs subsequent to the first year.

Table C–2.

AGGREGATE "ASSUMED" EXPERIENCE UNDERLYING PREMIUM ASSUMPTIONS COMPARED WITH "ACTUAL" EXPERIENCE (1) RECORDED THROUGH 1971 AND (2) PROJECTED TO 1980 BASED ON 1971 FACTS—ALL ORDINARY LIFE PLANS COMBINED—SELECTED MEASUREMENT ITEMS

Year	Insurance Sold (000,000)*	Insurance In Force (000,000) Assumed	Insurance In Force (000,000) Actual	Premiums (000) Assumed	Premiums (000) Actual	Present Value of Future Profits (000)** Assumed Discounted at Investment Earnings Rate	Present Value of Future Profits (000)** Assumed Discounted at 12%	Present Value of Future Profits (000)** Actual- Discounted at 12%	Change in 12% Present Values (000) Assumed	Change in 12% Present Values (000) Actual	Periodic Profits Using Full Adjusted Reserves - Assuming Distribution of Profits (000) Assumed	Periodic Profits Using Full Adjusted Reserves - Assuming Distribution of Profits (000) Actual
"ACTUAL"												
1941	$ 25	$ 25	$ 25	$ 844	$ 844	$ 173	$ 98	$ 390	$ 98	$ 390	$ 22	$ (14)
1942	35	55	55	1,848	1,837	401	229	962	131	572	49	10
1943	47	93	92	3,086	3,065	691	395	1,767	166	805	83	56
1944	56	135	135	4,474	4,450	1,019	584	2,746	189	979	122	159
1945	71	188	188	6,144	6,127	1,419	817	4,001	233	1,255	170	328
1946	83	247	247	8,017	8,012	1,871	1,081	5,577	264	1,576	224	506
1947	92	308	309	9,958	9,970	2,350	1,360	7,421	279	1,844	280	646
1948	90	361	363	11,572	11,607	3,224	1,875	8,961	515	1,540	390	769
1949	100	421	423	13,406	13,397	4,153	2,423	10,822	548	1,861	500	854
1950	109	485	487	15,234	15,147	5,138	3,007	12,970	584	2,148	619	1,017
1951	120	553	555	17,121	16,940	6,182	3,630	15,347	623	2,377	747	1,277
1952	128	623	625	18,864	18,598	6,903	4,049	17,930	419	2,583	821	1,510
1953	134	694	698	20,546	20,249	7,653	4,485	20,728	436	2,798	906	1,746
1954	135	760	766	22,064	21,747	8,374	4,906	23,702	421	2,974	990	1,943
1955	128	815	823	23,215	22,876	8,991	5,269	26,719	363	3,017	1,062	2,146
1956	116	853	864	23,926	23,591	9,451	5,544	29,617	275	2,898	1,116	2,377
1957	116	891	905	24,451	24,136	9,654	5,674	31,404	130	1,787	1,131	2,736
1958	126	939	950	25,181	24,806	9,949	5,855	33,139	181	1,735	1,166	3,045
1959	140	995	1,001	26,007	25,525	10,381	6,111	34,788	256	1,649	1,217	3,412
1960	157	1,064	1,061	27,038	26,417	10,964	6,450	36,465	339	1,677	1,283	3,711
1961	180	1,146	1,133	28,139	27,379	11,760	6,907	38,354	457	1,889	1,365	3,892
1962	216	1,256	1,229	29,228	28,296	12,528	7,399	40,699	492	2,345	1,458	3,942
1963	283	1,417	1,382	31,102	30,165	13,763	8,169	43,552	770	2,853	1,607	4,365
1964	340	1,613	1,576	33,527	32,692	15,430	9,163	46,857	994	3,305	1,792	4,744
1965	408	1,854	1,818	36,479	35,804	17,193	10,278	50,597	1,115	3,740	1,984	5,211
1966	476	2,134	2,103	40,080	39,590	19,368	11,647	54,928	1,369	4,331	2,222	5,650
1967	548	2,457	2,430	44,377	44,041	22,132	13,264	59,729	1,617	4,801	2,503	6,230
1968	616	2,813	2,788	48,992	48,674	24,996	15,142	63,855	1,878	4,126	2,839	7,055
1969	689	3,207	3,185	54,289	53,979	28,259	17,280	67,754	2,138	3,899	3,217	8,158
1970	774	3,650	3,631	60,292	60,078	33,429	21,029	70,858	3,749	3,104	3,903	9,546
1971	851	4,132	4,117	66,951	66,723	39,114	25,097	73,433	4,068	2,575	4,615	10,818

"PROJECTED"

Year												
1972	—0—	3,723	3,713	61,540	61,297	36,752	23,679	70,601	(1,418)	(2,832)	4,185	11,002
1973	—0—	3,450	3,446	57,899	57,677	34,561	22,385	67,374	(1,294)	(3,227)	3,908	11,055
1974	—0—	3,223	3,225	54,808	54,617	32,502	22,178	63,657	(1,207)	(3,717)	3,679	11,151
1975	—0—	3,019	3,026	52,023	51,874	30,558	20,045	59,548	(1,133)	(4,109)	3,472	11,101
1976	—0—	2,833	2,843	49,493	49,381	28,719	18,980	56,707	(1,065)	(2,841)	3,280	9,437
1977	—0—	2,681	2,693	47,207	47,149	26,948	17,945	55,405	(1,035)	(1,302)	3,129	7,660
1978	—0—	2,536	2,550	45,024	45,006	25,241	16,940	54,225	(1,005)	(1,180)	2,985	7,398
1979	—0—	2,400	2,415	42,958	42,962	23,594	15,960	53,166	(980)	(1,059)	2,847	7,150
1980	—0—	2,270	2,284	40,976	40,989	22,004	15,001	52,275	(959)	(891)	2,716	6,870

*Including term conversions.
**Full adjusted reserve basis.

Table C–3.

SELECTED PROFIT PATTERNS—ALL ORDINARY LIFE PLANS COMBINED

| | 000,000 Omitted | | | 000 Omitted | | | | | | | | |
| | | | | Present Value of Future Profits at 12% | | | Periodic Profits Assuming Distribution | | | Periodic Profits— Assuming Retention | | |
Year	Insurance Sold*	Insurance In Force	Premiums	Statutory Reserves	Full Adjusted Reserves	Modified Adjusted Reserves	Statutory Reserves	Full Adjusted Reserves	Modified Adjusted Reserves	Statutory Reserves	Full Adjusted Reserves	Modified Adjusted Reserves
"Actual"—1941	$ 25	$ 25	$ 844	$ 1,000	$ 390	$ 526	$ (778)	$ (14)	$ (244)	$ (790)	$ (14)	$ (247)
1942	35	55	1,837	2,261	962	1,271	(831)	10	(276)	(865)	9	(287)
1943	47	92	3,065	3,853	1,767	2,295	(880)	56	(295)	(941)	57	(315)
1944	56	135	4,450	5,663	2,746	3,528	(795)	159	(232)	(884)	163	(261)
1945	71	188	6,127	7,904	4,001	5,091	(784)	328	(137)	(899)	339	(172)
1946	83	247	8,012	10,535	5,577	7,018	(637)	506	(5)	(777)	530	(43)
1947	92	309	9,970	13,409	7,421	9,233	(415)	646	127	(575)	688	89
1948	90	363	11,607	14,643	8,961	11,138	869	769	294	709	834	261
1949	100	423	13,397	16,635	10,822	13,382	431	854	369	283	948	345
1950	109	487	15,147	19,151	12,970	15,908	339	1,017	564	195	1,145	553
1951	120	555	16,940	22,030	15,347	18,669	453	1,277	837	314	1,449	848
1952	128	625	18,598	26,215	17,930	21,624	(696)	1,510	1,111	(847)	1,738	1,155
1953	134	698	20,249	30,405	20,728	24,811	(112)	1,746	1,367	(285)	2,041	1,455
1954	135	766	21,747	34,654	23,702	28,151	392	1,943	1,640	216	2,316	1,783
1955	128	823	22,876	38,711	26,719	31,459	1,087	2,146	1,993	927	2,609	2,208
1956	116	864	23,591	42,400	29,617	34,559	1,855	2,377	2,396	1,737	2,954	2,704
1957	116	905	24,136	45,060	31,404	36,562	2,378	2,736	2,812	2,331	3,455	3,243
1958	126	950	24,806	47,731	33,139	38,519	2,673	3,045	3,128	2,720	3,936	3,710
1959	140	1,001	25,525	50,379	34,788	40,385	3,032	3,412	3,507	3,199	4,512	4,275
1960	157	1,061	26,417	53,238	36,465	42,314	3,143	3,711	3,766	3,455	5,054	4,753
1961	180	1,133	27,379	56,544	38,354	44,519	3,060	3,892	3,871	3,532	5,498	5,096
1962	216	1,229	28,296	58,721	40,699	47,126	4,637	3,942	3,898	5,307	5,819	5,369
1963	283	1,382	30,165	62,694	43,552	50,510	3,372	4,365	3,946	4,262	6,536	5,679
1964	340	1,576	32,692	68,047	46,857	54,588	2,618	4,744	4,042	3,695	7,251	6,058
1965	408	1,818	35,804	75,107	50,597	59,408	1,623	5,211	4,129	2,868	8,109	6,464
1966	476	2,103	39,590	83,460	54,928	65,068	1,340	5,650	4,316	2,753	9,035	7,035
1967	548	2,430	44,041	92,944	59,729	71,437	1,312	6,230	4,677	2,925	10,234	7,880
1968	616	2,788	48,674	105,218	63,855	77,382	(2,283)	7,055	5,279	(521)	11,846	9,094
1969	689	3,185	53,979	117,200	67,754	83,274	(837)	8,158	6,265	1,046	13,940	10,852
1970	774	3,631	60,078	128,311	70,858	88,640	(165)	9,546	7,325	1,913	16,542	12,862
1971	851	4,117	66,723	140,009	73,433	93,604	152	10,818	8,535	2,406	19,019	15,019
Cumulative	7,389	4,117	766,762	NA	NA	NA	25,553	97,845	79,005	39,409	148,592	117,465
"Projected"—1972	–0–	3,713	61,297	134,629	70,601	89,604	20,959	11,002	14,394			
1973	–0–	3,446	57,677	129,537	67,374	85,319	20,076	11,055	14,209			
1974	–0–	3,225	54,617	124,114	63,657	80,603	19,813	11,151	14,131			
1975	–0–	3,026	51,874	118,258	59,548	75,540	19,606	11,101	13,924			
1976	–0–	2,843	49,381	113,846	56,707	71,881	17,577	9,437	12,022		NOT TABULATED	
1977	–0–	2,693	47,149	111,211	55,405	69,869	15,399	7,660	10,052			
1978	–0–	2,550	45,006	108,488	54,225	68,003	15,183	7,398	9,686			
1979	–0–	2,415	42,962	105,727	53,166	66,275	14,910	7,150	9,343			
1980	–0–	2,284	40,989	102,901	52,275	64,734	14,659	6,870	8,972			

*Including term conversions.

Table C–4.

SELECTED PROFIT PATTERNS—ORDINARY PARTICIPATING WHOLE LIFE

		000,000 Omitted			Present Value of Future Profits at 12%			000 Omitted Periodic Profits—Assuming Distribution			Periodic Profits—Assuming Retention		
		Insur-ance Sold	Insurance In Force	Premiums	Statutory Reserves	Full Adjusted Reserves	Modified Adjusted Reserves	Statutory Reserves	Full Adjusted Reserves	Modified Adjusted Reserves	Statutory Reserves	Full Adjusted Reserves	Modified Adjusted Reserves
"Actual"—	1941	$ 2	$ 2	$ 65	$ 81	$ 31	$ 38	$ (53)	$ 1	$ (14)	$ (54)	$ 1	$ (14)
	1942	3	4	146	181	75	92	(52)	4	(15)	(54)	4	(15)
	1943	4	8	259	317	142	173	(59)	8	(19)	(63)	8	(20)
	1944	5	12	388	465	224	271	(42)	17	(13)	(48)	18	(15)
	1945	6	17	540	637	330	397	(21)	35	(1)	(27)	36	(3)
	1946	8	23	731	860	469	562	(23)	47	2	(31)	49	nil
	1947	8	29	929	1,093	631	752	6	57	11	(2)	62	9
	1948	9	36	1,142	1,170	750	916	98	67	(10)	91	73	(12)
	1949	11	44	1,405	1,345	904	1,126	31	76	(15)	26	85	(17)
	1950	12	53	1,676	1,564	1,076	1,358	20	95	2	16	107	(1)
	1951	13	62	1,962	1,817	1,261	1,609	26	120	24	21	136	21
	1952	14	71	2,223	2,212	1,410	1,831	(210)	143	58	(217)	164	57
	1953	15	81	2,485	2,585	1,578	2,072	(139)	153	73	(153)	180	74
	1954	15	90	2,721	2,949	1,761	2,323	(81)	162	97	(99)	196	101
	1955	13	96	2,876	3,248	1,944	2,556	32	165	134	12	207	142
	1956	11	100	2,986	3,526	2,132	2,782	95	170	162	76	221	176
	1957	11	104	3,064	3,776	2,298	2,979	138	187	192	122	249	214
	1958	13	109	3,168	4,059	2,466	3,181	138	217	219	126	291	250
	1959	15	116	3,332	4,417	2,649	3,409	99	249	235	91	340	279
	1960	17	125	3,523	4,823	2,846	3,660	94	272	251	89	381	309
	1961	20	135	3,757	5,310	3,083	3,960	66	283	252	64	412	325
	1962	24	147	4,009	5,452	3,273	4,178	293	194	213	299	341	300
	1963	28	164	4,343	5,736	3,492	4,441	147	192	189	163	356	291
	1964	33	185	4,780	6,170	3,757	4,770	(4)	175	146	16	357	261
	1965	36	206	5,242	7,158	4,052	5,218	(512)	293	136	(504)	499	265
	1966	42	233	5,811	8,222	4,385	5,736	(521)	303	115	(536)	539	260
	1967	49	264	6,475	9,353	4,732	6,296	(517)	336	121	(559)	610	286
	1968	55	299	7,223	10,524	5,051	6,853	(478)	407	177	(552)	730	368
	1969	61	338	8,064	11,687	5,304	7,365	(403)	508	264	(509)	895	490
	1970	68	382	8,953	12,256	5,082	7,462	(365)	670	349	(507)	1,138	620
	1971	75	429	9,933	12,828	4,706	7,421	(443)	766	436	(621)	1,318	754
Cumula-tive		696	429	104,211	NA	NA	NA	(2,640)	6,372	3,771	(3,324)	10,003	5,755
"Pro-jected"—	1972	–0–	398	9,264	12,025	4,377	6,938	2,213	845	1,298			
	1973	–0–	377	8,786	11,204	3,972	6,390	2,139	879	1,305			
	1974	–0–	359	8,370	10,285	3,482	5,763	2,139	913	1,317			
	1975	–0–	342	7,986	9,298	2,914	5,060	2,098	932	1,318			
	1976	–0–	327	7,627	8,558	2,515	4,546	1,754	707	1,059	NOT TABULATED		
	1977	–0–	312	7,283	8,102	2,319	4,254	1,401	471	792			
	1978	–0–	298	6,953	7,678	2,124	3,968	1,319	447	753			
	1979	–0–	285	6,637	7,286	1,931	3,686	1,241	424	716			
	1980	–0–	272	6,332	6,897	1,750	3,421	1,194	389	669			

adjusted reserves after development costs and overhead have been eliminated. The results reported using full adjusted reserves represent the results of using the rate-testing definition of acquisition costs. The results reported using modified adjusted reserves represent the results of using the accounting definition of acquisition costs.

Table C–4 shows the same information as Table C–3 for the participating whole life business sold by Crazy Quilt. The adjusted reserves treat dividends as a benefit in Table C–4. Dividend scales are updated periodically and generally are set in such a manner as to allocate profits before dividends 90 percent to participating policyholders and 10 percent to stockholders. This objective is, of course, not always attained.

While Crazy Quilt is domiciled in a state which restricts the stockholder charge against profits attributable to participating policies, that problem is not covered in Table C–4. The profits reported on any of the three bases in Table C–4 would require additional adjustment to reflect the stockholder charge limitation.

The statutory deficit arises from, among other things, early dividend scales which proved to be too liberal but which Crazy Quilt, for competitive reasons, was loath to change.

Table C–5 shows the same basic information as the preceding two tables for nonparticipating whole life business issued by Crazy Quilt. It will be observed that the net result of 31 years of selling this business is a statutory deficit of fairly substantial proportions. This is, of course, unusual, and is accounted for by thin margins in the premiums on this competitive product, rapid growth, and erratic reserve practices. From 1941 to 1947 net level methods were used; from 1948 to 1951, modified reserve methods; from 1952 to 1961, net level methods; from 1962 to 1967, modified methods, and from 1968 to 1971, net level methods.

Table C–6 shows selected profit patterns and other information for the 20-payment life business issued by Crazy Quilt. The reader will note a closer relationship between statutory profits and adjusted profits than was true of nonparticipating whole life business; this is due in large measure to the high level of the reserves under any reserve basis and the impact of interest earned on the related invested assets.

Again, in 1968 Crazy Quilt switched from modified to net level reserves, which accounts for the radical drop in statutory earnings in that year.

Table C–7 shows selected profit patterns for 20-year endowment business issued by Crazy Quilt, which stopped issuing such business in 1961. It will be noted that reported profits after 1961 increase under all three methods, due primarily to the high level of reserves on this business and the associated significant impact of excess interest.

Table C–8 shows selected profit patterns for 5-year renewable and convertible term insurance issued by Crazy Quilt.

It will quickly be noted that statutory profits exceed adjusted profits (assuming immediate distribution in both cases) in 13 of the 31 years shown in Table C–8, that the aggregate of such profits through 1971 exceeds the related aggregates of adjusted profits, but that the present value of future statutory profits in 1971 is nevertheless higher than the present value of future adjusted profits. The reason is that the adjusted reserves provide for (1) adverse selection on renewal and (2) adverse selection on conversion. Statutory practices do not require such extra mortality to be reserved for, although companies sometimes voluntarily provide term conversion reserves and, less frequently, term renewal reserves.

(The "out-of-pocket cost" of extra mortality on conversion is recognized in Table C–8 by transferring, at the time of conversion, the present value of the expected net cost of extra mortality to the plan to which the term insurance is converted.)

There is some difference of opinion as to whether term conversion reserves are needed, particularly where a company encourages conversion. In Crazy Quilt's case, experience (which in this case was patterned after that of a large company) indicated that such reserves were needed. The issue assumes greater significance when acquisition costs are deferred, since the cushion afforded by expensing acquisition costs is eliminated. Adjusted benefit reserves in 1971 are five times higher than statutory reserves, and even modified adjusted reserves are almost three times higher than statutory. When renewable and convertible term business is material, adjusted reserves on such business need special attention.

Table C–9 reports selected profit patterns on 25-year convertible decreasing term business issued by Crazy Quilt. In this case, adjusted benefit reserves are about 40 percent higher than statutory reserves in 1971, due in part to the conversion feature and in part to the fact that adjusted benefit reserves on decreasing term business are by their nature sometimes higher than statutory reserves.

Table C–5.

SELECTED PROFIT PATTERNS—ORDINARY NON-PARTICIPATING WHOLE LIFE

| | 000,000 Omitted | | | 000 Omitted | | | | | | | | |
| | | | | Present Value of Future Profits at 12% | | | Periodic Profits— Assuming Distribution | | | Periodic Profits— Assuming Retention | | |
Year	Insurance Sold	Insurance In Force	Premiums	Statutory Reserves	Full Adjusted Reserves	Modified Adjusted Reserves	Statutory Reserves	Full Adjusted Reserves	Modified Adjusted Reserves	Statutory Reserves	Full Adjusted Reserves	Modified Adjusted Reserves
"Actual"—1941	$ 6	$ 6	$ 163	$ 268	$ 109	$ 138	$ (216)	$ 3	$ (51)	$ (219)	$ 3	$ (51)
1942	9	14	376	643	281	351	(268)	10	(64)	(278)	10	(67)
1943	13	24	643	1,127	524	646	(301)	24	(70)	(320)	24	(74)
1944	15	36	949	1,686	816	1,000	(292)	57	(50)	(321)	59	(56)
1945	20	51	1,336	2,409	1,204	1,467	(298)	129	(3)	(336)	134	(10)
1946	23	67	1,761	3,225	1,661	2,013	(269)	172	28	(317)	182	21
1947	25	85	2,212	4,132	2,197	2,645	(226)	213	62	(283)	229	56
1948	29	104	2,682	4,636	2,769	3,335	164	253	71	104	277	66
1949	32	125	3,195	5,409	3,437	4,132	2	300	108	(59)	333	106
1950	35	148	3,740	6,355	4,191	5,026	(36)	363	166	(100)	408	168
1951	38	172	4,323	7,437	5,018	6,005	(18)	454	250	(87)	515	259
1952	41	197	4,921	9,250	6,061	7,193	(644)	511	310	(727)	591	328
1953	44	224	5,585	11,130	7,205	8,514	(462)	621	393	(569)	724	424
1954	44	250	6,219	13,066	8,435	9,924	(273)	692	482	(397)	823	530
1955	43	274	6,799	15,024	9,731	11,389	(54)	760	589	(191)	923	659
1956	39	292	7,251	16,870	11,005	12,806	266	834	729	123	1,038	827
1957	40	312	7,615	18,209	11,656	13,619	487	961	884	347	1,214	1,020
1958	45	335	8,052	19,631	12,372	14,500	557	1,023	947	426	1,335	1,130
1959	50	358	8,497	21,073	13,123	15,411	693	1,106	1,043	576	1,489	1,282
1960	57	386	9,039	22,709	13,972	16,446	658	1,165	1,075	561	1,629	1,380
1961	68	420	9,720	24,645	14,991	17,695	543	1,192	1,053	465	1,740	1,426
1962	86	467	10,583	26,206	16,542	19,520	1,398	1,300	1,020	1,357	1,937	1,462
1963	111	538	11,933	28,741	18,379	21,785	692	1,520	1,037	696	2,257	1,550
1964	134	629	13,656	32,099	20,498	24,479	234	1,729	1,077	259	2,583	1,668
1965	160	740	15,786	36,280	22,964	27,672	(138)	1,940	1,120	(108)	2,934	1,800
1966	188	871	18,301	41,258	25,791	31,372	(402)	2,165	1,202	(383)	3,335	1,991
1967	216	1,021	21,187	46,984	28,972	35,561	(542)	2,436	1,355	(544)	3,832	2,283
1968	236	1,181	23,946	54,457	31,477	39,119	(3,319)	2,741	1,674	(3,425)	4,428	2,783
1969	264	1,359	27,088	61,697	33,909	42,696	(2,496)	3,242	2,114	(2,777)	5,291	3,460
1970	296	1,558	30,623	68,572	36,092	46,151	(2,315)	3,903	2,599	(2,772)	6,412	4,246
1971	326	1,774	34,475	75,968	38,005	49,411	(2,415)	4,583	3,228	(3,051)	7,559	5,189
Cumulative	2,733	1,774	302,656	NA	NA	NA	(9,290)	36,402	24,378	(12,350)	54,248	35,856
"Projected"—1972	–0–	1,652	32,207	75,267	27,411	48,327	9,276	4,870	6,627			
1973	–0–	1,583	30,810	74,526	36,554	47,006	9,234	5,051	6,728			
1974	–0–	1,526	29,649	73,352	35,375	45,369	9,560	5,259	6,877			
1975	–0–	1,474	28,556	71,661	33,921	43,459	9,915	5,385	6,949			
1976	–0–	1,426	27,524	70,525	33,081	42,227	9,199	4,640	6,092	NOT TABULATED		
1977	–0–	1,380	26,535	70,294	33,061	41,888	8,216	3,770	5,108			
1978	–0–	1,335	25,575	69,940	33,083	41,598	8,305	3,728	5,024			
1979	–0–	1,293	24,650	69,460	33,139	41,347	8,384	3,698	4,954			
1980	–0–	1,252	23,756	68,751	33,258	41,158	8,547	3,646	4,867			

Table C–6.

SELECTED PROFIT PATTERNS—ORDINARY NON-PARTICIPATING 20-PAY LIFE

	000,000 Omitted			Present Value of Future Profits at 12%			Periodic Profits— Assuming Distribution			Periodic Profits— Assuming Retention		
Year	Insur- ance Sold	Insurance In Force	Premiums	Statutory Reserves	Full Adjusted Reserves	Modified Adjusted Reserves	Statutory Reserves	Full Adjusted Reserves	Modified Adjusted Reserves	Statutory Reserves	Full Adjusted Reserves	Modified Adjusted Reserves
"Actual"—1941	$ 7	$ 7	$ 233	$ 317	$ 103	$ 143	$ (283)	$ (4)	$ (71)	$ (287)	$ (4)	$ (72)
1942	9	15	483	690	248	337	(290)	(1)	(80)	(302)	(1)	(83)
1943	13	25	799	1,167	456	609	(330)	4	(95)	(352)	4	(101)
1944	15	36	1,158	1,724	718	945	(333)	21	(91)	(366)	21	(100)
1945	20	50	1,621	2,442	1,064	1,387	(397)	41	(99)	(442)	42	(111)
1946	23	66	2,124	3,306	1,536	1,965	(329)	115	(36)	(386)	118	(50)
1947	25	83	2,673	4,288	2,108	2,654	(300)	145	(14)	(368)	153	(30)
1948	16	89	2,871	4,344	2,492	3,087	480	142	103	412	154	88
1949	17	98	3,138	4,623	2,923	3,572	291	163	124	231	181	111
1950	19	107	3,445	5,066	3,414	4,120	187	194	151	131	218	142
1951	20	118	3,783	5,618	3,962	4,731	157	236	192	104	269	188
1952	20	128	4,069	6,556	4,496	5,333	(292)	254	202	(351)	297	205
1953	20	137	4,335	7,411	5,072	5,973	(92)	278	242	(159)	332	253
1954	19	145	4,557	8,251	5,682	6,635	34	302	289	(38)	368	309
1955	17	150	4,711	9,044	6,303	7,292	187	333	350	115	413	382
1956	14	153	4,789	9,776	6,910	7,915	345	375	426	278	474	475
1957	13	155	4,829	10,379	7,406	8,418	468	462	527	411	584	597
1958	13	157	4,876	10,977	7,894	8,907	550	529	601	507	681	699
1959	11	158	4,885	11,506	8,348	9,347	695	601	694	674	789	827
1960	12	160	4,942	12,074	8,809	9,794	718	665	752	725	896	927
1961	14	164	4,966	12,710	9,304	10,283	715	710	783	754	987	1,004
1962	17	171	4,969	13,130	9,790	10,744	1,050	744	842	1,131	1,071	1,112
1963	22	181	5,058	13,761	10,322	11,276	903	800	862	1,032	1,180	1,187
1964	27	195	5,201	14,532	10,905	11,878	847	851	886	1,024	1,291	1,269
1965	32	211	5,386	15,438	11,533	12,551	804	908	913	1,030	1,417	1,363
1966	37	232	5,629	16,464	12,192	13,279	794	988	965	1,076	1,582	1,495
1967	43	255	5,930	17,564	12,851	14,031	835	1,098	1,051	1,185	1,801	1,681
1968	48	281	6,383	19,374	13,566	14,954	102	1,318	1,125	514	2,162	1,881
1969	54	310	6,912	20,927	14,136	15,749	515	1,586	1,385	994	2,610	2,300
1970	61	342	7,520	22,340	14,535	16,387	781	1,904	1,696	1,355	3,153	2,812
1971	67	377	8,185	23,697	14,808	16,915	944	2,125	1,911	1,618	3,601	3,231
Cumula- tive	745	377	130,460	NA	NA	NA	9,756	17,887	16,586	12,250	26,844	23,991
"Pro- jected"—1972	–0–	342	7,243	22,792	14,307	16,219	3,542	2,152	2,575			
1973	–0–	324	6,667	21,992	13,712	15,462	3,340	2,184	2,555			
1974	–0–	309	6,194	21,140	13,024	14,624	3,298	2,205	2,544			
1975	–0–	296	5,780	20,165	12,227	13,690	3,318	2,230	2,541			
1976	–0–	284	5,420	19,481	11,691	13,032	2,933	1,893	2,175	NOT TABULATED		
1977	–0–	272	5,099	19,144	11,491	12,721	2,527	1,514	1,771			
1978	–0–	261	4,791	18,758	11,281	12,401	2,535	1,502	1,744			
1979	–0–	251	4,509	18,325	11,059	12,071	2,536	1,489	1,718			
1980	–0–	241	4,226	17,839	10,817	11,721	2,537	1,482	1,700			

Table C–7.

SELECTED PROFIT PATTERNS—ORDINARY NON-PARTICIPATING 20-YEAR ENDOWMENT

		000,000 Omitted			000 Omitted								
					Present Value of Future Profits at 12%			Periodic Profits—Assuming Distribution			Periodic Profits—Assuming Retention		
	Year	Insur-ance Sold	Insurance In Force	Premiums	Statutory Reserves	Full Adjusted Reserves	Modified Adjusted Reserves	Statutory Reserves	Full Adjusted Reserves	Modified Adjusted Reserves	Statutory Reserves	Full Adjusted Reserves	Modified Adjusted Reserves
"Actual"—	1941	$ 7	$ 7	$ 357	$ 283	$ 123	$ 178	$ (199)	$ (17)	$ (105)	$ (202)	$ (17)	$ (106)
	1942	9	15	769	624	296	418	(194)	(14)	(117)	(202)	(15)	(122)
	1943	11	24	1,249	1,016	527	728	(165)	(2)	(121)	(179)	(3)	(129)
	1944	13	35	1,779	1,448	806	1,095	(121)	23	(104)	(140)	22	(116)
	1945	15	46	2,375	1,932	1,138	1,526	(77)	55	(82)	(100)	55	(98)
	1946	17	59	3,050	2,497	1,549	2,048	(45)	80	(69)	(71)	82	(88)
	1947	18	72	3,721	3,087	2,019	2,630	33	108	(31)	7	114	(51)
	1948	19	85	4,402	3,499	2,344	3,090	21	169	19	(6)	178	(2)
	1949	21	97	5,059	4,039	2,791	3,662	(8)	153	21	(35)	168	(1)
	1950	20	107	5,561	4,626	3,299	4,260	44	163	83	16	184	62
	1951	19	115	5,991	5,229	3,844	4,875	130	211	165	103	239	146
	1952	18	121	6,335	5,863	4,442	5,524	285	323	310	263	361	299
	1953	16	126	6,581	6,475	5,033	6,144	368	369	391	356	422	391
	1954	15	130	6,771	7,096	5,631	6,761	426	415	457	427	484	471
	1955	11	130	6,797	7,605	6,166	7,284	556	464	553	573	551	585
	1956	8	128	6,677	7,973	6,601	7,679	688	528	659	729	639	715
	1957	8	126	6,612	8,329	6,985	8,029	748	634	753	820	775	841
	1958	8	125	6,545	8,601	7,274	8,282	863	756	878	972	937	1,004
	1959	7	124	6,468	8,763	7,444	8,412	989	886	1,010	1,146	1,116	1,186
	1960	6	122	6,375	8,802	7,497	8,417	1,110	997	1,126	1,324	1,286	1,362
	1961	5	118	6,171	8,746	7,459	8,327	1,186	1,062	1,195	1,465	1,417	1,499
	1962	–0–	108	5,686	8,363	7,207	7,970	1,353	1,084	1,281	1,706	1,508	1,658
	1963	–0–	100	5,258	7,954	6,899	7,572	1,335	1,108	1,280	1,769	1,606	1,737
	1964	–0–	92	4,851	7,511	6,551	7,141	1,321	1,111	1,266	1,840	1,688	1,807
	1965	–0–	84	4,448	7,031	6,164	6,677	1,305	1,108	1,248	1,919	1,774	1,883
	1966	–0–	77	4,044	6,488	5,727	6,167	1,310	1,112	1,239	2,035	1,883	1,983
	1967	–0–	69	3,648	5,854	5,216	5,585	1,335	1,132	1,249	2,194	2,033	2,126
	1968	–0–	61	3,205	5,134	4,618	4,922	1,345	1,157	1,260	2,369	2,215	2,299
	1969	–0–	52	2,749	4,357	3,946	4,192	1,316	1,159	1,248	2,535	2,406	2,478
	1970	–0–	44	2,331	3,547	3,225	3,421	1,260	1,128	1,204	2,701	2,593	2,655
	1971	–0–	37	1,938	2,778	2,533	2,684	1,128	1,020	1,084	2,763	2,674	2,727
Cumulative		271	37	137,803	NA	NA	NA	19,646	18,482	19,350	29,097	29,375	29,201
"Projected"—	1972	–0–	30	1,579	2,119	1,936	2,051	937	851	903			
	1973	–0–	24	1,262	1,566	1,434	1,519	763	694	735			
	1974	–0–	18	978	1,111	1,017	1,079	608	557	589			
	1975	–0–	14	756	737	674	717	479	439	464			
	1976	–0–	11	597	467	430	458	339	307	326	NOT TABULATED		
	1977	–0–	8	445	291	273	289	219	197	211			
	1978	–0–	6	308	158	151	159	160	146	156			
	1979	–0–	4	187	65	66	68	106	98	104			
	1980	–0–	2	84	13	16	16	56	55	57			

639

Table C–8.

SELECTED PROFIT PATTERNS—ORDINARY NON-PARTICIPATING 5-YEAR RENEWABLE AND CONVERTIBLE TERM

| | 000,000 Omitted | | | 000 Omitted | | | | | | | | |
| | | | | Present Value of Future Profits at 12% | | | Periodic Profits—Assuming Distribution | | | Periodic Profits—Assuming Retention | | |
Year	Insurance Sold	Insurance In Force	Premiums	Statutory Reserves	Full Adjusted Reserves	Modified Adjusted Reserves	Statutory Reserves	Full Adjusted Reserves	Modified Adjusted Reserves	Statutory Reserves	Full Adjusted Reserves	Modified Adjusted Reserves
"Actual"—1941	$ 3	$ 2	$ 26	$ 40	$ 24	$ 29	$ (26)	$ 3	$ (4)	$ (27)	$ 3	$ (4)
1942	4	6	63	124	61	74	(28)	10	1	(29)	11	1
1943	6	11	115	226	117	140	(24)	23	10	(26)	24	10
1944	8	17	175	340	183	217	(6)	41	26	(9)	43	27
1945	11	24	255	483	264	314	9	68	48	6	71	50
1946	14	32	343	641	358	425	32	93	70	30	99	74
1947	15	40	426	793	455	539	76	121	100	76	130	106
1948	17	49	493	970	587	688	108	136	112	110	150	121
1949	19	58	572	1,179	737	856	118	159	132	124	178	146
1950	24	71	684	1,481	946	1,092	129	200	163	139	225	182
1951	29	86	822	1,843	1,197	1,375	165	250	206	180	284	232
1952	34	105	973	2,203	1,429	1,639	185	273	231	207	318	266
1953	39	127	1,157	2,611	1,710	1,958	239	318	269	269	375	314
1954	42	148	1,341	3,028	2,014	2,303	310	362	313	351	434	371
1955	43	168	1,517	4,430	2,332	2,661	396	411	366	452	500	438
1956	42	184	1,663	3,778	2,641	3,008	494	453	417	569	564	508
1957	37	193	1,712	3,727	2,651	3,048	610	469	457	712	605	572
1958	40	204	1,791	3,668	2,643	3,078	605	484	467	739	650	610
1959	41	213	1,862	3,585	2,615	3,086	628	510	499	799	711	674
1960	40	218	1,912	3,463	2,572	3,074	656	520	519	868	760	730
1961	39	222	1,946	3,322	2,530	3,058	663	514	522	920	794	771
1962	39	224	1,968	3,190	2,556	3,093	691	490	512	994	809	799
1963	47	230	2,020	3,181	2,593	3,146	598	526	537	947	886	864
1964	43	233	2,042	3,130	2,601	3,168	628	544	563	1,026	950	935
1965	52	244	2,072	3,051	2,543	3,122	564	492	507	1,015	948	926
1966	56	258	2,126	3,040	2,527	3,124	521	469	476	1,033	983	952
1967	65	280	2,221	3,138	2,552	3,180	445	453	443	1,030	1,039	988
1968	73	304	2,320	3,210	2,524	3,206	435	446	409	1,106	1,118	1,035
1969	74	328	2,421	3,277	2,502	3,235	453	437	407	1,229	1,214	1,130
1970	83	360	2,590	3,448	2,498	3,297	353	434	387	1,245	1,330	1,218
1971	92	399	2,812	3,637	2,501	3,383	370	441	377	1,359	1,440	1,302
Cumulative	1,171	399	42,440	NA	NA	NA	10,397	10,150	9,542	17,444	17,646	16,348
"Projected"—1972	–0–	341	2,493	2,841	2,330	3,132	1,164	446	621			
1973	–0–	300	2,266	2,158	2,147	2,881	968	437	591			
1974	–0–	265	2,072	1,572	1,949	2,623	798	431	570			
1975	–0–	233	1,912	1,110	1,751	2,382	615	408	526			
1976	–0–	202	1,772	765	1,581	2,185	451	359	456	NOT TABULATED		
1977	–0–	182	1,649	393	1,439	1,994	438	313	428			
1978	–0–	162	1,530	50	1,314	1,827	369	282	384			
1979	–0–	143	1,419	(246)	1,205	1,682	285	252	344			
1980	–0–	125	1,322	(440)	1,121	1,575	155	216	292			

Table C–9.

SELECTED PROFIT PATTERNS—ORDINARY NON-PARTICIPATING 25-YEAR DECREASING CONVERTIBLE TERM

	000,000 Omitted			Present Value of Future Profits at 12%			Periodic Profits—Assuming Distribution			Periodic Profits Assuming Retention		
Year	Insurance Sold	Insurance In Force	Premiums	Statutory Reserves	Full Adjusted Reserves	Modified Adjusted Reserves	Statutory Reserves	Full Adjusted Reserves	Modified Adjusted Reserves	Statutory Reserves	Full Adjusted Reserves	Modified Adjusted Reserves
"Actual"—1957*	$ 5	$ 5	$ 32	$ 75	$ 32	$ 40	$ (49)	$ 5	$ (7)	$ (50)	$ 5	$ (7)
1958	7	11	71	165	71	91	(49)	13	(2)	(51)	13	(3)
1959	14	22	144	338	145	186	(87)	30	1	(93)	31	1
1960	22	39	254	596	256	332	(111)	58	15	(122)	61	15
1961	32	62	410	965	421	544	(137)	94	34	(154)	101	35
1962	48	98	645	1,481	701	895	(220)	85	(9)	(246)	96	(7)
1963	70	149	986	2,257	1,087	1,386	(323)	163	28	(362)	180	30
1964	97	219	1,451	3,334	1,597	2,043	(415)	267	82	(474)	295	87
1965	120	301	2,001	4,635	2,204	2,829	(409)	389	173	(490)	435	184
1966	145	396	2,639	6,202	2,956	3,794	(377)	522	276	(484)	592	299
1967	167	498	3,332	7,946	3,807	4,883	(263)	669	408	(396)	776	450
1968	194	610	4,105	9,956	4,819	6,162	(146)	853	574	(305)	1,012	647
1969	223	735	4,971	12,213	5,957	7,597	(17)	1,057	758	(197)	1,288	876
1970	250	869	5,948	14,669	7,294	9,254	352	1,285	971	160	1,615	1,155
1971	280	1,015	7,030	17,270	8,669	10,980	637	1,624	1,290	458	2,068	1,556
Cumulative	1,674	1,015	34,019	NA	NA	NA	(1,614)	7,114	4,592	(2,806)	8,568	5,318
"Projected"—1972	–0–	867	6,244	15,718	8,058	10,180	3,425	1,561	2,001			
1973	–0–	759	5,681	14,237	7,426	9,386	3,182	1,511	1,905			
1974	–0–	669	5,208	12,857	6,770	8,584	2,918	1,462	1,821			
1975	–0–	591	4,791	11,594	6,137	7,817	2,651	1,366	1,699			
1976	–0–	520	4,406	10,430	5,564	7,124	2,414	1,237	1,541	NOT TABULATED		
1977	–0–	467	4,162	9,394	5,005	6,463	2,162	1,159	1,432			
1978	–0–	418	3,933	8,359	4,487	5,845	2,042	1,057	1,317			
1979	–0–	372	3,711	7,357	4,017	5,274	1,895	954	1,202			
1980	–0–	328	3,489	6,451	3,599	4,755	1,691	850	1,089			

*First sold by Crazy Quilt in 1957.

It will be noted that statutory losses are generated in all years except 1970 and 1971, due to the great volume of sales. In 1970 Crazy Quilt switched from net level to modified valuation methods, and renewal profits on the older business finally began to emerge at the same time.

As in the case of 5-year renewable and convertible term business, the present value of the cost of net extra mortality on conversion is transferred to the plan to which the term insurance is converted at the time of conversion.

Table C–10 shows selected profit patterns for the whole life policies to which 5-year term and 25-year decreasing term policies are converted. Table C–10 reflects the receipt of conversion considerations from the term plans. Such considerations are established in such a manner as to produce an approximately normal profit on the converted plans, that is, the transfer represents the difference between the present value of expected future profits on standard policies and the present value of expected future profits on converted policies, after giving due regard to the cost of extra mortality and the expense savings associated with a conversion.

Table C–11 reports selected profit patterns for individual single-premium immediate non-refund annuities issued by Crazy Quilt.

It will be noted that the single-premium business is projected to develop reported losses on an adjusted

Table C–10.

SELECTED PROFIT PATTERNS—ORDINARY WHOLE LIFE PLANS RESULTING FROM TERM CONVERSION

| | 000,000 Omitted | | | 000 Omitted | | | | | | | | |
| | Term Insurance Converted | Insurance In Force | Premiums | Present Value of Future Profits at 12% | | | Periodic Profits— Assuming Distribution | | | Periodic Profits— Assuming Retention | | |
Year				Statutory Reserves	Full Adjusted Reserves	Modified Adjusted Reserves	Statutory Reserves	Full Adjusted Reserves	Modified Adjusted Reserves	Statutory Reserves	Full Adjusted Reserves	Modified Adjusted Reserves
1946	$ .1	$ .1	$ 4	$ 6	$ 4	$ 5	$ (3)	$ Nil	$ (1)	$ (3)	$ Nil	$ (1)
1947	.2	.3	9	17	11	13	(4)	1	(1)	(4)	1	(1)
1948	.3	.5	17	26	19	22	(3)	2	(1)	(3)	2	(1)
1949	.4	.8	28	40	29	34	(4)	3	Nil	(5)	3	Nil
1950	.5	1.3	41	59	44	51	(6)	4	Nil	(6)	4	Nil
1951	.6	1.8	59	86	65	74	(7)	5	Nil	(8)	5	Nil
1952	.7	2.4	78	131	91	105	(20)	6	Nil	(22)	7	Nil
1953	1.0	3.3	106	193	131	150	(26)	8	(1)	(28)	9	(1)
1954	1.2	4.3	137	264	179	204	(24)	10	1	(27)	11	1
1955	1.5	5.5	176	359	244	277	(29)	13	1	(33)	15	1
1956	1.8	7.0	225	477	326	369	(33)	17	3	(38)	19	3
1957	2.1	8.8	274	565	375	430	(25)	20	5	(32)	23	5
1958	1.5	9.8	303	629	418	481	9	24	18	1	28	18
1959	1.6	10.9	336	697	463	534	15	30	23	7	36	25
1960	1.8	12.2	372	770	512	591	18	34	27	10	42	30
1961	1.9	13.4	408	847	565	653	25	38	32	17	47	36
1962	1.8	14.5	437	898	630	725	71	44	40	65	56	45
1963	5.3	19.2	568	1,063	779	905	21	55	13	17	70	21
1964	6.0	24.3	711	1,271	947	1,109	8	69	22	4	87	31
1965	6.5	30.0	869	1,513	1,137	1,340	9	79	31	5	103	42
1966	7.1	36.0	1,041	1,786	1,349	1,596	16	92	43	12	121	56
1967	8.4	43.2	1,247	2,105	1,599	1,900	19	107	49	16	144	67
1968	10.6	52.4	1,492	2,563	1,801	2,167	(220)	133	60	(230)	180	82
1969	12.3	63.1	1,774	3,041	1,999	2,441	(206)	170	90	(228)	232	118
1970	14.8	75.9	2,111	3,481	2,132	2,668	(231)	222	120	(269)	303	159
1971	11.6	84.8	2,350	3,831	2,210	2,810	(69)	259	210	(119)	360	261
Cumulative	101.6	84.8	15,173	NA	NA	NA	(699)	1,445	784	(901)	1,908	997
"Projected"—1972	–0–	81.9	2,268	3,866	2,183	2,756	401	277	369			
1973	–0–	79.8	2,204	3,854	2,129	2,675	449	299	389			
1974	–0–	77.8	2,147	3,797	2,040	2,560	491	324	412			
1975	–0–	75.9	2,092	3,693	1,923	2,414	530	342	427			
1976	–0–	74.0	2,035	3,620	1,844	2,309	488	293	374		NOT TABULATED	
1977	–0–	72.1	1,976	3,592	1,817	2,259	435	235	309			
1978	–0–	70.0	1,915	3,544	1,785	2,205	453	236	307			
1979	–0–	67.8	1,850	3,480	1,750	2,147	463	236	305			
1980	–0–	65.4	1,780	3,389	1,715	2,089	480	231	298			

basis in 1977. The reason is that new money rates were used to price the annuities and develop adjusted reserves for them, but that portfolio rates were allocated to the line of business. (This was done intentionally to illustrate the problem of dealing with an emerging deficiency, among other things). In practice, where single-premiums are invested immediately in assets whose maturities are reasonably consistent with the maturities of the liabilities, a new money rate (graded to some extent to recognize the risk that the maturities may not precisely match, in which case capital losses might be incurred) can

Table C–11.

SELECTED PROFIT PATTERNS—INDIVIDUAL SINGLE-PREMIUM ANNUITIES

000 Omitted

Year	$100 Units of Monthly Income Sold	In Force	Premiums	Present Value of Future Profits at 12% Statutory Reserves	Full Adjusted Reserves	Modified Adjusted Reserves	Periodic Profits—Assuming Distribution Statutory Reserves	Full Adjusted Reserves	Modified Adjusted Reserves	Periodic Profits—Assuming Retention Statutory Reserves	Full Adjusted Reserves	Modified Adjusted Reserves
"Actual"—1952*	$ 1,780	$ 1,765	$ 2,831	$ 145	$ 83		$ 45	$ 167		$ 46	$ 169	
1953	1,865	3,581	2,967	325	197		53	171		55	180	
1954	1,880	5,371	2,991	534	341		64	176		69	191	
1955	1,780	7,016	2,831	757	502		80	176		87	198	
1956	1,600	8,434	2,545	977	665		102	179		113	209	
1957	1,596	9,799	2,439	1,107	761		138	185		155	224	
1958	1,752	11,273	2,677	1,261	867	SAME AS FULL ADJUSTED RESERVES	163	223	SAME AS FULL ADJUSTED RESERVES	186	273	SAME AS FULL ADJUSTED RESERVES
1959	1,932	12,878	2,952	1,442	986		191	263		224	328	
1960	2,172	14,666	3,319	1,658	1,127		224	307		269	389	
1961	2,496	16,713	3,814	1,921	1,302		262	358		320	460	
1962	3,000	19,183	4,263	2,152	1,387		181	367		253	492	
1963	3,900	22,455	5,542	2,495	1,540		188	432		272	582	
1964	4,680	26,390	6,650	2,964	1,768		201	500		299	680	
1965	5,625	31,134	7,993	3,595	2,092		228	594		342	810	
1966	6,570	36,660	9,336	4,388	2,516		290	712		426	977	
1967	7,575	43,002	10,764	5,321	3,023		410	877		577	1,207	
1968	8,478	50,028	11,223	6,366	3,009		(82)	1,086		110	1,504	
1969	9,495	57,819	12,569	7,384	2,911		128	1,277		344	1,810	
1970	10,640	66,469	13,708	8,275	2,318		66	1,617		314	2,300	
1971	11,704	75,860	15,058	9,010	1,541		250	1,736		529	2,576	
Cumulative	90,520	75,860	126,472	NA	NA		3,182	11,403		4,990	15,559	
"Projected"—1972	–0–	73,276	–0–	8,254	1,039		1,736	649				
1973	–0–	70,485	–0–	7,451	564		1,694	567		NOT TABULATED		
1974	–0–	67,485	–0–	6,560	90		1,687	511				
1975	–0–	64,294	–0–	5,582	(384)		1,667	458				
1976	–0–	60,955	–0–	4,836	(612)		1,338	172				
1977	–0–	57,523	–0–	4,386	(577)		974	(103)				
1978	–0–	54,029	–0–	3,956	(538)		904	(102)				
1979	–0–	50,489	–0–	3,547	(497)		835	(100)				
1980	–0–	46,923	–0–	3,158	(455)		769	(100)				

*First sold by Crazy Quilt in 1952.

logically be used in computing adjusted reserves, provided the assets are segregated for accounting purposes and no portion of the related investment income is credited to other lines of business. Where any one of these circumstances is lacking, a portfolio rate should be used in computing the reserves.

So the apparent emerging losses shown in Table C–11 are not quite what they seem.

Mortality assumptions used to compute the annuity natural reserves include a fairly healthy projection of improved mortality.

Modified adjusted reserves are the same as full adjusted reserves in the case of individual annuities because there are no deferred acquisition costs.

Table C–12 shows selected profit patterns for weekly-premium industrial business issued by Crazy Quilt. Adjusted reserves were computed in such a manner as to recognize the special characteristics of debit insurance. For example, first-year lapses are as high as 60 percent in the case of the model. One result is that adjusted benefit reserves are very close to statutory net level reserves at all durations. (In

Table C–12.

SELECTED PROFIT PATTERNS—INDUSTRIAL 20-PAY LIFE

	000,000 Omitted			Present Value of Future Profits at 12%			Periodic Profits—Assuming Distribution			Periodic Profits—Assuming Retention		
Year	Insurance Sold	Insurance In Force	Premiums	Statutory Reserves	Full Adjusted Reserves	Modified Adjusted Reserves	Statutory Reserves	Full Adjusted Reserves	Modified Adjusted Reserves	Statutory Reserves	Full Adjusted Reserves	Modified Adjusted Reserves
"Actual"—1941	$ 8	$ 5	$ 107	$ 142	$ 31	$ 47	$ (167)	$ (21)	$ (46)	$ (169)	$ (21)	$ (46)
1942	10	9	273	348	96	133	(220)	(45)	(76)	(228)	(47)	(78)
1943	13	14	452	582	186	246	(232)	(57)	(90)	(247)	(60)	(95)
1944	15	19	637	840	296	380	(233)	(61)	(95)	(256)	(66)	(104)
1945	17	24	834	1,145	445	557	(191)	(17)	(54)	(221)	(23)	(64)
1946	18	29	1,025	1,452	609	747	(156)	(7)	(41)	(192)	(14)	(53)
1947	18	34	1,202	1,753	783	945	(111)	8	(22)	(152)	1	(36)
1948	19	38	1,356	2,007	1,029	1,212	18	30	3	(26)	23	(12)
1949	19	42	1,502	2,250	1,240	1,448	63	97	68	18	92	54
1950	19	46	1,644	2,528	1,448	1,682	63	131	102	17	129	90
1951	20	50	1,782	2,819	1,664	1,925	86	152	127	41	155	118
1952	20	53	1,917	3,117	1,888	2,174	118	174	153	73	183	148
1953	20	57	2,046	3,374	1,997	2,313	(51)	135	100	(97)	149	99
1954	20	60	2,167	3,722	2,122	2,484	(103)	133	88	(154)	152	90
1955	20	63	2,276	4,041	2,264	2,667	(29)	132	98	(85)	157	103
1956	19	65	2,369	4,338	2,413	2,853	35	140	117	(24)	172	127
1957	19	67	2,459	4,647	2,587	3,060	123	198	182	62	239	198
1958	20	70	2,554	4,959	2,769	3,273	157	213	202	97	265	227
1959	20	73	2,656	5,271	2,956	3,491	193	230	224	134	295	260
1960	21	76	2,765	5,591	3,151	3,716	220	248	245	165	329	294
1961	22	79	2,869	5,940	3,369	3,963	271	296	295	223	395	359
1962	24	83	2,968	6,317	3,603	4,229	284	314	312	245	432	394
1963	27	88	3,093	6,754	3,860	4,525	269	336	328	240	476	429
1964	28	93	3,230	7,238	4,135	4,845	273	358	347	254	522	469
1965	30	99	3,365	7,803	4,487	5,245	258	359	347	251	550	493
1966	32	104	3,501	8,386	4,793	5,600	303	447	439	309	673	615
1967	33	110	3,641	8,956	5,054	5,911	380	529	525	403	800	742
1968	34	115	3,782	9,496	5,272	6,178	472	600	602	520	930	872
1969	35	121	3,923	9,978	5,442	6,393	583	673	682	667	1,078	1,021
1970	36	126	4,159	10,525	5,651	6,673	562	768	736	690	1,264	1,157
1971	36	131	4,402	11,061	5,804	6,907	630	847	813	805	1,433	1,317
Cumulative	692	131	70,956	NA	NA	NA	3,868	7,340	6,711	3,363	10,663	9,188
"Projected"—1972	–0–	113	4,024	10,620	5,570	6,615	1,671	879	1,060			
1973	–0–	103	3,509	9,869	5,327	6,261	1,913	861	1,084			
1974	–0–	97	3,137	9,187	5,072	5,908	1,763	845	1,044			
1975	–0–	91	2,848	8,510	4,795	5,541	1,682	836	1,016			
1976	–0–	86	2,598	7,950	4,595	5,261	1,494	733	893	NOT TABULATED		
1977	–0–	81	2,376	7,525	4,490	5,085	1,303	621	763			
1978	–0–	78	2,177	7,127	4,385	4,914	1,230	608	738			
1979	–0–	74	1,996	6,742	4,279	4,746	1,172	597	716			
1980	–0–	71	1,825	6,367	4,170	4,577	1,118	588	698			

Table C–13.

SELECTED PROFIT PATTERNS—INDIVIDUAL GUARANTEED RENEWABLE DISABILITY INCOME

000 Omitted

Year	$100 Units of Monthly Income Sold	In Force	Premiums	Present Value of Future Profits at 12% Statutory Reserves	Full Adjusted Reserves	Modified Adjusted Reserves	Periodic Profits—Assuming Distribution Statutory Reserves	Full Adjusted Reserves	Modified Adjusted Reserves	Periodic Profits—Assuming Retention Statutory Reserves	Full Adjusted Reserves	Modified Adjusted Reserves
"Actual"—1963*	$16,000	$16,000	$790	$1,330	$737	$863	$(724)	$117	$(50)	$(741)	$120	$(51)
1964	22,000	32,360	1,603	2,919	1,676	1,952	(615)	312	119	(663)	325	119
1965	28,000	50,767	2,521	4,848	2,808	3,262	(550)	538	319	(628)	571	329
1966	34,000	71,325	3,548	7,107	4,119	4,779	(433)	798	558	(540)	866	591
1967	46,000	99,943	4,976	10,177	5,864	6,803	(534)	1,133	816	(676)	1,256	886
1968	52,000	128,398	6,401	13,447	7,727	8,957	(174)	1,508	1,196	(350)	1,714	1,327
1969	58,000	157,981	7,884	16,961	9,713	11,246	161	1,890	1,584	(35)	2,215	1,809
1970	64,000	188,844	8,726	18,922	10,494	12,470	693	2,125	1,623	498	2,609	1,970
1971	64,000	218,166	9,702	21,059	11,191	13,585	735	2,294	1,861	566	2,950	2,340
Cumulative	384,000	218,166	46,151	NA	NA	NA	(1,441)	10,715	8,026	(2,569)	12,626	9,320
"Projected"—1972	–0–	181,197	8,193	19,652	10,268	12,407	3,718	2,141	2,654			
1973	–0–	161,930	7,365	18,704	9,472	11,411	3,124	1,917	2,348			
1974	–0–	148,030	6,746	17,820	8,727	10,494	2,956	1,778	2,160			
1975	–0–	136,199	6,210	16,951	8,036	9,643	2,841	1,643	1,994			
1976	–0–	125,477	5,722	16,116	7,412	8,878	2,712	1,501	1,817	NOT TABULATED		
1977	–0–	115,601	5,273	15,314	6,850	8,193	2,585	1,371	1,654			
1978	–0–	106,504	4,859	14,445	6,328	7,556	2,558	1,270	1,531			
1979	–0–	98,124	4,477	13,506	5,838	6,959	2,525	1,180	1,421			
1980	–0–	90,405	4,126	15,504	5,361	6,381	2,479	1,112	1,335			

*First sold by Crazy Quilt in 1963.

1971, for example, adjusted benefit reserves were $21,278,000; statutory reserves—all net level—were $21,820,000.)

One interesting characteristic of industrial insurance is that the value of the extended term insurance option—the usual automatic nonforfeiture option—is frequently much less than the cash value, due apparently to the fact that many policyholders, and hence their beneficiaries, are not aware that they have extended insurance. The related "savings" to the company are reflected in Table C–12.

Table C–13 reports selected profit patterns for the guaranteed renewable disability income business issued by Crazy Quilt. Statutory reserves are one-year preliminary term reserves.

In this case adjusted reserves (as well as statutory reserves) have been computed on the basis of earned premiums, that is unearned premium reserves are held in all cases. In theory there would seem to be no valid reason for not computing adjusted reserves on the basis of premiums received for this type of business. Alternative adjusted reserve calculations were made for the model in which the unearned premium reserve is eliminated; the practical effect is to release the "profit loading" contained in the increase in the gross unearned premium reserve. (The alternative calculations are not shown in Table C–13.)

Supplemental Benefits

Models for supplemental benefits—waiver of premium (active and disabled lines), accidental death, supplementary contracts not involving life contingencies, and supplementary contracts involving life contingencies—were developed from data provided by a large company. It was not deemed necessary to develop refined models for supplemental benefits because of their relative insignificance.

Such benefits as payor benefit and guaranteed insurability were ignored in the model.

For industrial business, supplemental benefits were provided for in the form of a "coupon".

Variable Annuities

The model for individual variable annuities was based on the separate account of a large writer of such business.

Commercial Individual Health Insurance

The model for commercial (i.e., cancellable) forms of individual health insurance was based on data provided by a large company.

Group Insurance and Annuities

Models for group life and health insurance (excluding credit insurance in both cases) and group annuities were based on data provided by a large writer of group insurance. Retention cases were traced through their life cycle; results of pooled group cases represent the contributing company's results on such business for the period studied.

Credit Insurance

Models for credit insurance were developed by staff members of Ernst & Ernst with advice and assistance from Mitchell & Kadoyama, Inc. Computer programs were also furnished by Mitchell & Kadoyama.

The credit models were based on data on California credit insurance rates and regulations. Loss ratios, commission rates, experience rating refund provisions, and administrative expense rates were based on the experiences of several credit insurers. Reserves were calculated on several bases: statutory (using an approximation of 130 percent of the 1958 CSO Table with interest at 3 1/2 percent in the case of life insurance and Rule-of-78 unearned premiums in the case of health insurance), Rule-of-78, modified Rule-of-78 (in this case, the mean of Rule-of-78 and full pro rata), and full adjusted reserves, i.e., reserves calculated as if the business were ordinary business.

A 24-month average duration was used for all contracts. Two basic types of business were modeled: auto-dealer/personal property broker type business and bank/finance company type business.

Appendix D

Mortality Fluctuation Reserves

Position Paper IN FAVOR of mortality fluctuation reserves prepared by Occidental Life Insurance Company of California for the Financial Accounting Standards Board in connection with the subject of "Accounting for Future Losses".

We are the fourth largest stock life insurance company in the United States. In anticipation of the issuance of an audit guide for life insurance companies, we changed our accounting methods to what we considered to be generally accepted accounting principles for the year ended December 31, 1970. We believe the methods we chose at that time conform to the Audit Guide for Stock Life Insurance Companies issued by the American Institute of Certified Public Accountants in December, 1972.

While we were not thinking precisely in terms of "provisions for adverse deviations" as referred to in the Guide, we did, and do, believe that the assumptions and methods used in adjusting statutory statements to GAAP should contain enough conservatism to be in keeping with the long-term nature of the contracts. Consequently, we adopted amortization periods of twenty (for term policies) and thirty (for permanent policies) years for acquisition costs instead of the premium paying period to provide for adverse variances in withdrawal assumptions, graded interest rates to non-inflationary rates over the same periods and set up a mortality fluctuation reserve. The latter is the subject of this position paper.

We first considered the use of simply a more conservative mortality table (such as the 1958 CSO generally used for current issues under statutory accounting). Assuming that the mortality actually assumed was realistic, this would have allowed some portion of our profits to flow into earnings as we were released from the risk involved. We did not adopt this approach for two basic reasons: (1) it would operate to release a predetermined amount of income in a given year without regard to whether or not there was adverse experience in that year, which would seem to be not only arbitrary but in violation of the matching concept and (2) it would ignore completely the fact that both adverse variances and favorable variances are usually temporary for a large company in a short period of time—a month, a quarter, or a year.

In the case of the latter (temporary favorable variations) we would be in the position of overstating earnings in the particular period with a subsequent understatement in subsequent (or previous) periods. To explain (or dismiss) these reversible fluctuations in earnings as due to "favorable" or "unfavorable" mortality in a particular short period of time does not seem to make good accounting sense. These fluctuations come from various causes, some natural such as disease epidemics, some company related such as retention limits and some completely random because of the limited number of lives compared to the number assumed in any recognized mortality table.

From our own experience, we have found that the shorter the period, the more violent these fluctuations tend to be. For example (and a typical example), using 100% as the level of "expected" mortality, our actual experience for 1973 and 1972 was as follows:

	1973	1972
January	115.3%	96.3%
February	122.8	95.2
March	103.2	108.7
1st quarter	108.3	100.2
April	76.7	111.7
May	99.2	110.7
June	94.8	101.7
1st half	99.2	104.0
July	130.0	85.2
August	94.2	111.0
September	113.8	101.5
1st nine months	103.8	102.5
October	93.3	100.7
November	124.2	84.5
December	73.8	83.8
Year	101.7	99.2

Our overall mortality statistics have indicated that the mortality table used in our present rate book, and our two preceding rate books is still valid—that is, over the extended future period, lasting generations, that currently issued policies will be in force, the actual mortality on these issues will be very close to that expected. Therefore, most short-term fluctuations and *all* material short-term fluctuations are expected to reverse over the long run.

With this in mind, we concluded that our "provision for adverse deviation"—our mortality fluctuation reserve—should consist of two elements. The first of these, which we call the "theoretical" part, is based upon the size and the structure of our "in force." This portion does follow the "release from risk" pattern in that amounts are added and released as business is put on and taken off the books. Operation of this portion of the formula resulted in about an $800,000 charge to earnings in 1973 based upon the increase in our amount at risk.

The second portion of the formula is called an "experience" adjustment and is made only in a period when a material deviation—favorable or unfavorable—occurs. In this connection, we have established a "band" of 5% in either direction of 100%—i.e., expected mortality. This band would not necessarily be the same for all companies, but it represents one "standard deviation" from the norm. Based on the statistics above, this portion of the formula produced no adjustment in 1972 and 1973 (and is never expected to result in a "material" adjustment).

Even though our statistics indicate that substantially all fluctuations will reverse over the lifetime of a block of business, we believe such a band is necessary for

the following reasons, among others: (1) it would be unrealistic from an accounting point of view to charge earnings with a "standard" amount (expected mortality) in any given period, let alone every period and (2) assuming that in the long run our experience is actually worse than expected, the band allows this experience to be reflected in the periods in which it occurs.

The "theoretical" portion of the reserve is based upon a branch of Ruin theory and uses an approximate formula developed in Scandinavia (described in some detail in a paper by T. Pentikainen). Essentially, it is the square root of the product of one year's expected claims on the current in force times the maximum retention on any one life times 3.61. Both it and the experience adjustment (if any) follow the "lock-in" concepts of both good accounting and the Audit Guide and are not subject to any "management manipulation."

While we do not contend that this is the only method to provide for "adverse deviation" in mortality as required by the Guide, we certainly feel it is better than an artificial mortality table (or any real table that has been discarded by the major portion of the industry as a basis for rate setting) and infinitely better than any simplistic approach, such as a percentage of the basic table.

/s/ David R. Carpenter
Vice President and Chief Actuary

/s/ A. R. Colles
Vice President and Chief
Accounting Officer

* * *

Memorandum OPPOSED to mortality fluctuation reserves prepared by The Lincoln National Life Insurance Company for the Financial Accounting Standards Board in connection with the subject of "Accounting for Future losses".

The Lincoln National questions the desirability of life insurance companies accruing provision for future losses through use of mortality fluctuation reserves. This memorandum is to discuss the nature of mortality fluctuation reserves and to explain the reasons for our position.

Life insurance claim reserves and policy reserves are based on expected present values. The amount established as reserves is equal to the present value of amounts which would be paid if actual future experience equaled that assumed in the actuarial assumptions upon which the reserves are based. It is possible, however, that actual losses over any given future time will be substantially greater or substantially less than this expected value. In fact, statistical theory can measure the possible degree of fluctuation, and that degree will tend to increase the longer the time period over which such fluctuations are measured. A few companies establish mortality fluctuation reserves against which unfavorable fluctuations are charged. The reserve may be built up out of uniform charges each year, or may be built up out of favorable mortality fluctuations, or both. Such reserves are the life insurance company's counterpart of the reserves for future self-insured losses which are discussed in the FASB memorandum. Life insurance policies written but not reinsured with other companies are, in fact, self-insured risks as far as the life insurer is concerned.

The avowed purpose of mortality fluctuation reserves is to avoid substantial impact on current earnings from a year of unfavorable mortality. Although actuarial risk theory may indicate the degree to which mortality fluctuations might be expected and may be useful as a guide for structuring a mortality fluctuation reserve, that theory falls far short of suggesting appropriate standards for developing such a reserve. In consequence, the standards used to establish and maintain such reserves must necessarily be arbitrary. In fact, theory indicates that that actual mortality will never approximate expected mortality (except coincidentally) over any time period and that the longer the time period, the greater the divergence in amount between actual and expected mortality. Hence, it is necessary to develop an arbitrary means of eventually grading the mortality charges to income to the actual mortality cost for the company. The result of such grading will necessarily result in the same claim experience resulting in different reported claims depending on the company's existing practice with regard to its fluctuation reserve.

It is true that the law of large numbers implies that the ratio of actual to expected mortality will approach unity as the amount of experience mea-

sured increases. However, the amount of difference between actual and expected mortality will tend to increase.

The Lincoln National believes that establishing fluctuation reserves of this type can lead to poor accounting practices. Because there is no theoretical standard which can be applied to such reserves and because of the necessity for eventually grading the total recognized claims to the amount which was actually incurred, the formulas for establishing fluctuation reserves must necessaily be arbitrary and therefore subject to a considerable amount of management control. We believe that the best accounting practice is to limit, as much as is practical, those situations where management has significant control of earnings.

A serious practical problem resulting under a system of charging mortality fluctuations against a reserve is that is is impossible to determine to what extent a fluctuation in mortality is a statistical fluctuation and to what extent it may be representative of a change in the basic mortality to which the insurance risks are exposed. Such a change may be the result of mortality changes in general or may be the result of change in the company's procedures for marketing and underwriting mortality risks. We are concerned that accounting procedures which fail to recognize unfavorable mortality when it occurs can result in delaying recognition of the underlying factors which may be causing the change in mortality and which may influence the long term profitability of the company.

Mortality fluctuation reserves are not now in common use in the life insurance industry. We believe that it would be unfortunate if accounting rules were changed to make such reserves more common.

Although life insurance companies are exposed to risks of catastrophic losses as from the loss of several insured policyholders in a single accident, the occurrence of such a loss of significant financial impact on a life insurance company is very rare. We know of no life insurance company which has established reserves specifically against this hazard.

Appendix E   Actuaries' Responsibilities

❧ "ACTUARIAL PRINCIPLES AND PRAC-
TICES IN CONNECTION WITH FINAN-
CIAL REPORTING OF LIFE INSURANCE
COMPANIES IN THE UNITED STATES"—
Interpretive Opinion S-6 to the guides to Pro-
fessional Conduct of the Society of Actuaries
(substantially similar to Opinion A–6 of The
American Academy of Actuaries)

Introduction

This opinion is intended to interpret and amplify
the application of sections 1, 2, 3 and 4 of the Society's
Guides to Professional Conduct, and their relation to
the financial reporting of life insurance companies,
including particularly their relation to the audit guide
entitled "Audits of Stock Life Insurance Companies"
published by the American Institute of Certified Public
Accountants, to any actuary who acts for a life insurance company in the preparation of a financial
statement or report, who contributes elements for inclusion in any such financial statement or report, or
who audits or reviews elements of any such financial
statement or report, when such statement or report
is to be presented as having been prepared in accordance with "Generally Accepted Accounting
Principles" as that term is understood in the United
States, and is intended for stockholders, policyowners,
taxing authorities, regulatory authorities, or the general
public, and is designed to show operating results or
solvency or other aspects of financial condition.

The Committee recognizes that it would be inappropriate to prescribe inflexible guides for the performance of the actuary's work in connection with the
financial reporting of life insurance companies. The
Committee also recognizes that the selection of assumptions and methods involves professional judgment
based on the circumstances applicable to a particular situation, including the purpose or purposes
which the actuary's work is intended to serve. The
promulgation of uniform procedures or practices which
fail to take into account such circumstances and variables would, in the opinion of the Committee, be
unprofessional.

On the other hand, the Committee believes that
there would be merit in adopting a statement of principles relating to the appropriate application of actuarial science to the financial reporting of life
insurance companies and to adequate disclosure of pertinent and material facts bearing on his work. It
is believed that the making and the observing of such
a statement of the basic responsibilities of the actuary
will tend to minimize the possibility of misunderstanding or misinterpretation by those relying on his
work and the likelihood of need for disciplinary
action under Article VII of the Society's Constitution.

Clarifying Statement

A requirement common to all actuarial procedures
is that assumptions and methods be selected and applied with integrity, informed judgment and perspective in relation to the purpose for which the results
are intended.

Assumptions and methods may appropriately be
different in calculations related to the same period
or moment in time but intended for different purposes;
for example, the statutory valuation of insurance
reserves for use in financial reports to state regula-

tory authorities or the valuation of insurance reserves for use in federal income tax returns may require different assumptions and methods from those used for reserve valuations and related calculations in connection with financial statements which are prepared in accordance with generally accepted accounting principles.

Determinations of various elements of a given related set of financial statements must be based upon assumptions and methods which are consistent among themselves, with due regard for the purpose of the statements and for the methods to be employed in the calculations.

Opinions

1. Guide 1(b) reminds the actuary that he will give actuarial advice only when he is qualified to do so. It is the opinion of the Committee that an actuary should undertake to prepare or verify reserves or other actuarial elements of financial statements only if he is familiar with the purposes and uses of such statements and, in the case of financial statements prepared in accordance with generally accepted accounting principles, with the application of generally accepted accounting principles to life insurance accounting.

2. Guide 2(a) relates to the relationship of the actuary to his client or employer. It is the opinion of the Committee that an actuary who is responsible for any part of financial statements which are subject to audit must make sure that the auditor is fully cognizant of his relationship with the company. If a formal actuarial opinion is made part of financial statements which are submitted to audit by a public accountant, the context of such opinion should make clear the relationship between the actuary and the company.

3. Guide 2(b) provides that an actuary will have due regard for the confidential nature of his work. It is the opinion of the Committee that when the actuary is required to make disclosures to the company's independent auditor and to support the assumptions and methods which he has used in the preparation of financial statements appropriate steps should be taken to preserve the confidential nature of any formal written report which contains any confidential material.

4. When an actuary's work relates to financial statements prepared in accordance with generally accepted accounting principles, it is the opinion of the Committee that Guide 2(c) requires that an actuarial report should be furnished to the company and to the company's independent auditor, if any. Such actuarial report should identify the actuary, his relationship with the company and the scope of his activity in relation to the financial statements involved. In situations where a number of actuaries who are responsible to a principal actuary participate in work relating to any such financial statement, the actuarial report may be signed by the principal actuary only. Any such actuarial report furnished by an independent actuarial firm may be signed with the name of the firm and the signature of the principal actuary appended.

5. Guide 3 relates to situations "in which there is or may be a conflict of interest involving the member's actuarial service" and states that "the member will not perform such actuarial service if the conflict makes or is likely to make it difficult for him to act independently". The service an actuary performs in reviewing financial statements for the purpose of forming, expressing and publishing an opinion which purports to be independent with regard to such financial statements is a type of service to which Guide 3 is intended to relate. It is the opinion of the Committee that Guide 3 does not inhibit the service an actuary performs for an insurance company in preparing or evaluating material for inclusion in financial statements of such company. If an actuary employed or engaged by the reporting company does express a professional opinion regarding any material in the financial statements of such company, Guide 3 requires that his relationship with the company be clearly described in the opinion.

6. Guide 4(a) states that "the member will customarily include in any report or certificate quoting actuarial costs, reserves, or liabilities a statement or reference describing or clearly identifying the data and the actuarial methods and assumptions employed". It is the opinion of the committee that Guide 4(a) as applied to the actuary's work in connection with published financial statements requires that the actuary disclose to the auditor the actuarial assumptions and methods, including, where apropriate, an appraisal of their suitability for the purposes at hand and reference to factors which have not been considered. In many instances, such disclosure may be supported by oral discussions between the auditor and the actuary. Approximations and approximate methods may be used provided the actuary has satisfied himself that the result does not differ materially from the result of using more precise methods.

7. It is the opinion of the Committeee that Guide 4(b) requires that the actuary, in selecting actuarial

assumptions and methods for use in any financial statement prepared in accordance with generally accepted accounting principles, take into consideration the published formal recommendations of the Committee on Financial Reporting Principles of the American Academy of Actuaries. An actuary who makes use in any such financial statement of any assumption or method which conflicts with such recommendations must be prepared to support his use of such assumption or method.

8. It is the opinion of the Committee that Guide 4(c) should be interpreted as requiring that an actuary who, for any reason, uses in a financial statement prepared in accordance with generally accepted accounting principles any assumption or method which in his opinion deviates materially from the requirements of Guide 4(b) or of Guide 4(d) will include in the report referred to in Opinion 4 above an appropriate and explicit qualification with respect to such deviation.

* * *

"ACTUARIAL REPORT AND STATEMENT OF ACTUARIAL OPINION" — Recommendation No. 3 of the Committee on Financial Reporting Principles of the American Academy of Actuaries

1. This Recommendation applies to the work of an actuary who acts for a stock life insurance company in the preparation of its financial statements, who contributes elements for inclusion in any such financial statement, or who audits or reviews elements of such a financial statement, when such financial statement is to be presented as having been prepared in accordance with "generally accepted accounting principles" as that term is understood in the United States.

2. As used in this Recommendation and related Interpretations, "Actuarial Report" means the actuary's report to management and auditor referred to in Number 4 of Opinion A-6 on the Academy's Guide to Professional Conduct, and "Statement of Actuarial Opinion" means a statement of the actuary's opinion prepared for publication with financial statements, referred to in Numbers 2 and 5 of Opinion A-6. A written plan of coordination or other working communication of a consulting actuary to an auditor as referred to in paragraph 3 of Recommendation 2 is not an "Actuarial Report" or a "Statement of Actuarial Opinion" within the meaning of this Recommendation.

3. Any judgment as to the appropriateness of the actuarial assumptions used in preparing data for financial statements must be formed in the light of the purpose for which the statements are being prepared. Financial statements which are primarily intended to reflect a matching of revenues and costs in accordance with generally accepted accounting principles may require the use of actuarial assumptions which differ from those which would be used in, for example, financial statements which give primary emphasis to solvency for the protection of policyholders, as is the case with statements based on standards prescribed by state regulatory authorities.

4. Guide 4 (d) provides, in part, that "When a member characterizes reserves as adequate, he shall either (i) assure himeslf that they meet any applicable statutory or regulatory standards or (ii) clearly qualify his characterization in this respect, including an explicit statement as to whether the reserves meet such statutory or regulatory standards".

Actuarial Report

5. Opinion A-6 provides (No. 4), "When an actuary's work relates to financial statements prepared in accordance with generally accepted accounting principles, it is the opinion of the (Professional Conduct) Committee that Guide 2 (c) requires as a minimum that an actuarial report should be furnished to the company and to the company's independent auditor, if any", and (No. 6), "It is the opinion of the (Professional Conduct) Committee that Guide 4 (a) as applied to the actuary's work in connection with financial statements prepared in accordance with generally accepted accounting principles requires that the actuary disclose to the auditor the actuarial assumptions and methods, including, where appropriate, an appraisal of their suitability for the purposes at hand and reference to factors which have not been considered".

6. An Actuarial Report should contain descriptions of the scope of the actuary's work and of the actuarial assumptions and methods used.

7. An Actuarial Report should contain expressions of the actuary's opinion as to whether the reserves and other actuarial items in the statements are based on assumptions which are appropriate to the purpose for which the statements were prepared, whether the methods employed are consistent with sound actuarial principles, and whether provision has been made for all actuarial reserves and related statement items which ought to be established. An Actuarial Report

should also include a statement of the actuary's opinion as to whether any amount carried in the balance sheet on account of unamortized acquisition expenses and the amount of liabilities carried on account of other future policy obligations and expenses are fairly stated (i.e., neither materially understated nor materially overstated) in accordance with sound actuarial principles (c.f., Recommendation 1).

8. If the actuary is unable to form an opinion in any respect defined in Paragraph 7, or if his opinion in any such report is adverse or qualified, the Actuarial Report should specifically state the reason.

9. Material changes in actuarial assumptions from those previously used should be disclosed in an Actuarial Report and their effects noted. Such disclosures should not be limited to factors explicitly assumed but should include reference to the handling, or absence of handling, of such other factors as the actuary in his judgment deems to have pertinence. The adoption for new issues of an actuarial assumption which differs from a corresponding assumption used for any prior issues is not a change in actuarial assumptions within the meaning of this paragraph.

10. The report should also compare (a) the amount of net liability for future policy obligations and expenses, less any amount of unamortized acquisition expenses, with (b) the amount of net liability for future policy obligations reported in financial statements filed with state regulatory authorities; and if (a) is less than (b) the report should state the amount of the difference. The "net liability" referred to in (a) and (b) above should re-

flect adjustments for deferred premiums and other related items.

Statement of Actuarial Opinion

11. Opinion A-6 states (No. 4) that the objective of Guide 2 (c) will be more fully satisfied if the auditor's opinion identifies the actuary or if published financial statements include a formal Statement of Actuarial Opinion.

12. A written Statement of Actuarial Opinion prepared for publication with financial statements of a life insurance company will normally include statements as to the scope of the actuary's participation in the preparation and the appraisal of the financial statements, his professional opinion as to the actuarial elements in the statements, and a statement of his relationship to the company. Such Statement of Actuarial Opinion should cover the subjects referred to in Paragraphs 6, 7, 8, 9 and 10 above, although normally without the supporting detail which would be appropriate in an Actuarial Report.

Other Actuarial Statements

13. In preparing any statement or report relating to a life insurance company, other than an Actuarial Report or Statement of Actuarial Opinion described in this Recommendation, the actuary should be aware of the Guides to Professional Conduct as interpreted by Opinions of the Professional Conduct Committee.

Chapter References

The references that follow are highly abbreviated. Enough information is given, however, that the details of a particular reference may be located by reference to the bibliography.

All references to the AICPA's life insurance audit guide are indicated by the word "guide".

CHAPTER 1

1. Surrey, p. 3
2. Ibid, p. 33
3. Ibid, p. 54
4. Raymond, p. 57
5. Ibid, p. 57
6. Surrey, p. 60
7. Raymond, p. 283
8. Ibid
9. Surrey, p. 146.
10. Ernst & Ernst, *Financial Reporting Trends* (Life), 1972, p. 3
11. Ibid, 1971, p. 142
12. *Response of the Joint Actuarial Committee on Financial Reporting to the December 1970 Exposure Draft of Audits of Life Insurance Companies,* May 14, 1971

CHAPTER 2

1. *Webster's,* p. 532

CHAPTER 3

1. Bassford, *TASA* XLIII 1942, p. 328

CHAPTER 4

1. AICPA, APB Accounting Principles, vol. 2, p. 9086
2. Ibid, p. 9085
3. Ibid, p. 9086
4. Ibid, p. 9087
5. Ibid, p. 6577
6. Ibid, p. 9063
7. Guide, p. 67, p. 70
8. AICPA, APB Accounting Principles, vol. 2, p. 9062

CHAPTER 5

1. Guide, p. 66
2. Ibid, p. 67
3. Ibid, p. 69
4. Ibid, p. 71
5. Ibid, p. 67
6. Ibid, p. 69
7. Ibid
8. Ibid
9. Ibid, p. 70
10. Ibid, pp. 69–70
11. Ibid, p. 71
12. Ibid
13. Ibid, p. 69
14. Ibid
15. Ibid, pp. 80–81
16. Ibid, p. 69
17. Ibid, p. 71
18. Ibid
19. Ernst & Ernst, *Financial Reporting Trends* (Life), 1972, p. 172
20. Ibid (Fire & Casualty), 1972, p. 69
21. Ibid (Life), p. 158
22. Guide, p. 66
23. Ernst & Ernst, *Financial Reporting Trends* (Life), 1972, p. 153
24. Guide, p. 75

CHAPTER 6

1. *Webster's Third New International Dictionary,* Springfield, Mass.: G & C Meriam Co., (1967), pp. 1930–1931
2. Guide, p. 68
3. Ibid, p. 67
4. Ibid, p. 68
5. Ibid
6. Ibid
7. Ibid, pp. 85–86
8. Ibid, p. 64
9. Ibid, p. 71
10. Ibid, p. 78
11. Ibid, p. 100
12. Ibid, p. 76
13. Ibid, p. 77
14. Ibid, p. 81
15. Ibid, p. 85
16. Ibid, p. 102
17. Ibid, p. 101
18. Horn, *TSA* XXIII p. 392
19. Ibid, p. 398
20. Ibid, p. 399
21. Ibid, p. 392
22. Ibid, p. 393
23. Ibid
24. Ibid
25. Ibid, p. 416
26. Ibid, p. 393
27. Ibid, pp. 417–418
28. Joint Actuarial Committee, *Response,* (September 29, 1972), pp. 2–3
29. American Academy of Actuaries Committee, Interpretation 1–a (July 19, 1973), pp. 1–2
30. Ibid
31. American Academy of Actuaries Committee, Interpretation 1–b, (July 19, 1973), p. 1
32. Guide, p. 76
33. Ibid, p. 142
34. Ibid, p. 64
35. Ibid, p. 86

36. Ibid, p. 64
37. Horn, *TSA* XXIII, p. 416
38. Guide, p. 86
39. Ibid, p. 76
40. Ibid, p. 101
41. Ibid
42. Ibid, p. 78
43. American Academy of Actuaries Committee Recommendation No. 1 (July 19, 1973), p. 2
44. Guide, p. 76
45. A. R. Colles, Interview (1970)
46. Guide, pp. 84–85
47. American Academy of Actuaries Committee, Interpretation 1–b, (July 19, 1973), p. 1

CHAPTER 7

1. Guide, p. 63
2. Ibid, p. 64
3. Ibid, p. 97
4. Ibid, p. 98
5. Ibid
6. American Academy of Actuaries Committee, Recommendation No. 1
7. Ibid, p. 1
8. Guide, p. 85, p. 178
9. Ibid, p. 85
10. Ibid, p. 86
11. Ibid
12. Ibid
13. Ibid
14. Ibid, p. 102
15. American Academy of Actuaries Committee, Recommendation No. 1
16. Ibid, p. 3
17. Guide, pp. 85–86
18. Ibid, p. 108

CHAPTER 8

1. Stuart Robertson, memorandum, April 12, 1965
2. Guide, p. 76
3. Ibid, p. 101
4. Ibid, p. 103
5. Ibid, p. 108
6. Ibid, p. 77
7. Ibid
8. Ibid, p. 101
9. Ibid, p. 103
10. Ibid, p. 77

CHAPTER 9

1. Guide, p. 75
2. Ibid
3. Ibid, p. 76
4. Ibid
5. Ibid, p. 100
6. Ibid
7. Ibid, p. 81
8. Ibid, p. 100
9. Ibid, p. 71

10. Ibid, p. 75, p. 100
11. Ibid, p. 153
12. Ibid, p. 93
13. Ibid, p. 88
14. Ibid, p. 89
15. Ibid, p. 94
16. Ibid, pp. 89–90

CHAPTER 10

1. Guide, p. 78
2. Ibid
3. Ibid, p. 80
4. Ibid, p. 109
5. Ibid

CHAPTER 13

1. Horngren, p. 69
2. Ibid, p. 49
3. Ibid, p. 75
4. Guide, p. 100
5. LOMA, Report No. 23, p. 1
6. LOMA, 1967 Proceedings, p. 87
7. LOMA, Report No. 23, p. 4
8. Ibid, p. 5
8a. LOMA, 1972 Instructions—Ordinary and Investment
9. Fraser, Study Notes, p. 10
10. Ibid, p. 1
11. Ibid, p. 17
12. Ibid, p. 1
13. Horngren, p. 522

CHAPTER 14

1. Guide, p. 71
2. Ibid, p. 72
3. Ibid, p. 141
4. Ibid, p. 72
5. Ibid, p. 74
6. Ibid, p. 72
7. Ibid
8. Horngren, p. 20
9. Ibid, pp. 21–22
10. Guide, p. 74

CHAPTER 15

1. Guide, p. 73
2. Ibid
3. Ibid

CHAPTER 16

1. Guide, p. 72
2. Ibid, p. 139
3. Ibid, p. 142
4. Ibid
5. Ibid, p. 141
6. Ibid, p. 142
7. Ibid, p. 87
8. Ibid, p. 107
9. Ibid, p. 108

CHAPTER 17

1. Guide, p. 100
2. Ibid, p. 74
3. AICPA, August 1972, exposure draft of audit guide
4. AICPA Accounting Research Study No. 7, p. 100
5. Ibid, p. 101
6. AICPA, APB Accounting Principles, vol. 2, p. 6662
7. Ibid, p. 665
8. Ibid
9. Guide, pp. 74–75
10. Ibid, p. 75
11. Ibid, p. 100
12. Ibid, p. 75

CHAPTER 19

1. Guide, p. 71
2. Ibid
3. Ibid, p. 83
4. Ibid, p. 84
5. Ibid, pp. 84–85
6. Ibid, p. 85
7. Ibid

CHAPTER 20

1. Guide, p. 69
2. Ibid, p. 71
3. Ibid, p. 81
4. Ibid, p. 80

CHAPTER 21

1. Guide, p. 82
2. Ibid, p. 83
3. Ibid

CHAPTER 22

1. Woody, *Reinsurance,* study note for Part 101 of the Actuarial Examinations
2. Ibid
3. Ibid
4. Committee on Financial Reporting Principles, American Academy of Actuaries, "Recommendation No. 4"
5. Guide, p. 92
6. Ibid
7. Ibid, p. 91

CHAPTER 23

1. Surrey, p. 103
2. Ibid, p. 91
3. Wightman, p. 45
4. Ibid, p. 581

CHAPTER 24

1. Guide, p. 73
2. Ibid, p. 75

3. Ibid, p. 103
4. Ibid, pp. 86–87
5. Ibid, p. 87
6. Finney and Miller, pp. 246–247
7. Guide, p. 87
8. Ibid
9. Ibid
10. Ibid

CHAPTER 25

1. Guide, p. 78
2. Ibid, p. 80
3. Ibid, p. 79
4. Ibid, p. 78
5. Ibid

CHAPTER 26

1. Guide, p. 88
2. AICPA, APB Accounting Principles, vol. 2, p. 6581
3. Ibid
4. Guide, p. 152
5. AICPA, APB Accounting Principles, vol. 2, p. 6586
6. Guide, p. 153
7. Ibid, p. 155
8. Ibid
9. Ibid, p. 153

10. Ibid
11. Ibid, p. 154

CHAPTER 27

1. AICPA, APB Accounting Principles (1972), vol. 2, p. 6645
2. Ibid, p. 6650
3. Ibid, p. 6653
4. Ibid, p. 6656
5. Ibid
6. Ibid, p. 6645
7. Ibid, p. 6673
8. Ibid, p. 6675
9. Guide, p. 91
10. Ibid

CHAPTER 29

1. Guide, p. 118
2. Ibid
3. Ibid, p. 107
4. Ibid, pp. 107–108
5. Ibid
6. Ibid
7. Ibid, p. 107
8. Ibid, p. 108
9. Ibid, p. 109
10. Ibid
11. Ibid, p. 110
12. Ibid, p. 111
13. Ibid, p. 112

14. Ibid
15. Ibid, p. 113
16. Ibid
17. Ibid, p. 112
18. Ibid, p. 89
19. Ibid, pp. 89–90
20. Ibid, p. 90
21. AICPA, APB Accounting Principles, vol. 2, p. 6783
22. Ibid
23. Ibid
24. Ibid, p. 6784
25. Ibid, p. 6785
26. Ibid
27. Ibid, p. 6786
28. Ibid

CHAPTER 30

1. Guide, p. 95
2. Ibid, p. 102
3. Ibid, p. 103
4. Ibid
5. Ibid, p. 64
6. Ibid
7. Ibid, p. 97
8. Ibid
9. Ibid, p. 99
10. Ibid, p. 122
11. Ibid, p. 98
12. Ibid
13. Ibid, p. 99
14. Ibid, p. 123

Selected Bibliography

BOOKS

Accounting Research and Terminology Bulletins. Final ed. New York: American Institute of Certified Public Accountants, 1961.

American Institute of Certified Public Accountants. *APB Accounting Principles.* 2 vols. Chicago: Commerce Clearing House, 1973.

_____. *Inventory of Generally Accepted Accounting Principles,* Accounting Research Study No. 7. New York.

_____. *Audits of Stock Life Insurance Companies.* New York: American Institute of Certified Public Accountants, 1972.

Armstrong, Dale E. *An Examination of External Financial Reporting Practices and Underlying Accounting Principles Applicable to Life Insurance Companies.* OSU College of Business Research Series No. 5. Stillwater: Publishing and Printing Department of Oklahoma State University, 1968.

Beardsley, Charles M. *Life Company Annual Statement Handbook.* Winston-Salem: Charles M. Beardsley, 1962.

Belth, Joseph M. *Participating Life Insurance Sold by Stock Companies.* Homewood, Illinois: Richard D. Irwin, 1965.

Best's Flitcraft Compend. Morristown, New Jersey: A.M. Best Co., 1971.

Best's Insurance Reports (Life-Health), 1973. 65th ed. Morristown, New Jersey: A.M. Best Co., 1973.

Black, Kenneth. *Group Annuities.* Philadelphia: University of Pennsylvania Press, 1955.

Davis, Malvin E. *Industrial Life Insurance in the United States.* New York: McGraw Hill Book Co., 1944.

Dickerson, O. D. *Health Insurance.* Homewood, Illinois: Richard D. Irwin, 1963.

Eilers, Robert D. and Robert M. Crowe (eds.). *Group Insurance Handbook.* Homebook, Illinois: Richard D. Irwin, 1965.

Ernst & Ernst, *GAAP Deferred Taxes,* Cleveland, 1974.

Ernst & Ernst, *Financial Reporting Trends* (Life Insurance), Cleveland. 1970, 1971, 1972, 1973.

Ernst & Ernst, *Financial Reporting Trends* (Fire and Casualty Insurance), Cleveland. 1972, 1973.

Finney, H. A. and Herbert E. Miller. *Principles of Accounting—Intermediate.* 5th ed. Englewood Cliffs, New Jersey: Prentice-Hall, 1961.

Fraine, Harold G. *Valuation of Securities Holdings of Life Insurance Companies.* Homewood, Illinois: Richard D. Irwin, 1962.

Grady, Paul. *Inventory of Generally Accepted Accounting Principles For Business Enterprises.* Accounting Research Study No. 7. New York: American Institute of Certified Public Accountants, 1965.

Gregg, Davis W. *Group Life Insurance.* 3rd ed. Homewood, Illinois: Richard D. Irwin, 1962.

_____. *Life and Health Insurance Handbook.* Homewood, Illinois: Richard D. Irwin, 1964.

Gushee, Charles H. (ed.). *Financial Compound Interest and Annuity Tables.* Boston: Financial Publishing Co., 1969.

Horngren, Charles. *Cost Accounting: A Managerial Emphasis.* Englewood Cliffs, N.J.: Prentice-Hall, Inc., 1962.

Life Insurance Fact Book. New York: Institute of Life Insurance, 1973.

Maclean, Joseph B. and Edward W. Marshall. *Distribution of Surplus.* Actuarial Study No. 6. New York: Actuarial Society of America, 1937.

McGill, Dan M. *Life Insurance.* Rev. ed. Homewood, Illinois: Richard D. Irwin, 1967.

Noback, Joseph C. *Life Insurance Accounting.* Homewood, Illinois: Richard D. Irwin, 1969.

Pickrell, Jesse F. *Group Health Insurance.* Rev. ed. Homewood, Illinois: Richard D. Irwin, 1961.

Source Book of Health Insurance Data. New York: Health Insurance Institute. 1972–1973.

Van House, Charles L. and W. Rogers Hammond. *Accounting for Life Insurance Companies.* Homewood, Illinois: Richard D. Irwin, 1969.

Wightman, E. C. *Life Insurance Statements and Accounts.* 1st ed. New York: Life Office Management Association, 1952. (Out of print.)

What Price Business? Hartford: Life Insurance Agency Management Association, 1953.

GOVERNMENT DOCUMENTS

California. Department of Insurance. *Rules and Regulations of the Insurance Commissioner Relating to Credit Life and Credit Disability Insurance.* Administrative Code, Title 10, Chapter 5, Subchapter 2, Article 6.7.

California. *Insurance Code.* (1965).

New York. Department of Insurance. *New York Insurance Law.* Albany: Williams Press, 1968. (Reprint.)

_____. *Regulation No. 33—Reporting and Allocation of Income and Expenses of Life Insurers.* January 1, 1955.

_____. *Regulation No. 48 (11 NYCRR 10).* March 24, 1969.

U.S. Congress. House. Committee on Interstate and Foreign Commerce, A Subcommittee. *Investor Protection.* Part 1. Hearings, 88th Cong., 1st Sess., April 3 and November 19, 20, 31, 1963. Washington: Government Printing Office, 1964.

_____. *Investor Protection.* Part 2. Hearings, 88th Cong., 1st and 2nd Sess., December 3, 4, and 5, 1963; January 21, 22, 23, February 4, 5, 18, and 19, 1964. Washington: Government Printing Office, 1964.

U.S. Securities and Exchange Commission. *Regulation S-X (Form and Content of Financial Statements).* Washington: Government Printing Office, 1968.

PERIODICALS

Anderson, James C. H. "Gross Premium Calculations and Profit Measurement for Nonparticipating Insurance," *Transactions of the Society of Actuaries,* Vol. XI (1959), pp. 357–420.

"Annual Statements of Life Insurance Companies in the United States," *Transactions of the Society of Actuaries,* Vol. XVIII (1966), pp. D554–D596.

Bartleson, Edwin L. and James J. Olsen. "Reserves for Individual Hospital and Surgical Expense Insurance," *Transactions of the Society of Actuaries,* Vol. IX (1957), pp. 334–417.

Bassford, Horace R. "Premium Rates, Reserves, and Nonforfeiture Values for Participating Policies," *Transactions of the Actuarial Society of America,* Vol. XLIII (1942), pp. 328–364.

Bittel, W. Harold. Discussion of "Valuation of Life Insurance Company Assets" by F. J. McDiarmid. *Transactions of the Society of Actuaries,* Vol. XVI (1964), pp. 409–435.

Blicksilver, Jack. "Future of Industrial Coverage Is Tied to Economic Growth of the South, Anti-Poverty Plans," *The National Underwriter,* February 3, 1968, p. 1.

Bowles, Thomas P., Lloyd S. Coughry, and Herbert E. Goodfriend. "Certain Actuarial Considerations in Determining Life Insurance Company Equity Values," *Transactions of the Society of Actuaries,* Vol. XVII (October, 1965), pp. 281–296.

J. C. Bradford & Co. "A Breakthrough in the Analysis of Life Insurance Earnings," *The Wall Street Journal,* September 19, 1969, p. 12.

Bragg, John M. "Prices and Profits," *Transactions of the Society of Actuaries,* Regional Meeting Number, April, 1968, pp. 44–84.

Clark, John N. "The Adjustment of Life Insurance Company Earnings," *Financial Analysts Journal,* September-October, 1966, pp. 71–73.

Connoly, Charles H. "The Effect of Varying Interest Rates," *Transactions of the Society of Actuaries,* Vol. IX (1957), pp. 135–139.

Dana, Franklin B. "Should Financial Reports Modify the Convention Blank?" *Actuarial Record,* December, 1966, pp. 3–5.

Davis, Shelby Cullom. "Only a Matter of Money," *Financial Analysts Journal,* September-October, 1966, pp. 67–70.

_____. "The Values in Insurance Stocks," *The Commercial and Financial Chronicle,* September 24, 1959. (Reprint.)

"Digest of Discussion of Subjects of General Interest," *Transactions of the Society of Actuaries,* Vol. XIX (1967), pp. D123–D517.

"Digest of Discussion of Subjects of Special Interest—New York Regional Meeting," *Transactions of the Society of Actuaries,* Vol. XIII (1961), pp. D56–D81.

Dineen, Robert E. and Jon S. Hanson. "Securities Laws and How They Relate to Insurance Regulation," *The National Underwriter,* May 18, 1968; May 25, 1968; June 1, 1968; June 8, 1968.

Discussions of "Adjusted Earnings," *Transactions of the Society of Actuaries,* Regional Meeting Number, April, 1968, pp. D353–D355 and D191–D234.

Discussions of "Projection of Operations" by Melvin Gold. *Transactions of the Society of Actuaries,* Vol. XVIII (1966), pp. 167–179.

Discussions of "Valuing a Life Insurance Company" by Melvin Gold. *Transactions of the Society of Actuaries,* Vol. XIV (1962), pp. 158–170.

Discussion of "Ordinary Insurance Premiums," *Transactions of the Society of Actuaries,* Vol. XIII (1961), pp. D57–D81.

Discussion of "Equity-Oriented Products," *Transactions of the Society of Actuaries,* Regional Meeting Number, March, 1969, pp. D715–D733.

Discussion of "Premiums and Dividends for Individual Ordinary Insurance," *Transactions of the Society of Actuaries,* Regional Meeting Number, April, 1968, pp. D235–D274.

Discussions of "Adjusted Earnings," *Transactions of the Society of Actuaries,* Regional Meeting Number, December, 1968, pp. D471–D485.

Discussions of "Life Insurance Accounting," *Transactions of the Society of Actuaries,* Regional Meeting Number, March, 1969, pp. D639–D664.

Duncan, Robert M. "A Retirement System Granting Unit Annuities and Investing in Equities," *Transactions of the Society of Actuaries*, Vol. IV (1952), pp. 317–342.

Elliott, John L. "John Elliott on Future of Debit Insurance —An Optimistic View," *The National Underwriter*, May 4, 1968, p. 1.

Flinn, Ellis D. and Franklin B. Dana. "Pricing A Life Insurance Company By Actuarial Methods," *Mergers & Acquisitions*, Vol. 5 (1970), pp. 17–32. (Reprint.)

Gold, Melvin. "A Critical Review of the New Life Insurance Companies," *Best's Insurance News (Life/Health Edition)*, June, 1966. (Reprint.)

————. "Expenses and the Small Company," *Best's Insurance News (Life/Health Edition)*, May, 1968. (Reprint.)

————. "Inflation and Life Insurance," *Transactions of the Society of Actuaries*, Vol. VIII (November, 1966), pp. 315–324.

————. "Projections of Operations," *Transactions of the Society of Actuaries*, Vol. XVIII (1966), pp. 148–166.

————. "Reviewing the New Life Companies," *Best's Insurance News (Life/Health Edition)*, March, 1967. (Reprint.)

————. "Statutory Earnings, Adjusted Earnings, and Net Worth," *Transactions of the Society of Actuaries*, Regional Meeting Number, April, 1968, pp. 13–38.

————. "Valuing a Life Insurance Company," *Transactions of the Society of Actuaries*, Vol. XIV (1962), pp. 139–157.

Goodfriend, Herbert E. "Adjustment and Projections of Life Insurance Company Earnings Utilizing a Computer," *Financial Analysts Journal*, November-December, 1966. (Reprint.)

————. "Two Approaches to Adjusted Earnings of Life Companies," *Best's Life News*, March, 1967, pp. 12–69.

Griffith, Reynolds. "A Note on Life Insurance Accounting," *Journal of Risk and Insurance*, June, 1964, pp. 207–215.

Guertin, Alfred N. "Notes on Valuation of Company Liabilities," *The Record of the American Institute of Actuaries*, Vol. XXXIII (1944), pp. 62–91.

Hanson, John S. and Duncan R. Farley, "New Life Insurance Companies: Their Promotion and Regulation," *Marquette Law Review*, Vol. 49, No. 2 (Fall, 1965), pp. 175–330.

"Higher Interest Earnings," *Transactions of the Society of Actuaries*, Vol. XI (1959), pp. 136–144.

Horn, Richard. "Life Insurance Earnings and the Release from Risk Policy Reserve System," *Transactions of the Society of Actuaries*, Vol. XXIII (1972), p. 392ff.

Hoskins, James E. "Asset Shares and Their Relation to Nonforfeiture Values," *Transactions of the Actuarial Society of America*, Vol. XL (1939), pp. 379–393.

"Industrial Insurance," *Transactions of the Society of Actuaries*, Vol. XII (1960), pp. 401–404.

"Insurance-Finance Category Was Leader in 1968 Merger Activity," *The National Underwriter*, January 18, 1969, p. 1.

Jackson, Paul H. "Experience Rating," *Transactions of the Society of Actuaries*, Vol. V (1953), pp. 239–267.

Kramer, Donald. "Current Accounting Practices," *Financial Analysts Journal*, January-February, 1969. (Reprint.)

————. "Life Insurance Profit Margins," *Financial Analysts Journal*, November-December, 1965. (Reprint.)

————. "The Outlook for Life Insurance Stocks," *Trusts and Estates Magazine*, July, 1966. (Reprint.)

Larson, Robert E. "A Method of Calculating Group Term Dividends," *Transactions of the Society of Actuaries*, Vol. IV (1952), pp. 308–316.

Leslie, Neale. "A New Approach to Life Insurance Evaluation," *Financial Analysts Journal*, September-October, 1966, pp. 75–78.

Lincoln, Owen C. "Should the Commissioners Reserve Valuation Method be Adopted by a Participating Company Which Has Traditionally Used the Net Level Premium Method?" *Transactions of the Actuarial Society of America*, Vol. XLVII (1946),

Lyons, Daniel J. "Expense Limitations in Section 213 of the New York Insurance Law," *Transactions of the Actuarial Society of America*, Vol. XLIX (1948), pp. 27–53.

McDiarmid, Fergus J. "Valuation of Life Insurance Company Assets," *Transactions of the Society of Actuaries*, Vol. XVI (1964), pp. 390–408.

Minor, Edward H. "Loss-of-Time Health Insurance Reserves Based on the 1964 Commissioners Disability Table," *Transactions of the Society of Actuaries*, Vol. XVII (1965), pp. 368–416.

Moorhead, Ernest J. "The Construction of Persistency Tables," *Transactions of the Society of Actuaries*, Vol. XII (1960), pp. 545–563.

————. "Mortality Investigation with Expected Mortality Estimated at Issue by Use of Persistency Factors," *Transactions of the Society of Actuaries*, Vol. XIII (1961), pp. 298–307.

Mullins, W. R. "An Actuary Looks at Term Insurance," *Best's Insurance News (Life/Health Edition)*, September, 1966, pp. 21–30.

Pedoe, Arthur. "Further Notes on the Trend of Life Insurance Company Expenses," *Transactions of the Society of Actuaries*, Vol. XIII (1961), pp. 1–30.

————. "Lidstone's Formula for the Present Value of the Profits of a Policy—Actuarial Note," *Transactions of the Society of Actuaries*, Vol. X (1958), pp. 531–538.

"Phoenix Mutual Establishes Reinsurance Pool," *Best's Weekly News Digest*, February 10, 1969, p. 1.

Pike, Bertram N. "Some Considerations in Determining Incurred Claims Used in the Computation of Dividends Under Group Accident and Health Insurance," *Transactions of the Society of Actuaries*, Vol. X (1958), pp. 630–654.

"Report on Society of Actuaries Meeting," *Transactions of the Society of Actuaries*, March, 1969, pp. 387–417.

Richardson, C. F. B. "Substandard Business," *Record of the American Institute of Actuaries*, Vol. XXX (1941), pp. 122–183.

Ryall, Peter. "An Analysis of the Rapidly Expanding Company," *Transactions of the Society of Actuaries,* Vol. XV (1963), pp. 113–150.

Shepherd, Bruce E. "Natural Reserves," *Transactions of the Actuarial Society of America,* Vol. XLI (1940), pp. 463–486.

Trowbridge, Charles L. "Funding of Group Life Insurance," *Transactions of the Society of Actuaries,* Vol. VII (1955), pp. 270–285.

"True (Adjusted) Values and Earnings by the Investment Yield Method," *The Key to Sound Management,* Vol. 69 (February, 1969), pp. 1–16.

"Voices Optimism Over Future of Industrial Cover," *The National Underwriter,* January 13, 1968, p. 1.

Weislander, Stanley. "Buy Term and Invest the Difference: A Mathematical Analysis," *Best's Insurance News (Life/ Health Edition),* December, 1966, pp. 32–42.

Winter, Bert A. "Modern Applications of Gross Premium Valuation to Participating Insurance," *Transactions of the Actuarial Society of America,* Vol. XLIX (1948), pp. 8–26.

UNPUBLISHED AND MISCELLANEOUS WORKS

American Academy of Actuaries. Recommendations No. 1, 2, 3, 4, and 5 and Interpretations, 1973 and 1974. (Mimeographed.)

American Institute of Certified Public Accountants. Minutes and documents relating to the work of the Committee on Insurance Accounting and Auditing, 1968–1973. (Mimeographed.)

Belth, Joseph M. "Life Insurance Reserves and the Regulatory Process." Bloomington, Indiana: June, 1967. (Mimeographed.)

Bowles, Thomas. Memorandum to Committee on Adjusted Earnings—Conference of Actuaries in Public Practice, November 8, 1967. (Internal memorandum.)

————. "The Status of Adjusted Earnings." Presentation to the Southwestern Actuaries Club. November 22, 1968. (Mimeographed.)

Corbett, Gary. "Adjusting Life Insurance Company Earnings." Paper circulated to actuaries and accountants, December 1969. (Mimeographed.)

Education and Examination Committee of the Society of Actuaries—Study Notes. Chicago: Society of Actuaries, 1968 (Mimeographed series.)

"Extracts from Report of the Committee to Study Nonforfeiture Benefits and Related Matters." National Association of Insurance Commissioners, September 10, 1941.

"Final Report from the Committee on Life Insurance Earnings Adjustments." New York: The Association of Insurance and Financial Analysts, November, 1969. (Mimeographed.)

Gustafson, Dale R. "Comments of the Joint Committee on Financial Reporting Principles of the American Life Convention and the Life Insurance Association of America on the Memorandum on Life Insurance Accounting Prepared by the AICPA Committee on Insurance Accounting and Auditing for Discussion with Representatives of the Life Insurance Industry." September 3, 1968. (Internal memorandum.)

"How Can the Conference Solve the Adjusted Earnings Dilemma?" Panel discussion, *Proceedings of the Conference of Actuaries in Public Practice,* Vol. XVII (1967–1968), pp. 97–101 and 127–135.

"Instructions, Intercompany Functional Comparison Analysis." New York: Intercompany Financial Comparison Committee, Life Office Management Association, January, 1972. (Mimeographed.)

"Instructions, Intercompany Functional Comparison Analysis, Selection Depth Study." New York: Intercompany Financial Comparison Committee, Life Office Management Association, January, 1969. (Mimeographed.)

"Instructions, Intercompany Functional Comparison Analysis, Selling Depth Study." New York: Intercompany Financial Comparison Committee, Life Office Management Association, January, 1969. (Mimeographed.)

Joint Actuarial Commitee on Financial Reporting. *Response to the 1970 Exposure Draft of Audits of Life Insurance Companies.* Chicago: Society of Actuaries, 1971.

————. *Response to the 1972 Exposure Draft.* (Mimeographed.)

Life Office Management Association, *Report No. 23* of the Financial Planning and Control Division.

————. 1967 *Proceedings.*

————. Special Report, 1972.

"Minutes of Meeting of Committee on Blanks." New York: National Association of Insurance Commissioners, March 20, 1969.

Noback, Joseph C. "Notes Prepared for Adjusted Earnings Workshop September 26, 1970." (Mimeographed.)

Potts, Robert W. "Review of Paper by Melvin Gold and Subsequent Discussion." Refers to "Valuing a Life Insurance Company" (*Transactions of the Society of Actuaries,* Vol. XIV). San Francisco: Coates, Herfurth & England, 1962. (Internal memorandum.)

Raymond, Robert Hugh. "Financial Statements of Life Insurance Companies." Unpublished doctoral dissertation, Michigan State University, 1964.

Richards, Alan. "Remarks before the Actuarial Club of the Pacific States." April 13, 1966. (Mimeographed.)

Robertson, Stuart A. "An Actuary Looks at Life Insurance Stocks." Talk presented before the Milwaukee Investment Analysts, May, 1967. (Mimeographed.)

————. Memorandum to all principals, April 12, 1965.

Society of Actuaries. "Interpretive Opinion 5–6 to the Guides to Professional Conduct", 1974. (Mimeographed.)

————. Study Notes for the 1968 Actuarial Examinations.

Surrey, Sterling. "The Development of the Convention Form of Life Insurance Statement." Unpublished doctoral dissertation, University of Pennsylvania, 1949.

"Valuation Procedures." Minutes of meeting of the Subcommittee on Valuation of Securities of the National Association of Insurance Commissioners, May 28, 1969.

Wolf, Herbert S. "Adjusted Accounting for Life Insurance Companies." Comments prepared for client managements, August, 1970. (Mimeographed.)

INTERVIEWS

Alper, M. L. New York, January 9, 1973; March 14, 1973.

Alpert, Alvin. New York, June 25, 1969; December 9, 1970.

Amos, William W. New York, January 30, 1969.

Anderson, James C. H. San Francisco, January 5, 1972; Atlanta, May 17, 1972; July 21, 1973.

Arenberg, J. T. New York, October 15, 1969; San Francisco, April 14, 1970; Chicago, June 3, 1970; March 27, 1971.

Arnold, Carl. Chattanooga, June 30, 1969.

Bagwell, James. Springfield, Mass., December 28, 1972; May 25, 1973.

Baldwin, William. Hamilton, January 23, 1973.

Barnhart, Lyle. Dallas, August 17, 1970.

Barr, Andrew. San Francisco, August 11, 1965; Washington, D.C., June 27, 1969.

Bartlett, Dwight. San Francisco, April 16, 1970.

Barton, G. S. San Francisco, July 28, 1970; August 14, 1970; January 6, 1971; April 6, 1971.

Beasley, Thomas. Des Moines, November 22, 1971; Cleveland, October 2, 1972.

Beers, Josephine. Los Angeles, September 15, 1971.

Belth, Joseph. Chicago, August 20, 1972.

Bellis, Gordon. San Francisco, September 20, 1970.

Bierschbach, R. A. Los Angeles, September 24, 1969; San Francisco, October 31, 1969; Denver, November 9, 1970; Los Angeles, January 20, 1971; February 12, 1971.

Biekel, Stephen. Houston, July 2, 1969; April 7, 1970.

Blazer, Barry L. New York, June 26, 1969; Denver, November 8, 1970; San Francisco, November 30, 1970.

Bloch, Lawrence. Washington, D.C., June 27, 1969.

Boe, Edmund. New York, January 29, 1969.

Bonnard, Fernand. Chattanooga, June 29, 1969.

Bourdeau, Paul. Des Moines, June 3, 1971; Miami, October 23, 1972.

Bowles, Thomas. Atlanta, July 1, 1969; San Francisco, October 14, 1970.

Bragg, John M. Miami, October 23, 1972; Atlanta, July 30, 1973.

Brodie, Norman. New York, December 11, 1970; New York, December 16, 1970; Des Moines, June 3, 1971; New York, December 6, 1972; January 2, 1973; March 24, 1973; July 1, 1973.

Brown, Robert. Denver, October 22, 1970.

Chapman, Peter. Baltimore, June 18, 1970; Denver, November 8, 1970.

Clark, Alex. New York, January 23, 1969; San Francisco, April 14, 1971.

Clement, Donald. Springfield, Mass., May 25, 1973; Atlanta, July 21, 1973.

Clennon, Barton H. Seattle, January 21, 1970; May 8, 1970; San Francisco, July 10, 1970; July 15, 1970; Seattle, October 16, 1970; Denver, November 9, 1970; San Francisco, March 11, 1971; Des Moines, June 3, 1971; New York, January 2, 1973; San Francisco, February 2, 1973.

Cody, Donald D. Denver, November 11, 1970; Boston, December 15, 1970; Boston, February 28, 1973.

Cohn, Howard T. Miami, October 23, 1972; New York, January 9, 1973.

Colles, A. R. Los Angeles, September 24, 1969; San Francisco, June 23, 1970; October 15, 1970; October 24, 1970; Los Angeles, January 20, 1971; February 12, 1971; Des Moines, June 3, 1971; New York, March 14, 1973.

Colton, Edward. New York, December 7, 1970; November 20, 1972.

Conklin, Harvey. Richmond, February 19, 1973.

Corbett, Gary. Seattle, January 23, 1970; San Francisco, April 14, 1970; Seattle, May 8, 1970; Chicago, June 4, 1970; Toronto, June 8, 1970; San Francisco, October 23, 1970; Denver, November 11, 1970; Atlanta, March 25, 1971; Des Moines, June 3, 1971; Miami, October 23, 1972; New York, January 11, 1973; March 22, 1973.

Cragoe, Arthur. Springfield, Illinois, June 18, 1969; April 28, 1971.

Crandall, Harold. Denver, November 10, 1969; Los Angeles, August 14, 1970; January 6, 1971; April 5, 1971.

Cullen, Charles. Boston, November 16, 1971.

Cushman, Allerton. New York, January 28, 1969; San Francisco, September 30, 1970.

Daly, Brian. Philadelphia, June 10, 1970.

Davidson, James. Seattle, October 15, 1970.

Davidson, Waid. Houston, April 7, 1970.

Deatsch, William. Sacramento, December 19, 1969.

Delaney, Andrew. Houston, July 2, 1969; April 7, 1970; San Francisco, April 14, 1970; Boston, November 27, 1972.

De Moss, Arthur. San Francisco, March 20, 1972.

Depolo, Gary. San Francisco, October 24, 1969; November 5, 1969; June 24, 1970.

Dickerson, Lamar. Atlanta, March 23, 1970; Dallas, June 19, 1970; August 18, 1970.

Diman, William. Boston, June 23, 1969; December 15, 1970; October 31, 1972.

Driscoll, Robert. New York, June 26, 1969.

Engstrom, Lloyd. Denver, October 22, 1970.

Espie, Robert. Hartford, June 21, 1969; Denver, November 11, 1970; Hartford, December 14, 1970.

Farley, Jarvis. San Francisco, April 14, 1970; Chicago, June 3, 1970.

Fee, Thomas. Toronto, June 9, 1970.

Finkel, Paul. New York, December 13, 1972; Hamilton, December 21, 1972; January 23, 1973; Atlanta, July 30, 1973.

Flournoy, Selwyn. Richmond, February 19, 1973.

Galban, Leandro S. New York, January 30, 1969.

Garber, Harry. New York, December 6, 1972; January 2, 1973.

Gliss, William. New York, January 22, 1969.

Gold, Melvin. Montclair, New Jersey, January 27, 1969; New York, December 19, 1970; January 3, 1973; March 28, 1973.

Goldberg, Alan. Atlanta, March 23, 1970; Chicago, June 4,

1970; Baltimore, Dallas, August 18, 1970; Des Moines, June 3, 1971.

Goldston, Harold. Richmond, February 19, 1972.

Goodfriend, Herbert. New York, January 29, 1969.

Greenberg, Herbert. Denver, October 22, 1970; November 12, 1970.

Groth, A. O. Des Moines, June 2, 1970.

Gustafson, Dale. San Francisco, February 14, 1969; Chicago, June 19, 1970; Des Moines, June 3, 1971; Chicago, August 21, 1972.

Hahn, Joseph. Houston, July 2, 1969.

Hammersla, W. D. Seattle, January 23, 1970.

Henss, John. San Francisco, April 14, 1970.

Hill, Frederick. San Francisco, January 10, 1969; March 7, 1969; October 23, 1969; April 16, 1970; Seattle, October 15, 1970; San Francisco, April 9, 1971; New York, November 12, 1972; March 22, 1973.

Hill, L. L. Des Moines, June 2, 1970; Cleveland, October 2, 1972.

Hochstadt, David. Newark, August 15, 1972; New York, March 20, 1973.

Hollenback, John. Sacramento, August 15, 1969; September 16, 1969; December 19, 1969; Atlanta, March 23, 1970; Toronto, June 9, 1970; Dallas, August 17, 1970; Des Moines, June 4, 1971; Sacramento, August 11, 1972.

Horn, Richard. Denver, October 22, 1970; March 30, 1972; Chicago, August 22, 1972.

Horn, Vincent. Denver, October 22, 1970.

Imus, Harry. Atlanta, March 23, 1970; Des Moines, June 1, 1970; Dallas, August 17, 1970.

Johnson, Glendon E. Houston, July 2, 1969.

Johnson, H. Clay. Chattanooga, June 30, 1969.

Johnson, Robert. San Francisco, March 5, 1969.

Johnston, Lynn. Atlanta, June 26, 1972.

Kadoyama, Mitsuru. Des Moines, June 2, 1971; Los Angeles, January 18, 1972.

Karp, Ronald. New York, March 20, 1973.

Kellogg, C. Burton. Morristown, New Jersey, January 27, 1969.

Kent, Morton. Chattanooga, June 29, 1969.

King, Frank. Denver, October 22, 1970; November 12, 1970.

Kirkpatrick, J. C. Chattanooga, June 29, 1969.

Knies, Paul H. San Francisco, October 25, 1970; New York, December 7, 1970; Des Moines, June 3, 1971; New York, November 20, 1972; January 5, 1973.

Kramer, Donald. New York, January 21, 1969.

Kristoff, Frank. Louisville, April 26, 1971; January 13, 1973.

Krowitz, Murray. New York, December 9, 1970.

Lake, Meno T. Los Angeles, September 24, 1969; Chicago, June 4, 1970; San Francisco, June 23, 1970; Denver, November 9, 1970; Des Moines, June 3, 1971; New York, March 14, 1973.

Lamb, James. Denver, November 9, 1970; Los Angeles, January 20, 1971; February 12, 1971; Des Moines, June 3, 1971.

Leong, Leonard. San Francisco, December 19, 1968.

Lewis, William. Fort Wayne, June 17, 1969; December 18, 1970; Miami, October 23, 1972.

Llorens, Hector. New York, January 28, 1969.

McCarty, R. W. Los Angeles, September 16, 1971.

McClean, Donald. Seattle, October 15, 1970.

Matz, Edward. Boston, October 31, 1972.

Mayeda, E. H. San Francisco, December 30, 1969.

Miller, Richard. Dallas, June 19, 1970.

Milliman, Wendell. Seattle, October 16, 1970.

Mitchell, Lawrence. San Francisco, January 9, 1969; Los Angeles, February 17, 1971; San Francisco, July 29, 1971; Los Angeles, January 18, 1972.

Mittelman, Jonas. San Francisco, May 10, 1971.

Moore, James. Newark, December 16, 1970.

Morton, James. Boston, June 24, 1969.

Murphy, Cecil. Dallas, June 19, 1970.

Murphy, J. P. Des Moines, June 2, 1970.

Nagle, William. Atlanta, March 23, 1970; Philadelphia, June 10, 1970.

Newton, Theodore. New York, January 31, 1969; Dallas, August 17, 1970; Des Moines, November 22, 1971; New York, June 26, 1973.

Nicol, W. K. San Francisco, April 14, 1970; Chicago, June 4, 1970; Denver, November 11, 1970; Atlanta, March 25, 1971; San Francisco, April 1, 1971.

Niles, Ralph. Los Angeles, January 26, 1971; San Francisco, January 27, 1971.

Noback, Joseph. Denver, November 10, 1970.

November, William J. Denver, November 9, 1970; New York, December 9, 1970.

Odell, W. H. Chicago, October 16, 1972.

O'Leary, George. Dallas, August 17, 1970.

Olshen, A. C. San Francisco, April 16, 1970.

Page, H. Clifford. Atlanta, March 23, 1970; New York, June 12, 1970.

Pharr, Joe B. Des Moines, June 3, 1971; Atlanta, May 17, 1972; Miami, October 24, 1972.

Pinola, Richard. Philadelphia, June 10, 1970.

Porter, Jay. Seattle, October 14, 1970; August 2, 1971.

Postle, Robert. Sacramento, December 19, 1969.

Powell, Robert N. Sacramento, August 11, 1969; Des Moines, June 2, 1971.

Pugmire, Robert. Seattle, October 16, 1970.

Ramsey, Henry. Philadelphia, June 10, 1970; Dallas, August 17, 1970; San Francisco, October 27, 1970; New York, October 13, 1972; Miami, October 23, 1972.

Rice, James. Denver, October 22, 1970.

Richards, Alan. San Francisco, November 23, 1970; Des Moines, June 1, 1971.

Richards, R. H. Des Moines, June 2, 1970.

Rickards, C. E. Philadelphia, June 10, 1970.

Robertson, Alex. Denver, October 22, 1970.

Robertson, Carl. Dallas, August 17, 1970.

Robertson, Richard. Fort Wayne, December 18, 1970; Indianapolis, April 2, 1971.

Robertson, Stuart. Seattle, June 16, 1969; January 21, 1970; October 16, 1970; Indianapolis, April 27, 1971.

Rosenberg, Leonard. Denver, November 12, 1970; San Francisco, July 28, 1971.

Ross, Seymour. New York, January 30, 1969.

Ruffing, Regis. Baltimore, June 18, 1970; Dallas, August 17, 1970.

Sahm, William. Boston, November 27, 1972.

Sanders, C. L. Worcester, Massachusetts, June 16, 1970.

Schutz, John. New York, March 28, 1973.

Shelly, George. New York, December 11, 1970; December 16, 1970.

Sherrill, Thomas. Atlanta, July 1, 1969.

Shoemaker, Charles. Denver, October 22, 1970.

Skinner, Jeffrey. Olympia, Wash., October 15, 1970; Denver, November 9, 1970.

Slater, Robert. San Francisco, March 21, 1972.

Smith, Guerdon D. New York, January 21, 1969.

Smith, Powell E. Los Angeles, September 24, 1969.

Smith, William. San Francisco, January 8, 1969.

Speas, R. A. Des Moines, June 1, 1970; November 22, 1971; Cleveland, October 2, 1972.

Stewart, Gathings. Fort Wayne, June 17, 1969; December 18, 1970; Miami, October 23, 1972.

Stonecipher, David. Atlanta, June 27, 1972.

Strickert, Roland. Atlanta, March 23, 1970; Dallas, August 17, 1970; Denver, November 10, 1970; Des Moines, June 3, 1971.

Strong, William. New York, October 16, 1969.

Sutton, W. F. Philadelphia, June 10, 1970.

Symes, George. Dallas, August 17, 1970.

Taylor, Robert. San Francisco, April 16, 1970; October 15, 1971.

Teske, Kenneth. Sacramento, December 19, 1969.

Tillinghast, John. Atlanta, May 17, 1972; London, January 21, 1973.

Tovian, Elizabeth. Hartford, December 14, 1970.

Townsend, Frederick S. Hartford, June 21, 1969; Miami, October 24, 1972; Hartford, May 24, 1973.

Turner, Samuel. Atlanta, July 1, 1969; May 17, 1972; Amsterdam, January 19, 1973.

Tuttle, David. New York, January 22, 1969.

Vanselow, A. C. Springfield, Illinois, June 18, 1969.

Wallach, Maximilian. Chicago, October 16, 1972.

Webster, David. San Francisco, April 14, 1970; Denver, November 8, 1970.

Weck, Frank. New York, December 7, 1970.

Whitcomb, Clifford H. San Francisco, October 26, 1970; Newark, December 10, 1970; February 5, 1973.

Wick, Merle. New York, January 29, 1969.

Williams, J. D. Worcester, Massachusetts, June 17, 1970; Portland, Maine, May 7, 1973.

Wilmeth, Harvey. Milwaukee, December 18, 1970.

Winter, Bert A. Newark, December 10, 1970.

Winters, Robert C. Newark, December 10, 1970; Des Moines, June 2, 1971; Miami, October 23, 1972.

Wirth, William. Richmond, February 19, 1973.

Woodson, Benjamin. San Francisco, February 3, 1972.

Yoder, Robert. Louisville, April 26, 1971.

Young, David. Springfield, Mass., December 28, 1972; May 25, 1973.

Znamerowski, Donald. New York, December 13, 1972.

Zunser, Andrew J. B. San Francisco, March 19, 1972; Boston, November 27, 1972.

LETTERS

Anderson, James C. H. September 9, 1966; May 1, 1970; May 12, 1970; August 8, 1973; August 14, 1973.

Arenberg, J. T. July 26, 1966.

Armstrong, David K. November 5, 1970.

Bach, Karl. September 10, 1966.

Bagwell, J. O. September 28, 1972.

Baitler, Simon C. November 13, 1969; November 21, 1969.

Barnes, J. Richard. September 6, 1966.

Barnhart, Lyle H. November 12, 1970.

Barr, Andrew. August 11, 1965.

Bartlett, Dwight K. September 25, 1970.

Belth, Joseph. May 20, 1971.

Bevan, John A. September 7, 1966.

Bierschbach, Raymond A. October 13, 1969; November 21, 1969; January 8, 1970; January 16, 1970.

Bittel, W. Harold. August 31, 1966.

Bleakney, Thomas. September 4, 1966.

Bowles, Thomas P. August 30, 1966.

Braddock, James H. September 7, 1966.

Bragg, John M. June 8, 1971; June 18, 1971; September 27, 1972.

Briggs, Mark. September 12, 1966.

Brodie, Norman. August 19, 1970; November 25, 1970; October 26, 1971.

Brunner, Edward P. October 23, 1970.

Buck, George B. October 13, 1966.

Burus, William R. September 19, 1966.

Bushnell, George A. August 26, 1966.

Campbell, Kenneth. August 29, 1966.

Chapman, Peter F. October 8, 1970; October 16, 1970.

Christian, D. H. September 23, 1966.

Clennon, Barton H. January 26, 1970; March 13, 1970; June 12, 1970; July 6, 1970; July 20, 1970; September 8, 1970; November 21, 1970.

Cody, Donald D. January 22, 1971; April 29, 1971; May 21, 1971; June 3, 1971; July 6, 1971; July 12, 1971; November 3, 1971; April 18, 1972; November 29, 1972; April 18, 1973.

Cody, Frank. October 12, 1966.

Colles, A. R. December 24, 1969; April 14, 1970.

Conklin, Max J. October 3, 1966.

Connor, Paul D. September 2, 1966.

Corbett, Gary. December 22, 1969; January 7, 1970; February 4, 1970; April 22, 1970; May 5, 1970; October 28, 1970; December 18, 1970; February 19, 1971; May 19, 1972; October 31, 1972.

Cullen, Spencer L. September 7, 1966.

Daskais, Richard. September 15, 1966.

Deering, Fred A. September 15, 1966.

Delaney, Andrew. January 8, 1971.

Dobbs, R. H. September 13, 1966.

Drury, G. J. August 31, 1966.

Eagle, E. R. September 2, 1966.

Economon, Gust P. August 30, 1966.

Espie, R. G. August 30, 1966; October 22, 1971; December 5, 1972; October 4, 1973.

Farley, Jarvis. July 2, 1970; October 28, 1971; January 4, 1972; January 28, 1972; March 6, 1972; May 5, 1972; May 10, 1972.

Farmer, Thurston P. August 29, 1966.

Fraser, John C. March 2, 1973.

Gold, Melvin L. September 27, 1966; December 31, 1970.

Goldberg, Alan. October 20, 1970.

Green, Sidney A. September 14, 1966.

Guertin, Alfred N. October 5, 1966.

Guglielmo, Dudley A. September 7, 1966.

Gustafson, Dale R. September 8, 1966.

Hollenback, John. July 28, 1969; November 28, 1969.

Horn, Richard. February 21, 1972; May 24, 1972.

Humphrey, P. L. August 30, 1966.

Humphries, Stanley C. August 6, 1970.

Kellogg, C. Burton. July 1, 1970; January 18, 1971.

Kendall, G. Preston. September 21, 1966.

Klein, Harold C. June 16, 1970.

Knies, Paul H. September 25, 1970; November 2, 1970; March 31, 1971; April 7, 1971; June 10, 1971; July 19, 1971; August 16, 1971; August 18, 1971; October 12, 1971; December 1, 1971; April 19, 1971.

Lake, Meno T. September 14, 1966.

Levy, Michael. August 26, 1966.

Liebtag, E. F. September 28, 1966.

MacRae, Earl. September 6, 1966.

McKee, Lawrence. September 14, 1966.

Marshall, R. E. August 31, 1966.

Mastos, Louis T. August 26, 1966.

Mims, Harnsby. August 25, 1966.

Moscovitch, Nathan. September 6, 1966.

Noback, Joseph C. October 1, 1970; July 14, 1971; March 2, 1973.

November, William J. January 12, 1971; January 28, 1971; March 16, 1971.

Odell, W. H., Jr. April 14, 1972.

O'Leary, George F. August 23, 1970.

Parker, John H. September 7, 1966.

Pharr, Joe B. November 5, 1971.

Pinola, Richard J. June 18, 1970.

Plumley, P. W. November 4, 1966.

Ramsey, Henry B. April 8, 1971; April 29, 1971; January 26, 1972.

Richards, Alan. September 26, 1966.

Rickards, E. E. September 20, 1966.

Robertson, Richard. August 23, 1973; November 5, 1973; May 23, 1974.

Robertson, Stuart. December 3, 1969; June 26, 1969; September 22, 1969; November 25, 1969; January 7, 1970; April 30, 1970; August 26, 1970; October 6, 1970.

Rosenberg, Leonard H. November 23, 1970; December 17, 1970; February 15, 1971.

Sanders, C. L. Various dates.

Sarnoff, Paul E. July 26, 1971; September 23, 1971.

Scott, David. September 16, 1966.

Shelly, George W. December 18, 1970; March 29, 1971.

Singletary, John N. October 3, 1966.

Skinner, Jeffrey S. December 15, 1970.

Smith, Philo. November 9, 1970.

Strong, William H. September 26, 1969.

Taylor, Robert H. October 22, 1970.

Thomas, B. R. September 13, 1966.

Tookey, C. H. September 9, 1966.

Townsend, Frederick S. September 17, 1970; June 7, 1971; July 9, 1971; February 2, 1972; May 3, 1972.

Turner, Samuel. June 14, 1971.

Unrue, John E. September 7, 1966.

Van Cleave, M. E. October 4, 1966.

Van House, Charles L. May 21, 1970; October 7, 1970; November 18, 1970; November 24, 1970; December 31, 1970; January 19, 1971; January 26, 1971; March 3, 1971.

Warren, Donald B. September 7, 1966.

Webb, H. A. September 2, 1966.

Weck, Frank A. January 11, 1971.

Weinstein, Louis. August 31, 1966.

Whitcomb, Clifford H. March 30, 1971; August 16, 1971.

White, William. September 1, 1966.

Whitehorn, Victor. August 26, 1966.

Whiting, D. B. August 25, 1966.

Wilmeth, Harvey D. October 30, 1970; November 6, 1970; January 20, 1971; February 26, 1971; March 2, 1971; January 4, 1972.

Winkle, Gary M. November 13, 1970.

Winters, Robert C. April 13, 1971; August 5, 1971; August 6, 1971; December 27, 1971; January 26, 1972.

Wood, David. February 23, 1972; March 3, 1972; October 5, 1973.

Woodbury, Charles. August 29, 1966.

DOCUMENTS OF THE COMMITTEE ON INSURANCE ACCOUNTING AND AUDITING OF THE AMERICAN INSTITUTE OF CERTIFIED PUBLIC ACCOUNTANTS (HEREINAFTER REFERRED TO AS "CIAA")

"Accounting for Marketable Securities." Position papers from the Symposium on Accounting for Marketable Securities, September 16, 1969.

"Accounting for Marketable Securities." Statement of the American Insurance Association, May, 1970.

"Accounting for Marketable Securities by Insurance Companies." Memorandum submitted to APB Subcommittee on Equity Accounting, February, 1969.

"Application of Generally Accepted Accounting Principles to Mutual Life Insurance Companies." Proposal of Joint LIAA-ALC Committee on Financial Reporting Principles, September 14, 1970. (Mimeographed.)

Arenberg, J. T. Draft of Report of the Acquisition Costs Subcommittee of the CIAA, June, 1968.

_____. Correspondence with T. J. Newton, Jr., July 11, 1968.

_____. Correspondence with R. A. Harden and the CIAA, July 22, 1968.

_____. Correspondence with David G. Scott of the ALC-LIAA Joint Committee on Financial Reporting Principles, April 7, 1969.

_____. Letter replying to F. Greenberg's paper (July 15), July 23, 1969.

_____. Comments regarding the audit of life reserves, October 8, 1969.

_____. Correspondence replying to Paul W. Pinkerton's January 14 letter, January 19, 1970.

_____. Correspondence with Paul W. Pinkerton on amortization of acquisition costs, February 3, 1970.

_____. Correspondence with Paul W. Pinkerton on non-forfeiture values and income recognition, February 4, 1970.

_____. Correspondence giving inventory of the status of the AICPA Life Insurance Audit Guide, February 7, 1970.

_____. Correspondence with Paul W. Pinkerton on income recognition, February 16, 1970.

_____. Correspondence on actuarial assumptions, February 19, 1970.

_____. Correspondence regarding ALC-LIAA participation, May 5, 1970.

_____. Correspondence with J. V. Bencivenga, Manager, Auditing Procedure, American Institute of Certified Public Accountants, May 21, 1970.

_____. Correspondence with J. R. Fritzemeyer, Director of Technical Services Division of the AICPA, regarding proposed Rule 2–06(a), October 2, 1970.

_____. Correspondence with Jarvis Farley, November 4, 1970.

_____. Correspondence on the proceedings of the APB Committee on Marketable Securities and the American Insurance Association Accounting Committee, December 10, 1970.

_____. Correspondence transmitting letters re "joint actuarial committee", February 15, 1971.

"Audits For Life Insurance Companies." Draft, April, 1969.

"Audits of Life Insurance Companies." Exposure draft, December, 1970.

Bencivenga, Joseph V. Correspondence with J. T. Arenberg inquiring re consulting actuaries for the AICPA Committee on Auditing Procedures, February 24, 1970.

CIAA "Letter to SEC re Rule 4–09 of Regulation S–X," August 1, 1967.

CIAA. Correspondence with Theodore J. Newton, Chairman, The Committee on Life Insurance Earnings Adjustments, the Association of Insurance and Financial Analysts, May 20, 1969.

"Consolidated Statements." Draft for the AICPA Life Insurance Guide, May 28, 1969.

Corbett, Gary. Correspondence with P. H. Knies replying to his May 4 letter, May 7, 1970.

Dunn, Bobby F. Draft on special reinsurance agreements for the AICPA Life Insurance Audit Guide, November 11, 1969.

Farley, Jarvis. Transmittal of Andrew Delaney's paper on discounting deferred taxes, July 27, 1970.

_____. Correspondence with J. T. Arenberg reporting on October 5 meeting of the ALC-LIAA Joint Committee on Financial Reporting Principles and the October 9 meeting of the LIAA Board of Directors, October 13, 1970.

_____. Report on the November 16, 1970 meeting of the Subcommittee on Accounting for Participating Insurance, addressed to the ALC–LIAA Joint Committee on Financial Reporting Principles, November 17, 1970.

_____. Correspondence with the ALC-LIAA Joint Committee on Financial Reporting Principles, January 19, 1971.

_____. Correspondence with J. T. Arenberg relaying comments of his joint committee on material points of substance re the exposure draft and related matters, March 3, 1971.

Greenberg, Frank. "Accounting For Marketable Securities by Insurance Companies," July 15, 1969.

_____. Correspondence regarding "Mechanics of Recording Transactions" (Bill Terry), October 26, 1970.

Gruber, George. "Deferred Taxes—Draft." For reporting chapter of the AICPA Life Insurance Audit Guide, December 1, 1968.

Hanley, Thomas R. Correspondence to "all AICPA Committees Drafting Audit Guides" regarding APB decisions on marketable securities and the fund statement, November 9, 1970.

_____. Correspondence regarding Leroy Layton's letter of November 12, 1970 regarding audits of life insurance companies, November 16, 1970.

Harden, R. A. Letter to J. T. Arenberg regarding policy acquisition costs, September 4, 1967.

Harris, Carl. Correspondence giving Paul Knies' views on "GAAP" and mutual companies, May 11, 1970.

_____. Correspondence re AICPA Life Insurance Audit

Guide draft of accounting for variable annuities, October 13, 1970.

Hart, John E. Correspondence regarding funds statements, February 8, 1971.

Henss, John L. Reply to F. Greenberg's paper (July 15), August 11, 1969.

———. Correspondence with Paul W. Pinkerton on adjusted life insurance earnings, February 19, 1970.

———. Correspondence on accounting for attorney-in-fact for a reciprocal insurance exchange, January 8, 1971.

Knies, Paul H. Correspondence with Gary Corbett regarding mutuals, May 4, 1970.

Lynch, Thomas M. Correspondence with the CIAA, August, 1968.

———. "Reserve Strengthening—Draft," December, 1968.

———. Correspondence with J. T. Arenberg, December 30, 1968.

———. "Report on Symposium on Marketable Securities," September 16, 1969.

———. "Reliance Upon Consulting Actuaries," September 25, 1969.

Mackay, A. E. Correspondence with the CIAA, August 28, 1968.

McMillan, R. H. Correspondence with J. T. Arenberg presenting a position paper on catastrophe losses, January 14, 1971.

"Major Changes Proposed in AICPA Audit Guidelines for Financial Reports of Life Insurance Companies," *Insurance Advocate,* January 16, 1971.

"Memorandum on Insurance Accounting Prepared by AICPA Committee on Insurance Accounting and Auditing for Discussion with Representatives of the Life Insurance Industry," April, 1968.

"Minutes" of CIAA Meetings—April 20–21, June 5, September 20, November 13, 1967; April 22, June 10, July 9, September 9–10, December 9, 1968; April 14–15, May 12–13, June 9–10, September 9–10, October 14–15, November 11–12, December 11–12, 1969; March 10–11, April 14–17, May 12–13, June 23–24, July 16, September 15–16, October 13–14, November 10–11, December 7–9, 1970; January 5–6, 1971.

"Minutes of AICPA's SEC Committee." Meeting on insurance matters, March 16, 1970.

N.A.I.C. Valuation Committee. Proposed changes in valuation of common stocks, July 7, 1969.

Norr, David. Correspondence with Robert Hampton regarding funds statement, November 4, 1970.

O'Leary, G. F. Correspondence with Jarvis Farley presenting the views of an ALC-LIAA member, April 28, 1970.

Pastore, Pat. "Reliance Upon Actuaries," October 9, 1969.

Pinkerton, Paul W. "An Approach to Income Recognition by Life Insurance Companies," April 8, 1968.

———. Correspondence with the CIAA, June 4, 1968.

———. Correspondence with the CIAA, July 9, 1968.

———. Correspondence with J. T. Arenberg commenting on April 1968 Memorandum, April 3, 1969.

———. "Consideration To Be Given to Nonforfeiture Provisions," April 8, 1969.

———. Memorandum on the effect of interest on reported profits from life insurance, May 1, 1969.

———. Correspondence regarding the May 14 meeting with representatives of the New York Stock Exchange Department of Stock List, May 22, 1969.

———. Correspondence regarding amortization of acquisition costs and nonforfeiture values, January 14, 1970.

———. Memorandum on GAAP and mutual life companies, January 22, 1970.

———. Correspondence with J. T. Arenberg on nonforfeiture values and income recognition, January 26, 1970.

———. Correspondence with J. T. Arenberg on amortization of acquisition costs, January 27, 1970.

———. Correspondence with J. T. Arenberg on income recognition, February 11, 1970.

———. Correspondence with J. T. Arenberg on timing of income recognition, February 17, 1970.

———. Correspondence with J. T. Arenberg on cash surrender values and reserves, February 23, 1970.

———. Correspondence with J. T. Arenberg, February 27, 1970.

———. "Effect on Changes in Estimates." Memorandum to the CIAA, July 10, 1970.

———. Correspondence regarding revision of the AICPA Life Insurance Audit Guide, December 2, 1970.

"Preliminary Report of Sub-committee on Financial Statement Presentation," November 2, 1970.

"Research Paper on Accounting for New Business Acquisition Costs." Chicago: Arthur Anderson & Co., July 21, 1967. (Internal memorandum.)

Revised drafts of "Nonadmitted Assets" and "Deferred Taxes" Sections of Chapter 6 of the AICPA Life Insurance Audit Guide, January 5, 1970.

Scott, David G. Letter from Joint ALC-LIAA Committee on Financial Reporting Principles to Donald Bevis, August 7, 1967.

Smith, Philo. Correspondence with F. W. Hausmann commenting on the AICPA Life Insurance Exposure Draft, November 25, 1970.

Smythe, William H. L. Correspondence regarding NAIC request for comments on rule change re valuation of subsidiaries, August 6, 1970.

Stewart, Richard C. Correspondence with the CIAA, November 27, 1968.

Terry, William H. "Analysis of 90 Life Insurance Company Annual Reports," August 30, 1968.

———. Correspondence presenting a draft "Mechanics of Recording Transactions" for the AICPA Life Insurance Audit Guide, October 5, 1970.

Waterfield, Randolph H. "Provision For Excess Losses," September 9, 1969.

———. "Reliance Upon Actuaries," September 14, 1969.

———. Correspondence with T. M. Lynch and P. L. Pastore regarding deferred income taxes, January 21, 1971.

———. Correspondence with T. M. Lynch and W. H. Terry regarding a meeting with David Isbell re reliance on actuaries. (n.d.)

List of Tables

CHAPTER 2

1. Summary of Growth of Crazy Quilt Life 1941–1971
2. Summary of Statutory Capital and Surplus Accounts of Crazy Quilt Life, 1961–1971
3. Crazy Quilt Life Organization Chart
4. Life Insurance Protection by Crazy Quilt Life's Agents, 1961–1971
5. Annuity and Health Insurance Production by Crazy Quilt Life's Agents, 1961–1971
6. Group Insurance Production by Crazy Quilt Life, 1956–1971
7. Distribution of Crazy Quilt Life's New Investments and New Money Yields, 1941–1971
8. Portfolio Yield Rates for Crazy Quilt Life, 1941–1971
9. Condensed Statutory Balance Sheet for Crazy Quilt Life at December 31, 1971
10. Condensed Summary of Operations and Statement of Capital and Surplus for Crazy Quilt Life for Year Ended December 31, 1971
11. After-Tax Statutory Gains from Operations for Crazy Quilt Life, 1941–1971
12. Entries to Statutory Unassigned Surplus for Crazy Quilt Life, 1941–1971

CHAPTER 3

1. Asset Share, Reserve, and Asset Share Surplus for Whole Life Policy Issued to Male Age 35—1948–51 Ratebook—per $1,000 Unit
2. Projection of Trial Premium and Assumed Experience for 20–Pay Life Issued to Male Age 45—1970–71 Ratebook per $1,000 of Original Issue
3. Asset Shares, Cash Values, and Reserves for Whole Life Policy Issued to Male Age 45—1948–51 Ratebook—per $1,000 of Insurance in Force
4. Comparison of Mortality Assumed for Renewable Term Policy (Renewable to Age 65) with Mortality Assumed for Whole Life Policy Issued Standard—Male Age 45—1968–69 Ratebook

5. 5-year Renewable and Convertible Term Gross Premiums and Cost of Extra Mortality on Renewal—Male Age 45—1968–69 Ratebook per $1,000 Originally Issued
6. Calculation of Cost Conversion of 5-Year Term Plan to Non-Participating Whole Life Policy at Age 50—1970–71 Ratebook per $1,000 Converted
7. Projection of Trial Premium and Assumed Experience for Male Age 35—1970-71 Ratebook—per $1,000 of Original Issue
8. Original Face Amounts and Insurance in Force for 25-Year Decreasing Term Business
9. Projection of Trial Premium and Assumed Experience for 25-year Convertible Decreasing Term—Composite of All Ages—1970–71 Ratebook—per $1,000 of Original Issue
10. Computation of 15th Year Dividend Illustrated for Participating Whole Life Policy Issued to Male Age 35—1968–69 Ratebook—per $1,000 in Force
11. Dividend Scale Illustrated for Participating Whole Life Policy Issued to Male Age 35—1968–69 Ratebook—per $1,000 in Force
12. Rate Test for Participating Whole Life Policy Issued to Male Age 35—1969–70 Ratebook—per $1,000 Originally Issued
13. Rate Test for Single-Premium Immediate No-Refund Annuity Issued to Male Age 65—1970–71 Ratebook—per Unit ($88.33 Monthly in Annual Income) Issued

CHAPTER 4

1. Present Value of Future Profits and Reported Profits (1) Using Statutory Reserves and (2) Using Adjusted Reserves for Business Issued by Crazy Quilt Life
2. Effect of Statutory Reserves on Adjusted Statements for Crazy Quilt Life

CHAPTER 5

1. Condensed Statements of Operations for the American Experience Block of Business

CHAPTER 6

1. Illustration of Effect of Changing Assumptions vs. Keeping Assumptions Constant—Whole Life Policy Issued to Male Age 35

CHAPTER 7

1. Summary of Crazy Quilt Life's Principal Ordinary Life and Annuity Ratebook Eras and Related Assumptions

2. Array of Ratebook Assumptions for 1948–1961 Issues of 20-year Endowment Policy and Review of Implicit Provisions for Adverse Deviation

3. Illustration of Various Relationships Among Gross Premiums and Valuation Premiums

4. Calculation of Trial Valuation Premium for 20-Year Endowment Policy Issued to Male Age 25—1948-1961 Ratebook

5. Comparison of average Gross Premiums and Trial Valuation Premiums per $1,000 for Crazy Quilt Life—Key Plan-Age Combinations

6. Comparison of Annualized Trial All-Inclusive Valuation Premiums and Annualized Gross Premiums for all Ordinary Life Insurance in Force at December 31, 1971

7. Illustration of Calculation of Valuation Premiums for 5-Year Renewable Term Issued to Male Age 25—1970–71 Ratebook

8. Calculation of Reserve Factors for 1948–61 Ratebook Edition of 20-Year Endowment Policy Issued to Male Age 25—per $1,000 in Force

9. Projection of Expected Book Profits from 1957 to 1977 for 20-Year Endowment Policy 1957 Issue Issued to Male Age 25 Using Proposed Adjusted Reserves—1948–61 Ratebook—per $1,000 Originally Issued

10. Summary of Ordinary Life and Annuity Net Level Statutory Reserves and Adjusted Benefit Reserves for Crazy Quilt Life at December 31, 1971

CHAPTER 8

1. Some Important Mortality Tables

2. Sample Accidental Death Rates per 1,000 Insured Lives from Two Widely-Used Tables

3. Statutory Reserves Classified by Mortality Table for 141 Stock Companies in 1968

4. Sample Assumed Deaths per 1,000 Individuals Insured

5. Sample Annuity Mortality Rates per 1,000 Annuitants

6. Effect of Varying Mortality Rates on Benefit Reserve Valuation Premiums for 1971 Issues of Selected Plans and Ages

7. Effect of Varying Mortality Rates on Benefit Reserve Factors at Selected Durations for 1971 Issues of Selected Plans and Ages

8. Present Values at Issue per $1,000 Originally Issued of Profits, Premiums, and Mortality

9. Selected Withdrawal Tables

10. Effect of Varying Withdrawal Rates on Benefit Reserve Valuation Premiums for 1971 Issues of Selected Plans and Ages

11. Effect of Varying Withdrawal Rates on Benefit Reserve Factors at Selected Durations for 1971 Issues of Selected Plans and Ages

12. Some Comparative Present Values Taking into Account Modified Withdrawal Estimates

CHAPTER 9

1. Effect of Varying Interest Rates on Benefit Reserve Valuation Premiums for 1971 Issues of Selected Plans and Issues—per $1,000

2. Effect of Varying Interest Rates on Benefit Reserve Factors at Selected Durations for 1971 Issues of Selected Plans and Ages

3. Summary of Distribution of Insurance Industry Assets and Liabilities, 1920–1972

4. Insurance Industry Average Interest Rates, 1930–1971

5. Summary of Interest Rates

6. Details of Grading Pattern for Interest Assumptions on Nonparticipating Products

7. Increase in Policy Loans as Percentage of Increase in Total Assets, 1967–1971

CHAPTER 10

1. Condensed Life Insurance Industry Statutory Summary of Operations for 1972

2. Calculation of Interest and Mortality Components of Dividend Scale

3. Details of Adjusted Reserve Calculation Where Dividends are Treated as Benefits

4. Asset Shares Before Loading Contribution, and Asset Shares After Contribution

5. Reserves and Income Statements for Participating 5-Year Endowment

6. Dividend Scale Revision and Effect on Income

7. Effect of Recalculating Reserves to Give Effect to Dividend Scale Revisions

8. Mortality and Interest Contributions to Dividends for 1966 Issues of Par Whole Life—Male Age 35

9. Loading Contribution to Dividends and Resulting Dividends Scale for 1966 Issues of Par Whole Life—Male Age 35

10. Summary of Profit Test per $1,000 Originally Issued for 1966 Issues of Participating Whole Life —Male Age 35

11. Reserves on Participating Business

CHAPTER 11

1. Illustrative Reserve Grading Patterns for 10-Year $1,000 Endowment (Interest Only; Zero Mortality and Withdrawals)

2. Comparison of Effect of Various Reserve Grading Patterns on Reserve Factors for 10-Year Term Policy

3. Comparison of Effect of Various Reserve Grading Patterns on 5% Adjusted Reserve Factors for Selected Ordinary Life Plans

4. Comparison of Effect of Various Grading Patterns on 6% Adjusted Reserve Factors for Single-Premium Immediate Annuities

5. Comparison of Effect of Various Reserve Grading Patterns on Crazy Quilt Life Adjusted Reserve Factors for Selected 1970–71 Ordinary Life Issues

6. Comparison of Effect of Various Reserve Grading Patterns on Crazy Quilt Life Adjusted Reserve Factors for 1970–71 Issues of Participating Whole Life

7. Comparison of Effect of Various Reserve Grading Patterns on Crazy Quilt Life Adjusted Factors for 1970–71 Term Issues

8. Comparison of Effect of Various Reserve Grading Patterns on Crazy Quilt Life Adjusted Reserve Factors for Selected Issues of Prior Years

9. Comparative Statutory and Adjusted Benefit Reserves at December 31, 1971

10. Changes in Comparative Statutory and Adjusted Benefit Reserves in 1971

11. 1971 Reserves and Reserve Changes for Different Grading Patterns for Selected Issues of Selected Years

12. Reserve Changes for Different Grading Patterns for All Ordinary Life Issues of Selected Years

13. Reserves and Reserve Changes for Different Grading Patterns for Selected Issues of All Years

14. Projection of Reserve Changes for Different Grading Patterns for Business in Force at December 31, 1971

15. Statutory and Adjusted Reserves for Two Supplemental Benefit Coverages

CHAPTER 12

1. Accumulation of Benefit Reserve Fund per $1,000 Issued and Calculation of Intermediate Benefit Reserve Factors Through Second Policy Year for Annual-Premium Case

2. Accumulation of Benefit Reserve Fund per $1,000 Issued and Calculation of Intermediate Benefit Reserve Factors Through Second Policy Year for Monthly-Premium Case

3. Accumulation of Expense Reserve Fund per $1,000 Issued and Calculation of Intermediate Expense Reserve Factors Through Second Policy Year Annual-Premium Case

CHAPTER 13

1. Schematic Flow of Functional Cost Data and Derivation of a Functional Cost

2. Condensed Summary of 1971 Expense Data for Crazy Quilt Life Based on Statutory Classifications of Expense

3. Summary of 1971 General Expenses of Crazy Quilt Life in the LOMA Format

4. Crazy Quilt Life's 1971 Functional Costs and Comparative Functional Costs of Selected Companies

5. Summary of Crazy Quilt Life's 1971 Functional Acquisition Costs in Format Used for Ratemaking

CHAPTER 14

1. Various Cost/Volume Relationships

2. Effect of Annualized Commission on Deferred Acquisition Costs Under (1) Agent's Balance Approach and (2) Immediate Charge-Off Approach

3. Illustration of Effect of "Leveling" All Commissions

4. Illustration of Effect of Accruing All Future Commissions at Time of Sale

5. Illustration of Effect of Agent Termination and Vesting Provisions on Effective Renewal Commission Rate

6. Illustrative Computation of Present Value of First-Year Acquisition Costs and Renewal-Year Commissions

CHAPTER 15

1. Summary of Expenses Allocated to Ordinary Life Lines of Business in Crazy Quilt's 1971 Convention Statement

2. Summary of First-Year Commissions in Excess of Commissions Payable at "Ultimate" Rate

3. Reconciliation of New Business Functional Costs with Total of General Insurance Expenses for Ordinary Line of Business

4. 1971 Commissions and Commissions Equivalents Deemed to Relate Primarily to Production

5. Details of Selling Functional Costs

6. Details of Adjustments Required to Derive 1971 Deferrable Sales Support Costs

7. Summary of 1971 Costs Deemed to Relate Primarily to Production—Ordinary Life Basic Plans

8. Costs Primarily Related to Production and New Business Volume for Ordinary Life Basic Plans, 1941–1971

9. Renewal-Year Acquisition Cost Commissions and Commission Equivalents Incurred in 1971

10. Renewal-Year Acquisition Costs Incurred 1941-1971

11. Comparison of Actual vs. Estimated Deferrals of Commissions and Commission Equivalents

12. Development of Estimated Deferrable First-Year Costs for Prior Years

13. Allocation of 1971 Acquisition Costs Between Permanent and Term, in Bulk

14. Computation of Percentages to be Applied to Ratebook Acquisition Cost Factors to Derive Deferrable Acquisition Cost Factors

15. Adjustment of Ratebook Nonacquisition Cost Factors to Obtain 1971 Deferrable Acquisition Cost Factors

16. Summary of 1971 Acquisition Costs After Allocation of Factors to Individual Plans

CHAPTER 16

1. Comparative Acquisition Cost Factors for 1971 Issues—Selected Plans (Age 35), Durations and Interest Rates

2. Summary of Acquisition Costs after Amortizing With and Without Interest

3. Development of Amortization Table for First-Year Acquisition Costs for 1971 Issues of 20-Pay Life—Excluding Interest

4. Development of Amortization Table for First-Year Acquisition Costs for 1971 Issues of 20-Pay Life—Recognizing Interest at 5%

5. Summary of Effect of Interest on Amortization of First-Year Acquisition Costs on 1971 Issues of 20-Pay Life

6. Modification of Amortization Table to Recognize Projected Renewal-Year Acquisition Costs—Excluding Interest

7. Modification of Amortization Table to Recognize Projected Renewal-Year Acquisition Costs—Recognizing Interest at 5%

8. Development of Estimated Amortization Rates for Issues of 1955

9. Summary Worksheet for Unamortized Acquisition Costs—Recognizing Interest and Renewal-Year Acquisition Costs

10. Effect of Varying Withdrawal Rates on Acquisition Cost Factors at Selected Durations for 1971 Issues (Age 35) of Selected Plans

11. Effect of Varying Mortality Rates on Acquisition Cost Factors at Selected Durations for 1971 Issues (Age 35) of Selected Plans

12. Percentages of First-Year Acquisition Costs Remaining Unamortized for Selected Plans, Years of Issue, and Durations—Ignoring Interest

13. Summary of Unamortized Balances of Acquisition Costs at December 31, 1971 Using Various Amortization Techniques

14. Decreases and (Increases) in Unamortized Balances of Acquisition Costs in 1971 Using Various Amortization Techniques

CHAPTER 17

1. Summary of Development Costs Applicable to Ordinary Line of Business, 1941–1971

2. Maintenance and Settlement Cost Reserves for Ordinary Plans

3. Effect of Varying Interest Rates on Maintenance and Settlement Cost Reserve Factors at Selected Durations for 1971 Issues (Age 35) of Selected Plans

4. Effect of Varying Withdrawal Rates on Maintenance Cost Reserve Factors at Selected Durations for 1971 Issues (Age 35) of Selected Plans

5. Effect of Inflation on Maintenance and Settlement Costs on 1971 Issues (Age 35) of 20-Pay Life

6. Elements of Single-Reserve Factors for Selected Plans (Age 35) at Selected Durations

CHAPTER 18

1. Summary of Principle Provisions of Combination Agents Contracts, 1941–1971

2. Assumed Industrial Mortality—Deaths per 1,000 Insured

3. Assumed Industrial Withdrawal Rates 1948–1971

4. Cash Values and Assumed Weighted Cost of Nonforfeiture Benefits for 1970–71 Issues of Industrial 20-Pay Life—per $1,000 of Insurance

5. Expense Assumptions for 1970-71 Issues of Industrial 20-Pay Life

6. Summary of Industrial Adjusted Reserve Assumptions

7. Statutory Reserves and Adjusted Benefit Reserves per $1,000 in Force for Industrial 20-Pay Life Policies—1970–71 Issues

8. Various Grading Patterns for Adjusted Benefit Reserves for Industrial 20-Pay Life Factors—1970–71 Issues—per $1,000 In Force

9. Effect of Grading on Adjusted Reserve Levels and Changes in Selected Financial Reporting Years—Industrial 20-Pay Life

10. Calculations of 1971 Deferrable Acquisition Costs for Industrial Line of Business

11. Selected Acquisition Cost Valuation Premiums and Factors for 1971 Issues of Industrial 20-Pay Life—per $1,000 In Force

12. Industrial Acquisition Costs Deferred and Amortized, 1941–1971

13. Maintenance and Settlement Reserves on Industrial 20-Pay Life

CHAPTER 19

1. Summary of Experience of Commercial Health Lines for Crazy Quilt Life 1960–1971

2. Pricing Assumptions for Noncancellable Disability Income Policy to Age 65 Issued to Male Age 45—2-Year Sickness, Lifetime Accident, 30-Day Elimination—1963 and 1970 Ratebooks

3. Disability Income Claim Cost Assumptions Associated with 1969 Morbidity Study

4. Profit Projection for Disability Income Policy Issued to Male Age 45—1970 Ratebook—per Unit of $100 Monthly Issued

5. Pre-Tax Impact on Statutory Summary of Operations of Disability Income Policy Issued to Male Age 45—1970 Ratebook—per Unit of $100 Monthly Issued

6. Disability Income Reserves for Male Age 35 Under 3 Different Claim Cost Assumptions—All Other Assumptions Held Constant

7. Net Level Adjusted Mid-Terminal Benefit Reserves Computed With and Without Interest—Noncancellable Disability Income Policy—1970 Ratebook

8. Summary of Calculation of Benefit Valuation Premiums on Two Bases—Noncancellable Disability Income Policy Issued to Male Age 45—1970 Ratebook

9. Calculation of First Two Benefit Reserve Factors on Two Bases—Noncancellable Disability Income Policy Issued to Male Age 45—1970 Ratebook

10. Selected Reserve Grading Patterns for Noncancellable Disability Income Policy

11. Ratios of Adjusted Benefit Reserves to Statutory Net Level Reserves for 3 Disability Income Plans of a Major Company

12. Benefit and Related Reserves on Various Bases for Noncancellable Disability Income Insurance Issued 1963–1971

13. 1971 Noncancellable Health Insurance First-Year Func-

tional Costs in Actuarial Format and Adjustments Required to Obtain Deferrable Amounts

14. Computation of Acquisition Cost Valuation Premiums and First Two Reserve Factors on Two Bases for Disability Income Policy Issued to Male Age 45—1970 Ratebook

15. Summary Worksheet for Amortizing First-Year and Renewal Acquisition Costs with Interest in Terms of Percentages Applied to First-Year Costs—Noncancellable Disability Income Issues, 1963–1971

16. Sum-of-the-Years' Premiums Amortization Rates for Disability Income Policy Composite on Cash Premium Basis and Earned Premium Basis

17. Comparative Unamortized Acquisition Costs for Noncancellable Disability Income Insurance Issued 1963–1971—Assuming Unearned Premiums are Held

18. Unit Claims Handling and Maintenance Expense Reserves for Noncancellable Disability Income Policy

19. Maintenance Expense Reserves for Noncancellable Disability Income Policy Under Selected Grading Patterns (Assuming Separate Unearned Premiums Are Held)

20. Comparison of Intermediate and Mid-Terminal Reserves per Unit of $100 Monthly Income for Noncancellable Income Policy—1970 Ratebook

21. Unearned Gross Premiums and Unearned Valuation Premiums for Noncancellable Disability Income Business, 1963–1971

22. Estimation of Unearned Valuation Premiums for Noncancellable Disability Income Business at December 31, 1971

CHAPTER 20

1. Comparison of Exposure (Measured by Outstanding Loan Balance) with Rule-of-78 and Modified Pro-Rata Earned Premium Patterns

2. Summary of Assumed Credit Insurance Experience Expressed in Terms of $1,000 of Single Premium Originally Issued—Aggregates for 24-Month Contracts—Auto Dealer/Personal Property Broker Type Business

3. Credit Life Cash Transactions and Statutory Pre-Tax Earnings per $1,000 of Single Premium Originally Issued—Auto Dealer/Personal Property Broker Type Business

4. Pure Casualty Approach—Credit Life Business—Auto Dealer/Personal Property Type—per $1,000 Single Premium Originally Issued

5. Credit Health Cash Transactions and Statutory Pre-Tax Earnings per $1,000 of Single Premium Originally Issued —Auto Dealer/Personal Property Broker Type Business

6. Pure Casualty Approach—Credit Health Business—Auto Dealer/Personal Property Broker Type—per $1,000 Single Premium Originally Issued

7. Summary of Assumed Credit Insurance Experience—Expressed in Terms of $1,000 of Single Premium Originally Issued—Aggregates for 24-Month Contracts—Bank Type Business

8. Credit Life Cash Transactions and Statutory Pre-Tax Income per $1,000 of Single Premium Issued—Bank Type Business

9. Pure Casualty Approach—Credit Life Business—Bank Type—per $1,000 Single Premium Originally Issued

10. Credit Health Cash Transactions and Statutory Pre-Tax Income—per $1,000 of Single Premium Originally Issued—Bank Type Business

11. Pure Casualty Approach—Credit Health Business—Bank Type—per $1,000 Single Premium Originally Issued

12. Coinsurance Ceded—Credit Health—Auto Dealer/Personal Property Broker Type Business—per $1,000 of Premium Originally Ceded

15. Coinsurance Ceded—Credit Life—Auto Dealer/Personal Property Broker Type Business—per $1,000 Single Premium Originally Ceded

14. Summary of Crazy Quilt Life's Credit Insurance Underwriting Experience for Auto Dealer/Personal Property Type Business, 1968–1971

15. Summary of Crazy Quilt Life's Credit Insurance Experience for Bank Type Business, 1968–1971

16. Details of Experience Rating for Retention Case No. 1, 1965–1971

17. Details of Experience Rating for Retention Case No. 2 for Selected Years

18. Summary of Experience on Group Retention Business, 1962–1971

19. Summary of Crazy Quilt Life's Pooled Group Experience, 1961–1971

20. Deferral and Amortization (5-Year Sum-of-the-Years'-Digits) of Acquisition Costs for Pooled Group Insurance, 1961–1971

21. Policyholders Memorandum Accounts for Immediate Participation Group Annuity Case and Related Financial Statement Effects in 1971

22. Policyholder Memorandum Accounts for Deposit Administration Group Annuity Case and Related Financial Statement Effects in 1971

CHAPTER 21

1. Operation of Crazy Quilt Life's Variable Annuity Separate Account, 1968–1971

2. Deferral and Amortization of Variable Annuity Acquisition Costs

3. Schematic Representation of Variable Life Transactions in General Account and Separate Account

4. General Account and Separate Account Transactions in Selected Years for $100,000 Original Amount of Participating Variable Whole Life Insurance Issued to Male Age 35

5. General Account Transaction (Assuming Zero General Account Interest) Under Varying Separate Account Yield Rates—per $1,000 Initial Face Amount of Variable Whole Life Issued to Male Age 35

6. Gross Premiums and Valuation Premiums for $1,000 Initial Amount Variable Life Insurance Issued to Male Age 35

7. Progression of General Account Reserves (Assuming

Zero Interest) for $1,000 Variable Whole Life Issued to Male Age 35

8. First Year Adjusted Income Statement for $1,000 Variable Whole Life Issued to Male Age 35

CHAPTER 22

1. Projection of Net YRT Reinsurance Costs per $1,000 of Reinsurance Ceded

2. YRT Reinsurance Premiums, Unearned Gross Premiums, and Statutory Mean Reserves per $1,000 of Reinsurance In Force

3. Coinsurance Proposal for Crazy Quilt Life

4. Illustration of YRT Experience Rating Calculation for One Year

5. Illustration of Coinsurance Experience Rating Calculation for One Year

6. Net Amount at Risk, Gross Reinsurance Premiums, and Projected Mortality Costs—YRT Reinsurance on Whole Life Policy Issued to Male Age 35

7. YRT Reinsurance Reserve Factors on 3 Bases—Age 35

8. Summary of YRT Reinsurance Ceded Transactions and Aggregate YRT Reinsurance Ceded Reserve Offsets on 4 Bases

9. Projected YRT Cash Transactions Including Estimated Refunds per $1,000 of Direct Business in Force

10. Effect of Coinsurance vs. Modified Coinsurance for $10,000,000 Whole Life Business Reinsured by Crazy Quilt Life in 1968 and 1969

11. Accumulation of Refund Premiums and Reinsurer's Experience Rating Accounts for $100,000 in Whole Life Coinsurance—Male Age 35—1968–69 Ratebook

12. Comparison of Cash Values Available on Surrender and Related Reinsurance Reserve Credits—Whole Life, Male Age 35, 1968–69 Ratebook—per $1,000 in Force.

CHAPTER 23

1. Possible Inconsistencies in Relationships Among Gross Premiums, Net Premiums, Direct Expenses, and Deficiency Reserves for 10-Pay Life Policy—Semi-Annual Mode

2. Statutory Deferred and Uncollected Premiums and Cost of Collection in Excess of Loading Thereon at December 31, 1971

3. Deferred and Uncollected Adjusted Reserve Valuation Premiums at December 31, 1971

4. Illustration of Preferred Method of Accounting for First-Year Deferred Premium (Ignoring Interest)

5. Financial Statement Effects of Accounting for First-Year Deferred Premium (Ignoring Interest)

6. Calculation of Adjusted Cost of Collection of Deferred and Uncollected Gross Premiums at December 31, 1971

7. Illustration of Effect of Amortization in Relation to Acquisition Costs Incurred as a Percentage of Premiums

8. Relationship Between Deferred Premiums to be Provided with Respect to Mean Reserves and Unearned Premiums to be Provided with Respect to Mid-Terminal Reserves

9. Comparison of Mean and Mid-Terminal Calculations of the Acquisition Cost Reserve

CHAPTER 25

1. Separation of Statutory Balance Sheet Accounts Between Par and Non-Par Branches at December 31, 1971

2. Separation of Statutory Operating and Surplus Accounts Between Par and Non-Par Branches in 1971

3. History of the Statutory Stockholder Charge Limitation, 1941–1971

4. Projection of Statutory Results for Participating Business In Force at December 31, 1971

5. Calculation of Stockholders' Share of Adjusted Par Surplus on 2 Bases at December 31, 1971

6. Illustrations of Methods of Accounting for Various Types of Restrictions

7. Par Net Gain and Surplus Components Under Varying Reserve Approaches, 1941–1971

8. Illustration of Timing Difference Problems Caused by Shifting Stockholder Charge Modes

9. Minority Interest Method of Recognizing Participating Policyholders' Interest in Income for Year Ended December 31, 1971

CHAPTER 26

1. Tax Calculations Under Three Different Situations

2. Illustration of Operation of Limits on Special Deductions Under Three Different Sets of Circumstances

3. Condensed 1971 Tax Return Calculations for Crazy Quilt Life

4. Summary Tax Calculations for Crazy Quilt Life, 1958–1971

5. Simplified Example of With-and-Without Calculation of Deferred Taxes

6. Illustration of Categories of Taxation as Defined by the Life Insurance Audit Guide

7. Taxable Income Under Several Different Situations

8. Illustrations of Impact of Future-Category Assumption

9. Illustration of Operation Loss Carryback and Carryforward Provisions

10. Comparison of Net Changes and Gross Change Method for Crazy Quilt Life

11. Deferred Taxes by the Net Change Method for Crazy Quilt Life, 1958–1971

12. Deferred Taxes by the Gross Change Method for Crazy Quilt Life, 1958–1971

13. Amortization of Originating Deferred Taxes Under the Gross Change Method

CHAPTER 27

1. Earnings, Market Values, and Acquisition Price (as of January 1, 1971) of McCabe Life

2. McCabe's Balance Sheet at December 31, 1970

3. Valuation of Investments of McCabe Life at January 1, 1971

List of Tables

4. McCabe Life's Reserve Liabilities on Three Bases as of January 1, 1971

5. Computation of Value (as of January 1, 1971) of McCabe Life's Insurance In Force

6. Amortization of Present Value of Future Statutory Profits of McCabe's Life Insurance In Force at January 1, 1971

7. Amortization with 4% Interest of Residual Acquisition Cost of McCabe's Life Insurance In Force

8. Computation of Value of McCabe Life's Agency Plant at January 1, 1971

9. Allocation of Purchase Price of McCabe Life, Computation of Charge to Crazy Quilt's Surplus, and Recording the Purchase as of January 1, 1971

10. Recording the Purchase of McCabe Life for Consolidation Purposes on January 1, 1971

11. McCabe Life's 1971 Income Statements Segregated Between Business Acquired in Purchase and New Business

CHAPTER 28

1. Timetable for Initial Conversation to Generally Accepted Accounting Principles

2. Diagram of a Reserve Model

3. Validation of a Reserve Model for Ordinary Life as Performed by a Medium-Sized Company in Connection with a 1973 Conversion

4. Reconciliation of Statutory and Adjusted Amounts for Crazy Quilt Life at December 31, 1971

5. Condensed Statutory and Adjusted Balance Sheets for Crazy Quilt Life at December 31, 1971

6. Condensed Statutory and Adjusted Statements of Operations and Retained Earnings for Year Ended December 31, 1971

CHAPTER 31

1. Mini-Quiz for Insurance Stock Analysts

2. New Business Interest Rate Assumptions for 30 Companies

3. Crazy Quilt Life's 1971 Adjusted Results by Line of Business

4. Pre-Tax GAAP Operating Income (Excluding Interest on Capital) as a Percentage of Premiums for 28 Companies in 1972

5. Pre-Tax GAAP Return on Equity for 29 Companies in 1972

6. Comparative Pre-Tax Results for Ordinary Life Model

7. Comparison of 1972 GAAP and AIFA Earnings for 31 Companies

APPENDIX A

1. Summary of Assumptions Underlying Illustrations of Present Values, etc., for a 20-Year Endowment Policy Issued to a Male Age 25

2. Calculation of Statutory Net Premiums (1941 CSO, 2 1/2%) for a 20-Year Endowment Policy Issued to a Male Age 25

3. Progression of a Net Level Statutory Reserve (1941 CSO, 2 1/2%) for a 20-Year Endowment Policy Issued to a Male Age 25

4. Calculation of Statutory Net Level Mean Reserves (1941 CSO, 2 1/2%) for a 20-Year Endowment Policy Issued to a Male Age 25

5. Calculation of CRVM Net Premiums (1941 CSO, 2 1/2%) for a 20-Year Endowment Policy Issued to a Male Age 25

6. Progression of a CRVM Statutory Reserve (1941 CSO, 2 1/2%) for a 30-Year Endowment Policy Issued to a Male Age 25

7. Calculation of Adjusted Premiums (1941 CSO, 2 1/2%) for a 20-Year Endowment Policy Issued to a Male Age 25

8. Progression of Cash Values (1941 CSO, 2 1/2%) for a 20-Year Endowment Policy Issued to a Male Age 25

9. Pattern of Assumed Deaths, Surrenders, and Maturities for a 20-Year Endowment Policy Issued to a Male Age 25

10. Present Value of Assumed Cash Flow for a 20-Year Endowment Policy Issued to a Male Age 25

11. Asset Shares for a 20-Year Endowment Policy Issued to a Male Age 25

12. Calculations of $1 Annuity Due that Contemplates Deaths, Surrenders, and Interest for a 20-Year Endowment Policy Issued to a Male Age 25

13. Present Value of a $1 Premium for a 20-Year Endowment Policy Issued to a Male Age 25

14. Progression of an Intermediate Natural Reserve for a 20-Year Endowment Policy Issued to a Male Age 25

15. Intermediate Natural Reserve Factors for a 20-Year Endowment Policy Issued to a Male Age 25

16. Interest (at 3%) on Natural Reserve and Reserve Increases for a 20-Year Endowment Policy Issued to a Male Age 25

17. Present Value at 3% and 12% of Book Profits (Using Natural Reserves) on a 20-Year Endowment Policy Issued to a Male Age 25

18. Present Value at 12% of Future Book Profits (Using Statutory Net Level Reserves) on a 20-Year Endowment Policy Issued to a Male Age 25

19. Progression of Present Value (at 3% of Future Book Profits (Natural Reserve Basis) on a 20-Year Endowment Policy Issued to a Male Age 25

20. Gross Premium Reserve Factors for a 20-Year Endowment Policy Issued to a Male Age 25

APPENDIX B

1. Source Data for Illustrations of Effects of Taxes on Investment Income

2. Illustration of Effect of Taxes on Investment Income on Reserves and Profits Where Company is Taxed on T

3. Illustration of Effect of Conventional Deferred Tax Procedures When Company is Taxed on G

APPENDIX C

1. Comparison of Selected Aggregate Financial Statement Items—"Assumed" vs. "Actual" Experience for Actual Production Volume—All Ordinary Life Plans Combined

2. Aggregate "Assumed" Experience Underlying Premium Assumptions Compared with "Actual" Experience (1) Recorded Through 1971 and (2) Projected to 1980 Based on 1971 Facts—All Ordinary Life Plans Combined —Selected Measurement Items

3. Selected Profit Patterns—All Ordinary Life Plans Combined

4. Selected Profit Patterns—Ordinary Participating Whole Life

5. Selected Profit Patterns—Ordinary Nonparticipating Whole Life

6. Selected Profit Patterns—Ordinary Nonparticipating 20-Pay Life

7. Selected Profit Patterns—Ordinary Nonparticipating 20-Year Endowment

8. Selected Profit Patterns—Ordinary Nonparticipating 5-Year Renewable and Convertible Term

9. Selected Profit Patterns—Ordinary Nonparticipating 25-Year Decreasing Convertible Term

10. Selected Profit Pattern—Ordinary Whole Life Plans Resulting from Term Conversion

11. Selected Profit Patterns—Individual Single-Premium Annuities

12. Selected Profit Patterns—Industrial 20-Pay Life

13. Selected Profit Patterns—Individual Guaranteed Renewable Disability Income

Index

The reader should also scan the detailed table of contents starting at page xiii in searching for references to particular topics.

A

Accidental death benefits, adjusted reserves, 200
Accounting Principles Board:
  Opinion No. 11, 507
  Opioion No. 16, 527
  Opinion No. 17, 316
  Opinion No. 28, 573
Acquisition costs:
  Amortization of—see *Amortization of acquisition costs*
  Composition of:
    Agent stock options, 251
    Agent terminations and vesting, effect of, 254
    Attribution, 246
    Audit guide criteria, 244
    Branch office expenses, 251
    Causality, 246
    Commissions and commission equivalents:
      First-year, 247
      Renewal, 252
    Field clerical expense, 254
    Field supervision expense, 256
    Financing expense, 255
    Finitude, 246
    Fixed costs, 244
    Home office agency administration expense, 254
    Indirect costs, 260
    Inflation, effect of, 244
    Issue costs, 259
    Linear relationships, 244
    Logic, 246
    Mail order solicitation costs, 256
    Measurement bases, 244
    Persistency bonuses, 254
    Precedence in accounting, 246
    Process costing concepts, applicability of, 247
    Recruiting expense, 255
    Salaries to assistant managers, 250
    Salaries to branch managers, 250
    Sales support expenses, 254
    Selection costs, 259
    Selling costs, 247
    Semi-fixed costs, 244
    Semi-variable costs, 244
    Step-cost relationships, 244
    Term renewals, costs of, 271
    Training expense, 255
    Variability, 244
  Deferral of:
    Allocations to blocks of business:
      Principles of, 278
      Reasons for, 276
      Techniques of, 279
    Comparisons of actual and assumed, 285
    Cost accumulation, 273
    Cost analysis, 262
    Income statement format, relationship to, 273
    Recoverability tests, 468
    Renewal year costs, 269
    Variability tests, 268
  Deferred and uncollected premiums, relationship to, 460
  Disclosure, 286
  Group insurance, 401
  Health insurance:
    Commercial forms, 350
    Noncancellable and guaranteed renewable forms, 364
    Return-of-premium business, 377
  Industrial insurance, 344
  Interim statements, 574
  Purchase accounting:
    Determination of acquisition cost, 537
    Negative acquisition cost, 545
  Variable annuities, 408
  Variable life insurance, 416
Actuaries:
  Crazy Quilt Life, 21
  Independent, 579
  Utilization of:
    Audit guide provisions, 578
    Certification of reserves, 579
    Coordination with auditors, 580
    Formulation of reserves, 578
    Guidelines for actuaries, 582
    Letters from actuaries, 581
Adjusted earnings:
  AIFA method, 591
  Dollars-per-thousand method, 590
  Pressure for, 7
Adjusted reserves:
  Disclosure, 109
  Terminology, 91
Administration:
  Conversion administration, 557
  Crazy Quilt Life, 28
Adverse deviation:
  Audit guide references, 71
  Interest, 138
  Interpretation of, 79
  Lock-in, relationship to, 82
  Mortality, 121
  Participating business, 173
  Purchase valuations, 544
  Recoverability tests, 468
  Release-from-risk concept, 73
  Surplus levels, relationship to, 81
  Withdrawals, 131
American Academy of Actuaries:
  Committee on Financial Reporting Principles, 75
  Recommendations:
    Adverse deviation, 76
  Lock-in, 82
    Reinsurance, 426
    Utilization of actuaries, Appendix E, 582
    Valuation premiums, 99
Amortization of acquisition costs:
  Comparison of methods, 309

Development costs, 315
Disclosure, 309
Factor method, 304
Grading, 307
Group insurance, 397
Health insurance, 366
Industrial insurance, 347
Interest on acquisition costs, 290
Nature of, 288
Persistency adjustments, 293
Purchase valuations, 541
Variable annuities, 410
Worksheet methods, 296
Agents and agencies:
  Combination agents, 18
  Development costs, 319
  Evaluation of agents, 594
  Ordinary agents, 17
  Value of agency force, 548
Anderson accumulation approach to
  pricing, 30
Annual reports, 572
Annuities:
  Acquisition cost factors, 307
  Group annuities, 404
  Individual fixed annuities, 47
  Reserve grading, 193
  Revenues, 61
  Single-premium annuities, interest as-
    sumption for, 154
  Variable annuities, 407
Asset share accumulation aproach to
  pricing, 30
Assumptions:
  Crazy Quilt Life, 95
  Dividends, 162
  General, 92
  Health insurance, 357
  Incidence, 201
  Industrial insurance, 337
  Interest, 138
  Maintenance expenses, 320
  Mortality, 112
  Nonforfeiture costs, 132
  Participating business, 172
  Renewal-year acquisition costs, 300
  Restricted participating business, 490
  Settlement expenses, 320
  Variable life insurance, 416
  Withdrawals, 131
Attribution criteria for acquisition costs,
  246, 265
Audit committees, role of in conversion,
  583
Audit guide:
  Acquisition costs, 244
  Actuaries, utilization of, 578
  Adverse deviation, 71
  Amortization of acquisition costs, 293
  Capital gains and losses, 156
  Credit insurance, 381
  Deferred taxes, 506
  Development of, 9
  Disclosure, 572
  Dividends, 159
  Exposure draft of 1970, 9
  Indirect costs, 261
  Interest, 138
  Lock-in, 82

Mortality, 112
Presistency adjustments for acquisi-
  tion costs, 293
Recoverability and loss recognition,
  465
Reinsurance special agreements, 443
Reserve grading, 179
Restricted participating business, 477
Revenue recognition, 60
Valuation premiums, 98
Withdrawals, 131
Audits, independent, 576

B

Benefit reserves—see *Reserves*
Business combinations:
  Consolidation policies, 555
  Disclosure, 556
  Equity method of accounting, 553
  Inter-company relationships, 553
  Mutual company subsidiaries, 555
  Poolings, 527
  Purchases, 530

C

Capital gains and losses, 156
Cash values, 32
Casualty-type business, 68
Categories of tax situations, 509
Claim cost assumptions for health in-
  surance, 357
Claim liabilities for health insurance,
  364
Coinsurance, 435
Combination agents, 18
Commercial health insurance, 349
  General, 349
  Loss recognition, 475
Commissions:
  Acquisition costs, 247
  Cost analysis, 266
Consolidation policies, 555
Contingency reserves:
  Group insurance, 400
  Reinsurance, 446
Continuous-premium intermediate re-
  serves, 206
Convention statement, 4
Conversions:
  Administering a GAAP conversion,
    557
  Term conversions:
    Acquisition costs, 272
    Cost of, 127
Convertibility, 38
Cost accounting:
  Actuarial approaches to, 237
  Basic concepts, 228
  Classification of costs, 230
  Costing objects, 229
  Cost centers, 230
  Functional costs, 232
  Group insurance, 395
  Industrial insurance, 340
  Inventoriable costs, 242
  Maintenance and settlement costs,
    320
  Management uses, 594
Cost accumulation, 273
Cost analysis, 262

Cost in excess of book value, 554
Cost of collection in excess of loading
  on deferred and uncollected pre-
  miums, 450
Cost of collection on adjusted deferred
  and uncollected valuation premi-
  ums, 455
Cost of reinsurance, 429
Cost of term conversions, 127
Cost-volume relationships, 244
Coupons and pure endowments, 177
Crazy Quilt Life, 13
Credit insurance:
  Adverse deviation, 388
  Audit guide provisions, 381
  Coinsurance, 386
  Disclosure, 390
  Level term business, 387
  Outstanding balance business, 387
  Single-premium business, 383
  Statutory reserves, 380
  Types of business, 379

D

Decreasing term insurance, 39
Decrement rates:
  General, 211
  Influence on grading, 181
  Use in recoverability tests, 468
Deferred and uncollected premiums:
  Calculation of, 453
  Cost of collection, 450, 455
  Intermediate reserves, relationship to,
    206
  Mean reserves, relationship to, 453
  Mid-terminal reserves, relationship to,
    462
  Nature of, 449, 451
  Percentage expenses, relationship to,
    462
  Statutory concepts, 449
  Uncollected group premiums, 464
  "When due" provision, relationship
    to, 464
Deferred tax accounting:
  APB Opinion No. 11, 507
  Calculations, 518
  Categories of tax situations, 509
  Changes in facts and circumstances,
    511
  Crazy Quilt Life, 524
  Disclosure, 524
  Grouping of similar transactions, 519
  Individual-transaction approach, 519
  Operations losses, 515
  Policyholders' surplus, 518
  Special deductions, 513
  Timing differences, 507
Deficiencies—see *Loss recognition* and
  Recoverability tests
Deficit in participating surplus, 494
Deposit-type revenue items, 70
Development costs, 315
Disclosure:
  Acquisition costs, 286
  Adjusted reserves, 109
  Amortization, 309
  Business combinations, 556
  Credit insurance, 390
  Deferred taxes, 524

Desirable disclosures, 572
Development costs, 320
Dividends, 177
Health insurance:
  Commercial forms, 352
  Noncancellable forms, 375
  Return-of-premium forms, 378
Industrial insurance, 348
Interest assumptions, 158
Investment expenses, 328
Investment income, 69
Loss recognition, 476
Maintenance and settlement costs, 326
Mortality, 127
Recoverability tests, 472
Reinsurance:
  Assumed, 446
  Normal agreements, 443
  Special agreements, 445
Required disclosures, 572
Reserve grading, 196
Restricted participating business, 495
Term conversions, 131
Variable annuities, 413
Variable life insurance, 422
Withdrawals, 137
Discount rates:
  Present value of profits, 57
  Purchase valuations, 539
Dividends:
  Assumptions, 162
  Audit guide provisions, 159
  "Benefit" concept of dividends, 170
  Changes in dividend scales, 166
  Disclosure, 177
  Dividend liabilities, 175
  Incidence assumption, 203
  Loss recognition, 170
  Options, 176
  Payable, 175
  Pricing, 44
  Recoverability, 170
  Restricted participating business, relationship to, 490
  Separation of dividend component, 173
  Significance of, 160
  Statutory reserves as approximation of adjusted, 169
  Variable life insurance, 416
Documentation of a conversion, 558
Dollars-per-thousand method, 590

E

Earnings, analysis of, 585
Economic value, 56
Endowment contracts, revenue on, 61
Equation approach to pricing, 29
Equation method of accounting, 553
Ernst & Ernst Life Insurance Accounting Research Project, 11
Estimates, changes in, 574
Established companies, audit guidelines, 576
Experience rating:
  Group insurance, 394
  Reinsurance, 428
Expense allowances under reinsurance agreements:

Normal agreements, 432
  Special agreements, 444
Expense reserves, 108
Expenses—see type of expense, e.g., *Investment expenses, Acquisition costs,* etc.

F

Factors:
  Amortization of acquisition costs, 304
  Calculation of, 107
  Intermediate reserve formulas, 212
  Reserve grading, 178
  "Single reserve," 326
Field, clerical, 254
Field supervision expense, 256
Financial statements, 571
Financing costs, 255
First-year costs—see *Acquisition costs*
Fixed annuities, 47
Formulas for intermediate reserves, 211
Fractional premiums, 204
Functional costs, 232

G

General account, variable life insurance, 414
General insurance expenses, 264
Goodwill, 551
Grading of reserves:
  Acquisition costs, 307
  Benefit reserves, 178
  Health insurance, 363
  Industrial insurance, 340
  Maintenance and settlement costs, 325
Gross change methods, 520
Group annuities, 404
Group conversions, 130
Group insurance:
  Cost accounting, 395
  Experience rating, 394
  Loss recognition, 476
  Pooled business, 404
  Products, 393
  Pricing, 393
  Reserves, 397
  Retention business, 397
Guaranteed renewable health insurance, 376

H

Health insurance:
  Cancellable forms—see *Commercial forms*
  Commercial forms:
    Acquisition costs, 350
    Casualty approach, 350
    Claim reserves, 352
    Disclosure, 352
    Loss recognition, 475
    Revenue, 62, 64, 349
  Credit health—see *Credit insurance*
  Group health—see *Group insurance*
  Guaranteed renewable forms, 376
  Loss recognition, 475
  Noncancellable forms:
    Acquisition costs, 364
    Amortization cutoff, 368
    Claim cost assumptions, 357

Claim liabilities, 364
    Disclosure, 375
    Grading to statutory reserve, 363
    Interest, 357
    Maintenance costs, 368
    Pricing, 353
    Reserve calculations, 358
    Revenue, 62, 356
    Statutory reserves as approximation of adjusted, 374
    Terminations, 357
    Uncollected premiums, 374
    Unearned premiums, 371
  Reserve models, 565
  Return-of-premium forms, 376
Hindsight, use of in implementing lock-in concept, 87
Home office "rent", 69

I

Incidence assumptions, 201
Independent actuaries, 579
Independent audits, 576
Index-linked products, 422
Indirect costs, 260
Individual fixed annuities—see *Annuities*
Industrial insurance:
  Acquisition costs, 344
  Amortization, 347
  Assumptions, 337
  Benefit reserves, 336
  Calculation techniques, 338
  Disclosure, 348
  Grading of reserves, 340
  Interest, 334
  Maintenance and settlement expenses, 347
  Mortality, 333
  Nonforfeiture costs, 334
  Paid-up business, 340
  Policy size, 335
  Pricing, 333
  Products, 331
  Supplementary benefits, 335
  "Times" system, 343
  Underwriting, 332
  Withdrawals, 333
Inflation:
  Interest assumption, 144
  Maintenance and settlement expenses, 325
  Variability measurements for acquisition costs, 244
Installment sales method of revenue recognition, 53
Inter-company relationships, 552
Interest:
  Acquisition costs, 290
  Adverse deviation, 143
  Annuities, 154
  Asset allocations, 144
  Asset-liability relationships, 143
  Audit guide provisions, 138
  Cost of collection adjustment, interest on, 461
  Convertible bonds, 145
  Credit insurance, 384
  Disclosure, 158
  Dividend accumulations, 155
  Dividend scales, 162

Expenses and taxes, 143
Gross investment income, 144
Group contracts, 155
Health insurance, 357
Incidence assumptions, 204
Industrial insurance, 334
Inflation, 144
Investment expenses, 146
Investments in subsidiaries and affiliates, 146
Loss recognition, 473
Maintenance and settlement costs, 324
Models, 153
Modified coinsurance reserves, 155
Nature of, 139
New money rates, 142
Nonparticipating products, 153
Participating business, 154
Plan differentiation, 153
Policy loans, 155
Portfolio rates, 142
Principal office deduction, 146
Purchase valuations, amortization of acquisition cost with interest, 543
Ratebook assumptions, 143
Reserve grading, 182
Self-rent, 145
Significance of, 141
Statutory rates, 142
Taxes on investment income, 147
Trends, 150
Type of business, 142
Variable life insurance, 416
Yield calculation, 150
Interim statements, 573
Intermediate reserve formulas, 211
Intermediate reserves, 204
Internal audits, 582
Inventoriable costs, 242
Investment expenses:
    Disclosure, 328
    Interest assumption, 146
    Nature, 328
    Revenue offset, 69
Investment income:
    Home office rent, 145
    Interest assumption, 144
    Principal office deduction, 146
    Revenue, 68
    Taxes on, 147
Investment in subsidiaries and affiliates, 146
Issue costs, 267

L
Level term insurance, 35
Life insurance audit guide—see *Audit guide*
Life insurance transaction, nature of, 50
Limited-payment life contracts, revenue on, 61
Line-of-business analysis, 586
Line-of-business cost allocations, 262
Loading in dividend scale, 162
Lock-in, adverse deviation, 86:
    American Academy references, 83
    Audit guide references, 82
    Exceptions, 87

Hindsight, 87
Implementation, 85
Practical reasons for, 84
Premium assumptions, 86
Problems with, 83
Theory of, 83
LOMA functional cost program, 233
Long-duration contracts, premium revenues, 60
Loss recognition, 473

M
Mail order solicitation costs, 256
Maintenance and settlement costs:
    Calculation of reserves, 321
    Cost accounting, relationship to, 321
    Deferred and uncollected premiums, 460
    Disclosure, 326
    Factors, 326
    Grading, effect of, 325
    Health insurance, 368
    Industrial insurance, 347
    Inflation, effect of, 325
    Interest, effect of, 324
    Nature of, 321
    New companies, 577
    Reasons for reserving, 321
    Recoverability tests, 326, 468
    Reserves, when needed, 321
    Unearned valuation premiums, 463
    Variable life insurance, 414
    Withdrawals, effect of, 324
Mandatory securities valuation reserve, 158
Management fee concept of participating restrictions, 480
Management uses of GAAP, 593
Mean reserves, 208, 453
Miscellaneous coverages, 200
Miscellaneous revenue items, 68
Mid-terminal reserves, 208, 463
Minimum death benefit guarantee under variable life coverages, 416
Models:
    Interest, 153
    Health insurance, 565
    Reserves, 559
Modified coinsurance:
    General, 426
    Interest on reserves, 155
    Normal reinsurance agreements, 436
    Reinsurance assumed, 445
Morbidity, 357
Mortality:
    Acquisition cost factors, effect on, 304
    Adverse deviation, 125
    Audit guide provisions, 112
    Disclosure, 127
    Dividend assumptions, 162
    Exposure base, effect of, 123
    Incidence assumption, 126, 202
    Industrial insurance, 333
    Loss recognition, 473
    New companies, 577
    Newer blocks of business, 123
    Older blocks of business, 121
    Profits, effect on, 117
    Reinsurance, effect of, 124

Reserves, effect on, 116
Select mortality savings, 41
Settlement options, 126
Tables, 113
Term renewal, 125
Variable life insurance, 416
Mortality fluctuation reserves, 137
Mutual companies, stock subsidiaries of, 555

N
Natural classifications of costs, 230
New companies:
    Audit guidelines, 577
    Recoverability tests, 469
New lines of business, costs of developing, 318
New money rates, 142
Newer blocks of business, provisions for adverse deviation, 123
Net change method of deferred tax accounting, 520
New York law on participating business sold by stock companies, 480
New York Stock Exchange, 9
Noncancellable health insurance—see *Health insurance*
Nonforfeiture benefits:
    Differential costs of, 203, 337
    Incidence of, 203
    Industrial insurance, 334
Non-life insurance companies—acquisition of by life companies, 527
Nonparticipating permanent insurance, 29
Nonparticipating term insurance, 35
Non-proportional reinsurance, 426, 443
Normal reinsurance agreements—see *Reinsurance*

O
Older blocks of business:
    Adverse deviation, 121
    Grading of reserves, 193
Operating ratios, 588
Operations loss carryforwards, recognition of tax benefits of, 517
Organization of a conversion effort, 557
Outstanding balance credit insurance, 387
Overhead, 328, 468

P
Paid-up additions, 177
Paid-up business, 197, 336
Participating permanent insurance:
    Adjustments to GAAP, 159
    Disclosure, 177
    Dividends:
        Assumptions, 162
        General, 44
        Interest contribution, 162
        Loading contribution, 162
        Mortality contribution, 162
    Interest assumptions, 154
    Loss recognition, 475
    Premiums, 43
    Rate tests, 46
    Recoverability tests, 471
    Reserve grading, 186, 193

Restricted participating business—see *Restricted participating business*
Stockholder charge limitations—see *Restricted participating business*
Permanent insurance—see *Nonparticipating permanent insurance* and *Participating permanent insurance*
Permanent tax differences, 507
Persistency bonuses, 254
Persistency adjustments, 293
Pervasive measurement principles, 55
Phases of taxation, 499
Plan differentiation in selecting interest assumptions, 153
Policy loans, 155
Policyholders' tax surplus, 518
Pooled group business, 404
Poolings:
Consistency and APB Opinion No. 16, 527
Consolidation policies, 529
Involving life companies only, 529
Involving non-life companies, 527
Portfolio interest rates, 142
Premiums:
Assumptions and lock-in, 86
Fractional, 204
Installment nature of, 53
Present value of gross, 283
Recoverability tests, 468
Revenues, 60
Uncollected, 464
Unearned—see *Unearned premiums*
Valuation (also see *Valuation premiums*):
General, 98
Recoverability tests, 469
Terminology, 92
"When due" provision, 65
Pricing:
Group insurance, 393
Health insurance, 353
Industrial insurance, 333
Ordinary insurance, 29
Variable life insurance, 414
Principal office deduction, 146
Process costing concepts, applicability of, 247
Products:
Credit insurance, 379
Group insurance, 393
Health insurance, 349
Index-linked, 422
Industrial insurance, 331
Ordinary insurance, 29
Return-of-premium health insurance, 376
Variable annuities, 407
Variable life insurance, 413
Profit recognition, 53
Projections in recoverability tests, 470
Purchase accounting:
APB Opinion No. 16, 537
Acquisition cost, determination of, 536
Agency plant, value of, 548
Amortization of acquisition costs, 541
General, 531
Goodwill, 551
Implications of not assigning part of

the purchase price to insurance in force, 547
Insurance in force, valuation of—special problems, 545
Negative acquisition costs, 545
Reserve valuation, 534
Pure endowments, 177

R

Ratebook development cost, 318
Reasonableness reviews, 577
Recapture under reinsurance agreements, 427, 441, 444
Reconciliations of statutory and GAAP amounts, 568
Recoverability tests:
Adverse deviation, treatment of, 468
Audit guide provisions, 465
Benefits, treatment of, 468
Calculating a deficiency, 470
Cancellable coverages, 472
Decrements, treatment of, 468
Development costs, treatment of, 468
Disclosure, 472
First-year deferred acquisition costs, treatment of, 468
General overhead, treatment of, 468
Gross premiums, treatment of, 468
Guaranteed renewable business, 471
Inventory analogy, 466
Loss leaders, 467
Maintenance and settlement costs, treatment of, 468
Methods of testing, 470
New companies, 469
Participating business, 170, 471
Practical considerations, 472
Recording a deficiency, 471
Renewal-year acquisition costs, treatment of, 468
Test frame, 466
Valuation premium comparisons, 469
Recruiting expense, 255
Reduced paid-up insurance, 176
Reinsurance:
Assumed, 445
Audit guide provisions, 443
Cost of, 430
Disclosure:
Assumed reinsurance, 446
Normal agreements, 443
Special agreements, 445
General:
Coinsurance, 425
Cost of reinsurance, 429
Experience rating, 428
Modified coinsurance, 426
Non-proportional reinsurance, 426
Recapture, 427
Special agreements, 429
Yearly renewable term, 424
Mortality assumption, effect on, 124
Normal agreements:
Coinsurance, 435
Coinsurance refunds, 438
Disclosure, 443
Expense allowances, 432
Modified coinsurance, 436
Non-proportional reinsurance, 443
Yearly renewable term, 430

YRT refunds, 433
Special agreements:
Assumed reinsurance, 446
Definition of, 444
Disclosure, 445
Expense allowances, 444
Limitation of risk, 444
Recapture, 444
Sale of business, 445
Unauthorized, 443
Release-from-risk concept, 73, 296
Renewability of term insurance, 36
Renewal year acquisition costs:
Approximation technique, 273
Commissions and commission equivalents, 252, 270
Term conversions, 272
Term renewals, 271
Worksheet methods, 300
Reserves:
Assumptions—see *Assumptions*
Benefit, 109
Credit insurance, 380
Deferred and uncollected premiums, relationship to, 453
Disclosure, 109
Expense, 108
Grading, 178
Group annuities, 404
Group insurance, 397, 403
Health insurance, 356
Industrial insurance, 336
Intermediate, 204
Maintenance and settlement cost, 321
Mean, 453
Mid-terminal, 462
Models, 558
Mortality fluctuation, 137
Participating business, 160, 170
Supplemental benefits, 198
Terminology, 91
Variable annuities, 412
Variable life insurance, 414
Restricted participating business:
Audit guide provisions, 477
Charter restrictions, 479
Company intent, 482
Contractual restrictions, 479
Cost allocations, 492
Deferred taxes, 493
Deficits, 494
Disclosure, 495
Dividends, treatment of, 490
Financial statement presentation, 495
Flat amount per $1,000, 478
Interpreting restrictions, 479
Management fee concept, 480
New York Law, 480
Ownership of surplus, 481
Percentage restrictions, 477
Regulatory restrictions, 479
Reserve assumptions, 490
Self-imposed restrictions, 479
Separation of statutory accounts, 483
Stockholder charge mode, 489
Retention group business, 397
Return on equity, 589
Return on sales, 588
Return-of-premium health insurance, 376

Revenue:
Deposit-type items, 70
Disclosure, 65
Installment sales method, 53
Investment income, 68
Long-duration contracts, 60
Recognition of, 53
Service method, 54
Short-duration contracts, 63
"When due" provision, 65
Rules of thumb for adjusted earnings, 589

S

Sale of business under reinsurance agreements, 445
Sales aspect of the life insurance transaction, 50
"Sales cores", 345
Sales support expenses, 254, 267
Securities valuation reserves, 158
Securities and Exchange Commission, 8, 575
Security analysts, 7, 585
Select mortality savings, 41
Selection costs, 259
Self-imposed restrictions on participating profits, 479
Selling costs, 247
Semi-fixed cost/production relationships, 244
Semi-variable cost/production relationships, 244
Separate accounts:
Participating business, 483
Variable life, 412
Variable annuities, 408
Service aspect of the life insurance transaction, 52
Settlement costs—*see Maintenance and settlement costs*
Short-duration contracts, revenues on, 63
Single-premium annuities—*see Annuities*
Single-premium credit insurance—*see Credit insurance*
Sources of earnings, 593
Society of Actuaries, 582
Special deductions, treatment of in deferred tax accounting, 513
Special reinsurance agreements, 429, 443
Specialty policies, 47
Statutory accounting:
Compared with GAAP, 6
Convention statement, 4
Objectives of, 5
Statutory reserves:
Credit insurance, 380
Grading to, 178
Health insurance, 374
Interest rates, 142
Paid-up business, 197
Participating business, 169
Step-cost relationships, 244

Stock options, 251
Stockholder charge on participating profits, 489
Subsidiaries:
Mutual company as owner, 555
Reserve models for, 565
Sale of, 555
Statement of, 553
Substandard adjusted reserves, 200
Sum-of-the-years'-premiums method of amortization, 289
Supplemental benefits, 47, 62, 198, 335
Surplus:
Adverse deviation, role in providing for, 81
Ownership of, 481
Statement of, 496

T

Taxes:
Deferred tax accounting, 506
Interim statements, 575
Investment income, taxes on, 147
Life Insurance Company Income Tax Act of 1959, 498
Variable life insurance, 416
Term conversions, 127, 136
Term dividend option, 175
Term insurance—see *Nonparticipating term insurance*
Term renewals, 125, 136, 271, 460
Terminations—see *Withdrawals*
Terminations of agents, 254
Tests of recoverability, 468
"Times" system, 343
Timetable for a conversion, 557
Timing differences, deferred taxes, 518
Training expense, 255
Trends, influence on the interest assumption, 150

U

Unauthorized reinsurance, 443
Uncollected premiums, 374, 464
Underwriting:
Group, 21
Industrial, 332
Ordinary, 20
Unearned premiums, 371, 463
Unit costs, 232

V

Valuation premiums:
Acquisition costs, 305
American Academy guidelines, 99
Audit guide references, 98
Incidence assumptions, 201
Lock-in, relationship to, 82
Recoverability tests, 469
Terminology, 91
Unearned, 463
Variable annuities:
Acquisition costs, 408

Amortization of acquisition costs, 410
Development costs, 412
Disclosure, 413
Product design, 407
Reserves, 412
Revenue, 408
Separate account, 408
Statutory reserves, 408
Variable life insurance:
Acquisition costs, 416
Assumptions, 416
Dividends, 416
Expenses, 416
Interest, 416
Investment earnings rate, 416
Maintenance and settlement expenses, 416
Minimum death benefit guarantee, 416
Mortality, 416
Separate account transfers, 416
Taxes, 416
Withdrawals, 416
Variability of costs, classifications, 230
Variability concept, 244
Variability tests for acquisition costs, 268
Vesting, 254
Volume credits for decreasing term insurance, 41

W

Waiver of premium reserves, 198
"When due" provision for revenue, 65, 464
Whole-life contracts, revenue on, 60
Withdrawal:
Acquisition cost factors, effect on, 305
Adverse deviation, 134
Audit guide provisions, 131
Disclosure, 137
Incidence assumptions, 203
Industrial insurance, 373
Loss recognition, 473
Maintenance and settlement costs, effect on, 324
New companies, 577
Nonforfeiture benefits, 132
Profits, effect on, 134
Reserves, effect on, 134
Tables of, 131
Term conversions, 136
Term renewals, 136
Variable life insurance, 416
"When terminated" assumption, 136
Working papers for recording conversion adjustments, 565
Worksheet methods of amortization, 296

Y

Yearly renewable term reinsurance, 424, 430, 445
Yield calculations, 150